what we call "civilization" is relatively recent, indeed, with the first permanent settlements occurring in the Middle East a scant 12,000 years ago. But the written record of our species' existence extends back only half this long, to the time humans invented writing and first farmed with animal-driven plows some 5,000 years B.P.

Sociology came into being in the wake of the many changes to society wrought by the Industrial Revolution over the last few centuries—ju... ...ary perspective. The lower ... ...k at the events and trends that have defined The Modern Era, most of which are discussed in this text. Innovations in technology are charted in the green panel below the line and provide a useful backdrop for viewing the milestones of social progress highlighted in the blue panel above the line. Major contributions to the development of sociological thought are traced along the very bottom of this time line.

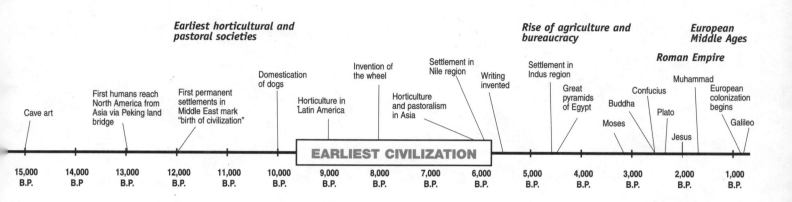

Earliest horticultural and pastoral societies

Rise of agriculture and bureaucracy

European Middle Ages

Roman Empire

Cave art

First humans reach North America from Asia via Peking land bridge

First permanent settlements in Middle East mark "birth of civilization"

Domestication of dogs

Horticulture in Latin America

Invention of the wheel

Horticulture and pastoralism in Asia

Settlement in Nile region

Writing invented

Settlement in Indus region

Great pyramids of Egypt

Moses

Buddha

Confucius

Plato

Jesus

Muhammad

European colonization begins

Galileo

EARLIEST CIVILIZATION

15,000 B.P.	14,000 B.P	13,000 B.P.	12,000 B.P.	11,000 B.P.	10,000 B.P.	9,000 B.P.	8,000 B.P.	7,000 B.P.	6,000 B.P.	5,000 B.P.	4,000 B.P.	3,000 B.P.	2,000 B.P.	1,000 B.P.

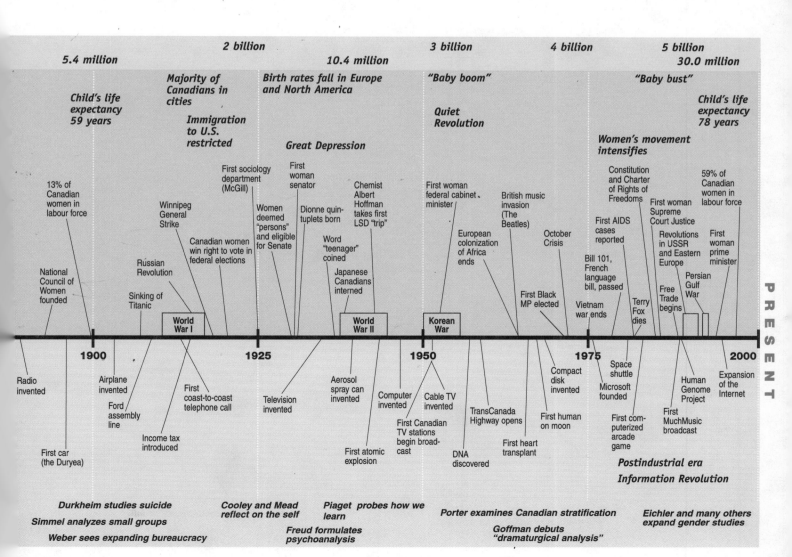

2 billion

5.4 million

10.4 million

3 billion

4 billion

5 billion
30.0 million

Majority of Canadians in cities

Birth rates fall in Europe and North America

"Baby boom"

"Baby bust"

Immigration to U.S. restricted

Child's life expectancy 59 years

Quiet Revolution

Child's life expectancy 78 years

Great Depression

Women's movement intensifies

13% of Canadian women in labour force

Winnipeg General Strike

Canadian women win right to vote in federal elections

First sociology department (McGill)

Women deemed "persons" and eligible for Senate

First woman senator

Dionne quin- tuplets born

Chemist Albert Hoffman takes first LSD "trip"

Word "teenager" coined

First woman federal cabinet minister

British music invasion (The Beatles)

October Crisis

Constitution and Charter of Rights of Freedoms

First AIDS cases reported

First woman Supreme Court Justice

Revolutions in USSR and Eastern Europe

59% of Canadian women in labour force

First woman prime minister

National Council of Women founded

Russian Revolution

Sinking of Titanic

Japanese Canadians interned

European colonization of Africa ends

First Black MP elected

Bill 101, French language bill, passed

Vietnam war ends

Terry Fox dies

Free Trade begins

Persian Gulf War

World War I

World War II

Korean War

Radio invented

1900

1925

1950

1975

2000

Airplane invented

Ford assembly line

First coast-to-coast telephone call

Television invented

Aerosol spray can invented

Computer invented

Cable TV invented

Compact disk invented

Space shuttle

Microsoft founded

Human Genome Project

Expansion of the Internet

First car (the Duryea)

Income tax introduced

First Canadian TV stations begin broad- cast

TransCanada Highway opens

First heart transplant

First human on moon

First com- puterized arcade game

First MuchMusic broadcast

First atomic explosion

DNA discovered

P R E S E N T

Postindustrial era

Information Revolution

Durkheim studies suicide

Cooley and Mead reflect on the self

Piaget probes how we learn

Porter examines Canadian stratification

Eichler and many others expand gender studies

Simmel analyzes small groups

Freud formulates psychoanalysis

Goffman debuts "dramaturgical analysis"

Weber sees expanding bureaucracy

SOCIOLOGY

This book is offered to teachers of sociology in the hope that it will help our students understand their place in today's society and, more broadly, in tomorrow's world.

SOCIOLOGY

THIRD CANADIAN EDITION

John J. Macionis

Kenyon College

Linda M. Gerber

University of Guelph

Prentice Hall Allyn and Bacon Canada
Scarborough, Ontario

Canadian Cataloguing in Publication Data

Macionis, John J.
  Sociology

3rd Canadian ed.
Includes index.
ISBN 0-13-095115-3

1. Sociology. I. Gerber, Linda Marie, 1944– .
II. Clarke, Juanne N. (Juanne Nancarrow), 1944– . III. Title.

HM51.M169 1999   301   C98-932313-7

 © 1999 Prentice-Hall Canada Inc., Scarborough, Ontario
A Division of Simon & Schuster/A Viacom Company

Prentice-Hall, Inc., Upper Saddle River, New Jersey
Prentice-Hall International (UK) Limited, London
Prentice-Hall of Australia, Pty. Limited, Sydney
Prentice-Hall Hispanoamericana, S.A., Mexico City
Prentice-Hall of India Private Limited, New Delhi
Prentice-Hall of Japan, Inc., Tokyo
Simon & Schuster Southeast Asia Private Limited, Singapore
Editora Prentice-Hall do Brasil, Ltda., Rio de Janeiro

ISBN 0-13-095115-3

Vice President, Editorial Director: Laura Pearson
Acquisitions Editor: Nicole Lukach
Marketing Manager: Kathleen McGill
Developmental Editor: Lisa Berland
Associate Editor: Lisa Phillips
Production Editor: Andrew Winton
Copy Editor: Susan Broadhurst
Production Coordinator: Sharon Houston
Permissions: Michaele Sinko
Photo Research: Susan Wallace-Cox
Cover and Interior Design: Sarah Battersby
Cover Image: Paul Watson
Page Layout: Hermia Chung

Original English Language edition published by Prentice-Hall, Inc., Upper Saddle River, New Jersey
Copyright © 1999, 1997, 1995, 1993, 1991, 1987.

1 2 3 4 5   CC   03 02 01 00 99

Printed and bound in the United States of America.

Visit the Prentice Hall Canada Web site! Send us your comments, browse our catalogues, and more at
www.phcanada.com. Or reach us through e-mail at **phabinfo_pubcanada@prenhall.com**.

BRIEF CONTENTS

PART I

THE FOUNDATIONS
OF SOCIOLOGY

PART II

THE FOUNDATIONS
OF SOCIETY

PART III

SOCIAL
INEQUALITY

PART IV

SOCIAL
INSTITUTIONS

PART V

SOCIAL
CHANGE

CONTENTS

PART IV   SOCIAL INSTITUTIONS

PART V   SOCIAL CHANGE

MAPS

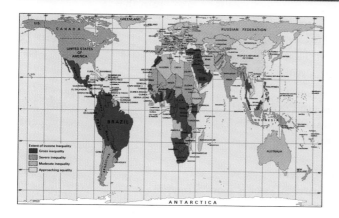
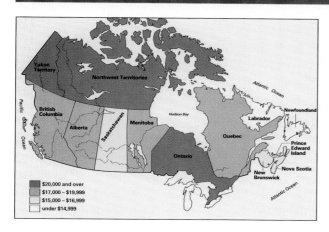

BOXES

GLOBAL SOCIOLOGY

SOCIAL DIVERSITY

EXPLORING CYBER-SOCIETY

CONTROVERSY & DEBATE

FEATURE ESSAYS
NEW INFORMATION TECHNOLOGY AND SOCIETY

cyber.scope

PREFACE

How much the world has changed in just the last few years! And nowhere is the change greater than with regard to new information technology. Back in 1996, when we were preparing the last edition of *Sociology*, this nation was just discovering the Internet. Now, as we stand at the brink of a new century, about half of Canadian adults—and a majority of men and women enrolled in college and university—have made computers a part of their everyday lives.

To mark the beginning of the new century—and to acknowledge the arrival of the Information Age—we are both proud and excited to present a new, groundbreaking edition of *Sociology*. As you surely have noticed, the third Canadian edition has a different look. This new appearance symbolizes the fact that *Sociology* will never stand still or be revised with only superficial changes. As in the past, this third Canadian edition of *Sociology* is authoritative, comprehensive, stimulating, and—as e-mail messages from students across the country testify—plain fun to read. This thoroughly updated edition elevates sociology's most popular text to a still higher standard of excellence, and offers an unparalleled resource to today's students as they learn about both our diverse society and the changing world.

But the book is just part of the learning package. All students using the third Canadian editon of *Sociology* can benefit from the full-featured Web site **www.prenticehall.ca/macionis**. For each chapter of the text, this site provides a chapter overview and learning objectives, suggested research paper topics, essay questions, multiple-choice and true-false questions that the server will immediately grade, chapter-relevant Web destinations with learning questions, and a chat room where students can discuss sociological issues with others taking the same course.

ORGANIZATION OF THIS TEXT

Part I of the textbook introduces the foundations of sociology. Underlying the discipline is the *sociological perspective*—the focus of Chapter 1, which explains how this invigorating point of view brings the world to life in a new and instructive way. Chapter 2 spotlights *sociological investigation*, or the "doing of sociology," and explains how to use the logic of science to study human society. We demonstrate major research strategies in action through well-known examples of sociological work. Learning how sociologists see the world and carry out research, passive readers become

active, critical participants in the issues, debates, and controversies that frame our discipline.

Part II surveys the foundations of social life. Chapter 3 focuses on the central concept of *culture*, emphasizing the cultural diversity that makes up our society and our world. Chapter 4 links culture to the concept of *society*, presenting four time-honoured models for understanding the structure and dynamics of social organization. This unique chapter provides students with the background to comprehend more deeply the ideas of important thinkers—including Emile Durkheim, Karl Marx, Max Weber, as well as Gerhard and Jean Lenski—that appear in subsequent chapters. The topic of Chapter 5 is *socialization*, an exploration of how we gain our humanity as we learn to participate in society. Chapter 6 provides a micro-level look at the patterns of *social interaction* that make up our everyday lives. Chapter 7 offers full-chapter coverage of *groups and organizations*, two additional and vital elements of social structure. Chapter 8 completes the unit by investigating how the operation of society generates both *deviance and conformity*.

Part III offers unparalleled discussion of social inequality, beginning with three chapters devoted to social stratification. Chapter 9, *social stratification*, introduces major concepts and presents theoretical explanations of social inequality. This chapter richly illustrates the historical changes in stratification and how patterns of inequality vary around the world today. Chapter 10 surveys *social inequality in Canada*, exploring common perceptions of inequality and assessing how well they square with research findings. Chapter 11 extends the analysis with a look at *global stratification*, revealing the gaps in wealth and power that separate rich and poor nations. Both Chapters 10 and 11 pay special attention to how global developments affect stratification in Canada, just as they explore our society's role in global inequality. Chapter 12, *sex and gender*, begins with the biological foundation of sex and sexuality, and goes on to explain how societies transform the distinction of sex into systems of gender stratification. *Race and ethnicity*, additional important dimensions of social inequality both in North America and the rest of the world, are detailed in Chapter 13. *Aging and the elderly*, a topic of increasing concern to "greying" societies such as our own, is addressed in Chapter 14.

Part IV includes a full chapter on each social institution. Chapter 15 leads off investigating *the economy and work*, because most sociologists recognize the economy as having the greatest impact on all other institutions. This chapter highlights the processes of industrialization and post-industrialization, explains the emergence of a global economy, and suggests what such transformations mean for the Canadian labour force. Chapter 16, *politics and government*, analyzes the distribution of power in Canadian society and surveys political systems around the world. Chapter 17, *family*, explains the central importance of families to social organization, and underscores the diversity of family life both here and in other societies. Chapter 18, *religion*, addresses the timeless human search for ultimate purpose and meaning, introduces major world religions, and explains how religious beliefs are linked to other dimensions of social life. Chapter 19, *education*, traces the expansion of schooling in industrial societies. Here again, schooling in Canada comes to life through contrasts with educational patterns in many other countries. Chapter 20, *health and medicine*, shows how health is a social issue just as much as it is a matter of biological processes. This chapter traces the historical emergence of medicine, analyzes current medical issues, and compares Canadian patterns to those found in other countries.

Part V examines important dimensions of global social change. Chapter 21 focuses on the powerful impact of *population growth and urbanization* in Canada and throughout the world. Chapter 22 explores forms of *collective behaviour* and explains how people seek or resist social change by joining *social movements*. Chapter 23 concludes the text with an overview of *social change* that contrasts *traditional, modern, and postmodern societies*. This chapter rounds out the text by explaining how and why world societies change and by critically analyzing the benefits and liabilities of traditional, modern, and postmodern ways of life.

CONTINUITY: ESTABLISHED FEATURES OF SOCIOLOGY

Everyone knows that introductory sociology texts have much in common; but they are not the same. The extraordinary success of *Sociology*—far and away the most widely adopted text of its kind—results from a combination of the following distinctive features:

Unsurpassed writing style. Most important, this text offers a writing style widely praised by students and faculty alike as elegant and inviting. *Sociology* is an enjoyable text that encourages students to read—even beyond their assignments.

Comprehensive coverage that lets instructors choose. No other text matches *Sociology's* twenty-three-chapter coverage of the field. We offer such breadth not with the expectation that instructors will assign every chapter, but so that instructors can choose exactly what they wish to teach.

Engaging and instructive chapter openings. One of the most popular features of earlier editions of *Sociology* has been the engaging vignettes that begin each chapter. These openings—for instance, using the tragic sinking of the *Titanic* to illustrate the life-and-death consequences of social inequality, citing the confrontation at Oka to highlight our ability to bring about intentional change, and visiting a vast city dump in the Philippines to bring home the desperate plight of many of the world's poor—spark the interest of readers as they introduce important themes. This revision retains the best chapter-opening vignettes from earlier editions and offers eleven new ones as well.

Instructive and varied examples. On virtually every page of *Sociology*, rich, illuminating examples bring concepts and theories to life, demonstrating to students the value of applying sociology to our everyday world.

A celebration of social diversity. *Sociology* invites students from all social backgrounds to discover a fresh and exciting way to see the world and understand themselves. Readers will discover in this text the diversity of Canadian society—people of African, Asian, European, and North and South American ancestry, as well as women and men of various class positions, in all parts of the country, and at all points in the life course. Just as important, without flinching from the problems that marginalized people confront, this text does not treat minorities as social problems but notes their achievements.

Inclusive focus on women and men. Beyond devoting a full chapter to the important concepts of sex and gender, *Sociology* mainstreams gender into *every* chapter, showing how the topic at hand affects women and men differently, and explaining how gender operates as a basic dimension of social organization.

A global perspective. *Sociology* has taken a leading role in expanding the horizons of our discipline beyond Canada. Each chapter of this text contains comparative material that explores the social diversity of the entire world. Moreover, this text explains that social trends in Canada—from musical tastes, to the price of wheat, to the growing disparity of income—are influenced by what happens elsewhere. Conversely, students will recognize ways in which social patterns and policies that characterize Canada and other rich countries affect poor nations around the world.

Theoretically clear and balanced. *Sociology* makes theory easy. Chapter 1 introduces the discipline's major theoretical approaches, which systematically reappear in the chapters that follow. The text highlights not only the social-conflict, structural-functional, and symbolic-interaction paradigms, but incorporates feminist theory, social-exchange analysis, ethnomethodology, cultural ecology, and sociobiology.

Chapter 4—unique to this text—provides students with an easy-to-understand introduction to important social theorists *before* they encounter their work in later chapters. The ideas of Max Weber, Karl Marx, Emile Durkheim, as well as Gerhard Lenski's historical overview of human societies, appear in distinct sections that instructors may assign together or refer to separately at different points in the course.

Emphasis on critical thinking. Critical thinking skills include the ability to challenge common assumptions by formulating questions, identifying and weighing appropriate evidence, and reaching reasoned conclusions. This text not only teaches but encourages students to discover on their own.

Recent sociological research. *Sociology* blends classical sociological statements with the latest research as reported in the leading publications in the field. Some 250 new studies inform this revision, and half of 1500 research citations used throughout the book were published since 1990. From chapter to chapter, the text's statistical data are the most recent available.

Learning aids. This text has many features to help students learn. In each chapter, **Key Concepts** are identified by boldfaced type and following each appears *a precise, italicized definition*. A complete **Glossary** is found at the end of the book. Each chapter also contains a numbered **Summary** and four **Critical-Thinking Questions** that help students to review material and assess their understanding. New to this revision is **Sociology Applied**, a list of learning exercises that provides students with activities to do on or near the campus and identifies interesting Web sites. At the end of each chapter are **Weblinks**, an additional list of Web sites relating to the topics of the chapter.

Outstanding images: photography and fine art. This book offers the finest and most extensive program of photography and artwork available in any sociology textbook. The third Canadian edition of *Sociology* displays more than one hundred examples of fine art as well as hundreds of colour photographs— more than ever before. Each of these images is carefully selected by the authors and appears with an insightful caption. Moreover, both photographs and artwork present people of various social backgrounds and historical periods. For example, alongside art by well-known Europeans such as Vincent Van Gogh and Canadian artists including William Kurelek and Emily Carr, this edition has paintings by outstanding Latino artists Frank Romero and Diego Rivera, and the engaging Australian painter and feminist Sally Swain.

Thought-provoking theme boxes. Although boxed material is common to introductory texts, *Sociology, Third Canadian Edition*, provides a wealth of uncommonly good boxes. Each chapter typically contains four boxes, which fall into four types that amplify central themes of the text. **Global Sociology** boxes provoke readers to think about their own way of life by examining the fascinating social diversity that characterizes our world. **Social Diversity** boxes focus on multicultural issues and amplify the voices of women and people of colour. **Exploring Cyber-Society** boxes, new to this edition, explore how computers and other new information technology are changing our lives. **Controversy & Debate** boxes conclude each chapter by presenting several points of view on an issue of contemporary importance; "Continue the debate" questions, which end each of these boxes, are sure to stimulate spirited class discussion.

Sociology, Third Canadian Edition, contains seventy-four boxes in all (on average, about three per chapter), revised and updated as necessary with nineteen boxes new to this revision. A complete listing of this text's boxes appears after the table of contents.

An unparalleled program of global and national maps. Another popular feature of *Sociology* is its program of global and national maps. **"Windows on the World"** global maps—many updated for this edition—are truly sociological maps offering a comparative look at income disparity, favoured languages and religions, the extent of prostitution, permitted marriage forms, the degree of political freedom, and a host of other issues. **Windows on the World** use a new, non-Eurocentric projection, devised by cartographer Arno Peters, that accurately portrays the relative size of all the continents. A complete listing of the **Windows on the World** global maps follows the table of contents.

"Seeing Ourselves" national maps help to illuminate the social diversity of Canada. These maps highlight suicide rates, median household income, foreign-born populations, divorce rates, unemployment rates, and other measures of the Canadian population. A complete listing of the **Seeing Ourselves** national maps follows the table of contents.

INNOVATION: CHANGES IN THE THIRD CANADIAN EDITION

Each new edition of *Sociology* has broken new ground, one reason that more than 2 million students have learned from this sociological best-seller. A revision raises high expectations, but, after several years of planning and work, we are excited to offer the most dramatically new and improved revision ever. Here is a brief overview of the innovations that define *Sociology, Third Canadian Edition:*

***Sociology*, Third Canadian Edition, offers interactive learning in sociology!** Computers and other new information technology are changing the way we learn, and *Sociology, Third Canadian Edition,* is now a twenty-first century textbook. The heart of the learning package—the book itself—comes with many new features, which are outlined below. In addition, the text is supported by a Web site.

The Web site. Students using *Sociology* have free access to a freshly revised and full-featured Web site: **http://www.prenticehall.ca/macionis**. Menu-driven and easy to use, this site follows the chapter flow of the text, providing learning objectives, essay questions and suggested paper topics, multiple-choice and true/false tests, additional Web destinations, and a chat room.

Cyber.Scopes. One of the innovations found within the text itself is the new series of Cyber.Scope essays spread throughout the text with one appearing after each of the book's five parts. Cyber.Scope essays explain what the Information Revolution is all about and show how computers and new information technology are altering the shape of people's lives here and around the world. The five Cyber.Scope essays are titled:

- Part I: Welcome to the Information Revolution!
- Part II: How New Technology Is Changing Our Way of Life
- Part III: New Information Technology and Social Stratification
- Part IV: New Information Technology and Social Institutions
- Part V: New Information Technology and Social Change

These essays, which contain photos and figures, provide an opportunity for instructors to pause at several points during the course to focus on new information technology or, alternatively, they can be read together as a "chapter" on new technology and society.

Exploring Cyber-Society boxes. The Cyber.Scopes are not the only place to find discussion of new information technology. A new series of Exploring Cyber-Society boxes highlights ways in which computer technology is linked to specific sociological topics. These new boxes—eleven in all—explore the spread of virtual culture (Chapter 3); imagine what Marx, Weber, and Durkheim might have to say about computer technology (Chapter 4); introduce the Internet as the world's largest network (Chapter 7); explore job patterns in the cyber-age (Chapter 15); examine the impact of modern communications on politics (Chapter 16); look at how religious organizations are utilizing the Internet (Chapter 18); and evaluate the prospects for on-line schools with no campuses at all (Chapter 19), among other themes. A complete listing of these and all third Canadian edition boxes appears after the Table of Contents.

Sociology Applied. *Sociology* is a text that helps transform students into active learners. This edition retains the Critical-Thinking Questions at the end of each chapter and the "Continue the debate" questions that conclude the Controversy & Debate boxes. Also, many of the captions for maps, photographs, and fine art are written as questions that provoke critical thinking.

And, in this third Canadian edition, *Sociology* includes a new feature: Sociology Applied, learning exercises at the end of each chapter. Some exercises direct students to explore engaging Web sites found around the world. But opportunities to use the sociological perspective are always close at hand (and, of course, many students do not have Internet access). Thus, most of the Learning Exercises involve familiar settings on and around the campus.

A small change in chapter ordering. In this revision, Chapters 12 and 13 have switched places. This change—prompted by suggestions from colleagues as well as our own classroom experiences—places the chapter on race and ethnicity *after* other stratification chapters, including sex and gender. Doing so gives students more experience discussing social inequality before they focus on race, a topic they sometimes find difficult to discuss in class.

A revised time line. Have you ever wished there was a way to locate at a glance important historical periods and key events? The last edition of *Sociology* introduced a time line found inside the front cover. This edition presents a more complete and improved time line that makes historical patterns even more clear to readers.

A thorough rewriting of the text. For every revision of this text, we have gone through the chapters page by page, line by line, updating and making the discussion as clear and engaging as possible. This time around, we performed this ritual twice, with the goal of identifying and replacing any language that presented unnecessary difficulties to students. The result is, by far, the most accessible and best-reading version of the text ever.

New topics. The third Canadian edition of *Sociology* is completely updated with new and expanded discussions in every chapter. Here is a partial listing, by chapter:

- **Chapter 1 The Sociological Perspective**: A new section entitled "Marginal Voices" highlights women's contribution to the development of sociology; see the added discussion of the contributions of Marshall McLuhan to Canadian sociology, and the expanded section on applied sociology.

- **Chapter 2 Sociological Investigation**: We've looked at how Florence Nightingale gathered statistics to support her case for better health care and expanded the discussion of research ethics.

- **Chapter 3 Culture**: We've added material on Canadian cultural diversity; a new section links culture to information technology; a new Cyber-Society box tracks the rise of virtual culture; and a new journal entry highlights child labour in Morocco.

- **Chapter 4 Society**: A new chapter opening describes the Tuareg nomads of the Sahara; a new Cyber-Society box imagines the classic theorists' view of the Information Revolution.

- **Chapter 5 Socialization**: There is a new discussion of Erik H. Erikson's theory of life course socialization and a new presentation of sexuality and violence in the mass media.

- **Chapter 6 Social Interaction in Everyday Life**: Beyond extensive rewriting, this chapter includes a new box on how a course conducted electronically affects class interaction and a box on humorous newspaper headlines.

- **Chapter 7 Groups and Organizations**: New research links organizational behaviour to size; notice a considerable increase in discussion of new information technology throughout the chapter as well as a new Cyber-Society box on the Internet; see the updated discussion of organizations, technology, and personal privacy.

- **Chapter 8 Deviance**: We have expanded discussion of gender and crime, added a discussion of projective labelling, added current Canadian cases as illustrations, and made statistical updates on crime and victimization.

- **Chapter 9 Social Stratification**: This chapter features an expanded discussion of the Kuznets curve; updates on inequality in South Africa and economic struggle in the former Soviet Union; there is a new Social Diversity box on social Darwinism that assesses the view of social stratification as "the survival of the fittest."

- **Chapter 10 Social Class in Canada**: A new opening looks at the effect of welfare reform; there are new data on Canadian income distribution; a new Exploring Cyber-Society box explores the relationship between computer skills and social class; and the chapter brings students up to date on poverty in Canada.

- **Chapter 11 Global Stratification**: A new chapter-opening vignette as well as a new section highlight the reality of global slavery; statistical updates document the extent of inequality among the world's people today; new United Nations data support discussion of world economic development; and a new Global Map shows which nations are making economic progress and which are not.

- **Chapter 12 Sex and Gender:** Note the new chapter ordering, switching gender and race; a new chapter-opening vignette deals with female circumcision; note the reorganized and expanded discussion of human sexuality; a new figure compares women's and men's athletic performance over time; a new Global Map explores women's political clout; there is a new box on the beauty myth, an update on women's political firsts, and a new box on women's hockey.

- **Chapter 13 Race and Ethnicity**: A new chapter-opening vignette highlights the experience of visible minorities in Canada; new tables and figures based on the 1996 Census provide the most complete picture ever of Canada's racial and ethnic composition.

- **Chapter 14 Aging and the Elderly**: See the new discussion contrasting the "young old" and the "old old" and the discussion of the ethical issues surrounding death; a new section explores the challenge of finding meaning in old age; a new Global Sociology box looks at euthanasia in the Netherlands; a new Global Map surveys the elderly population in global perspective.

- **Chapter 15 The Economy and Work**: A new chapter-opening vignette looks at changes to employment in an era of corporate downsizing; a new Cyber-Society box describes ways that work is changing in the Information Age; the section on corporations and the global economy has been updated and expanded.

- **Chapter 16 Politics and Government**: A new opening looks at politics in the midst of a natural disaster; a new Cyber-Society box explores how modern communications affect politics; a new section on the Marxist power-elite model has been added to the discussion of the different political models; and a new Controversy and Debate box assesses Canada's environmental record.

- **Chapter 17 Family**: Note how the new chapter-opening vignette leads into an updated and expanded discussion of the gay marriage debate; there are new data on the extent of cohabitation; a new Global Sociology box describes arranged marriages in India.

- **Chapter 18 Religion**: Another new chapter-opening vignette examines religious tensions on campus; there is an updated discussion of cults, and a new Cyber-Society box on religious organizations spreading their messages on the Internet.

- **Chapter 19 Education**: A new Cyber-Society box looks ahead to computer-based learning in the coming century; a new Global Snapshot focuses on functional illiteracy; there is a new discussion of the history of education in Canada; one of the chapter's new Sociology Applied exercises takes students to a Web site created by students in a sociology course.

- **Chapter 20 Health and Medicine**: A new box characterizes masculinity as a leading cause of death; a new national map examines smoking in Canada; and the chapter provides updates on HIV/AIDS as well as the "right-to-die" debate.

- **Chapter 21 Population and Urbanization**: A new chapter-opening vignette considers Japan's falling birth rate; discussion focuses on both underpopulation and overpopulation; new data and projections inform the section on global population; note the new discussion of urban political economy.

- **Chapter 22 Collective Behavior and Social Movements**: Discusses the mutiny on the slave ship *Amistad* as a case of mob behaviour or rebellion; investigates new information technology as a medium for rumour; and a Weblink takes students to the WebActive home page, a guide to political activism links on the World Wide Web.

- **Chapter 23 Social Change: Traditional, Modern, and Postmodern Societies**: The dis-

cussion of modernity and postmodernity are heavily rewritten to make theory clearer to students; and a new Cyber-Society box explores how the Information Revolution is changing Canadian culture.

The latest statistical data. The third Canadian edition of *Sociology* incorporates data from the 1996 Census and makes use of data from the Internet as well as conventional bound publications of various agencies and organizations. Finally, this revision is informed by some 250 new research findings and uses current events to illustrate discussions, elevating the interest of readers.

SUPPLEMENTS

Sociology, Third Canadian Edition, is the heart of a learning package that includes a wide range of proven instructional aids. As the authors of the text, we maintain a keen interest in all of the supplements to ensure their quality and integration with the text. The supplements for this revision have been thoroughly updated, improved, and expanded.

FOR THE INSTRUCTOR

Instructor's Manual. The instructor's manual provides more than detailed chapter outlines and discussion questions; it contains statistical profiles of Canada and other nations, summaries of important developments and significant research, and supplemental lecture material for every chapter of the text.

Test Item File. A completely revised test item file is available in both printed and computerized forms. The file contains 2300 items—100 per chapter—in multiple-choice, true-false, and essay formats. Questions are identified as simple "recall" items or more complex "inferential" issues; the answers to all questions are page-referenced to the text. It is a test generator designed to allow the creation of personalized exams. It is available in Windows and Macintosh formats.

CBC/Prentice Hall Canada Video Library for Sociology. Few will dispute that video is the most dynamic supplement you can use to enhance a class. The authors and editors of Prentice Hall Canada have carefully selected videos on topics that complement *Sociology, Third Canadian Edition*, and included notes on how to use them in the classroom. An excellent video guide carefully and completely integrates the videos into your lecture. The guide has a synopsis of each video showing its relation to the chapter and discussion questions to help students focus on how concepts and theories apply to real-life situations.

Colour Transparencies. Full-colour illustrations, charts, and other visual materials from the text have been selected to make up this useful in-class tool.

MEDIA SUPPLEMENTS

Companion Website. In tandem with the text, students and professors can now take full advantage of the World Wide Web to enrich their study of sociology. The Macionis Companion Website correlates the text with related material available on the Internet. Features of the Companion Website include chapter objectives and study questions, as well as links to interesting material and information from other sites on the Web that can reinforce and enhance the content of each chapter. **Address:**

> http://www.prenticehall.ca/macionis

FOR THE STUDENT

Study Guide. This complete guide helps students review and reflect on the material presented in *Sociology*. Each of the twenty-three chapters in the Study Guide provides an overview of the corresponding chapter in the student text, summarizes its major topics and concepts, offers applied exercises, and features end-of-chapter tests with solutions.

IN APPRECIATION

The conventional practice of designating just two authors obscures the efforts of dozens of women and men that have resulted in *Sociology, Third Canadian Edition.* We would like to express our thanks to the Prentice Hall Allyn and Bacon Canada editorial team.

We also have a large debt to the members of the sales staff, the men and women who have given this text such remarkable support over the years. Thanks also to those who have directed our marketing campaign.

Thanks, too, to Anne DeMarinis for providing the book's interior design. Developmental and copy editing of the manuscript was provided by Lisa Berland and Susan Broadhurst. Andrew Winton and Sharon Houston were heroic in seeing the book through production.

It goes without saying that every colleague knows more about some topics covered in this book than the authors do. For that reason, we are grateful to the hundreds of faculty and students who have written to offer comments and suggestions. More formally, we are grateful to the following people who have reviewed this manuscript:

Cecilia Benoit, University of Victoria; Valerie A. Haines, University of Calgary; Barbara Heather, Grant MacEwan University College; William A. Johnston, University of Alberta; Ron Joudrey, Red Deer College; Patricia Kachuk, University of British Columbia; John Metcalfe, Humber College; John Pestana, John Abbott College; Jacob Peters, University of Winnipeg; Ian Ritchie, Queen's University; Dale E. Schlenker, Concordia University College of Alberta; Edith Smith, University of Ottawa; Sheldon Ungar, University of Toronto.

John J. Macionis
Linda M. Gerber

The Prentice Hall Allyn and Bacon Canada

companion Website...

Your Internet companion to the most exciting, state-of-the-art educational tools on the Web!

The Prentice Hall Canada Companion Website is easy to navigate and is organized to correspond to the chapters in this textbook. The Companion Website is comprised of four distinct, functional features:

1) **Customized Online Resources**

2) **Online Study Guide**

3) **Reference Material**

4) **Communication**

Explore the four areas in this Companion Website. Students and distance learners will discover resources for indepth study, research and communication, empowering them in their quest for greater knowledge and maximizing their potential for success in the course.

A NEW WAY TO DELIVER EDUCATIONAL CONTENT

1) Customized Online Resources

Our Companion Websites provide instructors and students with a range of options to access, view, and exchange content.

- **Syllabus Builder** provides *instructors* with the option to create online classes and construct an online syllabus linked to specific modules in the Companion Website.

- **Mailing lists** enable *instructors* and *students* to receive customized promotional literature.

- **Preferences** enable *students* to customize the sending of results to various recipients, and also to customize how the material is sent, e.g., as HTML, text, or as an attachment.

- **Help** includes an evaluation of the user's system and a tune-up area that makes updating browsers and plug-ins easier. This new feature will enhance the user's experience with Companion Websites.

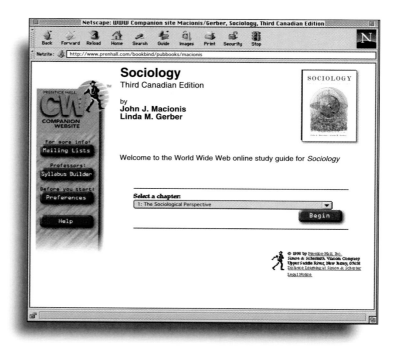

2) Online Study Guide

Interactive Study Guide modules form the core of the student learning experience in the Companion Website. These modules are categorized according to their functionality:

- True-False
- Multiple Choice

The True-False and Multiple Choice modules provide students with the ability to send answers to our grader and receive instant feedback on their progress through our Results Reporter. Coaching comments and references back to the textbook ensure that students take advantage of all resources available to enhance their learning experience.

3) Reference Material

Reference material broadens text coverage with up-to-date resources for learning. **Web Destinations** provides a directory of Web sites relevant to the subject matter in each chapter. **NetNews (Internet Newsgroups)** are a fundamental source of information about a discipline, containing a wealth of brief, opinionated postings. **NetSearch** simplifies key term search using Internet search engines.

4) Communication

Companion Websites contain the communication tools necessary to deliver courses in a **Distance Learning** environment. **Message Board** allows users to post messages and check back periodically for responses. **Live Chat** allows users to discuss course topics in real time, and enables professors to host online classes.

Communication facilities of Companion Websites provide a key element for distributed learning environments. There are two types of communication facilities currently in use in Companion Websites:

- **Message Board** – this module takes advantage of browser technology providing the users of each Companion Website with a national newsgroup to post and reply to relevant course topics.

- **Live Chat** – enables instructor-led group activities in real time. Using our chat client, instructors can display Website content while students participate in the discussion.

Companion Websites are currently available for:

- Boone/Kilgour/Kilgour: Contemporary Business Communication
- Baron/Earhard/Ozier: Psychology
- Wood/Wood/Wood/Desmarais: World of Psychology
- Troyka: Simon and Schuster Handbook for Writers

Note: CW '99 content will vary slightly from site to site depending on discipline requirements.

**PRENTICE HALL
ALLYN AND
BACON CANADA**

1870 Birchmount Road
Scarborough, Ontario M1P 2J7

To order:
Call: 1-800-567-3800
Fax: 1-800-263-7733

For samples:
Call: 1-800-850-5813
Fax: (416) 299-2539
E-mail: phabinfo_pubcanada@prenhall.com

The Companion Website can be found at:

www.prenticehall.ca/macionis

WE ARE PROUD TO BRING YOU THE

Third Canadian Edition of *Sociology*

Get ready! You are about to go on a fascinating trip to study the most amazing creatures on the face of the earth—human beings. People come in all shapes, sizes, colours, and creeds, and have created thousands of different ways of life all over the planet. Understanding our human world is the focus of sociology, which makes this one of the most important courses you can take in college or university.

As you begin this course, we would like to offer our own greeting to you. Just as important, let us offer a few suggestions about how you can get the most out of this text. There are three major themes to our story; keeping them in mind will help you organize all your reading assignments. The first theme is this: we must learn about others to understand ourselves. Sections of every chapter deal with societies around the world. As you read about another society, pay attention to not only how other people live, but think about how we live as well. The second theme is: we may be one nation, but we are many, diverse peoples. Pay attention to how social patterns differ for women and men, black people and white people, the young and the old, and people of high and low class standing. The third theme of the text is: good learning means being an active, critical reader. Don't be passive, accepting everything you read as true.

This text is part of an interactive learning package that will involve you in new information technology. You are invited to visit our Web site, www.prenticehall.ca/macionis, which offers for each text chapter, self-grading tests, suggested paper topics, still more interesting Weblinks, and a chat room. It's all there to help you, and it's all absolutely free.

Finally, we would like to hear from you. John Macionis teaches in the sociology department at Kenyon College in Gambier, Ohio, U.S.A. 43022. Linda Gerber teaches in the sociology department at the University of Guelph in Guelph, Ontario, N1G 2W1. But, in this new world of high technology, we are as near as your keyboard. Feel free to drop us a note to let us know what you think of our book or the Web site. Our e-mail addresses are macionis@kenyon.edu and lgerber@uoguelph.ca. And, if you wish, pass along suggestions for making them better. We will write back! Good luck and welcome to a new way of looking at the world.

Sincerely,
John J. Macionis
Linda M. Gerber

Begin each chapter by reading the engaging **chapter opening vignette**, a story that sparks interest as it raises a theme carried through the chapter. Eleven vignettes are new to this edition.

CHAPTER 6

SOCIAL INTERACTION IN EVERYDAY LIFE

Harold and Sybil are on their way to another couple's home in an unfamiliar section of Calgary, Alberta. They are now late because, for the last twenty minutes, they have travelled in circles looking for Creek View Drive. Harold, gripping the wheel ever more tightly, is doing a slow burn. Sybil, sitting next to him, looks straight ahead, afraid to utter a word. Both realize the evening is off to a bad start (adapted from Tannen, 1990:62).

Here we have a simple case of two people unable to locate the home of some friends. But Harold and Sybil are lost in more ways than one, since they fail to grasp why they are growing more and more enraged at their situation and at each other.

Consider the predicament from Harold's point of view. Like most men, Harold cannot tolerate getting lost. The longer he drives around, the more incompetent he feels. Sybil is seething, too, but for a different reason. She does not understand why

Harold does not pull over and ask someone where Creek View Drive is. If she were driving, she fumes to herself, they already would have arrived and would be comfortably settled with drinks in hand.

Why don't men ask for directions? Because men value their independence, they are uncomfortable asking for help (and also reluctant to accept it). To men, asking for assistance is an admission of inadequacy, a sure sign that others know something they don't. If it takes Harold a few more minutes to find Creek View Drive on his own—and to keep his self-respect in the process—he thinks the bargain is a good one.

If men pursue self-sufficiency and are sensitive to hierarchy, women are more attuned to others and strive for connectedness. Asking for help seems right to Sybil because, from her point of view, sharing information reinforces social bonds. Requesting directions seems as natural to Sybil as continuing to search on his own appears to Harold. But the two people will not resolve their situation as long as neither one understands the other's point of view.

Analyzing such examples of everyday life is the focus of this chapter. We begin by presenting many of the building blocks of common experience and then explore the almost magical way in which face-to-face interaction generates reality. The central concept is **social interaction**, *the process by which people act and react in relation to others*. Social interaction is the key to creating the reality we perceive. And we interact according to particular social guidelines.

SOCIAL STRUCTURE: A GUIDE TO EVERYDAY LIVING

October 21, 1994, Ho Chi Minh City, Vietnam. This morning we leave the ship and make our way along the docks towards the centre of Ho Chi Minh City—known to an earlier generation as Saigon. The government

Pay attention to **key concepts** presented in boldfaced type, each followed by *a precise, italicized definition*. A glossary of all key concepts is found at the end of the book.

Journal entries are short excerpts from the author's journals of travel to more than fifty countries. They offer first-hand observations that bring concepts to life and make useful cross-cultural comparisons.

How do the world's people differ? **Global Sociology** boxes provide a look at an unfamiliar culture and, in the process, help sharpen your understanding of our own way of life.

Early to Wed: A Report from Rural India

Sumitra Jogi was crying as her wedding was about to begin. Were they tears of joy? Not exactly: this "bride" is an eleven-month-old squirming in the arms of her mother. The groom? A boy of six.

estimate that thousands of children marry each year in ceremonies of this kind. "In rural Rajasthan," explains one social welfare worker, "all the girls are married by age fourteen. These are poor, illiterate families, and they don't

want to keep girls past their first menstrual cycle."

For the immediate future, Sumitra Jogi will remain with her parents. But by the time she is eight or ten, a second ceremony will mark the time for her to

The Bell Curve Debate: Are Rich People Really Smarter?

It is rare when the publication of a new book in the social sciences captures the attention of the public at large. But *The Bell Curve: Intelligence and Class Structure in American Life* by

and Murray use figures of 60 to 70 percent) is transmitted genetically from one generation to another; the remaining variability is due to environmental factors.

elite," who are, on average, not only better trained than most people but actually more intelligent.

6. Because more intelligent people are socially segregated on the col-

Do we duck the tough questions? No way! **Controversy & Debate** boxes present several points of view on many of today's most controversial issues. Use the "Continue the Debate" questions at the end of each box to assess your own views.

How is computer technology changing our way of life? A new series of **Exploring Cyber-Society** boxes gives some answers.

The Cyber-Church: Logging On to Religion

It takes only a few minutes on the Internet to discover that religion is alive and well on the World Wide Web, where you can find electronic

gious ideas, as clerics gathered in the universities of the largest cities of the day and people went to services in churches and other houses of worship

religious leaders, who founded "media congregations" no longer confined by the walls of a single building. During the 1990s, the Internet accelerated this

Is Getting Rich "the Survival of the Fittest"?

"The survival of the fittest." We have all heard this phrase, another way of saying "the law of the jungle." Actually, the words were coined by one of sociology's pio-

like a jungle, with the "fittest" people rising to wealth and power and the "deficient" gradually sinking to a state of miserable poverty.

It is no surprise that Spencer's

ability or unwillingness to measure up in a competitive world. Indeed, social Darwinism actually condemned social welfare programs as an evil because they penalized society's "best" mem-

Do you realize how much people differ right here "at home"? **Social Diversity Boxes** focus on multicultural issues and amplify the voices of people of colour and women.

How do people in this country differ from people in other countries? **Global Snapshots** offer a quick and insightful comparison between Canada and other nations of the world.

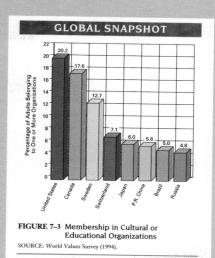

FIGURE 7–3 Membership in Cultural or Educational Organizations
SOURCE: World Values Survey (1994).

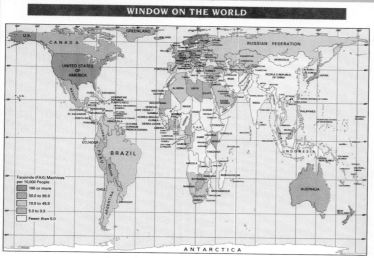

GLOBAL MAP 4–1 High Technology in Global Perspective

Countries with traditional cultures ignore or even resist technological innovation; nations with highly rationalized ways of life eagerly embrace such changes. Facsimile (fax) machines, one common form of technology, are numerous in high-income countries such as Canada, where millions of faxes fly along the "information superhighway" every day. In low-income nations, by contrast, fax machines are unknown to most people. Notice that, in Asia, fax machines are widely available only in Japan, South Korea, Taiwan, and the business centres of Hong Kong and Singapore.
SOURCE: *Peters Atlas of the World* (1990).

Would you like to learn more about the world? **Window on the World** global maps (twenty-six in all) highlight contrasts between rich and poor countries on issues such as income disparity, the lives of women, and HIV infection. All the maps use a non-Eurocentric projection by cartographer Arno Peters that accurately shows the relative size of the continents.

Do people in the Prairies really differ from those in the Maritimes? Find out by looking at the **Seeing Ourselves** national maps that offer a close-up look at life in Canada's provinces and territories, highlighting suicide rates, household income, unemployment, chance of divorce, and more.

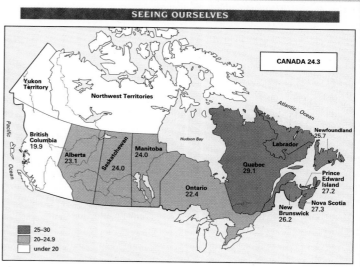

CANADA MAP 20–1 Percentage of the Population 11 Years and Over Smoking Cigarettes Daily, 1994–95
SOURCE: Caragata, 1998:30.

cyber.scope

PART II
HOW TECHNOLOGY IS CHANGING OUR WAY OF LIFE

Marshall McLuhan (1969) summed up his pioneering research in the study of communications this way: "Any new technology tends to create a new human environment." In other words, technology affects not just how we work, but it shapes and colours our entire way of life. In this second cyber.scope, we pause to reflect on some of the ways the Information Revolution is changing our culture and society.

The Information Revolution and Cultural Values

Chapter 3 ("Culture") noted the importance members of our society attach to material comfort. Throughout our history, many people have defined "success" to mean earning a good income and enjoying the things money will buy, including a home, car, and clothing.

But some analysts wonder if, as we enter the next century, our values may shift from a single-minded focus on the accumulation of "things" (the products of industrial technology) to gaining new kinds of "ideas" (the product of information technology). Such "new age" ideas range from "experiences" (including travel and countless experiences with virtual reality[1]) to "well-being," including the "self-actualization" that has become popular in recent decades (Newman, 1991).

Socialization in the Computer Age

Half a century ago, television rewrote the rule for socialization in Canada and, as Chapter 5 ("Socialization") explained, young people now spend more time watching TV than they do talking to their parents. Today, in the emerging Information Society, screens are not just for television, they are our windows into a cyber-world in which we look to computers to link, entertain, and educate us. But this trend towards "cyber-socialization" raises several important questions.

First, will the spread of computer-based information erode the regional diversity that has marked this country's history, setting off the west coast from Ontario and the prairies from Quebec? New information technology links Canada to the rest of the world. As a result we could see an enhanced Canadian culture as well as a more global culture. Marshall McLuhan predicts a weakening of national identities in response to new information technology.

Second, how will this "cyber-culture" affect our children? Will having computers at the centre of their lives be good for them? For most children, at least, computer-based images and information already play a significant role in the socialization process. Will this trend lessen the importance of parents in children's lives, as television did? Cyber-socialization can cer-

[1] For example, take the virtual Director's Tour of works in the Art Gallery of Ontario (http://www.ago.on.ca/), or visit Canada's capital city via Virtual Ottawa (http://www.intoronto.com/inottawa.html).

Almost unlimited access to information can be a mixed blessing, as parents can well understand. How can we prevent children from gaining access to pornography or other objectionable material on the Internet? Or, should we?

people: "MrMaine," "Ferret," and "RedWine."

The growing popularity of computer chat gives us a chance to highlight ways in which online interaction differs from more conventional modes of interaction. After studying online interaction, Dennis Waskul (1997) explains that the self transmitted via computer is "disembodied." Using Erving Goffman's dramaturgical approach (see Chapter 6), Waskul notes that computer technology screens out a host of "cues" about people's identities—where they are, what they look like, how they dress, and their age and sex—and conveys only the stylized identities they choose to present.

Cyberspace thus affords us great freedom to "try on" identities with few, if any, lasting consequences. As one chat-room participant ex-

... e ... I am"

... century, ... ho op- ... ution, ... g new ... could ... Lud- ... their ... at the ... would ... erally, ... 97). ... t their ... hange, ... le op- ... evolu- ... ites, as ... many ... at we ... into a ... ng to ... v new ... us. ... d us, ... er so- ... hology

does not simply exist *in* the world, it *changes* the world, pushing human lives in one direction while closing off other alternatives. As a people, we tend to venerate technology as good in and of itself, Theodore Roszak (1986) points out, but, in the process, we give up the power to decide for ourselves how we should live. Putting computers in the classroom is no substitute for good teaching, Roszak declares; we would do well to remember that no computer ever created a painting, penned a poem, or composed a symphony. And, perhaps most important of all, computers have no capacity to address ethical questions about right and wrong.

Living in a forward-looking culture, we easily imagine the benefits of new technology. But we need to remember that, just as technology can serve us, it also holds the potential to be destructive. After all, the Luddites were not anti-technology; they simply wanted to be sure that technology responded to human needs—and not the other way around. ▣

"On the Internet, nobody knows you're a dog."

Peter Steiner © 1993 from *The New Yorker* Collection. All rights reserved.

Have you noticed how rapidly the world is changing? **Cyber. Scopes** are a new series of five essays spread throughout the book (one follows each of the text's five parts) that explains new information technology and points out many of the ways the Information Revolution is involved in the issues raised in the chapters you have just finished reading. The Cyber. Scope essays highlight trends both in Canada and throughout the world.

SUMMARY

1. Science provides the logical foundation of sociological research and, more broadly, helps us to critically evaluate information we encounter every day.
2. Two basic requirements for sociological investigation are (1) viewing the world from a sociological perspective, and (2) being curious and asking questions about society.
3. Measurement is the process of determining the value of a variable in any specific case. Sound measurement is both reliable and valid.
4. A goal of science is discovering how variables are related. Correlation means that two or more variables change value together. Knowledge about cause-and-effect relationships is more powerful, however, because a researcher can use an independent variable to predict change in a dependent variable.
5. Although investigators select topics according to their personal interests, the scientific ideal of objectivity demands that they try to suspend personal values and biases as they conduct research.
6. Human curiosity and imagination must infuse the scientific method; moreover, researchers must always bring their data to life through interpretation.

CRITICAL THINKING QUESTIONS

1. What does it mean to state that there are various kinds of truth? What is the basic rationale for relying on science as a way of knowing?
2. What sorts of measures do scientists adopt as they strive for objectivity? Why do some sociologists consider objectivity an undesirable goal?
3. Identify several ways in which sociological research is similar to—and different from— research in the natural sciences.
4. What considerations lead a sociologist to select one method of research over another?

SOCIOLOGY APPLIED

1. During one class period, imagine that you are observing your instructor in an effort to assess that individual's skills as a teacher. How would you operationalize "good teaching"? What kinds of behaviours might you note as relevant to this task? Do you think you can evaluate a teacher after observing a single class?
2. Drop by to see at least three sociology instructors (or other social science instructors) during their office hours. Ask each the extent to which sociology is an objective science. Do they agree about the character of their discipline? Why or why not?
3. Read the "Code of Ethics" of the American Sociological Association, available on their Web site (www.asanet.org). Summarize the principles there by writing a description of a "professional sociologist."
4. Conduct a practice interview with a roommate or friend on the general topic of "What do you expect to gain from going to university?" Before the actual interview, prepare a list of specific questions or issues you think are relevant. Afterwards, give some thought to why carrying out an effective interview is much harder than it may initially seem.

WEBLINKS

www.d.umn.edu/cla/faculty/jhamlin/1400/weber.html
The Max Weber site contains a brief biography and an overview of Weber's sociological theories and methodology.

129.97.58.10/discipline/sociology/research.html
Maintained by the University of Waterloo library, Doing Research in Sociology contains links to information sources on how to do research in sociology, including searching CD-ROM databases, citing electronic sources, and steps to effective library research.

www.sociology.org/home.html
The *Electronic Journal of Sociology* has been publishing full-text articles online since September 1994 and provides a keyword search function to help readers locate references to specific topics.

www.statcan.ca/start.html
Statistics Canada offers a variety of resources, including Canada at a Glance, Latest News from Statistics Canada, Virtual Library, Internet Services at Statistics Canada, Electronic Marketplace, Other Canadian Government Servers, and Other Statistical Web Servers.

Albina Kosiec Felski, *The Circus*, 1971
Oil on canvas, 48 × 48 in. (121.9 × 121.9 cm). National Museum of American Art, Smithsonian Institution, Washington, DC/Art Resource, NY.

CHAPTER 1

THE SOCIOLOGICAL PERSPECTIVE

Imagine that a stranger walks into your classroom and announces he can tell you the income of your parents; whether or not you will marry and how long your marriage will last; how many children you will have; how much money you will make after graduation; how long you will live; and the cause of your death. Who is this? A psychic looking into a crystal ball? No, it's a sociologist. With their knowledge of patterns and trends, sociologists can draw certain conclusions about your past, present, and future. Let's take a closer look at some of these conclusions:

- If you are attending a Canadian university, your classmates probably come from families in the top half of the income ladder. If you are in a community college, your classmates probably come from families of more modest means.

- Almost 90 percent of your classmates will marry, half by the time they are thirty. About half of those who marry will go through a divorce, on average twelve years after tying the knot.

- You will have smaller families (one or two children) than your parents did. You or your spouse will likely choose to be surgically sterilized to prevent further childbirths.

- If you acquire a bachelor's degree, your annual income will be about 25 percent higher than if you had received a community college diploma; earning a master's or doctoral degree would increase your income by another 38 or 44 percent, respectively.

- On average, you and your classmates can expect to live into your seventies. Here, however, women have the edge: they will outlive men by about six years, with most women celebrating their eightieth birthday. When you die, the odds are that will happen in a hospital and as a result of heart disease, cancer, or a stroke.

These are the facts, but you are still left with the question of why—why do human lives seem to follow certain predictable patterns? The truth is that our lives do not unfold according to sheer chance; nor do people live in isolation, relying completely on what philosophers call "free will." On the contrary, although we make many important decisions every day, we do so within a larger arena called "society"—a family, a campus, a nation, an entire world.

The essential wisdom of sociology is that the social world guides our actions and values just as the seasons influence our activities and clothing. And, because sociologists know a great deal about how society works, they can analyze and predict our behaviour with surprising accuracy.

We can easily grasp the power of society over the individual by imagining how different our world would be had we been born in place of any of these children from, respectively, Guatemala, Sri Lanka, South Africa, Botswana, People's Republic of China, and El Salvador.

THE SOCIOLOGICAL PERSPECTIVE

Formally, the discipline of **sociology** is *the systematic study of human society*. At the heart of sociology is a distinctive point of view.

SEEING THE GENERAL IN THE PARTICULAR

Peter Berger (1963) characterized the sociological perspective as *seeing the general in the particular*. He meant that sociologists identify general patterns in the behaviour of particular individuals. While acknowledging that each individual is unique, in other words, sociologists recognize that society acts differently on various *categories* of people (say, children compared to adults, women versus men, the rich as opposed to the poor). We begin to think sociologically as we start to realize how the general categories into which we happen to fall shape our particular life experiences.

At a 1997 Toronto conference, sociology professor Donna Winslow illustrated this perspective in her report on a study commissioned by the federal government. Her 400-page tome, *The Canadian Airborne Regiment: A Socio-Cultural Inquiry*, attempts to explain the atrocities committed by Canadian peacekeepers in Somalia—not in terms of the characteristics of the individual soldiers who brutally murdered a Somali civilian but in terms of the combat or warrior culture within which they functioned. The culture of the Airborne regiment, which focused on war-making, was enhanced by recruitment, the chain of command, training, and even the nature of weapons at hand. Training for the peacekeeping role, in the areas of ethics and technique, was minimal: soldiers were unprepared in terms of recruitment, attitude, skill, or equipment to engage in problem-solving, negotiation, or dealing with high-stress civilian situations with milder force (perhaps riot gear and dogs). Despite Canada's commitment to peacekeeping, our military has continued to prepare soldiers for war instead of peace, thereby setting the scene for violence towards civilians (Skelton, 1997). The explanation lies in the position within a structural and cultural environment, not in individual personality.

Each chapter of this text illustrates the general impact of society on the actions, thoughts, and feelings of particular people. For instance, the differences that distinguish children from adults reflect not just biological maturity: by attaching meaning to age, society creates what we experience as distinct stages of life. Following these age-scripts, we expect children to be "dependent" and adults to behave "responsibly." And, further along the life course, our society defines old age as a time of diminished standing and withdrawal from earlier routines.

How do we know that society (and not simply biology) is at work here? Looking back in time or around the world today, we see that societies define the stages of life quite differently. The Hopi (an Arizona Pueblo people) confer surprising independence on children while in Abkhasia (part of the Russian Federation) elderly people enjoy tremendous social clout and esteem. Through storytelling, the Inuit elders of northern Canada have been responsible for transmitting historical knowledge, traditional culture, and legend to the younger members of their society.

A sociological look around us reveals the power of class position as well. Chapters entitled "Social Stratification" and "Social Class in Canada" provide ample evidence that how we live (and even how long we live) has a great deal to do with our ranking in the societal hierarchy.

Seeing the world sociologically also makes us aware of the importance of gender. As the chapter "Sex and Gender" points out, every society attaches meaning to being one sex or the other, according women and men different kinds of work and family responsibilities. Individuals experience the workings of society as they encounter advantages and opportunities characteristic of each sex.

SEEING THE STRANGE IN THE FAMILIAR

Especially at the beginning, using the sociological perspective amounts to *seeing the strange in the familiar*. This does not mean that sociologists focus on the bizarre elements of society. Rather, observing sociologically requires giving up the familiar idea that human behaviour is simply a matter of what people decide to do in favour of the initially strange notion that society guides our thoughts and deeds.

For individualistic North Americans, learning to "see" how society affects us may take a bit of practice. Asked why you "chose" to enrol at your particular

Whenever we come upon people whose habits differ from our own, we become more aware of social patterns. This is why travel is an excellent way to stimulate the sociological perspective. But even within Canada there is striking cultural diversity, which prompts us to become conscious of our social surroundings.

university or college, you might offer any of the following reasons:

I wanted to stay close to home.

This college has the best women's soccer team.

A journalism degree from this university ensures a good job.

My girlfriend goes to school here.

I wasn't accepted by the school I really wanted to attend.

Such responses are certainly grounded in reality for the people expressing them. But do they tell the whole story? The sociological perspective provides additional insights that may not be readily apparent.

Thinking sociologically about university and college attendance, we might first realize that for young people throughout most of the world, post-secondary education is all but out of reach. Moreover, had we lived a century or two ago, the "choice" to go to university or college probably would not have been an option. But even now, a look around your classroom suggests that social forces still have much to do with whether or not one pursues higher education. Typically, university and college students are relatively young—generally between eighteen and twenty-four years of age. Why? Because in our society university and college attendance is associated with this period of life. But more than age is involved, because the majority of university-age people in Canada is not enrolled in university.

Race is also involved. As the chapter dealing with race and ethnicity will point out, people of differing racial backgrounds vary in the likelihood of obtaining a post-secondary certificate. Moreover, the distinctions among racial or ethnic groups are large. For example, in Canada, adults of British and French origin are twice as likely to have achieved post-secondary certification than their aboriginal counterparts. However, people of Black[1] and especially of Asian origin are more likely to have achieved post-secondary certification than British- or French-origin individuals.

Another factor, alluded to in the opening of this chapter, is that higher education is costly, so that university students (and particularly those enrolled in professional programs such as medicine) tend to come from families with above-average incomes (Guppy and Arai, 1993).

Furthermore, while it's not necessarily the case, university graduates can expect to begin employment at and continue at a higher wage level than community college graduates. Since, in Canada, most college and university expenses are paid for by students and their families, those with modest means are likely to choose community colleges over universities. As a result, people from upper-middle-class and higher-class backgrounds tend to be overrepresented at universities (Levin, 1993). Older students with job and family responsibilities also favour community colleges, taking advantage not only of lower costs but of part-time and evening programs. Universities are typically the choice of younger, more affluent students who are able to study full-time. Although it initially may seem strange to explain personal choices in terms of social forces, the sociological perspective empowers us as we come to understand how our own experiences—including the opportunities and barriers we face—are linked to where we are placed in the vast society around us.

INDIVIDUALITY IN SOCIAL CONTEXT

The sociological perspective often challenges common sense by revealing that human behaviour is not as individualistic as we may think. For most of us, daily living carries a heavy load of personal responsibility, so that we pat ourselves on the back when we enjoy success and kick ourselves when things go wrong. Proud of our individuality, even in painful times, we resist the idea that we act in socially patterned ways.

---

[1] The labelling of people is a highly charged political issue. We use "Black" here because that is the designation used by Statistics Canada.

Perhaps the most compelling demonstration of how social forces affect human behaviour is the study of suicide. Why? Because nothing is a more personal "choice" than the decision to take one's own life. This is why Emile Durkheim (1858–1917), a pioneer of sociology writing a century ago, chose suicide as a topic of research. He was able to demonstrate that social forces figure in the apparently isolated act of self-destruction.

Durkheim began by examining suicide records in and around his native France. The statistics clearly showed that some categories of people were more likely than others to choose to take their own lives. Specifically, Durkheim found that men, Protestants, wealthy people, and the unmarried each had significantly higher suicide rates than women, Catholics and Jews, the poor, and married people. Durkheim deduced that these differences corresponded to people's degree of *social integration*. Low suicide rates characterized categories of people with strong social ties; high suicide rates were found among those who were more socially isolated and individualistic.

In the male-dominated societies studied by Durkheim, men certainly had more autonomy than women. Whatever freedom's advantages for men, concluded Durkheim, autonomy means lower social integration, which contributes to a higher male suicide rate. Likewise, more individualistic Protestants were more prone to suicide than Catholics and Jews, whose rituals foster stronger social ties. The wealthy clearly have much more freedom of action than the poor but, once again, at the cost of a higher suicide rate. Furthermore, single people, with weaker social ties than married people, are also at greater risk of suicide. Finally, rapid social change weakens the norms and values that define and stabilize the position of the individual within a social context.

A century later, statistical evidence continues to support Durkheim's analysis. Figure 1–1 shows the suicide rates for males and females from 1951 to 1995: the suicide rates are consistently higher for men than for women. The tendency for males to have higher suicides rates is true across all age groups and throughout the provinces and territories of Canada (Statistics Canada, 84-209, 1995). Following Durkheim's argument, we can conclude that the higher suicide rate among men is due to their greater affluence and autonomy in Canadian society. Interestingly, male suicide rates are highest (over 30 per 100 000 population) in Quebec and the Northwest Territories, where marriage rates are the lowest, and in the Yukon, where the divorce rate is the highest. In addition, these areas are still undergoing substantial social change. Young people in some of Canada's aboriginal communities have suicide rates five or more times higher than those of other Canadians—a shocking twenty times higher for young native females in some northern Ontario communities (Gray, 1996). Aboriginal communities are still experiencing massive social change and upheaval which, in turn, affect levels of integration.

Thus, we observe general social patterns in even the most personal actions of individuals. Social forces are complex, of course, but we can see that linked to gender they produce patterns with regard to suicide. Gender operates consistently: men are more prone to suicide than are women. The rates may change over time and across space, but even in the case of suicide we are able to see the impact of social conditions.

THE IMPORTANCE OF GLOBAL PERSPECTIVE

December 10, 1994, Fez, Morocco. This medieval city—its labyrinth of narrow streets and alleyways alive with the sounds and movements of playing children, veiled women, and men conducting business over donkeys laden with goods—has changed little over the centuries. We stand in northwest Africa, only a few hundred miles from the more familiar rhythms of Europe; yet this place seems a thousand years away. Never have we had such an adventure! Never have we thought so much about home!

In recent years, as even the farthest reaches of the earth have become more easily accessible through

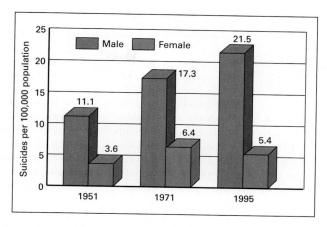

FIGURE 1–1 Suicide Rates by Sex, 1951, 1971, 1995
SOURCE: Colombo (1992:61); Statistics Canada 84-209, 1995.

advances in technology, many academic disciplines have incorporated a **global perspective**, *the study of the larger world and our society's place in it.* How does a global perspective enhance sociology?

First, global awareness is a logical extension of the sociological perspective. Sociology's basic insight is that our positions in our society profoundly affect our individual experiences. It stands to reason that the position of our society in the larger world system, in turn, affects everyone in Canada. The "Global Sociology" box provides a brief sketch of our "global village," indicating that people the world over are far from equal in terms of quality of life.

Global Map 1–1 provides a visual guide to the relative economic development of the world's countries. The world's **high-income countries** are *industrialized*

One important reason to gain a global understanding is that, living in a high-income society, we scarcely can appreciate the suffering that goes on in much of the world. The life of this Rwandan boy has been shredded by civil war. But even in more peaceful nations of Africa, children have less than a fifty-fifty chance to grow to adulthood.

The Global Village: A Social Snapshot of Our World

The planet Earth is home to some 5.8 billion people who reside in cities and across the countryside of 191 nations. To grasp the social "shape" of the world, imagine for a moment the planet's population reduced to a single settlement of 1000 people. A visit to this "global village" would reveal that more than half (575) of the inhabitants are Asians, including 200 citizens of the People's Republic of China. Next in terms of numbers we would find 130 Africans, 125 Europeans, and about 100 Latin Americans. North Americans—including people from Canada, the United States, and Mexico—would account for a scant 65 residents.

A study of the settlement's ways of life would yield some startling conclusions: the village is a rich place, with a seemingly endless array of goods and services for sale. Yet most of the inhabitants can do no more than imagine such treasures, since half of the village's total income is earned by just 150 individuals.

Food is the greatest concern of the majority. Every year, workers produce more than enough food to feed everyone; even so, half the village's people—including most of the children—are poorly nourished and many fall asleep hungry. The worst-off 200 residents, who lack food, safe drinking water, and secure shelter, do not have the strength to work and are vulnerable to life-threatening diseases.

Villagers boast of their community's many schools, including universities and colleges. About seventy-five inhabitants have completed a university degree and a few even have doctorates, but half of the village's people can neither read nor write.

As Canadians, we stand among the most prosperous people of the global village. The sociological perspective reminds us that many of the achievements we attribute to our personal abilities are also products of the privileged position we occupy in the worldwide social system.

SOURCE: United Nations data and calculations by John J. Macionis.

---

nations in which most people enjoy material abundance.[2] High-income countries include the United States and Canada, most of Western Europe, Israel, Japan, and Australia. Taken together, these forty societies generate most of the world's goods and services and control most of the planet's wealth. On average, individuals in these countries live well, not because they are particularly bright or exceptionally hard-working, but because they had the good fortune to be born in an affluent region of the world.

A second category of societies includes the world's **middle-income countries**, which are *nations characterized by limited industrialization and moderate personal income*. Individuals living in any of the roughly ninety nations at this level of economic development—which include the countries of Eastern Europe and most of Latin America—are more likely to live in rural areas than in cities; to walk or ride bicycles, scooters, or animals rather than to drive automobiles; and to receive only a few years of schooling. Most middle-income countries also have marked social

inequality, so that while some people are extremely rich (the sheiks of oil-producing nations in the Middle East, for example), many more lack safe housing and adequate nutrition.

Finally, about half of the world's people live in the sixty **low-income countries**, which are *nations with little industrialization in which severe poverty is the rule*. As Global Map 1–1 shows, most of the poorest societies in the world are in Africa and Asia. Here, again, a small number of people in each of these nations is rich, but the majority barely get by with poor housing, unsafe water, too little food, little or no sanitation, and, perhaps most seriously of all, little chance to improve their lives.

The disparity between the "haves" and "have-nots" in the world is presented in another way in Table 1–1, which lists the ten best countries in the world when ranked according to the Human Development Index formulated by the United Nations in 1990. This controversial standard measures the quality of life in a country by factoring together traditional measurements such as income and less quantifiable factors such as political freedom, the environment, and racial and gender equality. Canada ranks at the very top of the list of the best places to live in the world, followed by other industrial countries such as the United States, Japan, and Western European

---

[2] The text uses this terminology as opposed to the traditional, but outdated, terms "First World," "Second World," and "Third World." Chapter 11 ("Global Stratification") delves into the reasons for this shift.

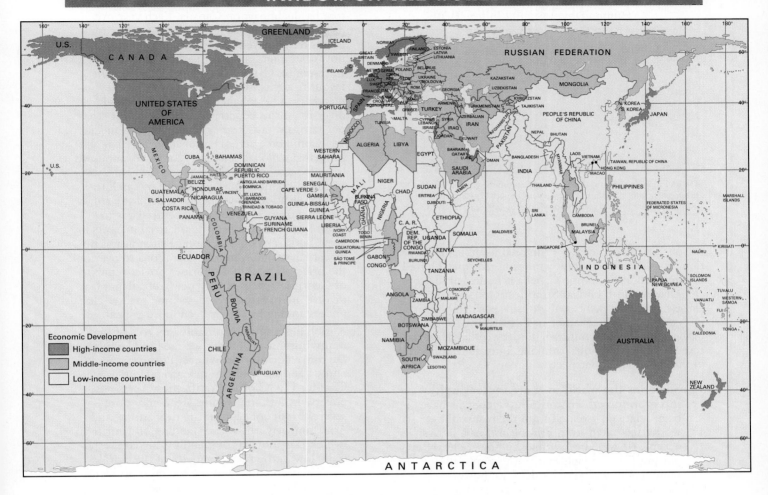

GLOBAL MAP 1–1 Economic Development in Global Perspective*

In high-income countries—Canada, the United States, most of the nations of Western Europe, Israel, Australia, and Japan—industrial technology provides people, on average, with material plenty. Middle-income countries—found throughout Latin America and including the nations of Eastern Europe—have limited industrial capacity and offer their people a standard of living that, while about average for the world as a whole, is far below that familiar to most people in Canada. The populations of these nations also encompass a significant share of poor people who barely scrape by with inadequate housing and diet. In the low-income countries of the world, poverty is severe and extensive. Although small numbers of elites live very well in these poorest nations, the majority of people struggle to survive on a small fraction of the income common in Canada.

*Note: Data for this map are provided by the World Bank and the United Nations. High-income countries have per-capita gross national product (GNP) of at least $10 000. Many are far richer than this, however; the figure for Canada stands at more than $20 000. Middle-income countries have a per-capita GNP ranging from $2500 to $10 000. Low-income countries have a per-capita GNP below $2500. Figures used here reflect the new United Nations "purchasing power parities" system. Rather than directly converting income figures to U.S. dollars, this calculation estimates the local purchasing power of each domestic currency.

Prepared by John J. Macionis using data from United Nations Development Programme (1995) and the World Bank (1995). Map projection from *Peters Atlas of the World* (1990).

TABLE 1–1 The Ten Best Places to Live in the World According to the United Nations Human Development Index (HDI)

Country	HDI Value
Canada	0.960
France	0.946
Norway	0.943
United States	0.942
Iceland	0.942
Netherlands	0.940
Japan	0.940
Finland	0.940
New Zealand	0.937
Sweden	0.936

SOURCE: United Nations Development Programme (1997), "Human Development Index," Human Development Report 1997 [online]. Available at www.undp.org/undp/hdro/hdi1.htm [1998, February 9].

nations. Needless to say, Prime Minister Jean Chrétien is pleased to draw attention to the United Nations report each time Canada is ranked at the top.

Chapter 11 ("Global Stratification") explores the causes and consequences of global wealth and poverty in detail. But every chapter of this text highlights life in the world beyond our own borders. Why? Here are three reasons why global thinking figures prominently in the sociological perspective.

1. **Societies the world over are increasingly interconnected.** Historically, Canadians have been relatively isolated from the rest of the world: separated from Europe and Asia by vast oceans, we have been influenced most clearly by our immediate neighbour to the south (the United States). In recent decades, however, Canada and the rest of the world have become linked as never before. People are whisked across continents or oceans in hours, while new electronic devices transmit pictures, sounds, and written documents around the globe in seconds. E-mail and Internet chat groups have freed social interaction from the constraints of geography. Economic, social, and cultural contact is instantaneous, intense, and global.

   One consequence of this new technology, as later chapters explain, is that people all over the world now share many tastes in music, clothing, and food. With their economic clout, high-income nations such as Canada and, especially, the United States cast a global shadow, influencing members of other societies who eagerly embrace Coke and McDonald's hamburgers, rock-and-roll music, and even the English language—which dominates in business, science, and entertainment.

As the North American way of life is projected onto much of the world, the larger world, too, has its impact on Canada. Each year over most of the past decade, 200 000 or more immigrants have arrived here, adding to the historical flow of immigration that has built our country. In response, Canada has adopted many of the favourite sights, sounds, and tastes of its new members. The enhanced racial and cultural diversity of this country is apparent in our streets, our festivals, our grocery stores, and the media.

Commerce across national borders has also propelled a global economy. Large corporations manufacture and market goods worldwide, just as global financial markets linked by satellite communications now operate around the clock. Today, no stock trader in Toronto dares to ignore what happens in the financial markets in New York, Tokyo, and Hong Kong, just as no wheat farmer in Manitoba can afford to overlook the price of grain in the former Soviet republic of Georgia. Because many new Canadian jobs involve international trade, gaining greater global understanding has never been more critical.

2. **A global perspective enables us to see that many human problems we face in Canada are far more serious elsewhere.** Poverty is certainly a serious problem in Canada, but, as Chapter 11 ("Global Stratification") explains, poverty is both more widespread and more severe throughout Latin America, Africa, and Asia. Similarly, the social standing of women (which is below that of men in Canada) is especially low in the poor countries of the world.

   Then, too, many of the toughest problems we grapple with at home are global in scope. Environmental decline is one example: the world is a single ecosystem in which the action (or inaction) of one nation has implications for all others.

3. **Thinking globally is an excellent way to learn more about ourselves.** We cannot walk the streets of a distant city without becoming keenly aware of what it means to live in Canada. Making these comparisons also leads to unexpected lessons. For instance, Chapter 11 ("Global Stratification") transports us to a garbage dump in Manila, the Philippines, that serves as a home for thousands of people. There, despite a desperate lack of basic material comforts, we are surprised to find children thriving in the love and support of family members. Such discoveries prompt us to think about why poverty in Canada so often involves isolation and anger, and whether material things—so crucial to our defin-

ition of a "rich" life—are the best way to gauge human well-being.

In sum, in an increasingly interconnected world, we fully know ourselves only to the extent that we understand others.

THE SOCIOLOGICAL PERSPECTIVE IN EVERYDAY LIFE

Encountering people who differ from ourselves—whether around the world or in our own home towns—inevitably reminds us of the power of social forces to shape our lives. But two other kinds of situations stimulate a sociological outlook, even before we take a first course in sociology.

SOCIOLOGY AND SOCIAL MARGINALITY

Sociological thinking is especially common among social "outsiders." Social marginality is something we all experience from time to time. For some categories of people, however, being an outsider is part of daily living. The more acute people's social marginality, the more likely they are to be keenly aware of their surroundings and to embrace the sociological perspective.

A Canadian aboriginal person, for example, soon learns how much race or visible minority status affects personal experience. But white people, who are the dominant majority, think about race only occasionally and often fail to recognize its impacts; if they do acknowledge that race has consequences, they may imagine that race affects only people of colour—not themselves as well.

Much the same is true of women, gay people, people with disabilities, and the very old. All those relegated to the outskirts of social life typically become aware of social patterns others take for granted. This means that one develops a sociological perspective by stepping back a bit from familiar routines and looking at one's life with new awareness and curiosity.

SOCIOLOGY AND SOCIAL CRISIS

Periods of massive social change or social crisis throw everyone a little off balance, and this, too, stimulates sociological vision. C. Wright Mills (1959), a noted U.S. sociologist, illustrated this principle by recalling the Great Depression of the 1930s. As the nation's unemployment rate soared to 25 percent, people out of work could not help but see general social forces at work in their particular lives. Rather than personalizing their plight by claiming, "Something is wrong with me; I can't find a job," they took a more socio-

logical approach, observing: "The economy has collapsed; there are no jobs to be found!"

Conversely, sociological thinking often fosters social change. The more we learn about the operation of "the system," the more we may wish to change it in some way. As women and men have confronted the power of gender, for example, many have actively tried to reduce the traditional differences that distinguish men and women.

In short, an introduction to sociology is an invitation to learn a new way of looking at familiar patterns of social life. At this point, we might well consider whether this invitation is worth accepting. In other words, what are the benefits of learning to use the sociological perspective?

BENEFITS OF THE SOCIOLOGICAL PERSPECTIVE

As we learn to use the sociological perspective, we can readily apply it to our daily lives. Doing so provides four general benefits.

1. **The sociological perspective challenges familiar understandings of ourselves and of others, so that we can critically assess the truth of commonly held assumptions.** Thinking sociologically, in other words, we may realize that ideas we have taken for granted are not always true. As we have already seen, a good example of a widespread but misleading "truth" is that Canada is populated with "autonomous individuals" who are personally responsible for their lives. Thinking this way, we are sometimes too quick to praise particularly successful people as superior to others whose more modest achievements mark them as personally deficient. A sociological approach prompts us to ask whether these beliefs are actually true and, to the extent that they are not, why they are so widely held.

2. **The sociological perspective enables us to assess both the opportunities and the constraints that characterize our lives.** Sociological thinking leads us to see that, for better or worse, our society operates in a particular way. Moreover, in the game of life, we may decide how to play our cards, but it is society that deals us the hands. The more we understand the game, then, the more effective players we will be. Sociology helps us to understand what we are likely and unlikely to accomplish for ourselves and how we can pursue our goals most effectively.

3. **The sociological perspective empowers us to be active participants in our society.** Without

an awareness of how society operates, we are likely to accept the status quo. The greater our understanding of the operation of society, however, the more we can take an active part in shaping social life. For some, this may mean embracing society as it is; others, however, may attempt nothing less than changing the entire world in some way. The discipline of sociology advocates no one particular political orientation, and sociologists themselves weigh in at many points across the political spectrum. But evaluating any aspect of social life—whatever one's eventual goal—depends on the ability to identify social forces and to assess their consequences.

Some forty years ago, C. Wright Mills (1959) wrote that the "sociological imagination," an understanding of the interplay between the individual and society, is a key source of change. By thinking sociologically, Mills maintained, people recognize that many others grapple with the same problems that they do. In this way, people can join together, turning personal problems into political issues.

4. **The sociological perspective helps us to recognize human diversity and to confront the challenges of living in a diverse world.** Sociological thinking highlights our world's remarkable social variety. North Americans represent a scant 5 percent of the world's population, and, as the remaining chapters of this book explain, many of our fellow human beings live in societies dramatically different from our own. Like people everywhere, we tend to define our own way of life as proper and "natural," and dismiss the lifestyles of those who differ from ourselves. But the sociological perspective encourages us to think critically about the relative strengths and weaknesses of all ways of life—including our own.

APPLIED SOCIOLOGY

The benefits of sociology go well beyond intellectual growth. Indeed, sociology is sound training for literally hundreds of jobs in various fields, including advertising, banking, criminal justice, education, government, health care, public relations, and research (Billson and Huber, 1993).

Sociology has played an important role in the development of Canadian social policy. For example, the medicare system arose out of the Royal Commission on Health Services (1964–65), which was strongly influenced by sociological research. Other royal commissions, including the Royal Commission on Bilingualism and Biculturalism (1963–69) and the Royal

Commission on the Status of Women in Canada (1967–70), were also based, in part, on the findings of sociologists. In Quebec, La Commission d'enquête sur l'enseignement au Québec (1963–66) drastically altered the educational system in that province. More recently, First Nations peoples are hoping that the Royal Commission on Aboriginal Affairs (which was completed in 1997, just in time for a new aboriginal affairs minister, Jane Stewart) will have positive effects on public policy. Many sociologists have done policy-relevant work outside the context of royal commissions: Raymond Breton (University of Toronto professor and former director of Montreal's Institute for Research on Public Policy) did influential work in the areas of ethnicity, cultural boundaries, Quebec nationalism, regionalism, and constitutional change.

Currently, most men and women who continue beyond a bachelor's degree to pursue advanced training in sociology go on to careers in teaching and research. But an increasing proportion of professional sociologists work in all sorts of applied fields. Evaluation research constitutes one type of applied sociology. In today's cost-conscious political climate, Canada's government and corporate administrators must evaluate the effectiveness of virtually every kind of program and policy. Sociologists—especially those with advanced research skills—are in high demand for this kind of work. Our criminal justice system employs numerous sociologists, as do the firms that engage in polling of opinion and voting intent. Journalists, in print or on screen, often produce good sociology while serving as Canada's "eyes" to the world: they are involved in data gathering, analysis, and presentation of results to a wide public.

THE ORIGINS OF SOCIOLOGY

Like the "choices" made by individuals, major historical events rarely just happen. They are typically products of powerful social forces that are always complex and only partly predictable. So it was with the emergence of sociology itself. Having described the discipline's distinctive perspective and surveyed some of its benefits, we can now consider how and why sociology emerged in the first place.

Although human beings have mused about society since the beginning of our history, sociology is of relatively recent origin. It is among the youngest academic disciplines—newer than history, physics, or economics, for example. Only in 1838 did the French social thinker Auguste Comte coin the term sociology to describe a new way of looking at the world. Comte (1798–1857) grew up in the wake of the French Revolution through the turbulent period that brought a sweeping transformation to his country. He felt that

This medieval drawing conveys the mix of apprehension and excitement with which early scientists began to question traditional understandings of the universe. Pioneering sociologists, too, challenged many ideas that people had long taken for granted, explaining that society is neither fixed by God's will nor human nature. On the contrary, Comte and other sociological pioneers claimed, society is a system that we can study scientifically and, based on what we learn, act deliberately to improve.

knowledge of how society operates, through what he called sociology ("the study of society"), would allow people to build a better future for themselves.

SCIENCE AND SOCIOLOGY

The nature of society was a major topic of inquiry for virtually all the brilliant thinkers of the ancient world, including the Chinese philosopher K'ung Fu-tzu, also known as Confucius (551–479 B.C.E.), and the Greek philosophers Plato (c. 427–347 B.C.E.) and Aristotle (384–322 B.C.E.).[3] Similarly, the Roman emperor Marcus Aurelius (121–180 C.E.), the medieval thinkers St. Thomas Aquinas (c. 1225–74) and Christine de Pizan (c. 1363–1431), and the English playwright William Shakespeare (1564–1616) all examined the state of human society. Yet, as Emile Durkheim noted almost a century ago, none of these social thinkers approached society from a sociological point of view.

> Looking back in history . . . we find that no philosophers ever viewed matters [from a sociological perspective] until quite recently. . . . It seemed to them sufficient to ascertain what the human will should strive for and what it should avoid in established societies. . . . Their aim was

[3] Throughout this text, the abbreviation B.C.E. designates "before the common era." We use this terminology in place of the traditional B.C. ("before Christ") in recognition of the religious plurality of our society. Similarly, in place of the traditional A.D. ("anno Domini," or "in the year of our Lord"), we employ the abbreviation C.E. ("common era").

not to offer us as valid a description of nature as possible, but to present us with the idea of a perfect society, a model to be imitated. (1972:57; orig. 1918)

What sets sociology apart from earlier social thought? Prior to the birth of sociology, philosophers and theologians mostly focused on imagining the ideal society. None attempted to analyze society as it really was. Pioneers of the discipline such as Auguste Comte and Emile Durkheim reversed these priorities. Although they were certainly concerned with how human society could be improved, their major goal was to understand how society actually operates.

The key to achieving this objective, according to Comte, was to look at society scientifically. But, Comte added, a scientific outlook is a recent development—the last of three distinct stages of history (1975; orig. 1851–54). The earliest era, extending from the beginning of human history through Europe's medieval period (until roughly 1350 C.E.), he termed the *theological stage*. During this period, thinking was guided by religion. More specifically, people regarded society as an expression of God's will—at least insofar as humans were capable of fulfilling a divine plan.

With the Renaissance, the theological approach to society gradually gave way to what Comte called the *metaphysical stage*. During this period, people came to understand society as a natural, rather than a supernatural, phenomenon. Human nature figured heavily in metaphysical visions of society: the English philosopher Thomas Hobbes (1588–1679), for example, posited that society reflected not the perfection of God as much as the failings of a rather selfish human nature.

What Comte heralded as the final, *scientific stage* in the long quest to understand society was propelled by scientists such as the Polish astronomer Copernicus (1473–1543), the Italian astronomer and physicist Galileo[4] (1564–1642), and the English physicist and mathematician Isaac Newton (1642–1727). Comte's contribution came in applying this scientific approach—first used to study the physical world—to the study of society.

Comte was thus a proponent of **positivism**, defined as *a means to understand the world based on science*. As a positivist, Comte believed that society conforms to invariable laws, much as the physical world operates according to gravity and other laws of nature.

Sociology emerged as an academic discipline in North America at the beginning of this century, with early sociologists such as the American Lester Ward (1841–1913) pursuing Comte's vision of a scientific sociology. Even today, most sociologists agree that science plays a crucial role in sociology. But, as Chapter 2 ("Sociological Investigation") explains, we now realize that human behaviour is often far more complex than natural phenomena. Human beings are creatures with considerable imagination and spontaneity, so that our behaviour can never be fully explained by any rigid "laws of society."

SOCIAL CHANGE AND SOCIOLOGY

Striking transformations in eighteenth- and nineteenth-century Europe drove the development of sociology. As the social ground trembled under their feet, people understandably focused their attention on society.

First came scientific discoveries and technological advances that produced a factory-based industrial economy. Second, factories drew millions of people from the countryside, causing an explosive growth of cities. Third, people in these burgeoning industrial cities soon entertained new ideas about democracy and political rights. We shall briefly describe each of these three changes.

A New Industrial Economy

During the European Middle Ages, most people tilled fields near their homes or engaged in small-scale *manufacturing* (a word derived from Latin words meaning "to make by hand"). But by the end of the

---

[4] Illustrating Comte's stages, the ancient Greeks and Romans viewed the planets as gods, while Renaissance metaphysical thinkers saw them as astral influences (giving rise to astrology). By the time of Galileo, scientists understood planets as natural objects behaving in orderly ways.

eighteenth century, inventors had applied new sources of energy—first water power and then steam power—to the operation of large machines, which gave birth to factories. Now, instead of labouring at home, workers became part of a large and anonymous industrial workforce, toiling for strangers who owned the factories. This drastic change in the system of production weakened families and eroded traditions that had guided members of small communities for centuries.

The Growth of Cities

Factories sprouting across much of Europe became magnets attracting people in need of work. This "pull" of work in the new industrialized labour force was accentuated by an additional "push" as landowners fenced off more and more ground, turning farms into grazing land for sheep—the source of wool for the thriving textile mills. This so-called enclosure movement forced countless tenant farmers from the countryside towards cities in search of work in the new factories.

Many villages were soon abandoned; at the same time, however, factory towns swelled rapidly into large cities. Such urban growth dramatically changed people's lives. Cities churned with strangers, in numbers that overwhelmed available housing. Widespread social problems—including poverty, disease, pollution, crime, and homelessness—were the order of the day. Such social crises further stimulated development of the sociological perspective.

Political Change

During the Middle Ages, as Comte noted, most people thought of society as the expression of God's will. Royalty claimed to rule by "divine right," and each person up and down the social hierarchy had some other part in the holy plan. This theological view of society is captured in lines from the old Anglican hymn "All Things Bright and Beautiful:"

> The rich man in his castle,
> The poor man at his gate,
> God made them high and lowly
> And ordered their estate.

With economic development and the rapid growth of cities, changes in political thought were inevitable. Starting in the seventeenth century, every kind of tradition came under spirited attack. In the writings of Thomas Hobbes (1588–1679), John Locke (1632–1704), and Adam Smith (1723–90), we see a distinct shift in focus: no longer was it people's moral obligation to remain loyal to their rulers; rather, these thinkers contended, society is the product of individ-

The birth of sociology was prompted by rapid social change. The discipline developed in those regions of Europe where the Industrial Revolution most disrupted traditional ways of life, drawing people from isolated villages to rapidly growing industrial cities.

ual self-interest. The key phrases in the new political climate, therefore, were *individual liberty* and *individual rights*. Echoing the thoughts of Locke, the Canadian constitution asserts that each individual has certain rights, freedoms, and protections. As section 2, "Fundamental Freedoms," puts it,

> Everyone has the following fundamental freedoms:
> (a) freedom of conscience and religion;
> (b) freedom of thought, belief, opinion and expression, including freedom of the press and other media of communication;
> (c) freedom of peaceful assembly; and
> (d) freedom of association.
>
> (The Canadian Charter of Rights and Freedoms, 1982)

The political revolution in France that began soon afterward, in 1789, constituted an even more dramatic break with political and social traditions. As the French social analyst Alexis de Tocqueville (1805–59) surveyed his society after the French Revolution, he exaggerated only slightly when he asserted that the changes we have described amounted to "nothing short of the regeneration of the whole human race" (1955:13; orig. 1856). In this context, it is easy to see why Auguste Comte and other pioneers of sociology soon developed the new discipline. Sociology flowered in precisely those societies—France, Germany, and England—where change was greatest.

Various sociologists reacted differently to the new social order then, just as they respond differently to society today. Some, including Auguste Comte, feared that people would be uprooted from long-established local communities and overpowered by change. So, in a conservative approach, Comte sought to shore up the family and traditional morality.

Taking a different view of these massive changes, the German social critic Karl Marx (1818–83) worried little about the loss of tradition, which he detested. But he could not condone the way industrial technology concentrated its great wealth in the hands of a small elite, while so many others faced hunger and misery. We examine his ideas at length in Chapter 4 ("Society").

Clearly, Comte and Marx advanced radically different prescriptions for the problems of modernity. Yet they had in common the conviction that society rests on much more than individual choice. The sociological perspective animates the work of each, revealing that people's individual lives are framed by the broader society in which they live. This lesson, of course, remains as true today as it was a century ago.

In subsequent chapters of this book, we delve into the major issues that concern sociologists. These pivotal social forces include culture, social class, race, ethnicity, gender, the economy, and the family. They all involve ways in which individuals are guided, united, and divided in the larger arena of society.

MARGINAL VOICES

Auguste Comte and Karl Marx stand among the giants of sociology. But, especially in recent years, sociologists have come to recognize the important contribution that others—pushed to the margins because they are women living in a male-dominated society—have made to their discipline.

Harriet Martineau (1802–76), born to a rich English family, first gained fame in 1832 when she published a monthly series *Illustrations of Political Economy*. In 1853, she translated Auguste Comte's *Positive Philosophy* from the French. Soon afterwards, she established her own reputation as a sociologist with studies of slavery, factory laws, and women's rights. She wrote a controversial sociological analysis of the United States, *Society in America* (1837), and a book on social science methodology called *How to Observe Morals and Manners* (1838). She also found time to write novels, travel widely, and pursue a full-time career as a journalist. She accomplished all this in spite of recurrent ill health and deafness (McDonald, 1994:164-75).

At that time, widespread beliefs in the social inferiority of women kept women such as Martineau at the margins of established sociology, causing many "established" sociologists to ignore their writings. Looking back with a sociological eye, we can see in their marginal standing how the forces of society were at work shaping even the history of sociology itself.

CANADIAN SOCIOLOGY: DISTINCTIVE TOUCHES

Canadian sociology arose from different traditions and continues to be, in many ways, distinct from U.S. sociology. As a discipline that reflects a country with two major cultures and linguistic communities, Canadian sociology includes a unique francophone component.

Sociology began in Canada, as in the United States, in the early part of the twentieth century. By 1920, sociology courses were being offered in a number of disciplines and sociology was included in the theology curricula. During this period the Canadian Political Science Association, formed in 1913, accepted sociologists as members. Teaching and research in sociology were undertaken earlier in Quebec—at Laval, the University of Montreal, and then later at the University of Quebec—than in the rest of the country. French-Canadian sociology was influenced initially by ties to the Roman Catholic Church and in the longer term by developments in Europe and France in particular, tending towards the investigation of economic and political trends and comparisons. English-Canadian sociology began both at McGill, following the U.S. tradition, and at the University of Toronto, following the British tradition.

Sociology did not have its own department at the University of Toronto until the 1960s. Before that time, social thinkers of the sociological cast worked out of the department of political economy. Sociology at the University of Toronto differed from the American-influenced social issues and community study approach that characterized studies at McGill. Modelled on British sociology, the University of Toronto tackled questions of political and economic history. The person who most influenced sociology in the early years was Harold A. Innis. His emphasis on the way Canadian economic development depended on resource extraction and exportation (known as the staple approach) formed the backdrop to the development of the sociological perspective in Canada. This perspective focused on economic developments in the country, particularly the branch-plant nature of the Canadian economy. Innis noted the role of communications and communications technology in the development of Canadian society.

Marshall McLuhan gained world renown for his insights into the impacts of electronic communication on culture, politics, and personal identities. In reality a social theorist, he provoked Canadians with his musings on the interplay of the media (the electronic media in particular) with human thought, behaviour, and the shape of society. He had Canadians chew on tidbits such as "the medium is the message" and "global village" while his thinking laid the groundwork for our understanding of the current concepts of cyberspace and virtual reality and their impacts on social cohesion and identity (Bendetti and DeHart, 1996; Goyder, 1997). Thirty years ahead of his time, McLuhan would have been very comfortable with the concepts of "cyberspace," "virtual reality," and "real time."

John Porter, in many minds, is Canada's leading sociologist. His book *The Vertical Mosaic* (1965) laid the groundwork for the focus on Canadian society in the context of development and underdevelopment (particularly as compared to the United States), inequality and inequity, elites, French–English relations, and bureaucratic structures.

Canada's massive size, its sparse but diverse population, its proximity to the United States, and its global situation (economic, cultural, and political) ensure that Canadian sociology will be concerned with questions of unity, political movements, economic development and inequality, regionalism, environment, identity, communications, diversity, as well as cultural expression and survival. (Brym and Fox, 1989; Helmes-Hayes, 1988; and Whyte and Vallee, 1988).

SOCIOLOGICAL THEORY

The task of weaving isolated observations into understanding brings us to another dimension of sociology:

Harold A. Innis (left) was best known as a political economist and a pioneer in communication studies—analyzing the impacts of modes of communication on social development. He was a member of the University of Toronto's political economy department from 1920 to his death in 1952. His first major work, The Fur Trade in Canada *(1930), introduced the staple thesis of development and established his reputation.*

John Porter (centre), a graduate of the London School of Economics, spent most of his career in Ottawa at Carleton University, as a faculty member, department chair, dean, and academic vice-president. He profoundly influenced his students, many of whom are important sociologists today (Vallee, 1988).

Marshall McLuhan (right) was a controversial figure who achieved international recognition in the 1960s and 1970s. His work fell out of favour for a while, but is being revisited as social scientists acknowledge the revolutionary impact of the electronic media. Trained in literature at Cambridge, McLuhan became a rather unconventional professor of English at the University of Toronto, where he simultaneously enthralled and enraged his students.

theory. A **theory** is *a statement of how and why specific facts are related.* Recall that Emile Durkheim observed that certain categories of people (men, Protestants, the wealthy, and the unmarried) have higher suicide rates than others (women, Catholics and Jews, the poor, and the married). He explained these observations by creating a theory: a high risk of suicide stems from a low level of social integration.

Of course, as Durkheim pondered the issue of suicide, he considered any number of possible theories. But merely linking facts together is no guarantee that a theory is correct. To evaluate a theory, as the next chapter explains, sociologists use scientific-research methods to gather evidence. Facts allow sociologists to confirm some theories while rejecting or modifying others. As a scientist, Durkheim was not content merely to identify a plausible cause of suicide; he set about collecting data to see precisely which categories of people committed suicide with the highest frequency. Poring over his data, Durkheim settled on a theory that best squared with all available evidence.

In attempting to develop theories about human society, sociologists face a wide range of choices. What issues should we study? How should we link facts together to form theories? In making sense of society, sociologists are guided by one or more theoretical "road maps" or paradigms (Kuhn, 1970). For them, a **theoretical paradigm** is *a basic image of society that guides thinking and research.*

We noted earlier that two of sociology's founders—Auguste Comte and Karl Marx—made sense of the emerging modern society in strikingly different ways. Such differences persist today as some sociologists highlight how societies stay the same, while others focus on patterns of change. Similarly, some sociological theorists focus on what joins people together, while others investigate how society divides people according to gender, race, ethnicity, or social class—and, in Canada, by region. Some sociologists seek to understand the operation of society as it is, while others actively promote what they view to be desirable social change.

In short, sociologists often disagree about what the most important questions are: even when they agree on the questions, they may still come up with a range of answers. Nonetheless, sociological theory is far from chaotic, because sociology has three major theoretical paradigms, or frameworks, that allow sociologists to effectively analyze virtually any dimension of society.

THE STRUCTURAL-FUNCTIONAL PARADIGM

The **structural-functional paradigm** is *a framework for building theory that envisions society as a complex system whose parts work together to promote solidarity and stability.* As its name suggests, this paradigm begins by

The approach of the structural-functional paradigm is conveyed by the painting St. Regis Indian Reservation *by Amy Jones (1937). Here we see society composed of major rounds of life, each serving a particular purpose that contributes to the operation of the entire system.*

Amy Jones, *St. Regis Indian Reservation*, 1937. Photo courtesy Janet Marqusee Fine Arts Ltd.

recognizing that our lives are guided by **social structure**, meaning *relatively stable patterns of social behaviour*. Social structure is what gives shape to the family, directs people to exchange greetings on the street, or steers events in a college classroom. Second, this paradigm leads us to understand social structure in terms of its **social functions**, or *consequences for the operation of society*. All social structure—from family life to corporate organization—contributes to the operation of society, at least in its present form.

The structural-functional paradigm owes much to the ideas of Auguste Comte who, as we have already explained, sought to promote social integration during a time of tumultuous change. A second architect of this theoretical approach was the influential English sociologist Herbert Spencer (1820–1903). Spencer was a student of both the human body and society, and he came to see that the two have much in common. The structural parts of the human body include the skeleton, muscles, and various internal organs. These elements are interdependent, with each contributing to the survival of the entire organism. In the same way, reasoned Spencer, various social structures are interdependent, working in concert to preserve society. The structural-functional paradigm, then, organizes sociological observations by identifying various structures of society and investigating the function of each one.

In France, several decades after Comte's death, Emile Durkheim continued the development of sociology. Durkheim was primarily concerned with the issue of social solidarity, how societies "hang together." Because of the extent of Durkheim's influence on sociology, his work is detailed in Chapter 4 ("Society").

As sociology developed in the United States, many of the ideas of Herbert Spencer and Emile Durkheim were carried forward by Talcott Parsons (1902–79). The major U.S. proponent of the structural-functional paradigm, Parsons treated society as a system, identifying the basic tasks any and all societies must perform to survive and the ways they accomplish these tasks.

Contemporary U.S. sociologist Robert K. Merton has expanded our understanding of the concept of social function in novel ways. Merton (1968) explains, first, that the consequences of any social pattern are likely to differ for various members of a society. For example, conventional families may provide crucial support for the development of children, but they also confer privileges on men while limiting the opportunities of women.

Second, Merton notes, people rarely perceive all the functions of a particular social structure. He described as **manifest functions** the *recognized and intended consequences of any social pattern*. By contrast, **latent functions** are *consequences that are largely unrecognized and unintended*. To illustrate, the obvious functions of North America's system of higher education include providing young people with the information and skills they need to perform jobs effectively. Perhaps just as important, although rarely acknowledged, is the way universities and colleges function as marriage brokers, bringing together people of similar social backgrounds in a social scene that operates as an ongoing setting for courtship. Another latent function of higher education is delaying the entry of millions of young people into the labour market where, presumably, many of them would fail to find jobs.

Merton makes a third point: not all the effects of any social structure turn out to be useful. Thus we designate as **social dysfunctions** *any social pattern's undesirable consequences for the operation of society*. And, to make matters still more complex, people may well disagree about what is useful or harmful. Some critics from the political right have criticized universities for promoting left-wing thinking that threatens traditional values. Critics on the left might dismiss such charges as trivial or simply wrong; yet, from their point of view, higher education is dysfunctional for conferring further privileges on the wealthy (who disproportionately attend university) while remaining out of the financial reach of most individuals from lower-income families.

Critical evaluation. The most salient characteristic of the structural-functional paradigm is its vision of society as comprehensible, orderly, and stable. Sociologists typically couple this approach with scientific methods of research aimed at learning "what makes society tick."

At mid-century, the structural-functional paradigm dominated sociology. In recent decades, however, its influence has waned. How can we assume that society has a "natural" order, critics ask, when social patterns vary from place to place and change over time? Further, by emphasizing social integration, structural-functionalism tends to gloss over inequality based on social class, race, ethnicity, and gender—divisions that may generate considerable tension and conflict. This focus on stability at the expense of conflict and change gives the structural-functional paradigm a conservative character. As a critical response to this approach, sociologists have developed another theoretical orientation: the social-conflict paradigm.

THE SOCIAL-CONFLICT PARADIGM

The **social-conflict paradigm** is *a framework for building theory that envisions society as an arena of inequality generating conflict and change.* This approach contrasts with that of the structural-functional paradigm by highlighting not solidarity but division based on inequality. Guided by this paradigm, sociologists investigate how factors such as social class, race, ethnicity, sex, and age are linked to unequal distribution of money, power, education, and social prestige. A conflict analysis points out that, rather than promoting the operation of society as a whole, social structure typically benefits some people while depriving others.

Working within the social-conflict paradigm, sociologists spotlight ongoing conflict between dominant and disadvantaged categories of people—the rich in relation to the poor, white people as opposed to visible minorities, men versus women. Typically, those on top strive to protect their privileges; the disadvantaged counter by attempting to gain more resources for themselves.

To illustrate, a conflict analysis of our educational system might highlight how schooling perpetuates inequality by helping to reproduce the class structure in every new generation. The process begins as secondary schools assign some students to university-preparatory programs while they provide vocational

The painting Dinner is Served *(1995), by Paul Marcus, presents the essential wisdom of social-conflict theory: Society operates in a way that conveys wealth, power, and privileges to some at the expense of others. Looking closely at the painting, what categories of people does the artist suggest are disadvantaged?*

training for others. From a functional point of view, such "streaming" may benefit all of society because, ideally, students receive the training appropriate to their academic abilities. But conflict analysis counters that "streaming" often has less to do with talent than with a student's social background, as well-to-do students are placed in higher streams and poor students end up in the lower ones. (Bob Rae's NDP government started to phase out streaming in Ontario as a result of these criticisms. Opposition effectively limited destreaming to grade 9—and Mike Harris's Conservative government will reverse it by 1999.)

Through streaming, privileged families gain favoured treatment for their children from schools and, subsequently, universities. With the best schooling behind them, these young people leave university to pursue occupations that confer both prestige and high income. As Maxwell and Maxwell (1994) point out, private schools are an effective channelling device towards elite social status. Furthermore, the advantages of private schools for women are even greater

Louis Schanker's Three Men on a Bench *captures a central insight of the symbolic-interaction paradigm. Society is never at rest: It is an ongoing process by which interacting people define and redefine reality.*

than for men; women graduating from private girls' schools will be the vanguard of women moving into high-status, male-dominated occupations. By contrast, the children of poor families are less prepared for university or college. So, like their parents before them, these young people typically move right from high school into low-paying jobs. In both cases, the social standing of one generation is passed on to another, with schools justifying the practice not in terms of privilege but in terms of individual merit.

Social conflict in Canada extends well beyond schools. Later chapters of this text highlight efforts by working people, women, and various racial and ethnic minorities to improve their lives. In each of these cases, the social-conflict paradigm helps us to see how inequality and the conflict it generates are rooted in the organization of society itself.

Finally, many sociologists who embrace the social-conflict paradigm attempt not just to understand society but to reduce social inequality. This was the goal of Karl Marx, the social thinker whose ideas underlie the social-conflict paradigm. Marx had little patience with those who sought merely to understand how society works. In a well-known declaration (inscribed on his monument in London's Highgate Cemetery), Marx asserted: "The philosophers have only interpreted the world, in various ways; the point, however, is to change it."

Feminism

Feminist sociology encompasses both the micro and the macro levels of analysis. Both levels focus on women's lives. The micro level examines the "re-production" of gender through such things as talk, body language, and emotion management. The macro level examines the myriad of constraints and forms of resistance in women's lives in such institutional realms as politics, economics, schooling, religion, and the family. The macro level of analysis has documented the patriarchal nature of the structure of societies, which characterizes virtually all realms of life.

In the past several decades, feminist sociology has been challenging the male-dominated discipline with critiques of methodology, theory, and all the substantive areas of the field. Feminist sociology, along with feminist analysis in other areas of academic life, has established a new field called women's studies. There are now women's studies programs in universities and colleges across Canada.

Critical evaluation. The social-conflict paradigm has developed rapidly in recent decades. Yet, like other approaches, it has come in for its share of criticism. Because this paradigm highlights inequality and division, it glosses over how shared values or interdependence generates unity among members of a society. For example, the shared values and economic or social bonds that unite Quebeckers and other Canadians might be overlooked. In addition, say critics, to the extent that the social-conflict approach explicitly pursues political goals, it relinquishes any claim to scientific objectivity. As Chapter 2 ("Sociological Investigation") explains in detail, conflict theorists are uneasy with the notion that science can be "objective." They contend, on the contrary, that the social-conflict paradigm as well as all theoretical approaches have political consequences, albeit different ones.

One additional criticism, which applies equally to both the structural-functional and social-conflict paradigms, is that these approaches envision society in very broad terms, describing our lives as a composite of "family," "social class," and so on. A third theoretical paradigm depicts society less in terms of abstract generalizations and more in terms of people's everyday, situational experiences.

THE SYMBOLIC-INTERACTION PARADIGM

Both the structural-functional and social-conflict paradigms share a **macro-level orientation**, meaning *a focus on broad social structures that characterize society as a whole.* Macro-level sociology takes in the big picture, rather like observing a city from high above in a helicopter, noting the way highways carry traffic from place to place and the striking contrasts between rich and poor neighbourhoods. The symbolic-interaction paradigm takes another tack by providing a **micro-level orientation**, meaning *a focus on social interaction in specific situations.* Exploring urban life in this way occurs at street level, perhaps observing how friends interact in public parks or how pedestrians respond to homeless people. The **symbolic-interaction paradigm**, then, is *a theoretical framework that envisions society as the product of the everyday interactions of individuals.*

How does "society" result from the ongoing experiences of tens of millions of people? One answer, detailed in Chapter 6 ("Social Interaction in Everyday Life"), is that society arises as a shared reality that its members construct as they interact with one another. That is, human beings attach meaning to everything; thus, we construct reality as we define our surroundings, our own identities, and our obligations towards others.

Of course, this process of definition varies a great deal from person to person. On a city street, for example, one person may define a homeless man as "just a bum looking for a handout" and ignore him. Another, however, may define him as a "fellow human being in need" and offer assistance. In the same way, one pedestrian may feel a sense of security passing by a police officer walking the beat, while another may be seized by a sense of nervous anxiety. Sociologists guided by the symbolic-interaction approach, therefore, view society as a mosaic of subjective meanings and variable responses.

The symbolic-interaction paradigm rests, in part, on the thinking of Max Weber (1864–1920), a German sociologist who emphasized the need to understand a setting from the point of view of the people in it. Weber's approach is presented at length in Chapter 4 ("Society").

On this foundation, others have devised their own micro-level approaches to understanding social life. Chapter 5 ("Socialization") examines the ideas of U.S. sociologist George Herbert Mead (1863–1931), who looked at how we build our personalities over time based on social experience. Chapter 6 ("Social Interaction in Everyday Life") presents the work of Canadian sociologist Erving Goffman (1922–82), whose dramaturgical analysis emphasizes how we resemble actors on a stage as we play out our various roles before others. Ethnomethodology is another micro-level analysis of the ways that people, as members of society, make sense of their social lives in order to carry out activities. Harold Garfinkel (1967), the founder of this perspective, showed how background understanding or assumptions are fundamental to the practice of social life through methods such as conversation analysis (see Chapter 6 for more information on this approach).

Other contemporary sociologists, including George Homans and Peter Blau, have developed *social-exchange analysis*. In their view, social interaction amounts to a negotiation in which individuals are guided by what they stand to gain and lose from others (Molm, 1997). In the ritual of courtship, for example, people typically seek mates who offer at least as much—in terms of physical attractiveness, intelligence, and social background—as they provide in return.

Critical evaluation. The symbolic-interaction paradigm helps to correct for a bias inherent in all macro-level approaches to understanding society. Without denying the usefulness of abstract social structures such as "the family" and "social class," we must bear in mind that society basically amounts to *people interacting.* Put another way, this micro-level approach helps convey more of how individuals actually experience society.

However, by focusing on day-to-day interactions, the symbolic-interaction paradigm can obscure larger social structures. Highlighting what is unique in each social scene risks overlooking the widespread effects of our culture, as well as factors such as class, gender, and race.

Table 1–2 summarizes the important characteristics of the structural-functional paradigm, the social-conflict paradigm, and the symbolic-interaction paradigm. As we have explained, each paradigm is especially helpful in answering particular kinds of questions. By and large, however, the fullest understanding of society comes from linking the sociological perspective to all three, as we shall now illustrate with an analysis of sports in Canada and the United States.

SPORTS: THREE THEORETICAL PARADIGMS IN ACTION

To people in North America, sports seem indispensable. Almost everyone has engaged in some type of sport, and athletics has evolved into a multibillion-dollar industry. What sociological insights about this

TABLE 1–2 The Three Major Theoretical Paradigms: A Summary

Theoretical Paradigm	Orientation	Image of Society	Illustrative Questions
Structural-functional	Macro-level	A system of interrelated parts that is relatively stable based on widespread consensus as to what is morally desirable; each part has functional consequences for the operation of society as a whole.	How is society integrated? What are the major parts of society? How are these parts interrelated? What are the consequences of each for the operation of society?
Social-conflict	Macro-level	A system characterized by social inequality; any part of society benefits some categories of people more than others; conflict-based social inequality promotes social change.	How is society divided? What are major patterns of social inequality? How do some categories of people attempt to protect their privileges? How do other categories of people challenge the status quo?
Feminist	Micro/macro	A gender-based hierarchy where men dominate women in all realms of social life, including knowledge, the polity, the economy, education, etc.	Why is there a gendered hierarchy? What have been the effects of male dominance on men and women? How can such a structure be overturned?
Symbolic-interaction	Micro-level	An ongoing process of social interaction in specific settings based on symbolic communications; individual perceptions of reality are variable and changing.	How is society experienced? How do human beings interact to create, sustain, and change social patterns? How do individuals attempt to shape the reality perceived by others? How does individual behaviour change from one situation to another?

familiar element of life can we derive from the three theoretical paradigms?

The Functions of Sports

A structural-functional approach directs attention to the ways sports help society to operate. The manifest functions include providing recreation, physical conditioning, and a relatively harmless way to let off steam. Sports have important latent functions as well, from fostering social relationships and teaching teamwork skills to generating tens of thousands of jobs. Perhaps most importantly, sports encourage competition and the pursuit of success, both of which are central to our way of life.

Sports also have dysfunctional consequences, of course. For example, North American colleges and universities intent on fielding winning teams sometimes recruit students for their athletic ability rather than their academic aptitude. Doing so can pull down the academic standards of a school and may shortchange the athletes themselves, as coaches denigrate academic endeavours so that student athletes concentrate all their energies on their sport.

Sports and Conflict

A social-conflict analysis begins by pointing out that sports are closely linked to social inequality. Some sports—including tennis, golf, and skiing—are expensive, so participation is largely limited to the well-to-do. By contrast, football, baseball, and basketball are accessible to people of all income levels. In short, the games people play are not simply a matter of choice but also reflect their social standing.

In Canada and the United States, sports are oriented primarily towards males. The first modern Olympic Games held in 1896, for example, excluded women from competition; until recently, moreover, even little league teams in most parts of Canada barred girls from the playing field. Such male-only practices have been defended by unfounded notions that girls and women lack the ability to engage in sports or risk losing their femininity if they do so. Thus, our society encourages men to be athletes, and expects women to be attentive observers and cheerleaders. More women now play professional sports than ever before—in women's hockey, Canada was the team to beat going into the 1998 Winter Olympics at Nagano, Japan—yet they continue to take a back seat to men, particularly in sports that yield the greatest earnings and social prestige.

Although North American society long excluded people of colour from "big league" sports, the opportunity to earn high incomes in professional sports has expanded in recent decades. Major league baseball first admitted African-American players when Jackie Robinson broke the "colour line" in 1947. Willie O'Ree, originally from Fredericton, New Brunswick, was the first Black player in the National Hockey League when he was brought up from the minor leagues to play for the Boston Bruins in 1958. By 1993, African-Americans—12 percent of the U.S. population—accounted for 17 percent of Major League Baseball players, 68 percent of National Football League players, and 77 percent of National Basketball Association players (Center for the Study of Sport in Society, 1993).

One reason for the increasing proportion of people of African descent in professional sports is the fact that precisely measured athletic performances cannot be diminished by white prejudice. There's no disputing the gold-medal Olympic performances of Canada's Donovan Bailey and the men's 4 × 100 metre relay team. Recently in North America, Black athletes have earned higher salaries, on average, than white players. But racial discrimination still taints professional sports in North America: Blacks figure prominently in only a handful of sports, and almost all managers, head coaches, and owners of sports teams are white.

Taking a wider view, who gains the greatest benefits from professional sports? Although millions of fans follow their teams, the vast numbers of dollars teams take in are controlled by the small number of people (predominantly white men) for whom teams are income-generating property. In sum, sports in Canada and the United States are bound up with inequalities based on gender, race, and economic power.

Sports as Interaction

At a micro level, a sporting event is a complex drama of face-to-face interaction. In part, play is guided by the players' assigned positions and, of course, everyone takes account of the rules of the game. But players are also spontaneous and unpredictable. Informed by the symbolic-interaction paradigm, then, we see sports less as a system than as an ongoing process.

From this point of view, too, we expect each player to understand the game a little differently. Some thrive in a setting of stiff competition while, for others, love[5] of the game may hold greater rewards than the thrill of victory.

Beyond different attitudes towards competition, team members will also shape their particular realities according to the various prejudices, jealousies, and ambitions they bring to the field. Then, too, the

Canada's pride and joy! Robert Esmie (Sudbury), Glenroy Gilbert (Ottawa), Bruny Surin (Montreal), and Donovan Bailey (Oakville, Ontario) celebrate another triumph—their gold-medal performance in the 4 × 100 metre relay at the world track and field championships in Athens.

---

[5] The ancient Romans recognized this fact, evident in the word "amateur," literally, "lover," which designates someone who engages in an activity for the sheer love of it.

behaviour of any single player also changes over time. A rookie in professional baseball, for example, may feel quite self-conscious during his first few games in the big leagues. In time, however, a comfortable sense of fitting in with the team usually emerges. Coming to feel at home on the field was slow and painful for Jackie Robinson, who was initially all too aware that many white players, and millions of white fans, resented his presence in Major League Baseball (Tygiel, 1983). In time, however, his outstanding ability and his confident and cooperative manner won him the respect of Canadians and Americans.

The three theoretical paradigms certainly offer different insights, but none is more correct than the others. Applied to any issue, each paradigm generates its own interpretations so that, to fully appreciate the power of the sociological perspective, you should become familiar with all three. Together, they stimulate fascinating debates and controversies, many of which are presented in the chapters that follow.

SUMMARY

1. The sociological perspective reveals "the general in the particular," or the power of society to shape our lives.

2. Because people tend to think in terms of individual choice, recognizing the impact of society on our lives initially seems like "seeing the strange in the familiar."

3. Emile Durkheim's research demonstrating that suicide rates are higher among some categories of people than others shows that society affects even the most personal of our actions.

4. Global awareness enhances the sociological perspective because, first, societies of the world are becoming more and more interconnected; second,

Is Sociology Nothing More Than Stereotypes?

"Protestants are the ones who kill themselves!"

"People in Canada? They're dull as dishwater and won't stand up for themselves!"

"Everyone knows that you have to be Black to play professional basketball!"

It can't be denied that sociologists make generalizations about categories of people. Recognizing this fact, some students who begin the study of sociology may wonder whether statements like those above are sociological insights or simply stereotypes. What, exactly, is the difference between the two?

All three statements at the top of this page illustrate the stereotype, an exaggerated description that one applies to all people in a given category. First, rather than describing averages, each statement paints every individual in a category with the same brush; second, each ignores facts and distorts reality (even though each does contain some element of truth); third, each sounds more like a "put down" than a fair-minded assertion.

Crafting a sociological insight, by contrast, does involve making generalizations, but with three important conditions. First, we do not indiscriminately apply these generalizations to individuals; second, we ensure that a generalization squares with available facts; third, we offer a generalization fair-mindedly, with an interest in getting at the truth.

First, recall that the sociological perspective reveals "the general in the particular;" therefore, a sociological insight is a generalization about some category of people. An example is the assertion, made earlier in this chapter, that the suicide rate among Protestants is higher than that among Catholics or Jews. However, the way the statement above is phrased—"Protestants are the ones who kill themselves!"—is unreasonable because in fact the vast majority of Protestants do no such thing.

Second, sociologists base their generalizations on available facts. A more factual and accurate version of the second statement above would be that historically Canadians have placed a high value on the role of consensus in deci-

sion-making, both among themselves and in their dealings with other nations.

Third, sociologists strive to be fair-minded; that is, they are motivated by a passion for learning and for truth. The third statement above about Blacks and basketball fails as good sociology not only because it doesn't square with the facts, but because it seems motivated by bias rather than truth-seeking or understanding.

Good sociology, then, stands apart from stereotyping. One of the most valuable aspects of a sociology course is that through it we learn how to collect the factual information that we need to assess the truth of popular wisdom.

Continue the debate . . .

1. *Are there stereotypes of sociologists? What are they? Are they valid?*

2. *Do you think taking a sociology course erodes people's stereotypes? Does it generate new ones?*

3. *Can you cite a stereotype of your own that sociology challenges?*

---

many social problems are most serious beyond Canada's borders; and, third, recognizing how others live helps us to better understand ourselves.

5. Socially marginal people are more likely than others to perceive the effects of society. For everyone, periods of social crisis or social change foster sociological thinking.

6. There are four general benefits to using the sociological perspective. First, it challenges our familiar understandings of the world, helping us to separate fact from fiction; second, it helps us appreciate the opportunities and constraints that frame our lives; third, it encourages more active participation in society; and, fourth, it increases our awareness of social diversity in the world as a whole.

7. Auguste Comte gave sociology its name in 1838. Whereas previous social thought had focused on

what society ought to be, Comte's new discipline of sociology used scientific methods to understand society as it is.

8. Sociology emerged as a reaction to the rapid transformation of Europe during the eighteenth and nineteenth centuries. Three dimensions of change—the rise of an industrial economy, the explosive growth of cities, and the emergence of new political ideas—each focused people's attention on the operation of society.

9. Building theory involves linking insights to gain understanding. Various theoretical paradigms guide sociologists as they construct theories.

10. The structural-functional paradigm is a framework for exploring how social structures promote the stability and integration of society. This approach minimizes the importance of social inequality, conflict, and change.

11. The social-conflict paradigm highlights social inequality, conflict, and change. At the same time, this approach downplays the extent of society's integration and stability.

12. In contrast to these broad, macro-level approaches, the symbolic-interaction paradigm is a micro-level theoretical framework that focuses on face-to-face interaction in specific settings.

13. Because each paradigm highlights different dimensions of any social issue, the richest sociological understanding is derived from applying all three.

14. Sociological thinking involves generalizations. But, unlike a stereotype, a sociological statement (a) is not applied indiscriminately to individuals, (b) is supported by facts, and (c) is put forward in the fair-minded pursuit of truth.

CRITICAL THINKING QUESTIONS

1. In what ways does using the sociological perspective make us seem less in control of our lives? In what ways does it give us greater power over our surroundings?

2. Consider this statement: Sociology would not have arisen if human behaviour were biologically programmed (like that of, say, ants); nor could sociology exist if our behaviour were utterly chaotic. Sociology thrives because human social life falls in a middle ground—as thinking people, we create social patterns, but those patterns are variable and changeable.

3. Give a sociological explanation of why sociology developed where and when it did.

4. Guided by the discipline's three major theoretical paradigms, what kinds of questions might a sociologist ask about (a) television, (b) war, (c) humour, and (d) universities and colleges?

SOCIOLOGY APPLIED

1. Spend several hours moving around your local community. Are there clear residential patterns? That is, does each neighbourhood contain certain categories of people? As best you can, identify who lives where. What social forces explain such patterns?

2. During a class, carefully observe the behaviour of the instructor and other students. What patterns do you see regarding use of space? Who speaks? What categories of people are there in the first place?

3. Observe a campus sporting event in sociological perspective. What functions do sports serve for your university or college? What patterns of inequality do they reflect and reinforce?

4. Think back to the 1998 Winter Olympics at Nagano, Japan. What are the functions of the Olympic Games for Canada and for the international community? Can you apply the structural-functional, social-conflict, and symbolic-interaction perspectives to the Olympic Games?

WEBLINKS

www.ixpres.com/lunatic/soc.html
WWW Virtual Library: Sociology provides links to research centres, resource directories, discussion groups of interest to sociologists, electronic journals and newsletters, organizations, a section on the sociology of the Web, and other resources.

www.sosig.ac.uk/welcome.html
A menu of worldwide sociology resources is provided at the *Social Science Information Gateway* (SOSIG), including an array of mailing lists, journals, associations, organizations, and archives.

weber.u.washington.edu/~hbecker/mills.html
An article about the life and work of the American sociologist Charles Wright Mills (1916–1962), by Howard S. Becker.

www.ccsd.ca/index.html
The Canadian Council on Social Development is a national, not-for-profit organization that focuses on the research and analysis of social and economic trends and their effects on the lives of Canadians.

www.solon.org/Constitutions/Canada/English/index.html
Canadian Constitutional Documents: A Legal History contains an extensive collection of constitutional documents, from the *Constitution Act* (1867) to the *Canada Act* (1982), including subsequent acts and amendments, plus relevant documents predating Confederation.

Alex Colville, *To Prince Edward Island,* 1965

SOCIOLOGICAL INVESTIGATION

It would be impossible to be a university student in the 1990s without knowing about AIDS. AIDS sprang into the consciousness of North Americans in the early to mid-1980s. Perhaps the first many people heard of this then-new disease was when Rock Hudson's name and death became associated with AIDS and with homosexuality. Since then, North Americans have become familiar with the disease through such different mechanisms as the highly successful film *Philadelphia*, and the Red Cross blood scandal in Canada, whereby many hemophiliacs and others who received blood in the early 1980s were infected with the HIV virus through transfused blood. Images of AIDS activists lying in front of trucks to force the U.S. government to provide costly and experimental drugs to AIDS patients, and of increasing activity often led by gay rights activists, are likely part of the everyday consciousness of Canadian citizens.

AIDS has raised a number of questions about civil and sexual rights, privacy, and confidentiality. Questions about mandatory HIV testing and the right of the public to know about infected persons are central to public discussions of AIDS (Callwood, 1995).

Michael Ornstein, a sociologist at York University in Toronto, set out to study public knowledge and policy attitudes with regard to AIDS. Because his goal was to portray the attitudes of Canadians, he surveyed a representative sample of 1250 Canadian adults. The survey included a list of open-ended questions regarding knowledge about and attitudes towards AIDS and public policy regarding AIDS. Table 2–1 lists some of the questions and briefly portrays the breakdown of answers from the sample.

Later in this chapter, we will take a closer look at Michael Ornstein's research. For the moment, notice how the sociological perspective helped him to spot broad social patterns operating in the lives of individuals. Just as importantly, Ornstein's work demonstrates the *doing* of sociology, the process of *sociological investigation*.

Many people think that scientists work only in laboratories, carefully taking measurements using complex equipment. But, as this chapter explains, sociologists also conduct scientific research in the familiar terrain of neighbourhood streets, in homes, at workplaces, and even in prisons, as well as in unfamiliar locales throughout the world—in short, wherever people can be found.

This chapter highlights the methods that sociologists use to conduct research. Along the way, we shall see that sociological research involves not just procedures for gathering information but controversies about whether that research should strive to be objective or to offer a bold prescription for change. Certainly, for example, sociological research on AIDS has important policy implications. We shall tackle questions of values after addressing the basics of sociological investigation.

27

TABLE 2–1 Responses to Questions About Attitudes on Public Policy Questions Relating to AIDS

Question	Percentage Distribution of Responses				
	Yes	Yes, qualified	No	No opinion	Total
This question is about a teacher who has been exposed to the AIDS virus. The teacher is in good health and shows NO symptoms of having the disease. If you had a child in this teacher's class, would you permit your child to go to the class?	69	8	15	7	100
Now let's say that an elementary school student is found to have been exposed to the AIDS virus through a blood transfusion. Medical authorities say that there is no risk at all to the other children in the class from the infected student. If your child was in this student's class, would you allow your child to attend that class?	73	8	13	6	100
Let's say that someone suspects that he or she has been infected with the AIDS virus and is considering whether to be tested.... Do you think a person should be able to have a test for the AIDS virus WITHOUT giving his or her name?	63	—	32	5	100
A doctor carries out a blood test and finds that a person has been infected with the AIDS virus. Do you think that the infected person should be required by law to name his or her sexual partners so that they can be traced and warned that they might have been exposed to the AIDS virus?	86	—	10	4	100
Suppose that someone is applying for a job. Do you think that the employer should be able to require that the job applicant undergo a test for the AIDS virus before being hired?	36	—	54	10	100
Someone answers an ad to rent an apartment. Now, what if the landlord discovers that the person is a carrier of the AIDS virus? Do you think that the landlord should have the legal right to refuse to rent the apartment?	16	—	78	6	100
People who inject themselves with drugs risk being infected with the AIDS virus if they share needles with other drug users. It might be possible to decrease the risk of infection by providing free needles to drug users. Do you think that free needles should be provided to drug users?	32	—	63	5	100
Say that the owner of a business learns that one of his workers is infected with the virus. The employee's work is completely satisfactory. Also, none of [his/her] work would expose other employees to infection.... Do you think the owner should have the legal right to fire the employee?	11	2	85	2	100
If a doctor thinks a patient has been exposed to the AIDS virus, should that patient be REQUIRED BY LAW to have a test for the virus?	80	—	17	3	100
Do you think that a life insurance company should be able to require that people taking out life insurance have a test to show they don't carry the AIDS virus?	51	—	41	8	100

SOURCE: Michael Ornstein (1992:250–51).

THE BASICS OF SOCIOLOGICAL INVESTIGATION

Sociological investigation begins with two simple requirements. The first was the focus of Chapter 1: *to look at the world using the sociological perspective.* Suddenly, from this point of view, we see all around us curious patterns of behaviour that call out for further study.

Michael Ornstein's sociological imagination prompted him to ask what social characteristics were associated with what social policy opinions regarding AIDS. This brings us to the second requirement for sociological investigation: to be curious and ask questions. Ornstein wanted to know what information Canadians had about AIDS and what their views were on the civil rights of people who had the disease. He wondered whether people who had more knowledge about AIDS held more progressive views on the rights of people with the disease. He wanted to know how people's attitudes towards gays and lesbians related to their level of information about AIDS and their attitudes towards people with AIDS.

These two requirements—seeing the world sociologically and asking questions—are fundamental to sociological investigation. Yet they are only the beginning. They draw us into the social world, stimulating our curiosity. But then we face the challenging task of finding answers to our questions. To understand the kind of insights sociology offers, we need to realize that there are various kinds of "truth."

People everywhere try to make sense of their surroundings. In his painting Whence Do We Come? *French artist Paul Gauguin (1848–1903) offers a mythic account of human origins. A myth (from Greek meaning "story") may or may not be factual in the literal sense, but it conveys some basic truth about the meaning and purpose of life. It is science, rather than art, that is powerless to address such questions of meaning.*

SCIENCE AS ONE FORM OF "TRUTH"

When we say we "know" something, we can mean any number of things. Most members of our society, a substantial 81 percent in fact, claim to believe in the existence of God (Bibby, 1995). Few would assert that they have direct contact with God, but they are believers all the same. We call this kind of knowing "belief" or "faith." A second kind of truth rests on the pronouncement of some recognized expert. Parents with questions about raising their children, for example, often consult child psychologists or other experts about which practices are "right." A third type of truth is based on simple agreement among ordinary people. We come to "know" that, say, sexual intercourse among young children is wrong, because virtually everyone in our society says it is.

People's "truths" differ the world over, and we often encounter "facts" at odds with our own. Imagine being a CUSO volunteer just arriving in a small, traditional village in Latin America. With the job of helping the local people to grow more food, you take to the fields, observing a curious practice: farmers carefully plant seeds and then place a dead fish directly on top of each one. In response to your question, they reply that the fish is a gift to the god of the harvest. A local elder adds sternly that the harvest was poor one year when no fish were offered as gifts.

From that society's point of view, using fish as gifts to the harvest god makes sense. The people believe in it, their experts endorse it, and everyone seems to agree that the system works. But, with scientific training in agriculture, you have to shake your head and wonder. The scientific "truth" in this situation is something entirely different: the decomposing fish fertilize the ground, producing a better crop.

Science, then, represents a fourth way of knowing. **Science** is *a logical system that bases knowledge on direct, systematic observation.* Standing apart from faith, the wisdom of "experts," and general agreement, scientific knowledge rests on **empirical evidence**, meaning *information we can verify with our senses.*

Our CUSO example does not mean, of course, that people in traditional villages ignore what their senses tell them, or that members of technologically advanced societies reject nonscientific ways of knowing. A medical researcher using science to seek an effective treatment for cancer, for example, may still practise her religion as a matter of faith; she may turn to experts when making financial decisions; and she may derive political opinions from family and friends. In short, we all embrace various kinds of truths at the same time.

COMMON SENSE VERSUS SCIENTIFIC EVIDENCE

Scientific evidence sometimes challenges our common sense. Here are six statements that many North Americans assume are "true," even though each is at least partly contradicted by scientific research.

1. **Poor people are far more likely than rich people to break the law.** Watching a television

Common sense suggests that, in a world of possibilities, people fall in love with that "special someone." Sociological research reveals that the vast majority of people select partners who are very similar in social background to themselves, as may be true of this couple from Alberta.

3. **Most poor people ignore opportunities to work.** Research included in Chapter 10 ("Social Class in Canada") suggests that this is true of some but not most poor people. Substantial majorities of the following categories are poor: unattached women over sixty-five are the most likely to be poor, followed by single-parent mothers with children under eighteen and unattached men over sixty-five. These are not people who are simply avoiding work.

4. **Differences in the behaviour of females and males reflect "human nature."** Much of what we call "human nature" is created by the society in which we are raised, as Chapter 3 ("Culture") details. Further, as argued in Chapter 12 ("Sex and Gender"), some societies define "feminine" and "masculine" very differently from the way we do.

5. **People change as they grow old, losing their former interests while focusing on their health.** Chapter 14 ("Aging and the Elderly") reports that aging actually changes our personalities very little. Problems of health increase in old age but, by and large, elderly people retain their distinctive personalities.

6. **Most people marry because they are in love.** To members of our society, few statements are so self-evident. But as surprising as it may seem, research shows that, in most societies, getting married has very little to do with love. Chapter 17 ("Family") explains why.

These examples confirm the old saying that "It's not what we don't know that gets us into trouble as much as things we do know that just aren't so." We have all been brought up believing conventional truths, bombarded by expert advice, and pressured to accept the opinions of people around us. As adults, we must learn to critically evaluate what we see, read, and hear, and sociology can help us to do that. Like any way of knowing, sociology has limitations, as we shall see. But scientific sociology gives us the tools to assess many kinds of information.

THE ELEMENTS OF SCIENCE

Sociologists apply science to the study of society in much the same way that natural scientists investigate the physical world. Whether they end up confirming a widely held opinion or revealing that it is way off base, sociologists use scientific techniques to gather empirical evidence. The following sections of this chapter introduce the major elements of scientific investigation.

show such as *Cops*, one might well conclude that police arrest only people from "bad" neighbourhoods. And, as Chapter 8 ("Deviance") explains, poor people are arrested in disproportionate numbers. But research also reveals that police and prosecutors are likely to treat apparent wrongdoing by well-to-do people more leniently. Further, some researchers argue that our society adopts laws designed to reduce the risk that affluent people will be criminalized.

2. **Canada is a middle-class society in which most people are more or less equal.** However, in the mid-1990s, close to 5 million Canadians had incomes below the poverty line: 1.5 million of these were children. Roughly 400 food banks across Canada help to feed these people. We may all be equal, but some, it seems, are much "more equal" than others.

CONCEPTS, VARIABLES, AND MEASUREMENT

A crucial element of science is the **concept**, *a mental construct that represents some part of the world, inevitably in a simplified form.* "Society" is itself a concept, as are the structural parts of societies, including "the family" and "the economy." Sociologists also use concepts to describe individuals, by noting, for example, their "sex," "race," "marital status," "sexual orientation," "education," "age," or "social class."

A **variable** is *a concept whose value changes from case to case.* The familiar variable "price," for example, changes from item to item in a supermarket. Similarly, people use the concept "social class" to evaluate people as "upper-class," "middle-class," "working-class," or "lower-class."

The use of variables depends on **measurement**, *the process of determining the value of a variable in a specific case.* Some variables are easy to measure, such as adding up our income at tax time. But measuring many sociological variables can be far more difficult. For example, how would you measure a person's "social class"? You might be tempted to look at clothing, listen to patterns of speech, or note a home address. In the interests of greater accuracy, you might ask about someone's income, occupation, and education.

Researchers know that almost any variable can be measured in more than one way. Having a very high income might qualify a person as "upper-class." But what if the income is derived from selling automobiles, an occupation most people think of as "middle-class"? And would having only an eighth-grade education make the person "lower-class?" To resolve such a dilemma, sociologists sensibly (if somewhat arbitrarily) combine these three measures—income, occupation, and education—into a single composite assessment of social class, called *socioeconomic status*, which is described in Chapter 9 ("Social Stratification") and Chapter 10 ("Social Class in Canada").

Sociologists also face the challenge of describing thousands or even millions of people according to some variable of interest such as income. Reporting an interminable stream of numbers would carry little meaning and tell us nothing about the people as a whole. Thus, sociologists use *statistical measures* (such as a mean or average) to describe people collectively.

Measurement is always a bit arbitrary since the value of any variable depends, in part, on how one defines it. **Operationalizing a variable** means *specifying exactly what one intends to measure in assigning a value to a variable.* If we were measuring people's social class, for example, we would have to decide if we were going to measure income, occupational prestige, education, or something else and, if we measured more

than one of these, how we would combine the scores. When reporting their results, researchers should specify how they operationalized each variable, so that readers can evaluate the research and fully understand the conclusions.

Reliability and Validity of Measurement

Useful measurement involves two further considerations. **Reliability** is *the quality of consistent measurement.* For a measure to be reliable, in other words, repeating the process should yield the same result. But consistency is no guarantee of **validity**, which is *the quality of measuring precisely what one intends to measure.* Valid measurement, in other words, means more than getting the same result time and again—it means obtaining a correct measurement.

To illustrate the difficulty of valid measurement, say you want to investigate how religious people are. A reasonable strategy would be to ask how often they attend religious services. But, in trying to gauge *religiosity* in this way, what you are actually measuring is *attendance at services*, which may or may not amount to the same thing. Generally, religious people do attend services more frequently, but people also participate in religious rituals out of habit or because of a sense of duty to someone else. Moreover, some devout believers shun organized religion altogether. Thus, even when a measurement yields consistent results (making it reliable), it can still miss the real, intended target (and lack validity). In sum, sociological research is no better than the quality of its measurement.

Relationships Among Variables

Once they achieve valid measurement, investigators can pursue the real payoff, which is determining how variables are related. The scientific ideal is **cause and effect**, *a relationship in which we know that change in one variable causes change in another.* A familiar cause-and-effect relationship occurs when a girl teases her brother until he becomes angry. *The variable that causes the change* (in this case, the teasing) is called the **independent variable**. *The variable that changes* (the behaviour of the brother) is known as the **dependent variable**. The value of one variable, in other words, is dependent on the value of another. Why is linking variables in terms of cause and effect important? Because doing so allows researchers to *predict*, that is, to use what they do know to predict what they don't know.

Because science puts a premium on prediction, people may be tempted to think that a cause-and-effect relationship is present any time variables change together. Consider, for instance, that the marriage rate tends to fall to its lowest point in January, exactly

Young people who live in the crowded inner-city are more likely than those who live in the spacious suburbs to have trouble with the police. But does this mean that crowding causes delinquency? Researchers know that crowding and arrest rates do vary together, but they have demonstrated that the connection is spurious: both factors rise in relation to a third factor—declining income.

the same month in which the death rate peaks. This hardly means that people die because they fail to marry (or that they don't marry because they die). In fact, it is the dreary weather during January (and perhaps also the post-holiday blahs) that causes both a low marriage rate and a high death rate. The flip side holds as well: the warmer and sunnier summer months have the highest marriage rate and the lowest death rate. Thus researchers often have to untangle cause-and-effect relationships that are not readily apparent.

To take a second case, sociologists have long recognized that juvenile delinquency is more common among young people who live in crowded housing. Say we operationalize the variable "juvenile delinquency" as the number of times (if any) a person under the age of eighteen has been arrested, and assess "crowded housing" by looking at the total square feet of living space per person in a home. We would find the variables related; that is, delinquency rates are, indeed, high in densely populated neighbourhoods. But should we conclude that crowding in the home (the independent variable) is what causes delinquency (the dependent variable)?

Not necessarily. **Correlation** is *a relationship by which two (or more) variables change together.* We know that density and delinquency are correlated because they change together, as shown in Part (a) of Figure 2–1. This relationship may mean that crowding causes misconduct, but often some third factor is at work causing change in both variables under observation. To see how, think what kind of people live in crowded housing: people with less money, power, and choice—the poor. Poor children are also more likely to end up with police records. Thus, crowded housing and juvenile delinquency are found together because both are caused by a third factor—poverty—as shown in Part (b) of Figure 2–1. In other words, the apparent connection between crowding and delinquency is "explained away" by a third variable—low income—that causes them both to change. So our original connection turns out to be a **spurious correlation**, *an apparent, although false, association between two (or more) variables caused by some other variable.*

Unmasking a correlation as spurious requires a bit of detective work, assisted by a technique called **control**, *holding constant all relevant variables except one in order to clearly see its effect.* In the example above, we suspect that income level may be behind a spurious connection between housing density and delinquency. To check, we control for income (that is, we hold it constant) by using as research subjects only young people of a single income level and looking again for a correlation between density and delinquency. If, by doing this, a correlation between density and delinquency remains (that is, if young people living in more crowded housing show higher rates of delinquency than young people with the same income in less crowded housing), we gain confidence that crowding does, in fact, cause delinquency. But if the relationship disappears when we control for income, as shown in Part (c) of Figure 2–1, we confirm that we have been dealing with a spurious correlation. Research has, in fact, shown that virtually all correlation between crowding and delinquency disappears if income is controlled (Fischer, 1984). So we have now sorted out the relationship among the three variables, as illustrated in Part (d) of Figure 2–1. Housing density and juvenile delinquency have a spurious correlation: evidence shows that both variables rise or fall according to people's income.

To sum up, correlation means only that two (or more) variables change together. Cause and effect rests on three conditions: (1) that there is a demonstrated correlation, but also (2) that the independent (or causal) variable precedes the dependent variable in time, and (3) that no evidence suggests that a third variable is responsible for a spurious correlation between the two.

Natural scientists identify cause-and-effect relationships more easily than social scientists because the laboratories used for study of the physical world allow control of many variables at one time. The sociologist, carrying out research in a workplace or on the streets, faces a considerably more difficult task. Often sociologists must be satisfied with demonstrating only correlation. In every case, moreover, human behaviour is highly complex, involving dozens of causal variables at any one time.

THE IDEAL OF OBJECTIVITY

Assume that ten writers who work for a magazine in Halifax, Nova Scotia, are collaborating on a story about that city's best restaurants. With their editor picking up the tab, they head out on the town for a week of fine dining. Later, they get together to compare notes. Do you think one restaurant would be everyone's clear favourite? That hardly seems likely.

In scientific terms, each of the ten reporters probably operationalizes the concept "best restaurant" differently. For one, it might be a place that serves delicious steaks at reasonable prices; for another, the choice might turn on a rooftop view of the city; for yet another, stunning decor and attentive service might be the deciding factors. Like so many other things in life, the best restaurant turns out to be mostly a matter of individual taste.

Personal values are fine when recommending restaurants, but they pose a challenge to scientific research. On the one hand, every scientist has personal opinions about the world. On the other hand, science endorses the goal of **objectivity**, *a state of personal neutrality in conducting research*. Objectivity in research depends on carefully adhering to scientific procedures in order not to bias the results. Scientific objectivity is an ideal rather than a reality, of course, since complete impartiality is virtually impossible to achieve. Even the subject a researcher selects to study and the framing of the questions are likely to grow out of personal interest. Ask your professor how his or her personal experiences have affected the choice of research question. Personal interest notwithstanding, scientists cultivate detachment and follow specific methods to minimize conscious or unconscious biases that distort their work. As an additional safeguard, researchers should try to identify and report their personal leanings to help readers evaluate their conclusions in the proper context.

Max Weber: Value-Free Research

The influential German sociologist Max Weber expected personal beliefs to play a part in a sociologist's

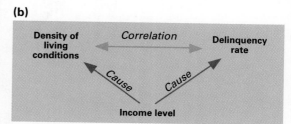

(a) If two variables vary together, they are said to be correlated. In this example, density of living conditions and juvenile delinquency increase and decrease together.

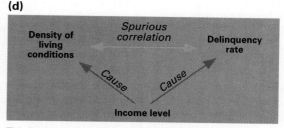

(b) Here we consider the effect of a third variable: income level. Low income level may cause *both* high-density living conditions *and* a high delinquency rate. In other words, as income level decreases, both density of living conditions and the delinquency rate increase.

(c) If we control income level — that is, examine only cases with the same income level — do those with higher-density living conditions still have a higher delinquency rate? The answer is *no*. There is no longer a correlation between these two variables.

(d) This finding leads us to conclude that income level is a cause of both density of living conditions and the delinquency rate. The original two variables (density of living conditions and delinquency rate) are thus correlated, but neither one causes the other. Their correlation is therefore *spurious*.

FIGURE 2–1 Correlation and Cause: An Example

selection of research topic. Why, after all, would one person study world hunger, another investigate the effects of racism, and still another examine one-parent families? But Weber (1958b; orig. 1918) admonished

A basic lesson of social research is that being observed affects how people behave. Researchers can never be certain precisely how this will occur; while some people resent public attention, others become highly animated when they think they have an audience.

researchers that even though they select topics that are *value-relevant*, they should conduct research that is *value-free* in their pursuit of conclusions. Only by being dispassionate in their work (as we expect any professional to be), can researchers study the world *as it is* rather than telling others how they think *it should be*. In Weber's view, this detachment is a crucial element of science that sets it apart from politics. Politicians, in other words, are committed to a particular outcome: scientists try to maintain an open-minded readiness to accept the results of their investigations, whatever they may be.

By and large, sociologists accept Weber's argument, although most concede that we can never be completely value-free or even aware of all our biases. Moreover, sociologists are not "average" people: most are white, highly educated, and more politically liberal than the population as a whole (Wilson, 1979). Sociologists need to remember that they, too, are affected by their own social backgrounds.

One strategy for limiting distortion caused by personal values is **replication**, *repetition of research by other investigators*. If other researchers repeat a study using the same procedures and obtain the same results, they gain confidence that the original research (as well as their own) was conducted objectively. The need for replication in scientific investigation is probably the reason that the search for knowledge is called research in the first place.

In any case, keep in mind that the logic and methodology of science hold out no guarantee that we will grasp objective, absolute truth. What science offers is an approach to knowledge that is self-cor-

recting so that, in the long run, researchers stand the best chance of overcoming their own biases and achieving greater understanding. Objectivity and truth, then, lie not in any particular research method, but in the scientific process itself.

SOME LIMITATIONS OF SCIENTIFIC SOCIOLOGY

The first scientists probed the operation of the natural world. Contemporary sociologists use science to study the social world; however, this application of the scientific method to sociological investigation has several important limitations.

1. **Human behaviour is too complex to allow sociologists to predict precisely any individual's actions.** Astronomers calculate the movement of planets with remarkable precision, announcing years in advance when a comet will next pass near the earth. But planets and comets are unthinking objects; humans, by contrast, have minds of their own. Because no two people react to any event in exactly the same way, the best sociologists can do is to show that categories of people typically act in one way or another. This is no failing of sociology; it is simply consistent with the nature of our mission—studying creative, spontaneous people.

2. **Because humans respond to their surroundings, the mere presence of a researcher may affect the behaviour being studied.** An

astronomer gazing at the moon has no effect whatever on that celestial body. But people usually react to being observed. Some may become anxious, angry, or defensive; others may try to "help" by providing the answers or actions they think researchers expect of them.

3. **Social patterns change constantly; what is true in one time or place may not hold true in another.** The laws of physics apply tomorrow as well as today, holding true around the world. But human behaviour is too variable for us to set down immutable sociological laws. In fact, some of the most interesting sociological research focuses on social diversity and social change.

4. **Because sociologists are part of the social world they study, being value-free when conducting social research can be difficult.** Barring a laboratory mishap, chemists are rarely personally affected by what goes on in test tubes. But sociologists live in their "test tubes"—the societies they study. Therefore, social scientists face a greater challenge in controlling—or even recognizing—personal values that may distort their work.

THE IMPORTANCE OF SUBJECTIVE INTERPRETATION

As we have explained, scientists tend to think of "subjectivity" as "bias"—a source of error to be avoided as much as possible. But there is also a good side to subjectivity, since creative thinking is vital to sociological investigation in three key ways.

First, science embodies a series of rules that guide research—rather like a recipe for cooking. But just as it takes more than a recipe to make a great chef, it takes more than scientific procedure to produce a great sociologist. Also needed is an inspired human imagination. After all, insight comes not from science itself but from the lively thinking of creative human beings (Nisbet, 1970). The genius of physicist Albert Einstein or sociologist Max Weber lay not only in his use of the scientific method but also in his curiosity and ingenuity.

Second, science cannot account for the vast and complex range of human motivations and feelings, including greed, love, pride, and despair. Science certainly helps us gather information about how people act, but it can never fully explain the complex meanings people attach to their behaviour (Berger and Kellner, 1981).

Third, we also do well to remember that scientific data never speak for themselves. After sociologists and other scientists "collect the numbers," they face the ultimate task of *interpretation*—creating meaning from

their observations. For this reason, good sociological investigation is as much art as science.

POLITICS AND RESEARCH

As Max Weber observed long ago, a fine line separates politics from science. Most sociologists endorse Weber's goal of value-free research. But a growing number of researchers are challenging the notion that politics and science can—or should—be distinct.

Alvin Gouldner (1970a; 1970b) was among the first to claim that the ideal of "value-free" research paints a "storybook picture" of sociology. Every element of social life is political, he argues, in that it benefits some people more than others. If so, Gouldner reasoned, the topics sociologists choose to study and the conclusions they reach also have political consequences.

If sociologists have no choice about their work being political, Gouldner continues, they do have a choice about *which* positions are worthy of support. Moreover, as he sees it, sociologists are obligated to endorse political objectives that will improve society. Although this viewpoint is not limited to sociologists of any one political orientation, it prevails among those with left-leaning politics, especially those guided by the ideas of Karl Marx. Recall Marx's (1972:109; orig. 1845) ringing assertion that the point is not simply to understand the world but to change it.

Such thinking, colliding with the value-free approach, has carried many universities and colleges into a spirited debate over "political correctness." In simple terms, this controversy pits advocates of Weberian value-free teaching and research against proponents of Marx's view that, since all knowledge is political, it should be used to promote positive societal change.

GENDER AND RESEARCH

One political dimension of research involves **gender,** *the significance members of a society attach to being female or male.* Sociologists have come to realize that gender often plays a significant part in their work. Margrit Eichler (1988) identifies five threats to sound research that relate to gender.

1. **Androcentricity**. Androcentricity (*andro* is the Greek word for "male;" *centricity* means "being centred on") refers to approaching an issue from a male perspective. Sometimes researchers enter a setting as if only the activities of men are important while ignoring what women do. For years, for example, researchers studying occupations focused on the paid work of men while overlooking the housework and child care

traditionally performed by women (Counts, 1925; Hodge, Treiman, and Rossi, 1966). When Matthews (1976) sought to understand the attitudes and values of three small Newfoundland communities that were being considered for relocation, he limited his interviews to a random sample of male household heads and all of the community leaders (who undoubtedly were also male). While seeking to understand human behaviour or community values, it has not been unusual to ignore half of humanity.

Eichler notes that the parallel situation of *gynocentricity*—seeing the world from a female perspective—is equally limiting to sociological investigation. However, in our male-dominated society, this narrowness of vision arises much less frequently.

2. **Overgeneralizing**. This problem occurs when researchers use data drawn from only people of one sex to support conclusions about both sexes. Historically, sociologists have studied men and then made sweeping claims about "humanity" or "society." For instance, gathering information about female managers and their productivity without examining the context of their work and its gender politics can lead to erroneous and sexist conclusions (Hale, 1987).

Here, again, the bias can occur in reverse. For example, in an investigation of child-rearing practices, collecting data only from women would allow researchers to draw conclusions about "motherhood" but not about the more general issue of "parenthood."

3. **Gender blindness**. This refers to the failure of a researcher to consider the variable of gender at all. As we note throughout this book, the lives of men and women generally differ in virtually every setting. A study of growing old in Canada that overlooked the fact that most elderly men live with spouses while elderly women generally live alone would be weakened by its gender blindness.

4. **Double standards**. Researchers must be careful not to distort what they study by applying different standards to men and women. For example, a family researcher who labels a couple as "man and wife" may define the man as the "head of household" and treat him accordingly, while assuming that the woman simply engages in family "support work."

5. **Interference**. In this case, gender distorts a study because a subject reacts to the sex of the researcher in ways that interfere with the research operation. While studying a small community in Sicily, for instance, Maureen Giovan-

nini (1992) found that many men responded to her as a woman rather than as a researcher, compromising her research efforts. Gender dynamics precluded her from certain activities, such as private conversations with men, that were deemed inappropriate for single women. In addition, local residents denied Giovannini access to places considered off-limits to women.

Of course, there is nothing wrong with focusing research on one sex or the other. But all sociologists, as well as people who read their work, should stay mindful of how gender can affect the process of sociological investigation.

FEMINIST RESEARCH

Sociology's pervasive attention to men in the past has prompted some contemporary researchers to make special efforts to investigate the lives of women. Advocates of feminist research embrace two key tenets: (1) that their research should focus on the condition of women in society, and (2) that the research must be grounded in the assumption that women generally experience subordination. Thus, feminist research rejects Weber's value-free orientation in favour of being overtly political—doing research in pursuit of gender equality.

There is no single feminist research strategy. On the contrary, feminists employ any and all conventional scientific techniques, including all of those described in this chapter. But some go further, claiming that feminist research must transform science itself, which they see as a masculine form of knowledge. Mainstream methodology, in the eyes of many modern feminists, is simply "malestream" methodology that is supportive of patriarchy and the status quo (McDonald, 1994:4). Whereas traditional notions about science demand detachment, feminists seek connections: a sympathetic understanding between investigator and subject. Moreover, conventional scientists take charge of the research agenda, deciding in advance what issues to raise and how to study them. Feminist researchers, by contrast, favour a more egalitarian approach that allows participants a chance to voice their needs and interests in their own words (Stanley and Wise, 1983; Nielsen, 1990; Stanley, 1990; Reinharz, 1992; Wolf, 1996).

Such alterations in research premises and methods have led more conventional sociologists to charge that feminist research is less science than simple political activism. Feminists respond that research and politics should not—indeed cannot—be distinct. Therefore, traditional notions that placed politics and science in separate spheres have now given way to some new thinking that merges these two dimensions.

Feminist research is not concerned simply with studying the social standing of women. It also transforms scientific research so that an investigator assumes a posture of social parity with others, working cooperatively towards solving their common problems.

University of Guelph professor Lynn McDonald (1994) has shaken up mainstream sociologists and feminists alike with her analysis of the role of women in the early development of sociology—and social science methodology in particular. McDonald argues that the feminists who reject empirical or scientific research and quantitative analysis—as serving the interests of men—are rejecting methodologies that women helped to develop in order to further their causes. Among the many women whose contributions are outlined in The Women Founders of the Social Sciences (McDonald, 1994) are Harriet Martineau (1802–76) and Florence Nightingale (1820–1910).

Martineau made her living as a writer and an investigative journalist, producing more than fifty books and 1600 feature articles on a wide range of issues. She also dealt with methodology in "Essays on the Art of Thinking" and an 1838 book entitled *How to Observe Morals and Manners.* Her *Society in America*, which appeared in 1837, made her the first to tackle comparative analysis applying an explicitly sociological approach. Martineau, an activist, supported the anti-slavery movement and worked for women's rights to education, divorce, occupations, the franchise (the right to vote), and freedom from violence.

The name Florence Nightingale is familiar to all of us. She was "the lady with the lamp," the humble nurse from a wealthy background who ministered to the needs of soldiers wounded in Crimea. McDonald (1994) reveals a Nightingale of such methodological and theoretical sophistication that one wonders if Durkheim was intellectually indebted to her. She was a "passionate statistician" who gathered data—often presented in pie charts that simultaneously compared data cross-sectionally and over time. She used her statistics to show that improved sanitation would reduce mortality in Crimean hospitals, in childbirth, and in British hospitals and would be cost-effective at the

same time. Her application of statistics to more general issues of public administration led her to "describe the laws of social science as God's laws for the right operation of the world" (p. 186). She noted that crime, suicide, mortality, accident, marriage, and poverty levels could be predicted with exact precision, despite individual free will. As an activist who believed that social and individual conditions could be changed, Nightingale fought for ameliorative changes to a wide range of laws, policies, and administrative budgets.

Feminist Research: Two Examples

How are women's lives affected by a capitalist and patriarchal social order? Dorothy Smith and Meg Luxton, two Canadian sociologists, have both done sociological research based on the description and analysis of this question.

In a series of essays (1977; 1979; 1983), Dorothy Smith notes the ways in which relations between men and women depend on economic conditions. Her argument begins with the idea that in the early homesteading period, the division of labour between the sexes was fairly evenly split. Men and women depended on one another for house-building, clearing land, growing and harvesting gardens, caring for livestock, and preserving foodstuffs for winter. This situation of approximate equality changed as the economic unit moved to cash production. As land speculation led to increased prices and expensive mortgages on houses and machinery, families had to produce more than they themselves needed for their own subsistence. They needed profits to pay off bank loans and to buy equipment and other goods. But, legally, only men could own property and borrow money at the bank. The labour of wives earned them nothing: the benefits went to their husbands (owners?). The result

Many women contributed to the emergence of sociology, although their achievements have long been unrecognized. Harriet Martineau (left) established her reputation as a sociologist with studies of slavery, factory laws, and women's rights. She also found time to write novels, travel widely, and pursue a full-time career as a journalist, in spite of recurrent ill health and deafness. Florence Nightingale (right) not only revolutionized the practice of nursing in the nineteenth century, she was also one of the first to use statistics and probability theory to reform public health laws.

was drudgery and a loss of power for the women. As late as 1973, the powerlessness of the farm wife was underscored in the Supreme Court decision regarding Irene Murdoch. Murdoch had worked on the family farm for twenty-five years. When she and her husband divorced, the court decided that she had no right to any of the farm property. Women's organizations in Canada rallied in opposition of this injustice; Murdoch took her case to the Supreme Court—and lost. Her case, however, was important. During the 1970s, province after province began to define marriage as a partnership of equals whose assets should be divided equally upon divorce (Anderson, 1991). By the late 1980s, Rosa Becker had won the right to the financial assets of a twenty-five-year common law partnership.

Women's work is still undervalued and women continue to play a subservient role to their husbands in the home and in corporations. Their services are used to maintain the labour power of their husbands and children. Meg Luxton's book *More Than a Labour of Love* (1980) describes the process whereby women work to "re-produce" labour power for a corporation in a single-industry mining town in Flin Flon, Manitoba. She describes the way in which the lives of the women are constrained by the requirements of the corporations. The rhythms of women's lives and the lives of their children revolve around the need of the husbands for sleep, food, rest, and relaxation, all in the interest of maintaining their employment. Luxton also documents the ways in which the husbands' frustrations at work are carried home to be vented on the wives. In extreme cases, wives contend not only with surplus anger and frustration but become the victims of violence, as their husbands act out their frustrations with the corporation.

Neither Dorothy Smith nor Meg Luxton is concerned with the explication and operationalization of concepts into quantitative variables. Causality is not determined mathematically on the basis of numerical measurements of variables, but from a subjective analysis of the situation. In their world view, exploitation and injustice in power, gender, class, and race

characterize social relations, and the relations among these conditions over time and place need explaining. Change towards justice is ultimately the goal. Sociology, in this tradition, is done very differently from positivist sociology.

RESEARCH ETHICS

Like all investigators, sociologists must be mindful that research can be harmful as well as helpful to subjects or communities. For this reason, the American Sociological Association—the major professional association of sociologists in North America—has established formal guidelines for the conduct of research (1997), as have the various bodies that fund social research, such as Canada's Social Sciences and Humanities Research Council.

The prime directive is that sociologists strive to be both technically competent and fair-minded in conducting their research. Sociologists must disclose all their findings, without omitting significant data, and they are ethically bound to make their results available to other sociologists, some of whom may wish to replicate the research.

Sociologists must strive to ensure the safety of subjects taking part in a research project. Should research develop in a manner that threatens the well-being of participants, investigators must terminate their work immediately. Furthermore, professional guidelines direct researchers to protect the privacy of anyone involved in a research project. Yet this is a promise that may be difficult to keep, since researchers sometimes come under pressure (say, from the police or courts) to disclose information. Therefore, researchers must think carefully about their responsibility to protect subjects, and they should discuss this issue with those who take part in research. An important principle in ethical research is obtaining the informed consent of participants, which means that subjects understand the responsibilities and risks that the research involves and agree—before the work begins—to take part.

Conducting Research with Aboriginal Peoples

A Royal Commission on Aboriginal Peoples was announced in 1991 with a mandate to do extensive research and provide baseline data on the lives of aboriginal peoples living in Canada. The ethical guidelines for the conduct of this research were published in the *Northern Health Research Bulletin*. As well as the standard principles for the conduct of ethical research, the royal commission established new guidelines with respect to the benefits of research to the community. As they stated under the heading "Community Benefit,"

- In setting research priorities and objectives for community-based research, the Commission and the researchers it engages shall give serious and due consideration to the benefit of the community concerned.

- In assessing community benefit, regard shall be given to the widest possible range of community interest, whether the groups in question be Aboriginal or non-Aboriginal, and also to the impact of research at the local, regional or national level.

Wherever possible, conflicts between interests within the community should be identified and resolved in advance of commencing the project. Researchers should be equipped to draw on a range of problem-solving strategies to resolve such conflicts as may arise in the course of research.

- Whenever possible research should support the transfer of skills to individuals and increase the capacity of the community to manage its own research.

The final, five-volume report of the royal commission covers every conceiv-

able issue related to aboriginal peoples—constitutional, political, social, medical, economic, demographic, and cultural. The report was based on the information acquired by the commission in meetings and hearings across the country, as well as from over 400 reports prepared by various organizations and individuals (aboriginal and nonaboriginal): sociologists and other social scientists were among those who submitted these reports. The report is also available on CD-ROM under the title *For Seven Generations: An Information Legacy of the Royal Commission on Aboriginal Peoples*. The CD-ROM has an elaborate search capacity (by subject, for example) that greatly increases access to the contents of the report. The Institute of Indigenous Government has made the report available on the Internet (www.indigenous.bc.ca/rcap/rcapeng.html). Thus, social scientists, politicians, and aboriginal communities can do research on the report itself.

SOURCE: Canada, The Royal Commission on Aboriginal Peoles, "Ethical Guidelines for Research," *Northern Health Bulletin*, 1993.

Taking this debate one step further, should researchers employ deception in their work? Obviously, if researchers tell people exactly what they are looking for, they will not observe natural behaviour. On the other hand, misleading subjects can generate understandable resentment. Researchers make decisions about how to proceed on a case-by-case basis, but they must avoid using deception if doing so threatens to bring any harm to subjects.

Another important guideline concerns funding. Sociologists must include in their published results the sources of any and all financial support. Furthermore, sociologists must seek to avoid any conflicts of interest (or even the appearance of such conflicts) that may compromise the integrity of their work. For example, researchers must never accept funding from any organization that seeks to influence the research results for its own purposes.

Ethical concerns extend well beyond the issues raised here and address the role of sociologists as teachers, administrators, and in clinical practice. Readers may review the current code of ethics by visiting the American Sociological Association's home page on the Internet (www.asanet.org).

At the broadest level, there are also global dimensions to research ethics. Before beginning research in other countries, investigators must become familiar enough with that society to understand what people there are likely to perceive as a violation of privacy or a source of personal danger. In a multicultural society such as ours, of course, the same rule applies to studying people whose cultural background differs from one's own. The "Social Diversity" box offers some tips about how outsiders can effectively and sensitively study aboriginal communities.

THE METHODS OF SOCIOLOGICAL RESEARCH

A **research method** is *a systematic plan for conducting research*. The remainder of this chapter introduces four commonly used methods of sociological investigation. None is inherently better or worse than any other. Rather, in the same way that a carpenter selects a particular tool for a specific task, researchers choose a method according to whom they choose to study and what they wish to learn.

TESTING A HYPOTHESIS: THE EXPERIMENT

The logic of science is most clearly expressed in the **experiment**, *a research method for investigating cause and effect under highly controlled conditions*. Experimental research is *explanatory*, meaning that it asks not just what happens but why. Typically, researchers turn to an experiment to test a specific **hypothesis**, *an unverified statement of a relationship between variables*.

Ideally, we evaluate a hypothesis in three steps: 1) the experimenter measures the dependent variable (the "effect"); 2) the investigator exposes the dependent variable to the independent variable (the "cause" or "treatment"); and 3) the researcher again measures the dependent variable to see if the predicted change took place. If the expected change did occur, the experiment lends support to the hypothesis; if not, the hypothesis is discounted.

But a change in the dependent variable may be due to something other than the assumed cause. To prevent this, researchers must carefully control any and all extraneous factors that might intrude into the experiment and affect what is being measured. Such control is most easily accomplished in a laboratory, an artificial setting specially constructed for research purposes. Another strategy for neutralizing outside influences is the random assignment of subjects into an *experimental group* and a *control group*. At the outset, the researcher measures the dependent variable for subjects in both groups but exposes only the experimental group to the independent variable or treatment (the control group typically gets a "placebo," an apparently comparable treatment known to have no experimental effect). Then the investigator measures the dependent variable for the subjects in both groups again. It is assumed that any factor (such as some news event) occurring during the course of the research that influences people in the experimental group would do the same to the control group subjects, thus neutralizing the factor. In short, the use of a control group "washes out" many extraneous factors; comparing before and after measurements of the two groups,

a researcher is able to assess how much of the observed change is due only to the independent variable.

The Hawthorne Effect

Subjects may alter their behaviour simply in response to a researcher's attention, as one classic experiment revealed. In the late 1930s, the Western Electric Company hired researchers to investigate worker productivity in its Hawthorne factory near Chicago (Roethlisberger and Dickson, 1939). One experiment examined whether increasing the available lighting would raise worker output. To test this idea, researchers measured initial productivity (the dependent variable); then they increased the lighting (the independent variable); finally, they measured productivity a second time. Productivity increased, supporting the hypothesis. But when the research team subsequently *reduced* the lighting, productivity again increased, contradicting the initial hypothesis. In time, the researchers realized that the employees were working harder (even if they could not see as well) simply because people were paying attention to them. From this research, social scientists coined the term **Hawthorne effect** to refer to *a change in a subject's behaviour caused simply by the awareness of being studied*.

An Illustration: The Stanford County Prison

Prisons are often violent institutions, but does the prison setting itself play a part in generating violence and disorder? This question prompted Philip Zimbardo to devise a fascinating experiment to investigate the causes of prison violence (Zimbardo, 1972; Haney, Banks, and Zimbardo, 1973).

Zimbardo's hypothesis was simple: prison violence is caused not so much by antisocial prisoners or guards as by the nature of prison itself. In other words, Zimbardo suspected that, once inside a prison, even emotionally healthy people become prone to violence. Thus Zimbardo treated the *prison setting* as the independent variable capable of causing *violence*, the dependent variable.

To test this hypothesis, Zimbardo's research team first constructed a realistic, artificial prison in the basement of the psychology building on the campus of Stanford University. Then they placed an ad in a Palo Alto newspaper, offering to pay young men for their help with a two-week research project. To each of the seventy men who responded they administered a series of physical and psychological tests, selecting the healthiest twenty-four for their experiment.

The next step was randomly designating half the men as "prisoners" and half as "guards." The plan called for the guards and prisoners to spend the next two weeks in the "Stanford County Prison." The "prisoners" began their part of the experiment soon afterwards when the Palo Alto police "arrested" them at their homes. After searching and handcuffing the men, the police took them to the local police station to be fingerprinted. Then they transported their captives to the Stanford "prison" where Zimbardo had the "guards" ready to secure them behind bars. Zimbardo then sat back with a video camera to see what would happen next.

The experiment quickly degenerated into more than anyone had bargained for. Both guards and prisoners soon became embittered and hostile towards one another. Guards humiliated the prisoners by assigning them tasks such as cleaning toilets with their bare hands. The prisoners, for their part, resisted and insulted the guards. Within four days, the researchers removed five prisoners who displayed "extreme emotional depression, crying, rage and acute anxiety" (Haney, Banks, and Zimbardo, 1973:81). Before the end of the first week, the situation had deteriorated so much that the researchers called off the experiment entirely. Zimbardo explains (1972:4): "The ugliest, most base, pathological side of human nature surfaced. We were horrified because we saw some boys (guards) treat others as if they were despicable animals, taking pleasure in cruelty, while other boys (prisoners) became servile, dehumanized robots who thought only of escape, of their own individual survival and of their mounting hatred for the guards."

The unfolding events in the "Stanford County Prison" supported Zimbardo's hypothesis that prison violence is rooted in the social character of jails themselves, rather than in the personalities of guards and prisoners. This finding also raises questions about how and why our society operates prisons, pointing towards the need for basic reform. But also note how this experiment reveals the potential of research to threaten the physical and mental well-being of subjects. Such dangers are not always as obvious as they were in this case. Therefore, researchers must carefully consider the potential harm to subjects at all stages of their work and end any study, as Zimbardo responsibly did, if subjects may suffer harm of any kind.

ASKING QUESTIONS: SURVEY RESEARCH

A **survey** is *a research method in which subjects respond to a series of items in a questionnaire or an interview.* The most widely used of all research methods, surveys are particularly well suited to studying attitudes that investigators cannot observe directly, including political and religious beliefs or the subjective effects of racism. Although surveys can shed light on cause and

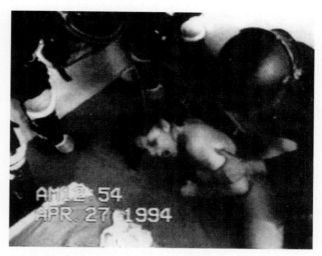

Philip Zimbardo's research helps to explain why violence is a common element in our society's prisons. At the same time, his work demonstrates the dangers that sociological investigation poses for subjects and the need for investigators to observe ethical standards that protect the welfare of people who participate in research.

effect, most often they yield *descriptive* findings, as researchers seek to paint a picture of subjects' views on some issue.

Population and Sample

The researcher begins a survey by designating a **population**, *the people who are the focus of research.* Ornstein, whose research was introduced at the beginning of this chapter, was interested in portraying the population of all adult Canadians. Political pollsters also try to predict election returns using surveys that treat every adult in the country as the population.

Obviously, however, contacting millions of people would overwhelm even the most well-funded and patient researcher. Fortunately, there is a far easier alternative that produces accurate results: Researchers collect data from a **sample**, *a part of a population that represents the whole.*

Although the term may be new to you, you use the logic of sampling all the time. If you look around the classroom and notice five or six heads nodding off, you might conclude that the class finds that day's lecture dull. Such a conclusion involves making an inference about *all* of the people (the "population") from observing *some* of the people (the "sample"). But how do we know if a sample actually represents the entire population?

One way to ensure this is through *random* sampling, in which researchers draw a sample from the

Most census data are obtained from questionnaires that officials send and receive back through the mail or deliver and pick up by hand. Although this strategy is generally quite efficient, it is likely to undercount the homeless or others who lack a customary street address. Olaf Solheim (above) was evicted from a rooming-house in Vancouver's West End to make room for tourist housing for Expo '86. Less than six weeks later, Solheim was dead. Modern sociologists are committed to research that does not rely solely on government statistics, but that also allows voices like Solheim's to be heard.

population in such a way that every element in the population has the same chance of ending up in the sample. If this is the case, the mathematical laws of probability dictate that the sample they select will, in the vast majority of cases, represent the population with a minimal amount of error. Seasoned researchers use special computer programs to generate random samples. Novice researchers, however, sometimes make the mistake of assuming that "randomly" walking up to people on the street produces a sample representative of an entire city. But such a strategy does not give every person an equal chance to be included in the sample. For one thing, any street—whether in a rich neighbourhood or a "university town"—contains more of some kinds of people than others. For another, any researcher is apt to find some people more approachable than others, again introducing a bias.

Although good sampling is no simple task, it offers a considerable savings in time and expense. We are spared the tedious work of contacting everyone in a population, while obtaining essentially the same results.

Questionnaires and Interviews

Selecting subjects is only the first step in carrying out a survey. Also needed is a plan for asking questions and recording answers. Surveys fall into two general categories: questionnaires and interviews.

A **questionnaire** is *a series of written questions a researcher supplies to subjects requesting their responses.* One type of questionnaire provides not only the questions but a series of fixed responses (similar to a multiple-choice examination). This *closed-ended format* makes the task of analyzing the results relatively easy, yet narrows the range of responses in a way that might distort the findings. By contrast, a second type of questionnaire, using an *open-ended format*, allows subjects to respond freely, expressing various shades of opinion. The drawback of this approach is that the researcher later has to make sense out of what can be a bewildering array of answers.

How to present questions to subjects forms another part of the research strategy. Most often, researchers employ a *self-administered survey*, in which they mail questionnaires to respondents with a request to complete the form and mail it back. Since no researcher is present when subjects read the questionnaire, it must be both inviting and clearly written. *Pretesting* a self-administered questionnaire with a small number of people before sending it to the entire sample can preclude the costly problem of finding out—too late—that instructions or questions are confusing.

Using the mail (or, more recently, electronic mail) has the advantage of allowing a researcher to contact a large number of people over a wide geographical area at minimal expense. But many people treat such questionnaires as "junk mail;" typically, no more than half are completed and returned. Researchers often send out follow-up mailings to coax reluctant subjects to fill out the questionnaire.

Finally, keep in mind that many people are not capable of completing a questionnaire on their own. Young children obviously cannot, nor can many hospital patients, as well as a surprising number of adults who simply lack the reading and writing skills needed to wade through a comprehensive questionnaire.

An **interview** is *a series of questions a researcher administers personally to respondents.* In a closed-ended format, researchers read a question or statement and then ask the subject to select a response from several choices. Generally, however, interviews are open-ended so that subjects can respond in whatever way they choose and researchers can probe with follow-up questions. In the ensuing conversation, however, the researcher must guard against influencing a subject, a problem that can creep in through such subtle gestures as the raising of an eyebrow when a person begins to answer.

Comparing the interview with the questionnaire, experienced investigators know that a subject is more likely to complete a survey if contacted personally by the researcher. Yet interviews have some disadvan-

TABLE 2–2 Sample and Population Characteristics: A Comparison

Variable	1986 Census of Canada*	Charter	1986 Census Quebec Only	Charter Sample Quebec Only
Mean age of respondents	42	43	42	41
Highest level of schooling				
High school graduation or less	55%	56%	58%	59%
College, technical school, some university, etc.	35%	28%	31%	30%
University degree(s)	10%	15%	9%	11%
Sex				
Female	51%	51%	52%	52%
Male	49%	49%	48%	48%
Marital status				
Married (living with partner)	65%	66%	64%	66%
Never been married	22%	23%	24%	22%
Separated, divorced, widowed	13%	11%	12%	12%
Employment status				
Employed	62%	63%	57%	55%
Not in labour force	31%	29%	35%	37%
Unemployed	7%	8%	8%	8%

SOURCE: Sniderman et al. (1993:246).

*Statistics Canada Public Use Sample Tapes.

tages: tracking people down and personally interrogating them is costly and time-consuming, especially if all subjects do not live in the same area. And while telephone interviews clearly allow far greater "reach," the impersonality of "cold calls" by telephone may result in a low completion rate.

In both questionnaires and interviews, the wording of questions has a significant effect on answers. Moreover, emotionally loaded language can easily sway subjects. For instance, the term "welfare mothers," as opposed to "women who receive public assistance," injects an emotional element into a survey and encourages respondents to answer more negatively. In still other cases, the wording of questions may hint at what other people think, thereby steering subjects. For example, people are more likely to respond positively to the question "Do you *agree* that the police force is doing a good job?" than to a similar question "Do you *think* that the police force is doing a good job?" Similarly, respondents are more likely to endorse a statement to "*not allow*" something (say, public speeches against the government) than a statement to "*forbid*" the same activity (Rademacher, 1992).

Finally, researchers may inadvertently confuse respondents by asking double questions such as "Do you think that the government should cut spending and raise taxes to reduce the deficit?" The problem here is that a subject could very well agree with one part of the question but reject the other, so that responding yes or no to the two-part question distorts the person's true opinion.

Surveys at Work: The Case of Anti-Semitism in Quebec

On September 17, 1991, Mordecai Richler, a prominent Canadian novelist with an international reputation (and a Jew), wrote an article on French-Canadian nationalism in the *New Yorker* in which he alleged that French Canadians are anti-Semitic. His statements were the beginning of passionately felt and argued controversy. Are French Canadians anti-Semitic? If so, are they more anti-Semitic than English Canadians? If they are more anti-Semitic, what is the explanation? A team of sociologists headed by Paul Sniderman attempted to answer these questions.

Sniderman used the data from an existing survey entitled the *Charter of Rights Study Survey*, carried out in 1993. The study used random digit dialling (RDD) of a random sample (2084 people) of the 97 percent of Canadian households that have telephones. The Quebec sampling strategy was specifically designed to yield a representative sample of the province. Care was taken that the Quebec response rate was equal to that in the rest of the country, and that those who responded filled the same demographic categories as those in the rest of Canada. In other words, the survey was designed to include the right proportions of male and female, older and younger, urban dwellers and rural dwellers, etc., in order to reflect the total population of both the country and Quebec. The accuracy of this method is demonstrated by the similarities between the sample and the population of Canada, as portrayed in Table 2–2. Notice, for example, that the

Fieldwork enables researchers to document fascinating rituals such as the one conducted by these Himba women in Namibia (left), who are seeking to rid themselves of the lion spirit sent by their dead husband to bring them to him in the afterlife. Fieldworkers often live for long periods with the people they are studying and form close bonds with their subjects, as Peggy Reeves Sanday, shown here in Indonesia (right), has clearly done with her namesake, Eggi.

average age of Canadians respondents in the 1986 Census was forty-two years, while the average age of the Charter sample was forty-three years.

The next problem for the researchers was the wording of the questions. A review of the literature on explanations for prejudice identified several common bases for prejudicial attitudes. These included

1. **Personality type** of the individual: apparently people with authoritative personalities are more likely to express prejudice.
2. **Normative prejudice**—prejudice widely taken for granted as acceptable—such as is found in South Africa, where prejudice was legislated into what were then the policies of apartheid.
3. **Normative conformity,** in which conformity itself is seen as an important norm.
4. **Nationalism.** With respect to Quebec, it has been suggested that one of the consequences of French nationalism may be a derogation of other groups.

These four competing hypotheses were operationalized through a series of questions and found reliable.

The questionnaire was designed to identify not only whether French-speaking Quebeckers held more anti-Semitic views than English-speaking Canadians (the dependent variable), but also to examine which of these factors was the underlying cause of those views (the independent variable). The five questions used were as follows (Sniderman et al., 1993:247):

> We realize no statement is true of all people in a group, but generally speaking, please tell me whether you agree or disagree with the following statements. Would you say you agree strongly, agree somewhat, disagree somewhat or disagree with this statement?

> Most Jews don't care what happens to people who aren't Jewish.

> Most Jews are pushy.

> Jews have made an important contribution to the cultural life of Canada.

> Jews are more willing than others to use shady practices to get ahead.

> Most Jews are warm and friendly people.

Note the carefully worded introduction, which was designed to make respondents feel comfortable expressing their views candidly by qualifying the responses. Given the sensitive nature of the topic, this was deemed necessary in order to combat what sociologists refer to as the social desirability effect, whereby respondents are unwilling to commit themselves to an opinion that might place them outside the "normal" range of opinion. By acknowledging that the statements could not be applied to all Jews, the researchers allowed respondents freer rein in expressing their attitudes. Even if respondents agreed strongly with one of the negative statements, they could rest assured that they fell within "acceptable norms," since the response was not going to be taken as a blanket condemnation of all Jews.

Findings. The researchers found that French-speaking Quebeckers were, in fact, more anti-Semitic than English-speaking Canadians. While the personality basis for anti-Semitism was conspicuously weak, the cultural basis for anti-Semitism was strong and related more to the high value placed on conformity in Quebec (normative conformity) than on nationalist sentiment, as had been suggested by some commentators. French-speaking Quebeckers were significantly more likely than English-speaking Canadians to express support for conformity as a value. "They place a greater priority on people learning to fit in and get along with others" and on the larger society being "a unified body pursuing a common goal" (Sniderman, 1993:264). They are therefore more likely to distrust and dislike those who try to be different.

Conclusions. The authors make the point that while francophone Quebeckers are overall more anti-Semitic than other Canadians, most are not anti-Semitic at all. Moreover, on every test but one, a majority expressed positive sentiments regarding Jews. "Quebeckers differ from other Canadians not so much in their readiness to submit to the full syndrome of anti-Semitic ideas but rather in their willingness to accept one or two negative characterizations of Jews" (265). Québécois were as tolerant as English-speaking Canadians and were as willing as anglophones to support such things as the rights of groups with unpopular points of view to hold public rallies, and the need for restrictions on the rights of Canada's security service to wiretap. Finally, the researchers warned that to say that anti-Semitism is more of a problem in Quebec is not to say that it does not exist elsewhere in Canada.

IN THE FIELD: PARTICIPANT OBSERVATION

Sociological investigation takes place not only in laboratories but "in the field"—or where people carry on their everyday lives. The most widely used strategy for field study is **participant observation**, *a method in which researchers systematically observe people while joining in their routine activities.*

Researchers choose participant observation in order to gain an inside look at social life in settings ranging from night clubs to religious seminaries. Cultural anthropologists commonly employ participant observation (which they call *fieldwork*) to study communities in other societies. They term their descriptions of unfamiliar cultures ethnographies; sociolo-

gists prefer to describe their accounts of people in particular settings as *case studies*.

At the outset of a field study, social scientists typically have just a vague idea of what they will encounter. Thus, most field research is *exploratory* and *descriptive*. Researchers might have hypotheses in mind, but just as likely they may not yet realize what the important questions will turn out to be.

As its name suggests, participant observation has two facets. On the one hand, gaining an "insider's" look depends on becoming a participant in the setting—"hanging out" with others, attempting to act, think, and even feel the way they do. Compared to experiments and survey research, then, participant observation has fewer hard-and-fast rules. But it is precisely this flexibility that allows investigators to explore the unfamiliar and to adapt to the unexpected.

Unlike other research methods, participant observation requires a researcher to become immersed in the setting, not for a week or two, but for months or even years. For the duration of the study, however, the researcher must maintain some distance as an "observer," mentally stepping back to record field notes and, eventually, to make sense of the action. The tension inherent in this method comes through in the name: playing the *participant* gains for the researcher acceptance and access to people's lives; yet, playing the observer affords the distance and perspective needed for thoughtful analysis. The twin roles of "insider" participant and "outside observer," then, often come down to a series of careful compromises.

Most sociologists carry out participant observation alone, so they must remain mindful that results depend on the interpretations of a single individual. Participant observation is typically **qualitative research**, meaning *investigation in which a researcher gathers impressionistic, not numerical, data.* Unlike experiments or surveys, participant observation usually involves little **quantitative research**, *investigation in which a researcher collects numerical data.* Some scientists disparage a "soft" method such as participant observation as lacking in scientific rigour. Yet its personal approach—relying so heavily on personal impressions—is also a strength; while a highly visible team of sociologists attempting to administer formal surveys would disrupt many social settings, a sensitive participant-observer can often gain considerable insight into people's natural, day-to-day behaviour.

An Illustration: Street Corner Society

In the late 1930s, a young graduate student at Harvard University named William Foote Whyte became fascinated by the lively street life of a nearby, rather run-down section of Boston. His curiosity ultimately led Whyte to carry out four years of participant observation in this neighbourhood, which he called "Cornerville," producing a sociological classic in the process.

At the time, Cornerville was home to first- and second-generation Italian immigrants. Many were poor and lived economically precarious lives, quite unlike the more affluent Bostonians familiar to Whyte. Popular wisdom in Boston held that Cornerville was a place to avoid: a poor, chaotic slum inhabited by racketeers. Unwilling to accept easy stereotypes, Whyte set out to discover for himself exactly what kind of life went on inside this community. His celebrated book, *Street Corner Society* (1981; orig. 1943), describes Cornerville as a highly organized community with a distinctive code of values, complex social patterns, and particular social conflicts.

Beginning his investigation, Whyte considered a range of research methods. Of course, he might have taken a pile of questionnaires to one of Cornerville's community centres and asked local people to fill them out. Or he could have asked members of the community to come to his Harvard office for interviews. But it is easy to see that such formal strategies would have prompted little cooperation from the local people and yielded few insights. Whyte decided, therefore, to ease into Cornerville life and patiently seek out the keys to understanding this rather mysterious place.

Soon enough, Whyte discovered the challenges of just getting started in field research. After all, an upper-middle-class Anglo-Saxon graduate student from Harvard did not exactly "fit in" to Cornerville life. And, as Whyte quickly found out, even what he intended as a friendly overture could seem pushy and rude to others. Early on, Whyte dropped in at a local bar, hoping to buy a woman a drink and encourage her to talk about Cornerville. He looked around the room, but could find no woman alone. Presently, he thought he might have an opportunity when a fellow sat down with two women. He gamely remarked, "Pardon me. Would you mind if I joined you?" Instantly, he realized his miscalculation:

> There was a moment of silence while the man stared at me. Then he offered to throw me down the stairs. I assured him that this would not be necessary, and demonstrated as much by walking right out of there without any assistance. (1981:289)

As this incident suggests, gaining entrée to a community—that is, becoming a participant—is the crucial (and sometimes hazardous) first step in this type of research. "Breaking in" typically depends on patience, ingenuity, and a little luck. For Whyte, a big break came in the form of a young man named "Doc," whom he met in a local social service agency. Listening to Whyte's account of his bungled efforts to make friends in Cornerville, Doc sympathetically decided to take Whyte under his wing and introduce him to others in the community. With Doc's help, Whyte soon became a "regular" in the neighbourhood.

Whyte's friendship with Doc illustrates the importance of a *key informant* in field research. Such people not only introduce a researcher to a community but often continue to be sources of help and information on a host of issues. But using a key informant also has its risks. Because any person has a particular circle of friends, a key informant's guidance is certain to introduce bias into the study. Moreover, in the eyes of others the reputation of the key informant—for better or worse—usually rubs off on the investigator. In sum, while relying on a key informant at the outset, a participant-observer soon must seek a broader range of contacts.

Now that he had entered the Cornerville world, Whyte began his work in earnest. But he soon realized that the careful field researcher needs to know when to speak up and when to simply listen, look, and learn. One evening, he joined a group of Cornerville people engaged in a discussion of neighbourhood gambling. Wanting to get the facts straight, Whyte asked naively, "I suppose the cops were all paid off?" In a heartbeat,

> The gambler's jaw dropped. He glared at me. Then he denied vehemently that any policeman had been paid off and immediately switched the conversation to another subject. For the rest of that evening I felt very uncomfortable.

The next day, Doc offered some sound advice:

> "Go easy on that 'who,' 'what,' 'why,' 'when,' 'where' stuff, Bill. You ask those questions and people will clam up on you. If people accept you, you can just hang around, and you'll learn the answers in the long run without even having to ask the questions." (1981:303)

In the months and years that followed, Whyte became familiar with life in Cornerville, and married a woman from the community. In the process, he learned that this neighbourhood was hardly the stereotypical slum. On the contrary, most immigrants were working hard, many had earned considerable success, and some could even boast of having sent children to college. In short, his book makes for fascinating reading about the dreams, deeds, and disappointments of one ethnic community, and it contains a richness of detail that only long-term participant observation can provide.

In Whyte's work, we also see that participant observation is a method rife with tensions and contrasts. Its flexibility helps a researcher respond to an unfamiliar setting but makes replication difficult for others. Insight depends on getting close to others, while scientific observation demands detachment. Participant observation calls for little expense, since no elaborate equipment or laboratory is needed, but a comprehensive community study does take time—typically a year or more. Perhaps this long-term commitment explains why participant observation is used less often than other methods described in this chapter. Yet the depth of understanding gained through research of this kind has greatly enriched our knowledge of many types of human communities.

USING AVAILABLE DATA: SECONDARY AND HISTORICAL ANALYSIS

Not all research requires investigators to collect their own data personally. In many cases, sociologists engage in **secondary analysis**, *a research method in which a researcher utilizes data collected by others.*

The most widely used statistics in social science are gathered by government agencies. Statistics Canada continuously updates information about the Canadian population, and offers much of interest to sociologists. Comparable data on the United States are available from the Bureau of the Census, a branch of the U.S. government. Global investigations benefit from various publications of the United Nations and the World Bank. In short, a wide range of data about the whole world is as close as the university or college library.

Clearly, using available data—whether government statistics or the findings of individual researchers—saves researchers time and money. Therefore, this approach holds special appeal to sociologists with low budgets. Just as important, the quality of government data is generally better than that of any data even well-funded researchers could hope to obtain on their own.

Still, secondary analysis has inherent problems. For one thing, available data may not exist in precisely the form one might wish; further, there are always questions about the meaning and accuracy of work done by others. For example, in his classic study of suicide, Emile Durkheim realized that he could not be sure that a death classified as an "accident" was not, in reality, a "suicide," and vice versa. And he also knew that various agencies used differing procedures and categories in collecting data, making comparisons difficult. In the end, then, using second-hand data is a little like shopping for a used car: bargains are plentiful, but you have to shop carefully to avoid being stuck with a lemon.

Content Analysis

Another type of secondary analysis is called content analysis. This entails the counting or coding of the content of written, aural, or visual materials, such as television and radio programming, novels, magazines, and advertisements. Content analysis has a long tradition in sociology. One of the best-known early content analyses of this century in North America is *The Polish Peasant in Europe and America* by Thomas and Znaniecki (1971; orig. 1919), which used diaries and letters written to and from Polish immigrants in America to describe the adjustment processes of new American immigrants. A 1977 study by the Montreal YWCA Women's Centre of gender roles in thirty-eight grade 1 readers used in Montreal's anglophone schools is another example of the use of content research. The study found that gender stereotypes were mirrored in the books. Males were portrayed as central characters and as active, competitive problem-solvers. Females were less often included and when they were included, tended to be portrayed in passive, domestic roles and occupations. Males were shown in seventy-eight different occupations; most females were housewives, and those who weren't were described as nurses, librarians, teachers, or cooks (Mackie, 1983). Recent research by Nancarrow Clarke (1991) on the "treatment" of cancer, heart disease, and AIDS in the media, described in Chapter 3 ("Culture"), provides another example of content analysis.

Historical Research: Open for Business

Since we are all trapped in the present, secondary analysis provides a key to investigating the past. Gordon Laxer's book *Open for Business: The Roots of Foreign Ownership in Canada* (1989) is an important contribution to the age-old Canadian debate about the reasons for the Canadian economy's high level of dependence on the United States and other foreign owners. Laxer rejected what have become the conventional explanations: geographical closeness to a powerful and expanding economy, our relative lack of technological development, the influence of merchant and banking elites, and a reliance on the export of raw materials. Focusing on forces beyond our control, he pointed out, tends to make Canadian failure to develop independently seem inevitable. Instead, Laxer chose to examine the internal social and political forces that have shaped Canada's development policies, by comparing Canada with other "late-followers" such as Germany, Japan, Sweden, and Russia (countries that were somewhat behind the United States and Great Britain in their economic development).

From Card Punching to Number Crunching:
Technological Advances in Research

How have technological advances changed research? When one of the authors of this text, Linda Gerber, began the research for her Ph.D. thesis around 1970, which in technological terms was the dinosaur era, she had to laboriously code about 80 variables for more than 600 aboriginal communities. These coded data were punched onto several thousand cards that had to be manually fed into the University of Toronto's huge mainframe computers every time a new piece of analysis was done. (These computers could be accessed most readily at 2:00 or 3:00 a.m.) Towards the end of the research period, these cards were read onto magnetic tape, which made the final analyses—"one more run, just one more run"—considerably less labour-intensive. Several drafts of that thesis were hammered out on a manual typewriter: since white-out was not allowed, mistakes on any of the 313 pages of the final document (Gerber, 1976) required that the entire page in question be retyped. Subsequent papers submitted to journals in hopes of publication were produced in the same plodding way.

By the mid-1980s, the Canadian census was arriving at the University of Guelph's library on paper *and* on magnetic tape. The tapes made secondary analysis infinitely easier for anyone who analyzed census data. In addition, the development and improvement of word processors made "keyboarding" (males do not "type") of manuscripts a breeze. Journal articles would be submitted on paper in duplicate for consideration by reviewers, but by the early 1990s the final copy of an "accepted" paper would be sent to most of the major journals on a floppy disk.

Today, data must still be coded, but the process is a lot less labour-intensive. Those who analyze census data pull the data directly off the Internet. The data are transferred onto microcomputer or mainframe files where they can be recoded and subjected to all kinds of sophisticated analysis using statistical software packages. Word processing produces "papers," which might never see anything but electronic form until they appear in the journals destined for our libraries. (This edition of your text was revised on disks.)

Computers can now be used for more than managing quantitative data: more and more qualitative applications are being developed. For example, if Gerber were preparing her Ph.D. thesis today, she could begin a survey of the literature by using a specially designed program that searches documents to find the terms "aboriginal," "community," and "migration" whenever they occur in close proximity to one another. Then she could have another program compare her newly found and coded data to help her find patterns and formulate theories on the subject (Neuman, 1997).

Increasingly, established journals are making the articles from their paper-based publications available on the Internet as well, with members paying for the right to read and print copies of the various papers. By 1996 a number of new sociology journals started appearing on the Internet and *on the Internet alone*. These journals have no paper copy available anywhere! Submission of papers to these journals is done electronically.

Just think of the implications for a moment. It is now possible to "collect" data, conduct sophisticated analysis, write a "paper," submit the paper, and have it "published" with instantaneous access around the world. All of this is accomplished electronically without ever putting ink or laser imprint to paper. Communications theorist Marshall McLuhan would have been quick to point out the revolutionary impact of these developments.

Laxer points out that at the turn of the century, Canada was the eighth largest manufacturing country in the world, a fact that was particularly surprising given its relatively small population. Early economic development was not due to American investment; rather, it was Canada's already developed industry, the nature of its labour force, and its standard of living that attracted American companies. Before Canada became a "branch-plant" economy, Canadians were exporting sophisticated industrial goods, developed and made by Canadian-owned businesses, to such markets as Britain, France, and Germany.

An important cause of the demise of Canadian economic independence, Laxer found, was the weakness of the organized farmers' movements from before Confederation to World War I. (Agrarian movements, because of their attachment to the land, were important elsewhere in protecting countries against economic penetration and the exploitation of the land and natural resources by foreign capitalists.) The weakness of the agrarian movements resulted partly from a loyalty to Britain and partly from internal divisions (e.g., French–English; Protestant–Catholic; and class divisions). As a result, banks did

TABLE 2–3 Four Research Methods: A Summary

Method	Application	Advantages	Limitations
Experiment	For explanatory research that specifies relationships among variables; generates quantitative data	Provides greatest ability to specify cause-and-effect relationships; replication of research is relatively easy	Laboratory settings have artificial quality; unless research environment is carefully controlled, results may be biased
Survey	For gathering information about issues that cannot be directly observed, such as attitudes and values; useful for descriptive and explanatory research; generates quantitative or qualitative data	Sampling allows surveys of large populations using questionnaires; interviews provide in-depth responses	Questionnaires must be carefully prepared and may produce a low return rate; interviews are expensive and time-consuming
Participant observation	For exploratory and descriptive study of people in a "natural" setting; generates qualitative data	Allows study of "natural" behaviour; usually inexpensive	Time-consuming; replication of research is difficult; researcher must balance roles of participant and observer
Secondary analysis	For exploratory, descriptive, or explanatory research whenever suitable data are available	Saves time and expense of data collection; makes historical research possible	Researcher has no control over possible bias in data; data may not be suitable for current research needs

not encourage Canadians to invest in their own country. Moreover, because of weak agrarian policies, the development of the West was delayed about twenty years, which in turn slowed the pace and scale of Canadian industrial development in the period immediately preceding the first major invasion of American branch plants. Finally, the weakness of agrarian and populist nationalism allowed open-door policies with regard to foreign investment.

Laxer concludes his book with a warning to Canadians. He states that internal problems resulting from anglophone–francophone tensions, regionalism, and ethnic, religious, and other divisions must be solved on an equitable basis of mutual respect so that Canadians form a united front for strong economic development policies. Looking at history, Laxer suggests, provides us with clues to the future development of the Canadian economy.

Table 2–3 summarizes the four major methods of sociological investigation. We now turn to some final considerations: the impact of technology on research and how to relate the specific facts, culled through sociological investigation, to theory.

TECHNOLOGY AND RESEARCH

In recent decades, new information technology has changed our lives considerably, and this applies to the practice of research as well. Personal computers—which came on the scene only about fifteen years ago—now give individual sociologists remarkable technical ability to randomly select samples, perform complex statistical analysis, and prepare written reports efficiently. Today's average office computer is far more powerful than even the massive mainframe devices that filled entire rooms on university campuses a generation ago.

The development of the Internet (the so-called "electronic superhighway") is certain to further enhance our research capabilities in the years to come. First, the Internet now links some 40 million computers in 160 countries of the world, allowing for an unprecedented level of communication. Contemporary sociologists are capable of building networks across the country and around the globe, which will facilitate collaboration and prompt comparative research. Second, both faculty and students can readily access a rapidly increasing amount of statistical information on the Internet. Statistics Canada opened a Web site on the Internet in 1994. Such developments—and other as-yet-unimagined forms of technological change—promise to transform sociological investigation as we enter the next century (Morton, 1995).

THE INTERPLAY OF THEORY AND METHOD

There are, of course, some research tasks that remain unaffected by technological change. No matter how we gather data, sociologists must ultimately transform facts into meaning by building theory.

Actually, sociological investigators move back and forth between facts and theory. **Inductive logical thought** is *reasoning that transforms specific observations into general theory.* In this mode, a researcher's thinking runs from the specific to the general, something like this: "I have some interesting data here; what are the data saying about human behaviour?"

A second type of logical thought works "downwards" in the opposite direction. **Deductive logical thought** is *reasoning that transforms general theory into specific hypotheses suitable for scientific testing.* This time, the researcher's thinking goes from the general to the specific: "I have this hunch about human behaviour; let's put it in a form we can test, collect some data, and see if it is correct." Working deductively, the researcher first states the theory in the form of a hypothesis and then selects a method by which to test it. To the extent that the data support the hypothesis, we conclude that the theory is correct; data that refute the hypothesis alert the researcher that the theory should be revised or perhaps rejected entirely.

Philip Zimbardo's Stanford County Prison experiment illustrates how this model operates. Zimbardo began with the general idea that prisons alter human behaviour. He then fashioned a specific, testable hypothesis: placed in a prison setting, even emotionally well-balanced young men would exhibit violent behaviour. Violence erupted soon after his experiment began, supporting this hypothesis. Had his experiment produced amicable behaviour between "prisoners" and "guards," his original theory would clearly have required reformulation.

Just as researchers commonly employ several methods over the course of one study, they typically make use of both types of logical thought.

PUTTING IT ALL TOGETHER: TEN STEPS IN SOCIOLOGICAL INVESTIGATION

Drawing together the threads of sociological investigation presented in this chapter, a typical project in sociology will include each of the following ten steps.

1. **Define the topic of investigation.** Being curious and looking at the world sociologically can generate ideas for social research anywhere. The issue you choose to study is likely to have some personal significance.

2. **Find out what others have learned about the topic.** You are probably not the first person to develop an interest in a particular issue. Spend time in the library to see what theories and methods researchers have applied to your topic

in the past. In reviewing existing research, note problems that may have come up before.

3. **Specify the research questions.** Are you seeking to explore an unfamiliar social setting? To describe some category of people? To investigate cause and effect among variables? If your study is exploratory, or descriptive, identify who you wish to study, where the research will take place, and what kinds of issues you want to explore. If it is explanatory, you almost must state the hypothesis to be tested and carefully operationalize each variable.

4. **Assess the requirements for carrying out the research.** How much time and money will the research require? What special equipment or skills are necessary? Can you do the work yourself? What sources of funding are available to support the research? You should answer all these questions before beginning to design the research project.

5. **Consider ethical issues.** Not all research raises serious ethical issues, but you should be sensitive to this matter throughout your investigation. Could the research harm anyone? How might you design the study to minimize the chances of injury? Do you plan to promise anonymity to the subjects? If so, how will you ensure that anonymity will be maintained?

6. **Devise a research strategy.** Consider all major research strategies—as well as innovative combinations of approaches. Keep in mind that the appropriate method depends on the kind of questions you are asking as well as the resources available to support your research.

7. **Gather the data.** The way you collect data depends on the research method you choose. Be sure to accurately record all information in a way that will make sense later (it may be some time before you actually write up the results of your work). Remain vigilant for any bias that may creep into the research.

8. **Interpret the data.** Scrutinize the data in terms of the initial questions and decide what answers they suggest. If your study involves a specific hypothesis, you should be able to confirm, reject, or modify the hypothesis based on the data. In writing up your research report, keep in mind that there may be several ways to interpret the results of your study, consistent with different theoretical paradigms, and you should delve into them all.

9. **State your conclusions.** As you write your final report, specify conclusions supported by the

Can People Lie with Statistics?

Is scientific research always as objective and "factual" as we think? Not according to the great English politician Benjamin Disraeli, who once noted wryly, "There are three kinds of lies: lies, damned lies, and statistics!" In a world that bombards us with numbers—often in the form of "scientific facts" and "official figures"—it is well worth pausing to consider that "statistical evidence" is not synonymous with truth. For one thing, as this chapter has explained, every method of data collection is prone to error; for another, because data do not speak for themselves, someone has to interpret them to figure out what they mean. And, sometimes, people (even social scientists) "dress up" their data almost the way politicians whip up a campaign speech—with an eye more to winning you over than to getting at the truth.

The best way to ferret out statistical manipulation is to understand how these tricks are performed. Here are three ways people can lie with statistics.

1. **People choose their data.** Many times, the data we confront are not wrong, they just do not tell the whole story. Let's say someone claims that television is ruining our way of life and, as evidence, offers statistics indicating that we watch more TV today than a generation ago and that standard mathematics and reading scores have fallen during that time. Such data are actually correct; however, they are selectively chosen. Another person could just as correctly counter that Canadian residents spend much more on books today than we did a generation ago, suggesting that there is no cultural crisis at all. In short, plenty of statistics are available for people on all sides of a political debate to use as ammunition to bolster their arguments.

2. **People interpret their data.** Another way people manipulate statistics is to "package" them inside a ready-made interpretation, as if to say "Here are the numbers, and this is what they mean." Usually several different slants can be put on any particular set of data. For example, take the table at the beginning of this chapter portraying responses to questions about attitudes to public policy questions relating to AIDS (Table 2–1). The fact that 36 percent of the sample indicated that an employer should have the right to require a job applicant to undergo an AIDS test can be seen optimistically or pessimistically depending, for example, on whether the writer says something like only 36 percent, or not.

3. **People use graphs to "spin" the "truth."** Especially in newspapers and other popular media, we often encounter graphic representations of statistical data. While graphs make comprehending data easy (showing, for example, an upward or downward trend), they also provide the designer with the opportunity to "spin" data in various ways. Where trends are concerned, one common technique for casting data in a particular light involves compressing or expanding the graph's time frame. A graph of the crime rate over the last several years, for example, would reveal a downward trend; shifting the time frame to the last few decades, however, would show a sharp increase.

Continue the debate . . .

1. *Why do you think people are so quick to accept "statistics" as true?*
2. *Max Weber's "value-free" approach to research would forbid "dressing up" one's data. What about a Marxist approach?*
3. *Can you cite a piece of research that you think presented biased data or conclusions? Specify the biases.*

data. Consider the significance of your work both for sociological theory and for improving research methods. Of what value is your research to people outside of sociology? Finally, evaluate your own work, noting problems that arose and questions left unanswered. Note ways in which your own biases may have coloured your conclusions.

10. **Share your results.** Consider submitting your research paper to a campus newspaper or magazine or making a presentation to a class, campus gathering, or perhaps a meeting of professional sociologists. The important point is to share what you have learned with others and to let others respond to your work.

SUMMARY

1. Science provides the logical foundation of sociological research and, more broadly, helps us to critically evaluate information we encounter every day.

2. Two basic requirements for sociological investigation are (1) viewing the world from a sociological perspective, and (2) being curious and asking questions about society.

3. Measurement is the process of determining the value of a variable in any specific case. Sound measurement is both reliable and valid.

4. A goal of science is discovering how variables are related. Correlation means that two or more variables change value together. Knowledge about cause-and-effect relationships is more powerful, however, because a researcher can use an independent variable to predict change in a dependent variable.

5. Although investigators select topics according to their personal interests, the scientific ideal of objectivity demands that they try to suspend personal values and biases as they conduct research.

6. Human curiosity and imagination must infuse the scientific method; moreover, researchers must always bring their data to life through interpretation.

7. Investigators should avoid examining issues from the point of view of only one sex or basing generalizations about humanity on data collected from only men or women.

8. Rejecting conventional ideas about scientific objectivity, some sociologists argue that research inevitably involves political values; with this in mind, research should be directed towards promoting desirable social change.

9. Because sociological research has the potential to cause discomfort and harm to subjects, sociological investigators are bound by ethical guidelines.

10. Experiments, which are performed under controlled conditions, attempt to specify causal relationships between two (or more) variables.

11. Surveys, which gather people's responses to statements or questions, may employ questionnaires or interviews.

12. Through participant observation, a form of field research, sociologists directly observe a social setting while participating in it for an extended period of time.

13. Secondary analysis, or making use of available data, is often preferable to collecting one's own data; it is also essential in the study of historical questions.

14. Theory and research are linked through two kinds of thinking. Deductive thought transforms general ideas into specific hypotheses suitable for testing. Inductive thought organizes specific observations into general ideas.

CRITICAL THINKING QUESTIONS

1. What does it mean to state that there are various kinds of truth? What is the basic rationale for relying on science as a way of knowing?

2. What sorts of measures do scientists adopt as they strive for objectivity? Why do some sociologists consider objectivity an undesirable goal?

3. Identify several ways in which sociological research is similar to—and different from—research in the natural sciences.

4. What considerations lead a sociologist to select one method of research over another?

SOCIOLOGY APPLIED

1. During one class period, imagine that you are observing your instructor in an effort to assess that individual's skills as a teacher. How would you operationalize "good teaching"? What kinds of behaviours might you note as relevant to this task? Do you think you can evaluate a teacher after observing a single class?

2. Drop by to see at least three sociology instructors (or other social science instructors) during their office hours. Ask each the extent to which sociology is an objective science. Do they agree about the character of their discipline? Why or why not?

3. Read the "Code of Ethics" of the American Sociological Association, available on their Web site (www.asanet.org). Summarize the principles there by writing a description of a "professional sociologist."

4. Conduct a practice interview with a roommate or friend on the general topic of "What do you expect to gain from going to university?" Before the actual interview, prepare a list of specific questions or issues you think are relevant. Afterwards, give some thought to why carrying out an effective interview is much harder than it may initially seem.

WEBLINKS

www.d.umn.edu/cla/faculty/jhamlin/1400/weber.html
The Max Weber site contains a brief biography and an overview of Weber's sociological theories and methodology.

129.97.58.10/discipline/sociology/research.html
Maintained by the University of Waterloo library, Doing Research in Sociology contains links to information sources on how to do research in sociology, including searching CD-ROM databases, citing electronic sources, and steps to effective library research.

www.sociology.org/home.html
The *Electronic Journal of Sociology* has been publishing full-text articles online since September 1994 and provides a keyword search function to help readers locate references to specific topics.

www.statcan.ca/start.html
Statistics Canada offers a variety of resources, including Canada at a Glance, Latest News from Statistics Canada, Virtual Library, Internet Services at Statistics Canada, Electronic Marketplace, Other Canadian Government Servers, and Other Statistical Web Servers.

minerva.acc.virginia.edu/surveys/code.htm
The Code of Ethics at the University of Virginia's Center for Survey Research includes guidelines for dealing responsibly with survey subjects.

cyber.scope

PART I
WELCOME TO THE INFORMATION REVOLUTION!

As we approach the new century (and the new millennium), we are witnessing astounding change brought on by a new kind of technology. For the last two centuries, the Industrial Revolution has given shape to our society, dictating the kind of work people do and defining the way we think about the world. But now a transformation is underway—dubbed the Information Revolution—that is already redefining our world in novel ways.

At the end of each of the five parts of this text, a special section we have named "cyber.scope" will review important themes from the chapters, highlighting the importance of computers and other new information technology. In this first cyber.scope section, we will briefly explain what the Information Revolution is all about, extending discussions of the sociological perspective (Chapter 1) and sociological investigation (Chapter 2).

The Age of Machines:
Industrial Society

The time line inside the front cover of this book places the onset of the "modern era" at about 250 years ago at the dawning of the Industrial Revolution. At that time—first in England, then soon after in North America—new sources of energy led imaginative people to create new products in new ways. First, rivers and then steam generated by coal furnaces provided the power to operate large machines. Soon afterwards, the Industrial Revolution was changing all aspects of social life: drawing people to work in the new factories, and demanding that they learn the skills needed to operate machines. As time went on, the increasing size and number of factories encouraged migration from the countryside to rapidly growing cities, where most people experienced a faster-paced, more impersonal life and, in time, enjoyed a higher material standard of living. As we have noted, these changes sparked people's interest in studying society, and played a key role in the birth of sociology itself.

The Age of Computers:
Information Society

The last half of the twentieth century has witnessed the unfolding of another technological transformation—the Information Revolution—which promises to change our world once again. The technology that will define the twenty-first century is based on *information*: the computer and related technology, including the Internet, facsimile machines, cellular telephones, and satellite communications. The fact that we already have shorthand names for these devices—the "Net," "fax," "cell phone," and "dish"—suggests how quickly they have become an established part of our lives.

The key to the Information Revolution is the computer. Since U.S. engineers first went "online" fifty years ago (with massive machines jammed with vacuum tubes and wires that did little more than today's ten-dollar hand-held calculator), computers have become more and more central to our way of life. By 1997 in Canada, virtually all new motor vehicles, the vast majority of businesses, many First Nations and Inuit communities, and more than a third of all households were outfitted with at least one computer to perform an expanding range of tasks—both instrumental and recreational. (Figure I–1 shows the growth of computers in the home over recent years.) But the biggest advantage of our new information technology is in communication: the Internet allows for instant communication between 100 million individuals and organizations in 90 percent of the world's countries. Eighteen percent of Canadians are on the Internet and have e-mail, but Finland leads the world as the "most wired" country, where 60 percent of the population has access to e-mail and the Internet—at home, at work, through Nokia cellular phones, or at public libraries (Ibrahim, 1997).

What's different about new information technology? Most basically, the change involves the kind of work people do. Yesterday's industrial technology empowered people to create more and more *things*; information technology leads us to work with *ideas*, creating and manipulating symbols. The Industrial Age was represented by the factory's assembly line, with workers toiling to make steel or to assemble cars. But the typical worker

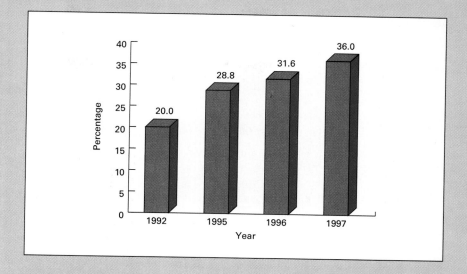

FIGURE I–1 Percentage of Canadian Households with a Computer

SOURCE: Statistics Canada, Catalogue no. 64-202-XPB.

in the Information Age is an individual peering at a computer screen, writing, calculating, drawing, or designing.

A second key change brought about by the Information Revolution is the declining importance of distance and physical space. Just as industrial technology demands that people work in centralized factories (where the machinery and energy sources are located), information technology allows people to work almost anywhere that they can carry a computer or flip a cell phone. Note, too, that when we use this technology to communicate with others, we often have no idea where they are. The popular term "cyberspace" itself suggests that our emerging world is less and less bounded by physical dimensions. Of course, just as we gauged the output of industrial engines with an obsolete reference to "horse-power," so we now cling to older, physical images in describing new realities: we talk about the "information superhighway,"[1] read "bulletin boards," and enter "chat rooms." Yet these "places" are a

"virtual reality," meaning that they are computer simulations that we see and interact with, and they have no physical existence at all. In fact, they exist only in the flow of electrons that illuminates our computer, electrons that can circle the world at the speed of light.

As later chapters of the text explain, this new technology is changing virtually every dimension of our lives: reshaping culture and how we learn about the world, connecting us to people in new ways, generating new kinds of crime and new ways of pursuing criminals, and even altering patterns of social inequality. There is little doubt that, as we enter the new century, the changes wrought by new information technology will continue to spark people's sociological imagination!

[1] The rapidly increasing numbers of people logging on the Internet has overwhelmed existing telephone lines, and sometimes results in long delays in transmitting and receiving information. For a while, at least, the information "superhighway" may remain more of a "dirt road."

New Information Technology: Thoughts on Theory

A key focus of Chapter 1 ("The Sociological Perspective") is sociology's three major theoretical paradigms. What insights can we gain using these paradigms to study new information technology?

A structural-functional analysis would point out that, because society is a system of countless interdependent elements, a development as important as a new form of technology is likely to cause changes in virtually all aspects of our lives. Since television was invented in 1939, some 1 billion TV sets have been built, and this electronic device has altered what we know, how we learn, patterns of recreation, and even the ways that family members interact. Computers will almost certainly change our lives even more. Their manifest (that is, intended and expected) effects will range from decentralizing the workplace to encouraging entire cities to spread outward, since talking to or working with others no longer requires being with them physically. The latent (that is, un-

FIGURE I–2 Cyber-Symbols: An Emerging Language

It all started with the "smiley" figure that shows that one is happy or telling a joke. Now a new language of gestures is emerging as creative people use computer keystrokes—called emoticons—to convey thoughts and emotions that no one, back in the days of typewriters, ever imagined. Here's a sampling of some recent examples:

:-)	I'm smiling at you.
:`-)	I'm so happy (laughing so hard) that I'm starting to cry.
:-O	Wow!
:-x	My lips are sealed!
:-‖	I'm angry at you!
:-P	I'm sticking my tongue out at you!
:-(	I feel sad.
:-l	Things look grim.
%-}	I think I've had too much to drink.
-:(	Somebody cut my hair into a mohawk!
@}——>	Here's a rose for you!
+O:-)	I've just been elected Pope!

Computers are as popular in Japan as they are in North America. And the Japanese have coined their own variants of emoticons.

(^_^)	I'm smiling at you.
(*^o^*)	This is exciting!
(^o^)	I am happy.
\(^x^)/	Banzai! This is wonderful!

How far will this new keyboard language go? If you're creative enough, anything is possible. Here's a routine that has been making the rounds on the Internet, titled Mr. Asciihead learns the Macarena!

```
   o    o    o    o    o   <o <o>  o>   o
  .l.   \l.   \l/   //   X    \    l   <l   <l>
   Ÿ   >\   /<   >\   /<   >\   /<   >\   /<
```

SOURCE: Pollak (1996); Krantz (1997); Mr. Asciihead is the creation of Leow Yee Ling.

intended) effects are certainly harder to foresee, but they may well include new kinds of human communities as people pay less attention to their physical neighbours and spend more time communicating with like-minded others "online."

A social-conflict analysis of the rise of new information technology offers other, contrasting insights, especially regarding social inequality. Here, we might note that the spread of new information technology has been rapid among afflu-ent people, but not among the poor. There is already evidence that the information age will be marked by two distinct classes: educated people with sophisticated symbolic skills (who are likely to prosper) and people without symbolic skills (who are likely to remain in low-income jobs). Statistical comparisons show that, among workers in the same job, those able to use a computer earn 15 percent more than those who cannot (Ratan, 1995).

The symbolic-interaction paradigm, too, makes a contribution here. On a micro-level, how does communication via electronic mail differ from face-to-face interaction? Obviously, lacking facial expression or tone of voice, electronic communication cannot convey emotion very well. For this reason, as shown in Figure I–2, people have creatively turned the characters found on their keyboards into new symbols, generating a new cyberlanguage!

New Information Technology: What About Research?

How is new information technology changing sociological research, the focus of Chapter 2? A generation of sociologists have now been trained to use computers to select random samples, to perform complex statistical analysis, and to prepare written reports efficiently. Obviously, electronic mail enables researchers to "travel" almost anywhere almost instantly and with minimal cost. In the coming years, more and more surveys will take place "online." And electronic surveys raise some interesting questions: Will this technology improve survey response rates or be discarded as electronic "junk mail"? Will cyber-surveys protect a respondent's anonymity or threaten people's privacy?

What seems sure is that new information technology will greatly enhance communication among researchers throughout the world. The Internet—highlighted in the next cyber.scope on pages 216 to 217—now links at least 100 million people in 160 countries, giving sociologists a powerful tool for building networks, sharing information, and joining together to conduct research. Just as important, faculty and students alike now have ready access to a rapidly increasing amount of statistical information. For example, Statistics Canada now publishes reports of all kinds "online" and responds to queries from individuals doing research on their own (visit their home page at www.statcan.ca).

Visit Us Online!

Please accept an invitation to visit the Web site that accompanies this text; our Internet address is http://www.phcanada.com/macionis. There, you will find learning objectives for each text chapter, self-scoring practice tests, recent news of sociological interest, a chat room in which you can share ideas with others, links to hundreds of other instructive and fascinating Web sites, and even a link that lets you send a note to the text authors. Welcome, and enjoy! ◉

Mike Larsen, *Generations*
Larsen & Larsen Studios, Inc.

CHAPTER 3

CULTURE

A belief in a life force—Ki or chi—pervades many people in China and Japan. It is taken so seriously that, for example, the Sony corporation in Japan has dedicated a four-person laboratory to studying Ki. At present, scientists are trying to measure the effects of Ki on skin temperature. Their ultimate goal is to discover the mind or consciousness that all of humanity, and the whole of creation, must possess to pursue the spirit, soul, or life force that exists in our universe (Pollack, 1995:D8).

Other foundations, with the support of the Ministry of International Trade, are currently investigating the artificial manufacturing of Ki to be used for healing "the sick."

Kosaku Iida, president of a Japanese drug importing firm and a Harvard Business School graduate, uses a Ki master to improve his health and business. In this process, he, in a ceremony along with perhaps a hundred other people at times, has been touched by Ki. Each person stands in front of the Ki Master and touches the back of his extended hand. Then, as if propelled by a powerful yet invisible force, the person reels back and crashes into a padded wall. Some people then collapse, screaming and writhing on the ground, before one of the Master's assistants helps them up. As Mr. Iida says, "When I had business trouble in the past, it put keen tension on my brain. Now I can think without much stress" (Pollack, 1995:D8).

The closest that North American business leaders come to such reliance on a spiritual force may be those who start business meetings with prayers. This is just one example of the enormous cultural differences between people even in the developed world.

The 5.9 billion people on earth today are members of a single biological species: *Homo sapiens*. Even so, the differences among people the world over can delight, puzzle, disturb, and sometimes even overwhelm us. Some differences in lifestyles are simply arbitrary matters of convention—the Chinese, for example, wear white at funerals, while people in Canada prefer black. Similarly, Chinese people associate the number four with bad luck, in much the same way that people in Canada think of the number thirteen. Or, take the practice of kissing: most people in Canada kiss in public at times, most Chinese kiss only in private; the French kiss publicly twice (once on each cheek), while Belgians kiss three times (starting on either cheek); for their part, most Nigerians don't kiss at all. At weddings, moreover, Canadian couples kiss, Koreans bow, and a Cambodian groom touches his nose to the bride's cheek.

Other cultural differences, however, are more profound. The world over, people wear much or little clothing, have many or few children, venerate or shunt aside the elderly, are peaceful or warlike, embrace different religious beliefs, and enjoy different kinds of art and music. In short, although we are all the same creatures biologically, the human beings on this planet have developed strikingly different ideas about what is pleasant and repulsive, polite and rude, beautiful and ugly, right and wrong. This capacity for startling difference is a wonder of our species: the expression of human culture.

Like so many elements of our lives, notions about kissing vary from place to place. People in Canada kiss in public; the Chinese do so only in private. Moreover, while we touch lips, the French kiss on the cheek, and New Zealand's Maoris, shown above, rub noses.

WHAT IS CULTURE?

Sociologists define **culture** as *the values, beliefs, behaviour, and material objects that constitute a people's way of life*. Culture includes what we think, how we act, and what we own. But as our social heritage, culture is also a bridge to the past as well as a guide to the future (Soyinka, 1991).

To begin to understand all that culture entails, it is helpful to distinguish between thoughts and things. What sociologists call **nonmaterial culture** is *the intangible world of ideas created by members of a society* that spans a wide range, from altruism to Zen. **Material culture**, on the other hand, constitutes *the tangible things created by members of a society*; here, again, the range is vast, running from armaments to zippers.

Not only does culture shape what we do, it also helps form our personalities—what we commonly (yet inaccurately) describe as "human nature." The warlike Yąnomamö of the Brazilian rain forest look on aggression as natural in their children, just as, halfway around the world, the Semai of Malaysia expect their young to be peaceful and cooperative. The cultures of Canada and Japan both stress achievement and hard work, but members of our society value individualism more than the Japanese, who place a stronger emphasis on tradition.

Given the extent of cultural differences in the world and the tendency of all of us to view our own way of life as "natural," it is no wonder that travellers commonly experience **culture shock**, *personal disorientation that comes from encountering an unfamiliar way of life*. People experience this kind of disorientation when they immigrate to a new country or, to a lesser extent, when they move between social environments within their own countries. A young person moving from rural Newfoundland to attend university in British Columbia or southern Ontario knows the feeling of culture shock.

No cultural trait is inherently "natural" to humanity, even though most people around the world view their own way of life that way. What is natural to our species is the capacity to create culture in our collective lives. Every other form of life—from ants to zebras—behaves in uniform, species-specific ways. To a world traveller, the enormous diversity of human life stands out in contrast to the behaviour of, say, cats, which is the same everywhere. Most living creatures are guided by instincts, biological programming over which animals have no control. A few animals—notably chimpanzees and related primates—have the capacity for limited culture, as researchers have noted by observing them use tools and teach simple skills to their offspring. But the creative power of humans far exceeds that of any other form of life; in short, *only humans rely on culture rather than instinct to ensure the survival of their kind* (Harris, 1987).

To understand how this came to be, we must briefly review the history of our species on earth.

CULTURE AND HUMAN INTELLIGENCE

In a universe some 15 billion years old, our planet is a much younger 4.5 billion years of age (see the time lines inside the front cover of the text). Not for a billion years after the earth was formed did any life at all appear on our planet. Several billion more years went by before dinosaurs ruled the earth and then disappeared. And then, some 65 million years ago, our history took a crucial turn with the appearance of the creatures we call primates.

What sets primates apart is their intelligence, based on their large brains (relative to body size). As primates evolved, the human line diverged from that of our closest relatives, the great apes, about 12 million years ago. But our common lineage shows through in the traits humans share with today's chimpanzees, gorillas, and orangutans: great sociability, affectionate and long-lasting bonds for child rearing and mutual protection, the ability to walk upright (normal in humans, less common among other primates), and hands that manipulate objects with great precision.

Studying fossil records, scientists conclude that, about 2 million years ago, our distant ancestors grasped cultural fundamentals such as the use of fire,

Human beings around the globe create diverse ways of life. Such differences begin with outward appearance: contrast the women shown here from Brazil, Kenya, New Guinea, and Morocco, and the men from Taiwan (Republic of China), Peru, India, and New Guinea. Less obvious, but of even greater importance, are internal differences, since culture also shapes our goals in life, our sense of justice, and even our innermost personal feelings.

tools, and weapons, created simple shelters, and fashioned basic clothing. Although these Stone Age achievements may seem modest, they mark the point at which our ancestors embarked on a distinct evolutionary course, making culture the primary strategy for human survival.

To comprehend that human beings are wide-eyed infants in the larger scheme of things, Carl Sagan

(1977) came up with the idea of superimposing the 15-billion-year history of our universe on a single calendar year. The life-giving atmosphere of the earth did not develop until the autumn, and the earliest beings who resembled humans did not appear until December 31—the last day of the year—at 10:30 at night! Yet not until 250 000 years ago, which is mere minutes before the end of Sagan's "year," did our own species finally emerge. These *Homo sapiens* (derived from Latin meaning "thinking person") have continued to evolve so that, about 40 000 years ago, humans who looked more or less like we do roamed the earth. With larger brains, these "modern" *Homo sapiens* produced culture at a rapid pace, as the wide range of tools and cave art from this period suggests.

Still, what we call "civilization," based on permanent settlements and specialized occupations, began in the Middle East (in what is today Iraq and Egypt) only about 12 000 years ago (Hamblin, 1973; Wenke, 1980). In terms of Sagan's "year," this cultural flowering occurred during the final seconds before midnight on New Year's Eve. And what of our modern, industrial way of life? Begun only 300 years ago, it amounts to a mere millisecond flash in Sagan's scheme.

Human culture, then, is very recent and was a long time in the making. As culture became a strategy for survival, our ancestors descended from the trees into the tall grasses of central Africa. There, walking upright, they discovered the advantages of hunting in groups. From this point on, the human brain grew larger, allowing for greater human capacity to create a way of life—as opposed to simply acting out biological imperatives. Gradually, culture pushed aside the biological forces we call instincts so that humans gained the mental power *to fashion the natural environment for ourselves*. Ever since, people have made and remade their worlds in countless ways, which explains today's extraordinary cultural diversity.

CULTURE, NATION, STATE, AND SOCIETY

At this point, we might well pause to clarify the proper use of several similar terms—"culture," "nation," "state," and "society." *Culture* refers to the ideas, values, and artifacts that make up a shared way of life. *Nation* is commonly used to refer to a political entity, a state or country; it also refers to a people who share a culture (including language), ancestry, and history. A *state* is a political entity in a territory with designated borders such as Canada, Argentina, or Zimbabwe. *Society* refers to organized interaction of people in a nation, state, or other boundary. Although it is a controversial idea, our fragile Canada can be said to encompass several nations—including francophone Quebec, the First Nations (the term applied to themselves by status Indian communities), and the Inuit. When Canadians talk of nation-building, they refer to the attempt to create a sense of nationhood—at the federal level—that supersedes our multicultural and regional loyalties.

In the world as a whole, how many cultures are there? The number of cultures making up the human record is a matter of speculation. Experts have docu-

mented the existence of more than five thousand human languages, suggesting that at least this many cultures have existed on the earth (Durning, 1993; Crispell, 1997). High-technology communication, rising international migration, and the expanding global economy have combined to lessen the cultural diversity of the contemporary world. Even so, at least one thousand distinct cultures continue to flourish, and hundreds of them thrive in Canada.

The tally of world nations has risen and fallen throughout history as a result of political events. The dissolution of the former Soviet Union and the former Yugoslavia, for example, added nineteen nations to the count. In 1997, there were 191 politically independent nations in the world.

THE COMPONENTS OF CULTURE

Although the cultures found in all the world's nations differ in many ways, they are all built on five major components: symbols, language, values, norms, and material objects. We shall consider each in turn.

SYMBOLS

Human beings not only sense the surrounding world as other creatures do, we build a reality of *meaning*. In doing so, humans transform elements of the world into **symbols**, *anything that carries a particular meaning recognized by people who share culture*. A whistle, a wall of graffiti, a flashing red light, and a fist raised in the air all serve as symbols. We can see the human capacity to create and manipulate symbols reflected in the very different meanings associated with the simple act of winking the eye. In some settings this action conveys interest; in others, understanding; in still others, insult.

We are so dependent on our culture's symbols that we take them for granted. Occasionally, however, we become keenly aware of a symbol when someone uses it in an unconventional way, as when political protesters in Brockville, Ontario, stomped on a Quebec flag. Entering an unfamiliar society also reminds us of the power of symbols: the resulting culture shock involves the inability to "read" meaning into one's surroundings. We feel lost and isolated, unsure of how to act, and sometimes frightened—a consequence of being outside the symbolic web of culture that joins individuals in meaningful social life.

Culture shock is a two-way process: it is something the traveller *experiences* when encountering people whose way of life is unfamiliar, and it is also what the traveller *inflicts* on others by acting in ways that may well offend them. For example, because North Americans consider dogs to be beloved household

As shown by Alighiero & Buetti's artwork Map, *each of the world's 191 nations has created as symbol of itself in the form of a flag. Around the globe, people are expected to treat a flag with respect because, in any cultural system, the flag is the nation.*

pets, travellers to northern regions of the People's Republic of China may be appalled to find people roasting dogs as a wintertime meal. On the other hand, a North American who orders a hamburger in an Indian restaurant causes offence to Hindus, who hold cows to be sacred and thus not available for human consumption.

Indeed, travel abroad provides almost endless opportunities for misunderstanding. When in an unfamiliar setting, we need to remember that even behaviour that seems innocent and quite normal to us may spark offence among others. The "Global Sociology" box takes a closer look.

Then, too, symbolic meanings vary even within a single society. A fur coat, prized by one person as a luxurious symbol of success, may represent to another the inhumane treatment of animals. Similarly, the Canadian flag, which to many Canadians embodies national pride, to separatist Quebeckers may symbolize Québécois oppression.

Cultural symbols also change over time. Blue jeans were created more than a century ago as sturdy and inexpensive clothing for people engaged in physical labour. In the liberal political climate of the 1960s, this working-class aura made jeans popular among affluent students—many of whom wore them simply to look "different" or perhaps to identify with working people. A decade later, "designer jeans" emerged as high-priced status symbols that conveyed quite a different message. In recent years, everyday jeans remain as popular as ever, simply as comfortable apparel.

In sum, symbols allow people to make sense of their lives, and without them human existence would be meaningless. Manipulating symbols correctly allows us to readily engage others within our own cultural system. In a world of cultural diversity, however, the use of symbols may give rise to embarrassment and even conflict.

LANGUAGE

Helen Keller (1880–1968) became an international celebrity because she overcame the daunting disability of being blind and deaf from infancy. The loss of two key senses cut off this young girl from the symbolic world, greatly limiting her social development. Only when her teacher, Anne Mansfield Sullivan, broke through Helen Keller's isolation by teaching her sign language did she begin to realize her human potential. This remarkable woman, who later became a renowned educator herself, recalls the moment she grasped the concept of language.

> We walked down the path to the well-house, attracted by the smell of honeysuckle with which it was covered. Someone was drawing water, and my teacher placed my hand under the spout. As the cool stream gushed over one hand, she spelled into the other the word water, first slowly, then rapidly. I stood still, my whole attention fixed upon the motions of her fingers. Suddenly I felt a misty consciousness as of something forgotten—a thrill of returning thought; and somehow the mystery of language was revealed to me. I knew then that "w-a-t-e-r" meant the wonderful cool something that was flowing over my hand. That living word awakened my soul; gave it light, hope, joy, set it free! (1903:21–24)

Language, the key to the world of culture, is *a system of symbols that allows members of a society to communicate with one another.* These symbols take the form of spoken and written words, which are culturally variable and composed of the various alphabets used around the world. Even conventions for writing differ: in general, people in Western societies write from left to right, people in northern Africa and western Asia write from right to left, and people in eastern Asia write from top to bottom.

Global Map 3–1 shows where in the world one finds the three most widely spoken languages. Chinese is the official language of 20 percent of humanity (about 1.2 billion people). English is the mother tongue of about 10 percent (600 million) of the world's people, with Spanish the official language of 6 percent (350 million). Notice, too, that one can travel virtually anywhere in the world other than much of western Africa and "get by" speaking English, which is fast becoming the favoured second language in most of the world and the international language of business and computer communication.

For people everywhere, language is the major means of **cultural transmission**, *the process by which one generation passes culture to the next.* Just as our bodies contain the genes of our ancestors, so our symbols carry our cultural heritage. Language gives us the power to gain access to centuries of accumulated wisdom.

Canadians are very familiar with the importance of language to culture. Although Canada is officially bilingual, in practice it is geographically unilingual, with a French-speaking majority in Quebec and northern New Brunswick and English predominant everywhere else. The controversial Bill 101, which regulates the use of English in Quebec and made French the only official language of the province, was an attempt to preserve the distinctive Québécois culture. To many French-speaking Quebeckers, Bill 101 is essential to their survival as a nation; to some English-speaking Canadians, the law seems like an infringement of the rights of the minority English-speaking Quebeckers. The heated debates over language that characterize Canadian (and especially Quebec) politics are evidence of how strongly people feel about their languages.

Throughout human history, people have transmitted culture through speech, a process sociologists call the *oral cultural tradition.* Only as recently as five thousand years ago did humans invent writing, and, even then, just a favoured few ever learned to read and write. It was not until this century that nations (generally the industrial, high-income countries) have boasted of nearly universal literacy. However, the International Adult Literacy Survey of 1994 revealed that 48 percent of Canadians over sixteen years of age either have severe reading difficulties (22 percent) or are able to read only simple, well-laid-out materials (26 percent). Limited literacy skills range from a high of 54 percent in Quebec to 42 percent in the western provinces (Literacy Secretariat, www.gc.ca). Clearly, a large number of Canadians face almost insurmountable barriers to opportunity in a society that increasingly demands symbolic skills.

Language skills not only link us with others and with the past, they also set free the human imagination. Connecting symbols in new ways, we can conceive of an almost limitless range of future possibilities. Language—both spoken and written—distinguishes human beings as the only creatures who are self-conscious, mindful of our limitations and aware of our ultimate mortality. Yet our symbolic power also enables us to dream, to envision a better world, and to work to bring that world into being.

Is Language Uniquely Human?

Creatures great and small direct sounds, smells, and gestures towards one another. In most cases, these signals are instinctive. But research shows that some animals have at least a rudimentary ability to use symbols to communicate with one another and with humans.

Consider the remarkable achievement of a twelve-year-old pygmy chimp named Kanzi. Chimpanzees lack the physical ability to mimic human speech. But researcher E. Sue Savage-Rumbaugh discovered that Kanzi was able to learn language by listening and observing people. Under Savage-Rumbaugh's supervision, Kanzi has amassed a vocabulary of several hundred words, and he has learned to "speak" by pointing to pictures on a special keyboard. Kanzi has correctly responded to requests like "Will you get a diaper for your sister?" or "Put the melon in the potty." More intriguing, Kanzi's abilities surpass mere rote learning because he can respond to requests he has not heard before. In short, this fascinating animal has the language ability of a two-and-a-half-year-old human child (Eckholm, 1985; Linden, 1993).

Despite such accomplishments, the language skills of chimps, dolphins, and a few other animals are limited. And even specially trained animals cannot, on their own, teach language skills to others of their kind. But the demonstrated language skills of Kanzi and others caution us against assuming that humans alone can lay claim to culture.

Does Language Shape Reality?

Do the Chinese, who think using one set of symbols, actually experience the world differently from North Americans who think in English, French, or Spanish? The answer is yes, since each language has its own distinct symbols that serve as the building blocks of reality.

Edward Sapir (1929; 1949) and Benjamin Whorf (1956; orig. 1941), two anthropologists who specialized in linguistic studies, noted that each language has words or expressions with no precise counterparts in other tongues. In addition, all languages fuse symbols with distinctive emotions. Thus, as multilingual people can attest, a single idea often "feels" different if spoken in, say, French rather than in English or Chinese (Falk, 1987).

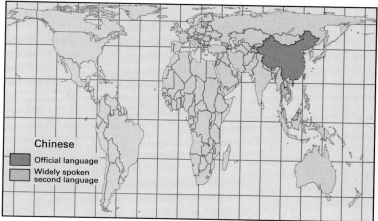

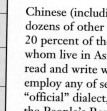

GLOBAL MAP 3–1 Language in Global Perspective

Chinese (including Mandarin, Cantonese, and dozens of other dialects) is the native tongue of 20 percent of the world's people, almost all of whom live in Asia. Although all Chinese people read and write with the same characters, they employ any of several dozen dialects. The "official" dialect, taught in schools throughout the People's Republic of China and the Republic of Taiwan, is Mandarin (the dialect of Beijing, China's historic capital city). Cantonese (the language of Canton, which differs in sound from Mandarin roughly the way French does from Spanish) is the second most common Chinese dialect.

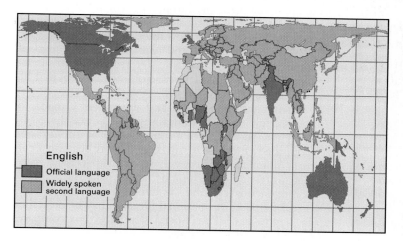

English is the native tongue or official language in several world regions and has become the preferred second language in most of the world.

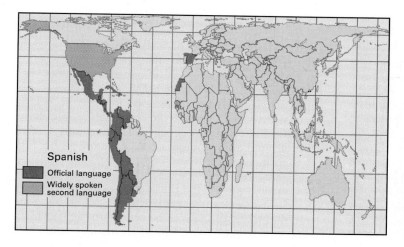

The largest concentration of Spanish speakers is in Latin America and, of course, in Spain. Spanish is also the preferred second language of the United States.

SOURCE: *Peters Atlas of the World* (1990).

Australian feminist artist Sally Swain alters a famous artist's painting to make fun of our culture's tendency to ignore the everyday lives of women. This spoof is entitled Mrs. Van Gogh Makes the Bed.

Formally, then, what we now call the **Sapir-Whorf hypothesis** states that *people perceive the world through the cultural lens of language*. Using different symbolic systems, a Filipino, a Turk, and a Brazilian and, indeed, English and French Canadians, actually experience "distinct worlds, not merely the same world with different labels attached" (Sapir, 1949:162).

Of course, the capacity to create and manipulate language also gives humans everywhere the power to alter how they experience the world. For example, the use of Ms. rather than Mrs. or Miss has allowed women to be introduced as women rather than as holders of a marital status. A system of language guides how we understand the world but does not preclude change.

VALUES AND BELIEFS

What accounts for the popularity of film characters such as James Bond, Dirty Harry, Rambo, and Thelma and Louise? Each is ruggedly individualistic, suspicious of "the system," and relies on personal skill and savvy. In applauding such people, we celebrate a sturdy strain of individualism, traditionally for men but increasingly for women, too.

Sociologists call these judgments **values**, *culturally defined standards by which people assess desirability, goodness, and beauty, and which serve as broad guidelines for social living*. From the standpoint of a culture, values are statements about what ought to be.

Values are broad principles that underlie **beliefs**, *specific statements that people hold to be true*. While values are abstract standards of goodness, in other words, beliefs are particular matters that individuals consider to be true or false.

Cultural values and beliefs not only colour how we perceive our surroundings, they also form the core of our personalities. We learn from families, schools, and religious organizations to think and act according to approved principles, to pursue worthy goals, and to believe a host of cultural truths while rejecting alternatives as false. Particular values and beliefs thus operate as a form of "cultural capital" that can spark in some people the optimistic determination to pursue success and, in others, a sense of hopelessness that little will ever change (Sowell, 1996).

In a nation as large and diverse as Canada, of course, few cultural values and beliefs are shared by everyone. In fact, with a long history of immigration from the rest of the world, Canada has become a cultural mosaic. In this regard, we stand apart from many nations (especially China or Japan), which have more homogeneous cultural systems. Even so, there is a broad shape to our national life that may be described as "key values." The "Social Diversity" box compares Canadian and U.S. values.

Values: Inconsistency and Conflict

Cultural values can be inconsistent and even outright contradictory (Lynd, 1967; Bellah et al., 1985). Living in Canada, we sometimes find ourselves torn between the "me first" attitude of an individualistic, success-at-all-costs way of life and the opposing need to belong and contribute to some larger community. Similarly, we affirm our belief in equality of opportunity only to turn around and promote or degrade others because of their race or sex.

Value inconsistency reflects the cultural diversity of Canadian society and the process of cultural change by which new trends supplant older traditions. One tradition that continues to be central to the Canadian winter and that elusive Canadian identity is hockey. The traditional hockey scene in Canada is being transformed by the arrival of women's hockey at the international level: young girls across the country now

Canadians and Americans: What Makes Us Different?

When asked about what it means to be Canadian or what factors contribute to a Canadian identity, the average person will shrug and say, "I don't really know." When pushed a little harder we might admit that we know we are Canadians because we are "not American." We share more attributes and attitudes with Americans than we realize, but there are significant differences as well; some of the differences are intriguing.

Seymour Martin Lipset argued in the 1950s that the traditional differences between Canadian and American values are rooted in the past. A central feature of the history of the United States was the war of independence from Great Britain. In a sense, Canada separated formally from Britain only in the 1980s with the repatriation of the Constitution. This difference is pivotal, Lipset argues, for cultural distinctions between the United States and Canada.

Canada, in Lipset's view, sits somewhere between the U.S. and Great Britain with respect to values. Americans place great value on freedom, individual initiative, achievement, and success; Canadians, on the other hand, stress conformity and obedience to the law. In the American West, outlaws such as Jesse James and Billy the Kid were lionized as heroes; in Canada it was the Mountie—the policeman—that was admired.

Practically speaking, the Canadian tendency to emphasize the good of the collectivity over the good of the individual has resulted in social programs such as universal medical care. Until now, Americans have cherished the individual right to choose (and pay for) medical care as desired—with various sorts and levels of medical coverage for people with varying abilities to pay.

Roger Sauvé (a futurist and former journalist) gathered comparable data for the early 1990s on American and Canadian characteristics and attitudes, providing us with the following insights:

- Americans are more likely to think that Canadians and Americans are essentially or mainly the same (78 to Canada's 56 percent)

- Americans are more likely to favour Canada becoming the fifty-first state (66 to our 14 percent)

- Canadians are more likely to turn out to vote in federal elections (73 to 54 percent)

- Americans believe in hell and the devil (60 and 52 percent) more than Canadians do (34 and 30 percent)

- Canadians are more inclined to allow gays in the military (67 to 57 percent)

- Canadians welcome more acceptance of sexual freedom (40 to 29 percent)

- Canadians are more likely than Americans to say that premarital sex is not wrong (70 to 54 percent)

- Canadians favour more restrictive gun laws (77 to 70 percent)

- Americans are more likely to own handguns (24 to 3 percent)

- Teenage girls in the U.S. have higher birthrates than Canadian teenagers (62 births per 1000 15- to 19-year-old girls in the U.S.; 27 per 1000 in Canada)

- American marriages are more likely to end in divorce (43 to 28 percent)

- Americans aged 25 to 64 are more likely to be university graduates (25 to 17 percent)

- Canadians are more likely to rate local health care as excellent or good (71 to 59 percent)

- Americans are more likely to think their children will be better off than they are (41 to 35 percent)

SOURCES: Lipset (1985;1990); Sauvé (1994)

have women hockey players as *their* role models. So central to our identity is hockey that our failure to win gold at the 1998 Winter Olympics in Nagano, Japan (a silver medal for the women and no medal at all for the men) unleashed anger, despair, and depressive slumps across the country. In some people's minds, we no longer "have" hockey as part of our identity.

Whether based on the ethnic mix of Canadian society or changes in our way of life, today's value inconsistency leads to strained and awkward balancing acts in how we view the world. Sometimes we pursue one value at the expense of another, supporting the principle of equal opportunity, say, yet opposing the acceptance of gays as elementary school teachers. As well, many Canadians feel that our shared values are too influenced by the U.S. In a recent poll, 50 percent of Canadians said that they felt that Canadians should be doing more to develop a cultural identity separate from Americans and 52 percent of Canadians felt that Canadian culture needs to be more protected from outside influence (Serrill, 1995).

Standards of beauty—including the colour and design of everyday surroundings—vary significantly from one culture to another. Members of the Ndebele in South Africa lavishly paint their homes. Members of North American and European societies, by contrast, make far less use of bright colours and intricate detail so that their neighbourhoods appear much more subdued.

Values in Action: The Games People Play

Cultural values affect every aspect of our lives. Children's games, for example, may seem like lighthearted fun, but through them we teach young people what our culture deems to be important.

Using the sociological perspective, James Spates (1976a) sees in the familiar game King of the Castle our cultural emphasis on achievement and success.[1]

> In this game, the King (winner) is the one who scrambles to the top of some designated area and holds it against all challengers (losers). This is a very gratifying game from the winner's point of view, for one learns what it is like (however brief is the tenure at the top before being thrown off) to be an unequivocal success, to be unquestionably better than the entire competition. (1976a:286)

Each player endeavours to become number one at the expense of all other players. But success has its price, and King of the Castle teaches that as well.

---

[1] The excerpt presented here has been slightly modified, on the basis of unpublished versions of the study, with the permission of the author.

The King can never relax in such a pressurized position and constant vigilance is very difficult to endure, psychologically, for long. Additionally, the sole victor is likely to feel a certain alienation from others: Whom can one trust? Truly, "it is lonely at the top." (1976a:286)

Just as King of the Castle conveys our cultural emphasis on winning, Tag, Hide and Seek, and Monkey in the Middle exemplify the dangers of being a "loser." Drawing on these sociological observations, we can better appreciate the prominence of competitive team sports such as hockey in Canadian culture and why star athletes such as Wayne Gretzky are often celebrated as cultural heroes.

NORMS

For most of our history, women and men in Canada generally held to the idea that sexual intercourse should occur only within the bounds of marriage. By the late 1960s, however, beliefs had changed so that sexual activity became widely viewed as a form of recreation, sometimes involving people who hardly knew each other. By the mid-1980s, however, the rules changed again. Amid growing fears of sexually transmitted diseases, especially the deadly acquired immune deficiency syndrome (AIDS), people began rethinking the wisdom of the "sexual revolution" (McKusick et al., 1985; Smilgas, 1987).

Such patterns illustrate the operation of **norms**, *rules and expectations by which a society guides the behaviour of its members*. Some norms are *proscriptive*, mandating what we should *not* do, as when health officials warn us to avoid casual sex. *Prescriptive* norms, on the other hand, spell out what we *should* do. Practising "safe sex," for example, has become one such norm in recent years.

The most important norms apply virtually anywhere and at any time. For example, parents expect obedience from children regardless of the setting. Many normative conventions, by contrast, are situation-specific. We expect audience applause at the end of a musical performance; we accept applause (although we do not expect it) when a classroom lecture is over; we discourage applause when a priest or a rabbi finishes a sermon.

Mores and Folkways

William Graham Sumner (1959; orig. 1906), an early U.S. sociologist, recognized that some norms are more crucial to our lives than others. Sumner used the term **mores** (pronounced MORE-ays) to refer to *a society's standards of proper moral conduct*. Sumner counted among the mores all norms essential to maintaining a way of life; because of their importance, he contended that people develop an emotional attachment to mores and defend them publicly. In addition, mores apply to everyone, everywhere, all the time. Violation of mores—such as our society's prohibition against sexual relations between adults and children—typically brings a swift and strong reaction from others.

Sumner used the term **folkways** to designate *a society's customs for routine, casual interaction*. Folkways, which have lesser moral significance than mores, include notions about proper dress, appropriate greetings, and common courtesy. In short, while mores distinguish between right and wrong, folkways draw a line between right and *rude*. Because they are less important than mores, societies afford individuals a measure of personal discretion in matters involving folkways and punish infractions leniently. For example, a man who does not wear a tie to a formal dinner party is, at worst, guilty of a breach of etiquette. If, however, the man were to arrive at the dinner party wearing only a tie, he would be challenging social mores and inviting more serious sanctions.

Social Control

As participants in cultural systems, we learn to accept mores and many folkways as the basic rules of everyday life, typically responding to the behaviour of others with *sanctions*, which take the form of either reward or punishment. Conforming to norms provokes praise and approval from others, just as norm violations prompt avoidance, contempt, or even a formal response from the criminal justice system. Taken together, all kinds of sanctions form the heart of a culture's system of **social control**, *various means by which members of a society encourage conformity to norms*.

As we internalize cultural norms, we develop the capacity to respond critically to our own behaviour. "Doing wrong" (say, downloading a term paper from the Internet) can provoke not only *shame*—the painful sense that others disapprove of our actions—but also *guilt*, a negative judgment we make of ourselves. Only cultural creatures experience shame and guilt: this is probably what Mark Twain had in mind when he quipped that human beings "are the only animals that blush . . . or need to."

"IDEAL" AND "REAL" CULTURE

Societies devise values and norms as moral guidelines for their members. As such, these cultural elements do not describe actual behaviour as much as they tell us how we *should* behave. We must remember, then, that **ideal culture**, *social patterns mandated by cultural values and norms*, is not the same as **real culture**, *actual social patterns that only approximate cultural expectations*.

To illustrate, most women and men acknowledge the importance of sexual fidelity in marriage. Even so, in a recent American study, about 25 percent of married men and 10 percent of married women reported being sexually unfaithful to their spouses at some point in the marriage (Laumann et al., 1994). Such discrepancies are common to all societies, since no one lives up to ideal standards all the time. But a culture's moral prodding is crucial to shaping the lives of individuals all the same, calling to mind the old saying "Do as I say, not as I do."

MATERIAL CULTURE AND TECHNOLOGY

In addition to intangible elements such as values and norms, every culture encompasses a wide range of tangible (from Latin meaning "touchable") human creations that sociologists term *artifacts*. The Chinese eat with chopsticks rather than knives and forks, the Japanese place mats rather than rugs on the floor, many men and women in India prefer flowing robes to the tighter clothing common in Canada. An unfamiliar people's material culture may seem as strange to us as their language, values, and norms.

The artifacts common to a society typically reflect cultural values. The fact that poison-tipped arrows are a prized possession of Yąnomamö males in the Amazon rain forest, for example, surely reflects the importance that society places on warfare and militaristic skills. Similarly, our own high regard for the automobile is rooted in cherished values of individuality and independence. Miles of freeways crisscross Canada and we own over 13 million cars! Figure 3–1 shows that, even compared to other industrial societies, Canada stands out as a car-loving nation.

In addition to reflecting values, material culture also reveals a society's **technology**, *knowledge that a society applies to the task of living in a physical environment*. In short, technology ties the world of nature to the world of culture. Among the most technologically simple people on earth, the Yąnomamö interfere little with the natural environment. They remain keenly aware of the cycles of rainfall and the movement of the animals they hunt for food. By contrast, technologically complex societies (such as those of North America) have an enormous impact on the natural world, reshaping the environment (for better or worse) according to their own interests and priorities.

Because we accord science such great importance and praise the sophisticated technology it has produced, members of our society tend to judge cultures with simpler technology as less advanced. Some facts would support such an assessment. For example, life

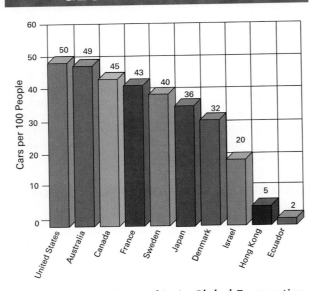

FIGURE 3–1 Car Ownership in Global Perspective

SOURCE: Author's calculations based on data from U.S. Bureau of the Census (1997).

expectancy for children born in Canada now exceeds seventy-five years; the lifespan of the Yąnomamö stands at only about forty years.

However, we must be careful not to make self-serving judgments about cultures that differ from our own. While our powerful and complex technology has produced work-reducing devices and seemingly miraculous forms of medical treatment, it has also contributed to unhealthy levels of stress, eroded the quality of the natural environment, and created weapons capable of destroying in a blinding flash everything that humankind has managed to achieve.

Finally, technology is another cultural element that varies substantially within Canada. Although many of us cannot imagine life without CD players, televisions, and the latest personal computers, many members of our society cannot afford such items, and others reject them on principle. The Old Order Mennonites, for example, live in small farming communities across southwestern Ontario, Alberta, and Manitoba. These people shun most modern conveniences as a matter of religious conviction. With their traditional black garb and horse-drawn buggies, the Old Order Mennonites may seem like a curious relic of the past. Yet their communities flourish, grounded in vibrant families and individuals with a strong sense of identity and purpose. And many of the thousands of outsiders who observe

them each year come away with the suspicion that these simple, stable communities may well suggest an attractive alternative to modern materialism and competitiveness.

NEW INFORMATION TECHNOLOGY AND CULTURE

Many industrial societies, including Canada, are now entering a post-industrial phase in which production is based on computers and new information technology. While industrial production centres on factories and machinery generating material goods, in other words, post-industrial production centres on computers and other electronic devices that create, process, store, and apply information.

The emergence of an information economy thus changes the skills that dominate a way of life, from the mechanical abilities to make things to the symbolic abilities to speak, write, compute, design, and create images in art, advertising, and entertainment. This transformation is likely to bring major change to our culture. In short, new information technology offers our society the capacity to *generate culture* on an unprecedented scale. The "Exploring Cyber-Society" box takes a closer look.

CULTURAL DIVERSITY: MANY WAYS OF LIFE IN ONE WORLD

Canada is a nation of striking cultural diversity. Perhaps this can best be appreciated by contrasting Canada with Japan, whose historic isolation has made it the most *monocultural* of all industrial nations. For Canada, on the other hand, heavy immigration over the past two centuries, especially over the last thirty years, has made it one of the most *multicultural* of all industrial nations.

The graph in Figure 3–2 gives not only some indication of how culturally diverse our country is, it also makes it clear that the *patterns* of immigration have changed over time. Before 1961, about 90 percent of immigrants to Canada hailed from Europe, especially the United Kingdom, and less than 5 percent came from countries in Asia and the Middle East. Since 1961, more and more immigrants have come from Asia and the Middle East. In the five-year period between 1991 and 1996, European immigrants made up only 19 percent of all immigrants, while those from Asia and the Middle East made up 57 percent of the total. This change in pattern, which has greatly increased the cultural diversity of our country, has been the result of a deliberate change in immigration policy on the part of the federal government.

Here Comes Virtual Culture!

The Information Revolution is now generating symbols—words, sounds, and images—at an unprecedented rate and rapidly spreading these symbols across the nation and around the world. What are the implications of new information technology for our way of life?

One key trend is that more and more of the cultural symbols that frame our lives are intentionally created. In the past, sociologists have described culture as a way of life transmitted over time from generation to generation. This traditional view envisions culture as a deeply rooted collective memory, a heritage passed along over the centuries and coming to us as something authentically our own because it belonged to our ancestors (Schwartz, 1996). But in the emerging cyber-society, more and more cultural symbols are new, intentionally generated by a small cultural elite of composers, writers, film makers, and others who work within the burgeoning information economy.

To illustrate this change, consider the changing character of cultural heroes, those people whose lives we celebrate and who represent an ideal we

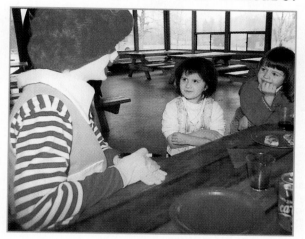

strive to live up to. Earlier in this century, the commonly recognized heroes were real men and women who made a difference in the life of this nation—people such as Laura Secord, Alexander Graham Bell, Grey Owl, Nellie McClung, John A. Macdonald, Louis Riel, Banting and Best, Maurice Richard, Mary Pickford, Barbara Ann Scott, Billy Bishop, and Dr. Norman Bethune. Of course, when we make a hero of someone (almost always well after the person has died) we "clean up" the person's biography, highlighting the successes and overlooking the shortcomings. But, although idealized, these people were authentic parts of our society's history.

Today's youngsters, by contrast, are fed a steady diet of virtual culture, images that spring from the mind of a contemporary culture-maker and that reach us through a screen: television, movies, or computer cyberspace. Today's "heroes" include the almost entirely American Power Rangers, Rug Rats, Ninja Turtles, Barney, Batman, Barbie, a continuous flow of Disney characters, Rambo, and the ever-smiling Ronald McDonald. No one doubts that many of these cultural icons embody at least some of the key cultural values that have shaped our way of life. But few of them have any historical reality and almost all of them have come into being for a single purpose: making money.

What do you think?

1. *As the Information Revolution proceeds, do you think "virtual culture" will become ever more important? Why or why not?*
2. *Will virtual culture erode or enhance our cultural traditions? For better or worse?*
3. *What effect do you think the predominance of U.S. movies and television shows has on Canada's self-image and its image abroad?*

Given this diversity, sociologists sometimes call Canada a cultural mosaic. To understand the reality of life in Canada, then, we must move beyond the notion of overarching cultural patterns to consider cultural diversity.

HIGH CULTURE AND POPULAR CULTURE

Much cultural diversity has roots in social class. In fact, in everyday conversation we usually reserve the term "culture" for sophisticated art forms such as classical literature, music, dance, and painting. We praise

symphony conductors, Shakespearean actors, or dance choreographers as "cultured," because they presumably appreciate the "finer things in life." The term "culture" itself has the same Latin root as the word "cultivate," suggesting that the "cultured" individual has cultivated or refined tastes.

By contrast, we speak less generously of ordinary people, assuming that everyday cultural patterns are somehow less worthy. In more concrete terms, we are tempted to judge the music of Mozart as "more cultured" than Motown, fine cuisine as better than fish sticks, and polo as more polished than ping-pong.

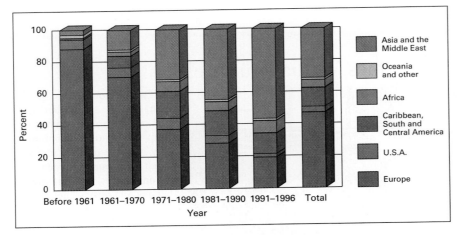

FIGURE 3–2 Immigrant Population by Place of Birth and Period of Immigration, 1996

SOURCE: Calculations by Gerber based on Statistics Canada, Catalogue 11–008E and www.statcan.ca.

Such judgments imply that many cultural patterns are readily accessible to some but not all members of a society (Hall and Neitz, 1993). Sociologists use the shorthand term **high culture**[2] to refer to *cultural patterns that distinguish a society's elite*; **popular culture**, then, designates *cultural patterns that are widespread among a society's population*. The publication of *Mondo Canuck: A Canadian Pop Culture Odyssey* (Pevere and Dymond, 1996) is a refreshing celebration of Canada's eye-level cultural creativity: the book itself is pop culture.

Common sense may suggest that high culture is superior to popular culture. After all, history chronicles the lives of elites much more than those of ordinary women and men. But sociologists are uneasy with such a sweeping evaluation and generally use the term "culture" to refer to *all* elements of a society's way of life, even as they recognize that cultural patterns vary throughout a population (Gans, 1974).

We should resist quick judgments about the merits of high culture as opposed to popular culture for two key reasons. First, neither elites nor ordinary people have uniform tastes and interests; people in both categories differ in numerous ways. Second, do we praise high culture because it is inherently better than popular culture, or simply because its supporters have more money, power, and prestige to begin with? For example, there is no difference between a violin and a fiddle; however, we refer to the instrument one way when it is used to produce a type of music typically enjoyed by people of higher social position, and the

other way when the musician is playing works appreciated by individuals with lower social standing.

SUBCULTURE

The term **subculture** refers to *cultural patterns that set apart some segment of a society's population*. Teenagers, native Canadians living on a reserve, homeless people, race-car drivers, jazz musicians, and maybe even sociologists all display subcultural patterns.

It is easy—but often inaccurate—to place people in subcultural categories. Almost everyone participates simultaneously in numerous subcultures, and we often have little commitment to many of them.

In some cases, however, important cultural traits such as ethnicity or religion do set off people from one another—sometimes with tragic results. Consider the former nation of Yugoslavia in southeastern Europe. The ongoing turmoil there has been fuelled by astounding cultural diversity. This one small country (which, before its breakup, was about the size of the Maritime provinces, with a population of 25 million—near the size of Canada's) made use of *two* alphabets, professed *three* religions, spoke *four* languages, was home to *five* major nationalities, was divided into *six* political republics, and absorbed the cultural influences of *seven* surrounding countries. The cultural conflict that plunged this nation into civil war reveals that subcultures are a source not only of pleasing variety but also of tensions and outright violence (cf. Sekulic et al., 1994).

Historically, we have been taught to view Canada as a "mosaic" with many nationalities contributing to a larger "Canadian" culture. But, considering the extent of our cultural diversity, how accurate is the "mosaic" description? One factor complicating this idealistic notion: cultural diversity involves not just *variety* but also *hierarchy*. Too often, what we view as

---

[2] The term "high culture" is derived from the more popular term "highbrow." Influenced by phrenology, the bogus nineteenth-century theory that personality was determined by the shape of the human skull, people a century ago contrasted the praiseworthy tastes of those they termed "highbrows" with the contemptible appetites of other they derided as "lowbrows."

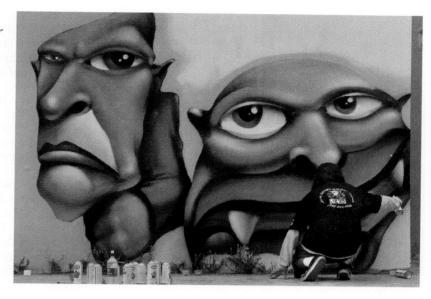

Whether visual expression in lines and colour is revered as "art' or dismissed as "graffiti" or even condemned as "vandalism" depends on the social standing of the creator. How would you characterize images such as this one? Is this art? Why or why not?

"dominant" or "highbrow" cultural patterns are those favoured by powerful segments of the population, while we relegate the lives of the disadvantaged to the realm of "subculture." This dilemma has led some researchers to highlight the experiences of less powerful members of our society in a new approach called multiculturalism.

MULTICULTURALISM

As well as being bilingual, Canadian society is officially multicultural. **Multiculturalism** is embodied in *social policy designed to encourage ethnic or cultural heterogeneity*. Historically, our society downplayed cultural diversity, defining our way of life primarily in terms familiar to the English or French immigrants who have socially dominated Canada.

Historians highlighted the role of descendants of the English and French, described events from their point of view, and pushed to the side the perspectives and accomplishments of other immigrants and of native peoples. The European way of life was set up as an ideal to which all should aspire and by which all should be judged. Multiculturalists describe this singular pattern in Canada as **Eurocentrism**, *the dominance of European cultural patterns*. The legacy of this practice is a spirited debate over whether we should continue to stress European, especially French and English, cultural contributions to the exclusion of those made by, for instance, the Chinese, Caribbean, Ukrainian, and East Indian peoples to this country. An interesting example of the continued presence of Eurocentric ideas in Canada was the widespread opposition to the decision to allow a Sikh, Baltej Singh Dhillon, to wear a turban as part of his RCMP uniform.

Although few deny that our culture has wide-ranging roots, multiculturalism has generated controversy because it requires us to rethink the norms and values at the core of our society. Not surprisingly, the battles over how to describe our culture now rage on many fronts.

One area of debate involves language. Although Canada is officially bilingual, the Canadian population is actually composed of people with many different mother tongues. Table 3–1 provides the distribution of Canadians by mother tongue. Despite the significant number of different languages spoken in this country, minority languages are not officially recognized. This has led some critics to charge that multiculturalism has a mostly symbolic significance in Canada. By this they mean that it allows minorities to maintain their cultures within their homes while forcing them to speak either French or English for any dealings outside the home. Gradually, minorities will lose the use of their mother tongues, and with them many of their distinctive cultural practices.

On the other hand, some people point out that each minority actually makes up a very small part of the total population of Canada. They claim that trying to accommodate every minority in Canada would lead to a fractured society, one with no sense of commonality or cohesiveness. The debate still rages, and important questions have been left unresolved. To what extent should Canada encourage those who speak languages other than French or English to maintain their mother tongues? Should Canadian taxpayers support heritage language schools and courses?

TABLE 3–1 Mother Tongues in Canada, 1996

Mother Tongue	Percent of Population
English	59.2
French	23.2
Chinese	2.5
Italian	1.7
German	1.6
Polish	0.7
Spanish	0.7
Portuguese	0.7
Punjabi	0.7
Ukrainian	0.6
Arabic	0.5
Dutch	0.5
Tagalog (Filipino)	0.5
Greek	0.4
Vietnamese	0.4
Cree	0.3
Inuktitut	0.1
Other nonofficial languages	4.2
Multiple languages	1.4

SOURCE: Statistics Canada, www.statcan.ca.

An additional issue is how our schools—from the early grades through university—should teach about culture. It is among educators that the clash over multiculturalism has been most intense. Four basic positions have emerged from this discussion.

Proponents defend multiculturalism, first, as a way to capture a more accurate picture of our past. Proposed educational reforms seek, for example, to temper the simplistic praise directed at European explorers by realistically assessing the tragic impact of the European conquest on the native peoples of this hemisphere. As detailed in Chapter 13 ("Race and Ethnicity"), from the point of view of the native peoples of North America, contact with Europeans unleashed centuries of domination and death from war and disease. In addition, a multicultural approach would recognize the achievements of many women and men whose cultural backgrounds up to now have kept them on the sidelines of history.

Second, proponents claim, multiculturalism is a means to come to terms with our country's even more diverse present. Children born in the 1990s can expect that, during their lifetimes, immigration from African, Asian, and Hispanic countries will increase significantly. Third, proponents assert that multiculturalism is a way to strengthen the academic achievement of immigrant and visible minority children and others who find little personal relevance in traditional educational programs. Fourth and finally, proponents see multiculturalism as worthwhile preparation for all people in Canada to live in a world that is increasingly interdependent. As various chapters of this book explain, social patterns in this country are becoming more closely linked to issues and events elsewhere in the world. Multiculturalism undermines nationalistic prejudices by pointing out global connectedness: it also makes Canadians more flexible in their international political and business dealings.

Although multiculturalism has found widespread favour in the last several years, it has provoked its share of criticism as well. The argument most commonly voiced by opponents of multiculturalism is that any society remains cohesive only to the extent that its cultural patterns are widely shared. Multiculturalism, say critics, fuels the "politics of difference," encouraging divisiveness as individuals identify with their subculture rather than with Canada as a whole. Opponents also charge that multiculturalism erodes the claim to common truth by maintaining that ideas should be evaluated according to the race (and sex) of those who present them. Are we to conclude that there is no common humanity, in other words, but only an "aboriginal experience," a "European experience," and so on? Further, critics are skeptical that multiculturalism actually benefits minorities as claimed. Multiculturalism, critics argue, demands precisely the kind of racial segregation that we claim to deplore. Furthermore, a heritage-centred curriculum may well deny children a wide range of knowledge and skills by encouraging study from a more limited point of view.

Is there any common ground in this debate? Virtually everyone agrees that all people in Canada need to gain greater appreciation of the extent of our cultural diversity. Further, because visible minorities are an increasingly large component of our population, efforts in this direction are needed now. But precisely where the balance is to be struck is likely to remain a divisive issue for some time to come.

COUNTERCULTURE

Cultural diversity also includes outright rejection of conventional ideas or behaviour. **Counterculture** refers to *cultural patterns that strongly oppose those widely accepted within a society.*

In many societies, countercultures spring from adolescence (Spates, 1976b, 1983; Spates and Perkins, 1982). Most of us are familiar with the youth-oriented counterculture of the 1960s that rejected the cultural mainstream as overly competitive, self-centred, and materialistic. Instead, hippies and other counterculturalists favoured a cooperative lifestyle in which "being" took precedence over "doing" and the capacity for personal growth—or "expanded consciousness"—was prized over material possessions such as homes and cars. Such differences led some people at that time to "drop out" of the larger society.

Counterculture may involve not only distinctive values, but unconventional behaviour (including dress and forms of greeting) as well as music. Many members of the 1960s counterculture, for instance, drew personal identity from long hair, headbands, and blue jeans; from displaying a peace sign rather than offering a handshake; and from drug use and the energy of ever-present rock-and-roll music.

Some countercultures, flourishing in North America, Europe, and beyond, seek to disrupt their societies. These highly significant countercultures may involve militaristic bands of men and women, deeply suspicious of government and willing to resort to violence. Canada's FLQ (Front de libération du Québec), which was active through the 1960s and early 1970s, resorted to bombings, kidnapping, and murder in its quest for an independent socialist Quebec. More recently, counterculture extremists bombed the Oklahoma City federal building in 1995, killing 168 people (including children in its day care centre).

CULTURAL CHANGE

Perhaps the most basic truth is that "All things shall pass." Even the dinosaurs, who dominated this planet for some 160 million years (see the time line), exist today only as fossils (and movie villains). Will humanity survive for millions of years to come? No one knows. All we can say with certainty is that, for as long as we do survive, the human record will be one of continuous cultural change.

Change in one dimension of a culture is usually associated with other transformations. For example, increased labour force participation among women occurs along with changing family patterns, including later age at first marriage, a rising divorce rate, and increasing numbers of children being raised in households without fathers. Such connections illustrate the principle of **cultural integration**, *the close relationship among various elements of a cultural system.*

But all elements of a cultural system do not change at the same speed. William Ogburn (1964) observed that technology moves quickly, generating new elements of material culture (such as "test-tube babies") faster than nonmaterial culture (such as ideas about parenthood) can keep up with them. Ogburn called this inconsistency **cultural lag**, *cultural elements changing at different rates, causing various degrees of disruption in cultural systems.* In a culture with the technical ability to allow one woman to give birth to a child by using another woman's egg, which has been fertilized in a laboratory with the sperm of a total stranger, how are we to apply the traditional notions of motherhood and fatherhood?

Cultural changes are set in motion in three ways. The first is *invention*, the process of creating new cultural elements. Invention has given us the telephone (1876), the airplane (1903), and the aerosol spray can (1941), all of which have had a tremendous impact on our way of life. The process of invention goes on constantly, as indicated by the numbers of applications submitted annually to the Canadian Patent Office.

Discovery, a second cause of cultural change, involves recognizing and understanding something not fully understood before—from a distant star, to the foods of another culture, to the athletic excellence of Canadian women like rower Silken Lauman and the members of our women's hockey team. Many discoveries result from scientific research. Yet discovery can also happen quite by accident, as when Marie Curie left a rock on a piece of photographic paper in 1898 and serendipitously discovered radium.

The third cause of cultural change is *diffusion*, the spread of cultural traits from one society to another. The technological ability to send information around the globe in seconds—by means of radio, television, facsimile, and computer—means that the level of cultural diffusion has never been greater than it is today. Insulin, developed first by Banting and Best at the University of Toronto in the 1920s, and the telephone, conceived by Alexander Graham Bell in Brantford, Ontario, in 1874, have spread around the world.

Certainly our own society has contributed many significant cultural elements to the world. But diffusion works the other way as well, so that much of what we assume is inherently "Canadian" actually comes from other cultures. Ralph Linton (1937) explained that many commonplace elements of our way of life—most clothing and furniture, clocks, newspapers, money, and even the English language—are all derived from other cultures.

ETHNOCENTRISM AND CULTURAL RELATIVITY

North American travellers are among the world's greatest shoppers. They delight in surveying hand-woven carpets in China, India, or Iran, inspecting finely crafted metals in Turkey, or collecting beautifully coloured porcelain tiles in Morocco. And, of course, all these items are wonderful bargains. But one major reason for the low cost is unsettling: many products from low- and middle-income countries of the world are produced by children, many as young as five or six, who work long days for extremely low wages.

We think of childhood as a time of innocence and freedom from adult burdens such as regular work. In poor countries throughout the world, however, families depend on income earned by children. So what

Most people in affluent Canada take for granted that childhood should be a carefree time of life devoted to learning and play. In low-income societies of the world, however, poor families depend on the income earned by children, some of whom perform long days of heavy physical labour. We may not want to accept all cultural practices as "natural" just because they exist. But what universal standards can be used to judge social patterns as either right or wrong?

people in one society think of as right and natural, people elsewhere find puzzling and even immoral. Perhaps the Chinese philosopher Confucius had it right when he noted that "All people are the same; it's only their habits that are different."

Just about every imaginable social habit is subject to at least some variation around the world, and such differences cause travellers excitement and distress in about equal measure. The tradition in Japan is to name intersections rather than streets, a practice that regularly confuses North Americans who do the opposite; Egyptians move very close to others in conversation, irritating North Americans used to maintaining several feet of "personal space;" bathrooms lack toilet paper throughout much of Morocco, causing great agitation among Westerners unaccustomed to using one's left hand for bathroom hygiene!

Because a particular culture is the basis for everyone's reality, it is no wonder that people everywhere

exhibit **ethnocentrism**, *the practice of judging another culture by the standards of one's own culture.* On one level, some ethnocentrism is inevitable if people are to be emotionally attached to a cultural system. On another level, however, ethnocentrism generates misunderstanding and sometimes conflict.

For example, take the seemingly trivial matter of people in North America referring to China as the "Far East." Such a term, which has little meaning to the Chinese, is an ethnocentric expression for a region that is far east *of Europe*. For their part, the Chinese refer to their country with a word translated as "Middle Kingdom," suggesting that, like us, they see their society as the centre of the world.

Is there an alternative to ethnocentrism? The logical alternative is to imagine unfamiliar cultural traits from the point of view of *them* rather than *us*. The casual observer of an Old Order Mennonite farmer tilling hundreds of acres with a team of horses rather than a tractor might initially dismiss this practice as hopelessly backward and inefficient. But, from the Old Order Mennonite point of view, hard work is a foundation of religious discipline. The Mennonites are well aware of tractors; they simply believe that using such machinery would be their undoing.

This alternative approach, called **cultural relativism**, is *the practice of judging a culture by its own standards.* Cultural relativism is a difficult attitude to adopt because it requires not only understanding the values and norms of another society but also suspending cultural standards we have known all our lives. But, as people of the world come into increasing contact with one another, we are confronting the need to more fully understand other cultures.

North American business is learning that success in the ever-expanding global economy depends on cultural sophistication. Consider the troubles several corporations had when they carelessly translated their advertising slogans into Spanish. General Motors soon learned that sales of its Nova were hampered by a product whose name in Spanish means "No Go." Coors' phrase "Turn It Loose" startled customers who read that the beer would make you "Suffer from Diarrhea." Braniff airlines turned "Fly in Leather" into clumsy Spanish reading "Fly Naked." Eastern Airlines transformed its slogan "We Earn Our Wings Daily" into words customers read as "We Fly Daily to Heaven." Or how about "It Takes a Tough Man to Make a Tender Chicken" translated into Spanish as "It Takes a Sexually Excited Man to Make a Chicken Affectionate"?

The world may need greater cultural understanding, but cultural relativity introduces problems of its own. Virtually any kind of behaviour is practised somewhere in the world; does that mean that everything is equally right? Just because Indian and Moroccan families benefit from having their children work long hours, does that justify such child labour?

Since we are all members of a single species, surely there must be some universal standards of proper conduct. But what are they? And, in trying to develop them, how can we avoid imposing our own standards of fair play on others? There are no simple answers. But here are some general guidelines to keep in mind when dealing with other cultures.

First, while cultural differences fascinate us, they can also be deeply disturbing. Be prepared to experience an emotional reaction when encountering the unfamiliar. Second, resist making snap judgments so that you can observe unfamiliar cultural surroundings with an open mind. Third, try to imagine the issue from their point of view rather than yours. Fourth, after careful thought, try to evaluate an unfamiliar custom. After all, there is no virtue in passively accepting every cultural practice. But, in reaching a judgment, bear in mind that—despite your efforts—you can never really experience the world as others do. Fifth, and finally, turn the argument around and think about your own way of life as others might see it. After all, what we gain most from studying others are insights into ourselves.

A GLOBAL CULTURE?

Today, more than ever before, we can observe many of the same cultural patterns the world over. Walking the streets of Seoul (South Korea), Kuala Lumpur (Malaysia), Madras (India), Cairo (Egypt), and Casablanca (Morocco), we find familiar forms of dress, hear well-known pop music, and see advertising for many of the same products we use at home. Just as importantly, as illustrated by Global Map 3–1, English is rapidly emerging as the preferred second language of most of the world. So, are we witnessing the birth of a global culture?

The world is still divided into 191 states or countries and thousands of different cultural systems. Further, as recent violence in the former Soviet Union, the former Yugoslavia, the Middle East, Sri Lanka, and elsewhere attests, many people are intolerant of others whose cultures differ from their own. Yet, looking back through history, we see that societies around the world now have more contact with one another, and enjoy more cooperation, than ever before. These global connections involve the flow of goods, information, and people.

1. **The global economy: the flow of goods.** The extent of international trade has never been greater. The global economy has introduced many of the same consumer goods (from cars to TV shows to T-shirts) the world over.

Canada's $580 billion in imports and exports (1997) suggest a complex web of production and distribution.

2. **Global communications: the flow of information.** A century ago, communication around the world depended on written messages delivered by boat, train, horse and wagon, or, occasionally, telegraph wire. Today's satellite-based communication system enables people to experience sights and sounds of events taking place thousands of miles away—often as they happen. When, in the 1960s, Marshall McLuhan conceived of "the global village" as a function of electronic (instantaneous) communication, we had only begun to scratch the surface of communications technology.

3. **Global migration: the flow of people.** Knowledge about the rest of the world motivates people to move where they imagine life will be better. Moreover, today's transportation technology—especially air travel—makes relocating easier than ever before. Canada, with one of the world's highest rates of immigration, has a population that is about 16 percent foreign-born. Travel, for business or pleasure, also contributes to interpersonal ties and global knowledge or awareness.

These global links have made the cultures of the world more similar at least in superficial respects. But there are three important limitations to the global culture thesis. First, the flow of goods, information, and people has been uneven throughout the world. Generally speaking, urban areas (centres of commerce, communication, and people) have stronger ties to one another, while rural villages remain more isolated. Then, too, the greater economic and military power of North America and Western Europe means that these regions influence the rest of the world more than the other way around.

Second, the global culture thesis assumes that people everywhere are able to afford various new goods and services. As Chapter 11 ("Global Stratification") explains, the grinding poverty in much of the world deprives millions of even the basic necessities of a safe and secure life.

Third, although many cultural traits are now found throughout the world, we should not conclude that people everywhere attach the same meanings to them. Do teenagers in Tokyo understand rap music the way their counterparts in New York or Los Angeles do? Similarly, we mimic fashions from around the world with little knowledge of the lives of people who first conceived of them. In short, people everywhere look at the world through their own cultural "lenses" (Featherstone, 1990; Hall and Neitz, 1993).

Travellers Beware!
The Meaning of Gestures in Other Societies

young man from Manitoba is enjoying a summer trip through the German countryside. He stands by the side of a county road hoping for a lift and, as a beautiful sports car approaches, he raises his right hand to flash the "A-OK!" sign (see Figure C below). The horn blares as the car speeds past, the angry driver hurling a few colourful words back at the hapless traveller.

What has happened here? Are Germans hostile to hitchhikers? No, except that, like people everywhere, they don't take kindly to insults. What the young Canadian meant as a sign of approval, Germans see as an offensive gesture—a crude word meaning "rectum."

Since much human communication involves not words but gestures and body language—especially when we encounter people whose language differs from our own—we need to be mindful that the innocent use of even a simple hand movement may provoke an angry response. Here are six bodily gestures that seem innocent enough to members

(A)

(B)

(C)

THEORETICAL ANALYSIS OF CULTURE

Culture allows us to understand ourselves and the world around us. Sociologists and anthropologists, however, have the special task of understanding culture. They do so by using various theoretical paradigms.

STRUCTURAL-FUNCTIONAL ANALYSIS

Recall from Chapter 1 ("The Sociological Perspective") that structural-functional analysis sees society as a relatively stable system of integrated parts devised to meet human needs. Thus, various cultural traits each help to maintain the overall operation of society.

The stability of cultural systems is rooted in core values (Parsons, 1964; Williams, 1970). In this way, structural-functionalism draws on the philosophical doctrine of idealism, the assertion that ideas (rather than, say, patterns of material production) are the basis of human reality. Expressed in a wide range of everyday activities, core values serve to bind all members of a society together.

Using a structural-functional approach, let us reconsider the Old Order Mennonite farmer plowing hundreds of acres with a team of horses. Within the Old Order Mennonite cultural system, rejecting tractors, automobiles, and electricity makes sense because it ensures that there is plenty of hard work. Continuous labour—usually outside the home for men and inside the home for women—functions to maintain

of our society but that may evoke a stern response from people elsewhere.

Figures A and B would each offend members of Islamic societies. Since Muslims typically perform bathroom hygiene with the left hand, they recoil at the sight of a person eating with that hand, illustrated in Figure A. Islam also holds that the sole of a shoe is unclean; therefore, any display of the bottom of the foot, as in Figure B, conveys insult. Figure C displays the common "A-OK" gesture by which people in North America express approval and pleasure.

In France, however, this symbol imparts the snub "You're worth zero," while Germans interpret this gesture as a crude word for "rectum." Figure D shows the simple curling of a finger, meaning "come here." Malaysians attach the same meaning to this gesture as we do, but they use it exclusively for calling animals; thus, they take no pleasure in being beckoned in this way. Figure E shows the familiar "thumbs up" gesture widely employed in North America to mean "Good job!" or "All right!" In Nigeria and also in Australia,

flashing this gesture (especially with a slight upward motion) transmits the insulting message "Up yours!" Finally, Figure F shows a gesture that members of our society read as "Stop!" or "No, thanks." But display this gesture to a motorist or street vendor anywhere in western Africa and you will probably have a fight on your hands. There it means "You have five fathers," or, more simply, "You bastard!"

SOURCES: Examples are drawn from Ekman, Friesen, and Bear (1984), and Axtell (1991).

(D)

(E)

(F)

the Old Order Mennonite value of discipline, which shapes their way of life. Long days of work, along with meals and recreation at home, define Old Order Mennonite culture and bind family members together. Their rejection of modern technology also has the function of making them self-sufficient (Fretz, 1989).

Of course, cultural traits have both functional and dysfunctional consequences. The Old Order Mennonite trait of "shunning," by which people cease social contact with anyone judged to have violated Mennonite mores, generates conformity but also provokes tension and, at the extreme, can cause a serious rift in the community.

Because cultures are strategies to meet human needs and were all devised by members of the same species, we would expect that cultures the world over

would have some elements in common. The term **cultural universals** refers to *traits found in every culture of the world*. Comparing hundreds of cultures, George Murdock (1945) found dozens of traits common to them all. One cultural universal is the family, which functions everywhere to control sexual reproduction and to oversee the care and upbringing of children. Another cultural universal, funeral rites, serves as a tellingly human response to the reality of death. Jokes, too, are found in all cultures, acting as a relatively safe means of releasing social tensions.

Critical evaluation. The strength of the structural-functional paradigm is showing how culture operates as an integrated system for meeting human needs. Yet, by emphasizing cultural stability, this approach

Funerals are often defined as a form of respect for the deceased. The social function of funerals, however, has much more to do with the living. For survivors, funerals reaffirm their sense of unity and continuity in the face of separation and disruption.

tem of economic production. "It is not the consciousness of men that determines their existence," Marx asserted, "it is their social existence that determines their consciousness" (1977:4; orig. 1859). This shows the social-conflict paradigm's link to the philosophical doctrine of materialism, the assertion that how people fashion their material world (for example, a capitalist economy) has a powerful effect on other dimensions of their culture. Such a materialist approach contrasts with the idealist leanings of structural-functionalism.

Social-conflict analysis, then, ties the competitive and individualistic values of capitalist societies to their economy, which serves the interests of those who own factories and other businesses. The culture of capitalism further teaches us to believe that the rich and powerful have more talent and discipline than others and therefore deserve their wealth and privileges. Viewing capitalism as somehow "natural," then, leads some people to distrust efforts to lessen the economic disparity.

Eventually, however, the strains fostered by social inequality exert continuous pressure towards change. The native rights movement and the women's movement exemplify the drive for change supported by disadvantaged segments of the Canadian population. Both, too, have encountered opposition from defenders of the status quo.

Critical evaluation. The strength of the social-conflict paradigm lies in showing that, if cultural systems address human needs, they do so unequally. Put otherwise, this orientation holds that cultural elements "function" to maintain the dominance of some people over others. This inequity, in turn, promotes change. Because the social-conflict paradigm stresses the divisiveness of culture, however, this approach understates the ways in which cultural patterns integrate all members of society. Thus, we should consider both social-conflict and structural-functional insights to gain a fuller understanding of culture.

downplays the extent to which societies change. Similarly, functionalism's assertion that cultural values are embraced by every member of a society overlooks the range of cultural diversity. Finally, the cultural patterns favoured by powerful people often dominate a society, while other ways of life are pushed to the margins. Thus, cultures typically generate more conflict than structural-functional analysis leads us to believe.

SOCIAL-CONFLICT ANALYSIS

The social-conflict paradigm views culture in a very different light. To social-conflict theorists, culture forms a dynamic arena of conflict generated by social inequality. This paradigm draws attention to the ways in which cultural traits serve the needs of some members of society at the expense of others.

Social-conflict analysis critically questions why certain values dominate in a society. What forces generate one set of values rather than another? Who benefits from these social arrangements? Many using this paradigm, especially sociologists influenced by Karl Marx, argue that values are shaped by a society's sys-

CULTURAL MATERIALISM

A fourth theoretical paradigm is derived from ecology, the natural science that delves into the relationship between a living organism and its environment. **Cultural materialism** (or cultural ecology), then, amounts to *a theoretical paradigm that explores the relationship of human culture to the physical environment.* This paradigm investigates how climate and the availability of food, water, and other natural resources shape cultural patterns.

Consider the case of India. This nation contends with widespread hunger and malnutrition, yet has cultural norms that prohibit the killing of cows. According to Hindu belief, cows are defined as sacred animals. To North Americans who enjoy so much beef, this is puzzling. Why should Indians not consume beef to supplement their diet?

Investigating India's ecology, Marvin Harris (1975) concluded that the importance of cows greatly exceeds their value as a food source. Harris points out that cows cost little to raise, since they consume grasses of no interest to humans. And cows produce two valuable resources: oxen (the neutered offspring of cows) and manure. Unable to afford expensive farm machinery, Indian farmers rely on oxen to power their plows. For Indians, killing cows would be as clever as farmers in Canada destroying factories that build tractors. Furthermore, each year millions of tonnes of cow manure are processed into building material and burned as fuel (India has little oil, coal, or wood). To kill cows, then, would deprive Indians of homes and a source of heat. In short, there are sound ecological reasons to culturally protect the cow.

Critical evaluation. Cultural materialism expands our understanding of culture by highlighting its interplay with the environment. This approach reveals how cultural patterns arise among human beings in response to particular natural conditions. However, this paradigm has several limitations. We can only rarely draw simple or direct connections between the environment and culture because cultural and physical forces interact in subtle and complex ways. Further, this approach has less application to technologically sophisticated societies that extensively manipulate the natural world.

SOCIOBIOLOGY

We know culture is a human creation; but does our biological humanity influence how this process unfolds? A third multidisciplinary paradigm, standing with one leg in biology and one in sociology, attempts to answer this question. **Sociobiology**, then, is *a theoretical paradigm that explores ways in which our biology affects how humans create culture.*

Sociobiology rests on the logic of evolution. In his treatise *On the Origin of the Species*, Charles Darwin (1859) asserted that living organisms change over long periods of time as a result of *natural selection*, a matter of four simple principles. First, all living things seek to reproduce themselves. Second, the blueprint for reproduction lies in the genes, the basic units of life that carry traits of one generation into the next. Genes vary randomly in each species; in effect, this genetic variation allows a species to "try out" new life patterns in a particular environment. Third, due to genetic variation, some organisms are more likely than others

to survive and to pass on their advantageous genes to their offspring. Fourth and finally, over thousands of generations, specific genetic patterns that promote reproduction survive and become dominant. In this way, as biologists say, a species adapts to its environment, and dominant traits emerge as the "nature" of the organism.

In the case of humans, culture itself emerged as human nature. That is, rather than being biologically "wired" for specific behaviour, humans developed the intelligence and sociability to devise life patterns for themselves. Such flexibility has allowed our species to flourish all over the planet. Even so, sociobiologists point out, we are all one species—a fact evident in the large number of cultural universals.

Consider, for example, the fact that, as sex researcher Alfred Kinsey put it, "Among all people everywhere in the world, the male is more likely than the female to desire sex with a variety of partners" (quoted in Barash, 1981:49). What insights does sociobiology offer into the so-called "double standard"?

To begin, we all know that children result from joining a woman's egg with a man's sperm. But the biological significance of a single sperm and a single egg differ dramatically. For healthy men, sperm represents a "renewable resource" produced by the testes throughout most of the life course. A man releases hundreds of millions of sperm in a single ejaculation—technically, enough to fertilize every woman in North America (Barash, 1981:47). A newborn female's ovaries, however, contain her entire lifetime allotment of follicles or immature eggs. A woman commonly releases a single mature egg cell from her ovaries each month. So, while a man is biologically capable of fathering thousands of offspring, a woman is able to bear only a relatively small number of children.

Given this biologically based difference, each sex is well served by a distinctive reproductive strategy. From a strictly biological perspective, a man reproduces his genes most efficiently by being promiscuous—readily engaging in sex. This scheme, however, opposes the reproductive interests of a woman, whose relatively few pregnancies demand that she carry the child for nine months, give birth, and provide care for long afterwards. Thus, efficient reproduction on the part of the woman depends on carefully selecting a mate whose qualities (beginning with the likelihood that he will simply stay around) will contribute to their child's survival and successful reproduction (Remoff, 1984).

The "double standard" certainly involves more than biology and is tangled up with the historical domination of women by men (Barry, 1983). But

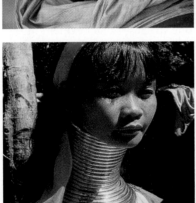

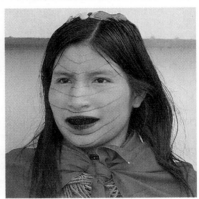

We claim that beauty is in the eye of the beholder, which suggests the importance of culture in setting standards of attractiveness. All of the people pictured here—from Morocco, South Africa, Nigeria, Myanmar (Burma), Japan, and Ecuador—are beautiful to members of their own society. At the same time, sociobiologists point out that, in every society on earth, people are attracted to youthfulness. The reason is that, as sociobiologists see it, attractiveness underlies our choices about reproduction, which is most readily accomplished in early adulthood.

sociobiology suggests that this cultural pattern, like many others, has an underlying bio-logic. Simply put, it has developed around the world because women and men everywhere tend towards distinctive reproductive strategies.

Critical evaluation. Sociobiology has generated intriguing theories about the biological roots of some cultural patterns, especially those that are universal. But sociobiology remains controversial for several reasons.

First, some critics fear that sociobiologists may revive biological arguments, common a century ago, touting the superiority of one race or sex. But defenders counter that sociobiology rejects the past pseudo-science of racial superiority. On the contrary, they continue, sociobiology actually unites all of humanity by asserting that all people share a single evolutionary history. With regard to sex, sociobiology does rest on

the assumption that men and women differ biologically in some ways that culture cannot overcome—if, in fact, any society intended to. But, far from asserting that males are somehow more important than females, sociobiology emphasizes how both sexes are vital to human reproduction.

Second, say the critics, sociobiologists have as yet amassed little evidence to support their theories. A generation ago, Edward O. Wilson (1975, 1978), generally credited as the founder of this field, optimistically claimed that sociobiology would reveal the biological roots of human culture. But research to date conclude that biological forces do not determine human behaviour in any rigid sense. Rather, abundant evidence supports the conclusion that human behaviour is *learned* within a cultural system. The contribution of sociobiology, then, lies in its explanation of why some cultural patterns seem "easier to learn" than others (Barash, 1981).

The Paparazzi: Villains or Our Eyes to the World?

Paparazzi! The word, which we heard repeatedly in the days and months following the tragic death of Princess Diana, is one that only then became part of the active vocabularies of most of us. The term comes from the classic film *La Dolce Vita*, directed by Federico Fellini, in which the main character, a journalist, was named Paparazzo.

The paparazzi are freelance photo journalists who indulge our passion for intimate glimpses into the lives of celebrities by relentlessly stalking them: their goal is to capture private moments on camera. Many celebrities are pursued by the paparazzi, but Diana—the most photographed woman in the world—had experienced more than her share of their attentions. Some of the paparazzi—among them Mark Saunders and Glenn Harvey, "hardest of the hard-core Diana paparazzi"—had devoted their whole careers to "doing Di:" taking rapid-fire pictures of her was referred to as "banging," "blitzing," "smudging," or "ripping" Di (Lyall and Pogrebin, 1997). The desperate quest for photos of Diana is understood better, perhaps, if one realizes that the right photo could be worth as much as a million dollars.

Princess Diana, sprinkled with the fairy dust of royalty, reached the heights of celebrity status in part because of her ambivalent relationship with the media, and the paparazzi in particular. The media propelled Diana—the beautiful, the vulnerable, the good, the irreverent—into the public eye, a process that she sometimes readily participated in and seemed to invite. For example, she did not hesitate to use the media as a means of presenting her own point of view, particularly concerning her relationship with Prince Charles and the rest of the royal family.

But at the same time, the media made her life a living hell. The cost of

Dr. Esther Konigsberg, a family physician in Burlington, Ontario, responded to the death of Princess Diana ("a wonderful champion of every human being") with a crusade to get merchants to stop selling the tabloids that publish pictures taken by the paparazzi. She circulated a petition asking consumers, merchants, and advertisers to stop buying, selling, and advertising in the tabloids. Dr. Konigsberg found it personally unsettling to realize that she is "part of a society whose curiosity and fascination with public figures have contributed to the unfortunate events" that led to Diana's death (Whitnell, 1997).

celebrity was the loss of her freedom and her privacy. She was stalked by the paparazzi, with their overwhelmingly intrusive cameras, but it was through their work that we came to know her so well. When she died, mourner after mourner would say, "I really felt that I knew her!" This kind of intimacy, which was predicted by Marshall McLuhan, illustrates the tremendous power of the media.

Shortly after Diana's death the British tabloids collectively suggested their own code of ethics regarding the purchase of paparazzi photos. Princes William and Harry are to be off limits until they are adults, and other photos of the private lives of celebrities are to

be obtained only with the permission of the subjects. Cynics point out that this voluntary code of ethics was devised to forestall action by the British government and that over time (a very short time at that) it will be discarded. What will happen, they ask, when Prince William begins to date?

The terrible accident that killed Princess Diana was the result of speed, alcohol, another car, bad judgment at several points, and the actions of the pursuing paparazzi. There are many who would add that the mass media as a whole and the general public, worldwide, must share responsibility and guilt for creating the circumstances that hastened Diana's death. After all, we have a voracious collective appetite for information about celebrities—the more personal the information the better. It could also be argued that the paparazzi were merely convenient scapegoats, soon forgotten when the public recovered from their initial shock over Diana's death.

It could be argued that celebrities need media exposure, and perhaps even the paparazzi, to keep them in the spotlight. If "the medium is the message" as Marshall McLuhan suggested, what does the existence of the paparazzi—and the media that support them—say about our culture?

Continue the debate . . .

1. *Should the relevant governments take steps to restrain the activities of the paparazzi? What possible impact could such restrictions have on freedom of speech?*
2. *What role do celebrities themselves play in encouraging the existence of the paparazzi? What role could they play in controlling them?*
3. *Why do we buy the magazines and tabloids that publish the paparazzi's pictures? Do we share responsibility for the activities of the paparazzi?*

CULTURE AS CONSTRAINT

Over the long course of human evolution, culture became the human strategy for survival. Truly, we cannot live without culture. But the capacity for culture does have some drawbacks. We may be the only animals who name ourselves; yet, as symbolic beings, we are also the only creatures who experience alienation. Moreover, culture is largely a matter of habit, limiting our choices and driving us to repeat troubling patterns, such as racial prejudice, in each new generation. And, in an electronic age, we may wonder at the extent to which the business-dominated media manipulate our cultural surroundings in pursuit of profits.

Moreover, while our society's insistence on competitive achievement urges us towards excellence, this same pattern also isolates us from one another. Material comforts improve our lives in many ways, yet our preoccupation with acquiring things distracts us from seeking the security and satisfaction of close relationships or cultivating spiritual strength. Our emphasis on personal freedom affords us privacy and autonomy, yet our culture often denies us the support of a human community in which to share life's problems (Slater, 1976; Bellah et al., 1985).

CULTURE AS FREEDOM

Human beings may seem to be prisoners of culture, just as other animals are prisoners of biology. But careful thought about the ideas presented in this chapter reveals a crucial difference. Biological instinct operates in a ready-made world: culture, by contrast, gives us the responsibility to make and remake a world for ourselves.

Therefore, although culture seems at times to circumscribe our lives, it always embodies the human capacity for hope, creativity, and choice. There is no better evidence of this than the fascinating cultural diversity of our own society and the far greater human variety of the larger world. Furthermore, far from being static, culture is ever-changing; it allows our imagination and inventiveness to come to the fore. The more we discover about the operation of our culture, the greater our capacity to use the freedom it offers us.

SUMMARY

1. Culture refers to a way of life shared by members of a society. Several species display a limited capacity for culture, but only human beings rely on culture for survival.

2. As the human brain evolved, the first elements of culture appeared some 2 million years ago; the development of culture reached the point we call "the birth of civilization" some 10 000 years ago.

3. Humans built culture on symbols by attaching meaning to objects and action. Language is the symbolic system by which one generation transmits culture to the next.

4. Values represent general orientations to the world around us; beliefs are statements people who share a culture hold to be true.

5. Cultural norms guide human behaviour. Mores consist of norms of great moral significance; folkways guide everyday life and afford greater individual discretion.

6. High culture refers to patterns that distinguish a society's elites; popular culture includes patterns widespread in a society.

7. Canada stands among the most culturally diverse societies in the world. Subculture refers to distinctive cultural patterns adopted by a segment of a population; counterculture means patterns strongly at odds with a conventional way of life. Multiculturalism is a social policy designed to encourage ethnic or cultural heterogeneity.

8. Invention, discovery, and diffusion all generate cultural change. When parts of a cultural system change at different rates, this is called cultural lag.

9. Because we learn the standards of one culture, we evaluate other cultures ethnocentrically. An alternative to ethnocentrism, cultural relativism, means judging another culture according to its own standards.

10. The structural-functional paradigm views culture as a relatively stable system built on core values. Cultural traits function to maintain the overall system.

11. The social-conflict paradigm envisions culture as a dynamic arena of inequality and conflict. Cultural patterns typically benefit some categories of people more than others.

12. Sociobiology studies the influence of humanity's evolutionary past on present cultural patterns.

13. Culture can constrain human needs and ambitions; yet, as cultural creatures, we have the capacity to shape and reshape the world to meet our needs and pursue our dreams.

CRITICAL THINKING QUESTIONS

1. What is the cultural significance of a carefully manicured lawn in a highly mobile and largely anonymous society? What does a well-tended (or untended) front yard say about a person?

2. How does a schoolroom activity such as a "spelling bee" embody Canadian cultural values? What cultural values are expressed by children's stories such as "The Little Train That Could" and popular board games such as "Snakes and Ladders," "Monopoly," and "Risk"?

3. Do you think Canadian cultural values are changing? If so, how and why?

4. Have there been protests in your province by aboriginal peoples regarding land claims? What do you know about this issue?

SOCIOLOGY APPLIED

1. Try to find someone on campus who has lived in another country. Ask for a chance to discuss how the culture of that other society differs from the way of life here. Try to identify ways in which the other person sees Canadian culture differently than most of us might.

2. Step back from your everyday thinking and look at several of your favourite television shows as you imagine someone from another country would. What cultural values do the shows reflect?

3. Play a game of "Monopoly" with several friends. As you play, comment to one another about what this popular game suggests about our way of life.

4. Approach someone in one of your classes who is of a different race or ethnicity than you are. Explain that you are doing an assignment for your sociology course, and see if you can strike up a discussion of how the two of you may experience campus life differently. To what extent does race and ethnicity give people a different "window" on campus culture?

WEBLINKS

http://iq.orst.edu/ethics/03cult01.html
Cultural Relativism discusses the moral lives of individuals in the context of their culture and deals with various topics in cultural relativism. It includes links to discussion activities.

http://infoservice.gc.ca/canadiana/faitc/fa26.html
Multiculturalism contains a brief history of multiculturalism in Canada, beginning with multiculturalism among the First Nations. The discussion includes immigration, multicultural programs, and multiculturalism in the media, business, the arts, and law and policy.

http://www.sciam.com/explorations/010697sagan/010697explorations.html
Scientific American's obituary for Carl Sagan—"A Pale Blue Planet Mourns the Passing of a Passionate Scientist"—contains links to many related sites on the Web, including earlier *Scientific American* articles.

http://www.symbols.com/
From ideograms carved in mammoth teeth by Cro-Magnon men to subway graffiti, *Symbols.com* contains more than 2500 Western signs, arranged according to their graphic characteristics, as well as 1600 articles about their histories, uses, and meanings.

http://tceplus.com/different.htm
How Are Canadians Different from Americans? is an article by Rae Corelli, originally published in *Maclean's* magazine.

Walter Greaves, *Hammersmith Bridge on Boat Race Day,* 1862

SOCIETY

Sididi Ag Inaka has never used a computer, sent a fax, or spoken on a cell phone. In today's high-technology world, this fact may seem strange enough. But how about this: neither Inaka nor anyone in his family has ever seen a television or even read a newspaper.

Are these people visitors from another planet? Prisoners on some remote island? Not at all. They are Tuareg nomads who wander the vastness of the Sahara Desert in western Africa, north of the city of Timbuktu in the nation we know as Mali. As unusual as Inaka's life seems to us, it is perfectly natural to him: "My father was a nomad, his father was a nomad, I am a nomad, my children will be nomads."

Thousands of people live the same life—raising camels, donkeys, goats, and sheep—in this desolate corner of the world. Tuaregs wear tattered clothes, sleep in camel-hide tents, and cook with charcoal. There are no schools for the children, and even toilets are unknown in the Tuareg world. Inaka and his family regularly endure unforgiving heat and push their way through blinding sandstorms in order to reach habitable spots offering water and grass for their herd of about thirty-five animals. At an inviting oasis, they may find others of their kind, with whom they sell or trade animals and cheese.

The Tuaregs are among the poorest people of the world, living a simple and difficult existence. When the rains fail to come, they and their animals are at risk of losing their lives. Inaka and his people are a society set apart, largely isolated from the rest of humanity and virtually untouched by modern ideas and advanced technology. To many, no doubt, they seem a curious throwback to the past. But Inaka does not complain: "This is the life of my ancestors. This is the life that we know" (Buckley, 1996).

Human societies have taken many forms throughout history, and remarkable diversity is still evident in the world today. But what is a society in the first place? What makes society "hang together"? How have societies changed over the course of human history? Why have they changed?

To begin, the concept of **society** refers to *people who interact in a defined territory and share culture.* In this chapter, we shall examine this deceptively simple term from four different angles. **Gerhard Lenski** and **Jean Lenski** describe the changing character of human society over the last ten thousand years. Focusing on how *technology* shapes social life, their analysis shows that a technological breakthrough often has revolutionary consequences for society as a whole. The remainder of the chapter presents classic visions of society developed by three of sociology's founders. Like the Lenskis, **Karl Marx** also understood human history as a long and complex process of social change. For Marx, however, the story of society spins around *social conflict*, which stems from inequality rooted in how people produce material goods. **Max Weber** recognized the importance of productive forces as well, but he sought to demonstrate the power of *ideas* to animate society. Weber was among the first to contrast the traditional thinking of many simple

In technologically simple societies, successful hunting wins men great praise. However, the gathering of vegetation by women is a more dependable and more easily available source of nutrition.

societies with the rational thought that animates our modern way of life. Finally, **Emile Durkheim** investigated patterns of *social solidarity*, noting that the bonds uniting traditional societies and their modern counterparts are strikingly different.

All four visions of society answer key questions: What makes people such as the Tuareg of the Sahara Desert so different from the society familiar to us? How and why do societies change? What forces divide a society? What forces hold it together? Are societies getting better or worse?

GERHARD LENSKI AND JEAN LENSKI: SOCIETY AND TECHNOLOGY

As people who take for granted schooling and medical care, and who enjoy rapid transportation and instant global communication, we must wonder at the nomads of the Sahara, who live as their ancestors did centuries ago. But sociologists who study the past (working with archaeologists and anthropologists) have learned quite a bit about our human heritage. Gerhard Lenski and Jean Lenski have chronicled the great differences among societies that have flourished and declined throughout human history. Just as important, the work of these researchers helps us better understand how we live today.

The Lenskis call the focus of their research **sociocultural evolution**, *the process of change that results from a society's gaining new information, particularly technology* (Lenski, Nolan, and Lenski 1995:75).

Rather like a biologist examining how a living species evolves over millennia, a sociologist employing this approach observes how societies change over centuries as they gain greater ability to manipulate their physical environments. Societies with rudimentary technology (such as the Tuareg, described at the beginning of this chapter) can support only a small number of people, who enjoy few choices about how to live. Technologically complex societies—while not necessarily "better" in any absolute sense—develop large populations characterized by diverse, highly specialized lives.

The Lenskis also explain that the greater the amount of technological information a society has in its grasp, the faster the rate at which it changes. Technologically simple societies, then, change very slowly; Sididi Ag Inaka says he "lives the life of his ancestors." By contrast, industrial, high-technology societies change so quickly that people witness dramatic transformations during their lifetimes. Consider some familiar elements of North American culture that would probably puzzle, delight, or even alarm people who lived just a few generations ago: beepers, phone sex, artificial hearts, "information superhighway," laser surgery, test-tube babies, genetic engineering, e-mail, fibre optics, smart bombs, the threat of nuclear holocaust, space shuttles, transsexualism, and "tell-all" talk shows.

As a society extends its technological reach, the effects ripple through the cultural system, generating countless repercussions. When our ancestors first harnessed the power of the wind by using a sail, they set the stage for building sailing ships, which took them to new lands, stimulated trade, and increased their power to make war. Consider, as a more recent example, the many ways modern life has been changed by the spread of computer technology.

Drawing on the Lenskis' work, we will describe five general types of societies distinguished by their technology: hunting and gathering societies, horticultural and pastoral societies, agrarian societies, industrial societies, and post-industrial societies.

HUNTING AND GATHERING SOCIETIES

Hunting and gathering refers to *simple technology for hunting animals and gathering vegetation*. From the emergence of our species until just ten thousand years ago, *all* humans were hunters and gatherers. Although hunting and gathering societies remained common several centuries ago, only a few persist today, including the Aka and Pygmies of central Africa, the Bushmen of southwestern Africa, the Aborigines of Australia, and the Batek and Semai of Malaysia.

With scarcely any technology to make food production efficient, most members of these societies must search continually for game and edible plants.

Only in lush areas where food is plentiful would hunters and gatherers have any leisure time. Moreover, foraging for food demands a large amount of land, so hunting and gathering societies comprise small bands of a few dozen people living at some distance from one another. These groups are also nomadic, moving on as they deplete vegetation in one area or in pursuit of migratory animals. Although periodically returning to favoured sites, they rarely form permanent settlements.

Hunting and gathering societies are based on kinship. The family obtains and distributes food, protects its members, and teaches the children. Most activities are common to everyone and centre on seeking their next meal; some specialization, however, corresponds to age and sex. The very young and the very old contribute only what they can, while healthy adults secure most of the food. The women gather vegetation—the more reliable food source—while men take on the less certain job of hunting. Although the two sexes have somewhat different responsibilities, then, most hunters and gatherers have probably accorded men and women comparable social importance (Leacock, 1978).

Hunting and gathering societies have few formal leaders. Most recognize a *shaman*, or spiritual leader, who enjoys high prestige but receives no greater material rewards than other members of the society and must help procure food like everyone else. In short, hunting and gathering societies are relatively simple and egalitarian.

Hunting and gathering societies rarely use their simple, hand-crafted weapons—the spear, the bow and arrow, and the stone knife—to wage war. Nonetheless they are often ravaged by the forces of nature. Storms and droughts can easily destroy their food supply, and they stand vulnerable to accident and disease. Such risks encourage cooperation and sharing, a strategy that increases everyone's odds of survival. Nonetheless, many die in childhood, and perhaps half perish before the age of twenty (Lenski, Nolan, and Lenski, 1995:104).

During this century, technologically complex societies have slowly closed in on the few remaining hunters and gatherers, reducing their landholdings and depleting game and vegetation. The Lenskis predict that the 1990s may well witness the end of hunting and gathering societies on earth. Fortunately, study of this way of life has already produced valuable information about human history and our fundamental ties to the natural world.

HORTICULTURAL AND PASTORAL SOCIETIES

Ten to twelve thousand years ago, a new technology began to change the lives of human beings (see the

Pastoralism historically has flourished in regions of the word where arid soil does not support crops. Pastoral people still thrive in northern Africa, living today much as they did a thousand years ago.

time line on the inside front cover). **Horticulture** is *a technology based on using hand tools to cultivate plants.* The most important tools of horticulturalists are the hoe to work the soil and the digging stick to punch holes in the ground for seeds. Humans first used these tools in fertile regions of the Middle East and, later, in Latin America and Asia. Cultural diffusion spread knowledge of horticulture throughout most of the world by about six thousand years ago.

Not all societies were quick to abandon hunting and gathering in favour of horticulture. Hunters and gatherers living amid plentiful vegetation and game probably saw little reason to embrace the new technology (Fisher, 1979). The Yąnomamö of the Brazilian rain forest (described in Chapter 3, "Culture") illustrate the common practice of combining horticulture with more traditional hunting and gathering (Chagnon, 1992).

Then, too, people in particularly arid regions (such as the Sahara region of western Africa or the Middle East) or mountainous areas found horticulture to be of little value. Such people turned to a different strategy for survival, **pastoralism**, which is *technology based on the domestication of animals.* Still others combined horticulture and pastoralism to produce a variety of foods. Today, many horticultural-pastoral societies thrive in South America, Africa, and Asia.

The domestication of plants and animals greatly increased food production, enabling societies to support not dozens but hundreds of people. Pastoralists remained nomadic, leading their herds to fresh grazing

Of Egypt's 130 pyramids, the Great Pyramids at Giza are the largest. Each of the three major structures stands more than forty stories high and is composed of three million massive stone blocks. Some 4500 years ago, tens of thousands of people laboured to construct these pyramids so that one man, the pharaoh, might have a godlike monument for his tomb. Clearly social inequality in this agrarian society was striking.

entire world. This view of God ("The Lord is my shepherd . . . ," Psalm 23) is widespread among members of our own society because Christianity, Islam, and Judaism originated as Middle Eastern, pastoral religions.

Expanding productive technology also intensifies social inequality. As some families produce more food than others, they assume positions of relative power and privilege. Forging alliances with other elite families ensures that social advantages endure over generations and a formal system of social inequality emerges. Along with social hierarchy, rudimentary government—backed by military force—is formed to shore up the power of elites. However, without the ability to communicate or to travel quickly, a ruler can control only a limited number of people, so empire-building proceeds on a small scale.

The domestication of plants and animals surely made simpler societies more productive. But advancing technology is never entirely beneficial. The Lenskis point out that, compared to hunters and gatherers, horticulturalists and pastoralists display more social inequality and, in many cases, engage in slavery, protracted warfare, and even cannibalism.

AGRARIAN SOCIETIES

About five thousand years ago, another technological revolution was under way in the Middle East and would eventually transform most of the world. This was the discovery of **agriculture**, *the technology of large-scale farming using plows harnessed to animals or, eventually, mechanical tractors.* The Lenskis state that the social significance of the animal-drawn plow, along with other technological innovations of the period—including irrigation, the wheel, writing, numbers, and the expanding use of metals—clearly qualifies this era as "the dawn of civilization" (1995:177).

Farmers with animal-drawn plows cultivated fields vastly larger than the garden-sized plots worked by horticulturalists. Plows have the additional advantage of turning, and thereby aerating, the soil to increase fertility. Such technology encouraged agrarian societies to farm the same land for decades, which, in turn, led to humanity's first permanent settlements. Large food surpluses, transported on animal-powered wagons, allowed agrarian societies to expand to unprecedented land area and population. As an extreme case, the Roman Empire at its height (about 100 C.E.) boasted a population of 70 million spread over some 2 million square miles (Stavrianos, 1983; Lenski, Nolan, and Lenski, 1995).

As always, increasing production meant greater specialization. Tasks once performed by everyone, such as clearing land and securing food, became distinct occupations. Specialization made the early barter

lands. Horticulturalists, by contrast, formed settlements, moving on only when they depleted the soil. These settlements, joined by trade, comprised multi-centred societies with overall populations often in the thousands.

Domesticating plants and animals generates a *material surplus*, more resources than necessary to sustain day-to-day living. A surplus frees some people from the job of securing food, allowing them to create crafts, engage in trade, cut hair, apply tattoos, or serve as priests. In comparison to hunting and gathering societies, then, horticultural and pastoral societies display more specialized and complex social arrangements.

Hunters and gatherers recognize numerous spirits inhabiting the world. Horticulturalists, however, practise ancestor worship and conceive of God as Creator. Pastoral societies carry this belief further, viewing God as directly involved in the well-being of the

Technology and the Changing Status of Women

In technologically simple societies of the past, women produced more food than men did. Hunters and gatherers valued meat highly, but men's hunting was not a dependable source of nourishment. Thus, vegetation gathered by women was the primary means of ensuring survival. Similarly, tools and seeds used in horticulture developed under the control of women, who already had primary responsibility for providing and preparing food. For their part, men engaged in trade and tended herds of animals. Only at harvest time did men and women work side by side.

About five thousand years ago, humans discovered how to mold metals.

This technology spread by cultural diffusion, primarily along trade networks forged by men. Thus it was men who devised the metal plow and, since they already managed animals, soon thought to hitch the implement to a cow.

This great innovation initiated the transition from horticulture to agriculture and, for the first time, thrust men into a dominant position in the production of food. Elise Boulding explains that this technological breakthrough thus undermined the social standing of women:

The shift of the status of the woman farmer may have happened

quite rapidly, once there were two male specializations relating to agriculture: plowing and the care of cattle. This situation left women with all the subsidiary tasks, including weeding and carrying water to the fields. The new fields were larger, so women had to work just as many hours as they did before, but now they worked at more secondary tasks. . . . this would contribute further to the erosion of the status of women.

SOURCES: Based on Boulding (1976) and Fisher (1979).

system obsolete and prompted the invention of money as a common standard of exchange. The appearance of money facilitated trade, sparking the growth of cities as economic centres with populations soaring into the millions.

Agrarian societies exhibit dramatic social inequality. In many cases, peasants or slaves constitute a significant share of the population and labour for elites: the seigneurial system of New France (part of Quebec) had its *habitants*, while slavery was practised coast to coast across what is now Canada from the 1750s through to the early 1800s. Thus freed from manual work, elites could devote their time to the study of philosophy, art, and literature. This helps to explain the historical link between "high culture," as noted in Chapter 3 ("Culture"), and social privilege.

Among hunters and gatherers and also among horticulturalists, women are the primary providers of food. The development of agriculture, however, appears to have propelled men into a position of social dominance (Boulding, 1976; Fisher, 1979). The "Social Diversity" box looks more closely at the declining position of women at this point in the course of sociocultural evolution.

Religion reinforces the power of agricultural elites. Religious doctrine typically propounds the idea that people are morally obligated to perform whatever tasks correspond to their place in the social order. Many of the "Wonders of the Ancient World," such as the Great Wall of China and the Great Pyramids of

Egypt, were possible only because emperors and pharaohs wielded virtually absolute power to mobilize their people to endure a lifetime of labour without pay.

In agrarian societies, then, elites gain unparallelled power. To maintain control of large empires, leaders require the services of a wide range of administrators. Along with the growing economy, then, the political system becomes established as a distinct sphere of life.

In relation to the societies described so far, the Lenskis conclude, agrarian societies have greater specialization and more social inequality. And, compared to horticultural and pastoral societies, agrarian societies differ more from one another because advancing technology increases human control over the natural world.

INDUSTRIAL SOCIETIES

Industrialism, as found in Canada, the United States, and other rich nations of the world, is *technology that powers sophisticated machinery with advanced sources of energy.* Until the industrial era, the major source of energy was the muscles of humans and other animals. At the dawning of the *Industrial Revolution*, about 1750, mills and factories relied on flowing water and then steam to power ever-larger and more efficient machinery.

Once industrial technology was at hand, societies began to change faster, as shown in Figure 4–1.

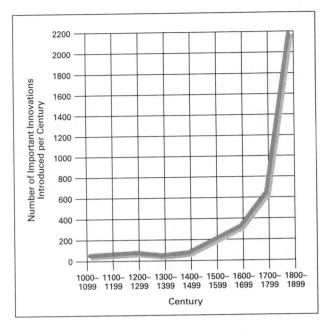

FIGURE 4–1 The Increasing Number of Technological Innovations

This figure illustrates the number of technological innovations in Western Europe after the beginning of the Industrial Revolution in the mid-eighteenth century. Technological innovation occurs at an accelerating rate because each innovation spins off existing cultural elements to produce many further innovations.
SOURCE: Lenski, Nolan, and Lenski (1995).

Industrial societies transformed themselves more in a century than they had in thousands of years before. As explained in Chapter 1 ("The Sociological Perspective"), this stunning change stimulated the birth of sociology itself. During the nineteenth century, railroads and steamships revolutionized transportation, and steel-framed skyscrapers recast the urban landscape, dwarfing the cathedrals that symbolized an earlier age.

As the twentieth century opened, automobiles further reshaped Western societies, and electricity was fast becoming the basis for countless "modern conveniences." Electronic communication, including the telephone, radio, and television, were mass producing cultural patterns and gradually making a large world seem smaller and smaller. More recently, transportation technology has given humanity the capacity to fly faster than sound and even to break the bonds of earth. During the last generation, computers have ushered in the *Information Revolution*, dramatically increasing humanity's capacity to process words and numbers.

Work, too, has changed. In agrarian societies, most men and women work in the home. Industrialization, however, creates factories near centralized machinery and energy sources. Lost in the process are close working relationships and strong kinship ties, as well as many of the traditional values, beliefs, and customs that guide agrarian life.

Occupational specialization, which expanded over the long course of sociocultural evolution, has become more pronounced than ever. Industrial people often size up one another in terms of their jobs rather than according to their kinship ties (as agrarian people do). Rapid change and movement from place to place also generate anonymity and cultural diversity, sparking the formation of numerous subcultures and counter-cultures, as described in Chapter 3 ("Culture").

Industrial technology recasts the family, too, diminishing its traditional significance as the centre of social life. No longer does the family serve as the primary setting for economic production, learning, and religious worship. And, as Chapter 17 ("Family") explains in detail, technological change also underlies the trend away from so-called traditional families to greater numbers of single people, divorced people, single-parent families, and stepfamilies.

The Lenskis explain that early industrialization concentrated the benefits of advancing technology on a small segment of the population, with the majority living in poverty. In time, however, the material benefits of industrial productivity spread more widely. Poverty remains a serious problem in industrial societies, but compared to the situation a century ago, the standard of living has risen fivefold, and economic, social, and political inequality has declined. Some social levelling, detailed in Chapter 9 ("Social Stratification"), occurs because industrial societies demand an educated and skilled labour force. While most people in agrarian societies are illiterate, industrial societies provide state-funded schooling and confer numerous political rights on virtually everyone. Industrialization, in fact, intensifies demands for political participation, as seen recently in South Korea, Taiwan, the People's Republic of China, the former Soviet Union, and the societies of Eastern Europe.

POST-INDUSTRIAL SOCIETIES

Many industrial societies, including Canada, now appear to be entering yet another phase of technological development, and we can briefly extend the Lenskis' analysis to take account of recent trends. A generation ago sociologist Daniel Bell (1973) coined the term **post-industrialism** to refer to *technology that supports an information-based economy*. While production in industrial societies centres on factories and

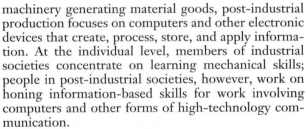

A century ago, industrial workers (most of whom were men) used their skills to manipulate things, often using massive machinery. Today, the postindustrial economy demands that workers (now as likely to be women as men) manipulate symbols in the forms of words, images or music often using computers.

machinery generating material goods, post-industrial production focuses on computers and other electronic devices that create, process, store, and apply information. At the individual level, members of industrial societies concentrate on learning mechanical skills; people in post-industrial societies, however, work on honing information-based skills for work involving computers and other forms of high-technology communication.

As this shift in key skills indicates, the emergence of post-industrialism dramatically changes a society's occupational structure. Chapter 15 ("The Economy and Work") examines this process in detail, explaining that a post-industrial society uses less and less of its labour force for industrial production. At the same time, the ranks of clerical workers, managers, and other people who process information (in fields ranging from academia and advertising to marketing and public relations) swell rapidly.

The Information Revolution is most pronounced in industrial, high-income societies, yet the reach of this new technology is so great that it is affecting the entire world. As explained in Chapter 3 ("Culture"), the unprecedented, worldwide flow of information originating in rich nations like our own has the predictable effect of tying far-flung societies together and fostering common patterns of global culture.

Another pivotal idea from Chapter 3—the concept of cultural lag—has an important application to post-industrial societies. Recall that cultural lag refers to the process by which some cultural elements (especially technology) change faster than others (such as values and norms). Even though information is fast replacing objects as the centre of our economy, our legal notions about property are still based on tangible things.

Consider, for example, the national practice by which government officials monitor the flow of property in and out of this country. Customs officers require travellers to declare all the property that they wish to carry with them when they arrive, and baggage is subject to physical search. Curiously, while people are lining up to discuss purchases of liquor, antiques, or oriental rugs, an individual in possession of valuable ideas or computer programs on a computer disk can easily and legally walk past customs officials announcing "Nothing to declare!" since our legal system has yet to fully recognize the value of nontangible property. In short, while recent decades have witnessed rapid technological change, many of our ways of thinking remain rooted in an earlier era.

Table 4–1 presents a summary of the contributions of technological innovation at various stages of sociocultural evolution.

THE LIMITS OF TECHNOLOGY

While technology remedies many human problems, by raising productivity, reducing infectious diseases, and sometimes simply relieving boredom, it provides no "quick fix" for many social problems. Poverty remains the plight of millions of women and men in this country (detailed in Chapter 10, "Social Class in Canada") and of 1 billion people worldwide (see Chapter 11, "Global Stratification"). Moreover, with the capacity to reshape the world, technology has

TABLE 4–1 Sociocultural Evolution: A Summary

Type of Society	Historical Period	Productive Technology	Population Size
Hunting and Gathering Societies	Only type of society until about 10 000 years ago; still common several centuries ago; the few examples remaining today are threatened with extinction	Primitive weapons	Twenty-five to forty people
Horticultural and Pastoral Societies	From about 10 000 years ago, with decreasing numbers after about 3000 B.C.E.	Horticultural societies use hand tools for cultivating plants; pastoral societies are based on the domestication of animals	Settlements of several hundred people, interconnected through trading ties to form societies of several thousand people
Agrarian Societies	From about 5000 years ago, with large but decreasing numbers today	Animal-drawn plow	Millions of people
Industrial Societies	From about 1750 to the present	Advanced sources of energy; mechanized production	Millions of people
Post-industrial Societies	Emerging in recent decades	Computers that support an information-based economy	Millions of people

created new problems that our ancestors (and people like Sididi Ag Inaka today) could hardly imagine. Industrial societies provide more personal freedom, often at the cost of the sense of community that characterized pre-industrial life. Further, although the most powerful societies of today's world engage in all-out warfare infrequently, international conflict now poses unimaginable horrors. Should nations ever unleash even a fraction of their present stockpiles of nuclear weapons, human society would almost certainly regress to a technologically primitive state if, indeed, we survived at all.

Another stubborn social problem involves humanity's relation to the physical environment. Each stage in sociocultural evolution has introduced more powerful sources of energy and accelerated our appetite for the earth's resources at a rate even faster than the population is growing. We now face a vital question: can humanity continue to pursue material prosperity without subjecting the planet to damage and strains from which it will never recover?

In some respects, then, technological advances have improved life and brought the world's people closer together within a "global village." Yet in technology's wake come daunting problems of establishing peace, ensuring justice, and sustaining a safe environment—problems that technology alone can never solve.

KARL MARX: SOCIETY AND CONFLICT

The first of our classic visions of society comes from Karl Marx (1818–83), one of the early giants of sociology. Few observed the industrial transformation of Europe as keenly as he did. Marx spent most of his adult life in London, then the capital of the vast British Empire. He was awed by the productive power of the new factories: not only were European societies producing more goods than ever before, but a global system of commerce was funnelling resources from around the world through British factories at a dizzying rate.

But what astounded Marx even more was the concentration of industry's riches in the hands of a few. A walk almost anywhere in London revealed dramatic extremes of splendid affluence and wretched squalor. A handful of aristocrats and industrialists lived in fabulous mansions well staffed by servants, where they enjoyed luxury and privileges. Most people laboured long hours for low wages, living in slums or even sleeping in the streets, where many eventually succumbed to poor nutrition and infectious disease.

Throughout his life, Marx wrestled with a basic contradiction: the rich societies he observed contained too many who were desperately poor. How, Marx asked, could this situation be changed? Many

TABLE 4–1 (continued)

Type of Society	Settlement Pattern	Social Organization	Examples
Hunting and Gathering Societies	Nomadic	Family centred; specialization limited to age and sex; little social inequality	Pygmies of central Africa Bushmen of southwestern Africa Aborigines of Australia Semai of Malaysia
Horticultural and Pastoral Societies	Horticulturalists form relatively small permanent settlements; pastoralists are nomadic	Family centred; religious system begins to develop; moderate specialization; increased social inequality	Middle Eastern societies about 5000 B.C.E. Various societies today in New Guinea and other Pacific islands Yąnomamö today in South America
Agrarian Societies	Cities become common, though they generally contain only a small proportion of the population	Family loses significance as distinctive religious, political, and economic systems emerge; extensive specialization; increased social inequality	Egypt during construction of the Great Pyramids Medieval Europe Numerous nonindustrial societies of the world today
Industrial Societies	Cities contain most of the population	Distinct religious, political, economic, educational, and family systems; highly specialized; marked social inequality persists, diminishing somewhat over time	Most societies today in Europe, North America, Australia, and Japan; these societies generate most of the world's industrial production
Post-industrial Societies	Population remains concentrated in cities	Similar to industrial societies with information processing and other service work gradually replacing industrial production	Industrial societies noted above are now entering post-industrial stage

people, no doubt, think of Karl Marx as a man determined to tear societies apart. But he was motivated by compassion for humanity and sought to help a society, already badly divided, forge what he hoped would be a new and just social order.

The key to Marx's thinking is the idea of **social conflict**, *struggle between segments of society over valued resources*. Social conflict can, of course, take many forms: individuals may quarrel, some colleges have long-standing rivalries, and nations sometimes go to war. For Marx, however, the most significant form of social conflict involved clashes between social classes that arise from the way a society produces material goods.

SOCIETY AND PRODUCTION

Living in the nineteenth century, Marx observed the early stage of industrial capitalism in Europe. This economic system, Marx noted, transformed a small part of the population into **capitalists**, *people who own factories and other productive enterprises*. A capitalist's goal is profit, which results from selling a product for more than it costs to produce. Capitalism transforms most of the population into industrial workers, whom Marx called the **proletariat**, *people who provide labour necessary to operate factories and other productive enterprises*. Workers sell their labour for the wages

they need to live. To Marx, an inevitable conflict between capitalists and workers has its roots in the productive process itself. To maximize profits, capitalists must minimize wages, generally their single greatest expense. Workers, however, want wages to be as high as possible. Since profits and wages come from the same pool of funds, ongoing conflict occurs. Marx argued that this conflict would end only when people fundamentally changed the capitalist system.

All societies are composed of **social institutions**, defined as *the major spheres of social life, or society's subsystems, organized to meet basic human needs*. In his analysis of society, Marx contended that one specific institution—the economy—dominates all others when it comes to steering the direction of a society. Drawing on the philosophical doctrine of *materialism*, which asserts that how humans produce material goods shapes the rest of society, Marx claimed that all the other major social institutions—the political system, family, religion, and education—operated more or less to shore up a society's economy. The Lenskis' argument, that technology shapes the contours of a society, echoes Marx's assertion that the economy is "the real foundation. . . . The mode of production in material life determines the general character of the social, political, and spiritual processes of life" (1959:43; orig. 1859).

Few names evoke as strong a response as that of Karl Marx. Is he genius and prophet or evil incarnate? Whatever the case, Marx's influence has been felt worldwide: today, more than one-fifth of humanity lives in societies that call themselves Marxist. The German-born Marx completed his doctorate in 1841 and went to work as a newspaper editor. So relentless was his social criticism that he was driven from Germany to live in Paris and from there to London. Marx did not merely observe society: he offered a rousing—in fact, revolutionary—prescription for social change.

Marx therefore viewed the economic system as the social *infrastructure* (*infra* is Latin for "below"). Other social institutions, including the family, the political system, and religion, which are built on this foundation, form society's *superstructure*. These institutions extend economic principles into other areas of life, as illustrated in Figure 4–2. In practical terms, social institutions reinforce the domination of the capitalists, by legally protecting their wealth, for example, and by transferring property from one generation to the next through the family.

Generally speaking, members of industrial-capitalist societies do not view their legal or family systems as hotbeds of social conflict. On the contrary, individuals come to see their rights to private property as "natural." We might think, for example, that affluent people have earned their wealth, whereas those

who are poor or out of work lack skills or motivation. Marx rejected this kind of reasoning as rooted in a capitalist preoccupation with the "bottom line" that treats human well-being as a market commodity. Poverty and unemployment are not inevitable; as Marx saw it, grand wealth clashing with grinding poverty represents merely one set of human possibilities generated by capitalism (Cuff and Payne, 1979).

Marx rejected capitalist common sense, therefore, as **false consciousness**, *explanations of social problems grounded in the shortcomings of individuals rather than the flaws of society.* Marx was saying, in effect, that industrial capitalism itself is responsible for many of the social problems he saw all around him. False consciousness, he maintained, victimizes people by obscuring the real cause of their problems and encouraging complacency.

CONFLICT IN HISTORY

Marx studied how societies have changed throughout history, noting that they often evolve gradually, although they sometimes change in rapid, revolutionary fashion. Marx observed (as do the Lenskis) that change is partly prompted by technological advance. But he steadfastly held that conflict between economic classes is the major engine of change.

To recast the Lenskis' analysis in Marxist terms, early hunters and gatherers formed primitive communist societies. The word *communism* refers to a social system in which the production of food and other material goods is a common effort shared more or less equally by all members of society. Because the resources of nature were available to all hunters and gatherers (rather than privately owned), and because everyone performed similar work (rather than dividing work into highly specialized tasks), there was little possibility for social conflict.

Horticulture, Marx noted, introduced significant social inequality. Among horticultural, pastoral, and early agrarian societies—which Marx lumped together as the "ancient world"—the victors in frequent warfare forced their captives into servitude. A small elite (the "masters") and their slaves were thus locked in an irreconcilable pattern of social conflict (Zeitlin, 1981).

Agriculture brought still more wealth to members of the elite, fuelling further social conflict. Agrarian serfs, occupying the lowest reaches of European feudalism from about the twelfth to the eighteenth centuries, were only slightly better off than slaves. In Marx's view, the power of both the church and the state defended feudal inequality by defining the existing social order as God's will. Thus, to Marx, feudalism amounted to little more than "exploitation, veiled by religious and political illusions" (Marx and Engels, 1972:337; orig. 1848).

Gradually, new productive forces undermined the feudal order. Commerce grew steadily throughout the Middle Ages as trade networks expanded and the power of guilds increased. Merchants and skilled craftsworkers in the cities formed a new social category, the *bourgeoisie* (a French word meaning "of the town"). Profits earned through expanding trade brought the bourgeoisie increasing wealth. After about 1800, with factories at their command, the bourgeoisie became true capitalists with power that soon rivalled that of the ancient, landed nobility. While the nobility regarded this upstart "commercial" class with disdain, their increasing wealth gradually shifted control of European societies to the capitalists. To Marx's way of thinking, then, new technology was only part of the Industrial Revolution; it was also a class revolution by which capitalists overthrew the agrarian elite to preside over the new industrial economy.

Industrialization also fostered the development of the proletariat. English landowners converted fields once tilled by serfs into grazing land for sheep to secure wool for the prospering textile mills. Forced from the land, serfs migrated to cities to work in factories, where they joined the burgeoning industrial proletariat. Marx envisioned these workers one day joining hands across national boundaries to form a unified class, setting the stage for historic confrontation, this time between capitalists and the exploited workers.

CAPITALISM AND CLASS CONFLICT

Much of Marx's analysis centres on destructive aspects of industrial capitalism—especially ways it promotes class conflict and alienation. In examining his views on these topics, we will come to see why he advocated the overthrow of capitalist societies.

"The history of all hitherto existing society is the history of class struggles." With this declaration, Marx and his collaborator Friedrich Engels began their best-known statement, the *Manifesto of the Communist Party* (1972:335; orig. 1848). The idea of social class suffuses Marx's critique of capitalist society. Industrial capitalism, like earlier types of society, contains two major social classes—the dominant and the oppressed—reflecting the two basic positions in the productive system. Capitalists and proletarians are the historical descendants of masters and slaves in the ancient world and nobles and serfs in feudal systems. In each case, one class controls the other as productive property. Marx used the term **class conflict** (and sometimes *class struggle*) to refer to *antagonism between entire classes over the distribution of wealth and power in society*.

Class conflict, then, dates back to civilizations long gone. What distinguishes the conflict in capitalist society, Marx pointed out, is how out in the open it has become. Agrarian nobles and serfs, for all their

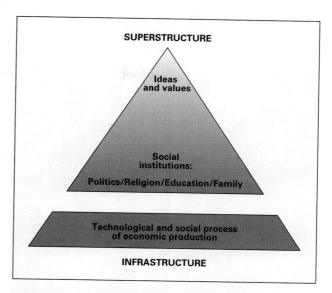

FIGURE 4–2 Karl Marx's Model of Society

This diagram illustrates Marx's materialist view that the process of economic production undergirds and shapes the entire society. Economic production involves both technology (industry, in the case of capitalism) and social relationships (for capitalism, the relationship between the capitalists, who control the process of economic production, and the workers, who are simply a source of labour). Upon this infrastructure, or foundation, are built the major social institutions as well as core cultural values and ideas. Taken together, these additional social elements represent the society's superstructure. Marx maintained that every part of a society operates in concert with the economic system.

differences, were bound together by long-standing traditions and a host of mutual obligations. Industrial capitalism dissolved those ties so that pride and honour were replaced by "naked self-interest" and the singular pursuit of profit. With no personal ties to their oppressors, Marx believed that the proletariat had little reason to stand for its subjugation.

But though industrial capitalism brought class conflict out in the open, Marx realized that fundamental social change would not come easily. First, he claimed, workers must *become aware* of their shared oppression and see capitalism as its true cause. Second, they must *organize and act* to address their problems. This means workers must replace false consciousness with **class consciousness**, *the recognition by workers of their unity as a class in opposition to capitalists and, ultimately, to capitalism itself*. Because the inhumanity of early capitalism was plain for him to see, Marx concluded that industrial workers would inevitably rise up en masse to destroy industrial capitalism.

Norbert Goenette's painting Pauper's Meal on a Winter's Day in Paris *suggests the numbing poverty common to migrants drawn to cities as the Industrial Revolution was getting underway. Karl Marx saw in such suffering a fundamental contradiction of modern society: industrial technology promises material plenty for all, but capitalism concentrates wealth in the hands of a few.*

And what of the workers' adversaries, the capitalists? The capitalists' formidable wealth and power, protected by the institutions of society, might seem invulnerable. But Marx saw a weakness in the capitalist armour. Motivated by a desire for personal gain, capitalists fear the competition of other capitalists. Thus, Marx thought that capitalists would be reluctant to band together, even though they, too, share common interests. Furthermore, he reasoned, capitalists keep employees' wages low in their drive to maximize profits. This strategy, in turn, bolsters the resolve of workers to forge an alliance against them. In the long run, Marx surmised, capitalists would only contribute to their own undoing.

CAPITALISM AND ALIENATION

Marx also condemned capitalism for producing **alienation**, *the experience of isolation resulting from powerlessness.* Dominated by capitalists and dehumanized by their jobs (especially monotonous and repetitive fac-

tory work), proletarians find little satisfaction and feel individually powerless to improve their situation. Herein lies another contradiction of capitalist society: as human beings devise technology to gain power over the world, the capitalist economy increasingly assumes power over human beings.

In practice, workers amount to only a commodity, a source of labour, bought by capitalists and discarded when no longer needed. Marx cited four ways in which capitalism alienates workers.

1. **Alienation from the act of working.** Ideally, people work both to meet immediate needs and to develop their long-range potential. Capitalism, however, tends to deny workers a say in what they produce or how they produce it. Furthermore, much work is tedious, involving countless repetitions of routine tasks. The modern-day replacement of human labour by machines would hardly have surprised Marx; as far as he was concerned, capitalism had turned human beings into machines long ago.

2. **Alienation from the products of work.** The product of work belongs not to workers but to capitalists, who sell it for profit. Thus, Marx reasoned, the more workers invest of themselves in their work, the more they lose.

3. **Alienation from other workers.** Through work, Marx claimed, people build bonds of community. Industrial capitalism, however, renders work competitive rather than cooperative.

4. **Alienation from human potential.** Industrial capitalism alienates workers from their human potential. Marx argued that a worker "does not fulfill himself in his work but denies himself, has a feeling of misery rather than well-being, does not freely develop his physical and mental energies, but is physically exhausted and mentally debased. The worker, therefore, feels himself to be at home only during his leisure time, whereas at work he feels homeless" (1964a:124–25; orig. 1844). In short, industrial capitalism distorts an activity that should express the best qualities in human beings into a dull and dehumanizing experience.

Marx viewed alienation, in its various forms, as a barrier to social change. But he hoped that industrial workers would eventually overcome their alienation by uniting into a true social class, aware of the cause of their problems and galvanized to transform society.

REVOLUTION

The only way out of the trap of capitalism, contended Marx, was deliberately to refashion society. He envi-

For years, the conventional wisdom in North America was that, once established, socialism stifled its opposition, rendering government immune to overthrow. But that notion collapsed along with the socialist regimes of Eastern Europe and the Soviet Union. The political transformation of this world region during the 1990s was symbolized, in city after city, by the removal of statues of Vladimir Lenin (1870–1924), architect of Soviet Marxism and Josef Stalin (1879–1953), shown here.

sioned a more humane and egalitarian productive system, one that would affirm rather than undermine our humanity. He called this system *socialism*. Marx knew well the obstacles to a socialist revolution; even so, he was disappointed that he never lived to see workers in England overthrow industrial capitalism. Still, convinced of the basic immorality of capitalist society, he was sure that, in time, the working majority would realize that they held the key to a better future in their own hands. This transformation would certainly be revolutionary, perhaps even violent. What emerged from the workers' revolution, however, would be a cooperative socialist society intended to meet the needs of all.

The discussion of social stratification in Chapter 9 ("Social Stratification") reveals more about changes in industrial-capitalist societies since Marx's time and why the revolution he championed has not taken place. Later chapters also delve into why people in the societies of Eastern Europe recently revolted against established socialist governments. But, in his own time, Marx looked towards the future with hope (1972:362; orig. 1848): "The proletarians have nothing to lose but their chains. They have a world to win."

MAX WEBER: THE RATIONALIZATION OF SOCIETY

With a broad understanding of law, economics, religion, and history, Max Weber (1864–1920) produced what many regard as the greatest individual contribution to sociology. This scholar, born to a prosperous family in Germany, generated ideas so wide ranging that we must limit ourselves to his vision of how modern society differs from earlier types of social organization.

Weber's sociology reflects the philosophical approach known as *idealism*, which emphasizes how human ideas shape society. Weber understood the power of technology, and he shared many of Marx's ideas about social conflict. But he departed from Marx's materialist analysis, arguing that societies differ primarily in terms of the ways in which their members think about the world. For Weber, ideas—especially beliefs and values—are the keys to understanding society. Weber saw modern society as the product, not just of new technology and capitalism, but of a new way of thinking. This emphasis on ideas contrasts with Marx's focus on material production, leading scholars to describe Weber's work as "a debate with the ghost of Karl Marx" (Cuff and Payne, 1979:73–74).

In all his work, Weber contrasted social patterns in different times and places. To sharpen comparisons, he relied on the **ideal type**, *an abstract statement of the essential characteristics of any social phenomenon*. He explored religion by contrasting the ideal "Protestant" with the ideal "Jew," "Hindu," and "Buddhist," knowing that these models precisely described no actual individuals. Note that Weber's use of the word *ideal* does not mean that something is "good" or "the best;" we could analyze "criminals" as well as "priests" as ideal types. We have already done so, of course, in comparing "hunting and gathering societies" and "industrial societies" as well as "capitalism" and "socialism."

TWO WORLD VIEWS: TRADITION AND RATIONALITY

Rather than categorizing societies in terms of technology or productive systems, Max Weber highlighted differences in the ways people view the world.

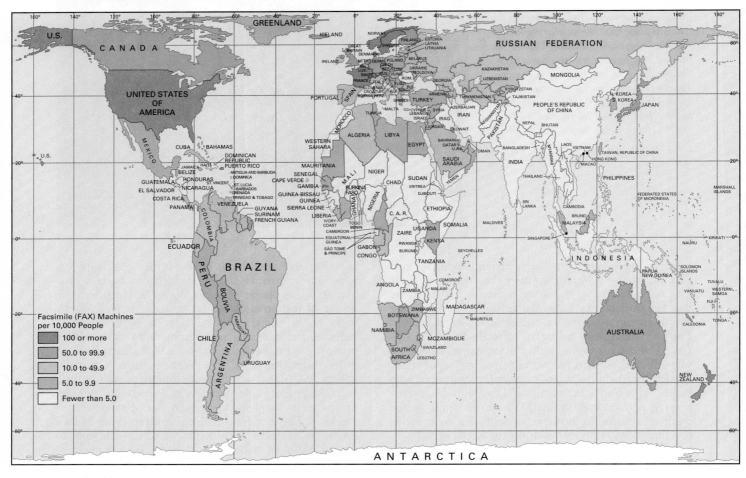

GLOBAL MAP 4–1 High Technology in Global Perspective

Countries with traditional cultures ignore or even resist technological innovation; nations with highly rationalized ways of life eagerly embrace such changes. Facsimile (fax) machines, one common form of technology, are numerous in high-income countries such as Canada, where millions of faxes fly along the "information superhighway" every day. In low-income nations, by contrast, fax machines are unknown to most people. Notice that, in Asia, fax machines are widely available only in Japan, South Korea, Taiwan, and the business centres of Hong Kong and Singapore.

SOURCE: *Peters Atlas of the World* (1990).

In simple terms, Weber concluded that members of pre-industrial societies adhere to *tradition*, while people in industrial-capitalist societies endorse *rationality*.

By **tradition**, Weber meant *sentiments and beliefs passed from generation to generation.* Thus traditional societies are guided by the past. Their members evaluate particular actions as right and proper precisely because they have been accepted for so long.

People in modern societies take a different view of the world, argued Weber, embracing **rationality**, *deliberate, matter-of-fact calculation of the most efficient means to accomplish a particular goal.* Sentiment has no place in a rational world view, which treats tradition simply as one kind of information. Typically, modern people choose to think and act on the basis of present and future consequences, evaluating jobs, schooling, and even relationships in terms of what we put into them and what we expect to receive in return.

Weber viewed both the Industrial Revolution and capitalism as evidence of a historical surge of rationality. He used the phrase **rationalization of society** to denote *the historical change from tradition to rationality as the dominant mode of human thought.* Modern society, he concluded, has been "disenchanted," as scientific thinking and technology have swept away sentimental ties to the past.

The willingness to adopt the latest technology, then, is one good indicator of how rationalized a society is. Indicating the global pattern of rationalization, Global Map 4–1 shows where in the world facsimile (fax) machines are found. In general, the high-income countries of North America and Europe use these devices to the greatest degree while they are quite rare in low-income nations.

Drawing on Weber's comparative perspective— and the data found in the map—we deduce that various societies place different values on technological advancement. What one society might herald as a breakthrough, another might deem unimportant, and a third might strongly oppose as a threat to tradition. The Tuareg nomads, described at the beginning of this chapter, shrug off the notion of using telephones: Why would anyone want such a thing in the desert? In Canada today, the Mennonites are guided by their traditions to staunchly oppose modern technology.

In Weber's view, then, technological innovation is promoted or hindered by the way people understand their world. He concluded that people in many societies discovered keys to technological change; however, only in the rational cultural climate of Western Europe did people exploit these discoveries to spark the Industrial Revolution (1958a; orig. 1904–05).

IS CAPITALISM RATIONAL?

Is industrial capitalism a rational economic system? Here, again, Weber and Marx came down on opposite sides of the issue. Weber considered industrial capitalism as the essence of rationality, since capitalists pursue profit in eminently rational ways. Marx, however, dismissed capitalism as the antithesis of rationality, claiming that it failed to meet the basic needs of most of the people (Gerth and Mills, 1946:49).

WEBER'S GREAT THESIS: PROTESTANTISM AND CAPITALISM

But, to look more closely at Weber's analysis, how did industrial capitalism emerge in the first place? Weber contended that industrial capitalism was the legacy of Calvinism—a Christian religious movement spawned by the Protestant Reformation. Calvinists, Weber explained, approached life in a highly disciplined and rational way. Moreover, central to the religious doctrine of John Calvin (1509–64) was *predestination*, the idea that an all-knowing and all-powerful God has preordained some people for salvation and others for damnation. With everyone's fate set before birth, Calvinists believed that people could do nothing to alter their destiny. Nor could they even know what their future would be. Thus the lives of Calvinists were framed by hopeful visions of eternal salvation and anxious fears of unending damnation.

For such people, not knowing one's fate was intolerable. Calvinists gradually came to a resolution of sorts. Why shouldn't those chosen for glory in the next world, they reasoned, see signs of divine favour in *this* world? Such a conclusion prompted Calvinists to interpret worldly prosperity as a sign of God's grace. Anxious to acquire this reassurance, Calvinists threw themselves into a quest for success, applying rationality, discipline, and hard work to their tasks. This pursuit of riches was not for its own sake, of course, since self-indulgently spending money was clearly sinful. Calvinists also were little moved to share their wealth with the poor, because they saw poverty as a sign of God's rejection. Their ever-present duty was to carry forward what they held to be their personal *calling* from God.

As they reinvested their profits for greater success, Calvinists built the foundation of capitalism. They piously used wealth to generate more wealth, practised personal thrift, and eagerly embraced whatever technological advances would bolster their efforts.

These traits, Weber explained, distinguished Calvinism from other world religions. Catholicism, the traditional religion in most of Europe, gave rise to a passive, "otherworldly" view of life with hope of greater reward in the life to come. For Catholics, material wealth had none of the spiritual significance that so motivated Calvinists. And so it was, Weber concluded, that industrial capitalism became established primarily in areas of Europe where Calvinism had a strong hold.

Weber's study of Calvinism provides striking evidence of the power of ideas to shape society (versus Marx's contention that ideas merely reflect the process of economic production). But, always skeptical of simple explanations, Weber knew that industrial capitalism had many roots. In fact, one purpose of this research was to counter Marx's narrow explanation of modern society in strictly economic terms.

As religious fervour weakened among later generations of Calvinists, Weber concluded, success-seeking personal discipline remained strong. A *religious* ethic became simply a "*work* ethic." From this point of

A key element of North American culture has long been a "work ethic," with its roots in the Calvinist thinking that fascinated Max Weber. This Currier and Ives lithograph from 1875 makes a statement that people should shun the stock market, race track, lotteries, and even labour strikes as ways to improve their lives in favour of climbing the "Ladder of Fortune" based on personal virtue and individual effort.

view, industrial capitalism emerged as "disenchanted" religion, with wealth now valued for its own sake. It is revealing that "accounting," which to early Calvinists meant keeping a daily record of moral deeds, now refers simply to keeping track of money.

RATIONAL SOCIAL ORGANIZATION

Weber contended that, by unleashing the Industrial Revolution and sparking the development of capitalism, rationality had defined the character of modern society. Rational social organization confers the following seven traits on today's social life.

1. **Distinctive social institutions.** Among hunters and gatherers, the family was the centre of virtually all activities. Gradually, however, other social institutions, including religious, political,

and economic systems, broke away from family life. In modern societies, institutions of education and health care have also appeared. The separation of social institutions—each detailed in a later chapter—is a rational strategy to address human needs more efficiently.

2. **Large-scale organizations.** Modern rationality is exemplified by a proliferation of large-scale organizations. As early as the horticultural era, political officials oversaw religious observances, public works, and warfare. In medieval Europe, the Catholic Church grew larger still with thousands of officials. In modern, rational societies, the employees of the federal government number in the millions and most people work for a large organization.

3. **Specialized tasks.** Unlike members of traditional societies, individuals in modern societies pursue a wide range of specialized activities. The enormous breadth of occupations can be seen in any city's "Yellow Pages™" telephone directory.

4. **Personal discipline.** Modern society puts a premium on self-directed discipline. For early Calvinists, of course, such an approach to life was rooted in religious belief. Although now distanced from its religious origins, discipline is still encouraged by cultural values such as achievement, success, and efficiency.

5. **Awareness of time.** In traditional societies, people measure time according to the rhythm of sun and seasons. Modern people, by contrast, schedule events precisely by the hour and minute. Interestingly, clocks began appearing in European cities some five hundred years ago just as commerce was starting to expand; soon, people began to think (to borrow Benjamin Franklin's phrase) that "time is money."

6. **Technical competence.** Members of traditional societies evaluate one another largely on the basis of *who* they are—how they are joined to others in the web of kinship. Modern rationality, by contrast, prompts us to judge people according to *what* they are—that is, with an eye towards their skills and abilities.

7. **Impersonality.** Finally, in a rational society technical competence takes priority over close relationships, rendering the world impersonal. Modern social life can be viewed as the interplay of specialists concerned with particular tasks, rather than people broadly concerned with one another. Weber explained that we tend to devalue personal feelings and emotions as "irrational" because they often are difficult to control.

Rationality and Bureaucracy

Although the medieval church grew large, Weber argued that it remained largely traditional. Truly rational organizations, with the principal focus on efficiency, appeared only in the last few centuries. The organizational type Weber called *bureaucracy* became pronounced along with capitalism as an expression of modern rationality.

Chapter 7 ("Groups and Organizations") explains that bureaucracy is the model for modern businesses, government agencies, labour unions, and universities. For now, note that Weber considered this organizational form to be the clearest expression of a rational world view because its chief elements—offices, duties, and policies—are intended to achieve specific goals as efficiently as possible. By contrast, the inefficiency of traditional organization is reflected in its hostility to change. In short, Weber asserted that bureaucracy transformed all of society in the same way that industrialization transformed the economy.

Still, Weber emphasized that rational bureaucracy has a special affinity to capitalism. He wrote:

> Today, it is primarily the capitalist market economy which demands that the official business of public administration be discharged precisely, unambiguously, continuously, and with as much speed as possible. Normally, the very large capitalist enterprises are themselves unequalled models of strict bureaucratic organization. (1978:974; orig. 1921)

Rationality and Alienation

Max Weber joined with Karl Marx in recognizing the unparalleled efficiency of industrial capitalism. Weber also shared Marx's conclusion that modern society generates widespread alienation, although for different reasons. For Weber, the primary problem is not the economic inequality that so troubled Marx, but the stifling regulation and dehumanization that comes with expanding bureaucracy.

Bureaucracies, Weber warned, treat people as a series of cases rather than as unique individuals. In addition, working for large organizations demands highly specialized and often tedious routines. In the end, Weber envisioned modern society as a vast and growing system of rules seeking to regulate everything and threatening to crush the human spirit.

An irony found in the work of Marx reappears in Weber's thinking: rather than serving humanity, modern society turns on its creators and enslaves them. In language reminiscent of Marx's description of the human toll of industrial capitalism, Weber portrayed the modern individual as "only a small cog in a

Max Weber agreed with Karl Marx that modern society is alienating to the individual, but the two thinkers identified different causes of this estrangement. For Marx, economic inequality is the culprit; for Weber, the issue is pervasive and dehumanizing bureaucracy. George Tooker's painting Landscape *echoes Weber's sentiments.*

ceaselessly moving mechanism that prescribes to him an endlessly fixed routine of march" (1978:988; orig. 1921). Thus, although he could see the advantages of modern society, Weber ended his life deeply pessimistic. He feared that the rationalization of society would end up reducing people to robots.

EMILE DURKHEIM: SOCIETY AND FUNCTION

"To love society is to love something beyond us and something in ourselves." These are the words of Emile Durkheim (1858–1917), another founding architect of sociology. This curious phrase (1974:55; orig. 1924) condenses another highly influential vision of human society.

STRUCTURE: SOCIETY BEYOND OURSELVES

Most significantly, Emile Durkheim recognized that society exists beyond ourselves. Society, as Durkheim saw it, is more than the individuals who compose it; society has a life of its own that stretches beyond our personal experiences. It was here long before we were born, it shapes us while we live, and it will remain long

Durkheim's observation that people with weak social bonds are prone to self-destructive behaviour stands as stark evidence of the power of society to shape individual lives. When rock and roll singers become famous they are wrenched out of familiar life patterns and existing relationships, sometimes with tragic results. The history of rock and roll contains many tragic stories of this kind, including Janis Joplin's death by drug overdose (1970) and Kurt Cobain's suicide (1994).

after we are gone. Patterns of human behaviour, Durkheim explained, are the basis of established *structures*: they are *social facts* that have an objective reality beyond the lives and perceptions of particular individuals. Cultural norms, values, religious beliefs—all endure as social facts.

Since society looms larger than individual lives, it has the *power* to shape our thoughts and actions, Durkheim noted. So studying individuals alone (as psychologists or biologists do) can never capture the essence of human experience. A classroom of first graders, a family sharing a meal, people milling about a country auction—all are examples of the countless situations that have an organization apart from any of the individuals who participate in them.

Once created by people, then, society takes on a momentum of its own, confronting its creators and demanding a measure of obedience. For our part, we experience society's influence as we come to see the order in our lives or as we face temptation and feel the tug of morality.

FUNCTION: SOCIETY AS SYSTEM

Having established that society has structure, Durkheim turned to the concept of *function*. The significance of any social fact, he explained, extends beyond individuals to how it helps society itself operate as a complex system.

To illustrate, consider crime. Most people think of lawbreaking as harmful acts that some individuals inflict on others. But, looking beyond individuals, Durkheim saw that crime has a vital function for the ongoing life of society itself. As Chapter 8 ("Deviance") explains, only by recognizing and responding to acts as criminal do people construct and defend morality, which gives purpose and meaning to our collective life. For this reason, Durkheim rejected

the common view of crime as "pathological." On the contrary, he concluded, crime is quite "normal" for the most basic of reasons: a society could not exist without it (1964a, orig. 1895; 1964b, orig. 1893).

PERSONALITY: SOCIETY IN OURSELVES

Durkheim contended that society is not only "beyond ourselves," it is also "in ourselves." Each of us, in short, builds a personality by internalizing social facts. How we act, think, and feel—our essential humanity—is drawn from the society that nurtures us. Moreover, Durkheim explained, society regulates human beings through moral discipline. Durkheim held that human beings are naturally insatiable, and in constant danger of being overpowered by our own desires: "The more one has, the more one wants, since satisfactions received only stimulate instead of filling needs" (1966:248; orig. 1897). Having given us life, then, society must also rein us in.

Nowhere is the need for societal regulation better illustrated than in Durkheim's study of suicide (1966; orig. 1897), detailed in Chapter 1 ("The Sociological Perspective"). Why is it that, over the years, rock stars have been so vulnerable to self-destruction? Durkheim had the answer long before anyone made electric music: it is the *least* regulated categories of people that suffer the *highest* rates of suicide. The greater licence afforded to those who are young, rich, and famous exacts a high price in terms of the risk of suicide.

Modernity and Anomie

Compared to traditional societies, modern societies impose fewer restrictions on everyone. Durkheim acknowledges the advantages of modern freedom, but he warned of a rise in **anomie**, *a condition in which society provides little moral guidance to individuals*. What so

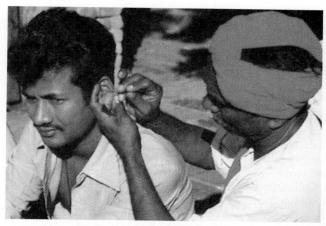

Historically, most members of human societies engaged in a narrow range of activities: searching out food and building shelters. Modern societies, explained Durkheim, display a rapidly expanding division of labour. Increasing specialization is evident on the streets of societies beginning to industrialize: providing people with their weight is the livelihood of this man in Istanbul, Turkey; on a Bombay street in India, another earns a small fee for cleaning ears.

many celebrities describe as "almost being destroyed by their fame," is one extreme example of the corrosive effects of anomie. Sudden fame or winning the lottery tears people away from their families and familiar routines, disrupting society's support and regulation of an individual, sometimes with fatal results. Durkheim instructs us, therefore, that the desires of the individual must be balanced by the claims and guidance of society—a balance that has become precarious in the modern world.

EVOLVING SOCIETIES: THE DIVISION OF LABOUR

Like Marx and Weber, Durkheim witnessed firsthand the rapid social transformation of Europe during the nineteenth century. Analyzing this change, Durkheim saw a sweeping evolution in the forms of social organization.

In pre-industrial societies, explained Durkheim, strong tradition operates as the social cement that binds people together. In fact, what he termed the *collective conscience* is so strong that the community moves quickly to punish anyone who dares to challenge conventional ways of life. Durkheim called this system **mechanical solidarity**, meaning *social bonds, based on shared morality, that unite members of pre-industrial societies*. In practice, then, mechanical solidarity springs from *likeness*. Durkheim described these bonds as "mechanical" because people feel a more or less automatic sense of belonging together.

Durkheim considered the decline of mechanical solidarity to be a defining trait of modern society. But this does not mean that society dissolves; rather, modernity generates a new type of solidarity that rushes into the void left by discarded traditions. Durkheim called this new social integration **organic solidarity**, defined as *social bonds, based on specialization, that unite members of industrial societies*. Where solidarity was once rooted in likeness, in short, it now flows from *differences* among people who find that their specialized pursuits—as plumbers, consultants, midwives, or sociology instructors—make them rely on one another.

For Durkheim, then, the key dimension of change is a society's expanding **division of labour**, or *specialized economic activity*. As Max Weber explained, modern societies specialize in order to promote efficiency. Durkheim fills in the picture by showing us that members of modern societies count on the efforts of tens of thousands of others—most of them complete strangers—to secure the goods and services they need every day.

So modernity rests far less on *moral consensus* (the foundation of traditional societies) and far more on *functional interdependence*. That is, as members of modern societies, we depend more and more on people we trust less and less. Why, then, should we put our faith in people we hardly know and whose beliefs may differ radically from our own? Durkheim's answer: "Because we can't live without them." In a world in which morality sometimes seems like so much shifting

The Information Revolution:
What Would Durkheim (and Others) Think?

Who can doubt that technological change is now reshaping society? If they were alive today, the founding sociologists discussed in this chapter would be eager observers of the current scene. Let's imagine for a moment the kind of questions Emile Durkheim, Max Weber, and Karl Marx might ask about the societal effects of computer technology.

To Emile Durkheim, what stands out about modern society is its increasing division of labour, as people pursue a host of specialized occupations. Durkheim would be quick to wonder if new information technology is pushing specialization even further. And there is good reason to think that it is. Because electronic communication (say, a Web site home page) gives any individual a vast market (there are already more than 100 million computers that can access a home page), people can specialize far more than they would working in a limited geographical area. For example, while most small-town lawyers have a general practice, an information-age lawyer (living anywhere) could become a specialist in, say, prenuptial agreements or electronic copyright law. In-

deed, as the electronic age unfolds, there is already a rapidly increasing number of highly specialized "micro-businesses" in all fields, some of which end up becoming quite large!

Max Weber, of course, held that modern societies are distinctive because their members share a rational world view. And, to Weber, nothing captured this way of thinking better than expanding bureaucracy. But will bureaucracy continue to dominate the social scene in the next century? Here is one reason to think it may not: while it may make sense for organizations to apply rules and regulations to workers performing the kinds of routine tasks that were common in the industrial era, more and more work in the post-industrial era involves imagination. Think, for instance, of "new age" work designing homes, composing music, or writing software. Certainly one cannot regulate creativity in the same way as, say, assembling automobiles on an assembly line. Perhaps this is why many high-technology companies have done away with the dress codes and even the time clocks found in factories of the past. In short, the character of "rational organi-

zation" may well be changing along with the nature of work.

Finally, what might Karl Marx make of the Information Revolution? To Marx, you will recall, the earlier Industrial Revolution was really a *class* revolution, which soon allowed the owners of industry to dominate society. As we enter the Information Age, Marx would probably question whether a new symbolic elite is coming to dominate society. Some analysts point out, for example, that film and television writers, producers, and performers now enjoy enormous wealth, international prestige, and unprecedented power (Lichter, Rothman, and Lichter, 1990). Similarly, just as those without industrial skills were held at the bottom of the class system in decades past, so people without symbolic skills are likely to become the new "underclass" in the next century.

Durkheim, Weber, and Marx greatly aided our understanding of industrial societies. As we move into the post-industrial age, there will be plenty of room for new generations of sociologists to carry on!

---

sand, then, we confront what might be called "Durkheim's dilemma:" the technological power and expansive personal freedom of modern society come only at the cost of receding morality and the ever-present danger of anomie.

Like Marx and Weber, Durkheim had misgivings about the direction society was taking. But, of the three, Durkheim was the most optimistic. Confidence in the future sprang from his hope that we could enjoy greater freedom and privacy while creating for ourselves the social regulation that had once been forced on us by tradition.

Finally, how might Durkheim respond to the increasing importance of new information technology in today's world? The Exploring Cyber-Society box argues that Durkheim—and the other theorists we

have considered in this chapter—would probably have much to say about the Information Revolution.

CRITICAL EVALUATION: FOUR VISIONS OF SOCIETY

This chapter opened with several important queries about human societies. We will conclude by summarizing how each of the four visions of society answers these questions.

What Holds Societies Together?

How is something as complex as society possible? The Lenskis claim that members of a society are united by

Is Our Society Getting Better or Worse?

Optimism has been a defining trait of Canadian society. As time goes on, life gets better—or so we thought. But a recent survey by Alberta sociologist Reginald Bibby suggests that optimism may be waning. Between 1975 and 1995, the proportion of people who believed that the "lot of the average person" is getting worse rose from 45 to 70 percent; the proportion who believed that racial and cultural minorities are experiencing discrimination increased from 55 percent in 1980 to 67 percent in 1995; and, in one decade (1985 to 1995), the proportion of respondents who agreed that "values in Canada have been changing for the worse" rose from 54 to 74 percent. In addition, when asked to identify their major concerns, Canadians placed the national debt, unemployment, and the economy at the top of their list—followed by crime, government incompetence, child abuse, AIDS, delinquency, family breakdown, and violence (Bibby, 1995:7, 52, 26, 94). Clearly, Canadians are worried.

What's going on here? After all, there are good reasons for optimism about Canada. Since the beginning of this century, educational attainment has increased dramatically so that larger proportions are university and college graduates. In addition, after taking inflation into account, average Canadians have enjoyed higher income and greater buying power. Almost every household has a telephone, television, and refrigerator, and more than 80 percent have automobiles, VCRs, and microwaves.

Most importantly, while people born in 1900 lived an average of about forty-seven years, children born today can expect to live about thirty years longer.

But some trends of the last decade or two are troubling. Members of our society are less certain that hard work pays off. Despite an increase in two-income couples, family earnings have increased only slightly. At the same time, divorce rates are climbing while marriage rates are decreasing, and a perception of rising crime rates has undermined people's sense of personal safety, even in their own homes. For 46 percent of Canadians, crime is a "very serious" concern, and 87 percent think the courts should be tougher on lawbreakers (Bibby, 1995:97, 116). Our relative affluence coupled with our capacity to move farther and faster than ever before seems to have eroded our sense of responsibility for others, unleashing a wave of individualism accompanied by a dramatic move to the right of the political spectrum.

Despite recent trends, an overwhelming and slightly increasing majority of Canadians claim to be "very happy" or "pretty happy"—87 and 92 percent in 1975 and 1995—and even more claim to have marriages in the two "happy" categories—92 and 94 percent in 1975 and 1995 (Bibby, 1995:5).

So, which is it? Is Canadian society getting better or worse?

The theorists highlighted in this chapter shed some light on this question. It is easy to equate "high tech"

with progress, but, the Lenskis maintain, we should make such assumptions cautiously; history shows us that, while advancing technology does offer real advantages, it is no guarantee of a "better" life. Marx, Weber, and Durkheim also acknowledged the growing affluence of societies over time, yet each offered a pointed criticism of modern society's dangerous tendency towards individualism. For Marx, capitalism is the culprit, elevating money to godlike status and fostering a culture of selfishness. Weber's analysis claims that the modern spirit of rationality wears away traditional ties of kinship and neighbourhood while expanding bureaucracy, which both manipulates and isolates people. In Durkheim's view, functional interdependence joins members of modern societies, who are less and less able to establish a common moral framework within which to judge right and wrong. Technological advances, it seems, are offset by the loss of human community. How well, one might ask, do the insights of these theorists describe Canadian society?

Continue the debate . . .

1. *Do you think life in Canada is getting better or worse? Why?*
2. *Is our society's level of affluence entirely good? What might Marx, Weber, and Durkheim say?*
3. *Do you think people in low-income countries generally look up to Canada? Why or why not?*

shared culture and that cultural patterns vary according to a society's level of technological development. But they note that inequality divides a society as technology becomes more complex; social stratification diminishes to some extent with the onset of industrialization. Marx spotlighted social division, not unity, treating class conflict as the hallmark of human societies throughout history. From his point of view, elites may force an uneasy peace between the classes, but true social unity would emerge only if production were to become a truly cooperative endeavour. To Weber, members of a society share a distinctive world view. Just as traditional beliefs joined people together in the past, so modern societies have created rational, large-scale organizations that fuse people's lives. Finally, Durkheim made solidarity the focus of his work, contrasting the morality-based mechanical solidarity of pre-industrial societies with modern society's organic solidarity based on specialization.

How Have Societies Changed?

According to the Lenskis' model of sociocultural evolution, societies differ primarily in terms of changing technology. Modern society stands out in this regard because of its enormous productive power. Karl Marx also stressed historical differences in productive systems, yet pointed to the persistence of social conflict throughout human history (except perhaps among simple hunters and gatherers). For Marx, modern society is distinctive only because it brings that conflict out in the open. Max Weber looked at this question from another perspective, tracing changes in the way people look at the world. Pre-industrial societies, he claimed, are guided by tradition, while modern societies espouse a rational world view. Finally, for Emile Durkheim, traditional societies are characterized by mechanical solidarity based on moral consensus. In industrial societies, mechanical solidarity gives way to organic solidarity based on productive specialization.

Why Do Societies Change?

As the Lenskis see it, social change is primarily a matter of technological innovation that, over time, may transform an entire society. Marx's materialist approach pointed to the struggle between social classes as the "engine of history," pushing societies towards revolutionary reorganization. Weber's idealist view argued that modes of thought also contribute to social change. He demonstrated how a particular world view—rational Calvinism—bolstered the Industrial Revolution, which, in turn, reshaped much of modern society. Finally, Durkheim pointed to an expanding division of labour as the key dimension of social change.

Like a kaleidoscope that shows us different patterns as we turn it, these four approaches reveal an array of insights into society. Yet no one approach is, in an absolute sense, right or wrong. Society is exceedingly complex, and we gain the richest understanding from using all of these visions, as we do in the "Controversy & Debate" box.

SUMMARY

Gerhard and Jean Lenski

1. Sociocultural evolution explores the societal consequences of technological advancements.

2. The earliest hunting and gathering societies were composed of a small number of family-centred nomads. Such societies have all but vanished from the earth.

3. Horticulture began some ten thousand years ago as people devised hand tools for the cultivation of crops. Pastoral societies domesticate animals and engage in extensive trade.

4. Agriculture, about five thousand years old, is large-scale cultivation using animal-drawn plows. This technology allows societies to expand into vast empires, characterized by more productivity, greater specialization, and increasing social inequality.

5. Industrialization began 250 years ago in Europe, as people harnessed advanced energy sources to power sophisticated machinery.

6. In post-industrial societies, production shifts from material things to information: computers and other information-based technology replace the heavy machinery of the industrial era.

Karl Marx

7. Marx's materialist analysis pointed up historical and contemporary conflict between social classes.

8. Conflict in "ancient" societies involved masters and slaves; in agrarian societies, it places nobles and serfs in opposition; in industrial-capitalist societies, capitalists confront the proletariat.

9. Industrial capitalism alienates workers in four ways: from the act of working, from the products of work, from fellow workers, and from human potential.

10. Once workers had overcome their own false consciousness, Marx believed they would overthrow capitalists and the industrial-capitalist system.

Max Weber

11. Weber's idealist approach revealed that modes of thought have a powerful effect on society.

12. Weber drew a sharp contrast between the tradition of pre-industrial societies and the rationality of modern, industrial societies.

13. Weber feared that rationality, embodied in efficiency-conscious bureaucratic organizations, would stifle human creativity.

Emile Durkheim

14. Durkheim explained that society has an objective existence apart from individuals.

15. His approach related social elements to the larger society through their functions.

16. Societies require solidarity: traditional societies are fused by mechanical solidarity based on moral consensus; modern societies depend on organic solidarity based on the division of labour or productive specialization.

CRITICAL THINKING QUESTIONS

1. Present evidence that supports and contradicts the notion that technological advance amounts to "progress."

2. As general approaches to understanding society, contrast Marx's concept of materialism with Weber's idealism.

3. Both Marx and Weber were concerned with modern society's ability to alienate people. How are their approaches different? Contrast their notions of alienation to Durkheim's concept of anomie.

4. How do these visions of society explain the changing standing of women? What issues might be raised by a feminist critique of these theories?

SOCIOLOGY APPLIED

1. Hunting and gathering people mused over stars, and we still know the constellations in terms that were relevant to them—mostly animals and hunters. As a way of revealing what's important to *our* way of life, write a short paper imagining, were we beginning the process from scratch, what meaning we would impose on the stars.

2. Spend an hour going around your home trying to identify every device that has a computer chip in it. How many did you find? Were you surprised by the number?

3. Rent or watch the television schedule for an old "Tarzan" movie or another film that portrays technologically simpler people. How are they portrayed in the film?

4. Over the next few days, ask a dozen people over the age of twenty-five whether they think our society is getting better or worse, and why they hold their opinion. See how much agreement you find.

WEBLINKS

eddie.cso.uiuc.edu/Durkheim
The *Durkheim Pages* contain a biography, critical summaries of his major works, some full texts, reviews, a glossary, a bibliography of primary and secondary sources, and more.

www.marx.org
The *Marx/Engels Internet Archive* houses an extensive collection of writings by and about Karl Marx and Friedrich Engels, as well as a photo gallery, and information about numerous other Marxist writers, from Rosa Luxemburg and Mao Tsetung to Leon Trotsky and Josef Stalin.

www.runet.edu/~lridener/DSS/Weber/PECAP. HTML
In this long excerpt from *The Protestant Ethic and the Spirit of Capitalism*—one of many documents from the *Dead Sociologists Society* site—Max Weber attempts to define his concept of "the spirit of capitalism."

history.hanover.edu/modern/indrev.htm
A small but significant collection of links to source texts about the Industrial Revolution, including works by Charles Dickens, Adam Smith, and Arnold Toynbee.

http://strategis.ic.gc.ca/SSG/ih01650e.html
Preparing Canada for a Digital World is the final report of the Information Highway Advisory Council, offering advice to policymakers on five key issues: economic growth, the Internet, access, Canadian content, and learning and the workplace.

Hale Woodruff, *Girls Skipping,* 1949

SOCIALIZATION

On a cold winter day in 1938, a social worker walked anxiously to the door of a rural Pennsylvania farmhouse. Investigating a case of possible child abuse, the social worker soon discovered a five-year-old girl hidden in a second-floor storage room. The child, whose name was Anna, was wedged into an old chair with her arms tied above her head so that she could not move. She was dressed in filthy garments, and her arms and legs—looking like matchsticks—were so frail that she could not use them.

Anna's situation can only be described as tragic. She was born in 1932 to an unmarried and mentally impaired woman of twenty-six who lived with her father. Enraged by his daughter's "illegitimate" motherhood, the grandfather did not even want the child in his house. Anna therefore spent her first six months in various institutions. But her mother was unable to pay for such care, so Anna returned to the hostile home of her grandfather.

At this point, her ordeal intensified. To lessen the grandfather's anger, Anna's mother moved the child to the attic room, where she received little attention and just enough milk to keep her alive. There she stayed—day after day, month after month, with essentially no human contact—for five long years.

Upon learning of the discovery of Anna, sociologist Kingsley Davis (1940) travelled immediately to see the child. He found her at a county home, where local authorities had taken her. Davis was appalled by Anna's condition. She was emaciated and feeble. Unable to laugh, smile, speak, or even show anger, she was completely unresponsive, as if alone in an empty world.

SOCIAL EXPERIENCE: THE KEY TO OUR HUMANITY

Here is a deplorable but instructive case of a human being deprived of virtually all social contact. Although physically alive, Anna hardly seemed human. Her plight reveals that, isolated in this way, an individual develops scarcely any capacity for thought, emotion, and meaningful behaviour. In short, without social experience, an individual is more an *object* than a *person*.

This chapter explores what Anna was deprived of—the means by which we become fully human. This process is **socialization**, *the lifelong social experience by which individuals develop their human potential and learn patterns of their culture.* Unlike other living species whose behaviour is biologically set, human beings rely on social experience to learn the nuances of their culture in order to survive.

Social experience is also the foundation of **personality**, *a person's fairly consistent patterns of thinking, feeling, and acting.* We build a personality by internalizing our social surroundings. As personality develops, we participate in a culture while remaining, in some respects, distinct individuals. But in the absence of social experience, as the case of Anna shows, personality does not emerge at all.

Because societies exist beyond the life span of any person, each generation must teach something of its way of life to the next. Socialization, then, amounts to the ongoing process of cultural transmission. In short, social experience is the vital foundation of our lives—individually and collectively.

HUMAN DEVELOPMENT: NATURE AND NURTURE

Virtually helpless at birth, the human infant depends on others for care and nourishment as well as learning. Although Anna's short life makes these facts very clear, a century ago most people mistakenly believed that human behaviour was the product of biological imperatives.

Charles Darwin: The Role of Nature

Charles Darwin, whose groundbreaking theory of evolution is summarized in Chapter 3 ("Culture"), held that each species evolves over thousands of generations as genetic variations enhance survival and reproduction. Biologically rooted traits that enhance survival emerge as a species' "nature." As Darwin's fame grew, people assumed that humans, like other forms of life, had a fixed, instinctive "nature" as well.

Such notions are still with us. People sometimes claim, for example, that our economic system is a reflection of "instinctive human competitiveness" (known as social Darwinism), that some people are "born criminals," or that women are "naturally" more emotional while men are "inherently" more rational (Witkin-Lanoil, 1984). We often describe familiar personality traits as *human nature* as if people were born with them, just as we are born with five senses. More accurately, however, our human nature leads us to create and learn cultural traits, as we shall see.

People trying to understand cultural diversity also misconstrued Darwin's thinking. Centuries of world exploration and empire building taught Western Europeans that the behaviour of people around the world differs from their own. They attributed such contrasts to biology rather than to culture. It was a simple—although terribly damaging—step to conclude that members of technologically simple societies were biologically less evolved and, therefore, less human. Such a self-serving and ethnocentric view helped justify colonial practices, including land seizures and slavery, since it is easier to exploit others if you are convinced that they are not truly human in the same sense that you are.

The Social Sciences: The Role of Nurture

In the twentieth century, social scientists launched a broad attack on biological explanations of human behaviour. Psychologist John B. Watson (1878–1958) devised a theory called *behaviourism*, which held that specific behaviour patterns are not instinctive but learned. Thus, people the world over have the same claim to humanity, Watson insisted; humans differ only in their cultural environment. For Watson, "human nature" was infinitely malleable:

> Give me a dozen healthy infants … and my own specified world to bring them up in, and I will guarantee to take any one at random and train him to become any type of specialist that I might select—doctor, lawyer, artist, merchant, chief, and yes, even beggar-man and thief—regardless of his talents, penchants, tendencies, abilities, vocations, and race of his ancestors. (1930:104)

Anthropologists weighed in on this debate as well, showing how variable the world's cultures are. An outspoken proponent of the "nurture" view, anthropologist Margaret Mead, summed up the evidence: "The differences between individuals who are members of different cultures, like the differences between individuals within a culture, are almost entirely to be laid to differences in conditioning, especially during early childhood, and this conditioning is culturally determined" (1963:280; orig. 1935).

The research on the relationship between race and intelligence by Professor Philippe Rushton of the University of Western Ontario is an example of modern "social Darwinism." In 1989 Rushton claimed to have demonstrated scientifically that Orientals (Rushton's term) were more intelligent than whites or Blacks, and that Blacks were the least intelligent of the three races. The widespread outrage in response to the presentation and publication of Rushton's work indicates the dramatic decline in the acceptance of social Darwinist theories today. Even the conceptualization of the hypothesis that there is a relationship between race and behaviour is seen today as racist.

However, most social scientists are cautious about describing any type of behaviour as instinctive. Even sociobiology, examined in Chapter 3 ("Culture"), holds that human behaviour is primarily guided by the surrounding culture. Of course, this does not mean that biology plays *no* part in human behaviour. Human life, after all, depends on the functioning of the body. We also know that children share many biological traits with their parents, especially physical characteristics such as height, weight, hair and eye colour, and facial features. Intelligence and various personality characteristics (for example, how one reacts to stimulation or frustration) probably have some genetic component, as does the potential to excel in such activities as art and music. But whether a person develops an inherited potential depends on the opportunities to develop it. Indeed, biologists point out that unless children *use* their brains in various

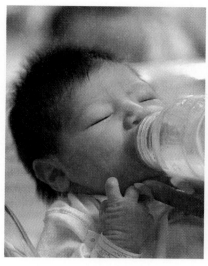 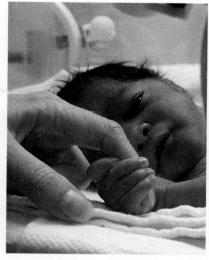 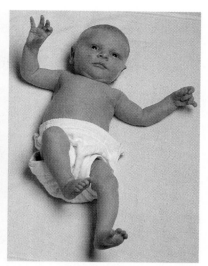

Human infants display various reflexes—biologically based behaviour patterns that enhance survival. The sucking reflex, which actually begins before birth, enables the infant to obtain nourishment. The grasping reflex, triggered by placing a finger on the infant's palm and causing the hand to close, helps the infant maintain contact with a parent and, later on, to grasp objects. The Moro reflex, activated by startling the infant, causes the infant to swing both arms outward and then bringing them together across the chest. This action, which disappears after several months of life, probably developed among our evolutionary ancestors so that a falling infant could grasp the body hair of a parent.

ways in early life, the brain itself will not fully develop (Herrnstein, 1973; Plomin and Foch, 1980; Goldsmith, 1983; Begley, 1995).

In sum, without denying the importance of nature, the evidence shows that nurture is far more important in determining human behaviour. Rather than thinking of nature as opposing nurture, it is more correct to say that nurture—social experience and the creation of culture—is our nature. For humans, then, nature and nurture are inseparable.

SOCIAL ISOLATION

For obvious ethical reasons, researchers cannot subject human beings to experimental isolation. Consequently, much of what we know about this issue comes from rare cases of abused children like Anna. Researchers have, however, studied the impact of social isolation on animals.

Effects of Social Isolation on Nonhuman Primates

Psychologists Harry Harlow and Margaret Harlow (1962) conducted a classic investigation of the effects of social isolation on nonhuman primates. They observed the consequences of various conditions of

isolation on rhesus monkeys, whose behaviour is in some ways remarkably similar to that of humans.

The Harlows found that complete social isolation for even six months (with adequate nutrition) seriously disturbed the monkeys' development. When these monkeys subsequently returned to their group, they were anxious, passive, and fearful.

The Harlows then isolated infant rhesus monkeys, but provided an artificial "mother" made of wire mesh with a wooden head and the nipple of a feeding tube where the breast would be. These monkeys survived, but they, too, subsequently displayed emotional damage.

But when the researchers covered the artificial "mother" with soft terry cloth, the infant monkeys would cling to it, apparently deriving emotional benefit from the closeness. Subsequently, these monkeys revealed less emotional distress. The Harlows thus concluded that normal emotional development requires affectionate cradling as part of parent-infant interaction.

The Harlows made two other discoveries. First, as long as they were surrounded by other infants, monkeys were not adversely affected by the absence of a mother. This finding suggests that deprivation of social experience, rather than the absence of a specific parent, is what causes devastating effects. Second, the

The personalities we develop depend largely on the environment in which we live. As William Kurelek shows in this painting, Prairie Childhood, *based on his childhood in the Alberta prairies, a young person's life on a farm is often characterized by periods of social isolation and backbreaking work. How would such a boy's personality be likely to differ from that of his wealthy cousin raised in Montreal?*

Harlows found that lesser periods of social isolation—up to about three months—caused emotional distress, but only temporarily. The damage of short-term isolation, then, can be overcome; longer-term isolation, however, appears to inflict on monkeys irreversible emotional and behavioural damage.

Effects of Social Isolation on Children

Unusual and tragic cases of children isolated by abusive family members demonstrate the catastrophic effects of depriving human beings of social experience. We will review three such cases.

Anna: The rest of the story. The case of Anna, described earlier, is the best-known instance of the extended social isolation of a human infant. After her discovery, Anna benefited from intense social contact and soon showed improvement. Visiting her in the county home after ten days, Kingsley Davis (1940) noted that she was more alert and even smiled with obvious pleasure. During the next year, Anna made slow but steady progress, showing greater interest in other people and gradually learning to walk. After a year and a half, she could feed herself and play with toys.

Consistent with the observations of the Harlows, however, it was becoming apparent that Anna's five years of social isolation had left her permanently damaged. At the age of eight her mental and social development was still less than that of a two-year-old. Not until she was almost ten did she begin to use words. Of course, since Anna's mother was mentally

retarded, perhaps Anna was similarly disadvantaged. The riddle was never solved, because Anna died at age ten from a blood disorder, possibly related to her years of abuse (Davis, 1940, 1947).

Another case: Isabelle. A second, quite similar case involved another girl, found at about the same time as Anna and under strikingly similar circumstances. After more than six years of virtual isolation, this girl—known as Isabelle—displayed the same lack of human responsiveness as Anna. Unlike Anna, though, Isabelle benefited from a special learning program directed by psychologists. Within a week, Isabelle was attempting to speak, and a year and a half later, her vocabulary included nearly two thousand words. The psychologists concluded that intensive effort had propelled Isabelle through six years of normal development in only two years. By the time she was fourteen, Isabelle was attending sixth-grade classes, apparently on her way to at least an approximately normal life (Davis, 1947).

A third case: Genie. Yet another case of childhood isolation involved a thirteen-year-old California girl victimized in a host of ways by her parents from the age of two (Curtiss, 1977; Pines, 1981). Genie's ordeal included extended periods of being locked alone in a garage. Upon discovery, her condition was similar to that of Anna and Isabelle. Genie was emaciated (weighing only 26.8 kg) and had the mental development of a one-year-old. She could not walk, chew food, speak, or even control her bladder. She received intensive treatment by specialists and thrived physically. Yet even after years of care, her ability to use language remains that of a young child.

Conclusion. All the evidence points to the crucial role of social experience in personality development. Human beings are resilient creatures, sometimes able to recover from even the crushing experience of abuse and isolation. But there is a point—precisely when is unclear from the limited number of cases—at which social isolation or other abuse in infancy results in irreparable developmental damage.

UNDERSTANDING THE SOCIALIZATION PROCESS

Socialization is a complex, lifelong process. The following sections highlight the work of six men and women who have made lasting contributions to our understanding of human development.

SIGMUND FREUD: THE ELEMENTS OF PERSONALITY

Sigmund Freud (1856–1939) lived in Vienna at a time when most Europeans considered human behaviour to be biologically fixed. Trained as a physician, Freud gradually turned to the study of personality and eventually developed the celebrated theory of psychoanalysis. Many aspects of this work bear directly on our understanding of socialization.

Basic Human Needs

Freud contended that biology plays an important part in social development, although not in terms of the simple instincts that guide other species. Humans, Freud theorized, respond to two general needs or drives. First, humans have a basic need for bonding, which Freud called the life instinct, or *eros* (from the Greek god of love). Second, opposing this need is an aggressive drive, which Freud termed the death instinct, or *thanatos* (from the Greek meaning "death"). Freud postulated that these opposing forces, operating primarily at the level of the unconscious mind, generate deeply rooted inner tensions.

Freud's Model of Personality

Freud incorporated basic drives and the influence of society into a model of personality with three parts: id, ego, and superego. The **id** represents *the human being's basic drives*, which are unconscious and demand immediate satisfaction. (The word *id* is Latin for "it," suggesting the tentative way in which Freud explored the unconscious mind.) Rooted in our biology, the id

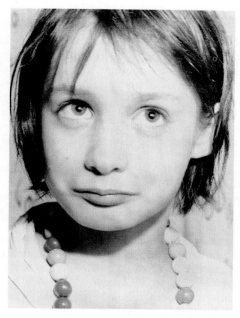

Like other children subjected to prolonged isolation, Genie never did develop a normal facility with language. Many researchers conclude that, unless a child learns language at an early age, this ability is permanently hindered. But others counter that children may well be intellectually damaged by such abuse. Thus, cases such as Genie do not settle "nature-nurture" debates about human development.

is present at birth, making a newborn a bundle of needs demanding attention, touching, and food. But society does not tolerate such a self-centred orientation, which is why one of the first words a child learns is "no."

To avoid frustration, the child learns to approach the world realistically. This accomplishment forms the second component of the personality, the **ego** (Latin for "I"), which is *a person's conscious efforts to balance innate, pleasure-seeking drives with the demands of society.* The ego arises as we gain awareness of our distinct existence; it reaches fruition as we come to understand that we cannot have everything we want.

Finally, the human personality develops the **superego** (Latin meaning "above" or "beyond" the ego), which is *the operation of culture within the individual.* With the emergence of the superego, we can see *why* we cannot have everything we want. The superego consists of cultural values and norms—internalized in the form of conscience—that define moral limits. The superego begins to emerge as children recognize parental control: it matures as they learn that their own behaviour and that of their parents—in fact, everyone's behaviour—reflect a broader system of cultural demands.

Personality Development

The id-centred child first encounters the world as a bewildering array of physical sensations. With gradual development of the superego, however, the child's comprehension extends beyond pleasure and pain to include the moral concepts of right and wrong. Initially, in other words, children can feel good only in the physical sense; but, after three or four years, they feel good or bad as they evaluate their own behaviour according to cultural standards.

Conflict between id and superego is ongoing; but, in a well-adjusted person, these opposing forces are managed by the ego. Unresolved conflicts, especially during childhood, typically result in personality disorders later on.

As the source of superego, culture operates to control human drives, a process Freud termed *repression*. All culture involves repression, since any society must coerce people to look beyond themselves. Often the competing demands of self and society are resolved through compromise. This process, which Freud called *sublimation*, transforms fundamentally selfish drives into socially acceptable activities. Sexual urges, for example, may lead to marriage, just as aggression gives rise to competitive sports.

Critical evaluation. Freud's work sparked controversy in his own lifetime, and some of that controversy still smoulders today. The world he knew vigorously repressed human sexuality, so that few of his contemporaries were prepared to concede that sex was a basic human need. More recently, Freud has come under fire for his depictions of humanity in allegedly male terms, thereby devaluing the lives of women (Donovan and Littenberg, 1982). But Freud provided a foundation that influenced virtually everyone who later studied the human personality. Of special importance to sociology is his notion that we internalize social norms and that childhood experiences have a lasting impact on socialization.

JEAN PIAGET: COGNITIVE DEVELOPMENT

Jean Piaget (1896–1980) is also among the foremost psychologists of the century. Much of his work centred on human *cognition*—how people think and understand. Early in his career, Piaget was fascinated by the behaviour of his three children, wondering not only what they knew but *how* they comprehended the world. His observations led him to conclude that children's thinking undergoes dramatic and patterned changes as they mature biologically and gain social experience. Piaget identified four stages of cognitive development.

The Sensorimotor Stage

Piaget's first step is the **sensorimotor stage**, *the level of human development at which individuals experience the world only through sensory contact*. At this stage, roughly the first two years of life, the infant explores the world with the five senses: touching, tasting, smelling, looking, and listening. Still unable to use symbols, "knowing" to infants amounts to direct, sensory experience.

The Preoperational Stage

The second plateau in Piaget's account of development is the **preoperational stage**, *the level of human development at which individuals first use language and other symbols*. At about age two, children begin to engage the world mentally; their capacity to *think* means reality moves beyond the senses. Children gain imagination and begin to appreciate the element of fantasy in fairy tales (Kohlberg and Gilligan, 1971; Skolnick, 1986). A child at this stage—roughly from age two to six—attaches names and meanings only to specific things. They can describe a favourite toy, for example, but cannot explain what kind of toy appeals to them.

Without abstract concepts, a child also cannot judge size, weight, or volume. In one of his best-known experiments, Piaget placed two identical glasses containing equal amounts of water on a table. He asked several children aged five and six if the amount in each glass was the same. They nodded that it was. The children then watched Piaget take one of the glasses and pour its contents into a taller, narrower glass, raising the level of the water. He asked again if each glass held the same amount. The typical five- and six-year-old now insisted that the taller glass held more water. But children of seven or eight, who are able to think abstractly, could comprehend that the amount of water remained the same.

We have all seen young children place their hands in front of their faces and exclaim, "You can't see me!" They assume that if they cannot see you, then you are unable to see them. This behaviour reveals that preoperational children maintain an egocentric view of the world: they cannot perceive yet that any situation may appear different to another person.

The Concrete Operational Stage

Next comes the **concrete operational stage**, *the level of development at which individuals first perceive causal connections in their surroundings*. At this level of development, typically between ages seven and eleven, children begin to grasp how and why things happen, gaining a far greater ability to manipulate their environments.

In addition, girls and boys now can attach more than one symbol to a particular event or object. For instance, if you say to a girl of five, "Today is Wednesday," she might respond, "No, it's my birthday!" indicating the ability to use just one symbol at a time. Within a few years, however, she would be able to respond, "Yes, this Wednesday is my birthday!"

Also during the concrete operational stage, children transcend earlier egocentrism so that they can now imagine themselves as others see them. As we shall explain shortly, the ability to "stand in another's shoes" is the key to participating in complex social activities, such as games.

The Formal Operational Stage

The final level in Piaget's model is the **formal operational stage**, *the level of human development at which individuals think abstractly and critically.* By about the age of twelve, children begin to reason in abstract terms rather than think only of concrete situations. If, for example, you were to ask a child of seven or eight, "What would you like to be when you grow up?" you might prompt a concrete response such as, "A teacher." But a teenager might well respond abstractly, saying "I would like a job that is exciting." At this point, young people's surging energy is matched by their creativity and imagination, sometimes evident in a passion for science fiction or poetry.

Also at this stage, children can comprehend metaphors. Hearing the phrase, "a penny for your thoughts," might lead a young child to ask for a coin, but the adolescent (preteen or teenager) will recognize a gentle invitation to intimacy. Then, too, adolescents begin to evaluate the world "in principle," a trait widely evident in teenagers.

Critical evaluation. While Freud envisioned personality as an ongoing battle between opposing forces of biology and society, Piaget viewed the human mind as active and creative. Piaget's contribution to understanding socialization lies in showing that the capacity to engage the world unfolds predictably as the result of biological maturation and increasing social experience.

Some challenge Piaget's scheme by questioning whether people in every society progress through all four of the stages he identified. For instance, living in a traditional society that changes very slowly is likely to inhibit the capacity for abstract and critical thought. Finally, even in modern society, as many as 30 percent of adults may never reach the formal operational stage at all (Kohlberg and Gilligan, 1971:1065). People exposed to little creative and imaginative thinking do not generally develop this capacity on their own.

In a well-known experiment, Jean Piaget demonstrated that children over the age of seven had entered the concrete operational stage of development because they could recognize that the quantity of liquid remained the same when poured from a wide beaker into a tall one.

LAWRENCE KOHLBERG: MORAL DEVELOPMENT

Lawrence Kohlberg (1981) used Piaget's theory as a springboard for a study of moral reasoning—the ways in which individuals come to judge situations as right or wrong. Following Piaget's lead, Kohlberg argues that moral development proceeds in stages.

Young children who experience the world in terms of pain and pleasure (Piaget's sensorimotor stage) are at the *preconventional* level of moral development. At this early stage, in other words, "rightness" amounts to "what serves my needs" or "what feels good to me."

The *conventional* level of moral development, Kohlberg's second stage, begins to appear among teenagers (corresponding to Piaget's last, formal operational stage). At this point, young people shed some of their selfishness and begin to define right and wrong in terms of what pleases parents and what is consistent with broader cultural norms. In reaching moral judgments, individuals at this stage try to assess intention in addition to simply observing what others do.

A final stage of moral development, the *postconventional* level, moves individuals beyond the specific norms of their society to ponder more abstract ethical principles. At this level, people philosophically reflect on the meaning of liberty, freedom, or justice. Individuals are now capable of actively criticizing their own society and of arguing, for instance, that what is traditional or legal still may not be right.

Critical evaluation. Like the work of Piaget, Kohlberg's model explains that moral development occurs in more or less definable stages. Thus, some of

Carol Gilligan, an educational psychologist at Harvard University, studies the personality development of young girls. In correcting the bias in research based on boys, she found that girls use different standards in making moral decisions. In later studies she found that self-esteem declines as girls go through adolescence.

the criticisms of Piaget's ideas also apply to Kohlberg's work. Whether this model applies to people in all societies, for example, remains unconfirmed. Then, too, many people apparently do not reach the postconventional level of moral reasoning, although exactly why is also, at present, an open question.

Another problem with Kohlberg's research is that his subjects were all boys. Kohlberg commits the research error, described in Chapter 2 ("Sociological Investigation"), of generalizing the results of male subjects to all of humanity. This problem prompted his colleague Carol Gilligan to investigate how gender affects moral reasoning.

CAROL GILLIGAN: BRINGING IN GENDER

Carol Gilligan, an educational psychologist at Harvard University, was disturbed that Kohlberg's research had overlooked girls. This narrow focus, as she sees it, is typical of much social science, which uses the behaviour of males as the norm for how everyone should act.

Therefore, Gilligan (1982) set out systematically to compare the moral development of females and males. Simply put, her conclusion is that the two sexes make moral judgments in different ways. Males, she contends, have a *justice perspective*, relying on formal rules and abstract principles to define right and wrong. Girls, on the other hand, have a *care and responsibility perspective*, judging a situation with an eye towards personal relationships and loyalties. Stealing, as boys see it, is wrong because it breaks the law and

violates common moral sentiments. Girls, however, are more likely to wonder why someone would steal, looking less severely upon an individual who felt forced to steal in order to, say, feed a hungry child.

Kohlberg treats the abstract male perspective as superior to the person-based female approach. Gilligan notes that impersonal rules have long dominated men's lives in the workplace. Concern for attachments, by contrast, has been more relevant to women's lives as wives, mothers, and caregivers. But, Gilligan asks, should we set male standards as the norms by which we evaluate everyone?

Gilligan's more recent work (1990) targets the issue of self-esteem. Her research team interviewed more than two thousand girls, ranging in age from six to eighteen years. Their responses made it clear that young girls start out with considerable confidence and self-esteem, only to find these vital resources slipping away as they pass through adolescence. An earlier Canadian survey by Bibby and Posterski (1985) had found that 35 percent of adolescent girls (compared to 23 percent of boys) said that they "felt inferior." Gilligan attributes the apparent lack of self-esteem among girls to our culture, which still defines the ideal woman as calm, controlled, and eager to please, and to the relative lack of women as teachers in later grades or as people in positions of authority.

Critical evaluation. Gilligan's work both sharpens our understanding of human development and highlights the problems related to gender in conducting and evaluating research. Yet what accounts for the differences she documents between females and males? Is it nature or nurture? Although it is impossible to rule out inherent differences between the sexes, Gilligan believes that these patterns reflect cultural conditioning.

GEORGE HERBERT MEAD: THE SOCIAL SELF

Our understanding of socialization stems in large part from the life work of George Herbert Mead (1863–1931), who described his approach as *social behaviourism* (1962; orig. 1934). While recognizing the power of the environment to shape human behaviour, Mead highlighted inward *thinking*, which he contended was humanity's defining trait.

The Self

Mead's central concept is the **self**, *a dimension of personality composed of an individual's self-awareness and self-image.* Mead's genius lay in seeing that the self is inseparable from society, a connection explained in a series of steps.

First, Mead asserted, *the self develops over time.* The self is not part of the body, and it does not exist at birth. Mead rejected the position that personality is guided by biological drives (as asserted by Freud) or biological maturation (as Piaget claimed). For Mead, the self develops *only* through social experience. In the absence of social interaction, as we see from the cases of isolated children, the body may grow but no self will emerge.

Second, Mead explained, *social experience is the exchange of symbols.* Using words, a wave of the hand, or a smile, people create meaning, which is a distinctively human experience. We can use reward and punishment to train a dog, after all, but the dog attaches no meaning to these actions. Human beings, by contrast, make sense of actions by inferring people's underlying intentions. In short, a dog responds to *what you do*; a human responds to *what you have in mind as you do it.*

Return to our friendly dog for a moment. You can train a dog to walk to the porch and return with an umbrella. But the dog grasps no meaning in the act, no intention behind the command. Thus, if the dog cannot find the umbrella, it is incapable of the *human* response of looking for a raincoat instead.

Third, says Mead, *to understand intention, you must imagine the situation from another person's point of view.* Using symbols, we can imaginatively place ourselves in another person's shoes and thus see ourselves as that person does. This capacity allows us to anticipate how others will respond to us even before we act. A simple toss of a ball requires stepping outside ourselves to imagine how another will respond to our throw. Social interaction, then, involves seeing ourselves as others see us, a process that Mead called *taking the role of the other.*

The Looking-Glass Self

In social life, other people represent the mirror or looking-glass in which we perceive ourselves. Charles Horton Cooley (1864–1929), one of Mead's colleagues, used the phrase **looking-glass self** to designate *the image people have of themselves based on how they believe others perceive them* (1964; orig. 1902). Whether we think of ourselves as clever or clumsy, worthy or worthless, depends in large measure on what we think others think of us. This insight goes a long way towards explaining Carol Gilligan's finding that young women lose self-confidence as they come of age in a society that discourages women from being too assertive.

The I and the Me

Our capacity to see ourselves through others implies that the self has two components. First, as we initiate

George Herbert Mead wrote: *"No hard-and-fast line can be drawn between our own selves and the selves of others."* The painting Manyness *by Rimma Gerlovinà and Valeriy Gerlovin conveys this important truth. Although we tend to think of ourselves as unique individuals, each person's characteristics develop in an ongoing process of interaction with others.*
Rimma Gerlovinà and Valeriy Gerlovin, *Manyness*, 1990. Courtesy Steinbaum Krauss Gallery, NY.

social action, *the self operates as a subject.* Humans are innately active and spontaneous, Mead claimed, dubbing this subjective element of the self the *I* (the subjective form of the personal pronoun).

Second, as we take the role of the other, *the self operates as an object.* Mead called this objective element of the self the *me* (the objective form of the personal pronoun). All social experience has both components: we initiate an action (the I-phase of self) and then we continue the action based on how others respond to us (the me-phase of self). Social experience is thus the interplay of the I and the me.

Mead stressed that thinking itself constitutes a social experience. Our thoughts are partly creative (representing the I), but in thought we also become objects to ourselves (representing the me) as we imagine how others will respond to our ideas.

Development of the Self

According to Mead, we gain a self as we learn to take the role of the other. Like Freud and Piaget, Mead regarded early childhood as the crucial time for this task, but the process goes on as long as we continue to have social experience.

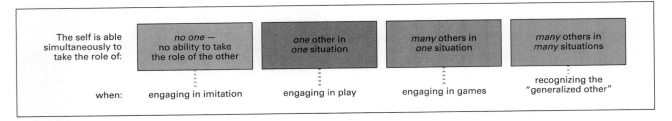

FIGURE 5–1 Building on Social Experience

George Herbert Mead described the development of the self as the process of gaining social experience. This is largely a matter of taking the role of the other with increasing sophistication.

Infants respond to others only in terms of *imitation*. They mimic behaviour without understanding underlying intentions. Unable to use symbols (thus, unable to take the role of the other), infants have no self.

Children first learn to use language and other symbols in the form of *play*, especially role playing. Initially, they model themselves on key people in their lives—such as parents—whom we call *significant others*. Playing "mommy and daddy," for example, helps children imagine the world from their parents' point of view.

Gradually, children learn to take the roles of several others at once. This skill is the key to moving from simple play (say, playing catch) involving one other to complex *games* (such as baseball) involving many others. Only by the age of seven or eight have most children acquired sufficient social experience to engage in team sports that demand taking the role of numerous others simultaneously.

Figure 5–1 shows the logical progression from imitation to play to games. But a final stage in the development of the self remains. A game involves taking the role of others in just one situation. But members of a society also need to see themselves as others in general might. In other words, we recognize that people in any situation throughout society share cultural norms and values, and we begin to incorporate these general patterns into the self. Mead used the term **generalized other** to refer to *widespread cultural norms and values that we use as references in evaluating ourselves*.

Of course, the emergence of the self is not the end of socialization. Quite the contrary: Mead claimed that socialization continues as long as we have social experience, so that changing circumstances can reshape who we are. The self may change, for example, with divorce, disability, or unexpected wealth. And we retain some control over this process as we respond to events and circumstances and thereby play a part in our own socialization.

At times people develop multiple selves. This process may be related to the experience of extreme abuse in children. Sylvia Fraser, a Canadian novelist, describes her own experience of sexual abuse and the development of another personality in the following passage:

> When the conflict caused by my sexual relationship with my father became too acute to bear, I created a secret accomplice for my daddy by splitting my personality in two. Thus, somewhere around the age of seven, I acquired another self with memories and experiences separate from mine, whose existence was unknown to me. My loss of memory was retroactive. I did not remember my daddy ever having touched me sexually. I did not remember ever seeing my daddy naked. I did not remember my daddy ever seeing me naked. In future, whenever my daddy approached me sexually I turned into my other self, and afterwards I did not remember anything that had happened. (Fraser, 1987:15)

Critical evaluation. The strength of Mead's work lies in exploring the nature of social experience itself. He succeeded in explaining how our use of symbols is the key that makes possible both self and society.

Some critics disparage Mead's view as radically social because it acknowledges no biological element in the emergence of the self. In this position, he stands apart from Freud (who identified general drives within the organism) and Piaget (whose stages of development are tied to biological maturation).

Mead's concepts of the I and the me are often confused with Freud's concepts of the id and the superego. But Freud rooted the id in the biological organism, while Mead rejected any link between the self and biology (although he never specified the origin of the I). Freud's concept of the superego and Mead's concept of the me both reflect the power of society to shape personality. But for Freud, superego and id are locked in continual combat. Mead, however, believed that the I and the me work closely and cooperatively together (Meltzer, 1978).

ERIK H. ERIKSON: EIGHT STAGES OF DEVELOPMENT

All of the thinkers we have discussed thus far highlight childhood as the crucial period during which personality emerges. Erik H. Erikson (1902–94) offered a broader view of socialization, claiming that personality continues to change throughout the life course as we face challenges linked to each stage of life. In Erikson's theory (1959), life holds eight key challenges.

Stage 1—Infancy: The challenge of trust (versus mistrust). Erikson explains that the first of life's challenges, faced by infants up to about eighteen months of age, is to gain a sense of trust that their world is a safe place. Family members play a key role in how the child addresses this challenge.

Stage 2—Toddler: The challenge of autonomy (versus doubt and shame). Up to about three years of age, young children must gain the skills to cope with the world in a confident way. Gaining self-control is a key part of this challenge.

Stage 3—Preschooler: The challenge of initiative (versus guilt). Four- and five-year-olds must learn to engage their surroundings—including people outside the family—or experience guilt at having failed to meet the expectations of parents and others.

Stage 4—Preadolescent: The challenge of industriousness (versus inferiority). Between about age six and thirteen, children enter school, establish peer groups, and strike out on their own more and more. They soon gain pride in their accomplishments or fear that they do not measure up.

Stage 5—Adolescence: The challenge of gaining identity (versus confusion). During the teenage years, young people struggle to establish their own identity. In part, we identify with others close to us; in part, we identify ourselves as unique. Almost all teens experience some confusion as they struggle to meet this challenge.

Stage 6—Young adulthood: The challenge of intimacy (versus isolation). A key challenge for young adults is establishing and maintaining intimate relationships with others. Falling in love (as well as keeping close friendships and working relationships) involves balancing the need to bond with the need to maintain a separate identity.

Stage 7—Middle adulthood: The challenge of making a difference (versus self-absorption). To Erikson, the key goal of middle age is contributing to the lives of others, in the family, at work, and in the larger world.

Failing to do so, we become stagnant, caught up in our limited concerns.

Stage 8—Old age: The challenge of integrity (versus despair). As we near the end of our lives, Erikson explains, we hope to look back on what we have accomplished with a sense of integrity and satisfaction. For those who have been self-absorbed (one thinks of the character Scrooge in Dickens' classic *A Christmas Carol*), old age brings only a sense of despair at missed opportunities.

Critical evaluation. Erikson's theory suggests that personality formation is an ongoing process, beginning in childhood and continuing until the end of one's life. Further, his model suggests that success at one stage (say, an infant gaining trust) sets the stage for happily resolving the challenge of the next stage of life.

One problem with a rigid model of stages is that everyone doesn't confront these challenges in the precise order noted by Erikson. Nor is it clear that failure to meet the challenge of one stage of life—say, forming intimate relationships in young adulthood—precludes experiencing success in later life by making a difference in the lives of others. A broader question, raised earlier in our discussion of Piaget's ideas, is whether people in other cultures and in other times in history would define a successful life in the same terms as Erikson does.

In short, then, Erikson's model helps us to make sense of the socialization process but may not be an actual description of how any of us experience the world. But his model suggests the need to examine how the family, the school, and other settings shape us, as well as how we change over the life course. We turn now to take a close look at these issues.

AGENTS OF SOCIALIZATION

Every social experience we have affects us in at least some small way. In modern industrial societies, however, several familiar settings have special significance in the socialization process.

THE FAMILY

The family is the most important agent of socialization because it represents the centre of children's lives. As we have seen, infants are almost totally dependent on others, and the responsibility of meeting their needs almost always falls on parents and other family members. At least until the onset of schooling, the family also shoulders the task of teaching children cultural values and attitudes about themselves and others.

Sociological research indicates that affluent parents tend to encourage creativity in their children while poor parents tend to foster conformity. While this general difference may be valid, parents at all class levels can and do provide loving support and guidance by simply involving themselves in their children's lives.

Family-based socialization is not all intentional. Children learn continuously from the kind of environment that adults create. Whether children learn to think of themselves as strong or weak, smart or stupid, loved or simply tolerated, and, as Erik Erikson suggests, whether they believe the world to be trustworthy or dangerous largely stem from this early environment.

Parenting styles aside, research points to the importance of parental *attention* in the social development of children. Physical contact, verbal stimulation, and responsiveness from parents and others all foster intellectual growth (Belsky, Lerner, and Spanier, 1984).

The family also confers on children a social position; that is, parents not only bring children into the physical world, they also place them in society in terms of race, ethnicity, religion, and class. In time, all these elements become part of a child's self-concept. Of course, some aspects of social position may change later on, but social standing at birth affects us throughout our lives.

Interestingly, children are aware from a very early age of the accessories of class. Canadian sociologists Bernd Baldus and Verna Tribe (1978) presented children in grades 1, 3, and 6 with sets of pictures of two men (one who was "well-dressed" and one who was casually dressed), two houses (one from a high-income area of the city), two dining rooms, and two cars (again reflecting expensive taste and less expensive taste). Children's ability to match person and appropriate taste level increased with their grade level, but it was not affected by gender, the school environment, or their own social class origin. Furthermore, the children were able to give "character" descriptions of the two men. The well-dressed man was described as cheerful, nice, smart, and likeable, while the casually dressed man was described as tough, lazy, and likely to swear, steal, drink, or be uncaring about his family. Clearly, when children learn about class, they are actually learning to assign different values to different people. This, in return, can have an effect on how they value themselves—in short, on their self-esteem.

SCHOOLING

Schooling enlarges children's social worlds to include people with social backgrounds that differ from their own. As children confront social diversity, they learn the significance society attaches to people's race and sex and often act accordingly. Studies document the tendency of children to cluster together in play groups composed of one race and gender (Lever, 1978; Finkelstein and Haskins, 1983).

Formally, schooling teaches children a wide range of knowledge and skills. But schools convey a host of other lessons informally through what sociologists call the *hidden curriculum*. Activities such as spelling bees and sports teach children key cultural values such as competitive achievement and success. Children also receive countless formal and informal messages promoting their society's way of life as morally good.

Moving beyond the personal web of family life, children entering school soon discover that evaluations of skills such as reading and arithmetic are based on impersonal, standardized tests. Here, the emphasis shifts from *who* they are to *how* they perform. Of course, the confidence or anxiety that children develop at home can have a significant effect on how well they perform in school (Belsky, Lerner, and Spanier, 1984).

School is also most children's first experience with rigid formality. The school day takes the form of a strict time schedule, subjecting children to impersonal regimentation and fostering punctuality. Perhaps not surprisingly, these are the same traits expected by most of the organizations that will employ them later in life.

Finally, schools socialize children with regard to gender. Raphaela Best (1983) points out that, in primary school, boys engage in more physical activities and spend more time outdoors, while girls tend to be more sedentary, sometimes even helping the teacher with various housekeeping chores. Gender distinctions continue in the higher grades and persist right through college or university. Women still tend to select degrees in the arts or humanities, while men tend towards the physical sciences, mathematics, and engineering. This remains the case even though, in some of Canada's medical, veterinary medicine and engineering programs, women are either a clear majority or a growing minority.

THE PEER GROUP

By the time they enter school, children have also discovered the **peer group**, *a social group whose members have interests, social position, and age in common*. A young child's peer group generally consists of neighbourhood playmates; later, peer groups are composed of friends from school or elsewhere.

Unlike the family and the school, the peer group allows young people to escape from the direct supervision of adults. With this newfound independence, members of peer groups gain valuable experience in forging social relationships on their own and developing a sense of themselves apart from their families. Peer groups also give young people the opportunity to discuss interests that may not be shared by adults (such as styles of dress and popular music) or tolerated comfortably by parents (such as drugs and sex).

For the young, the appeal of the peer group lies in the ever-present possibility of activity not condoned by adults. For the same reason, parents express concern about who their children's friends are. In a rapidly changing society, peer groups often rival parents in influence, as the attitudes of parents and children diverge along the lines of a "generation gap." The primacy of peer groups typically peaks during adolescence, as young people begin to break away from their families and think of themselves as responsible adults. At this stage of life, young people often display anxious conformity to peers because this new identity and sense of belonging eases some of the apprehension brought on by breaking away from the family.

The conflict between parents and peers may be more apparent than real, however, for even during adolescence children remain strongly influenced by their families. Peers may guide short-term concerns such as style of dress and musical taste, but parents retain greater sway over the long-term goals of their children. One study, for example, found that parents had more influence than even best friends on young people's educational aspirations (Davies and Kandel, 1981).

Finally, any neighbourhood or school operates as a social mosaic composed of numerous peer groups.

As we will see in Chapter 7 ("Groups and Organizations"), members tend to perceive their own peer group in positive terms while discrediting others. Moreover, individuals are also influenced by peer groups they would like to join, a process sociologists call **anticipatory socialization**, *social learning directed towards gaining a desired position*. In school, for example, young people may mimic the styles and banter of the group they hope to join. Or, at a later point in life, a young lawyer who hopes to become a partner in her law firm may conform to the attitudes and behaviour of the firm's partners to ease her way into this rarefied group.

THE MASS MEDIA

September 29, 1994, the Pacific Ocean nearing Japan. We have been out of sight of land for two weeks now, which renders this ship our entire social world. But more than land, many of the students miss television! Videotapes of Beverly Hills 90210 are a hot item.

The **mass media** are *impersonal communications directed to a vast audience*. The term "media" comes from Latin meaning "middle," suggesting that the media function to connect people. The development of *mass* media occurs as communications technologies (first newspapers and, more recently, radio and television) disseminate information on a mass scale.

In Canada today, the mass media have an enormous effect on our attitudes and behaviour. For this reason, they are an important component of the socialization process. Television, introduced in 1939, has rapidly become the dominant medium in Canada. About 98 percent of Canadians have colour televisions in their homes, about 80 percent have VCRs, and more than 75 percent have cable TV. Canadians spent almost $800 million on movies and video rentals in 1994, up from less than $200 million in 1979 (unfortunately, the vast majority of these expenditures, approximately $700 million, are on non-Canadian cultural products). By contrast, Canadians spent about $1.3 million on books, almost half of which was spent on books written and published in Canada (Serrill, 1995:41). As Figure 5–2 indicates, Canada has the second-highest rate of television ownership of the industrial countries.

Just how "glued to the television" are we? Television, on average, accounts for one of five waking hours of the typical Canadian (Young, 1990:231). Years before children learn to read, watching television becomes a regular routine and, as they grow up, young girls and boys spend as many hours in front of

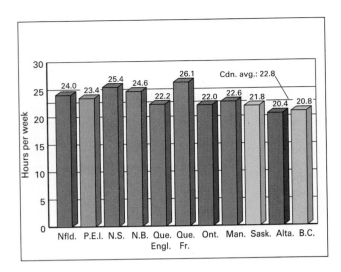

FIGURE 5–2 Television Viewing by Province, 1993

Source: Statistics Canada Catalogue No. 87–208.

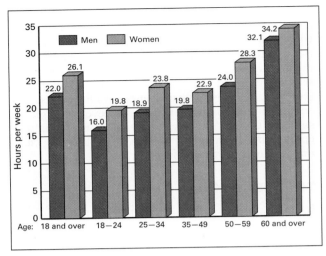

FIGURE 5–3 Television Viewing by Age and Sex, 1993

Source: Statistics Canada Catalogue No. 87–208.

a television as they do in school. Indeed, television consumes as much of children's time as interacting with parents does. The extent of television viewing by children is a concern to researchers who have found that television renders children more passive and less likely to use their imaginations (Singer and Singer, 1983; APA, 1993; Fellman, 1995).

Virtually everyone in Canada watches television, but not to an equal degree. Figures 5–3 and 5–4 show variation in television watching by province, age, and gender.

Comedian Fred Allen once quipped that we call television a "medium" because it is rarely well done. For a variety of reasons, television (as well as all mass media) has provoked plenty of criticism. Some cite biases in television programming: liberal (or left-leaning) critics maintain that television shows mirror our society's patterns of inequality and rarely challenge the status quo. That is, TV shows have traditionally portrayed men and women according to cultural stereotypes, placing men in positions of power and relegating women to the roles of mothers or subordinates. Moreover, television shows have long portrayed well-to-do people favourably, while depicting less affluent individuals (Archie Bunker is the classic example) as ignorant and wrongheaded. And, although racial and ethnic minorities in the United States tend to watch more television than the white majority, until recent decades minorities have been all but absent from U.S. TV programming (Gans, 1980; Cantor and Pingree, 1983; Ang, 1985; Parenti, 1986; Brown, 1990). The "Social Diversity" box on page 126 deals with the characterization of minorities in the television industry,

much of the programming of which originates in the U.S. In 1994, 53 percent of the television programs watched by Canadians originated in the United States, whereas only 36 percent originated in Canada.

On the other side of the fence, conservative critics charge that the television and film industries are dominated by a cultural elite that is far more liberal than the population as a whole. Especially in recent years, they maintain, the media have become increasingly "politically correct," advancing various socially liberal causes, including feminism and gay rights (Lichter, Rothman, and Rothman, 1986; Woodward, 1992; Prindle, 1994; Prindle and Endersby, 1993; Rothman, Powers, and Rothman, 1993).

A final issue concerns violence and the mass media. In 1996, the American Medical Association (AMA) expressed its concern that violence portrayed through the mass media—especially television and films—is a hazard to the public's well-being. An AMA survey (1996) found that three-fourths of U.S. adults have either walked out of a movie or turned off a television program due to objectionable levels of violence. A majority of parents also express concerns about sexual and violent content in popular music, video games, and on the Internet.

Two similar neighbouring towns in British Columbia provided a unique opportunity to study the impacts of television violence, as one of the towns had received television before the other. By measuring the level of aggressive behaviour in children in both communities, initially and two years after the arrival of television in the second town, Williams (1986) was able to demonstrate that, after the arrival of television, the children caught up—in terms of aggressiveness—to those in the neighbouring community that had had longer exposure.

The federal government turned its attention to the impact of television violence on the behaviour of children through a House of Commons committee. The committee concluded that the evidence of a link was inconclusive and contradictory: nonetheless, it recommended that legislation should be implemented to control extremely violent forms of entertainment and that a classification system to help parents to protect their children from exposure to television violence be developed (Canada, 1993).

The 1990s witnessed sustained activity on the part of the Canadian Radio-television and Telecommunications Commission (CRTC) regarding television violence. Two studies commissioned by the CRTC reported in 1992, concluding that there is a link between violence on television and violence in society, though it is not one of direct cause and effect. The Action Group for Violence on Television (AGVOT) was set up with representatives from advertisers, producers, broadcasters, and cable companies. This committee developed classification guidelines and worked with other groups to regulate programming and broadcasting. They have worked closely with American legislators and producers on regulation and in the development of the V-chip, which will allow parents to block unduly violent programming from their televisions. The Canadian Association of Broadcasters (CAB) decided that *Mighty Morphin Power Rangers* violated its violence code and was instrumental in getting YTV and Global to remove the program from their schedules in 1994. The CRTC Web site (www.crtc.gc.ca) provides a detailed chronology of reports, regulations, and actions taken on television violence.

Television and the other mass media have enriched our lives, generating a wide range of entertaining and educational programming. Moreover, the media increase our understanding of diverse cultures and provoke discussion of current issues. At the same time, the power of the media—especially television—to shape how we think continues to fuel controversy on many fronts. Computers and the Internet complicate the picture further because governments cannot censor or otherwise control the flow of information into or out of their countries.

Finally, other spheres of life beyond those just described also play a part in social learning. For most people in Canada, these include religious organizations, the workplace, and social clubs. As a result, socialization inevitably proceeds inconsistently as we absorb different information from disparate sources. In the end, socialization is not a simple learning process; it is a complex balancing act in which we

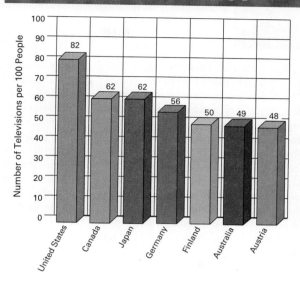

GLOBAL SNAPSHOT

FIGURE 5-4 Television Ownership in Global Perspective

SOURCE: U.S. Census Bureau (1996).

encounter a wide range of ideas as we try to form our own distinctive personalities and world views.

SOCIALIZATION AND THE LIFE COURSE

Although childhood is critical to the socialization process, learning continues throughout our lives. The following overview of the life course reveals that our society organizes human experience according to age, resulting in distinctive stages of life: childhood, adolescence, adulthood, and, finally, old age.

CHILDHOOD

Michael Jordan recently came under fire for endorsing Nike athletic shoes because the sneakers are made in Taiwan and Indonesia by children, who do not go to school but work full-time for roughly fifty cents an hour. Such wages are typical for workers in poor countries, which include perhaps 200 million of the world's children (Gibbs, 1996).

Today, we think of *childhood*—roughly the first twelve years of life—as a time of freedom from the burdens of the adult world. But until about a century ago, children in Europe and North America shouldered similar burdens to those of adults. According to

How Do the Media Portray Minorities?

On an old *Saturday Night Live* sketch, Ron Howard tells comedian Eddie Murphy about a new film, *Night Shift*, in which two mortuary workers decide to open their own sideline business—a prostitution ring. Murphy asks whether any Black actors are in the film; Howard shakes his head "no." Murphy then thunders, "A story about two pimps and there wasn't no brothers in it? I don't know whether to thank you or punch you in the mouth, man!"

Murphy's ambivalence points up twin criticisms of the mass media. The first is that films and television portray minorities in stereotypical fashion, the second is that they are excluded altogether (Press, 1993:219). Certainly, at the beginning of the television age in the 1950s, minorities were almost nowhere to be found on television and in films. Even the wildly successful 1950s comedy *I Love Lucy* was originally turned down by every major television studio because it featured Desi Arnaz—a Cuban—in a starring role. While the early Westerns presented stereotypical images of cowboys and "Indians," at least one of them starred an authentic Canadian aboriginal—Six Nations Jay Silverheels as Tonto, loyal sidekick of the Lone Ranger. Since then, the media have steadily included more minorities, so that the issue of visibility has declined in importance. Since a majority of the programming watched by Canadians is of U.S. origin, changes there have immediate impact here.

But the second issue is just as important: *how* the media portray minorities. The few African-Americans who managed to break into television in the 1950s (for example, the infamous Amos and Andy or Jack Benny's butler, Rochester) were confined to stereotypical roles portraying uneducated, low-status people. More recently, many television shows feature Black stars: some are situation comedies ("sitcoms") replete with crude humour and bumbling characters; others, though humorous, depict upper-status Black families; several soap operas (e.g., *The Young and the Restless, As the World Turns*) reveal Blacks as young professionals—among them physicians, hospital administrators, lawyers, fashion photographers, successful models, and corporate vice-presidents. Oprah Winfrey, host of her own talk show, is very successful, very wealthy, and in a position of power or authority relative to her guests.

The portrayal of aboriginal people has changed from the days when made-up white actors played "Indians" to American cowboys. Two aboriginal performers from Canada, Chief Dan George (B.C.) and Graham Greene (Ontario), helped to redefine the role of the native in the major U.S. films *Little Big Man* and *Dances with Wolves*. Greene continues to appear in a wide range of film and television roles. In the meantime, singer/actor Buffy Sainte-Marie (Saskatchewan) provided early exposure to youngsters through her long-term involvement with *Sesame Street*. The popular Canadian production *North of 60* depicts native people in the whole range of roles common to northern communities. Inuit singer Susan Aglukark (NWT) has changed the sound of Canadian music, just as Shania Twain (whose name means "on my way" in Ojibwa and who was raised for a time by an Ojibwa stepfather) has changed the sound of country music.

Significant change has taken place in news reporting on the CBC and other U.S. and Canadian television channels. Representation of social diversity today is greater than it was even a decade ago. In large measure, this stems from deliberate personnel policies responding to demands for political correctness and appealing to diverse audiences. Increasingly, the news is conveyed to us by women, members of visible minorities and, in Canada, people with names that are neither English or French. Even traditional white male areas such as sports, stock market coverage and business analysis, and war zone activity increasingly are reported by women and visible minorities.

Certainly, the mass media in Canada and the U.S. can boast of improvement in the portrayal of minorities: the perpetuation of old stereotypes has given way to a depiction of minority individuals (based on race, ethnicity, or gender) in a wide range of occupations and social class locations. Some critics would argue that depiction of minorities in high-status positions is unrealistic, masking the fact that minorities continue to face major barriers to full participation; on the other hand, such representation does reflect the fact that visible and ethnic minorities as well as women—in the *real* world—are to be found in all social class categories.

---

historian Philippe Ariès (1965), the whole idea of "childhood" is a fairly recent invention. Once children were able to survive without constant care, medieval Europeans expected them to take their place in the world as working adults. Although "child labour" is now prohibited in Canada, this historical pattern persists in poor societies today, especially in Africa and Asia. Global Map 5–1 shows that work is commonplace for children in low-income nations of the world.

Certainly, our notion of childhood is grounded in important biological differences that set youngsters apart from adults. But, as historical and global comparisons show us, the concept of "childhood" is also rooted in culture. In rich countries, not everyone has to work. In addition, societies with sophisticated technology extend childhood so that young people have time to learn the many complex skills required for adult activities.

Recently, some social scientists have declared that our conception of childhood is changing yet again. In an age of high divorce rates, mothers and fathers absorbed in the workforce, and an increasing level of "adult" programming on television, they point out, children are no longer protected from grown-up concerns as they were in the past. Rather, we are seeing the development of a "hurried child" syndrome, meaning that children have to grapple with sex, drugs, and violence as well as fend more and more for themselves (Elkind, 1981; Winn, 1983). Critics of this view, however, counter that there is no convincing evidence yet of any dramatic shift in our society's conception of childhood. Further, they note, the "hurried child" thesis overlooks the fact that children in the lower class have always assumed adult responsibilities sooner than their middle- and upper-class counterparts (Lynott and Logue, 1993).

ADOLESCENCE

As industrialization gradually framed childhood as a distinct stage of life, adolescence emerged as a buffer between childhood and adulthood. Corresponding roughly to the preteen and teenage years, this is the stage of life when young people establish some independence and learn specialized skills required for adult life.

We generally associate adolescence with emotional and social turmoil: young people experience conflict with their parents and struggle to develop their own, separate identities. Since adolescence commonly begins at the onset of puberty, we may be tempted to attribute teenage turbulence to physiological changes. However, comparative research indicates that, like childhood, adolescence is a variable product of culture. Studying the Samoan Islanders in the 1920s, Margaret Mead (1961; orig. 1928) found little evidence of stress among teenagers; there, children appeared to move easily to adult standing. Our society, however, defines childhood and adulthood more in opposing terms, making the transition between the two stages of life more difficult.

Consider the ambivalence our society displays towards young people on the brink of adulthood. Eighteen-year-olds can vote and they may face the adult responsibility of going to war; yet in some provinces we deny them the privilege of drinking alcohol. Similarly, our way of life also presents mixed

There is no better example of how parents can "hurry" their children into adulthood than beauty pageants for young girls. In this scene from a Georgia "baby beauty pageant," we see a girl not even old enough for school straining to embody traits usually associated with grown-up women. What are these traits? Would you want your daughter to compete in such pageants? Why or why not?

messages when it comes to adolescent sexuality. The mass media often encourage sexual activity, while parents urge restraint; for their part, schools try to discourage casual sex even as they hand out condoms to students (Gibbs, 1993).

As is true of all stages of life, the experience of adolescence varies according to social background. Most young people from working-class families move directly from high school into the adult world of work and parenting. Wealthier teens, however, have the resources to attend university and perhaps graduate school, which may extend adolescence into their late twenties and even their thirties. For different reasons, of course, poverty may also extend adolescence. Especially in the inner cities, many young members of minority groups cannot attain full adult standing because jobs are not available.

ADULTHOOD

Adulthood is the period during which most of life's accomplishments typically occur, including pursuing careers and raising families. And, too, especially in later adulthood, people reflect on what they have been able to accomplish, perhaps with great satisfaction or with the sobering realization that many of the idealistic dreams of their youth will never come true.

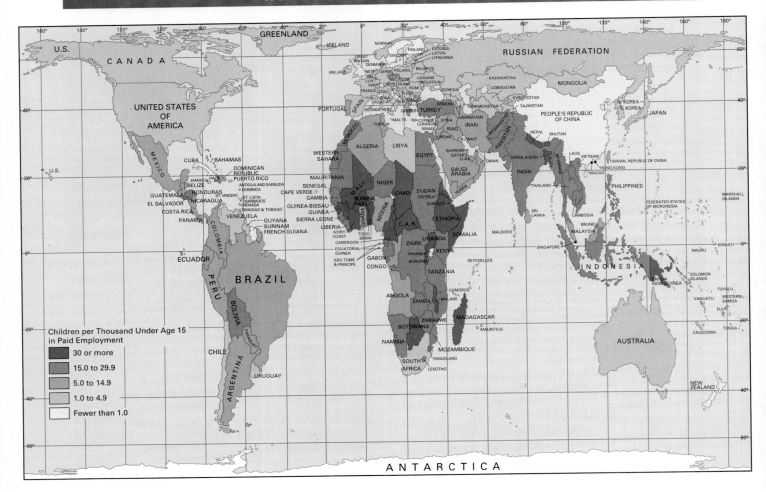

GLOBAL MAP 5–1 Child Labour in Global Perspective

Industrialization prolongs childhood and discourages children from engaging in work and other activities deemed suitable only for adults. Thus, child labour is relatively uncommon in Canada and other industrial societies. In less industrialized nations of the world, however, children serve as a vital economic asset, and they typically begin working as soon as they are able.

Source: *Peters Atlas of the World* (1990).

Early Adulthood

By the onset of adulthood, personalities are largely formed. Even so, a marked shift in an individual's life situation—brought on by unemployment, divorce, or serious illness—can result in significant change to the self (Dannefer, 1984).

Early adulthood—from age twenty to about age forty—is generally a time of pursuing many goals set earlier in life. Young adults break free of parents and learn to manage for themselves a host of day-to-day responsibilities. With the birth of children, parents draw on experiences from their own upbringing, although, as children, they may have only vaguely perceived what adult life entailed. In addition, young adults typically try to master patterns of intimate living with another person who may have just as much to learn.

Early adulthood is also a period of juggling conflicting priorities: parents, partner, children, schooling, and work (Levinson et al., 1978). Women, especially, confront the difficulty of "doing it all," since our culture still confers on them primary responsibility for child rearing and household chores, even if they have demanding occupations outside the home (Hochschild, 1989).

Middle Adulthood

Young adults usually cope optimistically with such tensions. But in middle adulthood—roughly age forty to age sixty—people begin to sense that marked improvements in life circumstances are less likely. The distinctive character of middle adulthood is the capacity to assess actual achievements in light of earlier expectations. At midlife, people also become more aware of the fragility of health, which the young typically take for granted.

Some women who have already spent many years raising a family find middle adulthood especially challenging. Children grow up and require less attention, husbands may become absorbed in their careers, leaving some women with spaces in their lives that they find difficult to fill. Women who divorce during middle adulthood may experience serious financial problems (Weitzman, 1985). For all these reasons, an increasing number of women mark middle adulthood by undertaking the challenge of returning to school and then launching careers.

Growing older means that both men and women face the reality of physical decline, but our society's traditional socialization has made this prospect more painful for women. Because good looks have been defined as more important for women, wrinkles, weight gain, and loss of hair are more traumatic for them. Men, of course, have their own particular difficulties. Some confront limited achievement, knowing that their careers are unlikely to change for the better. Others, now realizing that the price of career success has been neglect of family or personal health, harbour uncertainties about their self-worth even as they bask in the praise of others (Farrell and Rosenberg, 1981). Women, too, who devote themselves single-mindedly to careers in early adulthood may experience regrets about what they have given up in pursuit of occupational success.

Constance Beresford-Howe, a Canadian novelist, often writes about people who make immense changes during adulthood. Her novel *A Serious Widow* begins with the funeral of Rowena Hill's husband of thirty years, and Rowena's discovery that he was a bigamist. Over the course of the novel, as Rowena re-edits her biography and the history of her marriage, she makes a number of surprising changes in her lifestyle and relationships. In the following scene, she reviews her wardrobe, finds it inadequate, and sews herself a new outfit:

> Refreshed by this encounter, I wrap myself in a towel and cross to the bedroom to dress. But a survey of the cupboard (half empty, now, with most of Edwin's things packed away) does nothing to encourage the idea of rebirth. My clothes are all depressing reminders of many things, in particular my dressmaking inadequacies. The brown checked skirt that never did hang quite straight. The grey dress I made three years ago that looks even more boring whenever I try to brighten it up with a new scarf or belt. The beige skirt, baggy at the seat with age. Fretfully I push these dreary articles about on their hangers. Catching my eye in the mirror, it occurs to me that I look better in the bath towel pegged under my arms than in any of my clothes. The ruby colour and the soft pile are both pleasing. Turning first one way and then another, I look at my reflection thoughtfully. … Certainly it would take a bolder spirit than mine to wear such a rich red any place where other people could see it. But just to lounge around in at home … The longer I look at myself the better I like the way that ruby colour makes my hair look darker and my shoulders whiter.
>
> After a minute, I pull the matching towels out of the linen cupboard. There is enough material for a wraparound skirt and a sort of tabard top. Half furtively I uncover the sewing machine and sit down. A few hours with scissors and thread … Why not? It's not exactly fishing, Ethel, but maybe it's not far off. (Beresford-Howe, 1991:69–70)

Rowena Hill's midlife crisis may well have involved some of the personal transitions we have described. But her story also illustrates that the greatest productivity and personal satisfaction may occur after the middle of life. Socialization in our youth-oriented culture has convinced many people (especially the young) that life ends at forty. But as life expectancy in Canada has increased, such limiting notions have begun to dissolve. Major transformations may become less likely, but the potential for learning and new beginnings still infuses this stage of life with promise.

OLD AGE

Old age comprises the later years of adulthood and the final stage of life itself, beginning in about the

The world's cultures display strikingly different attitudes towards death. Chinese families in Manila, capital city of the Philippines, build tombs big enough to allow the living to gather for meals in the presence of the dead.

mid-sixties. Here again, societies attach different meanings to a time of life. Pre-industrial people typically grant elders great influence and prestige. As explained in Chapter 14 ("Aging and the Elderly"), traditional societies confer on older people control of most of the land and other wealth; moreover, since their societies change slowly, older people amass a lifetime of wisdom, which earns them great respect (Sheehan, 1976; Hareven, 1982).

In industrial societies, however, most younger people work apart from the family, becoming more independent of their elders. Rapid change and our society's youth orientation combine to define what is older as unimportant or even obsolete. To younger people, then, the elderly are dismissed as unaware of new trends and fashions, and their knowledge and experience are often deemed irrelevant.

No doubt, however, this anti-elderly bias will diminish as the proportion of older people increases. The proportion of our population over sixty-five has almost tripled since the beginning of this century and life expectancy is still increasing. Most men and women in their mid-sixties (the "young elderly") can look forward to decades more of life. Looking to the next century, Statistics Canada (1989a) predicts that the fastest-growing segment of our population will be those over eighty-five, whose numbers will soar sixfold.

At present, this final phase of the life course differs in an important way from earlier stages. Growing up typically means entering new roles and assuming new responsibilities; growing old, by contrast, entails the opposite experience of leaving roles that provided both satisfaction and social identity. Retirement, for example, sometimes fits the common image of being a period of restful activity. But it may mean the loss of valued activity and, sometimes, outright boredom. Like any life transition, retirement demands learning new and different patterns while simultaneously *un*learning familiar routines. A nearly equal transition is required of the nonworking wife or husband, who must now accommodate a partner spending more time at home.

DYING

Through most of human history, death caused by disease or accident came at any stage of life because of low living standards and primitive medical technology. Today, however, the average life span is seventy-seven years in Canada (Serrill, 1995:29). Therefore, although most senior citizens can look forward to more than another decade of life, growing old cannot be separated from eventual physical decline and ultimate death.

As the proportion of women and men in old age increases, we can expect our culture to become more comfortable with the idea of death. In recent years, for example, people in Canada and elsewhere have been discussing death more openly than decades ago, and the trend is to view dying as preferable to painful or prolonged suffering in hospitals or at home. Moreover, more married couples now anticipate their own deaths with legal and financial planning. This openness may ease the disorientation that generally accompanies the death of a spouse—a greater problem for women, who usually outlive their husbands.

The demand by guards that new prisoners publicly disrobe is more than a matter of issuing new clothing. Such a degrading ritual is also the first stage in the process by which the staff in a total institution attempts to break down an individual's established social identity.

THE LIFE COURSE: AN OVERVIEW

This brief examination of the life course points to two major conclusions. First and more important, although each stage of life is linked to the biological process of aging, the life course is largely a social construction. For this reason, people in other societies may experience a stage of life quite differently, or not at all. Second, each stage of any society's life course presents characteristic problems and transitions that involve learning something new and unlearning familiar routines.

Note, too, that although societies organize human experience according to age, age cannot be isolated from the effects of other forces, such as class, race, ethnicity, and gender. Thus, the general patterns we have described are all subject to further modification as they apply to various categories of people.

Finally, people's life experiences also vary depending on when, in the history of the society, they were born. A **cohort** is *a category of people with a common characteristic, usually age.* Age cohorts are likely to have been influenced by the same economic and cultural trends, so that members typically display similar attitudes and values (Riley, Foner, and Waring, 1988). The lives of women and men born at mid-century, for example, were framed by economic expansion that gave them a sense of optimism uncommon among today's college and university students, who have grown up in an age of economic uncertainty.

RESOCIALIZATION: TOTAL INSTITUTIONS

A final type of socialization involves people being confined—often against their will—in prisons or mental hospitals. This is the special world of the **total institution**, *a setting in which people are isolated from the rest of society and manipulated by an administrative staff.*

According to Canadian sociologist Erving Goffman (1961), total institutions have three distinctive characteristics. First, staff members supervise all spheres of daily life, including where residents (often called "inmates") eat, sleep, and work. Second, a rigid system provides inmates with standardized food, sleeping quarters, and activities. Third, formal rules and daily schedules dictate when, where, and how inmates perform virtually every part of their daily routines.

Total institutions impose such regimentation with the goal of **resocialization**, *radically altering an inmate's personality through deliberate manipulation of the environment.* The power of a total institution to resocialize is also enhanced by its forcible segregation of inmates from the "outside" by means of physical barriers such as walls and fences topped with barbed wire and guard towers, barred windows, and locked doors. With inmates cut off in this way, their entire world can be manipulated by the administrative staff to produce lasting change—or at least immediate compliance—in the inmates.

Resocialization is a two-part process. First, the staff tries to erode the new inmate's autonomy and

Ontario's First Boot Camp as a Total Institution

Resocialization in a total institution actually can change a human being, or so the theory goes. The rebuilding of the self is extremely difficult, however, and no two people are likely to respond to any program in precisely the same way. Resocialization is the goal of prisons, psychiatric hospitals and, in this case, Operation Turnaround, Strict Discipline Facility—otherwise known as boot camp. The key to the operation of a total institution, such as a boot camp, is complete control of the environment so that only desired behaviours are permitted.

Staff from military and social work backgrounds maintain discipline but are expected to treat inmates (staff call them "cadets") with respect. In return, inmates are expected to refer to staff as "Sir" or "Ma'am" (they are made do push-ups if they forget). The atmosphere is stern, but not brutal: inmates do not experience physical punishment or abuse.

Upon arrival, young offenders get military-style brush cuts and learn to make their beds and tie their shoes the required way. They are introduced to discipline and plenty of it! Up at 6 a.m., lights out at 10 p.m., tidiness in austere surroundings, and lots of marching to wherever they otherwise might have sauntered.

Other detention centres may allow inmates to play pool, watch television, play ping-pong or video games, and even to select their own food. Idle moments also may be part of one's day. None of these are on the agenda at the Strict Discipline Facility: plenty of military marching on the tarmac, more marching to and from various activities, calisthenics and some outdoor basketball and volleyball, three hours of school plus homework, and meals fill up the typical day.

Towards the end of their terms, the inmates build cedar canoes and then take those canoes, under staff supervision, on a wilderness adventure.

The program is designed, ultimately, to change cadet behaviour, attitudes, and values as well as to foster respect for themselves and for others. "Chins up. Look proud," they are told, in hopes that looking proud will make them *feel* proud. Those running the program believe that young people who respect themselves should be less inclined to return to a life of crime.

identity through what Goffman describes as "abasements, degradations, humiliations, and profanations of self" (1961:14). For example, inmates must surrender personal possessions, including clothing and grooming articles used to maintain their distinctive appearances. In their place, the staff provides standard-issue items that make everyone look alike. In addition, inmates all receive standard haircuts, so that, once again, what was personalized becomes uniform. The staff also subjects new inmates to "mortifications of self," including searches, medical examinations, fingerprinting, and then assigns them a serial number. Once inside the walls, individuals surrender the right to privacy; guards may demand that inmates undress publicly as part of the admission procedure, and they routinely monitor their living quarters.

The second part of the resocialization process includes efforts to systematically build a different self. The staff manipulates inmate behaviour through a system of rewards and punishments. The privilege of keeping a book, watching television, or making a telephone call may seem trivial to outsiders, but, in the rigid environment of the total institution, this can form a powerful motivation to conform. Bucking the system, on the other hand, means that privileges will be withdrawn or, in more serious cases, that the inmate will suffer further isolation or additional punishment. The duration of confinement in a prison or mental hospital also depends on an inmate's display of cooperation with official rules and regulations. Goffman emphasizes that the staff also seeks to win the hearts and minds of inmates, punishing even those who toe the line but have an "attitude problem."

In principle, total institutions can bring about considerable change in inmates. Yet the resocialization process is extremely complex, and no two people respond to such programs in precisely the same way (Irwin, 1980). Moreover, while some inmates are deemed "rehabilitated" or "recovered," others display little change at all, and still others only become confused, hostile, or bitter. Furthermore, over a long period of time, a rigidly controlled environment may destroy a person's capacity for independent living; such *institutionalized* personalities lose the capacity to deal with the demands of the outside world.

Continue the debate ...

1. *Do you feel that boot camp will actually turn around young offenders to the point where they will be less likely to reoffend?*
2. *Does the punishment fit the crime, or is it "cruel and unusual punishment" that occurs in this kind of setting?*
3. *If you were to be convicted of a crime, would you prefer to be sent to boot camp or a conventional youth detention centre (or secure-custody facility)? Why?*
4. *Does resocialization necessitate the repudiation of prior socialization?*

SOURCE: Edwards (1997).

Newly arrived young offenders or cadets (in black) march in front of their guards at Operation Turnaround, a strict discipline facility or "boot camp" in prime cottage country near Orillia, Ontario. The staff hopes that by the time inmates leave—in four to six months—they will have learned to like discipline and structure. In theory, the thirty-two repeat offenders will leave the facility with greater self-esteem, new attitudes and values, and a reduced likelihood of returning to crime.

SUMMARY

1. For individuals, socialization is the process of building our humanity and particular identity through social experience. For society as a whole, socialization is the means by which one generation transmits culture to the next.

2. A century ago, people thought most human behaviour was guided by biological instinct. Today, the nature-nurture debate has tipped the other way as we understand human behaviour to be primarily a product of a social environment. But the two concepts are not entirely opposed, since it is human nature to nurture.

3. The permanently damaging effects of social isolation reveal the importance of social experience to human development.

4. Sigmund Freud envisioned the human personality as composed of three parts. The *id* represents general human drives (the life and death instincts), which Freud claimed were innate. The *superego* embodies cultural values and norms internalized by individuals. The *ego* operates to resolve competition between the demands of the id and the restraints of the superego.

5. Jean Piaget believed that human development reflects both biological maturation and increasing social experience. In his view, socialization proceeds through four major stages of development: sensorimotor, preoperational, concrete operational, and formal operational.

6. Lawrence Kohlberg applies Piaget's approach to the issue of moral development. Individuals, he claims, first judge rightness in preconventional terms, according to their individual needs. Next, conventional moral reasoning takes account of the attitudes of parents and the norms of the larger society. Finally, postconventional moral reasoning allows for a philosophical critique of society itself.

7. Beginning with a critique of Kohlberg's reliance on male subjects, Carol Gilligan discovered that gender affects moral reasoning. Females, she asserts, look to the effect of decisions on relationships,

while males rely more on abstract standards of rightness.

8. To George Herbert Mead, socialization is based on the emergence of the self, which he viewed as partly autonomous (the I) and partly guided by society (the me). Mead contended that, beginning with imitation, the self develops through play and games and eventually recognizes the "generalized other."

9. Charles Horton Cooley used the term "looking-glass self" to underscore that the self is influenced by how we think others respond to us.

10. Erik H. Erikson identified characteristic challenges that individuals face at each stage of life from childhood to old age.

11. Commonly the first setting of socialization, the family has the greatest influence on a child's attitudes and behaviour.

12. School exposes children to greater social diversity and introduces the experience of impersonal evaluation. In addition to formal lessons, schools informally teach a wide range of cultural ideas, including attitudes about competitiveness and achievement.

13. Members of youthful peer groups are less subject to adult supervision than they are in the family or in school. Peer groups take on great significance among adolescents.

14. The mass media, especially television, have a considerable impact on the socialization process. The average Canadian child now spends about 22.5 hours a week watching television.

15. As with each phase of the life course, the characteristics of childhood are socially constructed. Medieval Europeans scarcely recognized childhood as a stage of life. In rich, industrial nations such as Canada, people define childhood as much different from adulthood.

16. Adolescence, the transition between childhood and adulthood, is considered a difficult period in our society. This is not the case in all societies, however.

17. During early adulthood, socialization involves settling into careers and raising families. Later adulthood is marked by considerable reflection about initial goals in light of actual achievements.

18. In old age, people make many transitions, including retirement. While the elderly typically enjoy high prestige in pre-industrial societies, industrial and post-industrial societies are more youth-oriented, relegating older people to the sidelines of life.

19. Members of rich societies typically fend off death until old age. Adjustment to the death of a spouse (an experience more common to women) and acceptance of one's own death are part of socialization for the elderly.

20. Total institutions, such as prisons and mental hospitals, strive for resocialization—radically changing the inmate's personality.

21. Socialization demonstrates the power of society to shape our thoughts, feelings, and actions. Yet, as free humans, we also have the capacity to act on society and, in so doing, shape our lives and our world.

CRITICAL THINKING QUESTIONS

1. What do cases of social isolation teach us about the importance of social experience to human development?

2. Describe the two sides of the nature-nurture debate. In what sense are human nature and nurture not opposed to one another?

3. What common themes are found in the theories of Freud, Piaget, Kohlberg, Gilligan, Mead, and Erikson? On what key points do they differ?

4. Proportionately speaking, television features far more physically attractive people than exist in the population as a whole. Develop arguments for and against this practice. How does this practice affect the way we think about others—and ourselves?

SOCIOLOGY APPLIED

1. Along with several members of your sociology class, gather some data: each person should ask a variety of classmates to identify traits they assume are elements of "human nature." Get together later to compare notes and assess the extent to which the traits noted are the product of "nature" or "nurture."

2. See if you can find a copy of the video (or book) *Lord of the Flies*, a tale by William Golding based

on a Freudian model of personality. Jack (and his hunters) represent the power of the id; Piggy consistently opposes them as the superego; Ralph stands between the two as the ego, the voice of reason. Golding wrote the book after participating in the carnage of the D-Day landing in France. Do you agree with his belief that the human proclivity for violence (as well as our capacity for cultural restraint) is basic to our nature?

3. Give some thought to your own personality. Think about the traits you think characterize you and, if you have the courage, ask several others who know you well what they think of you. To what extent did you learn these traits?

4. Watch several hours of prime-time programming on television. Keep track of every time any element of violence is shown. For fun, assign each program a "YIP rating," for the number of Years in Prison a person would serve for committing all the violent acts you witness (Fobes, 1996). On the basis of observing this small (and unrepresentative) sample of programs, what are your conclusions?

WEBLINKS

www.infidels.org/library/historical/charles_darwin/index.html
Fully searchable complete texts of Darwin's major works: *On the Origin of Species* (1859), *The Descent of Man* (1871), and *The Voyage of the Beagle* (1909).

plaza.interport.net/nypsan/
FreudNet, a site produced by the New York Psychoanalytic Institute, includes links to libraries, museums, and biographical materials, as well as many documents by and about Freud.

www.piaget.org/
The Web site for the *Jean Piaget Society* includes a brief biography of Swiss developmentalist Jean Piaget, information about publications and Piaget conferences, society information, and other links of interest.

www.nd.edu/~rbarger/kohlberg.html
"Kohlberg's Theory of Moral Development," an essay by Robert Barger, University of Notre Dame, summarizes Lawrence Kohlberg's theory about the stages of moral development.

paradigm.soci.brocku.ca/~lward/
George's Page is a large, well-organized document respository for the work of George Herbert Mead, with resources to support research on his contribution to social psychology.

Paul Cadmus, *Mask With False Noses: An Allegory on Promiscuity,* 1955

CHAPTER 6

SOCIAL INTERACTION IN EVERYDAY LIFE

Harold and Sybil are on their way to another couple's home in an unfamiliar section of Calgary, Alberta. They are now late because, for the last twenty minutes, they have travelled in circles looking for Creek View Drive. Harold, gripping the wheel ever more tightly, is doing a slow burn. Sybil, sitting next to him, looks straight ahead, afraid to utter a word. Both realize the evening is off to a bad start (adapted from Tannen, 1990:62).

Here we have a simple case of two people unable to locate the home of some friends. But Harold and Sybil are lost in more ways than one, since they fail to grasp why they are growing more and more enraged at their situation and at each other.

Consider the predicament from Harold's point of view. Like most men, Harold cannot tolerate getting lost. The longer he drives around, the more incompetent he feels. Sybil is seething, too, but for a different reason. She does not understand why Harold does not pull over and ask someone where Creek View Drive is. If she were driving, she fumes to herself, they already would have arrived and would be comfortably settled with drinks in hand.

Why don't men ask for directions? Because men value their independence, they are uncomfortable asking for help (and also reluctant to accept it). To men, asking for assistance is an admission of inadequacy, a sure sign that others know something they don't. If it takes Harold a few more minutes to find Creek View Drive on his own—and to keep his self-respect in the process—he thinks the bargain is a good one.

If men pursue self-sufficiency and are sensitive to hierarchy, women are more attuned to others and strive for connectedness. Asking for help seems right to Sybil because, from her point of view, sharing information reinforces social bonds. Requesting directions seems as natural to Sybil as continuing to search on his own appears to Harold. But the two people will not resolve their situation as long as neither one understands the other's point of view.

Analyzing such examples of everyday life is the focus of this chapter. We begin by presenting many of the building blocks of common experience and then explore the almost magical way in which face-to-face interaction generates reality. The central concept is **social interaction**, *the process by which people act and react in relation to others.* Social interaction is the key to creating the reality we perceive. And we interact according to particular social guidelines.

SOCIAL STRUCTURE: A GUIDE TO EVERYDAY LIVING

October 21, 1994, Ho Chi Minh City, Vietnam. This morning we leave the ship and make our way along the docks towards the centre of Ho Chi Minh City—known to an earlier generation as Saigon. The government

In any rigidly ranked setting, no interaction can proceed until people assess each other's social standing. Thus, military personnel such as these cadets at the Royal Military College in Kingston, Ontario, wear clear insignia to designate their level of authority. Don't we size up one another in much the same way in routine interaction, noting a person's rough age, quality of clothing, and manner for clues about social position?

security officers wave us through the security gates. Pressed against the fence are dozens of men who operate cyclos (bicycles with a small carriage attached to the front), the Vietnamese equivalent of taxicabs. We decline the offers of rides and spend the next twenty minutes fending off several persistent drivers, who cruise alongside us pleading for our business. The pressure is uncomfortable. We decide to cross the street but realize suddenly that there are no stop signs or signal lights—and no break at all in the steady stream of bicycles, cyclos, motorbikes, and small trucks. The locals don't

bat an eye—they just walk at a steady pace across the street, parting waves of vehicles that close in again immediately behind them. Walk right into traffic? Especially with our small children on our backs? Yup, we did it; that's the way it works in Vietnam.

Members of every society rely on social structure to make sense out of everyday situations. As one family's introduction to the streets of Vietnam suggests, the world can be disorienting—even frightening—when cultural norms are unclear. So what, then, are the building blocks of our daily lives?

STATUS

One basic element of social structure is **status**, *a recognized social position that an individual occupies*. Notice that the sociological meaning of the term "status" differs from its everyday meaning of "prestige." In common usage, a university president has more "status" than a professor. Sociologically, however, both "president" and "professor" are statuses because they represent socially defined positions, even though one does confer more power and prestige than the other.

Every status involves particular duties, rights, and expectations. The statuses people occupy thus guide their behaviour in any setting. In the university classroom, for example, professors and students have distinctive, well-defined responsibilities. Similarly, family interaction turns on the interplay of mother, father, daughters, sons, and others. In all these situations, statuses connect us to others, which is why, in the case of families, we commonly call others "relations." In short, a status defines who and what we are *in relation to* others.

Status is also a key component of social identity. Occupation, for example, is a major part of most people's self-concepts and is quickly offered as part of a social introduction. Even long after retirement, people continue to identify themselves in terms of their life's work.

STATUS SET

Everyone occupies many statuses simultaneously. The term **status set** refers to *all the statuses a person holds at a given time*. A girl may be a *daughter* to her parents, a *sister* to her siblings, a *friend* to members of her social circle, and a *goalie* to others on her hockey team. Just as status sets branch out in many directions, they also change over the life course. A child grows into an adult, a student becomes a lawyer, and people marry to become husbands and wives, sometimes becoming single again as a result of divorce or death. Joining an organization or finding a job enlarges our status set; withdrawing from activities diminishes it. Individuals gain and lose dozens of statuses over a lifetime.

ASCRIBED AND ACHIEVED STATUS

Sociologists classify statuses in terms of how people obtain them. An **ascribed status** is *a social position that someone receives at birth or assumes involuntarily later in life.* Examples of statuses that are generally ascribed include being a daughter, a native person, a teenager, or a widower. Ascribed statuses are matters about which people have little or no choice.

By contrast, an **achieved status** refers to *a social position that someone assumes voluntarily and that reflects personal ability and effort.* Among achieved statuses in Canada are being an honour student, an Olympic athlete, a spouse, a computer programmer, a Rhodes Scholar, or a thief. In each case, the individual has at least some choice in the matter.

In practice, of course, most statuses involve some combination of ascription and achievement. That is, people's ascribed statuses influence the statuses they achieve. Adults who achieve the status of lawyer, for example, are likely to share the ascribed trait of being born into relatively privileged families. And any person of a privileged sex, race, ethnicity, or age has far more opportunity to realize desirable achieved statuses than does someone without such advantages. By contrast, many less desirable statuses, such as criminal, drug addict, or being unemployed are more easily "achieved" by people born into poverty.

MASTER STATUS

Some statuses matter more than others. A **master status** is *a status that has exceptional importance for social identity, often shaping a person's entire life.* For many people, occupation is often a master status since it conveys a great deal about social background, education, and income. Family (of birth or marriage) can function this way, too. At the extreme, being "an Eaton," "a Vanier," "an Irving," or "a Southern" is enough by itself to push an individual into the limelight. Most societies of the world also limit the opportunities of women, whatever their abilities, making gender, too, a master status.

In a negative sense, serious disease also operates as a master status. Sometimes even lifelong friends shun cancer patients or people with AIDS simply because of their illness. Finally, we sometimes dehumanize people with physical disabilities by perceiving them only in terms of their impairments. In the

Elvis Stojko, from Richmond Hill, Ontario, is shown here with his silver medal for figure skating at the 1998 Winter Olympics in Nagano, Japan. Although many Canadians were disappointed that he did not win gold, it was revealed when competition was over that he had been concealing a painful injury. As much as Stojko is admired for his athletic skill, it is his perseverance and integrity that make him a role model for young people.

"Social Diversity" box, two people with physical disabilities describe this problem.

ROLE

A second major component of social interaction is **role,** *behaviour expected of someone who holds a particular status.* Think of a role as the dynamic expression of a status: individuals *hold* a status and *perform* a role (Linton, 1937). The obligations and privileges of being a student, for example, require you to fulfil that role by attending classes and completing assignments and, more generally, devoting much of your time to personal enrichment through academic study.

Both statuses and roles vary by culture. In Canada, the status "uncle" refers to a brother of either one's mother or father; in Vietnam, by contrast, specific terms designate uncles on each side of the family, and responsibilities differ accordingly. In every

Physical Disability as Master Status

Following are some comments from people with two very different diseases, both of which may have profound effects on the whole round of life, including self-concept, primary relationships, acquaintance relationships, and work life.

The first is a person with cancer. Among strangers, neighbours, and acquaintances, the term "cancer" is mentioned with particular care. One woman told of her trips to the hairdresser, to whom she had been going for many years, during her chemotherapy treatment. "My hairdresser said to me, 'Your hair is falling out,' and I was too shocked and ashamed to tell her the truth. So I just said, 'Oh, I don't know what it could be.'" This woman stopped going to the hairdresser. She couldn't face this individual with her pain and shame. They had always had a good but distant professional relationship and she had had her hair done there for ten years. She had told her hairdresser the things of which she was proud. Her hairdresser knew that she had three children, knew their names and ages, and knew the name of her husband. She didn't understand herself and was surprised by her reaction. She said,

I don't know why it is. Maybe it is something lacking in me. Maybe it's just my nature. I don't know. I'm not that open. I don't know what it is, but I can't go around telling everybody. I just can't do it. It's not really that I'm trying to keep it a secret. Or maybe I am. I don't know what it is.

Notice that the diagnosis of cancer is thought to be so overwhelming as to diminish the person with the disease. The irony, then, is that it is assumed to be a status of such proportions that its very naming is problematic. The same woman had been trying to sell her home. When people learned from the real estate agent that she had cancer, they lost interest.

We just had to change real estate companies and agents. And this time, we didn't tell. Soon several people looked at the house and then we finally sold it. (Nancarrow Clarke, 1985:30)

Second, listen to a person with chronic fatigue syndrome or myalgic encephalomyelitis (CFS or ME):

Well, when I first got diagnosed because there was such a stigma … you know, like it's a psychological thing and I felt embarrassed. I didn't really tell anybody other than my immediate family and my very closest friends, whereas now when I'm talking I'll just say what I have because how are people going to learn if they don't know what it is and how it affects us? So in the beginning, I felt embarrassed. I cried … I mean I didn't cry when I had the growth as much as I cried when I got diagnosed with CFS because it was such a negative … I felt … you know, and I went to a support group and I said why do I feel like we're a group that has … you know, where we should be shipped on an island all by ourself because …

I mean I wouldn't even say half of my complaints because they were so weird … like my fingers hurt, my joints hurt or I feel like I have arthritis but I'm too young to have arthritis. You know, half the time you didn't even tell them because you felt like you were a hypochondriac. (Nancarrow Clarke, unpublished research)

Notice here how the disease is seen as a threat to the very self of the sufferer. She experiences social isolation, embarrassment, and stigma. There is continuing debate about whether CFS is just an excuse for a break among hard-driving, ambitious young people (hence its early nickname, the "Yuppie flu"), a psychosomatic disorder, or a biologically based, and therefore "real," disease. Those with the disease suffer from the current lack of clarity as to its cause and treatment.

society, too, actual role performance varies according to an individual's unique personality, although some societies permit more personal latitude than others do.

ROLE SET

Because we occupy many statuses simultaneously—a status set—everyday life is a mix of multiple roles. Robert Merton (1968) introduced the term **role set** to identify *a number of roles attached to a single status.*

Figure 6–1 illustrates the status set and corresponding role sets of one individual. Four statuses are presented, each linked to a different role set. First, as a professor, this woman interacts with students (the "teaching role") as well as with other academics (the "colleague role"). Second, she also holds the status of "mother," with routine responsibilities for her children (the "maternal role") as well as obligations to their school and other organizations (the "civic role"). Third, her work as a researcher (the "laboratory role") generates the data she uses in her publications (the "author role"). Fourth, she occupies the status of "wife," with corresponding roles in relation to her husband ("conjugal roles" such as confidante and sexual partner), with whom she would share a "domestic role" in terms of maintaining the household. Of course, Figure 6–1 lists only some of this person's status and role sets, since an individual generally occupies several dozen statuses at one time, each linked to a role set. This woman might be, additionally, a daughter caring for aging parents and a member of the city council.

ROLE CONFLICT AND ROLE STRAIN

Members of industrial societies routinely juggle a host of responsibilities demanded by their various statuses and roles. As most mothers can testify, parenting as well as working outside the home taxes both physical and emotional strength. Sociologists thus recognize **role conflict** as *incompatibility among roles corresponding to two or more statuses.*

We experience role conflict when we find ourselves pulled in various directions while trying to respond to the many statuses we hold. Some municipal or provincial politicians, for example, decide not to run for federal office because the demands of a campaign would impoverish family life; in other cases, ambitious people defer having children or choose to remain childless in order to stay on the "fast track" for career success.

Even the roles linked to a single status may make competing demands on us. The concept of **role strain** refers to *incompatibility among roles corresponding to a single status.* A plant supervisor may enjoy being friendly with other workers. At the same time, however, the supervisor's responsibility for everyone's performance requires maintaining some measure of personal distance from each employee. In short, performing the roles attached to even one status may involve something of a balancing act.

Another strategy for minimizing role conflict is "compartmentalizing" our lives so that we perform roles linked to one status at one time and place, and carry out roles corresponding to another status elsewhere at another time. A familiar example of this scheme is heading home while leaving the job "at work."

ROLE EXIT

After she left the life of a Catholic nun to become a university sociologist, Helen Rose Fuchs Ebaugh (1988) began to study *role exit,* the process by which people disengage from important social roles. Studying a range of "exes," including ex-nuns, ex-doctors, ex-husbands, and ex-alcoholics, Ebaugh identified elements common to the process of "becoming an ex."

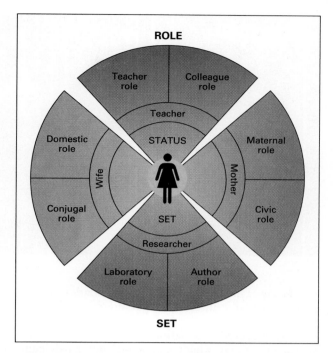

FIGURE 6–1 Status Set and Role Set

According to Ebaugh, people initiate the process of role exit by reflecting critically on their existing lives and grappling with doubts about their ability or willingness to persist in a certain role. As they imagine alternative roles, they ultimately reach a point when they decide to pursue a new life.

Even at this point, however, a past role may continue to influence their lives. "Exes" retain a self-image shaped by an earlier role, which may interfere with the drive to build a new sense of self. An ex-nun, for example, may hesitate to wear stylish clothing and makeup.

"Exes" must also rebuild relationships with people who may have known them in their earlier life and who may not realize just how new and unfamiliar their present role may be. And learning new social skills poses another challenge. For example, Ebaugh reports, ex-nuns who begin dating after decades in the church are often startled to learn that sexual norms are now vastly different from those they knew as teenagers.

THE SOCIAL CONSTRUCTION OF REALITY

While behaviour is guided by status and role, each human being has considerable ability to shape what happens moment to moment. "Reality," in other words, is not as fixed as we may think. The phrase **social construction of reality** identifies *the process by which people creatively shape reality through social*

Flirting is an everyday experience in reality construction. Each person offers information to the other, and hints at romantic interest. Yet the interaction proceeds with a tentative and often humorous air so that either individual can withdraw at any time without further obligation.

interaction. This idea stands at the foundation of sociology's symbolic-interaction paradigm, as described in earlier chapters.

Most everyday situations involve at least some agreement about what's going on, but participants perceive events differently to the extent that they are motivated by disparate interests and intentions. Social interaction, then, amounts to negotiating reality.

This short excerpt from "True Trash," a short story by internationally renowned Canadian author Margaret Atwood, illustrates one way that names and clothing styles construct a certain "type" of person.

> Eleven years later Donny is walking along Yorkville Avenue, in Toronto, in the summer heat. He's no longer Donny. At some point, which even he can't remember exactly, he has changed into Don. He's wearing sandals, and a white Indian-style shirt over his cut-off jeans. He has longish hair and a beard. The beard has come out yellow, whereas the hair is brown. He likes the effect: WASP Jesus or Hollywood Viking, depending on his mood. He has a string of wooden beads around his neck.
>
> This is how he dresses on Saturdays, to go to Yorkville; to go there and just hang around, with the crowds of others who are doing the same. Sometimes he gets high, on the pot that circulates as freely as cigarettes did once. He thinks he should be enjoying this experience more than he actually does.
>
> During the rest of the week he has a job in his father's law office. He can get away with the beard there, just barely, as long as he balances it with a suit. (But even the older guys are growing their sideburns and wearing coloured shirts, and using words like "creative" more than they used to.) He

doesn't tell the people he meets in Yorkville about this job, just as he doesn't tell the law office about his friends' acid trips. He's leading a double life. It feels precarious, and brave. (1991:30–31)

This situation reveals the drama—sometimes subtle, sometimes savage—by which human beings creatively build reality. There are limits, of course, to what even the most skilful and persuasive personality can achieve. And, of course, not everyone enters a negotiation with equal standing. The fact that Donny was the son of the lawyer in whose office he was working likely helped him bridge the two realities.

THE THOMAS THEOREM

Donny's impression management allowed him to be part of the Yorkville scene and his father's law office. W.I. Thomas (1966:301; orig. 1931) succinctly expressed this insight in what has come to be known as the **Thomas theorem**: *Situations we define as real become real in their consequences.*

Applied to social interaction, Thomas's insight means that although reality is initially "soft" as it is fashioned, it can become "hard" in its effects. In the case of Donny, having succeeded as a member in two very different groups, he is able to lead a double life.

ETHNOMETHODOLOGY

Rather than assuming that reality is something "out there," the symbolic-interaction paradigm posits that reality is created by people in everyday encounters. But how, exactly, do we define reality for ourselves? Answering this question is the objective of ethnomethodology, a specialized approach within the symbolic-interaction paradigm.

The term itself has two parts: the Greek *ethno* refers to people and how they understand their surroundings; "methodology" designates a set of methods or principles. Combining them makes **ethnomethodology**, *the study of the way people make sense of their everyday lives.*

Ethnomethodology is largely the creation of Harold Garfinkel (1967), who challenged the then-dominant view of society as a broad, abstract "system" (recall the approach of Émile Durkheim, described in Chapter 4, "Society"). Garfinkel wanted to explore how we make sense of countless familiar situations. On the surface, we engage in intentional speech or action; but these efforts rest on deeper assumptions about the world that we usually take for granted.

Think, for a moment, about what we assume in asking someone the simple question, "How are you?" Do we mean physically? Mentally? Spiritually? Financially? Are we even looking for an answer, or are we just being polite?

Ethnomethodology, then, delves into the sense-making process in any social encounter. Because so much of this process is ingrained, Garfinkel argues that the only effective way to expose how we make sense of events is to purposefully *break the rules.* Deliberately ignoring conventional rules and observing how people respond, he points out, allows us to tease out how people build a reality. Thus, Garfinkel (1967) directed his students to refuse to "play the game" in a wide range of situations. Some students living with their parents started acting as if they were boarders rather than children; others entered stores and insisted on bargaining for items; others recruited people into simple games (such as tic-tac-toe) only to intentionally flout the rules; still others initiated conversations while slowly moving closer and closer to the other person.

The students first noticed people's reactions. Typically, the "victims" of these rule violations became agitated, indicating that even if reality is taken for granted it is very important to us. Then the students tried to identify exactly *why* people were disturbed, leading to insights about the unspoken agreements that underlie family life, shopping, fair play, and the like.

Because of ethnomethodology's provocative character and its focus on commonplace experiences, some sociologists view it as less-than-serious research. Even so, ethnomethodology has succeeded in heightening awareness of many unnoticed patterns of everyday life.

REALITY BUILDING: SOME BROADER CONSIDERATIONS

Taking a broader view of reality construction, people do not build everyday experience out of thin air. In

Around the world, culture frames the reality people experience. Most people living in rich countries such as Canada rarely confront death. By contrast, these refugees in Rwanda—a poor nation shaken by violence and bloodshed—have been forced to accept death as a part of everyday life.

part, how we act or what we see in our surroundings depends on our interests. Scanning the night sky, for example, lovers discover romance, while scientists perceive the same stars as hydrogen atoms fusing into helium. Social background also directs our perceptions, since we build reality out of elements in the surrounding culture. For this reason, residents of, say, affluent Westmount in Montreal experience the city differently from those living in the city's east end, where the unemployment rate is one of the highest in Canada.

In global perspective, reality construction is even more variable. People waiting for a bus in London, England, typically "queue up" in a straight line; people in Quebec City wait in a much less orderly fashion. Constraints on the social experiences of women in Saudi Arabia would be incomprehensible to most Canadian women. Elvis lovers live in the rural and eastern regions of the U.S., while Elvis loathers predominate throughout most of the west. Though the birth rate is rising in Moscow, where women perceive increased economic security, it remains low in the rest of Russia, where economic turmoil persists.

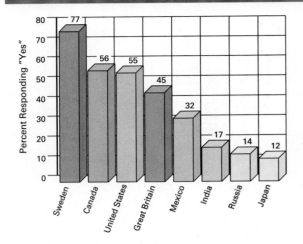

FIGURE 6–2 Global Happiness

Survey question: "We are interested in the way people are feeling these days. During the past few weeks, did you ever feel 'on top of the world,' feeling that life is wonderful?"

SOURCE: World Values Survey (1994).

From these examples, we conclude that people build reality from the surrounding culture. Chapter 3 ("Culture") explained how people the world over derive different meanings from specific gestures, so that travellers can find themselves building a most unexpected reality! Similarly, what we "see" in a book or a film also depends on the assumptions we make about the world. JoEllen Shively (1992) screened "Western" films for men of European descent as well as Native-American men. Both categories claimed to enjoy the films, but for different reasons. White men interpreted the films as praising rugged people striking out for the west to impose their will on nature. Native-American men, by contrast, saw in the same films a celebration of land and nature apart from any human ambitions.

If people the world over inhabit different realities, are some happier than others? Figure 6–2 suggests that, when asked if they had recently felt themselves to be "on top of the world," people in Sweden, Canada, and the U.S. were much more likely to respond in the affirmative than those in India, Russia, and Japan. Significantly, when asked about their wants, Canadians put "happiness" first (see Figure 6–3), followed closely by "freedom" and "family life"—both of which might contribute to happiness.

A brief pause is in order here. Before taking Figure 6–2 at face value, we should revisit our earlier dis-cussion of "cultural relativity" and the problems involved in translating advertisements. How, one might ask, does the concept or emotion of feeling "on top of the world" translate into different languages? Further, is the link between feeling "on top of the world" and "happiness" obvious in all cultural contexts? The World Values Survey, as you can see, faces some very complex translation problems.

DRAMATURGICAL ANALYSIS: "THE PRESENTATION OF SELF"

Erving Goffman (1922–82) enhanced the understanding of everyday life by noting that people interacting behave much like actors performing on a stage. By imagining ourselves as directors scrutinizing what goes on in some situational "theatre," we engage in what Goffman called **dramaturgical analysis**, *the investigation of social interaction in terms of theatrical performance.*

Dramaturgical analysis offers a fresh look at two now-familiar concepts. In theatrical terms, a status mirrors a part in a play, and a role serves as a script, supplying dialogue and action for each of the characters.

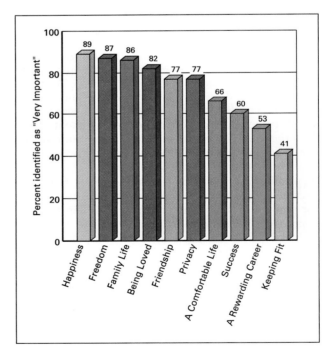

FIGURE 6–3 Top Ten Wants

What do Canadians want? This survey suggests that, more than anything, we want happiness. Does this strike you as a universal or a culturally specific trait?

SOURCE: Bibby (1995:2).

Moreover, in any setting, a person is both actor and audience. Goffman described each individual's "performance" as the **presentation of self**, *an individual's effort to create specific impressions in the minds of others.* Presentation of self, or impression management, contains several distinctive elements (Goffman, 1959, 1967).

PERFORMANCES

As we present ourselves in everyday situations, we convey information—consciously and unconsciously—to others. An individual's performance includes dress (costume), any objects carried along (props), and tone of voice and particular gestures (manner). In addition, people craft their performance according to the setting (stage). We may joke loudly on a sidewalk, for example, but assume a more reverent manner on entering a church. In addition, individuals design settings, such as a home or office, to enhance a performance by invoking the desired reactions in others.

An Illustration: The Doctor's Office

Consider how a physician's office conveys information to an audience of patients. Physicians enjoy substantial prestige and power in Canada, a fact immediately grasped by patients upon entering a doctor's office. First, the physician is nowhere to be seen. Instead, in what Goffman describes as the "front region" of the setting, the patient encounters a receptionist who functions as a gatekeeper, deciding if and when the patient can meet the physician. Who waits to see whom is, of course, a power game. A simple survey of the doctor's waiting room, with patients (often impatiently) awaiting their call to the inner sanctum, leaves little doubt that the medical team controls events.

The physician's private office and examination room constitute the "back region" of the setting. Here the patient confronts a wide range of props, such as medical books and framed degrees, which together reinforce the impression that the physician has the specialized knowledge necessary to call the shots. In the office, the physician usually remains seated behind a desk—the larger and grander the desk, the greater the statement of power—while the patient is provided with only a chair.

The physician's appearance and manner convey still more information. The usual costume of a white lab coat may have the practical function of keeping clothes from becoming soiled, but its social function is to let others know at a glance the physician's status. A stethoscope around the neck or a black medical bag in hand has the same purpose. A doctor's highly technical terminology—frequently mystifying—also emphasizes the hierarchy in the situation. The use of the title "Doctor" by patients who, in turn, are frequently

When we enter the presence of others, we "construct" ourselves and begin a "presentation of self" that has much in common with a dramatic performance. Such a presentation involves clothing (costume), other objects (props), certain typical behaviour (script), and it takes place in a particular setting (stage). No wonder the ancient Greeks, who understood the element of acting in everyday life, used the same word for "person" and "mask."

addressed only by their first names also underscores the physician's dominant position. The overall message of a doctor's performance is clear: "I will help you only if you allow me to take charge."

NONVERBAL COMMUNICATION

Novelist William Sansom describes a fictional Mr. Preedy, an English vacationer on a beach in Spain:

> ... He took care to avoid catching anyone's eye. First of all, he had to make it clear to those potential companions of his holiday that they were of no concern to him whatsoever. He stared through them, round them, over them—eyes lost in space. The beach might have been empty. If by chance a ball was thrown his way, he looked surprised; then let a smile of amusement lighten his face (Kindly Preedy), looked around dazed to see that there were people on the beach, tossed it back with a smile to himself and not a smile at the people. ...
>
> [He] then gathered together his beach-wrap and bag into a neat sand-resistant pile (Methodical and Sensible Preedy), rose slowly to stretch at ease his huge frame (Big-Cat Preedy), and tossed aside his sandals (Carefree Preedy, after all). (*A Contest of Ladies*, 1956, 230–32, quoted in Goffman, 1959:4–5)

GLOBAL SOCIOLOGY

Emotions in Global Perspective: Do We All Feel the Same?

On a Vancouver sidewalk, a woman reacts angrily to the skateboarder who zooms past her. Apart from a few choice words, her facial expression broadcasts a strong emotion that North Americans easily recognize. But would an observer from New Guinea be able to interpret her emotion? In other words, do people the world over share similar feelings, and do they express them in the same way?

Paul Ekman (1980b) and his colleagues studied emotions around the world, even among members of a small society in New Guinea. They concluded that people throughout the world experience six basic emotions: anger, fear, disgust, happiness, surprise, and sadness. Moreover, people everywhere recognize these feelings in the same distinctive facial gestures. To Ekman, this means that much of our emotional life is universal—rather than culturally variable—and that the display of emotion is biologically programmed in our facial features, muscles, and central nervous system.

But if the reality of emotions is rooted in our biology, Ekman and other researchers note three ways in which emotional life differs significantly in global perspective.

First, *what triggers an emotion varies from one society to another*. Whether people define a particular situation as an insult (causing anger), a loss (calling forth sadness), or a mystical event (provoking surprise and awe) depends on the cultural surroundings of the individual.

Second, *people display emotions according to the norms of their culture*. Every society has rules about when, where, and to whom an individual may exhibit certain emotions. People in Canada typically express emotions more freely in the home among family members than among colleagues in the workplace. Similarly, we expect children to express emotions to parents, although parents are taught to guard their emotions in front of children.

Third, *societies differ in terms of how people cope with emotions*. Some societies encourage the expression of feelings, while others belittle emotions and demand that their members suppress them. Societies also display significant gender differences in this regard. In Canada, most people regard emotional expression as feminine, expected of women but a sign of weakness in men. In other societies, however, this sex-typing of emotions is less pronounced or even reversed.

In sum, emotional life in global perspective has both common and variable elements. People around the world experience the same basic feelings. But what sparks a particular emotion, to whom someone expresses it, and whether people encourage or discourage the display of emotions are variable products of social learning.

SOURCES: Ekman (1980a, 1980b), Lutz and White (1986), and Lutz (1988).

Through his conduct, Mr. Preedy offers a great deal of information about himself to anyone caring to observe him. Notice that he does so without uttering a single word. This illustrates the process of **nonverbal communication**, *communication using body movements, gestures, and facial expressions rather than speech.*

Virtually any part of the body can be used to transmit nonverbal communication. Facial expressions form the most significant element of "body language." As noted in the "Global Sociology" box, smiling and other facial gestures express basic emotions such as pleasure, surprise, and anger the world over. Further, people project particular shades of meaning with their faces. We distinguish, for example, between the deliberate smile of Kindly Preedy on the beach, a spontaneous smile of joy at seeing a friend, a pained smile of embarrassment, and a full, unrestrained smile

of self-satisfaction that we often associate with the "cat who ate the canary."

Eye contact is another crucial element of nonverbal communication. Generally, we use eye contact to initiate social interaction. Someone across the room "catches our eye," for example, sparking a conversation. Avoiding the eyes of another, on the other hand, discourages communication. Hands, too, speak for us. Common hand gestures in our culture convey, among other things, an insult, a request for a ride, an invitation for someone to join us, or a demand that others stop in their tracks. Gestures also supplement spoken words. Pointing in a menacing way at someone, for example, intensifies a word of warning, just as shrugging the shoulders adds an air of indifference to the phrase "I don't know," and rapidly waving the arms lends urgency to the single word "Hurry!"

To most people in Canada, these expressions convey anger, fear, disgust, happiness, surprise, and sadness. But do people elsewhere in the world define them in the same way? Research suggests that all human beings experience the same basic emotions and display them to others in the same basic ways. But culture plays a part by specifying the situations that trigger one emotion or another.

Body Language and Deception

But, as any actor knows, the "perfect performance" is an elusive goal. In everyday performances, some element of body language often contradicts our intended meaning. A teenage boy offers an explanation for getting home late, for example, but his mother doubts his words because he avoids looking her in the eye. The movie star on a television talk show claims that her recent flop at the box office is "no big deal," but the nervous swing of her leg belies her casual denial. In practical terms, carefully observing nonverbal communication (most of which is not easily controlled) provides clues to deception, in much the same way that a lie detector records tell-tale changes in breathing, pulse rate, perspiration, and blood pressure.

Yet detecting lies is difficult, because no single bodily gesture directly indicates deceit the way, say, a

smile indicates pleasure. Even so, because any performance involves so many expressions, few people can confidently lie without allowing some piece of contradictory information to slip through, arousing the suspicions of a careful observer. Therefore, the key to detecting deceit is to scan the whole performance with an eye for inconsistencies and discrepancies.

Paul Ekman (1985) suggests scrutinizing four elements of a performance—words, voice, body language, and facial expressions—for clues to deception.

1. **Words.** Good liars can mentally rehearse their lines and manipulate words with ease. But they may not be able to avoid a simple slip of the tongue—something the performer did not mean to say in quite that way. For example, a young man who is deceiving his parents by claiming that his roommate is a male friend rather than a

female lover might inadvertently use the word "she" rather than "he" in a conversation. The more complicated the deception, the more likely a performer is to make a revealing mistake.

2. **Voice.** Tone and patterns of speech contain clues to deception because they are hard to control. A person trying to hide a powerful emotion, for example, cannot easily prevent the voice from trembling or breaking. Similarly, the individual may speak quickly (suggesting anger) or slowly (indicating sadness). Nervous laughter, inappropriate pauses between words, or non-words, such as "ah" and "ummm," also hint at discomfort.

3. **Body language.** A "leak" of *body language* may tip off an observer to deception as well. Subtle body movements, for example, give the impression of nervousness, as does sudden swallowing or rapid breathing. These are especially good clues to deception because few people can control them. Sometimes, *not* using the body in the expected way to enhance words—as when a person tries to fake excitement—also suggests deception.

4. **Facial expressions.** Because facial expressions, too, are hard to control, they give away many phony performances. A sad person feigning happiness, for example, generally "flashes" momentary frowns through a crooked smile. By contrast, raising and drawing together the eyebrows signals genuine fear or worry, since this expression is virtually impossible to make wilfully.

In sum, lies are detectable, but training is the key to noticing relevant clues. Another key to spotting deception is knowing the other person well, the reason that parents can usually spot deceit in their children. Finally, almost anyone can unmask deception when the liar is trying to cover up strong emotions.

GENDER AND PERSONAL PERFORMANCES

Because women are socialized to be less assertive than males, they tend to be especially sensitive to nonverbal communication. In fact, gender is a central element in personal performances. Based on the work of Nancy Henley, Mykol Hamilton, and Barrie Thorne (1992), we can extend the present discussion of personal performances to spotlight the importance of gender.

Demeanour

Demeanour—that is, general conduct or deportment—reflects a person's level of social power. Simply put, powerful people enjoy far greater personal dis-cretion in how they act; subordinates act more formally and self-consciously. Off-colour remarks, swearing, or casually removing shoes and putting feet up on the desk may be acceptable for the boss, but it rarely is for employees. Similarly, people in positions of dominance can interrupt the performances of others with impunity, while others are expected to display deference by remaining silent (Smith-Lovin and Brody, 1989; Henley, Hamilton, and Thorne, 1992; Johnson, 1994).

Since women generally occupy positions of lesser power, demeanour is a gender issue as well. As Chapter 12 ("Sex and Gender") explains, about half of all working women in Canada hold clerical or service jobs that place them under the control of supervisors, who are usually men. Women, then, craft their personal performances more carefully than men and display a greater degree of deference in everyday interaction.

Use of Space

How much space does a personal performance require? Here again, power plays a key role, since using more space conveys a nonverbal message of personal importance. According to Henley, Hamilton, and Thorne (1992), men typically command more space than women do, whether pacing back and forth before an audience or casually lounging on the beach. Why? Our culture traditionally has measured femininity by how *little* space women occupy (the standard of "daintiness"), while gauging masculinity by how *much* territory a man controls (the standard of "turf").

The concept of **personal space** refers to *the surrounding area in which an individual makes some claim to privacy.* In Canada, people typically position themselves several feet apart when speaking; throughout the Middle East, by contrast, people stand much closer when they converse. Throughout the world, gender further modifies these patterns. In daily life, men commonly intrude on the personal space of women. A woman's encroachment into a man's personal space, however, is likely to be construed as a sexual overture. Here again, women have less power in everyday interaction than men do.

Staring, Smiling, and Touching

Eye contact encourages interaction. Typically, women employ eye contact to sustain conversation more than men do. Men have their own distinctive brand of eye contact: staring. By making women the targets of stares, men are both making a claim of social dominance and defining women as sexual objects.

Although frequently signalling pleasure, *smiling* has a host of meanings. In a male-dominated world, women often smile to indicate appeasement or accep-

Near the end of his life, Erving Goffman (1979) studied the place of gender in advertising—that is, how advertising portrays the relative social position of men and women. Look at this Pepsi ad from an earlier era: What messages does it convey about women and men? Do you think today's advertising is different in this regard?

tance of submission. For this reason, Henley, Hamilton, and Thorne maintain, women smile more than men; in extreme cases, smiling may reach the level of nervous habit.

Finally, *touching* constitutes an intriguing social pattern. Mutual touching generally conveys intimacy and caring. Apart from close relationships, however, touching is generally something men do to women (although rarely, in our culture, to other men). A male physician touches the shoulder of his female nurse as they examine a report, a young man touches the back of his woman friend as he guides her across the street, or a male skiing instructor looks for opportunities to touch his female students. In these examples—as well as many others—touching may evoke little response, so common is it in everyday life. But it amounts to a subtle ritual by which men express their dominant position in an assumed hierarchy that subordinates women.

IDEALIZATION

Complex motives underlie human behaviour. Even so, according to Goffman, we construct performances to idealize our intentions. That is, we try to convince others (and perhaps ourselves) that what we do reflects ideal cultural standards rather than more selfish motives.

Idealization is easily illustrated by returning to the world of physicians and patients. In a hospital, physicians engage in a performance commonly described as "making rounds." Entering the room of a patient, the physician often stops at the foot of the bed and silently examines the patient's chart. Afterwards, physician and patient converse briefly. In ideal terms, this routine involves a physician making a personal visit to inquire about a patient's condition.

In reality, something less exemplary is usually going on. A physician who sees several dozen patients a day may remember little about most of them. Reading the chart gives the physician the opportunity to rediscover the patient's identity and medical problems. Openly revealing the actual impersonality of much medical care would undermine the culturally ideal perception of the physician as deeply concerned about the welfare of others.

Idealization is woven into the fabric of everyday life in countless ways. Physicians, university professors, lawyers, and other professionals typically idealize their motives for entering their chosen careers. They describe their work as "making a contribution to science," "helping others," "answering a calling from God," or perhaps "serving the community." Rarely do such people concede the less honourable, although common, motives of seeking the income, power, prestige, and leisure these occupations confer.

Taking a broader view, idealization underlies social civility, since we smile and make polite remarks to people we do not like. Such small hypocrisies ease our way through social interactions. Even when we suspect that others are putting on an act, rarely do we

Hand gestures vary widely from one culture to another. Yet people everywhere define a chuckle, grin, or smirk in response to someone's performance as an indication that one does not take another person seriously. Therefore, the world over, people who cannot restrain their mirth tactfully cover their faces.

openly challenge their performance, for reasons we shall explain next.

EMBARRASSMENT AND TACT

The eminent professor consistently mispronounces the dean's name; the visiting dignitary rises from the table to speak, unaware of the napkin that still hangs from her neck; the prime minister becomes ill at a state dinner. As carefully as individuals may craft their performances, slip-ups of all kinds frequently occur. The result is *embarrassment*, which, in dramaturgical terms, means the discomfort that follows a spoiled performance. Goffman describes embarrassment simply as "losing face."

Embarrassment looms as an ever-present danger because, first, all performances typically contain some measure of deception. Second, most performances involve a complex array of elements, any one of which, in a thoughtless moment, may shatter the intended impression.

Interestingly, an audience usually overlooks flaws in a performance, thereby allowing an actor to avoid embarrassment. If we do point out a misstep ("Excuse me, but do you know that your fly is open?"), we do it discreetly and only to help someone avoid even greater loss of face. In Hans Christian Andersen's classic fable "The Emperor's New Clothes," the child who blurts out that the emperor is parading around naked is telling the truth, yet is scolded for being rude.

But members of an audience usually do more than ignore flaws in a performance, Goffman explains; typically, they help the performer recover from them. Tact, then, amounts to helping another person "save face." After hearing a supposed expert make an embarrassingly inaccurate remark, for example, people may tactfully ignore the comment as if it were never spoken

at all. Alternatively, mild laughter may indicate that they wish to dismiss what they have heard as a joke. Or a listener may simply respond, "I'm sure you didn't mean that," acknowledging the statement but not allowing it to destroy the actor's performance.

Why is tact such a common response? Because embarrassment provokes discomfort not simply for one person but for *everyone*. Just as the entire audience feels uneasy when an actor forgets a line, people who observe awkward behaviour are reminded of how fragile their own performances often are. Socially constructed reality thus functions like a dam holding back a sea of chaos. Should one person's performance spring a leak, others tactfully assist in making repairs. Everyone, after all, jointly engages in building culture, and no one wants reality to be suddenly swept away.

In sum, Goffman's research shows that, while behaviour is spontaneous in some respects, it is more patterned than we like to think. Almost four hundred years ago, William Shakespeare captured this idea in memorable lines that still ring true:

> All the world's a stage,
> And all the men and women merely players:
> They have their exits and their entrances;
> And one man in his time plays many parts.
>
> (*As You Like It*, II.vii. 139-42)

INTERACTION IN EVERYDAY LIFE: TWO ILLUSTRATIONS

We have now examined many elements of social interaction. The final sections of this chapter illustrate key lessons by focusing on two important, yet quite different, elements of everyday life.

Social Interaction: Reaching across Cyberspace

> Whereas technology traditionally merely sustained human relationships already formed from face-to-face contact, an Internet relationship can be initiated technologically. Because they are so disembodied, so devoid of physical presence . . . divisions between man and woman, old and young, strong and weak, sick and healthy, cool dude and nerd begin to be bridged as in few other ways. (Goyder, 1997:186)

Social interaction based on electronic communication, and the Internet in particular, has become an increasingly important part of the experience of Canadians. While providing a new basis of interaction in ongoing relationships, this new medium has put us in contact with people around the world and given new meaning to the concept of social network. We are, in McLuhan's terms, disembodied and unconstrained in time and space to the point where we lose our old identities and become part of the world or global village (Benedetti and DeHart, 1996).

One of your authors, Linda Gerber, has students in second- and fourth-year Canadian society courses at the University of Guelph involved in computer conferencing. Students meet face-to-face in the classroom, but they also communicate electronically with the class as a whole and with smaller working groups as they report on their research activities, respond to current events, debate various issues, react to contributions by other group members, and prepare for class presentations. Since the conferencing begins early in each semester, most students "meet," or at least get to know, most of their classmates and study group members *first* via computer. Initially, one hears (and reads on the computer screen) rumblings of resistance and discontent as students complain about the impersonality of computer contact and try to arrange group meetings *in the flesh*. Later, these same students are involved in intensive electronic communication—effective communication that reaches all group members without the need to juggle schedules for face-to-face meetings restricted in time and place.

Their task at hand might be rewriting the Canadian constitution (by groups respresenting Canada's provinces or regions), designing social or economic policies and programs (as "consultants" to government departments), researching special topics and preparing for group presentations—or simply sharing reactions to current events. The conferencing system allows students to reach the whole class or their research group by simply logging on, from home or the computer lab, at any time of the day or night.

Over the course of the semester, discussion—and sometimes even argument—can become quite intense. Differences of opinion and interpersonal conflict are sorted out through computer conferences (as well as face-to-face contact). Some of the conference group members become almost "addicted," logging on several times a day with comments, references, or suggestions for areas to explore; others do the bare minimum. Comments on the conferences and in-course evaluations reveal that some students thoroughly enjoy the experience while others remain frustrated and unenthusiastic. Inevitably, at the end of the semester, conference messages turn to goodbyes and comment on the quality and emotional impact of the group work: "Let's keep in touch"; "I'm going to miss this"; "Hey, we really accomplished a lot!" One student noted, "I never thought I'd get emotionally attached to you all. This has been the best group experience I've had at university."

This experience with electronic communication is increasingly relevant to the world of work. Many people who work as teams through this medium may meet in person rarely or not at all. More and more people, including those highly placed in various corporations, are doing some or all of their work from home offices—electronically linked to their head offices and the rest of the world. Disembodied and unconstrained by time or place, students and workers alike are engaged in productive activity through cyberspace.

LANGUAGE: THE GENDER ISSUE

As Chapter 3 ("Culture") explains, language is the thread that ties members of a society together in the symbolic web we call culture. In everyday life, language conveys meaning on more than one level. Besides the obvious message in what people say, a host of additional meanings is embedded in our language. One such message involves gender. Language defines men and women differently in at least three ways, involving control, value, and attention (Henley, Hamilton, and Thorne, 1992).[1]

---

[1] The following sections draw primarily on Henley, Hamilton, and Thorne (1992). Additional material comes from Thorne, Kramarae, and Henley (1983) and others, as noted.

Language and Control

A young man astride his new motorcycle rolls proudly into the gas station, and eagerly says to the attendant, "Isn't she a beauty?" On the surface, the question has little to do with gender. Yet, curiously, a common linguistic pattern confers the female "she," and never the male "he," on a man's prized possessions.

The language men use often reveals their concern with competence and control. In this case, a man attaches a female pronoun to a motorcycle (car, yacht, or other object) because it reflects ownership.

A more obvious control function of language relates to people's names. Traditionally in Canada, and in many other parts of the world, a woman takes the family name of the man she marries. While few people consider this an explicit statement of a man's ownership of a woman, many believe that it reflects male dominance. When Joe Clark became Canada's prime minister in 1979, he encountered hostility and resistance from some quarters because his wife, Maureen McTeer, had retained her birth name: "If a man can't control his wife, how can he possibly run the country?" Over the years since McTeer was our prime minister's wife, an increasing proportion of married women have been retaining their own names or merging two family names. In Quebec, women are not merely encouraged to retain their original names: the law actually requires them to do so.

Language and Value

Language usually treats as masculine whatever has greater value, force, or significance. Although we may not think much about it, this pattern is deeply rooted in the English language. For instance, the positive adjective "virtuous," meaning "morally worthy" or "excellent," is derived from the Latin word *vir* meaning "man." By contrast, the derogatory adjective "hysterical" is derived from the Greek word *hyster*, meaning "uterus."

In numerous, more familiar ways, language also confers different value on the two sexes. Traditional masculine terms such as "king" or "lord" have retained their positive meaning, while comparable terms such as "queen," "madam," or "dame" have acquired negative connotations in contemporary usage. Language thus both mirrors social attitudes and helps to perpetuate them.

Similarly, use of the suffixes "ette" and "ess" to denote femininity generally devalues the words to which they are added. For example, a "major" has higher standing than a "majorette," as does a "host" in relation to a "hostess." And, certainly, men's groups with names such as the Saskatchewan Roughriders carry more stature than women's groups with names such as the Radio City Music Hall Rockettes.

Language and Attention

Language also shapes reality by directing greater attention to masculine endeavours. Consider our use of personal pronouns. In the English language, the plural pronoun "they" is neutral, as it refers to both sexes. But the corresponding singular pronouns "he" and "she" specify gender. According to traditional grammatical practice, we use "he" along with the possessive "his" and the objective "him" to refer to all people. Thus, we assume that the bit of wisdom "He who hesitates is lost" refers to women as well as to men. But this practice also reflects the traditional cultural pattern of ignoring the lives of women. Some research suggests that people continue to respond to allegedly inclusive male pronouns as if only males were involved (MacKay, 1983).

The English language has no gender-neutral, third-person-singular personal pronoun. In recent years, however, the plural pronouns "they" and "them" have increasingly gained currency as singular pronouns (e.g., "A person should do as they please"). This usage remains controversial because it violates grammatical rules. Yet, there is no doubt that English is now evolving to accept such gender-neutral constructions.

Even as the English language changes in response to social imperatives, gender is likely to remain a source of miscommunication between women and men. A booklet entitled *Words that Count Women ~~Out~~ In* (Ontario Women's Directorate, 1992) examines some of the most common assumptions and barriers that have made the transition to gender-inclusive language troublesome. Some of their suggestions for bias-free wordings are included in Table 6–1.

The authors point out that sexist language is so prevalent that it can even be found in the one piece of music that all Canadians hear and sing thousands of times over in their lifetimes:

> O Canada! Our home and native land!
> True patriot love in all thy sons command.

Our national anthem, the symbol of our democratic spirit, excludes half the population.

HUMOUR: PLAYING WITH REALITY

Some people think that comedy is Canada's greatest cultural export. Humour plays a vital part in everyday life. Comedians are among our favourite entertainers, most newspapers carry cartoons, and even professors and members of the clergy may include a joke or two in their performances. As with many aspects of social life, however, we largely take humour for granted. While everyone laughs at a joke, in other words, few people think about what makes something funny or

TABLE 6–1 Examples of Bias and Bias-Free Words

Biased	Bias-Free	Biased	Bias-Free
The Work World		**Stereotypes**	
alderman	municipal councillor	femme fatale	seducer
anchorman	anchor	kingmaker	power behind the throne,
career girl, career woman	professional, manager, executive		eminence grise
cleaning lady	cleaner	lady luck	luck
engineman	engine operator	maiden voyage	first voyage
foreman	supervisor	man of letters	scholar, writer, literary figure
longshoreman	dockhand, shorehand	one-upmanship	upstaging, competitiveness
newsman	journalist, reporter, newshound	workmanship	quality construction, expertise
World of Play		**Turns of Phrase**	
horseman, horsewoman	rider	All men are created equal.	We are all created equal.
sportsman	sports buff, sports enthusiast,	Boys will be boys.	Kids will be kids.
	athlete	A fool and his money are	Fools and their money are soon
		soon parted.	parted.
Roles People Play		Man does not live by	We don't live by bread alone.
alumni	graduates	bread alone.	
boys in blue	armed forces	A man's home is his castle.	Your home is your castle.
corporate wife	corporate spouse	no-man's-land territory	limbo, dead zone, unclaimed
layman	layperson, uninitiated,	to a man	to a one, to a person, without
	nonprofessional		exception
The Human Family		**Put-downs**	
brotherhood	kinship, community	fall guy	chump, dupe, scapegoat
common man	common person, average person	manhandle	abuse, mistreat
fatherland	native land	nervous Nellie	worrywart, worrier
fellowship	camaraderie	prodigal son	spendthrift, returned prodigal
sons of God	children of God	tomboy	rough-and-tumble child

SOURCE: Adapted from *Words That Count Women ~~Out~~ In* (1992).

why humans everywhere like to laugh. Many of the ideas developed in this chapter provide insights into the character of humour, as we shall now see.[2]

The Foundation of Humour

Humour is a product of reality construction; specifically, it stems from the contrast between two, incongruous realities. Generally, one reality is *conventional*, corresponding to what people expect in a specific situation. The other reality is *unconventional*, representing a significant violation of cultural patterns. Humour, therefore, arises from contradiction, ambiguity, and "double meanings" generated by two differing definitions of the same situation. Note how this principle works in this Woody Allen line: "I'm not afraid to die; I just don't want to be there when it happens."

In this example, the first phrase represents a conventional notion; the second half, however, interjects an unconventional—even absurd—meaning that col-

lides with what we are led to expect. This same simple pattern holds true for virtually all humour. Of course, there are countless ways to mix realities and, thereby, generate humour. In some cases, contrasting realities emerge simply from reordering syllables, as in the case of the (probably fictitious) country song "I'd Rather Have a Bottle in Front of Me Than a Frontal Lobotomy."

Of course, a joke can be built the other way around, so that the comic leads the audience to expect an unconventional answer but gives it a very ordinary one. When a reporter asked the famous desperado Willy Sutton why he robbed banks, for example, he replied dryly: "Because that's where the money is." However a joke is constructed, the greater the opposition or incongruity between the two definitions of reality, the greater the potential for humour.

The Dynamics of Humour: "Getting It"

If people fail to understand both the conventional and unconventional realities embedded in a joke, they usually say, with a puzzled expression, "I don't get it." To "get" humour, members of an audience must understand the two realities underlying the joke well enough to perceive their incongruity.

---

[2] The ideas contained in this section on humour are those of John J. Macionis (1987), except as otherwise noted. The general approach draws on work examined in this chapter, especially on the ideas of Erving Goffman.

Humorous treatment of shared experience is a way to express a common identity. On the television program This Hour Has 22 Minutes, *controversial issues, politicians, and other public figures are poked fun at in a news broadcast format.*

But getting a joke can be more challenging still, because comics may deliberately omit some of the information listeners must grasp. The audience, therefore, must pay attention to the stated elements of the joke, and then fill in the missing pieces on their own. As a simple case, consider the reflection of movie producer Hal Roach upon reaching his one-hundredth birthday:

> If I had known I would live to be one hundred, I would have taken better care of myself!

Here, "getting" the joke depends on realizing that Roach must have taken pretty good care of himself to live to be one hundred in the first place. Or take one of W.C. Field's lines: "Some weasel took the cork out of my lunch." "Some lunch," we think to ourselves to "finish" the joke.

Of course, some jokes demand more mental effort than others. *The Globe and Mail* (August 2, 1997:A1), under "Your Morning Smile," published a submission by Torontonian Poly O'Keefe, who must have at least an introductory sociology course in her background:

> What was the name of the first sociologist to study the impact of new communications technology on society? E-mail Durkheim.

To get this joke requires specialized knowledge about sociology. Of course, your recognition chuckle would have been more spontaneous had you encountered this tidbit out of context in the newspaper.

Why would an audience be required to make this sort of effort in order to understand a joke? Simply because our enjoyment of a joke is heightened by the pleasure of having completed the puzzle necessary to "get it." In addition, once we understand a complex joke, we gain favoured status as an "insider" in the larger audience. These insights explain the frustration that accompanies not getting a joke: the fear of mental inadequacy coupled with a sense of being socially excluded from a pleasure shared by others. Not surprisingly, "outsiders" in such a situation may fake "getting" the joke; sometimes, too, others may tactfully explain a joke to end another's sense of being left out.

But, as the old saying goes, if a joke has to be explained, it won't be very funny. Besides taking the edge off the language and timing on which the *punch* depends, an explanation completely relieves the audience of any mental involvement, substantially reducing its pleasure.

The Topics of Humour

People throughout the world smile and laugh, signifying humour as a universal human trait. But, living in diverse cultures, the world's people differ in what they find funny, so humour does not travel well.

October 1, 1994, Kobe, Japan: Can you share a joke with people who live halfway around the world? At dinner, I ask two Japanese college women to tell me a joke. "You know 'crayon'?" Asako asks. I nod. "How do you ask for a crayon in Japanese?" I respond that I have no idea. She laughs out loud as she says what sounds like "crayon crayon." Her companion Mayumi laughs too. Amy and I sit awkwardly straight-faced. Asako relieves some of our embarrassment by explaining that the Japanese word for "give me" is kureyo, which sounds like "crayon." I force a smile.

What is humorous to the Japanese, then, may be lost on the Chinese, Iraqis, or Canadians. To some degree, too, the social diversity of our own country means that people will find humour in different situations. Newfoundlanders, Québécois, and Westerners have their own brands of humour, as do Italians and Inuit, fifteen- and forty-year-olds, Bay Street brokers and hard hat construction workers.

But, for everyone, humour deals with topics that lend themselves to double meanings or *controversy*. For example, the first jokes many of us learned as children concerned the cultural taboo sex. The mere mention of "unmentionable acts" or even certain parts of the body can cause young faces to dissolve in laugh-

SOCIAL DIVERSITY

Double Take:
Real Headlines That Make People Laugh

Humor is generated by mixing two distinct and opposing realities. Here are several actual headlines from recent newspaper stories. Read each one and identify the conventional meaning intended by the writer as well as the unconventional interpretation that generates humor.

"Police Begin Campaign to Run Down Jaywalkers"

"Iraqi Head Seeks Arms"

"Panda Mating Fails: Veterinarian Takes Over"

"Squad Helps Dog Bite Victim"

"War Dims Hope for Peace"

"Drunk Gets Nine Months in Violin Case"

"Stud Tires Out"

"Soviet Virgin Lands Short of Goal Again"

"Miners Refuse to Work After Death"

"British Left Waffles on Falkland Islands"

"Survivor of Siamese Twins Joins Parents"

"Prostitutes Appeal to Pope"

"Teacher Strikes Idle Kids"

"Killer Sentenced to Die for Second Time in Ten Years"

"Stolen Painting Found by Tree"

SOURCE: Thanks to Kay Fletcher (1977).

---

ter. Are there jokes that do break through the culture barrier? Yes, but they must touch upon universal human experiences such as turning on a friend.

```
Journal entry continues ... I try a num-
ber of jokes, to little effect. So many
of our jokes are ethnic, and the two
Japanese women cannot connect. Inspira-
tion: "Two fellows are walking in the
woods and come upon a huge bear. One guy
leans over and tightens up the laces on
his running shoes. 'Jake,' says the
other, 'what are you doing? You can't out-
run this bear,' 'I don't have to outrun
the bear' responds Jake, 'I just have to
outrun you!'" Smiles all around.
```

The controversy inherent in humour often walks a fine line between what is funny and what is considered "sick." During the Middle Ages, the word *humours* (derived from the Latin *humidus*, meaning "moist") referred to a balance of bodily fluids that regulated a person's health. Today's researchers have provided scientific justification for the notion that "Laughter is the best medicine," because maintaining a sense of humour reduces a person's level of unhealthy stress (Robinson, 1983; Haig, 1988). At the extreme, however, people who always take conventional reality lightly risk being defined as deviant or

even mentally ill (a common stereotype depicts insane people laughing uncontrollably, and we have long dubbed mental hospitals "funny farms").

And then there are certain topics that every social group declares to be too sensitive for humorous treatment. Of course, one can joke about such things, but doing so courts criticism for telling a "sick" joke (and, therefore, being sick). People's religious beliefs, tragic accidents, or appalling crimes are the stuff of "sick" jokes.

The Functions of Humour

If humour is a cultural universal, it must make a significant contribution to social life. From a structural-functional perspective, humour serves as a social "safety valve," allowing people to release potentially disruptive sentiments safely. By means of humour, we can acceptably discuss a host of cultural taboos, from sex to prejudice to hostility towards parents.

Having strayed into controversy, an individual may also use humour to defuse the situation. Called to account for a remark an audience takes as offensive, a speaker may simply state, "I didn't mean anything by what I said; it was just a joke!" Likewise, an audience may use humour as a form of tact, smiling, as if to say, "We could take offence at what you said, but we'll assume you were only kidding."

As Canadians, we often use humour to express our common identity. By laughing at ourselves and

Is Technology Changing Our Reality?

Any technology tends to create a new human environment. ... Technological environments are not merely passive containers of people but are active processes that reshape people and other technologies alike. In our time the sudden shift from the mechanical technology of the wheel to the technology of electric circuitry represents one of the major shifts of all historical time.

—Marshall McLuhan, *The Gutenberg Galaxy*

When Alexander Graham Bell invented the telephone in 1874, and made the first long distance call between Brantford and Paris, Ontario, people were amazed that they suddenly had the ability to talk to others who were far away. No

doubt, people were just as astounded when Guglielmo Marconi received the first transatlantic wireless (radio) message on a hilltop at St. John's, Newfoundland (1901), or when the first airplane lifted off the ground (1903), or when the first television signal was broadcast (1939).

Is today's new information technology once again restructuring reality? Absolutely. We can cite at least three reasons why. First, computers and other information technology have already altered the Canadian economy: the production of material goods (such as paper and steel) that defined the Industrial Age is steadily being replaced by the creation of ideas and images. This trend is changing not only the nature of work, but the skills needed to find employment, and even our legal definition of property.

Second, new information technology is eroding the importance of place in our lives. Bell's telephone was able to "reshape people"—to borrow McLuhan's phrase—by greatly extending their ear's "reach;" however, because sound travelled along wires, Bell knew exactly where the call was going. Telephones remained basically unchanged for a century after that. Today, however, cellular technology allows a person to key in a number and reach another person who could be, quite literally, anywhere on the continent, moving in a car, or flying eight miles above the earth.

Similarly, technological advances are reconstructing the workplace so that "the new factory" is now any place one can position a computer terminal or fax machine, including one's home. Even the centuries-old concepts of na-

---

putting ourselves down, we reinforce a sense of our common bond. In the following joke, we are all being made fun of:

> After all, [Canada's] idea of a joke is spending a year debating a constitutional accord as if it were a matter of life and death, then changing the subject. Canada is a nation without a punch line. (Johnson, 1993:32)

In the midst of the deep divisions caused by the constitutional discussions, the joke reminds us that we have a common national identity. We are "insiders" to the joke, not only because we are familiar with the events being referred to, but also because we recognize in the situation as it is described a pattern that in some way characterizes our country. Because anglophones share constitutional angst with the Québécois, one can expect this joke to be funny in French translation. Would the joke seem as funny if the writer were an American?

Like theatre and art, humour allows a society to challenge orthodox ideas and to explore alternatives to the status quo. Sometimes, in fact, humour may actu-

ally promote social change by loosening the grip of convention.

Humour and Conflict

If humour holds the potential to liberate those who laugh, it can also be used to oppress others. Men who tell jokes about feminists, for example, typically are voicing some measure of hostility towards them (Powell and Paton, 1988; Benokraitis and Feagin, 1995). Similarly, jokes at the expense of gay people reveal the tensions surrounding sexual orientation in North America. Humour may be a sign of real conflict in situations where one or both parties choose not to bring the conflict out into the open (Primeggia and Varacalli, 1990).

"Put-down" jokes may function to make one category of people feel good at the expense of another. After collecting and analyzing jokes from many societies, Christie Davies (1990) concluded that conflict among ethnic groups is one driving force behind humour virtually everywhere. In the typical ethnic joke, the jokester and the audience label some disadvantaged category of people as stupid or ridiculous, thereby imputing greater wisdom and skills to people

tional boundaries and citizenship have grown fuzzy under the influence of new technology. Consider an employee who logs on to a computer terminal in Vancouver and, travelling the information highway, connects to a U.S. bank in Manhattan, where she processes transactions throughout the day. Is this "electronic immigrant" part of the labour force of Canada or the United States?

Third, there is no more basic foundation of our sense of reality than the timeless adage, "Seeing is believing." But digital imagery now allows photographers to combine and manipulate pictures to show anything; computer animation enables movie producers to have humans interact with lifelike dinosaurs, and the technology of "virtual reality" means that, connected to computers, we can see, hear, and even feel the "touch" of another person thousands of miles away.

Finally, new information technology is already reshaping the university and college scene. Historically, publishers have produced textbooks that augment the live instruction of a classroom teacher. But books are becoming a smaller and smaller part of publishers' offerings, as we witness a proliferation of images on tape, film, and computer disk. In the years to come, textbooks themselves gradually will be replaced by CD-ROMs. In a world of interactive computer-based instruction, will students still need to travel to classrooms to learn? Indeed, will the university or college campus itself eventually become obsolete?

Continue the debate . . .

1. *Over thirty years ago, Canadian media theorist Marshall McLuhan predicted that nations and their boundaries would not be able to survive the new electronic technologies, with their power of "totally involving all people in all other people." Under the influence of border-jumping technologies such as the Internet, will Canada survive as a separate country? What is your own prediction?*

2. *Do you see any dangers in the new information technology? Might this technology render life more impersonal or threaten our privacy?*

3. *As the "electronic age" unfolds, what changes would you predict in everyday routines involving school, recreation, entertainment, shopping, employment, and the economy?*

4. *If the university or college campus were to disappear, would the university or college as an institution disappear as well?*

like themselves. Given the Anglo-Saxon and French traditions of Canadian society, Poles and other ethnic and racial minorities have long been the butt of jokes, as have Newfoundlanders ("Newfies") in eastern Canada, the Irish in Scotland, Sikhs in India, Turks in Germany, Hausas in Nigeria, Tasmanians in Australia, and Kurds in Iraq.

Disadvantaged people, of course, also make fun of the powerful (although they usually do so discreetly). Women in North America have long joked about men, and poor people poke fun at the rich. Throughout the world, people target their leaders with humour, and officials in some countries take such jokes seriously enough to vigorously repress them.

In sum, the significance of humour is much greater than first impressions suggest. Humour amounts to a means of mental escape from a conventional world that is not entirely to our liking (Flaherty, 1984, 1990; Yoels and Clair, 1995). With that in mind, it makes sense that a disproportionate number of North America's comedians come from among the ranks of oppressed people, including Jews and African-Americans. As long as we maintain a sense of humour, then, we assert our freedom and are never prisoners of reality. And, in doing so, we change the world and ourselves just a little.

SUMMARY

1. Social structure provides guidelines for behaviour, rendering everyday life understandable and predictable.

2. A major component of social structure is status. Within an entire status set, a master status has particular significance.

3. Ascribed statuses are essentially involuntary, while achieved statuses are largely earned. In practice, however, many statuses incorporate elements of both ascription and achievement.

4. Role is the dynamic expression of a status. The incompatibility of roles corresponding to two or

more statuses generates role conflict; likewise, incompatible roles linked to a single status produce role strain.

5. The phrase "social construction of reality" conveys the important idea that we all build the social world through our interaction.

6. The Thomas theorem states, "Situations defined as real become real in their consequences."

7. Ethnomethodology seeks to reveal the assumptions and understandings people have of their social world.

8. Dramaturgical analysis studies how people construct their personal behaviour. This approach casts everyday life in terms of theatrical performances, noting how people try to foster impressions in the minds of others, the settings of interaction, and how performers often idealize their intentions.

9. Social power affects performances; our society's general subordination of women causes them to craft their behaviour differently than men do.

10. Social behaviour carries the ever-present danger of embarrassment. Tact is a common response to a "loss of face" by others.

11. Language is vital to the process of socially constructing reality. In various ways, language defines females and males differently, generally to the advantage of males.

12. Humour stems from the contrast between conventional and unconventional definitions of a situation. Because comedy is framed by a specific culture, people throughout the world find humour in very different situations.

CRITICAL THINKING QUESTIONS

1. Consider ways in which a physical disability can serve as a master status. How do people commonly characterize, say, a person with the physical disability cerebral palsy with regard to mental ability? With regard to sexuality?

2. George Jean Nathan once quipped, "I only drink to make other people interesting." What does this mean in terms of reality construction? Identify the elements of humour within this statement.

3. How does modern communications technology alter social interaction?

4. Here is a joke about sociologists: "Question—How many sociologists does it take to change a light-bulb? Answer—None, because there is nothing wrong with the light-bulb; it's the system that needs to be changed!" What makes this joke funny? What sort of people are likely to "get it"? What kind of people probably won't? Why?

SOCIOLOGY APPLIED

1. Write down as many of your own statuses as you can. Do you consider any statuses to be a master status? To what extent are each of your statuses ascribed and achieved?

2. During the next twenty-four hours, every time people ask "How are you?" stop and actually tell them. What happens when you respond to a "polite" question in an unexpected way? (Watch people's body language as well as noting what they say.) What does this experience suggest about everyday interactions?

3. This chapter illustrates Erving Goffman's ideas with a description of a physician's office. Investigate the offices of several professors in the same way. What furniture is there and how is it arranged? What "props" do professors use? How are the offices of physicians and professors different? Why are they different?

4. Spend an hour or two walking around the businesses of your town (or shops at a local mall). Observe the presence of women and men in each business. Based on your observations, would you conclude that physical space is "gendered"?

WEBLINKS

http://online.anu.edu.au/psychology/socpsych/socident.htm

Social Psychology at ANU—Social Identity Page contains an essay that describes social identity as having to do with categorization, identification, and comparison. We identify with groups to which we perceive ourselves to belong. Thinking of oneself as both a group member and as an individual is part of one's self-concept. This is an adaptation of a journal article.

http://www.ntu.ac.uk/soc/psych/miller/goffman.htm

Goffman on the Internet contains "The Presentation of Self in Electronic Life: Goffman on the Internet," a paper presented at the Embodied Knowledge and Virtual Space conference at the University of London in June 1995. Goffman's description of face-to-face interaction is discussed in relationship to interpersonal communication on the Internet.

http://www.bekkoame.or.jp/~mizukawa/EM/EMindex.html

The *unOfficial Ethnomethodology Homepage* contains a bibliography and links to various ethnomethodology sites, conferences, papers, journals, and a newsletter for researchers in ethnomethodology and conversation analysis.

http://mambo.ucsc.edu/psl/ekman.html

This site, which is dedicated to the publications of Paul Ekman, one of the leading researchers in the area of emotion, contains links to abstracts of several of his studies, as well as Ekman's complete research bibliography.

http://www.lumina.net/OLD/gfp/

Gender-Free Pronoun Frequently Asked Questions is a general information source for gender-free alternatives to gendered pronouns.

Ed McGowin, *Society Telephone Society*, 1989

CHAPTER 7

GROUPS AND ORGANIZATIONS

Sixty years ago, the opening of a new restaurant in Pasadena, California, attracted little attention from the local community and went unnoticed by the nation as a whole. Yet this seemingly insignificant small business, owned and operated by Mac and Dick McDonald, would eventually spark a revolution in the restaurant industry and provide an organizational model that would be copied by countless other businesses of all kinds.

The basic formula the McDonald brothers put into place—which we now call "fast food"—was to serve good quality food quickly and inexpensively to large numbers of people. They trained employees to perform highly specialized jobs, so that one person grilled hamburgers while others "dressed" them, made French fries, whipped up milkshakes, and presented the food to the customers.

As the years went by, the McDonald brothers prospered and they moved their single restaurant from Pasadena to San Bernardino.

It was there, in 1954, that events took an unexpected turn when Ray Kroc, a travelling blender and mixer merchant, paid a visit to the McDonalds.

Kroc was fascinated by the brothers' efficient system, and, almost immediately, saw the potential for a greatly expanded system of fast-food restaurants. Kroc launched his plans in partnership with the McDonald brothers. Soon, he bought out their interests and set out on his own to become one of the greatest success stories of all time. Today, twenty thousand McDonald's restaurants serve people in ninety-three countries around the world.

From a sociological point of view, the success of McDonald's reveals much more than the popularity of hamburgers. As this chapter explains presently, the larger importance of this story lies in the extent to which the principles that guide the operation of McDonald's are coming to dominate social life in North America and elsewhere.

We begin by examining social groups, the clusters of people with whom we associate in much of our daily lives. As we shall see, the scope of group life has expanded greatly during this century. From a world built on the family, the local neighbourhood, and the small business, the structure of our society now turns on the operation of vast businesses and other bureaucracies that sociologists describe as formal organizations. How this expanding scale of life came to be, and what it means for us as individuals, are the chapter's key objectives.

SOCIAL GROUPS

Virtually everyone moves through life with a sense of belonging; this is the experience of group life. A **social group** refers to *two or more people who identify and interact with one another*. Human beings continually come together to form couples, families, circles of friends, neighbourhoods, churches, businesses, clubs, and numerous large organizations. Whatever the form, groups encompass people with shared experiences, loyalties, and interests. In short, while maintaining their individuality, the members of social groups also think of themselves as a special "we."

Volunteers load a van with wood heading to Iberville-St-Hilaire, Quebec, where residents were without electricity after the ice storm of January 1998. Extraordinary circumstances such as storms, floods, or accidents can turn a crowd into a group, and strangers into neighbours.

GROUPS, CATEGORIES, AND CROWDS

People often use the term "group" imprecisely. Below, we distinguish the group from the similar concepts of category and crowd.

Category

A *category* refers to people who have some status in common. Women, single fathers, military recruits, homeowners, and Roman Catholics are all examples of categories.

Why are categories not considered groups? Simply because, while the individuals involved are aware that they are not the only ones to hold that particular status, the vast majority are strangers to one another.

Crowd

A *crowd* refers to a temporary cluster of individuals who may or may not interact at all. Students sitting together in a lecture hall do engage one another and share some common identity as college classmates; thus, such a crowd might be called a loosely formed

group. By contrast, riders hurtling along on a subway train or bathers enjoying a summer day at the beach pay little attention to one another and amount to an anonymous aggregate of people. In general, then, crowds are too transitory and too impersonal to qualify as social groups.

Circumstances, however, can turn a crowd into a group. As Torontonians learned so tragically in August 1995, people riding in a subway train that crashes under the city streets generally become keenly aware of their common plight and begin to help each other—often with heroic effort. Sometimes such extraordinary experiences become the basis for lasting relationships.

PRIMARY AND SECONDARY GROUPS

Acquaintances commonly greet one another with a smile and the simple phrase "Hi! How are you?" The response is usually a well-scripted "Just fine, thanks. How about you?" This answer, of course, is often more formal than truthful. In most cases, providing a detailed account of how you are *really* doing would prompt the other person to beat a hasty and awkward exit.

Sociologists classify social groups by measuring them against two ideal types based on members' level of genuine personal concern. This variation is the key to distinguishing *primary* from *secondary* groups.

According to Charles Horton Cooley (1864–1929), who observed the effects that urbanization and industrialization had on people's relationships over a century ago, a **primary group** is *a small social group whose members share personal and enduring relationships.* Bound together by *primary relationships,* individuals in these groups typically spend a great deal of time together, engage in a wide range of activities with one another, and feel that they know one another well. Although not without periodic conflict, members of primary groups display sincere concern for their mutual welfare. In every society, the family is the most important primary group.

Cooley characterized these personal and tightly integrated groups as *primary* because they are among the first groups we experience in life. In addition, the family and early play groups also hold primary importance in the socialization process, shaping attitudes, behaviour, and social identity.

The strength of primary relationships gives people a comforting sense of security. In the familiar social circles of family or friends, people feel they can "be themselves" without constantly worrying about the impressions they are making.

Members of primary groups generally provide one another with economic and other forms of assistance as well. But, as important as primary ties are, people generally think of a primary group as an end in itself rather than as a means to other ends. In other words, we prefer to think that kinship or friendship links people who "belong together," rather than people who expect to benefit from each other. For this reason, we readily call on family members or close friends to help us move into a new apartment, without expecting to pay for their services. And we would do the same for them. A friend who never returns a favour, by contrast, is likely to leave us feeling "used" and questioning the depth of the friendship.

Moreover, this personal orientation means that members of a primary group view each other as unique and irreplaceable. We typically do not care who cashes our cheque at the bank or takes our money at the supermarket checkout. Yet in the primary group—especially in the family—we are bound to specific others by emotion and loyalty. So even though brothers and sisters do not always get along, they remain siblings.

In contrast to the primary group, the **secondary group** is *a large and impersonal social group whose members pursue specific interests or activities.* In most respects, secondary groups have precisely the opposite characteristics of primary groups. *Secondary relationships* usually involve weak emotional ties and little personal knowledge of one another. Secondary groups vary in duration, but they are frequently short-term, emerging and disappearing without particular significance. Students in a university or college course, for instance, who may not see one another after the year or semester ends, exemplify the secondary group.

Weaker social ties permit secondary groups to include many more people than primary groups do. For example, dozens or even hundreds of people may work together in the same office, yet most of them pay only passing attention to one another. Sometimes the passing of time will transform a group from secondary to primary, as with co-workers who share an office for many years. Generally, however, people in a secondary group only occasionally think of themselves as "we," and the boundary separating members of a secondary group from nonmembers is far less clear than it is in primary groups.

Secondary groups lack strong loyalties and emotions because members look to one another only to achieve limited ends. So while members of primary groups display a *personal orientation,* people in secondary groups reveal a *goal orientation.* Secondary ties need not be aloof or cold, of course. Social interactions among students, co-workers, and business associates are often quite pleasant even if they are rather impersonal.

In primary groups, members define each other according to *who* they are, that is, in terms of kinship or unique, personal qualities. Members of secondary groups, by contrast, look to one another for *what* they

Around the world, families are the most important primary group. In industrial societies, however, numerous friendship groups stand alongside families, joining individuals on the basis of shared interests rather than kinship.

are or what they can do for each other. In secondary groups, in other words, we are always mindful of what we offer others and what we receive in return. For example, the people next door typically expect that a neighbourly favour will be reciprocated. Such "score-keeping" comes through most clearly in business relationships where exchange may be made explicit in contracts.

The goal orientation of secondary groups encourages individuals to craft their behaviour carefully. In these roles, we remain characteristically impersonal and polite. The secondary relationship, therefore, is one in which the question "How are you?" may be asked without really expecting a truthful answer.

Table 7–1 summarizes the characteristics that distinguish primary and secondary groups. Keep in mind that these traits define two types of social groups in ideal terms: actual groups in our lives may contain elements of both. By placing these concepts at each end of a continuum, however, we devise a useful scheme for describing and analyzing group life.

In general, primary relationships predominate in low-income, pre-industrial societies throughout Latin America, Africa, and Asia in which people's lives revolve around families and local villages. In these countries, especially in rural areas, strangers stand out in the social landscape. By contrast, secondary ties take precedence in high-income, industrial societies, in which people assume highly specialized social roles. Most Canadians, especially in cities, routinely engage in impersonal, secondary contacts with virtual strangers—people about whom we know very little and whom we may never meet again (Wirth, 1938).

TABLE 7–1 Primary Groups and Secondary Groups: A Summary

	Primary Group ◄──► Secondary Group	
Quality of relationships	Personal orientation	Goal orientation
Duration of relationships	Usually long-term	Variable; often short-term
Breadth of relationships	Broad; usually involving many activities	Narrow; usually involving few activities
Subjective perception of relationships	As an end in itself	As a means to an end
Typical examples	Families; close friendships	Co-workers; political organizations

GROUP LEADERSHIP

How do groups operate? One important dimension of group dynamics is leadership. Groups vary in the extent to which members recognize leaders. Large, secondary groups generally place leaders in a formal chain of command; a small circle of friends may have no leader at all. Parents assume leadership roles in families, although husband and wife may disagree about who is really in charge.

Two Leadership Roles

Groups typically benefit from two kinds of leadership (Bales, 1953; Bales and Slater, 1955). **Instrumental leadership** refers to *group leadership that emphasizes the completion of tasks*. Members look to instrumental leaders to get things done. **Expressive leadership**, by contrast, *focuses on collective well-being*. Expressive leaders take less of an interest in the performance goals of a group than in group morale and minimizing tension and conflict among members.

Concentrating on performance, instrumental leaders usually have formal, secondary relations with other group members: they give orders and reward or punish people according to their contributions to the group's efforts. Expressive leaders, on the other hand, cultivate more personal, primary ties. They offer sympathy to a member having a tough time, work to keep the group united, and lighten serious moments with humour. While successful instrumental leaders enjoy more distant *respect* from members, expressive leaders generally garner more personal *affection*.

In the traditional, North American family, this differentiation of leadership is linked to gender. Historically, cultural norms bestowed instrumental leadership on men so that, as fathers and husbands, they assume primary responsibility for earning income, making decisions, and disciplining children. By contrast, expressive leadership has been the traditional purview of women. Historically, mothers and wives have encouraged supportive and peaceful relationships among family members. This division of labour partly explains why many children have greater respect for their fathers but closer personal ties with their mothers (Parsons and Bales, 1955; Macionis, 1978).

Of course, increasing equality between men and women has blurred this gender-based distinction between instrumental and expressive leadership. In more group settings, women and men now assume both of these leadership roles.

Three Leadership Styles

Sociologists also characterize group leadership in terms of three orientations to power. *Authoritarian leadership* stresses instrumental concerns, taking personal charge of decision making and demanding strict compliance from subordinates. Although this leadership style may win little affection from group members, a fast-acting authoritarian leader often earns praise in a crisis situation.

Democratic leadership has a more expressive focus, with concern for including everyone in the decision-making process. Although less successful when crises afford little time for discussion, democratic leaders generally draw on the ideas of all members to forge reflective and imaginative responses to the tasks at hand.

Laissez-faire leadership (from the French phrase meaning, roughly, "to leave alone") allows the group to function more or less on its own. This style typically is the least effective in promoting group goals (White and Lippitt, 1953; Ridgeway, 1983).

GROUP CONFORMITY

Canadians across the country were shocked by news from Vancouver Island in November 1997. A group of teenagers on a riverbank had brutally beaten fourteen-year-old Reena Virk, whose body was found in the water a week later. Perhaps the most shocking element in this story was the fact that the teenagers who viciously attacked their classmate were, with one exception, girls. An incident that began with accusations that Reena had been spreading rumours about one of the girls escalated into brutal violence after the girl stubbed a cigarette out on Reena's forehead. Seven girls and one boy proceeded to assault Reena, while ten others watched and did nothing to intervene. Actions that would not have been contemplated by the *individuals* involved became possible in the group context—in fact, the actions became part of the process of belonging to the group or conformity to group expectations.

The fact that teens are anxious to fit in surprises no one, although many people might be amazed at the lengths to which some will go to gain acceptance. Social scientists confirm the power of group pressure to shape human behaviour and report that it remains strong into adulthood.

Asch's Research

Solomon Asch (1952) conducted a classic investigation that revealed the power of group conformity. Asch recruited students for an alleged study of visual perception. Before the actual experiment, however, he revealed to all but one member in each small group that their real purpose was to impose group pressure on the remaining subject. Placing all the students around a table, Asch asked each, in turn, to note the length of a "standard" line, as shown on Card 1 in Figure 7–1, and match it to one of three lines on Card 2.

Anyone with normal vision could easily see that the line marked "A" on Card 2 was the correct choice. Initially, as planned, everyone made the matches correctly. But then Asch's secret accomplices began answering incorrectly, making the naive subject (seated at the table in order to answer next to last) bewildered and uncomfortable.

What happened? Asch found that one-third of all subjects placed in this situation chose to conform to the others by answering incorrectly. His investigation indicates that many of us are willing to compromise our own judgment to avoid the discomfort of being different from others, even from people we do not know.

Milgram's Research

Stanley Milgram—a former student of Solomon Asch—conducted controversial conformity experiments of his own. In Milgram's initial study (1963, 1965; Miller, 1986), a researcher explained to male recruits that they were about to engage in a study of how punishment affects learning. One by one, he assigned them the role of "teacher" and placed another individual—an insider to the study—in a connecting room as the "learner."

The teacher saw the learner sit down in an ominous contraption resembling an electric chair. Before connecting an electrode attached to the learner's wrist, the researcher applied electrode paste to it, explaining that this would "prevent blisters and burns." The researcher explained to the teacher that leather straps holding the learner were "to prevent excessive movement while the learner was being shocked," and that, although the shocks would be painful, they would cause "no permanent tissue damage."

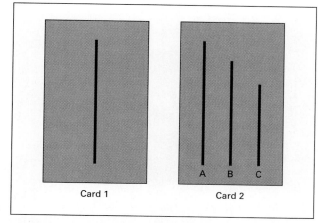

FIGURE 7–1 Cards Used in Asch's Experiment in Group Conformity

SOURCE: Asch (1952).

The researcher then led the teacher back into an adjoining room explaining that the "electric chair" was connected to a "shock generator," a bogus but forbidding piece of equipment (with a realistic-looking label that read "Shock Generator, Type ZLB, Dyson Instrument Company. Waltham, Mass."). Placed on a table in front of the teacher, this device included a shock switch and a dial marked to regulate electric current from 15 volts (labelled "slight shock") to 300 volts (marked "intense shock") to 450 volts (marked "Danger: Severe Shock" and "XXX").

Seated in front of the "shock generator," the teacher was told to begin reading aloud pairs of words. Then, the teacher repeated the first word of each pair and waited for the learner to recall the second word of the pair. Whenever the learner failed to respond correctly, however, the teacher was instructed to apply an electric shock from the "shock generator."

The researcher directed the teacher to begin at the lowest level (15 volts), and to increase the shock by 15 volts every time the learner made a mistake. And so they did. At 75, 90, and 105 volts, the teacher heard audible moans from the learner; at 120 volts, shouts of pain; at 270 volts, screams; at 315 volts, pounding on the wall; after that, deathly silence.

The results show just how readily authority figures can obtain compliance from ordinary people. None of forty subjects assigned the role of teacher during the initial research even questioned the procedure before 300 volts had been applied, and twenty-six of the subjects—almost two-thirds—went all the way to 450 volts.

Milgram (1964) then modified his research to see if Solomon Asch had documented such a high degree of group conformity only because the task of matching

In many traditional societies, children of the same age forge strong loyalties, generally with members of their own sex. These young men, members of the Massai in Kenya, sit with shaved heads listening to a blessing by the elders knowing they are about to pass together into adulthood.

lines seemed trivial. What if groups pressured people to administer electrical shocks?

To investigate, he varied the experiment so that a group of three teachers, two of whom were his accomplices, made decisions jointly. Milgram's rule was that each of the three teachers would suggest a shock level when the learner made an error and they would then administer the lowest of the three suggestions. This arrangement gave the naive subject the power to lessen the shock level regardless of the other two teachers' recommendations.

The accomplices called for increasing the shock level with each error, placing group pressure on the third member to do the same. Responding to this group pressure, subjects applied voltages three to four times higher than in control conditions in which subjects acted alone. Thus, Milgram's research suggests that people are surprisingly likely to follow the directions not only of "legitimate authority figures," but also of groups of ordinary individuals.

Janis's Research

Even the experts succumb to pressure for group conformity, according to Irving L. Janis (1972, 1989). Janis contends that a number of foreign policy errors made by the United States, including the failure to foresee the Japanese attack on Pearl Harbor in World War II, the disastrous U.S. invasion of Cuba's Bay of Pigs in 1961, and the ill-fated involvement in the Vietnam War, may have been the result of group conformity among the highest-ranking political leaders.

We often think that a group's "brainstorming" will improve decision making. However, Janis argues that group decision making sometimes backfires. First, rather than examining a problem from many points of view, groups often seek consensus, thereby narrowing the range of options. Second, groups may develop a distinctive language, adopting terms that favour a single interpretation of events. Third, having settled on a position, members of the group may come to see anyone with another view as the "opposition." Janis called this process "**groupthink**," *the tendency of group members to conform by adopting a narrow view of some issue.*

The effect of groupthink was apparent when federal and provincial leaders joined to campaign for the "yes" side during the constitutional referendum battle of October 1992 and assumed that Canadians would obediently follow suit: they failed to explain why the Charlottetown Accord would be good for Canada, opting instead for a slick advertising campaign. Anyone who pointed out that the hard-sell approach might backfire was dismissed as talking nonsense. The use of the term "enemies of Canada" to describe opponents of the accord who carefully explained their objections and fears is also consistent with groupthink.

A more recent illustration of the groupthink phenomenon was the inability of the federal "No" forces to see that they were in difficulty in the Quebec sovereignty referendum of October 1995. Assuming that Quebeckers would vote against sovereignty, Prime Minister Chrétien and his strategists appeared to have no plan for dealing with a victory by the "Yes" team. The dramatic takeover of the "Yes" forces by Bloc Québécois leader Lucien Bouchard, which took federal strategists by surprise, contributed to a razor-thin "No" victory (50.4 percent). Embarrassment and discomfort in the wake of the referendum led to attempts to assign or apportion blame. Quebec Liberal leader and head of the provincial "No" camp, Daniel Johnson, became the convenient scapegoat.

REFERENCE GROUPS

How do we assess our own attitudes or behaviour? Frequently, we make use of a **reference group**, *a social group that serves as a point of reference in making evaluations or decisions.*

A young man who imagines his family's response to a woman he is dating is using his family as a reference group. Similarly, a banker who assesses her colleagues' reactions to a new loan policy is using her co-workers as a standard of reference. As these examples illustrate, reference groups can be primary or secondary. In either case, the motivation to conform to a group means that the attitudes of others can greatly affect us.

We also use groups that we do not belong to for reference. People preparing for job interviews typically notice how those in the company they wish to join dress and act, adjusting their personal performances accordingly. The use of groups by nonmembers illustrates the process of anticipatory socialization, described in Chapter 5 ("Socialization"), by which individuals use conformity as a strategy to win acceptance by a particular group.

Stouffer's Research

Samuel A. Stouffer (1949) and his associates conducted a classic study of reference group dynamics during World War II. In a survey, researchers asked soldiers to evaluate the chances of promotion for a competent soldier in their branch of the service. One might guess that soldiers serving in outfits with a high promotion rate would be optimistic about their future advancement. Yet survey results supported the opposite conclusion: soldiers in branches of the service with low promotion rates were actually more optimistic about their own chances to move ahead.

The key to this paradox lies in sorting out the groups against which the soldiers measured their progress. Those in branches with low promotion rates looked around them and saw people making no more headway than they were. They had not been promoted, but neither had many others, so they did not feel unjustly deprived.

Soldiers in service branches with high promotion rates, however, could easily think of people who had been promoted sooner or more often than they had. With such people in mind, even soldiers who had been promoted themselves were likely to feel short-changed. So, these were the soldiers who voiced more negative attitudes in their evaluations.

Stouffer's research demonstrates that we do not make judgments about ourselves in isolation, nor do we compare ourselves with just anyone. Instead, we use specific social groups as standards in developing individual attitudes. Whatever our situation in absolute terms, then, we assess our well-being subjectively, *relative* to some specific reference group (Merton, 1968; Mirowsky, 1987).

Ingroups and Outgroups

Differences among groups in political outlook, social prestige, or even manner of dress, may lead us to embrace one while avoiding others. Across North America, for example, students wear high school jackets and place school decals on car windows to indicate that, to them, school serves as an important social group. Students attending another school may become the targets of derision simply because they belong to a rival group. The deep-seated, "friendly" rivalry between Dalhousie and Saint Mary's universities undoubtedly is matched by other pairs of universities across the country.

This illustrates an important process of group dynamics: the opposition of ingroups and outgroups. An ingroup is a social group commanding a member's esteem and loyalty. An ingroup exists in relation to an outgroup, a social group towards which one feels competition or opposition. Many social groups follow this pattern. A sports team, the Montreal Canadiens for example, is both an ingroup to its members and an outgroup for members of opposing teams such as the Calgary Flames. A town's active New Democrats are likely to think of themselves as an ingroup in relation to the local Tories. All ingroups and outgroups work on the principle that "we" have valued characteristics that "they" lack.

Tensions among groups often help to sharpen their boundaries and give people a clearer sense of social identity. However, this form of group dynamics also promotes self-serving distortions of reality. Specifically, research shows, members of ingroups construct overly positive views of themselves and hold unfairly negative views of various outgroups (Tajfel, 1982).

Power also guides intergroup relations. With greater power, members of one ingroup can define others as a lower-status outgroup; for their part, members of an outgroup may feel alienated from a system they feel victimizes them. For example, white people have historically viewed visible minorities in negative terms and subjected them to social, political, and economic disadvantages. Internalizing these negative attitudes, minorities often struggle to overcome negative self-images. In short, ingroups and outgroups foster loyalty but also generate tension and conflict.

GROUP SIZE

If you are the first person to arrive at a party, you are in a position to observe some fascinating group dynamics. Until about six people enter the room, everyone generally shares a single conversation. But as more people arrive, the group divides into two or more smaller clusters. It is apparent that size plays a crucial role in how group members interact.

To understand why, consider the mathematical connection between the number of people in a social group and the number of relationships among them. As Figure 7–2 shows, two people form a single relationship; adding a third person generates three relationships; adding a fourth person yields six. Increasing the number of people one at a time, then, boosts the

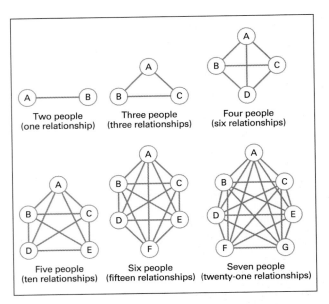

FIGURE 7–2 Group Size and Relationships

number of relationships much more rapidly since every new individual can interact with everyone already there. Thus, five people produce ten relationships and, by the time six people join one conversation, fifteen "channels" connect them. This leaves too many people unable to speak, which is why the group usually divides at this point.

The Dyad

German sociologist Georg Simmel (1858–1918) explored the social dynamics in the smallest social groups. Simmel (1950; orig. 1902) used the term **dyad** to designate *a social group with two members*. Throughout the world, most love affairs, marriages, and the closest friendships are dyadic.

What makes the dyad a special relationship? As Simmel explained, social interaction in a dyad is typically more intense than in larger groups since, in a one-to-one relationship, neither member shares the other's attention with anyone else. Thus, dyads have the potential to be the most meaningful social bonds we ever experience.

Simmel also notes that dyads, like two-legged stools, have a characteristic instability. Both members of a dyad *must* actively sustain the relationship: if either one withdraws, the dyad collapses. Because the stability of marriage is important to society, the marital dyad is supported with legal, economic, and often religious ties. Since a large group, such as the United Church women's auxiliary in Victoria, B.C., is inherently much more stable (as it can survive the loss of members), complex support mechanisms are not provided.

Marriage in our society is dyadic; ideally, we expect powerful emotional ties to unite husbands and wives. As we shall see in Chapter 17 ("Family"), however, marriage in other societies may involve more than two people. In that case, the household usually is more stable, although the marital relationships themselves may be weaker.

The Triad

Simmel also probed the **triad**, *a social group with three members*. A triad encompasses three relationships, each uniting two of the three people. A triad is more stable than a dyad because, should the relationship between any two members become strained, the third can act as a mediator to restore the group's vitality. This bit of group dynamics helps explain why members of a dyad (say, a married couple) often seek out a third person (a counsellor) to air tensions between them.

Nonetheless, two of the three can form a coalition to press their views on the third, or two may intensify their relationship, leaving the other feeling like a "third wheel." For example, two members of a triad who develop a romantic interest in each other will understand the old saying, "Two's company, three's a crowd": the potential for romance within a triad was the basis for much of the humour in the old TV sitcom *Three's Company*.

As groups grow beyond three members, they become progressively more stable because the loss of even several members does not threaten the group's existence. At the same time, increases in group size typically reduce the intense personal interaction possible only in the smallest groups. Larger groups are thus based less on personal attachments and more on formal rules and regulations. Such formality helps a large group persist over time, though the group is not immune to change. After all, their numerous members give large groups more contact with the outside world, opening the door to new attitudes and behaviour (Carley, 1991).

Does a social group have an ideal size? The answer depends on the group's purpose. A dyad offers unsurpassed emotional intensity, while a group of several dozen members is more stable, capable of accomplishing larger, more complex tasks, and better able to assimilate new members or ideas. People typically find more *personal pleasure* in smaller groups, while deriving greater *task satisfaction* from accomplishments in larger organizations (Slater, 1958; Ridgeway, 1983; Carley, 1991).

SOCIAL DIVERSITY

Social diversity affects group dynamics, especially the likelihood that members will interact with someone of another group. Peter Blau (1977, 1982; South and Messner, 1986) points out four ways in which the composition of social groups affects intergroup association.

1. **Large groups turn inward.** Extending Simmel's analysis of group size, Blau explains that the larger a group, the more likely its members are to maintain relationships exclusively among themselves. University of Toronto sociologist Raymond Breton (1964) studied this phenomenon among urban minorities, coining the term *institutional completeness* to account for the abilities of larger groups to meet their members' needs from within their own boundaries. In contrast, members of smaller groups reach beyond their immediate social circles. Generations ago, when the Montreal Jewish community was very small, young people could not find marriage partners from within: many migrated to centres with larger Jewish populations (New York, for example) or married non-Jews, thus threatening the viability of the Montreal community.

2. **Heterogeneous groups turn outward.** The more internally heterogeneous a group is, the more likely its members are to interact with members of other groups. We would expect, for example, that campus groups that recruit members of both sexes and people of various ethnic and geographic backgrounds would experience more intergroup contact than those that choose members of only one social type.

3. **Social parity promotes contact.** An environment in which all groups have roughly equal standing encourages people of all social backgrounds to mingle and form social ties. Thus, whether groups insulate their members or not depends on whether the groups themselves are dispersed within a social hierarchy.

4. **Physical boundaries foster social boundaries.** Blau contends that physical space affects the chances of contacts among groups. To the extent that a social group is physically segregated from others (by having its own dorm or dining area, for example), its members are less likely to interact with other people. The maintenance of social boundaries is enhanced by geographic separation as with First Nations reservations, Alberta's Hutterite colonies, or the province of Quebec.

NETWORKS

Formally, a **network** is *a web of social ties that links people who identify and interact little with one another*. Think of a network as a "fuzzy" group that brings people into occasional contact without a group's sense of boundaries and belonging. Computer networks, or other

Throughout the world, the most intense social bonds join two people. Even so, the dyad is also characteristically unstable, since withdrawal of either party causes the group to collapse.

high-technology links, now routinely connect people living all over the world. If we consider a group as a "circle of friends," then, we might describe a network as a "social web" expanding outward, often reaching great distances and including large numbers of people.

Some network contacts are regular, as among college friends who years later stay in touch by mail and telephone. More commonly, however, a network includes people we *know of*—or who *know of us*—but with whom we interact infrequently, if at all. As one woman with a widespread reputation as a community organizer explains, "I get calls at home, someone says, 'Are you Roseann Navarro? Somebody told me to call you. I have this problem . . . '" (quoted in Kaminer, 1984:94). For this reason, social networks amount to "clusters of weak ties" (Granovetter, 1973).

Network ties may be weak, but they serve as a significant resource. For example, many people rely on their networks to find jobs. Even the scientific genius Albert Einstein needed a hand in landing his first job. After a year of unsuccessful interviewing, he obtained employment only when the father of one of his classmates put him in touch with an office manager who hired him (Clark, 1971; cited in Fischer, 1977:19). This use of networks to one's advantage suggests that, as the saying goes, *who you know* is often just as important as *what you know*.

Today's university campuses value social diversity. One of the challenges of this movement is ensuring that all categories of students are fully integrated into campus life. This is not always easy. Following Blau's theory of group dynamics, as the number of minority students increases, these individuals are able to form a group unto themselves, perhaps interacting less with others.

Networks are based on people's colleges, clubs, neighbourhoods, political parties, and personal interests. Some networks encompass people with considerably more wealth, power, and prestige than others do, which is the essence of describing someone as "well connected." And some people have denser networks than others—that is, they are connected to more people—which is also a valuable social resource. Typically, the most extensive social networks are maintained by people who are young, well educated, and living in urban areas. Finally, size of community also affects who falls within social networks: people who live in small communities have more kin in their networks than people who live in large settlements (Marsden, 1987; Markovsky et al., 1993; Kadushin, 1995; O'Brien, Hassinger, and Dersham, 1996).

In a study of "intimate networks" in East York (a Toronto borough), Wellman (1979) found that almost everyone could name one to six intimates outside the home, only half of whom were kin. While most of their intimate contacts lived within Metropolitan Toronto, only 13 percent lived in the neighbourhood. In other words, Wellman's respondents felt close to people who were widely dispersed. Neither weak-tie networks nor the intimate variety are geographically bound.

Finally, new information technology has generated a global network of unprecedented size in the form of the Internet. The "Cyber-Society" box takes a closer look at the impacts of this twenty-first century form of communication. Global Map 7–1 shows access to the Internet around the world.

FORMAL ORGANIZATIONS

Throughout human history, most people lived in small groups of family members and neighbours; this pattern was still widespread in Canada a century ago. Today, families and neighbourhoods persist, of course, but our lives revolve far more around **formal organizations,** *large, secondary groups that are organized to achieve their goals efficiently.*

Formal organizations, such as corporations or government agencies, differ from families and neighbourhoods: their greater size renders social relationships less personal and fosters a planned, formal atmosphere. In other words, formal organizations operate to accomplish complex jobs rather than to meet personal needs.

When you think about it, organizing a society with thirty million members is a remarkable feat. Countless tasks are involved, from collecting taxes to delivering the mail. To meet most of these responsibilities, we rely on large, formal organizations. The Canadian government, our largest formal organization, employs about one million people in provincial, federal, and municipal government and the armed forces. Such vast organizations develop lives and cultures of their own, so that as members come and go, the statuses they fill and the roles they perform remain unchanged over the years.

TYPES OF FORMAL ORGANIZATIONS

Amitai Etzioni (1975) has identified three types of formal organizations, distinguished by why people participate—utilitarian organizations, normative organizations, and coercive organizations.

Utilitarian Organizations

Just about everyone who works for income is a member of a *utilitarian organization,* which pays its members for their efforts. Large business enterprises, for example, generate profits for their owners and income in the form of salaries and wages for their employees. Joining utilitarian organizations is usually a matter of individual choice, although most people must join one or another utilitarian organization to make a living.

Normative Organizations

People join normative organizations not for income but to pursue goals they consider morally worthwhile. Sometimes called *voluntary associations,* these include

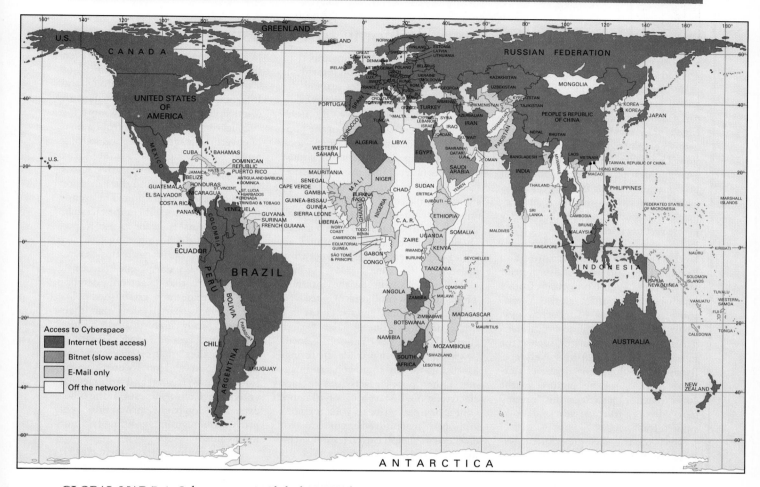

GLOBAL MAP 7–1 Cyberspace: A Global Network

While 175 of 191 world nations are connected to the Internet, a majority of the world's people have no access to this valuable resource. For one thing, computers are expensive, well out of reach of ordinary people in low-income countries, especially in Africa. Thus, the vast majority of Internet sites are in the United States, Canada, Western Europe, and Australia. But another barrier to global communication is language: born in the U.S., the Internet's software demands that users read and write in the Latin alphabet using English. But experts around the world are at work developing keyboards and interface programs that will link people using various languages. Perhaps, in the near future, the Internet may be as multicultural as the world it connects.

SOURCE: *N.Y. Times*, August 7, 1995.

community service groups (such as the Lions Club or Kiwanis), political parties, churches, and other organizations concerned with specific social issues. Historically, women played a greater role than men in voluntary and charitable organizations, in part because of their more limited involvement in the paid labour force.

Americans have long been characterized as "joiners" and still are involved, disproportionately, as members of voluntary associations (Curtis, Grabb, and Baer, 1992). Figure 7–3 provides a comparative glance at membership in cultural or educational organizations for selected countries, and reveals that Canadians are not too far behind their American neighbours.

The Internet: Welcome to Cyberspace!

Its origins seem right out of the 1963 Cold War film *Dr. Strangelove*. Three decades ago, government officials and scientists were trying to imagine how to run the country after an atomic attack, which, they assumed, would instantaneously eliminate telephones and television. The brilliant solution was to devise a communication system with no central headquarters, no one in charge, and no main power switch—in short, an electronic web that would link the country in one vast network.

It is worth noting that the brain behind it all, 1980 Web creator Tim Berners-Lee, still runs the nonprofit World Wide Web Consortium from a smallish, barren office at the Massachusetts Institute of Technology, where he helps maintain technical standards. Unlike his associates, such as the founders of Microsoft and Netscape, Berners-Lee does not drive a Mercedes-Benz or see his picture on the cover of major magazines: this "unsung hero" drives a thirteen-year-old Volkswagen Rabbit.

By 1985, the U.S. government was installing high-speed data lines around the country and the Internet was about to be born. Today, thousands of government offices, as well as universities and businesses around the world, are joined by the Internet. Many millions of other individuals connect their home computers to this "information superhighway" through a telephone-line modem and a subscription to a commercial "gateway" or server.

No one knows precisely how many people make use of the Internet. A rough estimate is that, by 1998, at least 100 million individuals in 175 (of 191) countries around the world were connected by the world's largest network in history. By 1997, Finland—where 60 percent of the population has access to the Internet—took over from Canada as the world's most "wired" country. Finns use the Internet to chat, do research, order postage stamps, bank, read newspapers, take university courses and do their grocery shopping. In addition, a new cellular phone combined with a computer allows Finns access to the Internet from the train or the sauna.

What is available on the Internet? There are now millions of sites—far more than anyone could ever list in a single directory. But popular "search engines" such as Yahoo! Canada (www.yahoo.ca) can provide site listings for just about any topic you can imagine. Other popular activities include electronic mail (start a cyber-romance with a pen pal, write to your textbook authors [macionis@kenyon.edu or lgerber@uoguelph.ca], check out sociological resources through our Web site [www.prenticehall.ca/macionis], or even send a message to the prime minister of Canada [http://pm.gc.ca]). Through the Internet, you can also participate in discussion groups, visit museums for "virtual tours," locate data from a host of government agencies (a good starting point is Statistics Canada at www.statcan.ca), and search libraries across your campus and around the world for books or other information. The excitement of the Internet lies in the fact that, given no formal rules for its use, its potential defies the imagination.

Ironically, it is precisely this chaotic quality that has many people up in arms. Pundits warn that "electronic democracy" may undermine established political practices, parents fear that their technologically sophisticated children can easily access any of the 20 000 or so "adult sites" that offer sexually explicit content, and purists bristle at the flood of advertising and commercial enterprise. Censorship and, at the other extreme, copyright protection will prove to be extremely difficult, if not impossible.

The "anything goes" character of the Internet only makes it more a virtual image of the real world. Not surprisingly, therefore, more and more users are now employing passwords, fees, and other "gates" to restrict access to subnetworks limited to people like themselves. As a result, a host of smaller social groups is emerging from the one vast network.

SOURCES: Elmer-DeWitt (1993, 1994); Haffner (1994); Ibrahim (1997); Wright (1997).

Coercive Organizations

In Etzioni's typology, *coercive organizations* are distinguished by involuntary membership. That is, people are forced to join the organization as a form of punishment (prisons) or treatment (psychiatric hospitals). Coercive organizations have extraordinary physical features, such as locked doors and barred windows, and are supervised by security personnel (Goffman, 1961). These are settings that segregate people as "inmates" or "patients" for a period of time and sometimes radically alter their attitudes and behaviour. Recall from Chapter 5 ("Socialization") the power of *total institutions* to transform a human being's overall sense of self.

From differing vantage points, any particular organization may fall into all of these categories. A psychiatric hospital, for example, serves as a coercive organization for a patient, a utilitarian organization for a psychiatrist, and a normative organization for a part-time hospital volunteer.

ORIGINS OF BUREAUCRACY

Formal organizations date back thousands of years. Elites who governed early empires relied on government officials to extend their power over millions of people and vast geographical regions. Formal organization allowed these rulers to collect taxes, undertake military campaigns, and construct monumental structures, from the Great Wall of China to the pyramids of Egypt.

The power of these early organizations was limited, however. This was not because elites lacked grandiose ambition, but, first, because they lacked the technological means to communicate quickly, to travel over large distances, and to collect and store information. Second, early organizations existed within a basically traditional setting. In pre-industrial societies, cultural patterns placed greater importance on preserving the past or carrying out "God's will" than on organizational efficiency. Only in the last few centuries did there emerge what Max Weber called a "rational world view," as described in Chapter 4 ("Society"). In the wake of the Industrial Revolution, the organizational structure called *bureaucracy* became commonplace in Europe and North America.

CHARACTERISTICS OF BUREAUCRACY

Bureaucracy is *an organizational model rationally designed to perform complex tasks efficiently.* In a bureaucratic business or government agency, officials deliberately enact and revise policy to make the organization as efficient as possible. To appreciate the power and scope of bureaucratic organization, consider that any one of more than 190 million phones in North America can connect you, within seconds, to any other phone—in homes, businesses, and automobiles, and even to a hiker on an Alberta mountain trail. Such instant communication is beyond the imagination of those who lived as recently as a century ago.

Of course, the telephone system depends on technological developments such as electricity, fibre optics, and computers. But neither could the system

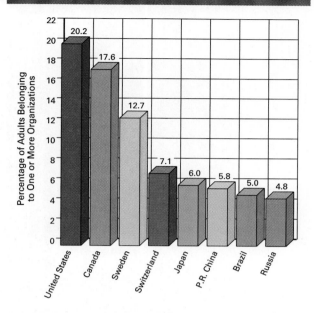

FIGURE 7–3 Membership in Cultural or Educational Organizations

SOURCE: World Values Survey (1994).

exist without the organizational capacity to keep track of every telephone call—noting which phone called which other phone, when, and for how long—and presenting all this information to many millions of telephone users in the form of monthly bills.

What specific traits promote organizational efficiency? Max Weber (1978; orig. 1921) identified six key elements of the ideal bureaucratic organization.

1. **Specialization.** Through most of human history, everyone pursued the basic goals of securing food and shelter. Bureaucracy, by contrast, assigns to individuals highly specialized duties.

2. **Hierarchy of offices.** Bureaucracies arrange personnel in a vertical hierarchy of offices. Each person is thus supervised by "higher-ups" in the organization while, in turn, supervising others in lower positions.

3. **Rules and regulations.** Cultural tradition holds scant sway in bureaucracy. Instead, operations are guided by rationally enacted rules and regulations. These rules control not only the organization's own functioning but, as much as possible, its larger environment. Ideally, a bureaucracy seeks to operate in a completely predictable fashion.

Although formal organization is vital to modern, industrial societies, it is far from new. Twenty-five centuries ago, the Chinese philosopher and teacher K'ung Fu-Tzu (known to Westerners as Confucius) endorsed the idea that government offices should be filled by the most talented young men. This led to what was probably the world's first system of civil service examinations. Here, would-be bureaucrats compose essays to demonstrate their knowledge of Confucian texts.

4. **Technical competence.** A bureaucratic organization expects officials to have the technical competence to carry out their official duties. Bureaucracies regularly monitor the performance of staff members. Such impersonal evaluation based on performance contrasts sharply with the custom, followed through most of human history, of favouring relatives—whatever their talents—over strangers.

5. **Impersonality.** In bureaucratic organizations, rules take precedence over personal whim. This impersonality encourages uniform treatment for each client as well as other workers. From this detached approach stems the notion of the "faceless bureaucrat."

6. **Formal, written communications.** An old adage states that the heart of bureaucracy is not people but paperwork. Rather than casual, verbal communication, bureaucracy relies on formal, written memos and reports. Over time, this cor-

respondence accumulates into vast *files*. These files guide the subsequent operation of an organization in roughly the same way that social background shapes the life of an individual.

These traits represent a clear contrast to the more personal character of small groups. Bureaucratic organization promotes efficiency by carefully recruiting personnel and limiting the unpredictable effects of personal tastes and opinions. In smaller, informal groups, members allow one another considerable discretion in their behaviour; they respond to each other personally and regard everyone as more or less equal in rank. Table 7–2 summarizes the differences between small social groups and large formal organizations.

ORGANIZATIONAL SIZE

Just as the character of social groups differs according to their size, so does the nature of formal organizations. Analyzing organizations of various sizes, Arne L. Kalleberg and Mark E. Van Buren (1996) found that "bigger is better" when it comes to many employee rewards. Typically, large organizations provide their workers with higher salaries, more fringe benefits, and greater opportunities for promotion.

On the other hand, the researchers conclude, "small is beautiful" when it comes to autonomy. Small organizations usually give their employees more autonomy about how they perform their jobs.

THE INFORMAL SIDE OF BUREAUCRACY

Weber's ideal bureaucracy deliberately regulates every activity. In actual organizations, however, human beings have the creativity (or the stubbornness) to resist conforming to bureaucratic blueprints. Sometimes informality helps to meet a legitimate need overlooked by formal regulations. In other situations informality may amount to simply cutting corners in one's job (Scott, 1981).

In principle, power resides in offices, not with the people who occupy them. Nonetheless, the personalities of officials greatly affect patterns of leadership. For example, studies of corporations document that the qualities and quirks of individuals—including personal charisma and interpersonal skills—have a tremendous impact on organizational outcomes (Halberstam, 1986). In Canada, the structure, operating style, and message of the Reform Party are a reflection of one man—its founder, Preston Manning.

Authoritarian, democratic, and laissez-faire types of leadership—described earlier in this chapter—also reflect individual personality as much as any organizational plan. Then, too, in the "real world" of organizations, leaders and their cronies sometimes seek to benefit personally through abuse of organizational power. And perhaps even more commonly, leaders take credit for the efforts of their subordinates. Many secretaries, for example, have far more authority and responsibility than their official job titles and salaries suggest (Yenerall et al., 1994).

Communication offers another example of how informality creeps into large organizations. Formally, memos and other written communications disseminate information through the hierarchy. Typically, however, individuals cultivate informal networks or "grapevines" that spread information much faster, if not always accurately. Grapevines—carried by both informal social networks as well as e-mail—are particularly important to subordinates because high officials often attempt to conceal important information from them.

Electronic mail is also inherently democratic, allowing even the lowest-ranking employee to bypass immediate superiors in order to communicate directly with the organization's president. Some leaders may find such "open-channel" communication unwelcome, of course. For this reason, Microsoft Corporation (whose leader, Bill Gates, has an "unlisted" address yet still receives hundreds of e-mail messages a day) is developing "screens" that will allow messages from only approved people to reach a particular computer terminal (Gwynne and Dickerson, 1997).

New information technology, as well as age-old human ingenuity, ensure that organizational members are likely to personalize their procedures and surroundings. Such efforts suggest that we turn now to take a closer look at some of the problems of bureaucracy.

PROBLEMS OF BUREAUCRACY

Despite our reliance on bureaucracy to manage countless dimensions of everyday life, many members of our society are ambivalent about this organizational form. The following sections review several of the problems associated with bureaucracy, ranging from its tendency to dehumanize and alienate individuals to the threats it poses to personal privacy and political democracy.

Bureaucratic Alienation

Max Weber touted bureaucracy as a model of productivity. Nonetheless, Weber was keenly aware of bureaucracy's potential to *dehumanize* those it purports to serve. That is, the same impersonality that fosters efficiency simultaneously denies officials and clients the ability to respond to each other's unique, personal needs. On the contrary, officials must treat each client impersonally as a standard "case."

TABLE 7–2 Small Groups and Formal Organizations: A Comparison

	Small Groups	Formal Organizations
Activities	Members typically engage in many of the same activities	Members typically engage in various highly specialized activities
Hierarchy	Often informal or nonexistent	Clearly defined, corresponding to offices
Norms	Informal application of general norms	Clearly defined rules and regulations
Criteria for membership	Variable, often based on personal affection or kinship	Technical competence to carry out assigned tasks
Relationships	Variable; typically primary	Typically secondary, with selective primary ties
Communications	Typically casual and face to face	Typically formal and in writing
Focus	Person-oriented	Task-oriented

The impersonal bureaucratic environment, then, gives rise to *alienation*. All too often, Weber contended, formal organizations reduce the human being to "a small cog in a ceaselessly moving mechanism" (1978:988; orig. 1921). The trend towards more and more formal organization, therefore, left him deeply pessimistic about the future of humankind. Although formal organizations are designed to benefit humanity, he feared that humanity might well end up serving formal organizations.

Bureaucratic Inefficiency and Ritualism

Then there is the familiar problem of inefficiency, the failure of a bureaucratic organization to carry out the work that it allegedly exists to perform. Perhaps the greatest challenge to a large, formal organization is responding to special needs or circumstances. Anyone who has ever tried to replace a lost driver's licence, return defective merchandise to a discount store, or change an address on a magazine subscription knows that bureaucracies sometimes can be maddeningly unresponsive.

The problem of inefficiency is captured in the concept of *red tape* (a phrase derived from the red tape used by eighteenth-century English administrators to wrap official parcels and records; Shipley, 1985). Red tape refers to a tedious preoccupation with organizational routines and procedures. Sociologist Robert Merton (1968) points out that red tape amounts to a new twist on the already-familiar concept of group

According to Max Weber, bureaucracy is an organizational strategy that promotes efficiency. Impersonality, however, also fosters alienation among employees, who may become indifferent to the formal goals of the organization. The behaviour of this municipal employee in Bombay, India, is understandable to members of formal organizations almost anywhere in the world.

conformity. He coined the term **bureaucratic ritualism** to designate *a preoccupation with rules and regulations to the point of thwarting an organization's goals.*

Ritualism impedes individual and organizational performance as it stifles creativity and imagination. In part, ritualism emerges because organizations, which pay modest, fixed salaries, give officials little or no financial stake in performing efficiently. Then, too, bureaucratic ritualism stands as another expression of the alienation that Weber feared would arise from bureaucratic rigidity (Whyte, 1957; Merton, 1968; Coleman, 1990; Kiser and Schneider, 1994).

Bureaucratic Inertia

If bureaucrats sometimes have little motivation to be efficient, they certainly have every reason to protect their jobs. Thus, officials typically strive to perpetuate their organization even when its purpose has been fulfilled. As Weber put it, "once fully established, bureaucracy is among the social structures which are hardest to destroy" (1978:987; orig. 1921).

Bureaucratic inertia refers to *the tendency of bureaucratic organizations to perpetuate themselves.* Formal organizations, in other words, tend to take on a life of their own beyond their formal objectives.

For example, as the need for service to veterans declined, Canadian War Amputations turned its attention to the needs of child amputees. Bureaucratic inertia usually leads formal organizations to devise new justifications for themselves after they have outlived their originally intended purpose.

Oligarchy

Early in this century, Robert Michels (1876–1936) pointed out the link between bureaucracy and political **oligarchy**, *the rule of the many by the few* (1949; orig. 1911). According to what Michels called "the iron law of oligarchy," the pyramidlike structure of bureaucracy places a few leaders in charge of vast and powerful government organizations.

Pre-industrial societies did not possess the organizational means for even the most power-hungry ruler to control everyone. But the power of elites increased over the centuries with the steady expansion of formal organizations and the development of technology.

Max Weber credited bureaucracy's strict hierarchy of responsibility with increasing organizational efficiency. By applying Weber's thesis to the organization of government, Michels reveals that this hierarchical structure concentrates power and thus endangers democracy. While the public expects organizational officials to subordinate personal interests to organizational goals, people who occupy powerful positions can—and often do—use their access to information and the media, plus numerous other advantages, to promote their personal interests.

Furthermore, bureaucracy also insulates officials from public accountability, whether in the form of a corporate president who is "unavailable for comment" to the local press or a national president seeking to control information by claiming "executive privilege." Oligarchy, then, thrives in the hierarchical structure of bureaucracy and undermines people's control over their elected leaders (Tolson, 1995).

Canada Map 7–1 on page 178 illustrates the extent to which government bureaucracy permeates Canadian society. While 6 percent of Canada's labour force is employed in public administration (federal, provincial, and municipal), regional variation is clearly evident—with levels ranging from 5.1 percent in Alberta to 20.8 percent in the Yukon.

Parkinson's Law and the Peter Principle

Finally, and on a lighter note, we acknowledge two additional insights concerning the limitations of bureaucratic organizations. The concerns of C. Northcote Parkinson and Laurence J. Peter are familiar to anyone who has ever been a part of a formal organization.

George Tooker's painting Government Bureau *is a powerful statement about the human costs of bureaucracy. The artist depicts members of the public in monotonous similitude—reduced from human beings to mere "cases" to be disposed of as quickly as possible. Set apart from others by their positions, officials are "faceless bureaucrats" concerned more with numbers than with providing genuine assistance (notice that the artist places the fingers of the officials on calculators).*

George Tooker, *Government Bureau*, 1956. Egg tempera on gesso panel, 19 ⅝ × 29 ⅝ inches. The Metropolitan Museum of Art, George A. Hearn Fund, 1956 (56.78).

Parkinson (1957) summed up his understanding of bureaucratic inefficiency with the assertion: *"Work expands to fill the time available for its completion."* Enough truth underlies this tongue-in-cheek assertion that it is known today as Parkinson's Law. To illustrate, assume that a bureaucrat working for New Brunswick's Department of Transportation processes fifty driver's licence applications in an average day. If one day this worker had only twenty-five applications to examine, how much time would the task require? The logical answer is half a day. But Parkinson's Law suggests that if a full day is available to complete the work, a full day is how long it will take.

Because organizational employees have little personal involvement in their jobs, few are likely to seek extra work to fill their spare time. Bureaucrats do strive to appear busy, however, and their apparent activity often prompts organizations to take on more employees. The added time and expense required to hire, train, supervise, and evaluate a larger staff make everyone busier still, setting in motion a vicious cycle that results in *bureaucratic bloat*. Ironically, the larger organization may accomplish no more real work than it did before.

In the same light-hearted spirit as Parkinson, Laurence J. Peter (Peter and Hull, 1969) devised the Peter Principle: *"Bureaucrats rise to their level of incompetence."* The logic here is simple: employees competent at one level of the organizational hierarchy are likely to earn promotion to higher positions. Eventually, however, they will reach a position where they are in over their heads; there, they perform poorly and thus are no longer eligible for promotions.

Reaching their level of incompetence dooms officials to a future of inefficiency. Adding to the problem, after years in the office they have almost certainly learned how to avoid demotion by hiding behind rules and regulations and taking credit for work actually performed by their more competent subordinates.

GENDER AND RACE IN ORGANIZATIONS

Rosabeth Moss Kanter, a professor of business administration at Harvard University, has analyzed how ascribed statuses such as gender and race figure in the power structure of bureaucratic hierarchies. To the extent that an organization has a dominant social composition, the gender- or race-based ingroup enjoys greater social acceptance, respect, credibility, and access to informal social networks.

As Figure 7–4 shows, much smaller proportions of women than men are in managerial occupations. Aboriginal and Black women have lower levels of representation than their British, French, and Asian counterparts, and the same holds true for men. Interestingly, though, if you consider the people employed at senior management level only (further calculations by Gerber) both aboriginal men and women (1.9 percent and 0.9 percent, respectively) are more likely to be senior managers than are their British, French, or Asian counterparts.

A smaller representation in the workplace, argues Kanter, may leave women, people of colour, and those from economically disadvantaged backgrounds feeling like members of socially isolated outgroups. They are often uncomfortably visible, taken less seriously, and

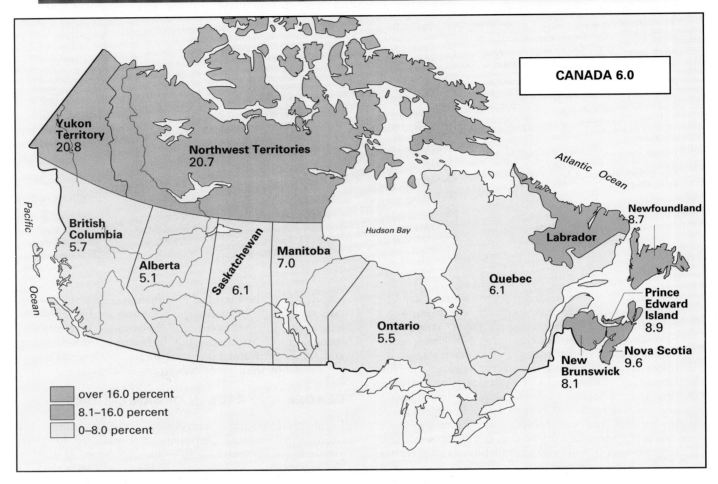

CANADA 6.0

Yukon Territory 20.8

Northwest Territories 20.7

British Columbia 5.7

Alberta 5.1

Saskatchewan 6.1

Manitoba 7.0

Ontario 5.5

Quebec 6.1

Labrador

Newfoundland 8.7

Prince Edward Island 8.9

Nova Scotia 9.6

New Brunswick 8.1

Hudson Bay

Atlantic Ocean

Pacific Ocean

over 16.0 percent
8.1–16.0 percent
0–8.0 percent

CANADA MAP 7–1 Employment in Government Service, 1996: Percent by Province and Territory

Note: Employment at federal, provincial, and municipal levels is shown as a percentage of all employment.

SOURCE: Compiled by Gerber from Statistics Canada Census Tables, www.statcan.ca.

given fewer chances for promotion. Understandably, minority individuals may conclude that they must work twice as hard as those in dominant categories to maintain their present positions, let alone advance to higher ones (Kanter, 1977; Kanter and Stein, 1979). Basset (1985) found a similar belief among Canadian career women and refers to this requirement as one of society's *double standards*.[1]

---

[1] Charlotte Whitton, the late mayor of Ottawa, put it as follows: "A woman has to be twice as good as a man to get ahead—fortunately, it's not difficult" (cited in Bassett, 1985:45).

Kanter (1977) finds that providing a structure of unequal opportunities has important consequences for everyone's on-the-job performance. A company with many "dead-end" jobs, she explains, only encourages workers to become "zombies" with little aspiration, poor self-concept, and little loyalty to the organization. Widespread opportunity, by contrast, motivates employees, turning them into "fast-trackers" with higher aspirations, greater self-esteem, and stronger commitment to the organization.

Finally, Kanter claims that in a corporate environment with wide-open opportunity for advance-

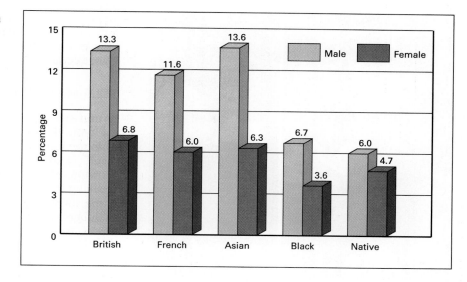

FIGURE 7–4 Representation in Management* for Selected Categories, 1991

*Percentage of employed population in managerial occupations.

SOURCE: Calculations by Gerber based on 1991 Census Public Use Microdata Files, Statistics Canada.

ment, leaders value the input of subordinates and seek to bolster their morale and well-being. It is officials with no real power, she maintains, who jealously guard their own privileges and rigidly ride herd over subordinates.

Organizational research in recent years has also spotlighted differences in management styles linked to gender. Deborah Tannen (1994) claims, for example, that women have a greater "information focus," and more readily ask questions in order to understand an issue. Men, she maintains, share an "image focus" that makes them hesitate in the same situation, wondering what effect asking questions will have on their reputations.

In another study of women executives, Sally Helgesen (1990) notes three additional gender-linked patterns. First, claims Helgesen, women tend to place greater value on communication skills and share information more than men do. Second, women are more flexible leaders who typically allow subordinates greater autonomy. Third, rather than emphasizing a narrow specialization, women are attentive to the interconnectedness of all organizational operations. Because many of today's leading business organizations operate more democratically and seek flexibility in order to contend with complex environments, Helgesen concludes that women bring a "female advantage" to the workplace.

In sum, one key conclusion drawn from recent research is that organizations that become more open and adaptable bring out the best in their employees. The flip side of this trend—in which women are playing a major part—is that, in more flexible environments, employees contribute the most to the organization.

BEYOND BUREAUCRACY: HUMANIZING ORGANIZATIONS

Humanizing organizations means *fostering a more democratic organizational atmosphere that recognizes and encourages the contributions of everyone.* Research by Kanter (1977, 1983, 1989; Kanter and Stein, 1980) and others (Peters and Waterman, Jr., 1982) suggests that "humanizing" bureaucracy produces both happier employees and healthier profits. In the post-industrial era, in other words, organizations need to foster initiative and creativity among their members. Based on the discussion so far, we can identify three paths to a more open and humane organizational structure.

1. **Social inclusiveness.** The social composition of the organization should, ideally, make no one feel "out of place" because of gender, race, or ethnicity. The performance of all employees will improve to the extent that no one is subject to social exclusion.

2. **Sharing of responsibilities.** Humanizing bureaucracy means reducing rigid oligarchical structures by spreading power and responsibility more widely. Managers cannot benefit from the ideas of employees who have no channels for expressing their opinions. Knowing that superiors are open to suggestions encourages all employees to think creatively, increasing organizational effectiveness.

3. **Expanding opportunities for advancement.** Expanding opportunity reduces the number of employees stuck in routine, dead-end jobs with little motivation to perform well. The organiza-

The recent trend is towards breaking down the rigid structure of conventional bureaucracy. One example of more flexible organizational form is the self-managed work team, whose members have the skills to carry out their tasks creatively and with minimal supervision.

tion should encourage employees at all levels to share ideas and try new approaches, defining everyone's job as the start of an upward career path.

Critical evaluation. Kanter's work takes a fresh look at the concept of bureaucracy and its application to business organizations. Rigid formality may have made sense in the past, when organizations hired unschooled workers primarily to perform physical labour. But today's educated workforce can contribute a wealth of ideas to bolster organizational efficiency—if the organization encourages and rewards innovation.

There is broad support for the idea that loosening up rigid organizations is the key to improved performance. Moreover, companies that treat employees as a resource to be developed rather than as a group to be controlled stand out as more profitable. But some critics challenge Kanter's claim that social heterogeneity necessarily yields greater productivity. In controlled comparisons, they maintain, it is homogeneous work groups that typically produce more, while heterogeneous groups are better at generating a diversity of ideas and approaches. Optimal working groups, then, appear to be those that strike a balance: team

members offer a variety of backgrounds and perspectives in outlook and goals, yet are similar enough that they can effectively coordinate their efforts (Hackman, 1988; Yeatts, 1994).

SELF-MANAGED WORK TEAMS

At mid-century, formal organizations in North America typically were conventional bureaucracies, run from the top down according to a stern chain of command. Today, especially as these businesses face growing global competition, rigid structures are breaking down. One important element of this trend is the increasing use of the *self-managed work team*. Members of these small groups have the skills necessary to carry out tasks with minimal supervision. By allowing employees to operate within autonomous groups, organizations enhance worker involvement in the job, generate a broader understanding of operations, and raise employee morale.

Even though it is difficult to compare the performance of organizations with disparate goals and operations, research indicates that self-managed work teams do boost productivity while heading off some of the problems—including alienation—of the traditional bureaucratic model. In the business world, many companies have found that decentralizing responsibility in this way also raises product quality and lowers rates of employee absenteeism and turnover (Yeatts, 1991, 1995; Maddox, 1995).

ORGANIZATIONAL ENVIRONMENT

How any organization performs depends not only on its internal structure but also on the **organizational environment,** *a range of factors external to an organization that affects its operation.* Such factors include technology, politics, population patterns, and the economy, as well as other organizations.

For example, modern organizations are shaped by the *technology* of computers, telephone systems, and copiers. Computers give employees access to more information and people than ever before. At the same time, computer technology also allows executive to closely monitor the activities of workers (Markoff, 1991).

A second dimension of the organizational environment is *political and economic trends*. All organizations are buoyed or burdened by economic growth or recession, and no organization today can afford to overlook increasing competition from abroad. Similarly, changes in law—such as environmental regulations—can dramatically alter the way an organization operates. Canadian sociologist Kathryn Schellenberg studied small companies that go through periodic boom-and-bust cycles. She found that the repeated

Is McDonaldization becoming a global trend? Yes and no. The spread of McDonald's around the world has been dramatic and the company now earns most of its revenues from operations outside the United States. But, in some nations, McDonald's has altered its menu to take account of local cultural norms. When McDonald's opened a restaurant in New Delhi, India, Hindu people were not about to begin eating beef. Thus, this restaurant company promotes "vegetable burgers" (with fries, of course).

restructuring of their bureaucracies is costly in that it undermines trust in and commitment to the organization, frequently leading to the loss of valued employees (Schellenberg, 1996; Schellenberg and Miller, 1998).

Third, *population patterns*—such as the size and composition of the surrounding populace—also affect organizations. The average age, typical education, and social diversity of a local community obviously shapes both the available workforce and the market for an organization's products or services.

Fourth, *other organizations* also contribute to the organizational environment. People who operate a hospital, for example, must be responsive not only to new government policies and regulations but also to the insurance industry and to organizations representing doctors, nurses, and other workers.

In sum, no organization operates in a social vacuum. But, just as formal organizations are shaped by their environment, organizations themselves have an impact on the surrounding society, as we shall now explain.

THE MCDONALDIZATION OF SOCIETY

October 9, 1994, Macau. Here I am half way around the world in the Portuguese colony of Macau—a little nub jutting from the Chinese coast. Few people here speak English, and life on the streets seems a world apart from the urban rhythms of New York, Chicago, or Los Angeles. Then we turn the corner and stand face to face with (who else?) Ronald McDonald! After

eating who-knows-what for so long, forgive our failure to resist the lure of the Big Mac! But the most amazing thing is that the food—the burgers, fries, and drinks—looks, smells, and tastes exactly the same as it does back home 16 000 kilometres away!

As noted in the opening to this chapter, McDonald's has enjoyed enormous success. From a single store in the mid-1950s, McDonald's now operates over eighteen thousand restaurants across North America and throughout much of the world. As of January 1996, McDonald's Restaurants of Canada Limited operated 907 outlets in Canada and five in Moscow. It was the Canadian branch that ventured into Moscow just as the Soviet Union crumbled, and the restaurant in Pushkin Square is the busiest McDonald's restaurant in the world (McDonald's Restaurants of Canada, 1996). The appeal of the burger has placed McDonald's Restaurants of Canada near the top of Canadian companies ranked by revenues—number 88 in 1997 (*The Financial Post 500*, 1998) with $1.8 billion in revenues and 68 000 employees.

McDonald's has become a symbol of the North American way of life, with polls suggesting that the gleeful clown Ronald McDonald is as much of a celebrity as Santa Claus. Even more importantly, the organizational principles that underlie McDonald's are beginning to dominate our entire society. Our culture is becoming "McDonaldized"—an awkward way of saying that we now model many aspects of life in the famous restaurant chain. Canadians, who love donuts more than Americans do, indulge their cravings at Tim Horton's or Country Style Donuts, where they know exactly what they'll get. We buy our household and automotive supplies at Canadian Tire, where inventory is continuously monitored for just-in-time replacement. More vacations take the form of resort and tour packages, television presents news in ten-second sound bites, and medical school applicants are screened on the basis of their MCAT results. The list goes on and on.

McDonaldization: Four Principles

What do all these developments have in common? According to George Ritzer (1993), the "McDonaldization of society" involves four basic organizational principles.

1. **Efficiency.** Ray Kroc, the marketing genius behind the expansion of McDonald's, set out with the goal of serving a hamburger, French fries, and a milkshake to a customer in fifty seconds. Today, one of the company's most popular items is the Egg McMuffin, an entire breakfast in a single sandwich. In the restaurant, customers bus their own trays or, better still, drive away from the pickup window taking the packaging and whatever mess they make with them.

   Efficiency is now a value virtually without critics in our society. Almost everyone believes that anything that can be done quickly is, for that reason alone, good.

2. **Calculability.** The first McDonald's operating manual declared the weight of a regular raw hamburger to be 1.6 ounces, its size to be 3.875 inches across, and its fat content to be 19 percent. A slice of cheese weighs exactly half an ounce. Fries are cut precisely 9/32 of an inch thick.

   Think about how many objects around the home, the workplace, or the campus are designed and mass-produced uniformly according to a calculated plan. Not just our environment but our life experiences—from travelling the nation's highways to sitting at home watching television—are now more deliberately planned than ever before.

3. **Uniformity and predictability.** An individual can walk into a McDonald's restaurant almost anywhere and receive the same sandwiches, drinks, and desserts prepared in precisely the same way. Predictability, of course, is the result of a highly rational system that specifies every course of action and leaves nothing to chance.

4. **Control through automation.** The most unreliable element in the McDonald's system is

human beings. People, after all, have good and bad days, sometimes let their minds wander, or simply decide to try something a different way. To eliminate the unpredictable human element as much as possible, McDonald's has automated its equipment to cook food at fixed temperatures for set lengths of time. Even the cash register at a McDonald's is little more than pictures of the items so as to minimize the responsibility of the human being taking the customer's order.

The scope of McDonaldization is expanding. Automatic teller machines are replacing banks, highly automated bakeries now produce bread with scarcely any human intervention, and chickens and eggs (or is it eggs and chickens?) emerge from automated hatcheries. In supermarkets, laser scanners are phasing out the work of (less reliable) human cashiers. Most North American shopping now occurs in malls, in which everything from temperature and humidity to the kinds of stores and products are subject to continuous control and supervision (Idle and Cordell, 1994).

Can Rationality Be Irrational?

No one would challenge the popularity or the efficiency of McDonald's and similar organizations. But there is another side to the story.

Max Weber viewed the increasing rationalization of the world with alarm, fearing that the expanding control of formal organizations would cage our imaginations and crush the human spirit. As he saw it, rational systems were efficient, but at the terrible cost of dehumanization. Each of the four principles noted above depends on reining in human creativity, discretion, and autonomy. Moreover, as George Ritzer contends, McDonald's products are not particularly good for people or the natural environment. Taking a broader perspective, Ritzer echoes Weber's concern, asserting that "the ultimate irrationality of McDonaldization is that people could lose control over the system and it would come to control us" (1993:145).

FORMAL ORGANIZATIONS IN JAPAN

We have described efforts to "humanize" formal organizations. Interestingly, however, organizations in some countries have long been more personal than those in North America. Organizations in Japan, a small nation that has had remarkable economic success, thrive within a culture of strong collective identity and solidarity. While most members of our society prize rugged individualism, the Japanese maintain traditions of cooperation.

The Japanese Model:
Will It Work in North America?

Who can argue with the economic success of the Japanese? Economic competition from Asia, and increasingly from Europe, is forcing North American companies to reconsider long-held notions about how corporate organizations should operate. Although the Japanese economy has suffered setbacks in recent years, Canadian and American companies have continued to incorporate Japanese business principles.

Among the most interesting examples of new organizations are Japanese manufacturing plants built here in Canada and in the United States. By and large, these "transplants" have been quite successful in terms of productivity, demonstrating the adaptive ability of organizations. Yet some voices in this country—workers, union leaders, and managers—speak as bitterly about transplanting Japanese organizational techniques as they do about importing Japanese cars.

Manufacturing plants operated in Canada by Honda and Toyota (in Alliston, Ontario, and Cambridge, Ontario), and in the United States by Honda, Nissan, and Toyota have achieved the same degree of efficiency and quality that have won these companies praise in Japan. However, these organizations have had to struggle to win the support of many North Americans for some traditional Japanese practices, especially the idea of broad worker participation. Our corporate culture, with its rigid hierarchy, its heritage of individualism, and its history of labour–management conflict makes proposals to enhance worker participation highly controversial.

Many workers in this country dislike the concept of worker participation because they see it as increasing their personal workloads. While still responsible for building cars, for instance, workers are now asked to worry about quality control, unit costs, and overall company efficiency—concerns usually shouldered by management. Some employees see the broad training favoured by the Japanese as a demanding routine of moving from job to job, always having to learn new skills. Many union leaders are also suspicious of new plans formulated by management, fearing an alliance between workers and managers may undermine union strength. Some managers, too, look cautiously on worker-participation programs. Sharing with employees the power to direct production and even schedule their own vacations does not come easily in light of past practices. Finally, North American corporations have a short-term outlook on profits, which discourages investing time and money in organizational restructuring.

Primarily due to rising global competition, however, worker-participation programs are slowly changing the North American workplace. While the Honda and Toyota plants here in Canada brought with them the Japanese organizational and management package, many other firms are adopting components of that package and are using them to modify their organizations. One of these, Total Quality Management (TQM), has been adopted at Culinar (Montreal), Cadet Uniform Services (Toronto), Reimer Express Lines (Winnipeg), and General Electric (Bromont, Quebec). Culinar, the Canadian pioneer of TQM, has discontinued its effort, but the other three companies are very enthusiastic about the results in terms of worker involvement and morale, customer satisfaction, and profits. The second approach, called Continuous Improvement or CI (*kaizen* in Japanese), has been responsible for a major comeback at a Schneider food processing plant in Kitchener, Ontario—the plant experienced improved efficiency, reduced waste, less absenteeism, and a dramatic increase in profits.

The successful implementation of either TQM or CI requires real commitment from senior management, a "friendly" or receptive corporate culture, highly motivated workers, willingness to change at all levels of the organization, and patience. The advantages go right to the bottom line: productivity and profits are usually higher when workers have a say in decision making. And most employees in worker-participation programs seem significantly happier about their jobs. Workers who have long used only their bodies are now enjoying the opportunity to use their minds as well.

While Canadian businesses adopted Japanese management principles to their benefit, Japan has been reeling from the effects of a prolonged recession, reduced competitiveness and efficiency, downsizing, unprecedented levels of unemployment, and, most recently, currency devaluation. The notion of lifelong bonds and loyalty between corporations and their employees suffered strain in some organizations and was abandoned in others. Despite what seemed to be superior business practices, Japan has joined the rest of the industrialized world in undergoing economic restructuring.

SOURCES: Hoerr (1989); Florida and Kenny (1991); Scott (1992); Fife (1992).

Because of Japan's social cohesiveness, formal organizations in that society approximate very large primary groups. William Ouchi (1981) highlights five distinctions between formal organizations in Japan and their counterparts in industrial societies of the West. In each case, the Japanese organization reflects that society's more collective orientation. The "Global Sociology" box looks at the application of these principles of Japanese organization in Canada.

1. **Hiring and advancement.** Organizations in North America hold out promotions and raises in salary as prizes won through individual competition. In Japanese organizations, however, companies hire new graduates together, and all employees of a particular age cohort receive the same salary and responsibilities. Only after several years is anyone likely to be singled out for individual advancement.

2. **Lifetime security.** Employees in North America expect to move from one company to another to advance their careers. Companies in turn are quick to lay off employees when economic setbacks strike. By contrast, most Japanese firms hire employees for life, fostering strong, mutual loyalties among members. Japanese companies avoid layoffs by retraining expendable workers for new jobs in the organization.

3. **Holistic involvement.** North American workers tend to see the home and the workplace as distinct spheres. Japanese organizations take a different tack, playing a broad role in their employees' lives by providing home mortgages, sponsoring recreational activities, and scheduling social events. Such interaction beyond the workplace strengthens collective identity and offers the respectful Japanese worker an opportunity to voice suggestions and criticisms informally.

4. **Broad-based training.** Bureaucratic organization in North America is based on specialization; many people spend an entire career at a single task. From the outset, a Japanese organization trains employees broadly in all phases of its operation, again with the idea that employees will remain with the organization for life.

5. **Collective decision making.** In our system, important decisions fall to key executives. Although Japanese leaders also take responsibility for their organization's performance, they involve workers in "quality circles" that discuss any decision that affects them. A closer working relationship is also encouraged by greater eco-

nomic equality between management and workers. The salary differential between executives and lower-ranking employees is about half that found in the United States.

These characteristics give the Japanese a strong sense of organizational loyalty. The cultural emphasis on *individual* achievement in our society finds its parallel in Japanese *groupism*. By tying their personal interests to those of their company, workers realize their ambitions through the organization.

GROUPS AND ORGANIZATIONS IN GLOBAL PERSPECTIVE

As this chapter has explained, formal organizations and their surrounding society interact, each influencing the other. Yet a global perspective reveals that bureaucracy does not take a consistent organizational form; formal organizations in Canada and Japan, for example, differ in a number of ways.

Organizations have also changed over time. Several centuries ago, most businesses in Europe and North America were small family enterprises. But the Industrial Revolution propelled large, impersonal organizations to the fore. Within this context, officials in the industrialized West came to define primary relationships at work (such as *nepotism*, favouritism shown to a family member) as an unethical barrier to organizational efficiency.

The development of formal organizations in Japan followed a different route. Historically, that society was even more socially cohesive, organized according to family-based loyalties. As Japan rapidly industrialized, people there did not discard primary relationships as inefficient, as Westerners did. Rather, the Japanese modelled their large businesses on the family, transferring traditional kinship loyalties to corporations.

From our point of view, then, Japan seems to be simultaneously modern and traditional, promoting organizational efficiency by cultivating personal ties. There are indications that Japanese workers are now becoming more individualistic. Yet the Japanese model still demonstrates that organizational life need not be so dehumanizing.

Economically challenged as never before, North American businesses are taking a closer look at organizational patterns elsewhere, especially in Japan. In fact, many efforts to humanize bureaucracy in North America are clear attempts to mimic the Japanese way of doing things.

Beyond the benefits for Western business organizations, there is another reason to study the Japanese

Are Large Organizations a Threat to Personal Privacy?

As he finishes dressing, Joe calls an 800 number to check the pollen count. As he listens to a recorded message, a Caller ID computer identifies Joe, records the call, and pulls up Joe's profile from a public records database. The profile, which now includes the fact that Joe suffers from allergies, is sold to a drug company, which sends Joe a free sample of a new allergy medication.

At a local department store, Nina uses her American Express card to buy an expensive new watch and some sleepwear. The store's computer adds Nina's name to its database of "buyers of expensive jewellery" and "buyers of sexy lingerie." The store trades its database with other companies. Within a month, Nina's mail includes four jewellery catalogues and a sex-videotape offer (Bernstein, 1997).

Are these cases of organizations providing consumers with interesting products, or violations of people's privacy? The answer, of course, is both: the same systems that help organizations operate predictably and efficiently also empower them to invade our lives and manipulate us. So, as bureaucracy has expanded in Canada, privacy has declined.

The problem reflects the enormous power of large organizations, their tendency to treat people impersonally, and their practice of collecting information. In recent decades, the danger to privacy has increased as organizations have acquired more and more computers and other new information technology that stores and shares information.

Consider some of the obvious ways in which organizations compile personal information. As they issue driver's licences, for example, provincial departments generate files that they can dispatch to police or other officials at the touch of a button. Similarly, Revenue Canada, Health and Welfare, and government programs that benefit veterans, students, the poor, and the unemployed all collect extensive information.

Businesses in the private sector now do much the same thing although, as the examples above suggest, people may not be aware that their choices and activities end up in someone's database. Most people find the use of credit cards a great convenience (people in North America now hold more than one billion of them, averaging more than five per adult), but few people stop to think that credit card purchases automatically generate electronic records that can end up almost anywhere.

We also experience the erosion of privacy in the surveillance cameras that monitor more and more public places, along main streets, in the shopping malls, and even across campuses. And then there is the escalating amount of junk mail. Mailing lists for this material grow exponentially as one company sells names and addresses to others. Bought a new car recently? If so, you probably have found yourself on the mailing lists of companies that market all kinds of automotive products. Have you ever rented an X-rated video? Many video stores keep records of the movie preferences of customers and pass them along to other businesses whose advertising soon arrives in the mailbox.

Of particular concern to Canadians is the information stored in connection with our Social Insurance Numbers (SINs), which in some organizations have become employee identification numbers as well. The amount of personal information associated with one's SIN, the multiple uses of the number, and the possibility of merging massive files make SINs a particularly sensitive issue. Access by one government department or agency, such as Revenue Canada or the RCMP, to SIN-related data or Statistics Canada files would also be a worrisome invasion of privacy. It is possible, as well, for unauthorized users—from anywhere in the world, in fact—to gain access to and link the various files containing personal information about us.

Concern about the erosion of privacy runs high. In response, privacy legislation has been enacted in Canada by provinces and the federal government. The federal *Privacy Act* (1978; amended in 1982) permits citizens to examine and correct information contained about them in government files. Canadians also have access to information (e.g., consultants' reports) that contributes to the making of government decisions and policy. But the fact is that so many organizations now have information about us that current laws simply can't address the scope of the problem.

Continue the debate . . .

1. *Which do you think represents a larger threat to personal privacy, government or businesses? Why?*
2. *Internet search engines such as Yahoo! Canada (www.yahoo.ca) have "people search" programs that let you locate almost anyone. Do you think such programs are, on balance, helpful or threatening to the public?*
3. *In our current age of large organizations and expanding computer technology, do you think the privacy problem will get worse or better? Why?*

SOURCES: Smith (1979); Rubin (1988); Miller (1991); and Bernstein (1997).

approach carefully. Our society is less socially cohesive now than the more family-based society Weber knew. A rigidly bureaucratic form of organization only further atomizes the social fabric. Perhaps by following the lead of the Japanese, our own formal organizations can promote—rather than diminish—a sense of collective identity and responsibility.

SUMMARY

1. Social groups—important building blocks of societies—foster personal development and common identity as well as performing various tasks.

2. Primary groups tend to be small and person-oriented; secondary groups are typically large and goal-oriented.

3. Instrumental leadership is concerned with realizing a group's goals; expressive leadership focuses on members' morale and well-being.

4. The process of group conformity is well documented by researchers. Because members often seek consensus, work groups do not necessarily generate a wider range of ideas than do individuals working alone.

5. Individuals use reference groups—both ingroups and outgroups—to form attitudes and make decisions.

6. Georg Simmel characterized the dyad relationship as intense but unstable; a triad, he noted, can easily dissolve into a dyad by excluding one member.

7. Peter Blau explored how the size, internal homogeneity, social standing, and physical segregation of groups all affect members' behaviour.

8. Social networks are relational webs that link people who typically have little common identity and limited interaction. The Internet, a vast electronic network, links millions of computers worldwide.

9. Formal organizations are large, secondary groups that seek to perform complex tasks efficiently. According to their members' reasons for joining, formal organizations are classified as utilitarian, normative, or coercive.

10. Bureaucratic organization expands in modern societies to perform many complex tasks efficiently. Bureaucracy is based on specialization, hierarchy, rules and regulations, technical competence, impersonal interaction, and formal, written communications.

11. Ideal bureaucracy may promote efficiency, but bureaucracy also generates alienation and inefficiency, tends to perpetuate itself beyond the achievement of its goals, and contributes to the contemporary erosion of privacy.

12. Formal organizations often mirror oligarchies. Rosabeth Moss Kanter's research has shown that the concentration of power and opportunity in large corporations can compromise organizational effectiveness.

13. Humanizing bureaucracy means recognizing people as an organization's greatest resource. To develop human resources, organizations should spread responsibility and opportunity widely. One way to put this ideal into action is through self-managed work teams.

14. Technology, politics, population patterns, the economy, and other organizations combine to form the environment in which a particular organization must operate.

15. The trend towards the "McDonaldization of society" involves increasing automation and impersonality.

16. Reflecting the collective spirit of Japanese culture, formal organizations in Japan are based on more personal ties than are their counterparts in North America.

CRITICAL THINKING QUESTIONS

1. What are the key differences between primary and secondary groups? Identify examples of each in daily life.

2. What are some of the positive functions of group conformity (for example, fostering team spirit)? Note several dysfunctions.

3. According to Max Weber, what are the six characteristic traits of bureaucracy? How do Japanese organizations differ from those common to North America?

4. What does the "McDonaldization of society" mean? Cite familiar examples of this trend beyond those discussed in this chapter.

SOCIOLOGY APPLIED

1. Visit a large, public building with an elevator. Observe groups of people as they approach the elevator and, entering the elevator with them, watch what happens next. What happens to the conversations? Where do people fix their eyes? Can you account for these patterns?

2. Make a list of ingroups on your campus, and also identify outgroups. What traits account for groups falling into each category? Ask several other people to comment on your list to see if group hierarchy is a matter of agreement.

3. The next time you arrive at a social gathering early, note how many people share the conversation. What happens to the single group as more people arrive? What seems to be the typical size of a group for conversation?

4. Using available publications (and some assistance from an instructor), try to draw an "organizational pyramid" for your college or university showing the key offices and how they supervise and report to other offices.

WEBLINKS

www.sociology.net/links/internetpostmodern. html
In "The Internet as a Postmodern Culture," a paper prepared by Allan Liska and Ilana Grune for presentation at the 1995 American Sociological Association Meetings, the authors argue that the Internet is a society that meets all of the traditional requirements for an anthropological/sociological definition of a culture.

insight.mcmaster.ca/org/efc/efc.html
Electronic Frontier Canada (EFC) was founded to ensure that the principles embodied in the Canadian *Charter of Rights and Freedoms* remain protected as new computing, communications, and information technologies are introduced into Canadian society.

www.airpower.maxwell.af.mil/airchronicles/apj/ apj94/waddell.html
Col. Donald E. Waddell, a professor of leadership studies at Air War College, writes about the art of leadership, a subject that may be studied more seriously in military schools than in civilian institutions,

given the life-and-death nature of military business. He discusses the evolution of leadership theory and the application of the situational leadership model to military leadership and management.

www.sociology.net/mcdonald/index.html
Dr. George Ritzer updates Max Weber's theories and extends his ideas to the fast food industry and today's society. Ritzer's book *The McDonaldization of Society* discusses how our society has become rationalized to such a point that there are very few escapes. This Web site outlines the theory of McDonaldization and provides some sources that relate to Ritzer's work.

www.anderson.ucla.edu/research/japan/
Created to enhance North American understanding of Japanese culture and business practices, *Global Window: A Guide to Business Success—Japan* provides introductory essays on the Japanese economy, how to conduct business, legal considerations, and other useful topics, as well as a glossary, bibliography, and discussion forum.

Fiona Smyth, *Untitled,* 1995

CHAPTER 8

DEVIANCE

Casablanca, Morocco, December 10, 1994. Casablanca! An exciting mix of African, European, and Middle Eastern cultures. Returning from a stroll through the medina, the medieval section of this coastal, north African city, we confront lines of police along one of Casablanca's breezy boulevards. Uniformed men stand between us and the harbour. Their presence has to do with the Islamic conference that has drawn many important leaders to one of the big hotels nearby. Are the streets closed? No one asks; people seem to halt at an invisible line some fifty feet from the police officers. I play the brash urbanite and start across the street to inquire (in broken French) if I can pass by; but I stop cold as several officers draw a bead on me with their eyes. Their fingers nervously tap at the grips to their automatic weapons. This is no time to strike up a conversation.

Every society demands a certain measure of conformity from its members. Sometimes—in Canada and elsewhere—this process involves the use of armed officers. But in the vast majority of cases we conform to cultural patterns for the simple reason that they seem right and natural, part of the reality we inhabit.

This chapter explores many questions dealing with deviance and conformity: Why do societies create cultural norms, including laws, in the first place? Why are some people more likely than others to be accused of violations? To what extent does our country succeed in controlling crime? We begin our investigation by defining several basic concepts.

WHAT IS DEVIANCE?

Deviance is *the recognized violation of cultural norms.* Norms guide virtually all human activities, so the concept of deviance covers a correspondingly broad spectrum. One distinctive category of deviance is **crime**, *the violation of norms a society formally enacts into criminal law.* Even criminal deviance is extensive, ranging from minor traffic violations to serious offences such as murder. A subcategory of crime, **juvenile delinquency**, refers to *the violation of legal standards by the young.*

Some instances of deviance barely raise eyebrows; other cases command a swift and severe response. Members of our society pay little notice to mild nonconformity such as boastfulness or being a "nerd"; we take a dimmer view of reckless driving or dropping out of school, and we dispatch the police in response to a violent crime like armed robbery.

Not all deviance involves action or even choice. For some categories of individuals, just *existing* may be sufficient to provoke condemnation from others. To the young, elderly people sometimes seem hopelessly "out of it"; to whites who are in the majority, the mere presence of people of colour may cause discomfort. Able-bodied people often view people with disabilities as an outgroup. And affluent people may view the poor as disreputable to the extent that they fall short by conventional middle-class standards.

Most examples of nonconformity that come readily to mind are negative instances of rule breaking, such as stealing from a convenience store, abusing a child, or driving while intoxicated. But, given our shortcomings, we also define especially righteous people—students who speak up too much in class or people who are enthusiastic about paying their taxes—as deviant, even if we accord them a measure of respect (Huls, 1987). What deviant actions or attitudes—

The kind of deviance people create reflects the moral values they embrace. The Berkeley campus of the University of California has long celebrated its open-minded tolerance of sexual diversity. Thus, in 1992, when Andrew Martinez decided to attend classes wearing virtually nothing, people were reluctant to accuse "The Naked Guy" of immoral conduct. However, in Berkeley's politically correct atmosphere, it was not long before school officials banned Martinez from campus—charging that his nudity constituted a form of sexual harassment.

whether negative or positive—have in common is some evaluation of difference that prompts us to regard another person as an "outsider" (Becker, 1966).

SOCIAL CONTROL

Members of a society try to influence each other's behaviour with various kinds of social control. Much of this process is informal, as when parents offer praise or criticism to their children or friends playfully comment on someone's latest romantic interest. Cases of serious deviance, however, may provoke a response from the **criminal justice system**, *a formal response to alleged violations of law on the part of police, courts, and prison officials.*

In sum, deviance is much more than a matter of individual choice or personal failing. *How* a society defines deviance, *whom* individuals brand as deviant, and *what* people decide to do about nonconformity are all issues of social organization. Only gradually,

however, have people recognized this essential truth, as we shall now explain.

THE BIOLOGICAL CONTEXT

Chapter 5 ("Socialization") explained that people a century ago understood—or, more correctly, misunderstood—human behaviour as an expression of biological instincts. Understandably, early interest in criminality emphasized biological causes as well. In 1876 Cesare Lombroso (1835–1909), an Italian physician who worked in prisons, characterized criminals as having a distinctive physique—low foreheads, prominent jaws and cheekbones, protruding ears, excessive hairiness, and unusually long arms that, taken together, made them resemble the apelike ancestors of human beings.

But Lombroso's work was flawed. Had he looked beyond prison walls, he would have realized that the physical features he attributed exclusively to prisoners actually were found throughout the entire population. We now know that no physical attributes of the kind described by Lombroso distinguish criminals from noncriminals (Goring, 1972; orig. 1913).

At midcentury, William Sheldon (1949) took a different tack, positing that body structure might predict criminality. He categorized hundreds of young men in terms of body type and, checking for any criminal history, concluded that delinquency occurred most frequently among boys with muscular, athletic builds. Sheldon Glueck and Eleanor Glueck (1950) confirmed Sheldon's conclusion, but cautioned that a powerful build does not necessarily cause or even predict criminality. The Gluecks postulated that parents tend to be more distant from powerfully built males so that they, in turn, grow up to display less sensitivity towards others. Moreover, in a self-fulfilling prophecy, people who expect muscular boys to act like bullies may provoke such aggressive behaviour.

Recent genetics research continues to seek possible links between biology and crime. To date, no conclusive evidence connects criminality to any specific genetic flaw. Yet people's overall genetic composition, in combination with social influences, may account for some variation in criminality. In other words, biological factors probably have a real, if modest, effect on whether individuals engage in criminal activity (Rowe, 1983; Rowe and Osgood, 1984; Wilson and Herrnstein, 1985; Jencks, 1987).

Critical evaluation. At best, biological theories that try to explain crime in terms of specific physical traits explain only a small proportion of all crimes. Recent sociobiological research—noting, for example, that violent crime is overwhelmingly committed by males or that parents are more likely to abuse foster children than natural children—is promising, but, at this point, we know too little about the links between genes and human behaviour to draw any firm conclusions (Daly and Wilson, 1988).

Then, too, because a biological approach looks just at the individual, it offers no insight into how some kinds of behaviours come to be defined as deviant in the first place. Therefore, although there is much to be learned about how human biology may affect behaviour, research currently places far greater emphasis on social influences (Gibbons and Krohn, 1986; Liska, 1991).

PERSONALITY FACTORS

Like biological theories, psychological explanations of deviance focus on cases of individual abnormality, this time involving personality. Some personality traits are hereditary, but most psychologists believe that temperament is shaped primarily by social experiences. Episodes of deviance, then, are viewed as the product of "unsuccessful" socialization.

The work of Walter Reckless and Simon Dinitz (1967) illustrates the psychological approach. These researchers began by asking teachers to categorize twelve-year-old boys as either likely or unlikely to engage in juvenile delinquency. Interviews with both categories of boys and their mothers allowed them to assess each boy's self-concept and how well he related to others. Analyzing their results, they concluded that the "good boys" displayed a strong conscience (or superego, in Sigmund Freud's terminology), coped well with frustration, and identified positively with cultural norms and values. The "bad boys," by contrast, had a weaker conscience, showed little tolerance for frustration, and felt less in tune with conventional culture.

Furthermore, the researchers found that the "good boys" went on to have fewer contacts with the police than the "bad boys." Since all the boys Reckless and Dinitz studied lived in areas where delinquency was widespread, the investigators attributed the tendency to stay out of trouble to a personality that reined in impulses towards deviance. Based on this conclusion, Reckless and Dinitz call their analysis containment theory.

Critical evaluation. Psychologists have demonstrated that personality patterns have some connection to delinquency and other types of deviance. Nevertheless, this approach suffers from one key limitation: the vast majority of serious crimes are committed by people whose psychological profiles are *normal*.

In sum, both biological and psychological approaches view deviance as an individual attribute without exploring how conceptions of right and wrong initially arise, why people define some rule

breakers but not others as deviant, and the role of social power in shaping a society's system of social control. To explore these issues, we now turn to a sociological analysis of deviance.

THE SOCIAL FOUNDATIONS OF DEVIANCE

Although we tend to view deviance in terms of the free choice or personal failings of individuals, all behaviour—deviance as well as conformity—is shaped by society. There are three social foundations of deviance, identified below.

1. **Deviance varies according to cultural norms.** No thought or action is inherently deviant; it becomes deviant only in relation to particular norms. The life patterns of rural Albertans, residents of Newfoundland fishing villages, and West Vancouverites differ in highly significant ways: as a result, their values and behavioural standards are different. Laws, too, differ from place to place. Quebeckers can drink at a younger age than Ontarians and are able to purchase wine and beer at corner stores, whereas only beer with 0.5 percent alcohol can be found in Ontario grocery stores. Casinos are now legal in Ontario—even on native reserves. They are also legal in Manitoba—but definitely not on native reserves.[1] In other words, what is deviant or even criminal is not uniform across the country.

   In global context, deviance is even more diverse. Albania outlaws any public display of religious faith, such as crossing oneself; Cuba can prosecute its citizens for "consorting with foreigners"; police can arrest people in Singapore for selling chewing gum; and–anywhere in Iran–police can arrest a woman for wearing makeup.

2. **People become deviant as others define them that way.** Each of us violates cultural norms regularly, occasionally to the extent of breaking the law. For example, most of us have at some time walked around talking to ourselves, or have "borrowed" supplies, such as pens and paper, from the workplace. Whether such activities are sufficient to define us as mentally ill or criminal depends on how others perceive, define, and respond to any given situation.

3. **Both rule making and rule breaking involve social power.** The law, Karl Marx asserted,

---

[1] Several reserve-based native communities have attempted to establish casinos, in part as a test of their sovereignty. While Manitoba closed down casinos that were opened illegally, Ontario gave its blessing to a casino on the Rama reserve near Orillia. Proceeds will be shared with the other bands of Ontario.

Artists have an important function in any society: to explore alternatives to conventional notions about how to live. For this reason, while we celebrate artists' creativity, we also accord them a mildly deviant identity. In today's more conservative political climate, some government officials have objected to art that seems to challenge traditional morality.

amounts to little more than a strategy by which powerful people protect their interests. For example, the owners of an unprofitable factory have a legal right to close their business, even if doing so throws thousands of people out of work. But if workers commit an act of vandalism that closes the same factory for a single day, they are subject to criminal prosecution.

Similarly, a homeless person who stands on a street corner denouncing the city government risks arrest for disturbing the peace; a mayoral candidate during an election campaign does exactly the same thing while receiving extensive police protection. In short, norms and their application are linked to social inequality.

STRUCTURAL-FUNCTIONAL ANALYSIS

We now turn to the structural-functional paradigm, which reveals how deviance contributes to the operation of society.

EMILE DURKHEIM: THE FUNCTIONS OF DEVIANCE

In his pioneering study of deviance, Emile Durkheim (1964a, orig. 1895; 1964b, orig. 1893) made the remarkable assertion that there is nothing abnormal about deviance; in fact, it supports the operation of society in four ways.

1. **Deviance affirms cultural values and norms.** Culture involves moral choices: unless our lives dissolve into chaos, people prefer some attitudes and behaviours to others. But any conception of virtue rests on an opposing notion of vice. Just as there can be no good without evil, there can be no justice without crime. Deviance, in short, is indispensable to the process of generating and sustaining morality.

2. **Responding to deviance clarifies moral boundaries.** By defining people as deviant, people draw a social boundary between right and wrong. For example, universities mark the line between academic honesty and cheating by imposing disciplinary procedures on those who commit plagiarism.

3. **Responding to deviance promotes social unity.** People typically react to serious deviance with collective outrage. In doing so, Durkheim explained, they reaffirm the moral ties that bind them. For example, the murder of fourteen female engineering students at Montreal's L'École Polytechnique on December 6, 1989, was met with reactions of horror and profound grief in the larger community. The fact that anniversaries of the massacre are still commemorated indicates the depth of its impact on our community.

4. **Deviance encourages social change.** Deviant people, Durkheim claimed, push a society's moral boundaries, suggesting alternatives to the status quo and encouraging change. Moreover, he declared, today's deviance sometimes becomes tomorrow's morality (1964a:71). In the 1950s, for example, many people denounced rock and roll as a threat to the morals of youth.

The most deadly episode of mass hysteria in U.S. history swept up the village of Salem, Massachusetts, in 1692. Fearing witches in their midst, villagers tried and executed twenty people within the year. Such cases of hysteria accompanied the declining strength of religion as the Middle Ages drew to a close.

Since then, however, rock and roll has been swept up in the musical mainstream, becoming a multibillion-dollar industry.

An Illustration: The Puritans of Massachusetts Bay

Kai Erikson's (1966) historical investigation of the early Puritans of Massachusetts Bay illustrates Durkheim's analysis. Erikson showed that even the Puritans—a disciplined and highly religious group—created deviance to clarify their moral boundaries. In fact, Durkheim might well have had the Puritans in mind when he wrote,

> Imagine a society of saints, a perfect cloister of exemplary individuals. Crimes, properly so called, will there be unknown; but faults which appear [insignificant] to the layman will create there the same scandal that the ordinary offense does in ordinary consciousness. ... For the same reason, the perfect and upright man judges his smallest failings with a severity that the majority reserve for acts more truly in the nature of an offense. (1964a:68–69)

Deviance, in short, is not a matter of how good or bad individuals are; it is a necessary condition of "good" social living.

But the *kind* of deviance people generate depends on the moral issues they seek to clarify. Over time, the Puritans confronted a number of "crime waves." In responding to them, the Puritans sharpened their views on crucial moral quandaries. Thus, they answered questions about how much dissent to allow or what their religious goals should be by celebrating some of their members while branding others as deviants.

And, most fascinating of all, Erikson discovered that, though the offences changed, the Puritans recognized a consistent proportion of their members as deviant over time. This stability, concludes Erikson, confirms Durkheim's contention that deviants serve as ethical markers, outlining a society's changing moral boundaries. By constantly defining a small number of people as deviant, the Puritans were able to maintain a certain "shape" to their society.

MERTON'S STRAIN THEORY

Some deviance may be necessary for a society to function, Robert Merton (1968a, 1968b) argues, but excessive violations arise from particular social arrangements. Specifically, the scope and character of deviance depend on how well a society makes cultural *goals* (such as financial success) accessible by providing the institutionalized *means* (such as schooling and job opportunities) to attain them.

The path to conformity, Merton begins, lies in pursuing conventional goals by approved means. The true success story, in other words, is someone who gains wealth and prestige through talent and hard work. But not everyone who desires conventional success has the opportunity to attain it. Children raised in poverty, for example, may see little hope of becoming successful if they play by the rules. As a result, they may seek wealth through one or another kind of crime—say, by dealing in drugs. Merton called this type of deviance innovation—the attempt to achieve a culturally approved goal (wealth) by unconventional means (drug sales). Figure 8–1 characterizes innovation

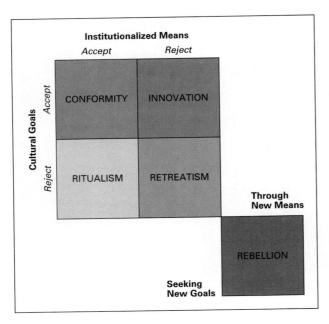

Institutionalized Means

	Accept	*Reject*
Cultural Goals *Accept*	CONFORMITY	INNOVATION
Cultural Goals *Reject*	RITUALISM	RETREATISM

Through
New Means

REBELLION

Seeking
New Goals

FIGURE 8–1 Merton's Strain Theory of Deviance

SOURCE: Merton (1968b).

as accepting the goal of success while rejecting the conventional means of becoming rich.

According to Merton, the "strain" between our culture's emphasis on wealth and the limited opportunity to get rich gives rise, especially among the poor, to theft, the selling of illegal drugs, or other forms of street hustling. In some respects, at least, a notorious gangster like Al Capone was quite conventional—he pursued the fame and fortune at the heart of the "American Dream." But, finding the usual doors to success closed to him as a minority member, he blazed his own trail to the top. In the meantime, a Canadian (with close ties to Capone) was establishing a parallel career.

When Prohibition outlawed the sale of liquor in Canada (1918), a young Hamilton, Ontario, grocer named Rocco Perri saw an opportunity to augment his income by selling bootleg liquor at the back of his store. By the time Prohibition was adopted in the United States (1920), "Perri had the organization and experience to take quick advantage of the opportunity . . . Before long, he was a major supplier to gangsters like Al Capone" (Carrigan, 1991:174). He had become "King of the Bootleggers." In the wake of Prohibition, Rocco Perri's "formidable criminal organization" expanded its links to U.S. gangs through a wide range of activities including gambling, prostitution, and extortion. Like Capone, Canada's innovator acquired wealth and power but never attained prestige in the larger society.

The inability to become successful by normative means may also prompt another type of deviance that Merton calls *ritualism* (see Figure 8–1). Ritualists resolve the strain of limited success by abandoning cultural goals in favour of almost compulsive efforts to live "respectably." In essence, they embrace the rules to the point where they lose sight of their larger goals. Lower-level bureaucrats, Merton suggests, often succumb to ritualism as a way of maintaining respectability.

A third response to the inability to succeed is *retreatism*—the rejection of both cultural goals and means so that one, in effect, drops out. Retreatists include some alcoholics and drug addicts, and some of the street people found in our cities. The deviance of retreatists lies in unconventional living and, perhaps more seriously, in accepting this situation.

The fourth response to failure is *rebellion*. Like retreatists, rebels reject both the cultural definition of success and the normative means of achieving it. Rebels, however, go one step further by advocating radical alternatives to the existing social order. Typically, they advocate a political or religious transformation of society, and often join a counterculture.

DEVIANT SUBCULTURES

Richard Cloward and Lloyd Ohlin (1966) extended Merton's theory in their investigation of delinquent youth. They maintain that criminal deviance results not simply from limited legitimate (legal) opportunity but also from available illegitimate (illegal) opportunity. In short, deviance or conformity grows out of the *relative opportunity structure* that frames young people's lives.

The life of Rocco Perri shows how an ambitious individual denied legitimate opportunity could organize a criminal empire to take advantage of the country's demand for alcohol during Prohibition. In other words, illegal opportunities foster the development of *criminal subcultures* that offer the knowledge, skills, and other resources people need to succeed in unconventional ways. Indeed, gangs may specialize in one or another form of criminality according to available opportunities and resources (Carrigan, 1991; Sheley et al., 1995).

But some poor and highly transient neighbourhoods may lack almost any form of opportunity—legal or illegal. Here, delinquency often surfaces in the form of *conflict subcultures* where violence is ignited by frustration and a desire for fame or respect. Alternatively, those who fail to achieve success, even by criminal means, may sink into *retreatist subcultures*, dropping out through abuse of alcohol or other drugs.

Albert Cohen (1971; orig. 1955) asserts that delinquency is most pronounced among lower-class youths because it is they who contend with the least opportunity to achieve success in conventional ways. Sometimes those whom society neglects seek self-respect by building a deviant subculture that "defines as meritorious the characteristics they *do* possess, the kinds of conduct of which they *are* capable" (1971:66). Having a notorious street reputation, for example, may win no points with society as a whole, but it may satisfy a youth's gnawing desire to "be somebody."

Walter Miller (1970) agrees that deviant subcultures typically develop among lower-class youths who encounter the least legitimate opportunity. He spotlights six focal concerns of these deviant subcultures: (1) *trouble*, arising from frequent conflict with teachers and police; (2) *toughness*, the value placed on physical size, strength, and athletic skills, especially among males; (3) *smartness* ("street smarts"), the ability to outthink or "con" others, and to avoid being similarly taken advantage of; (4) *excitement*, the search for thrills, risk, or danger to escape from a daily routine that is predictable and unsatisfying; (5) a preoccupation with *fate*, derived from the lack of control these youths feel over their own lives; and (6) *autonomy*, a desire for freedom often expressed as resentment of authority figures.

Critical evaluation. Durkheim's pioneering work on the functions of deviance remains central to sociological thinking. Even so, recent critics point out that a community does not always come together in reaction to crime; sometimes fear of crime drives people to withdraw from public life (Liska and Warner, 1991).

Derived from Durkheim's analysis, Merton's strain theory has also come under criticism for explaining some kinds of deviance (theft, for example) far better than others (such as crimes of passion or mental illness). In addition, not everyone seeks success in conventional terms of wealth, as strain theory implies. As we noted in Chapter 3 ("Culture"), members of our society embrace many different cultural values and are motivated by various notions of personal success.

The general argument of Cloward and Ohlin, Cohen, and Miller—that deviance reflects the opportunity structure of society—has been confirmed by subsequent research (Allan and Steffensmeier, 1989). However, these theories, too, fall short by assuming that everyone shares the same cultural standards for judging right and wrong. Moreover, we must be careful not to define deviance in ways that unfairly focus attention on poor people. If crime is defined to include stock fraud as well as street theft, offenders are more likely to include affluent individuals. Finally, all structural-functional theories imply that everyone who violates conventional cultural standards will be branded as deviant. Becoming deviant, however, is actually a highly complex process, as the next section explains.

SYMBOLIC-INTERACTION ANALYSIS

The symbolic-interaction paradigm analyzes the creation of deviance as a social process. From this point of view, definitions of deviance and conformity are surprisingly flexible.

LABELLING THEORY

The central contribution of symbolic-interaction analysis is **labelling theory**, *the assertion that deviance and conformity result, not so much from what people do, but from how others respond to those actions.* Labelling theory stresses the relativity of deviance, arguing that all reality is socially constructed so that the same behaviour may be defined in any number of ways. Howard S. Becker claims that deviance is, therefore, nothing more than "behaviour that people so label" (1966:9).

Consider these situations: a woman takes an article of clothing from a roommate; a married man at a convention in a city far from his home has sex with a prostitute; a member of parliament drives home intoxicated after a party. In each case, "reality" depends on the response of others. Is the first situation a matter of borrowing or is it theft? The consequences of the second case depend largely on whether news of the man's behaviour follows him back home. In the third situation, is the MP an active socialite or a dangerous drunk? The social construction of reality, then, is a highly variable process of detection, definition, and response.

Primary and Secondary Deviance

Edwin Lemert (1951, 1972) notes that many episodes of norm violation—say, skipping school or underage drinking—provoke little reaction from others and have little effect on a person's self-concept. Lemert calls such passing episodes *primary deviance*.

But what happens if other people take notice of someone's deviance and make something of it? If, for example, people begin to describe a young man as a "boozer," and push him out of their social circle, he may become embittered, drink even more, and seek the company of others who condone his behaviour. So the response to initial deviance can set in motion *secondary deviance*, by which an individual engages in repeated norm violations and begins to take on a

In Winnipeg, a born-again Christian gives visible expression to his faith. When the city council warned that his signs violated civic by-laws, the man vowed to challenge any charges in court.

deviant identity. The development of secondary deviance is one application of the Thomas Theorem, which states that situations defined as real become real in their consequences.

Stigma

The onset of secondary deviance marks the emergence of what Erving Goffman (1963) called a *deviant career*. As individuals develop a strong commitment to deviant behaviour, they typically acquire a **stigma**, *a powerfully negative social label that radically changes a person's self-concept and social identity.*

Stigma operates as a master status (see Chapter 6, "Social Interaction in Everyday Life"), overpowering other dimensions of social identity so that an individual is diminished and discounted in the minds of others and, consequently, socially isolated. Sometimes an entire community formally stigmatizes individuals through what Harold Garfinkel (1956) calls a *degradation ceremony*. A criminal prosecution is one example, operating much like a high school graduation except that people stand before the community to be labelled in a negative rather than a positive way.

Labelling: Past and Future

Once people have stigmatized a person, they may engage in **retrospective labelling**, *the interpretation of someone's past consistent with present deviance* (Scheff, 1984). For example, after discovering that a priest has sexually molested a child, others may rethink his past, perhaps musing, "He always did want to be around young children." Retrospective labelling distorts a person's biography, in a highly selective and prejudicial way, guided more by the present stigma than by any attempt to be fair. This process often deepens a person's deviant identity.

In the same way, people may engage in *projective labelling* of a stigmatized person. In this case, an audience remains mindful of an individual's deviant identity when assessing any future action. The result, of course, is that people continue to find evidence of deviance in the future actions of a stigmatized individual.

Labelling and Mental Illness

Is a woman who believes that Jesus rides the bus to work with her every day seriously deluded or merely expressing her religious faith in a highly graphic way? Is a homeless woman who refuses to allow police to take her to a city shelter on a cold night mentally ill or simply trying to live independently?

Psychiatrist Thomas Szasz charges that people apply the label of insanity to what is only "difference." Such reasoning has led Szasz to the controversial conclusion that the notion of mental illness should be abandoned (1961, 1970, 1994, 1995). Illness, Szasz argues, is physical and afflicts only the body; mental illness, then, is a myth. The world is full of people whose "differences" in thought or action may irritate us, but difference is no grounds on which to define someone as sick. To do so, Szasz claims, simply enforces conformity to the standards of people powerful enough to impose their will on others.

Many of Szasz's colleagues reject the notion that all mental illness is a fiction. But some have hailed his work for pointing out the danger of abusing medical practice in the interest of promoting conformity. Most of us, after all, experience periods of extreme stress or other mental disability from time to time. Such episodes, although upsetting, are usually of passing importance. If, however, others respond with labelling that forms the basis of a social stigma, the long-term result may be further deviance as a self-fulfilling prophecy (Scheff, 1984).

THE MEDICALIZATION OF DEVIANCE

Labelling theory, particularly the ideas of Szasz and Goffman, helps to explain an important shift in the way our society understands deviance. Over the last fifty years, the growing influence of psychiatry and medicine in North America has encouraged the **medicalization of deviance**, *the transformation of moral and legal issues into medical matters.*

In essence, medicalization amounts to swapping one set of labels for another. In moral terms, we evaluate people or their behaviour as "bad" or "good." However, the scientific objectivity of modern medicine passes no moral judgment, using instead clinical diagnoses such as "sick" and "well."

To illustrate, until the middle of this century, people generally viewed alcoholics as weak and morally deficient people easily tempted by the pleasure of drink. Gradually, however, medical specialists redefined alcoholism so that most people now consider it a disease, rendering individuals "sick" rather than "bad." Similarly, obesity, drug addiction, child abuse, promiscuity, and other behaviours that used to be moral matters are today widely defined as illnesses for which people need help rather than punishment.

The Significance of Labels

Whether we define deviance as a moral or medical issue has three profound consequences. First, it affects who responds to deviance. An offence against common morality typically provokes a reaction by ordinary people or the police. Applying medical labels, however, places the situation under the control of clinical specialists, including counsellors, psychiatrists, and physicians.

A second difference is *how people respond* to deviance. A moral approach defines the deviant as an "offender" subject to punishment. Medically, however, "patients" need treatment (for their own good, of course). Therefore, while punishment is designed to fit the crime, treatment programs are tailored to the patient and may involve virtually any therapy that a specialist thinks will prevent future deviance (von Hirsh, 1986).

Third, and most important, the two labels differ on the issue of *the personal competence of the deviant person*. Morally speaking, people take responsibility for their behaviour whether right or wrong. If we are sick, however, we are seen as lacking the capacity to control (or even comprehend) our behaviour. Those who are defined as incompetent are, in turn, subject to intense, often involuntary, treatment. For this reason alone, attempts to define deviance in medical terms should be made only with extreme caution.

SUTHERLAND'S DIFFERENTIAL ASSOCIATION THEORY

Learning any social pattern—whether conventional or deviant—is a process that takes place in groups. According to Edwin Sutherland (1940), any person's tendency towards conformity or deviance depends on the relative frequency of association with others who encourage conventional behaviour or norm violation. This is Sutherland's theory of *differential association*.

Many gangs constitute a peer group in which violence, drug use, and trafficking are "normal." Here members of the Hells Angels, identifiable by their hair and clothing, attend a funeral of one of their compatriots.

Sutherland's theory is illustrated by a study of drug and alcohol use among young adults at high school and university levels (Akers et al., 1979; Nawaz, 1978). Researchers have discovered close links between the extent of alcohol and drug use and the extent to which peer groups engage in or encourage such activity. The investigators concluded that young people embrace delinquent patterns as they receive praise and other rewards for defining deviance rather than conformity in positive terms. At the extreme, differential association can make drug use, trafficking, and brutal violence (including murder) seem acceptable or "normal," for example if one's peer group is the biker gang, Hells Angels.

HIRSCHI'S CONTROL THEORY

In his *control theory*, Travis Hirschi (1969, 1995) claims that the essence of social control lies in people's anticipation of the consequences of their behaviour. Hirschi assumes that everyone finds at least some deviance tempting. Imagining condemnation from family or friends is sufficient to deter most people from temptation; concerns about career consequences of transgressions will give others pause. By contrast, individuals who have little to lose from deviance are most likely to become rule breakers.

Hirschi asserts that conformity arises from four types of social controls.

1. **Attachment.** Strong social attachments encourage conformity; weak relationships in the family, peer group, and school leave people freer to engage in deviance.

2. **Opportunity.** The higher one's commitment to legitimate opportunity, the greater the advantages of conformity. A university-bound young person, with good career prospects, has a high stake in conformity. By contrast, someone with little confidence in future success may drift towards deviance.

3. **Involvement.** Extensive involvement in legitimate activities—such as holding a job, going to school and completing homework, or pursuing hobbies—inhibits deviance. People with few such activities—who simply "hang out" waiting for something to happen—have time and energy for deviant activity.

4. **Belief.** Strong beliefs in conventional morality and respect for authority figures restrain tendencies towards deviance. By contrast, people with a weak conscience (and those who spend a great deal of time without an authority figure's supervision) are more vulnerable to temptation (Osgoode et al., 1996).

Hirschi's analysis draws together a number of ideas presented earlier about the causes of deviant behaviour. Note that both relative social privilege and strength of moral character are crucial in generating a stake in conformity to conventional norms (Wiatrowski, Griswold, and Roberts, 1981; Sampson and Laub, 1990; Free, 1992).

Critical evaluation. The various symbolic-interaction theories share a focus on deviance as process. Labelling theory links deviance not to *action* but to the *reaction* of others. Thus some people come to be defined as deviant while others who think or behave in the same way are not. The concepts of stigma, secondary deviance, and deviant career demonstrate how people can incorporate the label of deviance into a lasting self-concept.

Yet labelling theory has several limitations. First, because it takes a highly relative view of deviance, this theory glosses over the fact that some kinds of behaviour, such as murder, are condemned virtually everywhere (Wellford, 1980). Labelling theory is thus most usefully applied to less serious deviance, such as sexual promiscuity or mental illness.

Second, the consequences of deviant labelling are unclear. Research is inconclusive as to whether deviant labelling produces subsequent deviance or discourages further violations (Smith and Gartin, 1989; Sherman and Smith, 1992).

Third, not everyone resists the label of deviance; some people may actually relish being defined as deviant (Vold and Bernard, 1986). For example, individuals may engage in civil disobedience leading to arrest to call attention to social injustice.

Both Sutherland's differential association theory and Hirschi's control theory have had considerable influence in sociology. But they provide little insight into why society's norms and laws define certain kinds of activities as deviant in the first place. This important question is addressed by social-conflict analysis, the focus of the next section.

SOCIAL-CONFLICT ANALYSIS

The social-conflict paradigm demonstrates how deviance reflects social inequality. This approach holds that who or what is labelled as deviant depends on the relative power of categories of people.

DEVIANCE AND POWER

Alexander Liazos (1972) points out that everyday conceptions of deviants—"nuts, sluts, and 'perverts'"— are people who share the trait of powerlessness. Bag ladies (not corporate polluters) and unemployed men on street corners (not arms dealers) carry the stigma of deviance.

Social-conflict theory links deviance to power in three ways. First, the norms—and especially the laws—of any society generally reflect the interests of the rich and powerful. People who threaten the wealthy, either by seizing their property or by advocating a more egalitarian society, come to be tagged as "common thieves" or "political radicals." As noted in Chapter 4 ("Society"), Karl Marx argued that the law (and all other social institutions) tends to support the interests of the rich. Echoing Marx, Richard Quinney makes the point succinctly: "Capitalist justice is by the capitalist class, for the capitalist class, and against the working class" (1977:3).

Second, even if their behaviour is called into question, the powerful have the resources to resist deviant labels. Corporate executives who order the dumping of hazardous wastes are rarely held personally accountable for these acts. As the very public, televised O.J. Simpson trial made clear, even when charged with violent crimes, the rich have the resources to vigorously resist being labelled as criminal. While wealth can provide similar advantages in

Canada, the absence of television cameras in the courtroom means that the drama is not enacted in our living rooms.

Third, the widespread belief that norms and laws are natural and good masks their political character. For this reason, we may condemn the unequal application of the law but give little thought to whether the *laws themselves* are inherently fair (Quinney, 1977).

DEVIANCE AND CAPITALISM

Also following the Marxist tradition, Steven Spitzer (1980) argues that deviant labels are applied to people who impede the operation of capitalism. First, because capitalism is based on private ownership of wealth, people who threaten the property of others—especially the poor who steal from the rich—are prime candidates for labelling as deviants. Conversely, the rich who exploit the poor are rarely called into question. Landlords, for example, who charge poor tenants high rents and evict those who cannot pay, are not considered a threat to society; they are simply "doing business."

Second, because capitalism depends on productive labour, those who cannot or will not work risk deviant labelling. Many members of our society think of people out of work—even if through no fault of their own—as deviant.

Third, capitalism depends on respect for figures of authority, so people who resist authority are labelled as deviant. Examples are children who skip school or talk back to parents and teachers; adults who do not cooperate with employers or police; and anyone who opposes "the system."

Fourth, anyone who directly challenges the capitalist status quo is likely to be defined as deviant. Into this category fall antiwar activists, environmentalists, and labour organizers.

To turn the argument around, society offers positive labels to those who enhance the operation of capitalism. Winning athletes, for example, have celebrity status because they express the values of individual achievement and competition vital to capitalism. Additionally, Spitzer notes, we condemn using drugs of escape (marijuana, psychedelics, heroin, and crack) as deviant, while espousing drugs that promote adjustment to the status quo (such as alcohol and caffeine).

The capitalist system also strives to control people who don't fit into the system. Those who are a "costly yet relatively harmless burden" on society, says Spitzer, include Robert Merton's retreatists (for example, those addicted to alcohol or other drugs), the elderly, and people with mental and/or physical disabilities. All are subject to control by social welfare agencies. But those who openly challenge the very underpinnings of the capitalist system, including the inner-city "underclass" and revolutionaries—Merton's innovators and rebels—come under the purview of the criminal justice system and, in times of crisis, military forces.

Prime Minister Pierre Trudeau invoked the War Measures Act in October 1970 to contain the threat posed by the Front de Libération du Québec (FLQ), which had planted numerous bombs and had kidnapped both the British trade commissioner and the Quebec labour and immigration minister. Civil rights were suspended and 465 people were arrested because Trudeau perceived a threat to Canadian stability from the violent, revolutionary FLQ.

Note that both the social welfare and the criminal justice systems apply labels that blame individuals and not the system for the control they exert over people's lives. Welfare recipients are deemed unworthy freeloaders; poor people who vent rage at their powerlessness are labelled rioters; anyone who actively challenges the government is branded a radical or a Communist; and those who attempt to gain illegally what they cannot otherwise acquire are called common thieves.

White-Collar Crime

"Reputable" Canadians have long been known to circumvent the law when doing so is likely to be immensely profitable (Carrigan, 1991:113–65). For example, during World War II, when consumer goods were being rationed in favour of the production of armaments, big and small businesses and helpful government officials were caught up in wartime racketeering, supplying illegal goods through the black market. More recently, Canada has had its share of stock and real estate fraud, bid-rigging, tax evasion, and the fencing of stolen goods—activities that have cost taxpayers and consumers many millions of dollars. But the perpetrators rarely find themselves in the criminal courts.

One recent example, the Bre-X case, involved tampering with (or "salting") ore samples and thus faking a massive gold find in Indonesia. The apparent suicide of the chief geologist, Michael de Guzman, followed by the collapse of Bre-X share prices, brought the scam to an end, costing investors about $3 billion (Waldie, 1998). It will be interesting to see if, in the end, only de Guzman is found guilty of fraud; executives David Walsh and John Felderhof may or may not be implicated.

The Bre-X case exemplifies **white-collar crime**, defined by Edwin Sutherland in 1940 as *crimes committed by persons of high social position in the course of their occupations* (Sutherland and Cressey, 1978:44). White-collar crime rarely involves uniformed police converg-

Laws regulate the operation of businesses just as they direct the actions of individuals. But, as social-conflict analysis points out, powerful corporate leaders who face allegations of wrong-doing are rarely thought of as "criminals," and rarely are they subject to the punishment accorded to ordinary people.

ing on a scene with drawn guns. Thus, it does not refer to crimes such as murder, assault, or rape that happen to be carried out by people of high social position. Instead, white-collar crimes are acts by powerful people making use of their occupational positions to enrich themselves or others illegally, often causing significant public harm in the process (Hagan and Parker, 1985; Vold and Bernard, 1986). In short, white-collar offences that occur in government offices and corporate boardrooms are commonly dubbed crime in the suites rather than crime in the streets.

The public harm wreaked by false advertising, marketing of unsafe products, embezzlement, and bribery of public officials extends far beyond what most people realize. Some researchers contend that white-collar crime causes greater public harm than the more visible "street crime" (Reiman, 1990). The marketing of unsafe products and the failure to implement workplace safety regulations have been responsible for many deaths in Canada. Immeasurable sums of money are stolen every year through fraud. Since much of it goes undetected, and the overburdened fraud units do not have the workforce necessary to prosecute all known cases, it is difficult to estimate the dollar value of white-collar crime. Among the roughly six hundred cases under investigation or prosecution

by the Ontario Provincial Police in 1989, frauds in the $10- to $15-million range were common. One Toronto developer alone defrauded investors and creditors of roughly $93 million in the late 1980s (Carrigan, 1991). Clearly, the losses from this kind of crime far exceed the economic losses through common theft.

Elite deviance rarely results in criminal labelling of powerful people. Even when their actions lead to extensive public harm, it is far from certain that officials will be prosecuted. And in the event that white-collar criminals do face the music, the odds are they will not go to jail. As well, Sutherland noted that the public voices less concern about white-collar crime than about street crime, partly because corporate crime victimizes everyone—and no one. White-collar criminals don't stick a gun in anyone's ribs, and the economic costs are usually spread throughout the population.

As the "backbone of capitalism," corporations have immense power, influencing both the mass media and the political process. High corporate officials are frequently graduates of prestigious universities and professional schools, belong to exclusive social clubs, and have well-developed networks linking them to other powerful people in all walks of life. Many government officials, drawn from the ranks of corporate executives, regulate the very corporate enterprises in which they have spent most of their working lives. Not surprisingly, then, serious episodes of white-collar crime only make headlines from time to time.

Critical evaluation. According to social-conflict theory, inequality in wealth and power guides the creation and application of laws and other norms. This approach asserts that the criminal justice and social welfare systems act as political agents, controlling categories of people who threaten the capitalist system.

Like other analyses of deviance, however, social-conflict theory has its critics. First, this approach implies that laws and other cultural norms are created directly by the rich and powerful. At the very least, this assumption is an oversimplification, since many segments of our society influence, and benefit from, the political process. Laws also protect workers, consumers, and the environment, sometimes in opposition to the interests of the rich.

Second, social-conflict analysis implies that criminality springs up only to the extent that a society treats its members unequally. However, as Durkheim noted, all societies generate deviance, whatever their economic system.

We have now presented various sociological explanations for crime and other types of deviance.

Table 8–1 summarizes the contributions of each approach.

DEVIANCE AND SOCIAL DIVERSITY

The shape of deviance in a society has much to do with the relative power and privilege of different categories of people. The following section offers an example of how gender is linked to deviance.

DEVIANCE AND GENDER

Virtually every society in the world applies more stringent normative controls to women than to men. Historically, our society has restricted the role of women to the home. Despite considerable change, Canadian women still face limitations to their opportunities in the workplace, in athletics, in politics, and in the military. Elsewhere in the world, the normative constraints placed on women are much greater. In Saudi Arabia, for example, women cannot vote or legally operate motor vehicles; in Iran, women who dare to expose their hair or wear makeup in public can be whipped.

Given the importance of gender to the social construction of deviance, we need to pause a moment to see how gender figures in some of the theories we have already discussed. Robert Merton's strain theory, for example, has a masculine cast in that it defines cultural goals in terms of financial success. Traditionally at least, this goal has had more to do with the lives of men, while women have been socialized to view success in terms of relationships, particularly marriage and motherhood (Leonard, 1982). A more woman-focused theory might recognize the "strain" caused by the cultural ideals of equality clashing with the reality of gender-based inequality.

Labelling theory, the major approach in symbolic-interaction analysis, offers greater insight into ways in which gender influences how we define deviance. To the extent that we judge the behaviour of females and males by different standards, the very process of labelling involves sex-linked biases. Further, because society generally places men in positions of power over women, men often escape direct responsibility for actions that victimize women. In the past, at least, men engaging in sexual harassment or other assaults against women have been tagged with only mildly deviant labels, if they have been punished at all.

By contrast, women who are victimized may have to convince an unsympathetic audience that they are not to blame for what happened. Research confirms an important truth: whether people define a situation as deviance—and, if so, whose deviance it is—depends on the sex of both the audience and the actors (King and Clayson, 1988). The "Controversy & Debate"

TABLE 8–1 Sociological Explanations of Deviance: A Summary

Theoretical Paradigm	Major Contributions
Structural-functional analysis	While what is deviant may vary, deviance itself is found in all societies; deviance and the social response it provokes sustain the moral foundation of society; deviance may also guide social change.
Symbolic-interaction analysis	Nothing is inherently deviant but may become defined as such through the response of others; the reactions of others are highly variable; the label of deviance may lead to the emergence of secondary deviance and deviant careers.
Social-conflict analysis	Laws and other norms reflect the interest of powerful members of society; those who threaten the status quo are generally defined as deviant; social injury caused by powerful people is less likely to be considered criminal than social injury caused by people who have little social power.

box takes a closer look at the issue of date rape, one example of how a double standard has proved harmful to women.

Ironically, social-conflict analysis—despite its focus on social inequality—virtually ignores the importance of gender. If, as conflict theory suggests, economic disadvantage is a primary cause of crime, why do women (whose economic position is worse than that of men) commit far fewer crimes than men do? The following section on crime examines crime rates in Canada and addresses this question.

CRIME

Crime is the violation of statutes enacted into criminal law. In Canada, criminal law (collected in the *Criminal Code*) is enacted by the federal government, though implementation details may vary from province to province.

THE COMPONENTS OF CRIME

Technically, crime is composed of two elements: the *act* itself (or, in some cases, the failure to do what the law requires) and *criminal intent* (in legal terminology, *mens rea*, or "guilty mind"). Intent is a matter of degree, ranging from wilful conduct to negligence in which a person does not deliberately set out to hurt

Date Rape: Exposing Dangerous Myths

Completing a day of work during a business trip to the courthouse in Tampa, Florida, thirty-two-year-old Sandra Abbott* pondered her return to her hotel. An attorney with whom she had been working—a pleasant enough man—made a kind offer of a lift. As his car threaded its way through the late afternoon traffic, their conversation was animated. "He was saying all the right things," Abbott recalled, "so I started to trust him." An invitation to join him for dinner was happily accepted. After lingering over an enjoyable meal, they walked together to the door of her hotel room. The new acquaintance angled for an invitation to come in, but Abbott hesitated, sensing that he might have something more on his mind. She explained that she was old-fashioned about relationships, but would allow him to come in, but only for a little while with the understanding that talking was *all* they would do.

Sitting on the couch in the room, soon Abbott was overcome with drowsiness. Feeling comfortable in the presence of her new friend, she let her head fall gently onto his shoulder and, before she knew it, she fell asleep.

*A pseudonym; the facts of this case are from Gibbs (1991a).

That's when the attack began. Abbott was startled back to consciousness as the man thrust himself sexually upon her. She shouted "No!" but he paid no heed. Abbott describes what happened next:

I didn't scream or run. All I could think of was my business contacts and what if they saw me run out of my room screaming rape. I thought it was my fault. I felt so filthy, I

Is a person who drinks alcohol to excess capable of making a responsible decision about having sex? What role does alcohol play in date rape on the campus?

washed myself over and over in hot water. Did he rape me?, I kept asking myself. I didn't consent. But who's gonna believe me? I had a man in my hotel room after midnight. (Gibbs, 1991a:50)

Abbott knew that she had said "No!" and thus had been raped. She notified the police, who conducted an investigation and turned their findings over to the state attorney's office. But the authorities backed away. In the absence of evidence such as bruises, a medical examination, and torn clothes, they noted, there was little point in prosecuting.

The case of Sandra Abbott is all too typical. Even today, in most incidences of sexual attack, a victim files no police report, and no offender is arrested. So reluctant are the victims of such attacks to come forward that, in Canada, "somewhere between 60 and 90 percent of rapes go unreported" (DeKeseredy and Hinch, 1991:94). Where charges are not laid, the victim faces the bitter reality of simply trying as best she can to put a traumatic experience behind her.

The reason for such appalling inaction is that many people have a misguided understanding of rape. Three false notions about rape are so common that they might be called "rape myths."

Myth #1: Rape involves strangers. A sexual attack brings to mind young men

---

anyone but acts (or fails to act) in a manner that may reasonably be expected to cause harm. Juries weigh the degree of intent in determining the seriousness of a crime and may find the person who kills another guilty of first-degree murder, second-degree murder, or manslaughter. In some cases (e.g., self-defence), homicide may be deemed justifiable.

Types of Crimes

In Canada, information on criminal offences is obtained from the Uniform Crime Reporting system

and reported in a Statistics Canada publication called *Canadian Crime Statistics*. Violent crime and property crime are recorded separately.

Violent crimes, *crimes against people that involve violence or the threat of violence*, include murder, manslaughter, infanticide, assault, sexual assault, abduction, and robbery.

Property crimes encompass *crimes that involve theft of property belonging to others*, including breaking and entering, motor vehicle theft, theft over $5000 (changed from $1000 in 1995), theft of $5000 and under, possession of stolen goods, and fraud.

lurking in the shadows who suddenly spring on their unsuspecting victims. But this pattern is the exception rather than the rule: experts report that only one in five rapes involves a stranger. For this reason, people have begun to speak more realistically about *acquaintance rape* or, more simply, *date rape*.

Myth #2: Women provoke their attackers. Surely, many people think, a woman claiming to have been raped must have done something to encourage the man, to lead him on, to make him think that she really wanted to have sex. In the case described above, didn't Sandra Abbott agree to have dinner with the man? Didn't she willingly admit him to her room? Such self-doubt often paralyzes victims. But having dinner with a man—or even inviting him into her hotel room—is hardly a woman's statement of consent to have sex with him any more than it is an invitation to have him beat her with a club.

Myth #3: Rape is simply sex. If there is no knife held to a woman's throat, or if she is not bound and gagged, then how can sex be a crime? The answer is that, under the law, forcing a woman to have sex without her consent is a *violent crime*. To accept the idea that rape is sex we would also have to see no difference between brutal combat and playful wrestling. "Having sex" implies intimacy, caring, and communication—none of which is present in cases of rape. Beyond the brutality of being physically violated, date rape also undermines a victim's sense of trust. This is especially serious in victims under eighteen, a significant percentage of whom are raped by their own fathers.

The more people believe these myths about rape, the more women will become victims of sexual violence. The ancient Babylonians stoned married women who became victims of rape, convinced that the women had committed adultery. Ideas about rape have not changed over thousands of years, which helps explain why, even today, most rapes go unreported to police and, even when authorities are notified, prosecutions and convictions are rare.

When women do report sexual attacks, police judgment as to whether or not a criminal act has occurred depends on the victim's reputation. When females referred to, by the Canadian police, as "women who can't be raped" or "open territory victims" filed complaints, 98 percent of them were dismissed as unfounded. "These women were prostitutes, known alcoholics, women who were drinking at the time of the offence, drug users, women on welfare, and unemployed women as well as women noted in police reports as 'idle'" (DeKeseredy and Hinch, 1991:66–67).

Nowhere has the issue of date rape been more widely discussed than at universities. The campus setting encourages trust, and young people often have much to learn about relationships and about themselves. While this open environment encourages communication, it also invites an alarming level of sexual violence. Studies in the U.S. estimate that one in six college women will be raped before she graduates. It is difficult to make estimates for Canada because of the limited amount of research on university rape done in this country. What is known is that university men who abuse their dates do so, quite often, with the support of male friends who encourage and legitimate female victimization (DeKeseredy and Hinch, 1991:53–55.).

To eliminate sexual violence we must begin by exposing the myths about rape. In addition, the campus must be transformed so that women and men interact with dignity and equality. Serious questions surround the role of alcohol in campus social life and the effect of cultural patterns that define sex as a sport. To address the crisis of date rape, everyone needs to understand two simple truths: forcing sex without a woman's consent is rape, and when a woman says "No," she means just that.

SOURCES: Gibbs (1991a, 1991b); Gilbert (1992); DeKeseredy and Hinch (1991).

A third category of offences includes **victimless crimes**, *violations of law in which there are no readily apparent victims*—such as prostitution and gambling. There is also a separate category of *Narcotic Control Act* offences regarding the use of illegal drugs, including cannabis or marijuana. However, "victimless crime" is often a misnomer. How victimless is a crime when a young runaway is lured into prostitution and then made to believe that that is her only way to live? And how victimless is the crime if a young pregnant woman smoking crack causes the death of or permanent injury to her baby? In many cases, the people who commit such crimes are themselves both offenders and victims.

Criminal Statistics

Canada's crime statistics show steady increases in both violent and property crime rates from 1962 to 1992, followed by clear declines. Figure 8–2 illustrates these trends in violent and property crimes over the period in question.

Canadians often pride themselves on having a much less violent society than the United States. A

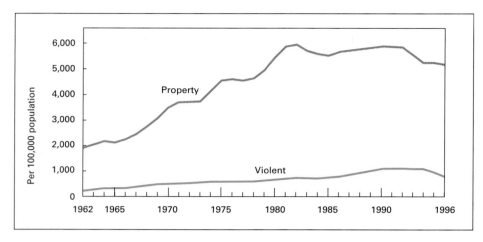

FIGURE 8–2 Violent and Property Crime Rates in Canada, 1962–96

SOURCE: Statistics Canada, Catalogue Nos. 85-205 and 85-002-XPE, Vol. 17, No. 8.

comparison of homicide rates in the two countries suggests that this is indeed the case. Since the early 1960s, the American homicide rate has been three to four times higher than that in Canada. Canada's homicide rate *dropped* from 2.7 per 100 000 population in 1992 to 2.1 in 1996. By contrast, the Americans had 9.5 homicides per 100 000 population in 1993.

Canada Map 8–1 suggests that homicide rates (per 100 000 population) differ not only between countries, but also among our own provinces. Note that the variation within Canada is greater than that between Canada and the United States.

Always read crime statistics with caution, however, since they include only crimes known to the police. The police learn about almost all homicides, but assaults—especially among acquaintances—are far less likely to be reported. The police record an even smaller proportion of property crimes, especially when losses are small. Some victims may not realize that a crime has occurred, or they may assume they have little chance of recovering their property even if they notify the police. And reports of rape, although rising over time, still grossly understate the extent of this crime.

One way to evaluate official crime statistics is through a *victimization survey*, in which a researcher asks a representative sample of people about their experience with crime. People do not always respond fully or truthfully to such surveys, experts acknowledge, but the results of these surveys indicate that actual crime occurs at substantially higher rates than suggested by official reports. Canada's first national survey on violence against women (1993) found that half of our women have experienced physical or sexual violence at least once since turning sixteen years of age. Among those who have been married or lived common-law, 29 percent have been physically or sexually assaulted by their partners. Victimization result-

ing from a wider range of criminal acts (measured by the General Social Survey) seems to have remained stable between 1988 and 1993, with 24 percent of the population each year experiencing at least one instance of criminal victimization (Statistics Canada, *Juristat*, March 1994).

THE "STREET" CRIMINAL: A PROFILE

Official statistics paint a broad-brush picture of people arrested for violent and property crimes. We now examine the breakdown of these arrest statistics by age, gender, social class, race, and ethnicity.

Age

Official crime rates rise sharply during adolescence and the early twenties, falling thereafter (Giffen, 1976; Hirschi and Gottfredson, 1983; Krisberg and Schwartz, 1983; Correctional Services Canada, 1991). Although people between the ages of twelve and twenty-four represent about 20 percent of the population, they account for about 60 percent of the people charged with property crimes and 35 percent of those charged with violent crimes. In contrast, those over forty-five years of age make up about 32 percent of the population, but are responsible for only 5 percent of the property crime and 10 percent of violent crime. Not surprisingly, twenty- to thirty-four-year-olds make up 25 percent of the Canadian population and 62 percent of the inmates in our prisons.

Gender

Although each sex constitutes roughly half of the population in Canada, about 85 to 90 percent of arrests involve males, and about 97 percent of prison inmates

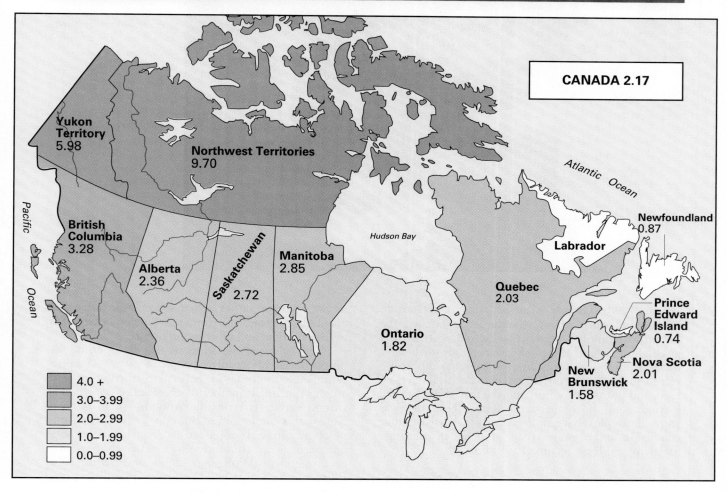

CANADA 2.17

Yukon Territory 5.98

Northwest Territories 9.70

British Columbia 3.28

Alberta 2.36

Saskatchewan 2.72

Manitoba 2.85

Ontario 1.82

Quebec 2.03

Labrador

Newfoundland 0.87

Prince Edward Island 0.74

Nova Scotia 2.01

New Brunswick 1.58

Hudson Bay

Atlantic Ocean

Pacific Ocean

4.0 +
3.0–3.99
2.0–2.99
1.0–1.99
0.0–0.99

CANADA MAP 8–1 Homicide Rates for Canada, Provinces and Territories, 1992–96 (Five-Year Averages, Rates Per 100 000 People)

SOURCE: Adapted by Gerber from Statistics Canada, Catalogue No. 85-002-XPE, Vol. 17, No. 9 (1997).

are male. The proportion of females arrested is always low but varies considerably from one country to another: one study found Finland had a low of 6.7 percent, Canada had 9.8, the U.S. had 13.7, and New Zealand had 20.5 (Simon and Sharma, 1979).

Historically, the low levels and typical patterns of crime committed by women have been linked to their subordinate social and economic status. Alberta sociologist Helen Boritch (1997), in one of the first comprehensive analyses of female criminality in Canada, asks if the changing position of women has led to increased rates and new patterns of crime. She finds that, "while women's participation in crime is increas-

ing, the overall pattern of female criminality has not changed dramatically . . . women's crimes continue to be primarily non-violent in nature, economically motivated, or victimless crimes" (1997:20). Prostitution, drug offences, and shoplifting still predominate. Women are more involved in violent crime than in the past, but usually in low-level assault. Very few women are charged with homicide in Canada, and there is no discernible change in women's homicide rate over recent decades.

Some of this gender difference stems from the reluctance of law enforcement officials to define women as criminals (Scott, 1992; Cluff, Hunter and

A police constable serves up a hot dog at a picnic organized to generate a sense of community among neighbours. The strategy of "community policing," by which law enforcement officials become involved in local communities, can be effective in preventing a crime before it occurs.

Hinch, 1998). Canada witnessed this reluctance to assume the worst about women as it watched the Bernardo-Homolka murder case unfold. Initially, the justice system and the public were ready to believe that Karla Homolka was an unwilling accomplice—a victim in effect—forced to participate in abduction, rape, and murder by a husband she feared. Before the incriminating videotapes were found, Homolka was allowed to plea bargain (receiving a manslaughter conviction and a twelve-year sentence) in exchange for giving evidence against Paul Bernardo.

Social Class

Although people commonly associate criminality with poverty, sociological research suggests that rich and poor alike commit crimes, albeit somewhat different kinds of offences. People arrested for violent and property crimes in North America and elsewhere disproportionately have low social standing (Wolfgang, Figlio, and Sellin, 1972; Clinard and Abbott, 1973; Elliot and Ageton, 1980; Braithwaite, 1981; Thornberry and Farnsworth, 1982; Wolfgang, Thornberry, and Figlio, 1987).

In part, this pattern reflects the historical tendency to view poor people as less worthy than those whose wealth and power confer "respectability" (Tittle and Villemez, 1977; Tittle, Villemez, and Smith, 1978; Elias, 1986). Even the strain theory discussed above contributes to the expectation that more lawbreakers will come from our less affluent neighbourhoods. Police officers, then, are conditioned to focus their search for crime and its perpetrators in the poor

sections of town rather than in the pristine office towers of business and government where embezzlement, insider trading, and bid-rigging occur.

The evidence also suggests that street crime disproportionately victimizes people of lower social position. Violent crime in particular is commonplace among the small number of chronically poor people living in inner-city neighbourhoods—or in our isolated native communities. But only a small proportion of less advantaged people are ever convicted of crimes; most crimes are committed by a relatively few hardcore offenders (Wolfgang, Figlio, and Sellin, 1972; Elliot and Ageton, 1980; Wolfgang, Thornberry, and Figlio, 1987; Harries, 1990).

Moreover, as John Braithwaite notes, the connection between social standing and criminality "depends entirely on what form of crime one is talking about" (1981:47). If the definition of crime is expanded beyond street crime to include white-collar crime, the average "common criminal" has a much higher social position.

Race and Ethnicity

Probing the relationship between race and criminality, we confront a raft of complex issues. Just as most people have long considered criminality the province of the poor, they have also associated crime with people of colour—despite clear evidence that most crimes are committed by whites.

In Canada, Blacks and particularly native people are arrested in disproportionate numbers. The effect of these arrest rates is apparent in the racial composition of our prison inmates: Black people represent roughly 1 percent of Canada's population, but make up 3.8 percent of federal inmates. Aboriginals make up about 2 percent of the population but 11.3 percent of inmates (Correctional Services Canada, 1991). This pattern is even more pronounced among female prisoners, where 8.8 percent are Black and 15.4 percent are aboriginal. More disturbing yet is the observation that, in the Prairie provinces, where natives make up about 6 percent of the population, 36 percent of male inmates and 47 percent of female inmates in federal prisons are aboriginal. The overrepresentation of native people in provincial prisons is even more pronounced.

The report of the Commission on Systemic Racism in the Ontario Criminal Justice System (January 1996) revealed that the imprisonment of Blacks increased by 204 percent between 1986 and 1994, while the comparable figure for whites was 23 percent. The report argues that at every stage of their contact with the justice system—from arrest through trial to imprisonment—Blacks are treated more harshly (Makin, 1996).

First, to the degree that prejudice related to colour prompts police to arrest natives and Blacks more readily than whites, and leads white citizens more readily to report members of these visible minorities to police as potential offenders, these two groups are overly criminalized. The same prejudices may work in the courtroom. In the long run, even small biases by law enforcement officials and the public substantially distort the official link between race and crime (Liska and Tausig, 1979; Unnever, Frazier, and Henretta, 1980; Smith and Visher, 1981).

Second, race in Canada closely relates to social standing, which, as we have already shown, affects the likelihood of engaging in street crimes. Several researchers claim that membership in lower-class gangs promotes criminality. American sociologists Judith and Peter Blau (1982) take a different tack, suggesting that criminality—especially violent crime—is promoted by the sting of poverty in the midst of affluence. Suffering the hardships of poverty in a rich society encourages people to perceive society as unjust and to disregard its laws.

Crime statistics tend to be biased against reporting white-collar crimes. In the U.S., these crimes are excluded from the official crime index. While Canadian statistics do include fraud and "theft over $5000" among property crimes, otherwise our society fails to recognize the range of white-collar crimes. Clearly, this omission contributes to the view of the typical criminal as not simply poor but a person of colour. If our definition of crime were broadened to include insider stock trading, toxic-waste dumping, embezzlement, bribery, and cheating on income tax returns,

The creators of this photograph, part of the "United Colors of Benetton" advertising campaign, intended to make the statement that people are linked together regardless of colour. But so strong are our notions about crime and race that many individuals mistakenly interpreted the photograph as a white police officer escorting a Black suspect. What can sociology contribute towards a more accurate understanding of the connection between crime and colour?

the proportion of white (and affluent) criminals would rise dramatically.

Crime in Global Perspective

By world standards, the United States has a lot of crime. Global comparisons fall short because nations define crimes differently and not every country collects data with care, but rough comparisons suggest that the homicide rate in the United States stands four times higher than in Canada and five times higher than in Europe, and that the rape rate is 2.6 times higher than Canada's and seven times higher than Europe's. The United States contends with more crime than virtually any other country in the world (Kalish, 1988). New York City led all U.S. cities with 1182 murders in 1995. Canada as a whole, with almost four times the population of New York City, had 732 murders in 1995.

Why does the U.S. have such high crime rates? Elliot Currie (1985) suggests that the problem stems from its cultural emphasis on individual economic success, frequently at the expense of family and community cohesion. Currie also notes that, unlike European nations, the United States neither guarantees families a minimum income nor publicly funds childcare programs. Such public policy decisions, he claims, erode the fabric of society, fuel frustration among society's have-nots, and thus encourage criminal behaviour. Furthermore, Currie asserts that the

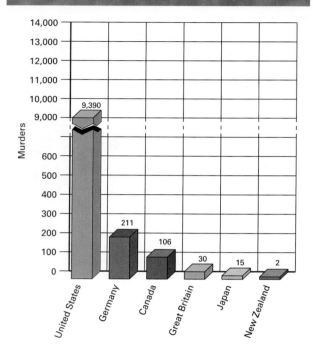

FIGURE 8–3 Deaths by Handguns, 1996

SOURCE: Handgun Control, Inc. (1998).

affect criminals, who almost always obtain guns illegally (Wright, 1995). Moreover, we should be cautious about assuming gun control is a magic bullet in the war on crime. Elliott Currie notes, for example, that the number of Californians killed each year by knives alone exceeds the number of Canadians killed by weapons of all kinds. Most experts do think, however, that gun control will help lower the level of violence.

This is clearly the intent of the gun control legislation enacted in Canada in the fall of 1995. CAVEAT (Canadians Against Violence Everywhere Advocating Its Termination) and other public-interest groups were instrumental in persuading the government to prohibit certain kinds of weapons and require the registration of others. Although very few Canadians have or want guns in their homes, collectors and rural people—including aboriginals—mounted significant resistance to the new regulations. Figure 8–4 shows Canadian firearm homicides by type of firearm.

Crime rates are soaring in some of the largest cities of the world, such as Manila, Philippines, and São Paulo, Brazil, which have rapid population growth and millions of desperately poor people. By and large, however, the traditional character of less economically developed societies and their strong family structure allow local communities to control crime informally (Clinard and Abbott, 1973; Der Spiegel, 1989).

One exception to this pattern is crimes against women. Rape is surging throughout the world, especially in poor societies. Moreover, traditional social patterns that curb the economic opportunities available to women also promote prostitution. Global Map 8–1 shows the extent of prostitution in various world regions.

Finally, as noted in earlier chapters, we are experiencing "globalization" on many fronts, including crime. Some types of crime have always been multinational, including terrorism, espionage, and arms dealing (Martin and Romano, 1992).

A more recent case in point is the illegal drug trade. In part, the proliferation of illegal drugs in North America stems from demand: there is a very profitable market for cocaine and other drugs in the U.S. and Canada, as well as legions of young people willing to risk arrest or even violent death by engaging in the lucrative drug trade. Montreal bikers, the Hells Angels or "Les Hells," are involved in a murderous gang war as they maneuver for international domination of the illegal drug trade—much of which passes through Canada on its way to the United States. But the "supply" side of the issue also propels drug trafficking. In the South American nation of Colombia, at least 20 percent of the population depends on cocaine production for their livelihood. Furthermore, not only is cocaine Colombia's most

high level of unemployment and underemployment tolerated in the United States helps create a category of perpetually poor people whose opportunities to make money are often limited to criminal pursuits. The key to reducing crime, then, lies in social change, not in hiring more police and building more prisons. Canada falls between Europe and the United States in the provision of social services and income support, but in recent years our "safety nets" have become increasingly frayed. According to Currie's reasoning, we can expect rising crime rates.

Another contributing factor to the relatively high level of violence in the United States is widespread private ownership of guns. Of 20 043 murder victims in the United States in 1995, 68 percent died from shootings. There are as many guns in the hands of private individuals as there are people in the United States. Figure 8–3 shows that the United States is the runaway leader in handgun deaths among industrial nations.

But as critics of gun control point out, waiting periods and background checks at retail gun stores (mandated by the 1993 Brady Bill) are unlikely to

profitable export, but it outsells all other exports combined (including coffee). Clearly, then, understanding crimes such as drug dealing requires analyzing social conditions both in this country and around the world.

THE CRIMINAL JUSTICE SYSTEM

The criminal justice system is a society's formal response to crime. In some countries, military police keep a tight rein on people's behaviour; in others, including Canada, police have more limited powers to respond to specific violations of criminal law. We shall briefly introduce the key elements of this scheme: police, the courts, and the punishment of convicted offenders.

POLICE

The police serve as the primary point of contact between the population and the criminal justice system. In principle, the police maintain public order by uniformly enforcing the law. Since Canada's police officers (1 per 523 people in 1995) cannot effectively monitor the activities of 30 million people, the police exercise considerable discretion about which situations warrant their attention and how to handle them.

How, then, do police carry out their duties? In a study of police behaviour in five U.S. cities, Douglas Smith and Christy Visher (1981; Smith, 1987) concluded that, because they must respond swiftly, police make several quick assessments that guide their actions. First, *how serious is the alleged crime?* The more serious police perceive a situation to be, the more likely they are to make an arrest. Second, *what is the victim's preference?* Generally, if a victim demands that police make an arrest, they are likely to do so. Third, *is the suspect cooperative or not?* Resisting police efforts increases a suspect's chance of arrest. Fourth, *have they arrested the suspect before?* Police are more likely to take into custody anyone whom they have arrested before, presumably because this suggests guilt. Fifth, *are bystanders present?* According to Smith and Visher, the presence of observers prompts police to take stronger control of a situation; arrests also move the encounter from the street (the suspect's turf) to the police department (where law officers have the edge). Sixth, *what is the suspect's race?* All else being equal, Smith and Visher contend, police are more likely to arrest people of colour than whites.

Similarly, factors that affect police discretion have been examined in Ontario (Schellenberg, 1995). Police officers are more likely to apply the rules regarding traffic offences, leaving less room for leniency, when their actions are being recorded by mobile video camera. More generally, when the police

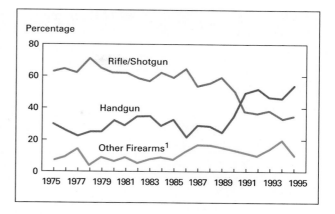

FIGURE 8–4 Firearm Homicides by Type of Firearm, Canada 1975–95

[1] Other firearms include sawed-off rifles/shotguns, fully automatic firearms (collected since 1991) and other firearm-like weapons.

SOURCE: Homicide Survey, Canadian Centre for Justice Statistics; Statistics Canada, Catalogue no. 85-002-XPE, Vol. 17, No. 7 (1997).

are considering making arrests, they are less likely to check an individual's record—even when they have computer access in their patrol cars—if they know the individual in question or if they feel that the individual is trustworthy. Race and class can easily enter into the decision-making process at this point.

In Canada, people of colour are arrested and eventually imprisoned in disproportionate numbers (Commission on Systemic Racism in the Ontario Criminal Justice System) but this observation does not apply equally to all visible minorities. While Blacks and aboriginals, respectively, are imprisoned at five and three times the rate for whites, those of Arab, East Indian, and Asian origin are imprisoned at two-thirds to half the rate for whites (Makin, 1996).

Finally, the greater numbers of police relative to population are found in areas with two key characteristics: high concentrations of minorities and large income disparities between rich and poor (Jacobs, 1979). Thus, the Northwest Territories and the Yukon have both the highest rates of violent crime, as indicated by homicide (see Canada Map 8–1), and the largest numbers of police officers relative to their populations (1 officer per 275 and 266 residents, respectively, in 1995). The higher crime rates in these areas may be partly alcohol-related and generated by underdevelopment or social disorganization; they may also reflect bias in police surveillance, arrests, and convictions as well as an emphasis on crime control and law enforcement rather than crime prevention (LaPrairie, 1983; Depew, 1992). Thus, police form an imposing presence where a volatile mix of social forces encourages social disruption.

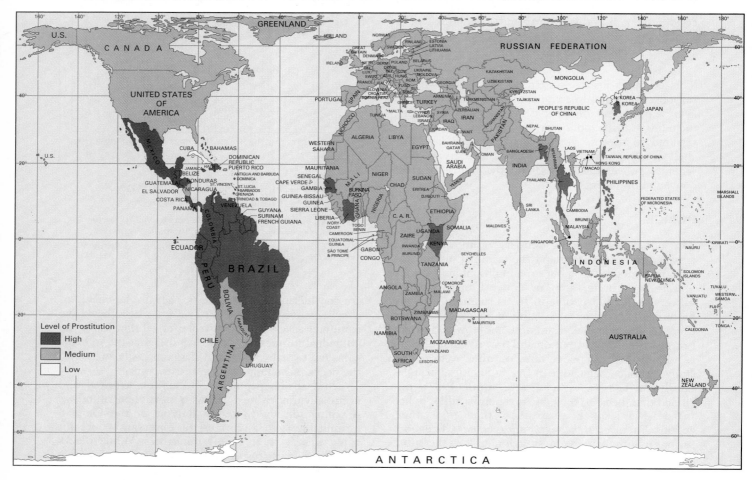

GLOBAL MAP 8–1 Prostitution in Global Perspective

Generally speaking, prostitution is widespread in societies of the world where women have low standing in relation to men. Officially, at least, the now-defunct socialist regimes in Eastern Europe and the former Soviet Union, as well as the People's Republic of China, boasted of gender equality, including the elimination of "vice" such as prostitution. By contrast, in much of Latin America, a region of pronounced patriarchy, prostitution is commonplace. In many Islamic societies patriarchy is also strong but religious forces restrain prostitution. Western, industrial societies display a moderate amount of this practice.
SOURCE: *Peters Atlas of the World* (1990).

COURTS

After arrest, a court determines a suspect's guilt or innocence. In principle, our courts rely on an adversarial process involving attorneys—who represent the defendant on the one side and the Crown on the other—in the presence of a judge who monitors adherence to legal procedures. In practice, however, a large percentage of criminal cases are resolved prior to court appearance through **plea bargaining**, *a legal negotiation in which the prosecution reduces a defendant's charge in exchange for a guilty plea.* For example, a defendant charged with burglary may agree to plead guilty to the lesser charge of possession of burglary tools; another charged with selling cocaine may go along with pleading guilty to possession.

What Can Be Done About Crime?

People across Canada are fearful of, and fed up with, crime. Guard dogs, special locks, and electronic security systems have never been more popular. By 1991, private security guards outnumbered police officers by more than two to one and Canadians have begun, though slowly, to copy the American practice of building gated communities. Although, as revealed by the General Social Survey, overall levels of victimization changed little between 1988 and 1993, 46 percent of Canadians think that crime levels have increased in their neighbourhoods—and 27 percent (42 percent of women) are afraid to walk alone at night near their homes (Statistics Canada 1994, Catalogue No. 85-002). The perception that we are increasingly vulnerable to crime leads to questions of what we can do about it.

Travis Hirschi, sociologist and author of the well-known "control theory," has offered his own version of a "community approach" to crime. Hirschi begins by pointing out two key traits that define today's criminals. The first is age; specifically, most offenders are young. Crime rates are high in the late teens and early twenties, and they fall quickly thereafter. Second, Hirschi continues, most offenders take a short-term view of their lives. Lawbreakers, in Hirschi's words, are people "relatively unable to sustain

a course of action toward some distant goal, whether that goal be education, friendship, employment, or criminal gain. In fact," he concludes, "the defining characteristic of offenders appears to be *low self-control*."

These two facts, he continues, are clues to suggest why the criminal justice system, on its own, can never control crime. For one thing, going to jail is too uncertain (most crimes go unpunished) and too far removed in time (catching, going to trial, and jailing criminals often takes a year or more) to deter the typical offender. Thus, Hirschi explains, popular calls for "stiffer sentences" actually have little effect in suppressing crime. Moreover, by the time many offenders are sent packing to prison, they are already moving beyond the "crime years" simply because they are growing older. Statistically speaking, then, offenders aging in prison represent a crime threat already shrinking on its own.

Therefore, rather than locking up adults, Hirschi argues that society needs to focus resources on younger people *before* they commit crimes. Hirschi calls for closer attention to teenagers—those at highest risk of criminal behaviour. Effective crime control, he explains, depends on keeping teens away not only from guns and drugs, but also alcohol, and, if necessary, cars and perhaps even each other.

A second suggestion comes even earlier in the life course. The most effective way to control crime, Hirschi concludes, is for us to teach our children the key trait of *self-control*. But this is a job ill-suited to government, Hirschi continues, and so the responsibility must fall on parents. But government can help by targeting seriously dysfunctional families for assistance and through any other strategy that fosters strong—preferably two-parent—families. Simply "delaying pregnancy among teenage girls," he predicts, "would probably do more to affect long-term crime rates than all the criminal justice programs combined."

Continue the debate . . .

1. *Do you think limiting teenagers' freedom would reduce crime? What civil rights issues are raised by such a plan?*
2. *Do you think ensuring two-parent households would cut the crime rate? Can society realistically shape families in this way?*
3. *Would economic programs directed at reducing poverty diminish the crime problem? What specific programs would you suggest?*

SOURCE: Based on Gottfredson and Hirschi (1995).

Plea bargaining is widespread because it spares the judicial system the time and expense of court trials. A trial is usually unnecessary if there is little disagreement about the facts of the case. By selectively trying only a small proportion of the cases, the courts can also channel their resources into those deemed most important (Reid, 1991).

But this process pressures defendants (who are presumed innocent) to plead guilty. A person can exercise the right to a trial, but only at the risk of receiving a more severe sentence if found guilty. In

essence, then, plea bargaining undercuts the rights of defendants as it circumvents the adversarial process. According to Abraham Blumberg (1970), defendants who have little understanding of the criminal justice system, as well as those unable to afford a good lawyer, are likely to suffer from this system of "bargain-counter justice." On the other hand, Canadians who felt that Karla Homolka got off too lightly asked to have her plea bargain reassessed. Her case will not be reopened because to do so would threaten the whole plea-bargaining system.

TABLE 8–2 Four Justifications of Punishment: A Summary

Retribution	The oldest justification for punishment still holds sway today. Punishment is atonement for a moral wrong by an individual; in principle, punishment should be comparable in severity to the deviance itself.
Deterrence	An early modern approach, deviance is considered as social disruption, which society acts to control. People are viewed as rational and self-interested; for deterrence to work, the pains of punishment must outweigh the pleasures of deviance.
Rehabilitation	A modern approach linked to the development of the social sciences. Deviance is viewed as the product of social problems (such as poverty) or of personal problems (such as mental illness). Social conditions are improved and offenders are subjected to intervention appropriate to their condition.
Social protection	A modern approach easier to effect than rehabilitation. If society is unable or unwilling to rehabilitate offenders or reform social conditions, people are protected from further deviance by incarceration or execution.

PUNISHMENT

In 1831 the officials in an English town hanged a nine-year-old boy who was found guilty of the crime of setting fire to a house (Kittrie, 1971:103). Canada, which had its last execution in 1962 and abolished the death penalty in 1976, has decided that young people under eighteen years of age have a diminished capacity for crime.

Clearly, approaches to punishment have changed over time and vary from country to country. Debate about the appropriateness of specific punishments as applied to adults and juvenile offenders raises the question of how and why societies should punish its wrongdoers. This leads us to consider four justifications for punishment.

Retribution

The celebrated justice of the U.S. Supreme Court Oliver Wendell Holmes stated, "The first requirement of a sound body of law is that it should correspond with the actual feelings and demands of the community." Because people react to crime with a passion for revenge, Holmes continued, "the law has no choice but to satisfy [that] craving" (quoted in Carlson, 1976).

One key reason to punish, then, is to satisfy a society's need for **retribution** or *moral vengeance by*

which society inflicts suffering on the offender comparable to that caused by the offence. Retribution rests on a view of society as a moral entity in balance. When criminality upsets this balance, punishment exacted in comparable measure restores the moral order, as suggested by the biblical dictum "An eye for an eye."

Retribution stands as the oldest justification for punishment. During the Middle Ages, most people viewed crime as sin—an offence against God as well as society—that warranted a harsh response. Today, although critics charge that retribution does little to reform the offender, this principle retains widespread support.

A recent Toronto case illustrates the importance of the perceived appropriateness of the judicial response. In October 1997 Gordon Stuckless, the equipment manager of Maple Leaf Gardens, was sentenced to two years less a day for the sexual abuse of young boys over a period of twenty-odd years. Stuckless had traded sexual favours for tickets to hockey games or opportunities to meet players. After Martin Kruse came forward with allegations of sexual abuse, police received a stream of phone calls from other men who had had similar experiences. Shortly after Stuckless was sentenced, Kruse committed suicide. Other victims, their families, and many in the general public felt that the lenient sentence did not fit the crime; Kruse's family felt that the light sentence was one of the reasons for his suicide.

Deterrence

A second justification for punishment, **deterrence**, amounts to *the attempt to discourage criminality through punishment.* Deterrence reflects the eighteenth-century Enlightenment notion that, as calculating and rational creatures, humans will forgo deviance if they perceive that the pain of punishment outweighs the pleasure of mischief.

Deterrence emerged as reform directed at the harsh punishments based on retribution. Why put someone to death for stealing, critics asked, if theft can be discouraged with a prison sentence? As the concept of deterrence gained acceptance, execution and physical mutilation of criminals in most industrial societies were replaced by milder forms of punishment such as incarceration.

Punishment may deter crime in two ways. *Specific deterrence* demonstrates to an individual offender that crime does not pay. Through *general deterrence*, the punishment of one person serves as an example to others.

Rehabilitation

The third justification for punishment is **rehabilitation**, *a program for reforming the offender to preclude sub-*

sequent offences. Rehabilitation paralleled the development of the social sciences in the nineteenth century. According to sociologists of that time (and also since), crime and other deviance spring from an unfavourable environment marked by poverty or a lack of parental supervision. Logically, then, if offenders learn to be deviant, they can also learn to obey the rules—the key is controlling the environment. *Reformatories* or *houses of correction* served as a controlled setting to help people learn proper behaviour (recall the description of total institutions in Chapter 5, "Socialization").

Rehabilitation resembles deterrence in that both motivate the offender towards conformity. But rehabilitation emphasizes constructive improvement, while deterrence (like retribution) inflicts suffering on an offender. In addition, while retribution demands that the punishment fit the crime, rehabilitation tailors treatment to the offender. Thus, identical crimes would prompt similar acts of retribution but might call for different programs of rehabilitation.

Social Protection

A final justification for punishment, **social protection**, refers to *rendering an offender incapable of further offences either temporarily through incarceration or permanently by execution.* One of the concerns expressed by the Canadian public is that dangerous offenders are given "life" sentences and then released on parole. After the murder of her daughter Nina in Burlington, Ontario, Priscilla DeVilliers (who founded CAVEAT) has been involved in a massive campaign to restrict parole and bail for dangerous offenders. Her campaign touched a responsive cord in an apprehensive public that does not feel adequately protected at present. When a dangerous man such as Clifford Olson is granted early release and kills eleven young people, as he did in British Columbia in 1980–81, people question the level of social protection afforded them.[2]

Table 8–2 summarizes these four justifications for punishment. Note, too, Figure 8–5, which shows that Russia and the United States incarcerate a larger share of their populations than most other countries in the world. Canada's rate, although the lowest shown here, is still well above those of most European countries.

Critical evaluation We have identified four justifications for punishment. Assessing the actual conse-

---

[2] At the time of Olson's release in 1980, he was serving a prison sentence for murder. He is now serving the maximum sentence of twenty-five years without the possibility of parole. He can expect to be released in the year 2007, when he will be sixty-seven years old. Peter Worthington wrote about the 1980–81 murders of which Olson was convicted, as well as about many others he claims to have committed, in *Saturday Night* (July/August 1993).

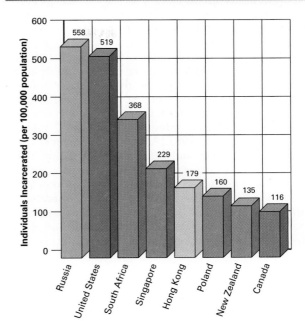

FIGURE 8–5 Incarceration Rates, 1993

SOURCE: Mauer (1994).

quences of punishment, however, is no simple task.

The value of retribution reminds us of Durkheim's contention that punishing the deviant person bolsters people's moral consciousness. To accomplish this objective, punishment was traditionally a public event. Public executions occurred in England until 1868; the last public execution in the United States took place in Kentucky in 1937. Even today, the American mass media ensure public awareness of executions carried out inside prison walls (Kittrie, 1971). We do not publicize executions in Canada (where they no longer occur), but we have television coverage when people like Paul Bernardo are taken away to prison.

Experts and the public as a whole agree that punishment deters some crime (Wright, 1994). Yet our society also has a high rate of **criminal recidivism**, *subsequent offences by people previously convicted of crimes.* Various studies of people released from prison show that substantial percentages have been rearrested and returned to prison within a few years, raising questions about the extent to which punishment actually deters crime. Then, too, only about one-third of all crimes are known to police, and of these, only about one in five results in an arrest. The old adage that "crime doesn't pay" rings rather hollow when we consider that such a small proportion of offences ever result in punishment.

General deterrence is even more difficult to investigate scientifically, since we have no way of knowing how people might act if they were unaware of punishments meted out to others. In the debate over capital punishment, critics of the practice point to research indicating that the death penalty has limited value as a general deterrent in the United States, which is the only Western, industrial society that routinely executes serious offenders (Sellin, 1980; van den Haag and Conrad, 1983; Archer and Gartner, 1987; Lester, 1987; Bailey and Peterson, 1989; Bailey, 1990; Bohm, 1991). Furthermore, an examination of the Canadian homicide rates compiled by Lenton (1989) from 1954 to 1986 reveals no sudden increase in homicide rates after 1962, when the last execution occurred, or after 1976, when capital punishment was abolished. In fact, the homicide rate went down for a few years after 1976.

Prisons accomplish short-term societal protection by keeping offenders off the streets, but they do little to reshape attitudes or behaviour in the long term (Carlson, 1976; Wright, 1994). Rehabilitation may be an unrealistic expectation, since, according to Sutherland's theory of differential association, locking someone up among criminals for months or years should simply strengthen criminal attitudes and skills. And because incarceration severs whatever social ties inmates may have in the outside world, individuals may be prone to further crime upon their release, consistent with Hirschi's control theory.

Ultimately, we should never assume that the criminal justice system—the police, courts, and prisons—can eliminate crime. The point, made strongly in the "Controversy & Debate" box as it has been throughout this chapter, is simple: crime and all other deviance are more than simply the acts of "bad people"; they are inextricably bound up in the operation of society itself.

SUMMARY

1. Deviance refers to normative violations ranging from mild breaches of etiquette to serious violence.

2. Biological investigation, from Cesare Lombroso's nineteenth-century observations of convicts to recent research in human genetics, offers little insight into the causes of crime.

3. Psychological study links deviance to abnormal personality stemming from either biological or environmental causes. Psychological theories help to explain some kinds of deviance.

4. Deviance has societal rather than individual roots because it is related to (1) cultural norms, (2) situational processes of social definition, and (3) patterns of social power.

5. Using the structural-functional paradigm, Durkheim asserted that responding to deviance affirms values and norms, clarifies moral boundaries, promotes social unity, and encourages social change.

6. The symbolic-interaction paradigm is the basis of labelling theory, which holds that deviance arises in the reaction of others to a person's behaviour. Acquiring a stigma of deviance can lead to secondary deviance and the onset of a deviant career.

7. Following the approach of Karl Marx, social-conflict theory holds that laws and other norms reflect the interests of powerful members of soci-

ety. Social-conflict theory also spotlights white-collar crimes, which cause extensive social harm even though the offenders are rarely branded as criminals.

8. Official statistics indicate that arrest rates peak in late adolescence, then drop steadily with advancing age. Three-fourths of those arrested for property crimes are males, as are almost nine of ten people charged with violent crimes.

9. People of lower social position commit more street crime than those with greater social privilege. When white-collar crimes are counted among criminal offences, however, this disparity in overall criminal activity diminishes.

10. More whites than Blacks are arrested for street crimes. However, Blacks are arrested more often than whites in proportion to their respective populations. Asian Canadians have lower-than-average rates of arrest.

11. The police exercise considerable discretion in their work. Research suggests that factors such as the seriousness of the offence, the presence of bystanders, and the accused being Black or aboriginal make arrest more likely.

12. Although ideally an adversarial system, Canadian courts resolve many cases through plea bargaining. While efficient, this method nevertheless places less powerful people at a disadvantage.

13. Justifications for punishment include retribution, deterrence, rehabilitation, and societal protection. Because its consequences are difficult to evaluate scientifically, punishment—like deviance itself—sparks controversy among sociologists and the public as a whole.

CRITICAL THINKING QUESTIONS

1. How does a sociological view of deviance differ from the common-sense notion that bad people do bad things?

2. Identify Durkheim's functions of deviance. From his point of view, could people create a society free from deviance? Why or why not?

3. How does social power affect deviant labelling? How do gender, race, and class figure in this process?

4. Why do you think crime rates have risen in Canada over the last fifty years? Do you agree or disagree with Travis Hirschi's prescription for crime control presented in the "Controversy & Debate" box? Why?

SOCIOLOGY APPLIED

1. Research the idea of computer crime. What new kinds of information are emerging in the Information Age? Is computer technology also generating new ways of tracking lawbreakers?

2. Watch an episode of the real-action police show *Cops*. From the perspective of the show, what kinds of people commit crimes?

3. Ask the security office for data about crime on your campus. How well does their view of campus crime square with your own?

WEBLINKS

www.acjnet.org/
Access to Justice Network is a bilingual site for Canadian justice and legal information and services. These resources are organized under headings such as aboriginal people, crime prevention, plain language, women, and youth.

www.crime-prevention.org/ncpc/
The National Crime Prevention Council is an independent, voluntary council whose mission is to develop strategies to empower individuals and their communities to improve their safety, security, and well-being. The site includes event listings, press releases, a publications archive, and links to crime prevention databases.

www.arf.org/
The *Addiction Research Foundation* is one of North America's pre-eminent facilities for research into alcohol, tobacco and other drug problems. The Foundation's mission is to help prevent and reduce the harm associated with alcohol, tobacco and other drugs in Ontario communities. The site includes journal articles, statistics, FAQs, and information about ARF, its library holdings, and training courses.

eserver.org/feminism/
This site publishes women's studies and feminist works, particularly focusing on issues of sex, gender, sexual identity and sexuality in cultural practices.

www.yorku.ca/faculty/osgoode/owp/racism/top.htm
The full text of the *Final Report of the Commission on Systemic Racism in the Ontario Criminal Justice System*, published in December 1995, is presented here by the Osgoode Web Press.

cyber.scope

PART II
HOW TECHNOLOGY IS CHANGING OUR WAY OF LIFE

Marshall McLuhan (1969) summed up his pioneering research in the study of communications this way: "Any new technology tends to create a new human environment." In other words, technology affects not just how we work, but it shapes and colours our entire way of life. In this second cyber.scope, we pause to reflect on some of the ways the Information Revolution is changing our culture and society.

The Information Revolution and Cultural Values

Chapter 3 ("Culture") noted the importance members of our society attach to material comfort. Throughout our history, many people have defined "success" to mean earning a good income and enjoying the things money will buy, including a home, car, and clothing.

But some analysts wonder if, as we enter the next century, our values may shift from a single-minded focus on the accumulation of "things" (the products of industrial technology) to gaining new kinds of "ideas" (the product of information technology). Such "new age" ideas range from "experiences" (including travel and countless experiences with virtual reality[1]) to "well-

---

[1] For example, take the virtual Director's Tour of works in the Art Gallery of Ontario (http://www.ago.on.ca/), or visit Canada's capital city via Virtual Ottawa (http://www.intoronto.com/inottawa.html).

being," including the "self-actualization" that has become popular in recent decades (Newman, 1991).

Socialization in the Computer Age

Half a century ago, television rewrote the rule for socialization in Canada and, as Chapter 5 ("Socialization") explained, young people now spend more time watching TV than they do talking to their parents. Today, in the emerging Information Society, screens are not just for television, they are our windows into a cyber-world in which we look to computers to link, entertain, and educate us. But this trend towards "cyber-socialization" raises several important questions.

First, will the spread of computer-based information erode the regional diversity that has marked this country's history, setting off the west coast from Ontario and the prairies from Quebec? New information technology links Canada to the rest of the world. As a result we could see an enhanced Canadian culture as well as a more global culture. Marshall McLuhan predicts a weakening of national identities in response to new information technology.

Second, how will this "cyber-culture" affect our children? Will having computers at the centre of their lives be good for them? For most children, at least, computer-based images and information already play a significant role in the socialization process. Will this trend lessen the importance of parents in children's lives, as television did? Cyber-socialization can cer-

Almost unlimited access to information can be a mixed blessing, as parents can well understand. How can we prevent children from gaining access to pornography or other objectionable material on the Internet? Or, should we?

tainly entertain and instruct, but can it meet the emotional needs of children? Will it contribute to their moral development?

Third, who will control cyber-socialization? Just as parents have long expressed concerns about what their children watch on television, they now worry about what kids encounter as they "surf the Web." To date, the federal courts have taken the position that the Internet should operate with minimal government interference. Do we—as citizens and as parents—have expectations for the content of "virtual culture"? Should the information industry operate for profit? With standards to ensure some measure of educational content? Who should decide?

The Cyber-Self

A person using the name "Veg-Diet" enters one of thousands of chat rooms found on the Internet, the vast global network described in Chapter 7 ("Groups and Organizations"). Within a few seconds, VegDiet is actively debating the state of the world with three other people: "MrMaine," "Ferret," and "RedWine."

The growing popularity of computer chat gives us a chance to highlight ways in which online interaction differs from more conventional modes of interaction. After studying online interaction, Dennis Waskul (1997) explains that the self transmitted via computer is "disembodied." Using Erving Goffman's dramaturgical approach (see Chapter 6), Waskul notes that computer technology screens out a host of "cues" about people's identities—where they are, what they look like, how they dress, and their age and sex—and conveys only the stylized identities they choose to present.

Cyberspace thus affords us great freedom to "try on" identities with few, if any, lasting consequences. As one chat-room participant ex-

plained, "On-line is a game . . . Only here, I play with who I am" (1997:21).

But Wait a Minute . . . The Neo-Luddites

In the early nineteenth century, groups of English weavers who opposed the Industrial Revolution, travelled about demolishing new machinery whenever they could gain access to a factory. The Luddites (named after Ned Ludd, their leader) were convinced that the new technology of their day would eliminate jobs and, more generally, make life worse (Zachary, 1997).

Although the Luddites lost their battle to stem the tide of change, their spirit lives on in people opposed to the Information Revolution today. These neo-Luddites, as they are called, speak with many voices. But they agree that we should not race headlong into a cyber-future without pausing to think critically about how new technology is likely to affect us.

The neo-Luddites remind us, first, that technology is never socially neutral. That is, technology

does not simply exist *in* the world, it *changes* the world, pushing human lives in one direction while closing off other alternatives. As a people, we tend to venerate technology as good in and of itself, Theodore Roszak (1986) points out, but, in the process, we give up the power to decide for ourselves how we should live. Putting computers in the classroom is no substitute for good teaching, Roszak declares; we would do well to remember that no computer ever created a painting, penned a poem, or composed a symphony. And, perhaps most important of all, computers have no capacity to address ethical questions about right and wrong.

Living in a forward-looking culture, we easily imagine the benefits of new technology. But we need to remember that, just as technology can serve us, it also holds the potential to be destructive. After all, the Luddites were not anti-technology; they simply wanted to be sure that technology responded to human needs—and not the other way around. ▣

"On the Internet, nobody knows you're a dog."

Antonio Ruiz, *Verano,* 1937
Oil on wood, 29 × 35 cm. Collection of Acervo Patrimonial, SHCP, Mexico.

CHAPTER 9

SOCIAL STRATIFICATION

On April 10, 1912, the ocean liner *Titanic* slipped away from the docks of Southampton, England, on its first voyage, across the North Atlantic to New York. A proud symbol of the new Industrial Age, the towering ship carried 2300 passengers, some enjoying more luxury than most travellers today could imagine. By contrast, poor immigrants crowded the lower decks, journeying to what they hoped would be a better life in the United States and Canada.

Two days out, the crew received radio warnings of icebergs in the area but paid little notice. Then, near midnight, as the ship steamed swiftly and silently westward, a lookout was stunned to see a massive shape rising out of the dark ocean directly ahead. Moments later, the *Titanic* collided with a huge iceberg, almost as tall as the ship itself, which split open its starboard side as if the grand vessel were nothing more than a giant tin can.

Seawater surged into the ship's lower levels, and within twenty-five minutes people were rushing for the lifeboats. By 2:00 in the morning the bow of the *Titanic* was submerged and the stern reared high above the water. Clinging to the deck, quietly observed by those in the lifeboats, hundreds of helpless passengers solemnly passed their final minutes before the ship disappeared into the frigid Atlantic (Lord, 1976).

The tragic loss of more than 1600 lives made news around the world. Looking back dispassionately at this terrible accident with a sociological eye, however, we see that some categories of passengers had much better odds of survival than others. In an age of conventional gallantry, women and children boarded the boats first, so that 80 percent of the casualties were men. Class, too, was at work. Of people holding first-class tickets, more than 60 percent were saved, primarily because they were on the upper decks, where warnings were sounded first and lifeboats were accessible. Only 36 percent of the second-class passengers survived, and of the third-class passengers on the lower decks, only 24 percent escaped drowning. (Linda Gerber's great aunt, Maria Panula, travelling from a small town in Finland to join her husband, was among the third-class passengers who perished, along with at least two of her children.) On board the *Titanic*, class turned out to mean much more than the quality of accommodations: it was truly a matter of life or death.

The fate of the *Titanic* dramatically illustrates the consequences of social inequality for the ways people live—and sometimes whether they live at all. This chapter explores the important concept of social

The personal experience of poverty is captured in Sebastiao Salgado's haunting photograph, which stands as a universal portrait of human suffering. The essential sociological insight is that, however strongly individuals feel its effects, our social standing is largely a consequence of the way in which a society (or a world of societies) structures opportunity and reward. To the core of our being, then, we are all the products of social stratification.

stratification. Chapter 10 ("Social Class in Canada") continues the story by highlighting social inequality in Canada, and Chapter 11 ("Global Stratification") examines how our country fits into a global system of wealth and poverty.

WHAT IS SOCIAL STRATIFICATION?

For tens of thousands of years, humans the world over lived in small hunting and gathering societies. Although members of these bands might single out one person as being swifter, stronger, or more skilled in collecting food, everyone had more or less the same social standing. As societies became more complex—a process detailed in Chapter 4 ("Society")—a monumental change came about. The social system elevated entire categories of people above others, providing one segment of the population with more money, power, and schooling than others.

Sociologists use the concept **social stratification** to refer to *a system by which a society ranks categories of people in a hierarchy*. Social stratification is a matter of four basic principles.

1. **Social stratification is a characteristic of society, not simply a reflection of individual differences.** Members of industrial societies consider social standing as a reflection of personal talent and effort, although we typically exaggerate the extent to which people control their destinies. Did a higher percentage of the first-class passengers survive the sinking of the *Titanic* because they were smarter or better swimmers than the second- and third-class passengers? Hardly. They fared better because of their privileged position on the ship. Similarly, children born into wealthy families are more likely than those born into poverty to enjoy health, achieve academically, succeed in their life's work, and live well into old age. Neither rich nor poor people are responsible for creating social stratification, yet this system shapes the lives of them all.

2. **Social stratification persists over generations.** To understand that stratification stems from society rather than from individual differences, note how inequality persists over time. In all societies, parents pass their social positions along to their children, so that patterns of inequality stay much the same from generation to generation.

   Especially in industrial societies, however, some individuals do experience **social mobility**, *change in a person's position in a social hierarchy*. Social mobility may be upward or downward. Our society celebrates the achievements of a Jean Chrétien, a Rita MacNeil, or a Wayne Gretzky, all of whom rose to prominence from modest beginnings. But we also acknowledge that people move downward as a result of business setbacks, unemployment, or illness. More often, people move *horizontally* when they exchange one occupation for another that is comparable. For most people, however, social standing remains much the same over a lifetime.

3. **Social stratification is universal but variable.** Social stratification is found everywhere. At the same time, whatever the basis of or extent of inequality, it varies from one society to another. Among the members of technologically simple societies, social differentiation is minimal and based mostly on age and sex. With the development of sophisticated technology for growing food, societies also forge complex and more rigid systems for distributing what people produce. As we shall see, industrialization has the effect of increasing social mobility and reducing at least some kinds of social inequality. On the other hand, there is evidence that, for the short term at least, the development of new information technology has had the opposite effect, increasing social inequality.

4. **Social stratification involves not just inequality but beliefs.** Any system of inequality not only gives some people more resources than others but defines certain arrangements as fair. Just as *what* is unequal differs from society to society, so too does the explanation of *why* people should

be unequal. Furthermore, virtually everywhere, people with the greatest social privileges express the strongest support for their society's system of social stratification, while those with fewer social resources are more likely to seek change.

CASTE AND CLASS SYSTEMS

In describing social stratification in particular societies, sociologists often use two opposing standards: "closed" systems that allow little change in social position and "open" systems that permit considerable social mobility (Tumin, 1985).

THE CASTE SYSTEM

A **caste system** amounts to *social stratification based on ascription* (a social status received at birth, described in Chapter 6). A pure caste system, in other words, is "closed" so that birth alone determines one's social destiny with no opportunity for social mobility based on individual efforts. In caste systems, then, categories of people are ranked in a rigid hierarchy and everyone is born, lives, and dies at the same social level.

Two Illustrations: India and South Africa

A number of the world's societies—most of them agrarian—approximate caste systems. One example is India, or at least India's traditional villages in which most people still live. The Indian system of castes (or *varna*, a Sanskrit word that means "colour") is composed of four major categories: Brahmin, Kshatriya, Vaishya, and Shudra. On the local level, however, each is composed of hundreds of subcaste (or *jati*) groups.

Caste has also played a key role in the history of South Africa. In this nation's former policy of *apartheid*, the five million South Africans of European ancestry enjoy a commanding share of wealth and power, dominating some thirty million Black South Africans. In a middle position are another three million mixed-race people, known as "coloureds," and about one million Asians. (See the "Global Sociology" box for a discussion of South Africa's caste system.)

In a caste system, birth determines the fundamental shape of people's lives in four crucial respects. First, traditional caste groups are linked to occupation, so that generations of a family perform the same type of work. In rural India, although some occupations (such as farming) are open to all, castes are identified with the work their members do (as priests, barbers, leather workers, street sweepers, and so on). In South Africa, whites still hold almost all the desirable jobs, while most Blacks are consigned to manual labour and other low-level service work.

A desire to better one's social position fuels immigration the world over, creating a flow of humanity from poorer countries to richer ones. The mix of fear and hope in the hearts of people seeking a better life is captured in the painting Los Emigrantes *by Argentine artist Antonio Berni.*

No rigid social hierarchy could persist if people married outside their own categories; if they did, what rank would their children hold? To shore up the hierarchy, then, a second trait of caste systems is mandating that people marry others of the same rank. Sociologists call this pattern *endogamous* marriage (*endo* stems from Greek, meaning "within"). Traditionally, Indian parents select their children's marriage partners, often before the children reach their teens. Until 1985, South Africa banned marriage and even sex between the races; even now, interracial couples are rare, since Blacks and whites continue to live in separate areas.

As well, caste guides everyday life so that people remain in the company of "their own kind." Hindus in India enforce this segregation with the belief that a rit-

Race as Caste: A Report from South Africa

At the southern tip of the African continent lies South Africa, a territory about the size of Ontario or Quebec with a 1997 population of some forty-six million. The indigenous African people were joined by Dutch traders and farmers who settled the region in the mid-seventeenth century. Early in the nineteenth century, a second wave of colonists—this time British—pushed the descendants of the Dutch settlers inland. By the beginning of the twentieth century, the British had gained control of the entire country, naming it the Union of South Africa.

In 1961, formal ties with the United Kingdom ended, making the Republic of South Africa a politically independent nation. But freedom was a reality only for the white minority who dominated the society by imposing the policy of apartheid, or racial separation. A common practice for many years, apartheid was enshrined in a 1948 law denying the Black

South African majority citizenship, ownership of land, and any formal voice in the government.

Apartheid rendered Blacks a subordinate caste, and offered them only the education needed to perform low-paying jobs deemed inappropriate for

Although imprisoned for twenty-seven years for opposing apartheid, Nelson Mandela went on to become president of South Africa and has taken major steps to reduce racial inequality.

whites. So separate were the races that white people earned four times the income of Black people and even whites of limited means became accustomed to having a Black household servant. A final plank in the platform of apartheid was the forcible resettlement of millions of Blacks to so-called homelands, poor districts that resembled the desolate reserves that are home to many natives in Canada.

The prosperous white minority defended apartheid, claiming that Blacks threatened their cultural traditions or, more fundamentally, were inferior beings. But resistance to apartheid rose steadily, prompting the government to resort to brutal military repression to maintain power. Under racially based law, the police could arrest and detain any Black person for any violation of or opposition to apartheid, and numerous instances of torture and murder have been documented.

Despite severe repression, violent confrontations became an al-

ually "pure" person of a higher caste will be "polluted" by contact with someone of lower standing. Apartheid in South Africa achieved much the same effect.

Finally, caste systems rest on powerful cultural beliefs. Indian culture is built on Hindu traditions that mandate accepting one's life work, whatever it may be, as a moral duty. And, although apartheid is no longer a matter of law, South Africans still cling to notions distinguishing "white jobs" from "Black jobs."

Caste and Agrarian Life

Caste systems are typical of agrarian societies, because the lifelong routines of agriculture depend on a rigid sense of duty and discipline. Thus, caste still persists in rural India half a century after being formally outlawed, though its grip is easing in the nation's more industrial cities, where most people exercise greater choice about their work and marriage partners (Bahl,

1991). Similarly, the rapid industrialization of South Africa elevated the importance of personal choice and individual rights, making the abolition of apartheid only a matter of time. In Canada, although elements of caste survive, treating people categorically on the basis of their race or ethnicity is now widely denounced as unjust, inviting charges of racism.

Note, however, that the erosion of caste with all of its rigidities does not signal the end of social stratification. On the contrary, it simply marks a change in its character, as the next sections explain.

THE CLASS SYSTEM

Agrarian life relies on the discipline wrought by caste systems; industrial societies, by contrast, depend on developing specialized talents. Industrialization thus erodes caste in favour of a **class system**, *social stratification based on individual achievement.*

most everyday occurrence, sparked primarily by younger Blacks impatient for a political voice and economic opportunity. Support for change also swelled outside the country as, during the 1980s, Canada and other countries severed direct economic ties with South Africa. This foreign divestiture staggered the South African economy and effectively pressured the government to make significant reforms.

In 1984, the government granted all South Africans the right to form labour unions, to enter various occupations once restricted to whites, and to own property. Soon afterward, officials abolished a host of "petty apartheid" regulations that segregated the races in public places, including beaches and hospitals.

In 1990, the legalization of the anti-apartheid African National Congress (ANC) and the release from prison of its leader Nelson Mandela raised the hope for more basic change. In 1992, a majority of white voters endorsed, in principle, an end to apartheid. Two years later, all South African adults—regardless of race—voted in a national election that swept Nelson Mandela

into office as South Africa's new president. In 1996, South Africa adopted a new constitution renouncing the racism of the past and declaring itself a "non-racial democracy" that grants equal rights to all regardless of colour.

In practice, however, these developments have actually brought about only minimal changes in social stratification. The five million white people—11 percent of the population—still earn half of all income. The legal right to own property means little to millions of Black people who are dirt poor; opening hospitals to people of every race is an empty gesture for those who cannot afford to pay for medical care; ending racial barriers to the professions offers scant real opportunity to men and women without much schooling. The harsh reality is that more than one-third of all Black adults cannot find any work at all, and half of all Black people live in desperate conditions.

The worst off are those called *ukuh-leleleka* in the Xhosa language, which means the marginal people. Some seven million Black South Africans fall into this category, living on the edge of society and on the edge of life itself. In

Soweto-by-the-Sea, an idyllic-sounding community, thousands of people live crammed into shacks built of packing crates, corrugated metal, cardboard, and other discarded materials. There is no electricity for lights or refrigeration. Without plumbing, people haul sewage in buckets, and a single tap provides water for more than one thousand people. Jobs are hard to come by, partly because Ford and General Motors closed their factories in nearby Port Elizabeth and partly because people keep migrating to the town from regions where life is even worse. Those who can find work are lucky to earn $200 a month.

South Africa has ended white minority rule and, most analysts agree, there is no turning back. Yet undoing centuries of racial caste cannot be accomplished by simple legal mandate. Even when deeply rooted notions about racial inequality are finally overcome, this still-divided society will face the daunting challenge of resolving the underlying problem of intense and persistent poverty among most of its people.

SOURCES: Fredrickson (1981), Wren (1991), and various news reports.

A class system is more "open," so that people who gain schooling and skills may experience some social mobility in relation to their parents and siblings. Mobility, in turn, blurs class distinctions. Social boundaries also break down as people immigrate from abroad or move from the country to the city, lured by greater opportunity for education and the promise of a brighter future (Lipset and Bendix, 1967; Cutright, 1968; Treiman, 1970). Typically, newcomers take low-paying jobs, thereby pushing others up the social ladder (Clark, 1978; Tyree, Semyonov, and Hodge, 1979).

People in industrial societies come to think that everyone—not just someone of high social standing—is entitled to "rights." The principle of equal standing before the law gradually assumes a central place in the political culture of industrial class systems.

Class systems are no different from caste systems in one basic respect: people remain unequal. But social stratification now rests on personal talent and effort

rather than the accident of birth. Careers become not a matter of moral duty but an issue of individual choice; likewise, class systems allow more individual freedom in the selection of marriage partners.

Status Consistency

Status consistency refers to *the degree of consistency of a person's social standing across various dimensions of social inequality*. In a caste system, limited social mobility generates high status consistency so that the typical person has the same relative ranking with regard to wealth, power, and prestige. By contrast, the greater mobility of class systems allows for less status consistency. In industrial nations such as Canada, a university professor (with his or her Ph.D.) might enjoy high social prestige while receiving a comparatively modest income. Such status inconsistency contributes to the fact that *classes* are less well defined than *castes*.

CASTE AND CLASS TOGETHER: THE UNITED KINGDOM

There are no pure caste or class systems; social stratification everywhere involves some combination of these two forms. This mix is particularly striking in the United Kingdom, an industrial nation with a long agrarian history.

The Estate System

In the Middle Ages, social stratification in England (which, together with Wales, Scotland, and Northern Ireland constitutes today's United Kingdom of Great Britain and Northern Ireland) took the form of a caste-like system of three groups or "estates." A hereditary nobility, or first estate, was composed of 150 families or barely 5 percent of the population (Laslett, 1984). These nobles exercised power and controlled wealth in the form of land. Typically, nobles had no formal occupation at all; to be "engaged in trade" or any other type of work for income was deemed "beneath" the aristocracy. Well tended by servants, many nobles used their leisure time to cultivate refined tastes in art, music, and literature.

The estate system depended on protecting vast landholdings from division by heirs. This was accomplished through the law of *primogeniture* (from Latin meaning "first born"), which mandated that a man's entire property be inherited by his eldest son or other nearest male relation. This process maintained a landed aristocracy, but primogeniture forced younger sons to seek out other sources of support. One possibility for such men was to enter the clergy—often dubbed the "second estate"—where spiritual power was supplemented by the church's extensive landholdings. Other young men of high birth became military officers, lawyers, or took up other "honourable" professions set aside for "gentlemen."

And what of women? In an age when no woman could inherit her father's property and few women had the opportunity to earn a living on their own, the daughter of a noble family depended for her security on marrying well.

Below the nobility and the clergy, the vast majority of men and women formed the third estate, or "commoners." With little property, most commoners were serfs working plots of land belonging to nobles. The phrase "one's lot in life" literally describes the daily focus of commoners during the Middle Ages. Unlike the nobility and the clergy, most commoners had little access to schooling and remained illiterate.

As the Industrial Revolution steadily enlarged England's economy, some commoners living in cities gained enough wealth to rival the power of the nobility. The increasing importance of money, along with the extension of schooling and legal rights to more and more people, blurred social rankings and gave rise to a class system. In a pointed illustration of how far the pendulum has swung, a descendant of nobility, now working for a living as a writer, was asked in an interview if Britain's caste-like estates had finally broken down. Playfully she retorted, "Of course they have, or I wouldn't be here talking to someone like you!" (*New Haven Journal-Courier*, November 27, 1986).

The United Kingdom Today

Social stratification in the United Kingdom today is more of a class system, but one that retains the mark of a long, feudal past. At the top of the hierarchy, a small cluster of British families continues to enjoy inherited wealth, attends expensive schools, and wields political influence. Queen Elizabeth II, who traces her ancestry back through a millennium of aristocracy, reigns as the United Kingdom's (and Canada's) head of state, while Parliament's House of Lords is composed of other "peers," most of noble birth. A sign of the times, however, is the fact that actual control of government resides in the House of Commons, where the prime minister and other commoners are more likely to have gained their position through achievement than by ascription. Looking beyond the government, most of the leading people in all sectors of British society today are individuals of extraordinary achievement rather than noble birth.

Moving down the hierarchy, roughly one-quarter of the population forms the British middle class. Some families are moderately wealthy, with high incomes from professions and business. These richer "commoners," along with the upper class, make up the 10 to 15 percent of Britons with significant financial holdings in the form of stocks and bonds. Most middle-class Britons, however, earn too little to accumulate substantial wealth.

Below the middle class, approximately half of all Britons think of themselves as "working class." As in Canada, members of the working class earn modest incomes, generally by performing manual labour. The decline of British industries such as coal mining and steel production has subjected many working-class families to chronic unemployment. Some have slipped into poverty, joining the remaining one-quarter of Britons who are socially and economically deprived. Lower-class people—or, more simply, the poor—are heavily concentrated in the northern and western regions of the United Kingdom, which are plagued by economic decline.

Today's class system affords the British people some opportunity to move upward or downward. One legacy of the estate system, however, is that social mobility occurs less often in the United Kingdom than in Canada or the United States. Compared with members of our society, therefore, Britons are relatively more resigned to remaining in the social position to which they were born (Snowman, 1977; Kerckhoff, Campbell, and Winfield-Laird, 1985).

The greater rigidity of British stratification is exemplified in the importance of accent as a mark of social position. Distinctive patterns of speech develop in any society as people are segregated from one another over time. While people in North America treat accent as a matter of geography (there is little mistaking the Newfoundland lilt or the southern drawl), a British accent identifies one as a person of high birth (speaking the "Queen's English") or someone of common ancestry. So different are these two accents that the British seem to be, as the saying goes, a single people divided by a common language.

ANOTHER EXAMPLE: JAPAN

Social stratification in Japan also mixes the traditional and the contemporary. Japan is at once the world's oldest continuously operating monarchy and a modern society in which wealth follows individual achievement.

Feudal Japan

As early as the fifth century B.C.E., Japan was an agrarian society with a rigid caste system composed of nobles and commoners and ruled by an "imperial family." Despite the widespread belief that the emperor ruled by divine right, limited government organization forced the emperor to delegate much authority to a network of regional nobles or *shoguns*.

Below the nobility stood the *samurai*, or warrior caste. The word *samurai* means "to serve," indicating that this second rank of Japanese society comprised soldiers who cultivated elaborate martial skills and pledged their loyalty to the nobility. To set themselves off from the rest of the commoners, the *samurai* dressed and behaved according to a traditional code of honour.

As in Great Britain, the majority of people in Japan at this time in history were commoners who laboured to eke out a bare subsistence. Unlike their European counterparts, however, Japanese commoners were not the lowest in rank. The *burakumin*, or "outcasts," stood further down on that country's hierarchy, shunned by lord and commoner alike. Much like the lowest caste groups in India, "outcasts" lived apart from others, engaged in the most distasteful occupations, and, like everyone else, had no opportunity to change their standing.

The Japanese ritual of bowing is more than just a greeting. It affirms people's ranking since the person with the higher social standing bends only slightly while the person of lower position bows more deeply.

Japan Today

Important changes in nineteenth-century Japan—industrialization, the growth of cities, and the opening of Japanese society to outside influences—combined to weaken the traditional caste structure. In 1871, the Japanese legally banned the social category of "outcast," although even today people look down on women and men who trace their lineage to this rank. After Japan's defeat in World War II, the nobility, too, lost legal standing, and, as the years have passed, fewer and fewer Japanese accept the notion that their emperor rules by divine right.

Thus, social stratification in contemporary Japan is a far cry from the rigid caste system in force centuries ago. Analysts describe the modern-day Japanese population in terms of social gradations, including "upper," "upper-middle," "lower-middle," and "lower." But since classes have no firm boundaries, they disagree about what proportion of the population falls in each category.

Today's Japanese class system also reveals this nation's fascinating ability to weave together tradition and modernity. Because many Japanese people revere the past, family background is never far from the surface in assessing someone's social standing. Therefore, despite legal reforms that assure everyone equal standing before the law and a modern culture that stresses individual achievement, the Japanese continue to perceive each other through the centuries-old lens of caste.

In recent years, the former Soviet Union has moved towards a market economy. These economic reforms have made some people quite wealthy, while others have been reduced to selling household goods in order to buy food.

This dynamic mix echoes from the university campus to the corporate boardrooms. The most prestigious universities—now gateways to success in the industrial world—admit students with outstanding scores on rigorous entrance examinations. Even so, the highest achievers and business leaders in Japan are products of privilege, with noble or *samurai* background. At the other extreme, "outcasts" continue to live in isolated communities cut off from opportunities to better themselves (Hiroshi, 1974; Norbeck, 1983).

Finally, traditional ideas about gender still shape Japanese society. Despite legal reforms that confer formal equality on the sexes, women are clearly subordinate to men in most important respects. Japanese parents are more likely to push sons than daughters towards university, and the nation thus retains a significant "gender gap" in education (Brinton, 1988). As a consequence, women predominate in lower-level support positions in the corporate world, only rarely assuming leadership roles. In this sense, too, individual achievement in Japan's modern class system operates in the shadow of centuries of traditional privileges.

THE FORMER SOVIET UNION

The former Union of Soviet Socialist Republics (USSR), which rivalled the United States as a military superpower through most of the twentieth century, was born out of revolution in 1917. The feudal estate system ruled by a hereditary nobility came to an abrupt end as the Russian Revolution transferred most farms, factories, and other productive property from private ownership to state control.

A Classless Society?

This transformation was guided by the ideas of Karl Marx, who asserted that private ownership of productive property was the basis of social classes (see Chapter 4, "Society"). As the state gained control of the economy, Soviet officials boasted that they had engineered a remarkable achievement: humanity's first classless society.

Analysts outside the Soviet Union were always skeptical about this claim of classlessness (Lane, 1984). The occupations of the people in the former Soviet Union, they pointed out, clustered into a four-level hierarchy. At the top were high government officials, or *apparatchiks*. Next came the Soviet intelligentsia, including lower government officials, university professors, scientists, physicians, and engineers. Below them stood the manual workers and, in the lowest stratum, the rural peasantry.

Since people in each of these categories enjoyed very different living standards—and levels of power—the former Soviet Union was never classless in the sense of having no social inequality. Nonetheless, placing factories, farms, universities, and hospitals under state control did rein in economic inequality to levels below those in capitalist societies such as the United States or Great Britain.

The Second Russian Revolution

November 24, 1994, Odessa, Ukraine. The first snow of our voyage flies about the decks as our ship puts in at Odessa, the former Soviet Union's southernmost port on the Black Sea. A short distance from the dock, we gaze up the Potemkin Steps—the steep stairway leading to the city proper where the first shots of the Russian Revolution rang out. It has been six years since our last visit and much has changed; indeed, the Soviet Union itself has collapsed. Has life improved? Obviously, for some people: there are now chic boutiques in which well-dressed shoppers spend cash for fine wines, designer labels, and imported perfumes. Outside, shiny new Volvos, Mercedes, and even a few Cadillacs stand out against the small Ladas from the "old days." But for most, life seems unmistakably worse. Flea markets line the curbs as families hawk home furnishings. Many are desperate in a town where meat sells for $4 a pound and the average person earns about $30 a month. Odessa has no lights after about eight o'clock in the evening—the city's strategy to save electricity. The spirits of most people seem as dim as the city streets.

After steady efforts to restructure Soviet society following the ideas of Karl Marx (and revolutionary Russian leader Vladimir Lenin, the Soviet Union underwent another sweeping transformation in the 1980s. Economic reforms accelerated when Mikhail Gorbachev came on the scene in 1985. His economic program, popularly known as *perestroika*, meaning "restructuring," sought to solve a dire problem. While the Soviet system had succeeded in minimizing economic inequality, everyone was relatively poor, and living standards lagged far behind those of other industrial nations. Simply put, Gorbachev hoped to stimulate economic expansion by reducing inefficient centralized control of the economy.

Gorbachev's reforms soon escalated into one of the most dramatic social movements in history as popular uprisings toppled one socialist government after another throughout Eastern Europe and, ultimately, brought down the Soviet system itself. In essence, people blamed their economic plight as well as their lack of basic freedoms on a repressive ruling class of Communist party officials.

From the founding of the Soviet Union in 1917 until its demise in 1991, the Communist party retained a monopoly of power, often brutally repressing any opposition. Near the end, eighteen million party members (6 percent of the Soviet people) still made all the decisions about Soviet life while enjoying privileges such as vacation homes, chauffeured automobiles, and access to prized consumer goods and elite education for their children (Zaslavsky, 1982; Shipler, 1984; Theen, 1984). The second Soviet revolution, then, mirrors the first in that it was nothing less than the overthrow of the ruling class.

The rise and fall of the Soviet Union demonstrate that social inequality involves more than economic resources. But elite standing in the former Soviet Union was based on power rather than wealth. Thus, even though both Mikhail Gorbachev and his successor Boris Yeltsin earned far less than Western prime ministers or presidents, they wielded awesome power.

And what about social mobility in the Soviet Union? Evidence indicates that during this century there was more upward social mobility in the Soviet Union than in Great Britain, Japan, or Canada. Why? For one thing, Soviet society lacked the concentrated wealth that families elsewhere pass from one generation to the next. Even more importantly, industrialization and rapid bureaucratization during this century pushed a large proportion of the working class and rural peasantry upward to occupations in industry and government.

In the last decade, however, the people of the Russian federation have experienced downward social mobility. A staggering fact is that, between 1990 and 1997, the average life span for Soviet men tumbled by eight years (two years in the case of women). Many factors are involved—including Russia's poor system of health care—but clearly the Russian people are suffering from a turbulent period of economic change (Róna-Tas, 1994; Specter, 1997). Sociologists describe such upward and downward trends as **structural social mobility**, *a shift in the social position of large numbers of people due more to changes in society itself than to individual efforts.* As we shall see in Chapter 10 ("Social Class in Canada"), much of the mobility of our society, too, follows from broad economic changes that have taken place over the course of the twentieth century.

IDEOLOGY: THE "STAYING POWER" OF STRATIFICATION

Looking around the world at the extent of social inequality, we might wonder how societies persist without distributing their resources more equally. Caste-like systems in Great Britain and Japan lasted for centuries, concentrating land and power in the hands of several hundred families. Even more strikingly, for

Medieval Europeans accepted rigid social differences as part of a divine plan for the world. This fifteenth-century painting by the Limbourg brothers shows a noble—the Duke of Berry—setting off on a hunt along with a group of his peers, while, in the background, serfs farm the land outside his castle.

two thousand years most people in India accepted the idea that they should be privileged or poor because of the accident of birth.

One key reason for the remarkable persistence of social hierarchies is that they are built on **ideology**, *cultural beliefs that serve to justify social stratification.* Any beliefs—for example, the claim that the rich are smart while the poor are lazy—are ideological to the extent that they bolster the dominance of wealthy elites and suggest that poor people deserve their plight.

Plato and Marx on Ideology

The ancient Greek philosopher Plato (427–347 B.C.E.) defined justice as agreement about who should have what. Every society, Plato explained, teaches its members to view some stratification system as "fair." Karl Marx, too, understood this process, although he was far more critical of inequality than Plato was. Marx took capitalist societies to task for channelling wealth and power into the hands of a few, all the while defining the practice as simply "a law of the marketplace." Capitalist law, Marx continued, defines the right to own property as a bedrock principle. Then, laws of inheritance, which are tied to kinship, funnel money and privileges from one generation to the next. In short, Marx concluded, ideas as well as resources are controlled by a society's elite, which helps to explain why established hierarchies are so difficult to change.

Both Plato and Marx recognized that ideology is rarely a simple matter of privileged people conspiring to propound self-serving ideas about social inequality. By contrast, ideology usually takes the form of cultural patterns that evolve over a long period of time. As people learn to embrace their society's conception of fairness, they may question the rightness of their own position but are unlikely to challenge the system itself.

Historical Patterns of Ideology

The ideas that shore up social stratification change along with a society's economy and technology. Early agrarian societies depended on slaves to perform burdensome manual labour. Aristotle (384–322 B.C.E.) defended the practice of slavery among the ancient Greeks, noting, for example, that some people with little intelligence deserve nothing better than life under the direction of their natural "betters."

Agrarian societies in Europe during the Middle Ages also required the daily farm labour of most people to support the small aristocracy. In this context, noble and serf learned to view occupation as rightfully determined by birth and any person's work as a matter of moral responsibility. In short, caste systems always rest on the assertion that social ranking is the product of a "natural" order.

The rise of industrial capitalism transformed wealth and power into prizes won by those who display the greatest talent and effort. Class systems celebrate individualism and achievement, so that social standing serves as a measure of personal worthiness. Thus poverty, which called for charity under feudalism, was transformed under industrial capitalism into a scorned state of personal inadequacy. Nowhere was this harsh view more clearly stated than by Herbert

Is Getting Rich "the Survival of the Fittest"?

"The survival of the fittest." We have all heard this phrase, another way of saying "the law of the jungle." Actually, the words were coined by one of sociology's pioneers, Herbert Spencer (1820–1903), who gave voice to a view of social stratification that is still widespread today.

Spencer, who lived in England, was fascinated by the work of the natural scientist Charles Darwin (1809–1882). Darwin developed a theory of biological evolution holding that species changed physically over many generations as they adapt to a particular natural environment. Spencer, however, did something Darwin would never have done: he applied the evolutionary model to the operation of society. That is, Spencer argued that society operates

like a jungle, with the "fittest" people rising to wealth and power and the "deficient" gradually sinking to a state of miserable poverty.

It is no surprise that Spencer's thinking was extremely popular among the rising industrialists a century ago as the new world of factories reached full speed. John D. Rockefeller (1839–1937), who made a vast fortune building the modern oil industry, often recited Spencer's "social gospel" to young children in Sunday school. As Rockefeller saw it, the growth of giant corporations—and the staggering wealth of their owners—was merely the "survival of the fittest," a basic fact of nature. Neither Spencer nor Rockefeller had any sympathy for the poor, viewing their plight as clear evidence of an in-

ability or unwillingness to measure up in a competitive world. Indeed, social Darwinism actually condemned social welfare programs as an evil because they penalized society's "best" members (through taxes) and rewarded society's "worst" members (through welfare benefits).

Almost a century has passed since Spencer spread his message. Today, sociologists are quick to point out that social standing is not simply a matter of personal effort, as Spencer contended. And it is simply not the case that the efforts that yield the most wealth are necessarily the most beneficial to society. Yet, given our individualistic culture, Spencer's basic view that people get more or less what they deserve in life remains very much with us today.

Spencer, whose ideas are described in the "Social Diversity" box.

Throughout human history, most people have regarded social stratification as unshakable. Especially as traditions weaken, however, people begin to question cultural "truths" and to unmask their political foundations and consequences.

For example, historic notions of a "woman's place" seem far from natural today and are losing their power to deprive women of opportunities. For the present, however, the contemporary class system still subjects women to caste-like expectations that they perform traditional tasks out of altruism while men are financially rewarded for their efforts. To illustrate, most chefs are men who work for income, while most household cooks are women who perform this role as a household duty.

Yet, while gender differences persist in countries such as Canada, there is little doubt that women and men are becoming steadily more equal in important respects. The continuing struggle for racial equality in South Africa also exemplifies widespread rejection of apartheid, which for decades shaped economic, political, and educational life in that nation. Apartheid, never widely accepted by Blacks, has lost its support as a "natural" system among whites who reject ideological racism (Friedrich, 1987; Contreras, 1992).

THE FUNCTIONS OF SOCIAL STRATIFICATION

Why are societies stratified at all? One answer, consistent with the structural-functional paradigm, is that social inequality plays a vital part in the operation of society. This influential—and controversial—argument was set forth some fifty years ago by Kingsley Davis and Wilbert Moore (1945).

THE DAVIS-MOORE THESIS

The **Davis-Moore thesis** is *the assertion that social stratification has beneficial consequences for the operation of a society.* How else, ask Davis and Moore, can we explain the fact that some form of social stratification has been found everywhere?

Davis and Moore describe our society as a complex system involving hundreds of occupational positions of varying importance. Certain jobs—say, changing spark plugs in a car—are fairly easy and can be performed by almost anyone. Other jobs—such as transplanting a human organ—are quite difficult and demand the scarce talents of people who have received extensive (and expensive) education. Positions of high day-to-day responsibility that demand special abilities are the most functionally significant.

Salaries: Are the Rich Worth What They Earn?

For an hour of work, a Canadian child-care worker earns about $6, a police officer earns about $27, a veterinarian earns about $32. The average worker—and even the prime minister and other high government officials—earn salaries that pale in comparison with those of popular athletes and entertainers.

In the United States, Barry Bonds garners about $40 000 per hour playing baseball for the San Francisco Giants. And what about the $100 000 Jim Carrey makes for every hour he spends making movies? Bill Cosby commands about $100 000 per hour to take the stage, and Oprah Winfrey earns about $200 000 for each hour she chats with guests before the television cameras. Many Canadians—among them Leslie Nielson, Michael J. Fox, Neve Campbell, Wayne Gretzky, and William Shatner—have gone to the U.S. in

Celine Dion is a multimillionaire, selling more than 20 million copies of her last album. Are her efforts for one album worth as much as two thousand average workers?

search of greater opportunity and remuneration.

According to the Davis-Moore thesis, rewards reflect an occupation's value to society. But are the talents of Julia Louis-Dreyfus, who earned about $13 million a year as a sidekick on *Seinfeld*, worth almost as much as the efforts of all one hundred U.S. senators (who, unlike Canada's, are elected and accountable to their constituencies)? Is Roger Clemens of the Toronto Blue Jays worth as much as thirty-five or forty of Canada's physicians or surgeons? In short, do earnings reflect the social importance of work?

Salaries in industrial-capitalist societies such as Canada are a product of market forces. Defenders of the laws of supply and demand claim that the market impartially evaluates worth, rewarding each worker according to the supply of the talent in question and the

In general, Davis and Moore explain, the greater the functional importance of a position, the more rewards a society will attach to it. This strategy pays off, since rewarding important work with income, prestige, power, and leisure encourages people to do these things. In effect, by distributing resources unequally, a society motivates each person to aspire to the most significant work possible, and to work better, harder, and longer. The overall effect of a system of unequal rewards—which is what social stratification amounts to—is a more productive society.

Davis and Moore concede that every society could be egalitarian. But, they caution, rewards can be equal only to the extent that people are willing to let anyone perform any job. Equality also demands that someone who carries out a job poorly be rewarded on a par with another who performs well. Logic dictates that such a system offers little incentive for people to make their best efforts, and thereby reduces a society's productive efficiency.

The Davis-Moore thesis points out why *some* form of stratification exists everywhere; it does not endorse any *particular* system of inequality. Nor do

Davis and Moore specify precisely what reward should be attached to any occupational position. They merely point out that positions a society deems crucial must yield sufficient rewards to draw talent away from less important work.

MERITOCRACY

The Davis-Moore thesis implies that a productive society is a **meritocracy**, *a system of social stratification based on personal merit.* Such societies hold out rewards to develop the talents and encourage the efforts of everyone. In pursuit of meritocracy, a society promotes equality of opportunity while, at the same time, mandating inequality of rewards. In other words, a pure class system would be a meritocracy, since it rewards everyone based on ability and effort. In addition, such a society would have extensive social mobility, blurring social categories as individuals moved up or down in the social system depending on their performance.

To the extent that caste societies speak of "merit" (from Latin, meaning "worthy of praise") they mean dutiful persistence in low-skill labour such as farming.

public demand for it. According to this view, movie and television stars, top athletes, skilled professionals, and many business executives have rare talents that are much in demand; thus, they may earn hundreds of times more than the typical worker. Executive salaries in Canada in 1994 included $13 million to Brian Hannan of Methanex and $41 million to Frank Stronach of Magna Corporation (Newman, 1996). Are these and other Canadian CEOs really worth the mega-million dollar incomes they earn each year?

Some critics claim that the market is not a good evaluator of occupational importance. First, critics maintain, the economy is dominated by a small proportion of people who manipulate the system for their own benefit. In Canada, thirty-two of our wealthiest families play "monopoly with the money of average Canadians" (Francis, 1986). In 1997, 19 of Canada's CEOs were compensated to the tune of $5 to 27 million (Globe and Mail, *Report on Business*, July 1998:87).

Corporate executives pay themselves multimillion dollar salaries and bonuses whether their companies do well or not. Gilbert Amelio, CEO of Apple Computer, laid off more than 4000 employees during 1996 and his company's stock price tumbled by almost 40 percent, yet he still paid himself more than $23 million for his efforts. In Canada, Paul Stern of Northern Telecom Ltd. was to have earned $5 million in 1992, despite serious mismanagement. His departure from the company, under a shadow, sent stock prices tumbling by almost 30 percent (Surtees, 1993). As noted by Newman (1996:183), these were "monumental pay-packets that had little connection with the success or failure of their enterprises."

A second problem with the idea that the market measures people's contributions to society is that many who make clear and significant contributions receive surprisingly little money. Tens of thousands of teachers, counsellors, and health-care workers enhance the welfare of others every day for little salary. The average teacher would have to work over a thousand years to earn what Amelio received in one year.

Using salary to measure social worth, then, only works to the extent that market forces actually gauge people's societal contribution. Some people view market forces as the most accurate measure of occupational worth. Others contend that lucrative activities may or may not be socially valuable. From this standpoint, the market system amounts to a closed game in which only a handful of people have the money to play.

Caste systems, in short, offer honour to those who remain "in their place."

Although caste systems waste human potential, they are quite orderly. And herein lies a clue to an important question: why do modern industrial societies resist becoming pure meritocracies by retaining many caste-like qualities? Simply because, left unchecked, meritocracy erodes social structure such as kinship. No one, for example, evaluates family members solely on the basis of performance. Class systems in industrial societies, therefore, retain some caste elements to promote order and social cohesion.

Critical evaluation. By investigating the functions of social stratification, Davis and Moore made a lasting contribution to sociological analysis. Even so, critics point to several flaws in their thesis. Melvin Tumin (1953) wonders, first, whether functional importance really explains the high rewards that some people enjoy. Can one even measure functional importance? Perhaps, he suggests, the high rewards our society accords to physicians at least partly result from deliberate efforts by medical schools to limit the supply of physicians and increase the demand for their services.

If so, income and other rewards may have little to do with an individual's functional contribution to society. Wayne Gretzky's hockey contract alone (apart from income earned through product endorsements) gives him twenty-one times the income of the prime minister, who earned a salary of $134 000 in 1996. What about the $65 million income reported for Celine Dion in 1997? Would anyone argue that, in societal significance, playing hockey or singing tops the responsibilities of the prime minister? Our "Controversy & Debate" box takes a critical look at the link between pay and societal importance.

A second charge made by Tumin is that the Davis-Moore thesis exaggerates social stratification's role in developing individual talent. Our society does reward individual achievement, but we also allow families to transfer wealth and power from generation to generation in caste-like fashion. Additionally, for women, people of colour, and others with limited opportunities, stratification still raises barriers to personal accomplishment. In practice, Tumin concludes, social stratification functions to develop some people's abilities to the fullest while barring others from ever reaching their potential.

This cartoon, titled "Capital and Labour," appeared in the English press in 1843, when the ideas of Karl Marx were first gaining attention. It links the plight of that country's coal miners to the privileges enjoyed by those who owned coal-fired factories.

CAPITAL AND LABOUR.

Third, by contending that social stratification benefits all of society, the Davis-Moore thesis ignores how social inequality promotes conflict and, sometimes, even outright revolution. This assertion leads us to the social-conflict paradigm, which provides a very different explanation for the persistence of social hierarchy.

STRATIFICATION AND CONFLICT

Social-conflict analysis argues that, rather than benefiting society as a whole, social stratification provides advantages to some people at the expense of others. This theoretical perspective draws heavily on the ideas of Karl Marx: additional contributions were made by Max Weber.

KARL MARX: CLASS AND CONFLICT

Karl Marx, whose approach to understanding social inequality is detailed in Chapter 4 ("Society"), identified two major social classes corresponding to the two basic relationships to the means of production: individuals either (1) own productive property, or (2) labour for others. In medieval Europe, the nobility and the church owned the productive land; peasants toiled as farmers. Similarly, in industrial class systems, the capitalists (or the bourgeoisie) control factories, which depend on the labour of workers (the proletariat).

Marx noted great disparities in wealth and power arising from the industrial-capitalist productive system, which, he contended, made class conflict inevitable. In time, he believed, oppression and misery would drive the working majority to organize and ultimately to overthrow capitalism.

Marx's analysis was grounded in his observations of capitalism in the nineteenth century, when great industrialists dominated the economic scene. Andrew Carnegie, J.P. Morgan, and John Jacob Astor (one of the few very rich passengers to perish on the *Titanic*) lived in fabulous mansions filled with priceless art and staffed by dozens of servants. Their fortunes were staggering: Andrew Carnegie reportedly earned more than $20 million a year as the twentieth century began (worth close to $100 million in today's dollars)—all at a time when the wages paid to the average worker totalled roughly $500 a year (Baltzell, 1964; Pessen, 1990).

According to Marx, the capitalist elite draws its strength from more than the operation of the economy. He noted that through the family, opportunity and wealth are passed down from generation to generation. Moreover, the legal system defends this practice through inheritance law. Similarly, exclusive schools bring children of the elite together, encouraging informal social ties that will benefit them throughout their lives. Overall, from Marx's point of view, capitalist society *reproduces the class structure in each new generation.*

Critical evaluation. Exploring how the capitalist economic system generates conflict between classes, Marx's analysis of social stratification has had enormous influence on sociological thinking in recent decades. Because it is revolutionary—calling for the overthrow of capitalist society—Marxism is also highly controversial.

One of the strongest criticisms of the Marxist approach is that it denies one of the central tenets of the Davis-Moore thesis: that motivating people to perform various social roles requires some system of unequal rewards. Marx separated rewards from performance, endorsing an egalitarian system based on the principle of "from each according to his abilities; to each according to his needs" (1972:388; orig. 1848). Critics argue that severing rewards from performance is precisely the flaw that generated the low productivity characteristic of the former Soviet Union and other socialist economies around the world.

Defenders of Marx rebut this line of attack by pointing to considerable evidence supporting Marx's general view of humanity as inherently social rather than unflinchingly selfish (Clark, 1991; Fiske, 1991). They counter that we should not assume that individual rewards (much less monetary compensation alone) are the only way to motivate people to perform their social roles.

In addition, although few doubt that capitalist society does perpetuate poverty and privilege as Marx asserted, the revolutionary developments he considered inevitable have failed to materialize. The next section explores why the socialist revolution Marx predicted and promoted has not occurred, at least in advanced capitalist societies.

WHY NO MARXIST REVOLUTION?

Despite Marx's prediction, capitalism is still thriving. Why have workers in Canada, the United States, and other industrial societies not overthrown capitalism? Ralf Dahrendorf (1959) pointed to four reasons.

1. **The fragmentation of the capitalist class.** First, the century since Marx's death has witnessed the fragmentation of the capitalist class in North America. A century ago, *single families* typically owned large companies; today, *numerous stockholders* have assumed much of that ownership. Moreover, day-to-day operation of large corporations is now in the hands of a large managerial class, who may or may not be major stockholders. With stock more widely held, an increasing number of people have a direct stake in preserving the capitalist system (Wright, 1985; Wright, Levine, and Sober, 1992).

2. **A rising standard of living.** As Chapter 15 ("The Economy and Work") details, a century ago most workers laboured either on farms or in factories performing **blue-collar occupations**, *lower-prestige jobs involving mostly manual labour*. By contrast, most workers today hold **white-collar occupations**, *higher-prestige work involving mostly mental*

activity. These occupations include positions in sales, management, and other service work, frequently in large, bureaucratic organizations.

While many of today's white-collar workers perform repetitive tasks, most do not think of themselves as an "industrial proletariat." Just as important, workers' overall standard of living in North America rose fourfold over the course of the twentieth century in dollars controlled for inflation, even as the work week decreased. Is it any wonder, then, that most white-collar workers now perceive their social positions as higher than those of their blue-collar parents and grandparents? This structural mobility has cooled revolutionary aspirations among working people (Edwards, 1979; Gagliani, 1981; Wright and Martin, 1987).

3. **More extensive worker organization.** Employees have organizational strengths they lacked a century ago. Workers have won the right to organize into labour unions that can and do make demands of management backed by threats of work slowdowns and strikes. If not always peaceful, then, worker-management disputes are now institutionalized.

4. **More extensive legal protections.** During the twentieth century, the government has extended laws to make the workplace safer and devised programs, such as unemployment insurance, disability protection, and social security, to provide workers with greater financial security.

Taken together, these four developments mean that, despite persistent stratification, our society has smoothed out many of capitalism's rough edges.

A Counterpoint

Advocates of social-conflict analysis, however, counter that Marx's analysis of capitalism is still largely valid (Matthews, 1983; Brym, 1985; Smith, 1987; Clement, 1990; Cuneo, 1990; Winson, 1990; Wotherspoon and Satzewich, 1993). They offer this counterpoint:

1. **Wealth remains highly concentrated.** As Marx contended, wealth remains in the hands of the few. By the mid-1980s, Canada had six billionaire families and another twenty-two worth $100 million or more, who according to Francis (1986) control an inordinate amount of Canada's wealth. In particular, the concentration of wealth and ownership of newspapers and cable TV (plus *Maclean's* magazine) by Conrad Black and Ted Rogers, respectively (Newman, 1996), is a source of tremendous concern to critics of capitalist industrial society.

TABLE 9–1 Two Explanations of Social Stratification: A Summary

Structural-Functional Paradigm	Social-Conflict Paradigm
Social stratification keeps society operating. The linkage of greater rewards to more important social positions benefits society as a whole.	Social stratification is the result of social conflict. Differences in social resources serve the interests of some and harm the interests of others.
Social stratification encourages a matching of talents and abilities to appropriate positions.	Social stratification ensures that much talent and ability within society will not be used at all.
Social stratification is both useful and inevitable.	Social stratification is useful to only some people; it is not inevitable.
The values and beliefs that legitimate social inequality are widely shared throughout society.	Values and beliefs tend to be ideological; they reflect the interests of the more powerful members of society.
Because systems of social stratification are useful to society as a whole and are supported by cultural values and beliefs, they are usually stable over time.	Because systems of social stratification reflect the interests of only part of the society, they are unlikely to remain stable over time.

SOURCE: Adapted in part from Arthur L. Stinchcombe, "Some Empirical Consequences of the Davis-Moore Theory of Stratification," *American Sociological Review*, Vol. 28, No. 5 (October 1963):808.

2. **White-collar work offers little to workers.** As defenders of Marx's thinking see it, the white-collar revolution has delivered little in the way of higher income or better working conditions compared to the factory jobs of a century ago. On the contrary, much white-collar work remains monotonous and routine, especially the low-level clerical jobs commonly held by women.

3. **Progress requires struggle.** Labour organizations may have advanced the interests of the workers over the last half-century, but regular negotiation between workers and management hardly signals the end of social conflict. In fact, many of the concessions won by workers came about precisely through the class conflict Marx described. Moreover, workers still strive to gain concessions from capitalists and, in the 1990s, struggle to hold on to the advances already achieved.

4. **The law still favours the rich.** Workers have gained some legal protections over the course of this century. Even so, the law still defends the overall distribution of wealth in Canada and the United States. Just as importantly, "average" people cannot use the legal system to the same advantage as do the rich.

In sum, according to social-conflict theory, the fact that no socialist revolution has taken place in Canada or the U.S. hardly invalidates Marx's analysis of capitalism. As we shall see in Chapter 10 ("Social Class in Canada"), pronounced social inequality persists, as does social conflict—albeit less overtly and violently than in the nineteenth century.

Finally, some defenders of capitalism cite the collapse of communist regimes in Eastern Europe and the former Soviet Union as proof of the superiority of capitalism over socialism. Most analysts agree that socialism failed to meet the needs of the people it purported to serve, either in terms of raising living standards or ensuring personal freedoms. But, to be fair, socialism's failings do not excuse flaws in capitalism. Many critics maintain that capitalism in North America has yet to demonstrate its ability to address problems of public education and desperate poverty, especially among the urban underclass (Uchitelle, 1991). Table 9–1 summarizes the contributions of the two contrasting sociological approaches to understanding social stratification.

MAX WEBER: CLASS, STATUS, AND POWER

Max Weber, whose approach to social analysis is described in Chapter 4 ("Society"), agreed with Karl Marx that social stratification sparks social conflict, but he thought Marx's two-class model was simplistic. Instead, he viewed social stratification as a more complex interplay of three distinct dimensions.

First, Weber took note of economic inequality—the issue so vital to Marx—which he termed *class* position. Weber's use of "class" refers not to crude categories but to a continuum on which anyone can be ranked from high to low. Second, Weber highlighted *status*, or social prestige. Third, Weber emphasized the importance of *power* in a social hierarchy.

The Socioeconomic Status Hierarchy

Marx believed that social prestige and power derived from economic position; thus, he saw no reason to treat them as distinct dimensions of social inequality. Weber disagreed, recognizing that status consistency in modern societies is often quite low: a local government official, say, might wield considerable power, yet have little wealth or social prestige.

Weber's key contribution in this area, then, lies in showing that social stratification in industrial societies resembles a multidimensional ranking rather than clearly defined classes. Following Weber's thinking, sociologists often use the term **socioeconomic status** (SES) to refer to a composite *ranking based on various dimensions of social inequality.*

A population that varies widely in class, status, and power—Weber's three dimensions of inequality—creates a virtually infinite array of social categories, all of which pursue their own interests. Thus, unlike Marx, who focused on conflict between two distinct classes, Weber considered social conflict as highly variable and complex.

Inequality in History

Weber also made a key historical observation, noting that each of his three dimensions of social inequality stands out at different points in the evolution of human societies. Agrarian societies, he maintained, emphasize status or social prestige, typically in the form of honour or symbolic purity. Members of these societies gain such status by conforming to cultural norms corresponding to their rank.

Industrialization and the development of capitalism level traditional rankings based on birth but generate striking material differences in the population. Thus, Weber argued, the crucial difference among people in industrial-capitalist societies lies in the economic dimension of class.

In time, industrial societies witness a surging growth of the bureaucratic state. This expansion of government, coupled with the proliferation of other types of formal organizations, means power gains importance in the stratification system. Power is also central to the organization of socialist societies, evident in their extensive government regulation of many aspects of life. The elite members of such societies are mostly high-ranking officials rather than rich people.

This historical analysis underlies a final disagreement between Weber and Marx. Looking to the future, Marx believed that social stratification could be largely eliminated by abolishing private ownership of productive property. Weber doubted that overthrowing capitalism would significantly diminish social stratification. It might lessen economic disparity, Weber reasoned, but socialism would simultaneously increase social inequality by expanding government and concentrating power in the hands of a political elite. Recent popular uprisings against entrenched bureaucracies in Eastern Europe and the former Soviet Union lend support to Weber's argument.

Critical evaluation. Weber's multidimensional analysis of social stratification retains enormous influence among sociologists. Some analysts (particularly those influenced by Marx's ideas) argue that while social class boundaries have blurred, striking patterns of social inequality persist in North America and elsewhere in the industrial world.

Moreover, as we shall see in Chapter 10 ("Social Class in Canada"), economic inequality has increased in recent years. Against this backdrop of economic polarization, the last decade of this century already has seen a renewed emphasis on "classes" in conflict rather than on subtle shadings of a "multidimensional hierarchy."

STRATIFICATION AND TECHNOLOGY IN GLOBAL PERSPECTIVE

We can weave together a number of observations made in this chapter by considering the relationship between a society's technology and its type of social stratification. This analysis draws on Gerhard Lenski's and Jean Lenski's model of sociocultural evolution, detailed in Chapter 4 ("Society").

HUNTING AND GATHERING SOCIETIES

Simple technology limits the production of hunting and gathering societies to only what is necessary for day-to-day living. Although some individuals produce more than others, the group's survival depends on all sharing what they have. Thus, no categories of people emerge as better off than others. Until quite recently, this would have been an accurate description of stratification among the majority of Inuit communities across northern Canada.

HORTICULTURAL, PASTORAL, AND AGRARIAN SOCIETIES

Technological advances generate surplus production, while intensifying social inequality. In horticultural and pastoral societies, a small elite controls most of the surplus. Large-scale agriculture generates even greater abundance, but marked inequality—as great as any time in history—means various categories of people lead strikingly different lives. Agrarian nobility wield godlike power over the masses.

INDUSTRIAL SOCIETIES

Industrialization reverses the historical trend, nudging social inequality downward. Prompted by the

In this stone carving created in Egypt some 5,000 years ago, we see King Narmer about to slay his enemies with a mace, his sandals carried behind him and other fallen enemies below. Next to the king, the falcon represents the god Horus, who holds a rope attached to a head that grows from the soil like other plants. The message is that the king and Horus are one and the same, with the power of life and death over others.

need to develop individual talents, caste rankings gradually erode in favour of greater individual opportunity. Then, too, the increasing productivity of industrial technology steadily raises the living standards of the historically poor majority. Specialized work also demands the expansion of schooling, sharply reducing illiteracy. A literate population, in turn, tends to press for a greater voice in political decision making, further diminishing social inequality and reducing the domination of women by men.

The net effect is that, over time, even wealth becomes somewhat less concentrated (countering the trend predicted by Marx). Estimates suggest that the proportion of all wealth controlled by the richest 1 percent of U.S. families peaked at about 36 percent just before the stock market crash in 1929, falling to about 30 percent by 1990 (Williamson and Lindert,

1980; Beeghley, 1989; *1991 Green Book*). Although Canada appears to have more billionaire families per capita than the United States—six here compared to twelve in the U.S. (Francis, 1986)[1]—it is likely that our overall pattern in control of wealth is very similar to that of the U.S.

THE KUZNETS CURVE

The trend described above can be distilled into the following statement: *in human history, technological progress first increases but then moderates the intensity of social stratification.* So if greater inequality is functional for agrarian societies, then industrial societies benefit from a more egalitarian climate. This historical shift, recognized by Nobel prize–winning economist Simon Kuznets (1955, 1966), is illustrated by the Kuznets curve, shown in Figure 9–1.

Current patterns of social inequality around the world generally square with the Kuznets curve. As shown in Global Map 9–1, industrial societies have somewhat less income inequality—one important measure of social stratification—than nations that remain predominantly agrarian. Specifically, mature industrial societies such as Canada, the United States, and the nations of Western Europe exhibit less income inequality than the less industrialized countries of Latin America, Africa, and Asia.

Yet income disparity reflects a host of factors beyond technology, especially political and economic priorities. Societies that have had socialist economic systems (including the People's Republic of China, the former Soviet Union, and the nations of Eastern Europe) display relatively little income inequality. Keep in mind, however, that an egalitarian society such as the People's Republic of China has an average income level that is quite low by world standards; further, on noneconomic dimensions such as political power, China's society reveals pronounced inequality.

And what of the future? Notice that we have extended the trend described by Kuznets (the broken line) showing an upturn in the intensity of inequality corresponding to the post-industrial era. That is, as the Information Revolution has begun transforming Canada, we have experienced rising economic polarization (highlighted in the next chapter). In sum, the long-term pattern may diverge from that observed by Kuznets almost half a century ago (Nielsen & Alderson, 1997).

---

[1] By 1996 the number of billionaire families in Canada had increased to eight, according to *The Financial Post Magazine* (Hamilton, 1996).

SOCIAL STRATIFICATION: FACTS AND VALUES

The year was 2081 and everybody was finally equal. They weren't only equal before God and the law. They were equal every which way. Nobody was smarter than anybody else. Nobody was better looking than anybody else. Nobody was stronger or quicker than anybody else. All this equality was due to the 211th, 212th, and 213th Amendments to the Constitution and the unceasing vigilance of agents of the Handicapper General.

With these words, novelist Kurt Vonnegut, Jr. (1968; orig. 1961) begins the story "Harrison Bergeron," an imaginary account of a future United States in which social inequality has been totally abolished. While some people find equality appealing in principle, Vonnegut warns that it can be a dangerous concept in practice. His story describes a nightmare of social engineering in which every individual talent that makes one person different from another has been systematically neutralized by high-handed government agents.

In order to neutralize differences that make one person "better" than another, the state mandates that physically attractive people wear masks that render them average looking, that intelligent people don earphones that generate distracting noise, and that the legs of the best athletes and dancers be precisely fitted with weights to make their movements just as cumbersome as everyone else's. In short, although we may imagine that social equality would liberate people to make the most of their talents, Vonnegut concludes that a truly egalitarian society could exist only by reducing everyone to a lowest common denominator.

This chapter's explanations of social stratification also involve value judgments. The Davis-Moore thesis, which finds social stratification universal, interprets this pattern as evidence that inequality is a necessary element of social organization. Class differences, then, reflect both variation in human abilities and the importance of occupational roles. From this point of view, the spectre of equality is a threat to a society of diverse people, since such uniformity could exist only as the product of the relentless and stifling efforts of officials like Vonnegut's fictitious Handicapper General.

Social-conflict analysis, advocated by Karl Marx, interpreted universal social inequality in a very different way. Rejecting the notion that inequality is in any sense necessary, Marx condemned social hierarchy as

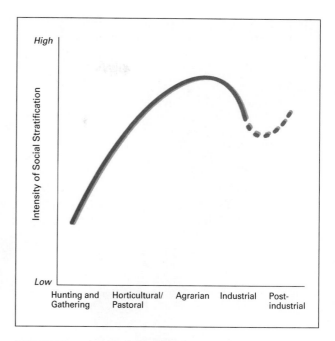

FIGURE 9–1 Social Stratification and Technological Development: The Kuznets Curve

The Kuznets curve reveals that greater technological sophistication is generally accompanied by more pronounced social stratification. The trend reverses itself, however, as industrial societies gradually become more egalitarian. Rigid caste-like distinctions are relaxed in favour of greater opportunity and equality under the law. Political rights are more widely extended, and there is even some levelling of economic differences. The Kuznets curve may also be usefully applied to the relative social standing of the two sexes.

a product of greed. Guided by egalitarian values, he advocated social arrangements that would enable everyone to share all important resources equally. Rather than undermining the quality of life, Marx maintained that equality would enhance human well-being.

The "Controversy & Debate" discussion addresses the link between intelligence and social class. This issue—also a mix of facts and values—is among the most troublesome in social science, partly because of the difficulty in defining and measuring "intelligence," but also because the idea that elites are inherently "better" than others challenges our democratic culture.

The next chapter ("Social Class in Canada") takes a close look at inequality in our own society. But, here

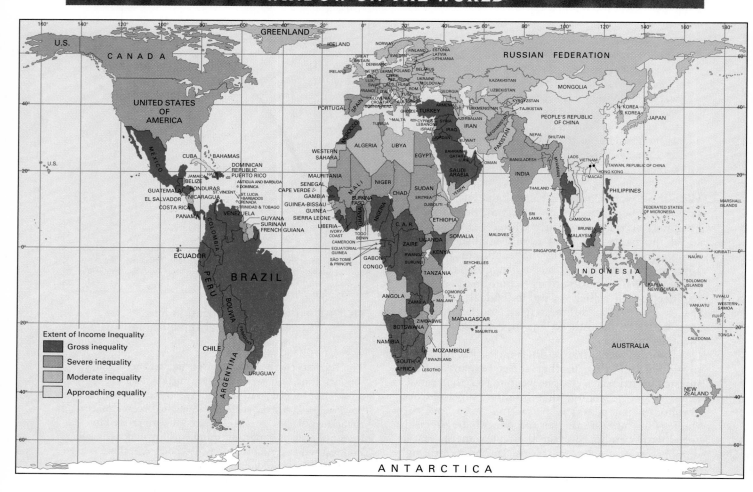

GLOBAL MAP 9–1 Income Disparity in Global Perspective

Societies throughout the world differ in the rigidity and intensity of social stratification, as well as in overall standard of living. This map highlights income inequality. Generally speaking, countries that have had centralized, socialist economies (including the People's Republic of China, the former Soviet Union, and Cuba) display the least income inequality, although their standard of living has been relatively low. Industrial societies with predominantly capitalist economies, including Canada, the United States, and most of Western Europe, have higher overall living standards, accompanied by severe income disparity. The low-income countries of Latin America and Africa (including Mexico, Brazil, and Zaire) exhibit the most pronounced inequality of income.

SOURCE: *Peters Atlas of the World* (1990).

---

again, even people who agree on the basic facts often interpret them quite differently. This lesson is repeated in Chapter 11 ("Global Stratification"), which examines inequality among the world's nations and offers two opposing explanations for it. At all levels, then, the study of social stratification involves a complex, ongoing debate that yields no single or simple truth.

SUMMARY

1. Social stratification refers to categories of people ranked in a hierarchy. Stratification is (1) characteristic of society, not something that merely arises from individual differences; (2) persistent over many generations; (3) universal, yet variable in form; and (4) supported by cultural beliefs.

2. Caste systems, typical of agrarian societies, are based on ascription and permit little or no social mobility. Caste hierarchy, which is supported by strong moral beliefs, shapes a person's entire life, including occupation and marriage.

3. Class systems, common to industrial societies, reflect a greater measure of individual achievement. Because the emphasis on achievement opens the way for social mobility, classes are less clearly defined than castes.

4. Historically, socialist societies have claimed to be classless, based on their public ownership of productive property. While such societies may exhibit far less economic inequality than their capitalist counterparts, they are notably stratified with regard to power.

5. Social stratification persists due to support from various social institutions and the power of ideology to define certain kinds of inequality as both natural and just.

6. The Davis-Moore thesis states that social stratification is universal because it contributes to the operation of society. In class systems, unequal rewards motivate people to aspire to the occupational roles most important to the functioning of society.

7. Critics of the Davis-Moore thesis note that (1) it is difficult to assess objectively the functional importance of any occupational position; (2) stratification prevents many people from developing their abilities; and (3) social stratification often generates social conflict–benefiting some at the expense of others.

8. Karl Marx, a key architect of social-conflict analysis, recognized two major social classes in industrial societies. The capitalists, or bourgeoisie, own the means of production in pursuit of profits; the proletariat, by contrast, offer their labour in exchange for wages.

9. The socialist revolution that Marx predicted has not occurred in industrial societies such as Canada and the United States. Some sociologists see this as evidence that Marx's analysis was flawed; others, however, point out that our society is still marked by pronounced social inequality and substantial class conflict.

10. Max Weber identified three distinct dimensions of social inequality: economic class, social status or prestige, and power. Taken together, these three dimensions form a complex hierarchy of socioeconomic standing.

11. Gerhard Lenski and Jean Lenski explained that, historically, technological advances have been associated with more pronounced social stratification. A limited reversal of this trend occurs in advanced, industrial societies, as represented by the Kuznets curve; recently, however, the emergence of a postindustrial economy in some societies has increased economic inequality once again.

12. Social stratification is a complex and controversial area of research because it deals not only with facts but also with values that suggest how society should be organized.

CRITICAL THINKING QUESTIONS

1. How is social stratification evident on university and college campuses? What categories of people are there? In what respects are they unequal?

2. Why are agrarian societies typically caste systems? Why does industrialization replace castes with classes?

3. According to the Davis-Moore thesis, why should a university president be paid more than a professor? Do you agree with this analysis?

4. In what respects have the predictions of Karl Marx failed? In what respects are they correct?

SOCIOLOGY APPLIED

1. Visit the Internet Web site www.paywatch.org to determine the compensation for chief executive officers of various large corporations. To see how their companies performed, check the corporate

The Bell Curve Debate: Are Rich People Really Smarter?

It is rare when the publication of a new book in the social sciences captures the attention of the public at large. But *The Bell Curve: Intelligence and Class Structure in American Life* by Richard J. Herrnstein and Charles Murray (1994) did that and more, igniting a firestorm of controversy over why pronounced social stratification divides U.S. society and, just as importantly, what to do about it. Note that had Herrnstein and Murray written about Canada, they would have reached very similar conclusions.

The Bell Curve is an 800-page book that addresses many critical issues and resists simple summary. But its basic thesis is captured in the following propositions:

1. There exists something we can describe as "general intelligence"; people with more of it tend to be more successful in their careers than those with less of it.

2. At least half the variation in human intelligence (Herrnstein and Murray use figures of 60 to 70 percent) is transmitted genetically from one generation to another; the remaining variability is due to environmental factors.

3. Over the course of the twentieth century—and especially since the Information Revolution—intelligence has become more necessary to the performance of our society's top occupational positions.

4. Simultaneously, the best U.S. colleges and universities have shifted their admissions policies away from favouring children of inherited wealth to admitting young people who perform best on standardized tests (such as the Scholastic Aptitude Test (SAT), American College Testing Program (ACT), and Graduate Record Examination (GRE)).

5. As a result of these changes in the workplace and higher education, American society is now coming to be dominated by a "cognitive elite," who are, on average, not only better trained than most people but actually more intelligent.

6. Because more intelligent people are socially segregated on the college campus and in the workplace, it is no surprise that they tend to pair up, marry, and have intelligent children, perpetuating the "cognitive elite."

7. Near the bottom of the social ladder, a similar process is at work: Increasingly, poor people are individuals with lower intelligence, who live segregated from others, and who tend to pass along their modest abilities to their children.

Resting on the validity of the seven assertions presented above, Herrnstein and Murray then offer, as a eighth point, a basic approach to public policy:

8. To the extent that membership in the affluent elite or the impoverished underclass is rooted in intelligence and determined mostly

stock price for that period (available from Yahoo!, click on the financial news link). What conclusions do you reach?

2. Read Kurt Vonnegut's short story "Harrison Bergeron" (in his collection of stories entitled *Welcome to the Monkey House*). Writing as an artist, what are Vonnegut's views of social stratification and the prospect of an egalitarian society? Do you agree with him or not? Why?

3. Sit down with parents, grandparents, or other relatives and try to assess the social class position of your own family over the last three generations. Have changes taken place? If so, what caused this mobility?

4. Identify the "seven deadly sins," human failings according to the medieval Christian church. These may be deadly to the agrarian caste system, but what about the modern, capitalist class system?

WEBLINKS

www.cudenver.edu/public/sociology/introsoc/topic4a.html
This article defines the *Basic Concepts in Social Stratification*, including social status, power, and systems of

stratification. Links are provided to the topic of inequality.

www.anu.edu.au/polsci/marx/marx.html
The Marxism Page contains the full text of *The Com-*

by genetic inheritance, programs to assist underprivileged people (from Head Start to Affirmative Action) will have few practical benefits.

Within weeks of the book's publication, analysts pro and con were squaring off on television news shows, including *Nightline*, and trading charges across the pages of practically every U.S. news magazine. Most social scientists tended to side with *The Bell Curve*'s critics. In response to the book's thesis, critics first questioned exactly what is meant by "intelligence," arguing that people's innate abilities can hardly be separated from the effects of socialization. Intelligence tests, they continue, don't measure cognitive *ability*, they measure certain kinds of cognitive *performance*. And we might well expect rich children to perform better on intelligence tests, since they have had the best schooling. Some critics dismiss the concept of "intelligence" outright as phony science. At the very least, we should not think of "intelligence" as a cause of achievement since research indicates that mental abilities and life experiences are *interactive*, each affecting the other.

In addition, while most researchers who study intelligence agree that genetics does play a part in transmitting intelligence, the consensus is that no more than 25 to 40 percent is inherited—only about half what Herrnstein and Murray claim. Therefore, critics conclude, *The Bell Curve* misleads readers into thinking that social elitism is both natural and inevitable. In its assumptions and conclusions, moreover, *The Bell Curve* amounts to little more than a rehash of the social Darwinism popular a century ago, which heralded the success of industrial tycoons as merely "the survival of the fittest."

Perhaps, as one commentator noted, the more society seems like a jungle, the more people think of stratification as a matter of blood rather than upbringing. But, despite its flaws and exaggerations, the book's success suggests that *The Bell Curve* raises many issues we cannot easily ignore. Can democratic systems tolerate the "dangerous knowledge" that elites (including not only rich people but also our political leaders) are at least somewhat more intelligent than the rest of us? What of *The Bell Curve*'s description—which few challenge—that our society's elites

are increasingly insulating themselves from social problems including crime, homelessness, and poor schools? As such problems have become worse in recent years, how do we counter the easy explanation that poor people are hobbled by their own limited ability? And, most basically, what should be done to ensure that all people have the opportunity to develop their abilities as fully as possible?

Continue the debate . . .

1. *Do you agree that "general intelligence" exists? Why or why not?*

2. *In general, do you think that people of higher social position are more intelligent than those of lower social position? If you think intelligence differs by social standing, which factor is cause and which is effect?*

3. *Do you think sociologists should study controversial issues such as differences in human intelligence? Why or why not?*

SOURCES: Herrnstein and Murray (1994); Duster (1995), Hauser (1995), Jacoby and Glauberman (1995), and Taylor (1995).

---

munist Manifesto, various introductions to Marxist politics, lyrics and a sound recording of "The Internationale," contemporary Marxist writings, and links to other resources on the Web.

www.worldbank.org/wdi/wdi/wdi.htm
This site presents samples from the World Bank annual publication *World Development Indicators*, including information about the effects of development on people, the economy, markets, and the environment.

www.theatlantic.com/unbound/aandc/trnscrpt/ lemtest.htm
In this transcript of a live online conference published in *The Atlantic Monthly Online*, Nicholas Lemann dis-

cusses how educational testing and the idea of meritocracy have shaped American society in the twentieth century.

www.truth.org.za/
The official home page of the *Truth and Reconciliation Committee* in South Africa includes statements and press releases, news reports from the South African Press Association, Amnesty decisions and statistics, written submissions to the TRC, transcripts of the Human Rights Violations Hearings and the Amnesty Hearings, background information, recommended reading, and more.

William Groppner, *Sweat Shop*
© Christie's Images.

CHAPTER 10

SOCIAL CLASS IN CANADA

Karen Moss, a twenty-two-year-old single mother, was packing up her belongings to move for the third time in seven months. Her dreams of improving her life with a college education were dashed when the Ontario government cut welfare payments by almost 22 percent in 1996. Moss was now receiving $957 per month—down from $1221—to support her three-year-old son Cameron and herself.

Moss had also lost government funding for school. She had been doing very well in a retail management course at a local community college, but bureaucratic mix-ups and problems with getting a work placement forced her to discontinue her studies. "If it wasn't for the welfare cuts," Moss said, "I'd still be living in my old apartment and I'd be two semesters away from completing my course."

The cuts meant that Moss could no longer afford the $700-a-month rent for her one-bedroom apartment. She tried sharing an apartment with another single mother, but when that didn't work she moved in with her parents. But living in their small condominium was too cramped and stressful for Moss and her son. So once again she found herself looking for another place to live.

Cameron's father, also on welfare, did not help support their son. So Moss decided that the best thing to do was to try a fresh start in a new city. "I just want to get off welfare and get back on my feet. Once that happens, I'll look into trying to finish school," she said (Monsebraaten, 1996).

The story of Karen Moss offers stark evidence of the pervasive power of social stratification to shape the lives of people throughout Canada. Whether individuals easily achieve great success, struggle simply to get by, or collapse with broken spirits is not a simple matter of people's talents and personal ambitions. For all of us, social standing reflects the distribution of wealth, power, and opportunity in our society.

DIMENSIONS OF SOCIAL INEQUALITY

We tend to think of ourselves as a "middle-class society," but in fact Canadian society is highly stratified. The rich not only control most of the money, they also benefit from more schooling, they enjoy better health, and they consume a greater share of almost all goods and services than others do. On the other end of the socioeconomic spectrum, poor families struggle from day to day simply to make ends meet. This chapter will explain that the popular perception of Canada as a society with a bulging middle class and a uniformly high standard of living does not square with many important facts.

Our egalitarian values suggest that we experience equality of opportunity and widespread upward mobility and that, at the very least, we provide a broad social safety net that catches those who fall through the cracks. We fail to recognize that, in reality, birth confers advantages and opportunities on some people that others who are less fortunate could never imagine.

Social inequality in Canada is not easily recognized because our primary groups—including family, neighbours, and friends—typically have the same social standing as we do. At work, we tend to mix with

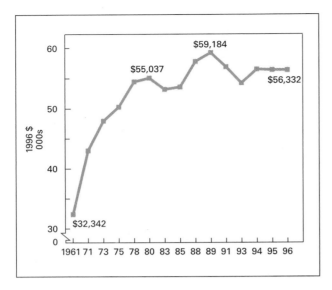

FIGURE 10–1 Average Family Income in Canada in Constant 1996 Dollars, 1961–1996

SOURCE: Calculations by Gerber based on Statistics Canada, Catalogue No. 13-208. Statistics Canada, various sources, various years.

others like ourselves. In effect, most of our daily interaction involves a narrow stratum of society, with only brief and impersonal encounters with people very different from ourselves. The mass media, even in their ads, project a largely middle-class picture of our social world, and recently governments have quoted statistics showing that Canadians, overall, have the highest standard of living in the world. The net effect of this bombardment with images of homogeneity is that the very rich and the very poor are largely invisible to the rest of us.

When people do acknowledge their differences, they often talk of inequality as if it were determined by a single factor such as money. More accurately, however, social class in Canada has several dimensions. *Socioeconomic status* (SES), examined in Chapter 9 ("Social Stratification"), amounts to a composite measure of social position that encompasses not only money but power, occupational prestige, and schooling.

INCOME

One important dimension of inequality involves **income**, *occupational wages or salaries, and earnings from investments.* As revealed in Figure 10–1, the average family income in Canada in 1996 was $56 332, marking a sustained, but partial recovery from a recent dip in 1993. Note that average family incomes—measured in 1996 dollars—rose from $32 000 to $55 000 through the 1960s and 1970s, dipped in the recession of the

early 1980s, climbed to a high in 1989, and dipped again in the recession of the early 1990s. By reporting incomes in constant dollars, Figure 10–1 reveals the fluctuation in buying power of the average family from 1961 to 1996, suggesting that the earlier rate of increase has essentially levelled off since about 1980. Note that an important contributor to rising family income was the increase in dual-income families through the 1960s and 1970s.

Table 10-1, which shows the distribution of income by quintiles (by fifths, or groups of 20 percent) among all Canadian families from 1951 to 1996, suggests remarkable stability over time. Taking 1996 as the point of reference, the 20 percent of families with the highest earnings received 40.6 percent of all income, while the bottom 20 percent made only 6.1 percent. In short, the bulk of the nation's income is earned by a small proportion of families, while the rest of the population makes do with far less.

A glance at the Canadian figures over a forty-five-year period suggests that little has changed in terms of the pattern of income distribution. The stability in the figures is quite surprising considering the fact that Canada experienced substantial economic growth during the period. In addition, our social welfare system, which is intended to redistribute income to those who are less well off, became firmly established during this interval. It would appear that increases in government transfer payments have been accompanied by decreases in primary income (Fréchette, 1988).

A comparison of the 1996 Canadian and 1990 U.S. figures in Table 10–1 reveals a substantial difference between the two countries that is probably attributable to the more broadly based social welfare programs in our country, which, however ineffectively, do indeed transfer income from the wealthy to the poor. Where our lowest quintile receives 6.1 per-

TABLE 10–1 Distribution of Family Income by Quintile* in Canada, 1951–96, and in the U.S., 1990

	Canada						U.S.
Quintile	**1951**	**1961**	**1971**	**1981**	**1991**	**1996**	**1990**
Lowest	6.1	6.6	5.6	6.4	6.4	6.1	3.9
Second	12.9	13.5	12.6	12.9	12.2	11.9	9.6
Middle	17.4	18.3	18.0	18.3	17.6	17.4	15.9
Fourth	22.4	23.4	23.7	24.1	23.9	24.0	24.0
Highest	41.1	38.4	40.0	38.4	40.0	40.6	46.6
Total	100.0	100.0	100.0	100.0	100.0	100.0	100.0

* Quintiles divide those with income into five equal categories. The distribution refers to the percentage of total income going to each category.

SOURCES: Fréchette (1988); Statistics Canada, Catalogue No. 13-207; U.S. Bureau of the Census (1991).

cent of all income, in the United States the comparable figure is 3.9 percent. In Canada, the highest quintile receives 40.6 percent of income where in the U.S. it receives 46.6 percent. Thus, the difference between rich and poor is more marked in the U.S., where income distribution is more clearly skewed towards the highest quintile. Furthermore, while the distribution of income within Canada has remained stable, income disparity actually increased in the U.S. during the 1980s as a result of changes in the economy, new tax policies, and cuts in social programs that assist low-income people (Levy, 1987; Reich, 1989). Figure 10–2 places Canada closer to Germany with respect to income distribution. In the United States, Switzerland, and Great Britain, the top 20 percent of income earners take home larger portions of their national incomes.

Canada Map 10–1 shows the median income for each province and territory within Canada, suggesting that 1995 incomes are lowest in Newfoundland and highest in the two territories and Ontario. Median incomes range from a low of $13 972 in Newfoundland to $24 970 in the Yukon.

WEALTH

Income is but one component of a person's or family's **wealth**, *the total amount of money and other assets, minus outstanding debts*. Wealth in the form of stocks, bonds, real estate, and other privately owned property is distributed even less equally than income. Paul Desmarais, for example, has to declare his "income" to Revenue Canada, but not the value of his mansions or business holdings. It is the control of these kinds of assets that really sets the wealthy apart from the average person or the poor in Canada. When the political left talks of establishing a wealth tax and an inheritance tax, it is this component of wealth that it seeks to redistribute.

POWER

In Canadian society, as elsewhere, wealth stands as an important source of power. Major owners of corporate stock, for example, make decisions that create jobs for ordinary people or scale back operations, throwing people out of work.

More broadly, the "super-rich" families who own most of the nation's wealth have a great deal of say about the national political agenda (Clement, 1975; Francis, 1986). Chapter 16 ("Politics and Government") raises a question that has engaged sociologists for decades: can a society maintain a political democracy if a small share of the population controls most of the wealth? Some analysts maintain that while the rich

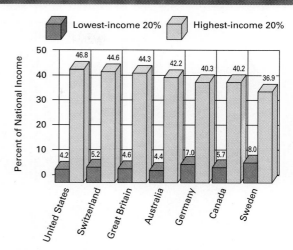

GLOBAL SNAPSHOT

Lowest-income 20%   Highest-income 20%

FIGURE 10–2 Income Disparities for Selected Industrial Countries

SOURCE: The World Bank (1997).

may have some advantages, they do not dominate the political process. Others argue that, in general, the political system represents the interests of the wealthy.

OCCUPATIONAL PRESTIGE

Occupation is a major determinant of income, wealth, and power. In addition, it serves as a key source of social prestige, since we commonly evaluate each other according to the kind of work we do, respecting some while looking down on others. Once we learn that Bonnie Shnier Monik is the President of Gesco Industries, Inc., we can make numerous assumptions about her lifestyle, education, and income. We are likely to treat her with respect and listen more closely to her opinions.

For more than half a century, sociologists have measured the relative social prestige of various occupations (Counts, 1925; Blishen, 1958; Hodge, Treiman, and Rossi, 1966; Blishen et al., 1987). Surveys asking respondents to rate occupations in terms of prestige produce a ranking that reflects both income and education. Physicians, lawyers, and engineers (high on income and education) are ranked near the top on prestige, while cashiers and janitors are ranked near the bottom. In global perspective, occupational prestige rankings tend to be roughly the same in all industrial societies (Ma, 1987). Almost everywhere, white-collar work that involves mental activity free from extensive supervision confers greater prestige

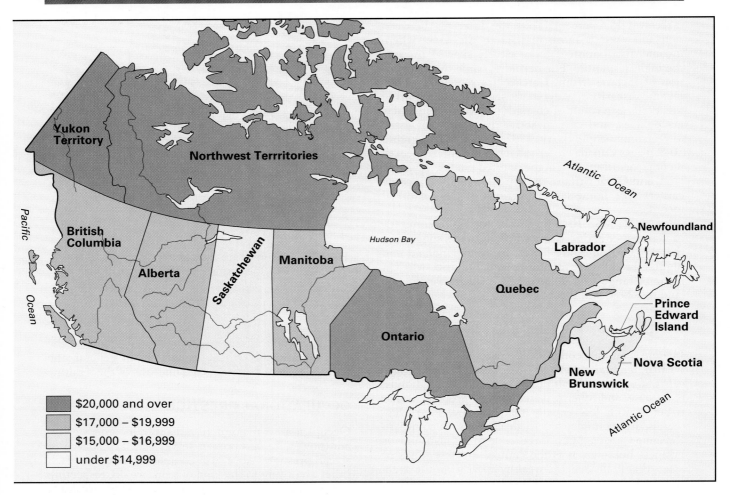

CANADA MAP 10–1 Median Incomes by Province and Territory, 1995

SOURCE: Data from Statistics Canada, www.statcan.ca.

than blue-collar occupations that require supervised, manual labour. There are exceptions to this pattern, however. For example, a blue-collar aircraft mechanic enjoys greater social prestige than a white-collar filing clerk.

Table 10–2 shows the ranking of various occupational categories in Canada in 1986, based on the Blishen scale, which uses income and education to assess socioeconomic status and produces a ranking very similar to the survey-based prestige scales. In a ranking of 514 census occupations, physicians and surgeons come out at the top with a score of 101.3, while newspaper carriers and vendors scored 17.8. Collapsing occupations into broader categories makes certain patterns apparent (Creese et al., 1991). In the middle range of occupations, the Blishen scores are lower for women than for men—particularly in the various white- and blue-collar categories. This is where the *pink ghetto* jobs—lower status and poorly paid—are concentrated. Women and men have similar educational levels across occupational categories, with the few differences usually resulting from higher educational attainment among women. There are, however, marked differences in the incomes of women and men: in most of the occupational categories, women earn about 60 percent of male income, but in the professional and semi-professional/technical categories, the figures are 72 and 84 percent respectively. Though not apparent in the table, Creese et al. (1991) note that self-employed profes-

TABLE 10–2 Occupational Categories by Average Blishen Scores, Years of Schooling, Income, and Sex, 1986

Occupation	Blishen Scores		Years of Schooling		Income ($)	
	Male	Female	Male	Female	Male	Female
1. High-level management	69	67	14.0	14.0	62,555	36,637
2. Professional	65	65	15.0	15.0	38,226	27,672
3. Middle management	52	52	13.0	13.0	36,935	21,894
4. Semi-professional/technician	52	51	13.6	14.0	30,784	25,732
5. Upper (skilled) white-collar	46	42	12.7	12.9	37,334	18,005
6. Upper (skilled) blue-collar	44	37	11.0	11.6	28,572	18,476
7. Lower (unskilled) white-collar	33	32	12.0	12.0	23,016	13,301
8. Lower (unskilled) blue-collar	32	28	10.5	10.0	22,186	13,444
9. Farmers	28	28	10.0	14.0	26,528	–13,147*
10. Farm labourers	24	24	10.0	11.0	14,774	8,830

* The negative income reflects net losses for some farmers. Since there are relatively few female farmers, a large net loss for a small number of individuals can produce a negative average income for the category as a whole.

SOURCE: Creese, Guppy, and Meissner (1991:37), based on analysis of data collected for the 1986 General Social Survey.

sional women fare best, earning 88 percent of the income earned by their male counterparts.

The important point here is that social stratification typically involves various dimensions of inequality (based on income and prestige as well as sex and race) *that are superimposed* on each other, forming a complex, and often steep, hierarchy.

SCHOOLING

Education is an important determinant of labour force participation, occupation, and income, so it is highly valued in industrial societies. Although industrial societies generally define schooling as everyone's right, the opportunity for formal education is not always equal. In Canada, traditionally, women did not pursue formal education as far as their male counterparts; however, in recent years, more than half of the undergraduate degrees and community college diplomas have been earned by women (though they have not caught up with men in earning master's and doctoral degrees). Table 10–2 suggests that while educational differences between men and women employed in similar jobs are minimal, overall, women have completed slightly more years of schooling than their male colleagues.

Schooling not only promotes personal development but also affects an individual's occupation and income. Individuals with higher levels of schooling are more likely to be in the labour force, to be employed rather than unemployed, and to earn higher incomes (Secretary of State, 1992).

ASCRIPTION AND SOCIAL STRATIFICATION

To a large extent, the class system in Canada rewards individual talent and effort. But, as explained in Chap-

ter 9 ("Social Stratification"), class systems still rest on ascription: who we are at birth greatly influences what we become later in life.

ANCESTRY

Nothing affects social standing in Canada as much as our birth into a particular family—an event over which we have no control. Ancestry determines our point of entry into the system of social inequality. Some Canadian families, including the Reichmans, Blacks, Bentleys, Irvings, and Campeaus, are known around the world. On a more modest scale, certain families in practically every Canadian community have wealth and power that have become well established over several generations.

Being born to privilege or poverty sets the stage for our future schooling, occupation, and income. Although there are numerous "rags to riches" stories in Canada, many of the richest individuals—those with hundreds of millions of dollars in wealth—derived their fortunes primarily through inheritance. By the same token, the "inheritance" of poverty and the lack of opportunity that goes with it just as surely shape the future of those in need. The family, in short, transmits property, power, and possibilities from one generation to the next, contributing to the persistence of social stratification.

GENDER

People of both sexes are born into families at every social level. Women born into families of high social standing, therefore, draw on many more social resources than men born into disadvantaged families. Yet, on average, women earn lower income, accumulate less wealth, enjoy lower occupational prestige,

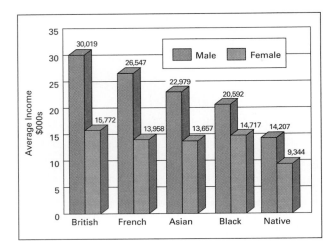

FIGURE 10–3 Average Income* in Canada by Gender for Selected Categories, 1990

* Figures based on populations fifteen years of age and over, including individuals with no income.

SOURCE: Compiled by Gerber from Canada Census 1991, Public Use Microdata.

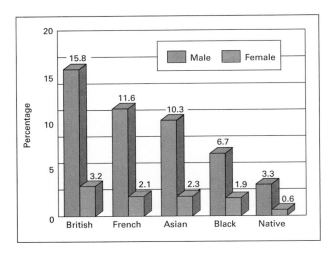

FIGURE 10–4 Percentage* in Canada with Incomes of $50 000 or More, by Gender for Selected Categories, 1990

* These figures refer to percentages of populations fifteen years of age and over.

SOURCE: Compiled by Gerber from Canada Census 1991, Public Use Microdata.

and rank lower in *some* aspects of educational achievement than men do (Bernard, 1981; Lengermann and Wallace, 1985; Creese, Guppy, and Meissner, 1991).

Later in the chapter, you will discover that women do not "inherit" the social position of their fathers to the extent that men do. You will also learn that households headed by women are many times more likely to be poor than are those headed by men. A full picture of the link between gender and social stratification is found in Chapter 12 ("Sex and Gender").

RACE AND ETHNICITY

Although we tend to think of our society as largely egalitarian, race and ethnicity remain important determinants of social position. In Chapter 19 ("Education") we shall see that, in Canada, people of Asian origin have higher levels of educational attainment than those of British and French origin and that Blacks are ahead on some educational measures and labour force participation. The native population, on the other hand, has not acquired the same levels of education or gained the same access to employment as have others in Canada. Figures 10–3 and 10–4 suggest that race and ethnicity have a bearing on income as well.

In Figure 10–3, we see that, for men, average incomes decline steadily as we move from the British through the French, Asian, Black, and native cate-

gories. Among men, the three visible minority categories have lower incomes than the British and the French. Among women, the differences are not as clear in that the average income of Black women is greater than those of women of French and Asian origin. This is in part the result of substantial education and high levels of labour force involvement (including full-time employment) among Black women.

Figure 10–4 reveals income differences based on a different measure. The bars in the graph indicate the proportion of the population (fifteen years of age and over) in each category with incomes of $50 000 or more—and on this measure the intercategory differences are much more dramatic. The proportion of British males in this high-income category is almost *five* times that of the native males. Women in each of the ethnic or racial categories have fewer members in the $50 000-plus income category than their male counterparts. Note that British women are *five* times as likely to be in the high-income category as are native women. In terms of entry into the highest income levels, the French are behind the British while the three visible minorities trail behind the French: clearly, natives are the most disadvantaged in terms of income.

While it is true that income is only one dimension of social class, race and ethnicity are clearly associated with differential placement in the socioeconomic hierarchy of Canada.

People often distinguish between the "new rich" and those with "old money." Men and women who suddenly begin to earn high incomes tend to spend on "status symbols" because they enjoy the new thrill of high-roller living and they want others to know of their success. Those who grow up surrounded by wealth, on the other hand, are used to a privileged way of life and are more quiet about it. Thus, the "conspicuous consumption" of the lower-upper class (left) can differ dramatically from the more private pursuits and understatement of the upper-upper class (right).

SOCIAL CLASSES IN CANADA

As Chapter 9 ("Social Stratification") explained, people living in rigid caste systems can tell anyone's social ranking at a glance. Assessing the social position in a more fluid class system, however, poses a number of challenges.

Consider the joke about the fellow who orders a pizza, asking that it be cut into six slices because he isn't hungry enough to eat eight. While sociologists acknowledge extensive social inequality in Canada, they have long debated precisely how to divide up this social hierarchy. Some who follow Karl Marx's thinking contend that there are two major classes; other sociologists suggest that North American society breaks down into as many as six categories (Warner and Lunt, 1941). Still others align themselves with Max Weber, believing that people form a multidimensional status hierarchy, rather than clear-cut classes.

Defining classes in Canada is difficult due to the relatively low level of status consistency. Especially towards the middle of the hierarchy, an individual's social standing on one dimension often contradicts that person's position on another (Tepperman, 1979; Gilbert and Kahl, 1987). A government official, for example, may control a multimillion-dollar budget yet earn a modest income. Similarly, members of the clergy typically enjoy ample prestige while possessing only moderate power and earning low pay. Or consider a lucky professional gambler who may win little respect but who accumulates considerable wealth.

Finally, the social mobility typical of class systems—again, most pronounced near the middle—means that social position often changes during one's lifetime. This mobility further blurs the lines between social classes.

Despite these problems of definition, it is useful to think of four general social classes in Canada: the upper class, the middle class, the working class, and the lower class. As we shall explain, however, some categories are more clear-cut than others.

THE UPPER CLASS

The upper class, encompassing perhaps 3 to 5 percent of the population, derives much of its income from inherited wealth, in the form of stocks and bonds, real estate, and other investments. And this income may be substantial. In January 1996, the *Financial Post* magazine profiled fifty of the richest individuals and families in Canada, each of them with a minimum net worth of at least $145 million and eight of them worth at least $1 billion. On the top is Kenneth R. Thompson with a net worth of $8.2 *billion* (Hamilton, 1996). The upper class thus comprises what Karl Marx termed "capitalists," those who own or control most of the nation's productive property.

Despite this immense wealth, many members of the upper class work as top executives in large corporations—often earning salaries of $500 000 or more: in 1994, CEOs Brian Hannan of Methanex Corp. and Frank Stronach of Magna International were rewarded to the tune of $13 million and $41 million, respectively (Newman, 1996:185). As corporate executives and as senior government officials, these

Computers and Social Class

In the past decade or so Canada ceased to be an industrial society and moved through to the post-industrial phase. This means that the service sector has expanded to include a high proportion of knowledge-based industries, and this in turn means that there is more and more reliance on information technology in a wide range of work environments. If computer literacy, in particular, is increasingly the key to opportunity in Canada, the question of *who* becomes comfortable with the technology is of considerable importance.

Schools across Canada (in rural or urban, affluent or poor communities) are gradually introducing computers into the classroom from the earliest grades: where available, special school networks and the Internet have ex-

panded horizons and revolutionized the learning process. But the number of computers available is usually limited,

so that individual students often have little opportunity to put new skills into practice. The most adept students (often the boys) tend to monopolize the equipment while the more reticent watch from the sidelines. As long as the supply of computers in the classroom is limited, additional exposure to computers in the home environment will play an important role in skill development. It is here that social class background has an impact.

John Goyder (1997) examined patterns of technology diffusion in Canada, comparing the presence of telephones in 1911 and personal computers (PCs) in 1994 in the homes of people in various occupational categories. Note that both of these technologies started off in offices and were later adopted in homes.

---

privileged individuals further enhance their power to shape events in the nation and, increasingly, the entire world.

Members of the upper class also attain the highest levels of education, typically in the most expensive and highly regarded schools and universities. Historically, though less so today, the upper class has been composed of people of British origin (Porter, 1975; Clement, 1975; Tepperman, 1979). Today, among the fifty most wealthy families or individuals noted above, about half are of British origin and the rest a mix of Jewish, French, other European, and one Asian. Over the next decade or two we can expect to find an increasing number of Asians represented in this highly select group.

Upper-Uppers

The *upper-upper class*, often described as "society" or "bluebloods," includes less than 1 percent of the Canadian population. Membership is usually the result of ascription or birth, as suggested by the old quip that the easiest way to break into "society" is to be born there. These families possess enormous wealth, primarily inherited rather than earned. For this reason, members of the upper-upper class are said to have *old money*.

Set apart by their wealth, members of the upper-upper class live in a world of exclusive affiliations. They inhabit elite neighbourhoods, such as Forest Hill in Toronto or Westmount in Montreal. Schools extend this privileged environment. Their children typically attend private schools such as Upper Canada College with others of similar background, completing their formal education at high-prestige universities such as Cambridge, Oxford, or Harvard. In the historical pattern of European aristocrats, they study liberal arts rather than vocationally directed subjects.

Women of the upper-upper class often maintain a full schedule of volunteer work for charitable organizations. For example, women from Toronto's upper-crust neighbourhoods are the backbone of the Toronto Symphony and the National Ballet: old-money families support these organizations, offering their time as well as funds. While helping the larger community, such charitable activities also build networks that put these families at the centre of this nation's power elite (Ostrander, 1980, 1984).

Lower-Uppers

The remaining 2 to 4 percent of the population that make up the upper class falls into the *lower-upper class*. From the point of view of the average Canadian, such

The more affluent homes were more likely to have both telephones and computers. Home telephone subscribers in 1911, in Kingston, Ontario, were overwhelmingly in the professional and managerial categories: 96 percent of professionals had telephones at home, compared with 3 percent of those in skilled and semi-skilled trades. In 1994 PCs were more evenly distributed in the homes of various occupational categories. Among professionals (employed and self-employed), 61 percent had computers at home, compared to 24 percent of unskilled craft and farm labourers. Considering the expense of computers, the fact that about 25 percent of households in the four lowest occupational categories have PCs is remarkable and indicative of the centrality of computers in modern Canadian life. The absence of computers in the homes of 39 percent of pro-

fessionals may be a function of age: some older professionals have not adopted computers either in the office or at home.

Goyder also looked at the relationships between schooling, age, and province of residence and the ownership of home computers. As one might expect, there is a clear and strong relationship between years of schooling and computer ownership: among those with one to five years of schooling, 2 percent have computers at home; at the opposite extreme, 55 percent of those with thirteen or more years of education have computers. (If university and graduate education had been measured, computer ownership might have been higher.) Among respondents fifteen to nineteen years of age, 48 percent have computers, while among those seventy years of age and over, only about 4 percent have computers in

their homes. PCs are most prevalent in Ontario and Alberta homes (38 percent) and least prevalent in the Atlantic provinces (about 20 percent)—a pattern that is consistent with relative income levels.

In a society in which economic development is focused on knowledge-based industries, computer technology is being applied very widely, even in underground mining. Computer literacy is increasingly distinguishing the highly employable from those who face multiple barriers to satisfactory employment. If the children of the affluent have more exposure to computers at school, and that exposure is augmented by the presence of computers in the home, social class position will be perpetuated in the younger generation.

people seem every bit as privileged as the upper-upper class. The major difference, however, is that "lower-uppers" are the "working rich" who depend on earnings rather than wealth as their primary source of income. Few people in this category inherit a vast fortune from their parents, although the majority do inherit some wealth.

Especially in the eyes of members of "society," the lower-upper class are merely the "new rich," people who can never savour the highest levels of prestige enjoyed by those with rich and famous grandparents. Thus, while the new rich typically live in expensive homes, they often find themselves excluded from the most prestigious clubs and associations maintained by old-money families.

Historically, the dream of great success has meant joining the ranks of the lower-upper class through exceptional accomplishment. The entrepreneurial individual who makes the right business moves with split-second timing, the athlete who accepts a million-dollar contract to play in the big leagues, the clever computer whiz who designs a new program that sets a standard for the industry—these are the lucky and talented achievers who reach the level of the lower-upper class. Their success stories fascinate most of us because this kind of upward social mobility has long stood as a goal that, however unlikely, is still within

the realm of the possible. A dual-earner family in which both wife and husband are professionals *can* make it into this lower-upper stratum of the upper 5 percent of families (as measured by income). Members of the upper-upper class, in contrast, move in rarefied circles far from the everyday reality of the rest of us: we know so little about them that we cannot emulate them.

THE MIDDLE CLASS

Encompassing about 40 to 50 percent of the Canadian population, the middle class exerts tremendous influence on patterns of North American culture. Television and other mass media usually portray middle-class people, and most commercial advertising is directed at these "average" consumers. The middle class encompasses far more racial and ethnic diversity than the upper class. While many upper-class people (especially "upper-uppers") know each other personally, such exclusiveness and familiarity do not characterize the middle class.

Upper-Middles

The top half of this category is often termed the *upper*-middle class, based on above-average income in

The life of this Newfoundland fisherman has been changed drastically by the moratorium on cod fishing. How do you think different classes are affected by this type of change in the local economy?

the range of $50 000 to $100 000 a year. Such income allows upper-middle-class families gradually to accumulate considerable property—a comfortable house in a fairly expensive area, several automobiles, and some investments. Virtually all upper-middle-class people receive university educations, and postgraduate degrees are common. Many go on to high-prestige occupations (physicians, engineers, lawyers, accountants, or business executives). Lacking the power of the upper class to influence national or international events, the upper-middle class often plays an important role in local political affairs.

Average-Middles

The rest of the middle class typically works in less prestigious white-collar occupations (as bank tellers, middle managers, and sales clerks) or in highly skilled blue-collar jobs (including electrical work and carpentry). Family income is sufficient to provide a secure, if modest, standard of living. Middle-class people generally accumulate a small amount of wealth over the course of their working lives, and most eventually own a house. Middle-class men and women are likely to be high-school graduates themselves. If they do send their children to university, it is more likely to be the one closest to home to save on accommodation expenses.

THE WORKING CLASS

Including about one-third of the population, the working class (sometimes called the "lower-middle class") refers to people who have lower incomes than those in the middle class and little or no accumulated wealth. In

Marxist terms, the working class forms the core of the industrial proletariat. The blue-collar occupations of the working class generally yield a family income that is somewhat below the national average, although unionized blue-collar workers can contribute to family incomes that are well above that level.

Many working-class jobs provide little personal satisfaction—requiring discipline but rarely imagination—and subject workers to continual supervision. These jobs also provide fewer benefits, such as dental insurance and pension plans. University is less likely to be part of the experience of children of working-class parents. The many working-class families who own their own homes are likely to own them in lower-cost neighbourhoods. Still, working-class families express a great deal of pride in what they do have, especially compared to people who are not working at all.

THE LOWER CLASS

The 20 percent of our population with the lowest family income makes up the lower class. A lack of work and little income renders life unstable and insecure. In 1996, over 5 million people (almost 18 percent of our population) were classified by the federal government as poor. While some of these people are supported entirely by social welfare payments, others are among the "working poor"—those whose incomes from working at full-time jobs fall short of what is required to cover necessities such as food, shelter, and clothing.

The working poor have low-prestige jobs that provide minimal income and little intrinsic satisfaction. Some have managed to complete high school, but university degrees and college diplomas are relatively rare. In fact, many lower-class men and women are functionally illiterate.

Lower-class families find themselves segregated into specific, less-desirable neighbourhoods—some of which are ethnically or racially distinct. Although there are many poor people in small towns and rural areas—where resource-based industries have collapsed or plants have closed—physical segregation of the poor is most starkly apparent in cities, where large numbers of poor people live in rental housing shunned by others.

Lower-class children quickly learn that many people consider them only marginal members of society. Observing their parents and other lower-class adults, they may conclude that their own futures hold little hope for breaking the cycle of poverty. Lower-class life, then, often generates self-defeating resignation, as these people are cut off from the resources of an affluent society: welfare dependency, as a lifestyle, can be passed from one generation to the next. Some of the poor simply give up, but others work sometimes at two or three jobs to make ends meet, going to great lengths to avoid going on welfare.

The policies of the Klein and Harris governments in Alberta and Ontario have led to reductions in welfare payments and tighter eligibility requirements. Fewer people are on welfare but no one yet knows where the missing welfare recipients have gone or how they are managing to survive.

CLASS, FAMILY, AND GENDER

Family life is closely related to social class. Because the typical individual marries someone of comparable social position, distinctive family patterns correspond to each class level. For example, because lower-class people marry earlier in life and make less use of birth control, they have more children than middle-class parents do.

Working-class parents encourage children to conform to conventional norms and remain obedient and respectful to authority figures. By contrast, parents of higher social standing transmit a different "cultural capital" to their children, motivating them to express their individuality and to use their imaginations more freely. This difference reflects parents' expectations about their children's future: the odds are that less-privileged children will take jobs demanding close adherence to specified rules, while most advantaged children will enter fields that call for more creativity (Kohn, 1977; McLeod, 1985).

Of course, it stands to reason that the more social resources a family has, the more parents can develop their children's talents and abilities. An affluent family will spend $300 000 or more in raising a child to the age of eighteen. Ballet, music lessons, summer camp, and (for some) private-school education provide opportunities about which poor families may not even dream. Such differences underline how privilege tends to beget privilege as family life reproduces the class structure in each generation.

Class also shapes the relationship between spouses. Elizabeth Bott (1971) documented that working-class couples maintain a rigid division of responsibilities according to gender. Middle-class marriages, by contrast, are more egalitarian, sharing more activities as well as greater intimacy. Keeping this insight in mind, we can understand why divorce is more common among disadvantaged couples, whose limited communication skills may be overwhelmed by the stress of low-income living (Kitson and Raschke, 1981; National Council of Welfare, 1990:60–61). Lack of love, poor communication, adultery, and alcohol and wife abuse are important contributors to marriage breakdown among the poor.

SOCIAL MOBILITY

Ours is a dynamic society marked by a significant measure of social mobility. As we noted in the last chapter, social mobility involves individuals moving upward or downward in the stratification system. Earning a university degree, securing a higher-paying job, or succeeding in a business endeavour contributes to *upward social mobility*, while dropping out of school, losing a job, or having a business enterprise fail may signal the onset of *downward social mobility*.

Over the long term, most social mobility is not a matter of individual decision as much as changes in society itself. During the first half of this century, for example, industrialization expanded the economy, dramatically raising living standards for the majority of Canadians. Even without being very good swimmers, so to speak, people were able to "ride a rising tide of prosperity." As explained presently, *structural social mobility* in a downward direction has more recently dealt many people economic setbacks.

In studying social mobility, sociologists distinguish between changes within a single generation and shifts between generations of a family. **Intragenerational social mobility** refers to *a change in social position occurring during a person's lifetime*. **Intergenerational social mobility**, *upward or downward social mobility of children in relation to their parents*, has special significance because it reveals long-term changes in society that affect virtually everyone.

MYTH VERSUS REALITY

Although the "American Dream" may be attributed to people south of the border, Canadians share the

Middle-Class Stampede?

Who participates in community festivals? Surely, the Calgary Stampede, for example, draws a cross-section of the community (and of Canadians from a wide geographic area) into a generalized tension-release ritual. Without a doubt "yahoos" and "yippees" will be part of the spontaneous vocabulary of people everywhere. Right?

Richard J. Ossenberg set out to show that while homogeneous communities might give rise to generalized participation, complex urban centres such as Calgary would elicit differentiated or selective participation. His research involved "a systematic pub-crawl on two evenings of the weeklong Stampede" held every July. He expected to find that members of the middle class, who are more "sensitive to legal and other restrictive norms," might be most likely to respond to the relaxation of social controls with "festival-related aggressive/expressive behaviour."

Ossenberg had already carried out extensive analysis of Calgary bar behaviour as a way of discovering the social class structure in Calgary, so he knew which nine of the city's beer parlours and lounges would represent a "cross-section of social-class-related drinking establishments." Those chosen for the study were close to the Stampede grounds; two were upper-class, three were middle-class, and four were lower-class. The establishments are described as follows:

The upper-class establishments are usually patronized by the elite oil

and ranching group as well as the nouveau riche and the occasional white-collar couple celebrating an anniversary. The middle-class bars are patronized by clerical workers, small businessmen, and generally middle-range employees of the larger local firms, with the occasional labourers drifting in. The lower-class bars are the clearest in definition. They are patronized by service personnel, labourers, winos and deprived Indians as well as by members of newly-arrived immigrant groups.

During the two evenings of observation "only about one in ten of the tipplers at the lower-class establishments wore Western cowboy costume, and most of those who did were completely ignored by the other patrons." The noise level was lower than usual, fights broke out less frequently, prostitutes were more in evidence, and patrons stuck to the normal men's parlour and "ladies and escorts" pattern, even though restrictions were lifted during the Stampede. And there were virtually no rodeo-related "yahoos" to be heard.

In the middle-class establishments—two cocktail lounges and one beer parlour in a posh hotel—90 percent or more of the patrons were in cowboy or Western costumes. In fact, the researchers were ridiculed for their lack of such attire. The noise levels were intolerable, "yippees" and "yahoos" filled the air, and back slapping and necking were the norm. Executives interacted freely with their secretaries

and tourists or strangers were readily accepted and even invited to house parties. Call girls, rather than streetwalkers, made their appearances.

The two upper-middle-class cocktail lounges in Calgary's plush, reputable hotels presented a very different picture. About 25 percent of patrons were costumed, but the noisy celebration was missing. Here, as in the working-class bars, it was business as usual. The few costumed patrons who tried to liven up the scene soon left in disgust: "Let's blow this joint—it's like a graveyard."

Ossenberg concluded that Stampede week is "functional" for people who are inhibited in their daily lives and "look forward to the 'green light' of tolerated deviance during a community festival." Behaviour during such festivals reflects the social structure of the city but does not reinforce solidarity across class lines. It is, in effect, a "middle-class 'binge.'"

Postscript: In January 1996, Calgary had its first (annual) cowboy convention, in opulent surroundings. Here cowboys and cowgirls—the authentic and the "wannabes"—gathered to share cowboy lore, paraphernalia, and music, or simply to celebrate a way of life. So central is the horse to the cowboy lifestyle that (to the dismay of the hotel staff who had to clean up the plush carpets in their wake), several of the better-known horses were invited to mingle with their fans.

SOURCE: Adapted from Ossenberg (1979).

belief that those who apply themselves can "get ahead" and that each new generation will do better than the last. But how much social mobility is there in Canada?

Data from the 1986 General Social Survey revealed that Canadians have been a little more likely

to experience upward than downward mobility (Creese et al., 1991). Compared with their fathers, 48 percent of women moved up, while 40 percent moved down; the comparable figures for men are 39 and 36 percent respectively. Only 12 percent of women and 26 percent of men experienced no mobility at all, meaning that they were in the same occupational category as their fathers.

Occupational inheritance, or "following in Dad's footsteps," occurs most commonly among men whose fathers are in the professional, white-collar, and farming categories. Specific occupational inheritance has been less common for women because of the types of occupations traditionally available to them.

Though overall educational levels are increasing, class background continues to affect educational attainment: the higher the level of education and occupation of one's father, the more years of schooling one is likely to complete. Furthermore, a person's first job is *principally* affected by his or her level of education. Therefore, parental education and occupation have an impact on occupational status, not directly but through their effects on the educational attainment of the younger generation. For example, a physician passes his occupation on to his child if he inspires that child to jump the educational hurdles required to gain admission to and complete medical school.

Education, then, is the key to occupational mobility in Canada. If family background has an impact, it is through its effect on schooling. But, as we saw earlier, it seems that francophones, visible minorities, and women have difficulty translating their educational accomplishments into higher-status, well-paid work.

Others have also noted the general lack of occupational inheritance in Canada. In a study of occupational mobility over four generations, Goyder and Curtis (1979) found that the occupations of great-grandfathers had no bearing whatsoever on those of their great-grandsons. Occupationally speaking, the descendants were all over the map. On the basis of their findings and those of others who have studied the extreme upper and lower ends of the spectrum, Goyder and Curtis conclude that the "two types of processes may well occur together: high over-all three-generation mobility in the general population along with low three-generation mobility in poverty and elite groups" (p. 229). In other words those at the very top and bottom of the socioeconomic ladder may experience substantial occupational inheritance, while those in the middle do not.

Historically, women have had less opportunity for upward mobility than men. As we shall see in Chapter 12 ("Sex and Gender"), the majority of working women hold clerical positions (think of secretaries) and low-paying service jobs (such as waitresses). These jobs offer little chance for advancement, which effectively limits upward social or economic movement. Divorce also commonly results in downward social mobility for women—but not for men—as Chapter 17 ("Family") explains. Data reflecting

Education is key to occupational mobility in Canada. As many provinces reverse or at least relax policies that improve financial accessibility to post-secondary education for people at lower-income levels, will there continue to be an upgrading of educational levels between generations?

income change during the 1980s and early 1990s reveal a narrowing of the gap between the earnings of women and men, with the female-to-male income ratio increasing from about 60 percent to over 70 percent.

THE GLOBAL ECONOMY AND CANADIAN CLASS STRUCTURE

For generations of immigrants as well as the Canadian-born, Canada has been a land of opportunity. In global perspective, the rates of social mobility in this country have been about the same as those of the United States and other industrial societies. As the economies of the world become more interrelated, we can expect that the structural shifts—both upward and downward—that occur in Europe and Japan will mirror those we experience here in North America.

In the last few years, Canada—in the company of much of the industrial world—has been going through economic restructuring and upheaval that will undoubtedly upset normal patterns of mobility. Some of the industrial production that provided highly paid jobs for Canadians has been transferred to the United States (partly in response to the Free Trade Agreement) and to developing countries overseas. Throughout the negotiation of the North American Free Trade Agreement (NAFTA), companies were already moving to Mexico from Canada and the U.S. in anticipation of more open borders. While industrial jobs migrate out of the country, a growing

North American culture has long held the idea that, through talent and hard work, people can make their dreams come true. Do you think that social position is more a matter of individual effort or more a matter of the social class into which we are born? Why?

proportion of the new jobs being created in Canada are in the service sector, which often requires lower skill levels and pays poorly. In the meantime, a large number of highly specialized jobs remain unfilled because Canada has not produced a workforce with the required skills.

The process of deindustrialization has hurt the standard of living of Canadians and shaken our confidence. Industrial jobs are giving way to service jobs, full-time employment is disappearing and being replaced by part-time work, and real income has declined since 1989. Compared to a generation ago, far fewer now expect to improve their social position, and a growing number of Canadians worry that their children will not be able to maintain the same standard of living as themselves. The standard of living in Canada has stopped rising, even though women and men are working harder than ever and more families have two or more people in the labour force.

The mixed performance of Canada's economy through the 1980s and 1990s, like that of other industrialized countries, has generated intense controversy and debate—particularly with respect to the role of government in the economy, job creation, income maintenance, and the alleviation of poverty.

POVERTY IN CANADA

Social stratification simultaneously creates "haves" and "have-nots." Poverty, therefore, inevitably exists within all systems of social inequality. Sociologists employ the concept of poverty in two different ways, however. **Relative poverty**, which is by definition universal and inevitable, refers to *the deprivation of some people in relation to those who have more*. The richest and most egalitarian of societies have some members who live in relative poverty. Much more serious is **absolute poverty**, or a *deprivation of resources that is life-threatening*. Defined in this way, poverty is a pressing, but solvable, human problem.

As the next chapter ("Global Stratification") explains, the global dimensions of absolute poverty place the lives of perhaps 800 million people—one in seven of the earth's entire population—at risk. Even in affluent Canada, with its social welfare safety net, families go hungry, live in inadequate housing, and endure poor health because of wrenching poverty.

THE EXTENT OF CANADIAN POVERTY

Poverty statistics are based on the "poverty line," also known as the "low-income cutoff." People who spend at least 55 percent of their pretax income on food, clothing, and shelter are considered to be below the poverty line. In 1995, the income cutoffs for families of four were $21 944 in rural areas and $31 753 in a city such as Vancouver. Accordingly, there were about 4.5 million Canadians in 1995 who had incomes below the poverty line (Colombo, 1997b:79)—17.8 percent of the Canadian population. The 1996 rate was 17.9 percent (Statistics Canada, *The Daily*, December 22, 1997).

Our lack of progress in eliminating poverty prompted a United Nations committee to sharply criticize the Canadian government "for allowing poverty and homelessness to persist at disturbing levels in one of the world's richest countries" (York, 1993:A1). We have been criticized by the UN committee because of the poverty of more than half of our single mothers and a million children, and dependence on voluntary food banks to deal with hunger. The report goes on to criticize Canada for the fact that, over the past decade, we have made "no measurable progress" in alleviating poverty.

Poverty means hunger, and many of the people at lower income levels are forced to rely on food banks and soup kitchens, both of which, in Canada, are run by voluntary organizations. The demand for food banks has increased substantially over the past few years to a point where, in 1992, Canada's 372 food banks were serving, on a regular basis, two million people, 40 percent of whom were under sixteen years of age (Colombo, 1992:88). The fact that so many people feel the need to resort to food banks, which function only because some people volunteer to staff them while others donate food, is particularly distressing in a country where we *have* the resources to alleviate poverty, if only we had the political will.

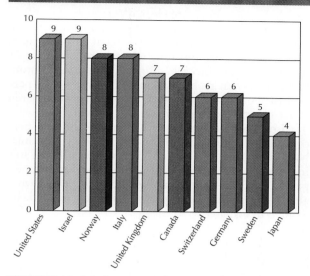

FIGURE 10–5 Infant Mortality Rates* for Selected Countries, 1993

* Number of deaths among infants under one year of age for every 1000 live births.

SOURCE: The World Bank (1995).

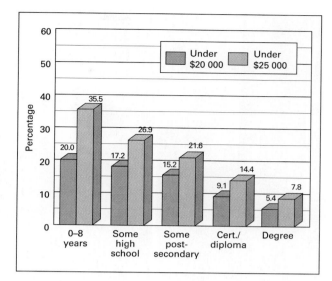

FIGURE 10–6 Low Income Among Canadian Families, 1996, by Education of Family Head

SOURCE: Adapted from Statistics Canada, *Income Distribution by Size in Canada*, 1991, Catalogue No. 13-207.

WHO ARE THE POOR?

Although no single description covers all poor people, poverty is pronounced among certain categories of our population. Children, women, certain visible minorities (specifically natives), and those who live in rural areas are all at higher risk of being poor. Regional disparities in economic development and income are also in evidence in that poverty is a particularly acute problem in the Atlantic provinces, Quebec, and the North. With any combination of the above factors, the problem of poverty is especially serious.

Age

The burden of poverty falls heavily on children. In 1995, almost 1.4 million young Canadians (21 percent of our children) were classified as poor. From another perspective, slightly more than three in ten poor Canadians are children and teenagers under the age of eighteen. Although there are no comparable data on child poverty available for other countries, selected infant mortality rates—shown in Figure 10–5—suggest that this problem is greater in the United States than in other industrial societies. In fact, despite having a high standard of living, the United States stands twentieth in global child mortality rates. Canada's rate is lower but still above that of certain European countries.

A generation ago, the elderly were at greatest risk for poverty. By 1990, the poverty rate for women and men over the age of sixty-five was 19.3 percent; by 1995, the rate was a slightly lower 18.7 percent. Although the situation of our elderly has improved over several decades, with better pension support from the government and private employers, the growing numbers of elderly people suggest that this category will increasingly contribute to the numbers of poor people in Canada. The appearance of the baby boomers among the retired, following difficult economic times and cutbacks in government services, means that in the future we are likely to see an increase in the number of the elderly poor.

Education

Education is another factor that determines the likelihood of having an income below the poverty line. People who have higher levels of education are less likely to be unemployed and more likely to have higher incomes. Not surprisingly, they are also less likely to fall below the poverty line—as indicated in Figure 10–6, where the incidence of poverty drops with each added level of education.

Race and Ethnicity

The likelihood of experiencing poverty is related to race and ethnicity in Canada, but the ranking of various

Three in ten poor Canadians are children. Researchers have linked rising rates of child poverty to the increasing share of single-parent households.

categories is not necessarily what we might expect. Those of British origin are not all at the top of the income hierarchy; in fact, in a ranking of sixty ethnic and racial categories by average male income for those employed full-time all year (Gerber, 1990:79), those of *English* origin rank twenty-fifth. The French, too, are near the middle. Canadians of Welsh and Scottish background appear in the top fifteen, along with those of Jewish and Japanese descent.

In the bottom fifteen categories we find Blacks, West Indians, Latin Americans, some of the Asian groups, and the Métis, Inuit, and North American Indians. The only categories that rank below the North American Indians are groups that tend to be recent immigrants and possibly refugees—Chileans and "other" Latin Americans, Vietnamese, Haitians, Laotians, and Cambodians. While male income for those employed full-time is only *one* indicator of economic well-being, the rank ordering by race or ethnicity is suggestive. We would expect to find that more of the individuals or families in the bottom fifteen categories have incomes below the poverty line.

Gender and Family Patterns

The disparity in male and female incomes and the fact that lone-parent families tend to be headed by females contribute to higher rates of poverty among women. The Statistics Canada Web site (www.statcan.ca) provides data that help account for the **feminization of poverty**, *the trend by which women represent an increas-ing proportion of the poor*. The effects of pay or employment inequity and family structure on the economic well-being of women are clear. Women are less likely to be employed—52 percent of adult women are employed, as compared to 66 percent of adult men. Women who work full-time all year are paid only 71 percent of male income. Further, women are more likely than men to be working part-time—29.4 percent of female workers work part-time, as compared to 10.5 percent of male workers.

Lone-parent families, which made up 14.5 percent of all families in 1995, are more likely than husband-wife families to fall below the official low income line, as Figure 10–7 shows. Women head 83 percent of lone-parent families. In 1995, there were almost a million lone-parent families headed by women in Canada.

In 1995, the average income for female-headed lone-parent families was 47 percent of that of two-parent families. Furthermore, 48 percent of female-headed lone-parent families fall below the poverty line, while that is true of only 12.6 percent of two-parent families, as Figure 10–8 illustrates.

It is clear, then, that lone-parent families have substantially lower incomes that two-parent families, and that female-headed lone-parent families are the most disadvantaged. Issues of pay equity, employment equity, and family structure combine to increase the incidence of poverty among women, thus contributing to the feminization of poverty.

EXPLAINING POVERTY

The presence of 4.5 million poor people in one of the world's most affluent societies raises serious social and moral concerns. It also sparks considerable controversy within Canada—and from abroad. Many Canadians concur with the UN committee mentioned earlier, arguing that our government should take a much more active role in eradicating poverty. Others feel that the poor must bear responsibility for themselves. It is also possible to argue, as some do, that *both* governments and the poor themselves need to contribute to the solution. We now turn to arguments underlying each of these two approaches to the problem of poverty, which together frame a lively and pressing political debate.

One View: Blame the Poor

Proponents of one side of the issue hold the following view: *the poor are primarily responsible for their own poverty*. In this land of immigration and once seemingly unlimited resources and opportunities, we have embraced the notion that people are largely responsi-

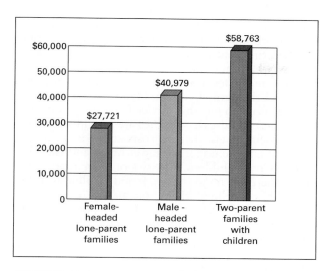

FIGURE 10–7 Average Family Income by Family Structure, 1995

SOURCE: Statistics Canada, *The Daily*, May 12, 1998.

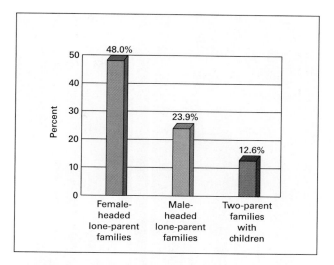

FIGURE 10–8 Percentage of Families with Low Income by Family Structure, 1995

SOURCE: Statistics Canada, *The Daily*, May 12, 1998.

ble for their own social standing. This approach assumes that our society offers considerable opportunity for anyone able and willing to take advantage of it. The poor, then, are those with fewer skills, less schooling, lower motivation, or, perhaps, a debilitating drug addiction—in sum, people who are somehow undeserving.

Anthropologist Oscar Lewis (1961) illustrates this approach in his studies of Latin American poverty. Lewis claims that the poor become entrapped in a *culture of poverty* that fosters resignation to one's plight as a matter of fate. Socialized in this environment, children come to believe that there is little point aspiring to a better life. The result is a self-perpetuating cycle of poverty.

Edward Banfield (1974) adds the contention that, where there is intense poverty, there exists a distinctive lower-class subculture that denigrates and erodes personal achievement. One element of this subculture, a present-time orientation, encourages living for the moment, rather than looking towards the future by engaging in hard work, saving, and other behaviour likely to promote upward social mobility. In Banfield's view, poor people who live largely for the moment perpetuate their own poverty; he defines this kind of behaviour as basically irresponsible, and he concludes that the poor reap more or less what they deserve.

Counterpoint: Blame Society

The other view of the issue follows this reasoning: *society is primarily responsible for poverty.* This alternative position, argued by William Ryan (1976), holds that society—not the poor—is responsible for poverty because of the way it distributes resources. Looking at this problem in global context, societies that distribute wealth very unequally face a significant poverty problem; societies that strive for more equality (such as Sweden and Japan) lack such extremes of social stratification.

Poverty, Ryan insists, is not inevitable: the problem is simply a matter of low incomes, not personal deficiencies. Ryan interprets any lack of ambition on the part of poor people as a *consequence* rather than a *cause* of their lack of opportunity. He therefore dismisses Banfield's analysis as little more than "blaming the victims" for their own suffering. In Ryan's view, social policies that empower the poor would give them real economic opportunity, and this should yield greater equality.

Critical evaluation. Each of these explanations of poverty has won its share of public support, and each has advocates among government policymakers. Some, particularly on the right of the political spectrum, believe that society should strive to encourage equality of opportunity, but should otherwise adopt a laissez-faire attitude towards the poor. Others, on the left, hold that society should actively reduce poverty by redistributing income in a more equitable manner through programs such as a comprehensive child-care package that would allow poor mothers to gain skills necessary to maintain jobs, or a guaranteed minimum income for every family. Canada has given serious consideration to national programs in both of these areas and might have moved ahead had we not

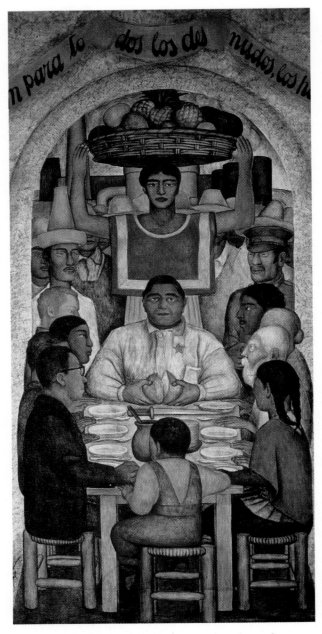

Mexican artist Diego Rivera captured the humility and humanity of poor people in his painting Our Bread. *This insight is important in a society like ours where many people tend to dismiss the poor as morally unworthy and deserving of their bitter plight.*

reflection on society as much as the individuals concerned. Middle-class women combine working and child rearing, but doing so is much harder for poor women who cannot afford child care.

In Canada, few employers provide child-care programs for their employees, and few low-income workers can afford to buy this service from the private sector. Where child-care subsidies are provided, parents may still find that, when all costs are taken into consideration, it is cheaper to stay at home and take care of one's own children. Most poor men report that either there are no jobs to be found, or illness or disability has sidelined them, or, in the case of the elderly, that they have retired. Overall, poor adults are poor, not by choice, but because they know of no alternatives.

The Working Poor

But not all poor people are jobless. At various points in this chapter, tables and figures refer to salaries of people who work full-time all year. Many of these salaries—for women, for certain occupations, and for specific ethnic and racial categories—are low relative to the official poverty line. If these people, working full-time, have incomes that are below the poverty line for individuals, what happens if they are single parents with two or three children? The *working poor* are the men and women who labour for at least fifty weeks of the year and yet cannot escape poverty. Since full-time jobs have decreased and have been replaced with part-time jobs, many people who involuntarily work part-time are also included among the working poor. Such "working poverty" places the poor in a bind: their jobs provide low wages that barely allow them to make ends meet, but consume the time and energy needed to obtain training or schooling that might open new doors. People in this situation are often reluctant or simply unable to risk the jobs they do have in hopes of finding something better. Even with minimum wages of $4.75 to $7.00 in 1995, depending on the province, a full-time worker could not support a family above the official poverty line.

Clearly, individual ability and initiative play a part in shaping everyone's social position. On balance, though, the weight of sociological evidence points to society—not individual character traits—as the primary cause of poverty. This is because the poor are *categories* of people, who contend with special barriers and limited opportunities.

HOMELESSNESS

Many low-income people in Canada cannot afford even basic housing; as a society, we have failed to

turned our attention to the national debt and deficit reduction.

Since the heads of many low-income families do not have jobs, their poverty is attributed to *not holding a job*. But the *reasons* that people do not work are a

ensure an adequate supply of affordable housing. In light of the enormous wealth of our country and its commitment to providing opportunity and/or social safety nets for everyone, homelessness may be fairly described as a societal scar that demands an effective response. The scar consists of thousands of people across the country, living on the streets, in various (often temporary) shelters, and even in our jails.

The familiar stereotypes of homeless people—men sleeping in doorways and women carrying everything they own in a shopping bag—have recently been undermined by the reality of the "new homeless," those thrown out of work because of plant closings; people forced out of apartments by rising rents, condominium conversions, or "gentrification" (e.g., converting rooming houses into expensive single-family homes); and others unable to meet mortgage or rent payments because they must work for low wages. Today, no stereotype paints a complete picture of the homeless.

But virtually all homeless people have one thing in common: *poverty*. For that reason, the explanations of poverty already offered also apply to homelessness. One side of the debate places responsibility on *personal* traits of the homeless themselves. Perhaps one-third of homeless people are mentally ill; others are addicted to alcohol or other drugs. Some, for whatever reason, seem unable to cope in a complex and highly competitive society (Bassuk, 1984; Whitman, 1989).

On the other side of the debate, advocates assert that homelessness results from *societal* factors, including a lack of low-income housing and the economic transition towards low-paying jobs described earlier (Kozol, 1988; Schutt, 1989). Supporters of this position are quick to point out that fully one-third of all homeless people are now entire families, and children are the fastest growing category of the homeless. The closing of a plant, making it necessary for an individual to take a job at McDonald's—at $950 per month, or $11 500 per year—makes it virtually impossible to support a family.

No one disputes that a large proportion of homeless people have personal difficulties to some degree, although how much is cause and how much effect is difficult to untangle. But structural changes in the Canadian economy coupled with declining government support for lower-income people have all contributed to homelessness.

In the winter of 1995–96, the Toronto churches that provide emergency overnight accommodation for the homeless were finding that more *families* were appearing on their doorsteps. Some of these families were evicted by landlords when reduced welfare payments could no longer cover the rent. In the same winter (a record cold one for Toronto), at least two homeless people froze to death while huddled in their

Social scientists debate the causes of poverty, some citing the failings of individuals and others pointing to flaws in society. Whatever side one takes in this controversy, it is impossible to turn away from the drama of children born into poor families. Noted photographer Mary Ellen Marks has followed this family for over a decade. She notes that the children have never known any life but poverty. Whatever their talents may be, are they destined to repeat the ordeal of their parents?

makeshift shelters. One man, who died under a highway ramp, did not even have shoes on his feet.

A comprehensive response to homelessness must consider both personal and societal dimensions of the problem. Increasing the supply of low-income housing (other than shelters) is one important step. Additionally, low-income people must have the opportunity to earn the income necessary to pay for housing. Homelessness, however, is not only a housing problem, it is also a *human* problem. People who endure months or years of insecure living come to need various types of social services.

CLASS AND WELFARE, POLITICS AND VALUES

This chapter has presented a great many facts about social class in Canada. In the end, however, our understanding of what it means to be wealthy and privileged or poor and perhaps homeless also turns on politics and values. Understandably, support for the notion that social standing reflects personal merit, effort, and responsibility is strongest among people who are well-off and support the political right. The idea that society should distribute wealth and other resources more equally finds greatest favour among

The Welfare Dilemma

The predicament of Karen Moss, described at the beginning of this chapter, highlights a remarkable consensus in this country regarding "welfare"—nobody likes it. The political left criticizes it as an inadequate response to poverty; conservatives charge that it is hurting the people it allegedly helps and driving the country to bankruptcy; and the poor themselves find welfare a complex, confusing, and often degrading program.

Conservative critics (those to the right on the political spectrum) contend that, rather than alleviating poverty, welfare has actually *worsened* the problem for two reasons. First, it has eroded the traditional family by making living as a single an attractive alternative to marriage. As conservatives see it, welfare makes it economically beneficial for women to have children outside of marriage and is a key reason for the rapid rise in out-of-wedlock births among poor people.

The second part of the conservative critique holds that government assistance undermines self-reliance among the poor and fosters dependency. Dependence on government "handouts," argue critics, is the main reason that so many poor heads of households do not have steady, full-time jobs. Clearly, conservatives say, welfare has strayed far from its original purpose of helping

nonworking women with children (typically, after the death or divorce of a husband) make the transition to self-sufficiency. On the contrary, welfare has become a way of life. Once trapped in dependency, poor women most often raise children who will themselves remain poor as adults.

The left charges its opponents with using a double standard for assessing government programs. Why, they ask, is there so much outrage at the thought of the government transferring money to poor mothers and children when most "welfare" actually goes to relatively rich people? The amounts spent on welfare across Canada, while they are not negligible, pale in comparison with the tax write-offs received by more affluent people for the registered retirement savings plans (RRSPs) they buy each year. And what about the billions of dollars in tax write-offs for corporations, many of which are enjoying record profits? As the left sees it, "wealthfare" costs the country a great deal more than "welfare," even though public opinion takes the opposite view.

Second, critics claim that conservatives (and much public opinion) distort the performance of public assistance. Images of irresponsible "welfare queens" mask the fact that most poor families who turn to public assistance are truly needy. For instance, Karen

Moss received only $1221 a month for herself and her son *before the rates were cut*, hardly enough to attract people to a "life of welfare dependency." And across Canada in recent years, the trend has been to slash welfare rates as a deficit-reduction measure. Overall, the left faults public assistance as a band-aid approach to the growing social problems of unemployment and poverty in Canada.

As for the charge that public assistance undermines families, the left concedes that the proportion of single-parent families is rising, but disputes the argument that welfare is to blame. Rather, single parenting is a widespread cultural trend found at all class levels in most industrial societies.

Thus, critics conclude, public assistance programs such as welfare have not been attacked because they have failed, but because they benefit poor people, a segment of the population long scorned as "undeserving." Our cultural tradition of equating wealth with virtue and poverty with vice allows rich people to display privilege as a "badge of ability" while poverty carries a negative stigma. Richard Sennett and Jonathan Cobb (1973) call this the "hidden injury of class."

Many on the right believe all welfare programs should be abolished. Those on the left, by contrast, want both to

those with relatively few advantages or those on the political left.

Although we may recognize that structural constraints place insurmountable barriers in the paths of some categories of people, we still share a general North American belief in a meritocracy. These cultural values encourage us to see successful people as personally meritorious and the poor as personally deficient. Richard Sennett and Jonathan Cobb (1973) called this judgment, applied to the poor, the *hidden injury of class*. In other words, poverty significantly lowers the self-image of disadvantaged people, while

the more fortunate display their affluence as a personal "badge of ability." Values supporting individual responsibility also contribute to negative views of social welfare programs and the people who rely on them. While advocates for the poor defend welfare programs as necessary for millions of people lacking opportunities and advantages, our cultural values promote the view that social welfare programs undermine initiative. Accepting assistance of this kind thus becomes personally demeaning, which helps explain why many people who are eligible for assistance are reluctant to apply for it.

improve and to expand them. Are there areas of common ground in this debate? The province of Ontario, as part of its welfare reform program, is instituting "workfare," which makes income assistance contingent on able-bodied recipients performing useful work and participating in occupational training. Under discussion, too, are proposals to limit the duration of public assistance to a fixed term. Other provinces are monitoring Ontario's program with great interest.

Continue the debate . . .

1. *Is it fair for provinces across the country to slash their welfare budgets and for the federal government to slash the transfer payments that support those budgets all in the name of deficit reduction, while at the same time no effort is made to recoup the tax write-offs that middle-class and wealthy people are awarded when they buy RRSPs? Is this just one more case of the poor being exploited because they are politically powerless?*

2. *Do you think public assistance has become a "way of life" for many people, as conservatives charge?*

3. *Do you feel that an expanded public assistance program would lessen the extent of poverty in Canadian society? Why or why not?*

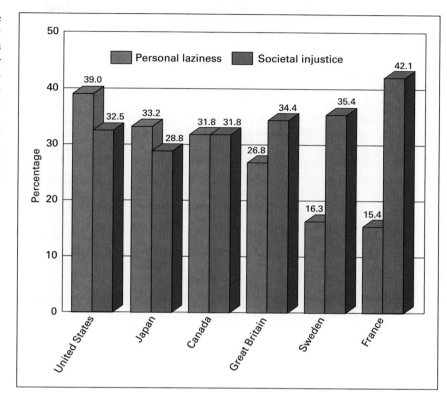

FIGURE 10–9 Assessing the Causes of Poverty

Survey Question: "Why are there people in this country that live in need?" Percentages reflect respondents' identification of either "personal laziness" or "societal injustice" as the primary cause of poverty.

Percentages for each country do not add up to 100 because less frequently identified causes of poverty were omitted from this figure.

SOURCE: World Values Survey (1994).

Finally, the drama of social stratification extends far beyond Canada's borders. The most striking social disparities are found not by looking inside one country but by comparing living standards in various parts of the world. In Chapter 11 ("Global Stratification"), we broaden our investigation of social stratification, focusing on global inequality.

SUMMARY

1. Social inequality in Canada involves disparities in a host of variables, including income, wealth, education, and power.

2. White-collar occupations generally confer more prestige and higher incomes than blue-collar jobs. The pink-collar occupations typically

held by women offer little social prestige or income.

3. Ascription exerts a powerful effect on stratification in Canada; ancestry, race or ethnicity, and gender are all related to social position.

4. The upper class, which is small (perhaps 4 or 5 percent of the population) includes the richest and most powerful families. Members of the upper-upper class, or the old rich, derive their wealth through inheritance over several generations; those in the lower-upper class, or the new rich, depend on earned income as their primary source of wealth.

5. The middle class encompasses 40 to 50 percent of the Canadian population. The upper-middle class may be distinguished on the basis of higher income, higher-prestige occupations, and more schooling.

6. The working class comprises about one-third of our population. With below-average income, working-class families have less financial security than those in the middle class. Few working-class people attain more than a high-school education, and they commonly work in blue-collar or lower-prestige white-collar jobs.

7. About one-fifth of the population belongs to the lower class and lives near or below the official poverty line.

8. Social class affects nearly all aspects of life, beginning with health and life expectancy, and encompassing a wide range of attitudes and patterns of family living.

9. Social mobility is common in Canada, as it is in other industrial societies. For only 12 percent of women and 26 percent of men is there no intergenerational mobility; typically, however, only small changes (upward or downward) occur from one generation to the next.

10. Since the early 1970s, changes in the Canadian economy have reduced the standard of living for low- and moderate-income families. In one important trend, manufacturing industries have declined in Canada, paralleling growth in low-paying service-sector jobs.

11. Some four million people in Canada are officially classified as poor. About one million of the poor are children and young people under the age of eighteen. Increasingly, poor families are headed by women: the elderly, natives, and certain other racial and ethnic categories are overrepresented among the poor as well.

12. Oscar Lewis and Edward Banfield advanced the "culture of poverty" thesis, suggesting that poverty can be perpetuated by the social patterns of the poor themselves. Opposing this view, William Ryan argues that poverty is caused by the unequal distribution of wealth in society. Although Banfield's view is consistent with our society's cultural pattern of personalizing social position, Ryan's view is supported by more evidence.

CRITICAL THINKING QUESTIONS

1. Assess your own social class. Does your family have consistent standing on various dimensions of social stratification (including income, education, and occupational prestige)? Why do most people find talking about their own social position awkward?

2. Identify some of the effects of Canadian social stratification on health, values, politics, and family patterns.

3. What categories of people are at high risk of poverty in Canada? What evidence supports the assertions 1) that the poor are responsible for their low social position, and 2) that society is primarily responsible for poverty?

SOCIOLOGY APPLIED

1. Develop several simple questions that, taken together, would let you measure someone's social class position. Try these on several adults—refine your questions as you proceed.

2. If you have access to the Internet, visit the Web site run by Statistics Canada (www.statcan.ca). Here you will find income data as well as a host of other statistics about social inequality. See what you can learn about the social standing in your part of the country.

3. During an evening of television viewing, assess the social class level of the characters you see in various shows. In each case, note precisely why you place someone in a particular social position. Do you discern any patterns?

www.ccsd.ca/facts.html
Maintained by the Canadian Council on Social Development, the *Statistics and Information* page publishes statistical information on family income, poverty lines, child poverty, welfare incomes, the estimated number of Canadians on welfare, and other related topics.

www.nald.ca/lithome.htm
Gimme Shelter: A Resource on Literacy and Homelessness Work is an online book written mostly for people who do, or would like to do, literacy and community development work with people who are transient or homeless. It defines literacy and homelessness, discusses critical issues including outreach, racism, and gender, offers instruction for literacy tutors, and provides resource materials.

www.napo-onap.ca
National Anti-Poverty Organization is a non-governmental, non-partisan advocacy organization of low-income Canadians and others concerned about issues affecting poor people. The site includes a poverty quiz, NAPO newsletters and research, facts about poverty, and ideas for action.

www.canoe.ca/FP/home.html
The online version of *The Financial Post* publishes daily reports and opinion, technology articles, investment information, profiles of Top 50 companies, and other business news.

www.calgary-stampede.ab.ca/
The official site of the *Calgary Stampede* offers news and FAQs, provides exhibit and event information, and sells souvenirs through the Stampede Store and tickets to the upcoming annual celebration.

Diego Rivera, *Formation of Revolutionary Leadership (Los Explotatores),* 1926–27

CHAPTER 11

GLOBAL STRATIFICATION

Standing against the burning sun at the edge of the North African desert, the two reporters nervously wait to meet their contacts. They have travelled thousands of miles in pursuit of a stunning story—that, in the 1990s, slavery still exists. To many people, slavery is a vestige of the 1800s, and an evil that has been eradicated from the world. But this is not the case. And Gilbert Lewthwaite and Gregory Kane (1996) are about to prove it. They have travelled from Baltimore to the nation of Sudan with case in hand to buy a human being.

Two men approach, carrying assault rifles. A few words pass between the men and the interpreter who accompanies the reporters. The interpreter then explains that the group will travel on foot to meet the slave trader. The sun climbs higher in the sky, and heat rises up from the ground. As they walk for one, two, three hours, the reporters drain their canteens, but the men with the rifles never drink at all.

Finally, up ahead stands a giant mango tree, where the group escapes from the pounding sun. Minutes later, seemingly out of nowhere, the slave trader appears, a small muscular figure with a close-fitting cap and a trimmed moustache. Calling himself Adam al Haj, he explains that he is in the business of trying to return to their families women and children seized by tribal raiders. Over the last five years, he claims, he has helped 473 slaves gain their freedom. His price is five cows or $500 per person. The reporters hand over $1000 in cash. From around the tree, the trader's associates come forward with a dozen young boys, most showing signs of malnutrition. The trader motions to the reporters: Pick any two.

The boys are fearful, imagining that they are being resold and not knowing what their new owners will expect of them. For most such boys—seized by raiders in intertribal warfare—life as a slave means tending animals or doing menial labour for scraps of food and enduring periodic abuse. In the case of girls, sexual assault is commonplace.

The boys have no idea that the reporters mean to return them to their families, and so they stand expressionless, eyes fixed on the ground. The reporters are struck by the enormity of the moment, paralyzed by the thought of picking out two boys as if they were shirts on a rack. They settle on the boy who seems to be the oldest. Nearby stands a cluster of anxious parents who have heard that children are to be freed. The reporters ask if the boy's parents are there. The interpreter points and a man named Deng Kuot

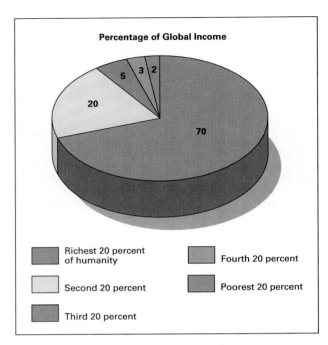

Percentage of Global Income

- Richest 20 percent of humanity
- Second 20 percent
- Third 20 percent
- Fourth 20 percent
- Poorest 20 percent

FIGURE 11–1 Distribution of World Income

SOURCES: Based on Sivard (1988) and The World Bank (1993).

Mayen steps forward towards his son. The father points to a second boy—also his son. The deal is struck. The father is jubilant, dancing about and praising God for the return of his sons. Twelve-year-old Akok Deng Kuot and ten-year-old Garang Deng Kuot stand silently. It has been six years since they were seized: they do not recognize their father and it will be days before they fully comprehend that their ordeal is over.

While the details vary, this story is far from unique. In fact, experts claim that tens of millions of children across Latin America, Africa, and Asia have been seized by raiders or sold into bondage by their desperately poor families.

The fact that slavery still exists as we come to the end of this century is a powerful sign of the extent of social inequality in the world. As this chapter explains, poverty is a reality in Canada, but the problem is both more widespread and more severe in the poor countries of the world.

GLOBAL INEQUALITY: AN OVERVIEW

Chapter 10 ("Social Class in Canada") detailed the income inequality that marks our own society. In global perspective, however, social stratification is even more pronounced. Figure 11–1 divides the world's total income by fifths of the population. Recall that the richest 20 percent of the Canadian population earns about 40 percent of the national income (see Table 10–1 on page 244); the richest 20 percent of the global population, however, receives about 70 percent of all income. At the other end of the social scale, the poorest 20 percent of the Canadian population earns 6.1 percent of our national income; the poorest fifth of the world's people, by contrast, struggles to survive on just 2 percent of global income.

Because global income is so concentrated, the average member of a rich society (such as Canada) lives extremely well by world standards. In fact, the living standard of even most people below our government's poverty threshold far surpasses that of the majority of the earth's people.

A WORD ABOUT TERMINOLOGY

Most people are familiar with the "Three Worlds" model for describing the unequal distribution of global income. Developed after World War II, this model has been in wide use ever since. Rich, industrialized countries are "First World" nations, less-industrialized socialist countries are the "Second World," and the remaining nonindustrialized and poor countries are called the "Third World."

Recently, however, the "Three Worlds" model has lost validity. For one thing, it was a product of Cold War politics by which the capitalist West (the First World) faced off against the socialist East (the Second World), while the rest of the world (the Third World) remained more or less on the sidelines. But the sweeping transformation of Eastern Europe and the former Soviet Union means that a distinctive Second World no longer exists. Even the superpower opposition that defined the Cold War has faded in recent years.

A second problem with the "Three Worlds" model is that it lumped together in the Third World more than one hundred countries at different levels of development. Some relatively better-off nations of the Third World (such as Chile in South America) have ten times the per-person productivity of the poorest countries of the world (including Ethiopia in eastern Africa).

Today's world calls for a modestly revised system of classification. We will, therefore, use the terms introduced in Chapter 1 ("The Sociological Perspec-

When natural disasters strike rich societies, as in the 1997 floods in southern Manitoba, property loss is great but the loss of life is low. In poor societies, the converse is true, evident in the aftermath of this cyclone that devastated coastal Bangladesh, killing tens of thousands of poor people who lived on land prone to flooding.

tive"): *high-income countries* are the richest forty nations with the most-developed economies and the highest overall standard of living for their people. Next, the world's roughly ninety *middle-income countries* are somewhat poorer nations whose economic development is more or less typical for the world as a whole. Finally, the remaining sixty *low-income countries* are marked by the lowest productivity and the most severe and extensive poverty.

Compared to the older "Three Worlds" system, this new form of classification has two main advantages. First, it focuses on the key issue of economic development rather than highlighting whether societies are capitalist or socialist. Second, this revision provides a more precise picture of the relative economic development of the world's countries because it does not lump together all less-industrialized countries into a single Third World.

Nonetheless, classifying the 191 nations on earth into any three categories (or, even more crudely, dividing them into the "rich North" and the "poor South") ignores pronounced differences in their ways of life. The countries at each of the three levels of economic development have rich and varied histories, speak hundreds of languages, and encompass diverse peoples who are proud of their cultural distinctiveness.

Keep in mind, too, that just as the world's nations form an economic hierarchy of very rich to very poor, so every country on earth is also internally stratified. In other words, the extent of global inequality is actually greater than national comparisons suggest, since the most well-off people in rich countries (such as Canada) live worlds apart from the poorest people in

low-income countries (such as Haiti, Sudan, and India). This striking contrast helps explain why, despite the affluence familiar to so many people in this nation, millions of the world's children fall victim to the horrors of slavery.

HIGH-INCOME COUNTRIES

High-income nations are rich because theirs were the first economies to be transformed by the Industrial Revolution more than two centuries ago, increasing their productive capacity one hundredfold. To grasp how this development enriched our own region of the world, consider that the small European nation of Holland is more productive than the vast continent of Africa below the Sahara Desert; likewise, tiny Belgium outproduces all of India.

A look back at Global Map 1–1 identifies the forty high-income countries of the world. They include most of the nations of Western Europe, including England, where industrialization first took hold about 1750. Canada and the United States are also rich nations; in North America, the Industrial Revolution was well under way by 1850. In Asia, one of the world's leading economic powers is Japan; recent economic growth also places Hong Kong and Singapore in this favoured category. Finally, to the south of Asia in the global region known as Oceania, Australia and New Zealand also rank as industrial, high-income nations.

Taken together, countries with the most-developed economies cover roughly 25 percent of the earth's land area—including parts of five continents—while lying mostly in the Northern Hemisphere. In mid-1998, the total population of these nations was barely 900 million, or 15 percent of the earth's people. By global standards, rich nations are not densely populated; even so, some countries (such as Japan) are crowded while others (such as Canada) are sparsely settled. Inside their borders, however, about three-quarters of the people in high-income countries congregate together in or near cities.

High-income countries reveal significant cultural differences—the nations of Europe, for example, recognize more than thirty official languages. But these countries share an industrial capacity that generates, on average, a rich material life for their people. Per-capita income in these societies ranges from about $10 000 annually (in Portugal and Cyprus) to more than $20 000 annually (in Canada, the United States, and Switzerland).[1] This prosperity is so great that residents of most-developed countries enjoy more than half the world's total income.

Finally, just as people in a single society perform specialized work, so various regions form a global division of labour. Generally speaking, high-income countries dominate the world's scientific efforts and employ the most complex and productive technology. Production in rich societies is capital-intensive, meaning high investments in factories and related machinery. High-income countries also stand at the forefront of the Information Revolution; the majority of the largest corporations that design and market computers, as well as most computer users, are found in rich societies. With the lion's share of wealth, high-income countries also control the world's financial markets; ups and downs on the financial exchanges of New York, London, and Tokyo affect people throughout the world.

MIDDLE-INCOME COUNTRIES

Middle-income countries are those with per-capita incomes ranging between $2500 and $10 000, or roughly the median for the world's *nations* (but higher than that of the world's *people*, since most individuals live in low-income countries). These nations have experienced limited industrialization, primarily centred in cities. But about half their people still live in rural areas and engage in agricultural production. Especially in the countryside, schooling, medical care, adequate housing, and sometimes even safe water are

---

[1] High-income countries have per-capita annual income of at least $10 000. For middle- and low-income countries the comparable figures are $2500 to $10 000, and below $2500, respectively. All data reflect the United Nations' concept of "purchasing power parities," which avoids distortion caused by exchange rates when converting all currencies to U.S. dollars. Instead, the data represent the local purchasing power of each nation's currency.

hard to come by. This represents a standard of living far below what members of high-income societies take for granted.

Looking back at Global Map 1–1 (page 9), we see that about ninety of the world's nations fall into the middle-income category, and they are a very diverse lot. At the high end are Chile (Latin America), the Czech Republic (Europe), and Malaysia (Asia) with about $9000 in annual income. At the low end are Guyana (Latin America), Albania (Europe), Swaziland (Africa), and China (Asia) with roughly $2500 annually in per-capita income.

One group of middle-income countries includes the former Soviet Union and the nations of Eastern Europe (in the past, also known as the Second World). The former Soviet Union and its satellite in Eastern Europe—including Poland, the German Democratic Republic (East Germany), Czechoslovakia, Hungary, Romania, and Bulgaria—had predominantly socialist economies until popular revolts between 1989 and 1991 swept aside their governments. Since then, these nations have begun to introduce market systems. This process, detailed in Chapter 15 ("The Economy and Work"), has yet to solve serious economic woes; on the contrary, in the short term at least, nations of the former Eastern Bloc are battling high inflation, and some people enjoy fewer consumer goods than ever.

In a second category of middle-income countries are most of the oil-producing nations of the Middle East (or, less ethnocentrically, western Asia). These nations, including Saudi Arabia, Oman, and Iran, are very rich, but their wealth is so concentrated that most people receive little benefit and remain poor.

The third, and largest, category of middle-income countries is found in Latin America and northern and western Africa. These nations (which might be termed the better-off countries of the Third World) include Argentina and Brazil in South America as well as Algeria and Botswana in Africa. Although South Africa's white minority lives as well as people in Canada, this country, too, must be considered middle-income because its majority Black population lives with far less income.

Together, middle-income countries span roughly 40 percent of the earth's land area. About two billion people, or one-third of humanity, call these nations home. Some countries (such as El Salvador) are far more crowded than others (such as Russia), but compared to high-income countries, these nations are densely populated.

LOW-INCOME COUNTRIES

Low-income countries of the world are primarily agrarian societies with little industry and very poor populations.

Japan represents the world's high-income countries, in which industrial technology and economic expansion have produced material prosperity. The presence of market forces is evident in this view of downtown Tokyo (above, left). The Russian Federation represents the middle-income countries of the world. Industrial development has been slower in the former Soviet Union, as socialist economies have performed sluggishly. Residents of Moscow, for example, chafe at having to wait in long lines for their daily needs (above, right). The hope is that the introduction of a market system will raise living standards, although it probably will also increase economic disparity. Bangladesh (left) represents the low-income countries of the world. As the photograph suggests, these nations have limited economic development and rapidly increasing populations. The result is widespread poverty.

These sixty nations, identified in Global Map 1–1 on page 9, are found primarily in central and eastern Africa, as well as Asia. Low-income countries (or the poorest nations within the so-called Third World) represent about 35 percent of the planet's land area but are home to half its people. Combining these facts, the population density for poor countries is generally high, although it is much higher in Asian countries (such as Bangladesh and India) than in more sparsely settled central African nations (such as Chad or Zaire).

In poor countries, barely 25 percent of the people live in cities; most inhabit villages and farm as their families have done for centuries. In fact, half the world's people are peasants, and most of them live in low-income countries. By and large, peasants are staunchly traditional, following the folkways of their ancestors. Living without industrial technology, peasants are not very productive; thus, many of them endure severe poverty. Hunger, minimal housing, and frequent disease all frame the lives of the world's poorest people.

This broad overview of global economic development gives us a foundation for understanding the problem of global inequality. For people living in affluent nations such as Canada, the scope of human want in much of the world is difficult to grasp. From time to time, televised scenes of famine in very poor countries such as Ethiopia and Bangladesh give us a shocking glimpse of the absolute poverty that makes every day a life-and-death struggle. Behind these images lie cultural, historical, and economic forces that we shall explore in the remainder of this chapter.

GLOBAL WEALTH AND POVERTY

To classify a country as "low income" does not mean that only poor people live there. On the contrary, the rich neighbourhoods of Manila (the Philippines) and Madras (India) testify to the high living standards of some. Indeed, given the low wages in most of these countries, the typical well-to-do household is staffed by several servants and served by a gardener and chauffeur. The following journal notes provide a sense of the dramatic inequality that marks poor nations.

October 14, 1994, Smokey Mountain, on the northern side of Manila, the Philippines. What caught my eye was how clean she was—

By and large, rich nations such as the United States wrestle with the problem of relative poverty, meaning that poor people get by with less than we think they should have. In poor countries such as Ethiopia, absolute poverty means that people lack what they need to survive. What kind of diet, medical care, and access to clean water do you think families like these have?

a girl no more than seven or eight years old, hair carefully combed and wearing a freshly laundered dress. Her eyes followed us as we walked past; camera-toting Americans stand out in this, one of the poorest neighbourhoods in the entire world.

Fed by methane from the decomposing garbage, the fires never go out on Smokey Mountain, Manila's vast garbage dump. Smoke envelopes the hills of refuse like a thick fog. But Smokey Mountain is more than a dump; it is a neighbourhood that is home to thousands of people. The residents of Smokey Mountain are the poorest of the poor, and one is hard pressed to imagine a setting more hostile to human life. Amid the smoke and the squalor, men and women do what they can to survive, picking plastic bags from the garbage and washing them in the river, stacking flattened cardboard boxes outside a family's plywood shack. And all over Smokey Mountain are children who must already sense the enormous odds against them. The girls and boys we see are the lucky ones, of course. What chance do they have, living in families that earn scarcely a few hundred dollars a year? With barely any opportunity for schooling? Year after year, breathing this air?

And, against this backdrop of human tragedy, one lovely little girl has put on a fresh dress and gone out to play. . . .

With Smokey Mountain behind us, our taxi driver threads his way through heavy traffic towards the other side of Manila. The change is amazing: the forbidding smoke and smells of the dump give way to the polished neighbourhoods that look like Miami or Los Angeles. In the distance, a cluster of yachts is visible on the bay. No more rutted streets; now we glide quietly along wide tree-lined boulevards filled with expensive Japanese cars. We pass shopping plazas, upscale hotels, and high-rise office buildings. At every block or so stands the entrance to an exclusive residential enclave set off by gates and protected by armed guards. Here, in large, air-conditioned homes, the rich of Manila live and many of the poor work.

Poor nations are home to both rich and poor people, but hardly in equal numbers. Indeed, for most people in the world's poor countries, poverty is the rule. Moreover, with incomes of only several hundred dollars a year, the burden of poverty is greater than among the poor of Canada. This does not mean that deprivation here at home is a minor problem. Especially in a rich society, the lack of food, housing, and health care for millions of people—almost half of them children—amounts to a national tragedy. Yet, even after years of recession and government cutbacks in Canada, poverty in poor countries remains both *more severe* and *more extensive* than in this country.

THE SEVERITY OF POVERTY

Poverty in poor countries is more severe than it is in rich nations such as Canada. The data in Table 11–1 provide a statistical picture of global stratification. The first column of figures shows the gross domestic product (GDP)[2] for countries at each level of economic development. Industrial societies have a high economic output primarily because of their industrial technology. A large, industrial nation such as the United States had a 1994 GDP of about $6.6 trillion; Japan's GDP stood at about $4.6 trillion; Canada's was about $0.5 trillion. Comparing GDP figures shows that the world's richest nations are thousands of times more productive than the poorest countries on earth.

The second column of figures in Table 11–1 indicates per-capita GDP in terms of what the United Nations (1995) calls "purchasing power parities," the value of people's income in terms of what it can buy in a local economy. The resulting figures for rich countries such as the United States, Switzerland, and Canada are very high—in the range of $20 000. Per-capita GDP for middle-income countries, including Brazil, Poland, and Iran, are much lower—in the $5000 range. And in the world's low-income countries, per-capita annual income is no more than just a few hundred dollars. In Ethiopia, for example, a typical person labours all year to make what the average worker in Canada earns in several days.

The last column in Table 11–1 indicates quality of life in the various nations. This index, calculated by the United Nations, combines income, education (extent of adult literacy and average years of schooling), and longevity (how long people typically live). Index values are decimals that fall between the hypothetical extremes of 1 (highest) and zero (lowest). By this calculation, Canadians enjoy the highest quality of life (.960), with residents of the United States close behind (.942). At the other extreme, people in the African nation of Sierra Leone have the world's lowest quality of life (.176).

---

[2] Gross domestic product refers to all the goods and services on record as produced by a country's economy in a given year. Income earned outside the country by individuals or corporations is excluded from this measure; this is the key difference between GDP and gross national product (GNP), which includes foreign earnings. For countries that invest heavily abroad (Kuwait, for example), GDP is considerably less than GNP; for countries in which other nations invest heavily (Hong Kong), GDP is much higher than GNP.

TABLE 11–1 Wealth and Well-Being in Global Perspective, 1994

Country	Gross Domestic Product ($ billion)	GDP per-Capita (PPP$)*	Quality of Life Index
High-income			
Canada	543	21,459	.960
United States	6,648	26,397	.942
Japan	4,591	21,581	.940
Sweden	169	24,967	.936
Australia	332	19,285	.931
United Kingdom	1,017	18,621	.931
Switzerland	260	24,967	.930
Germany	2,046	19,675	.924
South Korea	377	10,656	.890
Middle-income countries			
Eastern Europe			
Hungary	41	5,884	.857
Poland	93	5,002	.834
Russian Federation	377	4,828	.792
Lithuania	5	4,011	.762
Latin America			
Argentina	282	8,937	.884
Mexico	377	7,384	.853
Brazil	555	5,362	.783
Asia			
Thailand	143	7,104	.833
Malaysia	71	8,865	.832
Middle East			
Iran, Islamic Republic of	64	5,766	.780
Saudi Arabia	117	9,338	.774
Africa			
Algeria	42	5,442	.737
Botswana	4	5,367	.673
Low-income countries			
Latin America			
Honduras	3	2,050	.575
Haiti	2	896	.338
Asia			
China, P.R.	522	2,604	.626
India	294	1,348	.446
Africa			
Zaire (now Democratic Republic of Congo)	–	429	.381
Guinea	3	1,103	.271
Ethiopia	5	427	.244
Sierra Leone	1	643	.176

* These data are the United Nations' new "purchasing power parity" calculations, which avoid currency rate distortion by showing the local purchasing power of each domestic currency.

SOURCE: United Nations Development Programme, *Human Development Report, 1997* (New York: Oxford University Press, 1997).

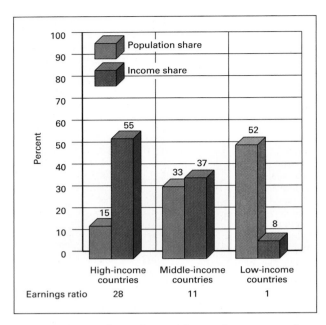

FIGURE 11–2 The Relative Share of Income and Population by Level of Economic Development

A key reason for marked disparities in quality of life is that economic productivity is lowest in precisely the regions of the globe where population growth is highest. Figure 11–2 shows the division of global population and global income for countries at each level of economic development. High-income countries are by far the most advantaged with 55 percent of global income supporting just 15 percent of the world's people. Middle-income nations contain about 33 percent of the global population; these people earn about 37 percent of the world's income. This leaves half the planet's population with just 8 percent of global income. Factoring together income and population, for every dollar received by individuals in the low-income countries, their counterparts in the high-income nations enjoy 28 dollars.

Relative Versus Absolute Poverty

The distinction made in the last chapter between relative and absolute poverty has an important application to global inequality. People living in rich societies typically focus on *relative poverty*, meaning that some people lack resources others take for granted. Relative poverty, by definition, cuts across every society, rich or poor.

Especially important in a global context is the concept of *absolute poverty*, a lack of resources that is life threatening. Human beings in absolute poverty commonly lack the nutrition necessary for health and long-term survival. To be sure, some absolute poverty exists in Canada. Inadequate nutrition that leaves children or elderly people vulnerable to illness and even outright starvation is a reality in this nation. But such immediately life-threatening poverty strikes only a small proportion of the Canadian population; in low-income countries, by contrast, one-third or more of the people are in desperate need.

Since absolute poverty threatens people with death, one indicator of the extent of the problem is the median age at death. Global Map 11–1 identifies the age by which half of all people born in a society die. In rich societies, most people die after reaching the age of seventy-five; in poor countries, however, half of all deaths occur among children who have not yet reached the age of ten.

THE EXTENT OF POVERTY

Poverty in poor countries is more extensive than it is in rich nations such as Canada. Chapter 10 ("Social Class in Canada") noted that the Canadian government officially classifies about one in six or seven people as poor. In low-income countries, however, most people live no better than the poor in our nation, and many live close to the edge of survival. As the high death rates among children suggest, the extent of absolute poverty is greatest in Africa, where half the population is malnourished. In the world as a whole, at any given time, 20 percent of the people (about one billion) lack the nutrition they need to work regularly. Of these, at least 800 million are at risk for their lives (Sivard, 1988; Helmuth, 1989; United Nations Development Programme, 1993).

Members of rich societies, such as Canada, tend to be overnourished. On average, a member of a high-income society consumes about 3 500 calories daily, an excess that contributes to obesity and related health problems. Most people in low-income countries not only do more physical work than we do, but they rarely consume more than 2 000 calories daily. In short, they lack sufficient food or, more precisely, enough of the right kinds of food.

Lack of necessary nutrition makes death a way of life in poor societies. In the ten minutes it takes to read through this section of the chapter, about three hundred people in the world will die from disease because they have been weakened by an inadequate diet. This amounts to about 40 000 people a day, or 15 million people each year. Worldwide, the annual loss of life due to poverty is ten times greater than the number of lives lost in all the world's armed conflicts. Clearly, easing world hunger is one of the most serious responsibilities facing humanity today.

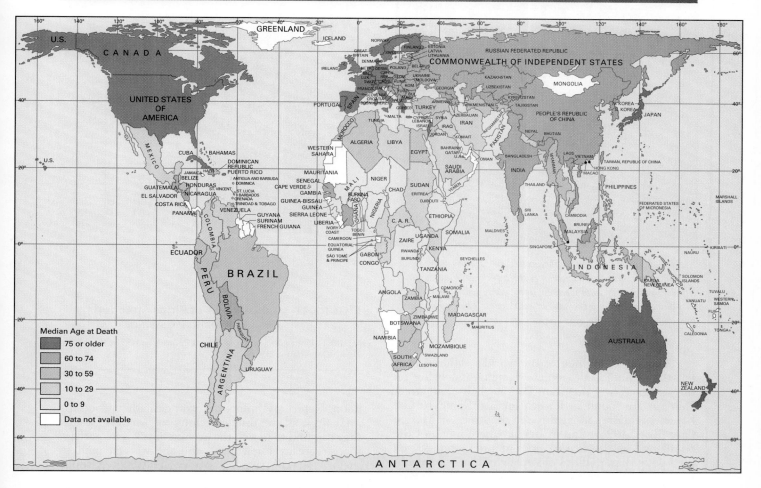

GLOBAL MAP 11–1 Median Age at Death in Global Perspective

This map identifies the age below which half of all deaths occur in any year. In the high-income countries of the world, including Canada, it is the elderly who face death—that is, people age seventy-five or older. In middle-income countries, including most of Latin America, most people die years or even decades earlier. In low-income countries, especially in Africa and parts of Asia, it is children who die, half of them never reaching their tenth birthday.

SOURCES: The World Bank (1993); map projection from *Peters Atlas of the World* (1990).

POVERTY AND CHILDREN

Death often comes early in poor societies, where families lack adequate food, safe water, secure housing, and access to medical care. In many cases, too, children in poor countries leave their families because their chances of surviving are better on the streets.

Organizations combating child poverty in the world estimate that poverty forces some 75 million city children in poor countries to beg, steal, sell sex, or serve as couriers for drug gangs in order to provide income for their families. Such a life almost always means dropping out of school and places children at high risk of illness and violence. Many street girls, with little or no access to medical assistance, become pregnant—a case of children who cannot support themselves having still more children.

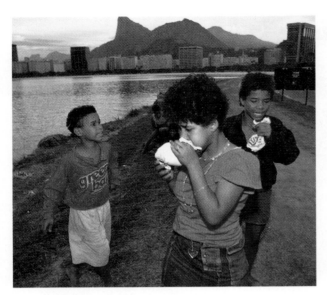

Rio de Janeiro is known as a playground for wealthy tourists. But many who live there know only stark poverty. Faced with little opportunity to improve their lives, many young people fall into despair and numb themselves with drugs. These youngsters breathe the fumes from glue almost every day.

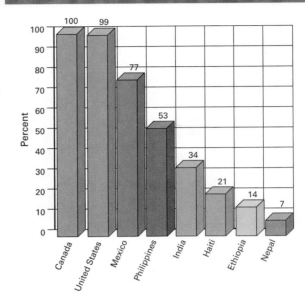

FIGURE 11–3 Percentages of Births Attended by Trained Health Personnel

SOURCE: United Nations Development Programme (1997); World Health Organization (1998).

Another 25 million of the world's children have left their families altogether, sleeping and living on the streets as best they can. Perhaps half of all street children are found in Latin America. Some 10 000 homeless children move through the streets of Mexico City (Ross, 1996). And in Brazil, where much of the population has flocked to cities in a desperate search for a better life, millions of street children—many not yet teenagers—live in makeshift huts, under bridges, or in alleyways. Public response to street children is often anger directed at the children themselves. In Rio de Janeiro, known to many of us as Brazil's beautiful seaside resort, police try to keep the number of street children in check; on occasion, death squads may sweep through a neighbourhood in a bloody ritual of "urban cleansing." In Rio, several hundred street children are murdered each year (Larmer, 1992; U.S. House of Representatives, 1992).

POVERTY AND WOMEN

Women in Sikandernagar, one of India's countless rural villages, begin work at 4:00 in the morning, lighting the fires, milking the buffalo, sweeping floors, and walking to the well for water. They care for other family members as they rise. By 8:00, when many people in Canada are just beginning their day, these women move on to their "second shift," working under the hot sun in the fields until 5:00 in the after-

noon. Returning home, the women gather wood for their fires, all the time searching for whatever plants they can find to enrich the evening meal. The buffalo, too, are ready for a meal, and the women tend to them. It is well past dark before their eighteen-hour day is through (Jacobson, 1993:61).

In rich societies, the work women do is typically unrecognized, undervalued, and underpaid; women receive less income for their efforts than men do. In low-income countries, this pattern is even more pronounced. Furthermore, although women do most of the work in poor nations, they are disproportionately the poorest of the poor.

Families in poor societies depend on women's work to provide income. At the same time, tradition bars many women from school, as it gives them primary responsibility for child rearing and maintaining the household. The United Nations estimates that in poor societies, men own 90 percent of the land, a far greater gender disparity in wealth than in industrial nations. Multilayered systems of tradition and law subordinate women in poor societies so that about 70 percent of the world's roughly one billion people near absolute poverty are women (Hymowitz, 1995).

Women in poor countries have limited access to birth control (which, obviously, raises the birth rate),

Infanticide and Sexual Slavery:
Gender Bias in Poor Societies

Rani, a young woman living in a remote Indian village, returned home from the hospital after delivering a baby girl. There was no joy in the family upon her arrival. On the contrary, upon learning of the birth, the men sombrely filed out of the mud house. Rani and her mother-in-law then set about the gruesome task of mashing oleander seeds into several drops of oil to make a poisonous paste, which they pushed down the baby's throat. The day came to an end as Rani returned from a nearby field where she had buried the child.

As she walked home, Rani felt not sadness at losing her daughter but bitterness at not bearing a son. Members of her village, like poor people throughout the world (and especially in Asia), favour boys, while defining girls as an economic liability. Why? Because, in poor societies, most power and wealth fall into the hands of men. Parents recognize that boys are a better investment of their meagre resources, because males have a better chance of surviving to adulthood and providing for the family. Then, too, custom dictates that parents of a girl offer a dowry to the family of her prospective husband. In short, given the exist-

ing social structure, families are better off with boys and without girls.

One consequence of the cultural preference for males is high rates of sex-selective abortion throughout rural India, China, and other Asian nations. In India, many villages that lack running water have a doctor who uses either high-tech amniocentesis or ultrasound to determine the sex of a fetus. Most women, upon hearing the results of the test, are either elated at carrying a boy or resolved to terminate the pregnancy quickly so they can "try again." There are no precise counts of abortion and female infanticide, but in some rural regions of Asia, men outnumber women by as many as ten to one.

Young girls await customers in a Bangkok brothel.

Gender bias is also evident in the explosion of sexual slavery that has spread across southeast Asia. Thailand alone now has one to two million prostitutes (perhaps 8 percent of the country's female population); about half of these are children. Bangkok, Thailand's capital, is now considered the sex-tourism capital of the world. In some cases, parents sell female infants to agents who pay others to raise them, then "harvest their crop" when the girls approach their teenage years and are old enough to work the sex trade. In other cases, girls who see little future in a rural village make their own way to the city, only to fall into the hands of pimps who soon have them working in brothels, soliciting in bars, or performing in sex shows. Pimps provide girls with clothes and housing, but at a price that exceeds the girls' salaries. The result is a system of debt bondage that keeps women virtual prisoners. Most suffer from a host of diseases brought on by abuse and neglect, and 40 percent are now infected with the virus that causes AIDS. The future for these girls and women is bleak.

SOURCES: Anderson and Moore (1993) and Santoli (1994).

and they typically give birth without the assistance of any trained health personnel. Figure 11–3 draws a stark contrast between high- and low-income countries in this regard.

Overall, gender inequality is strongest in low-income societies, especially in Asia where cultural traditions favour males. As the "Global Sociology" box explains, the cultural preference for males is evident in virtually every dimension of life, and has produced a stunning lack of females in some regions (Kishor, 1993).

SLAVERY

Poor societies are vulnerable to a host of related problems: hunger, illiteracy, warfare, and slavery. Anti-Slavery International (ASI) is an organization that helped bring an end to slavery in the British Empire in 1833; Upper Canada was the first to take action when, under John Graves Simcoe, it took steps to phase out slavery in 1793; the United States banned slavery in 1865. According to ASI, as many as 400 million men, women, and children (almost 7 percent of humanity) currently live in conditions that amount to slavery (Janus, 1996).

ASI distinguishes four types of slavery. First is *chattel slavery*, in which one person owns another. The number of chattel slaves is difficult to estimate because slavery violates laws almost everywhere. But slave trading—as portrayed in the opening of this chapter—takes place in many countries, mostly in Africa, the Middle East, and Asia. Second, *child slavery* refers to children abandoned by their families or boys and girls so poor that they take to the streets in an effort to survive. Perhaps 100 million children—many in poor countries of Latin America—fall into this category. Third, *debt bondage* refers to the practice, found in dozens of countries around the world, of paying people to work (sometimes as prostitutes), but charging them more than they earn for food and shelter. Never able to pay their debts, these workers are, for practical purposes, enslaved. Fourth, *servile forms of marriage* also amount to slavery. In India, Thailand, and some African nations, families marry off women against their will. Many end up as slaves to their husband's family; some are forced into prostitution.

In 1948, the United Nations issued the Universal Declaration of Human Rights, which states: "No one shall be held in slavery or servitude; slavery and the slave trade shall be prohibited in all their forms." Unfortunately, fifty years later, this social evil persists.

CORRELATES OF GLOBAL POVERTY

What accounts for the severe and extensive poverty throughout much of the world? The rest of this chapter weaves together explanations from the following facts about poor societies.

1. **Technology.** Almost two-thirds of people in low-income countries farm the land; the productive power of industrial technology is all but absent in these poorest nations. Energy from human muscles or beasts of burden falls far short of the force unleashed by steam, oil, gas, or nuclear fuels; this technological disparity limits the use of complex machinery. Moreover, poor societies' focus on farming, rather than on specialized production, inhibits development of human skills and abilities.

2. **Population growth.** As Chapter 21 ("Population and Urbanization") explains, countries with the least-developed economies have the world's highest birth rates. Despite the death toll from poverty, the populations of poor countries in Africa, for example, double every twenty-five years. In these countries, half the people are teenagers or younger. Because they are just entering their childbearing years, a wave of pop-

ulation growth will roll into the future. In recent years, for example, the population of Kenya has swelled by 4 percent; as a result, even with economic development, living standards actually fell.

3. **Cultural patterns.** Poor societies are typically very traditional. Kinship groups pass folkways and mores from generation to generation. Adhering to long-established ways of life, people resist innovations—even those that promise a richer material life.

    The members of poor societies often accept their fate, although it may be bleak, in order to maintain family vitality and cultural heritage. Such attitudes bolster social bonds, but at the cost of discouraging development.

4. **Social stratification.** Low-income societies distribute their wealth very unequally. Chapter 9 ("Social Stratification") explained that social inequality is more pronounced in agrarian societies than in industrial societies. In Brazil, for example, half of all farmland is owned by less than 1 percent of the people (Bergamo and Gerson, 1996).

5. **Gender inequality.** As we have already explained, poor societies subordinate women even more than industrial societies do. Moreover, women with few opportunities typically have many children, and the needs of a growing population, in turn, restrain economic development. As a result, many analysts conclude that raising living standards in much of the world depends on improving the social standing of women.

6. **Global power relationships.** A final cause of global poverty lies in the relationships among the nations of the world. Historically, wealth flowed from poor societies to rich nations by means of **colonialism**, *the process by which some nations enrich themselves through political and economic control of other nations.* Historical patterns of trade, some analysts claim, spurred certain nations to prosper economically while others simultaneously were made poor. The societies of Western Europe colonized much of Latin America for more than three hundred years and also controlled parts of Asia, notably India, for centuries. Africa, too, endured up to a century of colonization, most of which ended in the 1960s.

    Although 130 former colonies gained their independence during this century, exploitation continues through **neocolonialism** (*neo* is a Greek word for "new"), *a new form of global power relationships that involves not direct political control but economic exploitation by multinational corporations.* **Multinational corporations** are *large businesses that operate in many countries.*

The value of children in low-income countries includes their ability to earn income. This pattern is especially true in the case of girls. In India, families typically invest in the education of their sons, who may go on to higher earning. Girls, by contrast, are often kept out of school so they can work full days in factories. This factory offers little pay to girls who produce hand-cut wooden matches.

These corporations wield such clout that corporate decision makers can—and often do—impose their will on countries where they do business just as colonizers did in centuries past.

GLOBAL INEQUALITY: THEORETICAL ANALYSIS

There are two major explanations for the unequal distribution of the world's wealth and power—*modernization theory* and *dependency theory*. Each of these approaches suggests why so many of the world's people are poor and why members of rich societies enjoy such relative advantages.

MODERNIZATION THEORY

Modernization theory is a model of economic and social development that explains global inequality in terms of technological and cultural differences among societies. Modernization theory emerged in the 1950s, a decade of fascination with new technology in North America and a period of hostility towards U.S. interests in many poor societies. Socialist countries—especially the Soviet Union—were gaining influence among low-income nations by asserting that economic progress was impossible under the sway of rich, capitalist countries. In response, policymakers in the industrialized world framed principles of support for a free-market economy that have shaped official foreign policy towards poor nations ever since.[3]

---

[3] The following discussion of modernization theory draws primarily on Rostow (1960, 1978), Bauer (1981), and Berger (1986); see also Firebaugh (1996).

Historical Perspective

Modernization theorists point out that as recently as several centuries ago, the entire world was poor. Because poverty has been the norm throughout human history, it is *affluence* that requires an explanation.

Affluence came within reach of a growing share of people in Western Europe during the late Middle Ages as exploration of other parts of the world expanded trade. Soon, the Industrial Revolution was underway, transforming Western Europe and, shortly thereafter, North America. Industrial technology coupled with entrepreneurial innovation created new wealth on an unprecedented scale. At the outset, this new wealth benefited only a few. But industrial technology was so productive that gradually the standard of living of even the poorest people began to rise. Absolute poverty, which had cast a menacing shadow over society for its entire history, was finally being routed.

During this century, the standard of living in high-income countries, where the Industrial Revolution began, has jumped at least fourfold. Many middle-income nations in Asia and Latin America are now industrializing, and they, too, are becoming wealthier. But without industrial technology, low-income countries have changed little.

The Importance of Culture

Why didn't the Industrial Revolution sweep away poverty the world over? Modernization theory holds that not every society has been eager to seek out and use new technology. Doing so requires a cultural environment that emphasizes the benefits of innovation and materialism.

According to modernization theory, *tradition* is the greatest barrier to economic development. In societies with strong family systems and a reverence for the past, a "cultural inertia" discourages people from adopting new technologies that would improve their living standards. Even today, many people—from Canadian Mennonites to the Islamic people of Iran and the deeply traditional Semai of Malaysia—oppose technological advances as threats to their family relationships, customs, and religious beliefs.

As Max Weber (1958; orig. 1904–05) explained, at the end of the Middle Ages the cultural environment of Western Europe distinctly favoured change. The Protestant Reformation had reshaped traditional Catholicism to create a new progress-oriented way of life (see Chapter 4, "Society"). Material affluence—regarded with suspicion by the Catholic church—became a personal virtue, and the growing importance of individualism steadily undermined the emphasis on kinship and community. Taken together, these emerging cultural patterns nurtured the Industrial Revolution, which propelled one segment of humanity from poverty to prosperity.

Rostow's Stages of Modernization

Modernization theory holds that the door to affluence remains open to all. Indeed, as technological advances diffuse around the world, all societies are gradually becoming industrialized. According to W.W. Rostow (1960, 1978), the process of modernization occurs in four stages:

1. **Traditional stage.** Initially, cultural traditions are strong, so poor people resist change, including new technology. Socialized to venerate the past, most people in traditional societies cannot even imagine how life could be very different from what they know. Therefore, they build their lives around their families and local communities, following well-worn paths that allow for little individual freedom and few options to make life better. Life in such communities is often spiritually rich but lacking in material abundance.

   A century ago, much of the world was at this initial stage of economic development. And, because nations such as Bangladesh, Niger, and Somalia are still at the traditional stage, they remain impoverished to this day.

2. **Take-off stage.** As a society begins to shake off the grip of tradition, people start to use their talents and imagination, sparking economic growth. A market emerges as people produce goods not just for their own consumption but to trade with others for profit. The culture is marked by a developing spirit of individualism and a stronger achievement orientation, often at the expense of family ties and longstanding norms and values.

   Great Britain reached take-off by about 1800, the United States by 1820. Rostow determined that take-off in Canada occurred between 1890 and 1914 (Pomfret, 1981). Thailand, a middle-income country in eastern Asia, is now at this stage. Rich nations can help poor countries reach the take-off stage by supplying foreign aid, advanced technology, investment capital, and opportunities for schooling abroad.

3. **Drive to technological maturity.** By this time, "growth" has become a widely accepted concept that fuels a society's pursuit of higher living standards. An active, diversified economy drives a population eager to enjoy the benefits of industrial technology. At the same time, however, people begin to realize (and sometimes lament) that industrialization is eroding traditional family and community life. Great Britain reached stage three about 1840, the United States by 1860, and Canada between 1914 and 1950. Today, Mexico, the U.S. territory of Puerto Rico, and the Republic of Korea are among the nations driving to technological maturity.

   By this stage of economic development, absolute poverty has greatly declined. Cities swell with people who stream from the rural hinterland in search of economic opportunity, occupational specialization renders relationships less personal, and heightened individualism sparks movements pressing for expanded political rights. Societies approaching technological maturity also provide basic schooling to all their people, and advanced training for some. The newly educated consider tradition "backwards," opening the door to further change. The social position of women steadily becomes more equal to that of men. Even so, in the short term, the process of development may subject women to unanticipated problems, as the "Global Society" box explains.

4. **High mass consumption.** Economic development driven by industrial technology steadily raises living standards. This rise occurs, Rostow explains, as mass production stimulates mass consumption. Simply put, people soon learn to "need" the expanding array of goods that their society produces.

   The United States moved into this stage of development by 1900, and other high-income countries such as Canada were not far behind. Japan, for example, was sufficiently industrialized to become a military power early in the twentieth

Modernization and Women:
A Report from Rural Bangladesh

In global perspective, gender inequality is most pronounced where people are poorest. Economic development, then, gives women opportunities for schooling and work outside the home, reduces birth rates, and therefore weakens traditional male domination.

Along the way, however, the process of modernization often impedes women's progress. Investigating the lives of women in a poor, rural district of Bangladesh, Sultana Alam (1985) observed several hazards of development for women.

First, as economic opportunity draws men from rural areas to cities in search of work, women and children must fend for themselves. Some men sell their land and simply abandon their wives, who are left with nothing but their children.

Second, the waning strength of the family and neighbourhood leaves women who are deserted in this way with little assistance. The same holds true for women who become single through divorce or

the death of a spouse. In the past, Alam reports, kin or neighbours readily took in a Bangladeshi woman who found herself alone. Today, as Bangladesh struggles to advance economically, the number of poor households headed by women is increasing. Rather than enhancing women's autonomy, Alam argues, a new spirit of individualism has actually eroded the social standing of women.

In Rajshahi, Bangladesh, women meet to address their common problems.

Third, economic development—as well as the growing influence of Western movies and mass media—undermine women's traditional roles as wives, sisters, and mothers, defining them instead as objects of sexual attention. A new cultural emphasis on sexuality now encourages men in poor countries to abandon aging spouses for younger, more physically attractive partners. The same emphasis contributes to the world's rising tide of prostitution, noted earlier in this chapter.

Modernization, then, does not affect men and women in the same way. In the long run, evidence suggests that modernization gives the sexes more equal standing. In the short run, however, the economic position of many women actually declines, and women are also forced to contend with problems previously unknown in traditional societies.

SOURCES: Based on Alam (1985) and Mink (1989).

---

century. Then, after recovering from World War II, the Japanese entered an era of high mass consumption, and Japan's economic output is now second only to that of the United States. Now entering this fourth stage of economic development are two of the most prosperous small societies of eastern Asia, Hong Kong and Singapore. (The economic impacts of Hong Kong's 1997 return to Chinese control remain to be seen.)

The Role of Rich Nations

Modernization theory credits high-income countries with a crucial role in global economic development. More specifically, rich societies are the key to alleviating global inequality in the following ways:

1. **Assisting in population control.** We have already noted that population growth is greatest in the poorest societies of the world, where rising population easily overtakes economic advances and lowers the standard of living. As rich nations export birth control technology and promote its use, they help curb population growth, a crucial step in combating poverty. Integral to this process are programs that advance the social standing of women. Once economic development is under way, birth rates should decline as they have in industrialized societies.

2. **Increasing food production.** Modernization theory asserts that "high-tech" farming methods, exported from rich to poor nations, raise agricul-

tural yields. Such techniques, collectively referred to as the *Green Revolution*, involve the use of new hybrid seeds, modern irrigation methods, chemical fertilizers, and pesticides.

3. **Introducing industrial technology.** Technological transfers should involve industry as well as agriculture. Rich nations can accelerate economic growth in poor societies by introducing machinery and information technology, which moves the labour force to skilled industrial and service jobs.

4. **Instituting programs of foreign aid.** Investment capital from rich nations can boost the prospects of poor societies striving to reach the "take-off" stage. Foreign aid can purchase fertilizers and fund irrigation projects, which raise agricultural productivity, as well as build power plants and factories that improve industrial output.

Critical evaluation. Modernization theory, a sweeping analysis of how and why industrialization transforms societies, has influential supporters among social scientists (Parsons, 1966; W. Moore, 1977, 1979; Bauer, 1981; Berger, 1986; Firebaugh and Beck, 1994). Moreover, this model has guided the foreign policy of Canada and other rich nations for decades. Proponents point to rapid economic development in Asia as proof that the affluence created in Western Europe and North America is within reach of all regions of the world. With the assistance of rich countries, South Korea, Taiwan, Singapore, and Hong Kong have made impressive economic gains.

From the outset, however, modernization theory has come under fire from socialist countries (and left-leaning analysts in the West) as a thinly veiled defence of capitalism. According to its critics, modernization simply has not occurred in many poor countries. The United Nations recently reported that living standards in a number of nations—including Haiti and Nicaragua in Latin America, and Sudan, Ghana, and Rwanda in Africa—are actually lower than in 1960 (United Nations Development Programme, 1996).

A second criticism of modernization theory is that it fails to recognize how rich nations, which benefit from the status quo, often block paths to development for poor countries. Critics charge that rich countries industrialized centuries ago from a position of global *strength*; so how can we expect poor countries today to industrialize from a position of global *weakness*?

Third, critics continue, modernization theory treats rich and poor nations as worlds unto themselves, failing to see how international relations historically have affected all nations. It was colonization that boosted the fortunes of Europe to begin with; further, this economic windfall came at the expense of

countries in Latin America and Asia that are still reeling from the consequences.

Fourth, critics contend that modernization theory holds up the world's most-developed countries as the standard by which the rest of humanity should be judged, betraying an ethnocentric bias. As environmentalists point out, our Western conception of "progress" has led us to degrade the physical environment throughout the world. Moreover, not every culture buys into our notions about competitive, materialistic living.

Finally, modernization theory draws criticism for locating the causes of global poverty almost entirely in the poor societies themselves. Critics see this analysis as little more than "blaming the victims" for their own plight. Instead, they argue, an analysis of global inequality should focus as much attention on the behaviour of *rich* nations as on that of poor nations (Wiarda, 1987).

From all these concerns has emerged a second major approach to understanding global inequality. This is dependency theory.

DEPENDENCY THEORY

Dependency theory is a model of economic and social development that explains global inequality in terms of the historical exploitation of poor societies by rich ones. Dependency theory places primary responsibility for global poverty on rich nations. It holds that high-income countries have systematically impoverished low-income countries, making poor societies dependent on them. Moreover, this destructive process extends back for centuries and persists today.

Historical Perspective

Everyone agrees that before the Industrial Revolution there was little affluence in the world. Dependency theory asserts, however, that people living in poor countries were actually better off economically in the past than their descendants are now. André Gunder Frank (1975), a noted proponent of this approach, argues that the colonial process that helped develop today's rich nations simultaneously *underdeveloped* poor societies.

Dependency theory is based on the idea that the economic positions of the rich and poor nations of the world are linked and cannot be understood correctly in isolation from one another. This analysis maintains that poor nations are not simply lagging behind rich ones on a linear "path of progress." Rather, the increasing prosperity of the high-income countries came largely at the expense of low-income societies. In short, then, some nations became rich *only because other nations became poor.* Both are products of global commerce beginning five centuries ago.

The Importance of Colonialism

Late in the fifteenth century, Europeans began surveying the Americas to the west, the massive continent of Africa to the south, and the vast expanse of Asia to the east. When, for example, Christopher Columbus sailed westward from Spain in 1492 and reached the Americas, Europeans celebrated "the discovery of the New World." From the point of view of people on these shores, however, the arrival of Europeans can be described as the systematic conquest of one region of the world by another (Sale, 1990; Gray, 1991).

By the nineteenth century, most of the world had come under the domination of European nations. Spain and Portugal colonized nearly all of Latin America from the sixteenth until the mid-nineteenth centuries. A century ago, Great Britain controlled about one-fourth of the world's land and people, boasting that "the sun never sets on the British Empire." The United States, itself originally thirteen small British colonies on the eastern seaboard, pushed across the continent, purchased Alaska, and gained control of Haiti, Puerto Rico, Guam, the Philippines, the Hawaiian Islands, and part of Cuba.

Meanwhile, Europeans and Africans engaged in a brutal form of human exploitation—the slave trade—from about 1500 until 1850. But even as the world was rejecting slavery, Europeans gained control of Africa itself, as Figure 11–4 shows. European powers dominated most of the continent until the early 1960s.

Formal colonialism has almost disappeared from the world, but, according to dependency theory, political liberation has not translated into *economic* autonomy. Far from it: the economic relationship between poor and rich nations perpetuates a colonial pattern of domination. This neocolonialism is the essence of a capitalist world economy.

Wallerstein's Capitalist World Economy

Immanuel Wallerstein (1974, 1979, 1983, 1984) explains global stratification using a model of the "capitalist world economy."[4] The term *world economy* suggests that the prosperity or poverty of any country is the result of a global economic system. According to Wallerstein, today's global economy is rooted in the colonization that began five hundred years ago when Europeans first saw the wealth of the rest of the

In her mixed-media work Living in the Storm Too Long, *Canadian native artist Jane Ash Poitras shows Christopher Columbus's flagship, the Santa Maria, on a collision course with a buffalo, a symbol of North American native culture. In Poitras's view, the Age of Exploration meant nothing but exploitation to the indigenous peoples, who were left powerless politically and with a bankrupt culture.*

world. Since the world economy is based in the most-developed countries, it is capitalist in character.

Wallerstein considers rich nations the *core* of the world economy. Colonialism enriched this core by funnelling raw materials from around the globe to Western Europe. Over the longer term, this wealth helped to ignite the Industrial Revolution. Similarly, today, multinational corporations operate worldwide, but channel wealth to North America, Western Europe, Australia, and Japan.

Low-income countries, by contrast, represent the *periphery* of the world economy. Drawn into this system by colonial exploitation, poor nations continue to support rich ones by providing inexpensive labour, easy access to raw materials, and vast markets for

---

[4] While based on Wallerstein's ideas, this section also reflects the work of Frank (1980, 1981), Delacroix and Ragin (1981), Bergesen (1983), and Dixon and Boswell (1996).

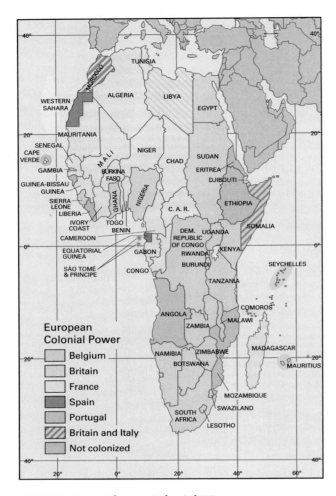

FIGURE 11–4 Africa's Colonial History

industrial products. The remaining countries are considered the *semiperiphery* of the world economy. They include prospering countries such as Portugal and South Korea that have closer ties to the global economic core.

According to Wallerstein, the world economy benefits rich societies (by generating profits) and harms the rest of the world (by perpetuating poverty). In short, the world economy imposes a state of dependency on poor nations, which remain under the control of rich ones. This dependency involves the following three factors:

1. **Narrow, export-oriented economies.** Unlike the diversified economies of core nations, production in poor countries focuses on a few raw materials or crops for export. Examples include coffee and fruits from Latin American nations, oil from Nigeria, hardwoods from the Philippines, and palm oil from Malaysia.

Replicating colonial-style patterns today, multinational corporations purchase raw materials cheaply in poor societies and transport them to core societies where factories process them for profitable sale. This practice discourages production of food or goods needed by local people in poor nations. These corporations also own a great deal of land and have transformed traditional farmers into low-paid farm labourers. Overall, then, rich nations effectively prevent poor ones from developing industries of their own.

2. **Lack of industrial capacity.** Without an industrial base, poor societies face a double bind. They count on selling their inexpensive raw materials to rich nations, from whom they buy whatever expensive manufactured goods they can afford. In a classic example of this dependency, British colonialists encouraged the people of India to raise cotton, but prohibited them from making their own cloth. Instead, the British shipped Indian cotton to textile mills in Birmingham and Manchester, wove it into cloth, and shipped the finished goods back for profitable sale in India.

Dependency theorists also blast the Green Revolution, widely praised by modernization theorists. To promote agricultural productivity, poor countries must buy expensive fertilizers, pesticides, and mechanical equipment from core nations. Typically, rich countries profit from this exchange more than the poor nations.

3. **Foreign debt.** Such unequal trade patterns have plunged poor countries deeper and deeper into debt to industrialized societies. Collectively, the poor nations of the world owe rich countries more than $1 trillion, including hundreds of billions of dollars to the United States alone. This staggering debt can paralyze a country, causing high unemployment and rampant inflation (Walton and Ragin, 1990; The World Bank, 1997).

The Role of Rich Nations

Nowhere is the difference between modernization theory and dependency theory sharper than in the role they assign to rich nations. Modernization theory maintains that rich societies *produce wealth* through capital investment and technological innovation. From this point of view, as poor nations adopt progrowth attitudes and policies and seek more productive technology, they, too, will prosper. By contrast, dependency theory sees global inequality in terms of the *distribution of wealth*, arguing that rich countries have *over*developed themselves as they have *under*developed the rest of the world.

Dependency theorists dismiss the idea that strategies proposed by rich countries to control population or to boost agricultural and industrial output will help raise living standards in poor countries. They contend that such programs provide profits to rich countries (through purchases of high technology), while rewarding not the poor majority but the ruling elites who maintain a favourable "business climate" for multinational corporations (Lappé, Collins, and Kinley, 1981).

Hunger activists Frances Moore Lappé and Joseph Collins (1986) claim that the capitalist culture of high-income countries encourages people to think of absolute poverty as somehow inevitable. Following this line of reasoning, poverty results from "natural" processes, including having too many children, and from natural disasters such as droughts. Global poverty is far from inevitable, they argue; rather, it results from deliberate policies. Lappé and Collins point out that the world produces enough food to allow every person on the planet to grow quite fat. Moreover, India and most of Africa actually *export* food, even though many of their own people go hungry.

According to Lappé and Collins, the contradiction of poverty amid plenty stems from the policy of producing food for profits, not people. That is, corporations in rich nations collaborate with elites in poor countries to grow and export profitable crops such as coffee while simultaneously limiting the production of staples such as corn and beans for local families. Governments of poor countries support the practice of "growing for export" because they need food profits to repay massive foreign debt. At the core of this vicious cycle, according to Lappé and Collins, is the capitalist corporate structure of the global economic system.

Critical evaluation. The main idea of dependency theory—that no nation develops (or fails to develop) in isolation—points out how the global economy shapes the destiny of all nations. Citing Latin America and other poor regions of the world, dependency theorists claim that development simply cannot proceed under the constraints presently imposed by rich countries. Rather, they call for radical reform of the entire world economy so that it operates in the interests of the majority of people.

Critics, however, charge that dependency theory incorrectly treats wealth as a zero-sum commodity, as if no one gets richer without someone else getting poorer. Not so, critics continue, since farmers, small business owners, and industrialists can and do create new wealth through their drive and imaginative use of new technology. After all, they point out, the entire world's wealth has swelled fivefold since 1950.

Second, critics continue, dependency theory is wrong in blaming rich nations for global poverty because many of the world's poorest countries (such as Ethiopia) have had little contact with rich nations. Similarly, a long history of trade with rich countries has dramatically improved the economies of nations, including Singapore and Hong Kong (both former British colonies), South Korea, and Japan. In short, an increasing body of evidence supports the conclusion that foreign investment by rich nations fosters economic growth, as modernization theory claims, not economic decline, as dependency theorists assert (Vogel, 1991; Firebaugh, 1992).

Third, critics view dependency theory as simplistic for pointing the finger at a single factor—world capitalism—as the cause of global inequality (Worsley, 1990). In doing so, dependency theory casts poor societies as passive victims and ignores factors *inside* these countries that contribute to their economic plight. Sociologists have long recognized the role of culture in shaping people's willingness to embrace or resist change. Iran's brand of fundamentalist Islam, for example, discourages ties with other countries. Capitalist societies, then, need hardly accept the blame for Iran's stagnation.

Nor can rich societies be saddled with responsibility for the reckless behaviour of some foreign leaders who engage in far-reaching corruption and self-serving military campaigns to enhance their own power (examples include Ferdinand Marcos in the Philippines, François Duvalier in Haiti, Manuel Noriega in Panama, Mobutu Sese Seko in Zaire, and Saddam Hussein in Iraq). Governments have even withheld food supplies for leverage in internal political struggles, a strategy that left the masses starving in the African nations of Ethiopia, Sudan, and Somalia. Other regimes throughout the world have done little to improve the status of women and to control population growth.

Fourth, critics chide dependency theorists for downplaying the economic dependency fostered by the former Soviet Union. The Soviet army seized control of most of Eastern Europe during World War II and subsequently dominated the Eastern Bloc nations politically and economically. Many consider the uprisings between 1989 and 1991 as a wholesale rejection of a Soviet colonial system by hundreds of millions of people.

A fifth criticism of dependency theory faults this approach for offering only vague solutions to global poverty. Most dependency theorists urge poor societies to sever economic ties to rich countries, and some call for nationalizing foreign-owned industries. Dependency theory implies that the path to ending global poverty begins with the overthrow of international capitalism. At its core, say the critics, depen-

After decades of war and communist rule, Vietnam is now attracting foreign investment, evident in the new high-rise hotels going up in Saigon (Ho Chi Minh City). Will this inflow of capital raise living standards, as modernization theory contends, or block development, as dependency theory maintains?

dency theory advocates some sort of world socialism. In light of the difficulties socialist societies have had in meeting the needs of their own people, critics ask, should we really expect such a system to lift the entire world towards prosperity?

Canada and Low-Income Countries

Canada's approach to development in low-income countries reveals tension between the modernization and dependency models on which it is based. In 1995, Canada spent $2.2 billion on aid to developing countries (0.29 percent of our GNP), most of which is distributed through the Canadian International Development Agency (CIDA).[5] In the past, CIDA has concentrated on encouraging industrial development, but it has recently started to emphasize self-sufficiency and improvement of the lives of the poor through enhancement of health care, housing, education, and agricultural methods. The involvement of women in development has also become a priority.

By the mid-1980s Canada had responded to changing conditions in low-income countries "with increasingly sophisticated social, cultural, and economic programs for human development and self-reliance" (Tomlinson, 1991), but there remains a tension between the goal of eliminating poverty and the desire to create an environment conducive to private-sector development and debt reduction through "economic structural adjustment" (CIDA, 1987). Despite its humanitarian goals, much of Canada's aid continues to be linked to trade or the perceived potential for

trade (that is, "*tied aid*"). Although in this sense Canada's role is similar to that of the U.S., some low-income countries are more comfortable accepting aid from Canada, which does not have the superpower status of the United States.

In addition to its aid and trade involvements with developing countries, Canada plays an active role in the generation and dissemination of knowledge in those societies. Several Canadian universities are involved in overseas research and development. For example, in 1995 Canada had 72 700 students from more than 200 countries, at all levels of education from elementary to graduate school. These figures reflect a 11.6 percent drop since 1991. Undergraduate university enrolment in 1995, 18 200, is down 16.2 percent since 1991 (Statistics Canada, *The Daily*, May 13, 1998). While on a trade mission to India with politicians and businesspeople in tow, Prime Minister Jean Chrétien proposed that recruitment centres be set up in various locations across the country. Their purpose would be to facilitate the applications of students from India to study at Canadian universities.

GLOBAL INEQUALITY: LOOKING AHEAD

Among the most important trends of recent decades is the development of a global economy, which is exacerbating inequality both within our country and around the world. Profitable investments, many of them in poor nations, and lucrative sales by North American companies to foreign interests have brought greater affluence to those who already have substantial wealth. At the same time, increasing industrial

---

[5] This is down from $3.2 billion (0.49 percent of GNP) in 1992.

TABLE 11–2   Modernization Theory and Dependency Theory: A Summary

	Modernization Theory	Dependency Theory
Historical pattern	The entire world was poor just two centuries ago; the Industrial Revolution brought affluence to high-income countries; as industrialization gradually transforms poor societies, all nations are likely to become more equal and alike.	Global parity was disrupted by colonialism, which made some countries rich while simultaneously making other countries poor; barring radical change in the world capitalist system, rich nations will grow richer and poor nations will become poorer.
Primary causes of global poverty	Characteristics of poor societies cause their poverty, including lack of industrial technology, traditional cultural patterns that discourage innovation, and rapid population growth.	Global economic relations—historical colonialism and the operation of multinational corporations—have enriched high-income countries while placing low-income countries in a state of economic dependency.
Role of rich nations	Rich countries can and do assist poor nations through programs of population control, technology transfers that increase food production and stimulate industrial development, and investment capital in the form of foreign aid.	Rich countries have concentrated global resources, conferring advantages on themselves while generating massive foreign debt in low-income countries; rich nations impede the economic development of poor nations.

production abroad has cut factory jobs in this country, exerting downward pressure on wages. The net result is gradual economic polarization.

As this chapter has noted, however, social inequality is far more striking in global context. The concentration of wealth among high-income countries, coupled with the grinding poverty typical of low-income nations, may well constitute the most important dilemma facing humanity in the twenty-first century. To some analysts, rich nations hold the keys to ending world poverty; to others, they are the cause of this tragic problem.

Faced with two radically different approaches to understanding global inequality, we might well wonder which one is correct. As with many controversies in sociology, each view has some merit as well as its own limitations. Table 11–2 summarizes important arguments made by advocates of each approach.

In searching for truth, we must consider empirical evidence. According to the recent survey of the world conducted by the United Nations (1996), people in about one-third of the world's countries are enjoying an unprecedented standard of living. These nations—identified in Global Map 11–2—include most of the high-income countries but also dozens of poorer countries, especially in Asia. These developing nations stand as evidence that the market forces endorsed by modernization theory can raise living standards.

In about one-third of the world's countries, however, living standards are actually lower today than they were in 1980. A rising wave of poverty, especially in the nations of sub-Saharan Africa, supports the dependency theory assertion that current economic arrangements are leaving hundreds of millions of people behind.

The picture now emerging calls into question arguments put forward by both modernization and dependency theories. Theorists for both camps are revising their views of the major "paths to development." On the one hand, few societies seeking economic growth now favour a market economy completely free of government control. This view challenges orthodox modernization theory, which endorses a free-market approach to development. On the other hand, recent upheavals in the former Soviet Union and Eastern Europe demonstrate that a global re-evaluation of socialism has been under way. These events, following decades of poor economic performance and political repression, make many poor societies reluctant to consider a government-mandated path to development. Because dependency theory has historically supported socialist economic systems, changes in world socialism will surely generate new thinking here as well.

Hunger is one critical problem caused by absolute poverty. As the "Controversy & Debate" box explains, many analysts wonder if we have the technological means and political will to address hunger effectively before it overwhelms much of the world.

Although the world's future is uncertain, we have learned a great deal about global stratification. One key insight, offered by modernization theory, is that world hunger is partly a *problem of technology*. A higher standard of living for a surging world population depends on raising agricultural and industrial productivity. A second insight, derived from dependency theory, is that global inequality is also a *political issue*. Even with higher productivity, the human community must address crucial questions concerning how resources are distributed—both within societies and around the globe.

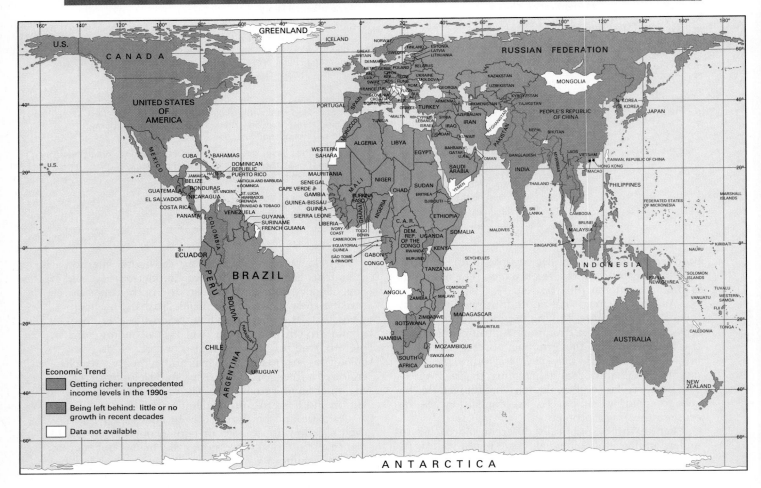

GLOBAL MAP 11–2 Prosperity and Stagnation in Global Perspective

In about sixty nations of the world, people are enjoying a higher standard of living than ever before. These prospering countries are found throughout the world, and include some rich nations (such as Canada) and some poor nations (especially in Asia). For most of the world's countries, however, living standards have remained steady or even slipped in recent decades. Especially in Eastern Europe and the Middle East, some nations have experienced economic setbacks since the 1980s. In sub-Saharan Africa, some nations are worse off than they were in 1960.

SOURCE: United Nations Development Programme (1996).

Note, too, that while economic development increases living standards, it also places greater strains on the natural environment. Imagine, for example, if almost one billion people in India were suddenly to become "middle class," with automobiles guzzling gasoline and spewing hydrocarbons into the atmosphere.

Finally, the vast gulf that separates the world's richest and poorest people puts everyone at greater risk of war, as the most impoverished people act to challenge the social arrangements that threaten their very lives. In the long run, we can achieve peace on this planet only by ensuring that all people enjoy a significant measure of dignity and security.

Will the World Starve?

The animals' feet leave their prints
on the desert's face.
Hunger is so real, so very real,
that it can make you walk around a
barren tree looking for
nourishment.
Not once,
Not twice,
Not thrice ...

These lines, by Indian poet Amit Jayaram, describe the appalling hunger found in Rajasthan, in northwest India. As this chapter has explained, however, hunger casts its menacing shadow not only over regions of Asia, but also over much of Latin America, most of Africa, and even parts of North America. Throughout the world, hundreds of millions of adults do not consume enough food to enable them to work. And, most tragically, some ten million of the world's children die each year because they do not get enough to eat.

At the closing of the nineteenth century, humankind took a major step forward by abolishing slavery almost everywhere on the planet. As we approach the twenty-first century, however, what are the prospects for eradicating the wretched misery of human beings enduring daily hunger?

It is easy to be pessimistic. For one thing, the population of poor countries is currently increasing by 90 million people annually—equivalent to adding another Mexico to the world every year. Poor countries can scarcely feed the people they have now; looking ahead a generation into the future, how will they ever feed *double* their current populations?

In addition, hunger forces poor people to exploit the earth's resources by using short-term strategies for food production that will lead to long-term disaster. For example, to feed the swelling populations of poor, tropical countries, farmers are cutting rain forests in order to increase their farmland. But, without the protective canopy of trees, it is only a matter of time before much of this land turns to desert.

Taken together, rising populations and ecological approaches that borrow against the future raise the spectre of hunger and outright starvation escalating well beyond current levels. Regarded pessimistically, the world's future is bleak: unprecedented hunger, human misery, and political calamity.

But there are also some grounds for optimism. Thanks to the Green Revolution, food production the world over is up sharply over the last fifty years, well outpacing the growth in population. Taking a broader view, the world's economic productivity has risen steadily, so that the average person on the planet has more income now to purchase food and other necessities than ever before.

This growth has increased daily calorie intake as well as life expectancy, access to safe water, and adult literacy, while around the world infant mortality is half of what it was in 1960.

So what are the prospects for eradicating world hunger—especially in low-income nations? Overall, we see less hunger in both rich and poor countries, and a smaller *share* of the world's people faces starvation now than, say, in 1960. But as global population increases, with 90 percent of children born in middle- and low-income countries, the *number* of lives at risk is as great today as ever before. Moreover, as noted earlier, although many low-income countries have made solid gains, many more are stagnating or even losing ground.

Also bear in mind that aggregate data mask different trends in various world regions. The "best-case" region of the world is eastern Asia, where incomes (controlled for inflation) have tripled over the last generation. It is to Asia that the "optimists" in the global hunger debate typically turn for evidence that poor countries can and do raise living standards and reduce hunger. The "worst-case" region of the world is sub-Saharan Africa, where living standards have actually fallen over the last decade, and more and more people are pushed to the brink of starvation. It is here that high technology is least evident and birth rates are highest. Pessimists typically look to Africa when they argue that poor countries are losing ground in the struggle to keep their people well nourished.

Television brings home the tragedy of hunger every year or so when news cameras focus on starving people in places like Ethiopia and Somalia. But hunger—and the early death from illness that it brings on—is the plight of millions all year round. The world does have the technical means to feed everyone; the question is: do we have the moral determination to do so?

Continue the debate . . .

1. *In your opinion, what are the primary causes of global hunger?*
2. *Do you place more responsibility for solving this problem on poor countries or on rich ones? Why?*
3. *Do you expect the extent of global hunger to increase or decrease? Why?*

SOURCES: United Nations (1994, 1995).

SUMMARY

1. In the world as a whole, social stratification is more pronounced than in Canada. About 15 percent of the world's people live in industrialized, high-income countries such as Canada and take in 55 percent of the earth's total income. Another one-third of humanity lives in middle-income countries with limited industrialization, receiving about 37 percent of all income. Half the world's population lives in low-income countries that have yet to industrialize; they earn only 8 percent of global income.

2. While relative poverty is found everywhere, poor societies contend with widespread, absolute poverty. Worldwide, the lives of some one billion people are at risk. About fifteen million people, most of them children, die every year from various causes because they lack proper nourishment.

3. Women are more likely than men to be poor nearly everywhere in the world. Gender bias against women is much greater in poor, agrarian societies than it is in industrial societies such as Canada.

4. The poverty found in much of the world is a complex problem reflecting limited industrial technology, rapid population growth, traditional cultural patterns, internal social stratification, male domination, and global power relationships.

5. Modernization theory maintains that development hinges on acquiring advanced productive technology. This approach views traditional cultural patterns as the key barrier to modernization.

6. Modernization theorist W.W. Rostow identifies four stages of development: traditional, take-off, drive to technological maturity, and high mass consumption.

7. Arguing that rich societies have the keys to creating wealth, modernization theory cites four ways rich nations can assist poor nations: bolstering population control strategies, providing crop-enhancing technologies, encouraging industrial technology, and providing investment capital and other foreign aid.

8. Critics of modernization theory maintain that this approach has produced limited economic development in the world, while ethnocentrically assuming that poor societies can follow the path to development taken by rich nations centuries ago.

9. Dependency theory claims that global wealth and poverty are directly linked to the historical operation of the capitalist world economy.

10. The dependency of poor countries on rich ones began five centuries ago with colonialism. Furthermore, even though most poor countries have won political independence, neocolonialism persists as a form of exploitation carried out by multinational corporations.

11. Immanuel Wallerstein views the high-income countries as the privileged "core" of the capitalist world economy; middle-income nations are the "semiperiphery"; poor societies form the global "periphery."

12. According to dependency theorists, three key factors—export-oriented economies, a lack of industrial capacity, and foreign debt—perpetuate poor countries' dependency on rich nations.

13. Critics of dependency theory argue that this approach overlooks the success of many nations in creating new wealth. Total global wealth, they point out, has increased fivefold since 1950. Furthermore, contrary to the implications of dependency theory, the world's poorest societies are not those with the strongest ties to rich countries.

14. Both modernization and dependency approaches offer useful insights into the development of global inequality. Some evidence supports each view. Less controversial is the urgent need to address the various problems caused by worldwide poverty.

CRITICAL THINKING QUESTIONS

1. Distinguish between relative and absolute poverty. How do the two concepts apply to social stratification in Canada and the world as a whole?

2. Why do many analysts argue that economic development in low-income countries depends on raising the social standing of women?

3. State the basic tenets of modernization theory and dependency theory, and then spell out several criticisms of each approach.

4. Based on what you have read here and elsewhere, what is your prediction about the extent of global hunger fifty years from now? Will the problem be more or less serious? Why?

SOCIOLOGY APPLIED

1. Keep a log book noting any advertising (for coffee from Colombia or exotic vacations to Egypt or India) that you see on television or in other media. What image of life in low-income countries does this advertising present? In light of the facts contained in this chapter, do you think this image is accurate?

2. On most campuses, there are students who have come to Canada from a poor country. Approach one such woman and one such man. Explain that you have been studying global stratification, and ask if they are willing to share their views of life in their countries. You may be able to learn quite a bit from them.

3. The university library should be able to provide a number of popular press accounts of the extent of slavery in today's world. Or you could visit the Web site of an organization opposing African slavery: the Coalition Against Slavery in Mauritania and Sudan (http://www.columbia.edu/~slc11/). These sources provide information about the problem of slavery that make for very interesting reading and, perhaps, the basis of a course paper.

4. Look over all the global maps in this text. As you examine them, identify the various social traits associated with the world's richest and poorest nations. Try to use both modernization theory and dependency theory to build theoretical explanations of the patterns you find.

WEBLINKS

www.igc.org/igc
The *Institute for Global Communications* is the U.S. member of the Association for Progressive Communications, a global partnership of computer networks that link activists around the world. The mission of IGC is to advance and inform movements for peace, economic and social justice, human rights and environmental sustainability around the world by promoting strategic use of appropriate computer networking technology.

www.fourmilab.ch/etexts/www/un/udhr.html
Adopted by the General Assembly of the United Nations on December 10, 1948, the *Universal Declaration of Human Rights* declares that "all human beings are born free and equal in dignity and rights," and that everyone is "entitled to all the rights and freedoms set forth in the Declaration, without distinction of any kind, such as race, colour, sex, language, religion, political or other opinion, national or social origin, property, birth or other status."

www.ciesin.org/docs/003-322/003-322a.html
This excerpt from *Global Environmental Change: Understanding the Human Dimensions* (1992) summa-

rizes the human causes and consequences of global change. The authors suggest that to understand global environmental change, it is necessary to focus on the interactions of environmental systems, including the atmosphere, the biosphere, the geosphere, and the hydrosphere, and human systems, including economic, political, cultural, and sociotechnical systems.

cil.andrew.cmu.edu/projects/World_History/Wall.html
This page summarizes Immanuel Wallerstein's *The Modern World System: Capitalist Agriculture and the Origins of the European World Economy in the Sixteenth Century*. Wallerstein develops a theoretical framework to understand the historical changes involved in the rise of the modern world.

vi.uh.edu/pages/mintz/primary.htm
This fascinating collection of excerpts from slave narratives includes writing by slave traders, physicians, military men, former slaves, and abolitionist Frederick Douglass.

Wendy Seller, *Magritte and Me,* 1944
© Wendy Seller, o/c 34" × 30". Photo courtesy of Pepper Gallery, Boston.

SEX AND GENDER

The little girl, just eighteen months old, huddled in the corner of the room, fighting back tears. Meserak Ramsey eyed her with concern. Ramsey, a friend of the child's mother, was there visiting. Both women had immigrated from Nigeria to the United States. The child was obviously in pain, and Ramsey crouched down to see what was wrong.

At that moment, the girl's mother entered the room. She explained that her daughter had just had a clitoridectomy, or female circumcision, whereby the clitoris is surgically removed. In Nigeria, Togo, Somalia, Egypt, and three dozen other nations in Africa and the Middle East, this painful procedure is commonly performed on young girls by midwives, tribal practitioners, or, sometimes, doctors, and typically without anesthesia. Meserak Ramsey swallowed hard. She, too, had suffered genital mutilation as a child.

Why would anyone want to subject young girls to pain, the risk of infection, and other complications? Because, according to the cultural tradition in some societies, women must be virgins at marriage and remain sexually faithful to their husbands. Genital mutilation eliminates sexual sensation so, the thinking goes, a female is less likely to violate sexual mores. Experts estimate that at least 100 million women in the world have suffered genital mutilation, and perhaps thousands of these procedures take place each year in North America.

In most cases, immigrant mothers and grandmothers who have themselves been mutilated expect young girls in their family to follow suit. Indeed, many immigrant families subject their daughters to genital mutilation because they believe social mores in the United States are lax. "I don't have to worry about her now," explains Ramsey's friend, looking at her daughter. "She'll be a good girl" (Crossette, 1995).

SEX AND GENDER

Many people think there is something "natural" about sexuality, and that sexual behaviour is simply an expression of the same biology that animates "the birds and the bees." But as we shall see, sex is bound up with culture, so that sexual practices—and our response to them—vary significantly from time to time and from place to place. Ideas about sexuality are also closely tied to the ways that societies expect girls to be "feminine" and boys to be "masculine." We can begin, then, by distinguishing between the key concepts of sex and gender.

SEX: A BIOLOGICAL DISTINCTION

Sex refers to *the biological distinction between females and males.* Sex is closely related to reproduction, in which both females and males play a part. The female ovum and the male sperm, which join to form a fertilized

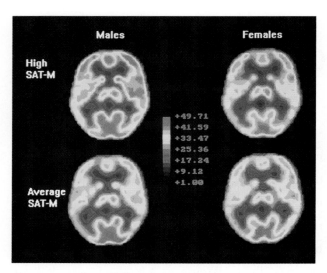

Do women and men differ in mental abilities? That is, do the two sexes think differently? Using high technology equipment that creates images such as these, physical scientists note slightly dissimilar patterns of brain activity in women and men when they are performing mathematical calculations. Sociologists link these small differences in mathematical aptitude (as well as other differences in interests and attitudes) to the social environment, which, right from birth, sets down different expectations for girls and boys.

embryo, each contain twenty-three pairs of chromosomes—biological codes that guide physical development. One of these chromosome pairs determines the child's sex. The mother always contributes an X chromosome; the father contributes either an X or a Y. A second X from the father produces a female (XX) embryo; a Y from the father yields a male (XY) embryo. A child's sex, then, is determined at conception.

Within weeks, the sex of an embryo starts to guide its development. If the embryo is male, testicular tissues begin producing testosterone, a hormone that stimulates the development of the male genitals. Without testosterone, the embryo develops female genitals. In Canada about 105 boys are born for every 100 girls, but a higher death rate among males (8.1 per 1000) than among females (6.5 per 1000) contributes to a slight female majority in the population by the time people reach their mid-thirties.

Sex and the Body

At birth, females and males are distinguished by **primary sex characteristics**, *the genitals,* organs used to *reproduce the human species.* Further sex differentiation occurs years later when children reach puberty and their reproductive systems become fully operational. At this point, humans exhibit **secondary sex charac-**

teristics, *bodily development, apart from the genitals, that distinguishes biologically mature females and males.* To accommodate pregnancy, giving birth, and nurturing infants, adolescent females develop wider hips, breasts, and soft fatty tissue, which provides a reserve supply of nutrition for pregnancy and breast-feeding. Usually slightly taller and heavier than females from birth, adolescent males typically develop more muscles in the upper body, more extensive body hair, and voices deeper in tone. These are general differences, however: some males are smaller, have less body hair, and speak in a higher tone than some females.

Hermaphrodites

Sex is not always a clear-cut matter. In rare cases, a hormone imbalance before birth produces a **hermaphrodite** (a word derived from Hermaphroditus, the offspring of the mythological Greek gods Hermes and Aphrodite, who embodied both sexes), *a human being with some combination of female and male genitalia.* Because our culture is uneasy about sexual ambiguity, people may respond to hermaphrodites with confusion and even disgust. But such need not be the case: the Pokot of eastern Africa are indifferent to what they consider a simple biological error, and the Navajo regard hermaphrodites with awe, viewing them as the embodiment of the full potential of both the female and the male (Geertz, 1975).

Transsexuals

Further complicating the story of human sexuality, some people deliberately change their sex. Hermaphrodites may undergo genital surgery to gain the appearance (and occasionally the function) of a sexually normal female or male. Surgery is also commonly considered by **transsexuals**, *people who feel they are one sex though biologically they are the other.* A number of transsexuals in Canada have had their genitals medically altered to escape the sense of being "trapped in the wrong body."

SEXUAL ORIENTATION

Sexual orientation refers to *an individual's preference in terms of sexual partners: same sex, other sex, either sex, neither sex* (Lips, 1993). For most living things, sexuality is biologically programmed. Of course, biology is at work in humans too, but for humans, sexual orientation is bound up in a complex web of cultural attitudes and rules. The norm in all industrial societies is *heterosexuality* (*hetero* is a Greek word meaning "the other of two"), by which a person is sexually attracted to someone of the other sex. However, *homosexuality* (*homo* is the Greek word for "the same"), by which a person is sexually attracted to people of the same sex, is not uncommon. Other sexual orientations, discussed presently, are *bisexuality* (attraction to either sex) or *asexuality* (attraction to neither sex).

Although all cultures endorse heterosexuality, many tolerate—and some have even encouraged—homosexuality. Among the ancient Greeks, for instance, elite men celebrated homosexuality as the highest form of relationship, shunning women, whom they considered their intellectual inferiors. As they saw it, heterosexuality was little more than a reproductive necessity, and men who did not engage in homosexuality were viewed as deviant. But because homosexual relations do not permit reproduction, no record exists of a society that has favoured homosexuality to the exclusion of heterosexuality (Kluckhohn, 1948; Ford and Beach, 1951; Greenberg, 1988).

The Origin of Sexual Orientation

How does a person develop a particular sexual orientation? There is no definitive answer to this question, but mounting evidence suggests that homosexuality and heterosexuality are rooted in biological factors present at birth and reinforced by hormone balance as well as social experiences as we grow (Gladue, Green, and Hellman, 1984; Weinrich, 1987; Troiden, 1988; Isay, 1989; Puterbaugh, 1990; Angier, 1992; Gelman, 1992). Noting that most adults who describe themselves as homosexuals have had some heterosexual experience (and many nominal heterosexuals have had at least some homosexual feelings), researchers conclude that sexual orientation is a highly complex human trait affected by both nature and nurture.

Moreover, there is no reason to think that sexual orientation is established in precisely the same way for everyone. Though physical and social scientists have discovered a great deal about sexual orientation, we still have much to learn.

The Gay Rights Movement

By the 1960s, homosexuals in North America became more visible and outspoken. By adopting the term *gay*, people were affirming their satisfaction with their sexual orientation. Gays also began to challenge stereotypes—pointing out that the personalities of gay people vary as much as those of "straights"—and to organize in opposition to pervasive discrimination.

In recent years, gay men have faced calamity in the form of acquired immune deficiency syndrome, or AIDS. Since 1980, this deadly disease has not only killed more than 5000 gay men and others in Canada, it also provoked a renewed outburst of prejudice, discrimination, and outright violence against gays. Today, however, Canadian attitudes towards abuse and AIDS are more liberal. Only 11 percent of Cana-

Svend Robinson, the first federal politician to publicly acknowledge his homosexuality, held a seat in Parliament for nine years before "coming out." His sexual orientation became a hot election issue in 1988 but, by 1997, was no longer of concern to voters. Nonetheless, most gay or lesbian politicians remain wary of going public (McDougall, 1997).

dians feel that an employer should be able to fire an AIDS-infected worker, and only 16 percent agree that a landlord should be able to deny accommodation (Ornstein, 1992:249). As late as 1990 a Canadian court ruled that a homosexual couple was not a family under workplace laws at the federal level. But by 1995, an Ontario court ruling made it possible for same-sex couples to adopt children (Bibby, 1995:64).

Until our society becomes more accepting of homosexuality, some gay people will understandably choose to remain "in the closet," fearfully avoiding public disclosure of their sexual orientation. Heterosexuals can begin to understand what this secrecy means by imagining never speaking about their romances to parents, roommates, or colleagues (Offir, 1982).

For their part, many gay men and gay women (commonly called *lesbians*) have adopted the term *homophobia* (with Greek roots meaning "fear of sameness") to describe the attitudes of their opponents. This word, first used in the late 1960s, designates an irrational fear of gay people (Weinberg, 1973). Instead of asking "What's wrong with gay people?" this label turns attention to society itself: "What's wrong with people who can't accept this sexual orientation?" Indeed, Canadians are becoming more accepting of homosexuality. In 1975, 14 percent of Canadians surveyed said that they regarded homosexuality as "not wrong at all"; by 1995, the number had risen to 32 percent (Bibby, 1995:72).

How Many Gay People?

The gay rights movement extends well beyond the gay community. But the movement has long pointed out that we all interact with many more gay people than we realize. So what share of our population is gay? Answering this question is difficult because, for one thing, people are not always willing to discuss their sexuality with strangers (or even family members); for another, sexual orientation is not a matter of neat, mutually exclusive categories. Pioneering sex researcher Alfred Kinsey (1948, 1953) described sexual orientation as a continuum, from exclusively homosexual at one end, through equally homosexual and heterosexual in the middle, to exclusively heterosexual at the other end. Kinsey contended that about 4 percent of males and 2 percent of females have an exclusively same-sex orientation, although he also estimated that at least one-third of men and one-eighth of women have had at least one homosexual experience leading to orgasm.

In the wake of the Kinsey studies, most social scientists settled on a figure of 10 percent to describe the proportion of gays in the U.S. population. But a comprehensive 1992 survey of sexuality in the United States indicates that precisely how one operationalizes "homosexuality" makes a big difference in the results (Laumann et al., 1994). About 9 percent of U.S. men and about 4 percent of women reported homosexual activity at some time in their lives. A second set of numbers suggests that a significant share of men (less so women) have a childhood homosexual experience that is not repeated after puberty. Finally, 2.8 percent of men and 1.4 percent of women define themselves as partly or entirely homosexual. Although a similar Canadian study is not available, there is no reason to suppose that Canadian figures would be significantly different.

Montreal has a reputation as a safe and comfortable place for gays. A gay bar scene took root in the 1930s—despite intolerance and frequent police raids—in part because the city's divided elite (French/English) failed to take full control. The work of photographer Alan B. Stone allowed drugstores and magazine stands in Quebec to provide gays with homegrown physique magazines through the 1950s and 1960s. The establishment (in 1983) of the *Archives gaies du Québec* (which is sorting through the Stone photograph collection) indicates a growing interest in exploring and documenting the history of gay Montreal. Capitalizing on this tolerant atmosphere, Montreal is making a bid to host the Gay Games in 2002 (Unland, 1997); Vancouver already hosted this international event in 1990.

Bisexuality

Alfred Kinsey and his colleagues treated sexual orientation as an "either/or" trait; to be more homosexual is, by definition, to be less heterosexual. But the evidence suggests that same-sex and other-sex attractions operate independently. At one extreme, *asexual* people experience little sexual attraction to people of either sex; at the other extreme, *bisexual* people feel strong attraction to people of both sexes.

In the 1992 U.S. sexuality survey discussed above, less than 1 percent of adults described themselves as bisexual. But bisexuality is far more popular (at least as a phase) among younger people (especially on university and college campuses) who reject rigid conceptions of proper relationships (Laumann, 1994; Leland, 1995). Many bisexuals, then, do not think of themselves as either gay or straight, and their behaviour reflects elements of both gay and straight living.

GENDER: A CULTURAL DISTINCTION

Gender refers to *the significance a society attaches to the biological categories of female and male.* Gender is a basic organizing principle of society that shapes how we think about ourselves and guides our interaction with others. But gender involves much more than difference; it also involves *hierarchy*, because it affects the opportunities and constraints we face throughout our lives (Ferree and Hall, 1996; Riley, 1997).

The inequality inherent in gender is no simple matter of biological differences between the two sexes. Females and males do differ biologically, of course, but, as Figure 12–1 suggests, the physical abilities of men and women are more alike than we may think.

What are the main biological differences between the sexes? Beyond the primary and secondary sex characteristics already noted, males around the world average 68 kg, compared to about 55 kg for females. In addition, males have more upper-body strength than women do, and men typically outperform women in short-term tests of physical endurance. Yet women outperform men in some tests of long-term endurance because they can draw on the energy derived from greater body fat. Females also outperform males in the ultimate game of life itself: the average life expectancy for men in Canada is 75.4 years, while women can expect to live 81.3 years (Columbo, 1995).

Adolescent males exhibit greater mathematical ability, while adolescent females outperform males in verbal skills, differences that researchers attribute to both biology and patterns of socialization (Maccoby, Emmons, and Jacklin, 1974; Baker et al., 1980; Lengermann and Wallace, 1985). But, according to research, there are no overall differences in intelligence between females and males.

Biologically, then, the sexes differ in limited ways, with neither one naturally superior. Nevertheless, the deeply rooted *cultural* notion of male superiority may seem so natural that we assume it is the inevitable consequence of sex itself. But society, much more than biology, is at work here, as several kinds of research reveal.

An Unusual Case Study

In 1963 a physician in a Canadian prairie town was performing a routine penis circumcision on seven-month-old identical twin boys. While using electro-cautery (surgery with a heated needle), the physician accidentally burned off the penis of one boy. Under-standably, the parents were horrified. After consulting with Dr. John Money of Johns Hopkins University, they decided to surgically change the boy's sex and to raise him as a girl.

The parents dressed Joan as a girl, let her hair grow long, and treated her according to cultural defi-nitions of femininity. Meanwhile, the twin brother—born an exact biological copy—was raised as a boy.

In the initial reports, the researchers reported that because of their different socialization, each child adopted a distinctive **gender identity**, *traits that females and males, guided by their culture, incorporate into their personalities.* In this extraordinary case, it was reported, one child learned to think of himself in terms that our culture defines as masculine, while the other child—despite beginning life as a male—soon began to think of herself as feminine.

The girl's development did not proceed smoothly, however, suggesting that some biological forces were coming into play. While feminine in some respects, later researchers reported that she began to display some masculine traits, including a desire to gain dominance among her peers. As she reached ado-lescence, she was showing signs of resisting her femi-nine gender identity (Diamond, 1982). By the spring of 1997, Diamond and Sigmundson suggested that the gender reassignment had been much less successful than previously reported. By age fourteen, Joan (who had been teased mercilessly by other children for her boyish looks and behaviour) was suicidal and refused to continue living as a girl. When the father broke down and told Joan the truth, she was relieved, as she could finally understand herself. Since then, Joan has become John—undergoing a mastectomy, hormone treatment, and surgical reconstruction of male geni-talia. Happy as a man, John has married and adopted his wife's children (Angier, 1997).[1] This complex case

---

[1] Joan/John was featured in a *Fifth Estate* documentary on gender reassignment (aired on September 23, 1997) in which he talked about the painful childhood he had endured because of rejection by his peers. His mother, who was interviewed as well, told of their experience from her perspective and, essentially, contradicted the statement attributed to her by researchers Money and Ehrhardt concerning the "feminine" qualities of the child.

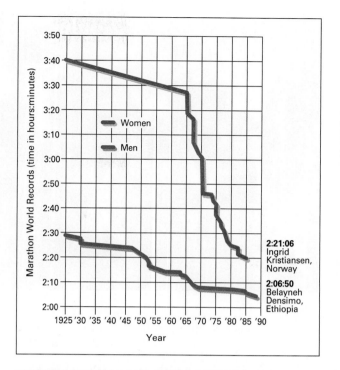

FIGURE 12–1 Men's and Women's Athletic Performance

Do men naturally outperform women in athletic competition? The answer is not obvious. Early in this century, men outdistanced women by many miles in marathon races. But as opportunities for women in athletics increased, women have been closing the performance gap. Less than fifteen minutes separates the current world marathon records for women (set in 1985) and for men (set in 1988).

SOURCE: 1995 Sports Almanac.

reveals that while gender (a social construct) is the product of the social environment, cultural condi-tioning does not operate free from the influence of biology.

GENDER IN GLOBAL PERSPECTIVE

The best way to see how gender is grounded in cul-ture is through global comparisons. Here, we briefly review three studies that highlight the global variety of gender.

The Israeli Kibbutzim

Some researchers investigating gender have focused on collective settlements in Israel called *kibbutzim*. The kibbutz (the singular form) is important for gender

In every society, people assume that certain jobs, patterns of behaviour, and ways of dressing are "naturally" feminine while others are just as obviously masculine. But, in global perspective, we see remarkable variety in such social definitions. These men, Wodaabe pastoral nomads who live in the African nation of Niger, are proud to engage in a display of beauty most people in our society would consider feminine.

research because its members historically have embraced social equality, with men and women sharing in both work and decision making.

In the kibbutzim, both sexes typically take care of children, cook, clean, maintain the buildings, and make decisions about the operation of the kibbutz. Boys and girls are raised in the same way, and from the first weeks of life, children live together in dormitories. Members of kibbutzim, then, do not consider sex relevant to most of aspects of everyday life.

There is evidence that women and men in the kibbutzim have never achieved complete social equality (Tiger and Shepher, 1975). But, even so, the kibbutzim stand as evidence of wide cultural latitude in defining what is feminine and masculine.

Margaret Mead's Research

Well-known anthropologist Margaret Mead also carried out groundbreaking research on gender. To the extent that gender reflects biological facts of sex, she reasoned, people everywhere should define the same traits as feminine and masculine; if gender is cultural, these conceptions should vary.

Mead studied three societies of New Guinea (1963; orig. 1935). In the high mountainous home of the Arapesh, Mead observed men and women with remarkably similar attitudes and behaviour. Both sexes, she reported, were cooperative and sensitive to others—in short, what our culture would label "feminine."

Moving south, Mead then studied the Mundugumor, whose culture of head-hunting and cannibalism stood in striking contrast to the gentle ways of the Arapesh. Both Mundugumor females and males were typically selfish and aggressive, traits we define as more "masculine."

Finally, travelling west to survey the Tchambuli, Mead discovered a culture that, like our own, defined females and males differently. Yet the Tchambuli reversed many of our notions about gender: Females tended to be dominant and rational, while males were submissive, emotional, and nurturing towards children. Based on her observations, Mead concluded that culture is the key to gender, since what one culture defines as masculine another may consider feminine.

Some critics consider Mead's findings "too neat," as if she saw in these three societies precisely the patterns she was looking for. Moreover, Deborah Gewertz (1981) challenged Mead's "reversal hypothesis," claiming that, in fact, Tchambuli males tend to be more aggressive and Tchambuli females tend to be more submissive. Gewertz explains that Mead visited the Tchambuli (who actually call themselves the Chambri) during the 1930s, after they had lost much of their property due to war, and observed men working in the home. But she maintains that this "domestic role" for Chambri men was just temporary.

George Murdock's Research

In a broader study of more than 200 pre-industrial societies, George Murdock (1937) found some global agreement about defining certain tasks as feminine and others as masculine. Hunting and warfare, Murdock found, generally fall to males, while home-centred tasks such as cooking and child care tend to be female work. With their simple technology, pre-industrial societies apparently assign roles to take advantage of men's and women's physical attributes: because of their greater size and short-term strength, men hunt game and protect the group; because women bear children, they assume domestic duties.

But beyond this general pattern, Murdock found significant variation. Consider agriculture: women did the farming in about the same number of societies as men did; but, in most societies, the two sexes divided this work. When it came to other tasks—from building shelters to tattooing the body—Murdock found societies of the world were as likely to turn to one sex as the other.

In Sum: Gender and Culture

Global comparisons show us that, by and large, societies do not consistently define most tasks as either feminine or masculine. As societies industrialize, which gives people more choices and decreases the significance of muscle power, gender distinctions become smaller and smaller (Lenski, Nolan, and Lenski, 1995). Gender, then, is simply too variable across cultures to be considered a simple expression of biology. Instead, as with many other elements of culture, what it means to be female and male is mostly a creation of society.

The cultural variability of gender also means that, anywhere in the world, the lives of women and men change over time. The "Global Sociology" box highlights change in the southern African nation of Botswana, and points out how and why gender is often controversial.

PATRIARCHY AND SEXISM

Although conceptions of gender certainly vary, a universal pattern among world societies is some degree of **patriarchy** (literally, "the rule of fathers"), *a form of social organization in which males dominate females*. Despite mythical tales of societies dominated by female "Amazons," the pattern of **matriarchy**, *a form of social organization in which females dominate males*, has never been documented in human history (Gough, 1971; Harris, 1977; Kipp, 1980; Lengermann and Wallace, 1985).

But while some degree of patriarchy may be universal, Global Map 12–1 shows significant variation in the relative power and privilege of females and males around the world. According to the United Nations, the Nordic nations (Norway, Sweden, and Finland) afford women the highest social standing; by contrast, women in the Asian nations of Pakistan and Afghanistan and the east African nation of Djibouti have the lowest social standing relative to men anywhere in the world. Out of 116 countries in the UN

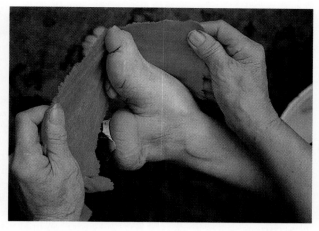

Among the most striking consequences of patriarchy in China is the ancient practice of "foot-binding," by which young girls' feet are tightly wrapped as they grow, with predictable results. Although this practice—now rare—produces what people deem "dainty" proportions, what effect would you imagine this deformity has on the physical mobility of women?

study, the U.S. ranked eighth and Canada ranked fifth in terms of gender equality (United Nations, 1995).

Sexism, *the belief that one sex is innately superior to the other*, is the ideological basis of patriarchy. In effect, sexism justifies men dominating women in much the same way that racism legitimizes whites dominating people of colour. Also like racism, sexism is more than a matter of individual attitudes. The idea that one sex is superior to the other is built into various institutions of our society. For example, *institutional sexism* pervades the economy, with women highly concentrated in low-paying jobs. Similarly, the legal system has historically winked at violence against women, especially when committed by boyfriends, husbands, and fathers (Landers, 1990).

The Costs of Sexism

Sexism, which is deeply entrenched in our society, has clear costs to women, who are denied opportunities, stand at increased risk of poverty, and endure sexual violence. Taking a broader view, sexism burdens all of society by stunting the talents and abilities of women, who are half the population. And even though men benefit in some respects from sexism, their privilege comes at a high price. Masculinity in our culture calls for men to engage in all sorts of high-risk behaviours, including smoking and chewing tobacco, drinking alcohol, participating in physically stressful sports, and even speeding on the road to the point that motor-vehicle accidents are the leading cause of death

Patriarchy Breaking Down: A Report from Botswana

As the judge handed down the decision, Unity Dow beamed, and people around her joined together in hugs and handshakes. Dow, then a thirty-two-year-old lawyer and citizen of the southern African nation of Botswana, had won the first round in her effort to overturn the laws that, she maintains, define women as second-class citizens.

The law that sparked Unity Dow's suit against her government specifies the citizenship rights of children. Botswana is traditionally patrilineal, meaning that people trace family membership through males, making children part of their father's—but not their mother's—family line. Citizenship law reflects this tradition, very important for anyone who marries a citizen of another country, as Dow did. Under the law, a child of a Botswanan man and a woman of another nationality is a citizen of Botswana, since legal standing passes through the father. But the child of a Botswanan woman and a man from another nation has no rights of citizenship. Thus, because she married a man from

the United States, Unity Dow's children had no citizen rights in the country in which they were born.

Ruling in Dow's favour, High Court Judge Martin Horwitz declared, "The time that women were treated as chattels [property] or were there to obey the whims and wishes of males is long past." In support of his decision, Horwitz pointed to the constitution of Botswana, which guarantees fundamental rights and freedoms to both women and men. Arguing for the government against Dow, Ian Kirby, a deputy attorney general, conceded that

Around the world, patriarchy is most pronounced in the economically poorest societies.

the constitution confers equal rights on the two sexes, but he claimed that the law can and should take account of sex where such patterns are deeply rooted in Botswanan culture. To challenge national traditions in the name of Western feminism, he continued, amounts to cultural imperialism by foreign influences.

Women from many African nations attended the Dow court case, suggesting that support for sexual equality is widespread. Many analysts on both sides of the issue agree that Dow's victory probably signals the beginning of historic change. Indeed, as a result of the Dow ruling, the government of Botswana amended its constitution to move women and men towards social equality.

To many people in Canada, the Dow case may seem strange, since the notion that men and women are entitled to equal rights and privileges is widely endorsed in our country.

SOURCES: John J. Macionis's personal communication with Unity Dow, and Shapiro (1991).

among young males. Moreover, as Marilyn French (1985) argues, patriarchy compels men to relentlessly seek control—not only of women but of themselves and the entire world. Thus, masculinity is closely linked not only to accidents but also to suicide and violence as well as to diseases related to stress. The so-called Type A personality—characterized by chronic impatience, driving ambition, competitiveness, and free-floating hostility—is a recipe for heart disease and almost perfectly matches the behaviour that our culture defines as masculine (Ehrenreich, 1983).

Finally, insofar as men seek control over others, they lose opportunities for intimacy and trust. As one

analyst put it, competition is supposed to separate "the men from the boys." In practice, however, it separates men from men—and from everyone else (Raphael, 1988).

Overall, when human feelings, thoughts, and actions are rigidly scripted according to a culture's conceptions of gender, people cannot develop and express the full range of their humanity. Society saddles males with the burden of being assertive, competitive, and always in control; simultaneously, society constrains females to be submissive, dependent, and self-effacing, regardless of their talents and inclinations.

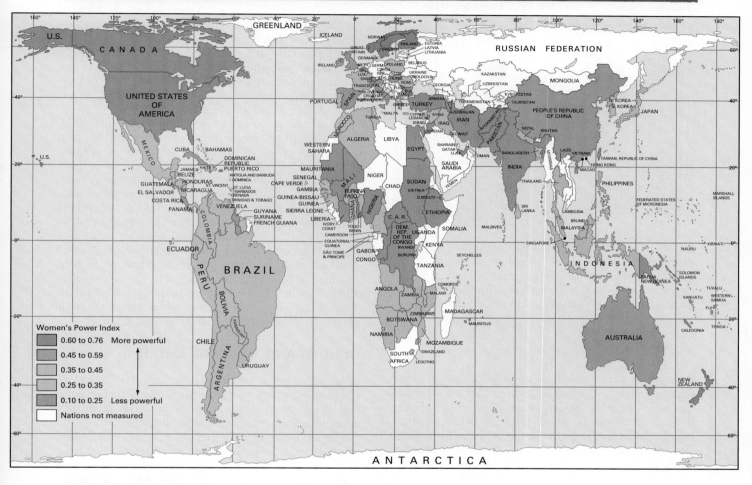

GLOBAL MAP 12–1 Women's Power in Global Perspective

A recent United Nations study ranked 116 nations on a scale of 0 (women have no power) to 1 (women have as much power as men). In general, women fare better in rich nations than they do in poor countries. Yet, some countries stand out: Scandinavian societies lead the world in promoting women's power.

SOURCE: United Nations (1997).

Is Patriarchy Inevitable?

In pre-industrial societies, women have little control over pregnancy and childbirth, which limits the scope of their lives. Similarly, men's greater height and physical strength are highly valued resources. But industrialization—including birth control technology—gives people choices about how to live. Today, then, in societies like our own, biological differences provide little justification for patriarchy.

But, legitimate or not, male dominance still holds sway in Canada and elsewhere. Does this mean that patriarchy is inevitable? Some sociologists claim that biological factors "wire" the sexes with different motivations and behaviours—specifically, more aggressiveness in males—that made the eradication of patriarchy difficult, perhaps even impossible (Goldberg, 1974, 1987; Rossi, 1985; Popenoe, 1993). Most sociologists, however, believe that gender is primarily a social construction that *can* be changed. Just because

TABLE 12–1 Traditional Notions of Gender Identity

Feminine Traits	Masculine Traits
Submissive	Dominant
Dependent	Independent
Unintelligent and incapable	Intelligent and competent
Emotional	Rational
Receptive	Assertive
Intuitive	Analytical
Weak	Strong
Timid	Brave
Content	Ambitious
Passive	Active
Cooperative	Competitive
Sensitive	Insensitive
Sex object	Sexually aggressive
Attractive because of physical appearance	Attractive because of achievement

no society has yet eliminated patriarchy does not mean that we must remain prisoners of the past.

To understand the persistence of patriarchy, we now examine how gender is rooted and reproduced in society, a process that begins in childhood and continues throughout our lives.

GENDER SOCIALIZATION

From birth until death, human feelings, thoughts, and actions reflect the social definitions that we attach to gender. Children quickly learn that their society defines females and males as different kinds of human beings; by about the age of three, they incorporate gender into their identities by applying society's standards to themselves (Kohlberg, 1966; Bem, 1981).

Table 12–1 sketches the traits that people in Canada and the United States traditionally have used to distinguish "feminine" and "masculine." Such oppositional thinking remains part of our way of life even though research suggests that most young people do not develop consistently feminine or masculine personalities (L. Bernard, 1980; Bem, 1993).

Just as gender affects how we think of ourselves, so it teaches us to *act* in normative ways. **Gender roles** (or sex roles) are *attitudes and activities that a society links to each sex.* Insofar as our culture defines males as ambitious and competitive, we expect them to engage in team sports and to aspire to positions of leadership. To the extent that we define females as deferential and emotional, we expect them to be good listeners and supportive observers.

GENDER AND THE FAMILY

The first question people usually ask about a newborn—"Is it a boy or a girl?"—looms large because the answer involves not just sex but the likely direction of the child's entire life.

In fact, gender is at work even before the birth of a child, since parents generally hope to have a boy rather than a girl. As we noted in Chapter 11 ("Global Stratification"), in China, India, and other strongly patriarchal societies, female embryos are at risk because parents may abort them, hoping later to produce a boy, whose social value is greater (United Nations Development Programme, 1991).

According to sociologist Jessie Bernard (1981), soon after birth, family members usher infants into the "pink world" of girls or the "blue world" of boys. Parents convey gender messages to children by how they themselves act and even unconsciously in the way they handle daughters and sons. One researcher at an English university presented an infant dressed as either a boy or a girl to a number of women; her subjects handled the "female" child tenderly, with frequent hugs and caresses, while treating the "male" child more aggressively, often lifting him up high in the air or bouncing him on their knees (Bonner, 1984). The lesson is clear: the female world revolves around passivity and emotion, while the male world places a premium on independence and action.

GENDER AND THE PEER GROUP

As children reach school age, their lives spill outside the family as they forge ties with others of the same age. Peer groups further socialize their members according to normative conceptions of gender.

Janet Lever (1978) spent a year observing fifth graders at play. She concluded that boys engage more in team sports—such as baseball and football—that involve many roles, complex rules, and clear objectives such as scoring a run or a touchdown. These games are nearly always competitive, separating winners from losers. Male peer activities reinforce masculine traits of aggression and control.

By contrast, girls play hopscotch or jump rope, or simply talk, sing, or dance together. Such spontaneous activities have few rules and rarely is "victory" the ultimate goal. Instead of teaching girls to be competitive, Lever explains, female peer groups promote interpersonal skills involving communication and cooperation—presumably the basis for family life.

To explain Lever's observations, recall Carol Gilligan's (1982) gender-based theory of moral reasoning in Chapter 5 ("Socialization"). Boys, Gilligan contends, reason according to abstract principles. For them, "rightness" amounts to "playing by the rules." Girls, by contrast, consider morality more a matter of their responsibilities to others. Thus, the games we play have serious implications for our later lives.

Some recent advertising reverses traditional gender definitions by portraying men as the submissive sex object of successful women. Although this reversal is new, the use of gender stereotypes to sell consumer products is very old indeed.

GENDER AND SCHOOLING

Even before children enter school, their reading tends to promote gender distinctions. A generation ago, the *Report of the Royal Commission on the Status of Women in Canada* (1970) analyzed a selection of children's texts and found that "versatile characters who have adventures are invariably males" (Mackie, 1983:185). Even math books represented males and females differently. For example, a problem focusing on the number of words typed per minute in forty-five minutes referred to the typist as female. The Commission concluded that "A woman's creative and intellectual potential is either underplayed or ignored in the education of children from their earliest years" (*Report of the Royal Commission on the Status of Women*, 1970:175).

More recently, a growing awareness among authors, publishers, and teachers of the limiting effects of gender stereotypes on young people has led to changes. Today's books for children portray females and males in a more balanced way.

Through primary and secondary school, despite many efforts at change, classroom curricula may still encourage children to embrace traditional gender patterns. For example, more young women take instruction in typing and home-centred skills such as nutrition and sewing. Classes in woodworking and auto mechanics, conversely, contain mostly young men.

In university, the pattern continues, with men and women tending towards different majors. Men are disproportionately represented in mathematics and the sciences, including physics, chemistry, and biology. Women cluster in the humanities (such as English), the fine arts (painting, music, dance, and drama), education courses, and the social sciences (including anthropology and sociology). New areas of study are also likely to be gender-typed. Computer science, for example, with its grounding in engineering, logic, and abstract mathematics, enrols mostly men, while courses in gender studies tend to enrol mostly women.

GENDER AND THE MASS MEDIA

Since television first captured the public imagination in the 1950s, white males have held centre stage. Racial and ethnic minorities were all but absent from television until the early 1970s; only in the last few decades have programs featured women in prominent roles.

Even when both sexes appear on camera, men generally play the brilliant detectives, fearless explorers, and skilled surgeons. Women, by contrast, play the less-capable characters, and are often important primarily for their sexual attractiveness.

Change has come most slowly to advertising, which sells products by conforming to widely established cultural norms. Advertising thus presents the two sexes, more often than not, in stereotypical ways. Historically, ads have shown women in the home, happily using cleaning products, serving foods, modelling clothing, and trying out new appliances. Men, on the other hand, predominate in ads for cars, travel, banking services, industrial companies, and alcoholic beverages. The authoritative "voice-over"—the faceless voice that promotes products on television and radio—is almost always male (Busby, 1975; Courtney and Whipple, 1983, Davis, 1993).

Pretty Is as Pretty Does: The Beauty Myth

The Duchess of Windsor once quipped, "A woman cannot be too rich or too thin." Perhaps the first half of this observation might apply to men as well, but certainly not the second half. It is no surprise that the vast majority of ads placed by the $20-billion-a-year cosmetics industry and the $40-billion-a-year diet industry target women.

Indeed, Naomi Wolf (1990) argues, women in our society are victimized by cultural patterns she terms the "beauty myth." The beauty myth arises, first, because society teaches women to measure themselves in terms of physical appearance (Backman and Adams, 1991). Yet, the standards of beauty (such as the *Playboy* centrefold or the one-hundred-pound fashion model) are unattainable for most women.

The beauty myth also derives from the way society teaches women to prize relationships with men, whom they

presumably attract with their beauty. Relentless pursuit of beauty not only

drives women towards being highly disciplined, but it also forces them to be highly attuned and responsive to men. Beauty-minded women, in short, try to please men and avoid challenging male power.

The beauty myth affects males as well, as men should want to possess beautiful women. In short, the concept of beauty reduces women to objects and motivates men to possess them as if they were dolls rather than human beings.

As Wolf explains, beauty is really more about behaviour than appearance. It should not be surprising, therefore, that the beauty myth surfaced in our culture during the 1890s, the 1920s, and the 1980s—all decades of heightened debate about the social standing of women.

SOURCE: Based on Wolf (1990).

In a systematic study of magazine and newspaper ads, Erving Goffman (1979) found other, more subtle biases. Men, he concluded, are photographed to appear taller than women, implying male superiority. Women are more frequently presented lying down (on sofas and beds) or, like children, seated on the floor. The expressions and gestures of men exude competence and authority, whereas women are more likely to appear in childlike poses. While men focus on the products being advertised, women direct their interest to men, conveying their supportive and submissive role.

Advertising also actively perpetuates what Naomi Wolf calls the "beauty myth." The "Social Diversity" box takes a closer look.

GENDER STRATIFICATION

Gender implies more than how people think and act. The concept of **gender stratification** refers to *a society's unequal distribution of wealth, power, and privilege between the two sexes*. In Canada, the lower social standing of women can be seen, first, in the world of work.

WORKING MEN AND WOMEN

In 1901, women comprised 13 percent of Canada's paid workforce and earned one-half of men's income (*Canada's 125th Anniversary Yearbook*, 1992). In 1996, 58.6 percent of women, compared with 72.7 percent of men, were active in the Canadian labour force (www.statcan.ca). So, the traditional view that earning an income is exclusively a "man's role" no longer holds true.

Among the factors at work in the changing Canadian labour force are the decline of farming, the growth of cities, shrinking family size, a rising divorce rate, and the fact that 65 percent of married couples depend on two incomes (*Women in Canada*, 1995:65).

In short, Canada and other industrial nations consider women working for income to be the rule rather than the exception. As Global Map 12–2 shows, however, this is not the case in many of the poorer societies of the world.

A common misconception (especially among middle-class people) holds that working women are

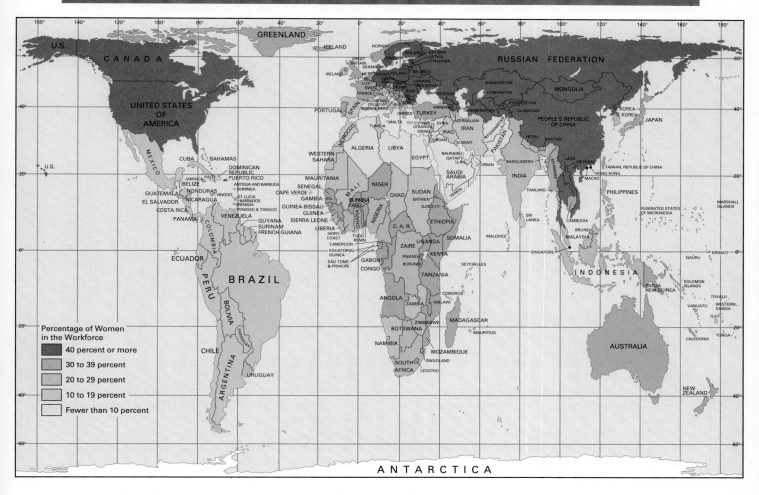

GLOBAL MAP 12–2 Women's Paid Employment in Global Perspective

In 1996, women comprised 45 percent of the labour force in Canada—up considerably from the last generation. Throughout the industrialized world, at least one-third of the labour force is made up of women. In poor societies, however, women work even harder than they do in this country, but they are less likely to be paid for their efforts. In Latin America, for example, women represent only about 15 percent of the paid labour force; in Islamic societies of northern Africa and the Middle East, the figure is even lower.

SOURCE: *Peters Atlas of the World* (1990).

childless. More and more women with children are entering the workforce, particularly over the last decade or so. In 1981, 50 percent of women with children under sixteen living at home belonged to the labour force; by 1994 the rate was 63 percent. By contrast, the employment rate for women without children under sixteen living at home grew from 46 percent to 50 percent (*Women in Canada*, 1995:64).

Gender and Occupations

While the proportions of men and women in the labour force have been converging—especially since 1970—the work they do remains distinct. As Table 12–2 shows, clerical work employs over 25 percent of all working women. In this category are secretaries, typists, stenographers, and other workers whose

TABLE 12–2 Distribution of Employment, by Occupation, 1982 and 1994

	1982			1994		
	Women	Men	Women as a % of occupation	Women	Men	Women as a % of occupation
Managerial/administrative	6.0	10.2	29.3	12.7	13.8	43.1
Professional:						
Natural sciences/engineering/mathematics	1.3	5.3	14.9	1.7	5.9	19.2
Social sciences/religion	2.0	1.8	42.7	3.3	2.1	56.8
Teaching	6.1	3.0	58.9	6.9	3.3	63.4
Doctors/dentists	0.3	0.8	18.3	0.5	0.9	32.1
Nursing/therapy/other health related	8.8	1.1	84.7	9.1	1.2	86.1
Artistic/literacy/recreational	1.4	1.6	38.6	2.2	2.1	46.4
Clerical	34.2	6.4	78.8	26.8	5.4	80.2
Sales	10.1	10.8	39.7	10.1	9.9	45.7
Service	18.1	10.7	54.2	17.1	11.0	56.2
Primary	2.8	8.0	19.6	2.1	6.4	21.3
Manufacturing	6.4	19.8	18.4	4.8	17.3	18.5
Construction	0.2	9.3	1.4	0.3	9.3	2.4
Material handling/other crafts	1.8	5.2	19.3	1.6	5.0	21.0
Total	100.0	100.0	41.2	100.0	100.0	45.2
Total employed (000s)	4544	6491	...	6002	7290	...

SOURCE: Adapted from *Women in Canada* (1995:76) from Statistics Canada, *Labour Force Survey*.

efforts typically support the work of men. Not surprisingly, over 80 percent of all such "pink-collar" jobholders are women. The second largest category is service work, performed by over 17 percent of employed women. These jobs include waiting tables and other food-service work. Both categories of jobs lie at the low end of the pay scale and offer limited opportunities for advancement.

Although increasing numbers of women, both married and single, are working, women remain highly segregated in the labour force because our society continues to link work to gender (Roos, 1983; Kemp and Coverman, 1989; *Women in Canada: A Statistical Report*, 1995).

Men predominate in most other job categories. Men overwhelmingly control the construction trades: 97.6 percent of brickmasons, stonemasons, structural metalworkers, and heavy-equipment mechanics are men. Men also hold the lion's share of positions that provide a great deal of income, prestige, and power. For example, more than 90 percent of engineers, 75 percent of judges and magistrates, 70 percent of physicians, 70 percent of corporate managers, and 65 percent of computer specialists are men (*Occupations*, 1993). Only a few women appear as top executives of the largest corporations in Canada. Even where men and women do much the same work, titles (and consequently pay) confer greater benefits on men. A "special assistant to the president," for example, is likely to

be a man, while an "executive secretary" is nearly always a woman.

Table 12–3 brings us up in time to 1990 and provides average income figures (based on the census) for men and women employed full-time, all year long in selected occupations. The occupations are ranked by male income. Physicians and surgeons have the highest incomes, although not as high as some of the negative publicity surrounding doctors would lead us to believe. Dentists are not too far behind doctors, but since their incomes do not come from public funds they are not as controversial (except in our incoherent private mutterings as we depart dentists' offices with frozen jaws and aching chequebooks). Elected members of legislative assemblies (also subject to loud public criticism) earn less than police officers and pharmacists. At the bottom of the income scale come housekeepers and child-care workers, with chefs, artists, musicians, and actors above them. Once again we see variation in the size of the gap between male and female incomes. In only *two* of the selected occupations (sociologists and radio and television announcers) do women actually make (slightly) more than men. Whatever the gender of the recipient, the range of average incomes for various occupations is substantial in Canada and implies vastly different lifestyles.

Overall, then, gender stratification permeates the workplace, where men tend to hold occupational positions that confer more wealth and power than those typically held by women. This gender-based hierarchy is easy to spot in the job setting: in most cases, female nurses assist male physicians, female secretaries serve male executives, and female flight attendants serve male airline pilots. Moreover, in any field, the greater the income and prestige associated with a job, the more likely it is to be held by a man.

HOUSEWORK: WOMEN'S "SECOND SHIFT"

One indicator of the global pattern of patriarchy, shown in Global Map 12–3, is the extent to which housework—cleaning, cooking, and caring for children—is the province of women. In North America, housework has always embodied a cultural contradiction: it is touted as essential for family life on the one hand, but it carries little prestige or reward on the other hand (J. Bernard, 1981).

Despite women's rapid entry into the labour force, the amount of housework performed by women has declined only slightly (and the proportion done by men has not changed at all). Although the typical couple shares in disciplining the children and managing finances, men routinely perform home repairs and yardwork while women see to most daily tasks of shopping, cooking, and cleaning. Consuming, on average, twenty-six hours a week, housework amounts to a "second shift" that women undertake after returning from the workplace each day (Schooler et al., 1984; Fuchs, 1986; Hochschild, 1989; Presser, 1993; Keith and Schafer, 1994; Benokraitis and Feagin, 1995).

In sum, men support the idea of women entering the labour force and most count on the money women earn. But men nonetheless resist modifying their own behaviour to help their partners in their careers by making their home lives more manageable (Komarovsky, 1973; Cowan, 1992; Robinson and Spitze, 1992; Lennon and Rosenfeld, 1994; Heath and Bourne, 1995).

GENDER, INCOME, AND WEALTH

In 1996, women working full-time earned an average of $30 717, while men working full-time earned $41 848. For every dollar earned by men, then, women earned about 73 cents.

In 1993, the average annual pretax income of women over age fifteen from all sources was $16 500—only 58 percent of the average income of men at that time. One part of the explanation for this discrepancy is that 11.9 percent of women had no source of personal income at all, compared to 4.5 percent of men (*Women in Canada*, 1995:84). Younger women, those fifty-four and under, have higher incomes than

TABLE 12–3 Average Income for Selected Occupations for Those Working Full-time, All Year Long, 1990 (Ranked by Male Income)

Occupation	Male	Female
Physicians and surgeons	$111,261	$73,071
Dentists	99,280	67,997
Lawyers and notaries	86,108	50,012
Athletes	75,358	n.a.
General managers and other senior officials	74,425	40,633
Osteopaths and chiropractors	68,404	45,368
University teachers	65,671	49,000
Veterinarians	57,542	39,262
Architects	53,083	36,083
Economists	52,739	51,369
Civil engineers	50,389	38,137
Police officers and detectives	49,497	38,415
Pharmacists	48,949	35,100
Biologists and related scientists	47,725	35,597
Members of legislative bodies	47,539	37,360
Secondary school teachers	47,385	41,667
Elementary and kindergarten teachers	45,471	37,694
Real estate sales	43,544	35,093
Systems analysts, computer programmers	43,025	35,932
Writers and editors	41,552	33,007
Sociologists	41,549	41,830
Radio and television announcers	36,614	37,563
Nurses	35,964	33,317
Secretaries and stenographers	33,839	23,880
Actors/actresses	33,359	22,879
Photographers and camera operators	31,323	22,949
Tool and die makers	30,646	25,860
Carpenters	29,565	19,512
Painters, paperhangers	28,763	23,483
Musicians and singers	27,036	20,066
Orderlies	24,984	23,599
Painters, sculptors, and related artists	22,396	14,533
Cashiers and tellers	21,913	17,243
Chefs and cooks	21,079	16,294
Child-care workers	20,987	13,252
Farmers	19,649	12,871
Housekeepers, servants	19,210	14,053

SOURCE: Statistics Canada, 1991, Catalogue No. 93-332.

women over fifty-five. Women with university degrees earn more money than those without one; in 1993, women with university degrees had an average annual income of $40 700. Women with non-university but post-secondary graduation earned an average of $28 000, and those who had graduated from high school and had some post-secondary training averaged $25 000. Finally, women without a high school diploma averaged $20 000 annually.

Furthermore, whatever women's educational levels, men earn more. Female university graduates who worked full-time, full-year earned three-quarters of the income of their male counterparts (*Women in Canada*, 1995:87).

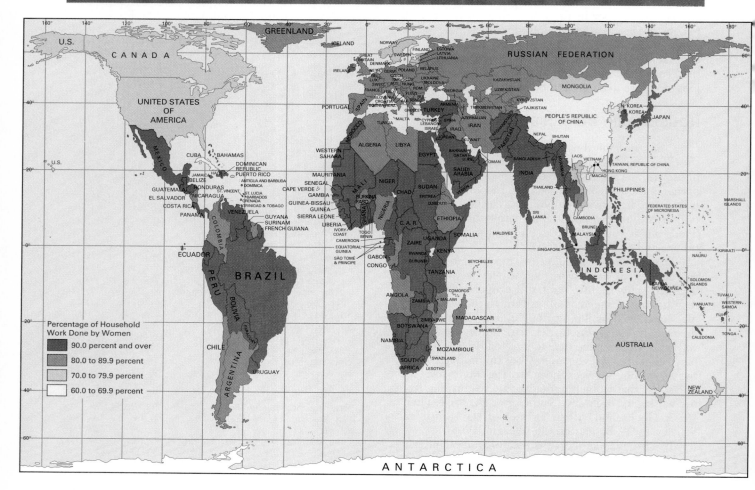

GLOBAL MAP 12–3 Housework in Global Perspective

Throughout the world, a major component of women's routines and identities involves housework. This is especially true in poor societies of Latin America, Africa, and Asia, where women are not generally in the paid labour force. But our society also defines housework and child care as "feminine" activities, even though a majority of Canadian women work outside the home. Married women spend almost twice as much time as married men on domestic work.

SOURCE: *Peters Atlas of the World* (1990), updated by John J. Macionis; *Women in Canada* (1995:83).

Differences in earnings between men and women in Canada have gradually declined in recent decades. Some of this change is due to increasing opportunities for working women; mostly, however, it reflects a *decline* in the earnings of men linked to a loss of manufacturing jobs.

The most important reason for the lower earnings of Canadian working women is the *kind* of work they do: largely clerical and service jobs. In effect, jobs and gender interact. People tend to perceive jobs with less clout as "women's work," and we devalue work simply because it is performed by women (Parcel, Mueller, and Cuvelier 1986; Blum, 1991; England, 1992; Bellas, 1994; Huffman et al., 1996).

During the 1980s, proponents of gender equality responded to this mind-set by proposing a policy of "comparable worth," which means that people should be paid, not according to the historical double standard, but based on the worth of what they actually do. Several nations, including Great Britain and Australia, and provinces such as Ontario under NDP Premier Bob Rae, have adopted such policies, although they have found limited acceptance in the United States.

A second cause of this gender-based income disparity has to do with the family. Both men and women have children, of course, but our culture defines parenting as more a woman's responsibility than a man's. Pregnancy and raising small children keep many younger women out of the labour force altogether at a time when their male peers stand to make significant occupational gains. As a result, women workers have less job seniority than their male counterparts (Fuchs, 1986; Stier, 1996; Waldfogel, 1997).

Moreover, women who choose to have children may be reluctant or unable to maintain fast-paced jobs that tie up their evenings and weekends. Career women with children may resolve this classic case of role strain by favouring jobs that offer a shorter commuting distance, more flexible hours, and employer-sponsored child-care services. Women seeking both a career and a family are torn between their dual responsibilities in ways that men are not. Consider this: among U.S. executives past the age of forty, about 90 percent of men—but only about 35 percent of women—have had a child (Schwartz, 1989). Women who do have children, in other words, start to fall behind childless women in terms of earnings.

Felice Schwartz (1989) also points out that corporate women risk their careers by having children. Rather than helping to meet the needs of working mothers, the typical corporation interprets a woman's choice to have a child as evidence that she may leave the company, taking with her a substantial investment in time and training. As an alternative, Schwartz calls on corporations to develop "mommy tracks" that allow women to meet family responsibilities while continuing their careers, with less intensity, for specified periods. This proposal has won praise, but it has also provoked strong criticism. Opponents of the "mommy-track" concept fear that it plays into the hands of corporate men who have long stereotyped women as being less attached to careers in the first place. Further, critics add, since companies are unlikely to apply such a plan to men, it can only hurt rather than help the career aspirations of corporate women.

The two factors noted so far—type of work and family responsibilities—account for about two-thirds of the earnings disparity between women and men. Researchers conclude that a third factor—discrimination against women—accounts for most of the remainder (Pear, 1987; Fuller and Schoenberger, 1991).

Because discrimination is illegal, it is often practised in subtle ways (Benokraitis and Feagin, 1995).

Diane McGarry, chairwoman, CEO, and president of Xerox Canada Inc., gets together for "girls' lunches" every three months with other executive women to talk about the pressures they share. These women agree that ambition has its price—at the expense of family and social life. Noting the small number of women at the top, McGarry points out the institutional and psychological obstacles women face—a plastic ceiling "because plastic is even harder to break than glass" (Maley, 1997).

Corporate women often encounter a so-called *glass ceiling*, a barrier that is hard to see and that is formally denied by high company officials, which effectively prevents women from rising above middle management.

For all these reasons, then, women earn less than men within all major occupational categories. As shown in Table 12–4, this disparity varies from job to job, but in only four of these major job classifications do women earn more than 70 percent of what men do.

GENDER AND EDUCATION

In the past, our society deemed schooling to be irrelevant for women, whose lives revolved around the home. But times have changed. In 1990, a majority of all bachelor's degrees (54 percent) were earned by women (*Women in the Labour Force*, 1990–91). Although the doors of universities and colleges have opened to women, the two sexes still tend to pursue different courses of study, although to a decreasing degree. In 1988, only 14.2 percent of those in engineering and 27.9 percent of those in the mathematical and physical sciences were women. On the other hand, women received over half of all degrees awarded in education (60.8 percent), fine and applied

TABLE 12–4 Earnings of Full-Time Canadian Workers, by Sex, 1990

Selected Occupational Categories	Income		Women's Income as a Percentage of Men's
	Men	Women	
Managerial, administrative, and related occupations	$47,446	$28,299	59.6%
Occupations in social sciences and related fields	$46,485	$22,634	48.7%
Teaching and related occupations	$40,600	$26,645	65.6%
Occupations in medicine and health	$57,424	$24,331	42.4%
Clerical and related occupations	$22,549	$16,831	74.6%
Sales occupations	$27,562	$13,968	50.7%
Service occupations	$20,146	$10,266	51.0%
Farming and horticultural occupations	$15,278	$ 9,561	62.6%
Machining and related occupations	$29,152	$17,458	59.9%
Mining and quarrying (including oil and gas field) occupations	$36,565	$20,814	56.9%

SOURCE: Employment by Income and Occupation: The Nation, Statistics Canada (1993).

arts (58.9 percent), and the humanities (56.5 percent) (*Women in the Labour Force*, 1990–91).

Women now enjoy more opportunities for postgraduate education, often a springboard to high-prestige jobs. In 1975 women in Canada earned 28.2 percent of all master's degrees; by 1988, the figure had risen to 44.9 percent. Women earned 30.6 percent of all doctoral degrees by 1988, but education was the only field of study in which women were awarded the majority of Ph.D.s—51.1 percent (*Women in the Labour Force*, 1990–91).

A growing number of women are pursuing academic programs that until recently were virtually all male. Women's share of degrees in medicine, engineering, applied sciences, mathematics, and physical sciences has grown since 1975. For instance, in medicine, the percentages of degrees awarded to women rose from 24.3 percent in 1975 to 40.5 percent in 1988 (*Women in the Work Force*, 1990–91).

Our society still defines high-paying professions (and the drive and competitiveness needed to succeed in them) as masculine; this helps to explain why women begin most pre-professional graduate programs in numbers equal to those of men but are less likely to complete their degrees (Fiorentine, 1987; Fiorentine and Cole, 1992). Nonetheless, the proportion of women in all these professions is steadily rising.

GENDER AND POLITICS

Before 1918, women could not vote in federal elections. Until 1919, no women were allowed to sit in the House of Commons, and until 1929, no women were allowed to sit in the Senate of Canada (*Canada's 125th Anniversary Yearbook*, 1992). It was not until 1940 that all eligible women in the country could vote in both federal and provincial elections. Table 12–5 cites milestones in women's gradual movement into Canadian political life.

Today, women are involved in all levels of politics in Canada. Still, the largest proportion of women politicians is found in the municipal arena. Women are also well represented on local school boards, where they can, again, act on their normative and institutionalized "responsibility" for their children.

There are, however, signs of change. An increasing proportion of our representatives in the House of Commons are women—moving up to 20 percent by 1997. The Canadian Advisory Council on the Status of Women stated that if the number of women in the House of Commons continued to increase at the rate it did between the 1984 and 1988 elections, in nine elections, or approximately forty-five years, there would be equal numbers of men and women in the House.

In 1989 the NDP became the first of Canada's major political parties to elect a woman leader—Audrey McLaughlin. In June 1993, Kim Campbell became Canada's first female prime minister by winning the leadership of the Conservative party when Brian Mulroney stepped down. Since 1997, Alexa McDonough has been the only female party leader in the House of Commons. In the Liberal party, Sheila Copps has been a starring member of the federal cabinet—and deputy prime minister for a term. Her brief resignation—because of an election promise to resign if the government did not eliminate the GST—may have reduced her chances of becoming the next Liberal leader.

A recent global survey found that while women are half the earth's population, they hold just 11.7 percent of seats in the world's 179 parliaments. While this represents a rise from 3 percent fifty years ago, only in the Nordic nations (Norway, Sweden, Finland, and Denmark) and the Netherlands does the share of parliamentary seats held by women (36.4 percent) even approach their share of the population (Inter-Parliamentary Union, 1997).

ARE WOMEN A MINORITY?

A **minority**[2] is *any category of people, distinguished by physical or cultural difference, that is socially disadvantaged.* Given the clear economic disadvantage of being a woman in our society, it seems reasonable to say that Canadian women are a minority.

Subjectively speaking, however, most white women do *not* think of themselves in this way (Hacker, 1951; Lengermann and Wallace, 1985). This is partly because, unlike racial minorities and ethnic minorities, white women are well represented at all levels of the class structure, including the very top.

Bear in mind, however, that women at every class level typically have less income, wealth, education, and power than men do. In fact, patriarchy makes women dependent for much of their social standing on men—first their fathers and later their husbands (J. Bernard, 1981).

MINORITY WOMEN

If women are defined as a minority, what about minority women? Are they doubly handicapped? Generally speaking, the answer is yes. First, there is the disadvantage associated with race and ethnicity. Aboriginal women have both the lowest labour force participation rate and the second-highest unemployment rate. Their unemployment level, at 28.2 percent, is well over twice that of nonaboriginal women. Aboriginal women who worked full-time in 1990 earned an average of $23 800, as compared to the $25 900 earned by nonaboriginal women. In addition, 33 percent of aboriginal women—compared to 17 percent of nonaboriginal women and 28 percent of aboriginal men—had incomes below Canada's low-income cutoff (Moore 1995:147).

As indicated in Figure 10–3 (p. 248), the average incomes of Asian and Black women are a little lower than that of British women—despite the fact that their levels of education and labour force participation are higher.

These disparities reflect minority women's lower positions on the occupational and educational hierarchies in comparison to white women (Bonilla-Santiago, 1990). Further, whenever the economy sags, minority women are especially likely to experience declining income and unemployment.

---

[2] We use the term "minority" rather than "minority group" because, as explained in Chapter 7 ("Groups and Organizations"), a minority is a category, not a group.

TABLE 12–5 Milestones for Women in Canadian Politics

Women's Rights

1916	Women in Manitoba, Alberta, and Saskatchewan gain right to vote in provincial elections.
1917	Women with property permitted to hold office in Saskatchewan. Women in British Columbia and Ontario gain right to vote in provincial elections.
1918	Women gain full federal franchise (right to vote). Women in Nova Scotia gain right to vote in provincial elections.
1919	Women in New Brunswick gain right to vote in provincial elections.
1920	Uniform franchise established through the *Dominion Election Act*, making permanent the right of women to be elected to Parliament.
1922	Women in Prince Edward Island gain right to vote and to hold elected office.
1925	Women over age twenty-five gain right to vote in Newfoundland.
1929	Women are deemed "persons" and can therefore be appointed to the Senate after the British Privy Council overturns Supreme Court of Canada's 1928 *Persons Case* decision, which had interpreted the BNA Act to mean women were not "persons" and could therefore not be appointed to the Senate.
1940	Women in Quebec gain right to vote in provincial elections, completing enfranchisement of women in Canada.
1983	*Canadian Human Rights Act* amended to prohibit sexual harassment and to ban discrimination on basis of pregnancy and family or marital status.

SOURCE: *Canada's 125th Anniversary Yearbook* (1992).

In short, gender has a powerful effect on our lives, but never operates alone. Class position, race and ethnicity, and gender form a multilayered system of disadvantage for some and privilege for others (Ginsberg and Tsing, 1990).

VIOLENCE AGAINST WOMEN

Perhaps the most wrenching kind of suffering that our society imposes on women is violence. As Chapter 8 ("Deviance") explained, official statistics paint criminal violence as overwhelmingly the actions of men—hardly surprising since aggressiveness is a trait our culture defines as masculine. Furthermore, a great deal of "manly" violence is directed against women, which we also might expect because North American society devalues what is culturally defined as feminine.

A 1993 Statistics Canada survey found that 51 percent of Canadian women had experienced at least one instance of sexual or physical violence. About 25 percent of women were subject to violence at the

Canadian Women in Hockey: Going for Gold

At the turn of the century, Canadian women were involved in hockey, doing battle in long, flowing skirts that made them look like sisters of the cloth rather than members of hockey teams. The Preston Rivulettes (from what is now part of Cambridge, Ontario) recorded an incredible win-loss record of 348–2 through the 1930s. But World War II intervened, draining attention and energies away from hockey so that by the 1950s, women's hockey had fizzled. The struggle to reestablish women's hockey—to get ice time, good equipment, sponsorships, public acceptance and support, media coverage, the attention of Don Cherry, and Olympic status—consumed the next forty to fifty years. In 1998 in Nagano, Japan, women's hockey would be an official Olympic sport for the first time.* With that announcement, and with Team Canada's *fourth* gold medal in the *fourth* world championship in Kitchener, On-

tario, in 1997, the world of Canadian women's hockey changed forever.

The game that originated in Canada, had become part of our collective identity, and continues to be our most popular sport, is now played by women—legitimately! Many of the women on Team Canada grew up playing on boys' teams and one, Manon Rhéaume, plays in the professional male leagues (for Tampa Bay Lightning). As a result of recent publicity (and the decision to prohibit body-checking in women's hockey), parents in large numbers are now willing to enrol their young daughters in girls' hockey leagues. Girls' teams—which often play against boys' teams—are springing up across Canada, and girls' participation in hockey has almost quadrupled in the last decade to 24 000 players nationally.

Without doubt, the image of girls and women as hockey players is inconsistent with our societal expectations of

femininity. Off the ice, most of these women conform to our cultural standards of feminine behaviour, dress, and makeup. However, when they don their protective hockey uniforms and helmets and step out onto the ice, they enter a world in which they exhibit aggression, speed, and impressive skill: power skating, strategic agility, and adroit handling of stick and puck become their tools. This transformation from "woman" to "athlete" (in a traditionally male or macho sport) is not easy for the women themselves, nor is it easy to accept for all members of the general public. There are still people who feel, strongly, that women should stick to ballet, gymnastics, and synchronized swimming (another Canadian "invention"). Ambivalence is apparent in embarrassment on the part of some Team Canada members about the fact that their first world championship (in Ottawa in 1990) was won in pink and white uniforms.

---

hands of an intimate partner (*Violence Against Women Survey*, 1993).

The most common location for gender-linked violence is the home. Richard Gelles (cited in Roesch, 1984) argues that, with the exception of the police and the military, the family is the most violent organization in the United States. There is no reason, given the statistics cited in the previous paragraph, to think that the picture is any different in Canada. Both sexes suffer from family violence, although, by and large, women sustain more serious injuries than men do (Straus and Gelles, 1986; Schwartz, 1987; Shupe, Stacey, and Hazlewood, 1987; Gelles and Cornell, 1990; Smolowe, 1994). Chapter 17 ("Family") delves more deeply into the problem of family violence.

Violence against women also occurs in casual relationships. As Chapter 8 ("Deviance") explained, most rapes involve not strangers but men known (and often trusted) by women. Dianne F. Herman (1992) argues that the extent of abuse suggests that sexual violence is built into our way of life. All forms of violence against women—from the wolf whistles that

intimidate women on city streets to a pinch in a crowded subway to physical assaults that occur at home—express what she calls a "rape culture" by which men try to dominate women. Sexual violence, then, is fundamentally about *power* rather than sex, and therefore should be understood as a dimension of gender stratification (Griffin, 1982).

Sexual Harassment

Sexual harassment refers to *comments, gestures, or physical contact of a sexual nature that are deliberate, repeated, and unwelcome.* During the 1990s, sexual harassment became an important North American issue that has already significantly redefined the rules for workplace interaction between the sexes.

Most victims of sexual harassment are women. Our culture encourages men to be sexually assertive and to perceive women in sexual terms; social interaction in the workplace, on campus, and elsewhere, then, can readily take on sexual overtones. Furthermore, most individuals in positions of power—includ-

Excitement about Team Canada's prospects was intense prior to the 1998 Winter Olympics. On January 20, our women's hockey team was ranked first among Canada's ten best bets for Olympic gold—ahead of Elvis Stojko (Christie, 1998). The media-driven gold fever contributed to a national groan of disappointment when our women's hockey team came home with "only" a silver medal—a feat that should have had Canadians bursting with pride.

Team Canada members celebrate a goal at the 1998 Winter Olympics in Nagano.

agents, being recognized on the street, and being the subject of sometimes overwhelming media attention. The dramatic change in the status of women's hockey is exciting for female players across the country and for the Canadian public as a whole. In their own way, these women have stretched the limits of and changed the definition of femininity.

Whatever the outcome, pre- and post-Olympic publicity has changed the lives of the women who play hockey for Team Canada. The quest for public awareness and support is over. Don Cherry's active support of women's hockey is now part of the public record. Major media in Canada, including *Maclean's*, *The Globe and Mail*, and the CBC, all provided extensive coverage of the exploits and victories of Team Canada, women's style. The team members have agents and contracts for product endorsements—from women's hockey apparel to soup (where Cassie Campbell appears with Don Cherry). Sports Canada helps cover their expenses and employers are willing to give the athletes time off to prepare for championship or Olympic competition. It will be a while before these young women become accustomed to having

* On January 16, 1998, the CBC ran a full-length edition of *The National Magazine* about women's hockey and our Olympic team. Among other guests, two of the women who had played for the Preston Rivulettes in the 1930s, and who would be watching Team Canada at Nagano, shared their thoughts on the dramatic changes in the world of women's hockey.

SOURCES: CBC (1998); Smith (1997a); Smith (1997b).

ing business executives, physicians, bureau chiefs, assembly-line supervisors, professors, and military officers—are men who oversee the work of women. Surveys carried out in widely different work settings confirm that half of women respondents report receiving unwanted sexual attention (Loy and Stewart, 1984; Paul, 1991).

Sexual harassment is sometimes blatant and direct, as when a supervisor solicits sexual favours from a subordinate, coupled with the threat of reprisals if the advances are refused. Courts have declared such *quid pro quo* sexual harassment (the Latin phrase means "one thing in return for another") to be an illegal violation of human or civil rights.

However, the problem of unwelcome sexual attention often involves subtle behaviour—sexual teasing, off-colour jokes, pinups displayed in the workplace—which an individual may not *intend* as harassment of another person. But, using the *effect* standard favoured by many feminists, such actions create a *hostile environment* (Cohen, 1991; Paul, 1991). Incidents of this kind are far more complex because

they involve different perceptions of the same behaviour. For example, a man may think that complimenting a co-worker on her appearance is simply a polite gesture; she, on the other hand, may deem his behaviour offensive and a hindrance to her job performance.

Pornography

Pornography, too, underlies sexual violence. Defining pornography has long challenged scholars and lawmakers alike. Unable to set a single, specific standard to distinguish what is, and what is not, pornographic, the Supreme Court allows provinces, cities, and counties to decide for themselves what violates "community standards" of decency and lacks any redeeming social value.

But few doubt that pornography (loosely defined) is popular: X-rated videos, 900 telephone numbers offering sexual conversation, and a host of sexually explicit movies, magazines, and Internet Web sites together constitute a multimillion-dollar-a-year industry.

Many public organizations and private companies have adopted policies to discourage forms of behaviour, conversation, or images that might create a "hostile or intimidating environment." In essence, such policies seek to remove sexuality from the workplace so that employees can do their jobs while steering clear of traditional notions about female and male relationships.

Traditionally, society has cast pornography as a *moral* issue, involving how people express their sexuality. A more recent view holds that pornography demeans women. That is, pornography is really a *power* issue because it fosters the notion that men should control both sexuality and women. Catharine MacKinnon (1987) has branded pornography as one foundation of male dominance because it portrays women in dehumanizing fashion as the subservient playthings of men. Worth noting, in this context, is that the term "pornography" is derived from the Greek word *porne*, meaning a harlot who acts as a man's sexual slave.

A related charge is that pornography promotes violence against women. While demonstrating a scientific cause-and-effect relationship between what people watch and how they act is difficult, research supports the contention that pornography gives men licence to think of women as objects rather than as people (Mallamuth and Donnerstein, 1984; Attorney General's Commission on Pornography, 1986). The public as a whole also voices concern about the effects of pornography, and many people hold the opinion that pornography encourages men to commit rape.

Like sexual harassment, pornography raises complex and sometimes conflicting issues. While everyone objects to material we find offensive, many also endorse the rights of free speech and artistic expression. But pressure to restrict this kind of material is building through the efforts of an unlikely coalition of conservatives (who oppose pornography on moral grounds) and progressives (who condemn it for political reasons).

THEORETICAL ANALYSIS OF GENDER

Although they come to differing conclusions, the structural-functional and social-conflict paradigms each point out the importance of gender in social organization.

STRUCTURAL-FUNCTIONAL ANALYSIS

The structural-functional paradigm views society as a complex system of many separate but integrated parts. From this point of view, gender functions as a way to organize social life.

As Chapter 4 ("Society") explained, members of hunting and gathering societies had little power over the forces of biology. Lacking effective birth control, women experienced frequent pregnancies, and the responsibilities of child care kept them close to home. Likewise, to take advantage of men's greater strength, norms guided men towards the pursuit of game and other tasks away from the home. Over many generations, this sexual division of labour became institutionalized and largely taken for granted (Lengermann and Wallace, 1985).

Industrial technology opens up a vastly greater range of cultural possibilities. Human muscle-power no longer serves as a vital source of energy, so the physical strength of men loses much of its earlier significance. At the same time, the ability to control reproduction gives women greater choice in shaping their lives. Modern societies come to see that traditional gender roles waste an enormous amount of human talent; yet change comes slowly, because gender is deeply embedded in social mores.

Talcott Parsons: Gender and Complementarity

As Talcott Parsons (1942, 1951, 1954) explained, gender differences help to integrate society—at least in its traditional form. Gender, Parsons noted, creates a *complementary* set of roles that link men and women together into family units that carry out various functions vital to the operation of society. Women take charge of family life, assuming primary responsibility for managing the household and raising children. Men, by contrast, connect the family to the larger world, primarily by participating in the labour force.

Parsons further argued that distinctive socialization teaches the two sexes their appropriate gender identity and skills needed for adult life. Thus, society teaches boys—presumably destined for the labour force—to be rational, self-assured, and competitive. This complex of traits Parsons termed *instrumental*. To prepare girls for child rearing, their socialization stresses what Parsons called *expressive* qualities, such as emotional responsiveness and sensitivity to others.

Society, explains Parsons, promotes gender conformity by instilling in men and women a fear that straying too far from accepted standards of masculinity or femininity courts rejection by members of the opposite sex. In simple terms, women learn to view nonmasculine men as sexually unattractive, while men learn to avoid unfeminine women.

Critical evaluation. Structural-functionalism advances a theory of complementarity by which gender integrates society both structurally (in terms of what people do) and morally (in terms of what they believe). Although influential at midcentury, this approach is rarely used today by researchers exploring the impact of gender.

For one thing, functionalism assumes a singular vision of society that is not shared by everyone. For example, many women have always worked outside the home as a matter of economic necessity, a fact not reflected in Parsons's conventional, middle-class view of family life. Second, critics charge that Parsons's analysis minimizes the personal strains and social costs of rigid, traditional gender roles (Wallace and Wolf, 1995). Third, for those who seek sexual equality, what Parsons describes as gender "complementarity" amounts to little more than male domination.

SOCIAL-CONFLICT ANALYSIS

From a social-conflict point of view, gender involves not just differences in behaviour but disparities in power. Conventional ideas about gender historically have benefited men while subjecting women to prejudice, discrimination, and sometimes outright violence, in a striking parallel to the treatment of racial and ethnic minorities (Hacker, 1951, 1974; Collins, 1971; Lengermann and Wallace, 1985). Thus, conflict theorists claim, conventional ideas about gender promote not cohesion but tension and conflict, with men seeking to protect their privileges while women challenge the status quo.

As earlier chapters noted, the social-conflict paradigm draws heavily on the ideas of Karl Marx. Yet Marx was a product of his time insofar as his writings focused almost exclusively on men. His friend and collaborator Friedrich Engels, however, did develop a theory of gender stratification (1902; orig. 1884).

Friedrich Engels: Gender and Class

Looking back through history, Engels noted that in hunting and gathering societies the activities of women and men, although different, had comparable importance. A successful hunt may have brought men great prestige, but the vegetation gathered by women constituted most of a society's food supply (Leacock, 1978). As technological advances led to a productive surplus, however, social equality and communal sharing gave way to private property and, ultimately, a class hierarchy. At this point, men gained pronounced power over women. With surplus wealth on their hands, upper-class men wanted to be sure of paternity, so they would be able to pass on property to their heirs; they could do this only by controlling women's sexuality. Women were then taught to remain virgins until marriage, to remain faithful to their husbands thereafter, and to build their lives around bearing and raising children.

According to Engels, capitalism intensifies this male domination. First, capitalism creates more wealth, which confers greater power on men as wage earners as well as owners and heirs of property. Second, an expanding capitalist economy depends on defining people—especially women—as consumers and convincing them that personal fulfilment derives from owning and using products. Third, to allow men to work, society assigns women the task of maintaining the home. The double exploitation of capitalism, as Engels saw it, lies in paying low wages for male labour and no wages for female work (Eisenstein, 1979; Barry, 1983; Jagger, 1983; Vogel, 1983).

Critical evaluation. Social-conflict analysis highlights how society places the two sexes in unequal positions of wealth, power, and privilege. As a result, the conflict approach is decidedly critical of conventional ideas about gender, claiming that society would be better off if we minimized or even eliminated this dimension of social structure.

But social-conflict analysis, too, has its critics. One problem, they suggest, is that this approach casts conventional families—defended by traditionalists as morally good—as a social evil. From a more practical standpoint, social-conflict analysis minimizes the extent to which women and men live together cooperatively and often quite happily. A third problem with this approach, for some critics, is its assertion that capitalism stands at the root of gender stratification. Agrarian countries, in fact, are typically more patriarchal than industrial-capitalist nations. And socialist

Dorothy Smith is a Canadian sociologist who has influenced a generation of feminist scholarship. Her work involves a radical revision of the way that knowledge, truth, and science are constructed—starting with the actual experiences of women. Her notion of bifurcated consciousness arose out of the discrepancies between her experiences as an academic and as a single mother of two. Combining elements of Marxism, ethnomethodology, and symbolic interaction, hers is a sociology of and for women.

societies, too—including the People's Republic of China—remain strongly patriarchal (Moore, 1992).

FEMINISM

Feminism is *the advocacy of social equality for the sexes, in opposition to patriarchy and sexism.* The "first wave" of the feminist movement in Canada began in the mid-1800s as Canadian women were influenced by writing such as Mary Woolstonecraft's *A Vindication of the Rights of Women*, published in 1792. The primary objective of the early women's movement was securing the right to vote, which was achieved for federal elections in Canada by 1918 with the passage of the *Women's Franchise Act*. Ironically, women were not "persons" before the law until 1929, and women living in Quebec could not vote in provincial elections until 1940.

BASIC FEMINIST IDEAS

Feminism views the personal experiences of women and men through the lens of gender. How we think of ourselves (gender identity), how we act (gender roles), and our sex's social standing (gender stratification) are all rooted in the operation of our society.

Although people who consider themselves feminists disagree about many things, most support five general principles:

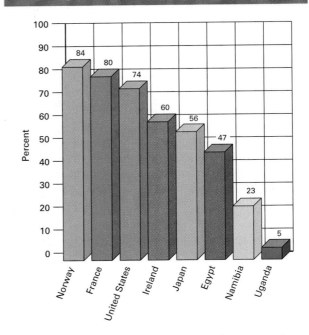

FIGURE 12–2 Use of Contraception by Married Women of Childbearing Age

SOURCE: The World Bank (1995).

1. **The importance of change.** Feminist thinking is decidedly political, linking ideas to action. Feminism is critical of the status quo, advocating change towards social equality for women and men.

2. **Expanding human choice.** Feminists maintain that cultural conceptions of gender divide the full range of human qualities into two opposing and limited spheres: the female world of emotion and cooperation and the male world of rationality and competition. As an alternative, feminists pursue a "reintegration of humanity" by which each person develops *all* human traits (French, 1985).

3. **Eliminating gender stratification.** Feminism opposes laws and cultural norms that limit the education, income, and job opportunities of women.

4. **Ending sexual violence.** Today's women's movement seeks to eliminate sexual violence. Feminists argue that patriarchy distorts the relationships between women and men, and encourages violence against women in the form of rape, domestic abuse, sexual harassment, and pornog-

raphy (Millet, 1970; J. Bernard, 1973; Dworkin, 1987).

5. **Promoting sexual autonomy.** Finally, feminism advocates women's control of their sexuality and reproduction. Feminists support the free availability of birth control information. As Figure 12–2 shows, contraceptives are much less available in most of the world than they are in Canada. In Canada, although information about birth control circulated from the early 1930s on, birth control became legal only in 1969 (Bishop, 1988). In addition, most feminists support a woman's right to choose whether to bear children or to terminate a pregnancy, rather than allowing men—as husbands, physicians, and legislators—to regulate sexuality. Many feminists also support gay peoples' efforts to overcome prejudice and discrimination in a predominantly heterosexual culture (Deckard, 1979; Barry, 1983; Jagger, 1983).

Violence against women is an important public issue of the 1990s. But, some analysts ask, isn't it men whose lives are built around the experience of violence? In pursuit of a less violent society, how would you change our culture's definitions of masculinity?

VARIATIONS WITHIN FEMINISM

People pursue the goal of sexual equality in different ways, yielding three general types of feminism: liberal, socialist, and radical (Barry, 1983; Jagger, 1983; Stacey, 1983; Vogel, 1983).

Liberal Feminism

Liberal feminism is grounded in classic liberal thinking that individuals should be free to develop their own talents and pursue their own interests. Liberal feminists accept the basic organization of our society but seek to expand the rights and opportunities of women. Liberal feminists support equal rights and oppose prejudice and discrimination that block the aspirations of women.

Liberal feminists also endorse reproductive freedom for all women. They respect the family as a social institution, but seek changes including widely available maternity leave and child care for women who wish to work. Moreover, while liberal feminists support the family as a social institution, they contend that families need to change to accommodate the ambitions of both women and men.

With their strong belief in the rights of individuals, liberal feminists do not think that all women need to move collectively towards any one political goal. Both women and men, through their individual achievement, are capable of improving their lives if society simply ends legal and cultural barriers rooted in gender.

Socialist Feminism

Socialist feminism evolved from Marxist conflict theory, partly as a response to Marx's inattention to gender (Philipson and Hansen, 1992). From this point of view, capitalism intensifies patriarchy by concentrating wealth and power in the hands of a small number of men.

Socialist feminists view the reforms sought by liberal feminism as inadequate. The bourgeois family fostered by capitalism must change, they argue, to replace "domestic slavery" with some collective means of carrying out housework and child care. This goal can only be realized through a socialist revolution that creates a state-centred economy to meet the needs of all. Such a basic transformation of society requires women and men to pursue their personal liberation together, rather than individually, as liberal feminists maintain.

Radical Feminism

Radical feminism, too, finds the reforms called for by liberal feminism inadequate. Moreover, radical feminists claim that even a socialist revolution would not end patriarchy. Instead, this variant of feminism holds that gender equality can be realized only by eliminating the cultural notion of gender itself.

The foundation of gender, say radical feminists, is the biological fact that only women bear children. Radical feminists, therefore, look towards new reproductive technology (see Chapter 17, "Family") to separate women's bodies from the process of childbearing. With the demise of motherhood, radical feminists reason, the entire family system could be left behind, liberating women, men, and children

Men's Rights! Are Men Really So Privileged?

"Anti-male discrimination has become far greater in scope, in degree, and in damage than any which may exist against women."
Richard F. Doyle

It is men, this chapter argues, who dominate society. Men enjoy higher earnings, control more wealth, exercise more power, do less housework, and get more respect than women do. The controversial assertion above, however, sums up an important counterpoint advanced by the "men's rights movement"—that the male world is not nearly as privileged as most people think.

If men are so privileged in our society, why do they turn to crime more often than women do? Moreover, the operation of the criminal justice system emphasizes the *lack* of special privileges accorded to men. When police make an arrest for a crime, approximately 85 percent of the time the handcuffs are slapped on a man (*Women in Canada*, 1995:101). Women make up 3 percent of those imprisoned in federal penitentiaries and 9 percent of those admitted to provincial facilities (*Women in Canada*, 1995:102).

Culture, too, is not always generous to men. Our way of life praises as "real men" those males who work and live hard, and who typically drink, smoke, and speed on the highways. Given this view of maleness, is it any wonder that men are twice as likely as women to suffer serious assault, three times more likely to fall victim to homicide, and four times more likely to commit suicide? Even more curious, in light of these statistics, is our national preoccupation with violence against *women*! Perhaps, critics suggest, we are in the grip of a cultural double standard: we expect males to commit self-destructive acts, while lamenting the far fewer cases in which brutality harms women. It is this same double standard, the argument continues, that moves women and children out of harm's way while expecting men to "go down with the ship" or to die defending their country on the battlefield.

Child custody is another sore point from the perspective of many men. Despite decades of consciousness-raising in pursuit of gender fairness, and clear evidence that men earn more income than women, courts across Canada routinely settle custody disputes by awarding primary care of children to mothers. And, to make matters worse, men separated from their children by the courts are then stigmatized as "runaway fathers" or "dead-beat dads."

Many men feel disadvantaged by affirmative action policies. Policies based on these laws give women, all objective criteria being equal, an edge in the workforce (where historic gaps between the sexes are slowly closing).

Even nature seems to have plotted against men by giving women, on average, a 10 percent bonus in longevity. But the controversial question is, when society plays favourites, who is favoured?

Continue the debate . . .

1. *Do you think that, overall, our culture benefits men or women? Why?*
2. *On the campus, do men's organizations (such as fraternities and athletic teams) enjoy special privileges? What about women's organizations?*
3. *On balance, do you agree or disagree with the "men's rights" perspective? Which specific points do you find convincing or objectionable? Why?*

SOURCES: Based on Doyle (1980) and Scanlon (1992).

---

from the tyranny of family, gender, and sex itself (Dworkin, 1987). Thus, radical feminism envisions a revolution much more far-reaching than that sought by Marx. It seeks an egalitarian and gender-free society.

Opposition to Feminism

Feminism provokes criticism and resistance from both men and women who hold conventional ideas about gender. Some men oppose feminism for the same reasons that many white people have historically opposed social equality for people of colour: they want to preserve their own privileges. Other men and women, including those who are neither rich nor powerful, distrust a social movement (especially its more radical expressions) that attacks the traditional family, rejecting what they see as time-honoured patterns that have guided male-female relationships for centuries.

Further, for some men, feminism threatens the basis of their status and self-respect: their masculinity. Men who have been socialized to value strength and dominance feel uneasy about the feminist notion that they can also be gentle and warm (Doyle, 1983). Similarly, women whose lives centre on their husbands and children may see feminism as trying to deprive them of cherished roles that give meaning to their lives (Marshall, 1985).

Resistance to feminism also comes from within academic circles. Some sociologists charge that feminism wilfully ignores a growing body of evidence that men and women do think and act in somewhat different ways (which may make gender equality impossible). Furthermore, say critics, with its drive to enhance women's presence in the workplace, feminism denigrates the crucial and unique contribution women make to the development of children—especially in the first years of life (Baydar and Brooks-Gunn, 1991; Popenoe, 1993).

Finally, there is the question of *how* women should go about improving their social standing. Although a large majority of people in Canada believe women should have equal rights, most also believe that women should advance individually, according to their abilities.

Thus, opposition to feminism is primarily directed at its socialist and radical variants; otherwise, there is widespread support for the principles of liberal feminism. Moreover, we are seeing an unmistakable trend towards greater gender equality. In 1942, during World War II, a Gallup poll asked Canadians, "If women take the place of men in industry, should they be paid the same wages as men?" Eighty-nine percent of women and 78 percent of men agreed. By 1995 the idea of equal pay for equal work was supported by 98 percent of a representative sample of Canadians (Bibby, 1995:4).

LOOKING AHEAD: GENDER IN THE TWENTY-FIRST CENTURY

Predictions about the future are, at best, informed speculation. Just as economists disagree about the inflation rate a year from now and political scientists can only guess at the outcome of upcoming elections, sociologists can offer only general observations about the likely future of gender and society.

Certainly, change has been remarkable. A century ago, women in Canada clearly occupied a subordinate position. Husbands controlled property in marriage, laws barred women from most jobs, from holding political office, and even from voting. Although women today remain socially disadvantaged, the movement towards equality has surged ahead. Note, further, that two-thirds of people entering the workforce during the 1990s have been women. Truly, today's economy *depends* on the earnings of women (Hewlett, 1990).

Many factors have contributed to this transformation. Perhaps most important, industrialization has both broadened the range of human activity and shifted the nature of work from physically demanding tasks that favoured male strength to jobs that require human thought and imagination, placing the talents of women and men on an even footing. Additionally, medical technology has afforded us control over reproduction, so women's lives are less constrained by unwanted pregnancies.

Many women and men have also made deliberate efforts in pursuit of social equality. Sexual harassment complaints, for example, now are taken much more seriously in the workplace. And as more women assume positions of power in the corporate and political worlds, social changes in the twenty-first century may turn out to be even greater than those we have already witnessed.

Yet strong opposition to feminism persists. Gender still forms an important foundation of personal identity and family life, and it is deeply woven into the moral fabric of our society. Therefore, efforts at changing cultural ideas about the two sexes will continue to provoke opposition, as the final box illustrates. On balance, however, while change is likely to proceed incrementally, the movement towards a society in which women and men enjoy equal rights and opportunities seems certain to gain strength.

SUMMARY

1. Sex is a biological concept; a human fetus is female or male from the moment of conception. Hermaphrodites represent rare cases of people who combine the biological traits of both sexes. Transsexuals are people who feel they are one sex though biologically they are the other, and who nowadays can choose to alter their sex surgically.

2. Heterosexuality is our species' dominant sexual orientation, although people with a bisexual or exclusively homosexual orientation make up a small percentage of the population everywhere.

3. Gender involves how cultures assign human traits and power to each sex. Gender varies historically and across cultures. Some degree of patriarchy, however, exists in every society.

4. Through the socialization process, people link gender with personality (gender identity) and actions (gender roles). The major agents of socialization—the family, peer groups, schools, and the mass media—reinforce cultural definitions of what is feminine and masculine.

5. Gender stratification entails numerous social disadvantages for women. Although most women are now in the paid labour force, a majority of working women hold low-paying clerical or service jobs. Unpaid housework also

remains a task performed predominantly by women.

6. On average, Canadian women earn about 70 percent as much as men do. This disparity stems from differences in jobs and family responsibilities as well as discrimination.

7. Women in Canada now earn a slight majority of all bachelor's degrees. Men still receive a majority of all master's degrees, doctorates, and professional degrees.

8. The number of women in politics has increased sharply in recent decades. Still, the vast majority of elected officials nationwide are men.

9. Minority women encounter greater social disadvantages than white women.

10. On the basis of their distinctive identity and social disadvantages, all women represent a social minority, although many do not think of themselves in such terms.

11. Violence against women is a widespread problem in Canada. Our society is also grappling with the issues of sexual harassment and pornography.

12. Structural-functional analysis holds that pre-industrial societies benefit from distinctive roles for males and females reflecting biological differences between the sexes. In industrial societies, marked gender inequality becomes dysfunctional and slowly decreases. Talcott Parsons claimed that complementary gender roles promote the social integration of families and society as a whole.

13. Social-conflict analysis views gender as a dimension of social inequality and conflict. Friedrich Engels tied gender stratification to the development of private property. He claimed that capitalism devalues women and housework.

14. Feminism endorses the social equality of the sexes and actively opposes patriarchy and sexism. Feminism also strives to eliminate violence against women and to give women control over their sexuality (and reproduction).

15. There are three variants of feminist thinking. Liberal feminism seeks equal opportunity for both sexes within current social arrangements; socialist feminism advocates abolishing private property as the means to social equality; radical feminism aims to create a gender-free society.

16. Because gender distinctions stand at the core of our way of life, feminism has encountered strong resistance.

CRITICAL THINKING QUESTIONS

1. In what ways are sex and gender related? In what respects are they distinct?

2. What techniques do the mass media use to "sell" conventional ideas about gender to women and men?

3. Why is gender a dimension of social stratification? How does gender interact with inequality based on race, ethnicity, and class?

4. What do feminists mean by asserting that "the personal is political"? Explain how liberal, socialist, and radical feminism differ from one another in their understanding of this phrase.

SOCIOLOGY APPLIED

1. Researchers have found that, when describing the performance of woman athletes compared to men athletes, sportscasters are much more likely to use phrases suggesting physical weakness or emotional fragility. Watch a televised tennis match involving men and women and see if you can detect any such pattern.

2. Take a walk through a business area of your local community. Which businesses are frequented almost entirely by women? By men? By both men and women?

3. Several of the research studies noted in this chapter would be easy to replicate on a small scale. Try spending several hours observing children at play. Do you find that boys and girls play different kinds of games, as Janet Lever's research suggests (see page 302)? Or, examine a sample of newspaper or magazine advertisements. Does gender figure in them the way Erving Goffman claims (see page 304)?

4. Do some research on the history of women's issues in your province or territory. When was the first woman sent to Parliament? What laws have existed restricting the work of women?

www.iglhrc.org/
Founded in 1990, the *International Gay and Lesbian Human Rights Commission* is an advocacy group that supports the fundamental human rights of gay men, lesbians, bisexuals, transgendered people, and people with HIV and AIDS through monitoring, documenting, advocating, and public policy development, as well as grassroots organizing and supporting groups in developing countries.

www.web.net/archives/
Containing more than 300 pages of information, this resource site published by the *Canadian Lesbian and Gay Archives* includes a description of its holdings, many online documents (guides, chronologies, lives, essays, reviews, and monographs), and links to other sites.

www.igc.org/Womensnet/dworkin/index.html
American writer Andrea Dworkin supports women's rights and crusades against pornography, sexual abuse,

and censorship. The *Andrea Dworkin Online Library* contains selections from her most important nonfiction books, excerpts from her novels and short stories, texts from some of her speeches, articles, interviews, and op-ed pieces, and an autobiography.

www.swc-cfc.gc.ca/direct.html
Status of Women Canada is the federal government agency that promotes gender equality and the full participation of women in the economic, social, cultural, and political life of the country. SWC focuses on improving women's economic autonomy and well-being, eliminating systemic violence against women and children, and advancing women's human rights.

www.feminist.org/gateway/vs_exec2.html
The *Feminist Majority Foundation* site provides a gateway to Internet resources about violence against women, including information networks, research, fact sheets, self-defence, and support organizations.

Harry Roseland, *Beach Scene, Coney Island,* 1891

CHAPTER 13

RACE AND ETHNICITY

"When you're brought up with discrimination," says Barbara Carter of Dresden, Ontario, "you know what you can do and what you can't do. So you just abide by the rules and it's not that bad. We knew we couldn't go into the restaurants with our white girlfriends after school, so we just didn't go. I never understood, however, why there were two churches. There were two Baptist churches in town. One for the whites and one for the Blacks."

"It was different for me," says Bruce. "I was a very bitter person when I was a teenager. At one time there was not one restaurant in town where I could get a cup of coffee. Toward the end of the war we had German prisoners of war around here. They were working in the sugar-beet fields under guard. The prisoners of war could go into the restaurants, but a negro soldier in a Canadian army uniform couldn't. It was pretty bad. My aunt taught in a segregated school. The last one closed in the sixties."

"We went to Disney World a while ago," says Bruce. "We went to the Canadian pavilion. They have a movie about Canada there. It's a tremendous movie—all in the round. But do you know what? There is not one Black person in the whole movie. I was watching it and I thought, 'Wait a minute, where am I?' So I sat through it a second time to make sure. It's like we're a non-people. We weren't even in the crowd scenes" (McLean, 1992:75).

Globally, the pattern of inequality and conflict based on colour and culture is even more pronounced. Ukrainians, Moldavians, Azerbaijanis, and other ethnic peoples in Eastern Europe are struggling to recover their cultural identities after the collapse of the Soviet Union. In the Middle East, deep-rooted friction between Arabs and Jews continues in much the same way that Blacks and whites strive to establish a just society in South Africa. In Rwanda, India, Sri Lanka, and elsewhere, racial and ethnic rifts frequently flare up into violent confrontation.

Surely one of the greatest ironies of the human condition is that colour and culture—traits that are the roots of our greatest pride—are also those that most often foment hatred and violence and propel us into war. This chapter examines the meaning of race and ethnicity, explains how these social constructs have shaped our history, and suggests why they continue to play such a central part—for better or worse—in the world today.

THE SOCIAL SIGNIFICANCE OF RACE AND ETHNICITY

People in Canada and elsewhere in the world frequently use the terms "race" and "ethnicity" imprecisely and interchangeably. For this reason, we begin with important definitions.

RACE

A **race** is *a category composed of people who share biologically transmitted traits that members of a society deem* *socially significant*. People may classify each other into races based on physical characteristics such as skin colour, facial features, hair texture, and body shape.

Racial diversity appeared among our human ancestors as a result of living in different geographical regions of the world. In regions of intense heat, for example, people developed darker skin (from the natural pigment, melanin) that offers protection from the sun; in regions with moderate climates, humans have lighter skin. But such differences are just skin deep because *every* human being the world over is a member of a single biological species.

The striking variety of racial traits found today is the product of migration and intermarriage over the course of human history, so that many genetic characteristics once common to a single place are now evident throughout the world. Especially pronounced is the racial mix found in the Middle East (that is, western Asia), a region that has long served as a crossroads of human migration. Notable racial uniformity, by contrast, characterizes more isolated peoples such as the island-dwelling Japanese. But no society lacks genetic mixture, and increasing contact among the world's peoples will ensure that racial blending will accelerate in the future.

RACIAL TYPOLOGY

Nineteenth-century biologists responded to the world's racial diversity by developing a three-part scheme of racial classifications. They labelled people with relatively light skin and fine hair as *Caucasian*; they called those with darker skin and coarser, curlier hair *Negroid*; and people with yellow or brown skin and distinctive folds on the eyelids were termed *Mongoloid*.

Sociologists consider such categories misleading, at best, since we now know that no society is composed of biologically pure individuals. In fact, the world traveller notices gradual and subtle racial variations from region to region. The people conventionally called "Caucasians" or "whites" actually display skin colour that ranges from very light to very dark, and the same variation occurs among so-called "Negroids" and "Mongoloids." Some "whites" (such as the Caucasians of southern India) actually have darker skin and hair than some "Blacks" (including the blond Negroid Aborigines of Australia).

Although we might think that we can readily distinguish between "Black" and "white" people, research confirms that Canadians, like people throughout the world, are genetically mixed. Over many generations, the genetic traits of Negroid Africans, Caucasian Europeans, and Mongoloid Native Americans (whose ancestors came from Asia) have spread widely throughout the Americas. Many "Black" people, therefore, have a large proportion of Caucasian genes, and many "white" people have at least some Negroid genes. Similarly, a significant proportion of the French Canadian population has some—largely unacknowledged—native ancestry. Some of these people identify themselves as Métis, while others are totally unaware of their biological roots. In short, there is a great deal of racial blending—in North America and elsewhere.

Despite the reality of biological mixing, however, people around the world place each other in racial classifications and rank these categories in systems of social inequality. People sometimes defend racial hierarchy, claiming that one category is inherently "better" or more intelligent than another, although no sound scientific research supports such assertions (see the "Social Diversity" box on p. 328). But because so much is at stake, it is no wonder that societies focus on racial labelling more than facts permit. Earlier in this century, for example, many of the southern U.S. states legally defined as "coloured" anyone who had at least one-thirty-second African ancestry (that is, one African-American great-great-great-grandparent or any closer ancestor). Today, with race less of a caste distinction in the United States, the law enables parents to declare the race of a child.

Although Canada has a long-standing interest in its ethnic composition, it was only in the 1996 census that an attempt was made to determine racial identification. In the past, our attempts to determine the size of our visible-minority population were based on declared country of origin (or ancestry) and self-definition. If someone claimed to be of Jamaican origin, for example, it was assumed (sometimes incorrectly) that he or she is Black. Similarly, and equally incorrectly at times, someone who declared British or U.S. origins was assumed to be Caucasian. Even status or treaty Indians, whose precise numbers are known because of registration, are of mixed racial ancestry. In other words, any attempt to describe Canada in terms of racial composition is an approximation only.

One admittedly rough measure of biological mixing is the proportion of people who claim to be of mixed racial origins. By 1986, almost half (48 percent) of those claiming aboriginal origin indicated that they had mixed or multiple origins. This was true of 33 percent who claimed Black origin and 13 percent of those of Asian origin (Statistics Canada, 1989b). Statistics Canada's Public Use Microdata Files suggest similar patterns for the three categories in 1991.

ETHNICITY

Ethnicity is *a shared cultural heritage*. Members of an ethnic category have common ancestors, language, or religion that, together, confer a distinctive social iden-

The range of biological variation in human beings is far greater than any system of racial classification allows. This fact is made obvious by trying to place all of the people pictured here into simple racial categories.

tity. For certain purposes, as in dealing with ethnic categories that are undergoing change, it is important to distinguish between *objective* and *subjective* criteria (Isajiw, 1985). Objective criteria are traits such as ancestry, cultural practices, dress, religion, and language. Subjective criteria involve the internalization of a distinctive social identity, whereby people identify themselves or are perceived by others as belonging to a different group. Subjective ethnic identities may persist beyond cultural assimilation, sometimes over many generations, without perpetuation of traditional ethnic culture (the objective components). Whatever the degree of assimilation, ethnicity remains an important basis of social differentiation in Canada.

Over three million Canadians (12 percent of the population) claim languages other than French and English as their mother tongues. About half that number still speak those languages at home. There are now more Catholics than Protestants in Canada (see Chapter 18, "Religion"), as Catholic French Canadians have been joined by immigrants from traditionally Catholic areas such as Italy, Poland, and Latin America. Canada's Jewish population (roughly 250 000 people) traces its ancestral ties to various countries, as do the Eastern Orthodox and Muslim people.

Race and ethnicity, then, are quite different: one is biological, the other cultural. But the two sometimes go hand in hand. Japanese Canadians, for example, have distinctive physical traits and—for those who

maintain a traditional way of life—cultural attributes as well. But ethnic distinctiveness should not be viewed as racial. For example, Jews are sometimes described as a race although they are distinctive only in their religious beliefs as well as their history of persecution (Goldsby, 1977).

Finally, people can *change* their ethnicity by adopting a different way of life. Polish immigrants who discard their cultural background over time may cease to have a particular ethnicity. In a similar vein, people of mixed native and non-native heritage may have blended into the dominant francophone or anglophone populations of their respective provinces to the point where many are completely unaware of their mixed ancestry. From time to time people actually re-establish ethnic ties and identities after two or three generations, making serious efforts to return to their Polish, Jewish, or native roots.

MINORITIES

As Chapter 12 ("Sex and Gender") described, a racial or ethnic *minority* is a category of people, distinguished by physical or cultural traits, that is socially disadvantaged. Distinct from the dominant "majority," in other words, minorities are set apart and subordinated. In recent years, the breadth of the term "minority" has expanded in meaning to include not only people with particular racial and ethnic traits but also people with physical disabilities, and, as the previous chapter explained, women.

Minorities have two major characteristics. First, they share a *distinctive identity*. Because race is highly visible (and virtually impossible for a person to change), most minority men and women are keenly aware of their physical differences. The significance of ethnicity (which people *can* change) is more variable. Throughout Canada's history, some people have downplayed their historic ethnicity, while others have maintained their cultural traditions and lived in distinctive ethnic neighbourhoods. Some go so far as to insulate themselves from potentially assimilating influences: Hasidic Jews in Montreal have been particularly successful in nurturing a lifestyle that effectively separates them from their neighbours. The Hutterite people of the Prairie provinces, who have the advantage of living in communal agricultural colonies, manage even more effectively to minimize contact with the "outside."

A second characteristic of minorities is *subordination*. Chapter 10 ("Social Class in Canada") explained that minorities in Canada may have lower incomes and less occupational prestige than those of British or French origin, even if, as in the case of Blacks and Asians, their levels of educational attainment are as high or higher. These facts mean that class, race, and ethnicity, as well as gender, are not mutually exclusive but overlapping and reinforcing dimensions of social stratification.

Of course, not all members of any minority category are disadvantaged. But even the greatest success rarely allows individuals to transcend their minority standing (Benjamin, 1991). That is, race or ethnicity often serves as a *master status* (described in Chapter 6, "Social Interaction in Everyday Life") that overshadows personal accomplishments.

The term "minority" suggests that these categories of people constitute a small proportion of a society's population. But this is not always the case. For example, Blacks form a numerical majority in South Africa although they are grossly deprived of economic and political power by whites. In Canada, women represent slightly more than half the population but are still struggling to gain opportunities and privileges long enjoyed by men.

PREJUDICE

Prejudice is a *rigid and irrational generalization about an entire category of people*. Prejudice is irrational to the extent that people hold inflexible attitudes that are supported by little or no direct evidence. Further, prejudice leads people to characterize an entire category, the vast majority of whom they have never even met. Prejudice may target a particular social class, sex, sexual orientation, age, political affiliation, race, or ethnicity.

Prejudices are *prejudgments* that may be positive or negative. Our positive prejudices tend to exaggerate the virtues of people like ourselves, while our negative prejudices condemn those who differ from us. Negative prejudice runs along a continuum, ranging from mild aversion to outright hostility. Because attitudes are rooted in our culture, everyone has at least some measure of prejudice.

STEREOTYPES

Prejudice often involves **stereotypes** (*stereo* is derived from Greek, meaning "hard" or "solid"), *prejudicial views or descriptions of some categories of people*. Because many stereotypes involve emotions such as love and loyalty (generally towards members of ingroups) or hate and fear (towards outgroups), they are hard to change even in the face of contradictory evidence. For example, some people have a stereotypical understanding of the poor as lazy and irresponsible freeloaders who would rather rely on welfare than support themselves (Waxman, 1983). As was explained in Chapter 10 ("Social Class in Canada"), however, this stereotype distorts reality, since more than half of the poor people in Canada are children, working adults (including single mothers), or elderly people.

Stereotypes have been devised for virtually every racial and ethnic minority, and such attitudes can become deeply rooted in a society's culture. In Canada, many white people stereotype native people and other visible minorities as lacking motivation to improve their own lives. Such attitudes assume that social disadvantage stems from personal deficiency. This stereotypical view ignores some key facts: most poor people in Canada are white and most members of visible minorities work as hard as anyone else and are not poor. In this case the bit of truth in the stereotype is that, proportionately, natives and members of some other visible minorities are more likely than whites to be poor. But by building a rigid attitude out of a few selected facts, stereotypes grossly distort reality.

RACISM

A powerful and destructive form of prejudice, **racism** refers to *the belief that one racial category is innately superior or inferior to another*. Racism has pervaded world history. The ancient Greeks, the peoples of India, and the Chinese—despite their many notable achievements—were all quick to view people unlike themselves as inferior.

Racism has also been widespread in Canada: at one point, the enslavement of people of African descent or of native people (called *Panis* in New France) was supported by notions of their innate inferiority—as was the placement of First Nations peoples on reserves under paternalistic administration by an Ottawa-based Indian Affairs department.

Although Canadians are by no means devoid of prejudice, there is evidence that Canadians are more tolerant of racial and ethnic minorities than are their American neighbours (Lipset, 1991:112). The fact that Toronto, in a very short period of time, went from being a largely Anglo-Saxon Protestant city to one with a substantial immigrant and visible-minority component without major violence or disruption suggests a fair degree of social tolerance (Artibise, 1988:244). Bibby (1995:52–54) reports that between 1980 and 1995, Canadian sensitivity to the fact that minorities are subject to discrimination had increased by about 10 percent. In the meantime, between 1975 and 1995, acceptance of interracial and interfaith marriage had increased by a similar amount: more than 80 percent approve of interracial marriage and 90 percent approve of interfaith marriage—remarkable levels in both cases.

Overt racism in this country has subsided to some extent because of a more egalitarian culture and is "checked by the state in order to preserve social harmony and order" (Li, 1988:49). Racism persists, though in less open and direct forms, and research continues to document the injury and humiliation that racism causes to people of colour (Ramcharan, 1982; Wotherspoon and Satzewich, 1993). As the box explains, however, racial differences in mental abilities are due to environment rather than to biology.

Historically, the assertion that certain categories of people are *innately* inferior has provided a powerful justification for subjecting others to social inferiority. By the end of the last century, European nations and the United States had forged vast colonial empires. (Canada has never acquired external colonies, being one itself, but it has established a system of *internal* colonialism with respect to aboriginals living on reserves.) Colonial exploitation often took the form of subjugating foreign peoples with the callous claim that they were somehow less human than the explorers who enslaved them.

Stanley Barrett (1987:5–6), an anthropologist who did field research among various white supremacist groups in Canada, notes that

> Racism constitutes an elaborate and systematic ideology; it acts as a conceptual tool to rationalize the division of the world's population into the privileged and the deprived. It is inherently a political phenomenon. It emerged with the advent of the colonization of the Third World by European nations, and thus coincided too with the development of capitalism.

In a legal effort to mitigate sharp patterns of social inequality, India reserves half of all government positions for members of castes deemed disadvantaged. Because the government is the largest employer, higher-caste college students fear that this policy will shut them out of the job market after graduation. So intense are these concerns that eleven students killed themselves recently—five by fire—in public protest over this controversial policy.

In this century, racism was central to the Nazi regime in Germany. Nazi racial doctrine proclaimed a so-called Aryan race of blond-haired, blue-eyed Caucasians that was allegedly superior to all others and destined to rule the world. This racist ideology was used to justify the murder of anyone deemed inferior, including some six million European Jews and millions of Poles, gypsies, homosexuals, and people with physical and mental disabilities.

More recently, racial conflict has intensified in Britain and Western European societies as whites confront millions of immigrants from former colonies and refugees from strife-torn Eastern Europe. Similarly, in Canada, one can observe signs of increasing racial tensions that are aggravated by tough economic times. Racism—in thought and deed—remains a serious social problem here and elsewhere.

THEORIES OF PREJUDICE

If prejudice does not represent a rational assessment of facts, what are its origins? Social scientists have offered various answers to this vexing question, citing the importance of frustration, personality, culture, and social conflict.

Scapegoat Theory

Scapegoat theory holds that prejudice springs from frustration. Such attitudes, therefore, are common among

Does Race Affect Intelligence?

Are Asians more intelligent than Europeans? Is the typical European smarter than the average African? Assertions painting one category of people as more intellectually gifted than another have been common throughout history. Moreover, people have used such thinking to justify the privileges of an allegedly superior category or even to bar supposedly inferior people from entering the country.

The distribution of human intelligence forms a classic "bell curve," shown in the figure. By convention, average intelligence is defined as an IQ score of 100 (technically, an IQ score is mental age as measured by a test, divided by age in years, with the result multiplied by one hundred; thus, an eight-year-old who performs like a ten-year-old has an IQ of 10/8 = 1.2 × 100 = 120).

Philippe Rushton, a psychology professor at the University of Western Ontario, became the centre of academic controversy in 1989, when he claimed that in terms of intelligence, conformity to the law, and sexual restraint Orientals are superior to whites who, in turn, are superior to Blacks. Other researchers and journalists were quick to point out the methodological flaws in his research, criticizing his basic assumptions, data collection, and causal inferences. So politically incorrect were his assertions in the current Canadian climate that many people across the country demanded that his tenure at Western be revoked.

In a controversial study of intelligence and social inequality, Richard Herrnstein and Charles Murray (1994) contend that overwhelming research evidence supports the conclusion that race is related to intelligence. More specifically, they place the IQ of people with European ancestry at 100. People of East Asian ancestry exceed that standard slightly, aver-aging 103; people of African descent fall below that standard, with an average IQ of 90.

Of course, assertions of this kind are explosive because they fly in the face of our democratic and egalitarian beliefs, by implying that people of one racial type are inherently "better" than another. In response, some people charge that intelligence tests are not valid, while others question whether what we call "intelligence" has much real meaning.

Most social scientists acknowledge that IQ tests do measure something important that we think of as "intelligence," and they agree that some *individuals* have more intellectual aptitude than others. But they reject the notion that any *category* of people, on average, is "smarter" than any other. That is, categories of people may show small differences on intelligence tests, but the crucial question is *why.*

Thomas Sowell, an African-American social scientist, has demonstrated that most of the documented racial differences in intelligence are not due to biology but to people's environment. In some skilful sociological detective work, Sowell tracked down IQ scores for various racial and ethnic categories from early in this century. He found that, on average, immigrants from European nations such as Poland, Lithuania, Italy, and Greece, as well as Asian countries including China and Japan, scored ten to fifteen points below the U.S. average. Sowell's critical discovery came next: people in these same categories *today* have IQ scores that are average or above average. Among Italian Americans, for example, average IQ jumped almost ten points in fifty years; among Polish and Chinese Americans, the rise was almost twenty points.

Because genetic changes occur over thousands of years and these people largely married among themselves, biological factors simply cannot explain such a rise in IQ scores. Rather, the evidence points to changing cultural patterns. As immigrants settled in the United States, their new surroundings affected them in ways that improved their intellectual performance as measured in intelligence tests.

Sowell found that the same pattern applies to African-Americans. Sowell explains that African-Americans living in the northern U.S. have historically outscored people living in the southern U.S. on IQ tests by about ten points. And, among African-Americans who migrated from the south to the north after 1940, IQ scores soon rose as they did among earlier immigrants. Thus, if environmental factors are the same for everyone, racial IQ differences largely disappear.

What IQ test score disparities do tell, according to Sowell, is that *cultural patterns* matter. Asians who score high on tests are no smarter than other people, but they have been raised to value learning and to pursue excellence. For their part, African-Americans are no less intelligent than anyone else, but they carry a legacy of disadvantage that undermines self-confidence and discourages achievement.

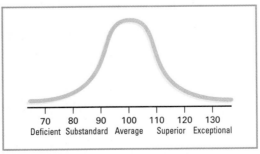

IQ: The Distribution of Intelligence

SOURCES: Knowles (1992); Herrnstein and Murray (1994); Sowell (1994, 1995).

people who are themselves disadvantaged (Dollard, 1939). A white woman earning low wages in a fish processing plant, for example, might understandably be unhappy about her situation. Directing hostility at the powerful people who operate the factory carries obvious risk; therefore, she may well attribute her low pay to the presence of minority co-workers. Her prejudice may not go far towards improving her situation, but it serves as a relatively safe way to vent anger and it may give her the comforting feeling that at least she is superior to someone.

A **scapegoat**, then, is a *person or category of people, typically with little power, whom people unfairly blame for their own troubles.* Because they often are "safe targets," minorities are frequently used as scapegoats. The Nazis painted the Jews as responsible for all of Germany's ills fifty years ago. As a less extreme example, while our economy struggles to respond to corporate restructuring, globalization, and national debt, one hears rumblings among Canadians about lax immigration laws and the immigrants and refugees who allegedly contribute to the shortage of jobs and the high costs of social welfare.

Authoritarian Personality Theory

According to T.W. Adorno (1950), extreme prejudice is a personality trait in certain individuals. This conclusion is supported by research showing that people who display strong prejudice against one minority are usually intolerant of all minorities. Such people exhibit *authoritarian personalities*, rigidly conforming to conventional cultural values, envisioning moral issues as clear-cut matters of right and wrong, and advocating strongly ethnocentric views. People with authoritarian personalities also look on society as naturally competitive and hierarchical, with "better" people (such as themselves) inevitably dominating those who are weaker.

Adorno also found that people tolerant towards one minority are likely to be accepting of all. They tend to be more flexible in their moral judgments and believe that, ideally, society should be relatively egalitarian. They feel uncomfortable in situations in which some people exercise excessive and damaging power over others.

Adorno claimed that people with little education who are raised by cold and demanding parents tend to develop authoritarian personalities. Filled with anger and anxiety as children, they grow into hostile and aggressive adults, seeking scapegoats whom they consider inferior.

Cultural Theory

A third theory contends that, while extreme prejudice may be characteristic of certain people, some preju-

Lincoln MacCauley Alexander was born to immigrant parents in 1922 and grew up in Hamilton, Ontario, where he developed street smarts. With a B.A. from McMaster University and a law degree from Osgoode Hall, Alexander practised law before entering federal politics as Canada's first Black MP. He was lieutenant-governor of Ontario from 1985–1991, and he has been chancellor of the University of Guelph since 1991. He is a Companion of the Order of Canada, and he has received honorary degrees from five universities and numerous outstanding citizen awards. Hamilton's new Lincoln Alexander Expressway is affectionately known as "The Linc." Throughout his career, he has sustained his interest in multicultural affairs.

dice is found in everyone because it is embedded in culture. Belief in the social superiority of some categories of people—the "charter" groups (British and French), the hard-working, reliable people of northern and western European roots—still colours Canadian culture to some extent despite Canada's multicultural policies and programs. Educational initiatives aim to broaden the traditionally Eurocentric attitudes by promoting appreciation of the culture and contributions of those of non-European backgrounds.

Emory Bogardus (1968) studied the effects of culturally rooted prejudices on interpersonal relationships for more than forty years. He devised the concept of *social distance* to assess how close or distant people feel in relation to members of various racial and ethnic categories. His research in the U.S., which documented widespread agreement among members of that society, found that they held the most positive views towards people of white English, Canadian, and Scottish background, even welcoming marriage with them. Attitudes are less favourable towards the French, Germans, Swedes, and the Dutch, and the

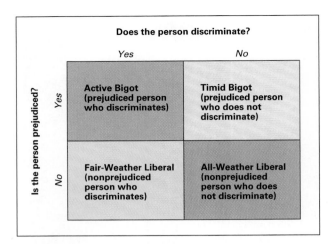

Does the person discriminate?

	Yes	No
Is the person prejudiced? Yes	**Active Bigot** (prejudiced person who discriminates)	**Timid Bigot** (prejudiced person who does not discriminate)
No	**Fair-Weather Liberal** (nonprejudiced person who discriminates)	**All-Weather Liberal** (nonprejudiced person who does not discriminate)

FIGURE 13–1 Patterns of Prejudice and Discrimination

SOURCE: Merton (1976).

most negative prejudices target people of African and Asian descent.

When Canadians were asked to rank various racial and ethnic categories on the Bogardus scale (Mackie, 1974), the ranking was very similar—with the British and Americans (white Anglo-Saxon Protestants, or WASPs) ranking first and second. Not only is there consistency within cultures but also between Canadian and American cultures, suggesting that such rankings are indeed normative.

According to Bogardus, then, prejudice is so widespread that we cannot explain it as merely a trait of a handful of people with authoritarian personalities, as Adorno suggests. Rather, Bogardus concludes, almost everyone expresses some bigotry because we live in a "culture of prejudice."

Conflict Theory

A fourth analysis views prejudice as the product of social conflict. According to this theory, powerful people use prejudice to justify their oppression of minorities. Canadians certainly did this with the Chinese labourers who were allowed to come to Canada to work—under appalling conditions—on the Canadian Pacific Railway in the 1870s and 1880s. Similarly, all elites benefit when prejudice divides workers along racial and ethnic lines and discourages them from working together to advance their common interests (Geschwender, 1978; Olzak, 1989).

A different conflict-based argument, advanced by Shelby Steele (1990), is that minorities themselves cultivate a climate of *race consciousness* in order to win greater power and privileges. In raising race consciousness, Steele explains, minorities argue that they are victims and that white people are their victimizers. Because of their historic disadvantage, minorities claim that they are entitled to special considerations based on their race. While this strategy may yield short-term gains, Steele cautions that such policies are likely to spark a backlash from white people and others who condemn "special treatment" for anyone on the basis of race or ethnicity.

The Québécois have made precisely that kind of claim on the basis of past injustices and the threat of assimilation in an English-speaking North America. Some non-Quebeckers feel that the wrongs of the past have now been redressed and that entrenching special status (that is, recognition as a "distinct society") in Canada's Constitution is going too far.

DISCRIMINATION

Closely related to prejudice is **discrimination**, *treating various categories of people unequally*. While prejudice refers to attitudes, discrimination is a matter of action. Like prejudice, discrimination can be either positive (providing special advantages) or negative (subjecting categories of people to obstacles). Discrimination also varies in intensity, ranging from subtle to blatant.

Prejudice and discrimination often occur together. A personnel manager prejudiced against members of a particular minority may refuse to hire them. Robert Merton (1976) describes such a person as an *active bigot* (see Figure 13–1). But prejudice and discrimination do not always occur together, as in the case of the prejudiced personnel manager who, out of fear of lawsuits, *does* hire minorities. Merton characterizes this person as a *timid bigot*. What Merton calls *fair-weather liberals* may be generally tolerant of minorities yet discriminate when it is to their advantage to do so, such as when a superior demands it. Finally, Merton's *all-weather liberal* is free of both prejudice and discrimination.

INSTITUTIONAL PREJUDICE AND DISCRIMINATION

We typically think of prejudice and discrimination as the hateful ideas or actions of specific individuals. But thirty years ago, Stokely Carmichael and Charles Hamilton (1967) pointed out that far greater harm results from **institutional prejudice or discrimination**, which refers to *bias in attitudes or action inherent in the operation of society's institutions*, including schools, hospitals, the police, or the workplace.

Anderson and Frideres (1981:208) describe this kind of process as follows:

> Bureaucracies have the job of establishing regulations and priorities as well as qualifications

for particular positions in our society. Only those individuals able to meet these initial qualifications will be able to participate in the ongoing institutional structure. For example, when Native people suggested that they be hired by the Department of Indian Affairs (with a staff of about 14 000), the response by the Minister of Indian Affairs was that placement was only possible for those belonging to a particular union, and having a particular position and level of seniority in the union. Unless these requirements were met, an Indian could not be hired, and if hired without these qualifications, the union would strike.

There was no need for the authors to point out that natives were *not* members of the appropriate union.

PREJUDICE AND DISCRIMINATION: THE VICIOUS CYCLE

Prejudice and discrimination frequently reinforce each other. In the Thomas theorem, W.I. Thomas offered a simple explanation of this fact (see Chapter 6, "Social Interaction in Everyday Life"): *Situations defined as real become real in their consequences* (1966:301; orig. 1931).

As Thomas recognized, stereotypes become real to those who believe them, sometimes even to those who are victimized by them. Power also plays a role here, since some categories of people with considerable social power can enforce their prejudices to the detriment of others.

Prejudice on the part of whites towards people of colour, for example, does not produce *innate* inferiority, but it can produce *social* inferiority, consigning minorities to poverty, inferior schooling, low-prestige occupations, and poor housing in racially segregated neighbourhoods. Then, if whites interpret social disadvantage as evidence that minorities do not measure up to their standards, they unleash a new round of prejudice and discrimination, giving rise to a *vicious cycle*, shown in Figure 13–2, as one wave of disadvantage generates another.

MAJORITY AND MINORITY: PATTERNS OF INTERACTION

Social scientists describe patterns of interaction among racial and ethnic categories in terms of four models: pluralism, assimilation, segregation, and genocide.

PLURALISM

Pluralism is *a state in which racial and ethnic minorities are distinct but have social parity.* In a pluralist society,

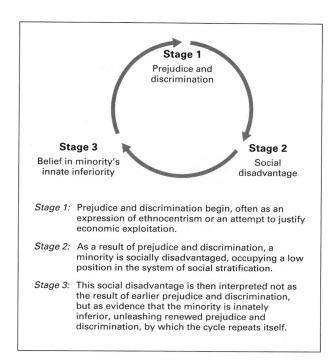

Stage 1: Prejudice and discrimination begin, often as an expression of ethnocentrism or an attempt to justify economic exploitation.

Stage 2: As a result of prejudice and discrimination, a minority is socially disadvantaged, occupying a low position in the system of social stratification.

Stage 3: This social disadvantage is then interpreted not as the result of earlier prejudice and discrimination, but as evidence that the minority is innately inferior, unleashing renewed prejudice and discrimination, by which the cycle repeats itself.

FIGURE 13–2 Prejudice and Discrimination: The Vicious Cycle

Prejudice and discrimination can form a vicious cycle, perpetuating themselves, as explained above.

categories of people are different, but they all share resources more or less equally. The relationship between Quebec—with its predominantly francophone population—and the rest of Canada provides an example of pluralism in action. Native peoples, while clearly distinct, would like to acquire social and political parity or equality.

Social diversity has long been a source of pride in Canada. Some argue that our multiculturalism not only acknowledges but actually celebrates our differences and encourages the perpetuation of countless "ethnic villages," communities where people proudly maintain the cultural traditions of their immigrant ancestors. These ethnic communities—the components of our cultural mosaic—add variety and colour to the urban and rural landscapes of our country. The viability of these communities is affected by their levels of **institutional completeness**, *the complexity of community organizations that meet the needs of members.* Where communities are institutionally complete, members are able to live, shop, pray, and sometimes work within the boundaries of their groups. Such communities might also have their own welfare and mutual aid societies, credit unions, newspapers, and radio stations. Breton (1964), who coined the term "institutional completeness," points out that the presence of these formal organizations keeps social relations within group boundaries and minimizes out-group contacts.

Canada embraces the ideal of multiculturalism, recognition of cultural heterogeneity, and mutual respect among culturally diverse groups. Through policies of multiculturalism, Canada supports the goal of allowing people to participate fully in all aspects of Canadian life without feeling that it is necessary to give up their ethnic identities and cultural practices. The aim of multiculturalism is to promote unity through diversity and to enhance a Canadian identity that embraces differences. We began to use the term "multiculturalism" in the 1960s, in recognition of the diverse backgrounds of Canadians, and adopted multiculturalism as government policy by 1971. The Canadian *Multiculturalism Act* of 1988 sought "to recognize all Canadians as full and equal partners in Canadian society" and in 1991 this goal was given explicit support through the creation of a new Department of Multiculturalism and Citizenship.

Multicultural programs provide education, consultative support, and funding for a wide range of activities, including heritage language training, race relations and cross-cultural understanding programs, the ethnic press, ethnic celebrations, policing and justice, and family violence programs.

Not everyone approves of the official goal of multiculturalism. Critics argue that it discourages immigrant adaptation and that it is divisive and detrimental to the development of a shared and coherent Canadian identity. And, while 85 percent of Canadians agree that we should make efforts to protect our racial and ethnic minorities, more than 60 percent *also* feel that immigrants should cling less to their old ways and try harder to be more like other Canadians (Fletcher, cited in *Muticulturalism and Citizenship Canada*, 1989:4). Writer Neil Bissoondath, who feels that continued ethnic identification weakens the social fabric of Canada, raised a few eyebrows, met with hostility, and caught the attention of the media when he made a plea to be accepted as an unhyphenated Canadian. Criticism of multiculturalism by this "person of colour" led to cries of "traitor" or "sell-out" from minority members and expressions of displeasure by mainstream defenders of the policy. Bissoondath (1994:5) suspects that these reactions have "more than a little to do with the psychology of the True Believer, who sees Canada's multicultural policy as the only one possible."

Questions about the impact of multiculturalism can be raised from other perspectives as well. Although they are not necessarily critical of multicultural policy, Reitz and Breton (1994) point out that Canada's "cultural mosaic" and the U.S. "melting pot" result in only minimal differences in assimilation, economic integration, or tolerance of ethnic distinctiveness. Therefore, they argue, the perception that Canada's minorities retain their cultural identities more than minorities in the United States is largely an illusion.

ASSIMILATION

Assimilation is *the process* by *which minorities gradually adopt patterns of the dominant culture.* Assimilation involves changing modes of dress, values, religion, language, and friends.

Although the United States has been seen as a "melting pot" in which different nationalities fuse into an entirely new way of life, this characterization is somewhat misleading. Rather than "melting" into some new cultural pattern, minorities have adopted the traits (the dress, the accent, and sometimes even the names) of the dominant culture established by the earliest settlers. Why? Assimilation is both the avenue to upward social mobility and the way to escape the prejudice and discrimination directed at visible foreigners (Newman, 1973).

The amount of assimilation varies by category. For example, Germans and Irish have "melted" more than Italians, and the Japanese more than the Chinese or Koreans. Multiculturalists, however, criticize the idea of assimilation for painting minorities as "the problem" and defining them (rather than elites) as the ones who need to do all the changing.

Among other things, minorities in the United States, until recently, have adapted to the use of the English language. The rapid growth of the Hispanic population in recent years has created areas where Spanish is the dominant language, encouraged the study of Spanish as a second language, and—as a counterforce—inspired a social movement seeking to establish English as the official language of the U.S. In fact, as they experience pressure to become officially bilingual—English and Spanish—Americans look to Canada to assess the possible effects of such a policy. Many Americans have concluded that the threat of Quebec separation clearly illustrates the dangers of bilingualism.

The fact that such ethnic enclaves still exist in the United States, where assimilation and the melting pot are the ideals, suggests that race and ethnicity endure as building blocks of American society (Glazer and Moynihan, 1970; Alba, 1985). In Canada, with its claim to be a colourful mosaic in which all the pieces make distinctive contributions, assimilation occurs as well. Immigrants learn to function in English and French, people from different ethnic backgrounds intermarry, ancestral cultural practices fall into disuse, and people acquire a set of shared attitudes and values that can only be called Canadian.

"Star Trek" has been a television favourite for more than thirty years. Compare the cast of the original show, which first aired in 1966, to the crew of the most recent "Star Trek: Voyager." What does the difference in casting suggest about our society's changing view of women? Of racial and ethnic minorities?

As a cultural process, assimilation involves changes in ethnicity but not in race. For example, many North Americans of Japanese descent have discarded their traditional way of life but still have their racial identity. However, distinguishing racial traits may diminish over generations as the result of **miscegenation**, *biological reproduction by partners of different racial categories*. Although resistance to such biological mixing remains strong, miscegenation (often outside of marriage) has occurred throughout Canadian and U.S. history.

SEGREGATION

Segregation refers to the *physical and social separation of categories of people*. Some minorities, especially religious orders such as the Hutterites, voluntarily segregate themselves. The concentration of various ethnic and racial groups in Canada's cities results, at least in part, from voluntary action. Mostly, however, majorities segregate minorities involuntarily by excluding them. Various degrees of segregation characterize residential neighbourhoods, schools, workplaces, hospitals, and even cemeteries. While pluralism fosters distinctiveness without disadvantage, segregation enforces separation to the detriment of a minority.

South Africa's system of apartheid (described in Chapter 9, "Social Stratification") illustrates rigid and pervasive racial segregation. Apartheid was created by the European minority it served, and it was historically enforced through the use of brutal power (Fredrickson, 1981). South Africa has now ended official apartheid but, as yet, its basic racial structure has changed little. The nation remains essentially two different societies that touch only when Blacks provide services for whites.

In the United States, too, racial segregation has a long history beginning with slavery and evolving into racially separated lodging, schooling, and transportation. Decisions such as the 1954 *Brown* case have reduced overt and *de jure* (Latin, meaning "by law") discrimination in the United States. However, *de facto* ("in fact") segregation continues to this day in the form of countless neighbourhoods that are home to people of a single race. Research points to modest declines in racial segregation in the United States during recent decades (Farley, 1997). Yet Douglas Massey and Nancy Denton (1989) have documented the *hypersegregation* of African-Americans in some inner cities. These people have little contact of any kind with people in the larger society. Hypersegregation affects about one-fifth of all African-Americans but only a small percentage of comparably poor whites (Jagarowsky and Bane, 1990).

Although Canadians might not want to think of themselves as a society that practises segregation, we have done so historically and we still do today. Early Black migrants—Loyalists in Nova Scotia and those brought via the Underground Railroad to Ontario—found themselves living in Africville (part of Halifax) or in small rural communities such as Buxton and Dawn in Ontario (as described at the beginning of the chapter). As a general rule, people in these communities did not receive the same kinds of land grants as

Black Citizens of Canada: A History Ignored

When the average Canadian thinks about slavery, the image that comes to mind is likely that of plantation slavery in the southern United States. Few of us are aware that Canada has its own history of slavery and that about 3500 freed slaves came to Nova Scotia and New Brunswick as United Empire Loyalists. They had fought on the side of the British during the American Revolution as members of the Black Pioneers (also known as the Black Loyalists). The 30 000 to 40 000 escaped American slaves who made it to Canada via the Underground Railroad between 1840 and 1865, when slavery was abolished in the United States, are unknown to most of us as well.

Slaves were on the scene in the earliest settlements of Canada (then New France). Olivier Le Jeune, who had been brought directly from Africa to Canada, was later sold in the first recorded slave sale in Canada, in 1629. By 1759, there were 3604 slaves in New France—1132 Blacks, the rest natives. In 1793, under the leadership of John Graves Simcoe,* Upper Canada became the first British colony to legislate the gradual abolition of slavery. While slavery remained legal through the rest of Canada until it was abolished throughout the British Empire in 1833, it had effectively died out by about 1810. Slavery was essentially un-

Harriet Tubman, known as "Moses," had been assisted in her escape from slavery by workers on the Underground Railroad. She returned to Maryland a year later (1850) to free members of her family and then became one of the most active "conductors" on the Railroad, repeatedly risking her life to guide more than three hundred slaves to freedom—many of them to Ontario, where she provided shelter for refugees in a rented house in St. Catharines.

other immigrants. They often attended segregated schools and were denied access to local restaurants. Residential and social segregation were a very real part of their lives.

The clearest example of segregation in Canada is found in our treatment of native peoples, through the system of reserves for status Indians administered by the Department of Indian and Northern Affairs. Prior to the late 1960s, most of the education of Indian children took place in separate residential schools or on the reserves themselves. The overall effect has been one of extreme physical and social segregation, especially when the reserves are located in remote areas.

GENOCIDE

Genocide is *the systematic annihilation of one category of people by another.* This brutal form of racism and ethnocentrism violates nearly every recognized moral standard; nonetheless, it has recurred time and again in human history.

Genocide figured prominently in centuries of contact between Europeans and the original inhabitants of the Americas. From the sixteenth century on, as the Spanish, Portuguese, English, French, and Dutch forcibly established vast colonial empires, they decimated the native populations of North and South America. Some native people fell victim to calculated killing sprees; most succumbed to diseases brought by Europeans to which they had no natural immunities (Cottrell, 1979; Butterworth and Chance, 1981; Matthiessen, 1984; Sale, 1990; Dickason, 1992). The Beothuk of Newfoundland, who experienced the earliest contact with Europeans, had completely disappeared by 1829. Feuding and open hunting season against the Beothuk, as well as tuberculosis, had taken their toll (Dickason, 1992:96).

Genocide has also occurred in the twentieth century. Unimaginable horror befell European Jews in the 1930s and 1940s, as the Nazi regime seized control of much of Europe. During Adolf Hitler's reign of terror, known as the Holocaust, the Nazis exterminated more than six million Jewish men, women, and children. Soviet dictator Josef Stalin murdered his country's people on an even greater scale, killing perhaps thirty million real and imagined enemies during his violent rule. Between 1975 and 1980, Pol Pot's Communist regime in Cambodia slaughtered anyone associated in any way with capitalist culture. Men and women able to speak a Western language and even

suited to agriculture as practised in Canada.

Fugitive slaves arrived in Ontario between the 1790s and 1860s. From about 1840 they used the Underground Railroad, an informal system of people and safe houses bringing escaped slaves to freedom in the northern United States and eventually Canada. These former slaves formed scattered rural settlements from Windsor to Barrie (or across the southern part of Ontario), where some farmed their own land while others hired themselves out as farm labourers. Some Black settlements, such as Buxton and Dawn,** were thriving communities with their own schools, blacksmith shops, and other businesses. Most of the residents of these communities and their descendants eventually abandoned their rural homes and moved, with other Canadians, to the cities. Some, however, stayed behind. Descendants of the residents of Dawn still live in Dresden, Ontario.

Though freed from slavery, Blacks in Ontario and other parts of Canada experienced economic hardship as well as prejudice and discrimination—suggesting that, despite a certain smugness, Canadians are not much more tolerant than our American neighbours. Nevertheless, immigration from many parts of the world, including the West Indies, has added to Canada's Black populations, now comprising 574 000 individuals living mainly in southern Ontario and Montreal.

The Black communities of Montreal are made up of immigrants, and their descendants, who come from French-speaking countries such as Algeria and Haiti, but shared language has not meant that social and economic integration have been painless. Racism and discrimination are as likely to appear in Montreal as in Toronto, where many Blacks encounter the combined barriers associated with recent immigration and visible minority status. Despite continued disadvantages in income, education, and employment, Blacks have made important contributions to Canada's economic and cultural life.

---

* When Governor Simcoe had dinner at the home of Mohawk leader and Loyalist Joseph Brant (Thayendanegea) in 1793, he was served by Brant's "Black slaves resplendent in scarlet uniforms with white ruffles, and with silver buckles on their shoes" (Walker, 1980:21).

** Dawn was founded in 1842 by Hiram Wilson and Josiah Henson. The latter, a "conductor" on the Underground Railroad who brought about a hundred slaves to freedom, is thought to be the model for Harriet Beecher Stowe's Uncle Tom in *Uncle Tom's Cabin*.

SOURCES: McClain (1979); Walker (1980); Ducharme (1985); Winks (1988); Nader, Milleron, and Conacher (1992); Merritt (1993).

---

individuals who wore eyeglasses, construed as a symbol of capitalist culture, were cut down. In all, some two million people (one-quarter of the population) perished in Cambodian "killing fields" (Shawcross, 1979).

These four patterns of minority-majority interaction exist together in our society. For example, we proudly point to patterns of pluralism and assimilation but only reluctantly acknowledge the degree to which our society has been built on segregation and genocide. The remainder of this chapter examines how these four patterns have shaped the history and present social standing of major racial and ethnic categories in Canada.

RACE AND ETHNICITY IN CANADA

Canada is a land of immigrants. Many thousands of years ago, the people we now call aboriginal or native peoples came to North America over a land bridge that once connected Alaska to Siberia across the Bering Strait. The first European explorers and settlers were met by fifty-five founding nations.

The French and then the British established permanent settlements in the 1600s and 1700s, conveniently ignoring the aboriginal nations, and declared themselves to be the two founding nations. Successive waves of immigration brought northern and then southern and eastern European people to our shores. More recently, in part as a result of changes in immigration laws, new Canadians have come from Asia, Africa, the Caribbean, and Latin America. In addition, refugees have come to Canada in unprecedented numbers over the last decade. These historic and more current flows have completely transformed our sociocultural landscape.

Table 13–1 shows the composition of Canada by ethnic origin (1996) for the twenty-five categories that are most heavily represented in Canada, based on responses to census questions about ethnic ancestry. The "total responses" category includes those who have the same ancestry on both maternal and paternal sides (single origin), as well as those who report mixed heritage (multiple origin). Further columns report the figures for single-origin and multiple-origin individuals separately. As a result of changes in the structure and wording of the census question on ethnic background, we see a dramatic increase in the number of people claiming "Canadian" ancestry (see the note in Table 13–1): almost a third of Canada's population claims Canadian ethnicity or cultural heritage. The

TABLE 13–1 The Top 25 Ethnic Origins* in Canada, Showing Single and Multiple Origin Responses,** 1996

Ethnic Origin	Total Responses	%	Single Responses	%	Multiple Responses	%
1. Canadian	8,806,275	30.9	5,326,995	18.7	3,479,285	34.0
2. English	6,832,095	23.9	2,048,275	7.2	4,783,820	46.8
3. French	5,597,845	19.6	2,665,250	9.3	2,932,595	28.7
4. Scottish	4,260,840	14.9	642,970	2.3	3,617,870	35.4
5. Irish	3,767,610	13.2	504,030	1.8	3,263,580	31.9
6. German	2,757,140	9.7	726,145	2.5	2,030,990	19.9
7. Italian	1,207,475	4.2	729,455	2.6	478,025	4.7
8. Aboriginal	1,101,955	3.9	477,630	1.7	624,330	6.1
9. Ukrainian	1,026,475	3.6	331,680	1.2	694,790	6.8
10. Chinese	921,585	3.2	800,470	2.8	121,115	1.2
11. Dutch (Netherlands)	916,215	3.2	313,880	1.1	602,335	5.9
12. Polish	786,735	2.8	265,930	0.9	520,805	5.1
13. South Asian	723,345	2.5	590,145	2.1	133,200	1.3
14. Jewish	351,705	1.2	195,810	0.7	155,900	1.5
15. Norwegian	346,310	1.2	47,805	0.2	298,500	2.9
16. Welsh	338,905	1.2	27,915	0.1	310,990	3.0
17. Portuguese	335,110	1.2	252,640	0.9	82,470	0.8
18. Swedish	278,975	1.0	31,200	0.1	247,775	2.4
19. Russian	272,335	1.0	46,885	0.2	225,450	2.2
20. Hungarian (Magyar)	250,525	0.9	94,185	0.3	156,340	1.5
21. Filipino	242,880	0.9	198,420	0.7	44,460	0.4
22. American	211,790	0.7	22,085	0.1	189,705	1.9
23. Spanish	204,360	0.7	72,470	0.3	131,895	1.3
24. Greek	203,345	0.7	144,940	0.5	58,405	0.6
25. Jamaican	188,770	0.7	128,570	0.5	60,200	0.6
Total Population	28,528,125		18,303,625		10,224,500	

* The 1996 census asked people to indicate the ethnic or cultural groups to which their *ancestors* belong. A list of examples, including "Canadian," was provided, and respondents were asked to write in up to four answers. The structure of this question produced a sevenfold increase in the number of people who identified themselves as single-origin "Canadian"—from 765 095 in 1991 to 5 326 995 in 1996.

** The "total responses" column includes those individuals who claim each ethnic background as a single origin or as part of a multiple-origin response. The single-response column includes those individuals whose parents share one ethnic background, while the multiple-origin individuals might have, for example, Italian, English, and Scottish ancestry. This hypothetical individual would be counted three times in the "total" or "multiple response" columns.

SOURCE: Adapted by Gerber from 1996 census tables (www.statcan.ca).

significance of this shift will be the subject of considerable debate, especially since between 1991 and 1996, 3.5 million fewer people declared themselves to be single-origin French.

Not surprisingly, considering the head start they had in settling this country, the largest ethnic categories in Canada (after those reporting Canadian ancestry) are the English and the French. Some 4.3, 3.8, and 2.8 million people are at least partly of Scottish, Irish, and German origin, respectively. Those with Italian, aboriginal, or Ukrainian roots also number more than one million each. The remaining ethnic categories among the top twenty-five drop off quickly in size, down to the roughly 189 000 people of Jamaican origin. The results give a picture of Canada as a country dominated by the British (mainly the English) and the French, but otherwise of remarkable diversity.

Comparing the numbers of people in each ethnic category reveals the extent of integration and intermarriage in Canada. While two million people claim English ancestry on both sides, more than double that number (4.8 million) have some English ancestry. Among German-origin Canadians, over two-thirds are of multiple origin; among the Swedish, the figure is 89 percent. The majority of aboriginal people have multiple origins as well (57 percent). The newer immigrant groups, many of which are visible minorities (Filipino, South Asian, or Jamaican), tend to have lower proportions claiming multiple origins. However, these proportions are likely to increase over the next few censuses. (Note that the choice of "Canadian" ancestry is also an indicator of cultural integration.)

Table 13–2 shows the top ten ethnic origins in the provinces and territories, revealing that ethnic and racial composition vary substantially from one part of the country to another. The proportion claiming "Canadian" background (either single or multiple origin) varies from 14 percent in the Northwest Territories to 47 percent in Quebec. The frequency of this designation in the 1996 census makes it difficult to observe the traditional predominance of the British

TABLE 13–2 Ethnic Origins for Canada, the Provinces and Territories, 1996 (rank order by percentage of population*)

	Canada	Nfld	PEI	NS	NB	Que	Ont	Man	Sask	Alta	BC	Yukon	NWT
1.	**Canadian** (30.9)	**English** (59.8)	**Scottish** (42.9)	**English** (37.5)	**Canadian** (41.0)	**Canadian** (47.2)	**English** (29.0)	*English* (24.7)	**German** (29.0)	**English** (28.3)	**English** (32.8)	**Canadian** (29.4)	**Aboriginal** (62.1)
2.	*English* (23.9)	**Canadian** (30.7)	**English** (38.5)	**Canadian** (36.1)	**French** (32.8)	**French** (40.7)	**Canadian** (25.4)	*Canadian* (19.4)	**English** (26.8)	**Canadian** (25.8)	*Canadian* (22.2)	**English** (29.2)	English (14.0)
3.	*French* (19.6)	*Irish* (22.2)	**Canadian** (29.9)	**Scottish** (33.3)	**English** (30.5)	Irish (4.5)	*Scottish* (17.7)	*German* (18.5)	*Canadian* (21.7)	*German* (19.9)	*Scottish* (20.4)	*Scottish* (22.2)	Canadian (13.7)
4.	Scottish	Scottish	**Irish**	Irish	Irish	English	Irish	Scottish	Scottish	Scottish	Irish	Aboriginal	Scottish
5.	Irish	French	French	French	Scottish	Italian	French	Ukrainian	Irish	Irish	German	Irish	Irish
6.	German	Aboriginal	German	German	German	Scottish	German	French	Ukrainian	French	French	German	French
7.	Italian	German	Dutch	Dutch	Acadian	Aboriginal	Italian	Irish	Aboriginal	Ukrainian	Chinese	French	German
8.	Aboriginal	Welsh	Aboriginal	Aboriginal	Aboriginal	German	Dutch	Aboriginal	French	Aboriginal	Aboriginal	Ukrainian	Ukrainian
9.	Ukrainian	Norwegian	Welsh	Welsh	Dutch	Jewish	South Asian	Polish	Norwegian	Dutch	Dutch	Dutch	Dutch
10.	Chinese	Dutch	Acadian	Italian	Welsh	Québécois	Chinese	Dutch	Polish	Polish	Ukrainian	Norwegian	Polish

* The first three ethnic categories for Canada and each province and territory include the percentage of population claiming each ethnic background (on the part of both parents, single origin, or just one parent, multiple origin). Categories with more than 25 percent of the population appear in bold, while those with 15 to 25 percent appear in italics. It is important to note that an individual with Scottish and Ukrainian background, for example, would be counted twice. The sum of these percentages therefore would be substantially more than 100.

SOURCE: Adapted by Gerber from 1996 census tables.

categories in the Maritimes and the European influence in the western provinces.

The most dramatic change is in the predominance of French origins in Quebec. In 1991, 75 percent of the Quebec population declared itself to be *single-origin* French. In 1996, only 41 percent declared either full or partial French ancestry. Aboriginal peoples appear among the top ten everywhere but in Ontario, but only in the Northwest Territories and the Yukon do they rank first and fourth by population, respectively. The Chinese rank tenth in Canada, but only appear in the top ten in Ontario (tenth) and B.C. (seventh). Despite the shift to "Canadian" identification, diversity and regional variation of backgrounds are still apparent.

Canada's 1996 census attempted to measure visible minority status (as distinct from ethnicity or aboriginal origins) to assess compliance with employment equity legislation. Respondents were asked to identify themselves as White, Chinese, South Asian, Black, Arab/West Asian, Filipino, Southeast Asian, Latin American, Japanese, Korean, or "Other." Black appeared as a choice among ethnic categories in the 1991 census, but now is part of a more direct question aimed at identifying visible minority populations.

Figure 13–3 provides a summary of aboriginal and other visible minority origins for Canada and the provinces and territories. Note that the totals for the Atlantic provinces are very low, while those in Ontario, Manitoba, British Columbia, and the Yukon are around 20 percent. The Northwest Territories population is close to two-thirds aboriginal, and aboriginals make up 12 percent of the population in Manitoba and 11 percent in Saskatchewan. People of Asian origin make up 8 to 16 percent of Alberta, Ontario, and British Columbia. In other words, as the Figure shows, the visible minority components of Canada's provinces and territories vary as clearly as their more general ethnic compositions.

SOCIAL STANDING

A great deal has been written about ethnic and racial inequality in Canada and its causes (Porter, 1965; Ramcharan, 1982; Gerber, 1983, 1990; Li, 1988; Driedger, 1989; Gerber, 1990; McAll, 1990; Frideres, 1993; Wotherspoon and Satzewich, 1993). The general consensus seems to be that the workings of our capitalist economy, along with racism, prejudice, and discrimination, contribute to socioeconomic inequality, with recent immigrants and visible minorities at the bottom of the scale. For a number of reasons, including a system of internal colonialism, native peoples are the most severely disadvantaged in this regard.

Table 13–3 compares selected ethnic categories—British, French, Asian, Black, and native—on a number of socioeconomic dimensions. The observations that we can make based on this table are surprising in some respects and consistent with expectations in others. Canadian Asians and Blacks—many of whom were educated elsewhere before coming here as immigrants—have higher levels of post-secondary certification than the British or French. They also have higher levels of labour force participation. However, despite higher levels of educational attainment and labour force participation, Asians and Blacks have

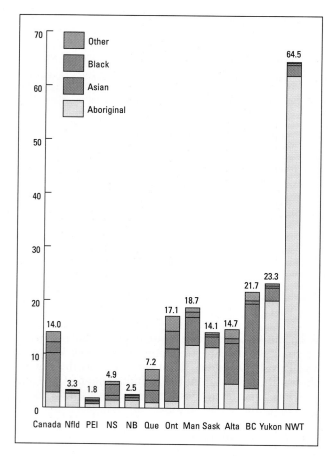

FIGURE 13–3 Visible Minority Populations for Canada, the Provinces and Territories, 1996 (percentages)

SOURCE: Calculations by Gerber from the 1996 census tables.

lower average incomes than the British and French. Blacks, in particular, are also more likely to be unemployed than the British.

The native population is disadvantaged on all of the measures in Table 13–3. They have lower levels of educational attainment coupled with both low levels of labour force participation and high unemployment—almost three times the British rate. The average income for aboriginal individuals is only half the British level.

On the basis of Table 13–3, one can conclude that the British are rewarded on income despite the fact that they have lower levels of post-secondary certification and labour force participation. The French, who are equal to the British on these measures, do not get the same financial rewards—in part, perhaps, because the economy of Quebec has been particularly sluggish. Asians and Blacks, with their high levels of

post-secondary education and labour force participation, should have the highest incomes—but they do not. This may be the result of racism, prejudice, and discrimination—as many analysts will be quick to point out—but date of entry into Canada also comes into the picture. Immigrants generally enter the Canadian labour market at a lower *entrance status* than they may have occupied in their countries of origin (Porter, 1965; Ujimoto, 1979; Reitz, 1980). Furthermore, recent immigrants are unlikely to have the seniority in their jobs that is associated with higher incomes.

While Blacks and Asians appear to have gained access to higher education and to the labour market (including full-time employment), they appear to face barriers to equity in remuneration. Natives, on the other hand, seem to face a host of barriers—in achieving higher education, in securing employment, and in earning decent wages or salaries. Something is clearly amiss when the First Nations (as some status Indians prefer to be called) find themselves systematically excluded from equal participation in our educational and economic institutions.

Although, as Wotherspoon and Satzewich (1993:51) point out, average incomes mask the fact that native people, as *individuals*, are distributed across all classes—including the wealthy business or capitalist class—there is socioeconomic stratification in Canada based on race and ethnicity (Porter, 1965; Breton, 1979; Li, 1988; McAll, 1990). It is also clear that, as we saw in Chapter 10 ("Social Class in Canada"), native peoples are particularly disadvantaged (Gerber, 1990; Frideres, 1993).

SPECIAL-STATUS SOCIETIES

On historical grounds, one might argue that the British have special status within Canada. We have a British parliamentary system, the majority of Canadians speak English, and the dominant culture is Anglo-Saxon. In the past, admission to Canada itself, to the economic elite, and to the most exclusive clubs was controlled, for the most part, by the British. It could also be argued that the policy of multiculturalism gives special status to all of the ethnic and cultural minorities that contribute to the Canadian mosaic. Nonetheless, two categories stand out because they have unique relationships with the federal government and other Canadians—the native peoples (Indian, Inuit, and Métis) and the Québécois.

NATIVE PEOPLES

The terms *native* and *aboriginal* refer to fifty-five or more sovereign peoples who had established them-

TABLE 13–3 Education, Employment, and Income Among Selected Ethnic and Racial Categories, 1991

	British	French	Asian	Black	Native
Total Population	5,618,661	6,145,027	1,452,265	319,300	450,233
Population aged 15+	4,732,962	4,962,228	1,131,899	236,866	294,166
% with less than secondary school certification	41.0	41.4	32.9	35.9	63.3
% with post-secondary certification	29.7	27.8	38.7	32.6	15.3
% in labour force*	62.1	64.4	68.7	72.3	51.8
Unemployment rate**	8.5	10.0	10.4	14.5	24.6
Mean income***	$22,798	$20,046	$18,216	$17,390	$11,676

* Percentages based on populations fifteen years of age or older.
** Percentage of the labour force unemployed.
*** Average income for all people with income.

SOURCE: Calculations by Gerber based on 1991 Census Public Use Microdata Files.

selves on the North American continent thousands of years before the arrival of European explorers and settlers. These include the Inuit, Cree, Ojibwa, Micmac, Blackfoot, Iroquois, Haida, and Slavey peoples, among others. The Métis are a sociocultural category of biracial descent—usually French and Indian. Among the Indian peoples there are numerous categories. Registered Indians, who come under the *Indian Act* and are the responsibility of the Department of Indian and Northern Affairs, may be "treaty" or "non-treaty," depending on whether their ancestors were party to treaties. In addition, there is an undetermined number of people who may be biologically and culturally Indian but are not legally so, because their ancestors, for whatever reasons, did not enter into agreements with the Crown.[1]

The 1991 Census identifies more than 470 000 individuals who claim to be single-origin aboriginal (i.e., Inuit *or* Métis *or* Indian on both sides—not an Inuit-Indian mix, for example). Within the aboriginal category, there are 30 000 Inuit, 75 000 Métis, and 365 000 Indians. Frideres (1993:31) estimates that there are over 1.5 million people in Canada—registered and unregistered—with native ancestry. In other words, almost 6 percent of the population of Canada is of native descent.

Registered Indians who live on reserves or settlements are the special responsibility of the Department of Indian and Northern Affairs. Their relationship with Ottawa over the years could be characterized as paternalistic and bureaucratic. For example, until the 1980s, Indian children were often removed from the reserves and taken to boarding schools. There they were punished for "talking Indian" among themselves, forced to speak English and taught that their own lan-

guages and cultures were of no value. Removed from their homes and communities for ten months of the year and deprived of parent-child relationships, these children were not prepared to live effectively in either the native or non-native worlds. Christianity was imposed on the communities and on the children in the boarding schools, and education beyond the level required for farming or raising livestock was discouraged. The effect of these measures was an erosion of the social and cultural fabric of community life. In January 1998, Jane Stewart, Canada's Minister of Indian Affairs and Northern Development, took the long overdue step of apologizing, formally, for the boarding school experiences of native youth—which often included physical and sexual abuse.

Because non-status Indians, the Métis, and the Inuit were never confined to reserves, they have escaped some of the negative effects of reserve life. Living in Canada's far north, the Inuit have not felt the same population pressures as native peoples in the rest of the country. However, they have experienced the same gradual erosion of traditional patterns of life. First, oil, gas, and uranium companies have degraded the environment in the north and reduced the game supply. Second, many Inuit families have moved into permanent settlements, both for employment and to meet the legal requirement of school attendance for their children. Consequently, extended families no longer establish winter camps in traditional hunting grounds or teach their children the old survival skills that used to foster a sense of self-worth.

It is important to realize that there is a great deal of diversity among native communities (Gerber, 1979), and native individuals, communities, and organizations have made real strides in dealing with the problems they face today. Where government policy once was based on the assumption that the "Indian problem" would solve itself through urban migration and assimilation, it is now recognized that native

---

[1] Frideres (1993:24–46) provides a detailed explanation of the various native and Indian categories.

Canada's native peoples have long been seeking self-determination, a struggle that has been more prominent in the media in recent years, but in fact has been going on throughout Canada's history. A sign in this protest on Parliament Hill hints at the frustration of many over another failed attempt at resolution.

communities on reserves and elsewhere are not only surviving but growing (Gerber, 1984). In addition, high-profile native leaders such as Ovide Mercredi, Elijah Harper, and George Erasmus have been effective in articulating their demands and thereby have gained public support for greater self-determination. National organizations, such as the Assembly of First Nations, Inuit Tapirisat, Native Council of Canada, and the Métis National Council were instrumental in negotiating recognition of the inherent right to self-government through the Charlottetown accord—which was rejected in the 1992 federal referendum (see the "Social Diversity" box on native self-government in Chapter 16, "Politics and Government," p. 410).

One dramatic result of the native quest for self-determination will be the creation in 1999 of a new territory, Nunavut, which is to be carved out of the present Northwest Territories. The new territorial government will be controlled by the Inuit majority, with support from an established system of cooperatives and the Inuit Broadcasting Corporation (IBC).

Political and administrative positions will bring new employment prospects, potentially stimulating greater educational achievement and enhancing pride. Returning control of Inuit communities to Inuit hands will not alleviate problems overnight; the hope on the part of native leaders, however, is that it will be one meaningful step towards dealing with a wide range of serious social problems.

THE QUÉBÉCOIS

The French presence in what is now Canada goes back to 1608, when the first permanent settlement in New France was established at Quebec City by Samuel de Champlain with twenty-eight settlers—eight of whom survived the first winter. France claimed a vast territory that extended west of the Thirteen Colonies and down to Louisiana, encompassing most of southern Ontario and the Great Lakes region. But New France grew slowly because of a lack of interest on the part of France in supporting the tiny settlement or in sending more settlers to the area. The population grew from eight in 1609 to just over 3000 in 1663—spread among Quebec City, Trois-Rivières, and Montreal—mainly because of an "extraordinary rate of child bearing" (Beaujot and McQuillan, 1982:4). Two centuries later, at the time of Confederation, The French formed 31 percent of Canada's population of 3.5 million people.

As a result of the size of the French population and its concentration in Quebec, the *British North America Act* of 1867 recognized the province's civil law tradition, Catholic schools, and language. Confederation was based on bilingualism, and assumed that English- and French-speaking communities would coexist and complement each other. English and French were to be the legislative and judicial languages in federal and Quebec institutions. Bilingualism was later strengthened and expanded by the *Official Languages Act* of 1969, which declared the equality of the two languages in Parliament and in the Canadian public service.

At the time of Confederation, the province of Quebec encompassed a traditional society based on the seigneurial system of land tenure—in which *habitants*, or tenants, worked the lands of the *seigneurs*, the landowners. In the political vacuum left by an ineffective provincial government, the Catholic Church took upon itself the task of administering many aspects of Quebec society, including education, health care, and social welfare. The Catholic Church, which had long dominated Quebec's major institutions, resisted change:

Uninterested in questioning the established
authorities and the excesses of industrialization,
and wary of new ideas, the Quebec church was

more concerned with maintaining its privileged position than with helping Quebeckers enter the twentieth century. It extolled the virtues of rural life, cautioned against the evils of the city and the dangers of education, and preached the need to accept one's lot in life (Latouche, 1988:1801).

At this time a British economic and industrial elite based in Montreal dominated the provincial economy. A clear linguistic class structure had developed with the unilingual English at the top, the unilingual French at the bottom, and bilingual people in the middle in supervisory positions. The unilingual French had few opportunities to better their social or financial standing, and even the French-origin bilinguals could rise only so far. Individuals who rejected church domination and moved to the cities to seek employment found that a linguistic ceiling restricted upward mobility.

The 1960s brought Quebec's "Quiet Revolution," which greatly diminished the political power and social influence of the Catholic Church. Newly elected premier Jean Lesage chose to expand the role of the state in the economic, social, and cultural life of the province. The Lesage government established a department of education (encouraging the study of engineering, maths, sciences, and business) and nationalized Hydro-Québec (to attract industry with the promise of cheap electricity). It also took over the administration of Quebec's pension funds. These and other changes served to integrate Quebec into the North American economic structure (Coleman, 1984).

Quebec was now characterized by a rapidly growing working class, a declining birth rate—eliminating "the revenge of the cradle" as a tool for maintaining or improving the linguistic balance in Canada—and a decline in the influence of the church. In other words, French-Canadian society was becoming more like the rest of North America—urban, secular, and industrialized. As a result, language became the primary defining characteristic of Québécois society, and francophone Quebeckers became even more aware of the relative numbers of French- and English-speaking people. They also realized that the continued existence of the small francophone minorities outside Quebec was threatened by assimilation. Reaching the conclusion that French language and culture could only be protected in the province of Quebec, many rejected their Canadian or French-Canadian identities and began to think of themselves as Québécois only. The desire to protect their distinct language and culture led them to seek institutional dominance in Quebec, and this in turn had profound implications for federal-provincial relations.

The logical extension of a demand for institutional control was the demand for sovereignty. The late 1960s and 1970s saw an increase in Québécois nationalism and in support for the independence movement. The sentiments that gave rise to the radical terrorist Front de libération du Québec (FLQ) became more widespread and eventually paved the way for the 1976 election of the separatist Parti Québécois, led by René Lévesque.

One of the first acts of the new Parti Québécois government in Quebec was to introduce Bill 101, making French the only official language of Quebec, including in business and education. Francophones were no longer excluded from the economic elite. In addition, the children of immigrants from other countries or from other provinces would be educated in French and assimilated into francophone society. In response to the election of a separatist government and the language laws, many anglophones and businesses, both large and small, left the province. From 1976 to 1981, Quebec's net loss through interprovincial migration was 156 000 people, double that of the previous five-year period.

In a 1980 referendum on "sovereignty-association," 60 percent of Quebeckers voted "No." The debate leading up the referendum was often divisive, especially in the city of Montreal. There, as elsewhere in the province, the referendum revealed a general pattern of increased support for sovereignty the further east one moved from the Ontario border (Gerber, 1992).

Under the Liberal government of Pierre Trudeau, Canada patriated its constitution and incorporated the *Charter of Rights and Freedoms* in 1982. The provincial government of Quebec did not agree to the conditions of patriation and did not sign the constitution at that point. Brian Mulroney and the Progressive Conservative party won the 1984 election with massive support in Quebec, in part because they promised amendments that would overcome Quebec's objections to the constitution.

For complex political reasons, the Meech Lake accord of 1987, which included recognition of Quebec as a "distinct society," was not ratified by all the provincial legislatures before its 1990 deadline. Among the reasons for public disenchantment with "Meech" was Quebec's 1988 sign law, which banned English from outdoor signs altogether. Anglophone Canadians perceived the sign law as a slap in the face. In turn, Quebeckers saw the failure of the Meech Lake accord as a symbol of rejection by English Canada. Such symbols, as Breton (1992) points out, can have powerful political impacts. Among other things, the failure of Meech spawned the separatist Bloc Québécois—a political party working at the federal level to promote the cause of separation.

The Charlottetown accord (discussed in Chapter 7, "Groups and Organizations") was rejected by

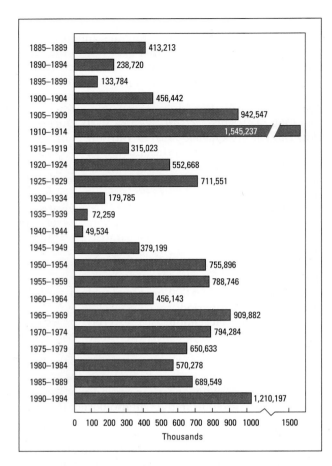

1885–1889	413,213
1890–1894	238,720
1895–1899	133,784
1900–1904	456,442
1905–1909	942,547
1910–1914	1,545,237
1915–1919	315,023
1920–1924	552,668
1925–1929	711,551
1930–1934	179,785
1935–1939	72,259
1940–1944	49,534
1945–1949	379,199
1950–1954	755,896
1955–1959	788,746
1960–1964	456,143
1965–1969	909,882
1970–1974	794,284
1975–1979	650,633
1980–1984	570,278
1985–1989	689,549
1990–1994	1,210,197

0 100 200 300 400 500 600 700 800 900 1000 1500
Thousands

FIGURE 13–4 Immigration to Canada, 1885–1994

SOURCE: Knowles (1992); Employment and Immigration Canada; Citizenship and Immigration Canada.

Canadians (including 55 percent of Quebeckers) in the referendum of October 26, 1992. Support for the separatist Bloc Québécois and Parti Québécois grew, at least in part because of the repeated failures in constitutional accommodation as well as the economic pain associated with a prolonged recession.

The success of the two separatist parties clearly reveals that the politics surrounding the quest for special status and related powers continues to have potentially explosive consequences for Canada. On October 30, 1995, Canadians were stunned by the razor-thin victory for the "No" side in Quebec's most recent referendum on "sovereignty"—50.6 percent voting "no" to 49.4 percent voting "yes." Quebec came dangerously close to giving its leaders the go-ahead to negotiate separation, which would have had incalculable costs for the country as a whole. The referendum alarm wakened federalist forces in Ottawa and Quebec City, reactivated the "unity" agenda and,

once again, raised the question of what can be done to keep Canada whole (see the "Controversy & Debate" box on page 346).

IMMIGRATION TO CANADA: A HUNDRED-YEAR PERSPECTIVE

Canada has been—and will remain—a land of immigrants. The ten-year period from 1905 to 1914 saw the arrival of 2.5 million people, making it the peak decade for Canadian immigration. (See Figure 13–4, which details our immigration history from 1885 to 1994.) At the height of immigration to Canada, in 1913, one in every seventeen people was a new-comer—not just an immigrant, but someone who had arrived within the past year. In contrast, we now admit about 225 000 immigrants per year into a population of 29 million: one in every 130 people today is a newly arrived immigrant of the current year. Knowing the numbers of immigrants absorbed by the tiny Canadian population of the early 1900s should give us encouragement regarding Canada's ability to absorb the numbers arriving in recent years. The 1990 to 1994 period was one of increased immigration, with the arrival of more than a million individuals.

Race and ethnicity retain their significance in part because of the continuous flow of immigrants into our country. The first wave of immigration after Confederation was driven by the desire to populate the West and to provide workers for the growing economy. This trend was encouraged by the controversial policies of Clifford Sifton, Minister of the Interior around the turn of the century (Hiller, 1991).

During the Sifton years, Canada was still trying to promote immigration from Britain—in part out of political necessity. "English Canadians took it for granted that the government would do everything possible to retain the British character of the country" (Knowles, 1992:67). By setting up an immigration office in London, England, Sifton was able to increase the flow from Britain to the point where, by 1905, about a third of our immigrants came from there. But because Sifton was primarily interested in attracting good farmers to populate the West, he also started a trickle of Ukrainian immigration that would peak in 1913, when 22 363 individuals arrived from that country (Knowles, 1992:73). These Ukrainians, along with a trickle of Doukhobors, Finns, Germans, and Scandinavians, were seen by many politicians and ordinary Canadians as ignorant, unassimilable aliens who would do irreparable damage to Canada.

In the early 1900s, policy severely restricted immigration to Canada to white people of Anglo-Saxon origin. Unsuitable, unassimilable southern and eastern Europeans, as well as the Chinese, the Japan-

TABLE 13–4 Immigrants by Geographic Region of Last Residence, 1996–1997

Region	Number	%
Europe	37,353	16.7
Africa	13,806	6.2
Asia	147,627	66.1
Australasia	1,332	0.6
North and Central America	8,912	4.0
West Indies	8,017	3.6
South America	5,502	2.5
Other	689	0.3
Total	223,238	100.0

SOURCE: Adapted from Canadian Statistics (www.statcan.ca).

TABLE 13–5 Top 10 Places of Birth for Immigrants* Arriving in 1991–1996

Country	Number	%
Hong Kong	108,915	10.5
People's Republic of China	87,875	8.5
India	71,335	6.9
Philippines	71,325	6.9
Sri Lanka	44,235	4.3
Poland	36,965	3.6
Taiwan	32,140	3.1
Vietnam	32,060	3.1
United States	29,020	2.8
United Kingdom	25,425	2.4
Total	1,038,995	100.0

* Non-permanent residents are not included in this table.
SOURCE: Census 1996 (www.statcan.ca).

ese, and African-American, were discouraged from entering. For example, the *Chinese Immigration Act* of 1923 barred all but a select few Chinese from entering Canada. Despite these efforts, immigration soared—in part because politicians and businessmen believed that economic prosperity depended on continued population growth. Immigration fell during World War I (1914–18), the Great Depression (1929–39), and World War II (1939–45). During a short boom in the 1920s, immigrants from Britain and Europe were admitted along with some Jews and Russian Mennonites. By 1931, however, Canada was to close her doors to refugees—especially Jewish refugees, in part because of widespread anti-Semitism.

After World War II there were mounting internal and international pressures to open the doors once again and accept large numbers of refugees. The immigrants—who, it was argued, were needed to meet labour needs, settle unpopulated areas, and expand the internal market for goods—were once again to come from "old" commonwealth countries and the United States. By the 1950s, Germany, Italy, and the Netherlands had become important sources of immigrants and our immigration laws had been liberalized to allow more Asians, as well as Palestinian and Hungarian refugees. Further liberalization would occur under the Conservative government of John Diefenbaker, who foresaw a population of forty million in the near future and argued that "Canada must populate or perish" (Knowles, 1992:137).

It was not until 1962, however, that Ellen Fairclough, Canada's first woman federal cabinet minister, put an end to our White Canada immigration policy. Education and occupational and language skills replaced race or national origin as the criteria of admission. After the Liberals won the 1965 election, they formalized the selection criteria through what we call the *points system*, which allocates specific numbers of points to education, occupation, facility in English or French, age, and the demand for the applicant's

skills in the Canadian labour market. The points system reduces reliance on the judgment of the individual immigration officer.

More recently, Canada has experienced waves of immigration from the West Indies and Asia (in the 1970s) and from Central and South America (in the 1980s). As Hiller (1991:173) points out, "these repeated waves of immigration reinvigorated ethnic groups already resident in Canada, and reminded residents of their own ethnicity."

The *Immigration Act* of 1976 recognized three classes of people as eligible for landed immigrant status: *family class* (immediate family and dependent children, parents and grandparents of Canadian citizens or landed immigrants), *humanitarian class* (refugees or persecuted and displaced persons), and *independent class* (those who apply as individuals and are admitted on the basis of the points system). These changes altered the countries of origin of the applicants, stimulated an unmanageable flow of refugees, and increased applications by family members, who now outnumber independent applicants. In recent years, Canada has made a concerted effort to attract people who are experienced in business or who have significant amounts of money to invest—and has had some success in doing so (2455 entrepreneurs with 7446 dependents in 1991).

Table 13–4 indicates the sources of our immigrants in 1996–97, by geographic region of last residence. Asia is by far the major source region, sending us 66 percent of our immigrants, while Europe—the source of almost all immigration in the first half of this century—has dropped down to 17 percent. Table 13–5 reveals that Great Britain now supplies 2.4 percent of our immigrants and ranks tenth among source countries. Hong Kong and China, which rank first and second, sent us 11 and 9 percent of our immigrants, respectively, between 1991 and 1996. Other

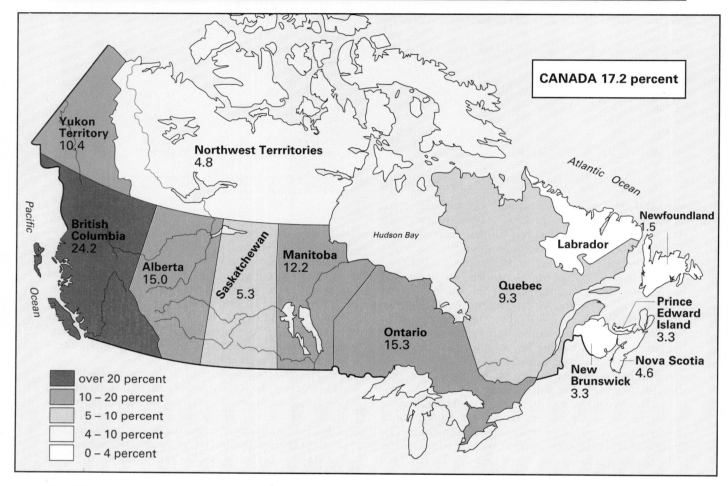

CANADA 17.2 percent

Yukon Territory 10.4

Northwest Terrritories 4.8

British Columbia 24.2

Alberta 15.0

Saskatchewan 5.3

Manitoba 12.2

Hudson Bay

Ontario 15.3

Quebec 9.3

Labrador

Newfoundland 1.5

Prince Edward Island 3.3

Nova Scotia 4.6

New Brunswick 3.3

Pacific Ocean

Atlantic Ocean

- over 20 percent
- 10 – 20 percent
- 5 – 10 percent
- 4 – 10 percent
- 0 – 4 percent

CANADA MAP 13–1 Percentage of Population Foreign-Born for Canada, the Provinces, and Territories, 1996

SOURCE: Adapted from 1996 census tables (www.statcan.ca).

Asian countries, including India, Philippines, Sri Lanka, Taiwan and Vietnam, rank among the top ten sources of Canadian immigrants.

Most of the immigrants who have come to Canada in recent decades have gone to Ontario and British Columbia. As Canada Map 13–1 reveals, Alberta and Manitoba have also attracted immigrants, while the Atlantic provinces have not. Not surprisingly, the metropolitan areas of Toronto and Vancouver have the largest immigrant components at 30 to 40 percent. Visible minorities made up about 20 percent of the populations of the two metropolitan areas. In Quebec, Montreal has attracted a significant immigrant component, whereas Quebec City has not.

Recent immigration has clearly touched some parts of Canada more than others.

RACE AND ETHNICITY: PAST AND FUTURE

Immigration has contributed to the development of a country which, though it started out native, British, and French at Confederation, is now quite rightly called multicultural. The characteristics of the newcomers have stimulated the continued, and often uneasy, awareness of race and ethnicity among Canadians. Their geographic distribution has contributed to regional diversity as people with different backgrounds found themselves concentrated in various parts of the country and in different cities, giving substance to the vision of Canada as what former prime minister Joe Clark would call a "community of communities."

Canada is an experiment in multilayered pluralism—multilayered because the British, the French, the native peoples, and the other ethnic and racial minorities have different kinds of relationships with each other and Canadian society as a whole. Each new wave of immigration will add to the complexity of the mosaic. Newly articulated demands and expectations on the part of the Québécois and the various native peoples will contribute to the definition and redefinition of our unique country. Our survival as a country depends on our success in forging an identity out of diversity.

SUMMARY

1. Race involves a cluster of biological traits that nineteenth-century biologists divided into three broad, overarching categories: Caucasians, Mongoloids, and Negroids. There are, however, no pure races. Ethnicity is based on shared cultural heritage. Minorities are categories of people who are socially distinctive—including those of certain races and ethnicities—and who have a subordinate social position.

2. Prejudice is an inflexible and distorted generalization about a category of people. Racism, a destructive form of prejudice, asserts that one race is innately superior or inferior to another.

3. Discrimination is a pattern of action by which a person treats various categories of people differently.

4. Pluralism refers to a state in which racial and ethnic categories, although distinct, have equal social standing. Assimilation is a process by which minorities gradually adopt the patterns of the dominant culture. Segregation means the physical and social separation of categories of people. Most segregation of minorities is involuntary. Genocide is the annihilation of a category of people.

5. Blacks have a long history in Canada, as free Loyalists, as slaves prior to 1810, and later as escaped slaves coming to Canada via the Underground Railroad. The past two decades have seen increased immigration of Blacks (from Africa, the Caribbean, and elsewhere) who have made their own cultural, economic, and political contributions to Canadian life.

6. The representation of racial and ethnic groups varies substantially from region to region in Canada, as does that of people who claim "Canadian" ancestry.

7. Blacks and Asians have higher levels of education than the British and French, but their incomes tend to be lower. Natives are low on both education and income scales.

8. The native peoples (or First Nations), who face numerous barriers to full participation in the larger society, seek self-government as a potential solution to some of their problems.

9. The Québécois feel that French language and culture can only be protected within Quebec and that they need to have maximum control of their institutions—perhaps through separation—in order to achieve this.

10. Canada, which has historically accepted large numbers of immigrants, is currently receiving most of its immigrants from Asia, especially Hong Kong.

CRITICAL THINKING QUESTIONS

1. Clearly differentiate between race and ethnicity. Do you think all nonwhite people should be considered minorities, even if they have above-average incomes?

2. In what ways do prejudice and discrimination reinforce each other?

3. Are *all* generalizations about minorities wrong? What distinguishes a fair generalization from an unfair stereotype?

4. Do you think Canadian society is colour-blind? Should we be? Does affirmative action reduce or exacerbate racial conflict?

SOCIOLOGY APPLIED

1. Give several of your friends or family members a quick quiz, asking them what share of the Canadian population is white, Black, aboriginal, or Asian (see Figure 13–3). Do they exaggerate the

CONTROVERSY & DEBATE

Distinct Societies and National Unity

Pluralism and diversity are so central to Canadian identity that we find them enshrined in our constitution. The French language (official bilingualism and minority language rights), civil law (in Quebec), Catholic or denominational schooling, existing aboriginal and treaty rights, and the right to preserve and enhance our multicultural heritage are guaranteed by our constitution and the *Charter of Rights and Freedoms*. Protection from the pressures of assimilation could be taken for granted in this country, yet some of us are so anxious to ensure the viability of our own cultures that we demand constitutional recognition as distinct societies.

The unwillingness or inability of Canadians across the country to respond positively to demands for such recognition by Quebec threatens the stability of our federation—as we learned so painfully on referendum day in October 1995, when the Québécois came within a hair's breadth of voting for sovereignty and separation. Because distinct society status is significant for both Quebec and Canada, the debate surrounding it receives a great deal of media attention.

The concept or symbol of a "distinct society" could have explosive consequences for Canada as a whole. Applying the concept to Quebec, people across Canada say, "But *of course* Quebec is a distinct society. It has its own language, legal system, political parties, and a vibrant French culture." Quebec leaders want to know why, if we so readily accept Quebec's distinctiveness, we cannot agree to include that recognition in our constitution.* The answer lies, in part, in the controversy surrounding the distinct society label.

Let's look at this concept. At one level, it implies that Quebec is *different*—and few would argue with that. (Aboriginal societies are different, too.) The controversy emerges with the argument that different or distinct implies *special* status. The notion that Quebec is not only different, but perhaps *special*, raises the issue of two classes of Canadians, one having special rights. It is this interpretation that raises the hackles of many Canadians and some provinces.

If we assume that the label "distinct society" is purely symbolic and merely implies the recognition of existing social and cultural differences, then putting it into the constitution would not have any significant effect. One way to restrict its potential impact on the constitution would be to define it carefully, so that the distinction implies no new powers, or no powers that substantially differentiate Quebec from other provinces.

However, to be acceptable to Quebec, "distinct society" must imply special powers, for it is through those that the Québécois hope to become "masters in their own house." To preserve and protect the small island of francophone culture, Quebec sovereigntists want unquestioned control over language (in business, education, social discourse, and government), immigration, employment, trade, natural resources, the economy, population policy and mobility, social services, and

share of all minorities and understate the white proportion? Does your place of residence affect perceptions?

2. There are probably people on your campus or in your local community who are immigrants from abroad. Have you ever thought about asking such people to tell you something about their homeland and their experiences since arriving in Canada? Most immigrants would be pleased to be asked and can provide a wonderful learning experience.

3. Does the ethnic diversity of Canada affect what you eat? Check out your grocery stores, the restaurants in town, your favourite snacks. What is your conclusion?

4. Visit the Web site of an organization working to improve the social standing of a Canadian minority: B'nai Brith Canada, Canadian Centre for Minority Affairs, or the Chinese Canadian National Council. What are the organization's strategies and goals?

WEBLINKS

www.interlog.com/~cccj/
The *Canadian Council of Christians and Jews* is a nonreligious organization dedicated to promoting cultural,

racial and religious harmony among the people of Canada. The council produces a nationwide market research study known as the "Harmony Barometer,"

more. Since other provinces do not want all these powers (mainly because of funding concerns), granting them to Quebec would give that province special status.

Another aspect of Quebec's relationship with the rest of the country is threatening to other provinces. Many Québécois see confederation as joining together *two founding nations*, while other Canadians see it as joining *ten equal provinces*. Is Quebec one of ten equal partners, or one of only two? Clearly, these are serious and potentially catastrophic clashes of vision.

In another attempt to circumvent the "distinct society" problem, Canada's premiers proposed constitutional recognition of Quebec's "unique characteristics" in the Calgary declaration of September 1997. Whatever words are used to describe different, special, or distinct status, with the implication of enhanced autonomy, the impact would not be neutral. The process itself is controversial and divisive, and even if we were able to deliver distinct society status, its implementation would generate its own strains. The heated debate that

erupts periodically around these powerful concepts is both inevitable and justifiable in the context of Canadian pluralism.

Postscript: When natural disasters occur in Canada, they can raise thorny political and constitutional questions. Many people wondered why it took the federal forces so long to arrive on the scene in the Montreal region during the crippling ice storm of January 1998 (the ice crisis was in its fourth day before federal soldiers made their appearance). In fact, before the Canadian Forces become involved, they need to be invited in by the provincial attorney-general—as they were during Oka (1990) and the flooding of the Saguenay (1996). The sovereigntist leaders of Quebec are particularly sensitive to admitting that their distinct and separatist society cannot look after its own. Canada's military and civilian response to the raging floods of the Saguenay led to a widespread positive reaction among Québécois. Quebec's leaders were not anxious for a repeat of such pro-Canada feelings as the Canadian Forces helped the Québécois cope with the ice and cold.

Continue the debate . . .

1. *Francophones outside of the province have been abandoned in Quebec's quest for greater autonomy and cultural protections. How might these francophones react to the granting of "distinct society" status to Quebec?*

2. *Native peoples claim distinctiveness and the right to self-government as well. What are the implications of granting "distinct society" status to Quebec for the aboriginal peoples in the province?*

3. *Both the status quo and constitutional recognition of "distinct society" status for Quebec results in strain or conflict within Canada. Why is this the case?*

---

*In early 1996, knowing that it would be almost impossible to get sufficient consensus to amend the constitution, the government of Prime Minister Chrétien (in the wake of the Quebec referendum) passed legislation recognizing Quebec as a distinct society and "loaning" the federal veto over future constitutional change to Quebec and other regions or provinces. It was hoped that this would pacify at least some Québécois, but the net effect of all the new vetoes is to make future constitutional change substantially more difficult.

---

which examines the attitudes and behaviours of Canadians towards people of different ethnic, religious, and racial backgrounds.

www.pathcom.com/~casnp/
Canadian Alliance in Solidarity with the Native Peoples' mandate is to actively involve and educate individuals on issues facing aboriginal peoples in Canada, North America, and around the world. The organization provides ways for native and non-native people to work together as allies to help create harmony among all peoples.

www.march21.com/
Maintained by the Canadian Department of Heritage, this site supports International Day for the Elimination of Racial Discrimination (March 21) activities by providing education and information resources.

canada.metropolis.globalx.net/main_e.html
Metropolis is a cooperative, international research initiative created to examine immigrant integration and the effects of international migration on urban centres. The project aims to provide all levels of government, community organizations, and business with solid information on which to anchor policy ideas and programs.

www.mensa.org/workout.html
Mensa is a society for people with a high IQ, in the top 2 percent of the population. The society is nonpolitical and free from all racial or religious distinctions, and offers culture-fair testing throughout the world. The Mensa workout is provided for entertainment purposes only—it is not an IQ test.

Deidre Schere, *Gifts,* 1966
From the Collection of St. Mary's Foundation, Rochester, N.Y.

CHAPTER 14

AGING AND THE ELDERLY

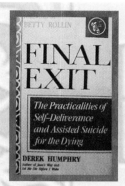

Almost as soon as it was released, the book *Final Exit* shot to the top of the best-seller list in 1991. This is a book about dying—not about the death of a famous person, nor a philosophical treatise on death, but a "how-to" manual explaining how to commit suicide. *Final Exit* gives specific instructions for killing yourself in a host of ways, from swallowing sleeping pills, to self-starvation, to suffocation with a plastic bag.

The author of *Final Exit*, Derek Humphry, is a founder and the executive director of the Hemlock Society, an organization that offers support and practical assistance to people who wish to die. Humphry argues that the time has come for people to have straightforward information about how to end their own lives. The immediate and remarkable popularity of *Final Exit*—especially among the elderly—suggests that millions of people agree with him.

Not surprisingly, *Final Exit* sparked controversy. While supporters view the work as a humane effort to assist people who are painfully and terminally ill, critics worry that it encourages suicide by people who, perhaps, are temporarily depressed (Angelo, 1991). Laws are being tested that prohibit doctors—and others—from assisting in the death of a patient. Sue Rodriguez brought the issue of euthanasia to national attention by fighting, right up to the Supreme Court of Canada, for the right to assisted suicide whenever she decided that her life with ALS was not worth living. She lost the case but was assisted to her chosen death by an anonymous doctor. Sue Rodriguez was supported through her legal battles and her final days by her friend (and MP) Svend Robinson.

The appearance of *Final Exit* also raises broader questions that are no less disturbing and controversial than the "right to die." As this chapter explains, the ranks of the elderly are swelling rapidly as more and more men and women live longer and longer. As a result, many younger people are uneasy about their responsibilities towards aging parents. For their part, many older people are alarmed at the prospect of losing control of their lives to a medical establishment driven to prolong life at any cost. And people of all ages worry whether the health care system must shortchange the young in order to meet the escalating needs of seniors.

Today, issues relating to aging and the elderly command the attention of policymakers as never before. In some respects, growing old in Canada has never been better: people live longer, have better health care, and experience less poverty than they did a generation ago. But stubborn problems persist. Older people, for example, continue to grapple with prejudice and discrimination. And, as unprecedented numbers of women and men enter old age, new problems loom on the horizon.

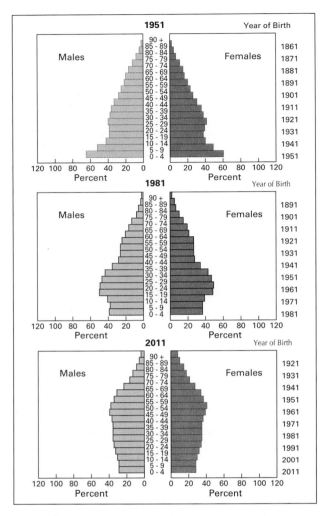

FIGURE 14–1 Age Pyramids of Canada for Selected Years Since 1951

SOURCE: Statistics Canada, *Report on the Demographic Situations in Canada*, Catalogue No. 91-209 (1992).

THE GREYING OF CANADA

A quiet but powerful revolution is reshaping Canada: the number of elderly people—women and men age sixty-five and over—is increasing more than twice as fast as the population as a whole. The effects of this "greying of Canada" promise to be profound.

Some statistics bring this change into sharp focus. The average annual growth of the youth population over the last 120 years has been 1.2 percent, and that of persons over sixty-five has been more than double that rate, at 2.7 percent (*Report on the Demographic Situation in Canada*, 1992). The 1996 census reveals that, in Canada, the population over sixty-five now makes up 12.2 percent of the whole (www.statcan.ca).

In just over a century, the life expectancy of Canadians has doubled and their average number of children has declined by a half. The age/sex pyramids for the Canadian population have shown and will continue to demonstrate dramatic shape changes (see Figure 14–1). By 2031, the proportion of the population age sixty-five and over will have increased to almost one-quarter of the whole, or 23.8 percent (*A Portrait of Seniors in Canada*, 1990). Already, the median age of Canadians has risen from 29.6 in 1981 to 31.6 in 1986 and 33.5 in 1991. Canada Map 14–1 shows the percentage of the population over sixty-five, by province and territory.

What is prompting the aging of our society? Two factors stand out. The first is the baby boom that began in the late 1940s. After World War II, men and women enthusiastically settled into family life and the bearing of children. The birth rate then took a sharp turn downward after 1965 (the so-called baby bust), so that our population will become increasingly "top-heavy" in the coming decades.

Global Map 14–1 shows that it is the rich nations, including Canada, in which the share of elderly people is rapidly increasing. Typically, two factors combine to drive up the elderly population: low birth rates (so there are fewer children) and increasing longevity (so people typically live well into old age).

LIFE EXPECTANCY: GOING UP

This century has witnessed a remarkable thirty-year increase in life expectancy. Females born in 1900 lived 50.2 years; males lived 47.2 years. By contrast, women now look forward to 81 years of life; men to about 75 years (Nancarrow Clarke, 1996:66; Colombo, 1997:62).

Our longer life spans are mainly due to medical advances that virtually eliminated infectious diseases such as smallpox, diphtheria, and measles, which killed many young people in the past. More recent medical strides fend off cancer and heart disease, afflictions common to the elderly (Wall, 1980). The decline in mortality rates means that of women born in 1950, only 5 percent will have died before becoming mothers. For every one hundred women born in the 1800s, forty died before giving birth to a child (*Report on the Demographic Situation in Canada*, 1992). In addition, a rising standard of living during this century has promoted the health of people of all ages. One clear indication of this change is that the fastest-growing segment of the entire population is people over eighty-five, who are already more than twenty times more numerous than they were at the beginning of this century. By 2011, about 20 percent of our elders (people over sixty-five) will be over eighty years of age (*Report on the Demographic Situation in Canada*, 1992).

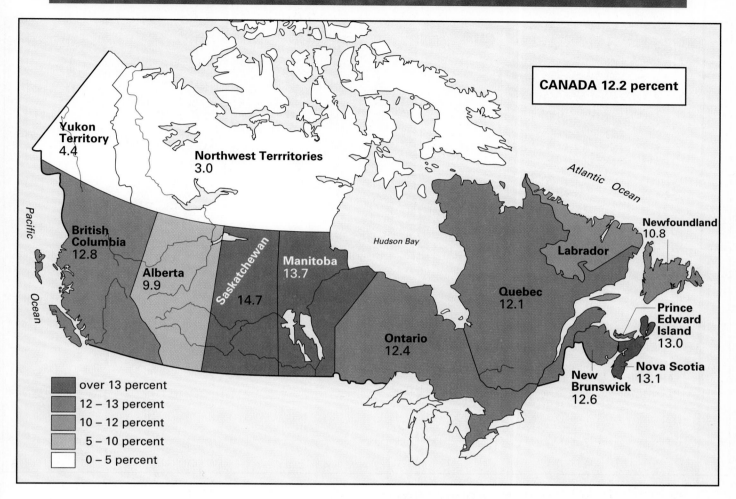

CANADA 12.2 percent

Yukon Territory 4.4

Northwest Terrritories 3.0

Atlantic Ocean

Newfoundland 10.8

British Columbia 12.8

Pacific Ocean

Alberta 9.9

Saskatchewan 14.7

Manitoba 13.7

Hudson Bay

Labrador

Quebec 12.1

Prince Edward Island 13.0

Ontario 12.4

Nova Scotia 13.1

New Brunswick 12.6

over 13 percent
12 – 13 percent
10 – 12 percent
5 – 10 percent
0 – 5 percent

CANADA MAP 14–1 Percentage of the Population Age 65 and Over for Canada, the Provinces and Territories, 1996

SOURCE: Adapted from www.statcan.ca

We can only begin to imagine the consequences of this massive increase in the elderly population. As elderly people steadily retire from the labour force, the proportion of nonworking adults—already about ten times greater than in 1900—will generate ever-greater demands for health care and other social resources. And the ratio of elderly people to working-age adults, which analysts call the old-age dependency ratio, will almost double in the next fifty years.

However, today's adults, especially women, are considerably different, in many important ways, from previous generations. They will not be entirely like the people who are over sixty-five today. The elderly of the future will tend to have greater levels of educa-

tion, fewer family responsibilities, better work and better conditions for saving, an improved health care system, and broader access to retirement alternatives. Predicting the use of services on the basis of current use is thus very complicated (*Report on the Demographic Situation in Canada*, 1992:144).

Presently, the elderly draw heavily on the health care system. A recent study indicated that health care spending is 4.5 times greater for Canadians over sixty-five and 6.5 times greater for those over seventy-five than for those under sixty-five (*Demographic Aging: The Economic Consequences*, 1991). Older people make the greatest use of physicians, hospitals, and prescription drugs. As Chapter 20 ("Health and Medicine")

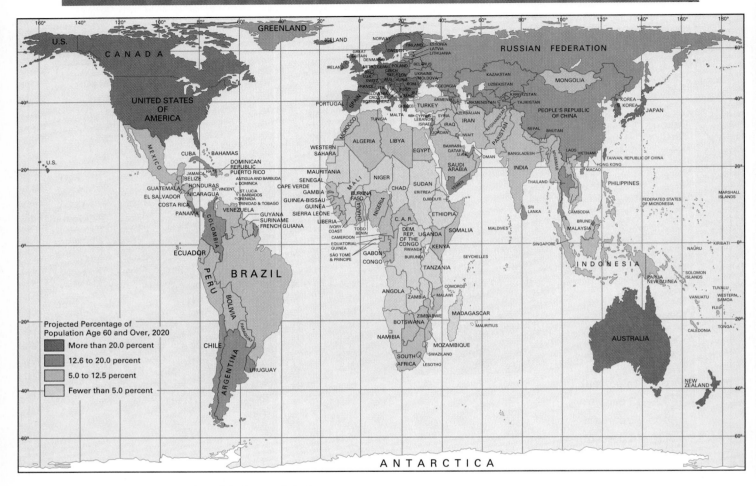

GLOBAL MAP 14–1 The Elderly in Global Perspective, 2020

Here we see projections for the share of population age sixty-five and older in the year 2020, one generation from now. What relationship do you see between a country's income level and its elderly population?

SOURCE: U.S. Bureau of the Census (1992).

explains, the costs of medical care have grown in recent years, a trend that shows little evidence of slowing. Unless steps are taken to address the real medical needs of millions of additional older people—at prices that Canadians (or taxpayers) can afford—our society will face a monumental health care crisis in the next century (Nancarrow Clarke, 1996).

AN AGING SOCIETY: CULTURAL CHANGE

As the number of people and the share of the population over sixty-five push upward, our way of life will change. In coming decades interacting with elderly people will become commonplace. Canadians are now accustomed to a considerable degree of age segregation. Young people rarely mingle in familiar settings with old people, so that most people know little about aging. In the twenty-first century, as the elderly population increases, age segregation will likely decline.

Will a "culture of aging" ever emerge? Probably not, for one key reason: the elderly are too diverse. After all, the elderly represent an open category in which all of us—if we are lucky—end up. Thus, elderly people in Canada represent not just the two sexes but all cultures, classes, and races.

THE "YOUNG OLD" AND THE "OLD OLD"

Analysts sometimes distinguish between two cohorts of the elderly. The "younger elderly," who are between sixty-five and seventy-five years of age, are typically autonomous, enjoy good health and financial security, and are likely to be living as couples. The "older elderly" who have passed age seventy-five, are more likely to be dependent on others because of health and money problems. Women outnumber men in the elderly population (due to their greater longevity), a discrepancy that increases with advancing age: among the "oldest old"—those over the age of eighty-five—about two-thirds are women.

While there are good reasons to be alert to population aging in Canada, there are scholars who argue that we have pressed the panic button fifteen years too early. The 1996 census suggests that the rate of growth in the elderly population has slowed down, and will not pick up substantially until the baby boomers hit retirement age. Susan McDaniel, a demographer at the University of Alberta, and David Foot, author of *Boom, Bust and Echo*, agree that we have started worrying too early about the social costs (health care and pensions included) of an elderly population now growing at a rate lower than anticipated (Mitchell, 1997).

GROWING OLD: BIOLOGY AND CULTURE

Tracking the greying of Canada is the special focus of **gerontology** (derived from the Greek word *geron*, meaning "an old person"), *the study of aging and the elderly*. Gerontologists explore the biological processes of aging, ask if personalities change as we grow older, and investigate how cultural assumptions about aging vary around the world.

BIOLOGICAL CHANGES

Aging amounts to a series of gradual, ongoing changes. How we think about life's transitions—whether we cheer our maturity or bemoan our physical decline—depends largely on whether our culture labels such changes as positive or negative. The youth-oriented way of life in Canada hails biological changes that occur early in life as positive. Through childhood and adolescence, we gain responsibility and look forward to expanded legal rights.

But our culture takes a dimmer view of the biological changes that unfold later in life. Few people receive congratulations for getting old. Rather, we commiserate with those entering old age and make jokes about aging to avoid the harsh conclusion that the elderly are on a slippery slope of physical and mental decline. We assume, in short, that by about age forty, people cease growing *up* and begin growing *down*.

Growing old does bring on certain physical problems. Grey hair, wrinkles, loss of height and weight, and an overall decline in strength and vitality all begin in middle age. After the age of fifty, bones become more brittle so that injuries take longer to heal, and the odds of suffering from chronic illnesses (such as arthritis and diabetes) as well as life-threatening conditions (such as heart disease and cancer) rise steadily. The sensory abilities—taste, sight, touch, smell, and especially hearing—also become less keen with age (Colloway and Dollevoet, 1977; Treas, 1995).

One of the most troublesome problems of old age is a group of illnesses called dementias. Dementias are characterized by progressive cognitive impairment including the loss of abilities such as attention span, concentration, orientation, and memory. While dementias can result from several distinct diseases that affect the brain, Alzheimer's disease is the best-known and the most common form of dementia (about 50 percent of dementia is Alzheimer's). Dementia is a serious and prevalent health problem among elderly Canadians, affecting between 5 and 10 percent of those over sixty-five and approximately 20 percent of those over eighty.

Without denying that health becomes more fragile with advancing age, the vast majority of older people are neither discouraged nor disabled by their physical condition. Only about one in ten seniors reports trouble walking, and fewer than one in twenty requires intensive care in a hospital or nursing home. No more than 1 percent of the elderly are bedridden. In a 1990 survey, less than 25 percent of people over the age of fifty-five characterized their health as "fair" or "poor," while about 75 percent described their overall condition as "good" or "excellent" (Keith and Landry, 1994:134).

Bear in mind, however, that patterns of well-being vary greatly within the elderly population. More health problems beset the "older elderly" past the age of seventy-five. Moreover, because women typically live longer than men, women spend more of their lives suffering from chronic disabilities such as arthritis. In addition, well-to-do people are likely to live and work in a healthful and safe environment, a fact that pays benefits well into old age. And, of course, richer people can afford much more preventive medical care. As well, happiness level does depend somewhat on income. In one survey, 56 percent of men and 49 percent of women over fifty-five reported being very happy. Very few happy men, only 4 percent, or women, only 9 percent, had incomes of less than $10 000. The greatest proportion of very happy

Jackrabbit (Herman Smith) Johannsen was born in Norway in 1875. Along with his skis, he left "an indelible mark on Canada: many kilometres of cross-country ski trails and jumps are directly attributable to him, and so are the thousands of skiers who have been inspired by his spirit of adventure and love for the Canadian winter." He promoted cross-country skiing through Quebec, Ontario, and parts of the U.S. He also was responsible for introducing skiing to the Crees in Northern Ontario—from whom he learned their language, his eighth, and who honoured him with the title Chief Jackrabbit. The Jackrabbit part stuck so well that many people never knew his Christian name. When asked, at 105 years of age, about his skiing, he said, "I'm steadier on skis with two poles to hold me up. But I'm not as good a skier as I was 100 years ago." (Norton, 1987)

men, 29 percent, fell into the highest income category (Keith and Landry, 1994:134).

PSYCHOLOGICAL CHANGES

Just as we tend to overstate the physical problems of aging, so it is easy to exaggerate the psychological changes that accompany growing old. Looking at intelligence over the life course, the conventional wisdom can be summed up in the simple rule: "What goes up must come down" (Baltes and Schaie, 1974).

If we operationalize intelligence to refer to skills such as sensorimotor coordination—the ability to arrange objects to match a drawing—we do find a steady decline as people grow old. The ability to learn new material and to think quickly also appears to diminish, although not until around age seventy. But the ability to apply familiar ideas holds steady with advancing age, and some studies actually show improvement in verbal and mathematical skills (Baltes and Schaie, 1974; Schaie, 1980).

We all wonder if we will think or feel differently as we get older. Gerontologists assure us that, for better or for worse, the answer is usually no. The only common personality change with advancing age is becoming more introspective. That is, people become more engaged with their own thoughts and emotions and less materialistic. Generally, therefore, two elderly people who were childhood friends would recognize in each other many of the same personality traits that distinguished them as youngsters (Neugarten, 1971, 1972, 1977; Wolfe, 1994).

AGING AND CULTURE

November 1, 1994, approaching Kandy, Sri Lanka. Our small van struggles up the steep mountain incline. Breaks in the lush vegetation offer spectacular views that interrupt our conversation about growing old. "Then there are no old-age homes in your country?" I ask. "In Colombo and other cities, I am sure," our driver responds, "but not many; we are not like you North Americans." "And how is that?" I counter, stiffening a bit. His eyes remain fixed on the road: "We would not leave our fathers and mothers to live alone."

When do people grow old? How do younger people regard society's oldest members? The range of answers to these questions demonstrates that, while aging is universal, the significance of growing old is a variable element of culture.

At one level, how well—and, more basically, how long—people live is closely linked to a society's technology and overall standard of living. Throughout human history, as English philosopher Thomas Hobbes (1588–1679) put it, people's lives were "nasty, brutish, and short" (although Hobbes himself persisted to the ripe old age of ninety-one). In his day, most people married and had children while in their teens, became middle-aged in their twenties, and began to succumb to various illnesses in their thirties and forties. It took several more centuries for a rising standard of living and advancing medical technology to curb deadly infectious diseases. Living to, say, age fifty became commonplace only at the beginning of this century. Since then, a rising standard of living coupled with medical advances has added over twenty years to people's longevity in industrial nations.

But living into what we call "old age" is not yet the rule in much of the world. Global Map 14–2 shows that, in the poorest countries, the average life span is still just fifty years.

The reality of growing old is as much a matter of culture as it is of biology. In Canada, being elderly is often synonymous with being inactive; yet, in Greece and other more traditional countries, old people commonly continue in many familiar routines.

Just as important as longevity is the importance societies attach to their senior members. As Chapter 9 ("Social Stratification") explains, all societies distribute basic resources unequally. We now turn to the importance of age in this process.

AGE STRATIFICATION: A GLOBAL ASSESSMENT

Like race, ethnicity, and gender, age is a basis for socially ranking individuals. **Age stratification**, then, is *the unequal distribution of wealth, power, and privileges among people at different stages in the life course.* As is true of other dimensions of social hierarchy, age stratification varies according to a society's level of technological development.

Hunting and Gathering Societies

As Chapter 4 ("Society") explains, without the technology to produce a surplus of food, hunters and gatherers are nomadic. Their survival depends on physical strength and stamina; thus, as members of these societies become elderly (in this case, reaching about age thirty) they become less active, leading others to consider them an economic burden (Sheehan, 1976).

Pastoral, Horticultural, and Agrarian Societies

With control over raising crops and animals, societies gain the capacity to produce a material surplus; consequently, individuals may accumulate considerable wealth over a lifetime. The most privileged members of these societies are typically the elderly, promoting **gerontocracy**, *a form of social organization in which the elderly have the most wealth, power, and prestige.* Old people, particularly men, are honoured (and sometimes feared) by their families and, as the "Global Sociology" box reports in the case of the Abkhasians, they remain active leaders of society until they die. This veneration of the elderly also explains the widespread practice of ancestor worship in agrarian societies.

Industrial Societies

Industrialization pushes living standards upward and advances medical technology, both of which, in turn, increase life expectancy. But these same forces simultaneously erode the power and prestige of the elderly. In part, this decline reflects a shift in the prime source of wealth from land (typically controlled by the oldest members of society) to factories and other goods (often owned or managed by younger people). The peak earning years among Canadian workers, for instance, occur around age fifty; after that, earnings generally decline.

Modern living also separates the generations physically as younger children move away to pursue their careers; therefore, they depend less on their parents and more on their own earning power. Furthermore, because industrial, urban societies change rapidly, the skills, traditions, and life experiences that served the old seem less relevant to the young. Finally, the tremendous productivity of industrial nations means that some members of society do not need to work; as a result, most of the very old and the very young remain in nonproductive roles (Cohn, 1982).

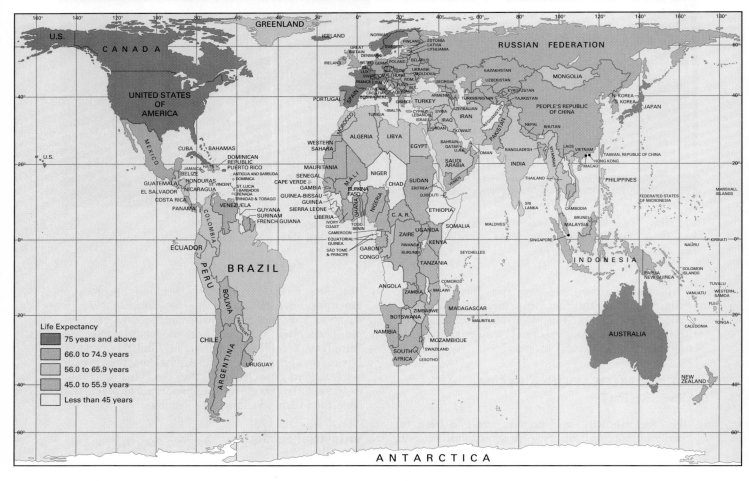

Life Expectancy

- 75 years and above
- 66.0 to 74.9 years
- 56.0 to 65.9 years
- 45.0 to 55.9 years
- Less than 45 years

GLOBAL MAP 14–2 Life Expectancy in Global Perspective

Life expectancy has shot upward over the course of this century in industrial countries including Canada, the United States, the nations of Western Europe, Japan, and Australia. A newborn in Canada can expect to live about seventy-five years, and our life expectancy would be greater still were it not for the high risk of death among infants born into poverty. Since poverty is the rule in much of the world, lives are correspondingly shorter, especially in parts of Africa where life expectancy may be as low as forty years.

SOURCE: *Peters Atlas of the World* (1990).

Over the long term, all these factors are transforming *elders* (a term with positive connotations) into the *elderly* (commanding far less prestige). In mature, industrial societies such as Canada and the United States, economic and political leaders are usually middle-aged people who combine seasoned experience with up-to-date skills. In rapidly changing sectors of the economy—especially high-tech fields—many key executives are much younger and sometimes barely out of university or college. Industrial societies often consign older people to marginal participation in the economy because these people lack the knowledge and training demanded by a fast-changing marketplace.

Certainly some elderly men and women remain at the helm of businesses they own but, more commonly, older people predominate in traditional occupations (such as barber, tailor, and seamstress) and jobs that involve minimal activity (night security guard, for instance) (Kaufman and Spilerman, 1982).

Growing (Very) Old: A Report from Abkhasia

Anthropologist Sula Benet was sharing wine and conversation with a man in Tamish, a small village in the Republic of Abkhasia, once part of the Soviet Union. Judging the man to be about seventy, she raised her glass and offered a toast to his long life. "May you live as long as Moses," she exclaimed. The gesture of goodwill fell flat: Moses lived to 120, but Benet's companion was already 119.

An outsider—especially an open-minded anthropologist who studies many of the world's mysteries—should be skeptical of the longevity claims made by some Abkhasians. In one village of 1200 visited by Benet, for example, 200 people declared their age to be over eighty. But government statistics confirm that, even if some Abkhasians exaggerate their longevity, most outlive the average North American.

What accounts for this remarkable life span? The answer certainly is not the advanced medical technology in which people in North America place so much faith; many Abkhasians have never seen a physician nor entered a hospital.

The probable explanation is cultural, including diet and physical activity. Abkhasians eat little saturated fat (which is linked to heart disease), use no sugar, and drink no coffee or tea; few smoke or chew tobacco. They consume large amounts of healthful fruits and vegetables and drink lots of buttermilk and low-alcohol wine. Additionally, Abkhasians maintain active lives built around regular physical work for people of all ages.

Moreover, Abkhasians live according to a well-defined and consistent set of traditional values, which confers on all a strong feeling of belonging and a clear sense of purpose. Here the elderly remain active and valued members of the community, in marked contrast to our own practice of pushing old people to the margins of social life. As Benet explains: "The old [in the United States], when they do not simply vege-tate, out of view and out of mind, keep themselves 'busy' with bingo and shuffleboard." For their part, the Abkhasians do not even have a word for old people and have no notion of retiring. Furthermore, younger people accord their senior members great prestige and respect since, in their minds, advanced age confers the greatest wisdom. Elders are indispensable guardians of culture and preside at important ceremonial occasions where they transmit their knowledge to the young. In Abkhasia, in short, people look to the old, rather than the young, for models of how to live life.

Given their positive approach to growing old, Abkhasians expect to lead long and useful lives. They feel needed because, in their own minds and everyone else's, they are. Far from being a burden, elders stand at the centre of society.

SOURCE: Based on Benet (1971).

Japan: An Exceptional Case

Japan stands out as an exception to the rule: with a slightly larger proportion of elderly people than Canada (14 percent versus 12.2 percent), Japan maintains a traditional culture that elevates the prestige of older people. Most aged people in Japan live with an adult son or daughter and continue to play a significant

TABLE 14–1 Self-reported Health and Happiness Status of Canadians Age 55 and Over, 1990

	Men	Women
Health Status		
Excellent	32%	27%
Good	46	48
Fair	17	19
Poor	4	6
Not stated	1	1
Happiness Status		
Very happy	56	49
Somewhat happy	39	43
Somewhat unhappy	2	5
Very unhappy	1	1
No opinion, not stated	3	2

SOURCE: Keith and Landry, *Canadian Social Trends* (1994:134).

role in family life. Elderly men in Japan are also more likely than their counterparts in North America to remain in the labour force and, in many Japanese corporations, the oldest employees enjoy the greatest respect. But even Japan is steadily becoming more like other industrial societies, in which growing old means giving up a large measure of social importance (Harlan, 1968; Cowgill and Holmes, 1972; Treas, 1979; Palmore, 1982; Yates, 1986).

TRANSITIONS AND PROBLEMS OF AGING

We confront change at each stage of life. People must unlearn self-concepts and social patterns that no longer apply to their lives and simultaneously learn to cope with new circumstances. Of all stages of the life course, however, old age presents the greatest challenges.

Physical decline in old age is less serious than most younger people think, but even small changes can cause emotional stress. Older people endure more pain, become resigned to limiting their activities, adjust to greater dependence on others, and see in the deaths of friends or relatives frequent reminders of their own mortality. Moreover, because our culture places such a premium on youth, aging often means added frustration, fear, and self-doubt (Hamel, 1990). As one retired psychologist commented about entering old age: "Don't let the current hype about the joys of retirement fool you. They are not the best of times. It's just that the alternative is even worse" (Rubenstein, 1991:13).

FINDING MEANING

Recall from Chapter 5 ("Socialization") Erik Erikson's (1963, 1980) theory that elderly people must resolve a tension of "integrity versus despair." No matter how much they still may be learning and achieving, older people recognize that their lives are nearing an end. Thus, the elderly spend much time reflecting on their past accomplishments and disappointments. To shore up their personal integrity, Erikson explains, older women and men must face up to past mistakes as well as savour their successes. Otherwise, this stage of life may turn into a time of despair—a dead end with little positive meaning.

Research suggests that most people who find satisfaction and meaning in earlier stages of life are likely to achieve personal well-being in old age.

Negative myths about the health, happiness, and sexuality of the elderly abound (McPherson, 1991). Some elderly people share this dim view of their plight, but most have a more positive outlook. As Table 14–1 indicates, a majority of men and women age fifty-five and over enjoy good health, and most consider themselves to be at least "somewhat happy." Married elderly people have advantages over single ones in a number of different areas of their lives, including morbidity (their rate of illness), mortality, and psychological well-being. Marriage appears to be particularly advantageous for elderly males because it unites them with a network of other people more easily than singlehood (Nett, 1993).

Overall, research suggests that, while personal adjustments are necessary, the experience of growing old in Canada often provides much cause for joy. However, a person's view does vary based on individual personality, family circumstances, social class, and financial position. People who adapt successfully to changes earlier in life can confidently look forward to deriving satisfaction and meaning from their lives later on (Neugarten, 1971; Palmore, 1979a).

SOCIAL ISOLATION

Being alone may provoke anxiety in people of any age; isolation, however, is most common among elderly people. Retirement closes off workplace social interaction, physical problems may limit mobility, and negative stereotypes depicting the elderly as "over the hill" may discourage younger people from close social contact with their elders.

The greatest cause of social isolation, however, is the inevitable death of significant others. Few human experiences affect people as profoundly as the death of a spouse. One study found that almost three-quarters of widows and widowers cited loneliness as their most serious problem (Lund, 1989). Widows and widowers must rebuild their lives in the glaring absence of people with whom, in many instances, they spent most of their adult lives. Some survivors choose not to live at all. One study of elderly men noted a sharp increase in mortality, sometimes by suicide, in the months following the deaths of their wives (Benjamin and Wallis, 1963).

The problem of social isolation falls most heavily on women, who typically outlive their husbands. As Table 14–2 shows, more men age sixty-five and over live with spouses and more women over age sixty-five (especially the "older elderly") live alone. More pronounced isolation among elderly women in Canada may account for the research finding that their mental health is not as strong as that of elderly men (Nett, 1993:307–40). Keep in mind, too, that living alone—which many older people value as a dimension of autonomy—presumes the financial means to do so (Mutchler, 1992).

For most older people, families provide the primary source of social support (McDaniel, 1994:129). However, older women reported more varied support than did men, who tended to rely more extensively on their wives. Men and women over sixty-five without spouses relied on family members, particularly daughters, but also on friends and others, as illustrated in Figure 14–2.

RETIREMENT

Work not only provides us with earnings, it also figures prominently in our personal identities. Retirement from paid work, therefore, generally entails some reduction in income, diminished social prestige, and some loss of purpose in life (Chown, 1977).

Some organizations strive to ease this transition. Universities and colleges, for example, confer the title of "professor emeritus" (from Latin, meaning "fully earned") on retired faculty members, who are permitted to maintain their library privileges, parking spaces, and e-mail accounts.

For many older people, fresh activities and new interests minimize the personal disruption and loss of prestige brought on by retirement. Volunteer work can be personally rewarding, allowing individuals to apply their career skills to new challenges and opportunities. Seventeen percent of men and 16 percent of women report that they engage in volunteer work after retirement. Others return to the labour force after retirement for part-time work, alternative careers, or as individual entrepreneurs.

Although the idea of retirement is familiar to us, it emerged only within the last century and only in industrial societies (Atchley, 1982). Advancing technology reduces the need for everyone to work, and places a premium on up-to-date skills. Retirement permits younger workers, who presumably have the most current knowledge and training, to predominate in the labour force. Then, too, the establishment of private and public pension programs offers the eco-

TABLE 14–2 Private Household Living Arrangements Among the Elderly,[1] 1991 (percentages)

	Men	Women
Living with spouse	70	38
Living alone	14	34
Living with others[2]	4	8

[1] The majority of the elderly (83.5 percent) maintain their own households.
[2] Includes both relatives and nonrelatives.

SOURCE: Adapted from Janet Chre-Alford, Catherine Allan, and George Butlin, *Focus on Canada: Families in Canada*, Catalogue No. 96-307E, Table 3.3 (Scarborough: Statistics Canada and Prentice Hall Canada Inc., 1994).

nomic foundation for retirement. In poor societies that depend on the labour of everyone, and where no pension programs exist, most people work until they can work no more.

Given how varied the elderly population is, we might wonder exactly when (or even if) we should expect people to retire. Vast differences in the interests and capacities of older people suggest that no one standard will serve the interests of all.

In Canada, retirement at sixty-five is closely tied to the development of pension plans. This is the age, too, when mandatory retirement comes into effect for some workers. There is an ongoing debate about whether mandatory retirement violates the individual's right to work as guaranteed under the *Canadian Charter of Rights and Freedoms*. But while about one-half of the Canadian workforce is currently subject to mandatory retirement regulations, only about 1 percent of the workforce would continue to work past sixty-five if given the choice (Tindale, 1991).

Today, with rapid transitions in the Canadian economy resulting from global economic restructuring, new free trade agreements, and a general move to the political right, more and more people are being forced out of work or encouraged to take early retirement. Many of those who have been given the "golden handshake" in this era of unprecedented numbers of employee buyouts are embarking on brand new careers. Severance packages, which may be as high as two years' salary, are often used as the initial investment for the new venture (Lipovenko, 1996).

AGING AND INCOME

On the whole, the image of the elderly as poverty-stricken is unfounded: the poverty rate among the elderly has declined from about 34 percent in 1980 to 19 percent in 1994 (www.statcan.ca). Among the elderly who live with their spouse or other family members, poverty levels have declined from 18 percent in 1980 to 6 percent in 1994. The unattached

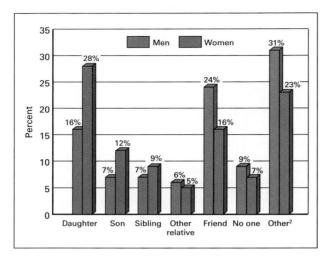

FIGURE 14–2 Sources of Emotional Support for Elderly Men and Women Without Spouses,[1] 1990

[1] Includes persons without sons, daughters, siblings, etc.

[2] Includes neighbours, co-workers, clergy, doctors, professional counsellors, others, and don't know. None of these specific sources exceeded 5 percent.

SOURCE: Statistics Canada, *General Social Survey, 1990*, cited in McDaniel (1994:130).

elderly endured low income at levels of 68 and 48 percent in 1980 and 1994, respectively. Overall, however, 80 percent of the elderly live above the low income level and some of them are affluent.

Nonetheless, for most people in Canada, retirement leads to a significant decline in income. For many, home mortgages and children's university expenses are paid off; yet the expenses for some medical and dental care, household help, and home utilities typically rise. Many elderly people do not have sufficient savings or pension benefits to be self-supporting; for this reason, various pension programs, including the Canada Pension Plan, are their greatest source of income. Because many retirees live with fixed incomes, inflation tends to affect them more severely than it does younger working people. Women and people of colour are especially likely to find that growing old means growing poorer.

Gender continues to shape the lives of people as they age. Elderly women are more likely to be poor than elderly men—one study found that 53.1 percent of elderly women who were unattached were poor, compared with 35 percent of elderly unattached men (Ross, Shillington, and Lochhead, 1994:119). Income inequality between different ethnic and racial groups is also not blunted by growing old.

What is distinctive about the privation of the elderly, however, is that it is often hidden from view.

Because of personal pride and a desire to maintain the dignity of independent living, many elderly people conceal financial problems even from their own families. It is often difficult for people who have supported their children for years to admit that they can no longer provide for themselves, even though it may be through no fault of their own.

ABUSE OF THE ELDERLY

In Canada, we seem to awaken to social problems in stages: we became aware of child abuse during the 1960s, spouse abuse in the 1970s, and abuse of the elderly in the 1980s. Abuse of older people takes many forms, from passive neglect to active torment, and includes verbal, emotional, financial, and physical harm. Most elderly people suffer from none of these things, but research suggests that, in Canada, Europe, and the United States, the incidence of elder abuse and neglect ranges from 3 to 5 percent. Like other forms of family violence, abuse of the elderly often goes unreported because victims are reluctant to talk about their plight. But as the proportion of elderly people rises, so does the incidence of abuse (Bruno, 1985; Clark, 1986; Pillemer, 1988; Holmstrom, 1994).

What motivates people to abuse the elderly? Often the cause lies in the stress—both financial and emotional—of caregiving. Today's middle-aged adults are a "sandwich generation" who may well spend as much time caring for their aging parents as for their own children. This caregiving responsibility is especially pronounced among adult women who not only look after parents and children but hold down jobs as well.

Even in Japan—where tradition demands that adult children care for aging parents at home—more and more people find themselves unable to cope. Abuse appears to be most common when the stress is greatest: in families with a very old person suffering from serious health problems. Here, family life may be grossly distorted by demands and tensions that caregivers simply cannot endure, even if their intentions are good (Douglass, 1983; Gelman, 1985; Yates, 1986).

AGEISM

In earlier chapters, we explained how ideology—including racism and sexism—serves to justify the social disadvantages of minorities. Sociologists use the parallel term **ageism** to designate *prejudice and discrimination against the elderly*.

Like racism and sexism, ageism can be blatant (as when a university decides not to hire a sixty-year-old professor because of her age) or subtle (as when a nurse speaks to elderly patients with a condescending tone, as if they were children) (Kalish, 1979). Also like racism and sexism, ageism builds physical traits into stereotypes; in the case of the elderly, people consider greying hair, wrinkled skin, and stooped posture as signs of personal incompetence. Negative stereotypes picture the aged as helpless, confused, resistant to change, and generally unhappy (Butler, 1975). Even sentimental notions of sweet little old ladies and charmingly eccentric old gentlemen gloss over people's individuality and ignore years of experience and accomplishment.

Sometimes, like other expressions of prejudice, ageism has some foundation in reality. Statistically speaking, old people are more likely than young people to be mentally and physically impaired. But we slip into ageism when we make unwarranted generalizations about an entire category of people, most of whom do not conform to the stereotypes.

Betty Friedan (1993), a pioneer of the contemporary feminist movement, believes ageism is central to our culture. Friedan points out that elderly people are still conspicuously absent in the mass media; only a small percentage of television shows, for example, include main characters over sixty. More generally, when most of us do think about older people, it is often in negative terms: this older man lacks a job, that older woman has lost her vitality, and seniors look back to their youth. In short, we tend to think about being old as if it were a disease—marked by decline and deterioration—for which there is no cure.

Rejecting such pessimism, Friedan points out that there are women and men who are discovering that they have far more to contribute than others give them credit for. Playing in orchestras, advising small business owners, designing housing for the poor, teaching children to read—there are countless ways in which older people can enhance their own lives and help others.

THE ELDERLY: A MINORITY?

No one doubts that, as a category of people in this country, the elderly do face social disadvantages. But sociologists disagree as to whether the aged form a minority in the same way as, say, native Canadians or women do.

Leonard Breen (1960) was the first to pronounce the elderly a minority, noting that older people have a clear social identity based on their age and are subject to prejudice and discrimination. Yet, Gordon Streib (1968) countered, minority status is usually both permanent and exclusive. That is, a person is a native Canadian or woman *for life* and cannot become part of the dominant category of white males. Being elderly, Streib continued, is an *open* status because, first, people are elderly for only part of their lives and, second, everyone who has the good fortune to live long enough grows old.

Sarah Abel, 101 years old, lived in the isolated village of Old Crow above the Arctic Circle in the northern tip of the Yukon until her death in August, 1998. Only at 100 years of age did she move out of the home in which she had raised seventeen children—on her own after her husband died of tuberculosis. She drove a dogsled, hunted moose and muskrat, and tanned her own hides: in other words, she did whatever had to be done. She had vivid memories of the past and told stories in person or on the CBC in her native tongue (Gwitchin). As someone who had never touched alcohol, she worried a great deal about the social costs of alcohol abuse in her community. (Brend, 1997)

Streib made a further point. The social disadvantages faced by the elderly are less substantial than those experienced by the minorities described in earlier chapters. For example, old people have never been deprived of the right to own property, to vote, or to hold office, as native Canadians and women have. Some elderly people, of course, do suffer economic disadvantages, but these do not stem primarily from old age. Instead, most of the aged poor fall into categories of people likely to be poor at any age. To Streib, it is less true that "the old grow poor" than it is that "the poor grow old."

In light of Streib's arguments and the rising economic fortunes of the elderly in recent decades, it seems reasonable to conclude that old people are not a minority in the same sense as other categories are. Perhaps the best way to describe the elderly is simply as a distinctive segment of our population with characteristic pleasures and challenges.

THEORETICAL ANALYSIS OF AGING

Each of sociology's major theoretical paradigms sheds light on the process of aging in Canada. We examine each in turn.

Women and men experience stages of the life course in different ways. Most men, for example, pass through their old age with the support of a woman. Women, who typically outlive men, endure much of their old age alone.

STRUCTURAL-FUNCTIONAL ANALYSIS: AGING AND DISENGAGEMENT

Drawing on the ideas of Talcott Parsons—an architect of the structural-functional paradigm—Elaine Cumming and William Henry (1961) point out that aging threatens to disrupt society as physical decline and death take their toll. Society's response, they claim, is to disengage the elderly—to gradually transfer statuses and roles from the old to the young so that tasks are performed with minimal interruption.

Disengagement is thus a strategy to promote the orderly functioning of society by easing aging people from productive roles while they are still able to perform them. Such disengagement has an added benefit in a rapidly changing society, since young workers typically bring the most up-to-date skills and training to their work. Formally, then, **disengagement theory** is *the proposition that society enhances its orderly operation by disengaging people from positions of responsibility as they reach old age.*

Disengagement may benefit elderly people as well as society. Aging individuals with diminishing capacities presumably look forward to relinquishing some of the pressures of their jobs in favour of new pursuits of their own choosing (Palmore, 1979b). Society also grants older people greater freedom, so that unusual behaviour on their part is construed as harmless eccentricity rather than dangerous deviance.

Critical evaluation. As a strategy for dealing with human decline, disengagement theory explains why rapidly changing, industrial societies typically define their oldest members as socially marginal. But there are also several limitations to this approach.

First, many workers cannot readily disengage from paid work because they do not have sufficient financial resources to fall back on. Second, many elderly people—regardless of their financial circumstances—do not wish to disengage from their productive roles. Disengagement, after all, comes at a high price, including loss of social prestige and social isolation. Third, it is far from clear that the benefits of disengagement outweigh its social costs. There is the loss of human resources on the one hand, and, on the other, the costs of increased care for people who might otherwise be able to fend for themselves. Indeed, as the numbers of elderly people swell, finding ways to help seniors remain independent will be a high priority. Fourth, a rigid system of disengagement does not allow for widely differing abilities among the elderly.

SYMBOLIC-INTERACTION ANALYSIS: AGING AND ACTIVITY

One rebuttal to disengagement theory draws heavily on the symbolic-interaction paradigm. **Activity theory** is *the proposition that a high level of activity enhances personal satisfaction in old age.* Because individuals build their social identities from statuses and roles, disengagement is bound to reduce satisfaction and meaning in elderly people's lives. What seniors need, in short, is not to be yanked out of roles, but a wider range of productive and recreational activities.

Activity theory does not reject the notion of disengagement; rather, it proposes that people substitute new roles and responsibilities for those they leave behind. After all, as members of a society that celebrates productivity, the elderly enjoy active lives as much as younger people do. Research confirms that elderly people who maintain high activity levels derive the most satisfaction from their lives.

Activity theory also recognizes that the elderly are no monolithic category. Older people have highly variable needs, interests, and physical abilities that guide their activities. Therefore, the activities people pursue and how vigorously they pursue them is always an individual matter (Havighurst, Neugarten, and Tobin, 1968; Neugarten, 1977; Palmore, 1979a; Moen, Dempster-McClain, and Williams, 1992).

Critical evaluation. Activity theory shifts the focus of analysis from the needs of society (as stated in disengagement theory) to the needs of the elderly themselves. It emphasizes the social diversity among elderly people, an important consideration in formulating any government policy.

A limitation of this approach, from a structural-functionalist point of view, is a tendency to exaggerate the well-being and competence of the elderly. Functionalist critics ask if we really want elderly people actively serving in crucial roles, say, as physicians or airline pilots. From another perspective, activity theory falls short by overlooking the fact that many of the problems that beset older people have more to do with how society, not any individual, operates. We turn now to that point of view, social-conflict theory.

SOCIAL-CONFLICT ANALYSIS: AGING AND INEQUALITY

A social-conflict analysis is based on the idea that different age categories have different opportunities and different access to social resources, creating a system of age stratification. By and large, middle-aged people in Canada enjoy the greatest power and the most opportunities and privileges, while the elderly (as well as children) contend with less power and prestige and a higher risk of poverty. Employers often replace elderly workers with younger men and women as a way of keeping down wages. Consequently, as conflict theorists see it, older people may well become second-class citizens (Atchley, 1982; Phillipson, 1982).

To conflict theorists, age-based hierarchy is inherent in industrial-capitalist society. Following the ideas of Karl Marx, Steven Spitzer (1980) points out that, because our society has an overriding concern with profit, we devalue those categories of people who are economically unproductive. Viewed as mildly deviant because they are less efficient than their younger counterparts, Spitzer reasons, the elderly are destined to be marginal members of a society consumed by material gain.

Social-conflict analysis also draws attention to social diversity in the elderly population. Differences of class, race, ethnicity, and gender splinter older people as they do everyone else. Thus the fortunate seniors in higher social classes have far more economic security, greater access to top-flight medical care, and more options for personal satisfaction in old age than others do. Likewise, elderly WASPs typically enjoy a host of advantages denied to older minorities. And women—who represent an increasing majority of the elderly population with advancing age—suffer the social and economic disadvantages of both sexism and ageism.

Critical evaluation. Social-conflict theory adds further to our understanding of the aging process by underscoring age-based inequality and explaining how capitalism devalues elderly people who are less productive. The implication of this analysis is that the aged fare better in noncapitalist societies, a view that has some support in research (Treas, 1979).

One shortcoming of this approach goes right to its core contention: capitalism is not to blame for the lower social standing of elderly people, say critics; industrialization is the culprit. Thus, socialism might not lessen age stratification. Furthermore, the notion that capitalism dooms the elderly to economic distress is challenged by the steady rise in the income and well-being among the North American elderly in recent decades.

DEATH AND DYING

> To every thing there is a season,
> And a time to every purpose under the heaven:
> A time to be born, and a time to die ...

These well-known lines from the Book of Ecclesiastes in the Bible state two basic truths about human existence: the fact of birth and the inevitability of death. Just as life varies in striking ways throughout history and around the world, so death, too, has many faces. We conclude this chapter with a brief look at the changing character of death—the final stage in the process of growing old.

HISTORICAL PATTERNS OF DEATH

Throughout most of history, confronting death was commonplace. No one assumed that a newborn child would live for long, a fact that led parents to delay naming children until they survived for a year or two. For those fortunate enough to survive infancy, illness, accident, and natural catastrophe combined to make life uncertain, at best.

Sometimes, in fact, societies facing food shortages have protected the majority by sacrificing the least productive members. Infanticide is the killing of newborn infants and geronticide is the killing of the elderly.

If death was routine, it was also readily accepted. Medieval Christianity assured Europeans, for example, that death fit into the divine plan for human existence. To illustrate, historian Philippe Ariès describes how Sir Lancelot, one of King Arthur's fearless Knights of the Round Table, prepared for his own death when he believed himself mortally wounded:

> His gestures were fixed by old customs, ritual gestures which must be carried out when one is

Our society has long been concerned with the "good life"; more recently, attention has turned to the idea of a good death. The hospice movement is an important part of this trend. In some cases, terminally ill patients move to a hospice facility, where a professional staff provides medical support and emotional comfort. In other cases, hospice workers provide care in the familiar surroundings of a person's home.

about to die. He removed his weapons and lay quietly upon the ground ...; He spread his arms out, his body forming a cross ... in such a way that his head faced east toward Jerusalem. (1974:7–8)

As societies gradually gained more knowledge about health, death became less of an everyday experience. Fewer children died at birth, and accidents and disease took a smaller toll among adults. Except in times of war or catastrophe, people came to view dying as quite extraordinary, except among the very old. In 1900, about one-third of all deaths in Canada occurred before the age of five, another third occurred before the age of fifty-five, and the remaining one-third of men and women died in what was then defined as old age. By 1995, 85 percent of our population died after the age of fifty-five. Thus, death and old age have become fused in our culture.

THE MODERN SEPARATION OF LIFE AND DEATH

Now removed from everyday experience, death appears as something unnatural. If social conditions prepared our ancestors to accept their deaths, modern society—with its youth culture and aggressive medical technology—has fostered a desire for immortality, or eternal youth. In this sense, death has become separated from life.

Death is also physically removed from everyday activities. The clearest evidence of this is that many of us have never seen a person die. While our ancestors typically died at home in the presence of family and friends, most deaths today occur in impersonal settings such as hospitals and nursing homes. Even hospitals commonly relegate dying patients to a special part of the building, and hospital morgues are located well out of sight of patients and visitors alike (Sudnow, 1967; Ariès, 1974).

ETHICAL ISSUES: CONFRONTING DEATH

Moral questions are more pressing than ever now that technological advances give humans the power to prolong life and, therefore, to draw the line separating life and death. We now grapple with how to use these new powers, or whether to use them at all.

When Does Death Occur?

Perhaps the most basic question is one of the most difficult: precisely how do we define death? Common sense suggests that life ceases when breathing and heartbeat stop. But the ability to revive or replace a heart and artificially sustain breathing renders such notions of death obsolete. Medical and legal experts now define death as an irreversible state involving no response to stimulation, no movement or breathing, no reflexes, and no indication of brain activity (Ladd, 1979; Wall, 1980).

The "Right to Die" Debate

The popularity of the book *Final Exit*, described in the opening to this chapter, suggests that many aging people are less terrified of death than the prospect of being kept alive at all costs. In other words, medical technology now threatens personal autonomy by letting doctors rather than the dying person decide when life is to end. In response, many people now seek control over their deaths just as they seek control over their lives.

Individuals are now taking the initiative and choosing not to employ medical technology to prolong life. After long deliberation, patients, families, and doctors may decide to forego "heroic measures" to resuscitate a person who is dying. Living wills—statements of which medical procedures an individual wants and does not want under specific conditions—are now widespread.

A more difficult issue involves mercy killing or euthanasia, assisting in the death of a person suffering from an incurable disease. Euthanasia (from the Greek, meaning "a good death") poses an ethical dilemma

Death on Demand: A Report from the Netherlands

Marcus Erich picked up the telephone and dialled his brother Arjen's number. In a quiet voice, thirty-two-year-old Marcus announced, "It's Friday at 5 o'clock." When the time came, Arjen was there, having driven to his brother's farmhouse an hour south of Amsterdam. They said their final goodbyes. Soon afterward, Marcus's physician arrived. Marcus and the doctor spoke for a few moments, and the doctor then prepared a "cocktail" of barbiturates and other drugs. As Marcus drank the mixture, he made a face, joking, "Can't you make this sweeter?"

As the minutes passed, Marcus lay back and his eyes closed. But, after half an hour, he was still breathing. At that point, according to their earlier agreement, the doctor administered a lethal injection. In a few minutes, Marcus's life came to an end.

Events like this take us to the heart of the belief that people should have a "right to die." Marcus Erich was dying from the virus that causes AIDS. For five years, his body wasted away so that he was suffering greatly and had no hope of recovery. It was then that he asked his doctor to end his life.

The Netherlands, a small nation in northwestern Europe, has gone further than any nation in the world in allowing mercy killing or euthanasia. A Dutch law, enacted in 1981, allows a physician to assist in a suicide if the following five conditions are met:

The patient must take a voluntary, well-considered, and repeated

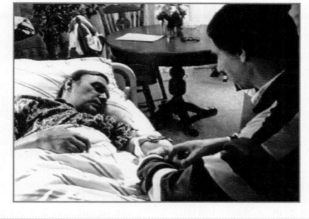

request to the doctor for help in dying.

The patient's suffering must be unbearable and without prospect of improvement.

The doctor and the patient must discuss alternatives.

The doctor must consult with at least one colleague who has access to the patient and the patient's medical records.

The assisted suicide must be performed in accordance with sound medical practice.

In 1995, according to official records, doctors ended the lives of 3600 people in the Netherlands. Since many such cases are never reported, the actual number is probably at least twice that many. A rough estimate is that, today, about 5 percent of the Dutch people die with the assistance of a physician.

SOURCES: Based on della Cava (1997) and Mauro (1997).

since it involves not just refusing life-extending treatment but actively taking steps to end life. In euthanasia, some see an act of kindness, while others find just a form of killing.

In Canada and the United States, euthanasia is illegal, including physician-assisted suicide for the elderly and terminally ill, but the issue continues to be hotly debated. The Netherlands, in contrast, has the most permissive euthanasia law in the world. The "Global Sociology" box takes a closer look.

Should Canada hold the line on euthanasia or follow the lead of the Dutch? Supporters of a "right to die" maintain that, faced with unbearable suffering, an individual should be able to choose to live or die. And, if death is the choice, medical assistance can help people achieve a "good death."

On the other side of the debate, opponents fear that opening the door to physician-assisted suicide invites abuse. Some point to the Netherlands: in about one-third of all cases, critics estimate, the five conditions noted in the box are not strictly met. In 1991, moreover, a Dutch doctor assisted in the death of a woman who was not dying at all, but was simply depressed over the death of her two sons. (The doctor was prosecuted, but not punished.) More generally, opponents fear that legalization will put society on a "slippery slope" towards more and more euthanasia. Can anyone deny, they ask, that ill people may be pushed into accepting death by doctors who consider suicide the "right" choice for the terminally ill or by family members who are weary of caring for them or who want to avoid the expenses of medical care?

Setting Limits: Must We "Pull the Plug" on Old Age?

Because death struck at any time, often without warning, our ancestors would have found the question, "Can people live *too long*?" to be absurd. In recent decades, however, a surge in the elderly population, widespread support for using technology to prolong life, and a dizzying increase in the costs of life-extending medical technology have prompted people to wonder how much old age we can now afford.

Currently, about half of the total lifetime medical costs of care for an individual are incurred during that individual's final years of life, and this share is projected to increase. Against the spiralling costs of prolonging life, then, we may well have to ask if what is technically possible is necessarily socially desirable. As we enter the next century, warns gerontologist Daniel Callahan, a surging elderly population ready and eager to extend their lives will eventually force us either to "pull the plug" on old age or to shortchange everyone else.

To even raise this issue, Callahan concedes, smacks of a lack of caring. But consider that the annual bill for the elderly's health care continues to grow substantially. This dramatic boost reflects our current policy of directing more and more medical resources towards studying and treating diseases and disabilities common to old age.

So Callahan makes a bold case for limits. He reasons, first, that to spend more on behalf of the elderly we must spend less on others. With a serious problem of poverty among children, he asks, can we continue to direct more money towards the needs of the oldest members of our society at the expense of those just growing up?

Second, Callahan reminds us, a *longer* life does not necessarily make for a *better* life. Costs aside, does stressful

However the debate over the "right to die" turns out in the future, our society has entered a new era when it comes to dying. Individuals, family members, and medical personnel often must face death not as a medical fact but as a negotiated outcome (Flynn, 1991; Humphry, 1991; Markson, 1992).

BEREAVEMENT

Chapter 5 ("Socialization") describes stages by which people usually confront their own death. Elisabeth Kübler-Ross (1969) claims that individuals initially react with *denial*, then swell with *anger*, try to *negotiate* a divine intervention, gradually fall into *resignation*, and, finally, reach *acceptance*. Those who will face the loss of a significant person must also adjust to the approaching death.

According to some researchers, bereavement parallels the stages of dying described by Kübler-Ross. Those close to a dying person, for instance, may initially deny the reality of impending death, reaching the point of acceptance only in time. Other investigators question the validity of any linear "stage theory," arguing that bereavement may not follow a rigid schedule (Lund, Caserta, and Dimond, 1986; Lund, 1989). But all the experts agree that how family and friends view a death influences the attitudes of the person who is dying. Specifically, acceptance by others of the approaching death helps the dying person do the same. Denial of an impending death may also isolate the dying person, who is then unable to share feelings and experiences with others.

One recent development intended to provide emotional and other support to dying people is the hospice. Unlike a hospital that is designed to cure disease, a hospice helps people have a good death by providing palliative care rather than active treatment. These care centres for dying people work to minimize pain and suffering—either there or at home—and encourage family members to remain close by (Stoddard, 1978). Similar palliative care centres have also been opened within hospitals.

Even under the most favourable circumstances, bereavement may involve profound grief and social disorientation that persist for some time. Research reveals that bereavement is less intense among people who accept the death of a loved one and feel that their relationship with the dying person has reached a satisfactory resolution. By taking the opportunity to bring an appropriate closure to their relationship with a dying person, in other words, family and friends are better able to comfort and support one another after the death has occurred (Atchley, 1983).

LOOKING AHEAD: AGING IN THE TWENTY-FIRST CENTURY

This chapter has explored a remarkable trend: the "greying" of Canada. Indeed, we can predict with

heart surgery that may prolong the life of an eighty-four-year-old woman for a year or two truly improve the quality of her life? Costs considered, would those resources yield more "quality of life" if used, say, to transplant a kidney into a ten-year-old boy?

Third, Callahan urges us to reconsider our notion of death. Today, many people rage against death as an enemy to be conquered at all costs. Yet, he suggests, a sensible health care program for an aging society must acknowledge death as a natural end to the life course. If we cannot make peace with death for our own well-being, limited financial resources demand that we do so for the benefit of others.

A compelling counterpoint, of course, is that those people who have worked all their lives to make our society what it is should, in their final years, enjoy society's generosity. Can we ethically deny an aging individual medical care as our medical care budget shrinks?

What is clear from everyone's point of view is that, in the next century, we will face questions that few would have imagined even fifty years ago: is optimum longevity good for everyone? Is it even possible for everyone?

Continue the debate . . .

1. Should doctors and hospitals devise a double standard, offering complete

care to the youngest people but more limited care to society's oldest members?

2. Do you think our cultural avoidance of death drives us to extend life at all costs?

3. Is the idea of rationing medical care really new? Hasn't our society historically done exactly this by allowing some people to amass more wealth than others?

SOURCE: Callahan (1987).

confidence that the ranks of the elderly will swell dramatically in the decades to come: by 2050, our elderly population alone will exceed the population of the entire country back in 1900. Just as important, one in five of these seniors will be over the age of eighty-five. Within the next fifty years, in other words, society's oldest members will gain unprecedented visibility and influence in our everyday lives. As this prediction is realized, gerontology, the study of the elderly, will also grow in stature as part of an expansion of research in all fields directed towards aging and the elderly.

The reshaping of the age structure of our society raises many serious concerns. With more people living to an advanced age (and living longer once they reach old age), will the support services they need be available? Remember, too, that as the elderly make unprecedented demands, our society will comprise proportionately fewer younger people to meet their needs. And what about the spiralling medical care costs of an aging society? As the baby boomers enter old age, some analysts paint a doomsday picture of their future.

But not all the signs are so ominous. For one thing, the health of tomorrow's elderly people (that is, today's young and middle-aged adults) is better than ever: smoking is decreasing and the consumption of healthy foods is increasing. Such trends probably mean that the elderly of the next century will be more

vigorous and independent than their counterparts are today. Moreover, tomorrow's old people will enjoy the benefits of steadily advancing medical technology although, as the "Controversy & Debate" box explains, seniors require a disproportionate share of our national resources, raising an issue that is already sparking heated debate.

Another positive sign is the surging financial strength of the elderly. Costs of living are certain to rise, but tomorrow's elderly will confront them with unprecedented affluence. Note, too, that the baby boomers will be the first cohort of Canadian seniors in which the vast majority of women have been in the labour force, a fact reflected in their substantial savings and pensions.

On balance, there are reasons for both concern and optimism as we look ahead. But there can be no doubt that younger adults will face a mounting responsibility to care for aging parents. Indeed, as the birth rate drops and the elderly population grows, our society is likely to experience a retargeting of caregiving from the very young to the very old.

Finally, an aging population will almost certainly bring change to the way we view death. In all likelihood, death will become less of a social taboo and more a natural part of the life course as it was in centuries past. Should this come to pass, both young and old alike may benefit.

SUMMARY

1. The proportion of elderly people in Canada has risen from 4 percent in 1900 to about 12 percent today; by the middle of the twenty-first century 25 percent of our society's members will be elderly.

2. Gerontology, the study of aging and the elderly, focuses on biological and psychological changes in old age, as well as cultural definitions of aging.

3. Growing old is accompanied by a rising incidence of disease and disability. Younger people, however, commonly exaggerate the extent of disability among the elderly.

4. Psychological research confirms that growing old results in neither overall loss of intelligence nor great change in individual personality.

5. The age at which people are defined as old has varied through history: until several centuries ago, old age began as early as thirty. In poor societies today, in which life expectancy is substantially lower than in North America, people become old at fifty or even forty.

6. In global perspective, industrialization fosters a decline in the social standing of elderly people.

7. As people age, they commonly experience social isolation brought on by retirement, physical disability, and the death of friends or spouse. Even so, most elderly people look to family members for social support.

8. Since 1980, poverty among the elderly has dropped sharply. The aged poor are categories of people—including single women and people of colour—who are likely to be poor regardless of age.

9. Ageism—prejudice and discrimination against old people—serves to justify age stratification.

10. Although many seniors are socially disadvantaged, the elderly encompass people of both sexes and all races, ethnicities, and social classes. Thus, older people do not qualify as a minority.

11. Disengagement theory, based on structural-functional analysis, contends that society disengages the elderly from positions of social responsibility before the onset of disability or death. In this way, society accomplishes the orderly transfer of statuses and roles from the older to the younger generation.

12. Activity theory, based on symbolic-interaction analysis, claims that a high level of activity affords people personal satisfaction in old age.

13. Age stratification is a focus of social-conflict analysis. The emphasis on economic output in capitalist societies leads to a devaluing of those who are less productive, including the elderly.

14. Modern society has set death apart from everyday life, prompting a cultural denial of human mortality. In part, this attitude is related to the fact that most people now die after reaching old age. Recent trends suggest that people are confronting death more directly and seeking control over the process of dying.

CRITICAL THINKING QUESTIONS

1. Why are the populations of industrial societies getting older? What are some of the likely consequences of this demographic shift?

2. Start with common phrases such as "little old lady" and "dirty old man" and identify ways in which our culture devalues old people.

3. Why does industrialization erode the social standing of the elderly?

4. What important insight about growing old is offered by each of sociology's three major theoretical paradigms?

SOCIOLOGY APPLIED

1. What practices and policies does your university or college have for helping older faculty pass through the transition of retirement? Ask several faculty nearing retirement—and several already retired—for their views. In what ways does retiring from an academic career seem harder or easier than ending other kinds of work?

2. Take a look through an issue of any popular magazine—say, *Maclean's*, *Time*, or *Newsweek*—and note images of men and women featured in stories and pictured in advertising. Are elderly people fairly represented in such publications?

3. Obtain a copy of a living will and try to respond to all the questions it asks. Does filling out such a

form help clarify your own thinking about confronting death?

4. Most communities have at least one hospice (check the telephone book). A call to the hospice can provide written material (and, perhaps, even a discussion with someone who works or volunteers there) on how these organizations help dying people.

WEBLINKS

www.hc-sc.gc.ca/seniors-aines
Aging and Seniors, a bilingual site maintained by Health Canada, provides resources on aging issues, including health, medication, injury prevention, seniors programs, government organizations, and various publications.

www.fifty-plus.net
The *Canadian Association of Retired Persons* provides news and information about retirement issues, including finances, health, lifestyles, safety, retirement communities, learning resources, and more.

library.utoronto.ca/www/aging/depthome.html
Based at University of Toronto, the *Institute for Human Development, Life Course and Aging* carries out research into the process of human development, life course and aging, population aging, and the aged, in the social, psychological, and health sciences. This site is also home to the Ontario Network for the Prevention of Elder Abuse.

ellesmere.ccm.emr.ca/wwwnais/select/aging/english/html/aging.html
Produced by the National Atlas Information Service, *Canada—The Aging Population* shows aspects of the age structure of Canada's population in 1986, based on the census. The map also shows population pyramids of age/sex distributions for 1961 and 1986 for each province and territory and for Canada.

www.cagacg.ca/
The *Canadian Association on Gerontology*, whose membership includes health care and social service providers and other professionals, researchers, educators, administrators, physicians, policy analysts, students, and retired adults, promotes the study of aging in all its aspects and the improvement in the well-being of older people.

cyber.scope

Change in technology transforms the nature of work. Just as important, such shifts alter the reward structure reshaping patterns of social inequality. This third cyber.scope considers several ways in which the spread of computer technology is linked to social stratification.

The Information Revolution and Stratification

Most analysts agree that recent decades have witnessed economic polarization in North America, with economic growth primarily enriching families that already had high incomes (Newman, 1996; Forcese, 1997; Persell, 1997). At the outset, at least, technological revolution typically concentrates income and wealth as a small number of people make key discoveries and, with the resulting products and services, establish and expand new markets. Just as John D. Rockefeller and Andrew Carnegie amassed great fortunes a century ago as captains of the Industrial Revolution, followed by Canadian entrepreneurs such as Timothy Eaton and K.C. Irving, the Information Revolution has created a new elite today.

For several years now, one of the world's richest people has been Bill Gates, a founder of Microsoft Corporation, which produces not oil or steel but the operating systems found on most of today's personal comput-

ers. More broadly, it is those with money to invest (the upper-middle and upper classes or, according to Karl Marx, the capitalist class) who reap the profits from successful new industries. During the 1990s, as the Information Revolution rolled ahead, key stock market indicators leaped fivefold, with new technology companies such as Microsoft (software), Intel (computer chips), Compaq (personal computers), and Dell (computer sales) making even more spectacular gains.

But the wave of technological change does not benefit everyone. As companies adopt new technology in their efforts to become more efficient and profitable, some people lose out. In recent decades, for

example, hundreds of thousands of jobs in Canada have simply disappeared. For each job lost, of course, a worker—and usually an entire family—suffers.

Another key link between new information technology and social inequality concerns the unequal spread of computing skills. The 1994 General Social Survey reveals that new technology diffuses first to the affluent and well-educated. Computer ownership is most common in professional, semi-professional, and management homes, and in the homes of the better educated. Sixty-six percent of families with incomes of $70 000 or more have home computers. In short, computer users are not "average" people.

Research suggests that, over time, computer users will come to mirror more closely the population as a whole. But there can be little doubt that, at least in the foreseeable future, new information technology is playing a role in rising levels of economic inequality as it creates a cyber-elite and generates a new underclass made up of those without crucial symbolic skills (Winter, 1995; Edmondson, 1997b; Forcese, 1997; Goyder, 1997).

The Information Revolution: Gender, Race, and Age

The Industrial Revolution ushered in a trend by which women and men are becoming more socially equal. Machinery eroded the link between work and physical strength, and more women entered the labor force as birth control technology helped lower the birth rate by making motherhood a matter of individual choice. The Information Revolution promises to continue this trend. Work in the computer age involves not making or moving *things* but manipulating *ideas*—activity that favours neither men nor women.

Note, too, that communication via computers obscures a person's sex—obvious in face-to-face interaction—placing men and women on an ever-more-equal footing. The same holds for race and ethnicity, so that the coming cyber-society may well be marked by greater contact among people of all colours and cultural backgrounds.

But an important counterpoint involves *access* to computer technology. To date, cultural biases within the new cyber-society have favoured males: most games that introduce children to computers are designed for boys, just as com-

Both blind and deaf, Georgia Griffith was able to communicate only through conversations traced out on her palms, until specially equipped computers opened up her life. Do you think that, in general, advances in information technology will improve the lives of all persons with disabilities? Or will these people be left behind by the Information Revolution?

puter science courses in universities and colleges enrol mostly men. Similarly, to the extent that racial and ethnic minorities are economically disadvantaged and have access to inferior schools, this segment of our population will be cut off from owning and operating computers—the key to success in the labour force of the twenty-first century.

Finally, the effects of computing on age stratification are likely to be mixed. On the one hand, the fact that computing demands mental more than physical vitality—and allows work to be performed almost anywhere—should expand opportunities for people to continue to work well past the standard age of "retirement" that emerged during the industrial era. On the other hand, new technology is almost always age-biased: readily adopted by the young, but regarded more cautiously by the old whose life experiences have been shaped by earlier ways. Unless our society expands programs of adult education, then, younger people are likely to predominate in, and benefit from, work and other activities involving new information technology.

The Information Revolution and Global Stratification

Worldwide, the elite pattern we have described holds even more:

the Information Revolution directly involves only a tiny share of the planet's people. A look back at Global Map 7–1, on page 171, shows that it is the rich regions of the world in which Internet access is readily available, at least to those who can afford it. But in most of Africa, by contrast, nations have, at best, only slow e-mail connections, and a dozen African countries have no network access at all. Moreover, the large number of African languages and alphabets will slow the spread of computing there.

While Internet access is found throughout most of Asia at present, a cultural and technical problem limits the spread of computing there: almost all computer keyboards use the Latin alphabet. In China and other Asian societies, while the technical elite is likely to speak and write English, most people use complex character sets that have yet to be incorporated into computer technology. Overall, then, the Information Revolution has come to that part of the world already benefiting from industrial technology: yet another case of the rich getting richer. ◉

Is computer software aimed more at males than females? Visit a local store and see for yourself.

Neil Osborne, *Money Maze,* 1996

CHAPTER 15

THE ECONOMY AND WORK

"When you compare what my dad looked forward to against what I'm looking forward to, he expected that things would be better for us and that my children would have it better than I have. But there isn't that feeling anymore." Ian Crump, a forty-five-year-old father of three, put three generations of experience in a nutshell as he pondered the situation of the descendants of Kitty and Henry Neville Compton Crump who had gathered at the old prairie homestead south of Regina. The family had felt the effects of the restructured economy, high taxes, and deficits that were contributing to a sense of economic malaise across the country.

Ian's cousin, Tom Crump, went through an experience that very clearly illustrates the changing job environment. As a hospital administrator in Vancouver he had been preparing to lay off fifty people when his boss came in and said that it would be fifty-one. A senior position and seventeen years with the same employer proved to be no protection from ongoing economic upheaval and no base for launching his children into middle-class security. Downsizing and restructuring were leading to layoffs at all levels, including middle management, and breaking the link that once bound company and employee for a much longer period—possibly through the entire working life of the employee. "By the standards of his parents, the job was a brief interlude; by the expectations of his children, an eternity" (Greenspon, 1993).

The experiences of Ian Crump and others in his extended family are shared by many Canadians: early (forced) retirements, layoffs, part-time employment instead of the desired full-time work, periods of unemployment, a series of jobs rather than a secure long-term career. Factory closings, mergers, downsizing, restructuring, globalization, freelancing, outsourcing, two recessions in the past twenty years, and a jobless recovery have all contributed to economic insecurity. All of these changes, coupled with more working from home (often for multiple employers), mean that, increasingly, people can look forward to finding "work" rather than "jobs." The traditional pattern, in parts of the economy, of working for decades for the same employer has been shaken to its core.

This chapter examines the economy as a social institution, explores the character of work in today's world, and explains some of the consequences of the emerging global marketplace for people in Canada.

We will see that a good deal of the conventional wisdom about economic life no longer applies in the face of sweeping changes in North America and around the world. Indeed, as we shall explain, sociologists debate how the economy ought to work, whose interests it ought to serve, and what companies and workers owe to each other.

THE ECONOMY: HISTORICAL OVERVIEW

The **economy** is *the social institution that organizes the production, distribution, and consumption of goods and services.* To call the economy an "institution" implies that it functions in an established manner that is predictable, at least in its general outlines. This is not to say the economy operates to everyone's liking, and, as we shall see, societies the world over organize their economies in various ways with various consequences. *Goods* are commodities ranging from necessities (such as food, clothing, and shelter) to luxury items (such as automobiles, swimming pools, and yachts). *Services* refer to valued activities that benefit others (including the work of religious leaders, physicians, police officers, hairdressers, and telephone operators).

We value goods and services because they ensure survival or because they make life easier, more interesting, or more aesthetically pleasing. The things we produce and consume are also important for our self-concepts and social identities. The distribution of goods and services, then, shapes the lives of everyone in basic ways. In Canada, more than in the United States, governments are involved in the distribution of a number of these services.

The complex economies that mark modern industrial societies are themselves the product of centuries of technological innovation and social change. The following sections highlight three technological revolutions that reorganized the means of production and, in the process, transformed many other dimensions of social life.

THE AGRICULTURAL REVOLUTION

Technologically simple societies of the past produced only what they immediately consumed. These small nomadic groups lived off the land—hunting game, gathering vegetation, and fashioning rudimentary clothing, tools, and shelters. Production, distribution, and consumption were all part of family life. As Chapter 4 ("Society") explained, the development of agriculture about five thousand years ago brought revolutionary change to these societies. Agriculture emerged as people harnessed animals to plows, increasing the productive power of hunting and gathering more than tenfold. The resulting surplus freed certain people in society from the demands of food production. Some people began to adopt specialized economic roles, forging crafts, designing tools, raising animals, and constructing dwellings.

Once agriculture was under way, towns emerged, soon to be linked by networks of traders dealing in food, animals, and other goods (Jacobs, 1970). These four factors—agricultural technology, productive specialization, permanent settlements, and trade—were the keys to a revolutionary expansion of the economy.

In the process, the world of work became distinct from family life, although production still occurred close to home. In medieval Europe, for instance, most people farmed nearby fields. Both country and city dwellers often laboured in their homes—a pattern called *cottage industry*—producing goods sold in frequent outdoor markets.

THE INDUSTRIAL REVOLUTION

By the mid-eighteenth century, a second technological revolution was proceeding apace, first in England and soon afterward elsewhere in Europe and North America. The development of industry was to transform societies even more than agriculture had done thousands of years before. Industrialization introduced five notable changes to the economies of Western societies.

1. **New forms of energy.** Throughout history, people derived energy from their own muscles or those of animals. Then, in 1765, English inventor James Watt pioneered the development of the steam engine. Surpassing muscle power a hundred times over, steam engines soon operated large machinery with unprecedented efficiency.

2. **The centralization of work in factories.** Steam-powered machinery soon rendered cottage industries all but obsolete. Factories—centralized and impersonal workplaces apart from the home—proliferated.

3. **Manufacturing and mass production.** Before the Industrial Revolution, most work involved cultivating and gathering raw materials, such as crops, wood, and wool. The industrial economy shifted that focus to manufacturing raw materials into a wide range of saleable products. For example, factories mass-produced lumber into furniture and transformed wool into clothing.

4. **Specialization.** Typically, a single skilled worker in a cottage industry fashioned a product from beginning to end. Factory work, by contrast, demands specialization, so that a labourer repeats a single task over and over, making only a small contribution to the finished product. Thus, as factories raised productivity, they also lowered the skill level of the average worker (Warner and Low, 1947).

The French Canadians of Manchester, New Hampshire

The Amoskeag Manufacturing Company, once the largest textile factory in the world, was the pillar of economic life in Manchester, New Hampshire. From its founding in 1837 to its closing in 1935, the Amoskeag plant provided the major source of employment in Manchester and controlled the development of the city as a whole. The company initially founded a community of young women, from rural New England, who worked together and lived together in boardinghouses with 10 p.m. curfews and compulsory church attendance. Irish immigrant families, willing to work for lower wages, eventually replaced the mill girls.

In the 1870s, French-Canadian immigrants who had been forced out of impoverished farming areas by a scarcity of land found their way in substantial numbers from rural Quebec to the Amoskeag mills. The mill owners soon concluded that French Canadians were the ideal labour force, and Amoskeag proceeded to recruit them actively. Mill agents scanned the Quebec countryside for possible recruits and advertisements in Quebec newspapers extolled the virtues of Amoskeag and Manchester.

French-Canadian workers were ideal in part because they had large families. Entire family groups were brought into the mills (including the children) and could be counted on to draw kinfolk as well as their own large families. So numerous were they, in the end, that the mill bosses were forced to learn a little French. This large group was appreciated by management because it proved to be a "docile," "industrious," and "stable" labour force with a family-based structure that discouraged union involvement. Despite their numbers, however, not one French Canadian was promoted into the supervisory ranks—these positions were filled by native-born Americans or immigrants of British and northern European stock.

Migration from Quebec to Manchester, a convenient stop on the railway linking Montreal and Boston, was so substantial that, by 1910, French Canadians made up 35 percent of the Amoskeag labour force and 38 percent of the population of Manchester. Some of the families that migrated to Manchester stayed only long enough to save some money before returning to their farms in Quebec. Others put down permanent roots and contributed to life with a French flavour in the section of Manchester that is still called Little Canada.

SOURCE: Based on Hareven and Langenbach (1978).

5. **Wage labour.** Instead of working for themselves or joining together as households, industrial workers entered factories as wage labourers. They sold their labour to strangers who often cared less for them than for the machines they operated. Supervision became routine and intense.

The impact of the Industrial Revolution gradually rippled outward from the factories to transform all of society. Greater productivity steadily raised the standard of living as countless new products and services filled an expanding marketplace. Especially at the outset, however, the benefits of industrial technology were shared very unequally. Some factory owners made vast fortunes, while the majority of industrial workers hovered perilously close to poverty. Children, too, worked in factories or deep in coal mines for pennies a day.

The post-industrial economy allows people to perform work almost anywhere, and many more people now choose to work at home. As the line between "the office" and "home" blurs, many children will see more of their parents, even if they don't always command their parents' attention.

THE INFORMATION REVOLUTION AND THE POST-INDUSTRIAL SOCIETY

By the middle of this century, the nature of production itself was changing once again. Canada was becoming a **post-industrial economy**, *a productive system based on service work and extensive use of information technology.* Automated machinery (and, more recently, robotics) reduced the role of human labour in factory production, while bureaucracy simultaneously expanded the ranks of clerical workers and managers. Between 1971 and 1991, manufacturing in Canada declined from 23 to 15 percent of the labour force, while the proportion involved in the service industries increased steadily. The service industries—such as public relations, health care, advertising, banking, and sales—now employ the bulk of Canada's workers. Distinguishing the post-industrial era, then, is a shift from industrial work to service jobs.

Driving this economic change is a third technological transformation: the development of the com-

puter. The Information Revolution in Canada and elsewhere is generating new kinds of information, new means of communication, and changing the character of work just as factories did two centuries ago. The Information Revolution has unleashed three major trends:

1. **From tangible products to ideas.** As we have discussed in earlier chapters, the industrial era was defined by the production of goods; in the post-industrial era, work involves creating and manipulating symbols. Computer programmers, writers, financial analysts, advertising executives, architects, editors, and all sorts of consultants make up the labour force of the Information Age.

2. **From mechanical skills to literacy skills.** Just as the Industrial Revolution required mechanical skills, the Information Revolution requires literacy skills—speaking and writing well, and, of course, using computers. People who can communicate effectively enjoy new opportunities; those who cannot face declining prospects.

3. **The decentralization of work away from factories.** Industrial technology drew workers into factories containing the machines and energy sources, but computer technology allows people to work almost anywhere. Indeed, laptop computers, cell phones, and portable facsimile (fax) machines now turn the home, car, or even an airplane into a "virtual office." New information technology, in short, blurs the line between work and home life, bringing about a return of cottage industries in the form of home-based offices and small businesses.

The need for face-to-face communication as well as the availability of supplies and information still keep most workers in the office. But the trend is clear, and many in today's more educated and skilled labour force no longer require—and often resist—the close supervision of yesterday's factories.

SECTORS OF THE ECONOMY

The three revolutions just described reflect a shifting balance among the three sectors of a society's economy. The **primary sector** is *the part of the economy that generates raw materials directly from the natural environment.* The primary sector, which includes agriculture, animal husbandry, fishing, forestry, and mining, predominates in pre-industrial societies. Figure 15–1 indicates that 63 percent of the economic output of low-income countries is from the primary sector. As a society develops economically, the primary sector becomes less important. Thus, this sector represents

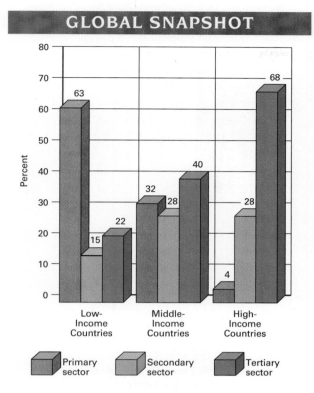

FIGURE 15–1 The Size of Economic Sectors by Income Level of Country

SOURCE: Estimates by John J. Macionis based on the World Bank (1995).

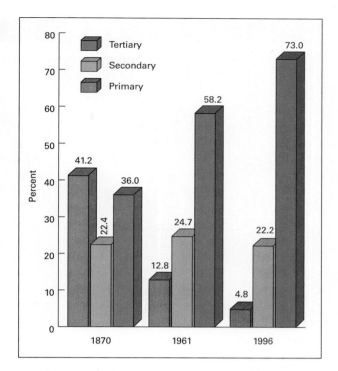

FIGURE 15–2 The Canadian Economic Structure, 1870–1996 (Percentages)

SOURCES: Adapted from www.statcan.ca; Watson (1988).

32 percent of economic activity among middle-income nations and just 4 percent of production among high-income countries. Figure 15–2 traces the decline of the primary sector in Canada from 41 percent of the economy in 1870 to less than 5 percent in 1996.

The **secondary sector** is *the part of the economy that transforms raw materials into manufactured goods.* This sector grows quickly as societies industrialize, just as manufacturing surged in Canada during the 1800s. Secondary sector production includes the refining of petroleum into gasoline and turning metals into tools and automobiles.

The **tertiary sector** is *the part of the economy that generates services rather than goods.* Accounting for just 22 percent of economic output in low-income countries, the tertiary sector grows with industrialization, and dominates the economies of high-income nations as they enter the post-industrial era. Today, about three-quarters of the Canadian labour force does some form of service work, including secretarial and clerical work and positions in food service, sales, law, accounting, advertising, and teaching.

THE GLOBAL ECONOMY

As technology draws people around the world closer together, another important economic transformation is taking place. Recent decades have witnessed the emergence of a **global economy,** *economic activity spanning many nations of the world with little regard for national borders.*

The development of a global economy has four main consequences. First, we are seeing a global division of labour by which each region of the world specializes in one sector of economic activity. As Global Map 15–1 shows, agriculture occupies more than 70 percent of the workforce in low-income countries. Global Map 15–2 indicates that industrial production is concentrated in the middle- and high-income nations of the world. The economies of the richest nations, including Canada, now specialize in service-sector activity.

Second, an increasing number of products pass through the economies of more than one nation. Consider, for instance, that workers in Taiwan may manufacture shoes, which a Hong Kong distributor sends to Italy, where they receive the stamp of an Italian designer; another distributor in Rome forwards

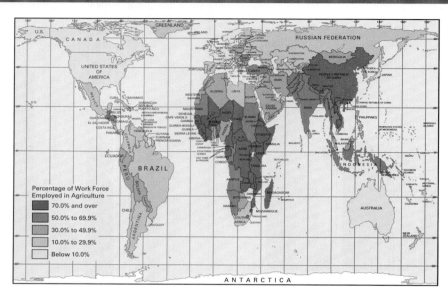

GLOBAL MAP 15–1 Agricultural Employment in Global Perspective

The primary sector of the economy predominates in societies that are least developed. Thus, in the poor countries of Africa and Asia, half, or even three-quarters, of all workers are farmers. This picture is altogether different among the world's most economically developed countries—including Canada, the United States, Great Britain, and Australia—which have less than 10 percent of their workforce in agriculture.

SOURCE: *Peters Atlas of the World* (1990).

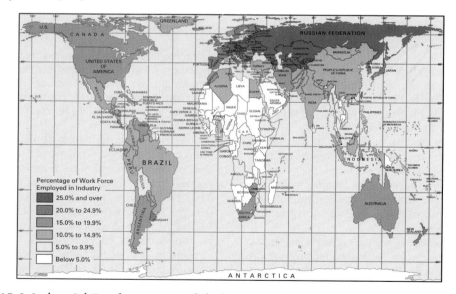

GLOBAL MAP 15–2 Industrial Employment in Global Perspective

Because the world's poor societies have yet to industrialize, only a small proportion of their labour force engages in industrial work. The nations of Eastern Europe and the Russian Federation have far more of their workers in industry. In the world's richest societies, we see workers moving from industrial jobs to service work. Thus, the post-industrial economy of Canada now has about the same share of workers in industrial jobs as the much poorer nation of Argentina.

SOURCE: *Peters Atlas of the World* (1990).

The productivity of capitalist Hong Kong (left) is evident in the fact that streets are choked with advertising and shoppers. Communist Beijing (right), by contrast, is dominated by government buildings rather than a central business district. Here bicyclists glide past the Great Hall of the People.

the shoes to Vancouver, where they are sold in a department store owned by a firm with its headquarters in Tokyo.

A third consequence of the global economy is that national governments no longer control the economic activity that takes place within their borders. In fact, governments cannot even regulate the value of their national currencies, since money is now traded around the clock in the financial centres of Tokyo, London, New York, and Toronto. Global markets are one consequence of satellite communications that forge information links among the world's major cities.

The fourth consequence of the global economy is that a small number of businesses, operating internationally, now control a vast share of the world's economic activity. One estimate concludes that the six hundred largest multinational companies account for fully half of the earth's entire total economic output (Kidron and Segal, 1991).

The world is still divided into 191 politically distinct nations—but, in light of the proliferation of international economic activity, "nationhood" has lost much of its former significance.

COMPARATIVE ECONOMIC SYSTEMS

Two overarching models—capitalism and socialism—have dominated analysis of economic systems during this century. No society has an economy that is purely capitalist or purely socialist; these models represent two ends of a continuum on which an actual economy can be placed. Further, societies towards each end of the continuum have undergone extensive change.

CAPITALISM

Capitalism *is an economic system in which natural resources and the means of producing goods and services are privately owned.* Ideally, a capitalist economy has three distinctive features.

1. **Private ownership of property.** In a capitalist economy, individuals can own almost anything. The more capitalist an economy is, the more private ownership there is of wealth-producing property such as factories, real estate, and natural resources.

2. **Pursuit of personal profit.** A capitalist society encourages the accumulation of private property and considers the profit motive natural, simply a matter of "doing business." Further, claimed the Scottish economist Adam Smith (1723–90), the individual pursuit of self-interest helps the entire society prosper (1937:508; orig. 1776).

3. **Free competition and consumer sovereignty.** A purely capitalist economy operates as a free-market system with no government interference (sometimes called a *laissez-faire* economy, from the French words meaning "to leave alone"). Adam Smith contended that a freely competitive economy regulates itself by the "invisible hand" of the laws of supply and demand.

   Smith maintained that a free-market system is dominated by consumers, who select goods and services that provide the greatest value. As producers compete with one another for the business of consumers, they provide the highest-quality goods and services at the lowest possible price. Thus, while entrepreneurs and consumers are motivated by personal gain, everyone benefits from more efficient production and ever-increasing value. This is what Smith had in mind when he declared that narrow self-interest produces "the greatest good for the greatest number of people." Any government control of the economy, he claimed, distorts market forces, reduces profit motivation, diminishes the quantity and quality of goods produced, and shortchanges consumers.

While Canada is a capitalist society, the guiding hand of government plays an extensive role in economic affairs. Through taxation and various regulatory agencies, the government influences what companies produce, the quality and cost of merchandise, the products that are imported and exported, and how we consume or conserve natural resources.

The federal and provincial governments own and operate a number of businesses including the Canadian Broadcasting Corporation, Via Rail, Atomic Energy of Canada, and Hydro-Québec. Governments regulate securities, step in to prevent the collapse of businesses (such as Algoma Steel), mandate minimum wages, enforce workplace safety standards, regulate corporate mergers, provide farm price supports, and administer unemployment insurance, welfare, and pensions. Not surprisingly, federal, provincial, and municipal governments employ 6 percent of Canada's labour force in public administration.

SOCIALISM

Socialism *is an economic system in which natural resources and the means of producing goods and services are collectively owned.* In its ideal form, a socialist economy is the exact opposite of capitalism.

1. **Collective ownership of property.** An economy is socialist to the extent that it limits the right to private property, especially property used to produce goods and services. Laws establish government ownership of property and make housing and other goods available to all, not just those of some privileged segment of society.

   Karl Marx claimed that private ownership of productive property generates social classes by which an economic elite serves its own interest at the expense of everyone else. Socialism, then, seeks to lessen economic inequality and create a classless society.

2. **Pursuit of collective goals.** The individualistic pursuit of profit is also at odds with the collective orientation of socialism. Socialist values and norms condemn the capitalist entrepreneurial spirit as simple "greed." For this reason, socialist nations outlaw private trading as "black market" activity.

3. **Government control of the economy.** Socialism rejects the idea that a free-market economy regulates itself. Instead of a laissez-faire approach, socialist governments oversee a *centrally controlled* or *command* economy.

Socialism also rejects the idea that consumers guide capitalist production. From this point of view, consumers lack the information necessary to evaluate products and are manipulated by advertising to buy what is profitable for factory owners rather than what consumers genuinely need. Commercial advertising thus plays little role in socialist economies.

Socialism and Communism

Most people equate the terms *socialism* and *communism*. More precisely, **communism** is a *hypothetical economic and political system in which all members of a society are socially equal.* Karl Marx viewed socialism as a transitory stage on the path towards the ideal of a communist society devoid of all class divisions. In many socialist societies today, the dominant political party describes itself as communist, but nowhere has the communist goal been achieved.

Why? For one thing, social stratification involves differences of power as well as wealth. In general, socialist societies have succeeded in reducing disparities in wealth only by expanding government bureaucracies and extensively regulating daily life. In the process, government did not "wither away" as Karl Marx imagined. On the contrary, socialist political elites have enormous power and privilege.

Probably Marx would have agreed that a communist society is a *utopia* (from Greek words meaning "not a place"). Yet Marx considered communism a worthy goal, and might well have disparaged reputedly "Marxist" societies such as North Korea, the former Soviet Union, the People's Republic of China, and Cuba for not fulfilling what he saw as the promise of communism.

WELFARE CAPITALISM AND STATE CAPITALISM

Some of the nations of Western Europe—including Sweden and Italy—have combined a market-based economy with extensive social welfare programs. Analysts call this "third way" **welfare capitalism**, *an economic and political system that combines a mostly market-based economy with government programs to provide for people's basic needs.*

Under welfare capitalism, the government owns some of the largest industries and services, such as transportation, the mass media, and health care. In Sweden and Italy, about 12 percent of economic production is "nationalized," or state controlled. That leaves most industry in private hands, although subject to extensive government regulation in the public interest. High taxation (aimed especially at the rich) funds a wide range of social welfare programs, including universal health care and child care (Olsen, 1996).

Yet another blend of capitalism and socialism is **state capitalism**, *an economic and political system in which companies are privately owned although they cooperate closely with the government.* Systems of state capitalism are common in the rapidly developing Asian countries along the Pacific Rim. Japan, South Korea, and Singapore, for example, are all capitalist nations, but their governments work in partnership with large companies, supplying financial assistance and controlling imports of foreign products to help their businesses compete in world markets. Countries in East Asia and Western Europe demonstrate that governments and companies can work cooperatively in many ways (Gerlach, 1992).

RELATIVE ADVANTAGES OF CAPITALISM AND SOCIALISM

In practice, which economic system works best? Comparing economic models is difficult because all countries mix capitalism and socialism to varying degrees. Moreover, nations differ in cultural attitudes towards work, available natural resources, level of technological development, and patterns of trade. Some also carry the burdens of war more than others (Gregory and Stuart, 1985).

Despite these complicating factors, some crude comparisons are revealing. The following sections contrast two categories of countries—those with predominantly capitalist economies and those with predominantly socialist economies. The supporting data reflect economic patterns prior to recent changes in the former Soviet Union and Eastern Europe.

Economic Productivity

One key dimension of economic performance is productivity. A common measure of economic output is gross domestic product (GDP), the total value of all goods and services produced annually by a nation's economy. Per capita (or per person) GDP allows us to compare societies of different population size.

Averaging the economic output of Canada, the United States, and the nations of Western Europe at the end of the last decade yields a per capita GDP of about $13 500. The comparable figure for the former Soviet Union and the nations of Eastern Europe was about $5000. In other words, capitalist countries outproduced socialist nations by a ratio of 2.7 to 1 (United Nations Development Programme, 1990).

Global comparisons indicate that socialist economies generate the greatest economic equality, although living standards remain relatively low. Capitalist economies, by contrast, engender more income disparity although living standards are typically higher. As the former Soviet Union has moved towards a market system, however, the majority of people have suffered a decline in living standards, while some people have become quite rich.

Economic Equality

The distribution of resources within a society is a second crucial test of an economy. A comparative study completed in the mid-1970s calculated income ratios by comparing the earnings of the richest and poorest 5 percent of the population (Wiles, 1977). This research found that societies with predominantly capitalist economies had an income ratio of about 10 to 1; the corresponding figure for socialist countries was 5 to 1.

This comparison of economic performance reveals that capitalist economies support a higher overall standard of living but generate greater income disparity. Or, put otherwise, *socialist economies create less income disparity but offer a lower overall standard of living.*

Personal Freedom

One final consideration in evaluating capitalism and socialism involves the personal freedoms a society accords its people. The capitalist concept of liberty is the *freedom to* act in pursuit of one's self-interest. A capitalist economy, after all, depends on the freedom of producers and consumers to interact without extensive interference from the state.

On the other hand, a socialist conception of liberty is *freedom from* basic want. Providing for the basic needs of everyone means promoting economic equality. This goal requires considerable state intervention in the economy, which limits the personal choices of citizens for the benefit of the public as a whole.

People have yet to devise a social system that both expands political freedoms and creates economic equality. In a capitalist system that guarantees many personal freedoms, are these freedoms worth as much to a poor person as a rich one? On the other side of the coin, socialist nations, while more economically equal, restrict the rights of their people to express themselves and move freely inside and outside their borders.

CHANGES IN SOCIALIST COUNTRIES

During the last decade, a profound transformation has taken place in many socialist countries of the world. Beginning in the shipyards of Poland's port city of Gdansk in 1980, workers began organizing in opposition to their socialist government. Despite setbacks, the Solidarity movement eventually dislodged the Soviet-backed party officials and elected its leader, Lech Walesa, as national president. Poland is now in the process of introducing market principles to its economy.

Other countries of Eastern Europe that had fallen under the political control of the former Soviet Union at the end of World War II also shook off repressive socialist regimes during 1989 and 1990. These nations—including the German Democratic Republic (East Germany), Czechoslovakia, Hungary, Romania, and Bulgaria—have likewise introduced capitalist elements into what had for decades been centrally controlled economies. In 1992, the Soviet Union itself formally dissolved; along the way, the Soviets liberated the Baltic states of Estonia, Latvia, and Lithuania and cast most of the remaining republics, except Georgia and Azerbaijan, into a new Commonwealth of Independent States (now named the Russian Federation).

The reasons for these sweeping changes are many and complex. In light of the preceding discussion, however, two factors stand out. First, these predominantly socialist economies grossly underproduced their capitalist counterparts. They were, as we have noted, somewhat successful in achieving economic equality; living standards for everyone, however, were low by Western European standards. Second, the Soviet brand of socialism made for heavy-handed and unresponsive government that rigidly controlled the media as well as the ability of Eastern Europeans to move about, even in their own countries.

In short, socialism did away with economic elites, as Karl Marx predicted. But, as Max Weber might have foreseen, this system *increased* the clout of political elites to gargantuan proportions.

At this stage, the market reforms are proceeding unevenly. Some nations (Czech Republic, Slovakia, Poland, and the Baltic states of Latvia, Estonia, and Lithuania) are faring well, but others (Romania, Bulgaria, and the former Soviet republics) are buffeted by price increases and falling living standards. Officials hope that in the longer term an expanding market will raise living standards through greater productivity. However, there is already evidence that if this happens, a rising standard of living will be accompanied by increasing economic disparity (Pohl, 1996; Buraway, 1997; Specter, 1997b).

WORK IN THE POST-INDUSTRIAL ECONOMY

Change is not restricted to the socialist world; the economy of Canada has also changed dramatically during the last century. The Industrial Revolution transformed the Canadian workforce a century ago; further changes are taking place today.

In 1996, fifteen million Canadians were in the labour force, representing two-thirds of those over the age of fifteen. As has been the case historically, a larger proportion of men (72.4 percent) than women (57.6 percent) are in the labour force. The gender gap in labour force participation has diminished in recent decades among Canadians. The figure for males has not increased since 1980, but the female rate is up from 46.7 percent.

Figure 15–3 provides labour force participation rates for selected racial and ethnic categories for the years 1986 and 1991, and reveals some very interesting patterns. For instance, labour force participation rates are very similar for the British and the French—between 62.1 and 64.4 percent for both categories in both 1986 and 1991. Note that the British rate declined slightly while the French rate rose by more than one percentage point. Participation among Asians is somewhat higher at almost 71 per cent, with a drop of two points by 1991. Blacks are even more likely to be involved in the labour force—75 percent in 1986, 72 percent in 1991—at a rate roughly ten percentage points higher than the British and French. It is worth noting that Asians and Blacks, with high proportions of immigrants, are the most active in the labour force.

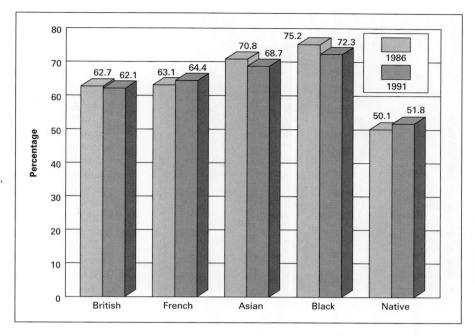

FIGURE 15–3 Labour Force Participation[1] for Selected Categories[2] 1986 and 1991

[1] Based on population fifteen years of age and older.

[2] Refers to single origin only—that is, those who are of the same origin on both paternal and maternal sides.

SOURCES: Adapted by Linda Gerber from Statistics Canada, *Profile of Ethnic Groups—Dimensions*, Catalogue No. 95-154, 1989, and 1991 Census, Individual Public Use Microdata.

In contrast, the native population exhibits markedly lower rates of participation in the labour force in both years—just over 50 percent. The comparison of native rates with those of Asians and Blacks suggests that race may not be the effective barrier to participation by natives; it may be the result of a history of internal colonialism, *de facto* segregation, rural isolation, lower levels of educational attainment, and cultural dislocation (Gerber, 1990; Frideres, 1993; Wotherspoon and Satzewich, 1993).

THE DECLINE OF AGRICULTURAL WORK

At the beginning of this century, about 35 percent of the Canadian labour force engaged in farming. By 1961, this proportion had fallen to almost 13 percent, and by 1991 to less than 5 percent. Still, because today's agriculture involves more machinery and fewer people, it is more productive than ever. A century ago, a typical farmer could feed five people; today, one farmer feeds seventy-five. This dramatic rise in productivity also reflects new types of crops, pesticides that promote higher yields, greater energy consumption, and other advances in farming techniques. The average Canadian farm has more than doubled in size from about 250 acres in 1950 to about 600 acres today.

This process signals the eclipse of "family farms," which are declining in number and produce only a small part of our agricultural yield; more and more production is carried out by corporate agribusinesses (Bakker and Winson, 1993). But, more productive or not, this transformation has brought painful adjustments for farming communities across the country, as a way of life is lost. The rest of us are affected indirectly by this change: prices have generally been kept low by the rising productivity of agribusiness, although a growing proportion of people are concerned about the effect of widespread use of pesticides and chemicals on crops.

THE DUAL LABOUR MARKET

Sociologists divide the jobs in today's economy into two categories. The **primary labour market** includes *occupations that provide extensive benefits to workers*. This segment of the labour market includes the traditional white-collar professions and upper management positions. These are jobs that people think of as *careers*. Work in the primary labour market provides high income and job security and is usually challenging and satisfying. Such occupations require a broad education rather than specialized training, and they offer solid opportunity for advancement.

But few of these advantages apply to work in the **secondary labour market**, *jobs that provide minimal benefits to workers*. This segment of the labour force is employed in low-skill, blue-collar assembly-line operations and low-level service-sector jobs, including clerical positions. Workers in the secondary labour market receive lower income, have less job security, and find fewer chances to advance. Not surprisingly,

D'Arcy Moses is a Gitksan native who grew up in Alberta. Incorporating aboriginal themes and issues in his creations, Moses has become a popular and highly successful fashion designer working out of Montreal.

then, these workers are more likely to experience alienation and dissatisfaction with their jobs (Mottaz, 1981; Kohn and Schooler, 1982).

Another term used to describe some of these workers is the **reserve army of labour**, *that part of the labour force that is last hired during expansion and first fired when the economy contracts.* These problems are especially serious for women, other minorities, and particularly natives, who tend to be overrepresented in this segment of the labour force (Kemp and Coverman, 1989; Gerber, 1990; Wotherspoon and Satzewich, 1993).

Most new jobs in our post-industrial economy fall within the secondary labour market. Like manufacturing jobs in factories a century ago, these positions involve unchallenging tasks, low wages, and poor working conditions (Edwards, 1979; Gruenberg, 1980).

LABOUR UNIONS

Labour unions are *worker organizations that seek to improve wages and working conditions through various strategies, including negotiations and strikes.* In Canada, union membership has been remarkably stable over

the last twenty years at just over one-third of the labour force, peaking at 35.1 percent in 1983. The involvement of women increased slightly while that of men decreased to the point where, in 1990, women constituted 40 percent of union membership in Canada (Statistics Canada, Catalogue No. 71-202, 1990). As well, the involvement of Canadian workers in international unions has dropped dramatically, while national unions have grown. The highest level of union membership is found in government or public administration at over 70 percent; the manufacturing and service sectors are both around the one-third mark, while mining and the trades lag behind. Most of the new service-sector jobs being created today are not unionized, and hardly any temporary workers belong to a labour union.

There is substantial interprovincial variation in levels of unionization. In Newfoundland, 55.1 percent of the labour force is unionized; at the other end of the spectrum is Alberta at 26.6 percent (Statistics Canada, Catalogue No. 71-202, 1990). The other relatively highly unionized provinces are Quebec, B.C., and Ontario. The differences are not entirely due to the economic structures of the various provinces, for even within the same industry there can be substantial variation: the level of unionization within the construction industry, for example, varies from 81 percent in Quebec to 25 percent in Prince Edward Island.

In global perspective, union membership in industrialized countries varies substantially—from a low of 16 percent of the workforce in the U.S. to about one-third in Canada, Switzerland, and Japan, one-half in Great Britain, and a high of more than 90 percent in Denmark and Sweden. Clearly, some cultures are more receptive to unions than others; those with social-democratic values tend to have higher levels of unionization. The United States, with its pro-capitalist values, has never been particularly supportive of the union movement.

PROFESSIONS

A **profession** is *a prestigious white-collar occupation that requires extensive formal education.* As distinct from *amateur* (from Latin meaning "lover," one who acts simply out of love for the activity itself), a professional pursues some task for a living. The term "profession" also suggests a public declaration to abide by certain principles. Traditional professions include the ministry, medicine, law, and academia (Goode, 1960). Today, we recognize more occupations as professions, to the extent that they have the following four characteristics (Ritzer, 1972):

1. **Theoretical knowledge.** Professionals have a theoretical understanding of their field rather

than mere technical training. Anyone can master first-aid skills, for example, but physicians claim a theoretical understanding of human health and illness.

2. **Self-regulated training and practice.** The typical professional is self-employed, "in practice" rather than working for a company. Professionals oversee their own work and observe a code of ethics.

3. **Authority over clients.** Many jobs—sales for example—require people to respond directly to the desires of customers. Based on their extensive training, however, professionals expect their clients to follow their direction and advice.

4. **Orientation to community rather than to self-interest.** The traditional "professing" of faith or duty is a professional's vow to serve the community rather than merely seek income. Some professionals, including physicians, are even barred by professional codes from advertising.

Many new service occupations in the post-industrial economy have also sought to *professionalize* their work. A claim to professional standing often begins by renaming the work to imply special, theoretical knowledge, which also distances the field from its previously less-distinguished reputation. Government bureaucrats, for example, become "public policy analysts," and stockroom workers are reborn as "inventory supply officials."

Interested parties may form a professional association to formally attest to their specialized skills. This organization then licenses people who perform the work and develops a code of ethics that emphasizes the occupation's contribution to the community. In its effort to win public acceptance, a professional association may also establish schools or other training facilities and perhaps start a professional journal (Abbott, 1988).

Not all occupations claim full professional status. Some *paraprofessionals*, including paralegals and medical technicians, possess specialized skills but lack the extensive theoretical education required of full professionals.

SELF-EMPLOYMENT

Self-employment—earning a living without working for a large organization—was once commonplace in North America. Rural farms were owned and operated by families, and self-employed workers in the cities owned shops and other small businesses or sold their skills on the open market. C. Wright Mills (1951) estimated that in the early nineteenth century about 80 percent of the U.S. labour force was self-employed, but, with the onset of the Industrial Revolution, that picture changed dramatically. Self-employment plummeted to one-third, one-fifth, and even lower in both Canada and the United States.

In recent years, Canada has experienced increases in self-employment. By 1998, self-employment accounted for roughly 16 percent of the labour force. The increasing importance of self-employment is illustrated by the fact that, between 1975 and 1987 in Canada, the number of self-employed workers grew by 60 percent, while the rest of the workforce grew by only 26 percent (Neill, 1990). The highest levels of self-employment are to be found in fishing, trapping, and agriculture. Not surprisingly, very little mining, manufacturing, or educating is done by the lone entrepreneur.

Professionals such as lawyers have always been well represented among the self-employed because their schooling and skills have high market value. But most self-employed workers in Canada have been small-business owners, plumbers, carpenters, freelance writers, editors, artists, and long-distance truck drivers. In the recent past, the self-employed have been more likely to be blue-collar than white-collar workers. Increasingly, women are joining the ranks of the self-employed—mainly, though not exclusively, in white-collar occupations.

Analysis of enumeration areas in Burlington, Ontario (Gerber, Statistics Canada Microdata, 1991) reveals that in one-quarter of the areas, 15 to 18 percent of men (fifteen years of age and over) were self-employed; only 6 percent of the areas had similar levels of female self-employment. The areas where larger proportions of men and women are self-employed tend to have higher levels of at-home work, home ownership, university degrees, and incomes—and more people who are currently married. By and large, self-employed people in Burlington are not marginal to the mainstream economy: they are numerous, well-educated, and relatively affluent. Undoubtedly, computers have facilitated the move to self-employment from home.

Our society has always painted an appealing picture of working independently: no time clocks to punch and no one looking over your shoulder. For those excluded from organizations by prejudice or discrimination, self-employment has served as a strategy to increase economic opportunity (Evans, 1989). Further, self-employment holds the potential of earning a great deal of money. But for all its advantages, self-employment presents workers with special problems. Many are vulnerable to fluctuations in the economy: during the recession of the early 1990s, small businesses filed for bankruptcy in alarming numbers. Another common problem is that the self-employed lack pension and health-care benefits generally provided to employees of large organizations.

Jose Clemente Orozco's painting The Unemployed *is a powerful statement of the personal collapse and private despair that afflicts men and women who are out of work. How does a sociological perspective help us to understand being out of work as more than a personal problem?*

Jose Clemente Orozco, *The Unemployed.* © Christie's Images. © Estate of Jose Clemente Orozco/Licensed by VAGA, New York, N.Y.

UNEMPLOYMENT

Some unemployment is found in every society. Few young people entering the labour force find a job immediately; some older workers leave the workforce temporarily while seeking a new job, to have children, or because of a strike; others suffer from long-term illnesses; and others who are illiterate or without skills find themselves locked out of the job market.

Although people may be quick to blame themselves if they find themselves out of work, unemployment is not just a personal problem; it is also a product of the economy itself. Capable and willing workers lose their jobs when economic recession occurs, if occupations become obsolete, or as factories close in the face of rising foreign competition. Mergers and "downsizing" can also lead to the dismissal of employees from all levels of an organization. The emerging post-industrial economy has shattered the job security of workers in many traditional blue-collar occupations as well (Kasarda, 1983).

In predominantly capitalist societies such as Canada, the unemployment rate rarely dips below 5 percent of the labour force. Public officials generally view this level of unemployment as natural, and sometimes even describe it as "full employment." An "unemployment problem" is publicly acknowledged only when the unemployment rate exceeds 7 or 8 percent (Albrecht, 1983). In principle, predominantly socialist societies consider work to be each person's right and obligation, so the government may create jobs to keep the unemployment rate low. In practice, however, unemployment is just as great a problem in these societies.

Canada's unemployment rate rose to over 11 percent in 1992 and 1993, before dropping to 9.5 percent in 1995 and 8.1 percent by December 1997. Throughout 1997, employment in Canada increased by 363 000 (+2.6 percent); most encouraging is the fact that the number of people working full-time hours increased by 377 000 (+3.4 percent) while the number working part-time declined by 14 000 (*The Daily*, January 9, 1998). While there have been gains in the numbers employed throughout the 1990s, economic restructuring has meant that hundreds of thousands of old jobs were lost as new ones were created. Many individuals who failed to make the transition from old to new jobs were casualties of this employment shift, contributing to the high unemployment rates of the early 1990s.

Part-time work currently accounts for 19 percent of all employment. In 1994, 5.4 percent of all workers (compared to 2.3 percent in 1981) were "involuntary part-timers," or people who have been unable to find full-time employment. In 1995, women held the bulk of part-time and shared jobs—72 and 84 percent, respectively (Columbo, 1997; Vardy, 1993; Wells, 1996). Some, but not all, of this part-time work can be classified as underemployment.

The national unemployment rate only tells part of the story, for unemployment in provinces such as Newfoundland and P.E.I. may approach twice the national rate. While Canada Map 15–1 reveals the regional pattern in unemployment rates, it is worth noting that cities or metropolitan areas have widely divergent rates: unemployment in Chicoutimi-Jonquière is roughly three times that of Toronto.

Unemployment rates differ for various segments of the Canadian population. In 1991, those of French origin had a higher unemployment rate (10.0 percent) than those of British origin (8.5 percent). The rate for Asian Canadians was similar to that of the French, while that of Black Canadians was substantially higher (14.5 percent). As has been the case over the past decade, the unemployment rate for natives is two to three times that of the other categories (24.6 percent). Note that these rates refer to the standard unemploy-

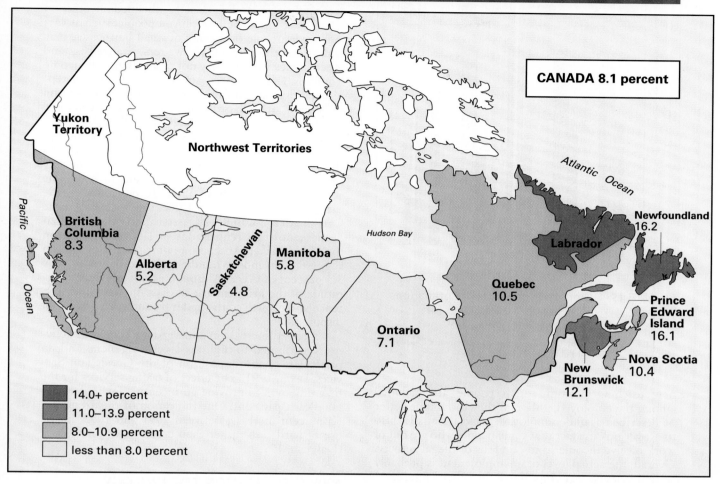

CANADA 8.1 percent

Yukon Territory

Northwest Territories

Pacific Ocean

British Columbia 8.3

Alberta 5.2

Saskatchewan 4.8

Manitoba 5.8

Hudson Bay

Ontario 7.1

Quebec 10.5

Labrador

Atlantic Ocean

Newfoundland 16.2

Prince Edward Island 16.1

Nova Scotia 10.4

New Brunswick 12.1

14.0+ percent
11.0–13.9 percent
8.0–10.9 percent
less than 8.0 percent

CANADA MAP 15–1 Unemployment Rates by Province, December 1997
SOURCE: Statistics Canada, *The Daily*, January 9, 1998.

ment rates measured as a percentage of the *labour force* that is unemployed and actively looking for work.

Figure 15–4 looks at employment or labour force involvement from a different perspective, indicating the proportion of *people fifteen years of age and over* who are (1) not in the labour force, (2) employed, or (3) unemployed. A comparison of the blue bars reveals that Asians and Black Canadians, at about 30 percent, are least likely to be classified as "not in the labour force." They are most likely to be employed (almost 62 percent of those over fifteen, red bars), but also more likely than the British or French to be unemployed (green bars). Native Canadian "adults" (that is, fifteen and over) have the highest percentage not in the labour force (48 percent), and are by far the least

likely to be employed and most likely to be unemployed. In other words, aboriginal people face barriers, initially, in becoming involved in the labour force and, then, in finding or retaining employment.

Official unemployment statistics, based on monthly national surveys, generally understate unemployment for two reasons. First, to be counted among the unemployed, a person must be actively seeking work. Especially during economic recessions, many people become discouraged after failing to find a job and stop looking. These "discouraged workers" are not counted among the unemployed. Second, many people unable to find jobs for which they are qualified take "lesser" employment: a former university teacher, for example, may drive a taxi while seeking a

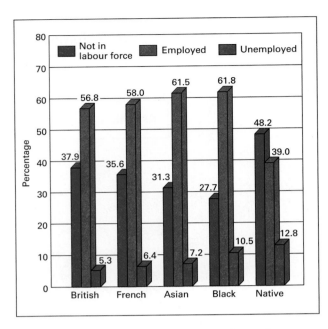

FIGURE 15–4 Employment Status of Populations
15 Years of Age and Over for
Selected Categories, 1991

SOURCE: Calculations by Linda Gerber based on Statistics Canada,
1991 Census, Individual Public Use Microdata.

new teaching position. Such people are included among the employed, although they too might better be described as underemployed. Official statistics also may overlook the fact that some people who are out of work receive income from odd jobs or illegal activity. Overall, the actual level of unemployment is probably several percentage points above the official figure.

THE UNDERGROUND ECONOMY

Government requires all businesses and individual workers to periodically report on their economic activity, especially earnings. Not reporting income received makes a transaction part of the **underground economy**, *economic activity involving income or the exchange of goods and services that is not reported to the government as required by law.*

On a small scale, evidence of the underground economy can be found everywhere: teenagers baby-sit for neighbours; a family makes some extra money by holding a garage sale without reporting the income to the government. Of course, far more of the underground economy is attributable to criminal activity such as illegal drug sales, cigarette smuggling, prostitution, bribery, theft, illegal gambling, and loan-sharking.

But the single largest segment of the underground economy involves "honest" people who fail to accurately report their legally obtained income on income tax forms. Self-employed people, such as various tradespeople or owners of small businesses, may understate their incomes; waiters, waitresses, and other service workers may not report their full income from tips. Even relatively small omissions and misrepresentations on individual income tax returns add up to billions of dollars in the underground economy (Simon and Witte, 1982; Dalglish, 1993).

Exactly how large is the underground economy? Roger Smith of the University of Alberta estimates that, in Canada, the underground economy accounted for some 15 to 20 percent of economic activity in 1990, up from about 10 percent a decade earlier (cited in Dalglish, 1993:20). A survey by the Canadian Home Builders' Association estimated that 55 percent of all renovations in 1992 were done on the black market. At the same time, Statistics Canada suggests that underground activity accounts for only 3.5 percent of GDP. Although estimates of the magnitude of the problem are all over the map, the existence and growth of the underground economy is not disputed.

A recent increase in underground economic activity is attributed to high tax levels in general and, in particular, to the imposition of the Goods and Services Tax in 1991. The effect of taxing services for the first time was to provide an incentive for under-the-table cash payment. One indication of this trend is a 57 percent increase, between 1991 and 1992, in the use of hard cash rather than credit cards or cheques (Dalglish, 1993).

NEW INFORMATION TECHNOLOGY AND WORK

Another key issue in the workplace of the twenty-first century is the central role of computers and other new information technology. The Information Revolution is changing the kind of work people do, as well as where they do it. Computers are also altering the character of work in four additional ways (Zuboff, 1982; Rule and Brantley, 1992; Vallas and Beck, 1996):

1. **Computers are "deskilling" labour.** Just as industrial machinery "deskilled" the master crafts workers of an earlier era, so computers now threaten the skills of managers. More and more business decisions are based not on executive decision making but on computer modelling. In other words, a machine determines whether to buy or sell a product, make an investment, or approve or reject a loan.

Working Through Cyberspace

The 1998 Winter Olympic Games in Nagano, Japan, gave IBM an opportunity to showcase its latest technology by transmitting, worldwide, millions of megabytes of data from the games to television viewers, radio listeners, newspaper readers, and Internet surfers. IBM makes the same technology available to business organizations that are involved in "e-business" or Internet-based commerce.

Business has become increasingly dependent on computers linked by intranets, extranets, and the World Wide Web. The number of people connected to the Web is expected to increase to 550 million by 2001; by then, the value of goods purchased *online* by businesses alone will have reached $231 billion (compared to $1.7 billion in 1996). But the Web is not limited to commercial transactions. Employees of a Vancouver firm can work—on data analysis, design, reports, or problem solving as part of an interactive group—from a home office in Winnipeg, Munich, or Helsinki. Work has invaded cyberspace—the McLuhanesque world that is free of the limitations of time and space.

Inco's Stobie mine in Sudbury, Ontario, is taking miners out of the underground tunnels and seating them at surface computer terminals from which they run automated drill rigs and scoop trams in various locations. Robo-operator Stan Holloway, who spent fifteen years in Inco's dangerous, dreary, diesel-fumed tunnels, is grateful to be comfortably seated, operating million-dollar scoop trams with a joystick and foot pedals and observing the otherwise back-breaking job through miniature cameras and microphones mounted on the machines.

Inco turned to this kind of high-tech mining in order to remain competitive at this particular mine, which has thirty to forty years' worth of low-grade ore left at the site. To remain in operation, Stobie must compete with mines that have high-grade ore and low labour costs. In Russia, a miner makes about $850 per year; Sudbury miners are employed at $85 000 to $100 000 per year. Robo-trams and drill rigs do a lot of dangerous, dirty work but displace large numbers of highly paid miners. Only a few miners will make the transition from hard manual labour to robo-operator.

The Department of Finance (http://www.fin.gc.ca) points out that many Canadian industries—beyond software, electronics, and aviation—are leaders in the development and adoption of new technology. New methods of inventory management are changing retailing and the skills needed by personnel, and satellite-generated images are used in resource exploration and development. So pervasive is this change that knowledge-based technology is now the major stimulus to economic growth and job creation. In the past decade, employment growth has been closely linked to intensity of information technology: employment has increased substantially (12 percent) in areas of high information technology intensity, increased moderately (8 percent) in areas of medium intensity, and declined (–9 percent) in sectors that make minimal use of information technology.

SOURCES: Canada, 1997; IBM, 1998; Robinson, 1998.

---

2. **Computers are making work more abstract.** Industrial workers typically have a "hands-on" relationship with their product. Post-industrial workers manipulate symbols in pursuit of abstract goals such as making a Web site more attractive, a company more profitable, or software more "user friendly."

3. **Computers limit workplace interaction.** The Information Revolution forces employees to perform most of their work at computer terminals, which isolates workers from one another.

4. **Computers enhance employers' control of workers.** Computers allow supervisors to monitor each worker's output precisely and continuously, whether employees are working at computer terminals or on an assembly line.

The changes wrought by computers remind us that technology is not socially neutral. Rather, it shapes the way we work and alters the balance of power between employers and employees. Understandably, then, people are likely to welcome some aspects of the Information Revolution while opposing others. See the "Exploring Cyber-Society" box for further discussion of the impacts of computers on the workplace.

CORPORATIONS

At the core of today's capitalist economies lies the **corporation**, *an organization with a legal existence including rights and liabilities apart from those of its members.* By incorporating, an organization becomes an entity unto itself, able to enter into contracts and own

Regional Economic Disparities

Although there is debate about the definition of "region" (Brodie, 1989), there is some justification for defining regions as units with institutional or political boundaries (Breton, 1981; Matthews, 1983). Furthermore, trying to measure regional disparities is easier if data (for example, census data) are collected regularly for the units in question. For these reasons, throughout this text, regions are defined in terms of provinces and territories.

Figure 15–5 shows the variation in the percentage of the labour force employed in manufacturing industries—considered by some to be the real wealth-creating engine of the economy—for Canada's regions or provinces. Despite consistent official efforts to promote regional development and to spread the manufacturing base more evenly across the country, Ontario and Quebec remain the manufacturing core of the Canadian economy, with 17 to 18 percent of their workers involved. Saskatchewan has the weakest manufacturing base of all the provinces, and B.C., for all its affluence, is still economically undiversified and overwhelmingly dependent on forestry (Marchak, 1986). Another way of looking at the manufacturing clout of Ontario and Quebec is to note that, with 62 percent of the population, they have 76 percent of the manufacturing jobs.

Brym points out that two explanations have been offered for these regional disparities: the "mainstream" approach and the "radical" or political economy approach. The mainstream approach focuses on the geographic causes of diversity: distance from markets, physical barriers (such as mountains), natural resources (generally in high demand), and population characteristics. From the radical perspective, inequities derive from human actions rather than nature. Confederation allowed "powerful central Canadian economic interests to drain wealth from the weak peripheral or hinterland regions, such as the prairies and the maritimes" (Brym, 1986:8).

Policies accentuate the disparities by concentrating capital, productive capacity, and jobs in a particular region. Population then flows to that region, which translates into political power (that is, increased representation in Parliament), and eventually into new policies that strengthen the economic centre. With one-half of Canada's population in the Windsor/Quebec City corridor, this trend is difficult to reverse.

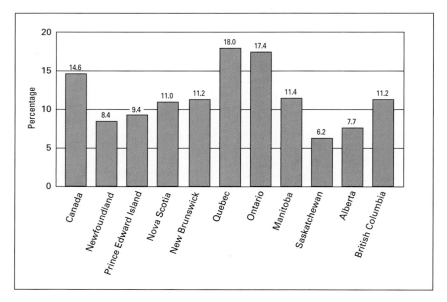

FIGURE 15–5 Percentage of Labour Force Employed in Manufacturing Industries for Canada and the Provinces, 1994

SOURCE: Statistics Canada data cited in Colombo, 1996.

SOURCE: Based on Brym (1986).

property. Incorporating, which arose about a century ago, protects the personal wealth of owners and top executives from lawsuits that might arise from business debts or harm to consumers.

Most large corporations operating in Canada (many of which are multinational) are owned by thousands of stockholders, including other corporations, rather than by single families. This dispersion of corporate ownership has to some extent spread wealth by making more people small-scale capitalists. Ralf Dahrendorf (1959) adds that the day-to-day operation of a corporation is the task of white-collar executives who are responsible to the stockholders. In practice, however, a great deal of corporate stock is

TABLE 15–1 The Top Companies in Canada Ranked by Revenues, 1997

Rank	Name	Revenues (1997, $000s)	Assets (1997, $000s)	Net Income (1997, $000s)	Employees
1	General Motors of Canada	34,249,489	n.a	n.a.	29,000
2	Bell Canada Enterprises	33,191,000	40,298,000	1,414,000	122,000
3	Ford Motor Company of Canada	27,911,591	9,572,319	684,785	24,402
4	The Seagram Company	17,160,728	28,902,148	685,883	30,000
5	Chrysler Canada	16,688,000	7,188,000	115,000	16,000
6	TransCanada Pipelines	14,242,800	14,571,600	457,000	3,042
7	George Weston	13,921,000	5,878,000	244,000	83,000
8	The Thomson Corp.	12,137,404	19,072,857	761,530	50,000
9	Onex Corp.	11,212,384	5,846,331	54,428	43,000
10	Alcan Aluminum	10,768,034	13,541,113	647,993	33,000
11	Imasco	10,008,000	50,258,000	790,000	27,000
12	Canadian Pacific	9,560,000	17,331,900	1,255,800	33,600
13	Imperial Oil	9,512,000	10,060,000	847,000	7,096
14	Power Corp. of Canada	8,615,000	55,888,000	331,000	15,505
15	Bombardier	8,508,900	10,575,200	420,200	47,000

SOURCE: *Financial Post 500 Magazine*, 1998.

owned by a small number of the corporation's top executives and directors who, in Canada, may be members of a very small number of families (Clement, 1975; Francis, 1986). These major stockholders comprise a small economic elite, which owns and operates the richest and most powerful Canadian businesses. Thus, the proliferation of corporations has not substantially changed how large businesses operate or affected the distribution of wealth in Canada.

ECONOMIC CONCENTRATION

Profit-making corporations range in size from one-person businesses to veritable giants, such as Bell Canada Enterprises (121 000 employees) and George Weston (76 180 employees). Many of Canada's corporations are small, with less than $100 000 in assets, but the largest of these corporations dominate the Canadian economy and periodically expand their empires through mergers and buyouts of smaller firms. In a pattern that differs from that of the U.S., Canada's banks and other financial institutions (though not always the largest employers) are well represented among the top corporations in terms of revenues and profits. The merger, announced in January 1998, of the Royal Bank and the Bank of Montreal not only enhances the position of the new bank within Canada, but places it among the top twenty-five banks in the world. With combined profits, in 1995, of over $2 billion, their two CEOs were compensated to the tune of $2.5 and $2.3 million (Forcese, 1997:53–55).

Canada's problems of corporate concentration stem from (1) the inordinate wealth and power of specific individuals, families, and corporations; (2) interlocking directorships that bind otherwise diverse corporations; (3) geographic centralization of investment in Ontario and Quebec; and (4) the tendency of corporations to expand or diversify by merging or buying existing firms instead of developing new productive capacity. The latter tendency was exacerbated by the free trade agreement with the United States, as evidenced by a $20-billion boom in acquisitions and mergers in the first few months of 1989 (Bronson, 1993:204). This has been referred to as "paper entrepreneurship," an activity which does nothing to contribute to Canada's wealth: "The pie remains the same size, but the pieces are cut differently" (Francis, 1986:229).

Table 15–1 ranks, by revenues, the top fifteen companies in Canada. General Motors, which employs 35 000 people, topped the list with over $30 billion in revenues. Note that the three major car manufacturers are all in the top four, and that Ontario Hydro and Hydro-Québec are among the major players in Canada.

FOREIGN OWNERSHIP

Concern about foreign investment was sparked in the early 1970s when a task force reported that foreign control of Canadian manufacturing had reached 60 percent overall, and as high as 90 percent in the rubber and petroleum industries. Since then, there has been some form of federal agency in place to review

The Irving Empire

Among the family dynasties Diane Francis examines in *Controlling Interest: Who Owns Canada?* is that of K.C. Irving, based in New Brunswick. "New Brunswick is a company town," claims Francis, "and its proprietor is K.C. Irving." She goes on to describe his empire:

The Irving group of companies is big by anybody's standards. It includes the country's largest shipyard and drydock facilities. Irving Oil is one of Canada's ten largest oil companies, with 3000 service stations in Atlantic Canada and the Ottawa Valley, the country's largest refinery, as well as untold holdings in oil and gas discoveries in western Canada. Irving's forestry business is world-scale, including half a dozen pulp and paper mills and sawmills and title to 1.5 million acres of timberlands in New Brunswick and Maine, an area equivalent to the size of Prince Edward Island. These land holdings, which Irving owns outright, make him the largest private landowner in the Maritimes. He also owns fleets of ships, trucks, buses, and railway cars, most of the media in the province, stores selling cars, food, hardware, drugs, and construction materials, and factories spewing out everything from pre-fab housing to concrete, steel, and hundreds more products. It is hard to get an exact picture of the scope of the Irving empire. None of the companies are publicly owned, and the Irvings fiercely protect their privacy through a complicated and impenetrable corporate structure.

Francis argues that corporate concentration is damaging to the Canadian economy. The Irvings' prosperity has been based, in part, on the ability to lobby politicians, on erecting barriers against competitors, and on a virtual media monopoly.

Since the death of K.C. Irving in 1992, Arthur Irving has taken over as CEO of this vast, privately owned empire. Though its revenues and net income are not disclosed, Arthur Irving is ranked among the 200 most powerful people in Canada—the Canadian corporate elite.

SOURCE: Francis (1986:16); *Financial Post Magazine* (November 1995:60).

---

foreign investment in Canada. Most of the foreign control has been American, a fact that has raised questions in many minds about Canada's economic and political sovereignty.

There are a large number of companies, with names familiar to most Canadians, that are not traded on Canadian stock exchanges because they are 100 percent American-owned (*Globe and Mail, Report on Business,* July 1993). Among them are General Motors, Chrysler, IBM, Safeway, Amoco, Proctor & Gamble, Mobil Oil, General Electric, McDonald's, Goodyear, Hewlett-Packard, Motorola, and John Deere. Honda Canada is held by Japanese (50.4 percent) and U.S. investors (49.6 percent). Concerns about these companies, as well as those owned by Japanese, British, Swiss, or other interests, revolve around profits leaving Canada, potential avoidance of Canadian taxes, the lack of research and development or high-level management functions on Canadian soil, and even political interference.

Concern about the extent of American investment in Canada, and the related processes of "integration, rationalization, and harmonization with the United States economically, socially, and politically" (Hurtig, 1992:4), even spawned a new political party.

The National Party of Canada promised, in the 1993 federal election campaign, to end the growth of foreign ownership and control as well as to reverse the growth of excessive corporate concentration (Hurtig, 1992:41). Failure to win any seats in 1993 and internal dissension led to the demise of the National Party before the next federal election in 1997.

CONGLOMERATES AND CORPORATE LINKAGES

The largest businesses are **conglomerates**, *giant corporations composed of many smaller corporations.* Conglomerates emerge as corporations enter new markets, spin off new companies, or take over other companies. Forging a conglomerate is also a way to diversify a company, so that new products can provide a hedge against declining profits in the original market. Sometimes these mergers are extremely diverse, as illustrated by the Irving empire, discussed in the "Social Diversity" box. Beatrice Foods, a Canadian company until it was purchased by American interests through Merrill Lynch Capital in 1991, is another corporate "umbrella," containing more than fifty smaller corporations that manufacture well-known products including Hunt's foods, Tropicana fruit juices, La Choy foods, Orville Redenbacher popcorn, Max Factor cosmetics, Playtex clothing, and Samsonite luggage.

Corporations are not only linked in conglomerates, but also by owning each other's stock. For example, in today's global economy, many companies invest heavily in other corporations commonly regarded as their competitors. In the automobile industry, Ford owns a significant share of Mazda, General Motors is a major investor in Isuzu, and Chrysler is part owner of Mitsubishi.

Besides conglomerates, corporations are also linked by extremely wealthy families who own their stock (Clement, 1975). Among the Canadian families who have large and varied corporate holdings in Canada (in addition to the Irvings) are the McCains, the Molsons, the Steinbergs, the Eatons, the Desmarais, the Campeaus, the Blacks, the Richardsons, the Mannixes, the Belzbergs, and the Bentleys (Francis, 1986). These families from across Canada know each other, interact socially, and have business interests in common.

Corporations are also linked through *interlocking directorates*, social networks of people serving simultaneously on the boards of directors of many corporations. These connections, which give corporations access to insider information about each other's products and marketing strategies (Clement, 1975; Marlios, 1975; Herman, 1981; Scott and Griff, 1985). Peter Bentley of Vancouver personally sits on more than a dozen "blue ribbon boards," has "titled Europeans on his boards and has served on theirs," and has "entered into countless partnerships with English and German firms" (Francis, 1986:193–94).

Not all corporate linkages are formal. Gwen Moore (1979) has described how social networks (discussed in Chapter 7, "Groups and Organizations") informally link members of the corporate elite. In other words, corporate executives travel in many of the same social circles, allowing them to exchange valuable information. Such networks enhance not only the economic clout of big businesses, they also expand the influence of corporate leaders in political, social, and charitable organizations (Clement, 1975; Useem, 1979; Francis, 1986).

Corporate linkages do not necessarily oppose the public interest, but they do concentrate power and they sometimes encourage illegal activity. Price-fixing, for example, is legal in much of the world (the Organization of Petroleum Exporting Countries—OPEC—meets regularly to try to set oil prices), but not in Canada and the United States. By their nature, however, linkages encourage price-fixing, especially when a few corporations control an entire market.

Corporations are often closely linked, even when they compete in the same market. In the automobile industry, for example, different manufacturers may actually be connected through ownership, as is the case with Ford and Mazda. How might this type of relationship between corporations in the same industry affect the consumer?

CORPORATIONS: ARE THEY COMPETITIVE?

The capitalist model suggests that businesses operate independently in a competitive market. But large corporations are not really competitive because, first, their extensive linkages mean that they do not operate independently. Second, a small number of corporations dominate many large markets. In Canada, the competitive sector is made up mostly of small businesses and the self-employed.

From a business point of view, a company establishing a **monopoly**, *domination of a market by a single producer*, could simply dictate prices. A century ago, the U.S. government saw the public danger in this and limited monopolies by law through the *Sherman Anti-Trust Act* of 1890. Canada does not have comparable legislation, but when it does allow monopolies, the companies have to submit to government regulation. For example, when Bell Canada had a monopoly, it had to apply to the government for permission to increase rates.

Although monopolies may be eliminated or at least controlled in North America, the **oligopoly**, or *domination of a market by a few producers*, is a common pattern. Oligopoly arises because the investment needed to enter a major product market, such as the

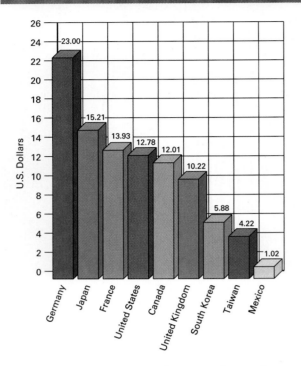

FIGURE 15–6 Average Hourly Wages for Workers in Manufacturing, 1996

SOURCE: Calculations by Macionis based on U.S. Bureau of the Census (1997).

auto industry, is beyond the reach of all but the biggest companies. Moreover, true competition means risk, which big business tries to avoid.

Corporate power is now so great—and competition among corporations so limited—that government regulation is the only way to protect the public interest. Yet the government is the corporate world's single biggest customer, and it frequently intervenes to support struggling companies. In truth, corporations and government often work together to make the entire economy more stable and to make businesses more profitable (Madsen, 1980). Paul Martin, as Minister of Finance, had the final say in the controversial Bank of Montreal/Royal Bank merger.

CORPORATIONS AND THE GLOBAL ECONOMY

Corporations have grown in size and power so fast that they account for most of the world's economic activity. In the process, the largest corporations, cen-

tred in the United States, Canada, Japan, and Western Europe, have spilled across national borders and now view the entire world as one vast marketplace.

Multinational corporations produce and market products in many different nations. Beatrice Foods operates factories in thirty countries and sells products in more than one hundred. Canada's Northern Telecom is among the huge corporations that earn much—and in some cases, most—of their profits outside their own countries.

Because most of the planet's resources and people are found in less-developed countries, multinational corporations spread their operations around the world in order to gain access to raw materials, inexpensive labour, and vast markets. As shown in Figure 15–6, labour costs are far lower in poor countries of the world: a manufacturing worker in Taiwan labours all week to earn what a German worker earns in a single day.

The impact of multinationals on poor societies is controversial, as Chapter 11 ("Global Stratification") explains in detail. On one side of the argument, modernization theorists claim that multinationals unleash the great productivity of the capitalist economic system, which will propel poor nations towards a higher standard of living. Specifically, corporations offer poor societies tax revenues, capital investment, new jobs, and advanced technology that act together to accelerate economic growth (Rostow, 1978; Madsen, 1980; Berger, 1986; Firebaugh and Beck, 1994).

On the other side, dependency theorists argue that multinationals intensify global inequality. Multinational investment, as they see it, actually creates few jobs in poor countries, inhibits the development of local industries, and pushes developing countries to produce goods for export rather than food and other products for local consumption. From this standpoint, multinationals make poor societies poorer and increasingly dependent on rich, capitalist societies (Vaughan, 1978; Wallerstein, 1979; Delacroix and Ragin, 1981; Bergesen, 1983; Walton and Ragin, 1990).

From this perspective, the growth of multinational corporations amounts to little more than an extension of historical colonialism: a neocolonialism now concerned with profit rather than direct political control. As one defender of multinationals asserted, "We are not without cunning. We shall not make Britain's mistake. Too wise to govern the world, we shall simply own it" (cited in Vaughan, 1978:20).

THE ECONOMY OF THE TWENTY-FIRST CENTURY

Social institutions are organizational strategies by which societies meet various needs of their members.

The global expansion of multinational corporations centred in high-income countries has altered consumption patterns almost everywhere, encouraging a homogeneous "corporate culture" that is—for better or worse—undermining countless traditional ways of life.

But, as we have seen, the Canadian economy only partly succeeds in this respect. Though highly productive, our economy distributes its products in a highly unequal fashion. Moreover, as we move into the new century, economic transformations in our society and the world present us with new opportunities and challenges.

As this chapter highlighted, the Information Revolution is driving much of this change. In the post-industrial era, the share of the Canadian labour force engaged in manufacturing has tumbled to two-thirds of what it was in 1960; service work—and especially computer-related jobs—have climbed just as quickly. For workers who depend on industrial skills to earn a living, this change has brought rising unemployment and declining wages. As we look to the coming century, our society must face up to the fact that millions of men and women lack the language and computer skills needed to participate in a post-industrial economy. Can we afford to consign these workers and their families to the margins of society? How can the government, schools, and families prepare young people to perform the kind of work their society makes available to them?

A second transformation that will define the next century is the emergence of a global economy. Two centuries ago, the ups and downs of a local economy reflected events and trends within a single town. One century ago, local communities throughout the country had become interconnected so that prosperity in once place depended on producing goods demanded by people elsewhere. We will enter the new century with powerful economic connections on the global level. In fact, it now makes little sense to speak of a national economy; what Saskatchewan farmers produce and consume may be affected more by what transpires in the wheat-growing region of Russia than by events in their own provincial capital. In short, Canadian workers and business owners are not only generating new products and services, but doing so in response to factors and forces that are distant and unseen.

Finally, change is causing analysts around the world to rethink conventional economic models. The emerging global system shows that socialist economies are less productive than their capitalist counterparts, one important reason for the recent collapse of socialist regimes in Eastern Europe and the former Soviet Union.

But capitalism, too, has seen marked changes, especially an increasing involvement of government in the economy. Moreover, productive enterprises have outgrown national boundaries with the emergence of multinational corporations. The world's societies are becoming increasingly interconnected, as illustrated by Canada's free trade agreements and the European Economic Community.

What will be the long-term effects of all these changes? Two conclusions seem inescapable. First, the economic future of Canada and other nations will be played out in a global arena. Second, we must face up to the issue of global inequality. Whether the world economy ultimately reduces or deepens the disparity between rich and poor societies may well be what steers our planet towards peace or war.

The Market: Does the "Invisible Hand" Serve Our Interests or Pick Our Pockets?

"The market" or "government planning"? Each is a means of economic decision making, determining what products and services companies produce and what people will consume. So important is this process that the degree to which the market or government directs the economy affects how nations define themselves, choose their allies, and identify their enemies.

Historically, the United States has relied on the market—the "invisible hand" of supply and demand—for most economic decisions. Canada has a tradition of greater government involvement in the economy in terms of both control and ownership. (The *North American Free Trade Agreement*, NAFTA, pushes Canada in the direction of reduced government interference in the economy.*)

Nevertheless, for the most part, both the U.S. and Canada allow the market to move prices for products upwards or downwards according to the supply of sellers and the demand of buyers. The market thus coordinates the efforts of countless people, each of whom—to return to Adam Smith's insight—is motivated only by self-interest.

Defenders also praise the market for discouraging racial and ethnic prejudice. Though one might restrict one's social contacts, in theory at least, one trades with whoever offers the best deal. Furthermore, as economists Milton and Rose Friedman remind us, a more-or-less freely operating market system provides capitalist countries with the highest standards of living, In effect, they argue, the market has produced economic prosperity.

But others point to the contributions government makes to the economy in Canada and, to a lesser extent, in the United States. First, government steps in to carry out tasks that no one would do for profit: even Adam Smith, for example, looked to government to defend the country against external enemies. Government also plays a role in constructing and maintaining public projects such as roads and utilities, as well as medical care, education, social security, public housing, and other social services. While Canada is privatizing many of these services, our government still plays a substantial role in the economy—a role that is supported by high levels of taxation.

High taxation and the proliferation of government services and regulation go hand in hand with our widely embraced philosophies of *collectivism* and *egalitarianism*. According to Gairdner (1990:3), these allow the central government to "control and engineer the condition of society" in an attempt to ensure *equality of outcome* for all. The effect of this social engineering is to break down traditional values such as "the primacy of honesty, freedom and hard work; respect for society, authority and private property; and all related matters built upon these values." Gairdner and other supporters of free markets believe that minimal state regulation serves the public interest best.

SUMMARY

1. The economy is a major social institution by which a society produces, distributes, and consumes goods and services.

2. In technologically simple societies, economic activity is subsumed within the family. In agrarian societies, most economic activity takes place apart from the home. Industrialization sparks significant economic expansion built around new sources of energy, factories, mass production, and specialization. In post-industrial economies, the majority of workers provide services rather than contribute to the manufacture of goods.

3. The post-industrial economy is characterized by a productive shift from tangible goods to services. Just as the Industrial Revolution propelled the industrial economy of the past, the Information Revolution is now advancing the post-industrial economy.

4. The primary sector of the economy generates raw materials; the secondary sector manufactures various goods; the tertiary sector focuses on providing services. In pre-industrial societies, the primary sector predominates; the secondary sector is of greatest importance in industrial societies; the tertiary sector prevails in post-industrial societies.

5. The emergence of a global economy means that nations no longer produce and consume products and services within national boundaries. Moreover, the six hundred largest corporations, operating internationally, now account for most of the earth's economic output.

But not everyone views the market as a positive force. For one thing, critics point out, the market has little incentive to produce anything that is not profitable. That is why few private companies set out to meet the needs of poor people since, by definition, they have little money to spend. A number of analysts are critical of a free-wheeling capitalist market economy, which by its nature erodes or threatens essential public services (Barlow and Campbell, 1991; Hurtig, 1991; Shields and McBride, 1994). American ownership of the Canadian economy, corporate power and control, and NAFTA (which pushes us into the embrace of American capitalism) threaten our values, our national identity, and the quality of life of all our citizens. In fact, since Canada is essentially an economic union, diminishing federal involvement in the economy and in the provision of social services even threatens national unity.

Second, critics look to government to curb what they see as the market system's self-destructive tendencies. Government takes a strong regulatory role, intervening in the market to control inflation (by setting interest rates), protect the well-being of workers (by imposing workplace safety standards), and benefit consumers (by mandating standards for product quality). Even so, advocates of a stronger role for government point out that the power of corporations in Canadian society is so great that the government still cannot effectively challenge the capitalist elite.

Third, critics support government's role in curbing the market's tendency to magnify social stratification. Since market economies concentrate income and wealth in the hands of a few, a government system of taxation that applies higher rates to the rich counters this tendency in the name of social justice.

For a number of reasons then, the market operating alone does not serve the public interest. While Canadians are largely supportive of the market, they also see benefits to the public through government involvement in the economy. In fact, government assists not only individual citizens but business itself by providing investment capital, constructing roads and other infrastructure, and shielding companies from foreign competition. Yet in Canada and around the world, people continue to debate the optimal balance of market forces and government decision making.

Continue the debate . . .

1. *How do visions of the market and government intervention in the economy fuel the debate during Canada's federal and provincial elections?*
2. *Why do defenders of the free market assert that "the government that governs best is the government that governs least"?*
3. *In your opinion, does a market system meet the needs of this country's people? Does it serve some better than others?*
4. *Does your family feel that income tax rates in Canada are too high? Too low? Why?*

---

*One notable exception to this trend is the treatment of Canada's poultry, egg, and milk marketing boards, which require trade barriers for their survival. NAFTA's five-member dispute panel—in a "smashing victory" for Canada—voted unanimously to allow Ottawa to maintain high border tariffs indefinitely, in spite of the NAFTA agreement to phase out tariffs between the U.S. and Canada over eighteen months (Fagan, 1996).

6. Social scientists describe the economies of today's industrial and post-industrial societies in terms of two models. Capitalism is based on private ownership of productive property and the pursuit of personal profit in a competitive marketplace. Socialism is based on collective ownership of productive property and the pursuit of collective well-being through government control of the economy.

7. Although the Canadian economy is predominantly capitalist, our government is widely involved in economic life. Government plays an even greater economic role in the democratic socialist societies of some Western European nations and the state capitalism of Japan. The former Soviet Union and the nations of Eastern Europe are gradually introducing some market elements into their historically centralized economies.

8. Capitalism is very productive, generally providing a high overall standard of living with extensive civil liberties. Socialism is less productive and restricts civil liberties, but does generate greater economic equality.

9. Agricultural work has declined in Canada during this century. The number of blue-collar jobs has also diminished; such work now involves only one-quarter of the labour force. Today, close to two-thirds of Canadian workers have white-collar service jobs.

10. A profession is a special category of white-collar work based on theoretical knowledge, occupational autonomy, authority over clients, and a claim to serve the community.

11. Work in the primary labour market provides far more rewards than work in the secondary labour

market. Most new jobs are in the secondary labour market's service sector.

12. Today, 14 percent of Canada's workers are self-employed. Although many professionals fall into this category, most self-employed workers have blue-collar occupations.

13. Capitalist societies tend to maintain an unemployment rate of at least 5 percent. Socialist societies, too, struggle with high unemployment.

14. The underground economy represents perhaps 15 to 20 percent of the economic activity in Canada, including most criminal business as well as legal income unreported on income tax forms.

15. Corporations form the core of the Canadian economy. The largest corporations, which are conglomerates, account for most corporate assets and profits.

16. The competitive sector of the Canadian economy encompasses smaller businesses. Large corporations dominate the noncompetitive sector.

17. Multinational corporations have grown in number and size during this century. The consequences for global economic development are a matter of continuing controversy.

CRITICAL THINKING QUESTIONS

1. What is a social institution? In principle, what is the economy supposed to do? How well do you think our economy does its job?

2. Identify several ways in which the Industrial Revolution reshaped the economy of Canada. How is the Information Revolution transforming the economy once again?

3. What key characteristics distinguish capitalism from socialism? Compare these two systems in terms of productivity, economic inequality, and their approach to personal freedoms.

4. Should Canada participate in the Multilateral Investment Agreement, which requires foreign investors within countries that are party to the agreement to operate under the same rules as domestic investors?

SOCIOLOGY APPLIED

1. The profile of the Canadian economy—75 percent of output in the tertiary sector, 16.5 in the secondary sector, and 4.6 percent in the primary sector—obscures great variety within this country. A trip to the library will allow you to profile your local economy (a city, region, or province).

2. Here are two interesting exercises involving the Internet. Statistics Canada makes available a wide range of data and reports on labour, employment, and unemployment at its Web site (www.statcan.ca). Learn more about Canadian farming at The Canadian Federation of Agriculture's site (www.cfa-fca.ca).

3. How are computers changing the character of the university or college campus? Meet with your sociology instructor or an official in the computer centre to find out the various ways computers are used on campus. Does the arrival of new information technology seem to be changing professional or personal relationships on the campus? How?

4. Visit a discount store such as Zellers or Wal-Mart and select an area of the store of interest to you. Do a little "fieldwork," inspecting products to see where they are made. Does your research support the existence of a global economy?

http://www.reflection.gc.ca/
This Government of Canada site includes the final report of the Advisory Committee on the Changing Workplace.

http://www.clc-ctc.com/
The Canadian Labour Congress (CLC) is the national voice of the labour movement, representing 2.3 million unionized workers. The CLC promotes decent wages and working conditions and improved health and safety laws, lobbies for fair taxes and strong social programs, and works for social equality.

http://www.statcan.ca/english/Pgdb/People/ labour.htm
Statistics Canada's collection of tables about the Canadian labour market, including information on age and sex, location, commuting, earnings, organized labour, and employment insurance.

http://www.ilo.org/
Founded in 1919, the International Labour Organization is a UN-specialized agency that seeks the promotion of social justice and internationally recognized human and labour rights.

http://www.wto.org/
Located in Geneva, Switzerland, the World Trade Organization arranges technical assistance and training for developing countries and provides a forum for international trade negotiations and disputes.

Christiane Pflug, *With the Black Flag,* 1971

CHAPTER 16

POLITICS AND GOVERNMENT

In April 1997, a sudden spring thaw and relentless rain brought the crest of a flood north from the United States—where it had already done extensive damage—through the farmlands and small towns of southern Manitoba, right into the city of Winnipeg. As the flood spread, volunteers from across the country and the Canadian Forces arrived to assist with building sandbag dykes and, as was too often necessary, with evacuation.

Intensive television coverage of the "flood of the century" allowed Canadians to monitor the height of the water and share the experiences of the victims as 27 000 people were evacuated and 180 000 hectares of farmland were wiped out. School children across the country engaged in a variety of fundraising activities, contributing to the $12 million raised by Canadians for flood relief.

While the rest of us watched and worried, Jean Chrétien and his Liberal government faced a dilemma: as the floodwaters rose, Canada was gearing up for a spring election set for June 2. Regulations regarding the length of federal campaigns made it necessary to decide on and call the election date in the week following the declaration of a state of emergency by Manitoba premier Gary Filmon. The prime minister visited the flood site, passed sandbags along the dyke, and worried about the political consequences of calling an election while part of the country was facing disaster. The pressures on him to postpone were considerable, but in the end—since the wheels were already in motion—he decided to go ahead with the election, while making arrangements for people in the flood area to go to the polls at a later date.

The Liberals won a second consecutive majority government in that election, although their total number of seats declined from 177 to 155 (a decline of 12 percent). In Manitoba, Liberal representation dropped by half—from 12 to 6 seats.

This chapter investigates the dynamics of power within societies and among nations, explaining the rules of the game and noting why people sometimes break them. **Politics**, or, more formally, "the polity," is *the institutionalized system by which a society distributes power, sets the society's agenda, and makes decisions.* Politics, in short, is about power, a topic about which there is considerable disagreement around the world as well as here at home.

POWER AND AUTHORITY

Every society rests on **power**, which sociologist Max Weber (1978; orig. 1921) defined as *the ability to achieve desired ends despite resistance.* To a large degree, the exercise of power is the business of **government**, *a formal organization that directs the political life of a society.* Yet, as Weber explained, few governments obtain compliance by openly threatening their people. Most

The powers that be have often disparaged popular opposition as a "mob." Such an argument was used to justify police violence against strikers—including ten who died—in a bloody confrontation near Chicago's Republic Steel Mill in 1936. Philip Evergood commemorates the event in his painting American Tragedy.

Philip Evergood, *American Tragedy*, 1936, oil on canvas, 29½ × 39½", Terry Dintenfass Gallery, New York.

of the time, people respect (or, at least, accept) their political system.

Practically speaking, it would be difficult for any large, complex society to persist if power derived *only* from sheer force, and life in such a society would be a nightmare of terror. Social organization, by contrast, depends on some degree of consensus about proper goals (often in the form of cultural values) and suitable means of pursuing them (cultural norms).

Every society, then, seeks to establish its power as legitimate. Weber therefore focused on the concept of **authority**, *power that people perceive as legitimate rather than coercive.* How is sheer power transformed into stable authority? There are three ways, Weber explained, and the one a society relies on most depends on its level of economic development.

TRADITIONAL AUTHORITY

Pre-industrial societies, Weber explained, rely on **traditional authority**, *power legitimized through respect for long-established cultural patterns.* In ideal terms, traditional authority is power woven into a society's collective memory, so that people consider social arrangements almost sacred. Chinese emperors in antiquity were legitimized by tradition, as were nobles in medieval Europe. In both cases, the power of tradition was strong enough that—for better or worse—people typically viewed members of the hereditary ruling family as almost godlike.

But traditional authority declines as societies industrialize. Hannah Arendt (1963) pointed out that traditional authority is compelling only as long as everyone shares the same heritage and world view. This form of authority, then, is undermined by the specialization demanded by industrial production, by modern, scientific thinking, and also by the social change and cultural diversity that accompany immigration. Thus, no prime minister of today's Canada, for example, would claim to rule by grace of God. However, we still have a monarch, Queen Elizabeth II, as our head of state, although today's more democratic culture has shifted real power to commoners popularly elected to office. On the recommendation of our prime minister, the queen appoints the governor general, who performs largely ceremonial functions such as opening Parliament. Despite this minimal role, many Canadians are uncomfortable with any attachment to the monarchy. The recent decline in prestige suffered by the British monarchy contributed to Canada's move from deference to defiance—the Canadian revolution described by Peter C. Newman (1995).

If traditional authority plays a smaller part in politics, it persists in other aspects of everyday life. Patriarchy, the domination of women by men, is a traditional form of power that remains widespread, even though it is increasingly challenged. Less controversial is the traditional authority parents exert over their children. The fact that traditional authority is linked to a person's status as parent is obvious every time a parent answers a doubting child with "Because I said so!" There is no debating the parent's decision because that would defeat traditional authority by putting parent and child on equal footing.

RATIONAL-LEGAL AUTHORITY

Weber defined **rational-legal authority** (sometimes called *bureaucratic authority*) as *power legitimized by* *legally enacted rules and regulations.* Rational-legal authority, then, is power legitimized in the operation of lawful government.

As Chapter 7 ("Groups and Organizations") explains, Weber viewed bureaucracy as the organizational backbone of rational-thinking, industrial societies. Moreover, just as a rational world view promotes bureaucracy, so it erodes traditional customs and practices. Instead of venerating the past, members of modern societies look to formally enacted rules—especially law—for principles of justice.

Rationally enacted rules also underlie many power relationships in everyday life. The authority of classroom teachers and deans, for example, rests on the offices they hold in bureaucratic universities and colleges. The police, too, are officers, within the bureaucracy of local government. In contrast to traditional authority, rational-legal authority flows not from family background but from organizational position. Thus, while a queen rules for life, a modern prime minister accepts and relinquishes power according to law; prime ministerial authority is in the office, not in the person.

CHARISMATIC AUTHORITY

Finally, Max Weber claimed power could be transformed into authority through charisma. **Charismatic authority** is *power legitimized through extraordinary personal abilities that inspire devotion and obedience.* Unlike tradition and rational law, then, charisma has less to do with social organization and is more a mark of an especially forceful and magnetic personality.

Throughout history, some members of societies have been regarded as charismatic. Charisma can enhance the stature of an established leader or strengthen the appeal of an outside challenger. Charismatics turn an audience into followers, often making their own rules and challenging the status quo: Vladimir Lenin guided the overthrow of feudal monarchy in Russia in 1917; Mahatma Gandhi inspired the struggle to free India from British colonialism after World War II; Martin Luther King, Jr., galvanized the civil rights movement in the United States; and, through her work ministering to the poor in Calcutta, India, Mother Teresa asked the world to confront stunning poverty.

The prospects of politicians in Canada rise or fall according to their degree of personal charisma. Among our more charismatic prime ministers, John Diefenbaker (1957–63) and Pierre Elliott Trudeau (1968–79, 1980–84) were able to inspire Canadians with oratory and a vision of Canada. The "Trudeaumania" that accompanied Trudeau into his first term of office is a phenomenon that has not been matched since. René Lévesque, Lucien Bouchard, and Jean Charest are among our other charismatic leaders.

Because charismatic authority emanates from a single individual, any charismatic movement faces a crisis of survival upon the loss of its leader. Thus, Weber explained, the persistence of a charismatic movement depends on the **routinization of charisma**, *the transformation of charismatic authority into some combination of traditional and bureaucratic authority.* Christianity, for example, began as a cult driven by the personal charisma of Jesus of Nazareth. After his death, the Roman Catholic church gradually emerged on the twin foundations of tradition and bureaucracy, and it continues to flourish today, two thousand years later.

POLITICS IN GLOBAL PERSPECTIVE

Political systems have taken many forms throughout history. The technologically simple hunting and gathering societies that once were found all over the planet operated like one large family. Leadership generally fell to a male with unusual strength, hunting skill, or personal charisma. But these leaders exercised little power, since they lacked the resources to control their own people, much less extend their rule outward. In the simplest societies, then, leaders were barely discernible from everyone else, and government did not exist as a distinct sphere of life (Lenski, Nolan, and Lenski, 1995).

Larger and more complex agrarian societies are characterized by specialized activity and material surplus. These societies become hierarchical, with a small elite gaining control of most wealth and power; politics moves outside the family to become a social institution in its own right. Leaders who manage to pass along their power over several generations may acquire traditional authority, perhaps even claiming divine right to govern. Such leaders also may benefit from Weber's rational-legal authority since they are served by a bureaucratic political administration and system of law.

As societies expand, politics eventually takes the form of a national government or *political state*. But the emergence of a political state depends on technology. Just a few centuries ago, armies moved slowly and communication over even short distances was uncertain. For this reason, early political empires—such as Mesopotamia in the Middle East about five thousand years ago—took the form of many small *city-states*.

More complex technology helped the modern world develop the larger-scale system of *nation-states*. Currently, the world has 191 independent nation-states, each with a somewhat distinctive political system. Generally speaking, however, the world's political systems can be analyzed in terms of four categories: monarchy, democracy, authoritarianism, and totalitarianism.

MONARCHY

Monarchy (with Latin and Greek roots meaning "one ruler") is *a political system in which a single family rules from generation to generation*. Monarchy is typical in the history of agrarian societies; the Bible, for example, tells of great kings such as David and Solomon. Today's British monarchy—the Windsor family—traces its lineage back roughly a thousand years. In Weber's terms, then, monarchy is legitimized primarily by tradition.

During the medieval era, *absolute monarchy*, in which hereditary rulers claimed a monopoly of power based on divine right, flourished from England to China and in parts of the Americas. Monarchs in some nations, such as Saudi Arabia, still exercise virtually absolute control over their people.

Over the course of this century, monarchs have gradually given way to elected officials. Europe's remaining monarchs—in Great Britain, Spain, Norway, Sweden, Belgium, Denmark, and the Netherlands—now preside over *constitutional monarchies*. They serve as symbolic heads of state while elected politicians led by a prime minister govern according to political principles embodied in a constitution. In these nations, then, the nobility may formally reign, but elected officials actually rule.

DEMOCRACY

The historical trend in the modern world is towards **democracy**, *a political system in which power is exercised by the people as a whole*. The members of democratic societies rarely participate directly in decision making; numbers alone make this an impossibility. Instead, a system of *representative democracy* places authority in the hands of elected leaders who are accountable to the people.

Most rich countries of the world claim to be democratic. Economic development and democratic government go together because both depend on a literate populace. Moreover, the traditional legitimization of power in a monarchy gives way, with industrialization, to rational-legal authority. A rational election process puts leaders in offices regulated by law. Thus, democracy and rational-legal authority are linked, just as monarchy and traditional authority are.

But countries such as Canada are not truly democratic for two reasons. First, there is the problem of bureaucracy. All democratic political systems rely on the work of large numbers of bureaucratic officials. The actual task of public administration in Canada involves close to one million people as federal, provincial, and municipal employees, making government Canada's largest employer. The vast majority of these bureaucrats are never elected by anyone and are not directly accountable to the people (Scaff, 1981; Edwards, 1985; Etzioni-Halevy, 1985).

The second problem involves economic inequality. In a highly stratified society, the rich will have far more political clout than the poor. Moreover, given the even greater resources of large organizations (such as billion-dollar corporations), how can we think our "democratic" system responds to—or even hears—the voices of "average people"?

Democracy and Freedom: Capitalist and Socialist Approaches

Despite the problems we have just described, rich capitalist nations such as Canada claim to operate as democracies. Of course, socialist countries such as Cuba and the People's Republic of China make the same claim. This curious fact suggests we need to look more closely at *political economy*: the interplay of politics and economics.

The political life of Canada, the United States, and the nations of Europe is largely shaped by the economic principles of capitalism. The pursuit of profit within a market system requires that "freedom" be defined in terms of people's rights to act in their own self-interest. Thus, the capitalist approach to political freedom translates into personal liberty—to act in whatever ways maximize profits or other forms of income. From this point of view, moreover, "democracy" means that individuals have the right to select their leaders from those running for office.

However, as we noted earlier, capitalist societies are marked by a striking inequality of wealth. If everyone acts in a self-interested way, in other words, the inevitable result is that some people accumulate far more wealth and power than others. It is this elite, then, that dominates the economic and political life of the society.

Socialist systems, by contrast, claim they are democratic because their economies meet everyone's basic needs for housing, schooling, work, and medical care. But critics of socialism counter that the extensive government regulation of social life in these countries can become oppressive. The socialist governments of China and Cuba, for example, do not allow their people to move freely inside or outside of their borders and do not tolerate organized political opposition.

These contrasting approaches to democracy and freedom raise an important question: are economic equality and political liberty compatible? To foster economic equality, socialism constrains the choices of individuals. Capitalism, on the other hand, provides broad political liberties, which, in practice, mean little to the poor. A look back at Global Map 9–1 on page 238 shows the extent of income inequality in the world's nations. Global Map 16–1 shows one organi-

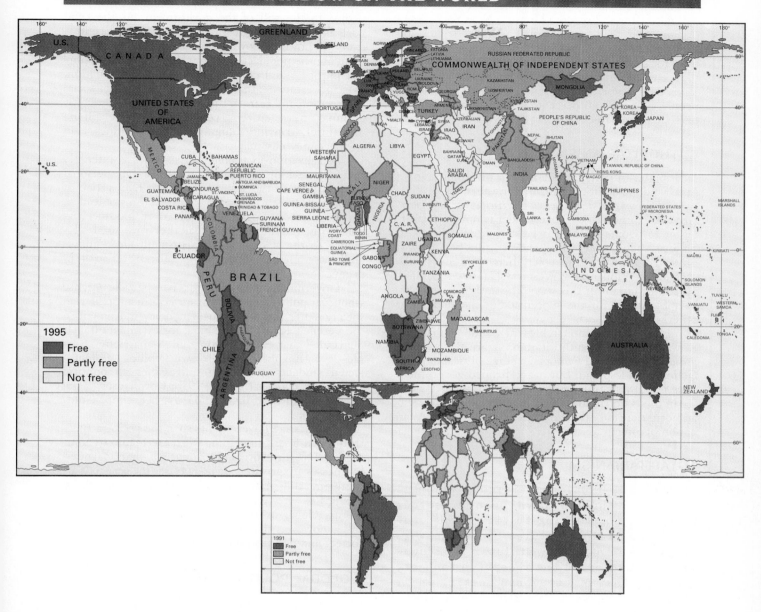

GLOBAL MAP 16–1 Political Freedom in Global Perspective

In 1995, seventy-six of the world's nations, containing 20 percent of all people, were politically "free"—that is, they offered their citizens extensive political rights and civil liberties. Another sixty-one countries that included 40 percent of the world's people were "partly free," with more limited rights and liberties. The remaining fifty-four nations, home to 40 percent of humanity, fall into the category of "not free." In these countries, government sharply restricts individual initiative. Between 1980 and 1991 democracy made significant gains, largely centred in Latin America and Eastern Europe. Since 1991, however, the world has witnessed an erosion of political freedom on all continents.

SOURCE: Freedom House (1995).

zation's assessment of the extent of political freedom around the world.

According to Freedom House, a New York–based organization that tracks global political trends, by 1991 more people in the world were "free" than "not free" for the first time in history. Since then, however, they say the tide has turned against democracy. In 1995, they characterized just 20 percent of the world's people as "free," 40 percent as "partly free," and 40 percent as "not free" (Karatnycky, 1995).

AUTHORITARIANISM

As a matter of policy, some nations give their people little voice in politics. **Authoritarianism** refers to *a political system that denies popular participation in government*. An authoritarian government is not only indifferent to people's needs, it lacks the legal means to remove leaders from office, and provides people with little or no way even to voice their opinions. Polish sociologist Wlodzimierz Wesolowski (1990:435) sums up authoritarianism this way: "the authoritarian philosophy argues for the supremacy of the state [over other] organized social activity."

The absolute monarchies in Saudi Arabia and Kuwait are highly authoritarian, as are the military juntas in Congo and Ethiopia, where political dissatisfaction is widespread. But heavy-handed government does not always breed popular opposition, as we can see in the "Global Sociology" box—a look at the "soft authoritarianism" that thrives in the small Asian nation of Singapore.

TOTALITARIANISM

October 22, 1994, near Saigon, Vietnam. Six U.S. students have been arrested, allegedly for talking to Vietnamese students and taking pictures at the university. The Vietnamese Minister of Education has cancelled the reception tonight, claiming that our students meeting their students threatens Vietnam's security.

The most restrictive political form is **totalitarianism**, *a political system that extensively regulates people's lives*. Totalitarian governments emerged only during this century, with the development of the technological means for rigidly regulating a populace. The Vietnamese government closely monitors the activities of its citizens as well as visitors to the country. Similarly, the government of North Korea uses surveillance equipment and sophisticated computers to store vast amounts of information and thereby manipulate an entire population.

Although some totalitarian governments claim to represent the will of the people, most seek to bend people to the will of the government. As the term itself implies, such governments are *total* concentrations of power, allowing no organized opposition. Denying the populace the right to assemble for political purposes and controlling access to information, these governments thrive in an environment of social atomization and fear. In the former Soviet Union, for example, most citizens could not own telephone directories, copying equipment, fax machines, and even accurate city maps.

Socialization in totalitarian societies is intensely political, seeking not just compliance but personal commitment to the system. In North Korea, one of the world's most totalitarian states, pictures of leaders and political messages broadcast over loudspeakers constantly remind citizens that they owe total allegiance to the state. Government-controlled schools and mass media present only official versions of events.

Government indoctrination is especially intense whenever political opposition surfaces in a totalitarian society. After the 1989 pro-democracy movement in the People's Republic of China, for example, officials demanded that citizens report all "unpatriotic" people—even members of their own families—and subjected students at Beijing universities to political "refresher" courses (Arendt, 1958; Kornhauser, 1959; Friedrich and Brzezinski, 1965; Nisbet, 1966; Goldfarb, 1989).

Totalitarian governments span the political spectrum from fascist (including Nazi Germany) to communist (North Korea). In some totalitarian states, businesses are privately owned (as was the case in Nazi Germany and, more recently, in Chile); in others, businesses are government-owned (as in North Korea, Cuba, or the former Soviet Union). In all cases, however, one party claims total control of the society and permits no opposition.

A GLOBAL POLITICAL SYSTEM?

Chapter 15 ("The Economy and Work") described the emergence of a global economy, by which more and more companies operate with little regard to national boundaries. Is there a parallel development of a global political system?

On one level, the answer is no. Although most of the world's economic activity now involves more than one nation, the planet remains divided into nation-states, just as it has been for centuries. The United Nations (founded in 1945) might seem like a step towards global government, but, to date, its political role has been limited.

"Soft Authoritarianism" or Planned Prosperity?
A Report from Singapore

To many, Singapore, a tiny nation on the tip of the Malay peninsula with a population of just over three million, seems an Asian paradise. Surrounded by poor societies grappling with rapidly increasing populations, squalid, sprawling cities, and rising crime rates, Singapore's affluence, cleanliness, and safety make North American visitors think more of a theme park than a country.

In fact, since its independence from Malaysia in 1965, Singapore has startled the world with its economic development; its per capita income now rivals that of the United States. But, unlike the United States, Singapore has scarcely any social problems such as crime, slums, unemployment, or children living in poverty. In fact, people in Singapore don't even contend with traffic jams, graffiti on subway cars, or litter in the streets.

The key to Singapore's orderly environment is the omnipresence of government, which actively promotes traditional morality and regulates just about everything. The state owns and manages most of the country's housing and has a hand in many businesses. It provides tax incentives for proper family planning and completing additional years of schooling. To keep traffic under control, the government slaps hefty surcharges on cars, pushing the price of a basic sedan up around $40 000.

Singapore has tough anti-crime laws that mandate death by hanging for drug dealing and permit police to detain a person suspected of a crime without charge or trial. The government has outlawed some religious groups (including Jehovah's Witnesses) and bans pornography outright. Even smoking in public brings a heavy fine. To keep the city streets clean, the state forbids smoking in public, bans eating on the subway, imposes stiff fines for littering, and has even outlawed the sale of chewing gum.

In economic terms, Singapore defies familiar categories. Government control of scores of businesses, including television stations, telephone service, airlines, and taxis seems socialist. Yet, unlike most socialist enterprises,

these businesses are operated efficiently and very profitably. Moreover, Singapore's capitalist culture applauds economic growth (although the government cautions people about the evils of excessive materialism), and this nation is home to hundreds of multinational corporations.

Singapore's political climate is as unusual as its economy. Members of this society feel the hand of government far more than their counterparts in Canada. Just as important, one political organization—the People's Action party—has ruled Singapore without opposition since the nation's independence thirty years ago.

Clearly, Singapore is not a democratic country in the conventional sense. But most people in this prospering nation wholeheartedly endorse their way of life. What Singapore's political system offers is a simple bargain: government demands unflinching loyalty from the populace; in return, it provides security and prosperity. Critics charge that this system amounts to a "soft authoritarianism" that stifles dissent and controls people's lives. Most of the people of Singapore, however, know the struggles of living elsewhere and, for now at least, consider the trade-off a good one.

SOURCE: Adapted from Branegan (1993).

On another level, however, politics has become a global process. In the minds of some analysts, multinational corporations represent a new political order, since they have enormous power to shape social life throughout the world. From this point of view, politics is dissolving into business as corporations grow larger than governments. (Critics argue that the proposed Multilateral Agreement on Investment, which would ensure a level playing field for international investment, would enhance the power of business over government.) As one multinational leader declared, "We are not without cunning. We shall not make Britain's mistake. Too wise to govern the world, we shall simply own it" (quoted in Vaughan, 1978:20).

Then, too, the Information Revolution has helped move national politics onto the world stage.

The members of the House of Commons represent the 301 electoral districts distributed across the country according to population. The daily "Question Period" gives members of the opposition parties a chance to grill the prime minister and cabinet ministers in front of the television cameras.

TABLE 16–1 Dates of Entry into Confederation

New Brunswick	July 1, 1867
Nova Scotia	July 1, 1867
Ontario	July 1, 1867
Quebec	July 1, 1867
Manitoba	July 15, 1870
North-West Territory*	July 15, 1870
British Columbia	July 20, 1871
Prince Edward Island	July 1, 1873
Newfoundland	March 31, 1949

*Rupert's Land (including central to northern Ontario and Quebec and the area west to B.C. and north to the Arctic) purchased from the Hudson's Bay Company.

SOURCE: Waite (1988).

Hours before the Chinese government sent troops to Tiananmen Square to crush the 1989 pro-democracy movement, officials "unplugged" the satellite transmitting systems of news agencies to keep the world from watching. Despite their efforts, news of the massacre flashed around the world in minutes via fax machines in universities and private homes.

Finally, several thousand nongovernmental organizations (NGOs) are now in operation, most with global membership and focus. Typically, these organizations seek to advance universal principles, such as human rights (Amnesty International) or an ecologically sustainable world (Greenpeace). In the twenty-first century, NGOs will almost certainly play a key part in forming a global political culture (Boli and Thomas, 1997).

In short, then, just as the economies of individual nations are linked globally, so are their politics. Today, no nation exists strictly within its own borders.

POLITICS IN CANADA

Canada's national existence comes from the other side of the political upheaval that gave birth to the United States. As Seymour Martin Lipset points out, "The United States is the country of the revolution, Canada of the counterrevolution." The Americans sought "a form of rule derived from the people and stressing individualism," while Canadians desired "free institutions within a strong monarchical state" (1991:1). Life, liberty, and the pursuit of happiness are the goals of our neighbours to the south; we chose peace, order, and good government.

Part of the impetus for Confederation was economic, but the leaders in various parts of what was to become Canada were watching nervously over their shoulders, fearing economic and political absorption, if not military conquest, by the increasingly populous and aggressive United States. The various parts of Canada came together somewhat reluctantly: Newfoundlanders initially rejected Confederation in an 1869 election, and the people of Nova Scotia would have done the same had they been asked to vote on the issue. Nowhere did political union occur without vigorous debate and passionate opposition. Table 16–1 reveals that Canada as we know it today was formed in bits and pieces from 1867 to 1949, when Newfoundland was enticed, at last, to vote "Yes" to Confederation in a referendum.

Because the provinces joined Canada at different times and through various kinds of agreements, they have never had uniform relationships with the federal government. Furthermore, Quebec was seen as unique from the beginning because of its French-speaking Catholic majority. Canada is a rather loose confederation in that important powers were left in provincial hands. Questions of federal-provincial jurisdiction—the centralization or decentralization of power—have been with us since 1867 and may never be fully resolved.

Canada's provincial structure, its geographic size and diversity, and its immigration and settlement history have added an important regional dimension to our collective identity and to Canadian politics. The presence of Quebec, the only entity with a French-speaking majority in North America, adds a special dimension to our "Canadian" experience in terms of identity, federal-provincial relations, and unity. Our existence as a "fragile federation" (Marsden and Harvey, 1979), ever mindful of the factors that divide and unite us, is expressed in our seemingly continuous constitutional navel-gazing.

Canadians are represented in Parliament by the Senate (an appointed body with 104 seats apportioned on a regional basis to the Maritimes, Ontario, Quebec, and the West[1]) and the House of Commons (with 301 seats distributed roughly on the basis of population). Quebec and Ontario together elect 59 percent, or 178, of the 301 members of Parliament, so they have a decisive impact on which party wins the most seats, and therefore on who becomes prime minister. In addition, the predominance of MPs from Ontario and Quebec reduces the likelihood that Parliament will pass legislation unfavourable to the interests of central Canada. The unhappiness of the peripheral provinces with the political clout of central Canada at both House of Commons and Senate levels was behind the quest for a *Triple-E senate* that is equal, effective, and elected. Equal representation for all provinces at the Senate level would counter the Quebec-Ontario dominance in the House.

CULTURE, ECONOMICS, AND POLITICS

Unlike Americans, who embrace individualism wholeheartedly, Canadians endorse it with ambivalence. Our individualism is tempered by a sense of communal responsibility, a recognition of legitimate *group* interests, and the realization that we are, in the words of former prime minister Joe Clark, a "community of communities." When the Trudeau government gave us our *Charter of Rights and Freedoms* in 1982, analysts pointed out that we had moved closer to embracing the individualism of the United States:

> The Canadian *Charter of Rights and Freedoms* is not the American *Bill of Rights*. It preserves the principle of parliamentary supremacy and places less emphasis on individual, as distinct from group, rights than does the American document. But the Charter brings Canada much closer to the American stress on protection of the individual and acceptance of judicial supremacy with its accompanying encouragement to litigiousness than is true of other parliamentary countries (Lipset, 1991:3).

In accordance with our emphasis on the collectivity, Canadians endorse a broadly interventionist government. Although in recent years Canadians have been increasingly worried about the costs of government activity, they nonetheless expect government to deal with national defence, law and order, international relations, radio and television broadcasting, sta-

[1] There are twenty-four seats in the Senate for each of the regions named, plus six for Newfoundland and one each for the Yukon and Northwest Territories.

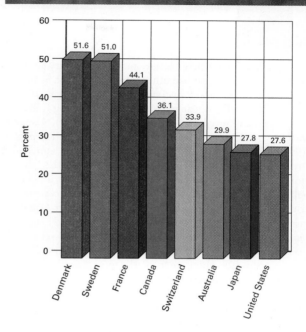

FIGURE 16–1 The Size of Government: Tax Revenues as Share of Gross Domestic Product, 1994

SOURCE: U.S. Bureau of the Census (1997).

bilization of the economy, regional development, pensions, employment insurance, welfare, transportation, education (right up through university), and medical care. In fact, to the extent that we can articulate a "Canadian" identity, it is based on some of the government services that make us a tolerant and caring society. The widespread anxiety about free trade with the United States arose partly from the fear of job loss, but also from the fear that resulting pressures to harmonize with our powerful neighbour to the south would threaten our social welfare programs and particularly our medicare system.

Government in Canada is more involved in the daily lives of its citizens than in the U.S., but this does not mean that Canadians are in complete agreement regarding the appropriateness of that involvement. Some people feel that governments should take an even *more* activist role in areas such as child care, job creation, minority rights, employment or pay equity, and environmental protection. Others feel that government already does far too much, at too great expense, and that it should be withdrawing many of its programs and encouraging privatization of services where feasible. These differences in perspective are in part a function of socioeconomic status and regional

Native Self-Government

Canada's native peoples have never been treated just like other Canadians—for good historical reasons. The first European explorers and settlers encountered fifty-five *founding nations* or *First Nations* (Dickason, 1992), distinct linguistic and cultural groups spread across the continent and north to the Arctic. The groups were self-governing within traditional territories and had formal relationships between tribes. The Iroquois, or Six Nations Confederacy,* had an elaborate constitution and federal structure. Fifty hereditary peace chiefs met yearly to deal with common problems and make new laws. "The laws and decisions of the Confederacy were passed on by word of mouth and recorded in wampum, arguably the world's oldest constitution, predating the American Constitution by 200 years" (Nader, Milleron, and Conacher, 1992). Some aspects of this constitution were incorporated into the federal structures of both the United States and Canada.

The First Nations taught the explorers and early settlers to survive on this harsh continent, introducing them to corn, squash, beans, potatoes, and tobacco. The fur trade would have been impossible without native expertise, labour, and the canoe, the design of which has not been improved (Nader et al., 1992). If most of the Six Nations, with their widespread reputation for

military prowess, had not sided with the British against the French in the 1750s and with the British and the Loyalists during the American Revolution (1777), Canada might now be either French or part of the U.S. As the Americans launched their attack on Canada in 1812, the British concluded that "Amerindian support was vital to the preservation of Britain's remaining North American colonies" (Dickason, 1992:217).

As settlers flowed into Canada, the old fur trade partners and military allies found themselves in conflict as pressures built up over land. To avoid the kind of native resistance to settlement that had occurred in the United States, a number of treaties were negotiated with some groups, dating from the pre-

Confederation period in the Maritimes through to 1921 in the Northwest Territories. The descendants of the natives who signed treaties are now called *treaty* or *status Indians*.

The terms of the treaties varied over time and across the country (Frideres, 1993), but most commonly they involved the surrender of lands in exchange for reserves and other guarantees. The interpretation of the treaties has been the subject of considerable debate for, in some cases, the actual wording of the treaties did not coincide with the understandings native people had about their contents. More importantly, in light of the current quest for self-government, there is debate about whether the existence of treaties implied recognition of native sovereignty. There are indications that sovereignty was recognized, and many native peoples believe that they were sovereign prior to the treaties and that the treaties did not extinguish that sovereignty.

Section 35 of Canada's Constitution (patriated in 1982) recognized and affirmed the existing aboriginal and treaty rights of aboriginal peoples, including Indian, Inuit, and Métis. Five years later, when the Meech Lake accord was negotiated in an effort to have Quebec sign on to the Constitution, native people's request for recognition of their right to self-government was ignored altogether. A technicality in

---

subculture, and are reflected in the policies and platforms of Canada's political parties.

The cost of government involvement in the lives of citizens is reflected in the level of taxation. Figure 16–1 shows that Canada falls between some European countries and the United States in terms of tax revenues.

POLITICAL PARTIES

Since about the time of Confederation, Canadians have joined to form **political parties**, *organizations*

operating within the political system that seek control of the government. Although we take political parties for granted today as part of a democracy, the party system had tentative beginnings here (and was hotly debated in the United States, where George Washington and Benjamin Franklin, among others, feared that parties would tear their fledgling nation apart).

The political parties that we know today trace their roots to the period after 1840, when the United Provinces of Upper and Lower Canada came into being. In fact, a "Liberal-Conservative" coalition of

Manitoba allowed a native member of the Legislative Assembly, Elijah Harper, the historic opportunity to scuttle "Meech" just before its ratification deadline in 1990.

Representatives of four native organizations participated in the next round of constitutional negotiation, with the result that the Charlottetown accord of August 1992 recognized the *inherent*** right to self-government of native people: "The Aboriginal peoples of Canada, being the first peoples to govern this land, have the right to promote their languages, cultures and traditions and to ensure the integrity of their societies, and their governments constitute one of three orders of government in Canada." The defeat of this accord in the referendum of October 26, 1992, was a bitter disappointment to the native negotiators. The likelihood is small that a combination of historic conditions, political personalities, and public mood will generate a similar compromise in the foreseeable future.

In the meantime, a number of native communities have proceeded to manage their own affairs, and the Royal Commission on Aboriginal Peoples (1997) declares that the right of aboriginal peoples to govern themselves predates Confederation, has a basis in Canadian law, and is already protected in our Constitution. A number of formal self-government agreements have already been negotiated between various native groups, the federal govern-

ment, and their respective provinces. For example, in the province of Manitoba, the functions of the Department of Indian Affairs and Northern Development will be taken over and carried out by First Nations organizations.

In a dramatic development, the Northwest Territories decided in a 1992 plebiscite to carve a new territory out of its eastern region. Although it is not self-government as the Assembly of First Nations would define it,*** Nunavut, with one-fifth of Canada's land mass and a population that is 80 percent Inuit, will become a distinct entity with its own territorial government in 1999. The development of Nunavut will be enhanced by the existence of the Inuit Broadcasting Corporation (IBC), numerous successful cooperatives, and experienced Inuit businesspeople, but the Inuit people will still face formidable challenges as they assume the tasks of territorial government.

In a report on self-determination, the Grand Council of the Crees (1995) concluded that Quebec has no right to secede from Canada nor to forcibly include the Crees and their territories in a sovereign Quebec. When Quebec held its sovereignty referendum in October 1995, the Crees conducted their *own* referendum in which they almost unanimously chose *not* to be part of an independent Quebec. A Grand Council report based on extensive research into international and Canadian law and precedent, combined with the Crees'

referendum, signal that others cannot continue to make decisions for the Crees.

In September 1997, Canada's premiers issued the "Calgary declaration," which recognized Quebec's unique characteristics and referred to native people and other ethnic minorities as "Canada's gift of diversity." Aboriginal leaders found this wording offensive and objected to being excluded from the Calgary talks. In November 1997, the premiers accepted a companion document, to be considered in constitutional deliberations, saying that natives constitute a distinct society and a separate order of government within Canada (Anderssen and Roberts, 1997).

---

*Known as the League of Five Nations (Mohawk, Cayuga, Onondaga, Oneida, and Seneca) until they were joined by the Tuscarora in 1722.

**This terminology is important because it implies that the right to self-government is neither granted by the Canadian government nor subject to repeal. Instead, the right is based on aboriginal status and granted by their Creator.

***The territorial government of Nunavut will be a *public* government serving all of its residents, Inuit and non-Inuit alike. An *ethnic* government, applying to the Inuit peoples (nations) alone, would be more in keeping with the principle of aboriginal self-determination.

---

factions under Sir George-Étienne Cartier and Sir John A. Macdonald provided sufficient political stability to allow for the negotiation of Confederation. The first House of Commons had, among others, "Tory" (Conservative) and "Grit" (Liberal) factions that, by 1867, were beginning to align themselves with specific sets of policies and supporters. The Tories were "firmly protectionist, expansionist, and pro-business," while the Grits were "anti-railroad, anti-protectionist, and pro-agrarian" (Van Loon and Whittington, 1981:326–27).

After World War I, a number of minor parties appeared on the scene, the most long-lived of which was the anti-capitalist Co-operative Commonwealth Federation (CCF), which became the New Democratic Party (NDP) after 1961.

In recent decades, about twenty different parties have registered at the federal level alone—some of them surviving only long enough to contest one election. Although each of these parties has fielded candidates in ridings across the country, only the Progressive Conservative, Liberal, New Democratic and

Some Canadian voters vote for particular candidates, but many remain loyal to the same political party from election to election. Party affiliation is often shown through signs on lawns and in windows, and a gathering of signs such as this one is a familiar sight during election campaigns. What affect do these signs have, if any, on the outcome of elections?

Social Credit parties have elected MPs over extended periods of time.

Functions of Political Parties

Political parties in Canada and elsewhere have the following key societal functions:

1. **Promoting political pluralism.** Political parties create centres of power independent of the government. This is why totalitarian governments routinely quash all political parties, save their own.

2. **Increasing political involvement.** Parties draw people into the political process by articulating various points of view about controversial issues. They function as reference groups that help people shape their individual opinions. Political campaigns encourage public debate, helping to make government more responsive to the people.

3. **Selection of political candidates.** Political parties nominate candidates to run for office. Through nomination meetings in each constituency, local party members choose the candidates who will run for office in the next election.[2] Whenever the national or provincial parties are selecting new leaders, the riding associations elect the delegates who go to the leadership conventions.[3]

4. **Forging political coalitions.** While parties can divide a society, they often forge broad coalitions among people interested in various specific issues. Party platforms usually incorporate a wide range of proposals so that the party will appeal to many people, making victory at the polls more likely. Many nations have dozens of narrowly based political parties. Canada has had two dominant federal parties fairly consistently (since Confederation) until the 1993 election introduced two new challengers that almost wiped out the Conservatives.

5. **Maintaining political stability.** By maintaining relatively consistent positions on a number of issues, the major parties promote political stability. For that reason, of course, those who seek radical change in Canada may lambast political parties in general.

Political Ideology

People commonly label their political views in terms of the political spectrum, a continuum ranging from communism on the left to extreme conservatism on the right. Many Canadians conclude that there are no ideological differences among our major political parties (at least not between the Liberals and Conservatives). William Christian (1983) disagrees, noting that there are some very clear and consistent ideological strains that have characterized our parties over time. Our parties and their ideological orientations are the result of our unique political history and European roots, as evidenced by the fact that they are very different from those in the United States. Furthermore, the ideological *mix* in our parties makes it difficult to accurately place them on a left-right continuum. For example, there are "Red"

---

[2] In the 1993 pre-election period, the Liberal party ruffled more than a few feathers by promoting and even appointing certain hand-picked candidates. In some cases, "stars" from outside the ridings were "parachuted" in despite bitter local protest. One of the goals of the Liberal party at that time was to have 25 percent female candidates. The Liberal government of Jean Chrétien was 21 percent female as of 1997.

[3] Another approach is to have members-at-large, throughout a province for example, vote for a new leader directly, rather than indirectly by electing delegates to a convention. The Alberta Conservatives used this approach in 1993 to elect Ralph Klein as their leader.

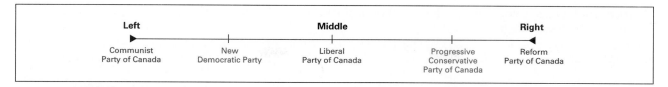

FIGURE 16–2 Selected Canadian Political Parties on a Left-Right Continuum

and "Pink" Tories in the Progressive Conservative party.

The political left in Canada can be described as anti-capitalist (or anti–big business), egalitarian, collectivist, and interventionist. It is supportive of a broad safety net of social welfare programs, including universal child care, education, and medicare. Government or public ownership and regulation of major industries, unionization, inheritance taxes, and progressive taxation (taxation rates that increase with income) are also part of its policy wish list. Free trade with the United States, or with the United States and Mexico, is opposed by the left because of its potential negative effects on employment (especially in manufacturing) and social programs.

As one might expect, those on the political right espouse a different set of values and goals. They are in favour of private enterprise, big business, and free markets. Although they might be elitist and individualistic in some respects, they also have collectivist sentiments. Competitiveness, globalization, restructuring, deficit reduction, and privatization of Crown corporations are laudable goals in the eyes of the right, as are private property rights, tax exemptions for capital gains, and free trade. Those on the right generally feel that, while government expenditures on social programs are necessary, they should be restricted by our ability to pay for them.

Parties on the Political Spectrum

As noted above, placing Canadian parties on a left-right continuum should be done with some hesitation, since each party is a mixed bag and there is always some movement in party positions. Our major parties have moved a little to the right in the past few years, in response to developments in the United States and widespread anxieties about government deficits and debt. Nevertheless, Figure 16–2 suggests the approximate location of some of our national parties on this scale.

It is difficult to place some of our other parties on the left-right axis in Figure 16–2. The Bloc Québécois has as its central aims disruption of the House of Commons and the political independence of Quebec, environmental or ecological issues are the *raison d'être*

of the Green party, and the Rhinoceros party[4] engages in generalized protest and fun.

Party Support

Although some Canadians support one particular political party throughout their lives, and may even come from families that have supported the same party for generations, most of us are considerably more fickle. As a result of changes in party platforms, leaders, dominant issues, or the general economic and political climate, as well as individual social or geographic mobility, there are people who have voted for three or more parties at some point in their lives. It is also common for Canadians to vote for different parties at the federal and provincial levels, even when the elections are only weeks or months apart. Many observers of the Quebec political scene argue that the Québécois hedge their bets by voting for a separatist party (Parti Québécois) at the provincial level and the Liberals or Conservatives federally, or the Bloc Québécois federally and the Liberals provincially. As strange as it might seem to an outside observer, this kind of split voting can be the result of cool calculation rather than confusion on the part of the voter.

Recently there have been dramatic changes in political alignment in this country, as Figure 16–3 reveals. In 1993, we turned away from the three parties with long-term representation across the country to embrace a mix with strong regional bases. In 1997, we confirmed the regionally based pattern of support.

As the figure shows, the 1993 election saw the near-collapse of the Conservatives and NDP, coupled with the sudden appearance of the Bloc Québécois and the Reform party. The 1997 results, with minor

---

[4] The Rhinoceros party was founded in 1963 with the express purpose of making fun of politicians and the political process. With their outrageous clothes and even more outrageously humorous election platforms, Rhinoceros party candidates provide an outlet to protest the political process without simply spoiling ballots; at the same time, they add to the entertainment value of Canadian politics for the rest of us. In the 1984 election, 89 Rhino candidates across the country won 99 207 votes, or an astounding 0.8 percent of the national vote. The largest chunk of this support came from a few ridings in the centre of Montreal.

FIGURE 16–3 Support for Canada's Federal Political Parties, 1988, 1993, and 1997 (percentage of votes)

SOURCE: Calculated by Gerber from the *Report of the Chief Electoral Officer*, 1988, 1993, 1997, (1997, www.elections.ca).

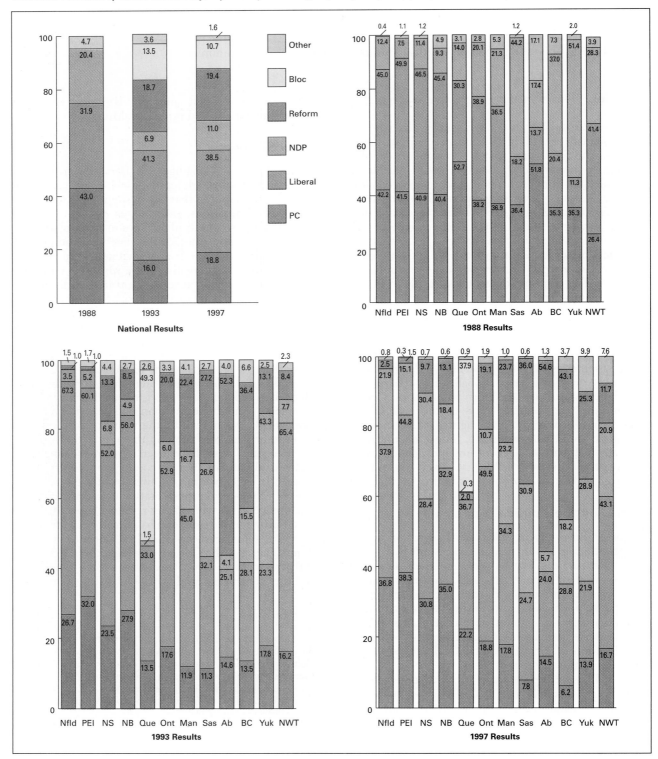

changes, suggest that Reform and the Bloc have staying power.

The federal election of 1988 revealed varying levels of support across the country for the Progressive Conservatives, Liberals, and New Democrats. People in Saskatchewan, British Columbia, and the Yukon were most likely to vote for the NDP, while the Liberals fared well in the Maritimes. Conservative support in Alberta was traditional, while that in Quebec was based on the policies and personal appeal of Prime Minister Mulroney.

The 1993 election results present a very different picture. Half of the vote in Quebec went to Lucien Bouchard's new party, the Bloc Québécois, at the expense of the Conservatives and, to a lesser extent, the NDP. Reform, with roots in Alberta, was most successful there, but also made substantial inroads into B.C., Saskatchewan, Manitoba, and even Ontario. The fact that the Bloc won 54 seats in Quebec, while 46 of Reform's 52 seats came from B.C. and Alberta, accentuated the regional aspect of this pivotal election.

Despite minor changes, including some revival in the fortunes of the Conservatives and the NDP—the latter most surprisingly in Nova Scotia—the overall pattern of the 1997 election results is very similar to that of 1993. Regionalism, once again, was reflected in the voting booth.

One of the peculiarities of our political system is that there is almost always a discrepancy between the level of popular support for each party and the number of seats the party wins. One of the more interesting examples occurred in the 1993 election, when the Reform and PC parties had similar levels of support measured nationally, but the Reform party won 52 seats while the PCs took only two. The key to this discrepancy is the existence of 301 separate races at the constituency or riding level. PC support was spread relatively evenly across the country, while Reform support was more concentrated regionally and *by riding*, leading to the high number of wins in local races. Figure 16–4 shows the distribution of the popular vote and seats by party for the 1997 election. Though discrepancies are clearly apparent, they are not as marked as they were in the 1993 election.

POLITICS AND THE INDIVIDUAL

The Canadian political system, being democratic, responds in principle to the needs and judgments of the electorate. But how do people acquire political attitudes in the first place? And to what extent do we use our right to participate in the political system?

Political Socialization

Pierre Trudeau and Brian Mulroney are among the prime ministers of Canada who raised young children

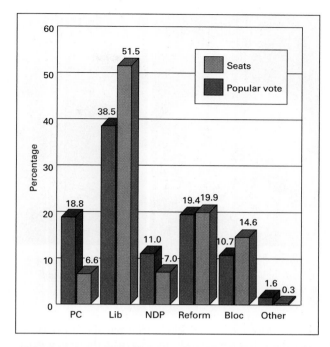

FIGURE 16–4 Distribution of Popular Vote and Seats in the House of Commons by Political Party, 1997 (percentages)

SOURCE: Calculations by Linda Gerber based on Report of the Chief Electoral Officer and www.elections.ca.

at 24 Sussex Drive and Harrington Lake, the prime minister's official summer residence. Although both of these parents probably shielded their offspring from many aspects of political life, their children undoubtedly learned the basic tenets of liberalism and conservatism from their fathers. These families are unusual in that they are intensely involved in politics; as a result of more intimate exposure, one would expect their children to be very much aware of politics and, at a tender age, to have clear party affiliations.

Political attitudes, like other elements of culture, are acquired through the socialization process. The major agents of socialization, which also shape our political views, are the family, the schools, and the mass media (see Chapter 5, "Socialization"). Of these, the family is in a position to exert the earliest influence.

The family is a powerful agent of socialization; not surprisingly, then, children typically come to share many opinions held by their parents. Because neighbourhoods and schools tend to be relatively homogeneous in socioeconomic terms, a child's initial peer groups are likely to reinforce ideas about the world learned at home. In Canada, a large minority of children express a partisan preference by grade 4, and by grade 8 a majority do so (Van Loon and Whittington, 1981:122).

About 75 percent of eligible voters actually vote in Canadian federal elections. Will increasing cynicism about politics and politicians reduce this number?

Children are more likely to learn about politics if their families are actively involved, if there is a great deal of political talk in the household, and if their families are of higher socioeconomic status. Also, male children absorb political information and identify political symbols at an earlier age than their female counterparts.

As described in Chapter 19 ("Education"), schools teach the culture's dominant political values, one of them being respect for authority. Our schoolchildren also learn to recognize political symbols, such as the flag, the prime minister, and the queen, and like children elsewhere, start off with positive feelings about these political icons. Interestingly, in grades 4 and 5, over 70 percent of children chose the queen as their favourite political figure (over the prime minister or governor general) and not until grade 8 do a majority (53 percent) realize that the prime minister is more powerful than the queen, whose role is entirely ceremonial (Van Loon and Whittington, 1981:121). Very few schools offer anything like the formal civics classes found in American schools. Our political socialization appears to be both more subtle and more informal than that in the U.S.

The mass media, too, convey values and opinions pertaining to politics. Conservatives sometimes charge the Canadian media with having a left-wing agenda, while critics on the left complain that what is packaged as "news" really amounts to support for the status quo. Specific newspapers are frequently identified as having Liberal or Conservative sympathies, and some of the francophone media in Quebec have been labelled as separatist.

Although it is not clear that the media convert their readers at a basic philosophical level, there is little doubt that the media are active players in the day-to-day conduct of politics and that their involvement has changed the way that politics is "done." Good "sound bites" and catchy phrases are gold to the politician, especially when uttered in time for the evening news. Advertising consumes a major part of election campaign budgets, and image takes precedence over substance.

The image projected on nightly television can help to make or break a political career, as our former short-term prime ministers Joe Clark, John Turner, and Kim Campbell learned. Televised debates between the leaders of political parties are almost mandatory in today's political climate, and can have a significant impact on the voters' impressions of the party leaders (Widdis Barr, 1991).

As we saw in Chapter 2 ("Sociological Investigation"), opinion polls are particularly worrisome to some observers of the political scene. Do polls reflect or shape public opinion? If Conservative fortunes seem to be rising, does the appearance of increasing support, in turn, pull more people onto the PC party wagon? Since the polls measure change as it is happening, it is very difficult to determine cause and effect.

Other agents of political socialization are the many organizations to which people belong. Some of these are professional, ethnic, or voluntary associations, unions, or special-interest organizations such as women's groups. From time to time, some churches attempt to mobilize their members behind a particular cause, such as fighting abortion or arranging for the sponsorship of refugees. Seniors clubs might form initially to encourage social interaction among elders, but find themselves marching on Ottawa to protest the de-indexing of pensions. Political parties themselves would normally recruit people already inclined to be political activists, but, having done so, they may increase participation levels, political knowledge and sophistication, and partisanship. Some of these organizations are founded for political purposes; others with a wide range of nonpolitical goals become political only as a result of specific circumstances.

Political Participation

Needless to say, socialization does not increase *everyone's* political involvement or enthusiasm for our system of government; on the contrary, significant segments of our population learn that the political system responds little, if at all, to their needs. Indifference or even hostility towards the political system is evident among those who are disadvantaged and feel powerless to remedy the situation. In other cases, those who become committed and actively involved in political action may turn away disillusioned when they see how the political system actually works. In fact, as the Spicer Commission reported in 1991, Canadians have become increasingly cynical about politicians and the political process in general. According to some observers, this is part of a general change in attitude involving Canadians in a move from deference to numerous elites to active defiance (Newman, 1995).

Lester Milbrath (1965) proposed a typology reflecting a *hierarchy of participation* in electoral politics. He classified individual participation as falling into *gladiatorial*, *transitional*, and *spectator* roles. At the gladiatorial level, participants are actually involved in the political fray, as in attending strategy meetings or running for political office. In a transitional role, one might contact a politician, contribute time to a campaign, or give money to a political party. As a spectator, one might express interest in politics, expose oneself to political information, and vote (and then sit back to watch the returns on television).

According to a 1974 survey, at most 5 percent of Canadians are involved at the gladiatorial level. Another 40 percent participate at the transitional level, most commonly attending a rally or an "all-candidates" meeting and trying to influence the votes of friends or co-workers. Only 5 percent said that they had *never* voted in a federal election, while 80 to 90 percent engage in informal discussion about elections with friends and follow the campaign to some extent through the media. Although people are a little less inclined to vote in provincial than federal elections, other types of participation seem to be similar at both levels of government (Van Loon and Whittington, 1981).

In any specific federal election about 75 percent or more of the eligible voters come out to the polls (compared to roughly 50 to 55 percent in the U.S.), though turnout in 1993 was a relatively low 70 percent. Turnout for provincial elections is generally a little lower and in municipal elections is lower still. To the extent that elections constitute spectator sport, turnout improves if it is a good race.

Canadians participated at every stage of the constitutional negotiations leading to the defeat of the Charlottetown accord in 1992. After the defeat of the Meech Lake accord, public demands for wider involvement in constitutional discussions led to the creation in November 1990 of the Spicer Commission, which conducted town-halls and home meetings and offered a toll-free phone line. In the end more than 400 000 Canadians participated in the sometimes painful, intensely introspective debate about our constitution.

Nellie McClung (left), Manitoba-born teacher, author, and activist was welcomed in many settings as an effective and humorous speaker. She fought for women's suffrage, prohibition, factory safety, and many other reforms. She was one of the chief activists in the "Persons Case," which involved a court battle to have women legally recognized as persons. Because of her efforts and those of her colleagues, women were given the right to vote, to sit in the House of Commons, and to be appointed to the Senate, in 1918, 1919, and 1929, respectively (Hallet, 1988).

Agnes Macphail (right) was the only woman elected to the House of Commons in 1921, the first federal election in which women could vote. Like her friend, Nellie McClung, Macphail was a teacher. She was involved in the agricultural cooperative movement of Ontario, various feminist causes, and prison investigation and reform. She founded the Elizabeth Fry Society of Canada and was the first woman appointed to Canada's delegation to the United Nations. Macphail was largely responsible for Ontario's first pay equity legislation in 1951 (Black, 1988).

The Participation of Women

As Chapter 12 ("Sex and Gender") discussed, the women's suffrage movement began in Canada in the 1880s, but since it had to function simultaneously at the provincial and federal levels, it was subject to all "the regional conflicts and divisions that characterized other Canadian social movements" (Bashevkin, 1993:4). Despite divisions that were especially damaging to this movement, women in Canada finally acquired the right to vote at the federal level in 1918. Manitoba was the first province to extend the vote to women (1916), while Quebec was the last (1940).

The extension of the vote to women set the scene for a series of political firsts. Agnes Macphail quickly ran for and won federal political office (1921), but she had to deal with numerous obstacles—including people who said "We can't have a woman." It was not until 1957 that Canada had its first female federal cabinet minister, Ellen Fairclough; and it was 1984 before women were given portfolios other than those deemed most "suited" to women, such as health, education, or the status of women. Brian Mulroney broke this pattern at the federal level by appointing Pat Carney to international trade, Barbara McDougall to junior finance, and Kim Campbell to the justice portfolio (Bashevkin, 1993:88). Audrey McLaughlin became the first federal party leader in 1989, and Kim Campbell's leadership win in 1993 automatically made her Canada's first female prime minister. Although, in ideological and practical terms, the NDP has been most persistent in the promotion of women, these firsts involve all three of the major parties.

Despite these highly visible firsts, overall women are underrepresented in politics. Women still tend to be on the support staff of the political party rather than to be candidates. The higher one goes within the party hierarchy, the smaller the representation of women. Most female candidates have run for minor parties or in ridings where a win would be unlikely. As well, the proportion of females running for office and winning is greatest at the municipal level, somewhat lower at the provincial level, and lower still at the federal level.

There has been a steady increase in the number of women elected at the federal level in recent years, from 5 percent winning in the 1980 election, to 10 percent in 1984, 13 percent in 1988, 18 percent in 1993, and 21 percent in 1997. These figures are high compared with the United States, Britain, and France, which have legislatures that are about 6 percent female, but low when compared with Finland, Sweden, Norway, and Denmark, where 32 to 38 percent of their legislatures are female (Bashevkin, 1993:87, 153–54).[5]

Among the barriers to women's participation are socialization, lack of financing or contacts, and the electoral system itself. To the extent that gender stereotypes contribute to resistance on the part of voters and reluctance on the part of potential female candidates, the appearance (even though temporary) of Kim Campbell in the prime minister's office and of Sheila Copps as deputy prime minister may expand horizons—but then Agnes Macphail thought that many women would immediately follow in her footsteps.

THEORETICAL ANALYSIS OF POWER IN SOCIETY

Sociologists and political scientists have long debated basic questions about power in society. How is power distributed? Who makes the decisions? Whose interests does government serve?

---

[5] The NDP government elected in Ontario in 1990 was 27 percent female.

Power is among the most difficult topics of scientific research because decision making is complex and often occurs behind closed doors. Moreover, as Plato recognized more than two thousand years ago, it is difficult to separate a theory of power from the theorist's personal beliefs and interests. Nevertheless, three competing models of power have emerged.

THE PLURALIST MODEL

The **pluralist model** is *an analysis of politics that views power as dispersed among many competing interest groups.* This approach is closely tied to structural-functional theory.

Pluralists claim, first, that politics is an arena of negotiation. There are thousands of interest groups in Canada, most of which seek narrow goals. The Canadian Association of University Teachers (CAUT), for example, involves itself in issues that affect university faculty, leaving to others debates over health policy, the death penalty, or gun control. But even with limited objectives, no organization holds sufficient power to realize all its goals. The political process, then, relies heavily on negotiating alliances and compromises among various interest groups so that policies gain wide support. In short, pluralists see power as widely dispersed throughout society so that all people have a voice in the political system (Dahl, 1961, 1982).

In *The Vertical Mosaic: An Analysis of Social Class and Power in Canada* (1965), John Porter addresses the question of who makes the major decisions (or exercises power) in Canada; on the basis of extensive research, he concludes that there are competing elites at the top of five major organizational clusters: economic, political, bureaucratic, labour, and ideological (that is, church, education, and the media). Of the five, the economic or corporate elite and the bureaucratic elite are the most powerful. While there is competition among these elites because of the opposing interests of their respective institutions, Porter points out that these powerful and wealthy elites are also highly integrated. To keep the system working, they are willing to accommodate each other. As a result, we have what one might call cooperative pluralism.

THE POWER-ELITE MODEL

The **power-elite model** is *an analysis of politics that views power as concentrated among the rich.* This second approach is closely allied with the social-conflict paradigm in sociology.

The term *power elite* is a lasting contribution of C. Wright Mills (1956), who argued that the upper-class holds the bulk of society's wealth, enjoys most of its

Who Decides? The Impact of Modern Communications

Parliamentary democracy in Canada involves political parties, party discipline, equal representation (in theory, at least), local constituencies (where the candidate with the most votes wins), a prime minister, cabinet (chosen by the prime minister), and a senate (appointed by prime ministers, present and past). In the wings, the Prime Minister's Office (PMO) controls physical access as well as the flow of information to the prime minister. The net effect of these interacting components, with imperfections* at each level of representation, is a system in which our prime minister—whom we do not elect directly—has more power in decision making and implementation than the U.S. president.

In times gone by, newspapers and the radio reported on the activities of our elected officials, undoubtedly affecting future electoral outcomes, but the speed with which news led to opinion change at the constituency level and, thereafter, to effective pressure on parliamentarians and their leaders was limited. In part because politicians were "in the know" and we were not, Canadians relied on and deferred to the political elite—expecting informed decisions.

Today there is almost constant communication between elected representatives and their constituents. Television, satellite transmission, the telephone, improved transportation, the Internet, e-mail, almost continuous opinion polling, and the potential for electronic voting ensure that the general public can be more quickly and completely informed about what is going on and that politicians can more quickly take the pulse of the public.

Electronic or televised town-halls do not always turn out as expected. The Reform party made an early attempt to establish its platform through an ultra-democratic process of electronic consultation, potentially with any member. Preston Manning soon learned that consensus is more difficult to achieve over cyberspace than in a crowded convention, where participants are subject to persuasion. Prime Minister Chrétien had a similarly disappointing experience with a televised town-hall—an informal conversation between prime minister and Canadians—when the situation became confrontational. Both of these experiments in communicative democracy were abandoned.

Politicians are very sensitive to public opinion and wary of offending potential voters. They are still subject to all of the traditional influences and constraints, but their responses to these must be tempered by their new instant and intimate relationship with the public. We know about Oka, the Manitoba flood, the ice storm disaster, or helicopter purchases *as events unfold*: we watch our political leaders and judge them—instantly and continuously.

Some people applaud this spirit of active citizen participation. After all, in a democratic system government *should* be aware of and responsive to public opinion, even as it changes between elections. Active participation through discussions, public meetings, electronic town-hall meetings, radio and TV talk shows, letters to the editor, referendums, and public opinion polls serves to keep politicians on their toes. Certainly, they counter the influence of big business, lobbyists, senior bureaucrats, and others.

On the other hand, governments are elected by much larger numbers of people on the basis of campaign promises. In that light, should less representative "activists" influence our politicians on an ongoing basis? Should the events of the day and shifting public moods divert government action? Some would argue that this kind of give and take between politicians and the general public—which clearly affects decision making—enhances the democratic process. Others argue that the effects, which are increasingly real and immediate, are actually ones of distortion.

---

*One complaint about our electoral system—usually voiced by political parties when they lose elections despite substantial support in the popular vote—is that it is possible to win a seat with 35 percent of the vote, while another party loses with 34.9 percent. Repeated across the country, this pattern can result in two parties with almost identical levels of popular support having vastly different numbers of seats in the legislature—as did the PCs and Reform in the 1993 election. Losing parties are bound to question the fairness of democratic representation in Canada.

---

prestige, and exercises the lion's share of power. Mills claimed that the power elite stands atop each of the three major sectors of society—the economy, the government, and the military. Thus, the power elite is made up of the "super-rich" (executives and large stockholders of major corporations), top officials in government, and the highest ranking officers in the military.

Further, Mills explained, these elites move from one sector to another, consolidating their power as they go. For example, Brian Mulroney was a labour lawyer and then vice-president of Iron Ore Company of Canada before becoming prime minister. Since he left political office, he has returned to Montreal to practise corporate law. It is not unusual for national political leaders to enter public life from powerful and

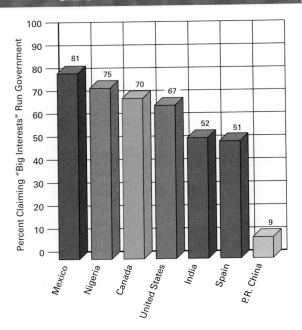

FIGURE 16–5 Who Runs the Government?

Survey Question: "Generally speaking, would you say this country is run by a few big interests looking out for themselves, or it is run for the benefit of all the people?"
SOURCE: World Values Survey (1990).

highly paid positions in business—and most return to the corporate world later on.

Wallace Clement (1975) argues that Canada is ruled by an economic or corporate elite that is becoming increasingly powerful. The members of this group are very likely to have upper-class origins and to have a vested interest in maintaining the capitalist system. As a result of the dense networks that bind the economic, political, and bureaucratic elites, they are blending into one group dominated by the corporate elite. Clement rejects the pluralist model, noting that the state and private capital are complementary and mutually dependent. In effect, the state and the capitalists act as one.

Power-elite theorists challenge the claim that Canada is a political democracy. They maintain that the concentration of wealth and power is simply too great for the average person's voice to be heard. They reject the pluralist idea that various centres of power serve as checks and balances on one another. Instead, the power-elite model maintains that those at the top encounter no real opposition. Figure 16–5 shows that a majority of Canadians favour the power-elite theory.

On the other hand, even the most powerful members of our society do not always get their way. As long as ordinary people continue to form political associations or express themselves in the context of various interest groups, our society will retain a substantial degree of pluralism. There are numerous examples of situations where Québécois, natives, environmentalists, labour unions, or feminists have won concessions and inspired policy changes that are anathema to big business. The Charlottetown accord was defeated in the 1992 referendum despite support by major political parties, big business, and the media: grassroots opposition and the Reform party spearheaded the "no" forces and staged an upset victory.

THE MARXIST MODEL: BIAS IN THE SYSTEM ITSELF

A third approach to understanding politics is the **Marxist political-economy model**, *an analysis that explains politics in terms of the operation of a society's economic system.* While the power-elite model focuses on the disproportionate wealth and power of certain individuals, the Marxist model highlights bias rooted within this nation's institutions, especially its economy. As noted in Chapter 4 ("Society"), Karl Marx claimed that a society's economic system (capitalist or socialist) goes a long way towards shaping how the political system operates. Power elites, therefore, do not simply appear on the scene; they are creations of capitalism itself.

From this point of view, reforming the political system—say, by limiting the amount of money that rich people can contribute to candidates—is unlikely to promote true democracy. The problem does not lie in the *people* who exercise great power or the *people* who don't vote, the problem is rooted in the *system* itself, what Marxists term the "political-economy of capitalism." In other words, within a predominantly capitalist economy, the majority of people will be shut out of politics just as surely as they are exploited in the workplace.

Critical evaluation. Which of the three different models of our political system is correct? Over the years, research has provided support for each model, suggesting that a case can be made for all three. In the end, how one views this country's political system, and how one thinks it ought to operate, turn out to be as much a matter of political values as scientific fact.

Table 16–2 summarizes the three political models. In the end, then, what are we to make of the Canadian political system? At one level, it affords almost everyone the right to participate in the political process through elections. This is an important opportunity, one that is not enjoyed by a majority of

TABLE 16–2 Three Models of Canadian Politics: A Summary

	Pluralist Model	Power-Elite Model	Marxist Model
How is power distributed in Canadian society?	Highly dispersed	Concentrated	Concentrated
Is Canada basically democratic?	Yes, because voting offers everyone a voice, and no one group or organization dominates society	No, because a small share of the people dominate the economy, government, and military	No, because the bias of the capitalist system is to concentrate both wealth and power
How should we understand voter apathy?	Apathy is indifference; after all, even poor people can organize for a greater voice if they wish	Apathy is understandable, given how difficult it is for ordinary people to oppose the rich and powerful	Apathy is alienation generated by a system that leaves most people powerless

the world's people. At the same time, however, the power-elite and Marxist models point out that, at the very least, the Canadian political system is far less democratic than most people think it is.

POWER BEYOND THE RULES

Politics always involves disagreement over a society's goals and the means to achieve them. Political systems, therefore, try to resolve controversy within a system of rules. But political activity sometimes exceeds—or tries to do away with—established practices.

REVOLUTION

Political revolution is *the overthrow of one political system in order to establish another.* In contrast to reform, which involves change *within* a system, revolution involves change *of the system itself.* Thus, even one leader deposing another—called a *coup d'état* (in French, literally, "stroke concerning the state")—falls short of revolution since it involves only a change at the top. And while reform rarely escalates into violence, revolution often does. The revolutions in Eastern Europe beginning in 1989 were surprisingly peaceful, with the exception of Romania, where violence claimed thousands of lives.

Closer to home, one sees revolutionary potential in Quebec's quest for greater autonomy. In the referendum on October 30, 1995, 49.4 percent of the people of Quebec voted "Yes" to Quebec becoming sovereign after making a formal offer of partnership with Canada. Had a few more people voted "Yes," they would have set in motion a process that would dismantle Canada as presently constituted and force the creation of two new and very different political entities, assuming that the rest of Canada survived in one piece.

No type of political system is immune to revolution; nor does revolution invariably produce any one kind of government. The American Revolution ended colonial rule by the British monarchy and produced a democratic government. French revolutionaries in 1789 also overthrew a monarch, only to set the stage for the return of monarchy in the person of Napoleon. In 1917, the Russian Revolution replaced the czarist monarchy with a socialist government built on the ideas of Karl Marx. In 1992, the Soviet Union was reborn as the Russian Federation, moving towards a market system and a greater political voice for its people.

Despite their striking variety, analysts claim, revolutions share a number of traits (Tocqueville, 1955, orig. 1856; also Davies, 1962; Brinton, 1965; Skocpol, 1979; Lewis, 1984; Tilly, 1986).

1. **Rising expectations.** Common sense suggests that revolution would be more likely when people are grossly deprived, but history shows that most revolutions occur when people's lives are improving. Rising expectations, rather than bitter resignation, fuel revolutionary fervour.

2. **Unresponsive government.** Revolutionary zeal gains strength if a government is unable or unwilling to reform, especially when demands for change are made by large numbers of people or powerful segments of society.

3. **Radical leadership by intellectuals.** The English philosopher Thomas Hobbes (1588–1679) observed that intellectuals often provide the justification for revolution, and universities frequently are the centre of sweeping political change. During the 1960s, students were at the forefront of much political unrest in North America and Western Europe. Students also played a critical role in China's recent pro-democracy movement and in the Eastern European uprisings.

4. **Establishing a new legitimacy.** Overthrowing a political system is not easy, but more difficult still is ensuring a revolution's long-term success. Some revolutionary movements are unified mostly by hatred of the past regime and fall apart once new

الاسلام
برئ منهم

They do not
belong to Islam

Because of highly publicized acts of violence by Middle Eastern people in recent years, some members of our society tend to link Islam with terrorism. More correctly, however, this religion (like Christianity) seeks harmony and justice. Officials in Egypt have countered a recent wave of terrorism by a few religious extremists by reminding citizens (and outsiders) of their religious responsibility to promote peace.

leaders are installed. Revolutionaries must also guard against counterrevolutionary drives led by the deposed leaders. This explains the speed and ruthlessness with which victorious revolutionaries dispose of previous rulers.

Scientific analysis cannot declare that a revolution is good or bad. The full consequences of such an upheaval depend on one's values and, in any case, become evident only after many years. In the wake of recent revolution, for example, the future of the former Soviet Union remains unsettled.

TERRORISM

Terrorism constitutes *random acts of violence or the threat of such violence employed by an individual or a group*

as a political strategy. Like revolution, terrorism is a political act beyond the rules of established political systems. According to Paul Johnson (1981), terrorism has four distinguishing characteristics.

First, terrorists try to paint violence as a legitimate political tactic, despite the fact that such acts are condemned by virtually every nation. Terrorists also bypass (or are excluded from) established channels of political negotiation. Terrorism is therefore a weak organization's strategy to harm a greater foe. The Front de libération du Québec (FLQ), which may have comprised fewer than thirty people, used terrorism to promote its goal of an independent, socialist Quebec. From 1963 to 1971, it was involved in two hundred or more bombings of increasing seriousness and in 1970 it kidnapped Pierre Laporte (a Quebec cabinet minister) and James Cross (the British trade commissioner) and murdered Laporte. The FLQ clearly caught the attention of the country.

Second, terrorism is employed not just by groups, but also by governments against their own people. *State terrorism* is the use of violence, generally without support of law, by a government or its agents. State terrorism may be lawful in some authoritarian and totalitarian states, which survive by inciting fear and intimidation. Saddam Hussein, for example, shores up his power in Iraq through state terrorism.

Third, democratic systems reject terrorism in principle, but they are especially vulnerable to terrorism because they afford extensive civil liberties to their people and have less extensive police networks. This susceptibility helps to explain the tendency of democratic governments to suspend civil liberties if officials think themselves under attack, as was done in 1970 when, in response to the murder of Pierre Laporte by the FLQ, Pierre Trudeau invoked the *War Measures Act* and arrested more than 450 people, many of whom were suspected of being FLQ members and sympathizers.

Hostage-taking and outright killing provoke popular anger, but responding to such acts is difficult. Before taking action, a government must identify those responsible. However, because most terrorist groups are shadowy organizations with no formal connection to any established state, a reprisal may be all but impossible. Yet, terrorism expert Brian Jenkins warns, the failure to respond "encourages other terrorist groups, who begin to realize that this can be a pretty cheap way to wage war" (quoted in Whitaker, 1985:29). At the same time, a forceful military reaction to terrorism may risk confrontation with other governments.

Fourth, and finally, terrorism is always a matter of definition. Governments claim the right to maintain order, even by force, and may brand opposition groups who use violence as "terrorists." Similarly, political differences may explain why one person's "terrorist" is another's "freedom fighter."

WAR AND PEACE

Perhaps the most critical political issue is **war**, *organized, armed conflict among the people of various societies.* War is as old as humanity, of course, but understanding it now takes on greater urgency. Because we have the technological capacity to destroy ourselves, war poses unprecedented danger to the entire planet. Most scholarly investigation of war aims to promote peace, which is *the absence of war* (but not necessarily the lack of all political conflict).

Many people think of war as an extraordinary occurrence; yet, for almost all of this century, nations somewhere on earth were in violent conflict. Most wars are localized, while others, like the two World Wars, are widespread. Canada's involvement in several of these wars cost Canadian lives: 60 661 Canadians were killed in World War I; 42 042 in World War II; and 312 in the Korean War. In the Vietnam War, some Canadian individuals signed up to fight in the American forces, but Canada's official role involved serving on truce commissions and supplying medical or technical assistance. Since Vietnam, Canada has generally been involved in the world's trouble spots as a peacekeeper.

THE CAUSES OF WAR

The frequency of war in human affairs might imply that there is something natural about armed confrontation. But while many animals are naturally aggressive, research provides no basis for concluding that human beings inevitably wage war under any particular circumstances. Indeed, governments around the world have to use considerable coercion to mobilize their people for war (Lorenz, 1966; Montagu, 1976).

Like all forms of social behaviour, warfare is a product of *society* that varies in purpose and intensity from culture to culture. The Semai of Malaysia, among the most peace-loving of the world's people, rarely resort to violence. By contrast, the Ya̧nomamö, described in Chapter 3 ("Culture"), are quick to wage war with others.

If society holds the key to war or peace, under what circumstances *do* humans go to battle? Quincy Wright (1987) identifies five factors that promote war.

1. **Perceived threats.** Societies mobilize in response to a perceived threat to their people, territory, or culture. The danger of armed conflict between the United States and the former Soviet Union, for example, has decreased as the two nations have become less fearful of each other.

2. **Social problems.** Internal problems that generate widespread frustration may prompt a society's leaders to divert attention by attacking an external "enemy" as a form of scapegoating. Some analysts see the lack of economic development in the People's Republic of China as underlying that nation's hostility towards Vietnam, Tibet, and the former Soviet Union.

3. **Political objectives.** Leaders sometimes use war as a political strategy. Poor nations, such as Vietnam, have fought wars to end foreign domination. For powerful countries such as the United States, a periodic "show of force" (such as the recent deployments of troops in Somalia and Haiti) may enhance global political stature.

4. **Moral objectives.** Rarely do nations claim to fight merely to increase their wealth and power. Leaders infuse military campaigns with moral urgency, rallying people around religious values or secular visions of "freedom." Although few doubted that the 1991 Persian Gulf War was largely about *oil*, U.S. strategists portrayed the mission as a drive to halt a Hitler-like Saddam Hussein.

5. **The absence of alternatives.** A fifth factor promoting war is the absence of alternatives. Although the United Nations has the job of maintaining international peace, the UN has had limited success in resolving tensions among self-interested societies.

In short, war is rooted in social dynamics on both national and international levels. Moreover, even combat has rules, and breaking them can lead to charges of war crimes.

THE COSTS AND CAUSES OF MILITARISM

The cost of armed conflicts extends far beyond battlefield casualties. Together, the world's nations spend some $5 trillion annually (almost $1000 for every person on the planet) for military purposes. Such expenditures, of course, divert resources from the desperate struggle for survival by hundreds of millions of poor people. If the world's nations could muster the will and the political wisdom to redirect their military spending, they could greatly reduce global poverty.

In recent years, defence has been the U.S. government's largest single expenditure, accounting for 19 percent of all federal spending, or $267 billion in 1997. This huge sum is the result of the *arms race*, a mutually reinforcing escalation of military power,

Although the two nuclear superpowers—the United States and the Russian Federation—have reduced their arsenals in recent years, global security is threatened by the spread of nuclear weapons. In 1998, both India and Pakistan tested atomic bombs, raising fears that long-time tensions between these neighbouring nations might in the future escalate into catastrophic warfare.

between the United States and the former Soviet Union. Canada, which in effect depends on the U.S. for its defence, allocates about 8 percent of government spending to defence.

Yet, even after the collapse of the Soviet Union in 1992, U.S. military expenditures remain high. Thus, analysts who support the power-elite theory say that the United States is dominated by a **military-industrial complex**, *the close association between the federal government, the military, and defence industries.* The roots of militarism, then, lie not just in external threats to that nation's security; they also grow from within the institutional structures of U.S. society (Marullo, 1987).

Another reason for persistent militarism in the post-Cold War world is regional conflict. Since the collapse of the Soviet Union, for example, localized wars have broken out in Bosnia, Chechneya, and Zambia, and tensions still run high in a host of other countries, including Northern Ireland, Iraq, and a divided Korea. Even wars of limited scope have the potential to escalate and involve other countries. And as more and more nations acquire nuclear weapons, the risk that regional conflicts will erupt into deadly wars goes up.

NUCLEAR WEAPONS

Despite the easing of superpower tensions, the world still contains almost twenty-five thousand nuclear warheads, a destructive force equivalent to five tonnes of TNT for every person on the planet. Should even a small fraction of this stockpile be used in war, life as we know it might cease on much of the earth. Albert Einstein, whose genius contributed to the development of nuclear weapons, reflected: "The unleashed power of the atom has changed everything *save our modes of thinking*, and we thus drift toward unparallelled catastrophe." In short, nuclear weapons make unrestrained war unthinkable in a world not yet capable of peace.

Great Britain, France, and the People's Republic of China all have a substantial nuclear capability, but the vast majority of nuclear weapons are held by the United States and the Russian Federation, which have agreed to reduce their stockpiles of nuclear warheads by 75 percent by the year 2003. But even as the superpower rivalry winds down, the danger of catastrophic war is increasing along with **nuclear proliferation**, *the acquisition of nuclear-weapons technology by more and more nations.* Most experts agree that Israel, India, Pakistan, and South Africa already possess some nuclear weapons, and other nations (including Argentina, Brazil, Iraq, North Korea, and Libya) are in the process of developing them. Early in the next century, as many as fifty nations could have the ability to fight a nuclear war, making any regional conflict much more dangerous (Spector, 1988).

INFORMATION WARFARE

As earlier chapters have explained, the Information Revolution is changing almost every dimension of social life. In the next century, how will computers reshape warfare?

For decades, scientists and military officials have studied how to use computers to defend against missiles and planes. More recently, however, the military

In recent years, the world has become aware of the death and mutilation caused by millions of land mines placed in the ground during wartime and left there afterward. Civilians, many of them children, maimed by land mines receive treatment in this Kabul, Afghanistan, clinic.

has recognized that new information technology can fundamentally transform warfare itself, replacing rumbling tanks and screaming aircraft with electronic "smart bombs" that would silently penetrate an enemy country's computer system and render it unable to transmit information. In such "virtual wars," soldiers seated at workstation monitors would dispatch computer viruses to shut down the enemy's communication links, causing telephones to fall silent, air traffic control and railroad switching systems to fail, computer systems to feed phony orders to field officers, and televisions to broadcast "morphed" news bulletins urging people to turn against their leaders.

Like the venom of a poisonous snake, the weapons of "information warfare" might quickly paralyze an adversary prior to a conventional military attack. Another more hopeful possibility is that new information technology might not just precede conventional fighting but prevent it entirely. If the "victims" of computer warfare could be limited to a nation's communication links—rather than its citizens and cities—wouldn't we all be more secure?

Yet so-called "infowar" also poses new dangers, since, presumably, a few highly skilled operators with sophisticated electronic equipment could also wreak communications havoc on Canada or the United States. The United Sates may be militarily without equal in the world, but given their increasing reliance on high technology, they are also more vulnerable to cyber-attack than any nation on earth. As a result, in 1996, the Central Intelligence Agency (CIA) began work on a defensive "cyberwar centre" to help prevent what one official termed an "electronic Pearl Harbor" (Waller, 1995; Weiner, 1996).

THE PURSUIT OF PEACE

How can the world reduce the danger of war? Here are the most recent approaches to promoting peace:

1. **Deterrence.** During the Cold War, from the end of World War II in 1945 to the dissolution of the Soviet Union in the early 1990s, the logic of the arms race linked security to a "balance of terror" between the superpowers. Based on the principle of mutually assured destruction (MAD)—meaning that whichever side launched a first-strike nuclear attack against the other would sustain massive retaliation—deterrence has kept the peace for almost fifty years. But it has three flaws. First, it has fuelled an exorbitantly expensive arms race. Second, as missiles become capable of delivering their warheads more and more quickly, computers are left with less and less time to react to an apparent attack, thereby increasing the risks of unintended war. Third, deterrence cannot curb nuclear proliferation, which poses a growing threat to peace.

2. **High-technology defence.** If technology created the weapons, some maintain, it can also deliver us from the threat of war. This was the idea behind the *strategic defence initiative* (SDI), proposed by the U.S. Reagan administration in 1981. Under SDI, satellites and ground installations provide a protective shield or umbrella against enemy missiles. In principle, the system would detect enemy missiles soon after launch and destroy them with lasers and particle beams before they could re-enter the atmosphere. If

CONTROVERSY & DEBATE

Environmentally Friendly Canada, Eh!

Many Canadians believe that our country and our provinces have come a long way on the environmental front. After all, we have recycling programs (including disposable diapers in some communities), environmental reviews for major resource developments, regulations governing the disposal of pollutants into waterways or the air, international agreements on emission reduction, a wonderful system of national and provincial parks, and an environmentally sensitive public.

We have an environmental movement, whose activists are quick to draw public attention to the clear-cutting of forests in B.C. or the slaughter of baby seals in Newfoundland. Our First Nations communities—

such as Walpole Island, Ontario—are attempting to achieve sustainable development (Jacobs, 1992; Nin.da.waab.jig, 1992) and organizations such as the

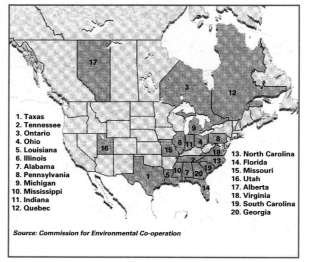

1. Taxas
2. Tennessee
3. Ontario
4. Ohio
5. Louisiana
6. Illinois
7. Alabama
8. Pennsylvania
9. Michigan
10. Mississippi
11. Indiana
12. Quebec
13. North Carolina
14. Florida
15. Missouri
16. Utah
17. Alberta
18. Virginia
19. South Carolina
20. Georgia

Source: Commission for Environmental Co-operation

Wendaban Stewardship Authority are being created to blend native and non-native environmental knowledge and to co-manage timber, land, and resource development in the Temagami area (Shute and Knight, 1995). Surely we can be forgiven if we are a little smug about our environmental record.

Looks can be deceiving, though! Behind the scenes, Canada and the provinces have been cutting budgets in the environmental protection area. In Ontario, "Virtually all of the province's environmental laws have been weakened, enforcement budgets have been cut and regulatory powers are being taken away." So lax is the enforcement of regulations that Ontario ranks third among North America's

---

perfected, advocates argue, such a "star wars" defence would render nuclear weapons obsolete.

But critics charge that even years of research costing trillions of dollars would yield at best a leaky umbrella. The collapse of the Soviet Union also calls into question the need for such an extensive and costly defence scheme. Furthermore, sophisticated technology raises not only new possibilities for defence, but also new strategies for waging war.

3. **Diplomacy and disarmament.** Still other analysts point out that the best path to peace is diplomacy rather than technology (Dedrick and Yinger, 1990). Diplomacy can enhance security by reducing, rather than building, weapons stockpiles.

But disarmament, too, has limitations. No nation wishes to become vulnerable by reducing its defences. Successful diplomacy, then, depends not on "soft" concession making or "hard" demands, but on everyone involved sharing responsibility for a common problem (Fisher and Ury, 1988).

While the United States and the former Soviet Union have managed to negotiate arms-reduction agreements, the threat from other nations such as Libya, North Korea, and Iraq—all of which desire to build a nuclear arsenal—remains great.

4. **Resolving underlying conflict.** Perhaps the best way to reduce the dangers of nuclear war is to resolve underlying conflicts. Even in the post–Cold War era, basic differences between the United States and Russia remain. Moreover, militarism also springs from nationalism, ethnic differences, and class inequality, which have fuelled regional conflicts in Latin America, Africa, Asia, and the Middle East. If peace depends on solving international disputes, why do nations around the world currently spend three thousand times as much money on militarism as they do on peacekeeping (Sivard, 1988)?

Ever since Canadian prime minister Lester B. Pearson proposed the creation of a United Nations peacekeeping force in 1956 (for which he was awarded the Nobel Peace Prize in 1957),

polluters, behind Texas and Tennessee, while Quebec ranks twelfth and Alberta ranks seventeenth (Fine, 1997). Ontario Hydro's nuclear energy program is in serious difficulty as it contemplates deactivating some of its plants amid daunting safety and pollution concerns (Mittelstaedt, 1997). As 1998 rolled in, Toronto was debating the merits of its household recycling program: it is extremely costly, ineffective in ensuring the reuse of materials, and some of the Blue Box deposits actually end up in landfill sites.

Decisions regarding environmental issues are inherently political—and controversial. Having failed to live up to its earlier promises regarding emission targets, Canada was expected to set new ones at the Kyoto environmental summit to deal with carbon emissions and the threat to global warming. The Vancouver-based David Suzuki Foundation took out full-page newspaper ads across the country aimed at stopping the global warming plague. In Alberta, fear-mongering reached a fever pitch because the proposed emission targets would reduce the demand for oil and natural gas, which it was claimed would be catastrophic for the province. The rumoured tax on carbon fuels as they come off the wells (to discourage fuel use) would transfer huge amounts of money out of the province. Premier Ralph Klein, the resource industries, and the Alberta public were up in arms and Chrétien felt the heat (Bercuson and Cooper, 1997).

Canadian governments, federal and provincial, are engaged in a high-wire act as they deal with environmental issues. Environmentalists, environmentally aware Canadians, and foreign interests exert considerable pressure on our elected leaders to protect our natural environment. Businesses, workers, and agencies in resource-dependent parts of the country (or economy) are equally persuasive. The people who design and implement our environmental policies and programs do so in the face of relentless cross-pressures.

Continue the debate . . .

1. *Are the people around you as concerned about environmental issues as they were five years ago?*
2. *Should we recycle cans, bottles, and newspapers, even if it proves to cost substantially more than other types of waste disposal? Who should bear these costs?*
3. *How much are you willing to give up, in terms of standard of living, to help Canada reach its emission targets?*

Canada has seen its international role mainly in terms of mediation and peacekeeping. Although we did participate in the Allied attack on Iraq during the Gulf War, after the war Canadians helped patrol the demilitarized zone. Our role in the former Yugoslavia has been largely limited to peacekeeping and medical assistance.

LOOKING AHEAD: POLITICS IN THE TWENTY-FIRST CENTURY

Just as economic systems——the focus of the last chapter—are changing, so are political systems. As we look ahead to the next century, several problems and trends command widespread attention.

Among these trends is the extension of global politics. The Information Revolution is changing politics just as it is reformulating the economy (although political change seems to be somewhat slower). Communications technology now allows news and political analysis to flow instantly from one point in the world to another. But will this global avalanche of information expand democracy by empowering individuals? Or will new information technology provide governments with new tools to manipulate their citizens?

Another major trend is the global rethinking of political models. The Cold War cast political debate in the form of two rigid political alternatives based on capitalism, on the one hand, and socialism, on the other. Today, in the post–Cold War era, analysts envision a broader range of political systems, linking government to economic production in various ways. "Welfare capitalism" as found in Sweden or "state capitalism" as found in Japan and South Korea are just two possibilities.

Finally, we still face the danger of war in many parts of the world. Even as tensions between the United States and the former Soviet Union have eased, vast stockpiles of weapons remain, and nuclear technology continues to proliferate around the world. New superpowers may arise in the century ahead (the People's Republic of China seems a likely candidate), just as regional conflicts will surely continue to fester. One can only hope that, in the century to come, world leaders will devise nonviolent solutions to the age-old problems that provoke war.

SUMMARY

1. Politics is the major social institution by which a society distributes power and organizes decision making. Max Weber explained that three social contexts transform coercive power into legitimate authority: tradition, rationally enacted rules and regulations, and the personal charisma of a leader.

2. Traditional authority is common to pre-industrial societies; industrial societies, by contrast, legitimize power through bureaucratic organizations and law. Charismatic authority, which arises in every society, sustains itself through routinization into traditional or rational-legal authority.

3. Monarchy is based on traditional authority and is common in pre-industrial societies. Although constitutional monarchies persist in some industrial nations, industrialization favours democracy based on rational-legal authority and extensive bureaucracy.

4. Authoritarian political regimes deny popular participation in government. Totalitarian political systems go even further, tightly regulating people's everyday lives.

5. The world remains divided into 191 politically independent nation-states; one dimension of an emerging global political system, however, is the growing wealth and power of multinational corporations. Additionally, new technology associated with the Information Revolution means that national governments can no longer control the flow of information across national boundaries.

6. The government of Canada is based on an elected House of Commons and an appointed Senate. Because representation in the House of Commons is based (roughly) on population, Quebec and Ontario together have 59 percent of the seats. This weighting in favour of central Canada is a source of concern for the other provinces.

7. Canada has traditionally had three major political parties at the federal level. The Progressive Conservative party leans to the right on social and economic issues, the Liberal party is closer to the centre, and the New Democratic party is farther to the left. Since each of the parties is a bit of a mixed bag, accurate placement on a left-right continuum is difficult.

8. One of the major political struggles going on in Canada involves the centralization versus the decentralization of power, or provincial versus federal power.

9. Canadian government takes an active role in the daily lives of its citizens. Canadian political culture supports widespread intervention in social and economic spheres.

10. Quebec separation, should it occur, would be a revolutionary act that would dismantle Canada as we know it today. The tradition of peaceful resolution of problems in Canada might make this a nonviolent transition but there are no guarantees.

11. Native self-government is a current issue that has deep historic roots. Many native groups are currently practising some level of self-government under a wide range of agreements, but constitutional recognition of an inherent right to self-government is still an important goal.

12. The pluralist model holds that political power is widely dispersed; the power-elite model takes an opposing view, arguing that power is concentrated in a small, wealthy segment of the population.

13. Revolution radically transforms a political system. Revolutions aim at different political objectives and meet with varied degrees of success.

14. Terrorism is the use of violence in pursuit of political goals. Although attention has long focused on group terrorism, state terrorism is potentially far more powerful.

15. War is armed conflict between governments. The development of nuclear weapons, and their proliferation, has increased the possibility of global catastrophe. Enhancing world peace ultimately depends on resolving social problems and the conflicts that underlie militarism.

CRITICAL THINKING QUESTIONS

1. What is the difference between authority and power? What forms of authority characterize pre-industrial and industrial societies? Why does democracy gradually replace monarchy as societies industrialize?

2. How would you describe the attitudes of the Canadian population on the political spectrum? How is class position linked to political opinions?

3. Contrast the pluralist, power-elite, and Marxist political-economy models of societal power. Which do you find more convincing?

4. Do you think that the dangers of war in the world are greater or less than in past generations? Why?

SOCIOLOGY APPLIED

1. Immediately after every federal election, newspapers publish an analysis of who voted and for whom. Visit the library to obtain a "scorecard" for the 1997 federal election. To what extent do men and women vote for different candidates? What about people of various racial categories? Different ages? Religions? Income levels? In short, what variables affect political attitudes the most?

2. The Internet provides enormous organizational potential, linking people who share an interest in some political issue. The goal of the www.women.ca Web site is to provide a community for women on the Internet. Visit the Web site: do you think such sites will make a difference in Canadian politics?

3. Along with several other people, make a list of leaders you think are or were charismatic. Discuss why someone is on the list. Do you think personal charisma is something more than "being good on television"? If so, precisely what is it?

4. Do a little research to trace the increase in the size of the federal government over the last fifty years. Try to discover how organizations at different points along the political spectrum (from socialist organizations on the left through the NDP, Liberal, Progressive Conservatives, and Reform parties, to right-wing groups) view the size of the current welfare state.

WEBLINKS

http://www.law-lib.utoronto.ca/law-review/utlr53-2/olynyk.htm
"Approaches to Sorting Out Jurisdiction in a Self-Government Context" by John M. Olynyk, published in the *University of Toronto Faculty of Law Review*, examines how First Nations jurisdiction might interact with and be distinguished from that of the federal and provincial governments.

http://www.statcan.ca/english/Pgdb/State/govern.htm
Statistics Canada's collection of tables about Canadian government, including information on elections, revenues and expenditures, and employment.

http://canada.gc.ca/howgoc/forsey/forsey_e.html
"How Canadians Govern Themselves" by Eugene A. Forsey, an essay on the Canadian system of government.

http://www.parl.gc.ca/
The Parliamentary Internet site, created and maintained jointly by the Senate, House of Commons, and Library of Parliament, offers information on the Canadian Parliament, including news updates and back issues of *Hansard*.

http://www.un.org/
The United Nations is an organization of sovereign nations. It provides the machinery to help find solutions to international problems or disputes, and to deal with pressing concerns that face people everywhere.

Frida Kahlo, *My Grandparents, My Parents, and I (Family Tree)*, 1936

Oil and tempera on metal panel, 12¹⁄₈ × 13⁵⁄₈ in. (30.7 × 34.5 cm). The Museum of Modern Art, New York. Gift of Allan Roos, MD, and B. Matthieu Roos. Photograph © 1996 The Museum of Modern Art.

CHAPTER 17

FAMILY

When you see a woman pushing a stroller, does it cross your mind that you might be watching a lesbian mother? In an article entitled "We Are Family: Lesbian Mothers in Canada," Katherine Arnup (1995) points out that, by some estimates, 10 percent of women are lesbians—and that 20 to 30 percent of those lesbians are mothers. Among these women, gaining recognition and acceptance as mothers (that is, as legitimate, good mothers) is not easy. The problems become especially apparent for lesbian mothers who leave a heterosexual relationship and try to gain custody of their children.

Many of these women choose not to contest custody in court because they fear defeat by a clearly homophobic legal system. Instead they hope to get liberal access rights. Despite the obstacles, other lesbian mothers are trying to get custody. In doing so, they have learned that there is an informal distinction between "good" and "bad" lesbian mothers. The "good" ones are those "who live quiet, discreet lives, who promise that they will raise their children to be heterosexual, [and] who

appear to the outside world to be heterosexual single parents"—in other words, those who are completely secretive about their identities. The "bad" ones are the women "who are politically active, who attend gay and lesbian demonstrations, and who view their lesbianism as one aspect of an entire challenge to society" (p. 331)—that is, those who have "come out."

Knowing the criteria the courts consider in determining "the best interests of the child," lesbian mothers face difficult choices. Most try to appear as "straight" as possible in court to increase the chances of gaining custody, rather than being open about their identities. "Such women have met with harsh criticism from some elements of the lesbian community, however, for sustaining an oppressive familial ideology, rather than standing up for their rights as open and proud lesbian mothers" (p. 333).

When they do have custody of their children, lesbian mothers have to decide whether to be open about their "unusual" family situations—in the community, at school, at church. By being forthright, they might find that they share all kinds of common concerns with heterosexual mothers and, gradually, they might stretch or expand the notion of what is acceptable family life.

In Canada, the state of the family is a hot topic. Indeed, a rising chorus of voices charges that families in Canada are fast becoming an endangered species. And some hard facts back up their case. The marriage rate within Canada is decreasing. The Canadian divorce rate has almost doubled since 1975 (Serrill, 1995:23), when only 7 percent of Canadians were "ever-divorced," to the present figure of 14 percent

In modern industrial societies, the members of extended families usually pursue their careers independently while living apart from one another. However, various nuclear families may assemble periodically for rituals such as weddings, funerals, and family reunions.

(Bibby, 1995:6). If the trend holds, over a third of today's marriages will end in divorce. Marital breakdown, coupled with the increase in the number of children born to unmarried women, means that half of Canadian children born today will live with a single parent for some time before reaching age eighteen. Not surprisingly, the proportion of Canadian children living in poverty has been rising steadily in recent years.

Taken together, these facts suggest a basic truth: families in Canada and in other industrial societies are changing dramatically. Not long ago, the cultural ideal of the family consisted of a working husband, a homemaker wife, and their young children. Today, fewer people embrace this singular vision of the family, and, at any given time, only a minority of Canadian households fits that description.

This chapter highlights important changes in family life, and offers some insights into these trends. Yet, as we shall also point out, changing family patterns are nothing new to this country. A century ago, for example, concern over the decline of the family swept the nation as the Industrial Revolution propelled men from farms to factories. Today, of course, many of the same concerns surround the rising share of women whose careers draw them away from home. In short, changes in other social institutions, especially the economy, are leaving their mark—for better or worse—on marriage and family life.

THE FAMILY: BASIC CONCEPTS

The **family** is *a social institution that unites individuals into cooperative groups that oversee the bearing and raising of children*. These social units are, in turn, built on **kin-**ship, *a social bond based on blood, marriage, or adoption, that joins individuals into families*. Although all societies contain families, just who is included under the umbrella of kinship has varied through history, and varies today from one culture to another.

During the twentieth century, most members of our society have regarded a **family unit** as *a social group of two or more people, related by blood, marriage, or adoption, who usually live together*. Initially, individuals are born into a family composed of parents and siblings, which is sometimes called the *family of orientation* because this group is central to socialization. In adulthood, people forge a *family of procreation* to have or adopt children of their own.

Throughout the world, families form around **marriage**, *a legally sanctioned relationship, usually involving economic cooperation as well as normative sexual activity and childbearing, that people expect to be enduring*. Our cultural belief that marriage is the appropriate context for procreation is apparent in the historical use of the term illegitimate for children born out of wedlock. Moreover, matrimony, in Latin, means "the condition of motherhood." The link between childbearing and marriage has weakened, however, as the proportion of children born to single women has increased.

Some people now object to defining only married couples and children as "families" because that implies that everyone should embrace a single standard of moral conduct. Yet many company and government programs designate benefits only for members of "families" as conventionally defined, excluding many unmarried, committed partners—whether heterosexual or homosexual. (Presently the government considers common-law heterosexual couples who have been

GLOBAL SOCIOLOGY

International Adoption

The rate of international adoption is rapidly increasing (Fulton, 1995:34) from ten per year in 1970 to about two thousand per year from forty-two different countries in the 1990s.

Formerly, Canadians usually adopted the children of unwed mothers. Abortion was illegal and infrequent, and women who bore and raised children outside of marriage were stigmatized. Now that abortion is legal and relatively available, women who give birth outside of marriage are increasingly likely to keep their babies. Between 1981 and 1990, adoptions of children born in Canada declined almost 50 percent.

In the low-income and war-torn countries of the world, out-of-country adoption of babies represents a potential benefit both to the individuals and to the nations who are unable to pro-

vide food, shelter, and schooling for these children. Canadians pay anywhere from $10 000 to $25 000 to adopt a child internationally. The money goes to adoption and state agencies for legal, medical, and transportation costs—not as payment for the child.

What does the future hold for these families? Often the adopted child has a different cultural heritage than the adoptive family. For instance, Vietnamese boat-lifts in 1971 unleashed the largest wave of international adoptions since after the Korean War in the 1950s. China's one-child policy, established in the 1980s, has led many Chinese couples to give daughters up for adoption so that they can try again for a son to carry on the family name.

One can only speculate about the adjustments of these children and their adoptive families. Fifty-seven percent

of Canadians say that they would prefer less immigration than presently occurs (Serrill, 1995:22), raising fears that these children may have to struggle with prejudice. On a more optimistic note, research in Canada by Westhues and Cohen (1994) indicates that most of these adoptions have many elements of success. Among the issues they considered are self-esteem, the degree of integration into the adoptive family, peer relations, and the children's comfort with their ethnic backgrounds. The unfolding stories of these adoptions and the children's adjustment to Canadian society will continue to hold great interest for Canadian researchers in the years to come.

SOURCES: Fulton (1995); Westhues and Cohen (1994).

---

living together for two years to be legally married.) As more and more people forge unconventional family ties, many are not thinking of kinship in terms of families of affinity, that is, people with or without legal or blood ties who feel they belong together and wish to define themselves as a family.

What does or does not constitute a family, then, is, in part, a moral matter that lies at the heart of the contemporary "family values" debate. Statistics Canada also plays a role in this discussion. It uses the conventional definition of family, and sociologists who rely on Statistics Canada data describing "families" must accept this definition. The trend in public opinion as well as in legal terms, however, favours a wider and more inclusive definition of the "family unit."

THE FAMILY: GLOBAL VARIETY

Members of pre-industrial societies take a broad view of family ties, recognizing the **extended family** as *a family unit including parents and children, but also other kin.* Extended families are also called *consanguine fam-*

ilies, meaning that they include everyone with "shared blood." With industrialization, however, increasing geographic and social mobility gives rise to the **nuclear family**, *a family unit composed of one or two parents and their children.* Because it is based on marriage, the nuclear family is also known as the *conjugal family.* Although many members of our society live in extended families, the nuclear family has become the predominant family form in Canada.

Many couples go to great lengths to become parents in pursuit of the model of the nuclear family. International adoption, discussed in the "Global Sociology" box, is one method used by adults to become parents.

MARRIAGE PATTERNS

Cultural norms, as well as laws, identify people as desirable or unsuitable marriage partners. Some marital norms promote **endogamy**, *marriage between people of the same social category.* Endogamy limits marriage prospects to others of the same age, race, religion, or social class. By contrast, **exogamy** mandates *marriage*

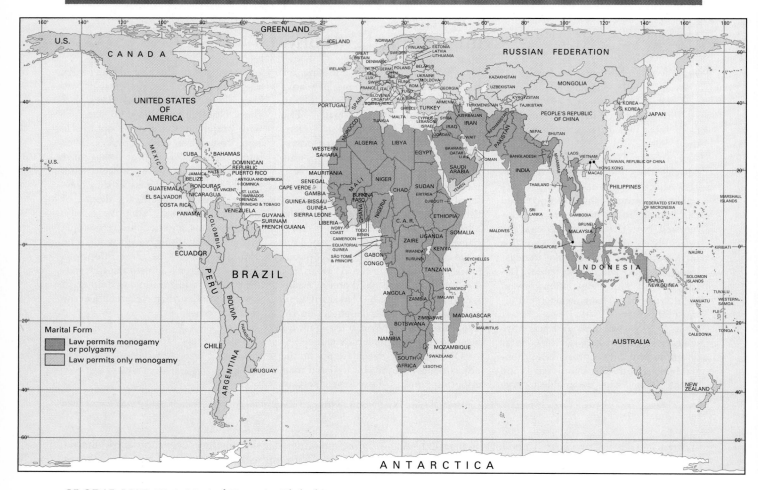

GLOBAL MAP 17–1 Marital Form in Global Perspective

Monogamy is the legally prescribed form of marriage in all industrial societies and throughout the Western hemisphere. In most African nations, as well as in southern Asia, however, polygamy is permitted by law. In many cases, this practice reflects the historic influence of Islam, a religion that allows a man to have up to four wives. Even so, most marriages in these traditional societies are monogamous, primarily for financial reasons.

SOURCE: *Peters Atlas of the World* (1990).

between people of different social categories. In rural India, for example, young people are expected to marry someone of the same caste (endogamy), but from a different village (exogamy). The logic of endogamy is that people of similar social position pass along their standing to offspring, thereby maintaining traditional social patterns. Exogamy, on the other hand, builds alliances and encourages cultural diffusion.

In industrial societies, laws prescribe **monogamy** (from Greek meaning "one union"), *a form of mar-*

riage joining two partners. Our high level of divorce and remarriage, however, suggests that *serial monogamy* is a more accurate description of Canada's marital practice.

Global Map 17–1 shows that while monogamy is the rule throughout the Americas and in Europe, many lower-income societies—especially in Africa and southern Asia—permit **polygamy** (from Greek, meaning "many unions"), *a form of marriage uniting three or more people.* Polygamy takes two forms. By far the more

434 CHAPTER 17 Family

common is **polygyny** (from Greek, meaning "many women"), *a form of marriage uniting one male and two or more females*. Islamic societies in Africa and southern Asia, for example, permit men up to four wives. Even so, most families in these societies are monogamous because few men have the wealth needed to support several wives and even more children.

Polyandry (from Greek, meaning "many men" or "many husbands") is *a form of marriage uniting one female with two or more males*. This pattern appears only rarely. One example is among people of Tibet, where agriculture is difficult. There, polyandry discourages the division of land into parcels too small to support a family and divides the work of farming among many men. Polyandry has also been linked to female infanticide—aborting female fetuses or killing female infants—because a decline in the female population forces men to share women.

Historically, most world societies have permitted more than one marital pattern; even so, most actual marriages have been monogamous (Murdock, 1965). This cultural preference for monogamy reflects two key facts of life: supporting multiple spouses is a heavy financial burden, and the number of men and women in most societies is roughly the same.

RESIDENTIAL PATTERNS

Just as societies regulate mate selection, so they designate where a couple resides. In pre-industrial societies, most newlyweds live with one set of parents, gaining economic assistance and security in the process. Most societies observe a norm of **patrilocality** (Greek for "place of the father"), *a residential pattern in which a married couple lives with or near the husband's family*. But some societies (such as the North American Iroquois) endorse **matrilocality** (meaning "place of the mother"), *a residential pattern in which a married couple lives with or near the wife's family*. Societies that engage in frequent, local warfare tend towards patrilocality since families want their sons close to home to offer protection. Societies that engage in distant warfare may be patrilocal or matrilocal, depending on whether sons or daughters have greater economic value (Ember and Ember, 1971, 1991).

Industrial societies show yet another pattern. When finances permit, at least, they favour **neolocality** (Greek meaning "new place"), *a residential pattern in which a married couple lives apart from the parents of both spouses*.

PATTERNS OF DESCENT

Descent refers to *the system by which members of a society trace kinship over generations*. Most pre-industrial societies trace kinship through only one side of the family—the father or the mother. The more prevalent pattern is **patrilineal descent**, *a system tracing kinship through men*. In a patrilineal system, children are related to others only through their fathers, and fathers typically pass property on to their sons. Patrilineal descent characterizes most pastoral and agrarian societies, since men produce the most valued resources. Less common is **matrilineal descent**, *a system tracing kinship through women*. Matrilineal descent, through which mothers pass property to their daughters, is found more frequently in horticultural societies where women are the primary food producers.

Industrial societies with greater gender equality recognize **bilateral descent** ("two-sided descent"), *a system tracing kinship through both men and women*. In this pattern, children recognize as relatives people on both the "father's side" and the "mother's side" of the family.

PATTERNS OF AUTHORITY

The predominance of polygyny, patrilocality, and patrilineal descent in the world reflects the universal presence of patriarchy. Without denying that wives and mothers exercise considerable power in every society, as Chapter 12 ("Sex and Gender") explains, no truly matriarchal society has ever existed.

In industrial societies such as Canada, more egalitarian family patterns are evolving, especially as increasing numbers of women enter the labour force. However, even here, men are typically heads of households. Parents in Canada also still prefer boys to girls, and (usually) give children their father's last name.

THEORETICAL ANALYSIS OF THE FAMILY

As in earlier chapters, several theoretical approaches offer a range of insights about the family.

FUNCTIONS OF THE FAMILY: STRUCTURAL-FUNCTIONAL ANALYSIS

The structural-functional paradigm contends that the family performs several vital tasks. From this point of view, the family operates as "the backbone of society."

1. **Socialization.** As explained in Chapter 5 ("Socialization"), the family is the first and most influential setting for socialization. Ideally, parents teach children to be well-integrated and contributing members of society (Parsons and Bales, 1955). Of course, family socialization continues throughout the life cycle. Adults change within marriage, and, as any parent

The family is a basic building block of society because it performs important functions such as conferring social position and regulating sexual activity. To most family members, however, the family (at least in ideal terms) is a "haven in a heartless world" in which individuals find a sense of belonging and emotional support, an idea conveyed in Marc Chagall's Scène Paysanne.

Marc Chagall, *Scène Paysanne*. © 1999 Artists Rights Society (ARS), New York/ADAGP, Paris.

knows, mothers and fathers learn as much from raising their children as their children learn from them.

2. **Regulation of sexual activity.** Every culture regulates sexual activity in the interest of maintaining kinship organization and property rights. One universal regulation is the **incest taboo,** *a cultural norm forbidding sexual relations or marriage between certain kin.* Precisely which kin fall within the incest taboo varies from one culture to another. The matrilineal Navajo, for example, forbid marrying any relative of one's mother. Our bilateral society applies the incest taboo to both sides of the family but limits it to close relatives, including parents, grandparents, siblings, aunts, and uncles. But even brother–sister marriages found approval among the ancient Egyptian, Incan, and Hawaiian nobility (Murdock, 1965).

Reproduction between close relatives can mentally and physically impair offspring. Yet, only human beings observe an incest taboo, suggesting that the real reason to control incest is social. Why? First, the incest taboo minimizes sexual competition within families by restricting legitimate sexuality to spouses. Second, it forces people to marry outside their immediate families, integrating the larger society. Third, since kinship defines people's rights and obligations towards each other, reproduction among close relatives would hopelessly confuse kinship ties and threaten social order.

3. **Social placement.** Families are not biologically necessary for people to reproduce, but they do help maintain social organization. Parents confer their own social identity—in terms of race, ethnicity, religion, and social class—on children at birth. This fact explains the long-standing preference for birth to married parents.

4. **Material and emotional security.** People view the family as a "haven in a heartless world," looking to kin for physical protection, emotional support, and financial assistance. To a greater or lesser extent, most families do all these things, although not without periodic conflict. Not surprisingly, then, people living in families tend to be healthier than those living alone.

Critical evaluation. Structural-functional analysis explains why society, at least as we know it, could not exist without families. But this approach overlooks the great diversity of Canadian family life. Also, it ignores ways in which other social institutions (say, government) could meet some of the same human needs. Finally, structural-functional analysis overlooks negative aspects of family life, including its support of patriarchy and the alarming extent of family violence.

INEQUALITY AND THE FAMILY: SOCIAL-CONFLICT ANALYSIS

Like the structural-functional approach, the social-conflict paradigm considers the family central to the operation of society, but rather than focusing on societal benefits, conflict theorists investigate how the family perpetuates social inequality. Families perpetuate social inequality in several ways:

1. **Property and inheritance.** Friedrich Engels (1902; orig. 1884) traced the origin of the family to the need to identify heirs so that men (especially in the higher classes) could transmit property to their sons. Families thus support the concentration of wealth and reproduce the class

structure in each succeeding generation (Mare, 1991).

2. **Patriarchy.** According to Engels, men determine their heirs by controlling the sexuality of women. Families therefore transform women into the sexual and economic property of men. A century ago in Canada, most wives' earnings belonged to their husbands. Today, despite striking economic gains, women still bear major responsibility for child rearing and housework (Nett, 1993) and still earn substantially less than men. Statistics Canada indicated that in 1992 employed women with at least one child under age five spent an average of 5.3 hours per day on housework, child care, and shopping, whereas the average man in this situation spent about 3 hours per day on domestic responsibilities (Steele, 1995:29). If this unpaid work were added to the economy, it would be worth at least $234 billion dollars (Philp, 1996:A8).

3. **Race and ethnicity.** Racial and ethnic categories will persist over generations only to the degree that people marry others like themselves. Thus, endogamous marriage also shores up the racial and ethnic hierarchy in our own society and elsewhere.

Critical evaluation. Social-conflict analysis reveals another side of family life: its role in maintaining social inequality. Engels condemned the family as part and parcel of capitalism. Yet noncapitalist societies have families (and family problems) all the same. While kinship and social inequality are deeply intertwined, as Engels argued, the family appears to carry out various societal functions that are not easily accomplished by other means.

CONSTRUCTING FAMILY LIFE: MICRO-LEVEL ANALYSIS

Both structural-functional and social-conflict analyses take a broad view of the family as a structural system. Micro-level approaches, by contrast, explore how individuals shape and experience family life day to day.

Symbolic-Interaction Analysis

People experience family life in terms of relationships, and these vary from person to person and change from day to day. In ideal terms, however, family living offers an opportunity for intimacy, a word with Latin roots meaning "sharing fear." That is, as a result of sharing a wide range of activities over a long period of time, members of families forge emotional bonds. Of course, the fact that parents act as authority figures often inhibits their communication with younger children. But, as young people reach adulthood, kinship ties typically "open up" to include confiding as well as turning to one another for emotional support and assistance with numerous tasks and responsibilities (Macionis, 1978).

Social-Exchange Analysis

Social-exchange analysis, another micro-level approach, depicts courtship and marriage as forms of negotiation (Blau, 1964). Dating allows each person the chance to assess the likely advantages and disadvantages of taking the other as a spouse, always keeping in mind the value of what one has to offer in return. In essence, exchange analysts contend, individuals seek to make the best "deal" they can in selecting a partner.

Physical attractiveness is one critical element of social exchange. Throughout history, patriarchal societies have made beauty a commodity offered by women on the marriage market. The high value assigned to beauty explains women's traditional concern with physical appearance and their sensitivity about revealing their age. Men, in turn, have traditionally been assessed according to their financial resources. Recently, however, because women are joining the labour force, they are less dependent on men to support them and their children. Thus, the terms of exchange have been converging for men and women.

Critical evaluation. Micro-level analysis offers a useful counterpoint to structural-functional and social-conflict visions of the family as an institutional system. Both the interaction and exchange viewpoints give a better sense of the individual's experience of family life and how people shape this reality for themselves.

This approach, however, misses the bigger picture, namely, that family life is similar for people in the same social and economic categories. Canadian families vary in predictable ways according to social class and ethnicity, and, as the next section explains, they typically evolve through distinct stages linked to the life course.

STAGES OF FAMILY LIFE

The family is dynamic, with marked changes across the life course. Typically, family life begins with courtship, followed by settling into the realities of married life. Next, for most couples at least, is raising children, leading to the later years of marriage after children have left home to form families of their own. We will look briefly at each of these stages.

Early to Wed: A Report from Rural India

Sumitra Jogi was crying as her wedding was about to begin. Were they tears of joy? Not exactly: this "bride" is an eleven-month-old squirming in the arms of her mother. The groom? A boy of six.

In a remote, rural village in India's western state of Rajasthan, two families gather at midnight to celebrate a traditional wedding ritual. It is May 2, an especially good day to marry according to Hindu tradition. Sumitra's father smiles as the ceremony begins; her mother cradles the infant, who, having just finished nursing, has now fallen asleep. The groom, dressed in a special costume with a red-and-gold turban on his head, gently reaches up and grasps the baby's hand. Then, as the ceremony reaches its conclusion, the young boy leads the child and mother three and a half times around the wedding fire—while the audience beams—marking the couple's first steps together as husband and wife.

Child weddings of this kind are illegal in India, but in the rural regions, traditions are strong and marriage laws are difficult to enforce. In fact, experts

estimate that thousands of children marry each year in ceremonies of this kind. "In rural Rajasthan," explains one social welfare worker, "all the girls are married by age fourteen. These are poor, illiterate families, and they don't want to keep girls past their first menstrual cycle."

For the immediate future, Sumitra Jogi will remain with her parents. But by the time she is eight or ten, a second ceremony will mark the time for her to move to the home of her husband's family, where her married life will begin.

If the responsibilities of marriage lie years in the future, why do families push their children to marry at such an early age? Parents of girls know that the younger the bride, the smaller the dowry offered to the groom's parents. Then, too, when girls marry this young, there is no chance that they will lose their virginity, which would spoil their attractiveness on the marriage market. But, of course, the entire system rests on the assumption that love has nothing to do with it. Marriage is an alliance between families, so no one worries that the children are too young to understand what is taking place.

SOURCE: Based on Anderson (1995).

COURTSHIP

November 2, 1994, Kandy, Sri Lanka. Winding our way through the rain forest of this beautiful island, the van driver Harry recounts to his audience how he met his wife. Actually, it was more of an arrangement: the two families were both Buddhist and of the same caste group. "We got along well, right from the start," recalls Harry. "We had the same background. I suppose she or I could have said 'no.' But 'love marriages' happen in the city, not in the village where I grew up."

People in Sri Lanka, and in pre-industrial societies throughout the world, generally consider courtship too important to be left to the young (Stone, 1977). Arranged marriages represent an alliance between two extended families of similar social standing, and usually involve not just an exchange of children, but also of wealth and favours. Romantic love has little to do with it, and parents may make such arrangements when their children are quite young. A century ago in Sri Lanka and India, for example, half of all girls married before reaching the age of fifteen (Mayo, 1927; Mace and Mace, 1960). And, as the "Global Sociology" box explains, in some parts of the world child marriage persists today.

Arranged marriages fit into Emile Durkheim's model of *mechanical solidarity* (see Chapter 4, "Society"). Because traditional societies are culturally homogeneous, almost any member of the opposite sex has been suitably socialized to perform the roles of spouse and parent. Thus, parents can arrange mar-

People in every society recognize the reality of physical attraction. But the power of romantic love, captured in Christian Pierre's painting, I Do, *holds surprisingly little importance in traditional societies. In much of the world, it would be less correct to say that individuals marry individuals and more true to say that families marry families. In other words, parents arrange marriages for their children with an eye to the social position of the kin groups involved.*

riages with little concern for whether the two individuals involved are *personally* compatible because they can be confident that virtually any couple will be *culturally* compatible.

Industrialization erodes the importance of extended families and weakens traditions while enhancing personal choice in courtship. Young people expect to choose their own mates, and usually delay doing so until they have financial security and the experience to select a suitable partner. Dating sharpens courtship skills and may serve as a period of sexual experimentation.

Romantic Love

Our culture celebrates *romantic love*—the experience of affection and sexual passion for another person—as the basis for marriage. We find it hard to imagine marriage without love, and popular culture—from remakes of traditional fairy tales such as "Cinderella" to today's paperback romance novels—portrays love as the key to a successful marriage.

Our society's emphasis on romance has some useful consequences. Passionate love motivates individuals to "leave the nest" to form new families of their own, and it can help a new couple through the difficult adjustments of living together (Goode, 1959). On the other hand, because feelings wax and wane, romantic love is a less stable foundation for marriage than social and economic considerations—an assertion supported by this country's high divorce rate compared to lower rates in societies that allow less choice in partners.

But even in a culture of more choice, sociologists know that Cupid's arrow is aimed by society more

than we like to think. Most people fall in love with others of the same race, comparable age, and similar social class. All societies "arrange" marriages to the extent that they encourage **homogamy** (literally, "like marrying like"), *marriage between people with the same social characteristics.*

In short, "falling in love" may be a strong personal feeling, but it is guided by social forces. Perhaps we exaggerate the importance of romantic love to reassure ourselves that we—not society—steer our own lives.

SETTLING IN: IDEAL AND REAL MARRIAGE

Our culture presents marriage to the young in idealized, "happily-ever-after" terms. One consequence of such optimistic thinking is the danger of disappointment, especially for women—who, more than men, are taught to see in marriage the key to future happiness.

Then, too, romantic love involves a good deal of fantasy. We fall in love with others, not necessarily as they are, but as we want them to be (Berscheid and Hatfield, 1983). Only after marriage do many spouses regularly confront each other as they carry out the day-to-day routines of maintaining a household.

Sexuality can also be a source of disappointment. In the romantic haze of falling in love, people may anticipate marriage as an endless sexual honeymoon, only to face the sobering realization that sex becomes a less than all-consuming passion. About two in three married people report that they are satisfied with the sexual dimension of their relationship, though marital sex does decline over time (Blumstein and Schwartz, 1983).

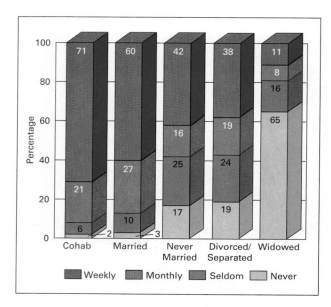

FIGURE 17–1 Sexual Activity by Marital Status

SOURCE: Bibby (1995:66).

Many experts agree that couples with the most fulfilling sexual relationships experience the greatest satisfaction in their marriages. This correlation does not mean that sex is the key to marital bliss, but, more often than not, that good sex and good relationships go together (Hunt, 1974; Tavris and Sadd, 1977; Blumstein and Schwartz, 1983). As Figure 17–1 shows, about 60 percent of married couples say that they are having sex weekly (Bibby, 1995:66).

Infidelity—sexual activity outside marriage—is another area in which the reality of marriage does not coincide with our cultural ideal. We strongly support traditional marriage vows "to forsake all others." In a survey, for example, three out of four adults said that extramarital sex is "always wrong" and only 4 percent believed that it was never wrong (Bibby, 1983). Even so, 17 percent of men and 9 percent of women indicated that they had been sexually unfaithful to their partners at least once (*Gallup Sexual Lifestyle Survey*, 1988). Moreover, the rates of premarital sex are increasing and may suggest even greater weakening of the bonds of fidelity within marriage (Herold, 1984:13).

CHILD REARING

Despite the substantial demands children make on the time and energy of parents, sometimes to the point of straining their marriage, almost all Canadians include at least one child in their conception of the ideal family, as Table 17–1 shows. Smaller families represent a

marked change from two centuries ago, when *eight* children was average!

Big families pay off in pre-industrial societies because children perform needed labour. Indeed, people generally regard having children as a wife's duty and, without reliable birth-control technology, child-bearing is a regular event. Of course, a high death rate in pre-industrial societies prevents many children from reaching adulthood; as late as 1900, a substantial minority of children born in Canada died in infancy or early childhood (*Canada Year Book*, 1994).

Economically speaking, industrialization trans-forms children from a vital asset to a burdensome lia-bility. Today, the expense of raising a child is sub-stantial, especially if the child acquires a university education. This expense helps to explain the steady drop in family size during the twentieth century to slightly more than one child per family in Canada today.

The trend towards smaller families also holds for all other industrial societies. But the picture differs sharply in low-income countries in Latin America, Asia, and especially Africa, where many women have few alternatives to bearing and raising children. In such societies, four to six children is the norm.

Not only is parenting expensive, it is a lifetime commitment. As our society has afforded its members more choice about family life, more adults have opted to delay childbirth or to remain childless. As Figure 17–2 shows, the median age of mothers giving birth to their first child rose by three years between 1971 and 1995; the age of mothers giving birth to their second child increased by four years in the same period. About two-thirds of parents in the United States claim they would like to devote more of their time to child rearing (Snell, 1990). The majority of Canadian par-ents would likely agree. But unless we are willing to accept some decline in our material standard of living, economic realities demand that most parents pursue careers outside the home. Thus, the child-rearing pat-terns we have described reflect ways of coming to terms with economic change.

As Chapter 12 ("Sex and Gender") explained, most women with young children now work for

TABLE 17–1 The Ideal Number of Children

	Two or less	Three	Four or more
1988	58%	29%	13%
1985	56	33	11
1980	59	27	14
1970	34	33	33
1957	22	23	55
1945	17	23	60

SOURCE: Gallup Canada Inc., *The Gallup Report*, June 6, 1988, p. 2.

income. In 1997, 76.6 percent of women age twenty-five to fifty-four were in the workforce; most mothers with children under eighteen worked for income outside the home. But while women and men share the burden of earning income, women continue to bear the traditional responsibility for raising children and doing housework. Many men in our society are eager parents, but most resist sharing responsibility for household tasks that our culture historically has defined as "women's work" (Hochschild, 1989; Presser, 1993; Keith and Schafer, 1994).

As more women join men in the labour force, parents have less time for parenting. Children of working parents spend most of the day at school. But many school-age youngsters perhaps are *latchkey kids* who fend for themselves after school. Traditionalists in the "family values" debate caution that mothers often work at the expense of children, who receive less parenting. Progressives counter that such criticism unfairly faults women for seeking the same opportunities men have long enjoyed.

THE FAMILY IN LATER LIFE

Increasing life expectancy in Canada means that, barring divorce, couples are likely to remain married for a long time. By about age fifty, most have completed the task of raising children. The remaining years of marriage bring a return to living with only one's spouse.

Like the birth of children, their departure (the "empty nest") requires adjustments, although the marital relationship often becomes closer and more satisfying in midlife. Years of living together may diminish a couple's sexual passion for each other, but mutual understanding and companionship are likely to increase.

Personal contact with children usually continues, since most older adults live a short distance from at least one of their children (Nett, 1993). Moreover, many Canadians are grandparents, and many help their daughters and sons with child care and a host of other responsibilities.

The other side of the coin, explained in Chapter 14 ("Aging and the Elderly"), is that more adults in midlife must care for aging parents. The "empty nest" may not be filled by a parent coming to live in the home, but parents living to eighty and beyond require practical, emotional, and financial care that can be more taxing than raising young children. The oldest of the "baby boomers"—now in their fifties—are often called the "sandwich generation" because they will spend as many years caring for their aging parents as they did for their own offspring.

The final, and surely the most difficult, transition in married life comes with the death of a spouse. Wives typically outlive their husbands because of

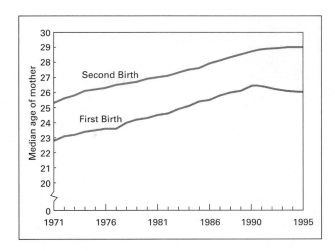

FIGURE 17–2 Median Age of Mothers Giving Birth to First or Second Child, 1971–95

SOURCE: Statistics Canada, Canadian Centre for Health Information, Health Status Section (1991); Columbo (1997).

women's longer life expectancy and the fact that wives are usually younger than husbands to begin with. Wives can thus expect to spend a significant period of their lives as widows. The bereavement and loneliness accompanying the death of a spouse are extremely difficult, and the experience may be worse for widowers, who usually have fewer friends than widows and may be unskilled at cooking and housework (Berardo, 1970).

CANADIAN FAMILIES: CLASS, RACE, AND GENDER

Dimensions of inequality—social class, ethnicity and race, and gender—are powerful forces that shape marriage and family life. This section addresses each factor separately, but bear in mind that they overlap in our lives.

SOCIAL CLASS

Social class frames a family's financial security and range of opportunities. Interviewing working-class women, Lillian Rubin (1976) found that wives deemed a good husband to be one who held a steady job and refrained from excessive drinking and violence. Rubin's middle-class informants, by contrast, never mentioned such things; these women simply *assumed* a husband would provide a safe and secure home. Their ideal husband was someone with whom they could communicate easily and share feelings and experiences.

Child Discipline, Child Abuse?

Is abuse the logical extension of socially acceptable punishment in Canada? Some researchers have found correlations between child abuse and rigid parenting styles, unrealistic expectations of children, a history of abuse in the early lives of the parents, and condoning high levels of physical punishment. A McMaster University study of parenting, based on home interviews, included a series of questions regarding child discipline (Lenton, 1990). Table 17–2 provides a brief overview of the common techniques the respondents used.

Notice how many mothers and fathers reported that they yelled at their children. The next two most frequently used strategies were slapping or spanking, followed by verbal threats. It is important to realize that these numbers may well be underrepresentations because, regardless of whether the practices are normative, the parents surveyed are still likely to be affected by the "social desirability effect" (the tendency to describe oneself in socially desirable terms).

Lenton also examined the extent to which parental discipline of children reflected the type of discipline they had received as children, or current norms favouring certain types of discipline. She found that parents generally used the type of discipline they had received as children, but only when social norms supported that type. However, when parents were particularly stressed, from unemployment or low family income, they were more likely to use violent discipline. Lenton found that unemployment is especially threatening to fathers and that low family income is particularly challenging to mothers.

At the structural level, the privacy of the family, the tradition of absolute parental authority, and the widespread acceptance of physical punishment as legitimate do support violence towards children.

TABLE 17–2 Aggressive Disciplinary Actions Tried by Parents, Ever and in Past Year (Percentages)

Ever Tried			Past Year	
Mothers	Fathers		Mothers	Fathers
99	94	yell	96	94
38	54	ridicule child	35	52
71	73	verbally threaten	65	71
18	33	withdraw emotionally	14	27
61	58	push, grab, shove	55	46
17	6	throw something at child	11	4
88	81	slap or spank with hand	75	58
20	19	hit child with object	15	10
10	10	withhold food	4	8
16	21	beat child	12	15

SOURCE: Lenton (1990:169).

SOURCE: Lenton (1990).

Such differences reflect the fact that people with higher social standing have more schooling, and most have jobs that emphasize verbal skills. In addition, middle-class couples share a wider range of activities, while working-class life is more divided along gender lines. As Rubin explains, many working-class men hold traditional ideas abut masculinity and self-control, so they stifle emotional expressiveness. Women then turn to each other as confidants.

What women (and men) think they can hope for in marriage—and what they end up with—is linked to their social class. Much the same holds for children: boys and girls lucky enough to be born into more affluent families enjoy better mental and physical health, develop higher self-confidence, and go on to greater achievement than children born to poor parents (Komarovsky, 1967; Bott, 1971; Rubin, 1976; Fitzpatrick, 1988; McLeod and Shanahan, 1993).

ETHNICITY AND RACE

As Chapter 13 ("Race and Ethnicity") discusses, ethnicity and race are powerful social forces, and the effects of both ripple through family life. Keep in mind, however, that all families are diverse and conform to no single stereotype.

Native Canadian Families

There are more than seven hundred native communities in Canada: about six hundred bands live on reserves, while there are dozens of Inuit and Métis villages and settlements as well. Over the past few decades, increasing numbers of First Nations (status Indian) people are living off reserve—42 percent in 1996 (Columbo, 1998). Residence in the major cities of Montreal, Vancouver, and Toronto is also

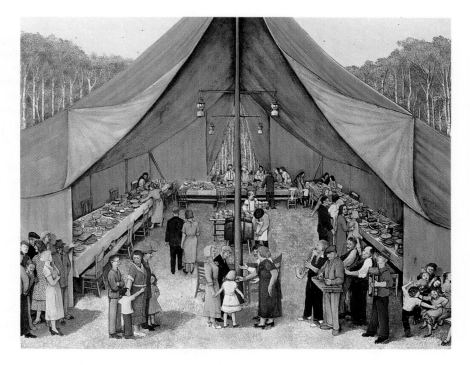

Prairie families, particularly those with a strong ethnic identity, traditionally tend to maintain kinship ties. William Kurelek's painting, Manitoba Party, *evokes the earthy gaiety of a Ukrainian family reunion.*

National Gallery of Canada, Ottawa, Courtesy: Mrs. Wm. Kurelek.

increasing—8, 5, and 3 percent for Indian, Métis, and Inuit people, respectively, in 1986 (Gerber, 1995). Given this diversity, it is impossible to discuss the family patterns of native Canadians as a homogeneous group.

Native Canadians are often among the most economically deprived members of our society, and suffer discrimination and prejudice resulting in high rates of unemployment, inadequate housing, and family instability. As one researcher says, "under these circumstances, identification with traditional cultures suffers, and their central familistic values of kin solidarity, respect for elders, and the welfare of children have been weakened" (Nett, 1993:101). Moreover, because of their political and economic subordination by Europeans, the family norms of many native people have been threatened.

Throughout the early 1900s, most native people lived on reserves or with extended families in isolated regions. Child care was the responsibility of the extended family and highly respected elders taught the young their languages and traditions. Christian missionaries, who had made concerted efforts to assimilate and Christianize native peoples, took children away from the reserves to church-run residential schools to learn another language, religion, and culture, while also learning to despise their own. Traditional family values began to erode: the elders lost their authority, and the extended families lost their responsibilities for nurturing and caretaking. Young

people raised outside of normal family settings failed to learn parenting skills to apply later on when raising their own children. In addition, resettlement programs broke up whole communities and diminished family ties even further (Shkilnyk, 1985).

The involvement of the church and the state in Canadian aboriginal life has been troublesome over the years. In the middle of this century until the mid-1970s, under the auspices of social workers employed by various Children's Aid Societies, children were taken away from parents who were no longer functioning as adequate parents because of poverty, unemployment, prejudice, alcohol abuse, and a variety of other social conditions. Many of these children were placed in non-native foster homes, where they lost contact with their remaining native traditions and culture; others were adopted by non-native families in Canada and even in the U.S. Having observed the severe adjustment problems of many of these children, authorities now focus on keeping children with their families whenever possible or placing them with other native Canadian families when it is necessary to remove them (Baker, 1991).

Mixed Marriages

Most spouses have similar social backgrounds with regard to class, race, and ethnicity, but over the course of this century, ethnicity has mattered less and less. Thus, a man of German and French ancestry might

Racially mixed couples are becoming more common, especially among the young. But do members of the white majority find people in all minorities equally attractive? Why? What patterns have you noticed on your campus?

readily marry a woman of Irish and English background.

Race remains a more formidable consideration, however. Since in 1996 African, Arab, Asian, and native Canadians represent about 13 percent of the Canadian population (www.statcan.ca), about that share of marriages would be "mixed" if people ignored race altogether in choosing marriage partners. The actual proportion is not as large, attesting to the continuing importance of race in social relations. Even so, the number of racially mixed marriages is rising steadily in the United States and will likely do so in Canada as the populations of "minority" Canadians increase. Table 17–3 shows that attitudes towards intergroup marriage in Canada have become more accepting over time. The vast majority, 80 to 92 percent, of Canadian adults are receptive to the idea of intermarriage across various racial and religious lines (Bibby, 1995:54).

GENDER

Among all races, said Jessie Bernard (1982), every marriage is actually *two* different relationships: a woman's marriage and a man's marriage. Although patriarchy has diminished, even today few marriages are composed of two equal partners. We still expect men to be older as well as taller than their wives and to have more important careers (McRae, 1986).

The persistence of the notion of man-as-breadwinner, wife-as-homemaker was illustrated in a study of steelworkers and their wives in Hamilton, Ontario. When, in 1979–80, the Women Back into Stelco Committee launched a successful discrimination complaint with the Ontario Human Rights Commission, the introduction of female co-workers into the masculine world of dangerous manual labour and big machinery was resisted among a majority of the steelworkers. In-depth interviews revealed that steelmaking was seen as men's work, strongly linked to the notion that men must be breadwinners. This attitude in turn was tied to men's "deeper sense of responsibility to provide for their families" (Livingstone and Luxton, 1995:187).

Such patriarchal values are associated with the persistent notion that marriage is more beneficial to women than to men (Bernard, 1982). The positive stereotype of the carefree bachelor contrasts sharply with the negative image of the lonely spinster. This image is rooted in a traditional view of women as being fulfilled only by being wives and mothers.

But, Bernard claimed, married women have poorer mental health, less happiness, and more passive attitudes towards life than do single women. Married men, however, live longer than single men, have better mental health, and report being happier. It is hardly surprising, then, that after divorce men are more eager than women to find a new partner.

Bernard concluded that there is no better guarantor of long life, health, and happiness for a man than a woman well socialized to perform the "duties of a wife" by devoting her life to caring for him and pro-

TABLE 17–3 Approval of Intergroup Marriage: 1975 Through 1995

	1975	1980	1985	1990	1995
Whites and natives	75%	80%	83%	84%	84%
Whites and Asians (Orientals)	66	75	78	82	83
Whites and East Indians/ Pakistanis	58	66	72	77	80
Whites and Blacks	57	64	72	79	81
Protestants and Roman Catholics	86	88	89	90	92
Protestants and Jews	80	84	84	86	90
Roman Catholics and Jews	78	81	82	85	89

SOURCE: Bibby (1995:54).

viding the security of a well-ordered home. She is quick to add that marriage *could* be healthful for women if husbands did not dominate wives and expect them to perform virtually all of the housework. Indeed, research confirms that husbands and wives with the best mental health deliberately share responsibilities for earning income, raising children, and doing housework (Ross, Mirowsky, and Huber, 1983; Mirowsky and Ross, 1984).

TRANSITION AND PROBLEMS IN FAMILY LIFE

Ann Landers (1984), a well-known observer of the North American scene, once remarked that "One marriage out of twenty is wonderful, four are good, ten are tolerable, and five are pure hell." Families can be a source of joy, but the reality of family life sometimes falls far short of this ideal.

DIVORCE

Our society strongly supports marriage, and more than nine out of ten people marry at some point, although the marriage rate is declining (Serrill, 1995:23). Moreover, many of today's marriages eventually unravel. Figure 17–3 shows the great increase in the Canadian divorce rate since 1968, followed by fluctuations between 1982 and 1996. Before 1968, divorces were granted only if one of the spouses was proven to have committed adultery; at that time the divorce rate was 40 per 100 000 population. The *Divorce Act* of 1968 allowed for divorce in certain other circumstances: if one of the spouses had committed a matrimonial offence (such as adultery or emotional or physical cruelty), if one spouse had deserted, or if the spouses had lived apart for at least three years. In 1985, the Act was rewritten, making "marriage breakdown" the only reason for divorce. (Marriage breakdown includes separation of at least one year, adultery, and physical and mental cruelty.) The divorce rate peaked in 1987 and has dropped off fairly steadily since then.

The increasing North American divorce rate has many causes (Huber and Spitze, 1980; Kitson and Raschke, 1981; Thornton, 1985; Waite, Haggstrom, and Kanouse, 1985; Weitzman, 1985; Gerstel, 1987; Furstenberg and Cherlin, 1991; Etzioni, 1993):

1. **Individualism is on the rise.** Today, members of our society spend less time together than in the past. We have become more individualistic and more concerned with personal happiness and success than with the well-being of families and children.

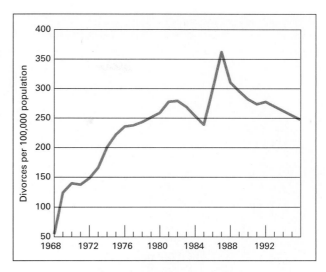

FIGURE 17–3 The Divorce Rate in Canada, 1968–1996

SOURCE: Statistics Canada, Catalogues 82-003S17 and 84-213, and Health Statistics Division, 1991; Statistics Canada, *The Daily*. January 29, 1998.

2. **Romantic love often subsides.** Our culture emphasizes romantic love as a basis for marriage, rendering relationships vulnerable as sexual passion fades. Many people end a marriage in favour of a new relationship that renews excitement and romance.

3. **Women are now less dependent on men.** Increasing participation in the labour force has reduced wives' financial dependence on husbands. As a practical matter, then, women find it easier to walk away from unhappy marriages.

4. **Many of today's marriages are stressful.** With both partners working outside the home in most cases, jobs consume time and energy that in the past were directed towards family life. Under such circumstances (and given the difficulty of securing good, affordable child care), raising children is a particular burden. Children stabilize some marriages, but divorce is most common during the early years of marriage when many couples have young children.

5. **Divorce is more socially acceptable.** Divorce no longer carries the powerful, negative stigma it did a century ago. Family and friends are now less likely to discourage couples in conflict from considering divorce.

6. **Divorce is legally easier to accomplish.** In the past, courts required divorcing couples to demonstrate that one or both were guilty of behaviour such as adultery or physical abuse. Today, as one

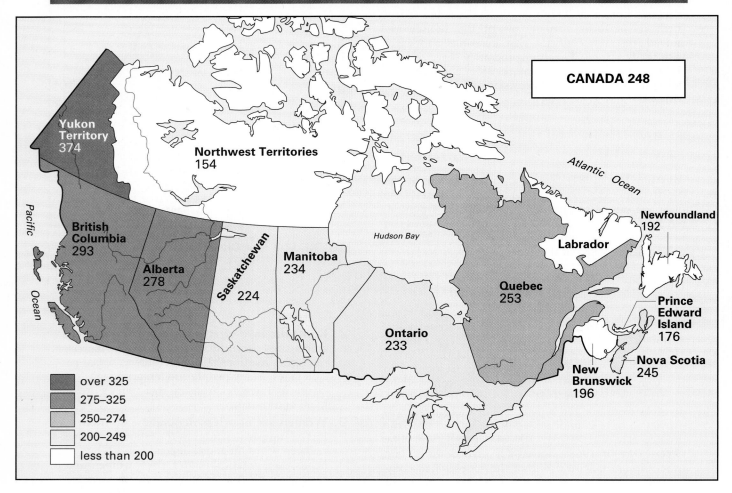

CANADA 248

Yukon Territory 374

Northwest Territories 154

British Columbia 293

Alberta 278

Saskatchewan 224

Manitoba 234

Ontario 233

Quebec 253

Labrador

Newfoundland 192

Prince Edward Island 176

Nova Scotia 245

New Brunswick 196

Pacific Ocean

Atlantic Ocean

Hudson Bay

- over 325
- 275–325
- 250–274
- 200–249
- less than 200

CANADA MAP 17–1 Divorce Rates Per 100 000 Population for Canada, the Provinces, and Territories, 1996

SOURCE: Adapted by Linda Gerber from Statistics Canada, *The Daily*, January 29, 1998.

law professor notes, "It is easier to walk away from a marriage than from a commitment to purchase a new car" (quoted in Etzioni, 1993).

The divorce rate has eased downwards slightly over the last decade for two reasons. First, the large baby-boomer cohort that was born shortly after the Second World War is now reaching middle age, when divorce is less common. Second, hard economic times discourage divorce, since living alone typically is more expensive than living in families.

Although the increase in divorces may have slowed down, Canada's rates remain a little higher than those of many European countries. Nonetheless,

it is roughly half of that of the U.S. (Columbo, 1997). Ed Kain (1990) cautions that we commonly exaggerate the stability of marriage in the past, when the early death of a spouse ended as many marriages after a few years as divorce does now.

Who Divorces?

At greatest risk of divorce are young spouses, especially those who marry after a brief courtship, have few financial resources, and have yet to mature emotionally. People of lower social position are also more likely to divorce, usually because of financial strains. At all social levels, the risk of divorce increases if a

Not all marriages thrive "til death do us part." Canada has one of the highest divorce rates in the world. The breakdown of communication that lies at the heart of failing relationships is clearly shown by Edward Hopper in his 1932 painting "Room in New York."

Edward Hopper (1882–1967), *Room in New York*, 1932. Oil on canvas. 29 × 36 in. Sheldon Memorial Art Gallery, University of Nebraska–Lincoln. F. M. Hall Collection. 1932. H–166.

couple marries in response to an unexpected pregnancy, or if one or both partners have alcohol- or other substance-abuse problems. People who are not religious divorce more readily than those who are.

Divorce also is more common if both the woman and the man have successful careers. This is partly due to the strains of a two-career marriage, and also because financially independent women are less inclined to remain in an unhappy marriage. Finally, men and women who divorce once are more likely to divorce again, presumably because problems follow them from one marriage to another (Booth and White, 1980; Yoder and Nichols, 1980; Glenn and Shelton, 1985).

Canada Map 17–1 takes a look at divorce rates across Canada. Divorce is pronounced where religious values are weaker and where people are more likely to move often, thus distancing themselves from family and friends. How would you characterize the West with regard to these factors?

Divorce as Process

Divorce is a form of role exit, as described in Chapter 6 ("Social Interaction in Everyday Life"). Paul Bohannan (1970) and others point to six distinct adjustments divorcing people make:

1. **Emotional divorce.** Distancing oneself from the former spouse usually begins before the formal break occurs. A deteriorating marriage can be fraught with indifference, disappointment, or outright hostility.

2. **Legal divorce.** Since marriage is a legal contract, divorce involves a legal change of status. Financial settlements are central to most divorce agreements.

3. **Psychic reorganization.** Many divorced people suffer not just from loneliness but from a sense that ending their marriage represents a personal failure.

4. **Community reorganization.** Ending a marriage requires both partners to reorganize friendships and adjust relations with parents and other family members who are accustomed to seeing them as a couple.

5. **Economic reorganization.** Divorce courts often require ex-spouses to sell homes and divide marital assets equally. No-fault divorce laws have reduced the amount of alimony and child support paid by men to their former wives. While divorce raises the living standards of many men (who no longer support wives and children), it can mean financial calamity to women whose earnings are lower than those of their husbands and who may be responsible for supporting children as well (Weitzman, 1985, 1996; Peterson, 1996).

6. **Parental reorganization.** More than half of all divorcing couples face the issue of child custody. Our society's conventional practice is still to award custody of children to mothers, based on the notion that women are more committed parents than men. A recent trend, however, is towards joint custody, whereby children divide

their time between both parents. Joint custody is difficult if divorced parents live far apart or do not get along, but it has the advantage of keeping children in regular contact with both parents (Roman and Haddad, 1978; Cherlin and Furstenberg, 1983).

Because mothers usually have custody of children but fathers typically earn more income, the well-being of children often depends on fathers making court-ordered child-support payments. Yet most children of divorced parents do not receive the financial support to which they are entitled by law. What has been called "an epidemic of nonsupport" has led to legislation mandating that employers withhold money from the paycheques of delinquent parents. Still, the legislation has proven very difficult to enforce (Nett, 1993).

In February 1998, British Columbia became the first North American jurisdiction to give gay and lesbian couples "the same privileges and obligations as heterosexuals for child support, custody and access" (Matas, 1998). British Columbia, North America's most progressive jurisdiction, has been extending rights and benefits to same-sex couples since the early 1990s.

Divorce may well be hardest on children. Divorce can tear young people from familiar surroundings, entangle them in bitter feuding, and distance them from a parent they love. And, most seriously of all, in their own minds, many children blame themselves for their parents' breakup. For many children, divorce changes the trajectory of their entire lives, increasing the likelihood of emotional and behavioural problems and the risk of dropping out of school and getting into trouble with the law. Some experts, however, point out that divorce can be better for children than staying in a family torn by tension or violence. In any case, parents must be mindful that, when deciding whether to divorce, much more than their own well-being is at stake (Wallerstein and Blakeslee, 1989; Adelson, 1996; Popenoe, 1996).

REMARRIAGE

Despite the rising divorce rate, marriage—and remarriage—remain as popular as ever. Four out of five people who divorce remarry, and most do so within three years (Ahlburg and De Vita, 1992). Nationwide, almost half of all marriages are now remarriages for at least one partner. Men, who derive greater benefits from wedlock, are more likely to remarry than women.

Remarriage often creates *blended families*, composed of children and some combination of biological parents and stepparents. Blended families thus have to define precisely who is part of the child's nuclear family (Furstenberg, 1984). Blended families also require

children to reorient themselves; an only child, for example, may suddenly find she has two older brothers. And, as already noted, the risk of divorce is high in remarriages. But blended families also offer both young and old the opportunity to relax rigid family roles.

FAMILY VIOLENCE

The ideal family serves as a haven from the dangers of the outside world. However, from the Biblical story of Cain's killing of his brother Abel to the recent Bernardo-Homolka case, the disturbing reality of many homes is **family violence**, *emotional, physical, or sexual abuse of one family member by another*. Sociologist Richard J. Gelles points to a chilling fact:

> The family is the most violent group in society with the exception of the police and the military. You are more likely to get killed, injured, or physically attacked in your home by someone you are related to than in any other social context. (Quoted in Roesch, 1984:75)

Violence Against Women

The common stereotype of a violent partner is a lower-class man who now and then drinks too much, loses control, and beats up his wife. In reality, although financial problems and unemployment do make the problem worse, violence against women in the home is perpetrated by men of all social classes, races, and ethnicities (Lupri, 1988:170). Furthermore, this violence often occurs at random. Family brutality frequently goes unreported to police, but researchers estimate that 20 percent of couples—or one in five—endure at least some violence each year (Lupri, 1988:171). Many of these couples experience serious incidents of violence, including kicking, biting, and punching.

Almost 30 percent of women who are murdered—as opposed to 6 percent of men—are killed by spouses, ex-spouses, or unmarried partners (Lupri, 1988). In 1989, 119 women in Canada were murdered by former husbands or partners (Begin, 1991). Overall, women are more likely to be injured by a family member than they are to be mugged or raped by a stranger or injured in an automobile accident.

Physically abused women have traditionally had few options. They may want to leave home, but many—especially those with children and without much money—have nowhere to go. Most wives are also committed to their marriages and believe (however unrealistically) that they can help abusive husbands to change. Some, unable to understand their husbands' violence, blame themselves. Others, raised in violent families, consider assault to be part of family life. Most abused women see no way out of the family violence that makes fear the centrepiece of their lives. In one study, researchers found that one-quarter of women who had entered a metropolitan hospital after attempting suicide had been victims of family violence (Stark and Flitcraft, 1979).

In 1990, Canada's solicitor general attempted to address the problem of crime and abuse against women by producing *Woman Alone*, a book of prevention advice. But this document ignored the situations that most frequently expose women to danger—domestic and private settings where they are threatened by men they know. One reason for this misjudgment is that victimization studies ask about "crime" and "many victims do not perceive their partners' violent actions as crimes in the legal sense" (DeKeseredy et al., 1995:479).

In the past, the law regarded domestic violence as a private, family matter. Now, even without separation or divorce, a woman can obtain court protection from an abusive spouse. "Stalker" legislation, introduced in 1993, protects women and children who are being threatened and followed. Some medical personnel are also more aware today of the tell-tale signs of spousal violence and are more likely to report such cases to police than they were in the past.

Communities across North America are establishing shelters that provide counselling as well as temporary housing for women and children driven from their homes by violence. In Ontario alone, in 1989, 78 transition houses accommodated 9838 women, accompanied by 11 000 children. Eighty-seven percent of these families were in shelters because of domestic violence. Some men and women who abuse their partners are also joining self-help groups in an effort to understand and control their own behaviour. In various ways, then, our society is beginning to mobilize against this serious problem.

Violence Against Children

Family violence also victimizes children. Perhaps 4 percent of all youngsters suffer abuse each year, including several hundred who die as a result. Child abuse entails more than physical injury because abusive adults misuse power and trust to undermine a child's emotional well-being. Child abuse is most common among the youngest and most vulnerable children (Straus and Gelles, 1986; Van Biema, 1994; Besharov and Laumann, 1996).

In 1996, children were reported missing at a rate of one every nine minutes—over 56 000 in that year. An alarming 78 percent of these youngsters are runaways; 57 percent of the runaways are girls; and the runaways are getting younger. Too many of these youngsters leave home because of abuse (psychologi-

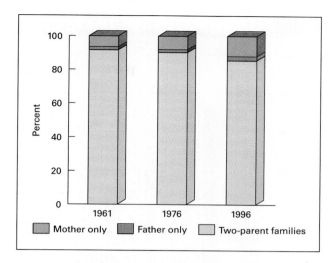

FIGURE 17–4 Single-Parent Families in Canada, 1961, 1976, and 1996

SOURCE: Statistics Canada, Household and Family Projections, 1976–2001, Catalogue No. 91-522, 1991; www.statcan.ca, 1998.

cal, sexual, or physical) and neglect. Recently, more of these children are leaving home because their parents say they can't afford to keep them, thereby repeating a pattern that appeared during the recession of the early 1980s. These numbers are described as an alarming sign of the increasing disintegration of the family (Mitchell, 1998, reporting on Statscan's *Juristat*, February 12).

Many abused children suffer in silence, believing that they are to blame for their own victimization. Abuse, compounded by years of guilt, can leave lasting emotional scars that prevent people abused as children from forming healthy relationships as adults.

About 90 percent of child abusers are men, but they conform to no simple stereotype. Most abusers, however, share one trait: having been abused themselves as children. Research shows that violent behaviour in close relationships is learned. In families, then, violence begets violence (Gwartney-Gibbs, Stockard, and Booftenhmer, 1987; Widom, 1996).

ALTERNATIVE FAMILY FORMS

Most families in Canada are still composed of a married couple who raise children. But, in recent decades, our society has displayed greater diversity in family life.

ONE-PARENT FAMILIES

As Figure 17–4 indicates, in 1961, 8.4 percent of Canadian families were headed by a single parent and

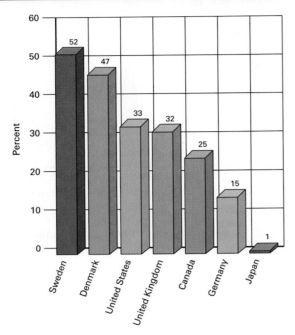

FIGURE 17–5 Percentage of Births to Unmarried Women, 1994

SOURCE: U.S. Bureau of the Census (1997).

91.6 percent were husband-wife families. By 1996, single-parent families had risen to 14.6 percent. Projections are that by 2011, two-parent families will decrease further to 83 percent (1993 *Corpus Almanac and Canadian Sourcebook*). Thus, the proportion of one-parent families is growing rapidly, and almost 12 percent of children in Canada now live in these families. One-parent families—about four times more likely to be headed by women than men—may result from divorce, the inability to find a suitable husband, or an unmarried woman's decision to have a child (Kantrowitz, 1985). Figure 17–5 compares the proportion of Canadian births out of wedlock to those of other industrial nations.

Single parenthood increases a woman's risk of poverty because it limits her ability to work and to further her education. The converse is also true: poverty raises the odds that a young woman will become a single mother (Trent, 1994).

Considerable research shows that growing up in a one-parent family usually disadvantages children. Some studies indicate that because a father and a mother each make distinctive contributions to a child's social development, it is unrealistic to expect one parent alone to do as good a job. But the most serious problem among families with one parent—especially if that parent is a woman—is poverty. Female lone-headed families have the highest rate of low income (*Women in Canada*, 1995:86).

On average, children growing up in a single-parent family start out poorer, get less schooling, and end up with lower incomes as adults. Such children are also more likely to be single parents themselves (Mueller and Cooper, 1984; McLanahan, 1985; Weisner and Eiduson, 1986; Wallerstein and Blakeslee, 1989; Astone and McLanahan, 1991; Li and Wojtkiewicz, 1992; Biblarz and Raftery, 1993; Popenoe, 1993; Shapiro and Schrof, 1995; Webster, Orbuch, and House, 1995; Wu, 1996).

COHABITATION

Cohabitation is *the sharing of a household by an unmarried couple.* A generation ago, widespread use of terms such as "shacking up" and "living in sin" indicated disapproval of cohabitation. But, as our society has grown more accepting of premarital sex, the number of cohabiting couples has increased sharply, from 8 percent of families in 1981 to 24 percent in 1996. Figure 17–6 shows the increases over this period, including variations among provinces. Quebec stands out as a province with a dramatic increase in common-law living.

In global perspective, cohabitation is common in Sweden and other Scandinavian societies as a long-term form of family life, with or without children. But it is rare in more traditional (and Roman Catholic) nations such as Italy. While cohabitation is gaining in popularity in Canada, such partnerships are still usually of short duration, with perhaps 40 percent of couples marrying after several years and the remainder splitting up (Blumstein and Schwartz, 1983; Macklin, 1983; Popenoe, 1988, 1991, 1992; Bumpass and Sweet, 1995).

GAY AND LESBIAN COUPLES

In 1989, Denmark became the first country to legalize same-sex marriages, thereby extending to gay and lesbian couples the legal advantages for inheritance, taxation, and joint property ownership. Norway (1993) and Sweden (1995) have followed suit. In Canada, while gays and lesbians cannot legally marry, there are churches that will sanctify such a union. The Metropolitan Community Church in Toronto is an ecumenical denomination that serves gays and lesbians with many of the rituals of the Christian church. The gay or lesbian marriage or "commitment" ceremony, for instance, is based on traditional Christian marriage vows. A number of institutions acknowledge homosexual partnerships in various spousal support and benefit schemes. The British Columbia government announced in 1998 that it would support legislation extending many rights to same-sex couples. Legal marriage may not be far behind.

Even though they are barred from legal marriage, many gay men and lesbians form long-term, committed partnerships and families (Bell, Weinberg, and Kiefer-Hammersmith, 1981; Gross, 1991). This is especially true of lesbian couples, who are more likely than gay couples to remain sexually exclusive (Blumstein and Schwartz, 1983). In 1995, members of gay and lesbian couples in Ontario won the right to adopt the biological children of their partners under the "stepparent adoption clause" of the *Child and Family Services Act*. In 1998, as already mentioned, B.C. gave separating same-sex parents equal privileges and obligations with respect to their children.

SINGLEHOOD

Because nine out of ten people in Canada marry, we tend to see singlehood as a transitory stage of life. In recent decades, however, more women and men have deliberately chosen the freedom and independence of living alone, remaining both single and childless (Nett, 1993).

Most striking is the rising number of single young women. In 1960 about one in four women aged twenty to twenty-four was single; by 1990 the proportion was nearing two-thirds. Underlying this trend is women's greater participation in the labour force. Women who are economically secure consider a husband a matter of choice rather than a financial necessity.

By midlife, however, women who have not married confront a lack of available men. Because our culture expects a woman to "marry up," the older a woman is, the more education she has, and the better her job, the more difficulty she has in finding a suitable husband (Leslie and Korman, 1989).

NEW REPRODUCTIVE TECHNOLOGY AND THE FAMILY

In 1991, Arlette Schweitzer, a forty-two-year-old librarian living in Aberdeen, South Dakota, became the first woman on record to bear her own grandchildren. Because her daughter was unable to carry a baby to term, Schweitzer agreed to have her daughter's fertilized embryos surgically implanted in her own womb. Nine months later, she gave birth to a healthy boy and girl (Kolata, 1991).

Such a case illustrates how *new reproductive technology* has created both new choices for families and new controversies for society as a whole. The benefits

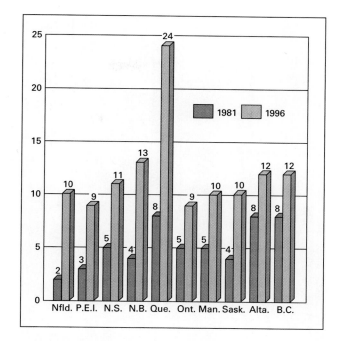

FIGURE 17–6 Couples Living Common Law by Province, 1981 and 1996 (percentage of all couples)[1]

[1] Includes married and common-law couples with and without children.
SOURCE: Statistics Canada, Catalogue Nos. 93-312 and 93-320, cited in Stout (1994:9); calculations based on census tables, www.statcan.ca.

of this rapidly developing technology are exciting, but it raises daunting ethical questions about the creation and manipulation of life itself.

A generation ago, England's Louise Joy Brown became the world's first "test-tube" baby; since then, tens of thousands of people have been conceived this way. Early in the twenty-first century, 2 or 3 percent of the children in industrial societies may result from new birth technologies.

Test-tube babies are the product of *in vitro fertilization*, a procedure whereby the male sperm and the female ovum are united "in glass" rather than in a woman's body. When successful, this complex medical procedure, undertaken by several thousand Canadian couples each year, produces embryos, which doctors either implant in the womb of a woman who is to bear the child or freeze for use at a later time.

At present, *in vitro* fertilization helps some couples who cannot conceive normally to have children. Looking ahead, new birth technologies may help reduce the incidence of birth defects. Genetically screening sperm and eggs allows medical specialists to increase the odds for the birth of a healthy baby. At the same time, new reproductive technology raises fascinating questions: Is Arlette Schweitzer the

For better or worse, the family is certainly changing. But the fact that young people still find marriage so attractive—even amid the most severe adversity—suggests that families will continue to play a central role in society for centuries to come.

mother of the children she bore? The grandmother? Both? Then, too, we need to consider that, when it comes to manipulating life, what is technically possible may not always be morally desirable (Vines, 1986; Ostling, 1987; Thompson, 1994).

LOOKING AHEAD: FAMILY IN THE TWENTY-FIRST CENTURY

Family life in Canada has changed in recent decades, and this change will continue. Change causes controversy, in this case pitting advocates of "traditional family values" against supporters of new family forms and greater personal choice. Sociologists cannot predict the outcome of this debate, but we can posit five probable future trends.

First, divorce rates are likely to remain high, even in the face of evidence that marital dissolution harms children. Yet, today's marriages are about as durable as they were a century ago, when many were cut short by death (Kain, 1990). The difference is that more couples now *choose* to end marriages that fail to live up to their expectations. Therefore, although the divorce rate has stabilized recently, it is unlikely that marriage will ever again be as durable as in the 1950s. But perhaps we should view the recent trend towards higher divorce rates less as a threat to families than as a sign of change in family form. After all, most divorces still lead to remarriage, so marriage is hardly becoming obsolete.

Second, family life in the twenty-first century will be highly variable. Cohabiting couples, one-parent families, gay and lesbian families, and blended families are all increasing in number. Most families, of course, still are based on marriage, and most married couples still have children. But, taken together, the variety of family forms implies a growing belief that family life is a matter of choice.

Third, men are likely to continue to play a limited role in child rearing. In the 1950s, a decade many people see as the "golden age" of families, men began to withdraw from active parenting (Snell, 1990; Stacey, 1990). Since then, the share of children growing up in homes without their fathers has risen steadily (Colombo, 1992:84). A counter trend is now emerging as some fathers—older, on average, and more established in their careers—eagerly jump into the parenting role. But, on balance, the high divorce rate and a surge in single motherhood point to more children growing up with weak ties to fathers. At the same time, evidence is building that the absence of fathers harms children, at the very least because such families are at high risk of being poor.

Fourth, we will continue to feel the effects of economic changes in our families (Hochschild, 1989). In many families, both household partners now work, making marriage the interaction of weary men and women who try to squeeze in a little "quality time" for themselves and their children (Dizard and Gadlin, 1990). Two-career couples may advance the goal of gender equality, but the long-term effects on families are likely to be mixed.

Fifth and finally, the importance of new reproductive technologies will increase. While ethical concerns surely will slow these developments, new methods of reproduction will continue to alter the traditional meanings of parenthood, as the "Controversy & Debate" box discusses.

Despite the social changes buffeting the family in Canada, most people still report being happy as partners and parents. Marriage and family life today may be more controversial than in the past, but both will likely remain the foundation of our society for some time to come.

The New Reproductive Technologies

Are "traditional families" virtually an arrangement of the past? Singlehood has increased, people often live together without marriage, divorce is on the increase, and a growing number of young women are having and keeping children as single parents. But perhaps the most revolutionary change to the family is the introduction of new reproductive technologies (NRTs), which have created a revolution in reproduction, in science, and in the family, with the potential for major social repercussions.

The very availability of these technologies raises important ethical questions about what kind of world we want to live in and how much control we want over that world. Among the new reproductive technologies are such alternatives as sex selection techniques, artificial insemination, *in vitro* fertilization, embryo transplants, and surrogate motherhood. At one time, it was not unusual to see ads in university newspapers in Canada in which a young woman would offer her services as a surrogate mother, or a young man would offer his sperm for sale.

NRTs carry with them a host of ethical questions and decisions. They have separated gestational, genetic, and social parenthood; eliminated the need for intercourse between a man and a woman for reproduction; and enabled men and women to purchase the necessities of reproduction (eggs and sperm) without the possibility of identification of the other parent.

Consider the following example. In his book *The Ethics of Genetic Control*, Joseph Fletcher argues for quality control in the creation of children. According to Fletcher, fetuses should be monitored, and those that show evidence of disease should be aborted. "We ought," he says, "to protect our families from the emotional and material burden of such diseased individuals and from the misery of their simply existing (not living) in a nearby 'warehouse' or public institution. ... Choosing high quality fetuses and rejecting low quality ones is not tragedy; sad, but not agonizing."

The question we face is this: once we decide to abort "low quality" fetuses, where do we draw the line? For Fletcher, all female fetuses that might carry a gene predisposing their children to hemophilia should automatically be aborted, even though today hemophiliacs can lead long and productive lives.

In Canada, the federal government has taken a hard line on regulating NRTs. In June 1996, legislation was tabled in the House of Commons that effectively banned many procedures. The bill would, however, still allow couples to practise "sex selection" by aborting female fetuses with the hemophilia gene.

But Madeline Boscoe, who works at a women's health clinic in Winnipeg, says that most Canadians support regulation in these areas. "I think it is important that we say as a society that you can't sell your eye to get through medical school. Why is this any different?" (McIlroy, 1996)

Continue the debate . . .

1. *Do you agree that NRTs should be regulated by the government? Should there be fines and jail sentences for men selling their sperm and women selling their eggs? Why or why not?*
2. *Do you agree with Joseph Fletcher that fetuses should be monitored so that society can exercise "quality control" over those allowed to take their place in it? Are there similarities between Fletcher's recommendations and Adolf Hitler's plan to develop a "Master Race"?*
3. *Is the sale of reproductive elements comparable to the sale of body parts? Why or why not?*

SUMMARY

1. All societies are built on kinship, although family forms vary considerably across cultures and over time.

2. In industrial societies such as Canada, marriage is monogamous. Many pre-industrial societies, however, permit polygamy, of which there are two types: polygyny and polyandry.

3. In global perspective, patrilocality is most common, while industrial societies favour neolocality and a few societies have matrilocal residence.

Industrial societies use bilateral descent, while pre-industrial societies tend to be either patrilineal or matrilineal.

4. Structural-functional analysis identifies major family functions: socializing the young, regulating sexual activity, transmitting social placement, and providing material and emotional support.

5. Social-conflict theories explore how the family perpetuates social inequality by transmitting divisions based on class, ethnicity, race, and gender.

6. Micro-level analysis highlights the variable nature of family life both over time and as experienced by individual family members.

7. Families originate in the process of courtship. Unlike Canada, few societies base the choice of a mate on romantic love. But even among members of our society, romantic love tends to join people with similar social backgrounds.

8. The vast majority of married couples have children, although family size has decreased over time. The key reason for this decline is industrialization, which transforms children into economic liabilities, encourages women to gain an education and to join the labour force, and reduces infant mortality.

9. Married life changes as children leave home to form families of their own. Many middle-aged couples, however, care for aging parents and are active grandparents. The final stage of this life course begins with the death of one spouse, usually the husband.

10. Families differ according to class position, race, and ethnicity. Some immigrant families, for example, tend to maintain extended kinship ties. Poorer families are more likely than others to be headed by women. Among all categories of people, well-to-do families enjoy the most options and the greatest financial security.

11. Gender affects family dynamics since husbands dominate in most marriages. Research suggests that marriage provides more benefits to men than to women.

12. The divorce rate today is ten times higher than it was a century ago; four in ten current marriages will end in divorce. Most people who divorce—especially men—remarry, often forming blended families that include children from previous marriages.

13. Most family violence victimizes women and children and is far more common than official records indicate. Most adults who abuse family members were themselves abused as children.

14. Our society's family life is becoming more varied. One-parent families, cohabitation, gay and lesbian couples, and singlehood have proliferated in recent years. While the law does not recognize homosexual marriages, many gay men and lesbians form long-lasting relationships and, increasingly, are becoming parents.

15. Although ethically controversial, new reproductive technology is altering conventional notions of parenthood.

CRITICAL THINKING QUESTIONS

1. How has the emerging post-industrial economy affected family life? What other factors are changing the family?

2. Why do some analysts describe the family as the "backbone of society"? How do families perpetuate social inequality?

3. Do you think that single-parent households do as good a job as two-parent households of raising children? Why or why not?

4. On balance, are families in Canada becoming weaker or not? What evidence can you cite?

SOCIOLOGY APPLIED

1. Parents and grandparents can be wonderful sources of information about changes in marriage and the family. Spend an hour or two with married people of two different generations and ask about when they married, what their married lives have been like, and what changes in today's world stand out to them.

2. Relationships with various family members differ. With which family member—mother, father, brother, sister—do you most readily and least readily share secrets? Why? Which family member would you turn to first in a crisis? Why?

3. Focus on the Family Canada is a conservative organization supporting what they call "traditional family values." Visit their Web site (www.fotf.ca) and find out what they consider to be a "traditional family." Why do they defend "traditional families"? What problems of families do they ignore?

4. Organize a debate for one class period with a team arguing each side of the "family-values" controversy. Present arguments for and against the following statement: "Resolved: The traditional family is necessary for the survival of our country's way of life."

www.cfc-efc.ca/

Initiated by the Canadian Child Care Federation, with the cooperation of forty-one non-profit organizations, *Child & Family Canada* is all about child care, child development, parenting, health, safety, literacy, media influences, nutrition, physical activities, play, family life, adolescence, learning activities, social issues and special needs.

www.divorce-online.com/

A resource for people involved in, or facing the prospect of, divorce, *Divorce Online* provides free articles and information on the financial, legal, psychological, real-estate, and other aspects of divorce.

www.famvi.com/

Dedicated to stopping domestic violence and child abuse, the *Family Violence Awareness Page* provides information about services for families in need of assistance, as well as articles and essays, facts, and statistics.

www.trinity.edu/~mkearl/family.html

Michael Kearl's *Guide to the Sociology of the Family* provides a useful sociological overview of family issues, including a survey of family relations across cultures and time, cultural factors (matters of age, gender, sex, and violence) that shape family structures and processes, parenting, genealogy, divorce, and so on.

www.lesbian.org/lesbian-moms/

Lesbian Mothers Support Society is a Canadian, non-profit group that provides peer support for lesbian parents and their children, as well as for lesbians considering parenthood. The site includes information about adoption, alternative fertilization, children's resources, coming out, legal issues, lesbian health, parenting, pregnancy, and a guide to lesbian baby-making.

Dinh Q. Le, *Interconfined*, 1994

© 1994 Dinh Le, c-print and linen tape, 55 × 39 in.

CHAPTER 18

RELIGION

Elisha Hack was elated at the news: highly prestigious Yale University had accepted him for the Class of 2001. But when he arrived on campus in the fall of 1997, his excitement turned to disappointment and confusion. In his dorm, Hack—an Orthodox Jew—was stunned to find only a short staircase separating men's and women's rooms. Copies of the "Safer Sex Menu" were prominently displayed in the lounges alongside bowls of condoms, and orientation that evening was a "safe-sex" seminar complete with a demonstration of how to use dental dams.

Was university life—at least at Yale—consumed by sin like the biblical cities of Sodom and Gomorrah? Hack wanted an education, but not if the living arrangements violated his religious principles. So Hack proposed what he viewed as a reasonable solution: he would enrol at Yale, but live off campus in an environment more to his liking. Yale, however, stuck to its requirement that all first-year students live in dorms, where they learn to interact with others who are different from themselves. The case now seems likely to end up in court (Cloud, 1997).

Religion has always played a central part in North American society, and conflicts like the one between Elisha Hack and Yale University are nothing new. Indeed, this dispute is merely one example of the long-standing debate over the proper role of religion in social life. This chapter explains what religion is, explores the changing face of religious belief throughout history and around the world, and examines the vital—yet sometimes controversial—place of religion in today's modern, scientific culture.

RELIGION: BASIC CONCEPTS

For French sociologist Emile Durkheim, whose ideas are discussed in detail in Chapter 4 ("Society"), the focus of religion is "things that surpass the limits of our knowledge" (1965:62; orig. 1915). As human beings, Durkheim explained, we organize our surroundings by defining most objects, events, or experiences as **profane** (from Latin meaning "outside the temple"), *that which is an ordinary element of everyday life.* But we set some things apart, Durkheim continued, by designating them as **sacred**, *that which is defined as extraordinary, inspiring a sense of awe, rever-*

ence, and even fear. Distinguishing the sacred from the profane is the essence of all religious belief. **Religion**, then, is *a social institution involving beliefs and practices based on a conception of the sacred.*

A global perspective reveals great variety in matters of faith, with no one thing sacred to everyone on earth. Although people regard most books as profane, Jews view the Torah (the first five books of the Hebrew Bible or Old Testament) as sacred, in the same way that Christians revere the Old and New Testaments of the Bible and Muslims exalt the Qur'an (Koran).

But no matter how a community of believers draws religious lines, Durkheim (1965:62) explained, people understand profane things in terms of their everyday usefulness: we log onto the Web with our computer or turn the key to start our car. What is sacred, however, we reverently set apart from everyday life and denote as "forbidden." Marking the boundary between the sacred and the profane, for example, Muslims remove their shoes before entering a mosque to avoid defiling a sacred place of worship with soles that have touched the profane ground outside.

The sacred is embodied in **ritual**, *formal, ceremonial behaviour.* Holy communion is the central ritual of

457

Religion is founded on the concept of the sacred: that which is set apart as extraordinary and which demands our submission. Bowing, kneeling, or prostrating oneself—shown in Fred Ehrlich's painting Facing Mecca—*are common elements in religious life that symbolize this surrender to a higher power.*

Christianity; the wafer and wine consumed during communion are sacred symbols of the body and blood of Jesus Christ, and are never treated in a profane way as food.

RELIGION AND SOCIOLOGY

Because religion deals with ideas that transcend everyday experience, neither sociology nor any other scientific discipline can verify or disprove religious doctrine. Religion is a matter of **faith**, *belief anchored in conviction rather than scientific evidence*. The New Testament of the Bible, for instance, describes faith as "the assurance of things hoped for, the conviction of things not seen" (Heb. 11:1) and exhorts Christians to "walk by faith, not by sight" (2 Cor. 5:7).

Through most of our history, human beings lived in small societies and attributed birth, death, and whatever happened in between to the operation of supernatural forces. Over the last several hundred years, however, science has emerged as an alternative way of understanding the natural world, and scientific sociology offers various explanations of how and why societies operate the way they do.

Some people with strong faith may be disturbed by the thought of sociologists turning a scientific eye to what they hold as sacred. In truth, however, a sociological study of religion is no threat to anyone's faith. Sociologists recognize that religion is central to virtually every culture on earth, and they seek to understand how religious beliefs and practices guide human societies. As sociologists, they cannot comment on the meaning and purpose of human existence or pass judgment on any religion as right or wrong. Rather, scientific sociology takes a more "worldly" approach by delving into why religions take particular forms in one society or another and how religious activity affects society as a whole.

THEORETICAL ANALYSIS OF RELIGION

Although, as individuals, sociologists may hold any number of religious beliefs—or none at all—they agree that religion plays a major role in the operation of society. Each theoretical paradigm suggests ways in which religion shapes social life.

FUNCTIONS OF RELIGION: STRUCTURAL-FUNCTIONAL ANALYSIS

Emile Durkheim (1965; orig. 1915) maintained that in religious life, people celebrate the awesome power of their society. Doesn't society, he asked, *have* an awesome power and an existence of its own beyond the life of any individual? Thus, some form of religion is found everywhere because society itself is "godlike." No wonder, too, that people in all societies transform certain everyday objects into sacred symbols of their collective life. Members of technologically simple societies, Durkheim explained, do this with the **totem**, *an object in the natural world collectively defined as sacred*. The totem—perhaps an animal or an elaborate work of art—becomes the centrepiece of ritual, symbolizing the power of collective life over any individual. In our society, the flag is a quasi-sacred totem. It is not to be used in a profane manner (say, as clothing) or allowed to touch the ground. The beaver, the maple leaf, and the *fleur de lis* are also quasi-sacred totems in Canada. Local communities across Canada also gain a sense of unity through totem-like symbolism attached to sports teams—from the Montreal Canadiens through the Toronto Blue Jays, the Calgary Stampeders, and the Vancouver Canucks.

The foundation of all religious life is ritual. Formal religious observances, such as this Buddhist ceremony in Seoul, South Korea, reveal the discipline needed in order to live out religious principles.

Why is the religious dimension of social life so important? Durkheim pointed out three major functions of religion:

1. **Social cohesion.** The shared symbols, values, and norms of religion unite people. Religious doctrine and ritual establish rules of "fair play" that make organized social life possible. Religion also involves *love* and *commitment*, which underscore both our moral and emotional ties to others (Wright and D'Antonio, 1980).

2. **Social control.** Every society uses religious imagery and rhetoric to promote conformity. Societies infuse many cultural norms—especially mores relating to marriage and reproduction—with religious justification. Religion even legitimizes the political system. In medieval Europe, in fact, monarchs claimed to rule by divine right. Few of today's political leaders invoke religion so explicitly, but many publicly ask for God's blessing, implying to audiences that their efforts are right and just.

3. **Providing meaning and purpose.** Religious beliefs offer the comforting sense that the vulnerable human condition serves some greater purpose. Strengthened by such convictions, people are less likely to despair when confronted by life's calamities. For this reason, major life-course transitions—including birth, marriage, and death—are usually marked by religious observances that enhance our spiritual awareness.

Critical evaluation. In Durkheim's structural-functional analysis, religion represents the collective life of society. The major weakness of this approach, however, is that it downplays religion's dysfunctions—especially the fact that strongly held beliefs can generate social conflict. During the early Middle Ages, for example, religious faith was the driving force behind the Crusades, in which European Christians battled Muslims for the Holy Lands that both religions considered to be sacred. Conflict among Muslims, Jews, and Christians is still a source of political instability in the Middle East today. Similarly, tensions continue to divide Protestants and Catholics in Northern Ireland; Dutch Calvinism historically supported apartheid in South Africa; and religious conflict persists in Algeria, India, Sri Lanka, and elsewhere. In short, many nations have marched to war under the banner of their god, and few analysts dispute that differences in faith have provoked more violence in the world than have differences of social class.

CONSTRUCTING THE SACRED: SYMBOLIC-INTERACTION ANALYSIS

"Society," asserts Peter Berger (1967:3), "is a human product and nothing but a human product, that yet continuously acts back upon its producer." In other words, from a symbolic-interactionist point of view, religion (like all of society) is socially constructed (although perhaps with divine inspiration). Through various rituals, from daily prayers to annual religious observances such as Easter or Passover, individuals sharpen the distinction between the sacred and profane. Further, Berger explains, by placing everyday events within a "cosmic frame of reference," people give their fallible, transitory creations "the semblance of ultimate security and permanence" (1967:35–36).

Religion and Patriarchy: Does God Favour Males?

Why do Canadians tend to envision God in male terms? Probably because we link "godly" attributes such as wisdom and power to men. Thus, it is hardly surprising that organized religions tend to favour males, a fact evident in passages from many of the sacred writings of major world religions.

The Qur'an (Koran)—the sacred text of Islam—asserts that men are to dominate women:

> Men are in charge of women.... Hence good women are obedient ... As for those whose rebelliousness you fear, admonish them, banish them from your bed, and scourge them (quoted in Kaufman, 1976:163).

Christianity—the major religion of the Western world—supports patriarchy. While many Christians revere Mary, the mother of Jesus, the New Testament also includes the following passages:

> A man ... is the image and glory of God; but woman is the glory of man. For man was not made from woman, but woman from man. Neither was man created for woman, but woman for man. (1 Cor. 11:7–9)

As in all the churches of the saints, the women should keep silence in the churches. For they are not permitted to speak, but should be subordinate, as even the law says. If there is anything they desire to know, let them ask their husbands at home. For it is shameful for a woman to speak in church. (1 Cor. 14:33–35)

> Wives, be subject to your husbands, as to the Lord. For the husband is the head of the wife as Christ is the head of the church. ... As the church is subject to Christ, so let wives also be subject in everything to their husbands. (Eph. 5:22–24)

Let a woman learn in silence with all submissiveness. I permit no woman to teach or to have authority over men; she is to keep silent. For Adam was formed first, then Eve; and Adam was not deceived,

---

Marriage is a good example. If two people look on marriage as merely a legal contract between them, they can end the marriage whenever they want to. But defined as holy matrimony, their relationship makes a far stronger claim on them. This fact, no doubt, explains why the divorce rate is lower among people who are more religious.

Especially when humans confront uncertainty and life-threatening situations—such as illness, war, and natural disaster—we turn to religion. Seeking sacred meaning helps people recover from life's setbacks and even face the prospect of death with strength and courage.

Critical evaluation. The symbolic-interaction approach views religion as a social construction, placing everyday life under a "sacred canopy" of meaning (Berger, 1967). Of course, Berger adds, the religion's ability to legitimize and stabilize society depends on its constructed character going unrecognized. After all, we would derive little strength from sacred beliefs that we saw as mere devices for coping with tragedy.

Then, too, this micro-level view pays scant attention to religion's part in maintaining social inequality, to which we now turn.

INEQUALITY AND RELIGION: SOCIAL-CONFLICT ANALYSIS

The social-conflict paradigm highlights religion's support of social hierarchy. Religion, claimed Karl Marx, serves ruling elites by legitimizing the status quo and diverting people's attention from social inequities.

Even today, for example, the British monarch is the nominal head of the Church of England, illustrating the close alliance between religious and political elites. In practical terms, working for political change may mean opposing the church and, by implication, God. Religion also encourages people to look with hope to a "better world to come," minimizing the social problems of this world. In one of his best-known statements, Marx offered a stinging criticism of religion as "the sigh of the oppressed creature, the sentiment of a heartless world, and the soul of soulless

but the woman was deceived and became a transgressor. Yet woman will be saved through bearing children, if she continues in faith and love and holiness, with modesty. (1 Tim. 2:11–15)

Judaism, too, traditionally supports patriarchy. Male Orthodox Jews include the following words in daily prayer:

Blessed art thou, O Lord our God, King of the Universe, that I was not born a gentile.

Blessed art thou, O Lord our God, King of the Universe, that I was not born a slave.

Blessed art thou, O Lord our God, King of the Universe, that I was not born a woman.

Major religions are also patriarchal in excluding women from the clergy. Even today, Islam and the Roman Catholic church continue to ban women from the priesthood. A growing number of Protestant denominations—including the Church of England—have overturned historical policies and now ordain women. Orthodox Judaism upholds the traditional prohibition against women serving as rabbis, but Reform and Reconstructionist Judaism look to both men and women as spiritual leaders since the early 1970s (and both these denominations ordain gay and lesbian people), and the first woman rabbi in the Conservative denomination of Judaism was ordained in 1985. Of the eighty religious denominations surveyed in Canada in 1986, only twenty-nine ordained women. The United Church of Canada reported the highest number, with 441 female clergy (11 percent of the total). Seven percent of Anglican clergy and 8 percent of Presbyterian clergy were women (Baril and Mori, 1991). The proportion of women among students in seminary schools across Canada has never been higher, evidence that change may be only a matter of time.

Challenges to the patriarchal structure of organized religion—from or-daining women to gender-neutral language in hymnals and prayers—has sparked heated controversy, delighting progressives while outraging traditionalists. Propelling these developments is a lively feminism in many religious communities. According to feminist Christians, for example, patriarchy in the church stands in stark contrast to the largely feminine image of Jesus Christ in the Scriptures as "non-aggressive, noncompetitive, meek and humble of heart, a nurturer of the weak and a friend of the outcast" (Sandra Schneiders, quoted in Woodward, 1989:61).

Feminists argue that unless traditional notions of gender are removed from our understanding of God, women will never be equal to men in the church. Theologian Mary Daly puts the matter bluntly: "If God is male, then male is God" (quoted in Woodward, 1989:58).

conditions. It is the opium of the people" (1964b:27; orig. 1848).

Religion and social inequality are also linked through gender. Virtually all the world's major religions reflect and encourage male dominance in social life, as the "Social Diversity" box explains.

During Marx's lifetime, powerful Christian nations of Western Europe justified the conquest of Africa, the Americas, and Asia by claiming that they were "converting heathens." In the United States, major churches in the South considered the enslavement of African-Americans to be consistent with God's will, and churches throughout the U.S. remain segregated to this day. In the words of African-American novelist Maya Angelou, "Sunday at 11:30 a.m., America is more segregated than at any time of the week."

Many would argue that for many years the Catholic church turned a blind eye to repeated complaints of child sex abuse by its members. According to Bibby (1993b), as many as fifteen thousand Canadian children were sexually abused in Quebec orphanages before 1960. Not until the child abuse by priests at Mount Cashel orphanage in Newfoundland came to light did Canadians see any significant acknowledgment of the problem or the beginnings of restitution.

Critical evaluation. Social-conflict analysis reveals the power of religion to legitimize social inequality. Yet critics of religion, Marx included, minimize the ways religion has promoted both change and equality. Nineteenth-century religious groups in the United States, for example, were at the forefront of the movement to abolish slavery. In Canada, the Social Gospel movement, active from the 1890s through the 1930s, created settlement houses and city missions and was instrumental in the development of Canada's social safety net.

RELIGION AND SOCIAL CHANGE

Religion is not just the conservative force portrayed by Karl Marx. At some points in history, as Max Weber (1958a; orig. 1904–05) pointed out, religion has promoted dramatic social transformation.

MAX WEBER: PROTESTANTISM AND CAPITALISM

Max Weber contended that new ideas are often the engines of change. It was the religious doctrine of Calvinism, for example, that sparked the Industrial Revolution in Western Europe.

As Chapter 4 ("Society") explains, John Calvin (1509–64), a leader in the Protestant Reformation, advanced the doctrine of predestination. According to Calvin, an all-powerful and all-knowing God predestines some people for salvation while condemning most to eternal damnation. With each individual's fate sealed before birth and known only to God, the only certainty is what hangs in the balance: eternal glory or hellfire.

Understandably anxious about their fate, Calvinists sought signs of God's favour in *this* world and gradually came to regard prosperity as a symbol of divine blessing. This conviction, and a rigid sense of duty, led Calvinists to work all the time, and many amassed great riches. But wealth was never to fuel self-indulgent spending or for sharing with the poor, whose plight Calvinists saw as a mark of God's rejection.

As agents of God's work on earth, Calvinists believed that they best fulfilled their "calling" by reinvesting profits and reaping ever-greater success in the process. All the while, they were thrifty and eagerly embraced technological advances that would enhance their efforts. Driven by religious motives, then, they laid the groundwork for the rise of industrial capitalism. In time, the religious fervour that motivated early Calvinists evaporated, leaving a profane Protestant "work ethic." In this sense, concluded Weber, industrial capitalism amounts to a "disenchanted" religion. Webster's analysis clearly demonstrates the power of religious thinking to alter the basic shape of society.

LIBERATION THEOLOGY

Christianity has a long-standing concern for poor and oppressed people, urging all to strengthen their faith in a better life to come. In recent decades, however, some church leaders and theologians have embraced **liberation theology**, *a fusion of Christian principles with political activism, often Marxist in character.*

This social movement started in the late 1960s in Latin America's Roman Catholic church. Today, in addition to the church's spiritual work, Christian activists are helping people in the least-developed countries to liberate themselves from abysmal poverty. The message of liberation theology is simple: social oppression runs counter to Christian morality and is also preventable. Therefore, as a matter of faith and social justice, Christians must promote greater social equality.

A growing number of Catholic men and women have taken up the cause of the poor in the liberation theology movement. The cost of opposing the status quo, however, has been high. Many church members—including Oscar Arnulfo Romero, the archbishop of San Salvador (the capital of El Salvador)—have been killed for seeking political change.

Liberation theology has also divided the Catholic community. Pope John Paul II condemns the movement for distorting traditional church doctrine with left-wing politics. But, despite the pontiff's objections, the liberation theology movement has become powerful in Latin America, where many people find that their Christian faith drives them to improve the condition of the world's poor (Boff, 1984; Neuhouser, 1989).

TYPES OF RELIGIOUS ORGANIZATION

Sociologists categorize the hundreds of different religious organizations that exist in Canada along a continuum, with *churches* at one end and *sects* at the other. We can describe any actual religious organization, then, in relation to these two ideal types by locating it on the church-sect continuum.

CHURCH AND SECT

Drawing on the ideas of his teacher Max Weber, Ernst Troeltsch (1931) defined a **church** as *a type of religious organization well integrated into the larger society.* Churchlike organizations usually persist for centuries and include generations of the same family. Churches have well-established rules and regulations and expect their leaders to be formally trained and ordained.

While concerned with the sacred, a church accepts the ways of the profane world, which gives it broad appeal. Church doctrine conceives of God in highly intellectualized terms (say, as a force for good), and favours abstract moral standards ("Do unto others as you would have them do unto you") over specific rules for day-to-day living. By teaching morality in safely abstract terms, a church can avoid social controversy. For example, many Christian churches that, in principle, celebrate the unity of all peoples, have, in practice, all-white memberships. Such duality minimizes conflict between a church and political life (Troeltsch, 1931).

December 11, 1994, Casablanca, Morocco. The waves of the Atlantic crash along the walls of Casablanca's magnificent coastline mosque, reputedly the largest in the world. From the top of the towering structure, a green laser points eastward towards Mecca, the holy city of Islam, towards which the faithful bow in prayer. To pay for this monumental house of worship, King Hassam II, Morocco's head of state and religious leader, levied a tax on every citizen in his realm, all of whom are officially Muslim. Our notion of the separation of church and state contrasts sharply with this "government religion."

A church generally takes one of two forms. Islam in Morocco represents an **ecclesia**, *a church formally allied with the state*. Ecclesias have been common in history; for centuries Roman Catholicism was the state religion of the Roman Empire, as was Confucianism in China until early in this century. Today, the Anglican Church is the official Church of England, as Islam is the official religion of Pakistan and Iran. State churches count everyone in a society as members; tolerance of religious difference, therefore, is severely limited.

A **denomination**, by contrast, is *a church, independent of the state, that accepts religious pluralism*. Denominations exist in nations that formally separate church and state, such as ours. Canada has dozens of Christian denominations—including Catholics, Baptists, Methodists, and Lutherans—as well as various branches of Judaism and other traditions. While members of a denomination hold to their own beliefs, they recognize the right of others to disagree.

A second general religious form is the **sect**, *a type of religious organization that stands apart from the larger society*. Sect members hold rigidly to their religious convictions, and discount the beliefs of others. In extreme cases, members of a sect may withdraw completely from society to practice their religion without interference from outsiders. The Old Order Mennonites are an example of a North American sect that has long isolated itself (Fretz, 1989). Since our culture views religious tolerance as a virtue, members of sects are sometimes accused of being narrow-minded in their insistence that they alone follow the true religion (Stark and Bainbridge, 1979).

In organizational terms, sects are less formal than churches. Thus, sect members may be highly spontaneous and emotional in worship, while members of churches tend to listen passively to their leader. Sects also reject the intellectualized religion of churches, stressing instead the personal experience of divine power. Rodney Stark (1985:314) contrasts a church's vision of a distant God—"Our Father, who art in Heaven"—with a sect's more immediate God—"Lord, bless this poor sinner kneeling before you now."

In global perspective, the range of human religious activity is truly astonishing. Members of this Christian cult in Guatemala observe Good Friday by vaulting over a roaring fire, an expression of their faith that God will protect them.

A further distinction between church and sect turns on patterns of leadership. The more church-like an organization, the more likely that its leaders are formally trained and ordained. Sect-like organizations, which celebrate the personal presence of God, expect their leaders to exhibit divine inspiration in the form of **charisma** (from Greek meaning "divine favour"), *extraordinary personal qualities that can turn an audience into followers*, infusing them with an emotional experience.

Sects generally form as breakaway groups from established churches or other religious organizations (Stark and Bainbridge, 1979). Their psychic intensity and informal structure render them less stable than churches, and many sects blossom only to disappear a short time later. The sects that do endure typically become more like churches, losing fervour as they become more bureaucratic and established.

To sustain their membership, many sects actively recruit, or *proselytize*, new members. Sects highly value the experience of *conversion*, a personal transformation or religious rebirth. Jehovah's Witnesses, for example, eagerly share their faith with others in hopes of attracting new members.

Finally, churches and sects differ in their social composition. Because they are more closely tied to the world, well-established churches tend to include people of high social standing. Sects, by contrast, attract more disadvantaged people. A sect's openness to new members and promise of salvation and personal fulfilment may be especially appealing to people who perceive themselves as social outsiders. However, as we shall explain presently, many established churches in Canada have lost membership in recent decades. For instance, the United Church membership has declined from 2 850 000 to 2 521 000 between 1985 and 1990, while the Anglican Church declined from 2 017 000 to 1 892 000. In the process, a number of sects now find themselves with more affluent members (Baril and Mori, 1991: 22).

CULT

A **cult** is *a religious organization that is substantially outside a society's cultural traditions.* Whereas a sect breaks off from a conventional religious organization, a cult represents something mostly new. Cults typically form around a highly charismatic leader who offers a compelling message of a new way of life.

Because some cult principles or practices may seem unconventional, the popular view is that they are deviant or even evil. The suicides of fifty-three members of the Order of the Solar Temple in 1994, and of five more members in 1997—in the belief that death on earth would allow transit to another planet where their lives would continue—confirmed the negative image the public holds of most cults. In short, according to some scholars, calling any religious community a "cult" amounts to dismissing its members as crazy (Richardson, 1990; Gleick, 1997).

This view of cults is unfortunate, because there is nothing intrinsically wrong with this kind of religious organization. Many long-standing religions—Christianity, Islam, and Judaism included—began as cults. Of course, not all or even most cults exist for very long. One reason is that they are even more at odds with the larger society than sects. Many cults demand that members not only accept their doctrine but embrace a radically new lifestyle. Such lifestyle changes sometimes prompt others to accuse cults of brainwashing their members, although research suggests that most people who join cults experience no psychological harm (Barker, 1981; Kilbourne, 1983).

RELIGION IN HISTORY

Religion shapes every society of the world. And, like other social institutions, religion shows considerable variation both historically and cross-culturally.

RELIGION IN PRE-INDUSTRIAL SOCIETIES

Religion predates written history. Archaeological evidence indicates that our human ancestors performed religious rituals some forty thousand years ago.

Early hunters and gatherers embraced **animism** (from Latin meaning "the breath of life"), *the belief that elements of the natural world are conscious life forms that affect humanity.* Animistic people view forests, oceans, mountains, even the wind as spiritual forces. Many First Nations societies are animistic, which accounts for their historical reverence for the natural environment. Hunters and gatherers conduct their religious life entirely within the family. Members of such societies may single out someone as a *shaman* with special religious skills, but there are no full-time, specialized religious leaders.

Belief in a single divine power responsible for creating the world arose with pastoral and horticultural societies. We can trace our society's conception of God as a "shepherd," directly involved in the world's well-being, to the roots of Christianity, Judaism, and Islam, all of whose original followers were pastoral peoples.

As societies develop more productive capacity, religious life expands beyond the family, and priests take their place among other specialized workers. In agrarian societies, religion becomes more important, evident in the huge medieval cathedrals in town centres throughout Europe.

RELIGION IN INDUSTRIAL SOCIETIES

The Industrial Revolution ushered in science as a way of knowing. Increasingly, people looked to physicians and scientists for the knowledge and comfort they had sought from religious leaders.

Even so, religious thought persists simply because science is powerless to address issues of ultimate meaning in human life. In other words, learning *how* the world works is a matter for scientists; but *why* we and the rest of the universe exist is a question about which science has nothing to say. Science may improve our material lives, but religion is uniquely suited to address the spiritual dimension of human existence.

WORLD RELIGIONS

The diversity of religious expression in the world is almost as wide-ranging as the diversity of culture itself. Many of the thousands of different religions are highly localized with few followers. *World religions,* by contrast, are widely known and have millions of adherents. We shall briefly describe six world religions, which together claim as adherents some four billion believers—almost three-quarters of humanity.

CHRISTIANITY

Christianity is the most widespread religion, with two billion followers, roughly one-third of the world's people. Most Christians live in Europe or the Americas; more than 85 percent of the people in Canada and the United States identify with Christianity. Moreover, as shown in Global Map 18–1, people who are at least nominally Christian represent a significant share of the population in many other world regions, with the notable exceptions of northern Africa and Asia. European colonization spread Christianity throughout much of the world over the last five hundred years. Its dominance in the West is evident in the practice of numbering years on the calendar beginning with the birth of Christ.

Christianity originated as a cult, incorporating elements of its much older predecessor, Judaism. Like many cults, Christianity was propelled by the personal charisma of a leader, Jesus of Nazareth, who preached a message of personal salvation. Jesus did not directly challenge the political powers of his day, calling on his followers to "Render therefore to Caesar the things that are Caesar's" (Matt. 22:21). But his message was revolutionary nonetheless, promising that faith and love would triumph over sin and death.

Christianity is one example of **monotheism**, *belief in a single divine power*. This new religion broke with the Roman Empire's traditional **polytheism**, *belief in many gods*. Yet Christianity has a unique vision of the Supreme Being as a sacred Trinity: God the Creator; Jesus Christ, Son of God and Redeemer; and the Holy Spirit, a Christian's personal experience of God's presence.

The claim that Jesus was divine rests on accounts of his final days on earth. Tried and sentenced to death in Jerusalem on charges that he was a threat to established political leaders, Jesus was executed by crucifixion. The cross therefore became a sacred Christian symbol. According to Christian belief, three days later Jesus arose from the dead, showing that he was the Son of God.

Jesus' apostles spread Christianity throughout the Mediterranean region. Although the Roman Empire initially persecuted Christians, by the fourth century Christianity had become an ecclesia—the official religion of what then became known as the Holy Roman Empire. What had begun as a cult four centuries before was now an established church.

Christianity took various forms, including the Roman Catholic church and the Orthodox church, based in Constantinople (now Istanbul, Turkey). Towards the end of the Middle Ages, the Protestant Reformation in Europe created hundreds of denominations, dozens of which now comprise about 30 percent of the adult Canadian population (as compared with the 45 percent that is Roman Catholic) (Baril and Mori, 1991).

William Kurelek's self-portrait, Lord That I Might See, *captures something of the painful perplexity of the Christian penitent seeking God's guidance and help.*

ISLAM

Islam has some 1.1 billion followers (about 20 percent of humanity); followers of Islam are called Muslims. A majority of people in the Middle East are Muslims, which explains our tendency to associate Islam with Arabs in that region of the world. But most Muslims live elsewhere; Global Map 18–2 shows that most people in northern Africa and western Asia are also Muslims. Moreover, significant concentrations of Muslims are found in Pakistan, India, Bangladesh, Indonesia, and the southern republics of the former Soviet Union. Although representing a small share of the population, North American Muslims number between five and ten million (Roudi, 1988; Weeks, 1988; University of Akron Research Center, 1993).

Islam is the word of God as revealed to the prophet Muhammad, who was born in the city of Mecca (now in Saudi Arabia) about the year 570. To Muslims, Muhammad is a prophet, not a divine being as Jesus is to Christians. The Qur'an (Koran), sacred to Muslims, is the word of God (in Arabic, "Allah") as transmitted through Muhammad, God's messenger. In Arabic, the word "Islam" means both "submission"

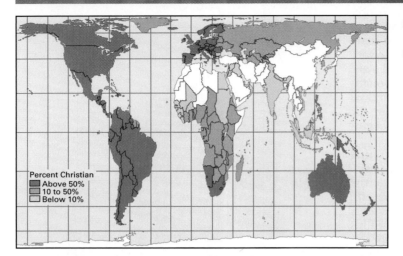

GLOBAL MAP 18–1 Christianity in Global Perspective

SOURCE: *Peters Atlas of the World* (1990).

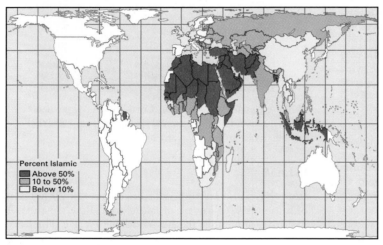

GLOBAL MAP 18–2 Islam in Global Perspective

SOURCE: *Peters Atlas of the World* (1990).

and "peace," and the Qur'an urges submission to Allah as the path to inner peace. Muslims express this personal devotion in a daily ritual of five prayers.

Islam spread rapidly after the death of Muhammad, although divisions arose, as they did within Christianity. All Muslims, however, accept the Five Pillars of Islam: (1) recognizing Allah as the one true God, and Muhammad as God's messenger; (2) ritual prayer; (3) giving alms to the poor; (4) fasting during the month of Ramadan; and (5) making a pilgrimage at least once to the Sacred House of Allah in Mecca (Weeks, 1988; El-Attar, 1991). Like Christianity, Islam holds people accountable to God for their deeds on earth. Those who live obediently will be rewarded in heaven, while evil-doers will suffer unending punishment.

Muslims are also obligated to defend their faith, which has led to holy wars against unbelievers (in roughly the same way that medieval Christians fought in the Crusades). Recently, in Algeria, Egypt, Iran, and elsewhere, some Muslims have sought to rid their society of Western influences that they regard as morally wrong (Martin, 1982; Arjomand, 1988).

To many Westerners, Muslim women are among the most socially oppressed people on earth. Muslim women do lack many of the personal freedoms enjoyed by Muslim men, yet many—and perhaps most—accept the mandates of their religion and find security in a rigid system that guides the behaviour of both women and men (Peterson, 1996). Moreover, patriarchy was well established in the Middle East long before the birth of Muhammad. Some defenders argue that Islam actually improved the social position of women by demanding that husbands deal justly with their wives. Further, although Islam permits a man to have up to four wives, it admonishes men to have only one wife if having more would encourage him to treat any woman unjustly (Qur'an, "The Women," v. 3).

JUDAISM

In terms of simple numbers, Judaism's fourteen million followers worldwide makes it something less than a world religion. Moreover, only in Israel do Jews represent a national majority. But Judaism has special significance in North America because the largest concentration of Jews (six million people) is found here.

Jews look to the past as a source of guidance in the present and for the future. And Judaism has deep historical roots that extend back some four thousand years before the birth of Christ to the ancient cultures of Mesopotamia. At this time, Jews were animistic; but this belief changed after Jacob—grandson of Abraham, the earliest great ancestor—led his people to Egypt.

Jews endured centuries of slavery in Egypt. In the thirteenth century B.C.E., a turning point came as Moses, the adopted son of an Egyptian princess, was called by God to lead the Jews from bondage. This exodus (this word's Latin and Greek roots mean "a marching out") from Egypt is commemorated by Jews today in the annual ritual of Passover. Once liberated, Jews became monotheistic, recognizing a single all-powerful God.

A distinctive concept of Judaism is the *covenant*, a special relationship with God by which Jews became the "chosen people." The covenant also implies a duty to observe God's law, especially the Ten Commandments as revealed to Moses on Mount Sinai. Jews regard the Bible (or, in Christian terms, the Old Testament) as both a record of their history and a statement of the obligations of Jewish life. Of special importance are the Bible's first five books (Genesis, Exodus, Leviticus, Numbers, and Deuteronomy), designated as the *Torah* (a word roughly meaning "teaching" and "law"). In contrast to Christianity's central concern with personal salvation, Judaism emphasizes moral behaviour in this world.

Judaism is composed of four main denominations. Orthodox Jews strictly observe traditional beliefs and practices, wear traditional dress, segregate men and women at religious services, and eat only kosher foods. Such traditional practices set off Orthodox Jews in Canada as the most sect-like. In the mid–nineteenth century, many Jews sought greater acceptance by the larger society, leading to the formation of more

Followers of Islam reverently remove their shoes—which touch the profane ground—before entering this sacred mosque in the southeast Asian nation of Brunei.

churchlike Reform Judaism. A third segment—Conservative Judaism—has since established a middle ground between the other two denominations. These were followed in the 1930s by the fourth and smallest denomination, Reconstructionist Judaism, which blends egalitarian and democratic thinking with traditional practices.

Whatever their denomination, Jews share a cultural history of considerable prejudice and discrimination. A collective memory of centuries of slavery in Egypt, conquest by Rome, and persecution in Europe has shaped Jewish identity. It was Jews in Italy who first lived in an urban ghetto (derived from the Italian word *borghetto*, meaning "settlement outside the city walls"), and this form of residential segregation soon spread to other parts of Europe.

Jewish immigration to North America began in the mid-1600s. Many early immigrants prospered, and many were also assimilated into largely Christian communities. But as larger numbers entered the country during the final decades of the nineteenth century, prejudice and discrimination against them—commonly termed *anti-Semitism*—increased. Jews were not allowed to work in certain institutions and others maintained quotas: for instance, there were quotas on the number of Jewish students who were to be admitted to universities (Abella, 1989). During World War II, some German Jewish refugees were refused admittance to Canada (Abella and Troper, 1982). And it was during World War II that anti-Semitism reached a vicious peak as the Nazi regime in Germany systematically annihilated six million Jews.

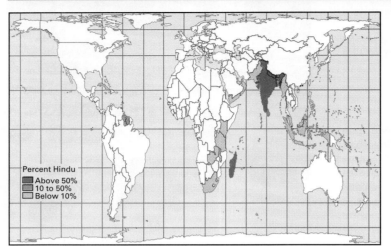

GLOBAL MAP 18–3 Hinduism in Global Perspective

SOURCE: *Peters Atlas of the World* (1990).

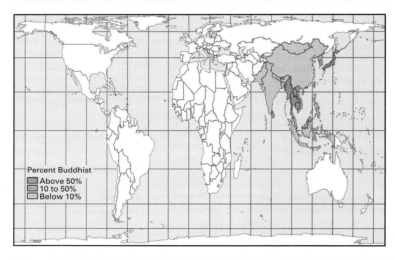

GLOBAL MAP 18–4 Buddhism in Global Perspective

SOURCE: *Peters Atlas of the World* (1990).

The University of Toronto, in its *National Report '97*, announced the endowment of two chairs in Jewish studies, an innovative and comprehensive program that reflects the belief that "the study of Jewish culture and history is critical to the understanding of Western civilization" and highly relevant to a "young, multicultural country like Canada."

HINDUISM

Hinduism is the oldest of all the world religions, originating in the Indus River Valley approximately 4500 years ago. Hindus number some 793 million (14 percent of humanity). Global Map 18–3 shows that Hinduism remains an Eastern religion, predominantly practiced in India and Pakistan, but with a significant presence in southern Africa and Indonesia.

Over the centuries, Hinduism and Indian culture have become intertwined, so that now one is not easily described apart from the other. This connection also explains why Hinduism, unlike Christianity, Islam, and Judaism, has not diffused widely to other nations. However, Hindus living in North America make this religion a significant part of the continent's cultural diversity.

Hinduism differs from most other religions by not being linked to the life of any single person. Hinduism also has no sacred writings comparable to the Bible or the Qur'an. Nor does Hinduism envision God as a specific entity. For this reason, Hinduism—like other Eastern religions, as we shall see—is sometimes described as an "ethical religion." Hindu beliefs and practices vary widely, but all Hindus recognize a moral force in the universe that presents everyone with responsibilities, termed *dharma*. Dharma, for example, calls people to observe the traditional caste system, described in Chapter 9 ("Social Stratification").

Another Hindu principle, *karma*, refers to the belief in the spiritual progress of the human soul. To a Hindu, all actions have spiritual consequences, and proper living contributes to moral development. Karma works through *reincarnation*, a cycle of death and rebirth, by which the individual is reborn into a spiritual state corresponding to the moral quality of their previous life. Unlike Christianity and Islam, Hinduism proclaims no ultimate judgment at the hands of a supreme god, although in the cycle of rebirth, people reap exactly what they have sown. *Moksha* is the sublime state of spiritual perfection: only when a soul reaches this level is it no longer reborn.

Hinduism stands as evidence that not all religions can be neatly labelled monotheistic or polytheistic. Hinduism is monotheistic insofar as it envisions the universe as a single moral system; yet Hindus see this moral order at work in every element of nature. Moreover, many Hindus participate in public rituals, such as the *Kumbh Mela*, which, every twelve years, brings some twenty million pilgrims to the sacred Ganges River to bathe in its purifying waters. At the same time, Hindus practise private devotions, which vary from village to village across the vast nation of India.

While elements of Hindu thought have characterized some cults in North America over the years, Hinduism is still unfamiliar to most Westerners. But, like religions better known to us, Hinduism is a powerful force offering both explanation and guidance in life (Pitt, 1955; Sen, 1961; Embree, 1972; Kaufman, 1976; Schmidt, 1980).

BUDDHISM

Some 2500 years ago, the rich culture of India also gave rise to Buddhism. Today more than 325 million people (6 percent of humanity) embrace Buddhism, and almost all are Asians. As shown in Global Map 18–4, Buddhists make up more than half the population of Myanmar (Burma), Thailand, Cambodia, and Japan; Buddhism is also widespread in India and the People's Republic of China. Of the world religions considered so far, Buddhism most resembles Hinduism in doctrine, but, like Christianity, its inspiration springs from the life of one individual.

Buddhists believe that a preoccupation with material things inhibits spiritual development, an idea that is also central to most Western religions. Buddhist monks, therefore, live a simple life devoted to meditation, music, and righteousness in everyday behaviour.

Siddhartha Gautama was born to a high-caste family in Nepal about 563 B.C.E. As a young man, he was preoccupied with spiritual matters. At the age of twenty-nine, he underwent a radical personal transformation, and set off for years of travel and meditation. His journey ended when he achieved what Buddhists describe as *bodhi*, or enlightenment. Understanding the essence of life, Gautama became a Buddha.

Energized by the Buddha's personal charisma, followers spread his teachings—the *dhamma*—across India. During the third century B.C.E., the ruler of India became a Buddhist and sent missionaries throughout Asia, making Buddhism a world religion.

Buddhists believe that much of life involves suffering. This idea is rooted in the Buddha's own travels in a society rife with poverty. But the Buddha rejected wealth as a solution to suffering; on the contrary, he warned that materialism inhibits spiritual development. Instead, Buddha taught that we must transcend our selfish concerns and desires through meditation, with the goal of obtaining *nirvana*, a state of enlightenment and peace.

Buddhism closely parallels Hinduism in recognizing no god of judgment; yet, each daily action has spiritual consequences. Another similarity is a belief in reincarnation. Here, again, only enlightenment ends the cycle of death and rebirth and finally liberates a person from the suffering of the world (Schumann, 1974; Thomas, 1975; Van Biema, 1997b).

When Western people perform religious rituals they typically do so collectively and formally as members of specific congregations. Eastern people, by contrast, visit shrines individually and informally, without joining a specific congregation. For this reason, Asian temples such as this one in Hong Kong receive a steady flow of people—families praying, individuals engaged in business, and foreign tourists just watching—that seems somehow inappropriate to the Western visitor.

CONFUCIANISM

From about 200 B.C.E. until the beginning of this century, Confucianism was an ecclesia—the official religion of China. Following the 1949 Revolution, religion was suppressed by the communist government of the new People's Republic of China. Today, though officials provide no precise count, hundreds of millions of Chinese are still influenced by Confucianism. Almost all Confucianists live in China, although Chinese immigration has spread this religion to other nations in Southeast Asia. Perhaps one hundred thousand followers of Confucius live in North America.

Confucius or, properly, K'ung-Fu-tzu, lived between 551 and 479 B.C.E. Like Buddha, Confucius was deeply concerned about people's suffering. The Buddha's response was a sect-like spiritual withdrawal from the world; Confucius, by contrast, instructed his followers to engage the world according to a strict code of moral conduct. Thus it was that Confucianism became fused with the traditional culture of China. Here we see a second example of what might be called a "national religion": as Hinduism has remained largely synonymous with Indian culture, Confucianism is enshrined in the Chinese way of life.

A central concept of Confucianism is *jen*, meaning humaneness. In practice, this means that we must always subordinate our self-interest to moral principle. In the family, the individual must be loyal and

considerate. Likewise, families must remain mindful of their duties towards the larger community. In this way, layer upon layer of moral obligation integrates society as a whole.

Most of all, Confucianism stands out as lacking a clear sense of the sacred. Recalling Durkheim's analysis, we might view Confucianism as the celebration of the sacred character of society itself. Alternatively, we might argue that Confucianism is less a religion than a model of disciplined living. Certainly the historical dominance of Confucianism helps to explain why Chinese culture is skeptical towards the supernatural. But even as a disciplined way of life, Confucianism shares with religion a body of beliefs and practices that have as their goal goodness, concern for others, and the promotion of social harmony (Kaufman, 1976; Schmidt, 1980; McGuire, 1987).

RELIGION: EAST AND WEST

This overview of world religions points up two general differences between the belief systems of Eastern and Western societies. First, Western religions (Christianity, Islam, Judaism) are typically deity-based, with a clear focus on God. Eastern religions (Hinduism, Buddhism, Confucianism) tend to be ethical codes; therefore, they make a less clear-cut distinction between the sacred and secular.

Second, the operational unit of Western religious organization is the congregation. That is, people worship in formal groups at a specific time and place. Eastern religious organization, by contrast, is informally fused with culture itself. For this reason, for example, a visitor finds a Japanese temple filled with tourists and worshippers alike, who come and go as they please and pay little attention to those around them.

These two distinctions do not overshadow the common element of all religions: a conception of a higher moral force or purpose that transcends the concerns of everyday life. In their global variety, religious beliefs give people of the world guidance and a sense of purpose in their lives.

RELIGION IN CANADA

In global perspective, Canada is a relatively religious nation. As Figure 18–1 shows, more than six in ten members of our society claim to gain "comfort and strength from religion," a proportion approximately in the middle of other industrial countries.

RELIGIOUS AFFILIATION

On national surveys, nearly 90 percent of Canadian adults claim a religious preference (Baril and Mori,

1991). Traditionally, Canada has been fairly evenly divided between Catholics and Protestants. For more than a century, until about 1971, Protestants outnumbered Catholics; now the reverse is true. Survey results show that Catholicism is embraced by approximately 45 percent of respondents, Protestants make up almost one-third of the population, 1 percent are Jewish, and just over 10 percent claim to have no religious affiliation (Baril and Moril, 1991:22).

About 24 percent of adults in Canada report that they attend religious services weekly, and about 8 percent go to church at least once a month (Baril and Mori, 1991:23). Almost a third of the adult population prays daily and more than half read the Bible or other religious literature at least occasionally (Nemeth, 1993).

An intriguing question related to religious affiliation is interfaith marriage. Bibby (1997) found that in an interfaith marriage, the children are more likely to embrace the religions of their mothers, especially when the mothers are Catholic or report no religion. Interestingly, when Catholic or Protestant women marry Jewish men, their children are most likely to report no religion (35 percent). This suggests that mothers are tremendously important in the transmission of religious values and identities.

Canadian society has no official religion, and the separation of church and state is enshrined in the Constitution. The population of Canada is also more religiously diverse than that of most other countries on earth—one result of our historically high level of immigration.

RELIGIOSITY

Religiosity refers to *the importance of religion in a person's life*. Identifying with a religion is only one measure of religiosity, of course, and a superficial one at that. How religious Canada turns out to be, therefore, depends on how we operationalize the concept.

Years ago, Charles Glock (1959, 1962) proposed five distinct dimensions of religiosity. *Experiential* religiosity refers to the strength of a person's emotional ties to a religion. *Ritualistic* religiosity refers to frequency of ritual activity such as prayer and church attendance. *Ideological* religiosity describes an individual's degree of belief in religious doctrine. *Consequential* religiosity has to do with how strongly religious beliefs figure in a person's daily behaviour. Finally, *intellectual* religiosity refers to a person's knowledge of the history and doctrines of a particular religion. Any person is likely to be more religious on some dimensions than on others, so assessing religiosity is a difficult task.

How religious, then, are members of our society? Canada Map 18–1 shows the percentage of respon-

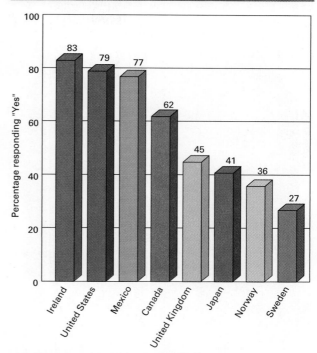

GLOBAL SNAPSHOT

FIGURE 18–1 Religiosity in Global Perspective

Survey Question: "Do you gain comfort and strength from religion?"

SOURCE: World Values Survey (1994).

dents in each province that stated they had "no religion" on the 1991 census, ranging from a low of 1.6 percent in Newfoundland to a high of 33.7 percent in the Yukon. In Canada as a whole, 12.3 percent claimed no religion, compared to 7 percent a decade earlier. This increase in the number of Canadians reporting no religion is mirrored by a drop in weekly church attendance, from close to 60 percent in the 1950s to about 25 percent in 1995 (Baril and Mori, 1981; Bibby, 1995). Bibby points out that the decline in attendance accelerated in the 1970s and has affected Catholics in Quebec in particular.

Nevertheless, 81 percent of Canadians believe in God. Seventy-four percent believe in miracle healing, 61 percent believe in angels, and 49 percent believe in hell (Bibby, 1995:131). Surprisingly, only 88 percent of Protestants believe in God (Bozinoff and MacIntosh, 1990). In terms of experiential religiosity, then, Canadians are still religious, although they tend to believe in the more positive doctrinal aspects, such as God and heaven, rather than the more negative aspects, such as hell. In addition, it seems

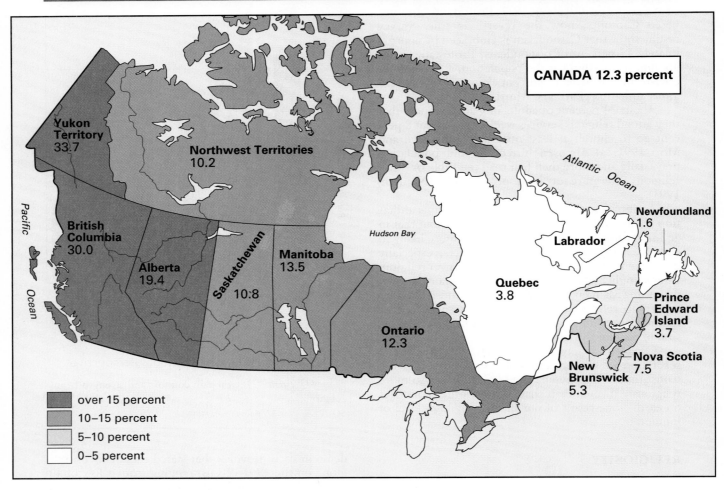

CANADA 12.3 percent

Yukon Territory 33.7

Northwest Territories 10.2

British Columbia 30.0

Alberta 19.4

Saskatchewan 10:8

Manitoba 13.5

Ontario 12.3

Quebec 3.8

Labrador

Newfoundland 1.6

Prince Edward Island 3.7

Nova Scotia 7.5

New Brunswick 5.3

Hudson Bay

Atlantic Ocean

Pacific Ocean

over 15 percent
10–15 percent
5–10 percent
0–5 percent

CANADA MAP 18–1 Canadians Claiming "No Religion" (by Province and Territory, 1991)
SOURCE: Data from Statistics Canada, Catalogue No. 93-319.

that "spirituality" is highly valued by 36 percent, religion by 26 percent (Bibby, 1995).

RELIGION AND SOCIAL STRATIFICATION

Sociologists who study religion have found that religious affiliation is related to other familiar social patterns. We shall consider three: social class, race, and ethnicity.

Social Class

Canada has historically been stratified along religious lines. By and large, Protestants with high social standing are people of northern European back-

ground. Members of the Anglican church, and later the other establishment Protestant churches, have long been among Canada's most affluent powerful people. Anglophone political and economic dominance, and traditional Catholic doctrine, kept Catholics in Quebec subordinate and poor. Jews command unexpectedly high social standing considering that they often contend with anti-Semitism from the Christian majority. The reason for this achievement is mostly cultural, since Jewish tradition places great value on education and achievement. Although a large proportion of Jews began life in North America in poverty, many—although certainly not all—improved their social position in subsequent generations.

Although income is only one dimension of social class, the ranking of various religious categories by income in Table 18–2 shows that stratification along religious lines is still with us. Jews have the highest average income, while members of the United Church, Anglicans, Presbyterians, and Lutherans also earn above-average incomes. Members of all other religions, including Christian fundamentalists and Roman Catholics, fall below the Canadian average. Despite massive changes in Canada's population after World War II, the old relationship between religion and economic well-being persists.

Ethnicity and Race

Throughout the world, religion is tied to ethnicity. Many religions predominate in a single nation or geographical region. Islam predominates in the Arab societies of the Middle East; Hinduism is fused with the culture of India, as is Confucianism with life in China. Christianity and Judaism, however, do not follow this pattern; while these religions are predominantly Western, Christians and Jews are found all over the world.

Religion and national identity come together in Canada as well. We have, for example, *Anglo-Saxon* Protestants, *Irish* Catholics, *Russian* Jews, and *Greek* Orthodox. This linking of nation and creed results from the influx of immigrants from nations with a single major religion, or from societies where large numbers of a particular religious group emigrated to escape persecution. Still, nearly every ethnic category displays some religious diversity. People of English ancestry, for instance, may be Protestants, Roman Catholics, Jews, or followers of other religions.

RELIGION IN A CHANGING SOCIETY

All social institutions evolve over time. Just as the economy, politics, and family life have changed over the course of this century, so has our society's religious life.

SECULARIZATION

One of the most important patterns of social change is **secularization**, *the historical decline in the importance of the supernatural and the sacred.* For society as a whole, secularization points to the waning influence of religion in everyday life. For religious organizations, becoming more secular means that they focus less on otherworldly issues (such as life after death) and more on worldly affairs (such as sheltering the homeless and feeding the hungry). Secularization also means that functions once performed by the church (such as charity) are now primarily the responsibility of businesses and government.

TABLE 18–2 Average Income by Selected Religious Affiliation, 1991

Religion	Average Income
Jewish	$34,488
United	24,096
Anglican	24,088
Presbyterian	23,668
No religion	22,536
Lutheran	22,365
Roman Catholic	20,523
Baptist	20,311
Greek Orthodox	17,863
Mennonite	17,691
Pentecostal	16,756
Jehovah's Witness	15,509
Other religions	16,086–20,237
Canadian average	21,524

SOURCE: Analysis by Gerber from Statistics Canada Census 1991, Individual Public Use Microdata

Secularization was at the core of the Quiet Revolution in Quebec during the 1960s. The Catholic church, which had administered welfare, health care, and education in addition to dealing with the spiritual needs of Quebec society, lost influence on the religious front, while giving up its social service involvement to the provincial government.

With Latin roots meaning "the present age," secularization is commonly associated with modern, technologically advanced societies (Cox, 1971; O'Dea and Aviad, 1983). Conventional wisdom holds that secularization results from the increasing role of science in understanding human affairs. Today, in other words, people perceive birth, illness, and death less as the work of a divine power than as natural stages in the life course. These events are now more likely to occur in the presence of physicians (scientific specialists) than religious leaders (whose knowledge is based on faith). As Harvey Cox explains:

> The world looks less and less to religious rules and rituals for its morality or its meanings. For some, religion provides a hobby, for others a mark of national or ethnic identification, for still others an aesthetic delight. For fewer and fewer does it provide an inclusive and commanding system of personal and cosmic values and explanations. (1971:3)

If Cox is correct, should we expect that religion will disappear completely some day? The consensus among sociologists is "no." The vast majority of people in Canada still profess a belief in God.

Secularization does not, then, signal the death of religion. More correctly, some dimensions of religiosity (such as belief in life after death) may have declined, but others (such as religious affiliation) have increased. A global perspective shows the same mixed pattern: religion is declining in importance in some regions (the Scandinavian countries, for example), but rising in others (such as Algeria) (Cox, 1990).

Our society is of two minds as to whether secularization is good or bad. Conservatives take any erosion of religion as a mark of moral decline. Progressives, however, think secularization liberates people from the all-encompassing beliefs of the past and allows them to choose what to believe. Secularization has also brought the practices of many religious organizations (for example, ordaining both men and women) in line with widespread social attitudes.

CIVIL RELIGION

One dimension of secularization is the rise of what Robert Bellah (1975) calls **civil religion**, a *quasi-religious loyalty binding individuals in a basically secular society*. In other words, although some dimensions of formal religion are weakening, our patriotism and citizenship retain many religious qualities.

Canada is a case in point. Just as religion presents a blueprint for leading a good life, a vast majority of people in Canada believe that their political, economic, and medical systems exemplify what is good, and that life in Canada is the best in the world.

Civil religion also involves a wide range of rituals, from rising to sing the national anthem at sporting events to sitting down to watch public parades. At all such events, like the Christian cross or the Jewish Star of David, the Canadian flag serves as a sacred symbol of our national identity that we expect people to treat with reverence.

Civil religion is not a specific religious doctrine. It does, however, incorporate many elements of traditional religion into the political system of a secular society.

RELIGIOUS REVIVAL

A great deal of change is going on in the world of organized religion. Membership in established, "mainstream" churches such as the Anglican and Presbyterian denominations has decreased. Between 1981 and 1991, Presbyterian membership decreased by 22 percent, United by 18 percent, Anglican and Lutheran by 10 percent, and Baptist by 5 percent. In the meantime, most of the smaller denominations—including the Spiritualist, Evangelical, Christian and Missionary Alliance, New Apostolic, and Missionary churches—grew significantly in the same time period. Jewish and Eastern Orthodox congregations grew by 7 percent. Secularization itself may be self-limiting so that as church-like organizations become more worldly, many people abandon them in favour of more sect-like religious communities that better offer a more intense religious experience (Bibby, 1987). Much the same pattern is found in other industrial societies. The "Global Sociology" box takes a look at changing religious affiliation in Great Britain.

RELIGIOUS FUNDAMENTALISM

One of the striking religious trends today is the growth of **fundamentalism**, *a conservative religious doctrine that opposes intellectualism and worldly accommodation in favour of restoring traditional, otherworldly spirituality*. Fundamentalism has made the greatest gains among Protestants, but fundamentalist groups have also proliferated among Roman Catholics and Jews.

In response to what they see as the growing influence of science and the erosion of the conventional family, religious fundamentalists defend what they call "traditional values." As they see it, liberal churches are simply too tolerant of religious pluralism and too open to change. Religious fundamentalism is distinctive in five ways (Hunter, 1983, 1985, 1987).

1. **Fundamentalists interpret sacred texts literally.** Fundamentalists insist on a literal interpretation of the Bible and other sacred texts to counter what they consider excessive intellectualism among more liberal religious organizations. Fundamentalist Christians, for example, believe that God created the world precisely as described in Genesis.

2. **Fundamentalists reject religious pluralism.** Fundamentalists believe that tolerance and relativism diminish personal faith. They maintain, therefore, that their religious beliefs are true while those of others are not.

3. **Fundamentalists pursue the personal experience of God's presence.** In contrast to the worldliness and intellectualism of other religious organizations, fundamentalism seeks a return to "good old-time religion" and spiritual revival. To fundamentalist Christians, being "born again" and having a personal relationship with Jesus Christ should be evident in a person's daily life.

4. **Fundamentalism opposes "secular humanism."** Fundamentalists believe that accommodation to the changing world undermines religious conviction. *Secular humanism* is a general term fundamentalists use to refer to our society's tendency to look to scientific experts (including sociologists) rather than to God for guidance about how to live.

The Changing Face of Religion: A Report from Great Britain

Although the Church of England enjoys the elite status of being that nation's official religious organization, only one-fifth of regular worshippers in Great Britain today are Anglicans. As in Canada, Britain's established, mainstream churches have lost members. The figure demonstrates that membership in the Anglican, Roman Catholic, Presbyterian, and Baptist churches is down significantly in recent years.

Overall, however, religiosity in Great Britain is holding steady (although at a lower level than that of Canada). Why? As the established churches lose members, newer religious organizations are showing surprising strength. Immigration is behind some of this religious revival, adding large numbers of

Muslims, Sikhs, and Hindus to the British population. Newly formed cults

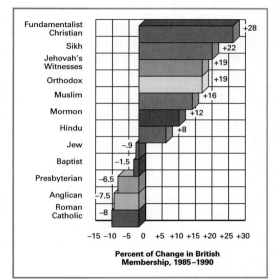

Percent of Change in British Membership, 1985–1990

are also a factor. Experts estimate that as many as six hundred cults exist in Britain at any one time.

But the most significant rise in British religious affiliation is among fundamentalist Christian organizations that embrace highly energetic and musical forms of worship, often under the direction of charismatic leaders. Like their counterparts in Canada, these religious communities typically seek and express the experience of God's presence in a much more intense and spontaneous way than the more staid, mainstream churches do.

SOURCES: Barker (1989) and *The Economist* (1993).

5. **Many fundamentalists endorse conservative political goals.** Although fundamentalism tends to back away from worldly concerns, some fundamentalist leaders have entered politics in recent years to oppose the "liberal agenda" of feminism and gay rights. Fundamentalists oppose abortion, gay marriages, and liberal bias in the media, while supporting the traditional two-parent family and seeking a return of prayer in schools (Viguerie, 1981; Hunter, 1983; Speer, 1984; Ostling, 1985; Ellison and Sherkat, 1993; Green, 1993; Thomma, 1997).

Opponents regard fundamentalism as rigid and self-righteous. But many find in fundamentalism—with its greater religious certainty and emphasis on the emotional experience of God's presence—an appealing alternative to the more intellectual, tolerant, and worldly mainstream denominations (Marquand, 1997).

Which religions are "fundamentalist"? This term is most correctly applied to conservative Christian organizations in the evangelical tradition, including

Pentecostals, Seventh-Day Adventists, and Assemblies of God.

The Electronic Church

In contrast to small village congregations of years past, some religious organizations—especially fundamentalist ones—have become electronic churches featuring "prime-time preachers" (Hadden and Swain, 1981). Electronic religion in the U.S. has propelled Oral Roberts, Pat Robertson, Robert Schuller, and others to greater prominence than all but a few clergy in the past. Canadian "televangelists" David Mainse and Terry Winter, true to the "Canadian personality," are relatively low-key and have exhibited fewer public "sins" (Bibby, 1987:34–36). About 5 percent of the national television audience regularly tune in to religious television. Moreover, the majority of people who watch religious programs on TV are also regular churchgoers. Almost 80 percent of them attend church either weekly (68 percent) or monthly (11 percent).

Recently, an increasing number of religious organizations are using computer technology to spread

Does Science Threaten Religion?

At the dawning of the modern age, the Italian physicist and astronomer Galileo (1564–1642) made a series of startling discoveries. Dropping objects from the Leaning Tower of Pisa, he discovered some of the laws of gravity; fashioning his own telescope, he surveyed the heavens and found that the earth orbited the sun, not the other way around.

For his discoveries, Galileo was denounced by the Roman Catholic church, which had preached for centuries that the earth stood motionless at the centre of the universe. In response, Galileo only made matters worse by declaring that religious leaders and Biblical doctrine had no place in the growing wave of science. Before long, he found his work banned and himself condemned to house arrest.

From its beginnings, science has had an uneasy relationship with religion. Indeed, as Galileo's life makes clear, the claims of one sometimes infringe on the other's truth.

Through the twentieth century, too, science and religion have had their battles, mostly over the issue of creation. In the wake of Charles Darwin's masterwork, *On the Origin of Species*, scientists concluded that humanity evolved from lower forms of life over the course of a billion years. Yet the theory of evolution seems to fly in the face of the Biblical account of creation found in Genesis, which states that "God created the heaven and the earth," introducing life on the third day and, on the fifth and sixth days, creating animal life, including human beings, who were fashioned in God's own image.

Galileo would certainly have been an eager observer of the famous "Scopes monkey trial" of 1925, in which the state of Tennessee prosecuted science teacher John Thomas Scopes. Scopes taught evolution in vio-

lation of a state law that forbade teaching "any theory that denies the story of the Divine Creation of man as taught in the Bible" and especially the idea that "man descended from a lower order of animals." Scopes was found guilty and fined $100. His conviction was reversed on appeal, perhaps to prevent the case from reaching the U.S. Supreme Court, and so the Tennessee law continued to ban the teaching of evolution until 1967. A year later, the U.S. Supreme Court struck down all such laws as an unconstitutional case of government-supported religion.

Today—almost four centuries after the silencing of Galileo—many people still ponder the apparently conflicting claims of science and religion. But a middle ground is emerging that the Bible may be inspired by God and contain important philosophical truth without being literally correct in a scientific sense. That is, science and religion represent two different levels of understanding that respond to different questions. Both Galileo and Darwin devoted their lives to investigating *how* the natural world operates. Yet only religion can address *why* humans and the natural world exist in the first place.

This basic difference between science and religion helps explain how our society can be at once actively scientific and devoutly religious. Moreover, the more scientists discover about the origins of the universe, the more awesome creation seems. Indeed, as one scientist recently pointed out, the mathematical odds that some cosmic "Big Bang" twelve billion years ago created the universe and led to the development of life on earth as we know it today are utterly infinitesimal—much smaller than the chance of one person winning a provincial lottery for twenty weeks in a row. Doesn't such a scientific fact allow for an intelligent and pur-

poseful power in our creation? Can't one be both a religious believer and scientific investigator?

There is another reason to appreciate both scientific and religious thinking: the rapid advances of science continue to present society with troubling ethical dilemmas. Latter-day Galileos have unleashed the power of atomic energy, yet we still struggle to find its rightful use in the world. And, discovering secrets of human genetics has brought us to the threshold of being able to manipulate life itself, a power that few have the moral confidence to use.

In 1992, a Vatican commission created by Pope John Paul II conceded that the church had erred in silencing Galileo. Most scientific and religious leaders agree that science and religion represent distinctive truths, and their teachings are complementary. And many believe that, in today's rush to scientific discovery, our world has never been more in need of the moral guidance afforded by religion.

Continue the debate . . .

1. *On what grounds do some scientists completely reject religious accounts of human creation? Why do some religious people reject scientific accounts?*
2. *Do you think the sociological study of religion challenges anyone's faith? Why or why not?*
3. *Does science sometimes develop outside of moral constraints? Is science too powerful? Where do science and religion conflict today?*

SOURCES: Based on Gould (1981), Hutchingson (1994), and Applebome (1996).

their message, a trend that Pope John Paul II has termed the "new evangelism." The "Exploring Cyber-Society" box takes a look at finding God online.

LOOKING AHEAD: RELIGION IN THE TWENTY-FIRST CENTURY

The popularity of media ministries, the rapid growth of religious fundamentalism, and the continuing adherence of millions more people to mainstream churches show that religion will remain a major institution of modern society. Moreover, high levels of immigration from many religious countries (in Asia, Africa, the Caribbean, and elsewhere) will intensify and diversify the religious character of Canadian society in the decades to come.

In addition, the pace of social change is accelerating. As the world becomes more complex, rapid change seems to outstrip our capacity to make sense of it all. But rather than undermining religion, this process fires the religious imagination of people who seek a sense of religious community and ultimate meaning in life. Tensions between the spiritual realm of religion and the secular world of science and technology will surely continue; the "Controversy & Debate" box takes a closer look at this dynamic relationship.

But science is simply unable to provide answers to the most basic human questions about the purpose of our lives. Moreover, new technology that can begin life and sustain life confront us with vexing moral

More and more religious organizations are making use of the Internet to spread their message. Do you think computer technology will serve to strengthen or weaken religion?

dilemmas as never before. Against this backdrop of uncertainty, it is little wonder that many people rely on their faith for assurance and hope.

SUMMARY

1. Religion is a major social institution based on distinguishing the sacred from the profane. Religion is a matter of faith, not scientific evidence, which people express through various rituals.

2. Sociology analyzes the consequences of religion for social life, but no scientific research can assess the truth of any religious belief.

3. Emile Durkheim argued that, through religion, individuals experience the power of their society. His structural-functional analysis suggests that religion promotes social cohesion and conformity and confers meaning and purpose on life.

4. Using the symbolic-interaction paradigm, Peter Berger explains that religious beliefs are socially constructed as a means of responding to life's uncertainties and disruptions.

5. Using the social-conflict paradigm, Karl Marx charged that religion promotes social inequality

and the status quo. On the other hand, Max Weber's analysis of Calvinism's contribution to the rise of industrial capitalism demonstrates religion's power to promote social change.

6. Churches, which are religious organizations well integrated into their society, fall into two categories—ecclesias and denominations.

7. Sects, the result of religious division, are marked by charismatic leadership and suspicion of the larger society.

8. Cults are religious organizations that embrace new and unconventional beliefs and practices.

9. Technologically simple human societies were generally animistic, with religion just one facet of family life; in more complex societies, religion emerges as a distinct social institution.

10. Followers of six world religions—Christianity, Islam, Judaism, Hinduism, Buddhism, and Con-

The Cyber-Church: Logging On to Religion

It takes only a few minutes on the Internet to discover that religion is alive and well on the World Wide Web, where you can find electronic Bibles for computer-assisted research, a proverb a day, prophecies related to the End of Time (from an online book entitled *In the Light of Biblical Prophecy*), as well as announcements of events, products, publications, and conventions. Chat groups, university or college courses, monthly magazines, and prayer groups provide opportunities for active participation. Internet Evangelism Central is a site designed to inspire Christians to evangelize the Web through the creation of further evangelical sites. New Age is also represented, with sites such as *New Age Web Works* or *The Cyberzine for the Open Minded*.

This is hardly the first time technological innovation has brought change to religion. Six hundred years ago in medieval Europe, face-to-face speaking was the major channel for transmitting religious ideas, as clerics gathered in the universities of the largest cities of the day and people went to services in churches and other houses of worship across the land. At that time, Bibles and other sacred texts were few and far between; monks in monasteries took years to complete the painstaking task of copying them by hand. But religion changed when Johann Gutenberg, a German inventor, built a movable-type press and published the first printed book—a Bible—in 1456. Within fifty years, millions of books were in print across Europe, and most of them were about religious matters. It is no coincidence that the spread of printed books was soon followed by a major religious transformation—the Protestant Reformation—as an expanding market of religious ideas prompted people to rethink established principles and practices.

In the twentieth century, radio (beginning in the 1920s) and television (after 1950) have extended the reach of religious leaders, who founded "media congregations" no longer confined by the walls of a single building. During the 1990s, the Internet accelerated this trend, as hundreds of thousands of Web sites offer messages from established churches, obscure cults, and "New Age" organizations.

How will computer technology affect religious life? With more to learn than ever before, some analysts anticipate a new "post-denominational" age in which people's religious ideas are not bound by particular organizations, as in the past. New information technology may also usher in an age of "cyber-churches." Television has already shown it can transmit the personal charisma and spiritual message of religious leaders to ever-larger audiences. Perhaps the Internet will lead to "virtual congregations," both larger in number and broader in background than any before.

SOURCE: Based on Ramo (1996); the World Wide Web

---

fucianism—represent three-quarters of all humanity.

11. Almost all adults in Canada identify with a religion; almost 90 percent claim to have a religious affiliation, with the largest number being Roman Catholic.

12. How religious we conclude our nation is depends on how we operationalize the concept of religiosity. The vast majority of people say they believe in God, but only a minority of the Canadian population attend religious services regularly.

13. Secularization refers to the diminishing importance of the supernatural and the sacred. In Canada, while some indicators of religiosity (such as membership in mainstream churches) have declined, others (such as membership in sects) are on the rise. Thus, it is doubtful that secularization will bring on the demise of religion.

14. Civil religion refers to the quasi-religious patriotism that ties people to their society.

15. Fundamentalism opposes religious accommodation to the world, favouring a more otherworldly focus. Fundamentalism advocates a literal interpretation of sacred texts, rejects religious diversity, and pursues the personal experience of God's presence. Some fundamentalist Christian organizations actively support conservative political goals.

16. Some of the continuing appeal of religion lies in the inability of science (including sociology) to address timeless questions about the ultimate meaning of human existence.

CRITICAL THINKING QUESTIONS

1. Explain the basic distinction between the sacred and the profane that underlies all religious belief.

2. Explain Karl Marx's contention that religion supports the status quo. Develop a counter-argument, based on Max Weber's analysis of Calvinism, that religion can be a major force for social change.

3. Distinguish between churches, sects, and cults. Is one type of religious organization inherently better than another? Why or why not?

4. What evidence points to a decline in religion in Canada? In what ways does religion seem to be getting stronger?

SOCIOLOGY APPLIED

1. Investigate the place of religion on your campus. Is your school affiliated with any religious organization? Was it ever? Is there a chaplain or other religious official? See if you can learn from sources on campus what share of students regularly attend any religious service.

2. Assessing people's religious commitment is very difficult. Develop several questions measuring religiosity that might be asked on a questionnaire or in an interview. Present them to several people; how well do they seem to work?

3. At first, only cults used the Internet. But, today, many religious organizations are online, and even

the Roman Catholic church has a Web page. Access Yahoo! Canada or another search engine and generate sites by searching on a key word such as "religion," "Judaism," "Hindu," or "cult." Visit several sites and see what you can learn about online religion.

4. Is religion getting weaker? To test the secularization thesis, go to the library or local newspaper office and obtain an issue of your local newspaper published fifty years ago and, if possible, one hundred years ago. Compare the attention to religious issues then and now.

WEBLINKS

www.utoronto.ca/stmikes/theobook.htm
The APS Guide to Resources in Theology is a collection of links to theological resources on the Web, maintained by the Faculty of Theology, University of St. Michael's College, Toronto.

bible.gospelcom.net/
The *Bible Gateway* site allows online searching of the Bible by word, by passage, or by topic, in nine languages and multiple Bible versions.

community.web.net/faith/index.html
Faith and Justice Network is a membership service for Canadians of all faiths who share a concern for justice and peace. The network provides space for issue-focused online discussion and publishes information about organizations, events, and more.

www.religioustolerance.org/
The *Ontario Consultants on Religious Tolerance* site includes an extensive library of more than 550 essays on different faiths, from Asatru to Christianity to Zoroastrianism, and controversial religious topics, from abortion to homosexuality to female clergy.

www.escape.ca/~jclong/
Created in conjunction with a 1998 conference at Carleton University School of Journalism, Ottawa, to explore how faith groups and the media can work together to improve faith coverage in Canada, *Faith and the Media* includes media reports about the conference, plenary session addresses, and selected readings.

Romare Bearden, *The Piano Lesson*, 1983
Collage and water colour, 29 × 22 in. © Romare Bearden Foundation/Licensed by VAGA, New York, N.Y.

CHAPTER 19

EDUCATION

Thirteen-year-old Naoko Matsuo returns from school to her home in suburban Yokohama, Japan. But instead of dropping off her books to begin an afternoon of fun, she settles in to do her homework. Several hours later, Naoko's mother reminds her that it is time to leave for the *juku*, a "cram school" that Naoko attends for three hours three evenings a week. Mother and daughter take the subway to an office building in downtown Yokohama where Naoko joins dozens of other girls and boys for intensive training in Japanese, English, math, and science.

Attending the *juku* costs the Matsuo family several hundred dollars a month. But the extra classroom hours are a good investment that will pay off when Naoko takes national examinations for high school placement. Later on, the challenge will be to gain admission to an exclusive national university, a prize earned by just one-third of Japanese students. Given the cutthroat competition for educational success in Japan, the Matsuos know that their daughter cannot work too hard or begin too early (Simons, 1989).

Why do the Japanese pay such attention to schooling? In this modern, industrial society, admission to an elite university all but ensures a high-paying, prestigious career. This chapter spotlights **education**, *the social institution guiding a society's transmission of knowledge—including basic facts, job skills, and also cultural norms and values—to its members.* In industrial societies, as we shall see, education is largely a matter of **schooling**, *formal instruction under the direction of specially trained teachers.*

EDUCATION: A GLOBAL SURVEY

Like people in Japan, we in Canada expect children to spend much of their first eighteen years of life in school. A century ago, however, only a small elite enjoyed the privilege of schooling. In the 1830s it is estimated that in Upper Canada about half of the children attended school—and only for an average of twelve months in total (Phillips cited in Johnson, 1968:27). In low-income countries, even today, the vast majority of people receive little or no schooling.

SCHOOLING AND ECONOMIC DEVELOPMENT

The extent of schooling in any society is closely tied to its level of economic development. Chapter 4 ("Society") explained that our hunting and gathering ancestors lived a simple life in families without governments, churches, or schools. For these people, "schooling" amounted to the knowledge and skills parents transmitted directly to their children (Lenski, Nolan, and Lenski, 1995).

In agrarian societies—in which most of the world's people live today—young people spend several years in school. By contrast, the opportunity to study literature, art, history, and science is a privilege generally available only to people freed by wealth from the need to work. The English word "school," in fact, comes down to us from the Greek word for "leisure." In ancient Greece, renowned teachers such as Socrates, Plato, and Aristotle concentrated their efforts on aristocratic men to the exclusion of everyone else. Similarly, in ancient China, the famous philosopher K'ung-Fu-tzu (Confucius) shared his wisdom with only a select few. During the Middle Ages, European education took a step forward as the church established the first colleges and universities. But, here again, the privilege of schooling remained largely restricted to ruling elites.

Today, schooling in low-income nations is very diverse because it reflects the local culture. In Iran, for example, education and religion are intertwined, so Islam figures prominently in schooling there. Elsewhere—including Bangladesh (Asia), Zimbabwe (Africa), and Nicaragua (Latin America)—distinctive cultural traditions have molded the process of schooling.

All low-income countries have one trait in common: limited access to schooling. In the poorest nations (including several in central Africa), only half of all elementary-aged children ever get to school; throughout the world, just half of all children attend secondary school (Najafizadeh and Mennerick, 1992). As a consequence, illiteracy disadvantages one-third of Latin Americans, almost half of Asians, and two-thirds of Africans. Global Map 19–1 displays the extent of illiteracy around the world.

Industrial, high-income societies embrace the principle of schooling for everyone. Industrial production demands that workers gain at least basic skills in the so-called three Rs—reading, 'riting, and 'rithmetic. For many industrial nations, literacy is also a necessary condition of political democracy.

The following national comparisons show how schooling is linked to economic development. Notice, too, how even industrial nations differ in their approach to educating their populations.

SCHOOLING IN INDIA

India is a low-income country in which people earn about 5 percent of the income standard in Canada. Consequently, many parents depend on children's earnings. Thus, even though India has outlawed child labour, many Indian children work in factories—weaving rugs or making handicrafts—up to sixty hours a week, which greatly limits their opportunity for schooling.

In recent decades, schooling in India has increased. Most children now receive some primary education, typically in crowded schoolrooms where one teacher attends to perhaps sixty children (more than twice as many as in Canadian classrooms). This is all the schooling most people ever acquire, since less than half pursue secondary education and very few enter university or college. The result is that about half of the people in this vast country are literate.

Patriarchy also significantly shapes Indian education. Indian parents are joyful at the birth of a boy,

since he and his future wife both will contribute income to the family. Girls are a financial liability, since parents must provide a dowry at the time of marriage, and a daughter's work will then benefit her husband's family. Because Indian society offers little incentive to invest in the schooling of girls, 45 percent of boys but only 30 percent of girls attend secondary school. Along with this cultural denigration of females, a large majority of the children working in Indian factories are girls—a family's way of benefiting from their daughter while they can (United Nations Development Programme, 1995).

SCHOOLING IN JAPAN

September 30, 1994, Kobe, Japan. Compared to us, the Japanese are, above all, orderly. Young people on the way to school stand out with their uniforms, their armloads of books, and their looks of seriousness and purpose.

Schooling has not always been part of the Japanese way of life. Before industrialization brought mandatory education to this country in 1872, only a privileged few enrolled in school. Today, Japan's educational system is widely praised for generating some of the world's highest achievers.

In the early grades, schools foster the cultural values long central to Japanese life, especially obligation to family. In their early teens, as illustrated by the account of Naoko Matsuo at the beginning of this chapter, students encounter Japan's system of rigorous and competitive examinations. Written evaluations are used to place the brightest students in the best schools. In terms of schooling, Japan is more of a meritocracy than Canada or the United States. Here, university or college admission is not limited only to the best students: a bigger barrier to advanced education is the high cost involved. In Japan, by contrast, government support covers most of the financial cost of higher education; however, without high examination scores, even the richest families cannot place their children in a good university.

More men and women in Japan graduate from high school (about 90 percent) than in Canada or the United States. But because of competitive examinations, only about 30 percent of high-school graduates end up entering university—compared to about 55 percent in Canada and about 65 percent in the U.S. Understandably, then, Japanese students view entrance examinations with the utmost seriousness, and about half attend *juku*, cram schools, to prepare for them.

Japanese women take such an active interest in their children's schooling that they have been dubbed

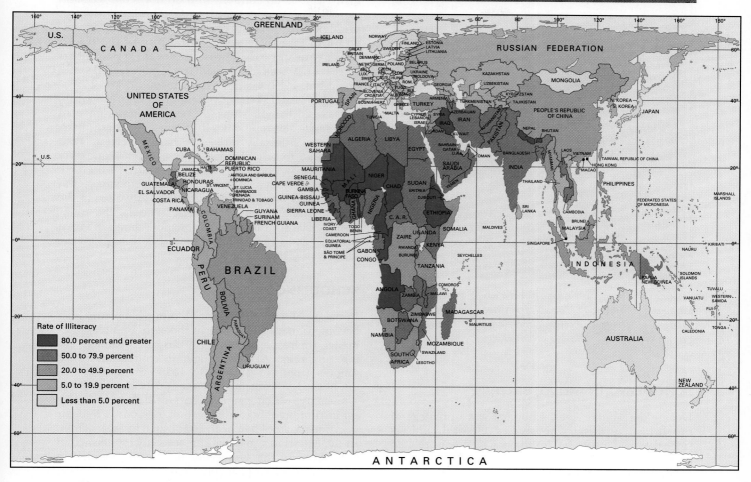

GLOBAL MAP 19–1 Illiteracy in Global Perspective

Reading and writing skills are widespread in every industrial society, with illiteracy rates generally below 5 percent. Throughout Latin America, however, illiteracy is more commonplace—one consequence of limited economic development. In about a dozen nations of the world—many of them in Africa—illiteracy is the rule rather than the exception. In such societies, people rely on what sociologists call the "oral tradition" of face-to-face communication rather than communicating by the written word.

SOURCES: The World Bank (1997); map projection from *Peters Atlas of the World* (1990).

koiku mamas (a mixture of Japanese and English that means "education mothers"). This maternal role reflects the stark reality that acceptance or rejection by a university shapes a student's career. In addition, most Japanese women, who are still not in the labour force, tend to devote themselves to the future success of their sons and, to a lesser extent, their daughters (Brinton, 1988; Simons, 1989). The payoff—or disappointment—after years of effort on the part of mother and child comes as they anxiously await the results of university examinations. So high is the suspense that observing the outcome has become something of a national pastime.

Because of the pressure it places on students, Japanese schooling produces impressive results. Especially in mathematics and science, Japanese students outperform students of every other industrial country, including Canada and the United States (Benedict, 1974; Hayneman and Loxley, 1983; Rohlen, 1983; Brinton, 1988; Simons, 1989).

Traditionally, the Japanese have placed a strong emphasis on fitting in with the group. This cultural value is evident in the widespread wearing of school uniforms—a practice that is also gaining favour in Canada as a means to improve school discipline.

SCHOOLING IN GREAT BRITAIN

During the Middle Ages, schooling was a privilege of the British nobility, who studied classical subjects since they had little need for the practical skills related to earning a living. But as the Industrial Revolution created a need for an educated labour force, and as working-class people demanded access to schools, a rising share of the British population entered the classroom. Law now requires every British child to attend school until age sixteen.

Traditional social distinctions, however, persist in British education. Many wealthy families send their children to what the British call *public schools*, the equivalent of Canadian private boarding schools. Such elite schools not only teach academic subjects, they also convey to children from wealthy (especially newly rich) families the distinctive patterns of speech, mannerisms, and social graces of the British upper class. These academies are far too expensive for most students, however, who attend state-supported day schools.

To lessen the influence of social background on schooling, the British expanded their university system and use competitive entrance examinations. For those who score the highest, the government pays most university costs. Compared with those in Japan, however, British examinations are less crucial, since many well-to-do children who do not score well still manage to attend Oxford or Cambridge, the most prestigious British universities. "Oxbridge" graduates go on to take their places at the core of the British power elite: more than two-thirds of the top members of the British government have "Oxbridge" degrees (Sampson, 1982; Gamble, Ludlam, and Baker, 1993).

These brief sketches of schooling in India, Japan, and Great Britain show the crucial importance of economic development. In poor countries, many children—especially girls—are more likely to work than to go to school. Rich nations adopt mandatory education laws both to forge an industrial workforce and to satisfy demands for political democracy. But rich nations vary among themselves, as we see in the intense competition of Japanese schools, the traditional social stratification that shapes schools in Great Britain, and the practical emphasis found in the schools of Canada.

SCHOOLING IN CANADA

Initial developments in education in what would later become Canada took place in the early French settlements, where the three Rs (in this case, reading, 'riting, and religion) were taught in church-controlled schools (Johnson 1968). By 1636, the Jesuits had established a "college" that eventually became Laval University, which claims to be North America's oldest institution of higher education. By 1668, a trade or vocational school had been established in St. Joachim. In the Maritimes, an Anglican academy established in 1785 became the University of New Brunswick in 1859. The earliest primary schools in Upper Canada, which were established in the 1780s, began receiving government funding in 1792. Elitist boarding schools started in 1807 were the first step in establishing our secondary school system.

Prior to Confederation (1867), governments in Canada had already created separate Catholic and Protestant school systems, embraced universal education and teacher training, and put texts and curricula under control of a department of education. In 1883, Toronto became the second North American city to establish kindergarten within the school system, and by about 1920, Canada had compulsory education to the end of elementary school or the age of sixteen in most provinces. (In the United States, all states had compulsory education by 1918.) In this period, secondary schools were being established and expanded across Canada. The principle of mass education had been firmly established, partly in response to the requirements of the Industrial Revolution for a literate and skilled workforce.

It is important to note that *official* literacy and *functional* literacy are not the same. Although Canada claims to have minimal illiteracy by international standards, educators and others have long voiced concerns about the extent to which Canadians have the literacy and numeracy skills required to cope with daily living and work—to say nothing of academic pursuits. A 1989 survey carried out by the National Literacy Secretariat concluded that 15 percent of Canada's adult population is not sufficiently literate to deal with normal everyday situations. More alarming still is the fact that the Economic Council of Canada estimated in 1992 that 28 percent of Canadians aged sixteen to twenty-four cannot read a simple newspaper article and that 44 percent are not functionally numerate. The Council estimated that one million functionally illiterate young people will join the labour force over the next ten years unless we establish and enforce stringent standards for graduation. It has even been suggested that university graduation should require passing a literacy test (*Toronto Star*, August 1, 1992:A1). We will revisit the problem of functional illiteracy in the "Academic Standards" section near the end of this chapter.

Levels of educational attainment have increased steadily over the last fifty years, so that over time larger percentages of the adult population have some post-secondary education or university degrees. Between 1961 and 1986, the proportion of Canadians twenty-five to forty-four years of age with some post-secondary education increased from 8 to about 55 percent: between 1971 and 1986—a mere fifteen years—the proportion with a university degree rose from 7 to 15 percent (Secretary of State, 1992:25–27). Clearly, Canadians are becoming aware of the educational requirements of the modern economy.[1]

In Canada, the school reformers of the late 1800s were concerned that the "classical curriculum did not reflect the realities of the new economic order. Education, thus, began to be viewed as an essential precondition for national economic growth" (Gilbert, 1989:105). Wide participation and universality were important goals. Canada also has a policy of universal, publicly supported primary and secondary schooling, including that in the "separate" or Catholic system. Canada has 273 publicly funded post-secondary institutions, 69 of which are classified as universities; tuition fees at our universities (none of which are pri-

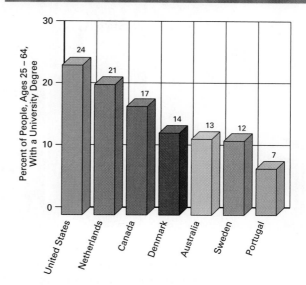

FIGURE 19–1 University Degrees in Global Perspective

SOURCE: U.S. Bureau of the Census (1997).

vate) cover about 15 percent of the costs, while government subsidies account for the rest.

Canada ranks second to the United States and well above the average of fourteen other developed countries in the proportion of twenty- to twenty-four-year-olds enrolled in post-secondary education. We rank above the U.S. (and below only Sweden) in terms of public expenditures on education—8 percent of our gross national product (Secretary of State, 1992). However, Figure 19–1 indicates that Canada falls substantially behind both the U.S. and the Netherlands in terms of the proportion of population aged twenty-five to sixty-four with university degrees.

Besides trying to make schooling more widely accessible, Canadian society has long favoured *practical* learning, that is, education that has a direct bearing on people's lives, and especially on their occupations. The educational philosopher John Dewey (1859–1952) advanced the idea that children would readily learn information and skills they found useful. Rejecting the traditional emphasis on teaching a fixed body of knowledge to each generation of students, Dewey (1968; orig. 1938) endorsed *progressive education* that reflected people's changing concerns and needs. With the Quiet Revolution in Quebec in the 1960s, the classical education favoured by the religious elite was replaced by a system encouraging the study of business, engineering, and science.

---

[1] The impact of education on unemployment rates is quite apparent. "In March, 1991, the rate of unemployment among those 25 years of age and older with a university degree was only 4.2 percent, compared to 18 percent for those without secondary schooling" (Secretary of State, 1992:27).

Schooling is a way of teaching the values and attitudes that a society deems important. It is also a means favoured by political regimes to instil conformity and compliance into children. These children in Taiwan are receiving a lesson in "political correctness."

Despite the overall trend towards applied or practical fields, Canada lags behind a number of other countries in terms of the proportion of its degrees awarded in engineering. In fact, in Canada the proportion of degrees granted in engineering—to men and women—is less than half that of Belgium, Portugal, Finland, Japan, Sweden, Germany, and Denmark (Oderkirk, 1993:10). Despite the rapid pace of technological change and increased interest in science and technology as fields of study, the proportion of graduates in these fields (17 percent) was the same in 1996 as in 1986. In 1996, 34 percent of Canada's science and technology graduates were women (Statistics Canada, *The Daily*, April 14, 1998).

THE FUNCTIONS OF SCHOOLING

Structural-functional analysis looks at how formal education enhances the operation and stability of society. Central to the socialization process, schooling serves as one cultural lifeline linking the generations.

SOCIALIZATION

Technologically simple societies transmit their ways of life informally from parents to children. As societies become more technologically complex, young people need rapidly expanding information and new skills, beyond the grasp of family members themselves, so other social institutions play a greater role in socialization. In industrial societies, schooling requires specially trained personnel to convey the knowledge needed for adult roles.

In primary school, children learn basic language and mathematical skills. Secondary school builds on this foundation and, for many, college or university allows further specialization. In addition, schools transmit cultural values and norms. Sometimes the operation of the classroom itself serves to teach important cultural lessons. However, where in the U.S. spelling bees and classroom drills are intended to foster a keen sense of competitive individualism, in Canada there is more emphasis on activities that encourage cooperation, sharing, and team effort. Competitiveness is actually discouraged in many Canadian classrooms because of potential damaging effects on the self-esteem of those who cannot compete successfully.

Nor is the political component of education as aggressively promoted in Canada as it is in other countries. In the United States, for example, the American political system and way of doing business are commonly championed in the classroom, and rituals such as saluting the flag and singing "The Star-Spangled Banner" foster patriotism. Although our children do sing "O Canada," we place less emphasis on Canadian history or the workings of our political system than do the Americans—and a consciousness of military purpose or presence is almost completely lacking here. Instead of espousing a unified cultural identity, our classrooms try to encourage respect for the many cultures that make up the Canadian mosaic.

CULTURAL INNOVATION

Educational systems create as well as transmit culture. Schools attempt to stimulate intellectual inquiry and critical thinking, which lead to the development of new ideas. Today, for example, most university professors not only teach but engage in research to expand our knowledge in countless areas. Medical research, carried on mainly at major universities, has helped to increase life expectancy, just as research by sociologists and psychologists has expanded our understanding of human social life and contributed to an improved quality of life.

Marshall McLuhan foresaw the radical cultural transformation and innovation that would accompany incorporating the electronic media into education. Suddenly, there would be classrooms without walls: teaching, educational content, and links with the wider world would change irrevocably. As McLuhan noted in 1972,

> The wired planet has no boundaries and no monopolies of knowledge. The affairs of the world are now dependent upon the highest information of which man is capable. The boundaries between the world of affairs and the community of learning have ceased to exist (Bendetti and Dettart, 1996:172).

SOCIAL INTEGRATION

Schooling helps to forge a mass of people into a unified society. This integrative function is especially important in nations characterized by great social diversity, where various cultures know little about—or may even be hostile to—one another. In the past, the Soviet Union and Yugoslavia relied on schools to unite their disparate peoples—without ultimately succeeding.

As we saw in Chapter 3 ("Culture"), Canada has had a long experience with the challenges of multiculturalism and linguistic dualism and has tried (not always successfully) to foster Canadian nationalism while accommodating a wide variety of interest groups. As a result, our educational policies have been sensitive to the problems of maintaining equality of access and unity in the face of diversity. We have been reluctant to push a national identity because of Quebec's sensitivities and our embrace of the mosaic model (Jaenen, 1981).

Societies in the Americas, Africa, and Asia similarly strive to foster social integration through schooling. Normally, schools try to meet this challenge by establishing a common language to encourage broad communication and to forge a national identity. Of course, some ethnic minorities resist state-sponsored schooling precisely for this reason. In the former Soviet Union, for example, Lithuanians, Ukrainians, and Azerbaijanis objected to learning Russian because they saw it as emblematic of their domination by outsiders and a threat to their own traditions. For similar reasons, the Hutterites, a culturally distinctive people in our Prairie provinces (mainly in Alberta), teach their children in schools within their own colonies (albeit using the provincial curriculum, and speaking in English for part of the day) and continue to speak a German dialect within their communities. Of course, the Québécois perceive a threat to their distinct culture, resent the need to learn English for economic survival, and insist on full provincial control of education—the current demand being for control of labour force training. Quebec has declared itself a unilingual province and only under special circumstances can a child be educated in English there. Native peoples in Canada have been struggling as well to establish greater control of their own schools. In each of the above cases, the peoples in question resist formal schooling in the language of the majority because of very real threats to linguistic and cultural survival.

Although there is understandable resistance to majority-controlled schooling by certain segments of the population, the striking cultural diversity of our country increases the importance of formal education as a path to social integration. The expansion of educational facilities and the enactment of mandatory education laws coincided with the arrival of hundreds of thousands of immigrants from a wide variety of origins who somehow had to be transformed into Canadians. Even today, formal education plays a major role in integrating disparate groups, as immigrants from Asia (roughly 50 percent of recent immigrants), the Caribbean, Eastern Europe, and Latin America—and roughly 35 000 refugees a year—blend their traditions with the existing cultural mix. Although our school systems seek to provide all of them with the linguistic and other skills needed for employment and daily life, Canada has not insisted that they give up their various identities completely.

The retention of other identities is assisted, where there are concentrations of people with shared backgrounds, through our heritage language programs, which provide formal education in traditional languages for ethnic minority children (where numbers warrant it). These programs sometimes attract other students, so that somewhere in Canada, young people of British or Ukrainian ancestry are studying Japanese or Italian. Furthermore, since our country is officially bilingual and since bilingualism is needed for certain types of jobs (that of prime minister, for example), the Trudeau government established French immersion schooling throughout the country. About 7 percent of nonfrancophone primary and secondary school students outside Quebec are enrolled in immersion programs. In 1992–93, enrolment in French immersion varied by province from 3 percent in the Northwest Territories to 17 percent in New Brunswick (Canada's only officially bilingual province). Quebec, which began reporting French immersion figures only recently, has 25.4 percent of nonfrancophone children enrolled (Statistics Canada, Cat. 81-528-XPB).

From a functionalist point of view, schooling provides children with the knowledge and skills they will need as adults. A conflict analysis adds that schooling differs according to the resources of the local community. When some schools offer children much more than others do, education perpetuates the class structure rather than increasing equality of opportunity.

SOCIAL PLACEMENT

Formal education helps young people assume culturally approved statuses and perform roles that contribute to the ongoing life of society. Ideally, schools accomplish this by identifying and developing each individual's aptitudes and abilities and then evaluating a student's performance in terms of achievement rather than social background.

In principle, teachers encourage the "best and the brightest" to pursue the most challenging and advanced studies, while others are guided into educational programs and occupations suited to their talents. Schooling, in short, enhances meritocracy by making personal merit a foundation of future social position (Hurn, 1978).

Meritocracy has always had special significance to people who begin life with social disadvantages based on ascribed traits such as sex, race, ethnicity, and social class. For this reason, schooling has historically been the major avenue of upward social mobility in Canada.

LATENT FUNCTIONS OF SCHOOLING

Besides these manifest functions of formal education, a number of latent functions are less widely recognized. One is child care. As the number of one-parent families and two-career couples rises, schools have become vital to relieving parents of some child-care duties.

For teenagers, too, schooling consumes considerable time and energy, in many cases fostering conformity at a time of life when the likelihood of unlawful behaviour is high. Also, because many students attend school well into their twenties, education engages thousands of young people for whom jobs may not be available.

Another latent function of schools is to establish social relationships and networks. Many people form lifelong friendships—as well as meet their future spouses—in high school, college, and university. Affiliation with a particular school also can create valuable career opportunities.

Critical evaluation. Structural-functional analysis of formal education identifies both manifest and latent functions of schooling. One key limitation of structural functionalism is that it overlooks how the quality of schooling is far better for some than for others. In the next section, social-conflict analysis places the spotlight squarely on this issue.

SCHOOLING AND SOCIAL INEQUALITY

Social-conflict analysis counters the functionalist view that schooling is a meritocratic strategy for developing people talent's and abilities. Rather, this approach argues that schools routinely provide learning according to students' social background, thereby perpetuating social inequality.

Throughout the world, people traditionally have thought that schooling is more important for males than for females. The education gap between women and men has been closing in recent decades, but many women still study conventionally "feminine" subjects such as literature, while men pursue mathematics and engineering. And by stressing the experiences of certain types of people (say, military generals) while ignoring the lives of others (such as farm women), schools reinforce the values and importance of dominant racial, cultural, and gender categories, to the detriment of minorities. Efforts have been made across Canada to provide gender-neutral texts and library materials and to remove materials that perpetuate negative stereotypes or are offensive to various ethnic, racial, and religious minorities. Schools are also attempting to incorporate a wide range of multicultural programs and materials into their curricula to increase tolerance and understanding among youngsters of different backgrounds. The intent, in part, is to eradicate stereotypes and to raise the aspiration levels of any people who may have felt themselves to be excluded by the system. Women and francophones are among those who now are spending more time in school and proceeding to university or college (Guppy and Arai, 1993).

It is also the case that affluence affects the extent to which Canadians take advantage of educational opportunities. Along with gender, social class is a strong predictor of aspirations to attend university (Porter, Porter and Blishen, 1982): in fact, one is much more likely to attend university or college if one's parents are white-collar with post-secondary education (Guppy and Arai, 1993).

Social class background is also an important determinant of familiarity with computers, which is increasingly important to education and employment. Home computer ownership rises (from below 30 percent) to well over 60 percent in the homes of those who are university educated, who have incomes of $70 000 or more and who are in professional occupations (Forcese, 1997:124). Children from these families have an advantage as they progress through the educational system.

Regional variations in affluence and economic structure give rise to marked differences in educational attainment across provinces. Canada Map 19–1 indicates the proportions of provincial and territorial populations, fifteen years or older, that have acquired a university degree. The levels range from 8.1 percent in Newfoundland to almost 15 percent in Ontario and the Yukon. British Columbia and Alberta are also above average in educational attainment. It is worth noting that the Yukon attracts much of its university-educated population from elsewhere to take jobs in government, natural resources, defence, and research.

SOCIAL CONTROL

Social-conflict analysis asserts that schooling acts as a means of social control, reinforcing acceptance of the status quo. In various, often subtle ways, schools reproduce the status hierarchy, although this process is not always evident to students or even to teachers.

Samuel Bowles and Herbert Gintis (1976) point out that public education grew exponentially in the late nineteenth century when capitalists were seeking a docile, disciplined, and literate workforce. Mandatory education laws ensured that schools would teach immigrants the English language[2] as well as cultural values that support capitalism. Compliance, punctuality, and discipline were—and still are—part of what is called the **hidden curriculum**, *subtle presentations of political or cultural ideas in the classroom.*

TESTING AND SOCIAL INEQUALITY

Here is a question of the kind traditionally used to measure the intelligence and academic ability of school-age children.

> Painter is to painting as _____ is to sonnet.
> Answers: (a) driver (b) poet (c) priest (d) carpenter

The correct answer is (b) *poet*: a painter creates a painting as a poet creates a sonnet. This question purports to measure logical reasoning, but demonstrating this skill depends on knowing what each term means. Unless students are familiar with sonnets as a form of written verse, they are not likely to answer the question correctly. An upper-middle-class student of European descent is likely to have more of the experiences rewarded by such tests. The same person, however, might not score as well on an intelligence test devised by the Ojibwa or the Inuit. Controversy surrounds the use of such tests, for they reflect our society's dominant culture, thereby placing the members of various minorities at a disadvantage. Children from less affluent backgrounds are also at a disadvantage because they face "tests of intelligence and cognitive skills weighted in favour of middle- and upper-class children" (Porter, Porter and Blishen, 1982:9). The motivations and attitudes transmitted to their children by middle- and upper-class parents also benefit them on these tests in the classroom.

Educational specialists claim that bias of this kind has been all but eliminated from standardized tests, since testing organizations carefully study response patterns and drop any question that favours one racial category over another. Critics, however, maintain that some bias based on class, race, or ethnicity is inherent

---

[2] Until Quebec passed Bill 101 in 1977, making French the sole official language in Quebec as well as the language of business, francophones had to be fluently bilingual to succeed economically. Even in Quebec, English was the language of business.

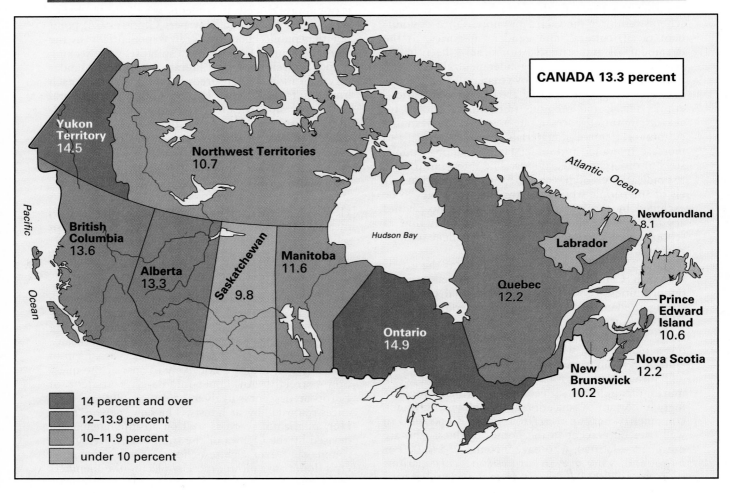

CANADA MAP 19–1 Population 15 Years or Older with University Degree (Percentage, by Province and Territory, 1996)

SOURCE: Calculations by Linda Gerber based on 1996 census tables (www.statcan.ca).

in any formal testing, because questions inevitably reflect our society's dominant culture and thereby put minorities at a disadvantage (Owen, 1985; Crouse and Trusheim, 1988; Putka, 1990).

One of the uses of such tests has been to place students in either a general or an academic (university-bound) stream, another controversial practice that is discussed below.

STREAMING AND SOCIAL INEQUALITY

Many Canadian schools practise **streaming**, *the assigning of students to different types of educational pro-grams*. Streaming is also a common practice in many other industrial societies, including the United States, Germany, Great Britain, France, and Japan.

The educational justification for streaming is to give students the kind of schooling appropriate to their individual aptitude. For a variety of reasons, including innate ability and level of motivation, some students are capable of more challenging work than others. Young people also differ in their interests, with some drawn to, say, the study of languages, while others seek training in art or science. Given this diversity of talent and focus, no single program for all students would serve any of them well.

But critics see streaming as a thinly veiled strategy to perpetuate privilege. Research shows that social background has as much to do with streaming as personal aptitude does. Students from affluent families generally do well in school and on tests and so are placed in university-bound streams, while students from modest backgrounds (including a disproportionate share of the poor) end up in programs that curb their aspirations and teach technical trades. Streaming, therefore, effectively segregates students—academically and socially—into different worlds.

Furthermore, most schools reserve their best teachers for students in the top streams. These teachers put more effort into teaching, show more respect to students, and expect more from them. By contrast, teachers in lower streams employ more memorization, classroom drill, and other unstimulating techniques. They also emphasize regimentation, punctuality, and respect for authority figures.

In light of these criticisms, many schools are now cautious about streaming. Recent initiatives in Ontario aimed at destreaming were met with opposition from school boards and teachers as well as from parents, who are concerned that their university-bound children will receive lower-quality education in destreamed classrooms.

Without streaming, less academically inclined children may be unable to compete with some of their classmates, and teachers face the difficult task of teaching students of differing abilities in one class; but these problems are not insurmountable. Rigid streaming, on the other hand, has a powerful impact on students' learning and self-concept. Young people who spend years in higher streams tend to see themselves as bright and able, whereas those in lower streams have less ambition and lower self-esteem (Bowles and Gintis, 1976; Persell, 1977; Rosenbaum, 1980; Oakes, 1982, 1985).

UNEQUAL ACCESS TO HIGHER EDUCATION

In industrial societies, higher education is the main path to occupational achievement. Not surprisingly, 79 percent of Canadians view education as "extremely important to one's future success" (Flower, 1984:27). Despite the decline in the proportion of the population that is eighteen to twenty-four years of age, enrolment in post-secondary education has risen dramatically throughout the post-war period and in recent decades. Between 1988 and 1994, while Canada's population grew by 8.8 percent, full-time post-secondary enrolment grew by 18.1 percent (Statistics Canada, 1996). Figure 19–2 reveals that in 1995 Canada ranked fifth among Organization for Economic Cooperation and Development (OECD) countries in university enrolment of those age seventeen to

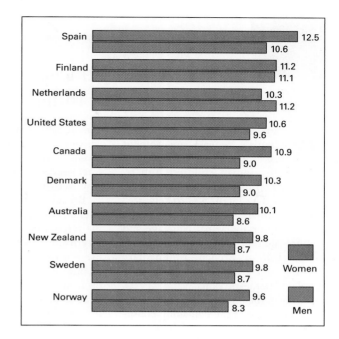

FIGURE 19–2 Ten OECD Countries with the Highest Percentage of Young Adults* Enrolled in University, 1995

*Percentage of persons 17 to 34 years of age enrolled at the university level. The rank order of countries is based on combined male and female figures.

SOURCE: OECD database, Table C5.2a (www.oecd.org/els/stats/eag97/C5.xls).

thirty-four—and ranked third in the enrolment of women. Note that the enrolment of women is ahead of that of men in all but one of these countries.

There are many reasons why most people in Canada do not attend and graduate from university or college. Some high-school students want to enter the labour force right away; others cannot afford to continue their education because of the costs of tuition and deferred income. Vast distances between homes and the nearest university are also major deterrents. In addition, the intellectual demands of the curriculum may dissuade some students with limited talents. Yet most of our young people would like to attend university or college, and doing so is certainly within the academic ability of the vast majority.

In one respect at least, we have moved closer to the goal of equal access to higher education in Canada: as noted above, women are now at least as likely as men to attend university. Low or moderate family income, however, remains a formidable barrier to enrolment: young people with lower family incomes or fathers in blue-collar occupations are much less likely to go to university (Wotherspoon,

"An Education of Oppression":
Canada's Indian Residential Schools

Around the turn of the century, Canada's federal government busily established residential schools for Indian children, run by Christian missionaries and their churches. The intent was to "civilize" and assimilate native children by stamping out aboriginal language and culture and replacing them with facility in English or French, rudimentary reading and arithmetic, and agricultural and domestic skills.

Only in the last two decades have we become aware of the damaging consequences of the residential school experience. Removed from their communities and families, native children were ill-prepared for life in the mainstream or for a return to their own communities. Inadequate and, in effect, damaging educational practices were accompanied in many of these schools by verbal, physical, and sexual abuse. By the time the residential schools were phased out in the early 1960s, several generations of native youngsters had paid a very heavy price.

Vicki English-Currie is one of many native people to describe her experience in a residential school—in this case, the Roman Catholic Indian Residential School at Brocket, Alberta—to which she was taken at the tender age of seven. Here the missionaries assumed total responsibility for—and total control over—the lives of Indian children.

Because of the different approaches to child rearing and education between the residential school and the community from which she had come, English-Currie experienced the transition as one of total shock, enormous setback, and "the beginning of a lifetime of cultural tragedy." In this setting, her formal education was overshadowed by accumulating "stress, anger, fear and hostility."

Here English-Currie describes the residential school experience in her own words:

I remember so well the first day of school in September of 1954. I was so excited and eager to get to school, because it meant reading, writing, games, children, and those Grey nuns who I thought were gods. I had wanted to become a nun so I would never sin and go to hell forever. My mother brought me to the door and left. A nun took me to a room and pushed me inside me to a room and pushed me inside with my bag and closed the door. This was one of the very first times I experienced violence. There was a lot more physical violence later at school, but this was one instance I was never able to forget....

This was the beginning of an education of oppression and the end to family life. We did not realize at that time the oppression and a limited education was an effective way of controlling the Indian people. In this way, the government could keep the Indian people divided and restrained. No matter how the parent felt or objected, the child was taken from age six to seventeen. They were kept undereducated, in poverty, and dependent upon the false charity of the Indian agent and the mission schools.

There was no way our parents could question the educational system. They did not know their rights under the law. In actuality, they had very few rights. They were told outright by the missionaries that they should be grateful for what they got. What was taught very well in residential school was

1991). Most universities provide financial assistance to students in the form of bursaries and scholarships, and governments make loans available to those of limited means. Nevertheless, many people cannot afford the remaining costs. The problem has been accentuated in recent years as cutbacks in government funding have forced tuition increases.

Figure 19–3 shows that overall the Asian and Black communities in Canada actually have *higher* levels of educational attainment than either the British or the French. However, it is important to note that the arrival of relatively well-educated immigrants in the Asian and Black categories may mean that the high levels of educational achievements are not necessarily characteristic of members of those minorities who are born or schooled in Canada. The figures for the native population suggest that we have failed, in a major way, to remove barriers to educational achievement by our first peoples.

Higher education, whether from university or college, expands career opportunities and increases earnings. Figure 19–4 shows that both labour force participation and income increase with educational attainment. The effect of education on labour force involvement is particularly evident in women; those with university degrees are four times as likely to be in the workforce as are those with less than grade 9, while male participation doubles. Average income also

how to feel guilty and to be grateful to the religious orders for "all they were doing" for us and our people....

The reason for these schools was not the betterment of the Indian child or to give that child an opportunity to excel in a formal educational setting. It was a way for the government to control the Indian people, using a religious order where the church was the instrument of the state. The way I see it, the missionaries were interested in converting people and the government was interested in keeping the Indian people quiet and out of the way. The two really did not care how it was done as long as they achieved the goals that they had set out to achieve....

The education so important in the first grades was so badly reduced by religious studies and by half-days in the kitchen for the girls or in the fields for the boys that many of the children had an inadequate basis upon which to attend successfully a provincial school system. Classroom work was modified to a cut-and-paste type of instruction. For art, we cut pictures out and constructed a scenery. In religion, we cut out people who served God and made a booklet. The curriculum was modified to what the teacher felt was important to teach Indian children.

All of the people in the pictures in our textbooks were white and middle-class; nurses, doctors, dentists, lawyers, and nuns were depicted, creating the impression that those were the only worthwhile persons in life. Native traditional leaders were never used. As a result the students' self-esteem, self-determination, self-worth, pride, and confidence slowly dwindled into a desire to be white. Indian culture taught us to have and to show respect for anyone in an authoritarian position. Indian people were not allowed by law to leave the reserve to attend higher educational institutions unless one joined a religious ministry. What possible point was there to use all these professional white, middle-class role models with the children during those primary years of schooling if they were to be denied by law ever achieving any of the roles of their models.

We were told outright that not only all Indian religion was heathen and should not be practiced but also that Indian culture and language were savagery. This further oppressed Native people and created a false belief that our culture, language, and religion were degrading and insignificant. (1993:114–16)

English-Currie goes on to say that native students were thought to be cognitively deficient and that psychological testing was used to legitimate their treatment. Not surprisingly, then, the core subjects of math, reading, and writing were not the major focus of their education. When the government decided to close the residential schools in the early 1960s, native youngsters were unprepared to cope with the integrated provincial schools to which they were sent. Finding themselves two or three grades behind their peers, native youth were degraded, dehumanized, and inclined to drop out.

The youngsters who were educated in "Indian" residential schools suffered the long-term consequences of being separated from their families and communities and of being wrenched from familiar cultural surroundings and thrust into an alien world where they felt themselves to be unwelcome. The cultural, economic, and political revival of native peoples across our country is all the more remarkable in the context of this background.

SOURCE: English-Currie (1993), abridged from Jeanne Perreault and Sylvia Vance, eds., *Writing the Circle* (Edmonton: NeWest Press, 1990).

increases with education for women and for men. Note the substantial increase in income for both sexes among those who have university degrees.

Obtaining a university degree, as opposed to a college diploma, also decreases the likelihood of unemployment two years after graduation: as one progresses from bachelor's through master's and doctoral degrees, the likelihood of being unemployed is further reduced (Secretary of State, 1992:40).

Certainly, many people find schooling to be its own reward, but the income figures shown here indicate that schooling is also a sound investment in financial terms, increasing income by hundreds of thousands of dollars over a person's working life. Bear in mind, of course, that the higher earnings of more educated people may stem from more than schooling. As we have seen, university graduates are likely to come from relatively well-to-do families and to enjoy social and economic advantages—including "old boy" networks, knowledge of how the system works, and a strong desire to achieve.

CREDENTIALISM

Sociologist Randall Collins (1979) calls ours a *credential society* because people view diplomas and degrees as evidence of ability to perform specialized occupational roles. In modern, technologically complex and

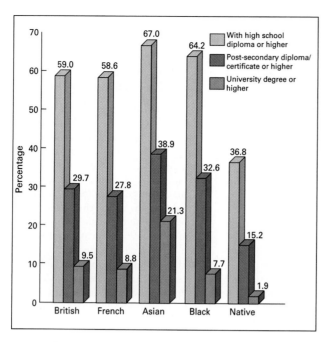

FIGURE 19–3 Educational Attainment for Selected Categories,* 1991

*Based on populations 15 years of age or older.

SOURCE: Compiled by Linda Gerber from 1991 Census, Individual Public Use Microdata.

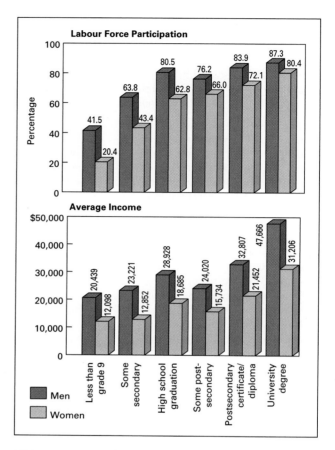

FIGURE 19–4 Labour Force Participation and Average Income by Educational Attainment and Sex,* 1993

* Percentages based on population 15 years of age and over.

SOURCES: Adapted from Statistics Canada, Catalogue Nos 81-229-XPB (Table 67) and 13-207 (Table 48); Hiller (1996).

socially mobile societies, credentials tell "who you are" as much as family background does.

Credentialism, then, is *evaluating a person on the basis of educational degrees.* Structural-functional analysis suggests that credentialism is simply the way our technologically complex society goes about filling jobs with well-trained people. By contrast, social-conflict analysis holds that credentials often bear little relation to the skills and responsibilities of a specific job. Collins argues that degrees serve as a shorthand way to sort out the people with the manners, attitudes, and even skin colour desired by many employers. Credentials, in short, work as a gatekeeping strategy, much like family background, that restricts important occupations to a small segment of the population.

PRIVILEGE AND PERSONAL MERIT

If, as social-conflict analysis suggests, attending university is a rite of passage for affluent men and women, then *schooling transforms social privilege into personal merit.* But given the North American cultural emphasis on individual achievement, we tend to see credentials as "badges of ability," as Richard Sennett

and Jonathan Cobb (1973) put it, rather than as symbols of family affluence. When we congratulate the typical new graduate, we often overlook the social resources that made this achievement possible. In the same way, we are quick to condemn the high-school dropout as personally deficient, with little thought for the social circumstances that surround that person's life.

Critical evaluation. Social-conflict analysis links formal education and social inequality, and shows how schooling transforms privilege into personal worthiness, and social disadvantage into personal deficiency. However, critics claim that social-conflict analysis minimizes the extent to which schooling provides upward social mobility for talented men and women—especially those from modest backgrounds.

Educators have long debated the proper manner in which to educate children with disabilities. On the one hand, such children may benefit from distinctive facilities and specially trained teachers. On the other hand, they are less likely to be stigmatized as "different" if included in regular classroom settings. What do you consider to be the ramifications of the "special education" versus "inclusive education" debate for the classroom experience of all children, not only those who have disabilities?

Further, despite the claims of many conflict theorists that schooling supports the status quo, "politically correct" educational curricula are challenging patterns of social inequality on many fronts.

PROBLEMS IN THE SCHOOLS

Although Canadians have long debated the quality of education, the debate has intensified over the past decade or two. Table 19–1 reveals that the percentage of people who are dissatisfied with the education their children are receiving has been increasing—from 41 percent in 1973 to 56 percent in 1992—and that the levels of dissatisfaction are greater in Ontario and British Columbia. Somewhat surprisingly, in light of current concerns with government deficits and taxes, a majority of Canadians (68 percent) favour increased government funding to all educational sectors (*Toronto Star*, September 7, 1992:A11). Many parents feel that formal education standards at all levels have declined in recent decades. Discipline appears to be lax and children go through school without learning "the basics." These concerns may explain part of the increase in private school attendance—from 2.4 to 4.8 percent of enrolments between 1971 and 1991 (Colombo, 1996:84).

SCHOOL DISCIPLINE

Canadians and Americans alike believe that schools should inculcate personal discipline and that the job is not being done properly. The U.S. government estimates that several hundred thousand students and at least one thousand teachers are physically assaulted on school grounds every year. This violence at school is blamed on poverty-stricken urban environments that breed drug use as well as violence on the street and at home. All too often in the U.S., violence in the community and at school involves the use of guns. The National Education Association estimates that 100 000 American students carry a gun to school (Hull, 1993:30).

Canada's school discipline problems are not of the same type or magnitude, but there have been many instances of assault on students and teachers; students have been found at school with knives—most often in specific violence-prone schools—but very rarely with guns. At the post-secondary level, the 1989 killing of fourteen female engineering students—by Marc Lepine at Montreal's l'Ecole Polytechnique—shocked Canadians across the country, driving home the realization that, even within our schools, we are not immune to deadly violence.

More commonly, however, the discipline problems in our schools involve students who display disdain for learning, are rude to their teachers or challenge their authority, skip classes, disrupt the classroom, or otherwise interfere with the formal education of themselves and others. "When I was young," parents will say, "we did what the teacher told us." Selective memory notwithstanding, there undoubtedly has been a gradual decline in classroom discipline over the past few decades related to larger societal trends. In teachers' college, discussion of educational theory and the finer points of pedagogy do nothing to prepare would-be teachers for their first field placements, where the most pressing question is one of how to "maintain *control* in the classroom."[3] Teachers,

---

[3] From a lecture by Ian Gomme of Memorial University.

TABLE 19–1 Parents' Dissatisfaction with Children's Education (percentage), 1973, 1978, 1992

Are you satisfied or dissatisfied with the education children are getting today?

Canada			
	Satisfied	Dissatisfied	Don't know
1992	35	56	9
1978	34	53	13
1973	51	41	8
Regional breakdown (1992)			
Atlantic	41	54	6
Quebec	37	55	8
Ontario	30	61	10
Prairies	49	45	6
B.C.	25	63	12

Note: Percentages may not add exactly to 100, due to rounding.

SOURCE: "Taking the Pulse—From Gallup Canada," *Toronto Star*, September 7, 1992, A11.

TABLE 19–2 Dropout Rate in Canada (Percentages)

	1970–71	1990–1991	1991
Canada	48	32	18
British Columbia	46	34	16
Alberta	40	35	14
Saskatchewan	32	24	16
Manitoba	45	27	19
Ontario	38	34	17
Quebec	54	28	22
New Brunswick	38	15	20
Nova Scotia	n/a	25	22
Prince Edward Island	43	24	25
Newfoundland	62	25	24

SOURCE: Fennell (1993:49), Gilbert et al. (1993).

who are trained to teach but find that their energies are diverted into policing students, experience frustration and disillusionment on the job.

DROPPING OUT

If many students are disruptive in class, others are not there at all. The problem of dropping out—quitting school before completing a high school diploma—leaves young people (many of whom are disadvantaged to begin with) ill-equipped for the world of work, and at high risk for poverty.

Numerous Canadian officials, business representatives, and educators have been very concerned about Canada's dropout rate, which seemed to be exceptionally high when compared to those of other countries. In 1970 and 1990, the U.S. rates were 12.2 and 10.7 percent, respectively, indicating a slight decline. Measured differently,[4] the Canadian rates were 48 and 32 percent in 1970–71 and 1990–91, respectively. A recently refined measure suggests that a more realistic dropout rate for Canada in 1991 was 18 percent, with considerable regional variation (see Table 19–2). Many who appear to be dropouts are really only stopouts, who leave and return at a later date to complete

their secondary school programs (Fennell, 1993:49). Detailed follow-up of such individuals by several school boards suggests that even the new numbers (in Table 19–2, column 3) are too high. Those numbers—based on Statistics Canada's *School Leavers Survey* (Gilbert et al., 1993)—are more reassuring than the earlier figures, but even at 18 percent or slightly less there is cause for concern.

In the report *Leaving School*, which compares school leavers and high school graduates, Gilbert et al. (1993) note that leavers are more likely

1. to be from single-parent or no-parent households
2. to have parents with lower educational attainment
3. to be married and to have dependent children (especially the women)
4. to have lower grade averages
5. to have failed a grade in elementary school
6. to have worked more than twenty hours per week during their final school year
7. to use alcohol (regularly) and drugs.

Aboriginal people have a very high dropout rate (40 percent), while immigrants have a low level (1 percent). In addition, it is noted that school leavers are currently more likely to be unemployed (34 percent) than are graduates (23 percent).

For young people who drop out of school in a credential-based society, the risks of unemployment or becoming stuck in a low-paying job are easy to imagine. Faced with this reality, many of those who leave school return to the classroom at a later time.

VALUE FOR OUR MONEY

Canada spends more than 7 percent of its gross national product on education. In terms of per-capita

---

[4] The American rates are based on the proportion of the population between fourteen and twenty-four that left school without a high school diploma (U.S. Bureau of the Census, 1991). The Statistics Canada figures reflect the number of students who did not enter and graduate from the same high school within four years (Fennell, 1993:49). Therefore, those who changed schools or who left and came back were counted as dropouts.

Welcome to Cyber-School

The wired planet has no boundaries and no monopolies of knowledge. The affairs of the world are now dependent upon the highest information of which man is capable . . . The boundaries between the world of affairs and the community of learning have ceased to exist. The workaday world now demands encyclopedic wisdom . . . Under these conditions, the old forms of specialized job has lost meaning. It was meaningful at very low speeds, but it has now been assumed into patterns of electric speeds. This change of pace from production-line to on-line computer programming has been ignored, just as the shift from hardware to software accelerates, making the old categories meaningless (McLuhan and Nevitt, quoted in Benedetti and DeHart, 1996:172).

Education is responding to the arrival of computer-literate children and the demands of a drastically altered, knowledge-based economy by integrating computers and the Internet throughout the education system—from kindergarten to Ph.D. The goal at primary and secondary levels is to have computers in every classroom; universities and colleges are placing more emphasis on computer-based, interactive, self-directed learning in the context of global, electronic information flow. Much of the computer access is arranged for the classroom or on-campus labs, but students are also linking up to school or campus,

by modem, from home. (On some campuses in Canada, it is compulsory for each student to have a computer and modem at home; on many, students are given e-mail addresses with their registration packages.) Expanded and more technologically sophisticated distance learning options and even virtual universities are being developed.

This new approach to learning begins in the early years. At the John D. Bracco School in northeast Edmonton, a third of the student body "skips classes." The students in question are studying from home via the school's home page. "We've pushed the walls of the school into the community," says principal Ron Bradley, who heads up the online program called LearnNet. The school walls now embrace students from all over Alberta and as far away as Sri Lanka and Holland. The program started in grades 7 to 9 at John D. Bracco (later in grades 10 to 12) and extended down to grade 2 at Kirkness School. The reasons for choosing LearnNet are varied, including the choice of home-schooling, a family move to a remote area, or attention deficit disorder. Internet-based learning has expanded the reach of John D. Bracco teachers into a geographically unbounded community (Gooderham, 1977).

Examples of computer-based learning and research abound. In Hamilton, Ontario, students of Scott Park High School have created YouthNet, an Internet-based student project, and YouthNet Mail, a homework hotline and a voting system for students to

rank their favourite movies, CDs, and computer games. A retired teacher in Summerland, B.C., created an Internet-based project called Global THINK: participants include about 1000 B.C. students along with others from as far away as Ontario and Alaska (Foss, 1997). SchoolNet is available in Ontario. The list is almost endless.

At the university level we see computer conferencing, online courses, multimedia distance education, and more complex virtual universities. Undergraduate and graduate students are relying increasingly on the Internet as a means of communication and a source of information. Statistics Canada data and "publications" increasingly are available only on the Internet or on CD-ROM; its *Daily*, among many other products, no longer appears in paper at all. Results of the 1997 federal election are available online, but have not yet appeared in the traditional print format. Academic journals in the sciences and social sciences are becoming available online. Most recently, purely electronic journals (several in the sociology area) have appeared. The researcher conducts computer analysis, writes a paper through word processing, submits the paper electronically, has it sent to reviewers via the Internet, and then sees it published in electronic form. Throughout this process, pen may never be set to paper. Access to information, as well as the production and dissemination of knowledge, has changed profoundly and irrevocably.

spending, this ranks us at the top of the G7 (Group of Seven) leading industrialized countries—and raises questions about the quality of the education we deliver for that money. Demographer David K. Foot, in a book fittingly entitled *Boom, Bust and Echo* (1996), looks at the effects of the baby boom, the subsequent

bust, and the smaller "echo boom" (the children of the boomers) on the economy, consumer habits, real estate, and the demand for social services, including education. Since schooling is compulsory to the age of sixteen in most Canadian provinces, we can predict enrolments at the primary and early secondary levels with considerable accuracy,[5] simply by keeping tabs on the numbers of babies born each year and watching them age. The baby boom, for example, caused peaks in elementary school enrolment in the late 1950s, and high school enrolment in the early 1970s. The inflated cost of our educational system, Foot concludes, is the result of the failure to analyze demographic trends (see Chapter 21, "Population and Urbanization") to predict demand at various levels and to adjust budgets, personnel, and policy accordingly.

Unfortunately, the inflated budgets left in the wake of the baby-boom cohort helped to raise our per-capita spending above that of the other G7 countries without improving the skills of students. As noted (and refuted) below, Canadian students do not fare well in international tests of scholastic achievement.

ACADEMIC STANDARDS

Canada and the U.S. share a growing concern with the quality of schooling or, more pointedly, with the quality of publicly funded schooling. *A Nation at Risk*, a comprehensive report on the quality of U.S. schools prepared in 1983 by the National Commission on Excellence in Education, noted that "nearly 40 percent of seventeen-year-olds cannot draw inferences from written material; only one-fifth can write a persuasive essay; and only one-third can solve mathematical problems requiring several steps" (1983:9). Furthermore, scores on the Scholastic Aptitude Test (SAT) have declined steadily since the early 1960s. Some of the decline may stem from the increasing share of students taking the standardized test, not all of whom are well prepared (Owen, 1985). But few observers of the North American scene doubt that schooling has suffered a setback.

A Nation at Risk noted with alarm the extent of **functional illiteracy**, *reading and writing skills insufficient for everyday living*. Roughly one in eight children in the United States completes secondary school without learning to read or write very well: for young African-Americans, the proportion is more than one in three. As indicated in the "Social Diversity" box, this concern has its parallel in Canada.

Canadians express concerns about the quality of our educational experience, in part because of observations about the skills (or lack thereof) of graduates, but also because of the lack of fit between these skills and the demands of the labour market (as indicated by unemployment levels). Concerns were heightened in 1992 when Canadian students appeared to do poorly in international mathematics tests involving a number of countries (including Japan). The media, special reports, and the business community were quick to criticize our public school system, thereby capitalizing on public disaffection and manipulating public opinion against schools (Barlow and Robertson, 1994). The provincial governments, being responsible for education, were quick to join in the criticism of schools and the search for solutions.

Using test scores in the international study of performance in mathematics—which, according to Barlow and Robertson, were misleading because they compared the performance of elite groups of students in some countries with a more broadly based Canadian cohort—arguments were made for a radical restructuring of education in Canada. Among the suggested solutions to our problems were many that were consistent with the political right and corporate interests: national testing and standards (to measure the quality of the "product"—that is, students); downsizing for greater efficiency (fewer school boards and teachers); vouchers (to allow students and families to shop for their choice of schools); privatization (schools run by the private sector); partnerships between corporations and schools or universities; corporate sponsorship of various programs (often involving overt advertising within the schools themselves); and harmonization with educational practices in the United States.

EDUCATION AND THE WORLD OF WORK

Recently, the province of New Brunswick took a novel approach to education in its utilitarian role of preparing people to participate in a changing and, hopefully, expanding labour market. While former premier Frank McKenna was actively recruiting businesses to establish in or relocate to New Brunswick, some of his province's schools were making a special, complementary offer. Their graduates would enter the workforce with "guaranteed" skills; if an employer found them wanting, they could be returned for upgrading at the schools' expense. Strategic spending in education has helped to decrease the overall dropout rate in New Brunswick as well. An appropriately educated, bilingual workforce is one of the factors allowing Moncton, New Brunswick, to entice a wide range of companies to relocate there. Moncton is attracting international attention, and has been chosen as one of the top five "Best Cities for Business" by the *Globe and Mail's Report on Business Magazine* (August 1993:55). Advanced telecommunications

---

[5] The internal migration of young families between districts and immigration, which expands the numbers of children in specific cities or regions, needs to be taken into account to make predictions in some parts of the country.

Functional Illiteracy: Must We Rethink Education?

Imagine being unable to read the labels on cans of food, the instructions for assembling a child's toy, the dosage on a medicine bottle, or even the information on your own paycheque. These are some of the debilitating experiences of *functional illiteracy*, reading and writing skills inadequate for carrying out everyday responsibilities.

As schooling became universal, the Canadian government confidently concluded that illiteracy had been all but eliminated. The truth of the matter, according to the National Literacy Secretariat, is that only 63 percent of Canadians have sufficient literacy and numeracy skills to deal adequately with everyday tasks; an additional 22 percent have some problems; and about 15 percent have difficulty recognizing familiar words or doing simple addition and subtraction (Montigny 1994:322). By 1994, another literacy survey revealed that the percentages in the two lower categories had increased to 25 and 22 percent, respectively (www.gc.ca). Canadians are not alone in this respect, though, for it is estimated that about one in four adults in the United States is functionally illiterate, and that the proportions are higher among the elderly and minorities.

Functional illiteracy is a complex social problem. It is caused partly by an educational system that passes children from one grade to the next whether they learn or not. Another cause is community indifference to local schools that prevents parents and teachers from working together to improve chil-

dren's learning. Still another cause is that millions of children grow up with illiterate parents who offer little encouragement to learn language skills.

Functional illiteracy costs the North American economy more than $100 billion a year. This cost includes decreased productivity (by workers who perform their jobs improperly) and increased accidents (by people unable to understand written instructions). It also reflects the costs of supporting those unable to read and write well enough to find work who then end up receiving public assistance or in prison.

Correcting this national problem requires one approach for young people and another for adults. To stop functional illiteracy before it happens, the

public must demand that children not be graduated from school until they have learned basic language skills. For adults, the answer begins with diagnosis—a difficult task since many feel shame at their plight and avoid disclosing their need for help. Once such people are identified, however, adult education programs must be provided and used. Canada has an elaborate set of literacy programs, but they are not reaching their target groups.

It should be noted that in some cases, illiteracy is not an inability to read at all, but an inability to read in English or French. In all the countries participating in the International Adult Literacy Survey, immigrants are disproportionately represented in the lower literacy levels as measured in the languages of the host countries (www.nald.ca). Canada has an active program teaching English as a second language (ESL) to the constantly replenished body of immigrant schoolchildren and adults.

Our society is one of the most affluent on earth, yet many other countries have more literate populations than we do, as Figure 19–5 illustrates. For those living in a world of incomprehensible symbols, functional illiteracy is a personal disaster; for all of us, it is an urgent national problem.

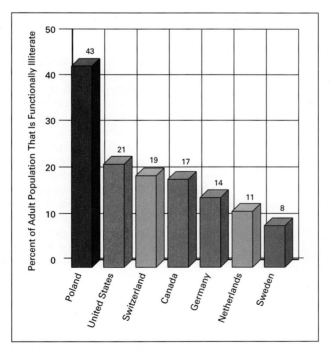

FIGURE 19–5 Functional Illiteracy in Global Perspective

SOURCE: Fiske (1997).

SOURCE: Based on Kozol (1980, 1985); Colombo (1992:76); Montigny (1994); www.nald.ca.

Currently, our society is debating many strategies for improving education. Some parents have kept their children out of formal education altogether, believing their youngsters can learn more at home, using information available not only in books, but also in cyberspace.

technology is one of the factors allowing many companies to move to an area without a large population base.

A large study, *Making the Match*, involving twenty companies and five universities (Evers, Rush, Krmpotic, and Duncan-Robinson, 1993) was designed to assess the skill development experiences of Canadian university students and graduates as well as the fit between these skills and the needs of corporations. The skills most in demand (and shortest in supply) were not technical skills (such as using a computer) but a skill composite: the ability to integrate and use information, adapt to change, take reasonable risks, and conceptualize the future. Leadership and conflict management are also scarce skills. The educational system must develop technical skills in its students as well as use innovative approaches to foster the skills needed by industry. Interestingly, there is a link between these skills and the educational "aims and objectives" espoused by many of our universities.

EDUCATION FOR TOMORROW

As a society, Canada is undergoing a series of changes with implications for our educational system.

First, we are dealing with increasing diversity as a result of steady immigration, cultural pluralism (partly in response to our policy of multiculturalism), and ethnic nationalism (most visibly among the Québécois and native peoples), as well as continuing regional and class divisions. In this context, the educational system is required (1) to promote equality of access, participation, and outcome, and (2) to play an integrative

role, in part by fostering a Canadian identity that overrides our differences.

Second, Canada is experiencing technological change involving the expanded use of computers and robots, which in turn has an impact on organizational patterns (for example, the possibility of working at home while "hooked up" to the office). The promise of this new technology goes beyond helping students to learn basic skills; computers actually may improve the overall quality of learning. Interacting with computers prompts students to be more active and allows them to progress at their own pace. For students with disabilities who cannot write using a pencil, computers permit easier self-expression. Using computers in schools—in some cases as early as kindergarten—also appears to increase significantly learning speed and retention of information (Fantini, 1986).

The numerous benefits of computers should not blind us to their limitations, however. Computers will never bring to the educational process the personal insight or imagination of a motivated human teacher. While the jury may be out on whether computers have improved teaching (Skinner, 1997), there is no doubt they have proliferated in the classroom. Computers have become central to the experience of students in many classes, from kindergarten to university. In some Canadian universities, all students are required to have computers and modems and, in some programs, they are required to bring lap-top computers to class. This type of requirement presents the danger of a new source of inequity in access to knowledge.

As our society enters the twenty-first century, we should not look to technology to solve many of the

CONTROVERSY & DEBATE

Is Political Correctness Undermining Education?

Are you "PC"? Is your teacher? What about this textbook? The last decade has seen a heightened level of political debate on the university campus. Around 1990, the term *political correctness* entered our language to refer to thinking and acting in accordance with liberal political principles. To be "politically correct," at least as opponents see it, implies that "truth" is less a matter of scientific evidence than having the "correct" politics. Surveying today's campus scene, James Davison Hunter (1991:211) concludes, "The cultural ethos of the modern university clearly favours a progressivist agenda," including support for feminism, gay rights, and various other movements towards social equality.

To some people, political correctness threatens the traditional open-mindedness of the university, at its worst transforming professors into political activists and teaching into indoctrination. Moreover, political correctness may have a chilling effect in the classroom, making students wary of expressing opinions about controversial issues (say, homosexuality or racial differences in measured intelligence) for fear of offending others who might, in turn, charge them with "homophobia" or "racism."

Professors, too, feel the pressure to be politically correct: Douglas Massey (1995) points out that a number of well-known researchers have been ostracized by their peers for publishing the results of research that is scientifically solid but that advances "unpopular notions" about race and gender.

But not everyone thinks "PC" is a problem. Many students and faculty defend a politically engaged campus on moral grounds. As they see it, there is much injustice in the world that cries out for redress. Richard Rorty (1994), for example, applauds the fact that some academic departments have become "sanctuaries for left-wing political views," because activist colleagues are "doing a great deal of good for people who have gotten a raw deal," namely, women, Blacks, gay men, and lesbians. By focusing on marginalized people, he continues, the politically engaged campus will help to make society "much more decent, more tolerant, and more civilized."

Keep in mind, too, that "political correctness" can be easily exaggerated. While it is probably fair to characterize academia (and sociologists, overall) as politically liberal, virtually every campus includes faculty, administrators, and students who continue to espouse a wide range of political opinions. Furthermore, charges of political correctness in academia are nothing new. Just sixty years ago, for example, a majority of U.S. states sought to keep teachers in check by requiring that they sign loyalty oaths before permitting them to speak in the classroom (Hunter, 1991). Perhaps it is true that "the more things change. . ."

Continue the debate . . .

1. *Overall, do you think that academia has a political bias? What is the bias?*
2. *Should teachers (or textbooks) take explicit political stands on controversial issues?*
3. *Have you or other students remained silent during class discussions for fear of sounding "politically incorrect"? Has a course ever led you to change attitudes you came to see as narrow-minded?*

---

problems that plague our schools. What we need is a broad plan for social change that refires this country's early ambition to provide quality universal schooling—a goal that has eluded us so far.

And third, we are facing a shrinking world of shifting political alliances, economic restructuring, multinational corporations, and global competition—in the context of which we strive to maintain our quality of life. Insofar as education is responsible for the development of skills relevant to the labour market, our schools must develop in students both technical skills and an ability to be innovative, flexible, and analytical.

Education is intricately involved with change as a catalyst, an adaptive mechanism, and a force for maintaining tradition and continuity. It is simultaneously an explosive irritant and one of the ingredients in the glue that binds us together.

SUMMARY

1. Education is a major social institution for transmitting knowledge and skills, as well as teaching cultural norms and values, to young people. In pre-industrial societies, education occurs informally within the family; industrial societies develop formal systems of schooling.

2. Structural-functional analysis highlights major functions of schooling, including socialization, cultural innovation, social integration, and placing people in the social hierarchy. Latent functions of schooling involve providing child care and building social networks.

3. Social-conflict analysis links schooling to hierarchy involving class, race, and gender. This approach also explains that schooling acts as a means of social control, instilling the value of discipline that produces compliant adult workers.

4. Standardized achievement tests are controversial: some see them as a reasonable measure of academic aptitude and learning, while others say they are culturally biased tools used to label less-privileged students as personally deficient.

5. Streaming, too, is controversial: some see streaming as the way schools provide instruction to students with different interests and aptitudes; others say streaming gives privileged youngsters a richer education.

6. Canada is a "credential society." By requiring degrees for higher-paying occupations, employers ensure that workers have learned norms and attitudes appropriate to the business setting.

7. Many people are critical of public schools. Lack of discipline and questionable standards are seen as problems. In addition, young women and men drop out of high school, thereby placing themselves at high risk of unemployment and poverty.

8. Declining academic standards are reflected in lower average scores on academic achievement tests and functional illiteracy among a significant proportion of high-school graduates.

9. The Information Revolution is changing schooling through the increasing use of computers. Although computers permit interactive, self-paced learning, they are not suitable for teaching every subject.

CRITICAL THINKING QUESTIONS

1. Why does industrialization lead societies to expand their system of schooling?

2. Referring to various countries, including Canada, describe ways in which schooling is shaped by economic, political, or cultural factors.

3. From a structural-functional perspective, why is schooling important to the operation of society? From a social-conflict point of view, how does formal education operate to reproduce social inequality in each generation?

SOCIOLOGY APPLIED

1. Arrange to visit a secondary school near your campus or home. Does it have a "streaming" policy? If so, find out how it works. How much importance does a student's social background have in making a stream assignment?

2. Most people agree that teaching our children is a vital task, yet most teachers earn relatively low salaries. What can you find out at the library about the average salaries of teachers compared to other workers? Can you explain this pattern?

3. To explore how new information technology is reshaping education, visit the Web site for the first "cyber-college" in the U.S. at http://www.westgov.org/smart/vu/vu.html. What do you see as the advantages and disadvantages of this type of schooling?

4. Policies and available funding for providing education to children with physical disabilities vary between provinces. Do some library research, or contact teachers or other officials, to determine the situation in your province.

http://www.statcan.ca:80/english/IPS/Data/ 89-552-MIE.htm
Primarily funded by Human Resources Development Canada, International Adult Literacy Survey creates comparable literacy profiles across national, linguistic, and cultural boundaries. The survey now encompass close to thirty countries around the world. Monographs focus on current policy issues and cover topics such as adult training, literacy skill match and mismatch in the workplace, seniors' literacy skills and health, and literacy and economic security.

http://www.cmec.ca/
Established in 1967, Council of Ministers of Education, Canada is the national voice for education in Canada. The site includes press releases and reports about education in Canada, as well as international issues.

http://www.oise.on.ca/~mpress/eduweb.html
Maintained by Marian Press, a reference librarian at Ontario Institute for Studies in Education, this site offers a comprehensive list of Canadian education-related resources on the Web.

http://www.acea.ca/
Canadian Education Association is a national, bilingual, not-for-profit organization committed to promoting the improvement of education. The association produces a variety of regular and special publications, and serves as a common meeting place for all sectors of education through its activities, special projects, and various committees.

http://www.umanitoba.ca/publications/cjeap/
Canadian Journal of Educational Administration and Policy is a peer-reviewed electronic journal that promotes debate on problems of educational practice and policy. Full-text articles are published online.

Li T'ang, *Itinerant Physician in Village, China,* c. 1100

CHAPTER 20

HEALTH AND MEDICINE

Nineteen-year-old Corey Smith squirms restlessly on a chair in the waiting room of the medical clinic at her west coast university. She is annoyed and uneasy; her roommate pressured her to see the doctor, and she is afraid her parents will find out. Her parents, both lawyers, expect her home for the weekend, but she is trying to think up an excuse for not going.

This young woman's problem is failing health due to starvation. Far from feeling that she is starving, however, she thinks of herself as fat. She knows that she weighs only eighty-seven pounds, and she expects the doctor to warn her that she weighs far too little for a woman five feet, three inches tall. But for over three years Corey has been preoccupied—her roommate would say obsessed—with being thin.

Corey Smith's problem is anorexia nervosa, a disorder that doctors describe as "severe caloric restriction," and university students know as intense, often compulsive dieting. Like most diseases, anorexia nervosa has social as well as biological causes: about 95 percent of the people with the disease are females, most of them white and from affluent families. Many women who contend with eating disorders feel pressured by their parents, the media, their peer group, advertisements, and other cultural and social structures to be both high achievers and have model-perfect bodies. Research suggests that up to half of university and college-aged women actively try to lose weight, although most of them are not, medically speaking, obese. About one in seven diet so much that doctors would say they have an eating disorder.

To appreciate the social foundation of eating disorders,[1] consider a comment once made by the Duchess of Windsor: "A woman cannot be too rich or too thin." Women fall victim to eating disorders because our culture places such emphasis on women's physical appearance, with slenderness the ideal of femininity (Parrott, 1987). Some researchers assert that our society socializes young women to believe that they are never "too thin to feel fat." Such an attitude pushes women towards a form of "mass starvation" or "hunger strike" (Orbach, 1986) that some critics claim "compares with foot-binding, lip-stretching, and other forms of woman mutilation" found in other cultures (Wooley, Wooley, and Dyrenforth, 1979; Levine, 1987; Robinson, 1987).

Health is obviously the concern of physicians and other medical professionals. But sociologists, too, study health because, as the case of Corey Smith illustrates and this chapter explains, social forces shape the well-being of everyone.

---

[1] This profile of victims of anorexia nervosa is based on Levine (1987). Another eating disorder, *bulimia*, involves binge eating coupled with induced vomiting to inhibit weight gain. The two diseases, which may be two expressions of the same intense concentration on dieting and weight control, have similar victim profiles (cf. Striegel-Moore, Silberstein, and Rodin, 1986).

Medieval medical practice was heavily influenced by astrology, so that physicians and lay people alike attributed disease to astral influence; this is the root of our word "influenza." In this woodcut by Swiss artist Jost Amman (1580), as midwives attend a childbirth, astrologers cast a horoscope for the newborn.

WHAT IS HEALTH?

The World Health Organization (1946:3) defines **health** as *a state of complete physical, mental, and social well-being.* This definition underscores the major theme of this chapter: *health is as much a social as a biological issue.*

HEALTH AND SOCIETY

Society shapes the health of people in five major ways.

1. **People judge their health as compared to others.** René Dubos (1980; orig. 1965) points out that early in the twentieth century yaws, a contagious skin disease, was so common in sub-Saharan Africa that people there considered it normal. In truth, then, health is sometimes a matter of having the same diseases as one's neighbours (Quentin Crisp, cited in Kirk and Madsen, 1989).

2. **People define as "healthy" what they hold to be morally good.** Members of our society (especially men) consider a competitive way of life to be "healthy" because it fits our cultural mores. This is so even though stress contributes to heart disease and many other illnesses. On the other hand, some people who object to homosexuality on moral grounds label this sexual orientation "sick" even though it is quite natural from a biological standpoint. In short, ideas about good health constitute a type of social control that encourages conformity to cultural norms.

3. **Cultural standards of health change over time.** Early in this century, some physicians condemned women for enrolling in college, claiming that higher education placed an unhealthy strain on the female brain. Others denounced masturbation as a threat to health. Today, on both counts, we know differently. Conversely, few physicians fifty years ago recognized the dangers of cigarette smoking, a practice that is now widely regarded as a health threat.

4. **Health relates to a society's technology.** In poor societies, infectious diseases are rampant because of malnutrition and poor sanitation. As industrialization raises living standards, people become more healthy. But industrial technology also creates new threats to health: for example, high-income countries threaten health by overtaxing the world's resources and creating pollution.

5. **Health relates to social inequality.** Every society on earth unequally distributes the resources that promote personal well-being. The physical, mental, and social health of wealthier women and men in Canada is far better than that of poor people, as we shall explain presently. This pattern starts at birth, with infant mortality highest among the poor. Affluent people also live years longer than poor people do.

HEALTH: A GLOBAL SURVEY

Because health is closely linked to social life, we find pronounced change in human well-being over the long course of history. Similarly, we see striking differences in health around the world today.

HEALTH IN HISTORY

With only simple technology, our ancestors could do little to improve health. Among hunters and gatherers, food shortages sometimes forced mothers to abandon children. Children fortunate enough to survive infancy were still vulnerable to a host of injuries and illnesses for which there were few effective treatments, and half died before age twenty. Few lived to forty (Lenski, Nolan, and Lenski, 1995).

One billion people on the planet suffer from various illnesses due to poverty. For most of these people, medical care is limited or nonexistent. In Tanzania, this physician flies a light plane to reach patients in remote areas, and depends on a computer and satellite links to get the latest information from medical centres around the world.

The agricultural revolution expanded the supply of food and other resources. Yet due to increasing social inequality, elites enjoyed better health while peasants and slaves faced hunger and endured crowded, unsanitary shelters. Especially in the growing cities of medieval Europe, human waste and other refuse fuelled infectious diseases, including plagues that periodically wiped out entire towns (Mumford, 1961).

HEALTH IN LOW-INCOME COUNTRIES

November 1, 1988, central India. Poverty is not just a matter of what you have; it shapes what you are. Probably most of the people we see in the villages here have never had the benefit of a doctor or a dentist. The result is easy to see: people look old before their time.

Abject poverty in much of the world cuts life expectancy far below the seventy or more years typical of rich societies. Global Map 14–2 (p. 356) shows that average life expectancy among Africans barely reaches fifty, and in the world's poorest nations, such as Ethiopia and Somalia, the figure falls to forty.

The World Health Organization reports that one billion people around the world—one in six—suffer from serious illness due to poverty. Poor sanitation and malnutrition kill people of all ages, especially children. Health is compromised not just by having too little to eat, but also by consuming only one kind of food, as the "Global Sociology" box explains.

In impoverished countries, sanitary drinking water may be as scarce as the chance for a balanced diet. Contaminated water breeds many of the infectious diseases that imperil both adults and children. The leading causes of death in Canada a century ago, including influenza, pneumonia, and tuberculosis, are still widespread killers in poor societies today and, until recently, among aboriginal peoples in Canada.

To make matters worse, medical personnel are few and far between, so that the world's poorest people—many of whom live in central Africa—never consult a physician. Global Map 20–1 illustrates the availability of doctors throughout the world.

Against this backdrop of poverty and minimal medical care, it is no wonder that 10 percent of children in poor societies die within a year of their birth. In some countries, half the children never reach adulthood—a pattern that parallels the death rates seen in Europe more than two centuries ago (George, 1977; Harrison, 1984).

Illness and poverty form a vicious cycle in much of the world: poverty breeds disease, which, in turn, undermines the ability to earn income. Moreover, when medical technology curbs infectious disease, the populations of poor nations soar. Without resources to ensure the well-being of the people they have now, poor societies can ill afford a larger population. Ultimately, programs to lower death rates in poor countries will succeed only if they can reduce birth rates as well.

HEALTH IN HIGH-INCOME COUNTRIES

Industrialization dramatically changed patterns of human health in Europe, although, at first, not for the better. By 1800, as the Industrial Revolution took hold, factories offered jobs that drew people from all over the countryside. Cities quickly became over-

Killer Poverty: A Report from Africa

Television images of famine in Africa bring home to people in affluent countries such as Canada the horror of starving children. Some of the children we see appear bloated, while others seem to have shrivelled to little more than skin drawn tightly over bones. Both of these deadly conditions, explains Susan George (1977), are direct consequences of poverty.

Children with bloated bodies are suffering from protein deficiency. In west Africa this condition is known as *kwashiorkor*, literally "one-two." The term derives from the common practice among mothers of abruptly weaning a first child on the birth of a second. Deprived of mother's milk, a baby may receive no protein at all.

Children with shrivelled bodies lack both protein and calories. This defi-

ciency is the result of eating little food of any kind.

Strictly speaking, starvation is rarely what kills children. Their weakened condition makes them vulnerable to

stomach ailments such as gastroenteritis or diseases such as measles. The death rate from measles, for example, is a thousand times greater in parts of Africa than in North America.

Eating just a single food also undermines nutrition, causing a deficiency of protein, vitamins, and minerals. Millions of people in low-income countries suffer from goitre, a debilitating, diet-related disease of the thyroid gland. Pellagra, common among people who consume mostly corn, is a serious disease that can lead to insanity. Similarly, people who eat only processed rice are prone to beriberi.

Health is obviously a social issue since diseases virtually unknown to people in rich societies are a common experience of life—and death—in poor nations around the world.

---

crowded, creating serious sanitation problems. Moreover, factories fouled the air with smoke—a health threat unrecognized until well into the twentieth century. Accidents in the workplace were common.

But industrialization gradually improved health in Western Europe and North America as rising living standards translated into better nutrition and safer housing for the majority of people. After 1850, medical advances also improved health, primarily by controlling infectious diseases. To illustrate, in 1854 John Snow noted the street addresses of London's cholera victims and traced the source of this disease to contaminated drinking water (Rockett, 1994). Soon after, scientists linked cholera to specific bacteria and developed a protective vaccine against the deadly disease. Armed with this knowledge, early environmentalists campaigned against age-old practices such as discharging raw sewage into rivers used for drinking water. As the twentieth century dawned, death rates from infectious diseases had fallen sharply.

Over the long term, then, industrialization has dramatically improved human health. In 1890, influenza and pneumonia prompted one-fourth of all death in Canada, and one-fourth of the population died before reaching ten years of age (Roberge, Berth-

elot, and Wolfson, 1995:15). Today, these diseases cause fewer than 3 percent of deaths in Canada. Life expectancy has increased and infant mortality rates have decreased, both dramatically, over the last century: we now die of diseases of "affluence," mainly cancer and heart disease, and die in old age (*Canada's 125th Anniversary Yearbook*, 1992). Nothing alters the reality of death, but industrial societies manage to delay death until old age.

HEALTH IN CANADA

Living in an affluent, industrial society, people in Canada are healthy by world standards. Some categories of people, however, enjoy far better health and well-being than others.

SOCIAL EPIDEMIOLOGY: THE DISTRIBUTION OF HEALTH

Social epidemiology is *the study of how health and disease are distributed throughout a society's population*. Just as early social epidemiologists examined the origin and spread of epidemic diseases, researchers today

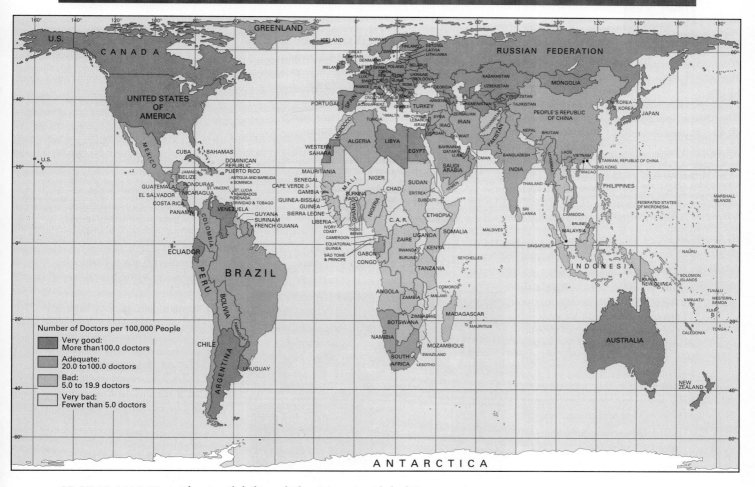

GLOBAL MAP 20–1 The Availability of Physicians in Global Perspective

Medical doctors, widely available to people in rich nations, are perilously scarce in poor societies. While traditional forms of healing do improve health, antibiotics and vaccines—vital for controlling infectious diseases—are often in short supply in poor societies. In these countries, therefore, death rates are high, especially among infants.

SOURCE: *Peters Atlas of the World* (1990).

find links between health and physical and social environments. Such analysis rests on comparing the health of different categories of people.

Age and Sex

Death is now rare among young people, with two notable exceptions: increases in mortality resulting from accidents and, more recently, from acquired immune deficiency syndrome (AIDS). Nonetheless,

sociocultural environments still affect the present and future health of youngsters: on February 8, 1998, the CBC's *National Magazine* reported that Canada's children, who are subject to poor diet, no exercise, and second-hand smoke, are the obese and the heart patients of tomorrow.

Across the life course, women live longer but spend more time without full health. Females have a slight biological advantage that renders them less likely than males to die before or immediately after

Masculinity: A Threat to Health?

What doctors call "coronary-prone behaviour," and psychologists call the "Type-A personality," sociologists describe as our cultural conception of masculinity. It is a combination of attitudes and behaviour—common among men in our society—that includes (1) chronic impatience ("C'mon! Go faster or get outta my way!"), (2) uncontrolled ambition ("I've gotta have it . . . I need that!"), and (3) free-floating hostility ("Why are so many people such *idiots*?").

This pattern, although quite normal from a cultural point of view, is one major reason why men who are driven to succeed are at high risk for heart disease. By acting out the "Type-A personality," we may get the job done, but we set in motion complex biochemical processes that are very hard on the human heart.

Here are a few questions to help you assess your own degree of risk (or that of someone important to you):

1. **Do you believe that a person has to be aggressive to succeed? Do you think** that "nice guys finish last"? For your heart's sake, try to remove hostility from your life. A starting point is eliminating profanity from your speech. Try to replace aggression with compassion, which can be surprisingly effective in dealing with other people. Medically speaking, compassion and humour—rather than irritation and aggravation—will enhance your life.

2. **How well do you handle uncertainty and opposition?** Do you have moments when you fume

"Why won't the waiter take my order?" or "Environmentalists are plain nuts"? We all like to know what's going on and we like others to agree with us, but the world often doesn't work this way. Accepting uncertainty and opposition makes us more mature and certainly healthier.

3. **Are you uneasy showing positive emotion?** Many men think giving and accepting love—from women, from children, and from other men—is a sign of weakness. But the medical truth is that love supports health while hate damages it.

As human beings, we have a great deal of choice about how to live. Think about the choices you make, and reflect on how our society's idea of masculinity often makes us hard on others (including those we love) and, just as important, hard on ourselves.

SOURCES: Based on Friedman and Rosenman (1974) and Levine (1990).

---

birth. Then, as socialization takes over, males become more aggressive and individualistic, resulting in higher rates of accidents, violence, and suicide. Our cultural conception of masculinity also pressures adult men to be more competitive, to repress their emotions, and to engage in hazardous behaviours such as smoking cigarettes and drinking alcohol to excess. As the "Sociology of Everyday Life" box explains, what doctors call "coronary-prone behaviour" is really a fairly accurate description of what our society defines as masculinity.

Social Class and Race

Infant mortality—the death rate among newborns—is almost twice as high among disadvantaged children as it is among children born to privilege. While the health of the richest children in our nation is the best in the world, our poorest children (especially aboriginal children) are as vulnerable to disease as those in many low-income countries, including Sudan and Lebanon.

Research by Wilkins and Adams (1983) shows that both life expectancy and life expectancy free of disability vary significantly by income level and by neighbourhood quality. Those at the highest income levels live longer than those at the lowest levels, and have more years free of disability. There is some debate about the causal direction in such findings (that is, whether people get sick because they are poor, or people are poor because they are sick). It appears that for the most part class is the independent variable

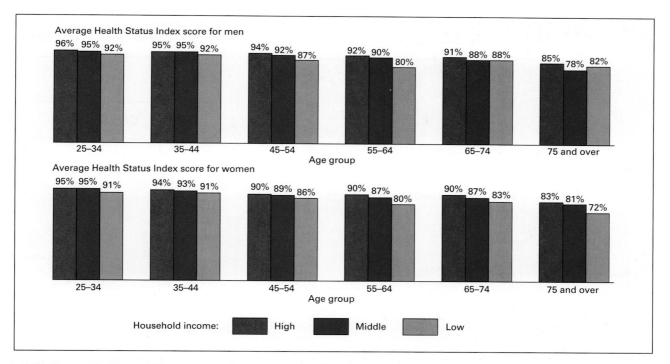

FIGURE 20–1 Adults with Low Household Incomes Have Lower Health Levels

SOURCE: Roberge, Berthelot, and Wolfson (1995:18), from Statistics Canada, Health Status Index (HSI) using the 1991 General Social Survey.

and health is the dependent variable. At times, however, sickness may lead to a decline in income over a long period of time. Also, members of low-income families miss more days of school or work each year due to illness than do higher-income people.

Figure 20–1 shows that for both men and women in almost every age group, health status declines as income declines. (Perfect health on the Health Status Index would result in a score of 100 percent, while any score measured at 80 percent or greater is considered a high level of health.)

Aboriginal Canadians continue to live shorter lives than their nonaboriginal counterparts. In 1990, the life expectancy for a native male was 66.9 years (compared to about 73 years for a non-native male), and for a native female was 74 years (compared to about 80 years for a non-native female) (*Canada's 125th Anniversary Yearbook*, 1992). Causes of death also tend to be different for aboriginal Canadians. Between 1982 and 1992, injury (violence and accidents) and poisoning were the major causes of death for aboriginals, although there were dramatic declines in these causes (43 percent since 1987). The second and third major causes of death parallel those for the nonaboriginal population: circulatory diseases and cancer (*Basic Departmental Data*, 1992).

In Canada, as elsewhere in the world, poverty condemns people to crowded, unsanitary environments that breed infectious diseases. Although tuberculosis is no longer a widespread threat to health in Canada, its rate is once again on the rise (Hurst, 1992). Their higher risk of poverty makes aboriginal people more likely than other Canadians to suffer from this disease.

Poor people also suffer from nutritional deficiencies. A large percentage of our population try to get by with a substandard diet and minimal medical care. The results are predictable: while wealthy women and men typically die in old age of chronic illnesses such as heart disease and cancer, poor people are likely to die younger from infectious diseases such as pneumonia.

There is some concern that AIDS may be spreading more quickly among aboriginal men and women, particularly women who live on reserves. According to the World Health Organization, by 1990, 960 aboriginal Canadians had AIDS and as many as 1500 carried the HIV infection (*Windspeaker*, 1991).

HEALTH AND SOCIETY: THREE EXAMPLES

Since we all make choices about how to live, we all have some control over our own health. But as the following sections indicate, dangerous behaviours such

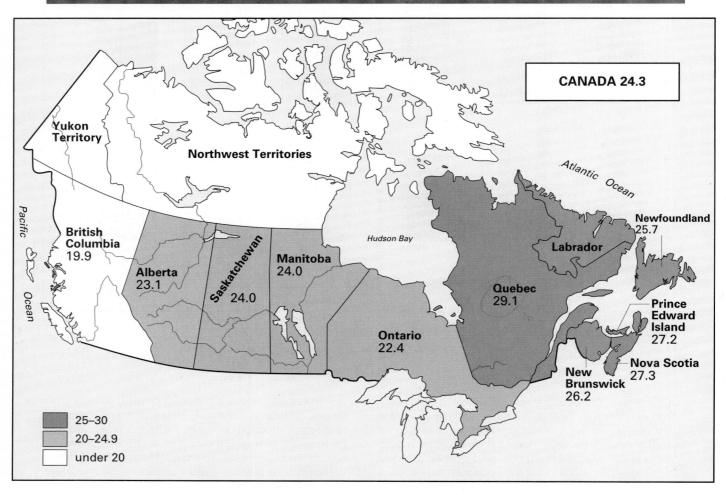

CANADA 24.3

Yukon Territory

Northwest Territories

Pacific Ocean

British Columbia
19.9

Alberta
23.1

Saskatchewan
24.0

Manitoba
24.0

Hudson Bay

Ontario
22.4

Atlantic Ocean

Labrador

Quebec
29.1

Newfoundland
25.7

Prince Edward Island
27.2

Nova Scotia
27.3

New Brunswick
26.2

25–30
20–24.9
under 20

CANADA MAP 20–1 Percentage of the Population 11 Years and Over Smoking Cigarettes Daily, 1994–95

SOURCE: Caragata, 1998:30.

as cigarette smoking and compulsive dieting are pronounced among certain categories of our population. Sexually transmitted diseases, too, reveal a distinctive social profile.

Cigarette Smoking

Cigarette smoking tops the list of preventable hazards to health. But we can see that smoking has a cultural dimension as well, because it was only after World War I that smoking became popular in Canada. Despite growing evidence of its dangers, smoking remained fashionable even a generation ago. Since

then, among adults—but not among young people—smoking has been falling out of favour and is now considered a mild form of social deviance.

As concern about the health effects of smoking has grown, consumption of cigarettes has fallen from its peak in 1960, when almost 45 percent of Canadian adults smoked. By 1994, only about 25 percent were smokers, as Canada Map 20–1 illustrates. Quitting is difficult because cigarette smoke contains nicotine, which is physically addictive. But people also smoke to cope with stress: divorced and separated people are especially likely to smoke, as are the unemployed and people in the armed forces.

Generally speaking, the less education people have, the greater their chances of smoking. Moreover, a larger share of men (35 percent) than women (31 percent) smoke. But cigarettes—the only form of tobacco popular among women—have taken a growing toll on women's health. Lung cancer competes with breast cancer as a leading cause of death among Canadian women.

Tens of thousands of Canadian men and women die prematurely each year as a direct result of cigarette smoking, which exceeds the combined death toll from alcohol, cocaine, heroin, homicide, suicide, automobile accidents, and AIDS (Mosley and Cowley, 1991). Smokers also endure frequent minor illnesses such as the flu, and pregnant women who smoke increase the likelihood of spontaneous abortion (miscarriage), prenatal death, and low-birth-weight babies. Even nonsmokers exposed to second-hand cigarette smoke have a higher risk of smoking-related diseases.

The tobacco industry, still a huge industry in Canada, maintained for years that because the precise link between cigarettes and disease has not been specified, the health effects of smoking remained "an open question." Nonetheless, laws mandating smoke-free environments are spreading rapidly. By 1997, the tobacco industry had conceded that cigarette smoking is harmful to health, and agreed to end marketing strategies that target the young. In 1998, Canada took steps to restrict advertising and the sponsorship of sporting and cultural events by the tobacco industry.

In response to the anti-smoking trend in Canada, the tobacco industry is selling more products abroad, especially in low-income countries where there is little legal regulation of tobacco sales and advertising. In Canada, however, more and more smokers are trying to break the habit, taking advantage of the fact that someone who has not smoked for ten years has about the same pattern of health as a lifelong nonsmoker.

Eating Disorders

An **eating disorder** is *an intense form of dieting or other kind of weight control in order to become very thin.* As the opening of this chapter suggests, eating disorders illustrate how cultural pressures shape human health.

Consider, first, that 95 percent of people who suffer from anorexia nervosa or bulimia are women, mostly from white, relatively affluent families. According to Michael Levine (1987), our culture equates slenderness in women with being successful and attractive to men. On the flip side, Levine adds, overweight people tend to be viewed as "lazy," "ugly," "stupid," and "sloppy."

Studies show that most university and college-age women (1) agree that "guys like thin girls," (2) think that being thin is the most crucial dimension of phys-

Evidence of the health hazards of smoking cigarettes first appeared in the 1930s. But cigarettes continued to increase in popularity, helped, in part, by celebrity advertising that was, at best, misleading.

ical attractiveness, and (3) believe that they are not as thin as men would like them to be. In fact, most university-age women want to be even thinner than university-age men say women should be. For their part, most men describe their actual body shape as just about what they want it to be; thus, compared to women, men display little dissatisfaction over body shape (Fallon and Rozin, 1985).

Chapter 12 ("Sex and Gender") explained that our culture embraces a "beauty myth" that teaches women to exaggerate the importance of physical attractiveness as well as to orient themselves towards pleasing men (Wolf, 1990). Such cultural patterns, Levine continues, pressure women to pursue thinness as a form of perfection. These messages about thinness come from mothers and fathers—especially affluent parents—who pressure a daughter to be "The Best Little Girl in the World." But television and other mass media also play a part in this process, almost exclusively casting actresses and models who are unnaturally thin and unrealistically beautiful. Paradoxically, as the emphasis on thinness has grown, so too has the second wave of the women's movement. This has resulted in a double bind for women, who are faced with an ideal woman who is both successful in the labour market (which often means competition with men) and beautiful and thin enough to be the wife of the very successful man.

The overall result of "gendered" images of women's roles and bodies is low self-image, since few women approach our culture's unrealistic standards of beauty. Just as important, those who do are likely to engage compulsively in dieting behaviour to the point of risking their health.

Sexually Transmitted Diseases

Sexual activity, though pleasurable and vital to the perpetuation of our species, can transmit more than fifty illnesses. Sometimes called *venereal diseases* (from Venus, the Roman goddess of love), these ailments date back to humanity's origins. Since our culture has long linked sex to sin, some people regard venereal disease not only as illness but also as a mark of immorality.

Sexually transmitted diseases (STDs) grabbed national attention during the "sexual revolution" of the 1960s, when people began sexual activity earlier and had a greater number of partners. As a result, STDs are an exception to the general decline in infectious diseases during this century. In recent years, the growing danger of STDs—and especially AIDS—has sparked a sexual counterrevolution that has discouraged casual sex, not necessarily for moral reasons, but out of self-interest (Kain, 1987; Kain and Hart, 1987). The following section provides a brief overview of several common STDs.

Gonorrhea and syphilis. Among the oldest diseases, gonorrhea and syphilis are caused by microscopic organisms almost always transmitted by sexual contact. Untreated, gonorrhea can cause sterility; syphilis damages major organs and can result in blindness, mental disorders, and death.

While 1441 cases of gonorrhea and syphilis were reported in Canada in 1990, the actual number may well be several times greater. Generally speaking, poorer people and particularly visible minorities have higher rates of various STDs than those from the higher social classes. Gonorrhea and syphilis can easily be cured with antibiotics, such as penicillin. Although some strains of these diseases resist efforts at treatment, neither disease currently represents a serious health threat in Canada.

Genital herpes. An estimated twenty to thirty million adults in the United States (one in seven) are infected with the genital herpes virus. Canadian data are not available, but based on differences in the pop-

ulation and in the degrees of inequality between Canadian and U.S. society, the proportion of Canadians infected could be expected to be smaller than that in the United States.

Although far less serious than gonorrhea and syphilis, herpes is incurable. People with genital herpes may exhibit no symptoms or they may experience periodic, painful blisters on the genitals accompanied by fever and headache. Although not fatal to adults, women with active genital herpes can transmit the disease during vaginal delivery to an infant, to whom it may be deadly. Infected women, therefore, usually give birth by Caesarean section.

AIDS. The most serious of all sexually transmitted diseases is AIDS. Identified in 1981, this disease is incurable and fatal. AIDS is caused by the human immunodeficiency virus (HIV), which attacks white blood cells, the core of the immune system. AIDS thus renders a person vulnerable to a wide range of other diseases that eventually cause death.

The first AIDS case in Canada was reported by the Laboratory Centre for Disease Control (LCDC) in February 1982. By December 1993 there had been 6187 reported deaths due to AIDS in Canada, and another 2896 people documented as living with AIDS. As of 1993 an estimated 1 in 1000 Canadians were infected with HIV, the virus linked to AIDS (*We Need to Know About Aids*, 1994:6). While Canada's widespread education campaign may have led to changes in sexual practices and drug and intravenous use, with resulting declines in rates of new HIV infection, it will be a while before we see a reduction in AIDS death rates. AIDS, which takes many years to develop, continues to cause more deaths: between 1990 and 1995, the death rate from AIDS grew from 3.6 to 5.6 per 100 000 population (calculations based on Columbo, 1995; 1998).

Women account for less than 7 percent of all AIDS cases reported in Canada. From 1982 to 1984, twenty women were diagnosed with AIDS. Between 1988 and 1989, 157 women contracted the disease. As of December 1993, there were ninety-three children under age fifteen diagnosed with AIDS; roughly three-quarters of them had contracted AIDS before or around the time of birth from their mothers. In 1989, AIDS had become one of the top four overall contributors to potential years of life lost (PYLL) for men in Canada, and presently contribute more PYLL in men than diseases such as diabetes and chronic lung and kidney disease (Remis, 1993).

In global perspective, HIV infects some thirty million people—half under age twenty-five—and the number is rising rapidly. Africa (more specifically, countries south of the Sahara Desert) has the highest HIV infection rate and currently accounts for two-thirds of all world cases. In central African nations such as Burundi, Rwanda, Uganda, and Kenya, roughly one-fifth of all young adults are infected (Tofani, 1991; Scommegna, 1996). North Americans account for less than 5 percent of global HIV cases.

Upon infection, people with HIV display no symptoms at all, so most are unaware of their condition. Not for a year or longer do symptoms of HIV infection appear. One-third of infected persons develop full-blown AIDS within five years, half develop AIDS within ten years, and almost all become sick within twenty years. Even though the number of AIDS deaths began to decline in 1997, the number of deaths so far makes AIDS potentially the most serious epidemic of modern times.

Today, all donated blood is checked for HIV before being transfused. However, the Canadian Hemophilia Society accused the Canadian Red Cross of "bureaucratic foot-dragging" that led to at least 750 hemophiliacs, and potentially many other transfusion recipients, becoming infected with the HIV virus in the mid-1980s. Several high-profile lawsuits were launched against the Red Cross. The Krever Commission, which was established to investigate the issue, found serious mismanagement and negligence and assigned responsibility to specific individuals. As a result, the Red Cross is no longer involved in the collection and management of our blood supplies.

AIDS is infectious but is not contagious. That is, HIV is transmitted through body fluids such as blood, semen, or breast milk but *not* through casual contact such as shaking hands, hugging, sharing towels or dishes, swimming together, or even by coughing and sneezing. The risk of transmitting AIDS through saliva (as in kissing) is extremely low. Infected women can pass HIV to their newborn children, although present evidence indicates that there is less than a 50 percent chance of this occurring. Moreover, the risk of transmitting HIV through sexual activity is greatly reduced by the use of latex condoms. But in the age of AIDS, abstinence or an exclusive relationship with an uninfected person is the only sure way to avoid infection.

Specific behaviours put people at high risk for HIV infection. The first is *anal sex*, which can cause rectal bleeding that allows easy transmission of HIV from one person to another. The practice of anal sex explains why homosexual and bisexual men comprise about 60 percent of those with AIDS in Canada.

Sharing needles used to inject drugs is a second high-risk behaviour. Casual sex sometimes accompanies drug use; therefore, having sex with an intravenous drug user also constitutes a high-risk behaviour. The association of this kind of drug use with people of lower socioeconomic levels is another reason that there are class correlates in the incidence of AIDS.

The ability to prolong life has led to increasingly complicated ethical considerations involving death. Nancy Marrison, a Halifax physician, was accused of killing a terminally-ill cancer patient in November 1996. Although a judge threw out the charges, the Crown is appealing that decision with the intention of proceeding with charges of manslaughter. Many are watching this ground-breaking case to see how the courts will handle "crimes of compassion."

Using any drug, including alcohol, also increases the risk of HIV infection to the extent that it impairs judgment. In other words, even people who understand what places them at risk of infection may act less responsibly once they are under the influence of alcohol, marijuana, or some other drug.

HIV prevalence among actively homosexual men is probably in the range of 10 to 15 percent. Approximately 22 500 among an estimated 200 000 to 300 000 gay and bisexual men may be infected with HIV in Canada. Some estimate that perhaps 9 percent of infected adults in North America contracted the disease through heterosexual contact (although heterosexuals, infected in various ways, account for more than 30 percent of AIDS cases) (Remis, 1993). But heterosexual activity does transmit AIDS, and the risk rises with the number of sexual partners, especially if they fall into high-risk categories. Worldwide, heterosexual relations are the primary means of HIV transmission, accounting for two-thirds of all infections (Eckholm and Tierney, 1990).

Treating a single person with AIDS costs hundreds of thousands of dollars, and this figure may rise as new therapies are developed. Added to the direct costs of treatment and research are tens of billions of dollars in lost earnings and productivity. Medicare, private insurance, and personal savings rarely cover more than a small fraction of the cost of treatment. In addition, there is the mounting cost of caring for children orphaned by AIDS. Overall, AIDS represents both a medical and a social problem of monumental proportions.

It has been suggested that governments responded slowly to the AIDS crisis, largely because gays and intravenous drug users are widely viewed as deviant. More recently, money allocated for AIDS research has increased rapidly, and researchers have identified drugs, including recent "protease inhibitors," that dramatically suppress symptoms and prolong life in many patients. Nevertheless, educational programs remain the most effective weapon against AIDS, since prevention is the only way to stop a disease that currently has no cure.

ETHICAL ISSUES: CONFRONTING DEATH

Health issues involve ethical considerations, especially now that technological advances have given human beings the power to draw the line separating life and death. Today we grapple with how to use these new powers, or whether to use them at all.

When does death occur? Common sense suggests that life ceases when breathing and heartbeat stop. But the ability to revive or replace a heart and to artificially sustain respiration have rendered such notions of death obsolete. Medical and legal experts in North America now define death as an *irreversible* state involving no response to stimulation, no movement or breathing, no reflexes, and no indication of brain activity (Ladd, 1979; Wall, 1980).

Do people have a right to die? Today, medical personnel, family members, and patients themselves face the agonizing burden of deciding when a terminally ill person should die. In 1992, Parliament abolished attempted suicide as a crime but retained the prohibition against assisting a suicide. Individuals periodically challenge this law, as did Sue Rodriguez, a British Columbia woman with Lou Gehrig's disease. Rodriguez eventually would have been unable to swallow, to speak, to walk, or even to turn over without assistance. She would have needed a respirator to breathe. As her condition worsened and she expected to lose the desire to live, her ability to end her life would have been reduced. She wanted permission for a doctor, at a given time in the future, to set up an intravenous tube filled with a lethal dose of medication. Her case spawned both widespread support and fer-

vent opposition from churches, anti-abortion activists, and provincial and federal governments (Wood, 1993). On September 30, 1993, the Supreme Court decided, with a vote of 5–4, that Rodriguez's rights were not violated by the federal law against assisting a suicide. The court ruled that the state's interest in protecting the sanctity of life took precedence over the individual's right to a dignified death (Wilson and Fine, *Globe and Mail*, October 1, 1993:1). In the end, Rodriguez was helped to die by an anonymous physician and a maverick member of Parliament, the long-sitting New Democratic party member Svend Robinson.

Generally speaking, the first responsibility of physicians and hospitals is to protect a patient's life. Even so, a mentally competent person in the process of dying may refuse medical treatment or even nutrition. Moreover, laws require hospitals, nursing homes, and other medical facilities to honour the desires of a patient made earlier in the form of a living will. Thus, most cases of death in Canada now involve a human decision about when and how death will occur.

What about mercy killing? *Mercy killing* is the common term for **euthanasia**, *assisting in the death of a person suffering from an incurable disease.* Euthanasia (from the Greek, meaning "a good death") poses an ethical dilemma, being at once an act of kindness and a form of killing.

Support for a patient's right to die (that is, *passive* euthanasia) is growing in North America. But assisting in the death of another person (*active* euthanasia) still provokes controversy and may violate the law. When Robert Latimer killed his badly disabled daughter by carbon monoxide poisoning, he was convicted of second degree murder. He felt that his daughter's life of constant pain was not worth living: he killed her because he loved her. A groundswell of public sentiment, both supportive and hostile, erupted. Though convicted, Latimer was released from prison provided that he remain on his farm. In 1997, the Supreme Court of Canada heard an appeal and convicted Latimer of murder, but gave him a very light sentence due to the special circumstances of his crime.

The debate on euthanasia breaks down roughly as follows. Those who categorically view life—even with suffering and disability—as preferable to death reject both passive and active euthanasia. People who recognize circumstances under which death is preferable to life endorse passive or perhaps active euthanasia, but they face the practical problem of determining just when life should be ended.

THE MEDICAL ESTABLISHMENT

Medicine is *a social institution concerned with combating disease and improving health.* Through most of human history, health care was the responsibility of individuals and their families. Medicine emerges as a social institution only as societies become more productive, assigning their members formal, specialized roles. Traditional medical practitioners use the healing properties of certain plants to address physical and emotional illness. From the point of view of some modern people, traditional healers such as acupuncturists and herbalists may seem unscientific, but, in truth, they improve human health throughout the world (Ayensu, 1981).

As a society industrializes, health care becomes the responsibility of specially schooled and legally licensed healers, from anesthesiologists to X-ray technicians. Today's medical establishment in Canada took form over the last 150 years.

THE RISE OF SCIENTIFIC MEDICINE

In colonial times, doctors, herbalists, druggists, midwives, and ministers all engaged in various forms of healing arts. But not all did so effectively: unsanitary instruments, lack of anesthesia, and simple ignorance made surgery a terrible ordeal in which doctors probably killed as many patients as they saved.

Gradually, however, specialists learned more about human anatomy, physiology, and biochemistry. Early in the nineteenth century, medical societies appeared in Canada as doctors established themselves as self-regulating professionals (Blishen, 1991). Formal colleges of medicine offered training in the field. The increase in the number of medical schools paralleled the growth in the number of hospitals (Stevens, 1971). Medical societies required those who wished to practise or teach medical skills to obtain licences, and these organizations enforced conformity to specific medical standards.

The standards that lay at the heart of this new profession were established largely through the efforts of the allopathic doctors (Blishen, 1991). The establishment in 1865 of the General Council of Medical Education and Registration in Upper Canada signified acceptance of the scientific model of medicine, and the organization widely publicized the medical successes of its members to further improve its own public image. Scientific researchers were touted for tracing the cause of life-threatening illnesses to bacteria and viruses, and also for developing vaccines to prevent disease.

Still, alternative approaches to health care, such as regulating nutrition, also had many defenders. The allopathic (conventional) doctors responded boldly— some thought arrogantly—by criticizing these alternative ideas about health. They established the Canadian Medical Association (CMA) in 1867. With control of the certification process, they were able to define what

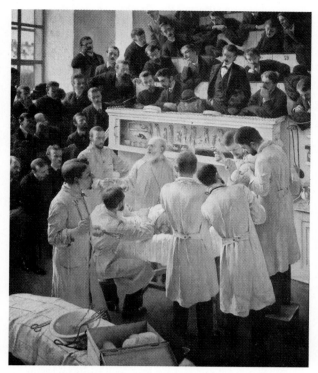

The rise of scientific medicine during the nineteenth century resulted in new skills and technology for treating many common ailments that had afflicted humanity for centuries. At the same time, however, scientific medicine pushed forms of health care involving women to the margins, and placed medicine under the control of men living in cities. We see this pattern in the A. F. Seligmann painting General Hospital, *showing an obviously all-male medical school class in Vienna in 1880.*

constituted medical acts and practice. Thus they, through the provincial colleges, could determine what the various "paramedical" occupations could and could not do. Before long, the practice of medicine was limited mainly to those with an MD degree. In the process, both the prestige and income of physicians rose dramatically. Men and women with MD degrees are among the highest-paid workers in Canada.

Other practitioners—such as naturopaths, herbal healers, and midwives—held to their traditional roles, but at a high cost: all have been relegated to fringe areas of the medical profession. With far less social prestige and income than physicians, such professionals now have a small, if devoted, following in Canada (Nancarrow Clarke, 1996; Blishen, 1991). Treatment by chiropractors is now partially covered by provincial health insurance, and midwives have recently been legalized as birth attendants in Ontario (Rajhathy and Roulard, 1994:40). Furthermore, more than one-third of North Americans use some form of "complementary medicine" (Eisenberg et al., 1993).

The rise of scientific medicine, taught in expensive, urban medical schools, also changed the social profile of doctors. There is and has long been an overrepresentation of medical students from higher-level social backgrounds. Their fathers have tended to have higher education than average, and to be employed in managerial and professional levels of the labour force (Blishen, 1991). Medicine is also a traditionally male-dominated profession. Women were long considered unfit to practise (Starr, 1982; Huet-Cox, 1984; Nancarrow Clarke, 1990). In 1992, more than 80 percent of physicians were men, while approximately 97 percent of nurses were women.

The result has been a shortage of physicians in rural areas, as well as a lack of physicians drawn from the ranks of women and other minorities.

HOLISTIC MEDICINE

The scientific model of medicine has recently been tempered by the more traditional notion of **holistic medicine**, *an approach to health care that emphasizes the prevention of illness and takes into account a person's entire physical and social environment.*

Some holistic practitioners agree with the use of drugs, surgery, artificial organs, and high technology, but they caution that these developments risk transforming medicine into narrow specialties focusing on symptoms rather than people, on disease instead of health. The following are foundations of holistic health care (Duhl, 1980; Ferguson, 1980; Gordon, 1980):

1. **Patients are people.** Holistic practitioners are concerned not only with symptoms but with how each person's environment and lifestyle affect health. For example, stress caused by poverty or intense competition at work increases the risk of illness. Holistic practitioners extend the bounds of conventional medicine by actively combating environmental pollution and other dangers to public health.

2. **Responsibility, not dependency.** In the scientific model, patients are dependent on physicians. Holistic medicine tries to shift some responsibility for health from physicians to patients themselves by helping them engage in health-promoting behaviour. Holistic medicine favours an *active* approach to *health*, rather than a *reactive* approach to *illness*.

3. **Personal treatment.** Conventional medicine locates medical care in impersonal offices and hospitals, which are disease-centred settings. By contrast, holistic practitioners favour, as much as possible, a personal and relaxed environment such as the home. Holistic medicine seeks to re-

establish the personal ties that united healers and patients before the era of specialists. The CMA currently recognizes approximately fifty specialized areas of medical practice, and a growing proportion of MDs are entering these high-paying specialties rather than family practice. Thus, there is a need for practitioners who are concerned with the patient in the holistic sense.

Clearly, holistic care does not oppose scientific medicine, but shifts its emphasis away from narrowly treating disease towards the goal of achieving the highest possible level of well-being for everyone.

PAYING FOR HEALTH: A GLOBAL SURVEY

As medicine has come to rely on high technology, the costs of health care in industrial societies have skyrocketed. Countries employ various strategies to meet these costs.

Medicine in Socialist Societies

In societies with predominantly socialist economies, the government provides medical care directly to the people. These nations hold that all citizens have the right to basic medical care. In practice, then, people do not pay physicians and hospitals on their own; rather, the government uses public funds to pay medical costs. The state owns and operates medical facilities and pays salaries to practitioners, who are government employees.

People's Republic of China. As a poor, agrarian society in the process of industrialization, the People's Republic of China faces the daunting task of attending to the health of more than one billion people. Traditional healing arts, including acupuncture and the use of medicinal herbs, are still widely practised in China. In addition, a holistic concern with the interplay of mind and body marks the Chinese approach to health (Sidel and Sidel, 1982b; Kaptchuk, 1985).

China has experimented with private medical care, but the government controls most health care. China's famed barefoot doctors, roughly comparable to North American paramedics, have brought some Western methods of medical care to millions of peasants in remote rural villages.

The former Soviet Union. The former Soviet Union is struggling to transform a state-dominated economy into more of a market system. For this reason, medical care is in transition. Nonetheless, the notion that everyone has a right to basic medical care remains widespread.

Currently, the government provides medical care funded from taxes. As is the case in the People's

The People's Republic of China has a long history of folk medicine, an effective strategy to meet the health-care needs of more than 1 billion people in a largely rural society. Here a "barefoot doctor" displays herbal remedies at a Sunday market.

Republic of China, people do not choose a physician but report to a local government health facility.

Physicians in the former Soviet Union have had lower prestige and income than their counterparts in Canada. Surprisingly, they receive about the same salary as skilled industrial workers (compared to an income six times higher in this country). Worth noting, too, is that about 70 percent of physicians in the Russian Federation are women, compared with about 20 percent in Canada, and, as in our society, occupations dominated by women yield fewer financial rewards.

In recent years, the new Russian Federation has suffered setbacks in health care, partly due to a falling standard of living. Rising demand for medical care has strained a bureaucratic system that, at best, provides highly standardized and impersonal care. The optimistic view is that, as market reforms proceed, both living standards and the quality of medical services will improve. In any case, what does seem certain is that disparities in medical care among various segments of the population will increase (Specter, 1995).

Medicine in Capitalist Societies

People living in nations with predominantly capitalist economies are more likely to provide for their own health care in accordance with financial resources and personal preferences. However, the high costs of medical care—beyond the reach of many people—mean that government programs underwrite a considerable proportion of health-related expenses.

Sweden. In 1891, Sweden instituted a compulsory, comprehensive system of government medical care. Citizens pay for this program with their taxes, which are among the highest in the world. In most cases,

physicians receive salaries from the government rather than fees from patients, and most hospitals are government managed. Because this medical system resembles that of socialist societies, it is often described as **socialized medicine**, *a health care system in which the government owns and operates most medical facilities and employs most physicians.*

Great Britain. In 1948, Great Britain, too, instituted socialized medicine. The British did not do away with private care, however; instead, they created a "dual system" of medical services. All British citizens are entitled to medical care provided by the National Health Service, but those who can afford to may purchase more extensive care from doctors and hospitals that operate privately.

Japan. Physicians in Japan operate privately, but a combination of government programs and private insurance pays medical costs. As shown in Figure 20–2, the Japanese approach health care much as the Europeans do, with most medical expenses paid through government.

The United States. The United States is unique among industrialized societies in having no government-sponsored medical program for every citizen. The government does pay most medical expenses, but only for some categories of people. For example, the Medicare program covers some of the medical expenses of men and women over age sixty-five. In 1993, about 14 percent of the U.S. population were covered under this program. During the same year Medicaid, a medical insurance program for the poor, provided benefits to nearly thirty million people, or about 12 percent of the population. An additional

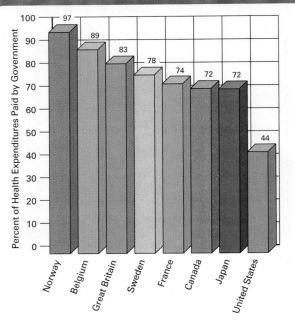

GLOBAL SNAPSHOT

Percent of Health Expenditures Paid by Government

Norway 97
Belgium 89
Great Britain 83
Sweden 78
France 74
Canada 72
Japan 72
United States 44

FIGURE 20–2 Extent of "Socialized Medicine" in Selected Countries

SOURCE: United Nations Development Programme (1997).

infants and adults in the United States (Fuchs, 1974; United Nations, 1995).

By 1994, there was strong public support for expanding government-based health care coverage in the United States. Congress considered a number of plans, ranging from a conservative Republican proposal to offer tax credits to people who purchase health insurance to a Canadian-type "single-payer" system sponsored by liberal Democrats.

President Clinton advocated something of a middle ground called "managed competition." The essence of the Clinton proposal was to shift medical care away from the traditional, private, fee-for-service system towards various types of health maintenance organizations (HMOs) and government-funded programs. In the process, supporters claimed, costs would fall even as coverage became universal. Critics, however, countered with a "pro-choice" argument that patients should be able to choose their own doctors without government interference. Further, because it would create new government bureaucracies, critics feared, the Clinton plan would raise—not lower—costs, eventually leading to rationing care.

After lengthy debate, Congress rejected the Clinton reforms, so that the status quo continues. Still, because public concern about health care runs high, this issue will hold centre stage for some time to come.

MEDICINE IN CANADA

The Canadian government pays doctors and hospitals—who operate privately—for the services they provide according to a schedule of fees set annually by the federal government and provincial governments in consultation with professional medical associations. Thus, Canada has government-funded and -regulated medical care but, because practitioners operate privately, not true socialized medicine.

Canada's system of universal medicare has a long history, with seeds in the pre-Confederation era. By 1884, Canada's *Public Health Act* required health boards and sanitary regulations at the local level. In 1919, Mackenzie King introduced the idea of universal health care as part of the Liberal party platform, but it wasn't until 1972 that all provinces were part of a federal program providing comprehensive medical insurance—eleven years after such a program was first implemented in Saskatchewan. Canada's law was shaped by recommendations of a Royal Commission on Health Services, instituted in 1961 under Supreme Court Justice Emmett Hall. The law was based on four basic premises:

1. **Universality.** All residents of Canada would be eligible on equal terms, regardless of such differ-

twenty-five million veterans (10 percent of the population) could obtain free care in government-operated hospitals. In all, 35 percent of U.S. citizens enjoy some medical care benefits from the government, but most are covered primarily through private insurance programs. Still, government expenditures for medical care in the United States amount to more per person than in any other industrial society, and double the figure in Australia and Japan.

In 1992, 71 percent were at least partially covered through a family member's employer or labour union, while 14 percent purchased medical insurance privately. Overall, three-quarters of the U.S. population have some private medical insurance, although few such programs pay all medical costs (U.S. Bureau of the Census, 1995).

For the most part, then, medicine in the United States is a private, profit-making industry in which more money buys better care. Called a **direct-fee system**, theirs is *a medical-care system in which patients pay directly for the services of physicians and hospitals.* Affluent people in the United States can purchase top-flight medical care, while the poor fare far worse than their counterparts in Europe and Canada. This translates into relatively high death rates among both

ences as previous health records, age, income, membership in a group, or other considerations. The federal government stipulated that at least 95 percent of the population was to be covered within two years of the provincial adoption of the plan.

2. **Portability.** The benefits were to be portable from province to province.

3. **Comprehensive coverage.** The benefits were to include all necessary medical services, and certain surgical services performed by a dental surgeon in hospital.

4. **Administration.** The plan was to be run on a nonprofit basis. (Nancarrow Clarke, 1996:256).

Canada's system has the advantage of providing care for everyone at a total cost that is significantly lower (as a percentage of GNP) than that needed to operate the (nonuniversal) medical system in the United States (see Table 20–1).

However, criticisms of the Canadian system include that it does not make effective use of state-of-the-art technology, as is done south of the border. However, in the United States such technology is available primarily for the wealthy and the well-insured. The vast majority of U.S. residents do not reap the benefits of these technological advances, and do not have access to the medical care that Canadians do. For example, death from cervical cancer is still a major threat in the U.S., especially for poor women. In contrast, because of the ready availability of Pap smears, Canada has all but eliminated death from cervical cancer.

Another current criticism of the Canadian system is that it is slower to respond and that people may have to wait long periods of time prior to treatment. Again, the counterargument is that at least people are not denied the possibility of treatment because they are unable to pay for it.

THEORETICAL ANALYSIS OF HEALTH AND MEDICINE

Each of the major theoretical paradigms in sociology provides a means of organizing and interpreting the facts and issues presented in this chapter.

STRUCTURAL-FUNCTIONAL ANALYSIS

Talcott Parsons (1951) viewed medicine as society's strategy to keep its members healthy. In this scheme, illness is dysfunctional, undermining the performance of social roles and, thus, impeding the operation of society.

TABLE 20–1 Health Expenditures as Percentages of GNP, Canada and the United States, 1960–91

Year	Canada	United States
1960	5.5	5.3
1965	6.0	5.9
1970	7.1	7.4
1975	7.2	8.4
1980	7.3	9.2
1985	8.5	10.5
1986	8.8	10.7
1987r	8.8	10.9
1988r*	8.7	11.1
1989r*	8.9	11.5
1990r*	9.4	12.2
1991*	9.9	13.2

r = Revised figures
*Provisional estimates

SOURCE: Policy, Planning and Information Branch, March 1993. *Health Expenditures in Canada Summary Report 1987–1991*, Health Canada, 1993. Reproduced with permission of the Minister of Supply and Services Canada, 1993.

The Sick Role

The normative response to disease, according to Parsons, is for an individual to assume the **sick role**, *patterns of behaviour defined as appropriate for people who are ill.* As explained by Parsons, the sick role has three characteristics.

1. **Illness suspends routine responsibilities.** Serious illness relaxes or suspends normal social obligations, such as going to work or attending school. To prevent abuse of this privilege, however, people do not simply declare themselves ill; they must enlist the support of others—especially a recognized medical expert—before assuming the sick role.

2. **A sick person must want to be well.** We assume that no one wants to be sick. Thus, people suspected of feigning illness to escape responsibility or to receive special attention have no legitimate claim to the sick role.

3. **An ailing person must seek competent help.** People who are ill must seek competent assistance and cooperate with health care practitioners. By failing to accept medical help or to follow doctor's orders, a person gives up any claim to the sick role's exemption from routine responsibilities.

The Physician's Role

The physician's role centres on assessing claims of sickness and restoring sick people to normal routines. This responsibility, Parsons explained, rests on spe-

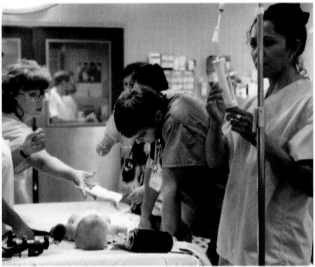

Our national view of medicine has changed during the last several decades. Television viewers in the 1970s watched doctors like Marcus Welby, M.D. confidently take charge of situations in a fatherly—and almost godlike—manner. By the 1990s, programs like "E.R." gave a more realistic view of the limitations of medicine to address illness, as well as the violence that wracks our society.

cialized knowledge. Physicians expect patients to follow "doctor's orders," and to provide whatever personal information may reasonably assist their efforts.

Although it is inevitably hierarchical, the doctor-patient relationship varies from society to society. Japanese tradition, for example, gives physicians great authority over their patients. Japanese physicians even take it upon themselves to decide how much information about the seriousness of an illness they will share with the patient (Darnton and Hoshia, 1989).

Until about thirty years ago, physicians in Canada acted in much the same way. But the patients' rights movement demands that physicians readily share more and more medical information and offer patients a choice of treatment options. A more egalitarian relationship between doctor and patient is also developing in European societies and, gradually, in Japan.

Critical evaluation. Parsons' analysis links illness and medicine to the broader organization of society. Others have extended the concept of the sick role to some nonillness situations such as pregnancy (Myers and Grasmick, 1989).

One limitation of the sick-role concept is that it applies to acute conditions (such as the flu) better than it does to chronic illness (such as heart disease), which may not be reversible. Moreover, a sick person's ability to regain health depends on available resources. Many poor people can ill afford either medical care or time off from work.

Critics also question the implication of Parsons' analysis that doctors—rather than people themselves—should bear the primary responsibility for health. Treatment-oriented physicians respond to acute illness, of course, but a more prevention-oriented approach makes physicians and patients equal partners in the pursuit of health.

SYMBOLIC-INTERACTION ANALYSIS

According to the symbolic-interaction paradigm, society is less a grand system than a series of complex, ever-changing realities. Both health and medical care are thus human constructions that people perceive subjectively.

The Social Construction of Illness

Since we socially construct our ideas of health and illness, members of a very poor society may view hunger and malnutrition as quite normal. Similarly, people in rich nations, such as our own, may give little thought to the harmful effects of spending leisure time passively watching television or consuming a rich diet.

How we respond to illness, too, is based on social definitions that may or may not square with medical knowledge. For instance, people with AIDS contend with fear and sometimes outright bigotry that has no medical basis.

Furthermore, whether we decide we are "sick" or "well" may rest on a host of nonmedical "contingencies." Canadian university students, for example, have been known to ignore signs of illness on the eve of a vacation, yet dutifully march into the infirmary hours before a difficult examination. Health, in short, is less an objective commodity than a negotiated outcome.

Moreover, how people define a medical situation may actually affect how they feel. Medical experts have long marvelled at *psychosomatic* disorders (a fusion of Greek words meaning "mind" and "body"), in which a state of mind leads to physical sensations (Hamrick, Anspaugh, and Ezell, 1986). As sociologist W.I. Thomas (1966, orig. 1931) pointed out, a situation defined as real becomes real in its consequences.

The Social Construction of Treatment

In Chapter 6 ("Social Interaction in Everyday Life"), we used the dramaturgical approach of Erving Goffman to explain how physicians craft their physical surroundings ("the office") and present themselves to others to foster specific impressions of competence and power.

Sociologist Joan Emerson (1970) further illustrates this process of reality construction by analyzing a situation familiar to women, a gynecological examination carried out by a male doctor. After observing seventy-five such examinations, she explains that this setting is especially precarious, because it is so vulnerable to misinterpretation. The man's touching of a woman's genitals—conventionally viewed as a sexual act and possibly even an assault—must, in this case, be defined as impersonal and professional.

To ensure that people construct reality in this way, doctors and nurses remove sexual connotations as completely as possible. They furnish the examination room with nothing but medical equipment; all personnel wear medical uniforms. Staff members act as if such examinations are simply routine, although, from the patient's point of view, they may be quite unusual.

Further, rapport between physician and patient is established before the examination begins. Once under way, the doctor's performance is strictly professional, suggesting to the patient that inspecting the genitals is no different from surveying any other part of the body. A female nurse is usually present during the examination, not only to assist the physician but to dispel any impression that a man and a woman are alone in a room.

The need to manage situational definitions has long been overlooked by medical schools. This omission is unfortunate because, as Emerson's analysis shows, understanding how people construct reality in the examination room is just as crucial as mastering the medical skills required for effective treatment.

Critical evaluation. One strength of the symbolic-interaction paradigm lies in revealing the relativity of sickness and health. What people view as normal or deviant, healthful or harmful, depends on a host of factors, many of which are not, strictly speaking, medical. This approach also shows that all medical procedures involve a subtle process of reality construction between patient and medical staff.

But it seems wrong to deny that there are some objective standards of well-being. Certain physical conditions do indeed cause specific negative changes in human capacities, whether we think so or not. People who lack sufficient nutrition and safe water, for example, suffer from their unhealthy environment, however they define their surroundings.

SOCIAL-CONFLICT ANALYSIS

Social-conflict analysis draws a connection between health and social inequality and, taking a cue from Karl Marx, ties medicine to the operation of capitalism. Researchers have focused on three main issues: access to medical care, the effects of the profit motive, and the politics of medicine.

The Access Issue

Personal health is the foundation of social life. Yet, from a Marxist perspective, capitalist societies make health a commodity, so that health follows wealth. As already noted, this problem is more serious in the United States than in other industrialized societies because that country has no universal health care system. However, as Canada's provincial and federal governments continue to wrangle about cost-sharing programs and as the federal deficit continues to be seen as a problem, even our most heralded medicare scheme is very vulnerable to cutbacks and growing inequality among the provinces, as well as among individual Canadians.

Most of the forty-two million people in the U.S. who lack any health care coverage at present have low incomes. Conflict theorists concede that capitalism does provide excellent health care for the rich; it simply does not provide very well for the rest of the population.

The Profit Motive

Some analysts go further, arguing that the real problem is not access to medical care but the character of capitalist medicine itself. The profit motive turns physicians, hospitals, and the pharmaceutical industry into multibillion-dollar corporations. The quest for ever-increasing profits also encourages questionable medical practices, including ordering needless tests, performing unnecessary surgery, and an overreliance on drugs (Kaplan et al., 1985).

Scientists are learning more and more about the genetic factors that prompt the eventual development of serious diseases. If offered the opportunity, would you want to undergo a genetic screening that would predict the long-term future of your own health?

One example of questionable medical practice involves more than two million women in the United States and Canada who have undergone silicone breast-implant surgery, under the assumption that the plastic packets of silicone were safe. Recently, however, it became clear that these implants are not safe enough, a fact apparently known to Dow Corning, their major manufacturer, for decades.

Most of the surgical operations performed annually in Canada are "elective," meaning that they promote a patient's long-term health rather then being prompted by a medical emergency. Critics charge that the decision to perform surgery often reflects the financial interests of surgeons and hospitals as much as the medical needs of patients (Illich, 1976). And, of course, any drugs or medical procedures prescribed for people subject them to risks, which harm between 5 and 10 percent of patients (Sidel and Sidel, 1982a; Cowley, 1995).

Finally, say social-conflict analysts, our society is all too tolerant of physicians having a direct, financial interest in the tests and procedures they order for their patients (Pear and Eckholm, 1991). In short, health care should be motivated by a concern for people, not profits.

Medicine as Politics

Although medicine declares itself to be politically neutral, scientific medicine frequently takes sides on significant social issues. For example, the medical establishment has often opposed government-operated health care programs. The history of medicine, critics contend, is replete with racial and sexual discrimination, defended by "scientific" opinions (Leavitt, 1984). Consider the diagnosis of "hysteria," a term that has its origins in the Greek word *hyster*, meaning uterus. In coining this word, medical professionals called on its resonances to suggest that being a woman was synonymous with being irrational.

Surveying the entire medical field, some critics see political mischief in today's scientific medicine. Scientists explain illness in terms of bacteria and viruses, ignoring the effects of social inequality on health. From a scientific perspective, in other words, poor people get sick because of a lack of sanitation and an unhealthy diet, even though poverty may be the underlying cause of these ills. In this way, critics charge, scientific medicine depoliticizes health by reducing complex political issues to simple matters of biology.

Critical evaluation. Social-conflict analysis offers another approach to the relationships among health, medicine, and our society. According to this view, social inequality is the reason some people have far better health than others.

The most common objection to the conflict approach is that it minimizes the overall improvement in health through the years and scientific medicine's contribution to our high standard of living today. Even though we could certainly do better, health indicators for our population have risen steadily over the course of the twentieth century and compare fairly well with those of other industrial societies.

In sum, sociology's three major theoretical paradigms convincingly argue that health and medicine are social issues. Indeed, as the "Controversy & Debate" box explains, advancing technology is forcing us to confront the social foundations of health and medicine. The famous French scientist Louis Pasteur (1822–95), who spent much of his life studying how bacteria cause disease, said just before he died that health depends much less on bacteria than on the social environment in which bacteria operate (Gordon, 1980:7). Explaining Pasteur's insight is sociology's contribution to human health.

LOOKING AHEAD: HEALTH IN THE TWENTY-FIRST CENTURY

At the beginning of the twentieth century, deaths from infectious disease were widespread, and scientists had yet to develop basic antibiotics such as penicillin. Thus, even common infections represented a deadly threat to health. Today, members of our soci-

The Genetic Crystal Ball: Do We Really Want to Look?

The clear liquid in the laboratory test tube seems ordinary enough, rather like a thick form of water. But this liquid represents perhaps the greatest medical breakthrough of all time: *the key to life itself.* The liquid is deoxyribonucleic acid, or DNA, the spiralling molecule found in each cell of the human body that contains the blueprint for making each one of us human as well as different from every other person.

In medical terms, the human body is composed of some 100 trillion cells, most of which contain a nucleus of twenty-three pairs of chromosomes (one of each pair comes from each parent). Each chromosome is packed with DNA, in segments called genes. Genes guide the production of proteins, the building blocks of the human body.

If genetics sounds complex (and it is), the social implications of genetic knowledge are more complex still. Scientists discovered the structure of DNA in 1952, and now an aggressive program is under way to "map" our genetic landscape. The ultimate goal of the Human Genome Project is to understand how each bit of DNA shapes our being. But do we really want to turn the key to understand life itself?

In the Human Genome Project, many scientists envision a completely new approach to medicine: rather than treating symptoms, physicians would address the basic causes of illness. Research, they point out, has already identified the genetic abnormalities that cause some forms of cancer, sickle cell anemia, muscular dystrophy, Huntington's disease, cystic fibrosis, and other crippling and deadly afflictions. In the twenty-first century, genetic screening—a scientific "crystal ball"—could let people know their medical destiny, and allow doctors to manipulate segments of DNA to prevent diseases before they appear.

But some people, both in and out of the scientific community, urge caution in pursuing such research, warning that genetic information can easily be abused. At its worst, genetic mapping opens the door to Nazi-like efforts at breeding a super-race. Indeed, in 1994, the People's Republic of China initiated a program of marriage regulation and forced abortion to prevent "new births of inferior quality."

It seems inevitable that some parents will seek to use genetic testing to evaluate the future health (or even the eye and hair colours) of their unborn children. Should people be permitted to abort a fetus that falls short of their standards? Or, further down the road when genetic manipulations become possible, should parents be able to create "designer children"?

Then there is the issue of "genetic privacy." Should a woman be able to request a genetic evaluation of her prospective fiancé before agreeing to marry? Should life or health insurance companies be allowed to demand genetic testing before writing policies? Should an employer be permitted to evaluate job applicants to weed out those whose future illnesses might drain their health care funds? Clearly, what is scientifically possible is not always morally desirable. Our society is already grappling with questions about how to use the ever-expanding knowledge about human genetics. These ethical dilemmas will only mount as genetic research pinpoints the roots of our makeup in the years to come.

Continue the debate . . .

1. *Traditional wedding vows join couples "in sickness and in health." Do you think individuals have a right to know the future health of their potential partners before tying the knot?*
2. *How do you feel about the desire of some parents to genetically design their children?*
3. *Where do we turn to devise standards for the proper use of genetic information?*

SOURCES: Elmer-Dewitt (1994); Thompson (1994); and Nash (1995).

---

ety take for granted the good health and long life that was the exception, not the rule, a century ago. There is every reason to expect that our health will continue to improve into the twenty-first century.

Another encouraging trend is that more people are taking responsibility for their own health (Caplow et al., 1991). Every one of us can live better and longer if we avoid tobacco, eat sensibly and in moderation, and exercise regularly.

Yet, certain health problems will continue to plague Canadian society in the decades to come. With no cure in sight, it seems likely that the AIDS epi-

demic will persist for some time. At this point, the only way to steer clear of contracting HIV is to make a personal decision to avoid all of the risky behaviours noted in this chapter.

But the changing social profile of people with AIDS—which increasingly afflicts the poor—reminds us that Canada falls short in addressing the health of marginalized members of our society. Even those among us who do not easily embrace the notion of serving as our "brother's keeper" should recognize the moral obligation that we as a people have to ensure that everyone has the security of medical care.

Finally, repeating a pattern seen in earlier chapters, we find that problems of health are far greater in the poor societies of the world than they are in Canada. The good news is that life expectancy for the world as a whole has been rising—from forty-eight years in 1950 to sixty-five years today—and the biggest gains have been in poor countries (Mosley and Cowley, 1991). But in much of Latin America, Asia, and especially in Africa, hundreds of millions of adults and children lack adequate food, safe water, and needed medical attention. Improving health in the world's poorest societies remains a critical challenge as we enter the twenty-first century.

SUMMARY

1. Health is a social as well as a biological issue, and well-being depends on the extent and distribution of a society's resources. Culture shapes both definitions of health and patterns of health care.

2. Through most of human history, health has been poor by today's standards. Health improved dramatically in Western Europe and North America in the nineteenth century, first because industrialization raised living standards and later because medical advances controlled infectious diseases.

3. Infectious diseases were the major killers at the beginning of the twentieth century. Today, most people in Canada die in or near old age of heart disease, cancer, or stroke.

4. Health in low-income countries is undermined by inadequate sanitation and hunger. Average life expectancy is about twenty years less than in Canada; in the poorest nations, half of the children do not survive to adulthood.

5. In Canada, more than three-quarters of children born today can expect to live to at least age sixty-five. Throughout the life course, however, people of high social position enjoy better health than the poor.

6. Cigarette smoking increased during this century to become the greatest preventable cause of death in Canada. Now that the health hazards of smoking are known, social tolerance for consumption of tobacco products is declining.

7. The incidence of sexually transmitted diseases has risen since 1960, an exception to the general decline in infectious disease.

8. The ability to prolong the lives of terminally ill people is forcing us to confront a number of ethical issues surrounding death and the rights of the dying.

9. Historically a family concern, health care is now the responsibility of trained specialists. The model of scientific medicine underlies the Canadian and U.S. medical establishments.

10. Holistic healing encourages people to assume greater responsibility for their own health and well-being, and urges professional healers to gain personal knowledge of patients and their environments.

11. Socialist societies define medical care as a right that governments offer equally to everyone. Capitalist societies view medical care as a commodity to be purchased, although most capitalist governments support medical care through socialized medicine or national health insurance.

12. Canada's health care system is a source of pride for Canadians and a major source of envy for many in the United States. Yet Canada's system was developed after, and in many ways is more restrictive than, those in Western Europe and Great Britain.

13. Structural-functional analysis links health and medicine to other social structures. A concept central to structural-functional analysis is the sick role, by which the ill person is excused from routine social responsibilities.

14. The symbolic-interaction paradigm investigates how health and medical treatments are largely matters of subjective perception and social definition.

15. Social-conflict analysis focuses on the unequal distribution of health and medical care. It criticizes the North American medical establishment for relying too heavily on drugs and surgery and for emphasizing the biological rather than the social causes of illness.

CRITICAL THINKING QUESTIONS

1. Explain why health is as much a social as a biological issue.

2. In global context, what are the "diseases of poverty" that kill people in poor countries? What are the "diseases of affluence," the leading killers in rich nations?

3. Sexually transmitted diseases represent an exception to the historical decline in infectious illness. What social forces are reflected in the rise in STDs since 1960?

4. Do you think the United States should follow the lead of Canada and other industrial countries by enacting a government program of health care for everyone? Why?

SOCIOLOGY APPLIED

1 In most communities, a trip to the local courthouse or to city hall is all it takes to find public records showing people's causes of death. Take a look at such records for people a century ago and recently. How do causes of death differ?

2. Visit the Web site for Health Canada at www.hc-sc. gc.ca. You will find health news, statistical data, and even travellers' health advisories. This site offers considerable evidence of the social dimensions of health.

3. Is there a medical school on or near your campus? If so, obtain a course catalogue and see how much (if any) of the medical curriculum involves the social dimensions of health care.

4. Arrange to speak with a midwife about her work helping women to give birth. How do midwives differ from medical obstetricians in their approach?

WEBLINKS

http://www.who.org/
World Health Organization is the directing and coordinating authority on international health work. Its responsibilities include assisting governments to strengthen health services; promoting improved nutrition, sanitation, and other living conditions; developing international standards for food and pharmaceutical products; and promoting cooperation among scientific and professional groups.

http://www.hc-sc.gc.ca/
The Ministry of Health publishes information on health issues, news headlines, advice for travellers, a food guide, reports, government regulations and policies, and more.

http://www.mrc.gc.ca/
Medical Research Council of Canada is the major federal agency responsible for funding biomedical research in Canada. Its role is to promote, assist, and undertake basic, applied, and clinical research in the health sciences, to support research training of health scientists, and to advise on health research to the federal Minister of Health.

http://www.hc-sc.gc.ca/hppb/hpo/
Developed by Health Canada's Health Promotion and Programs Branch, Health Promotion Online provides health promotion resources, including FAQs and publications about health issues, online discussion forums, a directory of health organizations, and a calendar of events.

http://www.nlm.nih.gov/
The U.S. National Library of Medicine site offers extensive health and medical information, including access to Medline and other databases, fact sheets and publications, images from the history of medicine, the Visible Human Project, and other resources.

cyber.scope

PART IV
NEW INFORMATION TECHNOLOGY AND SOCIAL INSTITUTIONS

Social institutions may change over time for many reasons. One source of change, highlighted in Chapters 15 through 20, is conflict over how social institutions ought to operate. We have highlighted debates, for example, about what kind of economy works best, how democratic our political system really is, the meaning of "the family," the role of religion in the modern world, the ways schools go about teaching young people, and how nations provide health care to their people.

Another source of change is technology. In the Information Age, all social institutions are in transition as computers and other communications equipment play a greater role in our lives. This fourth cyber.scope briefly reviews ways in which computer technology is reshaping several of the major social institutions.

The Symbolic Economy

The computer is at the centre of the new post-industrial economy. As Chapter 15 ("The Economy and Work") explained, work in the post-industrial economy is less likely to involve making *things* and more likely to involve manipulating *symbols*. Thus, gaining literacy skills is as crucial to success in the coming century as learning mechanical skills was to workers a century ago.

As the Industrial Age progressed, machines took over more and more of the manual skills performed by human workers. We might well wonder, then, if computers are destined to replace humans to perform many of the tasks that involve *thinking*. After all, the human brain is capable of only one hundred calculations per second; the most powerful computers process information a billion times faster.

Then, too, the expanding array of information available through the Internet to people with computer access may make many tradi-

As industrial production gives way to post-industrial work, fewer and fewer people are employed in factories. At the same time, new kinds of work are being invented by people clever at managing information. Tom and David Gardner started putting their views of stock market trends on the Internet and people paid attention. Soon they were in charge of a successful new business called "The Motley Fool." Of course, many new information companies don't succeed nearly this well. But the opportunities are bounded only by your imagination.

tional jobs obsolete. Will we need as many librarians when people can browse online catalogues of books? (Indeed, will we even need *libraries* as we have known them in the past?) Will there still be travel agents, when anyone can readily access flight schedules, shop for good fares, and purchase tickets as well as reserve hotel rooms and rental cars on the Internet? Even the shopping mall may lose much of its popularity in the century to come as computers purchase more products from online vendors.

Finally, computer technology seems sure to accelerate the expansion of a global economy as the Internet draws together businesses and computers into a worldwide market. Perhaps, in the computer-based economy of the twenty-first century, we will have to invent a new "virtual currency" to replace the outmoded idea of paper money.

Politics in the Information Age

Cyberspace, by its very nature, is both global and lacking centralized control. In the emerging Information Age, it is likely that the current system of dividing humanity into almost two hundred distinct nation-states will evolve into a new form. In other words, because the flow of information is unaffected by national boundaries, it makes less and less sense to think of people—who may work, shop, and communicate with others all over the world—as citizens of one geographically bounded nation.

And what effect will the global flow of information have on politics itself? By increasing the amount of available information and helping people to communicate more easily, it is reasonable to imagine that cyber-technology will be a force for political democracy. As long as computer-based communication remains free of government control, at least, how can a totalitarian political order persist?

On the other hand, should governments gain control of computer-based communication, they will have a powerful new tool for spreading propaganda and manipulating their populations. Or, more modestly, while governments bent on tyranny cannot control the global Internet, they may try to control access to computer technology within their borders. Such regulation of information would be a blow to democracy, of course. At the same time, however, any nation would pay a high price for isolating itself from the expanding world of computer-based information and trade.

Families of the Future

Over the centuries, new technology has shaped and reshaped the family. The Industrial Revolution moved work from farm and home to factories, making "the job" and "the family" separate spheres of life.

More recently, the Information Revolution is creating the opposite effect as new communications technology allows people to work at home (or, with portable computers and telephones, to work virtually anywhere). The trend towards *decentralizing* work means that, for more and more people, the line between "the office" and "the home" is disappearing.

In some respects, this trend should strengthen families, allowing parents, for example, to create more flexible work schedules and placing both fathers and mothers

New information technology is spreading ideas and images around the world as never before. These young women live in Malaysia, a relatively traditional society. How do you think the spread of culture via the Internet from Canada and other rich countries will affect the labour force, family patterns, and the desire for education in societies like this one? Will changes be for the better or worse? Why?

closer to children. Yet, in the Cyber Age, televisions and computers are playing a larger role in socializing the young. In short, families may be able to spend more time together in the coming century, but whether they will choose to do so is less certain.

Medicine and the Pursuit of Health

Just as computer technology is decentralizing work, so it is making medical care more readily available. In the years to come, many routine health checks (pulse rate, blood pressure, heart function) can be performed at home by people with computer access who transmit data via modem to specialists at medical centres.

Around the world, new information technology is making better health care available to more and more people. In North America, hospitals now rely on Internet sites to match patients and avail-

able organs, with the result of saving lives. In villages throughout poor nations, practitioners in clinics now log on to computers to consult with specialists in medical centres in the world's largest cities, gaining the information they need to provide more effective treatment. In 1995, for example, computer links were vital in helping physicians in central Africa share news, skills, and equipment while fighting the outbreak of the deadly Ebola virus.

New information technology is also making an important contribution to the lives of people with mental and physical disabilities. On one level, new computer programs allow officials to determine whether plans for new public buildings and private homes will include access to people with disabilities. On another level, specialists at numerous universities and hospitals now use computer simulations to train children to operate wheelchairs and to teach mentally retarded adults to ride the train or bus. More broadly, computers now allow people with various physical and mental limitations to enjoy and learn from virtual experiences, including travel, skiing, and even hang-gliding, that seemed impossible a generation ago (Biggs, 1996).

Institutions and Technology: Each Shaping the Other

New technology is bringing changes to all aspects of our lives. But although technology is a powerful agent of change, it does not determine the shape of society. On the contrary, technology alters the boundaries of what is possible. Therefore, *how* and even *if* we employ new information technology is an important decision that societies must make. And how we decide these questions comes back to our social institutions, which, after all, define *for whom* society should operate in the first place. ◉

Georgia Mills Jessup Rainy, *Night Downtown,* 1967

CHAPTER 21

POPULATION AND URBANIZATION

"We don't want to have children," declares Naomi Hamada, a twenty-eight-year-old Tokyo housewife. "My husband just doesn't like annoying things. And, since he won't help out raising them, I don't want kids either."

To hear his wife tell it, Mr. Hamada sounds like something of a grouch. But in today's Japan, he has a lot of company. In the city of Tokyo, with its small apartments, congested streets, living-room-sized parks, and sky-high prices, people are having fewer and fewer children. The city's birth rate, in fact, has fallen to just one child per couple—half the level necessary to replace the people alive now.

For the nation as a whole, the birth rate is only slightly higher. Should this trend continue, Japan's population will be cut in half by the end of the next century. To allay fears that the Japanese may "disappear," government officials have proposed new policies, ranging from paying cash incentives so couples will have large families to importing "mail-order" wives from the Philippines and restricting access to college and careers. Not surprisingly, such proposals have provoked a firestorm of controversy. But few are happy at the prospect of their nation's population skidding downward (Kristof, 1996).

As this chapter explains, a low birth rate is found in other industrial nations as well. But the picture is quite different in poor countries, where population is rising rapidly and cities are reaching unprecedented size. This chapter examines both population changes and urbanization, powerful forces that, together, are changing the face of our world.

DEMOGRAPHY: THE STUDY OF POPULATION

From the time the human species emerged about 200 000 B.C.E. until about 250 years ago, the population of the entire earth was only some 500 million—less than the number of Europeans today. Life for our ancestors was anything but certain; people were vulnerable to countless diseases, frequent injury, and periodic natural disasters. Looking back, one might well be amazed that our species has managed to survive for ten thousand generations.

About 1750, however, world population began to "spike" upward. We now add 80 million people to the planet each year, an increase that pushed the global total to 6 billion by 1998. Ironically, perhaps, human beings have been so successful in reproducing our species that the future well-being of humanity is again in doubt.

The causes and consequences of this growth form the core of **demography**, *the study of human population*. Demography (from the Greek, meaning "description of people") is closely related to sociology, but focuses on the size, age, and sex composition of a population as well as people's movements from place to place. Although much demographic research is quantitative, demography is more than a numbers game. The discipline poses crucial questions about the effects of population growth and how it may be controlled. The following section presents basic demographic concepts.

FERTILITY

The study of human population begins with how many people are born. **Fertility** is *the incidence of child-*

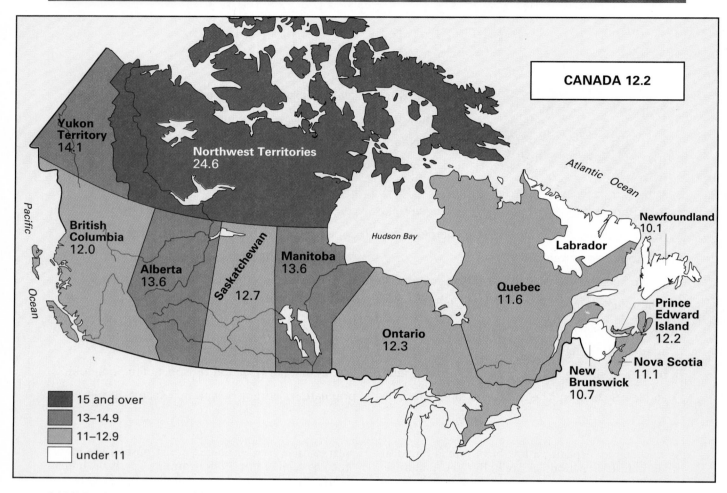

CANADA 12.2

Yukon Territory 14.1

Northwest Territories 24.6

Pacific Ocean

British Columbia 12.0

Alberta 13.6

Saskatchewan 12.7

Manitoba 13.6

Hudson Bay

Atlantic Ocean

Newfoundland 10.1

Labrador

Quebec 11.6

Ontario 12.3

Prince Edward Island 12.2

Nova Scotia 11.1

New Brunswick 10.7

15 and over
13–14.9
11–12.9
under 11

CANADA MAP 21–1   Birth Rates (by Province and Territory, 1996)

SOURCE: Data from Statistics Canada, Catalogue No. 91-213.

bearing in a country's population. Women are capable of childbearing from the onset of menstruation (typically in the early teens) to menopause (usually around fifty). During this time, a well-nourished noncontracepting woman could conceivably bear more than twenty children, but this *fecundity*, or potential childbearing, is sharply reduced for most people by health, financial concerns, cultural norms, and personal choice.

Demographers often measure fertility using the **crude birth rate**, *the number of live births in a given year for every thousand people in a population.* A crude birth rate is calculated by dividing the number of live births in a given year by a society's total population, and multiplying the result by 1000. In Canada in 1996

there were 379 295 live births in a population of 29 million. According to the formula, then, there were 12.7 live births for every thousand people, or a crude birth rate of 12.7.

This birth rate is "crude" because it is based on the entire population, not just women in their childbearing years. Making comparisons using crude birth rates can be misleading because one society may have a higher proportion of women of childbearing age than another. A crude birth rate also tells us nothing about how birth rates differ among people of various races, ethnicities, and religions. But this measure is easy to calculate and serves as a good indicator of a society's overall fertility. Figure 21–1 shows that, in

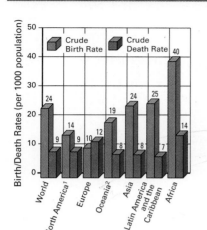
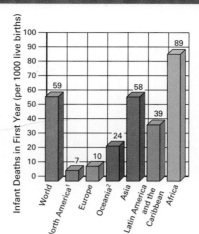
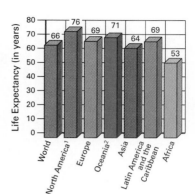

FIGURE 21–1 Crude Birth Rates and Crude Death Rates, Infant Mortality Rates, and Life Expectancy, 1997

[1] United States and Canada

[2] Australia, New Zealand, and South Pacific Islands

SOURCE: Population Reference Bureau (1997).

global perspective, the crude birth rate of North Americans is low. Canada Map 21–1 reveals that crude fertility rates within Canada vary dramatically—from a low of 10.1 in Newfoundland to a high of 24.6 in the Northwest Territories.

MORTALITY

Population size is also affected by **mortality**, the *incidence of death in a society's population*. To measure mortality, demographers use a **crude death rate**, *the number of deaths in a given year for every thousand people in a population*. The crude death rate is calculated as the number of deaths in a year divided by the total population and multiplied by 1000. In 1996, Canada's crude death rate was 7.2 per 1000 population. This rate, low by world standards, is even lower than that of the U.S. (8.8 in 1996).

A third, widely used demographic measure is the **infant mortality rate**, *the number of deaths among infants in the first year of life for each thousand live births in a given year*. This rate is derived from dividing the number of deaths of children under one year of age by the number of live births during the same year and multiplying the result by 1000. In 1996 Canada's infant mortality rate was 6.1 per 1000 live births. This is lower than the rate in the U.S. (6.7), but above that of most European and Scandinavian countries or Japan (4.4).

Like other demographic variables, this rate conceals considerable variation among segments of the Canadian population. For example, infant mortality rates are higher among the poor, in isolated communities, and among native peoples. Nonetheless, infant mortality offers a good general measure of overall quality of life and is therefore used as one indicator of socioeconomic development. The second part of Figure 21–1 shows that infant mortality in North America is low by world standards.

Societies with a low infant mortality rate have a high **life expectancy**, *the average life span of a society's population*. Canadian males born in 1996 can expect to live seventy-six years, while females can expect to live eighty-three years—three and four years longer than males and females in the United States. Life expectancy in rich, highly developed countries is about twenty years longer than it is in poor, less-developed societies, as the third part of Figure 21–1 shows.

MIGRATION

Population size is also affected by **migration**, *the movement of people into and out of a specified territory*. Migration is sometimes involuntary, as illustrated by the forcible transport of 10 million Africans to the Western Hemisphere as slaves (Sowell, 1981). Volun-

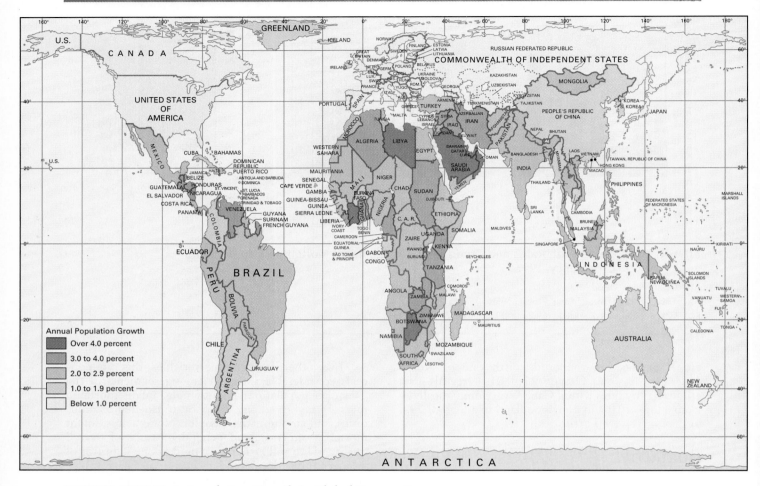

GLOBAL MAP 21–1 Population Growth in Global Perspective

The richest societies of the world—including Canada, the United States, and the nations of Europe—have growth rates below 1 percent. The nations of Latin America and Asia typically have growth rates approaching 2 percent, which double a population in thirty-five years. Africa has an overall growth rate of 2.6 percent, which cuts the doubling time to twenty-seven years. In global perspective, we see that a society's standard of living is closely related to its rate of population growth, meaning that population is rising fastest in the world regions that can least afford to support more people.

SOURCE: *Peters Atlas of the World* (1990), with statistics updated by John J. Macionis.

tary migration, however, is usually the result of complex "push-pull" factors. Dissatisfaction with life in a poor rural village may "push" people to begin the process of migration. A common "pull" factor is the attraction of a big city, where people assume opportunity is greater. As we shall explain later in this chapter, migration underlies much of rapid urban growth in less-developed countries.

The movement of people into a territory—commonly termed *immigration*—is measured as an *in-migration rate*, calculated as the number entering an area for every thousand people in the population. Movement out of a territory—or *emigration*—is measured as an *out-migration rate*, the number leaving for every thousand people. The two types of migration usually occur simultaneously; demographers describe

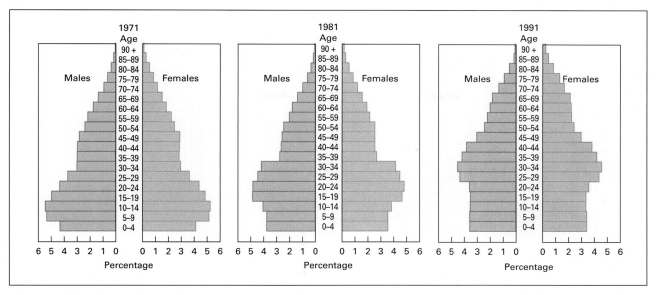

FIGURE 21–2 Age-Sex Population Pyramids for Canada, 1971–91*

* Note that, in 1971, the baby boom shows up in the 5 to 19 years age category; by 1991, the baby boom is in the 25 to 39 years age category.

SOURCE: Adapted from Statistics Canada, Catalogue No. 93-310, 1971, 1981, 1991.

the net result of in-migration and out-migration as the *net-migration rate*.

POPULATION GROWTH

Fertility, mortality, and migration all affect the size of a society's population. In general, rich nations (such as Canada) grow almost as much from immigration as from natural increase; less economically developed societies (such as Mexico) grow almost entirely from natural increase.

Demographers derive the *natural growth rate* of a population by subtracting the crude death rate from the crude birth rate. The natural growth rate of the Canadian population in 1996 was 5.5 per thousand (the crude birth rate of 12.7 minus the crude death rate of 7.2), or 0.55 percent annually. During the 1990s, demographers predict, the growth rate of the Canadian population will remain low, but this is not the case for many regions of the world, as is shown in Global Map 21–1.

Global Map 21–1 shows that population growth in Canada and other industrialized nations is well below the world average of 1.5 percent. The earth's low-growth continents include Europe (currently posting a slight decline of –0.1 percent annual growth), North America (0.6 percent), and Oceania (1.1 percent); Asia (1.6 percent) and Latin America (1.8 percent) stand slightly above the global average;

Africa (2.6 percent) is the high-growth region of the world.

Demographers have a handy rule of thumb for estimating population growth: divide a society's population growth rate into the number seventy to calculate the *doubling time* in years. Thus, annual growth of 2 percent (common in Latin America) doubles a population in thirty-five years, and a 3 percent growth rate (found in some of Africa) pares the doubling time to twenty-four years. The rapid population growth of the poorest countries is deeply troubling because they can barely support the populations they have now.

POPULATION COMPOSITION

Demographers also study the composition of a society's population at any point in time. One variable is the **sex ratio**, *the number of males for every hundred females in a given population*. In 1996 the sex ratio in Canada was 96.5 or 97 men for every 100 females. Sex ratios typically fall below 100 because, as was noted in Chapter 20 ("Health and Medicine"), women tend to outlive men. In India, however, the sex ratio is 107. There are more males than females in India because parents value sons more than daughters and may either abort a female fetus or, after birth, give more care to a male infant, raising the odds that a girl child will die.

A more complex measure is the **age-sex pyramid**, *a graphic representation of the age and sex of a population*.

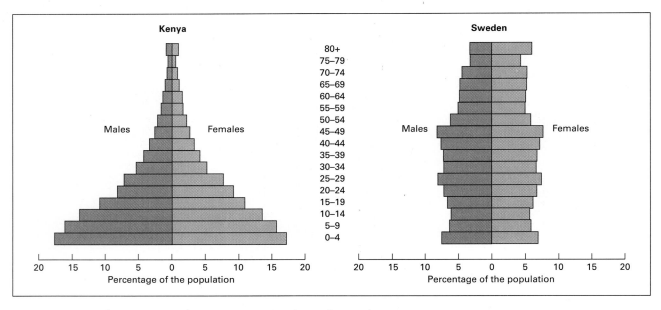

FIGURE 21–3 The Demographic Composition of Sweden and Kenya

SOURCE: Compiled by Linda Gerber from *Demographic Yearbook*.

Figure 21–2 presents the age-sex pyramids for Canada in 1971, 1981, and 1991. The left side indicates the distribution of males of different ages, while the right side shows the corresponding distribution of females. The rough pyramid shape of these figures results from higher mortality as people age. Also note that, after about age thirty, women increasingly outnumber men in Canada. The bulge that moves up the pyramid from 1971–91 represents the *baby boom* from the mid-1940s to 1970. The contraction just below age twenty shows that the baby boom was followed by a *baby bust* as the birth rate dipped from 28.2 in 1955 to a low of 12.7 in 1996. The bulges in the three pyramids in Figure 21–2 reveal the upward motion of the baby boom generation over a twenty-year period. See Figure 14–1 in Chapter 14 ("Aging and the Elderly") for projections to the year 2011.

By comparing the age-sex pyramids of two different societies, we can predict different demographic trends. Figure 21–3 compares the age-sex pyramids of a rich country, Sweden, and a poor one, Kenya. The age-sex pyramid for Kenya, like that of other low-income nations, is wide at the bottom (reflecting higher birth rates) and narrows quickly by what we would term middle age (due to higher mortality). The relatively box-like pyramid for Sweden reveals a birth rate that has long been very low, and that recently has dropped even further. With fewer women entering their childbearing years, population growth is likely to remain low. The Swedish pattern is more or less replicated by other industrial societies.

HISTORY AND THEORY OF POPULATION GROWTH

Through most of human history, people favoured large families since human labour was the key to productivity. Additionally, until the development of rubber condoms 150 years ago, preventing pregnancy was uncertain at best. But high death rates, resulting from widespread infectious diseases, put a constant brake on population growth.

As shown in Figure 21–4, a major demographic shift began about 1750 as the earth's population turned upward, reaching the one billion mark by 1800. This milestone (requiring all of human history) was repeated by 1930—barely a century later—when a second billion was added to the planet. In other words, not only did population increase, but the *rate* of growth accelerated. Global population reached three billion by 1962 (just thirty-two years later) and four billion by 1974 (a scant twelve years later). The rate of world population increase has recently slowed, but our planet passed the five billion mark in 1987 and will reach six billion before the year 2000. In no previous century did the world's population even double. In the twentieth century, it has increased *fourfold*.

Currently, global population is increasing by eighty million people each year, with 90 percent of this growth in poor societies. Looking ahead, experts predict, the earth's population will reach between eight and nine billion by 2050 (Wattenberg, 1997).

Given the world's troubles feeding its present population, such an increase has become a matter of urgent concern.

MALTHUSIAN THEORY

It was the sudden population growth two centuries ago that sparked the development of demography. Thomas Robert Malthus (1766–1834), an English clergyman and economist, warned that population increase would soon lead to social chaos.

Malthus (1926; orig. 1798) predicted that population would increase by what mathematicians call an *exponential progression*, illustrated by the series of numbers 2, 4, 8, 16, 32, and so on. At such a rate, Malthus concluded, world population would soon soar out of control.

Food production would also increase, Malthus reasoned, but only in *arithmetical progression* (as in the series 2, 3, 4, 5, 6) because, even with new agricultural technology, farmland is limited. Malthus's analysis yielded a troubling vision of the future: people reproducing beyond what the planet could feed, leading ultimately to catastrophic starvation.

Malthus acknowledged that artificial birth control or abstinence might change the equation. But he considered them either morally wrong or practically impossible. Thus, famine and war stalked humanity in Malthus's scheme, and he was justly known as "the dismal parson."

Critical evaluation. Fortunately, Malthus's prediction was flawed. By 1850 the birth rate in Europe began to drop, partly because children were becoming more of an economic liability than an asset, and partly because people *did* use birth control. Also, Malthus underestimated human ingenuity: irrigation, fertilizers, and pesticides have increased farm production far more than he imagined.

Some criticized Malthus for ignoring the role of social inequality in world abundance and famine. For example, Karl Marx (1967; orig. 1867) objected to viewing suffering as a "law of nature" rather than the curse of capitalism.

Still, we should not entirely dismiss Malthus. Habitable land, clean water, and fresh air are finite resources, and greater industrial productivity has taken a toll on the natural environment. In addition, as medical advances have lowered death rates, world population has risen even faster. Population growth is especially rapid in low-income countries, which are, in fact, experiencing much of the catastrophe Malthus envisioned.

In principle, of course, no level of population growth is sustainable indefinitely. Thus, people every-

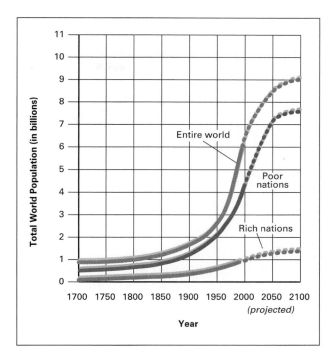

FIGURE 21–4 The Increase in World Population, 1700–2100

where must become aware of the dangers of population increase.

DEMOGRAPHIC TRANSITION THEORY

Malthus's rather crude analysis has been superseded by **demographic transition theory**, *a thesis linking demographic changes to a society's level of technological development*. Figure 21–5 shows the demographic consequences at four levels of technological development. Pre-industrial, agrarian societies—those at Stage 1—have high birth rates because of the economic value of children (many of whom will not survive until adulthood) and the lack of effective birth control. Death rates are also high, the result of low living standards and little medical technology, so that people fall victim to infectious diseases, including periodic outbursts of plague. Deaths thus neutralize births, so population rises and falls with only a modest overall increase. This was the case for thousands of years in Europe before the Industrial Revolution.

Stage 2—the onset of industrialization—brings a demographic transition as population surges. Technology expands food supplies and science combats disease. Death rates fall sharply while birth rates remain high, resulting in rapid population growth. It

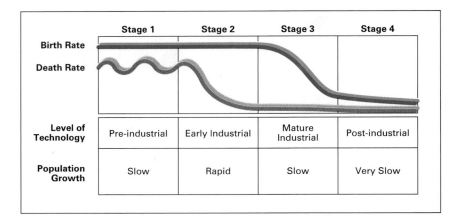

FIGURE 21-5 Demographic Transition Theory

was in a Stage 2 era that Malthus formulated his ideas, which explains his pessimistic view of the future. Most of the world's poorest countries today are in this high-growth stage.

In Stage 3—a mature industrial economy—birth rates drop, finally coming into line with death rates and, once again, curbing population growth. Fertility falls because most children survive to adulthood and rising living standards make raising children expensive. Thus, affluence transforms offspring from economic assets into economic liabilities. Smaller families, made possible by effective birth control, are also favoured by women working outside the home. As birth rates follow death rates downward, population growth slows further.

Stage 4 corresponds to a post-industrial economy. The birth rate continues to fall, partly because dual-income couples gradually become the norm and partly because the costs of raising children continue to rise. This trend, coupled with steady death rates, means that, at best, population grows only very slowly or even *decreases*. This is the case in Europe currently and, as noted in the opening to this chapter, may soon be true of Japan as well.

Critical evaluation. Demographic transition theory suggests that the key to population control lies in technology. Instead of the runaway population increase Malthus feared, this analysis foresees technology reining in population growth and ensuring material plenty.

Demographic transition theory dovetails with modernization theory, an approach to global development examined in Chapter 11 ("Global Stratification"). Modernization theorists are optimistic that poor countries will solve their population problems as they industrialize. But critics—notably dependency theorists—strongly disagree. Unless there is a significant redistribution of global resources, they maintain, our planet will become increasingly divided into industrialized "haves," enjoying low population growth, and nonindustrialized "have-nots," struggling in vain to feed soaring populations.

GLOBAL POPULATION TODAY: A BRIEF SURVEY

What demographic patterns characterize today's world? Drawing on what we have learned so far, we can highlight a number of key trends.

The Low-Growth North

When the Industrial Revolution began, population growth in Western Europe and North America peaked at 3 percent annually, doubling the population in little more than one generation. But, since then, growth rates have eased downward, dropping below 1 percent by 1970. As our post-industrial society enters Stage 4, the Canadian birth rate has fallen below the replacement level of 2.1 children per woman, a point at which we reach what demographers call **zero population growth**, *the level of reproduction that maintains population at a steady state.* Canada's fertility rate, which climbed to 3.9 during the baby boom, dropped to 1.7 between 1986 and 1991 (Hiller, 1996:37). A fertility rate that low means that, without immigration, Canada's population eventually would begin to decline.

Factors holding down population in these post-industrial societies include a high proportion of men and women in the labour force, the higher costs of raising children, and the growing number of people choosing to marry at a later age or to remain childless. Contraceptive use and voluntary sterilization have increased dramatically. Catholics, whose religious doctrine prohibits artificial birth control, no longer differ significantly from other Canadians in their con-

The Natomo family, pictured in the top photo, lives in the western African nation of Mali. The Hodson family, shown below, lives in England. What relationship do you see between a society's level of material affluence and its typical family size? Can you explain this pattern?

traceptive practices. (In fact, Quebec, which is more than 85 percent Catholic, has one of the lower fertility rates in Canada.) Abortion has been legal since 1969, and in each year in the 1990s, Canadian women have terminated more than 70 000 pregnancies in hospitals and another 20 000 in clinics.[1]

---

[1] In Canada, there is one abortion for every five live births. In the U.S. the ratio is 1 to 3.

The High-Growth South

Population growth is a critical problem in poor societies of the southern hemisphere. Only a few nations lack industrial technology altogether, placing them at demographic transition theory's Stage 1. Most of Latin America, Africa, and Asia are in Stage 2, with agrarian economies and some industry. In these nations, advanced medical technology (much supplied by rich societies) has sharply reduced death rates, but

Empowering Women:
The Key to Controlling Population Growth

Sohad Ahmad lives with her husband in a farming village fifty miles south of Cairo, Egypt's capital city. Ahmad lives a poor life, like hundreds of millions of other women in the world. Yet her situation differs in an important respect: she has had only two children and will have no more.

Why do she and her husband reject the conventional wisdom that children are an economic asset? One part of the answer is that Egypt's rising population has already created such a demand for land that her family could not afford more even if they had the children to farm it. Another part of the answer is that the Ahmads recognize that a bigger family means more bodies to feed, clothe, and house. In other words, if growing more food requires more hungry workers, how is a family better off? But the main reason is that Sohad Ahmad does not want her life defined by childbearing.

Like Sohad Ahmad, more women in Egypt are taking control of their fertility and seeking more opportunities. Indeed, this country has made great progress in reducing its annual population growth from 3.0 percent just ten years ago to 2.3 percent today. This success in reducing fertility is why the International Conference on Population and Development selected Cairo for its historic 1994 meeting.

The 1994 Cairo conference broke new ground, linking global efforts to control population to raising the standing of women. In the past, population

Dr. Nafis Sadik is in charge of United Nations efforts to monitor and control the growth of world population. In her view, success in controlling population growth depends directly on our ability to expand the opportunities for education and paid employment for women—especially in poor countries.

control programs focused on making birth control technology available to women. This is a crucial objective, since only half of the world's married women use birth control. But the larger picture shows that even when birth control is readily available, population continues to increase in societies that define women's primary responsibility as raising children.

Dr. Nafis Sadik, an Egyptian woman who heads the United Nations population control programs, sums up the new approach to lowering birth rates this way: *give women more life choices and they will have fewer children.* In other words, women with access to schooling and jobs, who can decide when and if they wish to marry, and who bear children as a matter of choice, will limit their own fertility. Schooling must be available to older women too, Dr. Sadik adds, since they often exercise great influence in local communities.

The lesson of Egypt and the Cairo conference—and mounting evidence from countries around the world—is that controlling population and raising the social standing of women are one and the same.

SOURCES: Linden (1994) and Ashford (1995).

birth rates remain high. This is why poor societies now account for two-thirds of the earth's people and 90 percent of global population increase.

In poor countries throughout the world, birth rates have fallen from an average of about six children per woman in 1950 to around four today. But even this level of increase will intensify global poverty if it continues. At a 1994 global population conference in Cairo, delegates from 180 nations agreed on the need for vigorous action to contain population growth. They also pointed out the crucial link between population control and the status of women. The "Social Diversity" box offers a closer look.

In the last decade, the world has made significant progress in lowering fertility. Yet the other half of the demographic equation—mortality—is also critical, and, worldwide, death rates are falling. Although few would oppose medical programs that save lives—mostly of children—lower death rates mean population increase. In fact, population growth in most low-income regions of the world is due *primarily* to declining death rates. Around 1920, Europe and North America began to export advances in scientific medicine, nutrition, and sanitation around the world. Since then, inoculations against infectious diseases and the use of antibiotics and insecticides have pushed down death rates with stunning effectiveness. For example, in Sri Lanka, malaria caused half of all deaths in the 1930s; a decade later, insecticides used to kill malaria-carrying mosquitoes cut the death toll from this disease in half. Although this is a great medical achievement, Sri Lanka's population began to soar. Similarly, India's infant mortality rate slid from 130 in 1975 to 74 in 1997, boosting that nation's population to one billion.

In short, in much of the world, fertility is falling. But so is mortality, especially among children. Thus, various strategies to control birth are now vital in poor countries where programs to fend off death have worked well in the past.

URBANIZATION: THE GROWTH OF CITIES

October 8, 1994, Hong Kong. The cable train grinds to the top of Victoria Peak where one of the world's most spectacular vistas awaits us: the Hong Kong harbour at night! A million bright, colourful lights ring the harbour as ships, ferries, and traditional Chinese "junks" churn by. Although the city seems almost asleep in the distance below, few settings match Hong Kong for sheer energy. This small city is as productive as the state of Wisconsin or the nation of Finland. One could sit here for hours entranced by the spectacle of Hong Kong.

For most of human history, the sights and sounds of great cities such as Hong Kong, New York, or Toronto were simply unimaginable. The world's people lived in small, nomadic groups, moving as they depleted vegetation or searched for migratory game. The small settlements that marked the emergence of civilization in the Middle East some 12 000 years ago held only a small fraction of the earth's people. Today, the largest three or four cities of the world together are home to as many people as the entire planet was then.

Urbanization is *the concentration of humanity into cities.* Urbanization both redistributes population within a society and transforms many patterns of social life. We will trace these changes in terms of three urban revolutions—the emergence of cities beginning ten thousand years ago, the development of industrial cities after 1750, and the explosive growth of cities in low-income countries today.

THE EVOLUTION OF CITIES

Cities are a relatively new development in human history. Only about 12 000 years ago did our ancestors found permanent settlements, setting the stage for the first urban revolution.

Preconditions of Cities

The first precondition of urban development is a *favourable ecology.* As glaciers drew back at the end of the last ice age, people congregated in warm regions with fertile soil. The second precondition is *advanced technology.* At about the same time, humans discovered how to domesticate animals and cultivate crops. Whereas hunting and gathering demanded continual movement, raising food required people to remain in one place (Lenski, Nolan, and Lenski, 1995). Domesticating animals and plants also yielded a *material surplus,* a third precondition for urban development. A surplus of food freed some people from concentrating on food production and allowed them to build shelters, make tools, weave clothing, and take part in religious rituals. Thus, the founding of cities was truly revolutionary, enhancing productive specialization and raising living standards as never before.

The First Cities

Historians identify Jericho as the first city. This settlement lies to the north of the Dead Sea in disputed land currently occupied by Israel. About 8000 B.C.E., Jericho contained about 600 people. By 4000 B.C.E., it was one of numerous cities flourishing in the Fertile Crescent between the Tigris and Euphrates rivers in present-day Iraq and, by 3000 B.C.E., along the Nile River in Egypt.

Some cities, with populations reaching fifty thousand, became centres of urban empires. Priest-kings wielded absolute power over lesser nobles, administrators, artisans, soldiers, and farmers. Slaves, captured in frequent military campaigns, laboured to build monumental structures such as the pyramids of Egypt (Kenyon, 1957; Hamblin, 1973; Stavrianos, 1983; Lenski, Nolan, and Lenski, 1995).

In at least three other areas of the world, cities developed independently. Several large, complex settlements bordered the Indus River in present-day Pakistan starting about 2500 B.C.E. Scholars date Chinese cities from 2000 B.C.E. And in Central and South America, urban centres began around 1500 B.C.E. In North America, only a few Native-American societies formed settlements; widespread urbanization did not take root here until the arrival of European settlers in the seventeenth century (Lamberg-Karlovsky, 1973; Change, 1977; Coe and Diehl, 1980).

Mont St. Michel, a French town that rises against the Atlantic Ocean, is a wonderful example of a medieval settlement: small and walled, with narrow, irregular streets that, even today, make walking seem like a delightful stroll back in time.

Pre-industrial European Cities

Urbanization in Europe began about 1800 B.C.E. on the Mediterranean island of Crete. Cities soon spread throughout Greece, resulting in more than one hundred city-states, of which Athens is the most famous. During its Golden Age, lasting barely a century after 500 B.C.E., some 300 000 people living within scarcely one square mile made lasting contributions to the Western way of life in philosophy, the arts, and politics. Yet Athenian society rested on the labour of slaves, who comprised one-third of the population. Their democratic principles notwithstanding, Athenian men denied the rights of citizenship to women and foreigners (Mumford, 1961; Gouldner, 1965; Stavrianos, 1983).

As Greek civilization faded, the city of Rome grew to almost one million inhabitants and became the centre of a vast empire. By the first century C.E., the militaristic Romans had subdued much of northern Africa, Europe, and the Middle East. In the process, Rome spread its language, arts, and technology. Four centuries later, the Roman Empire fell into disarray, a victim of its gargantuan size, internal corruption, and militaristic appetite. Yet, between them, the Greeks and Romans had founded cities across Europe, from the Atlantic Ocean all the way to Asia, including Vienna, Paris, London, and Istanbul.

The fall of the Roman Empire initiated an era of urban decline and stagnation lasting six hundred years. Cities became smaller as people drew back within defensive walls and competing warlords battled for territory. About the eleventh century, the "Dark Ages" came to an end as a semblance of peace allowed trade to bring life to cities once again.

Expanding trade prompted medieval cities to tear down their walls. Beneath the towering cathedrals, the narrow and winding streets of London, Brussels, and Florence soon teemed with merchants, artisans, priests, peddlers, jugglers, nobles, and servants. Typically, occupational groups such as bakers, keymakers, and carpenters clustered together in distinct sections or "quarters." Ethnic groups also inhabited their own neighbourhoods, often because people kept them out of other districts. The term *ghetto* (from the Italian word *borghetto*, meaning "outside the city walls") first described the segregation of Jews in medieval Venice.

Industrial European Cities

Throughout the Middle Ages, steadily increasing commerce enriched a new urban middle class or *bourgeoisie* (from the French meaning "of the town"). By the fifteenth century, the power of the bourgeoisie rivalled that of the hereditary nobility.

By about 1750, industrialization was well under way, triggering a *second urban revolution*, first in Europe and then in North America. Factories unleashed tremendous productive power, causing cities to grow to unprecedented sizes. London, the largest European city, swelled from 550 000 people in 1700 to 6.5 million by 1900 (A. Weber, 1963, orig. 1899; Chandler and Fox, 1974).

Cities not only grew but changed shape. Broad, straight boulevards replaced older irregular streets to accommodate the flow of commercial traffic and, eventually, motor cars. Steam and electric trolleys, too, crisscrossed the expanding cities. Lewis Mumford (1961) adds that, because land was a commodity to be bought and sold, developers divided cities into regular-sized lots. Before long, city life no longer revolved around the cathedrals; instead, bustling central business districts arose, filled with banks, retail stores, and ever-taller office buildings.

As cities focused on business, they became increasingly crowded and impersonal. Crime rates rose. Especially at the outset, a small number of industrialists lived in grand style, while for most men, women, and children, factory work proved exhausting and provided bare subsistence.

Organized efforts by workers to improve their plight led to legal regulation of the workplace, better housing, and the right to vote. Public services such as water, sewage, and electricity further enhanced urban living. Today some urbanites still live in poverty, but a rising standard of living has partly fulfilled the city's historical promise of a better life.

THE GROWTH OF NORTH AMERICAN CITIES

Most of the native North Americans who inhabited this continent over tens of thousands of years were migratory peoples, so there were few permanent settlements. Large numbers of villages and towns first sprang up as a product of European colonization. The Spanish made an initial settlement at St. Augustine, Florida, in 1565, and the English founded Jamestown, Virginia, in 1607. Samuel de Champlain founded a trading post at Québec in 1608. New Amsterdam, later called New York, was established by the Dutch in 1624, Montreal was founded by Maisonneuve in 1642, Halifax was founded in 1749 by the British (to counter the French influence in North America) and York (now Toronto) was founded in 1793 by John Graves Simcoe in a location where it could be protected from American invasion.

These tentative intrusions onto Indian lands were accompanied by an expanded fur trade, an invasion of rural settlers, colonial expansion, and a struggle for control over lands involving natives, the British, and the French—all of which led to massive immigration and gradual urbanization. By 1990, the United States contained 195 cities with a population of more than 100 000, while, according to the 1991 census, Canada had 35 cities of that size—and both countries have more than three-quarters of their populations living in areas that are designated as urban. How we became an urban society is explained in the brief history that follows.

Colonial Settlement in North America: 1624–1800

New York and Boston started out as tiny villages in a vast wilderness. Dutch New Amsterdam at the tip of Manhattan Island (1624) and English Boston (1630) developed along the lines of medieval towns of Europe, with narrow, winding streets that still curve through lower Manhattan and downtown Boston. New Amsterdam was walled on its north side, the site

TABLE 21–1 The Urban Population of Canada, 1871–1996

Year	Population (000s)	% Urban
1871	3,689	19.6
1881	4,325	25.7
1891	4,833	31.8
1901	5,371	37.5
1911	7,207	45.4
1921	8,788	49.5
1931	10,377	52.7
1941	11,507	54.5
1951	14,009	62.9
1961	18,238	69.6
1971	21,568	76.1
1981	24,343	75.7
1991	27,297	76.6
1996	28,847	77.9

SOURCE: Colombo (1998:42); Artibise and Stelter (1988).

of today's Wall Street. Boston, the largest colonial settlement, had a population of only 7000 in 1700.

Capitalism would soon transform these quiet villages into thriving towns with wide streets, usually built on a grid pattern. Figure 21–6 contrasts the traditional shape of colonial New Amsterdam with the regular design of Philadelphia, founded in 1680 after an additional half-century of economic development.

Toronto (York) was founded on July 30, 1793, by John Graves Simcoe, commander of the Queen's Rangers and later the first lieutenant-governor of Upper Canada. Montreal was already a bustling city of over 5500 by that time, but in Upper Canada there were only about fifteen settler families between Burlington Bay and the Bay of Quinte—a distance of 200 kilometres (Benn, 1993).

Simcoe's intent was to move the capital from its vulnerable location near Niagara Falls to one from which an American invasion could more easily be repelled. He also wanted to establish a civilian community and a naval base. The map of York Harbour in Figure 21–7 shows the location of "the Garrison" (now called Fort York) and the settlement of York. The grid-like settlement plan (similar to that of Philadelphia in Figure 21–6) is near the area where Toronto's St. Lawrence Market stands today (Benn, 1993). The north–south lines above Queen Street mark the parcels of land that Simcoe granted to some of his regimental comrades and others in an effort to entice them to settle in York as a local aristocracy. The members of that "Family Compact" dominated Upper Canada until the 1830s; the lines separating their land allotments still show up as major north–south arteries on Toronto road maps.

Even as the first settlements grew, North America remained overwhelmingly rural. In 1790 the

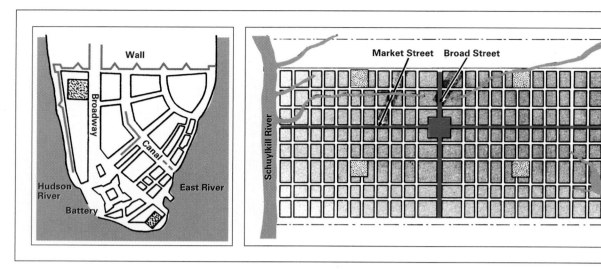

FIGURE 21–6 The Street Plans of Colonial New Amsterdam (New York) and Philadelphia

The plan of colonial New Amsterdam, shown at left, reflects the pre-industrial urban pattern of walls enclosing a city of narrow, irregular streets. Colonial Philadelphia, founded fifty years later, reflects the industrial urban pattern of accessible cities containing wide, regularly spaced, parallel and perpendicular streets to facilitate economic activity.

United States government's first census counted a national population of only four million, a scant 5 percent of whom lived in cities. Around the time of Confederation in Canada (1867), the U.S. population of about forty million was 20 percent urban, while Canada's population of about three million was almost as urban at 18 percent. The vast majority of people in both countries lived on farms and small villages. The small Canada–U.S. gap in levels of urbanization essentially disappeared by 1940 and, today, Canada has inched ahead of the U.S. (77 and 75 percent urban, respectively). Table 21–1 shows Canada's population growth and levels of urbanization from its first post-Confederation census to the present.

Urban Expansion

Early in the nineteenth century, towns sprang up across the North American continent—somewhat later in Canada than in the United States. Waterways as well as new roads and railway lines encouraged the growth of these towns and cities. British Columbia agreed to enter into Confederation in 1871 on the condition that a transcontinental railway would be completed within ten years. The last spike was not driven until 1885, but the Canadian Pacific Railway (CPR) gave a powerful boost to settlement and economic development, especially in towns and cities located on the railway line itself. Calgary was incor-

porated as a town in 1884 (one year after the arrival of the CPR) and by 1891 had a population of 3876; it became a city two years later.

Interestingly, urbanization took hold at different rates in various sectors of the continent. The Industrial Revolution proceeded far more rapidly in the northern states than in the American South, which experienced limited urbanization. By the time of the Civil War, New York City's population was ten times that of Charleston. The division of the United States into the industrial-urban North and the agrarian-rural South was a major cause of the Civil War (Schlesinger, 1969). In Canada, Ontario, and to a lesser extent Quebec, urbanized more rapidly than the Atlantic or Prairie provinces. Complaints about the political and economic power of industrialized central Canada (that is, Ontario and Quebec) have been common in the rest of the country and sometimes lead to talk of the separation of eastern or western provinces. Quebec has not had a monopoly on such sentiments.

By 1920 and 1931, respectively, American and Canadian censuses revealed that more than 50 percent of their populations were living in cities. To some, increased urbanization constituted progress towards better living, but others mourned the gradual passing of traditional agrarian life. Over time, rural-urban tensions grew more pronounced, with adversaries trading negative stereotypes that pitted "ignorant country cousins" against "shady city slickers" (Callow, 1969).

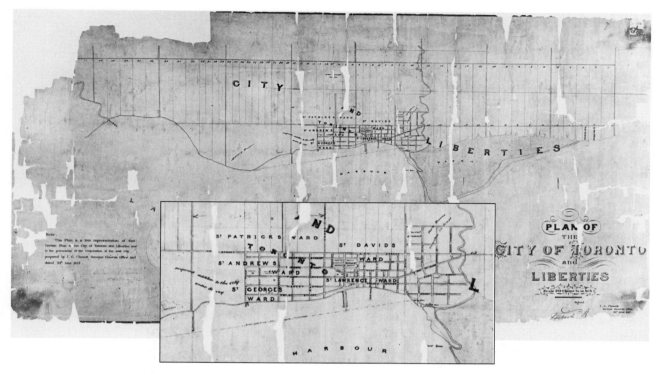

FIGURE 21–7 Map of York (Toronto), 1793

York was designed on a grid pattern as a temporary capital for Upper Canada. It was located on a protected bay where it could be shielded from potential attack by Americans.

The Great Metropolis

The American Civil War (1861–65) gave an enormous boost to industrialization in the U.S., as factories strained to produce the instruments of combat. Much later the First and Second World Wars stimulated war-related production in both Canada and the United States. These only added to structural economic changes that were encouraging rural-urban migration and paving the way for huge waves of immigrants, mostly from Europe. Throughout North America, tens of millions of newcomers were blending their various ways of life into the dynamic new urban mix.

As the Industrial Revolution picked up momentum, cities teemed with unprecedented numbers of people. In 1901 Montreal had a population of about 400 000, and Toronto was approaching 200 000. By 1991, Montreal and Toronto had grown to one million and 635 000, respectively. Table 21–2 ranks the ten largest Canadian cities in 1966 and 1996, indicating considerable change over time: only Montreal and Edmonton retain their ranks—first and fifth—over the thirty-year period involved.

The dizzying growth and concentration of population marked the coming of the **metropolis,** *a large city that socially and economically dominates the surrounding area.* This development began before 1900 in the U.S. and perhaps forty years later in Canada. The current Canadian definition of a Census Metropolitan Area (CMA) involves a population of at least 100 000 spread out among one or more municipalities with economic and commuting ties. These metropolises, and their counterparts in the U.S., became the manufacturing, commercial, and residential centres of North America.

As their populations grew, the physical shape of the metropolis continued to change as well. In 1850, few buildings could be found that exceeded three or four storeys. By the 1880s, industrial technology was producing steel girders and mechanical elevators so that builders were raising structures ten storeys above the ground. And this, of course, was only the beginning. In 1975, Toronto's CN Tower was completed. At 553.3 m, it is still the world's tallest free-standing structure. City centres contain these kinds of monuments as well as clusters of soaring buildings of glass, concrete, and steel, while public transit and roadways

TABLE 21–2 The Ten Largest Cities in Canada, 1966 and 1996 (Population in Thousands)

Rank	1966 City	Population	1996 City	Population
1	Montreal	1222.3	Montreal	1016.4
2	Toronto	664.6	Calgary	768.1
3	Vancouver	410.4	Toronto*	653.8
4	North York	399.5	Winnipeg	618.5
5	Edmonton	376.9	Edmonton	616.3
6	Calgary	330.6	North York*	589.7
7	Hamilton	298.1	Scarborough*	559.0
8	Ottawa	290.7	Vancouver	514.1
9	Scarborough	278.4	Mississauga	544.4
10	Winnipeg	257.0	Ottawa	323.3

* As of 1998, the Ontario government amalgamated a number of smaller cities surrounding Toronto (East York, Etobicoke, North York, Scarborough, and York) into the city of Toronto.

SOURCE: Statistics Canada, Catalogue No. 93-305; Colombo (1998)

The majority of Canada's urban population lives in suburban areas. While subdivisions such as the one pictured here provide desirable single-family dwellings, they can also have negative effects. Declining populations in central cities have reduced the tax base to fund city operations and social programs. As well, new housing construction often takes place at the expense of the environment, including loss of wilderness and agricultural land.

allow for lower-density city sprawl that stretches for miles.

Canada has twenty-five CMAs, ranging in size from Toronto at over 4 million population to Thunder Bay, Ontario, at 125 500 (see Table 21–3).

Urban Decentralization

The industrial metropolis reached its peak in about 1950 in the United States and in 1975 in Canada. Since then, something of a turnaround has occurred as people have deserted downtown areas in a process known as urban decentralization (Edmonston and Guterbock, 1984). Some of the largest cities stopped growing or actually lost population between 1976 and 1981, while a few showed further decline by 1986. But decentralization has not brought an end to urbanization: on the contrary, cities are evolving into a different form. In addition to our densely populated central cities, we now have vast urban regions encompassing expanded suburbs. Together, these city cores and their outlying suburban areas form metropolitan areas.

SUBURBS AND CENTRAL CITIES

Just as central cities flourished a century ago, we have recently witnessed the expansion of **suburbs**, *urban areas beyond the political boundaries of a city.* About a century ago, well-to-do people, imitating the pattern of the European nobility who shuttled between their town houses and country estates, became the first suburbanites (Baltzell, 1979). The popularity of suburbs also reflected racial and ethnic prejudice, as urbanites

fled central cities filled with immigrants for exclusive neighbourhoods beyond the financial reach of the masses.

During the economic boom of the late 1940s, less wealthy people also came to view a single-family house on its own piece of leafy suburban ground as the ideal lifestyle. The mobility provided by increasingly affordable automobiles made this dream come true for more and more people. After World War II, men and women eagerly returned to family life, igniting the baby boom described earlier in this chapter. Since central cities offered little space for new housing construction, suburbs blossomed almost overnight.

Today, well over half of Canada's urbanites live in municipalities outside the central cities, or in newer central cities, like those on the Prairies, which are largely suburban in style. As a result of the overall flight to the suburbs by young families and the fact that more people are living alone in their downtown homes, even vigorous construction in the central cities has not been sufficient to stem the decline in some central city populations (Michelson, 1988:86).[2] As population decentralized, businesses also began to migrate to the suburbs. Older people today can recall trips "downtown" to shop but, by the 1970s, the suburban mall had replaced "main

---

[2] The population of Toronto declined between 1976 and 1981, regained its losses by 1991, and increased more by 1996.

TABLE 21-3 Population of Census Metropolitan Areas* in Canada, 1956–96

	1956	1976	1996	Land Area (sq. km) 1996
Calgary, Alta	201,022	469,917	821,628	5083.28
Chicoutimi, Que.	90,987	128,643	160,454	1723.31
Edmonton, Alta	254,800	554,228	862,597	9536.63
Halifax, N.S.	164,200	267,991	332,518	2503.10
Hamilton, Ont.	338,294	529,371	624,360	1358.50
Kitchener, Ont.	128,772	272,158	382,940	823.64
London, Ont.	154,453	270,383	398,616	2105.07
Montreal, Que.	1,745,001	2,802,485	3,326,510	4024.21
Oshawa, Ont.	62,823	135,196	268,773	894.19
Ottawa-Hull, Ont./Que.	345,460	693,288	1,010,498	5686.45
Québec, Que.	311,604	542,158	671,889	3149.65
Regina, Sask.	89,755	151,191	193,652	3421.58
St. Catharines–Niagara, Ont.	85,025	301,921	372,406	1399.80
St. John's, Nfld	79,153	143,390	174,051	789.66
Saint John, N.B.	86,015	112,974	125,705	3509.34
Saskatoon, Sask.	72,858	133,750	219,056	5322.09
Sherbrooke, Que.	61,817	104,505	147,384	979.94
Sudbury, Ont.	97,945	157,030	160,488	2612.11
Thunder Bay, Ont.	N.A.	119,253	125,562	2295.27
Toronto, Ont.	1,502,253	2,803,101	4,263,757	5867.73
Trois-Rivières, Que.	75,446	98,583	139,956	871.91
Vancouver, B.C.	665,017	1,166,348	1,831,665	2820.66
Victoria, B.C.	133,829	218,250	304,287	633.44
Windsor, Ont.	185,865	247,582	278,685	861.66
Winnipeg, Man.	412,248	578,217	667,209	4077.64

* Census Metropolitan Areas are defined by Statistics Canada as very large urban areas together with neighbouring urban and rural areas that have a high degree of social and economic integration. Population is based on CMA boundaries at the time of each census.

N.A. = not available, as these areas had not yet reached the critical 100 000 population level.

SOURCE: *Census of Canada;* Colombo (1998:54).

street" as the centre of retail trade. Manufacturing interests, too, began to eye the suburbs where there was relief from high taxes, escalating property costs, and traffic congestion.

Decentralization was not good news for everyone, however. Rapid suburban growth meant financial difficulties for the older central cities. Population decline meant reduced tax revenues. Furthermore, cities that lost affluent residents to the suburbs were left to provide expensive social programs for the poor who remained.

In 1953, in response to this disparity between the core of the city and outlying areas, the Province of Ontario created "Metropolitan Toronto" by combining the central city of Toronto with twelve of its suburbs. The province had to impose the solution initially, as none of the municipalities was exactly enamoured of the prospect. But, as a result of the success of Metropolitan Toronto, other urban regions across Canada have followed suit. Note that the creation of the new city of Toronto through the amalgamation of six cities is distinct from the creation of metropolitan areas.

The benefits of this model of urban development are clear when we compare Canada's situation to that of the United States. Since American cities rarely adopt a metropolitan-type government, they tend to suffer much more from decaying inner cities. "Canadian metropolitan areas suffer fewer of the glaring contrasts in welfare, infrastructure, and supportive services differentiating American central cities and suburbs" (Michelson, 1988:97).

When several adjacent metropolitan regions get so large that they bump up against each other and form a continuous urban band, they form what is called a **megalopolis**, *a vast urban region containing a number of cities and their surrounding suburbs.* Gottman (1961) first coined the term *megalopolis* in reference to the area between and including Boston and Washington. In Canada, our closest equivalent is the area known as the Golden Horseshoe, which stretches from Oshawa in the east, through Toronto, and west to St. Catharines; the Windsor–Quebec City corridor forms another, looser version. The political and economic dominance of this region is quite apparent from the fact that the Golden Horseshoe alone con-

TABLE 21–4 Net Interprovincial Migration* in Canada, 1956–96

	Nfld	PEI	NS	NB	Que	Ont	Man	Sask	Alta	BC
1957–1961	–4,671	–1,099	–15,295	–5,270	–7,756	34,345	–15,957	–33,557	16,787	33,230
1962–1966	–15,213	–2,969	–27,124	–25,680	–19,859	85,369	–23,471	–42,094	–1,983	77,747
1967–1971	–19,344	–2,763	–16,396	–19,599	–122,736	150,712	–40,690	–81,399	32,005	114,964
1972–1976	–1,857	3,754	11,307	16,801	–77,610	–38,560	–26,827	–40,752	58,571	92,285
1977–1981	–18,983	–829	–7,140	–10,351	–156,496	–57,826	–42,218	–9,716	186,364	122,625
1982–1986	–15,051	751	6,895	–65	–81,254	121,767	–2,634	–2,974	–31,676	7,382
1987–1991	–15,282	–885	–5,302	–3,798	–39,934	68,730	–35,417	–63,155	–43,282	141,077
1992–1996	–26,937	3,045	–6,803	–3,080	–50,114	–38,440	–19,203	–18,385	3,499	157,750

* The number of persons moving into a province minus the number of persons moving out of that province.

SOURCE: Statistics Canada data from Colombo (1992; 1998).

tains about one-third of Canada's population, while the larger Windsor–Quebec City corridor contains about one-half.

INTER-REGIONAL POPULATION MOVEMENT

Any country, but particularly any large country, is likely to experience population shifts from one of its regions to another. In the United States, the major shift is taking population from the cities of the northeast and the midwest and redistributing it in the south. Southern cities such as San Diego, San Antonio, and Phoenix are growing rapidly, while cities in the north such as Detroit, Chicago, and Baltimore are losing population.

Canada—alas—does not have a sunbelt, but that does not stop us from moving from one part of the country to another in search of opportunities. Table 21–4 shows the net gains and losses through interprovincial migration for each province in each five-year period between 1956 and 1996. When Canadians move from one province to another, it tends to be directly related to economic conditions. This was most apparent from 1976–81 when the resource boom in Alberta caused a large influx there from other provinces. But falling international oil prices in the early 1980s led to a reversal of this trend as Canadians moved east, especially to Ontario.

In some parts of the country, the losses are consistent and large: the Atlantic provinces, overall, lost population in every five-year period except 1971–76. Quebec lost population in every period, but most dramatically in 1966–71 and 1976–81. The separatist Parti Québécois was elected in 1976 and in 1977 passed Bill 101, making French the language of business and restricting English-language schooling. Several head offices moved out of Montreal at that time, an outflow of anglophones took place, and real estate prices plummeted.

As Table 21–4 shows, Manitoba and Saskatchewan suffered consistent losses, while Ontario and Alberta lost in some periods and gained in others. In recent years, those moving to another province have tended to head to British Columbia. The only province to show consistent gains in every five-year interval, B.C. is the equivalent of our sunbelt in that there is lifestyle and retirement migration taking place, with British Columbia as the destination.

URBANISM AS A WAY OF LIFE

Early sociologists in Europe and the United States focused a great deal of attention on the rise of cities. We will briefly present their accounts of urbanism as a way of life.

FERDINAND TOENNIES: GEMEINSCHAFT AND GESELLSCHAFT

In the late nineteenth century, the German sociologist Ferdinand Toennies studied how life in the new industrial metropolis differed from life in traditional rural settings. From this contrast, he developed two concepts that have become an established part of sociology's terminology.

Toennies (1963; orig. 1887) used the German word ***Gemeinschaft*** (roughly meaning "community") to refer to *a type of social organization in which people are bound closely together by kinship and tradition*. The *Gemeinschaft* of the rural village, Toennies explained, joins people into what amounts to a single primary group.

By and large, argued Toennies, *Gemeinschaft* is absent in the modern city. On the contrary, urbanization enhances ***Gesellschaft*** (roughly meaning "association"), *a type of social organization in which people come together only on the basis of individual self-interest*. As part of *Gesellschaft*, individuals are motivated by their own needs and desires rather than by a desire to advance

The painting Peasant Dance *(c.1565), by Pieter Breughel the Elder, conveys the essential unity of rural life forged by generations of kinship and neighbourhood. By contrast, Fernand Léger's* The City *(1919) communicates the disparate images and discontinuity of experience that are commonplace in urban areas. Taken together, these paintings capture Toennies's distinction between* Gemeinschaft *and* Gesellschaft.

Pieter Breughel the Elder (c. 1525/30–1569), *Peasant Dance*, c. 1565, Kunsthistorisches Museum, Vienna/Superstock. Fernand Léger, *The City*, 1919, oil on canvas, Philadelphia Museum of Art, A. E. Gallatin Collection.

the well-being of everyone. City dwellers display little sense of community and look to others mostly as the means of achieving their individual goals. Thus Toennies saw in urbanization the erosion of close, enduring social relations in favour of the fleeting and temporary ties typical of business.

EMILE DURKHEIM: MECHANICAL AND ORGANIC SOLIDARITY

The French sociologist Emile Durkheim (see Chapter 4, "Society") agreed with much of Toennies's thinking about cities. But Durkheim did not think urban people lacked social bonds, but that they simply organize social life differently than rural people do.

Durkheim described traditional, rural life as *mechanical solidarity*, social bonds based on common sentiments and shared moral values. Durkheim's concept of mechanical solidarity, with its emphasis on conformity to tradition, bears a striking similarity to Toennies's *Gemeinschaft*.

Urbanization erodes mechanical solidarity, Durkheim explained, but it also generates a new type of bonding, which he termed *organic solidarity*, social bonds based on specialization and interdependence. This concept parallels Toennies's *Gesellschaft*, but there is a key difference between the two thinkers. Both thought the expansion of industry and cities would undermine traditional social patterns, but Durkheim took a more optimistic view of this historical transformation. Where societies had been built on

likeness, Durkheim observed, social organization was now based on *difference*.

For Durkheim, urban society offers more individual choice, moral tolerance, and personal privacy than people find in rural villages. In short, Durkheim concluded, something may be lost in the process of urbanization, but much is gained.

GEORG SIMMEL: THE BLASÉ URBANITE

German sociologist Georg Simmel (1858–1918) offered a microanalysis of cities, studying how urban life shapes people's attitudes and behaviour. According to Simmel, individuals experience the city as a crush of people, objects, and events. To prevent being overwhelmed by all this stimulation, urbanites develop a *blasé attitude*, tuning out much of what goes on around them. Such detachment does not mean that city dwellers lack compassion for others, although they may sometimes seem "cold and heartless." Rather, as Simmel saw it, a blasé attitude is simply a strategy for social survival by which people devote their time and energy to what really matters to them.

OBSERVING THE CITY: THE CHICAGO SCHOOL

Sociologists in the United States (there were no sociology departments in Canada yet) soon joined their European colleagues in exploring the rapidly growing cities. The first major sociology program in the

United States took root at the University of Chicago. In the late nineteenth century, Chicago was a major metropolis bursting with population and cultural diversity. Chicago's social life was the focus for generations of sociologists, who provided a rich understanding of many dimensions of urban life. The work of the Chicago School had a major impact on Canadian urban sociologists.

Robert Park, a leader of the Chicago School, sought to give urban studies a street-level perspective by studying real cities. He found the city to be an organized mosaic of distinctive ethnic communities, commercial centres, and industrial districts. Over time, he observed, these "natural areas" develop and change in relation to each other. To Park, then, the city was a living organism—a human kaleidoscope.

Another major figure in the Chicago School of urban sociology was Louis Wirth (1897–1952). Wirth (1938) is best known for blending the ideas of Toennies, Simmel, Park, and others into a comprehensive theory of urban life. Wirth began by identifying the city as a setting with a large, dense, and socially diverse population. These features, he argued, make urban life impersonal, superficial, and transitory. Sharing the teeming streets, urbanites have contact with many more people than rural residents. Thus, if city residents notice others at all, they know them not in terms of *who they are* but *what they do*: bus driver, florist, or grocery store clerk, for instance.

Specialized, urban relationships are sometimes quite pleasant for all concerned. But we should remember that self-interest rather than friendship is the main reason for the interaction. Finally, limited interpersonal involvement and great social diversity make city dwellers more tolerant than rural villagers. Rural communities often jealously maintain their narrow traditions, but the heterogeneous population of a city rarely shares any single code of moral conduct (T. Wilson, 1985, 1995).

Critical evaluation. Both in Europe and in the United States, early sociologists presented a mixed view of urban living. On the one hand, rapid urbanization was troubling. Toennies and Wirth, especially, saw the personal ties and traditional morality of rural life lost in the anonymous rush of the city. On the other hand, Durkheim and Park emphasized urbanism's positive face, including greater personal autonomy and a wider range of life choices.

What about Wirth's specific claims about urbanism as a way of life? Decades of research support only some of his conclusions. Wirth was correct in thinking that, compared to rural areas, cities have a weaker sense of local community. But conflict is found in the countryside as well as in the city. Furthermore, while urbanites treat most people impersonally, they also

typically welcome such privacy and maintain close personal relationships with select others, often not their neighbours (Keller, 1968; Cox, 1971; Macionis, 1978; Wellman, 1979; Lee et al., 1984).

Another problem is that Wirth and others painted urbanism in broad strokes that overlook the effects of class, race, and gender. There are many kinds of urbanites: rich and poor, white and Black, women and men—all leading distinctive lives (Gans, 1968). In fact, cities often intensify social differences; that is, we see the extent of social diversity most clearly in cities where different categories of people live in close proximity (Macionis and Parrillo, 1998).

URBAN ECOLOGY

Sociologists (especially members of the Chicago School) also developed **urban ecology**, *the study of the link between the physical and social dimensions of cities*. Consider, for example, why cities are located where they are. The first cities emerged in fertile regions where the environment favoured raising crops and, thus, settlement. Pre-industrial societies, concerned with defence, built their cities on mountains (Athens was situated on an outcropping of rock) or surrounded by water (Paris and Mexico City were founded on islands). After the Industrial Revolution, the unparallelled importance of economics led to the founding of cities near rivers and natural harbours that facilitated trade.

Urban ecologists also study the physical design of cities. In 1925, Ernest W. Burgess described land use in Chicago in terms of *concentric zones* that look rather like a bull's-eye. City centres, Burgess observed, are business districts bordered by a ring of factories, followed by residential rings with housing that becomes more expensive the farther it stands from the noise and pollution of the city's centre.

Homer Hoyt (1939) refined Burgess's observations by noting that distinctive districts sometimes form *wedge-shaped sectors*. For example, one fashionable area may develop next to another along a major road, or an industrial district may extend outward from a city's centre along a railroad line.

Chauncy Harris and Edward Ullman (1945) added yet another insight: as cities decentralize, they lose their single-centre form in favour of a *multicentred model*. As cities grow, residential areas, industrial parks, and shopping districts typically push away from one another. Few people wish to live close to industrial areas, for example, so the city becomes a mosaic of distinct districts.

Social area analysis investigates what people in specific neighbourhoods have in common. Three factors seem to explain most of the variation—family pat-

Every year, some 90 million people are added to the earth's population. Do you think this rate of growth can be sustained? What are the likely consequences of continuing population increase for the future of our planet?

terns, social class, and race and ethnicity (Shevky and Bell, 1955; Johnston, 1976). Families with children gravitate to areas with large apartments or single-family homes and good schools. The rich generally seek high-prestige neighbourhoods, often in the central city near cultural attractions. People with a common social heritage tend to cluster in distinctive communities.

Finally, Brian Berry and Philip Rees (1969) tie together many of these insights. They explain that distinct family types tend to settle in the concentric zones described by Ernest Burgess. Specifically, households with few children tend to cluster towards the city's centre, while those with more children live farther away. Social class differences are primarily responsible for the sector-shaped districts described by Homer Hoyt because, for instance, the rich occupy one "side of the tracks" and the poor, the other. And racial and ethnic neighbourhoods are found at various points throughout the city, consistent with Harris and Ullman's multicentred model.

Critical evaluation. After almost a century of research, urban ecologists have succeeded in linking the physical and social dimensions of urban life. But, as the researchers themselves concede, their conclusions paint an overly simplified picture of urban life. Critics chime in that urban ecology errs to the extent that it implies that cities take shape simply from the choices ordinary people make. Rather, they assert, urban development responds more to powerful elites than to ordinary citizens (Molotch, 1976; Feagin, 1983).

A final criticism holds that urban ecologists have studied only North American cities during a single historical period. Little of what we have learned about industrial cities applies to pre-industrial towns; similarly, even among industrial cities, socialist settlements differ from their capitalist counterparts. In sum, there is good reason to doubt that any single ecological model will account for the full range of urban diversity.

URBAN POLITICAL ECONOMY

As urban problems—rioting, crime, poverty, and unemployment—proliferated, most visibly in the United States, some analysts turned away from the ecological approach to a social-conflict understanding of city life. Urban political economy is influenced by the thinking of Karl Marx, although the scene of social conflict shifts from the workplace to the city (Lindstrom, 1995).

The ecological approach of the Chicago School sociologists saw the city as a "natural" organism, with particular districts and neighbourhoods developing according to an internal logic. Political economists disagree, claiming that city life is defined mostly by people with power: corporate leaders and the political elite. In Canada, U.S. multinational corporations, foreign investors, and the global capitalist system are seen as important players as well. These powerholders make the economic and political decisions that determine the location, size, shape, and character of major cities.

For example, deindustrialization of the Maritime provinces and shifts in political and economic clout up the St. Lawrence River to Montreal and then to Toronto caused an inordinate concentration of capital, industry, population, and political power in southern

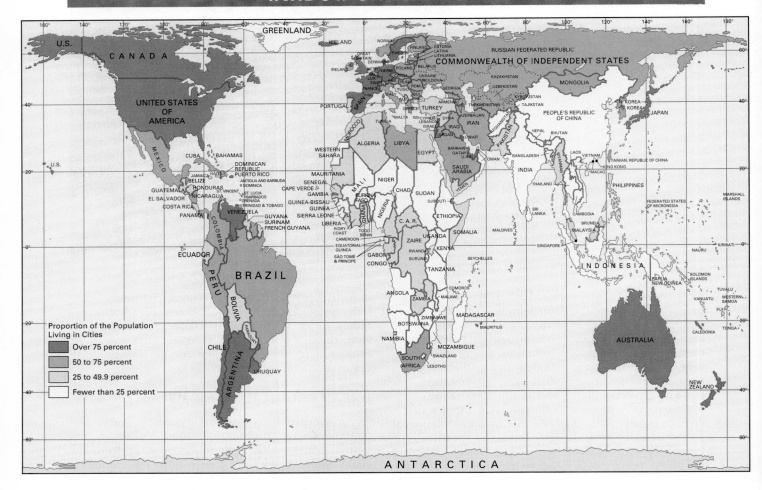

GLOBAL MAP 21–2 Urbanization in Global Perspective

Urbanization is closely linked to economic development. Thus, in rich nations—including Canada and the United States—more than three-fourths of the population cluster in cities, while in the poorest countries of the world—found in Africa and Asia—fewer than one-fourth of the people live in urban centres. Urbanization is now rapid in poor countries, however, with emerging "supercities" of unprecedented size.

SOURCE: *Peters Atlas of the World* (1990).

Quebec and Ontario. This relatively small area, and Metropolitan Toronto in particular, emerged as the core to the peripheral areas or hinterland across the rest of the country. The industrialized core dominates weaker areas, rural and urban, that are dependent on natural resources. This relationship accounts for regional inequalities, regionalism, and even threats to national unity (Matthews, 1983; Brym, 1986; Goyder, 1990; Hiller, 1996).

Critical evaluation. The urban political economy paradigm has gained much attention in recent years. For one thing, compared to the older urban ecology approach, the political economy view seems better able to address the harsh realities of urban life. But analysis based on the political economy perspective has been largely limited to capitalist societies in the modern era. Furthermore, capitalism and industrialization are assumed to cause the problems of urban life, while the environment and physical structure of cities are ignored. Jane Jacobs (1984), a highly esteemed expert on urban development and urban life who lives in Toronto, argues that urban social problems are the result of economic stagnation, but sustaining economic development is not a simple function of the availability of capital and political will. Cities are crucial to developing economies, but conditions including environment, population growth, economic differentiation, and a crucial mix of industries are required to sustain economic health. It is unlikely that any single model of cities can account for the full range of urban diversity that we find in the world today.

URBANIZATION IN POOR SOCIETIES

November 16, 1988, Cairo, Egypt. People call the vast Muslim cemetery in Old Cairo "The City of the Dead." In truth, it is very much alive: tens of thousands of squatters have moved into the mausoleums, making this place an eerie mix of life and death. Children run across the stone floors, clotheslines stretch between the monuments, and an occasional television antenna protrudes from a tomb roof. In a city gaining one thousand people a day, families live where they can.

Twice in human history the world has experienced a revolutionary expansion of cities. The first urban revolution began around 8000 B.C.E. with the first urban settlements, and continued as permanent settlements later appeared on different continents. The second urban revolution took hold about 1750 and lasted for two centuries as the Industrial Revolution touched off rapid growth of cities in Europe and North America.

A third urban revolution is now under way. As Global Map 21–2 shows, 75 percent of people are already city dwellers. But extraordinary urban growth is now occurring in poor societies. In 1950, about 25 percent of the people in low-income countries inhabited cities; by 1995, the proportion had risen to 42 percent; by 2005, it will exceed 50 percent.

Moreover, in 1950, just seven cities in the world had populations over five million, and only two of these were in low-income countries. By 1995, thirty-three cities had passed this mark, and twenty-five of them were in less-developed nations (U.S. Bureau of the Census, 1996).

Table 21–5 looks back to 1980 and ahead to 2015, locating the world's ten largest urban areas

TABLE 21–5 The World's Ten Largest Urban Areas, 1980 and 2015

1980	
Urban Area	**Population (in millions)**
New York, U.S.A.	16.5
Tokyo–Yokohama, Japan	14.4
Mexico City, Mexico	14.0
Los Angeles–Long Beach, U.S.A.	10.6
Shanghai, China	10.0
Buenos Aires, Argentina	9.7
Paris, France	8.5
Moscow, U.S.S.R.	8.0
Beijing, China	8.0
Chicago, U.S.A.	7.7

2015 (projected)	
Urban Area	**Population (in millions)**
Tokyo–Yokohama, Japan	28.8
Bombay, India	26.2
Lagos, Nigeria	24.6
Saõ Paulo, Brazil	20.3
Mexico City, Mexico	19.2
Shanghai, China	18.0
New York, U.S.A.	17.6
Calcutta, India	17.3
Delhi, India	16.9
Beijing, China	15.6

SOURCES: U.S. Bureau of the Census (1997). and *The World Almanac and Book of Facts, 1998* (1998).

(cities and surrounding suburbs). In 1980, six of the top ten were in industrialized societies, including three in the United States. By early in the next century, however, only two of the ten will be in industrialized nations: one in Japan and one in the United States. The majority will be in less economically developed societies.

Not only will these urban areas be the world's largest, but their populations will explode. Relatively rich countries such as Japan may have the resources to provide for cities with upwards of thirty million people, but for poor nations, such as Mexico and Brazil, such supercities will tax resources that are already severely strained.

A third urban revolution is taking place because many poor societies have now entered the high-growth Stage 2 of demographic transition. Falling death rates continue to fuel population growth in Latin America, Asia, and, especially, Africa. For urban areas, the rate of population increase is *twice* as high because, in addition to natural increase, millions of people leave the countryside each year in search of jobs, health care, education, and conveniences such as running water and electricity.

Will People Overwhelm the Earth?
The Environmental Challenge

Are you worried about the world's increasing population and the ability of the planet to sustain that growth? Think about this: by the time you finish reading this box, more than 1000 people will be added to our planet. By this time tomorrow, global population will have increased by 180 000. As the table shows, there are about two and a half births for every death on the planet, pushing the world's population upward by 90 million annually. Put another way, global population growth amounts to adding another Mexico to the world every year.

It is no wonder that many population analysts are deeply concerned about the future. The earth has an unprecedented population. The two billion people we have *added* since 1974 alone exceeds the planet's total in 1900. Might Thomas Robert Malthus—who predicted that population would outstrip the earth's resources and plunge humanity into war and suffering—be right after all?

Lester Brown, a *neo-Malthusian* population and environmental activist, sees a coming apocalypse if we do not change our ways. Brown concedes that Malthus failed to imagine how much technology (especially fertilizers and altering plant genetics) could boost the planet's agricultural output. But he maintains that the earth's burgeoning population is rapidly outstripping its finite resources. Families in many poor countries can find little firewood; members of rich societies are depleting oil reserves; everyone is draining global reserves of clean water.

Global Population Increase

	Births	Deaths	Net Increase
Year	141,000,000	51,000,000	90,000,000
Month	11,750,000	4,250,000	7,500,000
Day	391,000	141,000	250,000
Hour	16,300	5,875	10,425
Minute	270	98	172
Second	4.5	1.6	2.9

Cities do offer more opportunities than rural areas, but they provide no quick fix for the massive problems of escalating population and grinding poverty. Many cities in less-developed societies—Mexico City is a good example—are simply unable to meet the basic needs of much of their population. Thousands of rural people stream into Mexico City every day, even though more than 10 percent of the *current* 25 million residents have no running water in their homes, 15 percent lack sewerage facilities, and the city can process only half the trash and garbage produced. To make matters worse, exhaust from factories and cars chokes everyone, rich and poor alike (Friedrich, 1984; Gorman, 1991).

Like other major cities throughout Latin America, Africa, and Asia, Mexico City is surrounded by wretched shanty towns—settlements of makeshift homes built from discarded materials. As noted in Chapter 11 ("Global Stratification"), even city dumps are home to thousands of poor people, who pick through the waste hoping to find enough to survive for another day.

LOOKING AHEAD: POPULATION AND URBANIZATION IN THE TWENTY-FIRST CENTURY

The demographic analysis presented in this chapter points to some disturbing trends. We see, first of all, that the earth's population is unprecedented because birth rates remain high in poor nations and death rates have fallen just about everywhere. The numbers lead us to the sobering conclusion—the focus of the "Controversy & Debate" box—that controlling global population in the next century will be a monumental task. Some cause for optimism comes from recent reductions in birth rates that have at least slowed the rate of global population increase.

But population growth remains greatest in the poorest countries of the world, those that lack productive capacity to support their present populations, much less their future ones. Most of the privileged inhabitants of high-income nations are spared the trauma of poverty. But supporting about 90 million

Just as important, according to the neo-Malthusians, humanity is steadily poisoning the planet with waste. There is a limit to the earth's capacity to absorb pollution, they warn, and, as the number of people continues to increase, our quality of life will decline.

But another camp of analysts—the *anti-Malthusians*—sharply disagrees. Asks Julian Simon, "Why the doom and gloom?" Two centuries ago, he points out, Malthus predicted catastrophe. Today, however, there are almost six times as many people on the earth and, on average, they live longer, healthier lives than ever before. As Simon sees it, the current state of the planet is cause for great celebration.

Simon argues that the neo-Malthusians err in assuming that the world has finite resources that are spread thinner and thinner as population increases. Rather, the anti-Malthusians counter, people have the capacity to control population growth and to improve their lives in numerous ways. Furthermore, we do not know how many people the earth can support because humans keep rewriting the rules, in effect, by developing new fertilizers, new high-yield crops, and new forms of energy. Simon points out that today's global economy makes available more resources and products than ever (including energy and consumer goods), at increasingly low prices. He looks optimistically to the future because technology, economic investment, and—above all—human ingenuity have consistently proven the doomsayers wrong. And he is betting they will continue to do so. The assumption here is that substitutes for finite resources (such as oil) will be found, while waste management technology will allow human habitation and industry that do not result in irrevocable contamination or pollution of air, soil, and water.

Continue the debate . . .

1. *Where do you place your bet? Do you think the earth can support 8 or 10 billion people? Why or why not?*
2. *Ninety percent of current population growth is occurring in poor countries. What does this mean for rich nations? For poor ones?*
3. *Does the world population problem only affect people in low-income countries? What must people in rich societies do to ensure our children's future?*
4. *How do environment and population interact?*

SOURCES: Based, in part, on Brown et al. (1993, 1995), and Simon (1994).

additional people on our planet each year—80 million of them in poor societies—will require a global commitment to provide not only food but housing, schools, and employment. The well-being of the entire world may ultimately depend on resolving the economic and social problems of poor, overly populated countries and bridging the widening gulf between the "have" and "have-not" societies.

Great concentrations of people have always had the power to intensify the triumphs and tragedies of human existence. Thus, the world's demographic, environmental, and social problems are most pronounced in cities, especially in poor nations. In Mexico City, Saõ Paulo (Brazil), Kinshasa (Democratic Republic of Congo), Bombay (India), and Manila (the Philippines), urban problems now seem to defy solution, as people stream into the cities from rural areas where life is even worse.

Earlier chapters suggested different answers to the population problem. According to modernization theory, as poor societies industrialize, greater productivity will simultaneously raise living standards and reduce population growth (as happened in Western Europe and North America a century ago). Dependency theory, however, argues that progress will elude poor societies as long as they remain locked in economically dependent trading relationships with rich countries.

Throughout history, the city has improved people's living standards more than any other type of settlement. The question facing humanity now is whether cities in poor countries will be able to meet the needs of larger populations in the coming century. The answer—which depends on issues of technology, international relations, global economic ties, and simple justice—will affect us all.

SUMMARY

1. Fertility and mortality, measured as crude birth rates and crude death rates, are major components of population growth. In global terms, North American population growth is low.

2. Migration, another key demographic concept, has special importance to the historical growth of cities.

3. Demographers use age-sex pyramids to graphically represent the composition of a population and to project population trends. The sex ratio refers to a society's balance of females and males.

4. Historically, world population grew slowly because high birth rates were largely offset by high death rates. About 1750, a demographic transition began as world population rose sharply, mostly due to falling death rates.

5. Thomas Robert Malthus warned that population growth would outpace food production, resulting in social calamity. Demographic transition theory, however, contends that technological advances gradually prompt a drop in birth rates.

6. Research shows that lower birth rates and improved economic productivity in poor societies both result from improving the social position of women.

7. World population is expected to reach between eight and nine billion by 2050. Such an increase will likely overwhelm many poor societies, where most of the increase will take place.

8. Closely related to population growth is urbanization. The first urban revolution began with the appearance of cities some 10 000 years ago; by the start of the Common Era, cities had emerged in most regions of the world except for North America.

9. Urbanization is associated with a dramatic increase in the division of labour, as people assume a wide range of highly specialized, productive roles in society.

10. Pre-industrial cities are characterized by low-rise buildings; narrow, winding streets; and personal social ties.

11. A second urban revolution began about 1750 as the Industrial Revolution propelled rapid urban growth in Europe. The physical form of cities changed as planners created wide, regular streets to facilitate trade. The emphasis on commercial life and the increasing size of urban areas rendered city life more anonymous.

12. Urbanism came to North America with European settlers. A string of colonial towns dotting the Atlantic coastline gave way by 1850 to hundreds of new cities from coast to coast.

13. By 1931, a majority of the Canadian population lived in urban areas: twenty-five metropolises encompassing 100 000 to four million residents now dominate the urban scene.

14. Since 1950, Canadian cities have decentralized, moving out of central cities into suburban settings. This decentralization has generated vast urban areas, metropolises, that Statistics Canada calls Census Metropolitan Areas. As urban areas expand and bump up against each other they form what is called a megalopolis.

15. Rapid urbanization in Europe during the nineteenth century led early sociologists to contrast rural and urban life. Ferdinand Toennies built his analysis around the concepts of *Gemeinschaft* and *Gesellschaft*, and Emile Durkheim devised parallel concepts of mechanical solidarity and organic solidarity. Georg Simmel claimed that the overstimulation of city life produced a blasé attitude in urbanites.

16. At the University of Chicago, Robert Park hailed cities for permitting greater social freedom. Louis Wirth reasoned that large, dense, heterogeneous populations generated a way of life characterized by impersonality, self-interest, and tolerance of people's differences.

17. Urban ecology studies the interplay of social and physical dimensions of the city. Urban political economy employs the social-conflict perspective to understand city life in terms of economic and political inequality.

18. A third urban revolution is now occurring in poor societies of the world, where most of the world's largest cities will soon be found.

CRITICAL THINKING QUESTIONS

1. Explain the meaning of fertility and mortality rates. Change in which of these two has been of greater importance in increasing global population? Why?

2. How does demographic transition theory link population patterns to technological development?

3. Over the course of history, how have economic and technological changes transformed the physical shape of cities?

4. According to Ferdinand Toennies, Emile Durkheim, Georg Simmel, and Louis Wirth, what characterizes urbanism as a way of life?

5. What are the environmental impacts of population growth and urbanization?

SOCIOLOGY APPLIED

1. Check in the library for *World Population Prospects: The 1996 Revision*, a United Nations report. Why is population increase in many poor countries slower than a decade ago? Which countries are making the greatest progress towards population control?

2. Access New York University's Taub Urban Research Center on the Internet at www.nyu.edu/urban/main.html. Look over recent reports of urban studies research. Does doing research of this kind appeal to you?

3. Apply Toennies's concepts of *Gemeinschaft* and *Gesellschaft* to social life on your campus. What living, eating, or recreational arrangements add an element of *Gemeinschaft* to college life?

4. Draw a "mental map" of a city familiar to you with specific places, districts, roads, and transportation facilities that come to mind. Compare your map to a "real" one, or, better yet, one drawn by someone else. Try to account for the differences.

WEBLINKS

http://coombs.anu.edu.au/ResFacilities/ DemographyPage.html
CERN/ANU Demography and Population Studies is an enormous resource site containing 155 links to demographic information facilities throughout the world.

http://www.zpg.org/
Zero Population Growth is the largest grassroots organization in the United States concerned with the impacts of rapid population growth and wasteful consumption. Included here are many related links.

http://callisto.worldonline.nl/~marcelp/
Urban Issues in Developing Countries contains papers, information, and links to sites concerned with urbanization, habitat, and urban poverty in developing nations.

http://www.udel.edu/uaa/
The *Urban Affairs Association* is the international professional organization for urban scholars, researchers, and public service providers. You can find out more about the organization and the *Journal of Urban Affairs* at this Web site.

http://riceinfo.rice.edu/~lda/Sprawl_Net/ Home.html
Based at the Rice University School of Architecture in Houston, Texas, the *Sprawl Net* is a forum devoted to the topic of urban sprawl. This site uses the resources of the Internet to collect information, ideas, and opinions about the contemporary sprawling landscape, and to encourage interested people from a wide variety of fields to work together.

Anatoly Shdanow, *Warning,* 1991

CHAPTER 22

COLLECTIVE BEHAVIOUR AND SOCIAL MOVEMENTS

The summer of 1990 was pivotal for Canada's First Nations: after Elijah Harper and Oka, the relationship between native peoples and other Canadians would never be the same. The Meech Lake Accord was to have been ratified by each of the provinces by June 23, to allow amendments to the constitution that would satisfy Quebec (and thereafter, many fear, to block constitutional changes sought by aboriginal leaders). Newfoundland appeared to be poised to vote and Manitoba was trying to go through the procedural steps required for ratification. The snag came in the form of Elijah Harper, a native MLA (member of the Legislative Assembly) who, through dramatic delaying tactics, was able to prevent ratification by the Manitoba legislature—thereby "killing" the accord.

In the meantime, the town of Oka, Quebec, was ensuring its international visibility by introducing plans to expand a golf course onto lands that the people of Kanesatake considered to be a sacred burial ground. A barricade erected across a rural road in response to this threat gave rise to a five-month armed confrontation between the residents of Kanesatake (aided by Mohawk Warriors) and the Quebec police—and, later on, the Canadian forces.

The significance of these events lay not in the fact that native people and their leaders were taking decisive action to defend their interests—for that had happened many times before—but in the fact that their struggle had captured the attention of both the media (in Canada and abroad) and native individuals across the country. Suddenly, there was an outpouring of support for Elijah Harper and the people of Kanesatake in the form of letters, donations, marches, a run to bring a peace feather from British Columbia to Oka, a peace camp at Oka, and the barricade of the Mercier Bridge into Montreal. Daily, if not hourly, coverage of the Manitoba legislature and the tense, armed confrontation at Oka hypnotized Canadians across the country and mobilized native people in support of a cause. A growing sense of solidarity emerged as native individuals across the country watched events unfold. Many people, who had paid little attention to their aboriginal roots, were suddenly both intensely interested, proud, and somehow empowered by this new sense of movement and common cause. Consciousness had been raised and bonds had been forged in ways that would have profound effects on relations between native peoples and other Canadians or their governments. A social movement has gained momentum.

As this chapter explains, a **social movement** is an organized activity that encourages or discourages social change. Social movements are the most important type of **collective behaviour**, activity involving a large number of people, often spontaneous, and usually in violation of established norms. Other forms of collective behaviour—also controversial and sometimes provoking change—are crowds, mobs, and riots, rumour and gossip, public opinion, panic and mass hysteria, and fashions and fads.

For most of this century, sociologists focused on established social patterns such as the family and social stratification. They paid little attention to collective behaviour, considering most of it unusual or deviant. But numerous social movements that burst on the scene during the tumultuous 1960s ignited sociological interest in the field of collective behaviour (Weller and Quarantelli, 1973; G. Marx and Wood, 1975; Aguirre and Quarantelli, 1983; Turner and Killian, 1987; McAdam et al., 1988).

STUDYING COLLECTIVE BEHAVIOUR

Despite its importance, collective behaviour is difficult for sociologists to study for three main reasons:

1. **Collective behaviour is wide-ranging.** Collective behaviour encompasses a sometimes bewildering array of human actions. The traits common to fads, rumours, and mob behaviour, for example, are far from obvious.

2. **Collective behaviour is complex.** A rumour seems to come out of nowhere and circulates in countless different settings. For no apparent reason, one new form of dress "catches on" while another does not. And, historically speaking, why in the spring of 1998 did Quebeckers resist yet another referendum, telling pollsters they are quite comfortable as both Québécois *and* Canadian?

3. **Much collective behaviour is transitory.** Sociologists can readily study the family because it is an enduring element of social life. Since fashions, rumours, and riots tend to arise and dissipate quickly, they are difficult to investigate systematically.

Some researchers point out that these problems apply not just to collective behaviour but to *most* forms of human behaviour (Aguirre and Quarantelli, 1983). Moreover, collective behaviour is not always so elusive: no one is surprised by the crowds that form at sports events and music festivals, and sociologists can study these gatherings firsthand or by reviewing

videotapes. Sometimes researchers can even anticipate natural disasters and study the human response they provoke. We know, for example, that tornadoes occur in particular regions of Canada and the U.S. each year; some sociologists interested in how such disasters affect behaviour can be prepared to initiate research on short notice (Miller, 1985). Researchers can also use historical documents to reconstruct the details of a past natural disaster or riot.

Sociologists now know a great deal about collective behaviour, but they still have much to learn. The most serious shortcoming, according to Benigno Aguirre and E.L. Quarantelli (1983), is that sociologists have no theory that ties together all the diverse actions that fall under the umbrella of "collective behaviour."

At the least, all collective behaviour involves the action of some **collectivity**, *a large number of people whose minimal interaction occurs in the absence of well-defined, conventional norms.* Collectivities are of two kinds. A *localized collectivity* involves physical proximity and is illustrated by crowds and riots. A *dispersed collectivity* or *mass behaviour* involves people who influence one another even though they are separated by great distances; examples here include rumours, public opinion, and fashion (Turner and Killian, 1993).

It is important to distinguish collectivities from the already familiar concept of social groups (see Chapter 7, "Groups and Organizations"). Here are three key differences:

1. **Collectivities are based on limited social interaction.** Group members interact directly and frequently. Interaction in localized collectivities such as mobs is limited and temporary. People participating in dispersed collectivities such as a fad typically do not interact at all.

2. **Collectivities have no clear social boundaries.** Group members share a sense of identity that is usually missing among people engaged in collective behaviour. Localized crowds may have a common object of attention (such as someone on a ledge threatening to jump), but they exhibit little sense of unity or coherence. Individuals involved in dispersed collectivities, such as "the public" that turns out to vote in an election, have almost no awareness of shared membership. Of course, some issues divide the public into well-defined factions, but it is often difficult to tell who falls within the ranks of, say, the environmentalist or feminist movements.

3. **Collectivities engender weak and unconventional norms.** Conventional cultural norms usually regulate the behaviour of group members. Some collectivities, such as people travelling on

an airplane, observe conventional norms, but these rules usually amount to little more than respecting the privacy of people sitting in nearby seats. Other collectivities—such as emotional soccer fans who destroy property as they leave a stadium—spontaneously develop decidedly unconventional norms (Weller and Quarantelli, 1973; Turner and Killian, 1993).

LOCALIZED COLLECTIVITIES: CROWDS

A key form of collective behaviour is the **crowd**, a temporary gathering of people who share a common focus of attention and who influence one another. Historian Peter Laslett (1984) points out that crowds are a modern development; in medieval Europe, about the only time large numbers of people assembled in one place was when armies faced off on the battlefield. Today, however, crowds reaching 25 000 or more are common at sporting events, rock concerts, and even the registration halls of large universities.

But all crowds are not alike. Herbert Blumer (1969) identified four categories of crowds. A *casual crowd* is a loose collection of people who interact little, if at all. People at the beach or at the scene of an automobile accident have only a passing awareness of one another.

A *conventional crowd* results from deliberate planning, as with a country auction, a college lecture, or a funeral. In each case, most interaction conforms to norms appropriate to the situation.

An *expressive crowd* forms around an event with emotional appeal, such as a religious revival, a wrestling match featuring Hulk Hogan, or the Stanley Cup parade. Excitement is the main reason people join expressive crowds, which makes this experience relatively spontaneous and exhilarating for those taking part.

An *acting crowd* is a collectivity motivated by an intense, single-minded purpose, such as an audience rushing the doors of a concert hall or fleeing from a theatre that is on fire. Acting crowds are ignited by very powerful emotions, which can reach a feverish intensity and sometimes erupt into mob violence.

Any gathering can change from one type of crowd to another. In 1985, for example, a conventional crowd of 60 000 fans assembled in a soccer stadium to watch the European Cup Finals between Italy and Great Britain. Once the game started, some drunk British fans began taunting the Italians sitting nearby. At this point, the crowd became expressive. The two sides began to throw bottles at each other; then, the British surged in a human wave towards the Italians. An estimated 400 million television viewers watched in horror as what was now an acting crowd trampled

Much of the exuberance of Beatlemania, which swept up millions of young fans in Europe and North America beginning in the early 1960s, can be traced to the music and personal charisma of the Beatles. But being "part of the crowd" is itself appealing, because collective life generates its own emotional intensity.

hundreds of helpless spectators. In minutes, 38 people were dead and another 400 were injured (Lacayo, 1985).

Deliberate action by a crowd is not simply the product of rising emotions. Participants in *protest crowds*—a fifth category we can add to Blumer's list—may stage strikes, boycotts, sit-ins, and marches for political purposes (McPhail and Wohlstein, 1983). For example, students in a protest crowd vary in emotional intensity; some display the low-level energy characteristic of a conventional crowd, while others are emotional enough to be an acting crowd. Sometimes a protest gathering begins peacefully, but its members become aggressive when confronted with counter-demonstrators. In July 1990, during the Oka crisis, an unexpectedly violent clash occurred between the police and 4000 residents of Quebec's South Shore when the latter came out to protest the Mohawk takeover of the Mercier Bridge into Montreal.

MOBS AND RIOTS

When an acting crowd turns violent, we may witness the birth of a mob, a highly emotional crowd that pursues a violent or destructive goal. Despite, or perhaps because of, their intense emotion, mobs tend to dissipate quickly. The duration of a mob incident also depends on whether its leadership tries to inflame or stabilize the crowd, and on the mob's precise objectives.

This picture is a good illustration of a riot that developed from high spirits rather than from a sense of grievance or hatred. In 1993 thousands of hockey fans went on a rampage through the streets of Montreal to celebrate their team's victory over the Los Angeles Kings in the Stanley Cup final.

Lynching is the most notorious example of mob behaviour. This term is derived from Charles Lynch, a Virginia colonist who sought to maintain law and order in his own way before formal courts were established. The word soon became synonymous with violence and murder outside the legal system.

Lynching has always been coloured by race. After the Civil War in the U.S., lynch mobs became a terrorist form of social control over emancipated African-Americans. African-Americans who challenged white superiority risked hanging or being burned alive by hateful whites.

Lynch mobs—typically composed of poor whites threatened by competition from freed slaves—reached a peak between 1880 and 1930. About 5000 lynchings were recorded by police in that period; no doubt, many more occurred. Most of these crimes were committed in the Deep South, where an agrarian economy still depended on a cheap and docile labour force, but lynchings took place in virtually every state and victimized every minority. For example, on the western frontier, lynch mobs frequently targeted people of Mexican and Asian descent. In only about 25 percent of the cases did whites lynch other whites. Lynchings of women were rare; only about a hundred such instances are known, almost all involving women of colour (W. White, 1969, orig. 1929; Grant, 1975).

A frenzied crowd without any particular purpose is a riot, a social eruption that is highly emotional, violent, and undirected. Unlike the action of a mob, a riot usually has no clear goal. Long-standing anger generally fuels riots, which are sparked by some minor incident (Smelser, 1962). Rioters then indulge in seemingly random violence against property or persons. Whereas a mob action usually ends when a specific violent goal has been achieved (or decisively prevented), a riot tends to disperse only as participants run out of steam or as community leaders or the police gradually bring them under control.

Riots often serve as collective expressions of social injustice. Industrial workers, for example, have rioted to vent rage at their working conditions, and race riots have occurred with striking regularity. In Canada, in response to steady migration from China (of what seemed to be unfairly competitive cheap labour) and a sudden influx of over 8000 Japanese in 1907, a riot broke out, during which the people of Vancouver lashed out violently against the Japanese and looted their businesses. In Los Angeles in 1992, an especially destructive riot was triggered by the acquittal of police officers involved in the beating of Rodney King. The turmoil left more than fifty dead and caused thousands of injuries and millions of dollars' worth of property damage. These riots were followed almost immediately by race riots on the streets of Toronto.

Riots are not always fired by hate. They can also stem from positive feelings, such as the celebration of the 1993 Stanley Cup victory in Montreal, which turned into a night of looting and violence. Days later, in anticipation of further violence, the Montreal Canadiens were protected during their victory parade by hundreds of police officers and the riot squad.

CROWDS, MOBS, AND SOCIAL CHANGE

Ordinary people typically gain power only by acting collectively. Historically, because crowds have been able to effect social change, they have also provoked controversy. Defenders of the established social order fear "the mob." In countries around the world, elites know that the masses—when well organized—pose a threat to their power. However, the collective action condemned by some people is supported by others as rightful protest. In 1839, fifty-three Africans rose up and seized the ship *Amistad* off the coast of Cuba to prevent landing in the Americas and being sold into slavery. Were these men a vicious mob? Not according to the U.S. Supreme Court, which, after the ship put in to New York Harbor, ruled that the men were fighting for their freedom and were entitled to be released.

Moreover, crowds share no single political cast: some call for change—others resist it. Judeans rallying to the Sermon on the Mount by Jesus of Nazareth, traditional weavers destroying new industrial machines that were threatening their jobs, masses of marchers carrying banners and shouting slogans for or against abortion—these and countless other cases across the centuries show that crowds can challenge or support their society (Rudé, 1964; Canetti, 1978; Tarrow, 1994).

EXPLAINING CROWD BEHAVIOUR

What accounts for the behaviour of crowds? Social scientists have developed several different explanations.

Contagion Theory

An early explanation of collective behaviour was formulated by French sociologist Gustave Le Bon (1841–1931). According to Le Bon's *contagion theory* (1960; orig. 1895), crowds exert a hypnotic influence over their members. Shielded by the anonymity of a crowd, people evade personal responsibility and surrender to the contagious emotions of the crowd. A crowd thus assumes a life of its own, stirring up emotions and driving people towards irrational, perhaps violent, action.

Critical evaluation. Le Bon's assertion that crowds foster anonymity and sometimes generate emotion is surely true. Yet, as Clark McPhail (1991) points out, systematic research reveals that "the madding crowd" does not take on a life of its own, apart from the thoughts and intentions of members. For example, Norris Johnson (1987), investigating panic at a 1979 Who concert in Cincinnati, identified specific factors that led to the deaths of eleven people, including an inadequate number of entrance doors, an open-seating policy, and insufficient police supervision. Far from an episode of collective insanity, Johnson concluded, that crowd was composed of many small groups of people valiantly trying to help each other.

Convergence Theory

Convergence theory holds that crowd behaviour is not a product of the crowd itself, but is carried into the crowd by individual participants. Thus, crowds amount to a convergence of like-minded individuals. In other words, while contagion theory states that crowds cause people to act in a certain way, convergence theory says the opposite: that people who wish to act in a certain way come together to form crowds.

For example, whites in various U.S. communities have banded together to keep African-Americans from moving into their neighbourhoods. In such instances, convergence theorists contend, the crowd itself does not generate racial hatred or violence; in all likelihood, hostility has been simmering for some time among many local people. A crowd then arises from a convergence of people who oppose the presence of Black residents.

Critical evaluation. By linking crowds to broader social forces, convergence theory claims that crowd behaviour is not irrational, as Le Bon maintained. Rather, people in crowds express existing beliefs and values (Berk, 1974).

But, in fairness to Le Bon, people sometimes do things in a crowd that they would not have the courage to do alone, because crowds can intensify a sentiment simply by creating a critical mass of like-minded people.

Emergent-Norm Theory

Ralph Turner and Lewis Killian (1993) developed the *emergent-norm theory* of crowd dynamics. These researchers concede that social behaviour is never entirely predictable, but neither are crowds as irrational as Le Bon thought. If similar interests may draw people together, distinctive patterns of behaviour may emerge within a crowd itself.

According to Turner and Killian, crowds begin as collectivities in which people have mixed interests and motives. Especially in the case of less stable crowds—expressive, acting, and protest crowds—norms may be vague and changing, as when, say, one member at a rock concert holds up a lit cigarette lighter to signal praise for the performers, and others follow suit. In short, people in crowds make their own rules as they go along.

Critical evaluation. Emergent-norm theory represents a symbolic-interaction approach to crowd dynamics. Turner and Killian (1972:10) explain that crowd behaviour is neither as irrational as contagion theory suggests, nor as deliberate as convergence theory implies. Certainly, crowd behaviour reflects the desires of participants, but it is also guided by norms that emerge as the situation unfolds.

Decision making, then, plays a significant role in crowd behaviour, even though it may escape the notice of casual observers. For example, frightened people clogging the exits of a burning theatre may appear to be victims of irrational panic but, from their point of view, fleeing a life-threatening situation is entirely sensible.

Further, emergent-norm theory points out that people in a crowd take on different roles. Some assume leadership roles, while others become lieutenants, rank-and-file followers, inactive bystanders, or even opponents (Weller and Quarantelli, 1973; Zurcher and Snow, 1981).

The Rumour Mill: Paul Is Dead!

Everyone knows the Beatles. The music of John Lennon, Paul McCartney, George Harrison, and Ringo Starr caused a cultural revolution in the 1960s. Not everyone today, however, knows the rumour that circulated about Paul McCartney at the height of the group's popularity.

On October 12, 1969, a young man telephoned a Detroit disk jockey to say that he had discovered "evidence" that Paul McCartney was dead:

1. If you filtered out background music at the end of the song "Strawberry Fields Forever" on the *Magical Mystery Tour* album, you would hear a voice saying, "I buried Paul!"

2. The phrase "Number 9, Number 9, Number 9" from the song "Revolution 9" on the *White Album*, when played backward, seems to intone, "Turn me on, dead man!"

Two days later, the University of Michigan student newspaper ran a story entitled "McCartney Is Dead: Further Clues Found." It sent millions of Beatles fans scurrying for their albums.

3. A picture inside the *Magical Mystery Tour* album shows John, George, and Ringo wearing red carnations, while Paul is sporting a black flower.

4. The cover of the *Sergeant Pepper's Lonely Hearts Club Band* album shows a grave with yellow flowers arranged in the shape of Paul's bass guitar.

5. On the inside of that album, McCartney wears an arm patch with the letters "OPD." Was this the insignia of some police department, or confirmation that Paul had been "Officially Pronounced Dead"?

6. On the back cover of the same album, three Beatles are facing forward while McCartney has his back to the camera.

7. On the album cover of *Abbey Road*, John Lennon is clothed as a clergyman, Ringo Starr wears an undertaker's black tie, and George Harrison is clad in worker's attire as if ready to dig a grave. For his part, McCartney is barefoot, which is how Tibetan ritual prepares a corpse for burial. Behind Paul, a Volkswagen

nearby displays the licence plate "28 IF," indicating that McCartney would have been *28 if* he had not met his demise.

The report in the University of Michigan newspaper provided details of McCartney's alleged "death" in an automobile accident early in November 1966, and included a photograph allegedly of the musician's bloodied head. After the accident, the story continued, music company executives had secretly replaced Paul with a double.

Of course, Paul McCartney is very much alive and still jokes about the episode. Few doubt that the Beatles intentionally fabricated some of the "clues" to pique the interest of their fans. But the incident has a serious side, revealing how quickly rumours can arise and persist in a climate of distrust. During the late 1960s, many disaffected young people had no trouble believing that the media and other powerful interests would conceal McCartney's death.

McCartney himself denied the rumour in a 1969 *Life* magazine interview. But thousands of suspicious readers also noticed that the back of the page containing McCartney's picture had an advertisement for an automobile: If they held this page up to the light, the car lay across McCartney's chest and blocked his head! Another clue!

SOURCES: Based on Rosnow and Fine (1976) and Kapferer (1992).

DISPERSED COLLECTIVITIES: MASS BEHAVIOUR

It is not just people in physical proximity who participate in collective behaviour. **Mass behaviour** refers to *collective behaviour among people dispersed over a wide geographical area.*

RUMOUR AND GOSSIP

A common type of mass behaviour is **rumour**, *unsubstantiated information people spread informally, often by word of mouth.* People pass along rumours through face-to-face communication, of course, but today's modern technology—including telephones, the mass media, and now the Internet—spreads rumours faster and farther than ever before.

Rumour has three essential characteristics:

1. **Rumour thrives in a climate of ambiguity.** Rumours arise among people who lack definitive information about a topic of concern. For example, workers fearing a massive layoff, and hearing little official news from management, will usually find themselves awash in rumours.

2. **Rumour is unstable.** People change a rumour as they pass it along, usually giving it a "spin" that serves their own interests. Before long, many competing variations exist.

3. **Rumour is difficult to stop.** The number of people aware of a rumour increases exponentially as each person relays information to several others. Rumours dissipate with time; but, in general, the only way to control rumours is for a believable source to issue a clear and convincing statement of the facts.

Rumour can trigger the formation of crowds or other collective behaviour. Thus, authorities often establish rumour-control centres in times of crisis to manage information. Yet some rumours persist for years despite incontrovertible evidence to the contrary; the "Social Diversity" box provides a notable example.

Gossip is *rumour about people's personal affairs.* Charles Horton Cooley (1962; orig. 1909) explained that, while rumour involves issues or events of interest to a large segment of the public, gossip concerns a small circle of people who know a particular person. While rumours spread widely, then, gossip is more localized.

Communities use gossip as a means of social control, praising or scorning someone to encourage conformity to local norms. Moreover, people gossip about others to elevate their own standing as social "insiders." Yet no community wants gossip to get out of control, which may be the reason why people who gossip *too* much are criticized as "busybodies."

PUBLIC OPINION AND PROPAGANDA

Another form of highly dispersed collective behaviour is *public opinion*, widespread attitudes about controversial issues. Exactly who is, or is not, included in any "public" depends on the issue involved. Over the years in Canada, "publics" have formed over issues such as water fluoridation, air pollution, the social standing of women, handguns, Quebec separatism, immigration, health care, and even the Constitution. As this list indicates, public issues are important matters about which people disagree (Lang and Lang, 1961; Turner and Killian, 1993).

What explains the behaviour of crowds? Although people once thought a crowd takes on a "mind of its own." it is more correct to say that people are brought together by some shared interest. In the case of this protest crowd in Quebec City, the participants are demanding that the province not cut funding to education or raise tuition fees. Exactly what happens next, however, depends on many factors that unfold as the protest proceeds.

On any given issue, anywhere from 2 to 10 percent of people will offer no opinion because of ignorance or apathy. Moreover, over time, public interest in issues rises and falls. For example, interest in the social position of women in Canada was strong during the decades of the women's suffrage movement but declined after women won the right to vote—federally in 1918 and provincially when Quebec became the last province to extend the vote to women in 1940. Since the 1960s, a second wave of feminism has again created a public with strong opinions on gender issues.

On any issue, not everyone's opinion carries the same clout. Some categories of people have more social influence than others because they are wealthier, more powerful, or better educated. Many special-interest groups shape public policy even though they represent only a small fraction of the population. In general, privileged people make use of their affluence, prestige, and social contacts to promote their opinions more effectively than others.

Political leaders, special-interest groups, and businesses all seek to influence public tastes and attitudes by using propaganda, *information presented with the intention of shaping public opinion*. Although the term has negative connotations, propaganda is not necessarily false. A thin line separates information from propaganda; the difference depends mostly on the presenter's intention. We offer *information* to enlighten others; we use *propaganda* to sway an audience towards some viewpoint. Political speeches, commercial advertising, and even some university lectures may disseminate propaganda with the goal of making people think or act in some specific way. Input from Canada's business community during the 1987 debate over free trade with the U.S. was denounced by opponents as propaganda, as were all of the pronouncements of the three major federal political parties during the 1992 referendum on the Charlottetown accord.

PANIC AND MASS HYSTERIA

A **panic** is a form of localized collective behaviour by which people react to a threat or other stimulus with irrational, frantic, and often self-destructive behaviour. The classic illustration of a panic is people responding to a fire in a crowded theatre. As they flee in fear, they trample one another and block exits so that few actually escape.

Closely related to panic is **mass hysteria**, *a form of dispersed collective behaviour by which people respond to a real or imagined event with irrational, frantic, and often self-destructive behaviour*. Whether the cause of the hysteria is real or not, a large number of people think it is and take it seriously. Parents' fears that their children may become infected with HIV by a schoolmate who has AIDS may stir as much hysteria in a community as the very real danger of an approaching hurricane. Moreover, actions of people in the grip of mass hysteria generally make the situation worse. At the extreme, mass hysteria leads to chaotic flight and sends crowds into panic. People who see others overcome by fear may become more afraid themselves, as hysteria feeds on itself.

During the evening before Hallowe'en in 1938, CBS radio broadcast a dramatization of H.G. Wells's novel *War of the Worlds* (Cantril, Gaudet, and Herzog, 1947; Koch, 1970). It started with a typical program of dance music. Suddenly, a voice interrupted the music with a "special report" of explosions on the surface of the planet Mars, and, soon after, the crash landing of a mysterious cylinder near a farmhouse in New Jersey. The program then switched to an "on-the-scene reporter" who presented a chilling account of giant monsters equipped with death-ray weapons emerging from the spaceship. An "eminent astronomer" sombrely informed the audience that Martians had begun a full-scale invasion of Earth. Back then, most people relied on radio for factual news; thus, there was an announcement to clarify that the broadcast was fiction. But about one million of the ten million listeners across the United States and Canada missed the announcement and actually believed the report.

By the time the show was over, thousands were hysterical, gathering in the streets to spread news of the "invasion," while others flooded telephone switchboards with warnings to friends and relatives. Many simply jumped into their cars and fled.

FASHIONS AND FADS

Two additional types of collective behaviour—fashions and fads—affect people dispersed over a large area. A **fashion** is *a social pattern favoured by a large number of people*. Some fashions last for years, while others change after just a few months. The arts (including painting, music, drama, and literature), automobiles, language, architecture, and public opinion all change as ideas go in and out of fashion.

Lyn Lofland (1973) suggests that, in pre-industrial societies, clothing and personal adornment reflect traditional *style*, which changes very little. Categories of people—women and men, and members of various social classes and occupations—wear distinctive clothes and hairstyles that visibly mark their social standing.

In industrial societies, however, style gives way to changing fashion. For one thing, modern people are less tied to tradition and often eagerly embrace new ways of living. Then, too, high social mobility means that people use their "looks" to make a statement about themselves. German sociologist Georg Simmel (1971; orig. 1904) explained that affluent people are typically the trendsetters, since they have the money to spend on luxuries that bespeak privilege. In the lasting phrase of Thorstein Veblen (1953; orig. 1899), fashion involves *conspicuous consumption*, meaning that people buy expensive products simply to display wealth to one another.

Less affluent people who want to appear wealthy often snap up less expensive copies of what the rich make fashionable. In this way, a fashion moves downward in society. But the fashion loses its prestige when too many average people now share "the look," so the wealthy move on to something new. Fashions, in short, are born at the top of the social hierarchy, rise to mass popularity in bargain stores across the country, and soon are all but forgotten by everyone.

Because change in industrial societies is so rapid, we can see differences in personal appearance—one important kind of fashion—over short periods of time. The five photographs (beginning with the top left) show hair styles commonly worn by women in the 1950s, 1960s, 1970s, 1980s, and 1990s.

A reversal of this pattern sometimes occurs when rich people mimic a fashion found among people of lower social position. In the 1960s, for example, affluent university students began buying blue jeans, or dungarees (from a Hindi word for a coarse fabric). For decades, manual labourers had worn blue jeans, but in the era of civil rights and anti-war movements, jeans became the uniform of political activists and were soon popular on university campuses across the country. Author Tom Wolfe (1970) coined the phrase "radical chic" to satirize the desire of the rich to look fashionably poor.

A **fad** is *an unconventional social pattern that people embrace briefly but enthusiastically*. Fads, sometimes called *crazes*, are commonplace in rich industrial societies where many people have the money to spend on amusing, if often frivolous, products. During the 1950s, two young entrepreneurs in California produced a brightly coloured plastic version of a popular Australian toy, a three-foot-diameter hoop that one swung around the body by gyrating the hips. Dubbed the hula hoop, this odd device soon became a North American craze. But in less than a year, hula hoops vanished from the scene.

Streaking—running naked in public—had an even briefer moment in the sun, lasting only a few months in early 1974. Their fleeting existence suggests that fads happen almost at random, although national fads are usually begun by high-prestige people (Aguirre, Quarantelli, and Mendoza, 1988).

How do fads differ from fashions? Fads are passing fancies that capture the mass imagination but quickly burn out and disappear. Fashions, by contrast, reflect fundamental cultural values such as individuality and sexual attractiveness and tend to evolve over time. Therefore, a fashion—but rarely a fad—is incorporated into a society's culture. The fad of streaking, for instance, came out of nowhere and soon vanished; the fashion of wearing blue jeans, on the other hand, originated in the rough mining camps of Gold Rush California more than a century ago and still influences clothing designs today. This staying power explains

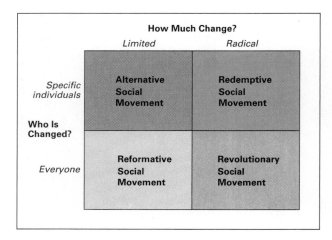

FIGURE 22–1 Four Types of Social Movements

SOURCE: Based on Aberle (1966).

the positive connotation of being called *fashionable*, in contrast to the mildly insulting label *faddish* (Blumer, 1968; Turner and Killian, 1987).

SOCIAL MOVEMENTS

Social movements are different from crowds, rumours, and other types of collective behaviour we have examined so far in three ways: they are deliberately organized, they have lasting importance, and they seek to change or defend some social pattern.

Social movements are far more common today than in the past. Pre-industrial societies are tightly integrated by tradition, making the emergence of social movements extremely rare. Industrial societies, however, foster diverse subcultures and countercultures so that social movements develop around a wide range of public issues. In recent decades, for example, homosexual men and women—supported by heterosexuals sympathetic to their political aims—have organized to win economic and legal parity with everyone else. Like any social movement that challenges conventional practices, this one has sparked a countermovement as traditionalists try to block greater social acceptance of homosexuality. Rightwing organizations in Canada, including the Ku Klux Klan and the Western Guard, are opposed to any extension of privileges to Blacks, immigrants, Jews—or homosexuals (Barrett, 1987). In today's society, almost every important public issue gives rise to a social movement favouring change and an opposing countermovement resisting it (Lo, 1982; Meyer and Staggenborg, 1996).

In the spring of 1996, the Liberal government undertook to add protection against discrimination on the basis of sexual orientation to the *Human Rights Act*. So bitterly divided was his own party on this issue that Prime Minister Chrétien relaxed party discipline and allowed a free vote. Though the bill did pass, more than twenty Liberals joined Reform MPs to vote against it on each of its readings.

There are three major dynamic sources of social change in Canada: class relations, regional identity, and the bilingual and multicultural nature of our society (Marsden and Harvey, 1979:4). Many of Canada's social movements arise from one of four sources:

1. **Quebec**, as its francophone majority seeks to reshape its relationship with the rest of the country or possibly to establish its sovereignty.

2. **The regions**, as they respond to economic and political inequities and numerous cultural differences.

3. **Native peoples**, as they struggle to gain recognition of an *inherent* right to self-government.

4. **Ethnic and racial minorities** that want to participate as equals within the larger society without completely losing their identities.

TYPES OF SOCIAL MOVEMENTS

Sociologists classify social movements according to several criteria (Aberle, 1966; Cameron, 1966; Blumer, 1969). Since some movements target selected people while others try to change everyone, one variable deals with *who is changed?* A second variable looks at *how much change?* Some movements attempt to foster only superficial changes in how we live, while others pursue a radical transformation of society. Combining these variables, we can identify four types of social movements, shown in Figure 22–1.

Alternative social movements are the least threatening to the status quo because they seek limited change in only some narrow segment of the population. Planned Parenthood, one example of an alternative social movement, encourages individuals of childbearing age to take the consequences of sexual activity more seriously by practising birth control.

Redemptive social movements also have a selective focus, but they seek radical change in those they engage. For example, Alcoholics Anonymous is an organization that helps alcoholics to achieve a sober life.

Reformative social movements, which generally work within the existing political system, seek only limited social change but encompass the entire society. They can be progressive (promoting a new social pattern) or reactionary (countermovements trying to preserve the status quo or to return to past social patterns). In the ongoing debate about abortion in

Canada, both the pro-life and pro-choice organizations are reformative social movements. Right-wing movements such as the Western Guard, the National Citizen's Coalition, and the Ku Klux Klan are examples of reactionary countermovements.

Revolutionary social movements are the most extreme of all. They seek basic transformation of a society. Sometimes pursuing specific goals, sometimes spinning utopian dreams, these social movements reject existing social institutions as flawed while promoting radically new alternatives. The nationalist or sovereigntist (i.e., separatist) movement in Quebec is revolutionary because it seeks, at the very least, a radical restructuring of federal institutions to give Quebec more political and economic autonomy; failing that, Quebec nationalists would argue, the need to protect their distinct society requires the establishment of an independent state and the complete overthrow of existing institutions.

EXPLAINING SOCIAL MOVEMENTS

Because social movements are intentional and long-lasting, sociologists find this form of collective behaviour somewhat easier to explain than fleeting incidents of mob behaviour or mass hysteria. Several theories have come to the fore.

Deprivation Theory

Deprivation theory holds that social movements arise among people who feel deprived. People who feel they lack sufficient income, satisfactory working conditions, important political rights, or basic social dignity may engage in organized collective behaviour to bring about a more just state of affairs (Morrison, 1978; Rose, 1982).

The rise of the Ku Klux Klan and the push for so-called Jim Crow laws to enforce segregation throughout the American South in the wake of the Civil War exemplify deprivation theory. With the end of slavery, white people lost a source of free labour and the claim that they were socially superior to African-Americans. Many whites reacted to this "deprivation" by trying to keep all people of colour "in their place" (Dollard et al., 1939). African-Americans had experienced much greater deprivation, of course, but as slaves they had little opportunity to organize. During the twentieth century, however, African-Americans have organized successfully in pursuit of racial equality.

As Chapter 7 ("Groups and Organizations") explained, deprivation is a relative concept. Regardless of how much money and power someone accumulates, people feel either well off or deprived compared to some category of others—a reference group. **Relative**

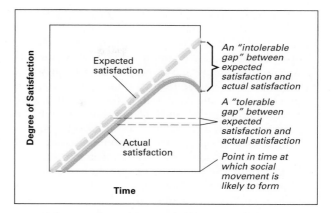

FIGURE 22–2 Relative Deprivation and Social Movements

In this diagram, the solid line represents a rising standard of living over time. The dotted line indicates the expected standard of living, which is typically somewhat higher. James C. Davies describes the difference between the two as "a tolerable gap between what people want and what they get." If the standard of living suddenly drops in the midst of rising expectations, however, the gap becomes intolerable. At this point, we can expect social movements to form.

SOURCE: Davies (1962).

deprivation, then, is *a perceived disadvantage arising from some specific comparison* (Stouffer et al., 1949; Merton, 1968).

More than a century ago Alexis de Tocqueville (1955; orig. 1856) studied the French Revolution. Why, he asked, did rebellion occur in progressive France rather than in more traditional Germany, where peasants were, by any objective measure, worse off? De Tocqueville's answer was that, as bad as their condition was, German peasants had known nothing but feudal servitude and thus had no basis for feeling deprived. French peasants, by contrast, had seen improvements in their lives that whetted their appetites for more. Thus, the French—not the Germans—felt a keen sense of relative deprivation. In analyzing this apparent paradox, de Tocqueville pinpointed one of the notable ironies of human history: increasing prosperity, far from satisfying the population, is likely to promote a spirit of unrest (1955:175; orig. 1856).

James C. Davies (1962) agrees that, as life gets better, people may take their rising fortunes for granted and expect even more. But what happens if the standard of living suddenly stops improving, or, worse, begins to drop? As Figure 22–2 illustrates, relative deprivation is the result, generating unrest and social movements aimed at change.

Critical evaluation. Deprivation theory challenges our common-sense assumption that the worse-off people are the most likely to organize for change. People do not organize simply because they are suffering in an absolute sense; rather, they form social movements because of *relative* deprivation. Indeed, both Tocqueville and Marx—as different as they were in many ways—agreed on the importance of relative deprivation in the formation of social movements.

Since most people experience some discontent all the time, one wonders why social movements emerge among certain categories of people and not others. Further, deprivation theory has a tendency towards circular reasoning: we assume that deprivation causes social movements, but often the only evidence of deprivation is the social movement itself (Jenkins and Perrow, 1977). Another limitation of this approach is that it focuses exclusively on the cause of a social movement and tells us little about movements themselves (McAdam et al., 1988). Lastly, some researchers claim that relative deprivation has not turned out to be a very good predictor of social movements (Muller, 1979).

Mass-Society Theory

William Kornhauser's *mass-society theory* (1959) argues that social movements attract socially isolated people who feel personally insignificant. From this point of view, social movements characterize large, complex *mass* societies. Further, social movements are more *personal* than *political*, in that they confer a sense of purpose and belonging on people otherwise adrift in society (Melucci, 1989).

This theory holds that categories of people with weak social ties are most readily mobilized into a social movement. People who have a strong sense of social integration, by contrast, are unlikely to join the ranks of a movement for change.

Like Gustave Le Bon, discussed earlier, Kornhauser offers a conservative view of social movements. He regards activists as psychologically vulnerable individuals who eagerly join groups and are often manipulated by group leaders. Social movements, in Kornhauser's view, are unlikely to be very democratic.

Critical evaluation. The strength of Kornhauser's theory lies in its explanation of social movements both in terms of the characteristics of the people who join them and the nature of the larger society. However, from a practical standpoint, if we try to evaluate the notion that mass societies foster social movements, we find it extremely difficult to specify what constitutes a "mass society."

A more political criticism holds that placing the roots of social movements in human psychology tends to dismiss the importance of social justice, by suggesting that flawed people, rather than a flawed society, underlie the emergence of social movements.

And what does research show about mass-society theory? The record is mixed. On the down side, some studies conclude that the Nazi movement in Germany did not draw heavily from socially isolated people (Lipset, 1963; Oberschall, 1973). Similarly, urban rioters during the 1960s typically had strong ties to their communities (Sears and McConahay, 1973). Evidence also suggests that young people who join religious cults do not have particularly weak family ties (Wright and Piper, 1986). Finally, researchers who have examined the biographies of 1960s political activists find evidence of deep and continuing commitment to political goals rather than isolation from society (McAdam, 1988, 1989; Whalen and Flacks, 1989).

On the up side, research by Frances Piven and Richard Cloward (1977) supports this approach. Piven and Cloward found that a breakdown of routine social patterns has encouraged poor people to form social movements. Also, in a study of the New Mexico State Penitentiary, Bert Useem (1985) found that when prison programs that promoted social ties among inmates were suspended, inmates displayed higher levels of protest.

Structural-Strain Theory

One of the most influential theories about social movements was developed by Neil Smelser (1962). *Structural-strain theory* identifies six factors that foster social movements. Smelser's theory also offers clues as to which situations spark unorganized mobs or riots and which create highly organized social movements. The prodemocracy movement that transformed Eastern Europe during the late 1980s serves to illustrate Smelser's six factors.

1. **Structural conduciveness.** Social movements arise as people come to think their society has some serious problems. In Eastern Europe, these problems included low living standards and political repression by socialist governments.

2. **Structural strain.** People begin to experience relative deprivation when their society fails to meet their expectations. Eastern Europeans joined the prodemocracy movement because they knew their living standards were far lower than living standards in Western Europe and much below what years of propaganda about prosperous socialism had led them to expect.

3. **Growth and spread of an explanation.** Any coherent social movement must formulate a

clear statement of a problem, its causes, and likely solutions. If people are confused about their suffering, they are likely to express their dissatisfaction in an unorganized way such as rioting. In Eastern Europe, intellectuals played a key role in the prodemocracy movement by pointing out economic and political flaws in the system and proposing strategies to increase democracy.

4. **Precipitating factors.** Discontent frequently festers for a long time, only to be galvanized into collective action by a specific event. In Eastern Europe, such an event occurred in 1985 when Mikhail Gorbachev came to power in the Soviet Union and implemented his sweeping program of *perestroika* (restructuring). As Moscow relaxed its rigid control over Eastern Europe, people there saw a historic opportunity to reorganize political and economic life.

5. **Mobilization for action.** Widespread concern about a public issue sets the stage for collective action in the form of rallies, distributing leaflets, and building alliances with sympathetic organizations. The initial success of the Solidarity movement in Poland—covertly aided by the Reagan administration in the United States and by the Vatican—mobilized people throughout Eastern Europe to press for change. The rate of change accelerated as reform movements gained strength: what took a decade in Poland required only months in Hungary and only weeks in other Eastern European nations.

6. **Lack of social control.** The responses of established authorities, such as political officials, police, and the military, largely determine the outcome of any social movement. Firm repression by the state can weaken or even destroy a social movement, as demonstrated by the crushing of prodemocracy forces in the People's Republic of China. By contrast, Gorbachev adopted a policy of nonintervention in Eastern Europe, thereby increasing the possibility for change. Ironically, the forces his program unleashed in these neighbouring nations soon spread to the Soviet Union itself, ending the historic domination of the Communist party and producing a new political confederation in 1992.

Critical evaluation. Smelser's approach—distinctly social, rather than psychological, in focus—recognizes the complexity of social movements and suggests how various factors encourage or inhibit their development. Structural-strain theory also explains how social problems may give rise to either organized social movements or more spontaneous mob action or rioting.

How can we explain a change as monumental as the fall of Soviet-backed governments throughout Eastern Europe at the beginning of the 1990s? At the outset, this movement was simply a strike by shipyard workers, led by Lech Walesa, in the Polish city of Gdansk. But within a decade, discontent and collective action had toppled the Polish government, made Walesa the nation's new president, and spilled throughout the region, ultimately bringing an end to the Soviet Union itself.

Yet Smelser's theory contains some of the same circularity of argument found in Kornhauser's analysis. A social movement is caused by strain, says Smelser, but the only evidence of this underlying strain appears to be the social movement itself. Finally, structural-strain theory overlooks the important role that resources such as the mass media or international alliances play in the success or failure of a social movement (Oberschall, 1973; Jenkins and Perrow, 1977; McCarthy and Zald, 1977; Olzak and West, 1991). Canada's native peoples have been particularly adept at gaining media coverage and winning support for their cause in the United States, Europe, the United Nations, and among the Canadian public.

These people in San Francisco's Marina Park are protesting the 1992 execution of convicted murderer Robert Alton Harris. Many of those shown here have engaged in similar protests at prison executions in other states. Mass-society theory suggests that people join social movements in order to gain a sense of meaning and purpose in their lives. How well do you think this theory explains the behaviour of such people? Why?

Resource-Mobilization Theory

Resource-mobilization theory points out that no social movement is likely to succeed—or even get off the ground—without substantial resources, including money, human labour, office and communications facilities, access to the mass media, and a positive public image. In short, any social movement rises or falls on its ability to attract resources, mobilize people, and forge alliances. The collapse of socialism in Eastern Europe was largely the work of dissatisfied people in those countries. But assistance from outside, in the form of fax machines, copiers, telecommunications equipment, money, and moral support, was critical in allowing first the Poles and then people in other countries to successfully oppose their leaders.

In other words, according to resource-mobilization theory, outsiders are as important as insiders to the victory of a social movement, often playing a crucial role in supplying resources. Socially disadvantaged people, by definition, lack the money, contacts, leadership skills, and organizational know-how that a successful movement requires, and it is here that sym-

pathetic outsiders fill the resource gap (Snow et al., 1980; Killian, 1984; Snow et al., 1986; Baron et al., 1991; Burstein, 1991; Meyer and Whitter, 1994; Valocchi, 1996). In Canada, people with all manner of skills, resources, and contacts have been involved in CASNP (the Canadian Alliance in Solidarity with Native Peoples). Well-to-do whites and university students performed a vital service to the Black civil rights movement in the U.S. in the 1960s.

On the other side of the coin, a lack of resources limits efforts to bring about change. The history of the AIDS epidemic offers a case in point. Initially, the U.S. government made a minimal response as the incidence of AIDS rose in the early 1980s. To a large extent, gay communities in cities such as San Francisco and New York were left to shoulder the responsibility for treatment and educational programs. Gradually, as the general public in both Canada and the U.S. began to grasp the dimensions of the problem, various levels of government in both countries started to allocate more resources. Galvanizing the public, members of the entertainment industry lent not only money and visibility but their prestige and credibility to the movement to combat the disease. These resources were crucial in transforming a fledgling social movement into a well-organized, global coalition of political leaders, educators, and medical specialists.

Critical evaluation. Resource-mobilization theory recognizes that resources as well as discontent are necessary to the success of a social movement. Research has confirmed that forging alliances to gain resources is especially important, and notes that movements with few resources may, in desperation, turn to violence to call attention to their cause (Grant and Wallace, 1991).

Critics of this theory maintain that even relatively powerless segments of a population can promote change if they are able to organize effectively and have strongly committed members. Research by Aldon Morris (1981) shows that Blacks drew largely on their own skills and resources to fuel the American civil rights movement of the 1950s and 1960s. Further, this theory overstates the extent to which powerful people are willing to challenge the status quo. Some rich white people did provide valuable resources to the civil rights movement but, probably more often, elites were indifferent or opposed to significant change (McAdam, 1982, 1983; Pichardo, 1995).

Overall, the success or failure of a social movement is decided by political struggle. A strong and united establishment, perhaps aided by a counter-movement, decreases the chances that any social movement will effect meaningful change. If, however, the established powers are divided, a movement's chances for success multiply. This is very clearly apparent in the native struggle for constitutional recognition in Canada. For close to two decades, native peoples faced a united front of provincial leaders who were unwilling to give in to demands for native participation in constitutional negotiations. However, by 1991, the election of several new premiers who were more open to native involvement set the stage for natives' active participation in the negotiations leading up to the Charlottetown accord.

New Social Movements Theory

A final, more recent theoretical approach addresses the changing character of social movements. *New social movements theory* emphasizes the distinctive features of recent social movements in post-industrial societies of North America and Western Europe (Melucci, 1980; McAdam et al., 1988; Kriesi, 1989; Pakulski, 1993).

Most of today's social movements are international, focusing on global ecology, the social standing of women and gay people, reducing the risks of war, and animal rights, among other issues. As the process of globalization connects the world's nations in more and more ways, in other words, social movements, too, are becoming global.

While traditional social movements, such as labour organizations, are concerned primarily with economic issues, new social movements tend to focus on cultural change and improving our social and physical surroundings. The international environmental movement, for example, opposes practices that aggravate global warming and other threats to the environment.

Lastly, whereas most social movements of the past drew strong support from working-class people, new social movements, with their noneconomic agendas, usually draw support from the middle-class. Furthermore, in Canada and other rich nations, the number of highly educated professionals—the people who most support "new social movements"—is increasing, which suggests that these movements will grow (Jenkins and Wallace, 1996).

Critical evaluation. One clear strength of this theory is its recognition that social movements are increasing in scale in response to the development of a global economy and international political connections. This theory also spotlights the power of the mass media to unite people around the world in pursuit of political goals.

Critics, however, claim that this approach exaggerates the differences between past and present social movements. The women's movement, for example, focuses on many of the same issues—workplace conditions and pay—that have concerned labour organizations for decades.

Each of the five theories we have presented offers some explanation for the emergence of social movements; no single theory, it seems, can stand alone (Kowalewski and Porter, 1992). Table 22–1 summarizes the theories.

GENDER AND SOCIAL MOVEMENTS

Gender figures prominently in the operation of social movements. In keeping with traditional notions about gender in Canada, men more than women tend to take part in public life—including spearheading social movements.

Investigating "Freedom Summer," a 1964 voter registration project in Mississippi, Doug McAdam (1992) found that most people viewed the job of registering African-American voters in the midst of considerable opposition and even hostility from whites to be dangerous, and therefore "men's work" unsuitable for women. Similarly, he discovered, project leaders were likely to assign women volunteers to clerical and teaching positions, leaving the actual field activities to men. This was so even though women who partici-

TABLE 22–1 Theories of Social Movements: A Summary

Deprivation Theory	People experiencing relative deprivation begin social movements. The social movement is a means of seeking change that brings participants greater benefits. Social movements are especially likely when rising expectations are frustrated.
Mass-Society Theory	People who lack established social ties are mobilized into social movements. Periods of social breakdown are likely to spawn social movements. The social movement gives members a sense of belonging and social participation.
Structural-Strain Theory	People come together because of their shared concern about the inability of society to operate as they believe it should. The growth of a social movement reflects many factors, including a belief in its legitimacy and some precipitating event that provokes action.
Resource-Mobilization Theory	People may join for all the reasons noted above and also because of social ties to existing members. The success or failure of a social movement depends largely on the resources available to it. Also important is the extent of opposition within the larger society.
New Social Movements Theory	People who become part of social movements are motivated by "quality of life" issues, not necessarily economic concerns. Mobilization is national or international in scope. New social movements arise in response to the expansion of the mass media and new information technology.

pated in Freedom Summer were more qualified than their male counterparts in terms of years of activism and organizational affiliations. McAdam concluded that only the most committed women were able to overcome the movement's gender barriers. In short, while women have played leading roles in many social movements (including the feminist movements in Canada and the U.S.), male dominance has been the norm even in social movements that otherwise oppose the status quo.

STAGES IN SOCIAL MOVEMENTS

Despite the many differences that set one social movement apart from others, all unfold in similar stages. Researchers have identified four phases in the life of the typical social movement (Blumer, 1969; Mauss, 1975; Tilly, 1978).

Stage 1: Emergence. Social movements are driven by the perception that all is not well. Some, such as the civil rights and women's movements, are born of widespread dissatisfaction. Others emerge only as a small vanguard group increases public awareness of some issue, as gay activists did with respect to the threat posed by AIDS. As Jean Charest left federal politics to lead the Quebec Liberals, an underlying social movement seemed to be emerging, creating the conditions for effective charismatic leadership on his part. The raising of the Canadian flag in front of city hall in Quebec City in April 1998—for the first time since the failure of the Meech Lake Accord in 1990—was a visible symbol of a growing willingness among francophones to embrace dual Québécois/Canadian identities. Opinion polls at the time suggested a surge of pro-Canadian sentiment and a reluctance to choose between the two identities. Perhaps most significant is the fact that three million Québécois who had claimed French origins in the 1991 census called themselves Canadian in 1996.

Stage 2: Coalescence. After emerging, a social movement must define itself clearly and develop a strategy for "going public." Leaders must determine policies, select tactics, build morale, and recruit new members. At this stage, the movement may engage in collective action such as rallies or demonstrations to attract media attention and public notice. The movement may also form alliances with other organizations to gain necessary resources.

Stage 3: Bureaucratization. To become an established political force, a social movement must assume bureaucratic traits, described in Chapter 7 ("Groups and Organizations"). As it becomes routinized, a social movement depends less on the charisma and talents of a few leaders and relies more on a capable staff. When social movements do not become established in this way, they risk dissolving. For example, many activist organizations on university campuses during the late 1960s were energized by a single charismatic leader and, consequently, did not last long. On the other hand, the National Action Committee on the Status of Women (NAC), despite changing leadership, is well-established and offers a steady voice on behalf of feminists in Canada.

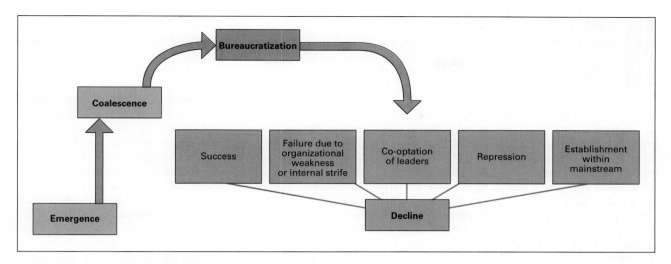

FIGURE 22–3 Stages in the Lives of Social Movements

Stage 4: Decline. Eventually, most social movements lose their influence. Frederick Miller (1983) suggests four reasons why this may occur.

First, if members have met their goals, decline may simply signal success. For example, the women's suffrage movement declined after it won the right to vote for women in Canada and the United States. Such clear-cut successes are rare, since few social movements have a single goal. More commonly, winning one victory leads to new campaigns. Because gender issues extend far beyond voting, the women's movement has recast itself time and again.

Second, a social movement may flag due to organizational factors, such as poor leadership, loss of interest among members, insufficient funds, or repression by authorities. Some people lose interest when the excitement of early efforts is replaced by formal routines. Fragmentation due to internal conflicts over goals and tactics is another common problem. Political parties with radical goals like those of the Parti Québécois (formed in 1968 with sovereignty as its central aim) can lose some of their more committed and activist members when they have to modify their platforms, however temporarily, to govern or to ensure re-election, as the PQ did in 1984.

Third, a social movement can fall apart if the established power structure, through offers of money, prestige, and other rewards, diverts leaders from their goals. Co-optation—that is, "selling out"—is one facet of the iron law of oligarchy discussed in Chapter 7 ("Groups and Organizations"). In other words, organizational leaders may use their positions to enrich themselves. For example, the former head of the Daily Bread food bank in Toronto, Gerard Kennedy, may take a different approach to poverty issues now that he is a Liberal MPP in Ontario and a political "insider." But this process can also work the other way: some people leave lucrative, high-prestige occupations to become activists. Cat Stevens, a rock star in the 1970s, became a Muslim, changed his name to Yusuf Islam, and now promotes his religion.

Finally, a social movement can collapse because of repression. Officials may crush a social movement by frightening away participants, discouraging new recruits, and even imprisoning leaders. In general, the more revolutionary the social movement, the more officials try to repress it. In the 1960s, the Front de libération du Québec (FLQ)—a revolutionary movement whose aim was an independent socialist Quebec—used bombs, kidnapping, and murder to promote its cause. In 1970, Prime Minister Trudeau invoked the *War Measures Act* in peacetime to suspend civil liberties and facilitate the arrest of FLQ members and sympathizers. By 1971, the FLQ had folded.

Another reason, beyond those noted by Miller, is that a social movement may "go mainstream." Some movements become an accepted part of the system (typically after realizing some of their goals) to the point that they no longer challenge the status quo. Until 1990, the government of South Africa, for example, banned the African National Congress (ANC), a political organization seeking to overthrow the state-supported system of apartheid. Even suspected members of the ANC were subject to arrest. In 1990, the government lifted the decades-old ban and released ANC leader Nelson Mandela from prison; in 1994, Mandela became president of a country now moving away from apartheid.

Figure 22–3 provides a graphic summary of the various stages of social movements.

CONTROVERSY & DEBATE

Are You Willing to Take a Stand?

Are you satisfied with our society as it is? Surely, everyone would change some things about our way of life. Indeed, despite the fact that 92 percent of Canadians claim to be "very happy" or "pretty happy" (Bibby, 1995), there are many things that people would change. Pessimism about our society is widespread. Seventy percent of Canadians believe that, in financial terms, the lot of the average person is getting worse. Only 25 and 22 percent of us have "a great deal" or "quite a bit" of confidence, respectively, in our federal and provincial leaders. We feel that the rich, corporations, and politicians have too much power, and that politicians are paid too much. We fear crime and 85 percent of us believe that the "courts do not deal harshly enough with criminals" (Bibby, 1995).

But are we willing to take a stand to bring about social change? How many of us are willing to serve on the picket lines or barricades, march in protest or in a Gay Pride parade, vote against our own parties in the House of Commons, or tie ourselves to trees to stop clear-cutting?

Certainly, there are good reasons to avoid political controversy. Any time we challenge the system—whether on campus, at work, or in the larger political arena—we risk making enemies, losing a job, or perhaps even sustaining physical injury. Challenging the status quo, by definition, means stepping on powerful toes. For Canadians, who, traditionally, have deferred to authority more readily than Americans, such challenges in themselves may seem to question basic values.

While it may be the case that only a small percentage of Canadians are willing to take a stand, publicly, on specific issues, there have been some highly visible and well-publicized instances of Canadians joining in collective action to address social problems. For example, in October 1995, three days before the referendum on sovereignty in Quebec, an estimated 150 000 Canadians gathered at a massive "No" rally in Montreal, including many thousands from across Canada, to express their solidarity with the people of Quebec. Despite the fact that airlines and buses offered cut rates (fare subsidies, in effect), participation required families to disrupt their routines and people to take time off from work or school. (Some analysts felt that the outpouring

"No" rally in Montreal, October 1995.

of support from the rest of Canada touched Quebeckers and may have helped to bring about the photo-finish in favour of the "No" side. In any case, Quebec's chief electoral officer declared that the politicians and corporations who organized the rally acted in contravention of Quebec's referendum laws and, therefore, illegally.)

Some may argue, in light of cultural values emphasizing the responsibility of individuals for their own well-being, that collective action is no remedy for social ills. Sociology, of course, poses a counterpoint to this cultural individualism. As C. Wright Mills (1959) pointed out decades ago, many of the problems we encounter as individuals are caused by the structure of society. Thus, he maintained, solutions to many of life's challenges depend on collective effort—that is, people willing to join together to take a stand for what they believe in.

Continue the debate . . .

1. *Does the reluctance of Canadians to address problems through collective action mean that they are basically satisfied with their lives and their society? Or does it mean that they think individuals acting together can't make a difference?*

2. *Have you ever participated in a political demonstration? What were its goals? What did it accomplish?*

3. *Identify ways that life today has been affected by people who took a stand in the past. Think about race and ethnic relations, the environment, the status of women, and conditions of employment.*

SOCIAL MOVEMENTS AND SOCIAL CHANGE

Social movements exist to encourage—or to resist—social change. Whatever the intention, their success varies from case to case. Gender equality, still only a partially realized goal, has been advanced by the actions of numerous women's groups in Canada and elsewhere. Environmentalists, as well, have experienced some major successes and changed public awareness dramatically.

Sometimes we overlook the success of past social movements and take for granted the changes that other people struggled so hard to win. Beginning a century ago, workers' movements fought to end child labour in factories, limit working hours, make the workplace safer, and establish the right to bargain collectively with employers. And women today have greater legal rights and economic opportunities won by earlier generations of women.

Seen one way, major social transformations such as the Industrial Revolution and the rise of capitalism give rise to social movements, including those involving workers and women. On the other hand, the efforts of workers, women, racial and ethnic minorities, and gay people have sent ripples of change throughout our society. Thus, social change is both the cause and the consequence of social movements.

LOOKING AHEAD: SOCIAL MOVEMENTS IN THE TWENTY-FIRST CENTURY

Especially since the turbulent decade of the 1960s—a decade marked by widespread social protests—Canadian society has been pushed and pulled by many social movements and countermovements. Sometimes tension explodes into violence, as with the Oka standoff described at the beginning of this chapter. In other cases, the struggles are more restrained, as with political debate for and against the free trade agreements. Yet people on all sides of controversial issues agree that many of this nation's most pressing problems—national unity, regionalism, poverty—remain unresolved. In addition, of course, new issues—including the state of the family and gay rights—have moved to centre stage.

Social movements have always been part of our society, although their focus, tactics, and intensity change with time. There is little doubt, therefore, that social movements will continue to shape our way of life. Indeed, for three reasons, the scope of social movements is likely to increase. First, protest should increase as women and other historically excluded categories of people gain a greater political voice. Thus, the twenty-first century should be marked by more social movements here at home. Second, at a global level, the technology of the Information Revolution means that anyone with a satellite dish, personal computer, or fax machine can stay abreast of political events, often as they happen. Third, new technology and the emerging global economy mean that social movements are now uniting people throughout the entire world—or throughout Marshall McLuhan's *global village*. Moreover, since many problems are global in scope, only international cooperation can solve them.

SUMMARY

1. A collectivity differs from a social group in its limited social interaction, vague social boundaries, and weak and often unconventional norms.

2. Crowds, an important type of collective behaviour, take various forms: casual crowds, conventional crowds, expressive crowds, acting crowds, and protest crowds.

3. Crowds that become emotionally intense and even violent spawn mobs and riots. Mobs pursue a specific goal; rioting involves undirected destructiveness.

4. Crowds have figured heavily in social change throughout history, although the value of their action depends on one's political outlook.

5. Contagion theory views crowds as anonymous, suggestible, and subject to escalating emotions. Convergence theory links crowd behaviour to the traits of participants. Emergent-norm theory holds that crowds may develop their own behavioural norms.

6. One form of mass behaviour is rumour, which thrives in a climate of ambiguity. While rumour involves public issues, gossip deals with personal issues of local interest.

7. Public opinion consists of people's positions on issues of widespread importance. Some people's attitudes carry more weight than others and, on any given issue, a small proportion of the population claims to hold no opinion at all.

8. A panic (in a local area) or mass hysteria (across an entire society) are types of collective behaviour by which people respond to a significant event, real or imagined, with irrational, frantic, and often self-destructive behaviour.

9. In industrial societies, people adopt fashion to enhance social prestige. A fad, which is more unconventional than a fashion, is of shorter duration but is embraced with greater enthusiasm.

10. Social movements exist to promote or discourage change. Sociologists classify social movements according to the range of people they seek to engage and the extent of change they seek.

11. According to deprivation theory, social movements arise in response to relative deprivation more than the lack of well-being in an absolute sense.

12. Mass-society theory holds that people join social movements to gain a sense of belonging and social significance.

13. Structural-strain theory explains the development of social movements as a cumulative consequence of six factors. Well-formulated grievances and goals encourage the organization of social movements; undirected anger, in contrast, promotes rioting.

14. Resource-mobilization theory ties the success or failure of a social movement to the availability of resources such as money, human labour, and alliances with other organizations.

15. New social movements theory notes that contemporary movements focus on quality-of-life issues that are typically national or international in scope.

16. A typical social movement proceeds through consecutive stages: emergence (defining the public issue), coalescence (entering the public arena), bureaucratization (becoming formally organized), and decline (brought on by failure or, sometimes, success).

17. Past social movements have shaped society in ways that people now take for granted. Just as movements produce change, so change itself sparks social movements.

CRITICAL THINKING QUESTIONS

1. The concept of collective behaviour encompasses a broad range of social patterns. What traits do they all have in common?

2. Imagine the aftermath of a hockey game in which the revelry of university students turns into a destructive rampage. What insights into this event do contagion theory, convergence theory, and emergent-norm theory provide? Is the trashing of rooms by the U.S. Olympic hockey team a similar phenomenon?

3. The 1960s was a decade of both great affluence and widespread social protest. What sociological insights help to explain this apparent paradox?

4. In what respects do some recent social movements (those concerned with the environment, animal rights, and gun control) differ from older crusades (focusing on, say, civil rights and gender equality)?

SOCIOLOGY APPLIED

1. Visit the Web site for Hemp Nation at www.hempnation.com. What are the goals of this organization? How is it trying to expand the social movement in favour of legalizing marijuana use?

2. With ten friends, try a fascinating experiment: One person writes down a detailed "rumour" about someone important and then whispers it to the second person, who whispers it to a third, and so on. When the rumour comes full circle, the first person writes it down again. Compare the two versions of the rumour.

3. With other members of the class, identify "fad" products, from hula hoops to Beanie Babies. What makes people want them? Why do they drop from favour so quickly?

4. What social movements are represented by organizations on your campus? Your class might invite several leaders to describe their groups' goals and strategies.

http://www.deadlists.com/nathan/thesis/
From Whence These Rumblings? is a long essay by Nathan Wolfson that examines how particular social structures foster movements for change.

http://www.ic.org/
The *Intentional Communities* page provides information and access to resources for seekers of community. Intentional Community is an inclusive term for eco-villages, cohousing, residential land trusts, communes, student co-ops, urban housing cooperatives, and other related projects and dreams.

http://www.webactive.com/
WebActive is a guide to political activism links on the World Wide Web, with a well-organized topic index.

http://carmen.artsci.washington.edu/propaganda/home.htm
This site contains an extensive analysis of propaganda, with contemporary examples.

http://www.uni.ca/index_e.html
The Unity Link is a pro-federalist site for supporters of Canadian national unity, containing news items and anti-separatist documents.

Joan Truckenbrod, *Sociotechture*, 1991
Courtesy of The Williams Gallery, Princeton, N.J. © Joan Truckenbrod, 1997.

CHAPTER 23

SOCIAL CHANGE: TRADITIONAL, MODERN, AND POST-MODERN SOCIETIES

The firelight flickers in the gathering darkness as Chief Kanhonk sits, as he has done at the end of the day for many years, ready to begin an evening of animated talk and storytelling (Simons, 1995). This is the hour when the Kaiapo, a small society in Brazil's lush Amazon region, celebrate their heritage. Because the Kaiapo are a traditional people with no written language, the elders rely on evenings by the fire to teach their culture and instruct the grandchildren. In the past, evenings like this have been filled with tales of brave Kaiapo warriors fighting off Portuguese traders in pursuit of slaves and gold.

But as the minutes pass, only a few older villagers assemble for the evening ritual. "It is the Big Ghost," one man grumbles, explaining the poor turnout. The Big Ghost has indeed descended upon them, its bluish glow spilling from windows of homes throughout the village. The Kaiapo children—and many adults as well—are watching television. Installing a satellite dish in the village several years ago has had greater consequences than anyone imagined. In the end, what their enemies failed to do with guns, the Kaiapo may well do to themselves with prime-time programming.

The Kaiapo are among the 230 000 native peoples who inhabit the country we call Brazil. They stand out because of their striking body paint and ornate ceremonial dress. Recently, they have become rich from gold mining and harvesting mahogany trees. Now they must decide if their newfound fortune is a blessing or a curse.

To some, affluence means the opportunity to learn about the outside world through travel and television. Others, like Chief Kanhonk, are not so sure. Sitting by the fire, he thinks aloud, "I have been saying that people must buy useful things like knives and fishing hooks. Television does not fill the stomach. It only shows our children and grandchildren white people's things." Bebtopup, the oldest priest, nods in agreement: "The night is the time the old people teach the young people. Television has stolen the night" (Simons, 1995:471).

The Kaiapo story raises profound questions about the causes of change and whether change is always for the better. The Kaiapo may be edging towards modernity, but is a higher standard of living necessarily better than their traditional way of life? Moreover, the drama of the Kaiapo is being played out around the globe as more and more traditional cultures are being lured away from their heritage by the materialism and affluence of rich societies.

Within Canada's own boundaries there are people grappling with the same kinds of concerns about the influence of television in particular. In the part of the Northwest Territories that in 1999 will become the separate territory of Nunavut, the Inuit people have long been concerned about the damaging effects of television programming originating in the U.S. and southern Canada. With financial assistance from the federal government, they have created the Inuit Broadcasting Corporation (IBC), which produces news, documentaries, children's programs (including cartoons and puppet shows), and talk shows that deal with issues of relevance to the region—in its own language, Inuktitut. Through the IBC, the Inuit people have been able to mitigate some of the intrusive and damaging impacts of television on their culture.

This chapter examines social change as a process with both positive and negative consequences. Of particular interest to us is what sociologists call *modernity*, changes brought about by the Industrial Revolution, and *post-modernity*, recent transformations sparked by the Information Revolution and the post-industrial economy.

WHAT IS SOCIAL CHANGE?

Earlier chapters have examined relatively *static* social patterns, including status and roles, social stratification, and social institutions. The *dynamic* forces that have shaped our way of life range from innovations in technology to the growth of bureaucracy and the expansion of cities. These are all dimensions of **social change**, *the transformation of culture and social institutions over time*. The process of social change has four key characteristics.

1. **Social change is inevitable.** "Nothing is constant except death and taxes," goes the old saying. Yet even our thoughts about death have changed dramatically as life expectancy in Canada has doubled over the past century. Taxes, meanwhile, were unknown through most of human history, and only emerged with complex social organization several thousand years ago. In short, one is hard-pressed to identify anything that is not subject to the twists and turns of change.

   Still, some societies change more quickly than others. As Chapter 4 ("Society") explained, hunting and gathering societies change quite slowly; members of modern, complex societies, on the other hand, experience significant change within a single lifetime.

   Moreover, in a given society, some cultural elements change faster than others. William Ogburn's (1964) theory of *cultural lag* (see Chapter 3, "Culture") states that material culture (that is, things) usually changes faster than nonmaterial culture (ideas and attitudes). For example, medical technology that prolongs life has developed more rapidly than ethical standards for deciding when and how to use it.

2. **Social change is sometimes intentional but often unplanned.** Industrial societies actively promote many kinds of change. For example, scientists seek more efficient forms of energy, and advertisers try to convince consumers that life is incomplete without some new gadget. Yet rarely can anyone envision all the consequences of the changes they set in motion.

   Early automobile manufacturers understood that cars would allow people to travel, in a single day, distances that had previously required weeks or months. But no one foresaw how profoundly the mobility provided by automobiles would reshape our society, scattering family members, threatening the environment, and reshaping cities and suburbs. Nor did anyone foresee the three to four thousand deaths in car accidents in Canada alone each year.

3. **Social change is controversial.** As the history of the automobile demonstrates, most social change yields both positive and negative consequences. Capitalists welcomed the Industrial Revolution because advancing technology increased both productivity and profits. Many workers, however, feared that machines would make their skills obsolete and resisted the push towards "progress."

   Changing patterns of social interaction between white Canadians and aboriginal peoples or other racial or ethnic minorities, between anglophones and francophones, between women and men, and between gays and heterosexuals give rise to both celebration and backlash as people disagree about how we ought to live.

4. **Some changes matter more than others.** Some social changes (such as clothing fads) have only passing significance, whereas other innovations (such as computers) unleash changes that transform the entire world and resonate for generations. Looking ahead, will the Information Revolution turn out to be as pivotal as the Industrial Revolution? Like the automobile and television, computers will have both beneficial and deleterious effects, providing new kinds of jobs while eliminating old ones, isolating people in offices while joining people together in global electronic networks, offering vast amounts of information while threatening personal privacy.

CAUSES OF SOCIAL CHANGE

Social change has many causes. And in a world linked by sophisticated communication and transportation technology, change in one place often begets change elsewhere.

Today, most of the people with access to computers live in rich countries such as Canada. But the number of people in agrarian societies going "online" is on the rise. How do you think the introduction of new information technology will change more traditional societies? Are all the changes likely to be for the good?

CULTURE AND CHANGE

Chapter 3 ("Culture") identified three important sources of cultural change. *Invention* produces new objects, ideas, and social patterns. Rocket propulsion research, which began in the 1940s, has produced spacecraft that can reach towards the stars. Today, we take such technology for granted; during the twenty-first century, a significant number of people may well travel in space.

Discovery occurs when people first take note of certain elements or learn to see them in a new way. Medical advances, for example, offer a growing understanding of the human body. Beyond their direct effects on human health, medical discoveries have stretched life expectancy, setting in motion "the greying of Canada" (see Chapter 14, "Aging and the Elderly").

Diffusion creates change as trade, migration, and mass communication spread cultural elements throughout the world. Ralph Linton (1937) recognized that many familiar elements of our culture came from other lands. For example, cloth (developed in Asia), clocks (invented in Europe), and coins (devised in Turkey) have all become part of our way of life. Generally, material things diffuse more readily than nonmaterial cultural traits. The Kaiapo, described at the beginning of this chapter, have been quick to adopt television, but they have been reluctant to embrace the materialism and individualism at the core of Western commercial programming.

During its entire history, immigrants have brought change to Canada. In recent decades, people from Southern and Central Europe, Asia, Latin America, and the Caribbean have introduced new cultural patterns, clearly evident in the tastes, sights, smells, and sounds of cities across the country. Little Italies, Chinatowns, Caribana parades, ethnic festivals such as Toronto's Caravan, outdoor cafés, reggae music, pizza, perogies, fajitas, and sushi have become part of the fabric of life for many Canadians.

CONFLICT AND CHANGE

Tension and conflict within a society also produce change. Karl Marx saw class conflict as the engine that drives societies from one historical era to another (see Chapter 4, "Society," and Chapter 9, "Social Stratification"). In industrial-capitalist societies, he maintained, struggle between capitalists and workers propels society towards a socialist system of production.

In the century since Marx's death, this model has proven simplistic. Yet, he correctly foresaw that social conflict arising from inequality (involving race and gender as well as social class) would force changes in every society, including our own.

IDEAS AND CHANGE

Max Weber, too, contributed to our understanding of social change. While Weber acknowledged the importance of conflict based on material production, he traced the roots of most social change to ideas. He illustrated his argument by showing how people with charisma can convey a message that sometimes changes the world.

CHAPTER 23 Social Change: Traditional, Modern, and Post-Modern Societies **583**

Weber highlighted the importance of ideas by showing how the religious beliefs of early Protestants set the stage for the spread of industrial capitalism (see Chapter 4, "Society"). The fact that industrial capitalism developed primarily in areas of Western Europe where the Protestant work ethic was strong proved to Weber (1958a; orig. 1904–05) the power of ideas to bring about change.

Ideas also direct social movements. Chapter 22 ("Collective Behaviour and Social Movements") explained how change comes from the determination of people acting together to, say, clean up the environment, or make the world more just. The international gay rights movement, for example, draws strength from people who believe that lesbians and gay men should enjoy the same rights and opportunities as the heterosexual majority. Opposition to the gay rights movement, moreover, reveals the power of ideas to inhibit as well as to advance social change.

THE NATURAL ENVIRONMENT AND CHANGE

Human societies are closely connected to their natural environment. For this reason, change in one tends to produce change in the other.

By and large, our culture casts nature as a force to be tamed and reshaped to human purposes. From the outset, European settlers systematically cut down forests to create fields for farming and to make materials for building; they established towns, extended roads in every direction, and dammed rivers as a source of water and energy. Such human construction not only reflects our cultural determination to master the natural environment, it also points up the centrality of the idea of "growth" in our way of life.

But the consequences of this thinking have placed increasing stress on the natural environment. Our society contends with problems of solid waste and air and water pollution, all the while consuming a disproportionate share of global resources. A growing awareness that such patterns are not sustainable in the long term is forcing us to confront the need to change our way of life in some basic respects.

DEMOGRAPHIC CHANGE

Population growth not only places escalating demands on the natural environment, but it alters cultural patterns. In the Netherlands, a high-density nation, homes are small and narrow compared to those in Canada, with extremely steep staircases to make efficient use of space. In Tokyo, bus drivers routinely negotiate city streets that many Canadian drivers would consider dangerously narrow for even a car. Although Canada enjoys a bounty of physical space, urbanization and industrialization have changed our way of life and will continue to do so. Over three-quarters of Canadians live in cities, which cover only a small percentage of the land surface.

Profound change is also taking place as our population, collectively speaking, grows older. As Chapter 14 ("Aging and the Elderly") explained, in 1996, more than 12 percent of Canadians were over sixty-five, more than double the proportion in 1901. Statistics Canada estimates that by the year 2036, seniors will account for almost *one-quarter* of the population. Medical research and health care services will increasingly focus on the elderly, and life will change in countless additional ways as homes and household products are redesigned to meet the needs of older consumers.

Migration within and among societies is another demographic factor that promotes change. Since the early 1800s, tens of millions of immigrants have come to Canada, initially to participate in the fur trade or to establish farming homesteads, but more recently to seek a better life in the growing urban areas. Immigrants to Canada's urban centres were joined by a steady flow of migrants from rural Canada, where high fertility and changes in the structure of agriculture resulted in surplus population. As a result of immigration and rural–urban migration, Canada's urban population grew from 18 to 78 percent of the total population between 1871 and 1996. In a mere 125 years, Canada was transformed from a nation of settlers to an urban-industrial society with one of the world's largest economies.

MODERNITY

A central concept in the study of social change is **modernity**, *social patterns linked to industrialization*. In everyday usage, modernity (its Latin root means "lately") designates the present in relation to the past. Sociologists include within this catch-all concept the many social patterns set in motion by the Industrial Revolution, beginning in Western Europe in the mid–eighteenth century. **Modernization**, then, is *the process of social change initiated by industrialization*. The time line inside the front cover of this text highlights important events that mark the emergence of modernity.

KEY DIMENSIONS OF MODERNIZATION

Peter Berger (1977) notes four major characteristics of modernization:

1. **The decline of small, traditional communities.** Modernity involves "the progressive weakening, if not destruction, of the concrete and rel-

In response to the accelerated pace of change in the late nineteenth century, Paul Gauguin (1848–1903) left his native France for the South Seas, where he was captivated by a simpler and seemingly timeless way of life. He romanticized this environment in his 1894 painting Mahana no Atua (The Day of the God).

Paul Gauguin, *The Day of the God (Mahana no Atua)*, 1894, oil on canvas (68.3 × 91.5 cm), Helen Birch Bartlett Memorial Collection, 1926. Photograph © 1994, The Art Institute of Chicago. All rights reserved.

atively cohesive communities in which human beings have found solidarity and meaning throughout most of history" (Berger 1977:72). For thousands of years, in hunting and gathering camps and in the agrarian villages of Europe and North America, people lived in small-scale settlements. Traditional worlds—based on sentiments and beliefs passed from generation to generation—afford each person a well-defined place. These primary groups conferred a limited range of experience with a strong sense of identity, belonging, and purpose.

Since Canada has a land mass of close to 10 million square kilometres (the second largest in the world) and a population density of only 2.8 persons per square kilometre, and since about 80 percent of its population lives within 160 kilometres of the U.S. border, there is a great deal of space through which to scatter isolated communities. Small, isolated communities—many of them with far fewer than 100 members—still exist in Canada, but they are now home to only a small percentage of our population. Many of these people are Indian, Métis, or Inuit. Even so, cars, telephones, and television give most rural families the pulse of the larger society and connect them to the entire world.

2. **The expansion of personal choice.** To people in traditional, pre-industrial societies, life is shaped by forces beyond human control—gods, spirits, or, simply, fate. But as the power of tradition erodes, people come to see their lives as a series of options, a process Berger calls *individu-*

alization. Many people in Canada, for example, adopt one "lifestyle" or another, showing an openness to change.

3. **Increasing social diversity.** In pre-industrial societies, strong family ties and powerful religious beliefs enforce conformity while discouraging diversity and change. Modernization promotes a more rational, scientific world view, in which tradition loses its force and morality becomes a matter of individual attitude. The growth of cities, the expansion of impersonal bureaucracy, and social interaction among people from various backgrounds combine to foster a diversity of beliefs and behaviour. Increasing secularization, or decline in the importance of religion, goes hand in hand with modernization.

4. **Future orientation and growing awareness of time.** While pre-modern people focus on the past, people in modern societies think more about the future. Modern people are not only forward-looking but optimistic that discoveries and new inventions will enhance their lives.

Modern people also organize daily routines according to precise units of time. With the introduction of clocks in the late Middle Ages, Europeans began to think not in terms of sunlight and seasons but in terms of hours and minutes. Preoccupied with personal gain, modern people calculate time to the moment and generally believe that "Time is money!" Berger points out that one key indicator of a society's degree of modernization is the proportion of people wearing wristwatches.

CHAPTER 23 Social Change: Traditional, Modern, and Post-Modern Societies **585**

TABLE 23–1 Canadian Mobility by Age Group (Percentage Changing Residence over a Five-Year Period)

Age Group	1991–96
5–14	45.1
15–24	47.3
25–34	70.8
35–44	46.8
45–54	31.9
55–64	25.5
65 and over	20.2
Total	43.3

SOURCE: Calculations from 1996 census tables (www.statcan.ca).

Finally, recall that modernization touched off the development of sociology itself. As Chapter 1 ("The Sociological Perspective") explained, the discipline originated in the wake of the Industrial Revolution in Western Europe, where social change was proceeding most rapidly. Early European and U.S. sociologists tried to analyze and explain modernization and its consequences—both good and bad—for human beings.

FERDINAND TOENNIES: THE LOSS OF COMMUNITY

The German sociologist Ferdinand Toennies produced a lasting account of modernization in his theory of *Gemeinschaft* and *Gesellschaft* (see Chapter 21, "Population and Urbanization"). Like Peter Berger, whose work he influenced, Toennies (1963; orig. 1887) viewed modernization as the progressive loss of *Gemeinschaft*, or human community. As Toennies saw it, the Industrial Revolution weakened the strong social fabric of family and tradition by introducing a businesslike emphasis on facts, efficiency, and money. European and North American societies gradually became rootless and impersonal as people came to associate mostly on the basis of self-interest—the condition Toennies dubbed *Gesellschaft*.

Early in this century, at least some North American areas approximated Toennies's concept of *Gemeinschaft*. Families that had lived for generations in small towns and villages were tightly integrated into a hard-working, slow-moving way of life. Telephones (invented in 1876) were rare; the first coast-to-coast call was placed only in 1915 (see the time line inside the front cover of this book). Before television (introduced in 1939, widespread after 1950), families entertained themselves, often gathering with friends in the evening—much like Brazil's Kaiapo—to share stories, sorrows, or song. Before the onset of rapid transportation (although Henry Ford's assembly line began in 1908, cars became commonplace only after World War II), many people viewed their home town as their entire world.

Inevitable tensions and conflicts—sometimes based on race, ethnicity, and religion—characterized past communities. According to Toennies, however, because of the traditional ties of *Gemeinschaft*, people were "essentially united in spite of all separating factors" (1963:65; orig. 1887).

Modernity turns societies inside out so that, as Toennies put it, people are "essentially separated in spite of uniting factors" (1963:65). This is the world of *Gesellschaft* where, especially in large cities, most people live among strangers and ignore each other as they pass on the street.

Our high level of geographic mobility is one important cause of a sense of rootlessness. Over one year, about one in six individuals changes his or her place of residence. Close to half of all Canadians move over a five-year interval. Seven percent of the population moves from outside the province or country; 23 percent move within the same municipality. Table 23–1 shows that people between the ages of 25 and 34 are the most mobile, with 70.8 percent having moved within the last five years. The relatively high level of mobility in the youngest age category in the table is probably due to the search for more suitable accommodation by the 25- to 34-year-old parents of these children. In the General Social Survey (1985), the most frequently stated reasons for moving are (1) to purchase or build a home; (2) to live in a larger home; (3) to live in a better neighbourhood; (4) to live near work; and (5) to establish an independent household. Each of these top-ranked reasons is consistent with movement among 25- to 34-year-olds, who are leaving the homes of their parents, getting married, and having children.

Critical evaluation. Toennies's theory of *Gemeinschaft* and *Gesellschaft* is the most widely cited model of modernization. The theory's strength lies in its synthesis of various dimensions of change—growing population, the rise of cities, and increasing impersonality in social interaction.

One problem with Toennies's theory, however, is that modern life, while often impersonal, is not completely devoid of *Gemeinschaft*. Even in a world of strangers, modern friendships can be strong and lasting. Traditions are especially pronounced in many ethnic neighbourhoods, where residents maintain close community ties.

Another criticism is that Toennies's approach says little about which factors (industrialization, urbanization, weakening of families) are cause and which are effect. Critics also assert that Toennies favoured—perhaps even romanticized—traditional

George Tooker's 1950 painting The Subway *depicts a common problem of modern life: Weakening social ties and eroding traditions create a generic humanity in which everyone is alike yet each person is an anxious stranger in the midst of others.*

George Tooker, *The Subway*, 1950, egg tempera on composition board, 18⅛ x 36⅛", Whitney Museum of American Art, New York. Purchased with funds from the Julianna Force Purchase Award, 50.23.

societies while overlooking bonds of family, neighbourhood, and friendship in modern societies.

EMILE DURKHEIM: THE DIVISION OF LABOUR

The French sociologist Emile Durkheim, whose work is examined in Chapter 4 ("Society"), shared Toennies's interest in the profound social changes wrought by the Industrial Revolution. For Durkheim, modernization is marked by an increasing *division of labour*, or specialized economic activity (1964b; orig. 1893). Whereas every member of a traditional society engages in more or less the same daily round of activities, modern societies rely on people assuming highly distinctive roles.

Durkheim contended that pre-industrial societies are held together by *mechanical solidarity*, or shared moral sentiments. Thus, members of pre-industrial societies view everyone as basically alike, doing the same kind of work, and belonging together. Durkheim's concept of mechanical solidarity is virtually the same as Toennies's *Gemeinschaft*.

With modernization, the division of labour becomes more and more pronounced. To Durkheim, this change means *less* mechanical solidarity, but *more* of another kind of tie: *organic solidarity*, or the mutual dependency among people who engage in specialized work. Put simply, modern societies are integrated not by likeness but by difference: all of us must depend on others to meet most of our needs. Organic solidarity corresponds to Toennies's concept of *Gesellschaft*.

Despite obvious similarities in their thinking, Durkheim and Toennies interpreted modernity somewhat differently. To Toennies, the change from *Gemeinschaft* to *Gesellschaft* amounts to the loss of social solidarity because modern people lose the "natural" and "organic" bonds of the rural village, leaving only the "artificial" and "mechanical" ties of the big city. Durkheim had a different take on modernity,

even reversing Toennies's language to bring home the point. Durkheim labelled modern society "organic," arguing that modern society is no less natural than any other, and he described traditional societies as "mechanical" because they are so regimented. Thus, Durkheim viewed modernization not as the loss of community but as a change from community based on bonds of likeness (kinship and neighbourhood) to community based on economic interdependence (the division of labour). Durkheim's perspective on modernity is both more complex and more positive than that of Toennies.

Critical evaluation. Durkheim's work stands alongside that of Toennies, which it closely resembles, as a highly influential analysis of modernity. Of the two, Durkheim is the more optimistic; still, he feared that modern societies might become so diverse that they would collapse into a state of *anomie*, a condition in which norms and values are so weak and inconsistent that society provides little moral guidance to individuals. Without strong moral ties to society, modern people tend to be egocentric and find little purpose in life.

Evidence supports Durkheim's contention that anomie plagues modern societies. Suicide rates, which Durkheim considered a prime index of anomie, have risen during this century in both Canada and the U.S.; in Canada, the rates have doubled.

Even though modernization is associated with numerous indicators of stress or distress, shared norms and values are still strong enough to give the majority of people a sense of meaning and purpose. Despite the hazards of anomie and atomization, most people seem to value the privacy and personal autonomy that modern society affords.

MAX WEBER: RATIONALIZATION

For Max Weber, whose work is also detailed in Chapter 4 ("Society"), modernity means replacing a

Max Weber maintained that the distinctive character of modern society was its rational world view. Virtually all of Weber's work on modernity centred on types of people he considered typical of their age: the scientist, the capitalist, and the bureaucrat. Each is rational to the core: the scientist is committed to the orderly discovery of truth, the capitalist to the orderly pursuit of profit, and the bureaucrat to orderly conformity to a rational system of rule.

traditional world view with a rational way of thinking. In pre-industrial societies, tradition acts as a constant brake on change. To traditional people, Weber explains, "truth" is roughly synonymous with "what has always been" (1978:36; orig. 1921). In modern societies, by contrast, people see truth as the result of rational calculation. Because efficiency is valued more than reverence for the past, individuals adopt whichever social patterns allow them to achieve their goals.

Echoing the claim of Toennies and Durkheim that industrialization weakens tradition, Weber declared modern society to be "disenchanted." The unquestioned truths of an earlier time have been challenged by rational, scientific thinking: in short, modern society turns away from the gods. Throughout his life, Weber explored various modern "types"—the capitalist, the scientist, the bureaucrat—all of whom share the rational world view that Weber believed was coming to dominate humanity.

Critical evaluation. Compared with Toennies, and especially Durkheim, Weber was critical of modern society. He recognized that science could produce technological and organizational wonders, yet worried that it was carrying us away from more basic questions about the meaning and purpose of human existence. Weber feared that rationalization, especially in bureaucracies, would erode the human spirit with endless rules and regulations.

However, some of Weber's critics think that the alienation he attributed to bureaucracy is actually a product of social inequality. That contention leads us to the ideas of Karl Marx.

KARL MARX: CAPITALISM

For Karl Marx, modern society was synonymous with capitalism: he saw the Industrial Revolution primarily as a *capitalist revolution*. Marx traced the emergence of the bourgeoisie in medieval Europe to expanding commerce. The bourgeoisie gradually displaced the feudal aristocracy as the Industrial Revolution placed a powerful new system of production under its control.

Marx agreed that modernity weakened small-scale communities (as described by Toennies), sharpened the division of labour (as noted by Durkheim), and fostered a rational world view (as asserted by Weber). But he considered these factors simply as conditions necessary for capitalism to flourish. Capitalism, according to Marx, draws people from farms and small towns into an ever-expanding market system centred in cities; specialization is needed for efficient factories; and rationality is exemplified by the capitalists' relentless quest for profits.

Earlier chapters have painted Marx as a spirited critic of capitalist society, but his vision of modernity also incorporates a considerable measure of optimism. Unlike Weber, who viewed modern society as an "iron cage" of bureaucracy, Marx believed that social conflict within capitalist societies would sow the seeds of revolutionary social change, leading to an egalitarian socialism. Such a society, as he envi-

TABLE 23–2 Traditional and Modern Societies: The Big Picture

Elements of Society	Traditional Societies	Modern Societies
Cultural Patterns		
Values	Homogeneous; sacred character; few subcultures and countercultures	Heterogeneous; secular character; many subcultures and countercultures
Norms	High moral significance; little tolerance of diversity	Variable moral significance; high tolerance of diversity
Time orientation	Present linked to past	Present linked to future
Technology	Pre-industrial; human and animal energy	Industrial; advanced energy sources
Social Structure		
Status and role	Few statuses, most ascribed; few specialized roles	Many statuses, some ascribed and some achieved; many specialized roles
Relationships	Typically primary; little anonymity and privacy	Typically secondary; considerable anonymity and privacy
Communication	Face-to-face	Face-to-face supplemented by mass media
Social control	Informal gossip	Formal police and legal system
Social stratification	Rigid patterns of social inequality; little mobility	Fluid patterns of social inequality; considerable mobility
Gender patterns	Pronounced patriarchy; women's lives centred in the home	Declining patriarchy; increasing number of women in the paid labour force
Economy	Based on agriculture; some manufacturing in the home; little white-collar work	Based on industrial mass production; factories become centres of production; increasing white-collar work
State	Small-scale government; little state intervention in society	Large-scale government; considerable state intervention in society
Family	Extended family as the primary means of socialization and economic production	Nuclear family retains some socialization functions but is more a unit of consumption than of production
Religion	Religion guides world view; little religious pluralism	Religion weakens with the rise of science; extensive religious pluralism
Education	Formal schooling limited to elites	Basic schooling becomes universal, with growing proportion receiving advanced education
Health	High birth and death rates; brief life expectancy because of low standard of living and simple medical technology	Low birth and death rates; longer life expectancy because of higher standard of living and sophisticated medical technology
Settlement patterns	Small scale; population typically small and widely dispersed in rural villages and small towns	Large scale; population typically large and concentrated in cities
Social Change	Slow; change evident over many generations	Rapid; change evident within a single generation

sioned it, would harness the wonders of industrial technology to enrich people's lives and also rid the world of social classes, the prime source of social conflict and dehumanization. While Marx's evaluation of modern capitalist society was highly negative, then, he imagined a future of human freedom, creativity, and community.

Critical evaluation. Marx's theory of modernization is a complex theory of capitalism. But he underestimated the dominance of bureaucracy in modern societies. In socialist societies, in particular, the stifling effects of bureaucracy turned out to be as bad as—or even worse than—the dehumanizing aspects of capitalism. The recent upheavals in Eastern Europe and the former Soviet Union reveal the depth of popular opposition to oppressive state bureaucracies.

THEORETICAL ANALYSIS OF MODERNITY

The rise of modernity is a complex process involving many dimensions of change, described in previous chapters and summarized in Table 23–2. How can we make sense of so many changes going on all at once?

Many people marvelled at new industrial technology that was changing the world a century ago. But some, including Norwegian painter Edvard Munch, could see that the social consequences of the Industrial Revolution were not all positive. Looking at Workers on Their Way Home, *which Munch completed in 1915, what do you think are his criticisms of modern industrial society?*

Sociologists have devised two overarching explanations of modern society, one derived from the structural-functional paradigm and one based on the social-conflict approach.

STRUCTURAL-FUNCTIONAL THEORY: MODERNITY AS MASS SOCIETY

One broad approach—drawing on the ideas of Ferdinand Toennies, Emile Durkheim, and Max Weber—depicts modernization as the emergence of *mass society* (Dahrendorf, 1959; Kornhauser, 1959; Nisbet, 1966, 1969; Stein, 1972; Berger, Berger, and Kellner, 1974; Pearson, 1993). A **mass society** is *a society in which industry and expanding bureaucracy have eroded traditional social ties.* A mass society is marked by weak kinship and impersonal neighbourhoods, so that individuals are socially isolated. In their isolation, members of mass societies typically experience feelings of moral uncertainty and personal powerlessness.

The Mass Scale of Modern Life

Mass-society theory argues, first, that the scale of modern life has greatly increased. Before the Industrial Revolution, Europe and North America constituted an intricate mosaic of countless rural villages and small towns. In these small communities, which inspired Toennies's concept of *Gemeinschaft*, people lived out their lives surrounded by kin and guided by a shared heritage. Gossip was an informal, yet highly

effective, way to ensure conformity to community standards. These small communities, with their strong moral values, tolerated little social diversity—the state of mechanical solidarity described by Durkheim.

For example, in England before 1690, both law and local custom demanded that all people regularly participate in the Christian ritual of Holy Communion (Laslett, 1984). On this continent, only Rhode Island among the New England colonies tolerated any religious dissent. Because social differences were repressed, subcultures and countercultures rarely flourished and change proceeded slowly.

Increasing population, the growth of cities, and specialized economic activity driven by the Industrial Revolution gradually altered this pattern. People came to know one another by their jobs (for example, as the "doctor" or the "bank clerk") rather than by their kinship group or home town. People looked on most others simply as strangers. The face-to-face communication of the village was eventually replaced by the mass media—newspapers, radio, television, and, more recently, computer networks. Large organizations steadily assumed more and more responsibility for daily tasks that had once been fulfilled by family, friends, and neighbours; public education drew more and more people to schools; police, lawyers, and formal courts supervised a formal criminal justice system. Even charity became the work of faceless bureaucrats working for various social welfare agencies.

Geographical mobility, mass communication, and exposure to diverse ways of life erode traditional values. People become more tolerant of social diversity, defending individual rights and freedom of choice. Subcultures and countercultures multiply. Treating people differently based on their race, sex, or religion comes to be defined as backward and unjust. In the process, minorities at the margins of society gained greater power and broader participation in public life. Yet, mass-society theorists fear that transforming people of various backgrounds into a generic mass may end up dehumanizing everyone.

The Ever-Expanding State

In the small-scale, pre-industrial societies of Europe, government amounted to little more than a local noble. A royal family formally reigned over an entire nation but, without efficient transportation or communication, the power of even absolute monarchs fell far short of that wielded by today's political leaders.

Technological innovation allowed government to expand, and the centralized state grew in size and importance. At the time of Confederation, government, either federal or provincial, had limited functions. Since then, government in Canada has entered more and more areas of social life—establishing publicly owned enterprises in the areas of transportation, communication, and natural resources, regulating wages and working conditions, establishing standards for products of all kinds, educating the population, delivering medical care, protecting the environment, and providing financial assistance to the ill, the aged, and the unemployed. To pay for such programs, taxes have soared, so that today's average worker labours for six months a year just to pay for the broad array of services the government provides.

In a mass society, power resides in large bureaucracies, leaving people in local communities little control over their lives. For example, public officials mandate a standardized educational program for local schools, local products must earn government certification, and every citizen must maintain extensive tax records. While such regulations may protect people and enhance social equality, they force us to deal more and more with nameless officials in distant and often unresponsive bureaucracies, and they undermine the autonomy of families and neighbourhoods.

Critical evaluation. The theory of mass society concedes that the transformation of small-scale communities has positive aspects, but only at the cost of losing our cultural heritage. Modern societies increase individual rights, tolerate greater social differences, and raise standards of living. But they are prone to what

Weber feared most—excessive bureaucracy—as well as Toennies's self-centredness and Durkheim's anomie. Their size, complexity, and tolerance of diversity all but doom traditional values and family patterns, leaving individuals isolated, anxious, and materialistic. Voter apathy is growing in Canada: should we be surprised that individuals in vast, impersonal societies think no one person can make a difference?

Critics of mass-society theory contend that it romanticizes the past. They remind us that many people in small towns were actually eager to set out for the excitement and higher standard of living found in cities. Moreover, mass-society theory ignores problems of social inequality. Critics say this theory attracts social and economic conservatives who defend conventional morality and are indifferent to the historical plight of women and other minorities.

SOCIAL-CONFLICT THEORY: MODERNITY AS CLASS SOCIETY

The second interpretation of modernity derives largely from the ideas of Karl Marx. From a social-conflict perspective, modernity takes the form of a **class society**, *a capitalist society with pronounced social stratification.* That is, while acknowledging that modern societies have expanded to a mass scale, this approach views the heart of modernization as an expanding capitalist economy, rife with inequality (Miliband, 1969; Habermas, 1970; Clement, 1975; Polenberg, 1980; Blumberg, 1981; Harrington, 1984; Brym, 1985).

Capitalism

Class-society theory follows Marx in claiming that the increasing scale of social life in modern society results from the insatiable appetite of capitalism. Because a capitalist economy pursues ever-increasing profits, both production and consumption steadily rise.

According to Marx and Engels, capitalism rests on "naked self-interest" (1972:337; orig. 1848). This self-centredness erodes the social ties that once cemented small-scale communities. Capitalism also treats people as commodities: as a source of labour and a market for capitalist production.

Capitalism also supports science, not just as the key to greater productivity but also as an ideology that justifies the status quo. That is, modern societies encourage people to view human well-being as a *technical* puzzle to be solved by engineers and other experts rather than through the pursuit of *social* justice (Habermas, 1970). A capitalist culture, for example, seeks to improve health through scientific medicine rather than by eliminating poverty, which threatens many people's health in the first place.

Mass-society theory attributes feelings of anxiety, isolation, and lack of meaning in the modern world to rapid social change that washes away tradition. Edvard Munch captured this vision of modern emptiness in his painting The Scream. *Class-society theory, by contrast, ties such feelings to social inequality, by which some categories of people have power and privileges denied to others. Paul Marcus portrays modern injustice in the painting* Musical Chairs.

Edvard Munch, *The Scream*, Oslo, National Gallery (left); © Paul Marcus, *Musical Chairs*, oil painting on wood, 48 in. × 72 in. (right).

Business also raises the banner of scientific logic, trying to increase profits through greater efficiency. As Chapter 15 ("The Economy and Work") explains, capitalist corporations have reached enormous size and control almost unimaginable wealth as a result of "going global" as multinationals. From the class-society point of view, then, the expanding scale of life is less a function of *Gesellschaft* than it is the inevitable and destructive consequence of capitalism.

Persistent Inequality

Modernity has gradually eroded the rigid categories that set nobles apart from commoners in pre-industrial societies. But class-society theory maintains that elites persist—albeit now as capitalist millionaires rather than as nobles born to wealth and power. Canada has more billionaire families per capita than the United States: in the early 1980s Canada had six, while the U.S., with an economy twelve times larger, had only double that number (Francis, 1986). Furthermore, the distribution of family income is skewed in Canada: from 1951 to 1985, with minor fluctuations, families in the top 20 percent earned about 40 percent of all income while the bottom fifth earned just over 6 percent of all income (Fréchette, 1988). When measured in terms of individual income, the pattern is accentuated, with the top quintile earning

46.5 percent of income and the lowest quintile earning 3.4 percent (Statistics Canada, Cat. No. 96 13-207).

What of the state? Mass-society theorists contend that the state works to increase equality and combat social problems. Marx was skeptical that the state could accomplish more than minor reforms because, as he saw it, the real power lies in the hands of capitalists who control the economy. Other class-society theorists add that, to the extent that working people and minorities enjoy greater political rights and a higher standard of living today, these changes are the fruits of political struggle, not expressions of government goodwill. Thus, they conclude, despite our pretensions of democracy, power still rests primarily in the hands of those with wealth.

Critical evaluation. Table 23–3 summarizes the interpretations of modernity offered by mass-society theory and class-society theory. While the former focuses on the increasing scale of life and the growth of government, the latter stresses the expansion of capitalism and the persistence of inequality.

Class-society theory also dismisses Durkheim's argument that people in modern societies suffer from anomie, claiming instead that they suffer from alienation and powerlessness. Not surprisingly, then, the class-society interpretation of modernity enjoys widespread support among the political left, who call for greater equality and extensive regulation (or abolition) of the capitalist marketplace.

A basic criticism of class-society theory is that it overlooks the many ways in which modern societies have grown more egalitarian. For example, discrimination based on race, ethnicity, and gender is now illegal and widely regarded as a social problem. Further, most people in Canada favour unequal rewards, at least insofar as they reflect differences in personal talent and effort.

Moreover, few observers think a centralized economy would cure the ills of modernity in light of socialism's failure to generate a high overall standard of living. Many other social problems in Canada—from unemployment, homelessness, and industrial pollution to unresponsive government—have also been commonplace in socialist nations such as the former Soviet Union.

MODERNITY AND THE INDIVIDUAL

Both mass- and class-society theories focus on broad patterns of social change since the Industrial Revolution. Each "macro-level" approach also offers "micro-level" insights into how modernity shapes individual lives.

Mass Society: Problems of Identity

Modernity liberated individuals from the small, tightly knit communities of the past. Most people in modern societies, therefore, have privacy and freedom to express their individuality. Mass-society theory suggests, however, that extensive social diversity, isolation, and rapid social change make it difficult for many people to establish any coherent identity at all (Wheelis, 1958; Riesman, 1970; Berger, Berger, and Kellner, 1974). Canadians have had considerable difficulty articulating a national identity—and, indirectly, personal identities—to the point where Lipset (1991:42) states that national identity "is the quintessential Canadian issue." Proximity to the United States, regional tensions, ethnic and cultural diversity, bilingualism, and rapid social change make clear self-definition more difficult for Canadians (Hiller, 1996; Taras, Rasporich, and Mandel, 1993).

Chapter 5 ("Socialization") explained that people's personalities are largely a product of their social experiences. The small, homogeneous, and slowly changing societies of the past provided a firm (if narrow) foundation for building a meaningful identity. For example, the Hutterite communities that still flourish in Canada's Prairie provinces (especially in Alberta) teach young men and women "correct" ways to think and behave—and most learn to embrace this

TABLE 23–3 Two Interpretations of Modernity: A Summary

	Process of Modernization	Effects of Modernization
Mass-society theory	Industrialization; growth of bureaucracy	Increasing scale of life; rise of the state and other formal organizations
Class-society theory	Rise of capitalism	Expansion of the capitalist economy; persistence of social inequality

life as "natural" and right. Everything is shared—property, work, meals—in these tiny communal societies that have perpetuated the Hutterite way of life, largely unchanged, for over 400 years. Under these circumstances, which contrast sharply with those of modern mass society, it is relatively easy to establish a coherent and secure sense of personal identity.

Mass societies, with their characteristic diversity and rapid change, provide only shifting sands on which to build a personal identity. Left to make their own life decisions, many people—especially those with greater affluence—confront a bewildering range of options. Autonomy has little value without standards for making choices; in a tolerant mass society, people may find one path no more compelling than the next. Not surprisingly, many people shuttle from one identity to another, changing their lifestyle, relationships, and even religion in search of an elusive "true self." Beset by the widespread "relativism" of modern societies, people without a moral compass lack the security and certainty once provided by tradition.

For David Riesman (1970; orig. 1950), modernization brings changes in **social character**, *personality patterns common to members of a particular society.* Preindustrial societies promote what Riesman terms **tradition-directedness**, *rigid conformity to time-honoured ways of living.* Members of traditional societies model their lives on what has gone before so that what is "good" is equivalent to "what has always been."

Tradition-directedness corresponds to Toennies's *Gemeinschaft* and Durkheim's mechanical solidarity. Culturally conservative, tradition-directed people think and act alike. Unlike the conformity found in modern societies, this uniformity is not an attempt to mimic one another. Instead, people are alike because everyone draws on the same solid cultural foundation. Hutterite women and men exemplify tradition-directedness; in Hutterite culture, tradition ties everyone to ancestors and descendants in an unbroken chain of communal living as ordained by God.

Members of diverse and rapidly changing societies define a tradition-directed personality as deviant because it seems so rigid. Modern people, by and large, prize personal flexibility and sensitivity to others. Riesman calls this type of social character **other-directedness**, *a receptiveness to the latest trends and fashions, often expressed in the practice of imitating others.* Because their socialization occurs within societies that are continuously in flux, other-directed people develop fluid identities marked by superficiality, inconsistency, and change. They try on different roles and identities, sometimes like so many pieces of new clothing, and engage in various "performances" as they move from setting to setting (Goffman, 1959). In a traditional society, such "shiftiness" marks a person as untrustworthy, but in a modern society, the ability to fit in virtually anywhere is a valued personal trait (Wheelis, 1958).

In societies that value the up-to-date rather than the traditional, people anxiously solicit the approval of others, looking to members of their own generation rather than to elders as significant role models. "Peer pressure" can be irresistible to people with no enduring standards to guide them. Our society urges individuals to be true to themselves. But when social surroundings change so rapidly, how can people develop the self to which they should be true? This problem is at the root of the identity crisis so widespread in industrial societies today. "Who am I?" is a question that many of us struggle to answer. In truth, this problem is not so much psychological as sociological, reflecting the inherent instability of modern mass society.

Class Society: Problems of Powerlessness

Class-society theory paints a different picture of modernity's effects on individuals. This approach maintains that persistent social inequality undermines modern society's promise of individual freedom. For some, modernity delivers great privilege, but for others, modern life means coping every day with economic uncertainty and a gnawing sense of powerlessness (Newman, 1993).

For visible minorities, and Canada's native population in particular, the problem of relative disadvantage looms even larger. Similarly, although women enjoy increasing participation in modern societies, they continue to run up against traditional barriers of sexism. Elderly people encounter the impediment of *ageism*. In short, this approach rejects mass-society theory's claim that people suffer from too much freedom. Instead, class-society theory holds that our society still denies a majority of people full participation in social life.

On a global scale, as Chapter 11 ("Global Stratification") explained, the expanding scope of world capitalism has placed more of the earth's population in the shadow of multinational corporations. As a result, more than half of the world's income is concentrated in the richest societies, which contain only about 15 percent of its people. Is it any wonder, class-society theorists ask, that people in poor nations seek greater power to shape their own lives?

The problem of widespread powerlessness led Herbert Marcuse (1964) to challenge Max Weber's contention that modern society is rational. Marcuse labels modern society irrational because it fails to meet the basic needs of so many people. While modern capitalist societies produce unparallelled wealth, poverty remains the daily plight of more than a billion people. Moreover, Marcuse argues, technological advances further reduce people's control over their own lives. High technology confers great power on a corps of specialists—not the vast majority of people themselves—who now control events and dominate the public agenda, whether the issue is computing, energy production for communities, or health care. Countering the common view that technology *solves* the world's problems, Marcuse believed that science actually *causes* them. In sum, class-society theory asserts that people suffer because modern, scientific societies concentrate both wealth and power in the hands of a privileged few.

MODERNITY AND PROGRESS

In modern societies, most people expect—and applaud—social change. People link modernity to the idea of *progress* (from Latin, meaning "moving forward"), a state of continual improvement. By contrast, we denigrate stability as a form of stagnation.

This chapter began by describing the Kaiapo of Brazil, for whom affluence has broadened opportunities but weakened traditional heritage. In examining the Kaiapo, we notice that social change, with all its beneficial and detrimental consequences, is too complex to simply equate with progress.

More precisely, whether we see a given change as progress depends on our values. A rising standard of living among the Kaiapo—or, historically, among people in Canada—has helped to make lives longer and more comfortable. In global context, as Figure 23–1 shows, people in the United States and Canada have considerable confidence in science to improve our lives.

Social change is both complex and controversial. Modern society's recognition of basic human rights is valued by most people. The assertion that individuals have rights simply by virtue of their humanity is a distinctly modern idea that can be found in the Canadian Charter of Rights and Freedoms, the American Declaration of Independence, and the United Nations' Declaration of Human Rights. But, as Chapter 3 ("Culture") explained, we now have something of a "culture of rights" that often overlooks the duties and obligations we have to one another.

In principle, almost everyone in our society supports the idea that individuals should have considerable autonomy in shaping their own lives. Yet, as people exercise their freedom of choice, they inevitably challenge social patterns cherished by those who maintain a more traditional way of life. For example, people may choose not to marry, to live with someone without marrying, perhaps even to form a partnership with someone of their own sex. To those who support individual choice, such changes symbolize progress; to those who value traditional family patterns, however, these developments signal societal decay.

New technology, too, provokes controversy. Rapid transportation and efficient communication have improved our lives in many respects, but complex technology has also weakened traditional attachments to home towns and even to families. Industrial technology has also unleashed an unprecedented threat to the natural environment and, in the form of nuclear weapons, imperilled the future of humanity. In short, we all know that social change comes faster all the time, but we may disagree about whether a particular change is progress or a step backwards.

MODERNITY: GLOBAL VARIATION

October 1, 1994, Kobe, Japan. Riding the computer-controlled monorail high above the streets of Kobe or the 200-mile-per-hour bullet train to Tokyo, we see in Japan the society of the future, in love with high technology. Yet the Japanese remain strikingly traditional in other respects: few corporate executives and almost no senior politicians are women, young people still accord seniors considerable respect, and public orderliness contrasts to the turmoil of North American cities.

Japan is a nation at once traditional and modern. This contradiction reminds us that, while it is useful to contrast traditional and modern societies, the old and the new often co-exist in unexpected ways. In the People's Republic of China, ancient Confucian principles are mixed with contemporary socialist thinking. Similarly, in Mexico and much of Latin America, people observe centuries-old Christian rituals even as they struggle valiantly to pursue economic development.

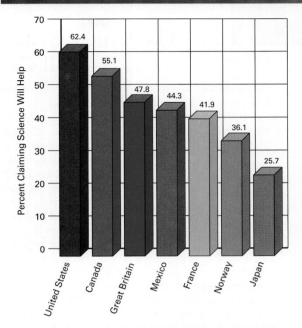

GLOBAL SNAPSHOT

FIGURE 23–1 Support for Science: A Global Survey

Survey Question: "In the long run, do you think the scientific advances we are making will help or harm humankind?"

SOURCE: World Values Survey (1994).

The description of Brazil's Kaiapo that opened this chapter points up the tension that typically accompanies the introduction of modern social patterns in a traditional society. The broader point is that combinations of traditional and modern patterns are far from unusual—indeed, they are found around the world.

POST-MODERNITY

If modernity was the product of the Industrial Revolution, is the Information Revolution creating a post-modern era? A number of scholars think so, and use the term **post-modernity** to refer to *social patterns characteristic of a post-industrial society.*

Precisely what post-modernism is remains a matter of debate. The term has been used for decades in literary, philosophical, and even architectural circles. It moved into sociology on a wave of social criticism that has been building since the spread of left-leaning politics in the 1960s. Although there are many variants of post-modern thinking, all share the following

The United States: A Nation in Decline?
Will Canada Follow?

Asked what was his greatest concern about the future of his country, the U.S. novelist Walker Percy responded:

> Probably the fear of seeing America, with all its great strength and beauty and freedom . . . gradually subside into decay and be defeated . . . from within by weariness, boredom, cynicism, greed and in the end helplessness before its great problems. . . .

Is the United States, which stood as the world's leading economic and political power during the twentieth century, now a nation in decline? Clearly, by some measures, the United States is thriving. Between 1960 and 1995, for example, the nation's economic output tripled and median family income (controlled for inflation) climbed by more than one-third. During the same time span, the official poverty rate dropped by half.

Nonetheless, William J. Bennett contends, a number of other indicators of well-being paint a very different—and disturbing—picture of life in the United States as it nears the end of this century. Between 1960 and 1995, violent crime shot up fourfold; the number of children born to single mothers as well as the number of children supported by welfare rose more than fivefold; the divorce rate doubled; and teen suicide tripled. Television viewing has increased by 35 percent and College Board scores have fallen by an average of 75 points.

Government expenditures (in constant dollars) rose fivefold between 1960 and 1995, while U.S. population increased by just 45 percent. Clearly, then, a wide range of serious social problems continues to plague the United States despite (or, perhaps, because of) government efforts to address them. As a result, Bennett concludes that the nation's decline is primarily moral—a matter of weakening individual character:

> [American] society now places less value than before on what we owe to others as a matter of moral obligation; less value on sacrifice as a moral good; less value on social conformity and respectability; and less value on correctness and restraint in matters of physical pleasure and sexuality.

The current dilemma—that even as governments are made bigger and more powerful, many social problems are getting worse—stems from the fact that government can do little to build individual character. Bennett continues:

---

five themes (Bernstein, 1992; Borgmann, 1992; Crook et al., 1992; Hall and Neitz, 1993):

1. **In important respects, modernity has failed.** The promise of modernity was a life free from want. As post-modernist critics see it, however, the twentieth century was unsuccessful in eradicating social problems such as poverty or even ensuring financial security for many people.

2. **The bright light of "progress" is fading.** Modern people typically look to the future expecting that their lives will improve in significant ways. Members (even leaders) of a post-modern society, however, have less confidence about what the future holds. Furthermore, the buoyant optimism that swept society into the modern era more than a century ago has given way to stark pessimism; most Canadian adults think that life is getting worse (Bibby, 1995:8).

3. **Science no longer holds the answers.** The defining trait of the modern era was a scientific outlook and a confident belief that technology would make life better. But post-modern critics contend that science has not solved many old problems (such as poor health) and has even created new problems (such as degrading the environment).

   More generally, post-modernist thinkers discredit the foundation of science: that objective reality and truth exist at all. Reality amounts to so much social construction, they say; moreover, we can "deconstruct" science to show how it has been widely used for political purposes, especially by powerful segments of society.

4. **Cultural debates are intensifying.** Modernity was to be an era of enhanced individuality and expanding tolerance. But it has fallen short here as well. Feminism asserts that patriarchy continues to limit the lives of women, while multiculturalism seeks to empower minorities who remain at the margins of social life.

[American] social institutions—families, churches, schools, neighborhoods, and civic associations—have traditionally taken on the responsibility of providing our children with love, order, and discipline—of teaching self-control, compassion, tolerance, civility, honesty, and respect for authority. . . . The social regression of the past thirty years is due in large part to the enfeebled state of our social institutions and their failure to carry out these critical and time-honored tasks.

From Bennett's point of view, the primary values of any society are set not by government but by people living in communities and, especially, by families raising their children. In effect, he concludes, we must not assume that affluence is the best—or even the only—measure of a society's well-being. Moreover, we cannot afford to ignore—nor can we hand over to the government—our basic responsibility to sustain civilization.

If asked, many Canadians would raise a similar list of concerns regarding our society. We are not confident about our economy—at least with respect to job creation and job security. Once inflation is taken into account, our average family income has actually declined, in real terms, over the past decade, and about 15 percent of our families continue to fall below the poverty line. Violent crime rates have almost doubled over the past decade (though homicide rates actually declined between 1991 and 1995), so that Canadians are increasingly fearful about the safety of themselves and their children. We are cynical about politicians (despite the prolonged "honeymoon" of Jean Chrétien's Liberal government) and worried about the quality of our schools and the survival of the family in its present form. Our political will to ensure universal access to medical care is even in question. To many people, it seems as though we are simply a few steps behind the United States with respect to the growth of social problems.

Despite these changes, which include a decline in church attendance, Canadians seem to have retained certain moral and social values. Honesty and reliability are "very important" to about 90 percent of Canadians, and family life to 86 percent. Intermarriage (cultural, racial, and religious) is approved by 80 to 90 percent, suggesting that we have become quite tolerant. Furthermore, our level of social compassion has remained quite high as evidenced by our beliefs that people who are poor deserve adequate income and medical care (84 and 96 percent, respectively). If ours has become a more cynical and dangerous society, it is clear that we have not rejected many of our basic social values. Of course, professing such beliefs and values is not the same as putting them into action.

SOURCES: Bennett (1993), Sauvé (1994), and Bibby (1995).

5. **Social institutions are changing.** Just as Industrialization brought sweeping transformation to social institutions, the rise of a post-industrial society is remaking society once again. For example, just as the Industrial Revolution placed *material things* at the centre of productive life, now the Information Revolution emphasizes *ideas*. Similarly, the post-modern family no longer conforms to a single formula; on the contrary, individuals are choosing among many new family forms.

Critical evaluation. Analysts who claim that Canada and other high-income societies are entering a post-modern era criticize modernity for failing to meet human needs. Yet few think that modernity has failed completely; after all, we have seen marked increases in longevity and living standards over the course of this century. Moreover, even if we accepted post-modernist criticism that science is bankrupt and traditional notions about progress are a sham, what are the alternatives?

LOOKING AHEAD: MODERNIZATION AND OUR GLOBAL FUTURE

In Chapter 1, we imagined the entire world reduced to a village of one thousand people. About 150 residents of this "global village" live in high-income countries, while about half receive less than ideal nourishment. Most seriously, 200 people are so poor that they are at risk for their lives.

Chapter 11 ("Global Stratification") presented two competing views of why one billion people the world over are poor. *Modernization theory* claims that in the past the entire world was poor and that technological change, especially the Industrial Revolution, enhanced human productivity and raised living standards. From this point of view, the solution to global poverty is to promote technological development in poor nations.

For reasons suggested earlier, however, global modernization may be difficult. Recall that David

The Canadian Revolution through the Information Revolution: The Point of No Return

Journalist and author Jeffrey Simpson opened his book *Faultlines* (1993) with the following passage:

Canada's traditional political culture in the 1980s cracked like river ice in spring. No single current produced the crack-up; it arose from the confluence of powerful new economic, demographic and political factors and the resurgence of older currents. By the early 1990s, a country that had always been at heart a political arrangement—for it had never been a cultural union or a natural economic entity—found its governmental institutions discredited and indebted, its national parties widely reviled, its political leaders mocked, its Constitution the source of division rather than pride, its economy battered by pressures from abroad, its habitual optimism dimmed.

The relative stability of the past, based on elite accommodation, brokerage politics, and deference to authority had been shattered. Peter C. Newman traced this radical transformation of Canada's political, social, cultural, and economic landscape in *The Canadian Revolution: From Deference to Defiance* (1995). Political scientist Neil Nevitte used the World Values Survey to reveal changes in Canadian values during the volatile 1980s, in a book entitled *The Decline of Deference* (1996). Each of these authors agree that Canada and Canadians have changed profoundly.

Through the 1980s and early 1990s, Canadians lost faith in many of the country's major institutions: organized religion, marriage, the Canada Pension Plan, the monarchy, political parties, the Red Cross, the military and peacekeepers, the Grey Cup, Canada Post, the railways, Ontario Hydro, banks, and corporations. Canadians are less inclined to believe in the inevitability of progress, in the ability of governments to solve our problems, or in corporations as the basis for investment or long-term careers. We are confused about our identities and worry that Lucien Bouchard may be right when he says that "Canada is not a country."

Refusing to defer to traditional leadership and authority, Canadians have turned to themselves as individuals for solutions to their problems, seeking information and making decisions often in defiance of the elite. For example, a majority said "no" to the Charlottetown accord, "no" to the Conservatives and the NDP in the 1993 federal election, and "no" to Ontario's Harris government regarding its initial compensation offer to the surviving Dionne quintuplets. The Québécois are saying "no" to the separatist leadership of Quebec and to perpetual economic and political turmoil based on the "neverendum referendum." Influential pollster Allan Gregg (1998) notes that over the past fifteen years, Canadians have gone from being perhaps *the* most deferential people in the Western world to the point where we now seek new rights and powers to take decision making away from our leaders.

Marshall McLuhan predicted this kind of radical transformation of Canadian society in the 1960s and early 1970s (Bendetti and DeHart, 1996) as the result of the development of the electronic media. Television was invading homes and classrooms during

---

Riesman portrayed pre-industrial people as *tradition-directed* and likely to resist change. So modernization theorists advocate that the world's rich societies help poor countries to grow economically. Specifically, industrial nations can export technology to poor regions, welcome students from abroad, and provide foreign aid to stimulate economic growth.

The discussion of modernization theory in Chapter 11 points to some limited success for these policies in Latin America and, especially, in the small Asian countries of Taiwan, South Korea, Singapore, and Hong Kong. But jump-starting development in the poorest countries of the world poses greater challenges. And even where dramatic change has occurred, modernization entails a trade-off. Traditional people, such as Brazil's Kaiapo, may gain wealth through economic development, but they lose their cultural identity and values as they are drawn into global "McCulture," based on Western materialism, pop music, trendy clothes, and fast food. One Brazilian anthropologist expressed hope about the future of the Kaiapo: "At least they quickly understood the consequences of watching television. . . . Now [they] can make a choice" (Simons, 1998:495).

But not everyone thinks that modernization is really an option. According to a second approach to global stratification, *dependency theory*, today's poor societies have little ability to modernize, even if they want to. From this point of view, the major barrier to economic development is not traditionalism but global domination by rich, capitalist societies. Initially, this dominance took the form of colonialism

that period and computers (room-sized monstrosities) were changing information processing. We moved into a world of instantaneous all-at-onceness. "Time, in a sense, has ceased as space has vanished . . . we now live in a global village of our own making, a simultaneous happening . . . created by instant electronic information movement" (p. 40). McLuhan foresaw the walls coming down between families, nations, and economies as people became intensely involved in the affairs of everyone else—everywhere. He predicted that electronic data would become indispensable to all decision making in business, politics, and education; education would be completely transformed; students from around the world would develop a sense of unity; people would forge personal identities in the context of the new simultaneous world; violence would escalate in the quest for identity and people (even children) would kill to find out if they are real; privacy would be a thing of the past; and one could be superhuman and nobody simultaneously.

As early as 1971, McLuhan said that the "wired planet has no boundaries and no monopolies of knowledge," that specialized jobs had lost meaning, and that we might return to a "cottage economy" again because one could run the world's largest factory from a kitchen computer. *Individuals* now have instant access to information, data, or knowledge, at the same time that these are available to the traditional elites—decision-makers and leaders in business, government, education, and religion. Deference to these traditional authorities is difficult to maintain under these conditions. Knowledge is power, and knowledge—through the electronic media—is available to the masses.

Peter C. Newman also sees the electronic media as a central force for social change:

> The invisible hand of technology had provided citizens with the ammunition for their Revolution. The advent of saturation television coverage of real-time news events, such as the raw footage of the aboriginal standoff at Oka, Quebec, left politicians with no place to hide. The new rules expected open covenants be openly negotiated. But by the decade's end television, which had been the dominant technological force at the beginning of the decade, was being supplanted by the computer. A full-scale rout

of authority was guaranteed by the advent of the power of the Internet. Unregulated access to unlimited, cheap information meant the computer channel that was signing up thousands of Canadian recruits daily had changed their world—and ours—by dramatically empowering its users (1995:xxi).

Information technology is so central to the transformation we have experienced that a new basis for social class appears to be evolving. Control of "the means of production" (using Marxist terms) in the post-industrial world means access to information, primarily through the use of computers. Affluent families are more likely to have computers, and children who grow up using computers have a head start as they further develop their computer skills at school. Growth in employment is taking place almost entirely in the knowledge-based sector. The result is a new privileged class made up of superbly educated, computer literate men and women (Newman, 1995; also Forcese, 1997; Goyder, 1997). The revolution is indeed profound.

whereby European societies seized much of Latin America, Africa, and Asia. Trading relationships soon enriched England, Spain, and other colonial powers, and their colonies became poorer and poorer. Almost all societies that were colonized are now politically independent, but economic ties persist in the form of multinational corporations operating throughout the world.

In effect, dependency theory asserts that rich nations achieved their modernization at the expense of poor ones, by plundering poor nations' natural resources and exploiting their human labour. Even today, the world's poorest countries remain locked in a disadvantageous economic relationship with rich nations, dependent on wealthy countries to buy their raw materials and in return sell them whatever manufactured products they can afford. Overall, dependency theorists conclude, continuing ties with rich societies only perpetuate current patterns of global inequality.

Whichever approach is more convincing, we can no longer isolate changes in our own society from those in the rest of the world. At the beginning of the twentieth century, most people in today's high-income countries lived in relatively small settlements with limited awareness of the larger world. At the threshold of the twenty-first century, the entire world has become one human village because the lives of all people are increasingly linked.

The twentieth century has witnessed unprecedented human achievement. Yet solutions to many problems of human existence—including finding meaning in life, resolving conflicts between nations, and eradicating poverty—have eluded us. To this list of pressing matters new concerns have been added, such as controlling population growth and establishing a sustainable society by living in harmony with the natural environment. In the twenty-first century, we must be prepared to tackle such problems with imagination, compassion, and determination. The challenge is great, but our wide-ranging understanding of human society gives us reason to look to the task ahead with optimism.

SUMMARY

1. Every society changes continuously, although at varying speeds. Social change often generates controversy.

2. Social change results from invention, discovery, and diffusion as well as from social conflict.

3. Modernity refers to the social consequences of industrialization, which, according to Peter Berger, include the erosion of traditional communities, expanding personal choice, increasingly diverse beliefs, and a keen awareness of the future.

4. Ferdinand Toennies described modernization as the transition from *Gemeinschaft* to *Gesellschaft*, which signifies the progressive loss of community amid growing individualism.

5. Emile Durkheim saw modernization as a function of a society's expanding division of labour. Mechanical solidarity, based on shared activities and beliefs, gradually gives way to organic solidarity, in which specialization makes people interdependent.

6. According to Max Weber, modernity replaces tradition with a rational world view. Weber feared the dehumanizing effects of rational organization.

7. Karl Marx saw modernity as the triumph of capitalism over feudalism. Viewing capitalist societies as fraught with social conflict, Marx advocated revolutionary change to achieve a more egalitarian, socialist society.

8. According to mass-society theory, modernity increases the scale of life, enlarging the role of government and other formal organizations in carrying out tasks previously performed by family members and neighbours. Cultural diversity and rapid social change make it difficult for people in modern societies to develop stable identities and to find meaning in their lives.

9. Class-society theory states that capitalism is central to Western modernization. This approach charges that, by concentrating wealth, capitalism generates widespread feelings of powerlessness.

10. Social change is too complex and controversial simply to be equated with social progress.

11. Post-modernity refers to cultural traits of post-industrial societies. Post-modern criticism centres on the failure of modernity, and specifically science, to fulfil its promise of prosperity and well-being.

12. In a global context, modernization theory links global poverty to the power of tradition. Therefore, some modernization theorists advocate intentional intervention by rich societies to stimulate the economic development of poor nations.

13. Dependency theory explains global poverty as the product of the world economic system. The operation of multinational corporations ensures that poor societies will remain economically dependent on rich nations.

CRITICAL THINKING QUESTIONS

1. How well do you think Toennies, Durkheim, Weber, and Marx predicted the character of modern society? How do their visions of modernity differ?

2. What traits render Canada a "mass society"? Do you consider yourself and most of your friends to be "other-directed"?

3. What is the difference between *anomie* (a trait of mass society) and *alienation* (a characteristic of class society)? Among which categories of Canadians would you expect each to be pronounced?

4. What developments lead some analysts to claim that ours has become a post-modern society?

1. Have you an elderly relative or friend? If asked, most older people will be happy to tell you about the social changes they have seen in their lifetimes.

2. Ask people in your class or your friends to make five predictions about Canadian society in the year 2050, when today's twenty-year-olds will be senior citizens. Compare notes. On what issues is there agreement?

3. Visit the Web site for the Communitarian network at www.gwu.edu/~ccps/. Explore the changes this organization is seeking and how they propose to achieve them.

4. Finally, on a personal note, we hope this book has helped you and will be a useful resource for courses later on. Please feel free to send an e-mail message (macionis@kenyon.edu and lgerber@uoguelph.ca) with your thoughts and suggestions. And, yes, we *will* write back!

WEBLINKS

http://community.web.net/
Web Networks, the Canadian affiliate of the Association for Progressive Communications, hosts a community of several hundred Canadian activists, artists, and non-profits devoted to social change, including WomensWeb, EcoWeb, UnionNet, the Faith and Justice Network, and more.

http://weber.u.washington.edu/~jamesher/barb.htm
This essay by Barbara Epstein examines the history and strategies of the grassroots environmentalist movement in the United States.

http://weber.u.washington.edu/~jamesher/herrick.htm
This essay by James Herrick offers a critical examination of empowerment theory and its relationship to social change.

http://www.utoronto.ca/utopia/
The *Society for Utopian Studies* is an international, interdisciplinary association devoted to the study of utopianism in all its forms, with a particular emphasis on literary and experimental utopias. The society publishes the journal *Utopian Studies* and a newsletter.

http://www.halcyon.com/FWDP/fwdp.html
Organized by the Center for World Indigenous Studies, the *Fourth World Documentation Project*'s mission is to document and make available important documents relating to the social, political, strategic, economic, and human rights situations being faced by developing countries and create a historical archive of the political struggles waged by indigenous peoples to assert their rights as sovereign nations.

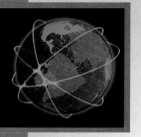

cyber.scope

PART V
NEW INFORMATION TECHNOLOGY AND SOCIAL CHANGE

There seems to be no end to the list of changes that new information technology is bringing to our world. This final cyber.scope highlights how the age of computers is altering the shape of cities, bringing people together the world over to form social movements, and, more than ever, encouraging us to reflect on the direction and pace of change to our way of life.

The New Shape of Cities

The metropolis, as Chapter 21 ("Population and Urbanization") explains, stands as the greatest monument to the Industrial Era. Within the largest cities a century ago, factories full of huge machines offered jobs that drew people from across the countryside. Industrial cities such as New York, Chicago, Montreal, and Toronto churned with activity, and their buildings of mortar, steel, and glass stretched skyward, in some cases reaching up a hundred storeys or more.

These cities became so busy and dense because industrial technology operated to centralize people. Businesses formed a "central business district," where executives and managers could easily establish face-to-face communication. Similarly, factories were sited together near rivers and railroads, which brought them fuel and raw materials and took away their finished products.

By 1950, about the time scientists had built the first computers, the industrial cities of North America reached their peak populations.

Computer technology helped push the economy from industry to service and information work, and this shift spurred the decentralization of cities. Population began radiating farther away from the central city so that, by 1970, most city-dwellers were actually living in suburbs. Businesses followed suit, deserting the downtowns for industrial parks and outlying shopping malls.

Why has the central city lost so much of its attraction? One important reason is that, with new information technology, people can communicate efficiently without working in the same area. Thus, the new shape of cities is sprawling and decentralized; that is, cities are growing "out" more than "up." The urban scene at the end of the twentieth century shows modest central-city populations surrounded by swelling suburbs, as well as new "edge cities," clusters of office buildings, shopping malls, hotels, and entertainment complexes miles from the old "downtowns."

Social Movements:
New Ways to Connect

The formation and growth of any social movement depends on people connecting with people. Today, anyone with an interest in some issue and a computer can access the Web pages of countless people and organizations seeking to change the world in some way. Along the Information Superhighway, people are making contact, asking questions, spreading ideas, and creating new social movements.

Just as important, this process of making connections is going on on a global scale. Take the students at the Redemptorist Vocational School in Pattaya, Thailand. These young men and women have physical disabilities, which, before the Information Age, might have kept them from learning at all. But by using their school's computers, the students have established contact with hundreds of other people with disabilities in dozens of countries, including Canada. From these contacts, as well as from the Web sites of national and international organizations that represent people with disabilities, the students have received a rich education. They have been surprised to learn that many countries have laws that protect people with disabilities from discrimination and that mandate access ramps for sidewalks and buildings; they have discovered that cities abroad feature buses that "kneel" to permit entry by people in wheelchairs, as well as public restrooms designed to accommodate everyone. Armed with their new knowledge, the students at the Redemptorist Vocational School are now taking the lead in their own country, educating people about disabilities and lobbying government officials to make changes in Thailand's laws.

The Internet represents a powerful communication resource for anyone. But it is especially important for people whose ability to make contact with others is otherwise limited, including people with disabilities. As one Thai student reports, "On the 'net, I don't feel like a handicapped person" (Smolan and Erwitt, 1996:150). And even though computer access is far from equal around the world, the Internet is providing a "global reach" to an increasing number of people in poor countries.

Social Change:
The Good, the Bad, and the Unexpected

In Chapter 3 ("Culture") we presented William Ogburn's (1964) concept of *cultural lag*, the pattern by which some elements of culture change faster than others. In general, Ogburn explained, technology changes the fastest; adapting to new technology, on the other hand, takes much longer. Cultural lag is evident in our use of old terminology to describe new developments, such as measuring the "horsepower" of gasoline engines or, more recently, exploring the "superhighway" of cyberspace (Newmann, 1991).

The fact that developments in science and technology outpace our ability to comprehend them makes many people uneasy about social change. But the majority of people are optimistic, believing that new technology will improve our lives.

In truth, any change is both bad and good, involving disruption of established social patterns as well as creating new possibilities. After the invention of the telephone in 1876, even though some people were awed that individuals separated by great distances could now speak as if they were in the same room, others worried that this new device would bring an end to the strong ties that had linked neighbour to neighbour. So it is with computer technology today. The staggering range of information and entertainment available on the World Wide Web will surely enrich our lives in many ways; but, will computers (like television) lure people into paying less attention to those in their immediate surroundings?

Consider the dramatic changes taking place at Dartmouth College, one of the most academically competitive schools in the U.S., located in Hanover, New Hampshire. Since wiring all dormitories—sometimes called the "one plug per pillow" model—life has not been the same. Take Arthur Desrosiers, who claims that he has fewer and fewer reasons to ever leave his room. This sophomore browses the college library, writes papers, questions professors, keeps up with old high school friends and his new girlfriend, and even orders pizza to eat while joining in 2 a.m. bull sessions—all using his personal computer. Perhaps strangest of all, Desrosiers often fires messages back and forth to his two roommates, even though they are sitting silently nearby in the same room staring at screens of their own.

Perhaps it is a sign of the times that a once-popular restaurant just down the street from dorms that house 3000 students has closed its doors. Similarly, the student union is far less busy than it was just a few years ago; some of the space once used for socializing now can accommodate—you guessed it—computer terminals for those who want to check their e-mail without going all the way back home.

At Dartmouth, computers have never been more popular, with 8000 students, faculty, and staff receiving some 250 000 messages each day. And no one doubts that new information technology has opened up new possibilities for contacting people around the world or right down the hall. But, some people are beginning to wonder, what is being lost in the process? Some faculty worry that they see less and less of their students. And some students are beginning to think that they ought to see more of each other. As senior Abigail Butler puts it, "I know people who sit home Friday and Saturday night and e-mail back and forth to people they only know by nick-names, while the rest of the world is going by. After a while it starts to be really unfulfilling. It's easier to just meet someone in person and actually talk. . ." (Gabriel, 1996). The more things change. . . ▣

With access to the Internet, these Thai students have joined an international social movement to advance the opportunities of people with disabilities.

GLOSSARY

absolute poverty a deprivation of resources that is life-threatening

achieved status a social position that someone assumes voluntarily and that reflects personal ability and effort

activity theory the proposition that a high level of activity enhances personal satisfaction in old age

ageism prejudice and discrimination against the elderly

age-sex pyramid a graphic representation of the age and sex of a population

age stratification the unequal distribution of wealth, power, and privileges among people at different stages in the life course

agriculture the technology of large-scale farming using plows harnessed to animals or more powerful sources of energy

alienation the experience of isolation resulting from powerlessness

animism the belief that elements of the natural world are conscious life forms that affect humanity

anomie a condition in which society provides little moral guidance to individuals

anticipatory socialization social learning directed toward gaining a desired position

ascribed status a social position that someone receives at birth or assumes involuntarily later in life

assimilation the process by which minorities gradually adopt patterns of the dominant culture

authoritarianism a political system that denies popular participation in government

authority power that people perceive as legitimate rather than coercive

beliefs specific statements that people hold to be true

bilateral descent a system tracing kinship through both men and women

blue-collar occupations lower-prestige work involving mostly manual labour

bureaucracy an organizational model rationally designed to perform complex tasks efficiently

bureaucratic inertia the tendency of bureaucratic organizations to perpetuate themselves

bureaucratic ritualism a preoccupation with rules and regulations to the point of thwarting an organization's goals

capitalism an economic system in which natural resources and the means fo producing goods and services are privately owned

capitalists people who own factories and other productive enterprises

caste system a system of social stratification based on ascription

cause and effect a relationship in which we knw that change in one variable causes change in another

charisma extraordinary personal qualities that can turn an audience into followers

charismatic authority power legitimized through extraordinary personal abilities that inspire devotion and obedience

church a type of religious organization well integrated into the larger society

civil religion a quasi-religious loyalty binding individuals in a basically secular society

class conflict antagonism between entire classes over the distribution of wealth and power in society

class consciousness the recognition by workers of their unity as a social class in opposition to capitalists and, ultimately, to capitalism itself

class society a capitalist society with pronounced social stratification

class system a system of social stratification based on individual achievement

cohabitation the sharing of a household by an unmarried couple

cohort a category of people with a common characteristic, usually age

collective behaviour activity involving a large number of people, often spontaneous, and typically in violation of established norms

collectivity a large number of people whose minimal interaction occurs in the absence of well-defined and conventional norms

colonialism the process by which some nations enrich themselves through political and economic control of other countries

communism a hypothetical economic and political system in which all members of society are socially equal

concept a mental construct that represents some part of the world, inevitably in a simplified form

concrete operational stage the level of human development at which individuals first perceive causal connections in their surroundings

conglomerates giant corporations composed of many smaller corporations

control holding constant all relevant variables except one in order to clearly see its effect

corporation an organization with a legal existence including rights and liabilities apart from those of its members

correlation a relationship by which two (or more) variables change together

counterculture cultural patterns that strongly oppose those widely accepted within a society

credentialism evaluating a person on the basis of eduational degrees

crime the violation of norms a society formally enacts into criminal law

criminal justice system a formal response to alleged violations of law on the part of police, courts, and prison officials

criminal recidivism subsequent offences committed by people previously convicted of crimes

crowd a temporary gathering of people who share a common focus of attention and whose members influence one another

crude birth rate the number of live births in a given year for every thousand people in a population

crude death rate the number of deaths in a given year for every thousand people in a population

cult a religious organization that is substantially outside a society's cultural traditions

cultural integration the close relationship among various elements of a cultural system

cultural lag cultural elements changing at different rates, causing various degrees of disruption in cultural systems

cultural materialism (or cultural ecology) a theoretical paradigm that explores the relationship of human culture to the physical environment

cultural relativism the practice of judging a culture by its own standards

cultural transmission the process by which one generation passes culture to the next

cultural universals traits found in every culture of the world

culture the values, beliefs, behaviour, and material objects that constitute a people's way of life

culture shock personal disorientation that comes from encountering an unfamiliar way of life

Davis-Moore thesis the assertion that social stratification has beneficial consequences for the operation of a society

deductive logical thought reasoning that transforms general theory into specific hypotheses suitable for scientific testing

democracy a political system in which power is exercised by the people as a whole

demographic transition theory a thesis linking demographic changes to a society's level of technological development

demography the study of human population

denomination a church, independent of the state, that accepts religious pluralism

dependency theory a model of economic and social development that explains global inequality in terms of the historical exploitation of poor societies by rich ones

dependent variable the variable that changes

descent the system by which members of a society trace kinship over generations

deterrence the attempt to discourage criminality through punishment

deviance the recognized violation of cultural norms

direct-fee system a medical care system in which patients pay directly for the services of physicians and hospitals

discrimination treating various categories of people unequally

disengagement theory the proposition that society enhances its orderly operation by disengaging people from positions of responsibility as they reach old age

division of labour specialized economic activity

dramaturgical analysis the investigation of social interaction in terms of theatrical performance

dyad a social group with two members

eating disorder an intense form of dieting or other kind of weight control in order to become very thin

ecclesia a church formally allied with the state

economy the social institution that organizes the production, distribution, and consumption of goods and services

education the social institution guiding a society's transmission of knowledge—including basic facts, job skills, and cultural norms and values—to its members

ego a person's conscious efforts to balance innate, pleasure-seeking drives with the demands of society

empirical evidence information we can verify with our senses

endogamy marriage between people of the same social category

ethnicity a shared cultural heritage

ethnocentrism the practice of judging another culture by the standards of one's own culture

ethnomethodology the study of the way people make sense of their everyday lives

Eurocentrism the dominance of European cultural patterns

euthanasia (mercy killing) assisting in the death of a person suffering from an incurable disease

exogamy marriage between people of different social categories

experiment a research method for investigating cause and effect under highly controlled conditions

expressive leadership focuses on collective well-being

extended family (consanguine family) a family unit including parents and children, but also other kin

fad an unconventional social pattern that people embrace briefly but enthusiastically

faith belief anchored in conviction rather than scientific evidence

false consciousness Marx's term for explanations of social problems grounded in the shortcomings of individuals rather than the flaws of society

family a social institution that unites individuals into cooperative groups that oversee the bearing and raising of children

family unit a social group of two or more people, related by blood, marriage, or adoption, who usually live together

family violence emotional, physical, or sexual abuse of one family member by another

fashion a social pattern favoured by a large number of people

feminism the advocacy of social equality for the sexes, in opposition to patriarchy and sexism

feminization of poverty the trend by which women represent an increasing proportion of the poor

fertility the incidence of childbearing in a country's population

folkways a society's customs for routine, casual interaction

formal operational stage the level of human development at which individuals think abstractly and critically

formal organization large, secondary groups that are organized to achieve their goals efficiently

functional illiteracy reading and writing skills insufficient for everyday living

fundamentalism a conservative religious doctrine that opposes intellectualism and worldly accommodation in favour of restoring a traditional, otherworldly spirituality

Gemeinschaft a type of social organization in which people are bound closely together by kinship and tradition

gender the significance members of a society attach to being female or male

gender identity traits that females and males, guided by their culture, incorporate into their personalities

gender roles (sex roles) attitudes and activities that a society links to each sex

gender stratification a society's unequal distribution of wealth, power, and privilege between the two sexes

generalized other widespread cultural norms and values that we use as references in evaluating ourselves

genocide the systematic annihilation of one category of people by another

gerontocracy a form of social organization in which the elderly have the most wealth, power, and prestige

gerontology the study of aging and the elderly

Gesellschaft a type of social organization in which people typically have weak social ties and a great deal of self-interest

global economy economic activity spanning many nations of the world with little regard for national borders

global perspective the study of the larger world and our society's place in it

gossip rumour about the personal affairs of others

government a formal organization that directs the political life of a society

groupthink the tendency of group members to conform by adopting a narrow view of some issue

Hawthorne effect a change in a subject's behaviour caused simply by the awareness of being studied

health a state of complete physical, mental, and social well-being

hermaphrodite a human being with some combination of female and male genitalia

hidden curriculum subtle presentations of political or cultural ideas in the classroom

high culture cultural patterns that distinguish a society's elite

high-income countries industrialized nations in which most people enjoy material abundance

holistic medicine an approach to health care that emphasizes prevention of illness and takes into account a person's entire physical and social environment

homogamy marriage between people with the same social characteristics

horticulture technology based on using hand tools to cultivate plants

humanizing organizations fostering a more democratic organizational atmosphere that recognizes and encourages the contributions of everyone

hunting and gathering simple technology for hunting animals and gathering vegetation

hypothesis an unverified statement of a relationship between variables

id the human being's basic drives

ideal culture (as opposed to real culture) social patterns mandated by cultural values and norms

ideal type Weber's term for an abstract statement of the essential characteristics of any social phenomenon

ideology cultural beliefs that serve to justify social stratification

incest taboo a cultural norm forbidding sexual relations or marriage between certain kin

income occupational wages or salaries and earnings from investments

independent variable the variable that causes the change inductive

industrialism technology that powers sophisticated machinery with advanced sources of energy

infant mortality rate the number of deaths among infants in the first year of life for each thousand live births in a given year

ingroup a social group commanding a member's esteem and loyalty

institutional completeness the complexity of community organizations that meet the needs of members

institutional prejudice or discrimination bias in attitudes or action inherent in the operation of society's institutions

instrumental leadership group leadership that emphasizes the completion of tasks

intergenerational social mobility upward or downward social mobility of children in relation to their parents

interlocking directorate social networks of people serving simultaneously on the boards of directors of many corporations

interview a series of questions a researcher administers personally to respondents

intragenerational social mobility a change in social position occurring during a person's lifetime

juvenile delinquency the violation of legal standards by the young

kinship a social bond based on blood, marriage, or adoption, that joins individuals into families

labelling theory the assertion that deviance and conformity result, not so much from what people do, as from how others respond to those actions

labour unions worker organizations that seek to improve wages and working conditions through various strategies, including negotiations and strikes

language a system of symbols that allows members of a society to communicate with one another

latent functions consequences that are largely unrecognized and unintended

liberation theology a fusion of Christian principles with political activism, often Marxist in character

life expectancy the average life span of a society's population

logical thought reasoning that transforms specific observations into general theory

looking-glass self the image people have of themselves based on how they believe others perceive them

low-income countries nations with little industrialization in which severe poverty is the rule

macro-level orientation a focus on broad social structures that characterize society as a whole

manifest functions the recognized and intended consequences of any social pattern

marriage a legally sanctioned relationship, involving economic cooperation as well as normative sexual activity and childbearing, that people expect to be enduring

Marxist political-economy model an analysis that explains politics in terms of the operation of a society's economic system

mass behaviour collective behaviour among people dispersed over a wide geographical area

mass hysteria a form of dispersed collective behaviour by which people respond to a real or imagined event with irrational, frantic, and often self-destructive behaviour

mass media impersonal communications directed to a vast audience

mass society a society in which industry and expanding bureaucracy have eroded traditional social ties

master status a status that has exceptional importance for social identity, often shaping a person's entire life

material culture the tangible things created by members of a society

matriarchy a form of social organization in which females dominate males

matrilineal descent a system tracing kinship through women

matrilocality a residential pattern in which a married couple lives with or near the wife's family

measurement the process of determining the value of a variable in a specific case

mechanical solidarity social bonds, based on shared morality, that unite members of pre-industrial societies

medicalization of deviance the transformation of moral and legal issues into medical matters

medicine a social institution concerned with combating disease and improving health

megalopolis a vast urban region containing a number of cities and their surrounding suburbs

meritocracy a system of social stratification based on personal merit

metropolis a large city that socially and economically dominates the surrounding area

micro-level orientation a focus on social interaction in specific situations

middle-income countries nations characterized by limited industrialization and moderate personal income

migration the movement of people into and out of a specified territory

military-industrial complex the close association between the federal government, the military, and defence industries

minority a category of people, distinguished by physical or cultural traits, that is socially disadvantaged

miscegenation biological reproduction by partners of different racial categories

mob a highly emotional crowd that pursues some violent or destructive goal

modernity social patterns linked to industrialization

modernization the process of social change initiated by industrialization

modernization theory a model of economic and social development that explains global inequality in terms of differing levels of technological development among societies

monarchy a political system in which a single family rules from generation to generation

monogamy a form of marriage joining two partners

monopoly domination of a market by a single producer

monotheism belief in a single divine power

mores a society's standards of proper moral conduct

mortality the incidence of death in a society's population

multiculturalism a social policy designed to encourage ethnic or cultural heterogeneity

multinational corporation a large corporation that operates in many different countries

neocolonialism a new form of global power relationships that involves not direct political control but economic exploitation by multinational corporations

neolocality a residential pattern in which a married couple lives apart from the parents of both spouses

network a web of social ties that links people who identify and interact little with one another

nonmaterial culture the intangible world of ideas created by members of a society

nonverbal communication communication using body movements, gestures, and facial expressions rather than speech

norms rules and expectations by which a society guides the behaviour of its members

nuclear family (conjugal family) a family unit composed of one or two parents and their children

nuclear proliferation the acquisition of nuclear-weapons technology by more and more nations

objectivity a state of personal neutrality in conducting research

oligarchy the rule of the many by the few

oligopoly domination of a market by a few producers

operationalizing a variable specifying exactly what one intends to measure in assigning a value to a variable

organic solidarity social bonds, based on specialization, that unite members of industrial societies

organizational environment a range of factors external to an organization that affects its operation

other-directedness a receptiveness to the latest trends and fashions, often expressed in the practice of imitating others

outgroup a social group toward which one feels competition or opposition

panic a form of localized collective behaviour by which people react to a threat or other stimulus with irrational, frantic, and often self-destructive behaviour

participant observation a method in which researchers systematically observe people while joining in their routine activities

pastoralism technology based on the domestication of animals

patriarchy a form of social organization in which males dominate females

patrilineal descent a system tracing kinship through men

patrilocality a residential pattern in which a married couple lives with or near the husband's family

peace the absence of war

peer group a social group whose members have interests, social position, and age in common

personality a person's fairly consistent patterns of thinking, feeling, and acting

personal space the surrounding area in which an individual makes some claim to privacy

plea bargaining a legal negotiation in which the prosecution reduces a defendant's charge in exchange for a guilty plea

pluralism a state in which racial and ethnic minorities are distinct but have social parity

pluralist model an analysis of politics that view power as dispersed among many competing interest groups

political parties organizations operating within the political system that seek control of the government

political revolution the overthrow of one political system in order to establish another

politics the institutionalized system by which a society distributes power, sets the society's agenda, and makes decisions

polyandry a form of marriage uniting one female with two or more males

polygamy a form of marriage uniting three or more people

polygyny a form of marriage joining one male and two or more females

polytheism belief in many gods

popular culture cultural patterns that are widespread among a society's population

population the people who are the focus of research

positivism a means to understand the world based on science

post-industrial economy a productive system based on service work and extensive use of information technology

post-industrialism technology that supports an information-based economy

post-modernity social patterns characteristic of post-industrial societies

power the ability to achieve desired ends despite resistance

power-elite model an analysis of politics that views power as concentrated among the rich

prejudice a rigid and irrational generalization about an entire category of people

preoperational stage the level of human development at which individuals first use language and other symbols

presentation of self an individual's effort to create specific impressions in the minds of others

primary group a small social group whose members share personal and enduring relationships

primary labour market occupations that provide extensive benefits to workers

primary sector the part of the economy that generates raw materials directly from the natural environment

primary sex characteristics the genitals, organs used to reproduce the human species

profane that which is defined as an ordinary element of everyday life

profession a prestigious, white-collar occupation that requires extensive formal education

proletariat people who provide labour necessary to operate factories and other productive enterprises

propaganda information presented with the intention of shaping public opinion

property crimes crimes that involve theft of property belonging to others

qualitative research investigation in which a researcher gathers impressionistic, not numerical, data

quantitative research investigation in which a researcher collects numerical data

questionnaire a series of written questions a researcher supplies to subjects requesting their responses

race a category composed of people who share biologically transmitted traits that members of a society deem socially significant

racism the belief that one racial category is innately superior or inferior to another

rationality deliberate, matter-of-fact calculation of the most efficient means to accomplish a particular goal

rationalization of society the historical change from tradition to rationality as the dominant mode of human thought

rational-legal authority (bureaucratic authority) power legitimized by legally enacted rules and regulations

real culture (as opposed to ideal culture) actual social patterns that only approximate cultural expectations

reference group a social group that serves as a point of reference in making evaluations or decisions

rehabilitation a program for reforming the offender to preclude subsequent offences

relative deprivation a perceived disadvantage arising from some specific comparison

relative poverty the deprivation of some people in relation to those who have more

reliability the quality of consistent measurement

religion a social institution involving beliefs and practices based on a conception of the sacred

religiosity the importance of religion in a person's life

replication repetition of research by other investigators

research method a systematic plan for conducting research

reserve army of labour the part of the labour force that is last hired during expansion and first fired when the economy contracts

resocialization radically altering an inmate's personality through deliberate manipulation of the environment

retribution moral vengeance by which society inflicts suffering on an offender comparable to that caused by the offence

retrospective labelling the interpretation of someone's past consistent with present deviance

riot a social eruption that is highly emotional, violent, and undirected

ritual formal, ceremonial behaviour

role behaviour expected of someone who holds a particular status

role conflict incompatibility among roles corresponding to two or more statuses

role set a number of roles attached to a single status

role strain incompatibility among roles corresponding to a single status

routinization of charisma the transformation of charismatic authority into some combination of traditional and bureaucratic authority

rumour unsubstantiated information spread informally, often by word of mouth

sacred that which is defined as extraordinary, inspiring a sense of awe, reverence, and even fear

sample a part of a population that represents the whole

Sapir-Whorf hypothesis the hypothesis that people perceive the world through the cultural lens of language

scapegoat a person or category of people, typically with little power, whom people unfairly blame for their own troubles

schooling formal instruction under the direction of specially trained teachers

science a logical system that bases knowledge on direct, systematic observation

secondary analysis a research method in which a researcher utilizes data collected by others

secondary group a large and impersonal social group whose members pursue specific interests or activities

secondary labour market jobs that provide minimal benefits to workers

secondary sector the part of the economy that transforms raw materials into manufactured goods

secondary sex characteristics bodily development, apart from the genitals, that distinguishes biologically mature females and males

sect a type of religious organization that stands apart from the larger society

secularization the historical decline in the importance of the supernatural and the sacred

segregation the physical and social separation of categories of people

self a dimension of personality composed of an individual's self-awareness and self-image

sensorimotor stage the level of human development at which individuals experience the world only through sensory contact

sex the biological distinction between females and males

sexism the belief that one sex is innately superior to the other

sex ratio the number of males for every hundred females in a given population

sexual harassment comments, gestures, or physical contact of a sexual nature that are deliberate, repeated, and unwelcome

sexual orientation an individual's preference in terms of sexual partners: same sex, other sex, either sex, neither sex

sick role patterns of behaviour defined as appropriate for people who are ill

social change the transformation of culture and social institutions over time

social character personality patterns common to members of a particular society

social conflict struggle between segments of society over valued resources

social-conflict paradigm a framework for building theory that envisions society as an arena of inequality generating conflict and change

social construction of reality the process by which people creatively shape reality through social interaction

social control various means by which members of a society encourage conformity to norms

social dysfunctions any social pattern's undesirable consequences for the operation of society

social epidemiology the study of how health and disease are distributed throughout a society's population

social functions consequences for the operation of society

social group two or more people who identify and interact with one another

social institution major spheres of social life, or society's subsystems, organized to meet basic human needs

social interaction the process by which people act and react in relation to others

socialism an economic system in which natural resources and the means of producing goods and services are collectively owned

socialization the lifelong social experience by which individuals develop their human potential and learn patterns of their culture

socialized medicine a health-care system in which the government owns and operates most medical facilities and employs most physicians

social mobility change in a person's position in a social hierarchy

social movement organized activity that encourages or discourages social change

social protection rendering an offender incapable of further offences either temporarily through incarceration or permanently by execution

social stratification a system by which a society ranks categories of people in a hierarchy

social structure relatively stable patterns of social behaviour

society people who interact in a defined territory and share culture

sociobiology a theoretical paradigm that explores ways in which our biology affects how humans create culture

sociocultural evolution the process of change that results from a society's gaining new information, particularly technology

socioeconomic status (SES) a composite ranking based on various dimensions of social inequality

sociology the systematic study of human society

spurious correlation an apparent, although false, association between two (or more) variables caused by some other variable

state capitalism an economic and political system in which companies are privately owned although they cooperate closely with the government

state terrorism the use of violence, generally without support of law, by a government or its agents

status a recognized social position that an individual occupies

status consistency the degree of consistency of a person's social standing across various dimensions of social inequality

status set all the statuses a person holds at a given time

stereotype prejudicial views or descriptions of some categories of people

stigma a powerfully negative social label that radically changes a person's self-concept and social identity

streaming the assigning of students to different types of educational programs

structural-functional paradigm a framework for building theory that envisions society as a complex system whose parts work together to promote solidarity and stability

structural social mobility a shift in the social position of large numbers of people due more to changes in society itself than to individual efforts

subculture cultural patterns that set apart some segment of a society's population

suburbs urban areas beyond the political boundaries of a city

superego the operation of culture within the individual in the form of internalized values and norms

survey a research method in which subjects respond to a series of items in a questionnaire or an interview

symbol anything that carries a particular meaning recognized by people who share culture

symbolic-interaction paradigm a theoretical framework that envisions society as the product of the everyday interactions of individuals

technology knowledge that a society applies to the task of living in a physical environment

terrorism random acts of violence or the threat of such violence employed by an individual or group as a political strategy

tertiary sector the part of the economy that generates services rather than goods

theoretical paradigm a basic image of society that guides thinking and research

theory a statement of how and why specific facts are related

Thomas theorem situations we define as real become real in their consequences

total institution a setting in which people are isolated from the rest of society and manipulated by an administrative staff

totalitarianism a political system that extensively regulates people's lives

totem an object in the natural world collectively defined as sacred

tradition sentiments and beliefs passed from generation to generation

traditional authority power legitimized through respect for long-established cultural patterns

tradition-directedness rigid conformity to time-honoured ways of living

transsexuals people who feel they are one sex though biologically they are the other

triad a social group with three members

underground economy economic activity involving income or the exchange of goods and services that is not reported to the government as required by law

urban ecology the study of the link between the physical and social dimensions of cities

urbanization the concentration of humanity into cities

validity the quality of measuring precisely what one intends to measure

values culturally defined standards by which people assess desirability, goodness, and beauty, and which serve as broad guidelines for social living

variable a concept whose value changes from case to case

victimless crimes violations of law in which there are no readily apparent victims

violent crimes crimes against people that involve violence or the threat of violence

war organized, armed conflict among the people of various societies

wealth the total amount of money and other assets, minus outstanding debts, that a person or family controls

welfare capitalism an economic and political system that combines a mostly market-based economy with government programs to provide for people's basic needs

white-collar crime crimes committed by persons of high social position in the course of their occupations

white-collar occupations higher-prestige work involving mostly mental activity

zero population growth the level of reproduction that maintains population at a steady state

REFERENCES

ABBOTT, ANDREW. *The System of Professions: An Essay on the Division of Expert Labor.* Chicago: University of Chicago Press, 1988.

ABELLA, IRVING. *A Coat of Many Colours: Two Centuries of Jewish Life in Canada.* Toronto: Lester and Orpen Dennys, 1989.

ABELLA, IRVING and HAROLD TROPER. *None Is Too Many: Canada and the Jews in Europe, 1933–1948.* Toronto: Lester and Orpen Dennys, 1982.

ABERLE, DAVID F. *The Peyote Religion Among the Navaho.* Chicago: Aldine, 1966.

ABRAHAMSON, PAUL R. "Postmaterialism and Environmentalism: A Comment on an Analysis and a Reappriasal." *Social Science Quarterly.* Vol. 78, No. 1 (March 1997):21–23.

ADELSON, JOSEPH. "Splitting Up." Article on divorce in the Sept 1996 issue of *Commentary.*

ADLER, JERRY. "When Harry Called Sally . . ." *Newsweek* (October 1, 1990):74.

ADORNO, T.W., ET AL. *The Authoritarian Personality.* New York: Harper & Brothers, 1950.

AGUIRRE, BENIGNO E., and E.L. QUARANTELLI. "Methodological, Ideological, and Conceptual-Theoretical Criticisms of Collective Behavior: A Critical Evaluation and Implications for Future Study." *Sociological Focus.* Vol. 16, No. 3 (August 1983):195–216.

AGUIRRE, BENIGNO E., E. L. QUARANTELLI, and JORGE L. MENDOZA. "The Collective Behavior of Fads: Characteristics, Effects, and Career of Streaking." *American Sociological Review.* Vol. 53, No. 4 (August 1988):569–84.

AHLBURG, DENNIS A., AND CAROL J. DE VITA. "New Realites of the American Family." *Population Bulletin.* Vol. 47, No. 2 (1992):1–44.

AIDS (1997). Data cited in Gorman, Christine, "When Did AIDS Begin?" *Time* (February 16, 1998):64.

AKERS, RONALD L., MARVIN D. KROHN, LONN LANZA-KADUCE, and MARCIA RADOSEVICH. "Social Learning and Deviant Behavior." *American Sociological Review.* Vol. 44, No. 4 (August 1979):636–55.

ALAM, SULTANA. "Women and Poverty in Bangladesh." *Women's Studies International Forum.* Vol. 8, No. 4 (1985):361–71.

ALBA, RICHARD D. *Italian Americans: Into the Twilight of Ethnicity.* Englewood Cliffs, N.J.: Prentice Hall, 1985.

———. *Ethnic Identity: The Transformation of White America.* Chicago: University of Chicago Press, 1990.

ALBAS, DANIEL, AND CHERYL ALBAS. "Disclaimer Mannerisms of Students: How to Avoid Being Labelled as Cheaters." *Canadian Review of Sociology and Anthropology.* Vol. 30, No. 4 (1993):457-67.

ALBON, JOAN. "Retention of Cultural Values and Differential Urban Adaptation: Samoans and American Indians in a West Coast City." *Social Forces.* Vol. 49, No. 3 (March 1971):385–93.

ALBRECHT, WILLIAM P., JR. *Economics.* 3d ed. Englewood Cliffs, N.J.: Prentice Hall, 1983.

ALFORD, RICHARD. "The Structure of Human Experience: Expectancy and Affect; The Case of Humor." Unpublished paper, Department of Sociology, University of Wyoming, 1979.

ALLAN, EMILIE ANDERSEN, and DARRELL J. STEFFENSMEIER. "Youth, Underemployment, and Property Crime: Differential Effects of Job Availability and Job Quality on Juvenile and Young Adult Arrest Rates." *American Sociological Review.* Vol. 54, No. 1 (February 1989):107–23.

ALLEN, MICHAEL PATRICK, and PHILIP BROYLES. "Campaign Finance Reforms and the Presidential Campaign Contributions of Wealthy Capitalist Families." *Social Science Quarterly.* Vol. 72, No. 4 (December 1991):738–50.

ALLEN, WALTER R. "African American Family Life in Social Context: Crisis and Hope." *Sociological Forum.* Vol. 10, No. 4 (December 1995):569–92.

ALLSOP, KENNETH. *The Bootleggers.* London: Hutchinson and Company, 1961.

ALTER, JONATHAN. "Down to Business." *Newsweek* (May 12, 1997):58–60.

ALTMAN, DREW, ET AL. "Health Care for the Homeless." *Society.* Vol. 26, No. 4 (May–June 1989):4–5.

AMERICAN COUNCIL ON EDUCATION. "Thirteenth Annual Status Report on Minorities in Higher Education." Washington, D.C.: The Council, 1995.

———. Response to telephone inquiry, 1996.

AMERICAN MEDICAL ASSOCIATION (AMA). Executive Summary of Media Violence Survey Analysis. [Online] Available http://www.ama-assn.org/ad-com/releases/1996/mvan1909.htm, 1997.

AMERICAN SOCIOLOGICAL ASSOCIATION. "Code of Ethics." Washington, D.C.: 1984.

ANDERSON, ALAN B. AND JAMES S. FRIDERES. *Ethnicity in Canada: Theoretical Perspectives.* Toronto: Butterworths, 1981.

ANDERSON, DORIS. *The Unfinished Revolution.* Toronto: Doubleday Books, 1991.

ANDERSON, JOHN WARD. "Early to Wed: The Child Brides of India." *Washington Post* (May 24, 1995):A27, A30.

ANDERSON, JOHN WARD, and MOLLY MOORE. "World's Poorest Women Suffer in Common." *Columbus Dispatch* (April 11, 1993):4G.

ANDERSSEN, ERIN, AND DAVID ROBERTS. "Natives win input into unity declaration." *The Globe and Mail* (November 19, 1997):A10.

ANDO, FAITH H. "Women in Business." In Sara E. Rix, ed., *The American Woman: A Status Report 1990–91.* New York: Norton, 1990:222–30.

ANG, IEN. *Watching Dallas: Soap Opera and the Melodramatic Imagination.* London: Methuen, 1985.

ANGELO, BONNIE. "The Pain of Being Black" (an interview with Toni Morrison). *Time.* Vol. 133, No. 21 (May 22, 1989):120–22.

———. "Assigning the Blame for a Young Man's Suicide." *Time.* Vol. 138, No. 2 (November 18, 1991):12–14.

ANGIER, NATALIE. "Scientists, Finding Second Idiosyncracy in Homosexuals' Brains, Suggest Orientation is Physiological." *New York Times* (August 1, 1992):A7.

ANGIER, NATALIE. "Sexual identity predominates: Case of boy raised as girl underscores importance of prenatal events, MDs say." *The Globe and Mail* (March 14, 1997):A1.

APA. *Violence and Youth: Psychology's Response.* Washington, D.C.: American Psychological Association, 1993.

APPLEBOME, PETER. "70 Years After Scopes Trial, Creation Debate Lives." *New York Times* (March 10, 1996):1, 10.

ARCHER, DANE, and ROSEMARY GARTNER. *Violence and Crime in Cross-National Perspective.* New Haven, Conn.: Yale University Press, 1987.

ARENDT, HANNAH. *The Origins of Totalitarianism.* Cleveland, Ohio: Meridian Books, 1958.

———. *Between Past and Future: Six Exercises in Political Thought.* Cleveland, Ohio: Meridian Books, 1963.

ARIÈS, PHILIPPE. *Centuries of Childhood: A Social History of Family Life.* New York: Vintage Books, 1965.

———. *Western Attitudes Toward Death: From the Middle Ages to the Present.* Baltimore, Md.: Johns Hopkins University Press, 1974.

ARJOMAND, SAID AMIR. *The Turban for the Crown: The Islamic Revolution in Iran.* New York: Oxford University Press, 1988.

ARMEY, DICK. "How Taxes Corrupt." *Wall Street Journal* (June 19, 1996):A20.

ARNUP, KATHERINE. " 'We Are Family': Lesbian Mothers in Canada." Pp. 330–45 in E.D. Nelson and B.W. Robinson (eds.), *Gender in the 1990s: Images, Realities and Issues.* Scarborough, Ontario: Nelson Canada 1995.

ARTIBISE, ALAN F.J. "Canada as an Urban Nation." *Daedalus.* Vol. 117 (Fall 1988).

———, AND GIL STELTER. "Urbanization." *The Canadian Encyclopedia.* 2d ed. Edmonton: Hurtig Publishers, 1988:2235–36.

ASANTE, MOLEFI KETE. *The Afrocentric Idea.* Philadelphia: Temple University Press, 1987.

———. *Afrocentricity.* Trenton, N.J.: Africa World Press, 1988.

ASCH, SOLOMON. *Social Psychology.* Englewood Cliffs, N.J.: Prentice Hall, 1952.

ASHFORD, LORI S. "New Perspectives on Population: Lessons From Cairo." *Population Bulletin.* Vol. 50, No. 1 (March 1995).

ASTONE, NAN MARIE, and SARA S. McLANAHAN. "Family Structure, Parental Practices and High School Completion." *American Sociological Review.* Vol. 56, No. 3 (June 1991):309–20.

ATCHLEY, ROBERT C. "Retirement as a Social Institution." *Annual Review of Sociology.* Vol. 8. Palo Alto, Calif.: Annual Reviews, 1982:263–87.

———. *Aging: Continuity and Change.* Belmont, Calif.: Wadsworth, 1983; 2d ed., 1987.

ATWOOD, MARGARET. "True Trash." In *Wilderness Tips.* Toronto: McClelland & Stewart, 1991: 1-30.

AUSTER, CAROL J., and MIND MacRONE. "The Classroom as a Negotiated Social Setting: An Empirical Study of the Effects of Faculty Members' Behavior on Students' Participation." *Teaching Sociology.* Vol. 22, No. 4 (October 1994):289–300.

AXTELL, ROGER E. *Gestures: The DOs and TABOOs of Body Language Around the World.* New York: Wiley, 1991.

AYENSU, EDWARD S. "A Worldwide Role for the Healing Powers of Plants." *Smithsonian.* Vol. 12, No. 8 (November 1981):87–97.

BABBIE, EARL. *The Practice of Social Research.* 7th ed. Belmont, Calif.: Wadsworth, 1995.

BACHMAN, RONET. *Violence Against Women.* U.S. Bureau of Justice Statistics. Washington, D.C.: U.S. Government Printing Office, 1994.

BACHRACH, PETER, and MORTON S. BARATZ. *Power and Poverty.* New York: Oxford University Press, 1970.

BACKMAN, CARL B., and MURRAY C. ADAMS. "Self-Perceived Physical Attractiveness, Self-Esteem, Race, and Gender." *Sociological Focus.* Vol. 24, No. 4 (October 1994):283–90.

BAHL, VINAY. "Caste and Class in India." Paper presented to the Southern Sociological Society, Atlanta, April 1991.

BAILEY, WILLIAM C. "Murder, Capital Punishment, and Television: Execution Publicity and Homicide Rates." *American Sociological Review.* Vol. 55, No. 5 (October 1990):628–33.

BAILEY, WILLIAM C., and RUTH D. PETERSON. "Murder and Capital Punishment:

A Monthly Time-Series Analysis of Execution Publicity." *American Sociological Review*. Vol. 54, No. 5 (October 1989):722–43.

BAKER, MARY ANNE, CATHERINE WHITE BERHEIDE, FAY ROSS GRECKEL, LINDA CARSTARPHEN GUGIN, MARCIA J. LIPETZ, and MARCIA TEXLER SEGAL. *Women Today: A Multidisciplinary Approach to Women's Studies*. Monterey, Calif.: Brooks/Cole, 1980.

BAKER, MAUREEN. Pp. 353–81 in *The Social World: An Introduction to Sociology*, Lorne Tepperman and R. Jack Richardson, eds. Toronto: McGraw Hill Ryerson, 1991.

BAKER, ROSS. "Business as Usual." *American Demographics*. Vol. 19, No. 4 (April 1997):28.

BAKKER, J.I. (HANS), AND ANTHONY WINSON. "Rural Sociology." Pp. 500–17 in Peter S. Li and B. Singh Bolaria, eds. *Contemporary Sociology: Critical Perspectives*. Toronto: Copp Clark Pitman, 1993.

BALDUS, BERND AND VERNA TRIBE. "The Development of Perceptions and Evaluations of Social Inequality Among Public School Children." *Canadian Review of Sociology and Anthropology*. Vol. 15, No. 1 (1978):50–60.

BALES, ROBERT F. "The Equilibrium Problem in Small Groups." In Talcott Parsons et al., eds., *Working Papers in the Theory of Action*. New York: Free Press, 1953:111–15.

BALES, ROBERT F., and PHILIP E. SLATER. "Role Differentiation in Small Decision-Making Groups." In Talcott Parsons and Robert F. Bales, eds., *Family, Socialization and Interaction Process*. New York: Free Press, 1955:259–306.

BALTES, PAUL B., and K. WARNER SCHAIE. "The Myth of the Twilight Years." *Psychology Today*. Vol. 7, No. 10 (March 1974):35–39.

BALTZELL, E. DIGBY. *The Protestant Establishment: Aristocracy and Caste in America*. New York: Vintage Books, 1964.

———. "Introduction to the 1967 Edition." In W. E. B. Du Bois, *The Philadelphia Negro: A Social Study*. New York: Schocken, 1967; orig. 1899.

———, ED. *The Search for Community in Modern America*. New York: Harper & Row, 1968.

———. "The Protestant Establishment Revisited." *The American Scholar*. Vol. 45, No. 4 (Autumn 1976):499–518.

———. *Philadelphia Gentlemen: The Making of a National Upper Class*. Philadelphia: University of Pennsylvania Press, 1979; orig. 1958.

———. *Puritan Boston and Quaker Philadelphia*. New York: Free Press, 1979.

———. "The WASP's Last Gasp." *Philadelphia Magazine*. Vol. 79 (September 1988):104–7, 184, 186, 188.

———. *Sporting Gentlemen: From the Age of Honor to the Cult of the Superstar*. New York: Free Press, 1995.

BANDON, ALEXANDRA. "Longer, Healthier, Better." *New York Times Magazine* (March 9, 1997):44–45.

BANFIELD, EDWARD C. *The Unheavenly City Revisited*. Boston: Little, Brown, 1974.

BARASH, DAVID. *The Whispering Within*. New York: Penguin Books, 1981.

BARBER, JOHN. "The Legacy of Wally Neshkiwe." *The Globe and Mail* (September 17, 1997):A2.

BARBERIS, MARY. "America's Elderly: Policy Implications." *Population Bulletin*. Vol. 35, No. 4 (January 1981). Population Reference Bureau.

BARIL, ALAIN AND GEORGE A. MORI. "Leaving the Fold: Declining Church Attendance." *Canadian Social Trends* (Catalogue no. 11-008E). No. 22 (1991):21–24.

BARKER, EILEEN. "Who'd Be a Moonie? A Comparative Study of Those Who Join the Unification Church in Britain." In Bryan Wilson, ed., *The Social Impact of New Religious Movements*. New York: The Rose of Sharon Press, 1981:59–96.

———. *New Religious Movements: A Practical Introduction*. London: Her Majesty's Stationery Office, 1989.

BARLOW, MAUDE, AND BRUCE CAMPBELL. *Take Back the Nation*. Toronto: Key Porter Books, 1991.

BARLOW, MAUDE, AND HEATHER-JANE ROBERTSON. *Class Warfare: The Assault on Canada's Schools*. Toronto: Key Porter Books, 1994.

BARON, JAMES N., BRIAN S. MITTMAN, and ANDREW E. NEWMAN. "Targets of Opportunity: Organizational and Environmental Determinants of Gender Integration Within the California Civil Service, 1979–1985." *American Journal of Sociology*. Vol. 96, No. 6 (May 1991): 1362–1401.

BARONE, MICHAEL, and GRANT UJIFUSA. *The Almanac of American Politics*. Washington, D.C.: Barone and Co., 1981.

BARRY, KATHLEEN. "Feminist Theory: The Meaning of Women's Liberation." In Barbara Haber, ed., *The Women's Annual 1982–1983*. Boston: G. K. Hall, 1983:35–78.

BASHEVKIN, SYLVIA B. *Toeing the Lines: Women and Party Politics in Canada*. 2d ed. Toronto: Oxford University Press, 1993.

BASIC DEPARTMENTAL DATA. Department of Indian Affairs & Northern Development. Ottawa: Statistics Canada, 1992.

BASSETT, ISABEL. *The Bassett Report: Career Success and Canadian Women*. Toronto: Collins, 1985.

BASSUK, ELLEN J. "The Homelessness Problem." *Scientific American*. Vol. 251, No. 1 (July 1984):40–45.

BAUER, P.T. *Equality, the Third World, and Economic Delusion*. Cambridge, Mass.: Harvard University Press, 1981.

BAYDAR, NAZLI, and JEANNE BROOKS-GUNN. "Effect of Maternal Employment and Child-Care Arrangements on Preschoolers' Cognitive and Behavioral Outcomes: Evidence From Children From the National Longitudinal Survey of Youth." *Developmental Psychology*. Vol. 27 (1991):932–35.

BEAUJOT, RODERIC AND KEVIN MCQUILLAN. *Growth and Dualism: The Demographic Development of Canadian Society*. Toronto: Gage, 1982.

BECKER, HOWARD S. *Outside: Studies in the Sociology of Deviance*. New York: Free Press, 1966.

BEDELL, GEORGE C., LEO SANDON, JR., and CHARLES T. WELLBORN. *Religion in America*. New York: Macmillan, 1975.

BEEGHLEY, LEONARD. *The Structure of Social Stratification in the United States*. Needham Heights, Mass.: Allyn & Bacon, 1989.

BEGIN, PATRICIA. *Violence Against Women: Current Response*. Cat. no. 1391B67. Ottawa: Ministry of Supply and Services, September 1991.

BEGLEY, SHARON. "Gray Matters." *Newsweek* (March 7, 1995):48–54.

———. "How to Beat the Heat." *Newsweek* (December 8, 1997):34–38.

BEINS, BARNEY, cited in "Examples of Spuriousness." *Teaching Methods*. No. 2 (Fall 1993):3.

BELL, ALAN P., MARTIN S. WEINBERG, and SUE KIEFER-HAMMERSMITH. *Sexual Preference: Its Development in Men and Women*. Bloomington: Indiana University Press, 1981.

BELL, DANIEL. *The Coming of Post-Industrial Society: A Venture in Social Forecasting*. New York: Basic Books, 1973.

BELLAH, ROBERT N. *The Broken Covenant*. New York: Seabury Press, 1975.

BELLAH, ROBERT N., RICHARD MADSEN, WILLIAM M. SULLIVAN, ANN SWIDLER, and STEVEN M. TIPTON. *Habits of the Heart: Individualism and Commitment in American Life*. New York: Harper & Row, 1985.

BELLAS, MARCIA L. "Comparable Worth in Academia: The Effects on Faculty Salaries of the Sex Composition and Labor-Market Conditions of Academic Disciplines." *American Sociological Review*. Vol. 59, No. 6 (December 1994):807–21.

BELSKY, JAY, RICHARD M. LERNER, and GRAHAM B. SPANIER. *The Child in the Family*. Reading, Mass.: Addison-Wesley, 1984.

BEM, SANDRA LIPSITZ. "Gender Schema Theory: A Cognitive Account of Sex-Typing." *Psychological Review*. Vol. 88, No. 4 (July 1981):354–64.

———. *The Lenses of Gender: Transforming the Debate on Sexual Inequality*. New Haven, Conn.: Yale University Press, 1993.

BENEDETTI, PAUL AND NANCY DEHART, eds. *On McLuhan: Forward Through the Rearview Mirror*. Scarborough, Ontario: Prentice Hall Canada, 1996.

BENEDICT, RUTH. "Continuities and Discontinuities in Cultural Conditioning." *Psychiatry*. Vol. 1 (May 1938):161–67.

———. *The Chrysanthemum and the Sword: Patterns of Japanese Culture*. New York: New American Library, 1974; orig. 1946.

BENET, SULA. "Why They Live to Be 100, or Even Older, in Abkhasia." *New York Times Magazine* (December 26, 1971):3, 28–29, 31–34.

BENETEAU, RENÉE. "Trends in Suicide." in Craig McKie and Keith Thompson, eds., *Canadian Social Trends*. Toronto: Thompson Educational Publishing, 1990.

BENJAMIN, BERNARD, and CHRIS WALLIS. "The Mortality of Widowers." *The Lancet*. Vol. 2 (August 1963):454–56.

BENJAMIN, LOIS. *The Black Elite: Facing the Color Line in the Twilight of the Twentieth Century*. Chicago: Nelson-Hall, 1991.

BENN, CARL. *Historic Fort York, 1793–1993*. Toronto: Natural Heritage, 1993.

BENNETT, NEIL G., DAVID E. BLOOM, and PATRICIA H. CRAIG. "The Divergence of Black and White Marriage Patterns." *American Journal of Sociology*. Vol. 95, No. 3 (November 1989):692–722.

BENNETT, STEPHEN EARL. "Left Behind: Exploring Declining Turnout Among Noncollege Young Whites, 1964–1988." *Social Science Quarterly*. Vol. 72, No. 2 (June 1991):314–33.

BENNETT, WILLIAM J. "Quantifying America's Decline." *Wall Street Journal* (March 15, 1993).

———. "Redeeming Our Time." *Imprimis*. Vol. 24, No. 11 (November 1995). Hillsdale, Mich.: Hillsdale College.

———. "School Reform: What Remains to Be Done." *Wall Street Journal* (September 2, 1997):A18.

BENOKRAITIS, NIJOLE, and JOE FEAGIN. *Modern Sexism: Blatant, Subtle, and Overt Discrimination*. 2d ed. Englewood Cliffs, N.J.: Prentice Hall, 1995.

BERARDO, F. M. "Survivorship and Social Isolation: The Case of the Aged Widower." *The Family Coordinator*. Vol. 19 (January 1970):11–25.

BERESFORD-HOWE, CONSTANCE. *A Serious Widow*. Toronto: McClelland & Stewart, 1991.

BERCUSON, DAVID AND BARRY COOPER. "A new tax on energy is unacceptable." *The Globe and Mail* (November 8, 1997):D2.

BERGAMO, MONICA, and GERSON CAMAROTTI. "Brazil's Landless Millions." *World Press Review*. Vol. 43, No. 7 (July 1996):46–47.

BERGEN, RAQUEL KENNEDY. "Interviewing Survivors of Marital Rape: Doing Feminist Research on Sensitive Topics." In Claire M. Renzetti and Raymond M. Lee, *Researching Sensitive Topics*. Thousand Oaks, Calif.: Sage, 1993.

BERGER, PETER L. *Invitation to Sociology*. New York: Anchor Books, 1963.

———. *The Sacred Canopy: Elements of a Sociological Theory of Religion*. Garden City, N.Y.: Doubleday, 1967.

———. *Facing Up to Modernity: Excursions in Society, Politics, and Religion*. New York: Basic Books, 1977.

————. *The Capitalist Revolution: Fifty Propositions About Prosperity, Equality, and Liberty.* New York: Basic Books, 1986.

BERGER, PETER, BRIGITTE BERGER, and HANSFRIED KELLNER. *The Homeless Mind: Modernization and Consciousness.* New York: Vintage Books, 1974.

BERGER, PETER L., and HANSFRIED KELLNER. *Sociology Reinterpreted: An Essay on Method and Vocation.* Garden City, N.Y.: Anchor Books, 1981.

BERGESEN, ALBERT, ED. *Crises in the World-System.* Beverly Hills, Calif.: Sage, 1983.

BERK, RICHARD A. *Collective Behavior.* Dubuque, Iowa: Wm. C. Brown, 1974.

BERNARD, JESSIE. *The Female World.* New York: Free Press, 1981.

————. *The Future of Marriage.* New Haven, Conn.: Yale University Press, 1982; orig. 1973.

BERNARD, LARRY CRAIG. "Multivariate Analysis of New Sex Role Formulations and Personality." *Journal of Personality and Social Psychology.* Vol. 38, No. 2 (February 1980):323–36.

BERNHARDT, ANNETTE, MARTINA MORRIS, and MARK S. HANDCOCK. "Women's Gains or Men's Losses? A Closer Look at the Shrinking Gender Gap in Earnings." *American Journal of Sociology.* Vol. 101, No. 1 (September 1995):302–28.

BERNSTEIN, NINA. "On Frontier of Cyberspace, Data Is Money, and a Threat." *New York Times* (June 12, 1997):A1, B14–15.

BERNSTEIN, RICHARD J. *The New Constellation: The Ethical-Political Horizons of Modernity/Postmodernity.* Cambridge, Mass.: MIT Press, 1992.

BERRILL, KEVIN T. "Anti-Gay Violence and Victimization in the United States: An Overview." In Gregory M. Herek and Kevin T. Berrill, *Hate Crimes: Confronting Violence Against Lesbians and Gay Men.* Newbury Park, Calif.: Sage, 1992:19–45.

BERRY, BRIAN L., and PHILIP H. REES. "The Factorial Ecology of Calcutta." *American Journal of Sociology.* Vol. 74, No. 5 (March 1969):445–91.

BERSCHEID, ELLEN, and ELAINE HATFIELD. *Interpersonal Attraction.* 2d ed. Reading, Mass.: Addison-Wesley, 1983.

BERTON, PIERRE. *The Dionne Years: A Thirties Melodrama.* Toronto: McClelland & Stewart, 1977.

BESHAROV, DOUGLAS J., and LISA A. LAUMANN. "Child Abuse Reporting." *Society.* Vol. 34, No. 4 (May/June 1996):40–46.

BEST, JOEL. "Victimization and the Victim Industry." *Society.* Vol. 34, No. 2 (May/June 1997):9–17.

BEST, RAPHAELA. *We've All Got Scars: What Boys and Girls Learn in Elementary School.* Bloomington: Indiana University Press, 1983.

"The Best and Worst Places to Live." *Report on Business Magazine* (January 1996):18–19.

BIANCHI, SUZANNE M., and DAPHNE SPAIN. "Women, Work, and Family in America." *Population Bulletin.* Vol. 51, No. 3 (December 1996).

————. "U.S. Women Make Workplace Progress." *Population Today.* Vol. 25, No. 1 (January 1997):1–2.

BIBBY, REGINALD W. "The Persistence of Religious Identification in Canada." *Canadian Social Trends* (Spring 1997):24.

————. *The Bibby Report: Social Trends Canadian Style.* Toronto: Stoddart, 1995.

————. *Unknown Gods.* Toronto: Stoddart Publishing, 1993.

————. *Fragmented Gods: The Poverty and Potential of Religion in Canada.* Toronto: Irwin, 1987.

————. "Secularization and Change." In W.E. Hewitt, ed., *The Sociology of Religion: A Canadian Focus.* Toronto: Butterworths, 1993.

————. "The Moral Mosaic: Sexuality in Canada 80s." *Social Indicators Research.* Vol. 13 (1983): 171–84.

BIBLARZ, TIMOTHY J., and ADRIAN E. RAFTERY. "The Effects of Family Disruption on Social Mobility." *American Sociological Review.* Vol. 58, No. 1 (February 1993):97–109.

BILLSON, JANET MANCINI, and BETTINA J. HUBER. *Embarking Upon a Career With an Undergraduate Degree in Sociology.* 2d ed. Washington, D.C.: American Sociological Association, 1993.

BISHOP, MARY F. "Birth Control." In *The Canadian Encyclopedia*, 2d ed., Vol. 1:231-32. Edmonton: Hurtig Publishers, 1988.

BISSOONDATH, NEIL. *Selling Illusions: The Cult of Multiculturalism in Canada.* Toronto: Penguin Books, 1994.

BLACK, NAOMI. "Agnes MacPhail." In *The Canadian Encyclopedia*, 2d ed. Vol. 2:1281. Edmonton: Hurtig Publishers, 1988.

BLANKENHORN, DAVID. *Fatherless America: Confronting Our Most Urgent Social Problem.* New York: HarperCollins, 1995.

BLAU, JUDITH R., and PETER M. BLAU. "The Cost of Inequality: Metropolitan Structure and Violent Crime." *American Sociological Review.* Vol. 47, No. 1 (February 1982):114–29.

BLAU, PETER M. *Exchange and Power in Social Life.* New York: Wiley, 1964.

————. *Inequality and Heterogeneity: A Primitive Theory of Social Structure.* New York: Free Press, 1977.

BLAU, PETER M., TERRY C. BLUM, and JOSEPH E. SCHWARTZ. "Heterogeneity and Intermarriage." *American Sociological Review.* Vol. 47, No. 1 (February 1982):45–62.

BLAU, PETER M., and OTIS DUDLEY DUNCAN. *The American Occupational Structure.* New York: Wiley, 1967.

BLAUSTEIN, ALBERT P., and ROBERT L. ZANGRANDO. *Civil Rights and the Black American.* New York: Washington Square Press, 1968.

BLISHEN, BERNARD R. "The Construction and Use of an Occupational Class Scale." *Canadian Journal of Economics and Political Science.* Vol. XXIV (1958):519–525.

————. *Doctors in Canada.* Toronto: University of Toronto Press, 1991.

————, W. Carroll and C. Moore. "The 1981 socio-economic index for occupations in Canada." *Canadian Review of Sociology and Anthropology.* Vol. 24 (1987):465–488.

BLOOM, LEONARD. "Familial Adjustments of Japanese-Americans to Relocation: First Phase." In Thomas F. Pettigrew, ed., *The Sociology of Race Relations.* New York: Free Press, 1980:163–67.

BLUM, LINDA M. *Between Feminism and Labor: The Significance of the Comparable Worth Movement.* Berkeley: University of California Press, 1991.

BLUMBERG, ABRAHAM S. *Criminal Justice.* Chicago: Quadrangle Books, 1970.

BLUMBERG, PAUL. *Inequality in an Age of Decline.* New York: Oxford University Press, 1981.

BLUMER, HERBERT G. "Fashion." In David L. Sills, ed., *International Encyclopedia of the Social Sciences.* Vol. 5. New York: Macmillan and Free Press, 1968:341–45.

————. "Collective Behavior." In Alfred McClung Lee, ed., *Principles of Sociology.* 3d ed. New York: Barnes & Noble Books, 1969:65–121.

BLUMSTEIN, PHILIP, and PEPPER SCHWARTZ. *American Couples.* New York: William Morrow, 1983.

BOBO, LAWRENCE, and VINCENT L. HUTCHINGS. "Perceptions of Racial Group Competition: Extending Blumer's Theory of Group Position to a Multiracial Social Context." *American Sociological Review.* Vol. 61, No. 6 (December 1996):951–72.

BODENHEIMER, THOMAS S. "Health Care in the United States: Who Pays?" In Vicente Navarro, ed., *Health and Medical Care in the U.S.: A Critical Analysis.* Farmingdale, N.Y.: Baywood Publishing Co., 1977:61–68.

BOERNER, CHRISTOPHER, and THOMAS LAMBERT. "Environmental Injustice." *The Public Interest.* Vol. 118 (Winter 1995):61–82.

BOFF, LEONARD and CLODOVIS. *Salvation and Liberation: In Search of a Balance Between Faith and Politics.* Maryknoll, N.Y.: Orbis Books, 1984.

BOGARDUS, EMORY S. "Comparing Racial Distance in Ethiopia, South Africa, and the United States." *Sociology and Social Research.* Vol. 52, No. 2 (January 1968):149–56.

BOHANNAN, CECIL. "The Economic Correlates of Homelessness in Sixty Cities." *Social Science Quarterly.* Vol. 72, No. 4 (December 1991):817–25.

BOHANNAN, PAUL. *Divorce and After.* Garden City, N.Y.: Doubleday, 1970.

BOHM, ROBERT M. "American Death Penalty Opinion, 1936–1986: A Critical Examination of the Gallup Polls." In Robert M. Bohm, ed., *The Death Penalty in America: Current Research.* Cincinnati: Anderson Publishing Co., 1991:113–45.

BOLI, JOHN, and GEORGE M. THOMAS. "World Culture in the World Polity: A Century of International Non-Governmental Organization." *American Sociological Review.* Vol. 62, No. 2 (April 1997):171–90.

BONCZAR, THOMAS P., and ALLAN J. BECK. *Lifetime Likelihood of Going to State or Federal Prison.* Washington, D.C.: U.S. Bureau of Justice Statistics, 1997.

BONILLA-SANTIAGO, GLORIA. "A Portrait of Hispanic Women in the United States." In Sara E. Rix, ed., *The American Woman 1990–91: A Status Report.* New York: Norton, 1990:249–57.

BONNER, JANE. Research presented in "The Two Brains." Public Broadcasting System telecast, 1984.

BOO, KATHERINE. "Two Women, Two Responses to Change." *Washington Post* (December 15, 1996):A1, A28–29.

BOOTH, ALAN, and LYNN WHITE. "Thinking About Divorce." *Journal of Marriage and the Family.* Vol. 42, No. 3 (August 1980):605–16.

BORGMANN, ALBERT. *Crossing the Postmodern Divide.* Chicago: University of Chicago Press, 1992.

BORITCH, HELEN. *Fallen Women: Female Crime and Criminal Justice in Canada.* Toronto: ITP Nelson, 1997.

BORMANN, F. HERBERT. "The Global Environmental Deficit." *BioScience.* Vol. 40 (1990):74.

BORMANN, F. HERBERT, and STEPHEN R. KELLERT. "The Global Environmental Deficit." In Bormann, F. Herbert and Stephen R. Kellert, eds., *Ecology, Economics, and Ethics: The Broken Circle.* New Haven, Conn.: Yale University Press, 1991:ix–xviii.

BOSWELL, TERRY E. "A Split Labor Market Analysis of Discrimination Against Chinese Immigrants, 1850–1882." *American Sociological Review.* Vol. 51, No. 3 (June 1986):352–71.

BOSWELL, TERRY E., and WILLIAM J. DIXON. "Marx's Theory of Rebellion: A Cross-National Analysis of Class Exploitation, Economic Development, and Violent Revolt." *American Sociological Review.* Vol. 58, No. 5 (October 1993): 681–702.

BOTT, ELIZABETH. *Family and Social Network.* New York: Free Press, 1971; orig. 1957.

BOULDING, ELISE. *The Underside of History.* Boulder, Colo.: Westview Press, 1976.

BOWLES, SAMUEL, and HERBERT GINTIS. *Schooling in Capitalist America: Educational Reform and the Contradictions of Economic Life.* New York: Basic Books, 1976.

BOYER, ERNEST L. *College: The Undergraduate Experience in America*. Prepared by The Carnegie Foundation for the Advancement of Teaching. New York: Harper & Row, 1987.

BOZINOFF, LORNE, AND PETER MACINTOSH. "Vast Majority of Canadians Believe in God and Heaven." Toronto: Gallup Report, August 30, 1990.

BRAITHWAITE, JOHN. "The Myth of Social Class and Criminality Reconsidered." *American Sociological Review*. Vol. 46, No. 1 (February 1981):36–57.

BRANEGAN, JAY. "Is Singapore a Model for the West?" *Time*. Vol. 141, No. 3 (January 18, 1993):36–37.

BREEN, LEONARD Z. "The Aging Individual." In Clark Tibbitts, ed., *Handbook of Social Gerontology*. Chicago: University of Chicago Press, 1960:145–62.

BREND, YVETTE. "Why history lives in Old Crow." *The Globe and Mail* (November 11, 1997):A2.

BRETON, RAYMOND. "Institutional completeness of ethnic communities and the personal relations of immigrants." *American Journal of Sociology*. Vol. 70 (1964): 193–205.

——. "Ethnic Stratification Viewed from Three Theoretical Perspectives." In James E. Curtis and William G. Scott, eds., *Social Stratification: Canada*. 2d ed. Scarborough, Ont.: Prentice Hall, 1979: 270–94.

——. "Regionalism in Canada." In David Cameron, ed. *Regionalism and Supranationalism*. Montreal: Institute for Research on Public Policy, 1981.

——. *Why Meech Failed: Lessons for Canadian Constitutionmaking*. Toronto: C.D. Howe Institute, 1992.

BRIGHTMAN, JOAN. "Why Hillary Chooses Rodham Clinton." *American Demographics*. Vol. 16, No. 3 (March 1994):9–11.

BRINTON, CRANE. *The Anatomy of Revolution*. New York: Vintage Books, 1965.

BRINTON, MARY C. "The Social-Institutional Bases of Gender Stratification: Japan as an Illustrative Case." *American Journal of Sociology*. Vol. 94, No. 2 (September 1988):300–34.

BRODER, JOHN M. "Big Social Changes Revive False God of Numbers." *New York Times* (August 17, 1997): section 4, pp. 1, 4.

BRONSON, HAROLD. "Economic Concentration and Corporate Power." In Peter S. Li and B. Singh Bolaria, eds., *Contemporary Sociology: Critical Perspectives*. Toronto: Copp Clark Pitman, 1993: 203–22.

BROUGH, JAMES. *We Were Five: The Dionne Sisters*. New York: Simon & Schuster, 1964.

BROWN, CLAIR, and JOSEPH PECHMAN, eds. *Gender in the Workplace*. Washington, D.C.: Brookings, 1987.

BROWN, LESTER R. "Reassessing the Earth's Population." *Society*. Vol. 32, No. 4 (May–June 1995):7–10.

BROWN, LESTER R., ET AL., EDS. *State of the World 1993: A Worldwatch Institute Report on Progress Toward a Sustainable Society*. New York: Norton, 1993.

BROWN, MARY ELLEN, ED. *Television and Women's Culture: The Politics of the Popular*. Newbury Park, Calif.: Sage, 1990.

BROWNMILLER, SUSAN. *Femininity*. New York: Linden Press, Simon and Schuster, 1984.μ

——. *Against Our Will: Men, Women and Rape*. New York: Simon & Schuster, 1975.

BRUNO, MARY. "Abusing the Elderly." *Newsweek* (September 23, 1985):75–76.

BRYM, ROBERT J, ED. *Regionalism in Canada*. Toronto: Irwin, 1986.

——. "An Introduction to the Regional Question in Canada." In Robert J. Brym (ed.), *Regionalism in Canada*. Toronto: Irwin Publishing, 1986:2–45.

——. "The Canadian Capitalist Class, 1965–1985." In Robert J. Brym (ed.), *The Structures of the Canadian Capitalist Class*. Toronto: Garamond, 1985:1–20.

BRYM, ROBERT J., AND BONNIE J. FOX. *From Culture to Power: The Sociology of English Canada*. Don Mills, Ont.: Oxford University Press, 1989.

BUCKLEY, STEPHEN. "A Spare and Separate Way of Life." *Washington Post* (December 18, 1996):A1, A32–33.

BUMPASS, LARRY, and JAMES A. SWEET. 1992–1994 National Survey of Families and Households. Reported in "Report From PPA." *Population Today*. Vol. 23, No. 6 (June 1995):3.

BURAWAY, MICHAEL. "Review Essay: The Soviet Descent Into Capitalism." *American Journal of Sociology*. Vol. 102, No. 5 (March 1997):1430–44.

BURCH, ROBERT. Testimony to House of Representatives Hearing in "Review: The World Hunger Problem." October 25, 1983, Serial 98–38.

BURKE, TOM. "The Future." In Sir Edmund Hillary, ed., *Ecology 2000: The Changing Face of the Earth*. New York: Beaufort Books, 1984:227–41.

BURSTEIN, PAUL. "Legal Mobilization as a Social Movement Tactic: The Struggle for Equal Employment Opportunity." *American Journal of Sociology*. Vol. 96, No. 5 (March 1991):1201–25.

BUSBY, LINDA J. "Sex Role Research on the Mass Media." *Journal of Communications*. Vol. 25 (Autumn 1975):107–13.

BUTLER, ROBERT N. *Why Survive? Being Old in America*. New York: Harper & Row, 1975.

BUTTERFIELD, FOX. "Prison: Where the Money Is." *New York Times* (June 2, 1996):E16.

——. "The Wisdom of Children Who Have Known Too Much." *New York Times* (June 8, 1997): section 4, pp. 1, 4.

BUTTERWORTH, DOUGLAS, and JOHN K. CHANCE. *Latin American Urbanization*. Cambridge: Cambridge University Press, 1981.

CAHNMAN, WERNER J., and RUDOLF HEBERLE. "Introduction." In *Ferdinand Toennies on Sociology: Pure, Applied, and Empirical*. Chicago: University of Chicago Press, 1971:vii–xxii.

CALLAHAN, DANIEL. *Setting Limits: Medical Goals in an Aging Society*. New York: Simon & Schuster, 1987.

CALLOW, A.B., JR., ED. *American Urban History*. New York: Oxford University Press, 1969.

CALLWOOD, JUNE. *Trial Without End: A Shocking Story of Women and AIDS*. Toronto: Knopf, 1995.

CALMORE, JOHN O. "National Housing Policies and Black America: Trends, Issues, and Implications." In *The State of Black America 1986*. New York: National Urban League, 1986:115–49.

CAMERON, WILLIAM BRUCE. *Modern Social Movements: A Sociological Outline*. New York: Random House, 1966.

CANADA. *The Economic and Fiscal Update*. Ottawa: Department of Finance, October 1997.

——. House of Commons. Standing Committee on Communications and Culture. *Television Violence: Fraying our Social Fabric*. Issue no. 6. Ottawa: Supply and Services Canada, 1993.

——. Royal Commission on Aboriginal Peoples. *Ethical Guidelines for Research*. 8 pp. Ottawa: Supply and Services Canada, 1993.

Canada Year Book. Ottawa: Statistics Canada, 1994.

CANADIAN BROADCASTING CORPORATION. *The National Magazine*. January 16, 1998.

CANADIAN INTERNATIONAL DEVELOPMENT AGENCY (CIDA). *Sharing our Future: Canadian International Development Assistance*. Ottawa: Ministry of Supply and Services Canada, 1987.

CANCIO, A. SILVIA, T. DAVID EVANS, and DAVID J. MAUME, JR. "Reconsidering the Declining Significance of Race: Racial Differences in Early Career Wages." *American Sociological Review*. Vol. 61, No. 4 (August 1996):541–56.

CANETTI, ELIAS. *Crowds and Power*. New York: Seabury Press, 1978.

CANTOR, MURIAL G., and SUZANNE PINGREE. *The Soap Opera*. Beverly Hills, Calif.: Sage, 1983.

CANTRIL, HADLEY, HAZEL GAUDET, and HERTA HERZOG. *Invasion From Mars: A Study in the Psychology of Panic*. Princeton, N.J.: Princeton University Press, 1947.

CAPLOW, THEODORE, ET AL. *Middletown Families*. Minneapolis: University of Minnesota Press, 1982.

CAPLOW, THEODORE, HOWARD M. BAHR, JOHN MODELL, and BRUCE A. CHADWICK. *Recent Social Trends in the United States, 1960–1990*. Montreal: McGill-Queen's University Press, 1991.

CARAGATA, WARREN. "Healthy habits, longer life." *Maclean's* (June 15, 1998):30–31.

CARLEY, KATHLEEN. "A Theory of Group Stability." *American Sociological Review*. Vol. 56, No. 3 (June 1991):331–54.

CARLSON, MARGARET. "The Real Money Train." *Time*. Vol. 146, No. 24 (December 11, 1995):93.

CARLSON, NORMAN A. "Corrections in the United States Today: A Balance Has Been Struck." *The American Criminal Law Review*. Vol. 13, No. 4 (Spring 1976):615–47.

CARMICHAEL, STOKELY, and CHARLES V. HAMILTON. *Black Power: The Politics of Liberation in America*. New York: Vintage Books, 1967.

CARR, LESLIE G. "Colorblindness and the New Racism." Paper presented at the annual meeting, American Sociological Association, Washington, D.C., 1995.

CARRIGAN, D. OWEN. *Crime and Punishment in Canada: A History*. Toronto: McClelland & Stewart, 1991.

CARROLL, GINNY. "Who Foots the Bill?" *Newsweek*. Special Issue (Fall–Winter 1990):81–85.

CASTELLS, MANUEL. *The Urban Question*. Cambridge, Mass.: MIT Press, 1977.

——. *The City and the Grass Roots*. Berkeley: University of California Press, 1983.

CASTRO, JANICE. "Disposable Workers." *Time*. Vol. 131, No. 14 (March 29, 1993):43–47.

CENTER FOR MEDIA AND PUBLIC AFFAIRS. 1991 report by Robert Lichter, Linda Lichter, and Stanley Rothman.

CENTER FOR RESPONSIVE POLITICS. *The Big Picture*. [Online] Available http://www.crp.org/crpdocs/bigpicture/default.htm, February 12, 1998.

CENTER FOR THE STUDY OF SPORT IN SOCIETY. *1997 Racial Report Card: A Study in the NBA, NFL, and Major League Baseball*. Boston: Northeastern University, 1998.

CHAGNON, NAPOLEON A. *Yanomamö: The Fierce People*. 4th ed. New York: Holt, Rinehart & Winston, 1992.

CHANDLER, TERTIUS, and GERALD FOX. *3000 Years of Urban History*. New York: Academic Press, 1974.

CHANGE, KWANG-CHIH. *The Archaeology of Ancient China*. New Haven, Conn.: Yale University Press, 1977.

CHAPPELL, NEENA L., and BETTY HAVENS. "Old and Female: Testing the Double Jeopardy Hypothesis." *The Sociological Quarterly*. Vol. 21, No. 2 (Spring 1980):157–71.

CHARLES, MARIA. "Cross-National Variation in Occupational Segregation." *American Sociological Review*. Vol. 57, No. 4 (August 1992):483–502.

CHAVES, MARK. "Ordaining Women: The Diffusion of an Organizational Innovation." *American Journal of Sociology*. Vol. 101, No. 4 (January 1996):840–73.

CHERLIN, ANDREW. *Marriage, Divorce, Remarriage*. Rev. ed. Cambridge, Mass.: Harvard University Press, 1990.

CHERLIN, ANDREW, and FRANK F. FURSTENBERG, JR. "The American Family in the Year 2000." *The Futurist*. Vol. 17, No. 3 (June 1983):7–14.

———. *The New American Grandparent: A Place in the Family, A Life Apart*. New York: Basic Books, 1986.

CHESNAIS, JEAN-CLAUDE. "The Demographic Sunset of the West?" *Population Today*. Vol. 25, No. 1 (January 1997):4–5.

CHILDREN'S DEFENSE FUND. *The State of America's Children Yearbook, 1995*. Washington, D.C.: Children's Defense Fund, 1995.

CHISHOLM, PATRICIA. "To Celebrate Our Love Publicly." *Maclean's* (June 28, 1993): 29.

CHOWN, SHEILA M. "Morale, Careers and Personal Potentials." In James E. Birren and K. Warner Schaie, eds., *Handbook of the Psychology of Aging*. New York: Van Nostrand Reinhold, 1977:672–91.

CHRISTIAN, WILLIAM. "Innis, Harold Adams." In *The Canadian Encyclopedia* (1988): 1069.

———. "Ideology and Politics in Canada." In John H. Redekop, ed., *Approaches to Canadian Politics*. 2nd ed. Scarborough, Ont.: Prentice Hall, 1983.

THE CHRISTIAN SCIENCE MONITOR. *Women and Power* (September 6, 1995):1, 9, 10, 11.

CHRISTIE, JAMES. "Calgary fuelled our Olympic flame." *The Globe and Mail* (January 20, 1998):S1.

CHURCH, GEORGE J. "Unions Arise—With New Tricks." *Time*. Vol. 143, No. 24 (June 13, 1994):56–58.

———. "Ripping Up Welfare." *Time*. Vol. 148, No. 8 (August 12, 1996):18–22.

CLARK, CURTIS B. "Geriatric Abuse: Out of the Closet." In *The Tragedy of Elder Abuse: The Problem and the Response*. Hearings before the Select Committee on Aging, House of Representatives (July 1, 1986):49–50.

CLARK, JUAN M., JOSE I. LASAGA, and ROSE S. REGUE. *The 1980 Mariel Exodus: An Assessment and Prospect: Special Report*. Washington, D.C.: Council for Inter-American Security, 1981.

CLARK, MARGARET S., ED. *Prosocial Behavior*. Newbury Park, Calif.: Sage, 1991.

CLARK, S.D. *The New Urban Poor*. Toronto: McGraw-Hill Ryerson, 1978.

CLARK, THOMAS A. *Blacks in Suburbs*. New Brunswick, N.J.: Rutgers University Center for Urban Policy Research, 1979.

CLARKE, JAMES W. "Black-on-Black Violence." *Society*. Vol. 33, No. 5 (July/August 1996):46–50.

CLARKE, JUANNE NANCARROW. *Health, Illness & Medicine in Canada*. Toronto: McClelland & Stewart, 1990.

———. "Media Portrayal of Disease from the Medical, Political Economy and Life Style Perspectives." *Qualitative Health Research*. Vol. 1, No. 3 (1991):287–308.

———. "Cancer, Heart Disease and AIDS: What Do the Media Tell Us About These Diseases?" *Health Communication*. Vol. 4, No. 2 (1992):105–120.

———. *It's Cancer: The Personal Experiences of Women Who Have Received a Cancer Diagnosis*. Toronto: IPI, 1985.

CLARKE, ROBIN. "Atmospheric Pollution." In Sir Edmund Hillary, ed., *Ecology 2000: The Changing Face of the Earth*. New York: Beaufort Books, 1984a:130–48.

———. "What's Happening to Our Water?" In Sir Edmund Hillary, ed., *Ecology 2000: The Changing Face of the Earth*. New York: Beaufort Books, 1984b:108–29.

CLARKSON, STEPHEN, AND CHRISTINA MCCALL. *Trudeau and Our Times. Vol. 1, The Magnificent Obsession*. Toronto: McClelland & Stewart, 1990.

CLEMENT, WALLACE. *The Canadian Corporate Elite: Economic Power in Canada*. Toronto: McClelland & Stewart, 1975.

———. "Comparative Class Analysis: Locating Canada in a North American and Nordic Context." *Canadian Review of Sociology and Anthropology*. Vol. 27, No. 4 (1990).

CLINARD, MARSHALL, and DANIEL ABBOTT. *Crime in Developing Countries*. New York: Wiley, 1973.

CLOWARD, RICHARD A., and LLOYD E. OHLIN. *Delinquency and Opportunity: A Theory of Delinquent Gangs*. New York: Free Press, 1966.

CLYMER, ADAM. "Class Warfare? The Rich Win by Default." *New York Times* (August 11, 1996): section 4, pp. 1, 14.

COE, MICHAEL D., and RICHARD A. DIEHL. *In the Land of the Olmec*. Austin: University of Texas Press, 1980.

COHEN, ADAM. "A New Push for Blind Justice." *Time*. Vol. 145, No. 7 (February 20, 1995):39–40.

COHEN, ALBERT K. *Delinquent Boys: The Culture of the Gang*. New York: Free Press, 1971; orig. 1955.

COHEN, LLOYD R. "Sexual Harassment and the Law." *Society*. Vol. 28, No. 4 (May–June 1991):8–13.

COHN, RICHARD M. "Economic Development and Status Change of the Aged." *American Journal of Sociology*. Vol. 87, No. 2 (March 1982):1150–61.

COLEMAN, JAMES S. "Rational Organization." *Rationality and Society*. Vol. 2, (1990):94–105.

———. "The Design of Organizations and the Right to Act." *Sociological Forum*. Vol. 8, No. 4 (December 1993):527–46.

COLEMAN, JAMES S., and THOMAS HOFFER. *Public and Private High Schools: The Impact of Communities*. New York: Basic Books, 1987.

COLEMAN, JAMES, THOMAS HOFFER, and SALLY KILGORE. *Public and Private Schools: An Analysis of Public Schools and Beyond*. Washington, D.C.: National Center for Education Statistics, 1981.

COLEMAN, RICHARD P., and BERNICE L. NEUGARTEN. *Social Status in the City*. San Francisco: Jossey-Bass, 1971.

COLEMAN, RICHARD P., and LEE RAINWATER. *Social Standing in America*. New York: Basic Books, 1978.

COLEMAN, WILLIAM D. *The Independence Movement in Quebec 1945–1980*. Toronto: University of Toronto Press, 1984.

COLLINS, RANDALL. "A Conflict Theory of Sexual Stratification." *Social Problems*. Vol. 19, No. 1 (Summer 1971):3–21.

———. *The Credential Society: An Historical Sociology of Education and Stratification*. New York: Academic Press, 1979.

———. *Sociological Insight: An Introduction to Nonobvious Sociology*. New York: Oxford University Press, 1982.

COLLOWAY, N. O., and PAULA L. DOLLEVOET. "Selected Tabular Material on Aging." In Caleb Finch and Leonard Hayflick, eds., *Handbook of the Biology of Aging*. New York: Van Nostrand Reinhold, 1977:666–708.

COLUMBO, JOHN ROBERT. *1998: The Canadian Global Almanac*. Toronto: Macmillan Canada, 1997.

———, ed. *The 1996 Canadian Global Almanac*. Toronto: MacMillan, 1996.

———, ed. *The 1995 Canadian Global Almanac*. Toronto: MacMillan, 1994.

———. *The Canadian Global Almanac 1993: A Book of Facts*. Toronto: Macmillan, 1992.

COMTE, AUGUSTE. *Auguste Comte and Positivism: The Essential Writings*. Gertrud Lenzer, ed. New York: Harper Torchbooks, 1975.

CONNETT, PAUL H. "The Disposable Society." In F. Herbert Bormann and Stephen R. Kellert, eds., *Ecology, Economics, and Ethics: The Broken Circle*. New Haven, Conn.: Yale University Press, 1991:99–122.

CONTRERAS, JOSEPH. "A New Day Dawns." *Newsweek* (March 30, 1992):40–41.

COOK, RHODES. "House Republicans Scored a Quiet Victory in '92." *Congressional Quarterly Weekly Report*. Vol. 51, No. 16 (April 17, 1993):965–68.

COOLEY, CHARLES HORTON. *Social Organization*. New York: Schocken Books, 1962; orig. 1909.

———. *Human Nature and the Social Order*. New York: Schocken Books, 1964; orig. 1902.

COONEY, MARK. "From Warfare to Tyranny: Lethal Conflict and the State." *American Sociological Review*. Vol. 62, No. 2 (April 1997):316–38.

CORLEY, ROBERT N., O. LEE REED, PETER J. SHEDD, and JERE W. MOREHEAD. *The Legal and Regulatory Environment of Business*. 9th ed. New York: McGraw-Hill, 1993.

COSER, LEWIS A. *Masters of Sociological Thought: Ideas in Historical and Social Context*. 2d ed. New York: Harcourt Brace Jovanovich, 1977.

COTTLE, THOMAS J. "What Tracking Did to Ollie Taylor." *Social Policy*. Vol. 5, No. 2 (July–August 1974):22–24.

COTTRELL, JOHN, and the EDITORS OF TIME-LIFE. *The Great Cities: Mexico City*. Amsterdam: 1979.

COUNCIL ON FAMILIES IN AMERICA. *Marriage in America: A Report to the Nation*. New York: Institute for American Values, 1995.

COUNCIL ON INTERNATIONAL EDUCATIONAL EXCHANGE. *Educating for Global Competence: The Report of the Advisory Committee for International Educational Exchange*. New York: The Council, 1988.

COUNTS, G. S. "The Social Status of Occupations: A Problem in Vocational Guidance." *School Review*. Vol. 33 (January 1925):16–27.

COURTNEY, ALICE E., and THOMAS W. WHIPPLE. *Sex Stereotyping in Advertising*. Lexington, Mass.: D.C. Heath, 1983.

COURTWRIGHT, DAVID T. *Violent Land: Single Men and Social Disorder From the Frontier to the Inner City*. Cambridge, Mass.: Harvard University Press, 1996.

COVINGTON, JEANETTE. "Racial Classification in Criminology: The Reproduction of Racialized Crime." *Sociological Forum*. Vol. 10, No. 4 (December 1995):547–68.

COWAN, CAROLYN POPE. *When Partners Become Parents*. New York: Basic Books, 1992.

COWGILL, DONALD, and LOWELL HOLMES. *Aging and Modernization*. New York: Appleton-Century-Crofts, 1972.

COWLEY, GEOFFREY. "The Prescription That Kills." *Newsweek* (July 17, 1995): 54.

COX, HARVEY. *The Secular City*. Rev. ed. New York: Macmillan, 1971; orig. 1965.

———. *Turning East: The Promise and Peril of the New Orientalism*. New York: Simon & Schuster, 1977.

———. "Church and Believers: Always Strangers?" In Thomas Robbins and Dick Anthony, *In Gods We Trust: New Patterns of Religious Pluralism in America*. 2d ed. New Brunswick, N.J.: Transaction, 1990:449–62.

CREESE, GILLIAN, NEIL GUPPY AND MARTIN MEISSNER. *Ups and Downs on the Ladder of Success*. Ottawa: Statistics Canada, 1991.

CRENSHAW, EDWARD M., and J. CRAIG JENKINS. "Social Structure and Global Climate Change: Sociological Propositions Concerning the Greenhouse Effect." *Sociological Focus*. Vol. 29, No. 4 (October 1996):341–58.

CRISPELL, DIANE. "Grandparents Galore." *American Demographics*. Vol. 15, No. 10 (October 1993):63.

———. "Speaking in Other Tongues." *American Demographics*. Vol. 19, No. 1 (January 1997):12–15.

———. "Lucky to be Alive." *American Demographics*. Vol. 19, No. 4 (April 1997):25.

CROOK, STEPHAN, JAN PAKULSKI, and MALCOLM WATERS. *Postmodernity: Change in Advanced Society*. Newbury Park, Calif.: Sage, 1992.

CROSSEN, CYNTHIA, and ELLEN GRAHAM. "Good News—and Bad—About America's Health." *Wall Street Journal* (June 28, 1996):R1.

CROSSETTE, BARBARA. "Female Genital Mutilation by Immigrants Is Becoming Cause for Concern in the U.S." *New York Times International* (December 10, 1995):11.

CROUSE, JAMES, and DALE TRUSHEIM. *The Case Against the SAT*. Chicago: University of Chicago Press, 1988.

CUFF, E. C., and G. C. F. PAYNE, EDS. *Perspectives in Sociology*. London: Allen and Unwin, 1979.

CULLETON, BEATRICE. *In Search of April Raintree*. Winnipeg: Pemmican Publications Inc, 1983.

The Cultural Readings in Sociology. 2d ed. Englewood Cliffs, N.J.: Prentice Hall, 1992: 27–32.

CUMMING, ELAINE, and WILLIAM E. HENRY. *Growing Old: The Process of Disengagement*. New York: Basic Books, 1961.

CURRIE, ELLIOTT. *Confronting Crime: An American Challenge*. New York: Pantheon Books, 1985.

CURRY, GEORGE E., ed. *The Affirmative Action Debate*. Reading, Mass.: Addison-Wesley, 1996.

CURTIS, JAMES E., EDWARD G. GRABB, and DOUGLAS BAER. "Voluntary Association Membership in Fifteen Countries: A Comparative Analysis." *American Sociological Review*. Vol. 57, No. 2 (April 1992):139–52.

CURTISS, SUSAN. *Genie: A Psycholinguistic Study of a Modern-Day "Wild Child."* New York: Academic Press, 1977.

CUTLER, DAVID M., and LAWRENCE F. KATZ. "Rising Inequality? Changes in the Distribution of Income and Consumption in the 1980s." Working Paper No. 3964. Cambridge, Mass.: National Bureau of Economic Research, 1992.

CUTRIGHT, PHILLIP. "Occupational Inheritance: A Cross-National Analysis." *American Journal of Sociology*. Vol. 73, No. 4 (January 1968):400–16.

CYLKE, F. KURT, JR. *The Environment*. New York: HarperCollins, 1993.

DAHL, ROBERT A. *Who Governs?* New Haven, Conn.: Yale University Press, 1961.

———. *Dilemmas of Pluralist Democracy: Autonomy vs. Control*. New Haven, Conn.: Yale University Press, 1982.

DAHRENDORF, RALF. *Class and Class Conflict in Industrial Society*. Stanford, Calif.: Stanford University Press, 1959.

DALGLISH, BRENDA. "Cheaters." *Maclean's* (August 9, 1993):18–21.

DALY, MARTIN, and MARGO WILSON. *Homicide*. New York: Aldine, 1988.

DANIELS, ROGER. "The Issei Generation." In Amy Tachiki et al., eds., *Roots: An Asian American Reader*. Los Angeles: UCLA Asian American Studies Center, 1971:138–49.

DANNEFER, DALE. "Adult Development and Social Theory: A Reappraisal." *American Sociological Review*. Vol. 49, No. 1 (February 1984):100–16.

DARNTON, JOHN. "The Battle Cry of 'Reform' Rocks the House of Lords." *New York Times* (April 21, 1996):1, 8.

DARNTON, NINA, and YURIKO HOSHIA. "Whose Life Is It, Anyway?" *Newsweek*. Vol. 113, No. 4 (January 13, 1989):61.

DAVIDSON, JAMES D., RALPH E. PYLE, and DAVID V. REYES. "Persistence and Change in the Protestant Establishment, 1930–1992." *Social Forces*. Vol. 74, No. 1 (September 1995):157–75.

DAVIES, CHRISTIE. *Ethnic Humor Around the World: A Comparative Analysis*. Bloomington: Indiana University Press, 1990.

DAVIES, JAMES C. "Toward a Theory of Revolution." *American Sociological Review*. Vol. 27, No. 1 (February 1962):5–19.

DAVIES, MARK, and DENISE B. KANDEL. "Parental and Peer Influences on Adolescents' Educational Plans: Some Further Evidence." *American Journal of Sociology*. Vol. 87, No. 2 (September 1981):363–87.

DAVIS, DONALD M., cited in "T.V. Is a Blonde, Blonde World." *American Demographics*, special issue: Women Change Places. Ithaca, N.Y.: 1993.

DAVIS, KINGSLEY. "Extreme Social Isolation of a Child." *American Journal of Sociology*. Vol. 45, No. 4 (January 1940):554–65.

———. "Final Note on a Case of Extreme Isolation." *American Journal of Sociology*. Vol. 52, No. 5 (March 1947):432–37.

DAVIS, KINGSLEY. "The Myth of Functional Analysis as a Special Method in Sociology and Anthropology." *American Sociological Review*. Vol. 24, No. 1 (February 1959):75ff.

DAVIS, KINGSLEY, and WILBERT MOORE. "Some Principles of Stratification." *American Sociological Review*. Vol. 10, No. 2 (April 1945):242–49.

DAVIS, NANCY, and ROBERT V. ROBINSON. "Are the Rumors of War Exaggerated? Religious Orthodoxy and Moral Progressivism in America." *American Journal of Sociology*. Vol. 102, No. 3 (November 1996):756–87.

DAVIS, SHARON A., and EMIL J. HALLER. "Tracking, Ability, and SES: Further Evidence on the 'Revisionist-Meritocratic Debate.'" *American Journal of Education*. Vol. 89 (May 1981):283–304.

DE TOCQUEVILLE, ALEXIS. *Democracy in America*. Garden City, N.Y.: Doubleday Anchor Books, 1969; orig. 1834–40.

———. *The Old Regime and the French Revolution*. Stuart Gilbert, trans. Garden City, N.Y.: Anchor/Doubleday Books, 1955; orig. 1856.

DECKARD, BARBARA SINCLAIR. *The Women's Movement: Political, Socioeconomic, and Psychological Issues*. 2d ed. New York: Harper & Row, 1979.

DEDRICK, DENNIS K., and RICHARD E. YINGER. "MAD, SDI, and the Nuclear Arms Race." Manuscript in development. Georgetown, Ky.: Georgetown College, 1990.

DEKESEREDY, WALTER S. AND RONALD HINCH. *Woman Abuse: Sociological Perspectives*. Toronto: Thompson Educational Publishing, 1991.

———, HYMAN BURSHTYN, AND CHARLES GORDON. "Taking Woman Abuse Seriously: A Critical Response to the Solicitor General of Canada's Crime Prevention Advice." Pp. 478–89 in E.D. Nelson and B.W. Robinson (eds.), *Gender in the 1990s: Images, Realities, and Issues*. Scarborough, Ontario: Nelson Canada, 1995.

DELACROIX, JACQUES, and CHARLES C. RAGIN. "Structural Blockage: A Crossnational Study of Economic Dependency, State Efficacy, and Underdevelopment." *American Journal of Sociology*. Vol. 86, No. 6 (May 1981):1311–47.

DELLA CAVA, MARCO R. "For Dutch, It's as Easy as Asking a Doctor." *USA Today* (January 7, 1997):4A.

DEMERATH, N. J., III. "Who Now Debates Functionalism? From System, Change, and Conflict to 'Culture, Choice, and Praxis'." *Sociological Forum*. Vol. 11, No. 2 (June 1996):333–45.

Demographic Aging: The Economic Consequences. Ottawa: Ministry of Supply and Services, 1991.

DEMOTT, JOHN S. "Wreaking Havoc on Spring Break." *Time*. Vol. 127, No. 14 (April 7, 1986):29.

DENMARK, FLORENCE A., ED. *Who Discriminates Against Women?* Beverly Hills, Calif.: Sage, 1974.

DENT, DAVID J. "African-Americans Turning to Christian Academies." *New York Times*, Education Life supplement (August 4, 1996):26–29.

DEPARLE, JASON. "Painted by Numbers, 1980s are Rosy to G.O.P., While Democrats See Red." *New York Times* (September 26, 1991a):B10.

DEPEW, ROBERT. "Policing Native Communities: Some Principles and Issues in Organizational Theory." *Canadian Journal of Criminology*. Vol. 34 (1992).

DERSHOWITZ, ALAN. *The Vanishing American Jew*. Boston: Little, Brown, 1997.

DER SPIEGEL. "Third World Metropolises Are Becoming Monsters; Rural Poverty Drives Millions to the Slums." In *World Press Review* (October 1989).

DEVINE, JOEL A. "State and State Expenditure: Determinants of Social Investment and Social Consumption Spending in the Postwar United States." *American Sociological Review*. Vol. 50, No. 2 (April 1985):150–65.

DEWEY, JOHN. *Experience and Education*. New York: Collier Books, 1968; orig. 1938.

DIAMOND, MILTON. "Sexual Identity, Monozygotic Twins Reared in Discordant Sex Roles and a BBC Follow-Up." *Archives of Sexual Behavior*. Vol. 11, No. 2 (April 1982):181–86.

DICKASON, OLIVE PATRICIA. *Canada's First Nations: A History of Founding Peoples from the Earliest Times*. Toronto: McClelland & Stewart, 1992.

DICKENS, CHARLES. *The Adventures of Oliver Twist*. Boston: Estes and Lauriat, 1886; orig. 1837–39.

DIMAGGIO, PAUL, JOHN EVANS, and BETHANY BRYSON. "Have Americans' Social Attitudes Become More Polarized?" *American Journal of Sociology*. Vol. 102, No. 3 (November 1996):690–755.

DIXON, WILLIAM J., and TERRY BOSWELL. "Dependency, Disarticulation, and Denominator Effects: Another Look at Foreign Capital Penetration." *American Journal of Sociology*. Vol. 102, No. 2 (September 1996):543–62.

DIZARD, JAN E., and HOWARD GADLIN. *The Minimal Family*. Amherst: The University of Massachusetts Press, 1990.

DOBSON, RICHARD B. "Mobility and Stratification in the Soviet Union." *Annual Review of Sociology*. Vol. 3. Palo Alto, Calif.: Annual Reviews, 1977:297–329.

DOBYNS, HENRY F. "An Appraisal of Techniques with a New Hemispheric Estimate." *Current Anthropology*. Vol. 7, No. 4 (October 1966):395–446.

DOLLARD, JOHN, ET AL. *Frustration and Aggression*. New Haven, Conn.: Yale University Press, 1939.

DOMHOFF, G. WILLIAM. *Who Rules America Now? A View of the '80s*. Englewood Cliffs, N.J.: Prentice Hall, 1983.

DONOVAN, VIRGINIA K., and RONNIE LITTENBERG. "Psychology of Women: Feminist Therapy." In Barbara Haber, ed., *The Women's Annual 1981: The Year in Review*. Boston: G. K. Hall, 1982.:211–35.

DOUGLASS, RICHARD L. "Domestic Neglect and Abuse of the Elderly: Implications for Research and Service." *Family Relations*. Vol. 32 (July 1983):395–402.

DOYLE, JAMES A. *The Male Experience*. Dubuque, Iowa: Wm. C. Brown, 1983.

DOYLE, RICHARD F. *A Manifesto of Men's Liberation*. 2d ed. Forest Lake, Minn.: Men's Rights Association, 1980.

———, ED. 1989. *The Ethnic Factor: Identity in Diversity*. Toronto: McGraw-Hill Ryerson.

DU BOIS, W. E. B. *Dusk of Dawn*. New York: Harcourt, Brace & World, 1940.

———. *The Philadelphia Negro: A Social Study*. New York: Schocken Books, 1967; orig. 1899.

DUBOS, RENÉ. *Man Adapting*. New Haven, Conn.: Yale University Press, 1980; orig. 1965.

DUHL, LEONARD J. "The Social Context of Health." In Arthur C. Hastings et al., eds., *Health for the Whole Person: The Complete Guide to Holistic Medicine*. Boulder, Colo.: Westview Press, 1980:39–48.

DUNLAP, DAVID W. "Fearing a Toehold for Gay Marriages, Conservatives Rush to Bar the Door." *New York Times* (March 3, 1996):A13.

DUNLAP, RILEY E., GEORGE H. GALLUP, JR., and ALEC M. GALLUP. *The Health of the Planet Survey*. Princeton, N.J.: The George H. Gallup International Institute, 1992.

DUNLAP, RILEY E., and ANGELA G. MERTIG. "The Evolution of the U.S. Environmental Movement From 1970 to 1990: An Overview." In Riley E. Dunlap and Angela G. Mertig, eds., *American Evironmentalism: The U.S. Environmental Movement, 1970–1990*. New York: Taylor & Francis, 1992:1–10.

DUNN, ASHLEY. "Ancient Chinese Craft Shifts Building Designs in the U.S." *New York Times* (September 22, 1994):A1, B4.

DUNN, JOHN. "Peddling Big Brother." *Time*. Vol. 137, No. 25 (June 24, 1991):62.

DURKHEIM, EMILE. *The Division of Labor in Society*. New York: Free Press, 1964a; orig. 1895.

———. *The Rules of Sociological Method*. New York: Free Press, 1964b; orig. 1893.

———. *The Elementary Forms of Religious Life*. New York: Free Press, 1965; orig. 1915.

———. *Suicide*. New York: Free Press, 1966; orig. 1897.

———. *Selected Writings*. Anthony Giddens, ed. Cambridge: Cambridge University Press, 1972.

———. *Sociology and Philosophy*. New York: Free Press, 1974; orig. 1924.

DURNING, ALAN THEIN. "Supporting Indigenous Peoples." In Lester R. Brown et al., eds., *State of the World 1993: A Worldwatch Institute Report on Progress Toward a Sustainable Society*. New York: Norton, 1993:80–100.

DWORKIN, ANDREA. *Intercourse*. New York: Free Press, 1987.

Earnings of Men and Women. 1991. Ottawa: Statistics Canada.

EBAUGH, HELEN ROSE FUCHS. *Becoming an EX: The Process of Role Exit*. Chicago: University of Chicago Press, 1988.

ECKHOLM, ERIK. "Malnutrition in Elderly: Widespread Health Threat." *New York Times* (August 13, 1985):19–20.

ECKHOLM, ERIK, and JOHN TIERNEY. "AIDS in Africa: A Killer Rages On." *New York Times* (September 16, 1990):A1, 14.

THE ECONOMIST. "Worship Moves in Mysterious Ways." Vol. 326, No. 7802 (March 13, 1993):65, 70.

———. "Cockfighting: 'Til Death Us Do Part." Vol. 330, No. 7851 (February 19, 1994):30.

———. "Japan's Missing Children." Vol. 333, No. 7889 (November 12, 1994):46.

EDIN, KATHRYN, and LAURA LEIN. "Work, Welfare, and Single Mothers' Economic Survival Strategies." *American Sociological Review*. Vol. 62, No. 2 (April 1996):253–66.

EDMONDSON, BRAD. "The Great Money Grab." *American Demographics*. Vol. 17, No. 2 (February 1995):2.

———. "Fountains of Youth." *American Demographics*. Vol. 18, No. 7 (July 1996):60.

———. "The Facts of Death." *American Demographics*. Vol. 49, No. 4 (April 1997):47–53.

———. "The Wired Bunch." *American Demographics*. Vol. 49, No. 6 (June 1997):10–15.

EDMONSTON, BARRY, AND THOMAS M. GUTERBOCK. "Is Suburbanization Slowing Down? Recent Trends in Population Deconcentration in U. S. Metropolitan Areas." *Social Forces*. Vol. 62, No. 4 (June 1984):905–25.

EDWARDS, DAVID V. *The American Political Experience*. 3d ed. Englewood Cliffs, N.J.: Prentice Hall, 1985.

EDWARDS, PETER. "Boot campers get cool welcome." *The Toronto Star* (August 1, 1997): A1.

EDWARDS, RICHARD. *Contested Terrain: The Transformation of the Workplace in the Twentieth Century*. New York: Basic Books, 1979.

EGGEBEEN, DAVID J., and DANIEL T. LICHTER. "Race, Family Structure and Changing Poverty Among American Children." *American Sociological Review*. Vol. 56, No. 6 (December 1991):801–17.

EHRENREICH, BARBARA. *The Hearts of Men: American Dreams and the Flight From Commitment*. Garden City, N.Y.: Anchor Books, 1983.

EHRENREICH, JOHN. "Introduction." In John Ehrenreich, ed., *The Cultural Crisis of Modern Medicine*. New York: Monthly Review Press, 1978:1–35.

EICHLER, MARGRIT. *Nonsexist Research Methods: A Practical Guide*. Winchester, Mass.: Unwin Hyman, 1988.

———. *Families in Canada Today: Recent changes and their policy consequences*. 2d ed., Toronto: Gage, 1988.

EISEN, ARNOLD M. *The Chosen People in America: A Study of Jewish Religious Ideology*. Bloomington: Indiana University Press, 1983.

EISENBERG, DAVID M., ET AL. "Unconventional Medicine in the United States - Prevalence, Costs and Pattern of Use." *New England Journal of Medicine*. Vol. 328, No. 4 (1993):246–52.

EISENSTEIN, ZILLAH R., ED. *Capitalist Patriarchy and the Case for Socialist Feminism*. New York: Monthly Review Press, 1979.

EISLER, BENITA. *The Lowell Offering: Writings by New England Mill Women 1840–1845*. Philadelphia and New York: J. B. Lippincott, 1977.

EKMAN, PAUL. "Biological and Cultural Contributions to Body and Facial Movements in the Expression of Emotions." In A. Rorty, ed., *Explaining Emotions*. Berkeley: University of California Press, 1980a:73–101.

———. *Face of Man: Universal Expression in a New Guinea Village*. New York: Garland Press, 1980b.

———. *Telling Lies: Clues to Deceit in the Marketplace, Politics, and Marriage*. New York: Norton, 1985.

EKMAN, PAUL, WALLACE V. FRIESEN, and JOHN BEAR. "The International Language of Gestures." *Psychology Today* (May 1984):64–69.

EL-ATTAR, MOHAMED. Personal communication, 1991.

ELIAS, ROBERT. *The Politics of Victimization: Victims, Victimology and Human Rights*. New York: Oxford University Press, 1986.

ELKIND, DAVID. *The Hurried Child: Growing Up Too Fast Too Soon*. Reading, Mass.: Addison-Wesley, 1981.

ELLIOT, DELBERT S., and SUZANNE S. AGETON. "Reconciling Race and Class Differences in Self-Reported and Official Estimates of Delinquency." *American Sociological Review*. Vol. 45, No. 1 (February 1980):95–110.

ELLISON, CHRISTOPHER G., JOHN P. BARTKOWSKI, and MICHELLE L. SEGAL. "Do Conservative Protestant Parents Spank More Often? Further Evidence From the National Survey of Families and Households." *Social Science Quarterly*. Vol. 77, No. 3 (September 1996):663–73.

ELLISON, CHRISTOPHER G., and DARREN E. SHERKAT. "Conservative Protestantism and Support for Corporal Punishment." *American Sociological Review*. Vol. 58, No. 1 (February 1993):131–44.

ELMER-DEWITT, PHILIP. "The Revolution That Fizzled." *Time*. Vol. 137, No. 20 (May 20, 1991):48–49.

———. "First Nation in Cyberspace." *Time*. Vol. 142, No. 24 (December 6, 1993):62–64.

———. "The Genetic Revolution." *Time*. Vol. 143, No. 3 (January 17, 1994):46–53.

———. "Battle for the Internet." *Time*. Vol. 144, No. 4 (July 25, 1994):50–56.

EMBER, MELVIN, and CAROL R. EMBER. "The Conditions Favoring Matrilocal Versus Patrilocal Residence." *American Anthropologist*. Vol. 73, No. 3 (June 1971):571–94.

———. *Anthropology*. 6th ed. Englewood Cliffs, N.J.: Prentice Hall, 1991.

EMBREE, AINSLIE T. *The Hindu Tradition*. New York: Vintage Books, 1972.

EMERSON, JOAN P. "Behavior in Private Places: Sustaining Definitions of Reality in Gynecological Examinations." In H. P. Dreitzel, ed., *Recent Sociology*. Vol. 2. New York: Collier, 1970:74–97.

Employment by Income and Occupation: The Nation. Ottawa: Statistics Canada, April 1993.

ENDICOTT, KAREN. "Fathering in an Egalitarian Society." In Barry S. Hewlett, ed., *Father-Child Relations: Cultural and Bio-Social Contexts*. New York: Aldine, 1992:281–96.

ENGELS, FRIEDRICH. *The Origin of the Family*. Chicago: Charles H. Kerr & Company, 1902; orig. 1884.

ENGLAND, PAULA. *Comparable Worth: Theories and Evidence*. Hawthorne, N.Y.: Aldine, 1992.

ENGLISH-CURRIE, VICKIE. "The Need for Re-Evaluation in Native Education." In David Taras, Beverly Rasporich, and Eli Mandel, eds., *A Passion for Identity: An Introduction to Canadian Studies*, 2d ed., 111-19. Scarborough, Ont.: Nelson Canada, 1993.

EPPS, EDGAR G. "Race, Class, and Educational Opportunity: Trends in the Sociology of Education." *Sociological Forum*. Vol. 10, No. 4 (December 1995):593–608.

ERIKSON, ERIK H. *Childhood and Society*. New York: Norton, 1963; orig. 1950.

———. *Identity and the Life Cycle*. New York: Norton, 1980.

ERIKSON, KAI T. *Wayward Puritans: A Study in the Sociology of Deviance*. New York: Wiley, 1966.

ERIKSON, ROBERT, and JOHN H. GOLDTHORPE. *The Constant Flux: A Study of Class Mobility in Industrial Societies*. Oxford: Clarendon Press, 1992.

ERIKSON, ROBERT S., NORMAN R. LUTTBEG, and KENT L. TEDIN. *American Public Opinion: Its Origins, Content, and Impact*. 2d ed. New York: Wiley, 1980.

ETZIONI, AMITAI. *A Comparative Analysis of Complex Organization: On Power, Involvement, and Their Correlates*. Rev. and enlarged ed. New York: Free Press, 1975.

———. "Too Many Rights, Too Few Responsibilities." *Society*. Vol. 28, No. 2 (January–February 1991):41–48.

———. "How to Make Marriage Matter." *Time*. Vol. 142, No. 10 (September 6, 1993):76.

———. "The Responsive Community: A Communitarian Perspective." *American Sociological Review*. Vol. 61, No. 1 (February 1996):1–11.

ETZIONI-HALEVY, EVA. *Bureaucracy and Democracy: A Political Dilemma*. Rev. ed. Boston: Routledge & Kegan Paul, 1985.

EVANS, M. D. R. "Immigrant Entrepreneurship: Effects of Ethnic Market Size and Isolated Labor Pool." *American Sociological Review*. Vol. 54, No. 6 (December 1989):950–62.

EVERS, FREDERICK T., JAMES C. RUSH, JASNA A. KRMPOTIC, JOANNE DUNCAN-ROBINSON. *Making the Match: Phase II* (Final Technical Report), Universities of Guelph and Western Ontario, 1993.

EXTER, THOMAS G. "The Costs of Growing Up." *American Demographics*. Vol. 13, No. 8 (August 1991):59.

FAGAN, DREW. "Canada Triumphs in Tariff Battle." *The Globe and Mail* (July 16, 1996):A1.

FALK, GERHARD. Personal communication, 1987.

FALKENMARK, MALIN, and CARL WIDSTRAND. "Population and Water Resources: A Delicate Balance." *Population Bulletin*. Vol. 47, No. 3 (November 1992). Washington, D.C.: Population Reference Bureau.

FALLON, A. E., and P. ROZIN. "Sex Differences in Perception of Desirable Body Shape." *Journal of Abnormal Psychology*. Vol. 94, No. 1 (1985):100–5.

FALLOWS, JAMES. "Immigration: How It's Affecting Us." *The Atlantic Monthly*. Vol. 252 (November 1983):45–52, 55–62, 66–68, 85–90, 94, 96, 99–106.

FANTINI, MARIO D. *Regaining Excellence in Education*. Columbus, Ohio: Merrill, 1986.

FARLEY, CHRISTOPHER JOHN. "Winning the Right to Fly." *Time*. Vol. 146, No. 9 (August 28, 1995):62–64.

FARLEY, REYNOLDS, and WILLIAM H. FREY. "Changes in the Segregation of Whites From Blacks During the 1980s: Small Steps Toward a More Integrated Society." *American Sociological Review*. Vol. 59, No. 1 (February 1994):23–45.

FARRELL, MICHAEL P., and STANLEY D. ROSENBERG. *Men at Midlife*. Boston: Auburn House, 1981.

FEAGIN, JOE. *The Urban Real Estate Game*. Englewood Cliffs, N.J.: Prentice Hall, 1983.

———. "The Continuing Significance of Race: Antiblack Discrimination in Public Places." *American Sociological Review*. Vol. 56, No. 1 (February 1991):101–16.

———. "Death By Discrimination?" *Newsletter, Society for the Study of Social Problems*. Vol. 28, No. 1 (Winter 1997):15–16.

FEATHERMAN, DAVID L., and ROBERT M. HAUSER. *Opportunity and Change*. New York: Academic Press, 1978.

FEATHERSTONE, MIKE, ED. *Global Culture: Nationalism, Globalization, and Modernity*. London: Sage, 1990.

FEDARKO, KEVIN. "Who Could Live Here?" *Time*. Vol. 139, No. 3 (January 20, 1992):20–23.

———. "Land Mines: Cheap, Deadly, and Cruel." *Time*. Vol. 147, No. 20 (May 13, 1996):54–55.

FELLMAN, BRUCE. "Taking the Measure of Children's T.V." *Yale Alumni Magazine* (April 1995):46–51.

FENNELL, MARY C. "The Effects of Environmental Characteristics on the Structure of Hospital Clusters." *Administrative Science Quarterly*. Vol. 29, No. 3 (September 1980):489–510.

FENNELL, TOM. "A Measure of Hope." *Maclean's* (June 14, 1993):48–49.

FERGUSON, TOM. "Medical Self-Care: Self Responsibility for Health." In Arthur C. Hastings et al., eds., *Health for the Whole Person: The Complete Guide to Holistic Medicine*. Boulder, Colo.: Westview Press, 1980:87–109.

FERGUSSON, D. M., L. J. HORWOOD, and F. T. SHANNON. "A Proportional Hazards Model of Family Breakdown." *Journal of Marriage and the Family*. Vol. 46, No. 3 (August 1984):539–49.

FERREE, MYRA MARX, and ELAINE J. HALL. "Rethinking Stratification From a Feminist Perspective: Gender, Race, and Class in Mainstream Textbooks." *American Sociological Review*. Vol. 61, No. 6 (December 1996):929–50.

FIFE, SANDY. "The Total Quality Muddle." *The Globe and Mail: Report on Business* (November 1992):64–74.

FIND/SVP. *The 1997 American Internet Users Survey: Realities Behind the Hype*. Reported in *Society*, Vol. 43, No. 5 (July/August 1997):2.

FINKELSTEIN, NEAL W., and RON HASKINS. "Kindergarten Children Prefer Same-Color Peers." *Child Development*. Vol. 54, No. 2 (April 1983):502–8.

FIORENTINE, ROBERT. "Men, Women, and the Premed Persistence Gap: A Normative Alternatives Approach." *American Journal of Sociology*. Vol. 92, No. 5 (March 1987):1118–39.

FIORENTINE, ROBERT, and STEPHEN COLE. "Why Fewer Women Become Physicians: Explaining the Premed Persistance Gap." *Sociological Forum*. Vol. 7, No. 3 (September 1992):469–96.

FIREBAUGH, GLENN. "Growth Effects of Foreign and Domestic Investment." *American Journal of Sociology*. Vol. 98, No. 1 (July 1992):105–30.

———. "Does Foreign Capital Harm Poor Nations? New Estimates Based on Dixon and Boswell's Measures of Capital Penetration." *American Journal of Sociology*. Vol. 102, No. 2 (September 1996):563–75.

FIREBAUGH, GLENN, and FRANK D. BECK. "Does Economic Growth Benefit the Masses? Growth, Dependence, and Welfare in the Third World." *American Sociological Review*. Vol. 59, No. 5 (October 1994):631–53.

FIREBAUGH, GLENN, and KENNETH E. DAVIS. "Trends in Antiblack Prejudice, 1972–1984: Region and Cohort Effects." *American Journal of Sociology*. Vol. 94, No. 2 (September 1988):251–72.

FISCHER, CLAUDE S., ET AL. *Networks and Places: Social Relations in the Urban Setting*. New York: Free Press, 1977.

FISCHER, CLAUDE W. *The Urban Experience*. 2d ed. New York: Harcourt Brace Jovanovich, 1984.

FISHER, ELIZABETH. *Woman's Creation: Sexual Evolution and the Shaping of Society*. Garden City, N.Y.: Anchor/Doubleday, 1979.

FISHER, ROGER, and WILLIAM URY. "Getting to YES." In William M. Evan and Stephen Hilgartner, eds., *The Arms Race and Nuclear War*. Englewood Cliffs, N.J.: Prentice Hall, 1988:261–68.

FISKE, ALAN PAIGE. "The Cultural Relativity of Selfish Individualism: Anthropological Evidence That Humans Are Inherently Sociable." In Margaret S. Clark, ed., *Prosocial Behavior*. Newbury Park, Calif.: Sage, 1991:176–214.

FISKE, EDWARD B. "Adults: The Forgotten Illiterates." *Christian Science Monitor* (May 30, 1997):18.

FITZPATRICK, JOSEPH P. "Puerto Ricans." In *Harvard Encyclopedia of American Ethnic Groups*. Cambridge, Mass.: Harvard University Press, 1980:858–67.

FITZPATRICK, MARY ANNE. *Between Husbands and Wives: Communication in Marriage*. Newbury Park, Calif.: Sage, 1988.

FLAHERTY, MICHAEL G. "A Formal Approach to the Study of Amusement in Social Interaction." *Studies in Symbolic Interaction*. Vol. 5. New York: JAI Press, 1984:71–82.

———. "Two Conceptions of the Social Situation: Some Implications of Humor." *The Sociological Quarterly*. Vol. 31, No. 1 (Spring 1990).

FLETCHER, FREDERICK J., ED. *Media and Voters in Canadian Election Campaigns*. Toronto: Dundurn Press, 1991.

FLORIDA, RICHARD, and MARTIN KENNEY. "Transplanted Organizations: The Transfer of Japanese Industrial Organization to the U.S." *American Sociological Review*. Vol. 56, No. 3 (June 1991):381–98.

FLOWER, G.E. *Speaking Out: The 1984 CEA poll of Canadian opinion on education*. Toronto: Canadian Education Association, 1984.

FLYNN, PATRICIA. "The Disciplinary Emergence of Bioethics and Bioethics Committees: Moral Ordering and its Legitimation." *Sociological Focus*. Vol. 24, No. 2 (May 1991):145–56.

FOBES, RICHARD. "Creative Problem Solving." *The Futurist*. Vol. 30, No. 1 (January–February 1996):19–22.

FOOT, DAVID K. *Boom, Bust and Echo: How to Profit From the Coming Demographic Shift*. Toronto: Macfarlane, Walter & Ross, 1996.

FORBES. "Forbes 400." Vol. 160, No. 8 (October 13, 1997):418–22.

FORCESE, DENNIS. *The Canadian Class Structure*. 4th ed. Toronto: McGraw-Hill Ryerson, 1997.

FORD, CLELLAN S., and FRANK A. BEACH. *Patterns of Sexual Behavior*. New York: Harper & Row, 1951.

FORREST, HUGH. "They Are Completely Inactive . . ." *The Gambier Journal*. Vol. 3, No. 4 (February 1984):10–11.

FORTUNE. "The Fortune 500." Vol. 131, No. 9 (May 15, 1995): Special issue.

FORTUNE 500. [Online] Available http://www.pathfinder.com/fortune/fortune500/, January 19, 1998.

FOST, DAN. "American Indians in the 1990s." *American Demographics*. Vol. 13, No. 12 (December 1991):26–34.

FRANCIS, DIANE. *Bre-X: The Inside Story*. Toronto: Key Porter Books, 1997.

———. *Controlling Interest: Who Owns Canada?* Toronto: Macmillan, 1986.

FRANK, ANDRÉ GUNDER. *On Capitalist Underdevelopment*. Bombay: Oxford University Press, 1975.

———. *Crisis: In the World Economy*. New York: Holmes & Meier, 1980.

———. *Reflections on the World Economic Crisis*. New York: Monthly Review Press, 1981.

FRANKLIN, JOHN HOPE. *From Slavery to Freedom: A History of Negro Americans*. 3d ed. New York: Vintage Books, 1967.

FRANKLIN ASSOCIATES. *Characterization of Municipal Solid Waste in the United States, 1960–2000*. Prairie Village, Kans.: Franklin Associates, 1986.

FRASER, SYLVIA. *In My Father's House*. Toronto: Collins Paperback, 1987.

FRAZIER, E. FRANKLIN. *Black Bourgeoisie: The Rise of a New Middle Class*. New York: Free Press, 1965.

FRÉCHETTE, PIERRE. "Income Distribution." *The Canadian Encyclopedia*. 2d ed. Vol. 2. Edmonton: Hurtig Publishers, 1988:1051–1052.

FREDRICKSON, GEORGE M. *White Supremacy: A Comparative Study in American and South African History*. New York: Oxford University Press, 1981.

FREE, MARVIN D. "Religious Affiliation, Religiosity, and Impulsive and Intentional Deviance." *Sociological Focus*. Vol. 25, No. 1 (February 1992):77–91.

FREEDOM HOUSE. *Freedom in the World*. New York: Freedom House, 1998.

FRENCH, MARILYN. *Beyond Power: On Women, Men, and Morals*. New York: Summit Books, 1985.

FRETZ, WINFIELD. *The Waterloo Mennonites: A Community in Paradox*. Waterloo: Wilfrid Laurier Press, 1989.

FRIDERES, JAMES S. *Native Peoples in Canada: Contemporary Conflicts*. 4th ed. Scarborough, Ontario: Prentice Hall, 1993.

FRIEDAN, BETTY. *The Fountain of Age*. New York: Simon and Schuster, 1993.

FRIEDMAN, MEYER, and RAY H. ROSENMAN. *Type A Behavior and Your Heart*. New York: Fawcett Crest, 1974.

FRIEDRICH, CARL J., and ZBIGNIEW BRZEZINSKI. *Totalitarian Dictatorship and Autocracy*. 2d ed. Cambridge, Mass.: Harvard University Press, 1965.

FRIEDRICH, OTTO. "A Proud Capital's Distress." *Time*. Vol. 124, No. 6 (August 6, 1984):26–30, 33–35.

———. "United No More." *Time*. Vol. 129, No. 18 (May 4, 1987):28–37.

FRUM, DAVID, and FRANK WOLFE. "If You Gotta Get Sued, Get Sued in Utah." *Forbes*. Vol. 153, No. 2 (January 1994):70–73.

FUCHS, VICTOR R. "Sex Differences in Economic Well-Being." *Science*. Vol. 232 (April 25, 1986):459–64.

———. *Who Shall Live*. New York: Basic Books, 1974.

References **617**

FUGITA, STEPHEN S., and DAVID J. O'BRIEN. "Structural Assimilation, Ethnic Group Membership, and Political Participation Among Japanese Americans: A Research Note." *Social Forces*. Vol. 63, No. 4 (June 1985):986–95.

FUJIMOTO, ISAO. "The Failure of Democracy in a Time of Crisis." In Amy Tachiki et al., eds., *Roots: An Asian American Reader*. Los Angeles: UCLA Asian American Studies Center, 1971:207–14.

FULLER, REX, and RICHARD SCHOENBERGER. "The Gender Salary Gap: Do Academic Achievement, Intern Experience, and College Major Make a Difference?" *Social Science Quarterly*. Vol. 72, No. 4 (December 1991):715–26.

FULTON, E. KAYE. "Bringing Home Baby." *Maclean's* (May 21, 1995):34–42.

FUMENTO, MICHAEL. *The Myth of Heterosexual AIDS*. New York: Basic Books, 1989.

FURSTENBERG, FRANK F., JR. "The New Extended Family: The Experience of Parents and Children After Remarriage." Paper presented to the Changing Family Conference XIII: The Blended Family. University of Iowa, 1984.

FURSTENBERG, FRANK F., JR., J. BROOKS-GUNN, and S. PHILIP MORGAN. *Adolescent Mothers in Later Life*. New York: Cambridge University Press, 1987.

FURSTENBERG, FRANK F., JR., and ANDREW CHERLIN. *Divided Families: What Happens to Children When Parents Part*. Cambridge, Mass.: Harvard University Press, 1991.

FUSFELD, DANIEL R. *Economics: Principles of Political Economy*. Glenview, Ill.: Scott, Foresman, 1982.

GABRIEL, TRIP. "Computers Help Unite Campuses but Also Drive Some Students Apart." *New York Times* (November 11, 1996).

GAGLIANI, GIORGIO. "How Many Working Classes?" *American Journal of Sociology*. Vol. 87, No. 2 (September 1981):259–85.

GALLUP, GEORGE, JR. *Religion in America*. Princeton, N.J.: Princeton Religion Research Center, 1982.

GALLUP POLL. *The Gallup Poll Monthly*. December 1993.

Gallup Sexual Life Style Survey. Toronto: Gallup Report, September 3, 1988.

GALSTER, GEORGE. "Black Suburbanization: Has It Changed the Relative Location of Races?" *Urban Affairs Quarterly*. Vol. 26, No. 4 (June 1991):621–28.

GALSTON, WILLIAM A., and DAVID WASSERMAN. "Gambling Away Our Moral Capital." *The Public Interest*. Vol. 123 (Spring 1996):58–71.

GAMBLE, ANDREW, STEVE LUDLAM, and DAVID BAKER. "Britain's Ruling Class." *The Economist*. Vol. 326, No. 7795 (January 23, 1993):10.

GAMORAN, ADAM. "The Variable Effects of High-School Tracking." *American Sociological Review*. Vol. 57, No. 6 (December 1992):812–28.

GANS, HERBERT J. *People and Plans: Essays on Urban Problems and Solutions*. New York: Basic Books, 1968.

———. *Popular Culture and High Culture*. New York: Basic Books, 1974.

———. *Deciding What's News: A Study of CBS Evening News, NBC Nightly News, Newsweek and Time*. New York: Vintage Books, 1980.

———. *The Urban Villagers: Group and Class in the Life of Italian-Americans*. New York: Free Press, 1982; orig. 1962.

GARDNER, WILLIAM D. *The Trouble With Canada*. Toronto: Stoddart Publishing, 1990.

GARFINKEL, HAROLD. "Conditions of Successful Degradation Ceremonies." *American Journal of Sociology*. Vol. 61, No. 2 (March 1956):420–24.

———. *Studies in Ethnomethodology*. Cambridge: Polity Press, 1967.

GARREAU, JOEL. *Edge City*. New York: Doubleday, 1991.

GEERTZ, CLIFFORD. "Common Sense as a Cultural System." *The Antioch Review*. Vol. 33, No. 1 (Spring 1975):5–26.

GEIST, WILLIAM. *Toward a Safe and Sane Halloween and Other Tales of Suburbia*. New York: Times Books, 1985.

GELLES, RICHARD J., and CLAIRE PEDRICK CORNELL. *Intimate Violence in Families*. 2d ed. Newbury Park, Calif.: Sage, 1990.

GELMAN, DAVID. "Who's Taking Care of Our Parents?" *Newsweek* (May 6, 1985):61–64, 67–68.

———. "Born or Bred?" *Newsweek* (February 24, 1992):46–53.

GEORGE, SUSAN. *How the Other Half Dies: The Real Reasons for World Hunger*. Totowa, N.J.: Rowman & Allanheld, 1977.

Gerber, Linda M. *Minority Survival: Community Characteristics and Out-Migration from Indian Communities Across Canada*. Ph.D. thesis. Toronto: University of Toronto Press, 1976.

———. "The Development of Canadian Indian Communities: A Two-Dimensional Typology Reflecting Strategies of Adaptation to the Outside World." *Canadian Review of Sociology and Anthropology*. Vol. 16, No. 4 (1979):123–50.

———. "Ethnicity Still Matters: Socio-Demographic Profiles of the Ethnic Elderly in Ontario." *Canadian Ethnic Studies*. Vol. XV, No. 3 (1983):60–80.

———. "Community characteristics and out-migration from Canadian Indian communities: path analyses." *Canadian Review of Sociology and Anthropology*. Vol. 21 (1984):145–165.

———. "The Federal Election of 1968: Social Class Composition and Party Support in the Electoral Districts of Ontario." *Canadian Review of Sociology and Anthropology*. Vol. 23, No. 1 (1986):118-35.

———. "Multiple Jeopardy: A Socio-economic Comparison of Men and Women among the Indian, Métis and Inuit Peoples of Canada." *Canadian Ethnic Studies*. Vol. XXII, No. 3 (1990):69–84.

———. "Referendum Results: Defining New Boundaries for an Independent Quebec." *Canadian Ethnic Studies*. Vol. XXIV, No. 2 (1992):22–34.

———. "Indian, Métis, and Inuit Women and Men: Multiple Jeopardy in a Canadian Context." Pp. 466–77 in E.D. Nelson and B.W. Robinson (eds.), *Gender in the 1990s: Images, Realities, and Issues*. Scarborough, Ontario: Nelson Canada, 1995.

GERLACH, MICHAEL L. *The Social Organization of Japanese Business*. Berkeley and Los Angeles: University of California Press, 1992.

GERSTEL, NAOMI. "Divorce and Stigma." *Social Problems*. Vol. 43, No. 2 (April 1987):172–86.

GERTH, H. H., and C. WRIGHT MILLS, EDS. *From Max Weber: Essays in Sociology*. New York: Oxford University Press, 1946.

GESCHWENDER, JAMES A. *Racial Stratification in America*. Dubuque, Iowa: Wm. C. Brown, 1978.

GEWERTZ, DEBORAH. "A Historical Reconsideration of Female Dominance Among the Chambri of Papua New Guinea." *American Ethnologist*. Vol. 8, No. 1 (1981):94–106.

GHALAM, NANCY ZUKEWICH. "Women in the Workplace." Pp. 141–45 in *Canadian Social Trends*, 2d ed. Craig McKie and Keith Thompson. Toronto: Thompson Educational Publishing, 1994.

GIBBONS, DON C., and MARVIN D. KROHN. *Delinquent Behavior*. 4th ed. Englewood Cliffs, N.J.: Prentice Hall, 1986.

GIBBS, NANCY. "When Is It Rape?" *Time*. Vol. 137, No. 22 (June 3, 1991a):48–54.

———. "The Clamor on Campus." *Time*. Vol. 137, No. 22 (June 3, 1991b):54–55.

———. "How Much Should We Teach Our Children About Sex?" *Time*. Vol. 141, No. 21 (May 24, 1993):60–66.

———. "The Vicious Cycle." *Time*. Vol. 143, No. 25 (June 20, 1994):24–33.

———. "The Blood of Innocents." *Time*. Special Issue. No. 25 (June 1, 1995):57–64.

———. "Cause Celeb." *Time*. Vol. 147, No. 25 (June 17, 1996):28–30.

GIDDENS, ANTHONY. *Sociology: A Brief but Critical Introduction*. New York: Harcourt Brace Jovanovich, 1982.

GIELE, JANET Z. "Gender and Sex Roles." In Neil J. Smelser, ed., *Handbook of Sociology*. Newbury Park, Calif.: Sage, 1988:291–323.

GIFFEN, P.J. "Official rates of crime and delinquency." In W.T. McGrath, ed., *Crime and Its Treatment in Canada*. Toronto: Macmillan, 1976.

———. "Clark, Samuel Delbert." In *The Canadian Encyclopedia* (1988): 433.

GIGLIOTTI, RICHARD J., and HEATHER K. HUFF. "Role Related Conflicts, Strains, and Stresses of Older-Adult College Students." *Sociological Focus*. Vol. 28, No. 3 (August 1995):329–42.

GILBERT, DENNIS, AND JOSEPH A. KAHL. *The American Class Structure: A New Synthesis*. 3d ed. Homewood, Ill.: The Dorsey Press, 1987.

GILBERT, NEIL. "Realities and Mythologies of Rape." *Society*. Vol. 29, No. 4 (May–June 1992):4–10.

GILBERT, S.N. "The Forgotten Purpose and Future Promise of University Education." *Canadian Journal of Community Mental Health*. Vol. 8, No. 2 (1989):103–122.

GILBERT, SID, LYNN BARR, WARREN CLARK, MATTHEW BLUE AND DEBORAH SUNTER. *Leaving School: Results from a national survey comparing school leavers and high school graduates 18 to 20 years of age*. Ottawa: Government of Canada (LM-294-07-93E), 1993.

GILBERTSON, GRETA A., and DOUGLAS T. GURAK. "Broadening the Enclave Debate: The Dual Labor Market Experiences of Dominican and Colombian Men in New York City." *Sociological Forum*. Vol. 8, No. 2 (June 1993):205–20.

GILL, RICHARD T. "What Happened to the American Way of Death?" *The Public Interest*. Vol. 127 (Spring 1996):105–17.

GILLIGAN, CAROL. *In a Different Voice: Psychological Theory and Women's Development*. Cambridge, Mass.: Harvard University Press, 1982.

———. *Making Connections: The Relational Worlds of Adolescent Girls at Emma Willard School*. Cambridge, Mass.: Harvard University Press, 1990.

GILLIS, A.R. "High-Rise Housing and Psychological Strain." *Journal of Health and Social Behaviour*. Vol. 18 (1977):418–31.

GIMENEZ, MARTHA E. "Silence in the Classroom: Some Thoughts About Teaching in the 1980s." *Teaching Sociology*. Vol. 17, No. 2 (April 1989):184–91.

GINDA, JOHN J. "Teaching 'Nature Versus Nurture': The Case of African American Athletic Success." *Teaching Sociology*. Vol. 23, No. 4 (October 1995):389–95.

GINSBURG, FAYE, and ANNA LOWENHAUPT TSING, EDS. *Uncertain Terms: Negotiating Gender in American Culture*. Boston: Beacon Press, 1990.

GIOVANNINI, MAUREEN. "Female Anthropologist and Male Informant: Gender Conflict in a Sicilian Town." In John J. Macionis and Nijole V. Benokraitis, eds., *Seeing Ourselves: Classic, Contemporary, and Cross-Cultural Readings in Sociology*. 2d ed. Englewood Cliffs, N.J.: Prentice Hall, 1992:27–32.

GLAAB, CHARLES N. *The American City: A Documentary History*. Homewood, Ill.: Dorsey Press, 1963.

GLADUE, BRIAN A., RICHARD GREEN, and RONALD E. HELLMAN. "Neuroendocrine Response to Estrogen and Sexual Orientation." *Science*. Vol. 225, No. 4669 (September 28, 1984):1496–99.

GLAZER, NATHAN, and DANIEL P. MOYNIHAN. *Beyond the Melting Pot*. 2d ed. Cambridge, Mass.: MIT Press, 1970.

GLEICK, ELIZABETH. "The Marker We've Been Waiting For." *Time*. Vol. 149, No. 14 (April 7, 1997):28–42.

GLEICK, SHARON. "Who Are They?" *Time*. Special Issue (June 1, 1995):44–51.

GLENN, NORVAL D., and BETH ANN SHELTON. "Regional Differences in Divorce in the United States." *Journal of Marriage and the Family*. Vol. 47, No. 3 (August 1985):641–52.

GLOCK, CHARLES Y. "The Religious Revival in America." In Jane Zahn, ed., *Religion and the Face of America*. Berkeley: University of California Press, 1959:25–42.

———. "On the Study of Religious Commitment." *Religious Education*. Vol. 62, No. 4 (1962):98–110.

GLUCK, PETER R., and RICHARD J. MEISTER. *Cities in Transition*. New York: New Viewpoints, 1979.

GLUECK, SHELDON, and ELEANOR GLUECK. *Unraveling Juvenile Delinquency*. New York: Commonwealth Fund, 1950.

GOETTING, ANN. "Divorce Outcome Research." *Journal of Family Issues*. Vol. 2, No. 3 (September 1981):350–78.

———. Personal communication, 1989.

GOFFMAN, ERVING. *The Presentation of Self in Everyday Life*. Garden City, N.Y.: Anchor Books, 1959.

———. *Asylums: Essays on the Social Situation of Mental Patients and Other Inmates*. Garden City, N.Y.: Anchor Books, 1961.

———. *Stigma: Notes on the Management of Spoiled Identity*. Englewood Cliffs, N.J.: Prentice Hall, 1963.

———. *Interactional Ritual: Essays on Face to Face Behavior*. Garden City, N.Y.: Anchor Books, 1967.

———. *Gender Advertisements*. New York: Harper Colophon, 1979.

GOLDBERG, STEVEN. *The Inevitability of Patriarchy*. New York: William Morrow, 1974.

———. Personal communication, 1987.

GOLDEN, FREDERIC. "Here Come the Microkids." *Time*. Vol. 119, No. 18 (May 3, 1982):50–56.

GOLDFARB, JEFFREY C. *Beyond Glasnost: The Post-Totalitarian Mind*. Chicago: University of Chicago Press, 1989.

GOLDFARB, WILLIAM. "Groundwater: The Buried Life." In F. Herbert Bormann and Stephen R. Kellert, eds., *Ecology, Economics, and Ethics: The Broken Circle*. New Haven, Conn.: Yale University Press, 1991:123–35.

GOLDFIELD, MICHAEL. *The Decline of Organized Labor in the United States*. Chicago and London: University of Chicago Press, 1987.

GOLDSBY, RICHARD A. *Race and Races*. 2d ed. New York: Macmillan, 1977.

GOLDSMITH, H. H. "Genetic Influences on Personality From Infancy." *Child Development*. Vol. 54, No. 2 (April 1983):331–35.

GOODE, WILLIAM J. "The Theoretical Importance of Love." *American Sociological Review*. Vol. 24, No. 1 (February 1959):38–47.

———. "Encroachment, Charlatanism, and the Emerging Profession: Psychology, Sociology and Medicine." *American Sociological Review*. Vol. 25, No. 6 (December 1960):902–14.

GORDON, JAMES S. "The Paradigm of Holistic Medicine." In Arthur C. Hastings et al., eds., *Health for the Whole Person: The Complete Guide to Holistic Medicine*. Boulder, Colo.: Westview Press, 1980:3–27.

GORING, CHARLES BUCKMAN. *The English Convict: A Statistical Study*. Montclair, N.J.: Patterson Smith, 1972; orig. 1913.

GORMAN, CHRISTINE. "Mexico City's Menacing Air." *Time*. Vol. 137, No. 13 (April 1, 1991):61.

GOTTFREDSON, MICHAEL R., and TRAVIS HIRSCHI. "National Crime Control Policies." *Society*. Vol. 32, No. 2 (January–February 1995):30–36.

GOTTMANN, JEAN. *Megalopolis*. New York: Twentieth Century Fund, 1961.

GOUGH, KATHLEEN. "The Origin of the Family." *Journal of Marriage and the Family*. Vol. 33, No. 4 (November 1971):760–71.

GOULD, STEPHEN J. "Evolution as Fact and Theory." *Discover* (May 1981):35–37.

GOULDNER, ALVIN. *Enter Plato*. New York: Free Press, 1965.

———. "The Sociologist as Partisan: Sociology and the Welfare State." In Larry T. Reynolds and Janice M. Reynolds, eds., *The Sociology of Sociology*. New York: David McKay, 1970a:218–55.

———. *The Coming Crisis of Western Sociology*. New York: Avon Books, 1970b.

GOYDER, JOHN. *Technology and Society: A Canadian Perspective*. Peterborough, Ontario: Broadview Press, 1997.

———. *Essentials of Canadian Sociology*. Toronto: McClelland and Stewart, 1990.

GOYDER, JOHN C. AND JAMES E. CURTIS. "Occupational mobility in Canada over four generations." In James E. Curtis and William G. Scott, eds., *Social Stratification: Canada*. 2d ed. Scarborough, Ont.: Prentice Hall, 1979.

GRAHAM, JOHN W., and ANDREA H. BELLER. "Child Support in Black and White: Racial Differentials in the Award and Receipt of Child Support During the 1980s." *Social Science Quarterly*. Vol. 77, No. 3 (September 1996):528–42.

GRAND COUNCIL OF THE CREES. *Sovereign Injustice: Forcible Inclusion of the James Bay Crees and Cree Territory Into a Sovereign Quebec*. Nemaska, Que.: Grand Council of the Crees, 1995.

GRANOVETTER, MARK. "The Strength of Weak Ties." *American Journal of Sociology*. Vol. 78, No. 6 (May 1973):1360–80.

GRANT, DON SHERMAN, II, and MICHAEL WALLACE. "Why Do Strikes Turn Violent?" *American Journal of Sociology*. Vol. 96, No. 5 (March 1991):1117–50.

GRANT, DONALD L. *The Anti-Lynching Movement*. San Francisco: R and E Research Associates, 1975.

GRANT, KAREN R. "The Inverse Care Law in the Context of Universal Free Health Insurance in Canada: Toward Meeting Health Needs Through Public Policy." *Sociological Focus*. Vol. 17, No. 2 (April 1984):137–55.

GRAY, JOHN. "A Disaster among Native Youth." *The Globe and Mail* (November 16, 1996):D3.

GRAY, PAUL. "Whose America?" *Time*. Vol. 137, No. 27 (July 8, 1991):12–17.

GREELEY, ANDREW M. *Ethnicity in the United States: A Preliminary Reconnaissance*. New York: Wiley, 1974.

———. *Religious Change in America*. Cambridge, Mass.: Harvard University Press, 1989.

GREEN, JOHN C. "Pat Robertson and the Latest Crusade: Resources and the 1988 Presidential Campaign." *Social Sciences Quarterly*. Vol. 74, No. 1 (March 1993):156–68.

GREENBERG, DAVID F. *The Construction of Homosexuality*. Chicago: University of Chicago Press, 1988.

GREENHOUSE, LINDA. "Justices Uphold Stiffer Sentences for Hate Crimes." *New York Times* (June 12, 1993):1, 8.

GREENSPON, EDWARD. "The Incredible Shrinking Middle Class." *The Globe and Mail* (July 31, 1993):D1.

GREENWALD, JOHN. "The New Service Class." *Time*. Vol. 144, No. 20 (November 14, 1994):72–74.

GREER, SCOTT. *Urban Renewal and American Cities*. Indianapolis, Ind.: Bobbs-Merrill, 1965.

GREGG, ALLAN R. "Brave New Epoque." *Maclean's* (April 6, 1998):56–60.

GREGORY, PAUL R., and ROBERT C. STUART. *Comparative Economic Systems*. 2d ed. Boston: Houghton Mifflin, 1985.

GREGORY, SOPHFRONIA SCOTT. "The Knife in the Book Bag." *Time*. Vol. 141, No. 6 (February 8, 1993):37.

GROSS, JANE. "New Challenge of Youth: Growing Up in a Gay Home." *New York Times* (February 11, 1991):A1, B7.

GRUENBERG, BARRY. "The Happy Worker: An Analysis of Educational and Occupational Differences in Determinants of Job Satisfaction." *American Journal of Sociology*. Vol. 86, No. 2 (September 1980):247–71.

GUP, TED. "What Makes This School Work?" *Time*. Vol. 140, No. 25 (December 21, 1992):63–65.

GUPPY, NEIL AND A. BRUCE ARAI. "Who Benefits from Higher Education? Differences by Sex, Social Class, and Ethnic Background." In James E. Curtis, Edward Grabb, and Neil Guppy, eds. *Social Inequality in Canada: Patterns, Problems, Policies*. 2d ed. Scarborough, Ont.: Prentice Hall Canada, 1993: 214–232.

GUTFELD, ROSE. "Eight of Ten Americans are Environmentalists." *Wall Street Journal* (August 2, 1991):A1.

GUTMAN, HERBERT G. *The Black Family in Slavery and Freedom, 1750–1925*. New York: Pantheon Books, 1976.

GWARTNEY-GIBBS, PATRICIA A. "The Institutionalization of Premarital Cohabitation: Estimates From Marriage License Applications, 1970 and 1980." *Journal of Marriage and the Family*. Vol. 48, No. 2 (May 1986):423–34.

GWARTNEY-GIBBS, PATRICIA A., JEAN STOCKARD, and SUSANNE BOHMER. "Learning Courtship Agression: The Influence of Parents, Peers, and Personal Experiences." *Family Relations*. Vol. 36, No. 3 (July 1987):276–82.

GWYNNE, S. C., and JOHN F. DICKERSON. "Lost in the E-Mail." *Time*. Vol. 149, No. 15 (April 21, 1997):88–90.

HA, TU THANH. "Canadian confirmed as oldest person." *The Globe and Mail* (August 15, 1997):A1.

HABERMAS, JÜRGEN. *Toward a Rational Society: Student Protest, Science, and Politics*. Jeremy J. Shapiro, trans. Boston: Beacon Press, 1970.

HACKER, HELEN MAYER. "Women as a Minority Group." *Social Forces*. Vol. 30 (October 1951):60–69.

———. "Women as a Minority Group: 20 Years Later." In Florence Denmark, ed., *Who Discriminates Against Women?* Beverly Hills, Calif.: Sage, 1974:124–34.

HACKEY, ROBERT B. "Competing Explanations of Voter Turnout Among American Blacks." *Social Science Quarterly*. Vol. 73, No. 1 (March 1992):71–89.

HACKMAN, J. R. "The Design of Work Teams." In J. Lorch, ed., *Handbook of Organizational Behavior*. Englewood Cliffs, N.J.: Prentice Hall, 1988:315–42.

HADAWAY, C. KIRK, PENNY LONG MARLER, and MARK CHAVES. "What the Polls Don't Show: A Closer Look at U.S. Church Attendance." *American Sociological Review*. Vol. 58, No. 6 (December 1993):741–52.

HADDEN, JEFFREY K., and CHARLES E. SWAIN. *Prime Time Preachers: The Rising Power of Televangelism*. Reading, Mass.: Addison-Wesley, 1981.

HAFNER, KATIE. "Making Sense of the Internet." *Newsweek* (October 24, 1994):46–48.

HAGAN, JOHN, and PATRICIA PARKER. "White-Collar Crime and Punishment: The Class Structure and Legal Sanctioning of Securities Violations." *American Sociological Review*. Vol. 50, No. 3 (June 1985):302–16.

HAGAN, JOHN, A.R. GILLIS, AND JOHN SIMPSON. "The Class Structure of Gender and Delinquency: Toward a Power-control Theory of Common Delinquent Behavior." *American Journal of Sociology*. Vol. 90, No. 6 (May 1985): 1151–78.

HAIG, ROBIN ANDREW. *The Anatomy of Humor: Biopsychosocial and Therapeutic Perspectives*. Springfield, Ill.: Charles C. Thomas, 1988.

HALBERSTAM, DAVID. *The Reckoning*. New York: Avon Books, 1986.

HALE, SYLVIA. "The Documentary Construction of Female Mismanagement" *Canadian Review of Sociology and Anthropology*. Vol. 24, No. 4 (November 1987):489–513.

HALEDJIAN, DEAN. "How to Tell a Businessman From a Businesswoman." Annandale, Va.: Northern Virginia Community College, 1997.

HALL, JOHN R., and MARY JO NEITZ. *Culture: Sociological Perspectives*. Englewood Cliffs, N.J.: Prentice Hall, 1993.

HALLETT, M.E. "Nellie McClung." In *The Canadian Encyclopedia*. 2d ed. Vol. 2. Edmonton: Hurtig Publishers, 1988:1257.

HALLINAN, MAUREEN T. "The Sociological Study of Social Change." *American Sociological Review*. Vol. 62, No. 1 (February 1997):1–11.

HALLINAN, MAUREEN T., and RICHARD A. WILLIAMS. "Interracial Friendship Choices in Secondary Schools." *American Sociological Review*. Vol. 54, No. 1 (February 1989):67–78.

HAMBLIN, DORA JANE. *The First Cities*. New York: Time-Life Books, 1973.

HAMEL, RUTH. "Raging Against Aging." *American Demographics*. Vol. 12, No. 3 (March 1990):42–45.

HAMILTON, DWIGHT. "50 Richest Canadians: It's So Much Better to Be Rich." *The Financial Post Magazine* (January 1996):1257.

HAMMOND, PHILIP E. "Introduction." In Philip E. Hammond, ed., *The Sacred in a Secular Age: Toward Revision in the Scientific Study of Religion*. Berkeley: University of California Press, 1985:1–6.

HAMRICK, MICHAEL H., DAVID J. ANSPAUGH, and GENE EZELL. *Health*. Columbus, Ohio: Merrill, 1986.

HANDGUN CONTROL, INC. Data cited in *Time* (December 20, 1993) and various newspaper reports (March 2, 6, 1994).

——. [Online] Available http://www.handguncontrol.org, 1998.

HANDLIN, OSCAR. *Boston's Immigrants 1790–1865: A Study in Acculturation*. Cambridge, Mass.: Harvard University Press, 1941.

HANEY, CRAIG, CURTIS BANKS, and PHILIP ZIMBARDO. "Interpersonal Dynamics in a Simulated Prison." *International Journal of Criminology and Penology*. Vol. 1 (1973):69–97.

HARBERT, ANITA A., and LEON H. GINSBERG. *Human Services for Older Adults*. Columbia: University of South Carolina Press, 1991.

HAREVEN, TAMARA K. "The Life Course and Aging in Historical Perspective." In Tamara K. Hareven and Kathleen J. Adams, eds., *Aging and Life Course Transitions: An Interdisciplinary Perspective*. New York: Guilford Press, 1982:1–26.

HARLAN, WILLIAM H. "Social Status of the Aged in Three Indian Villages." In Bernice L. Neugarten, ed., *Middle Age and Aging: A Reader in Social Psychology*. Chicago: University of Chicago Press, 1968:469–75.

——, and Randolph Langenbach. *Amoskeag: Life and Work in an American Factory City*. New York: Pantheon Books, 1978.

HARLOW, CAROLINE WOLF. *Female Victims of Violent Crime*. Bureau of Justice Statistics report. Washington, D.C.: U.S. Government Printing Office, 1991.

HARLOW, HARRY F., and MARGARET KUENNE HARLOW. "Social Deprivation in Monkeys." *Scientific American*. Vol. 207 (November 1962):137–46.

HARRIES, KEITH D. *Serious Violence: Patterns of Homicide and Assault in America*. Springfield, Ill.: Charles C. Thomas, 1990.

HARRINGTON, MICHAEL. *The New American Poverty*. New York: Penguin Books, 1984.

HARRIS, CHAUNCEY D., and EDWARD L. ULLMAN. "The Nature of Cities." *The Annals*. Vol. 242 (November 1945):7–17.

HARRIS, JACK DASH. Lecture on cockfighting in the Philippines. Semester at Sea (October 27, 1994).

HARRIS, MARVIN. *Cows, Pigs, Wars and Witches: The Riddles of Culture*. New York: Vintage Books, 1975.

——. "Why Men Dominate Women." *New York Times Magazine* (November 13, 1977):46, 115–23.

——. *Cultural Anthropology*. 2d ed. New York: Harper & Row, 1987.

HARRISON, PAUL. *Inside the Third World: The Anatomy of Poverty*. 2d ed. New York: Penguin Books, 1984.

HARRON, DON. *Debunk's Illustrated Guide to the Canadian Establishment*. Toronto: Macmillan, 1984.

HARTMANN, BETSY, and JAMES BOYCE. *Needless Hunger: Voices From a Bangladesh Village*. San Francisco: Institute for Food and Development Policy, 1982.

HARVEY, DAVID. "Labor, Capital, and Class Struggle Around the Built Environment." *Politics and Society*. Vol. 6 (1976):265–95.

HAVIGHURST, ROBERT J., BERNICE L. NEUGARTEN, and SHELDON S. TOBIN. "Disengagement and Patterns of Aging." In Bernice L. Neugarten, ed., *Middle Age and Aging: A Reader in Social Psychology*. Chicago: University of Chicago Press, 1968:161–72.

HAYNEMAN, STEPHEN P., and WILLIAM A. LOXLEY. "The Effect of Primary-School Quality on Academic Achievement Across Twenty-nine High- and Low-Income Countries." *American Journal of Sociology*. Vol. 88, No. 6 (May 1983):1162–94.

HEALTH INSURANCE ASSOCIATION OF AMERICA. *Source Book of Health Insurance Data*. Washington, D.C.: The Association, 1991.

HEATH, JULIA A., and W. DAVID BOURNE. "Husbands and Housework: Parity or Parody?" *Social Science Quarterly*. Vol. 76, No. 1 (March 1995):195–202.

HEILBRONER, ROBERT L. *The Making of Economic Society*. 7th ed. Englewood Cliffs, N.J.: Prentice Hall, 1985.

HELGESEN, SALLY. *The Female Advantage: Women's Ways of Leadership*. New York: Doubleday, 1990.

HELIN, DAVID W. "When Slogans Go Wrong." *American Demographics*. Vol. 14, No. 2 (February 1992):14.

HELMES-HAYES, R. *A Quarter-Century of Sociology and the University of Toronto. 1963–1988*. Toronto: Canadian Scholars' Press, 1988.

HELMUTH, JOHN W. "World Hunger Amidst Plenty." *USA Today*. Vol. 117, No. 2526 (March 1989):48–50.

HENLEY, NANCY, MYKOL HAMILTON, and BARRIE THORNE. "Womanspeak and Manspeak: Sex Differences in Communication, Verbal and Nonverbal." In John J. Macionis and Nijole V. Benokraitis, eds., *Seeing Ourselves: Classic, Contemporary, and Cross-Cultural Readings in Sociology*, 2d ed. Englewood Cliffs, N.J.: Prentice Hall, 1992:10–15.

HENRY, WILLIAM A., III. "Gay Parents: Under Fire and On the Rise." *Time*. Vol. 142, No. 12 (September 20, 1993):66–71.

HERMAN, DIANNE. "The Rape Culture." In John J. Macionis and Nijole V. Benokraitis, eds., *Seeing Ourselves: Classic, Contemporary, and Cross-Cultural Readings in Sociology*. 4th ed. Upper Saddle River, N.J.: Prentice Hall, 1998.

HERMAN, EDWARD S. *Corporate Control, Corporate Power: A Twentieth Century Fund Study*. New York: Cambridge University Press, 1981.

HEROLD, E.S. *Sexual Behaviour of Canadian Young People*. Markham, Ont.: Fitzhenry and Whiteside, 1984.

HERRNSTEIN, RICHARD J. *IQ and the Meritocracy*. Boston: Little, Brown, 1973.

HERRNSTEIN, RICHARD J., and CHARLES MURRAY. *The Bell Curve: Intelligence and Class Structure in American Life*. New York: Free Press, 1994.

HERRSTROM, STAFFAN. "Sweden: Pro-Choice on Child Care." *New Perspectives Quarterly*. Vol. 7, No. 1 (Winter 1990):27–28.

HERSCH, JONI, and SHELLY WHITE-MEANS. "Employer-Sponsored Health and Pension Benefits and the Gender/Race Wage Gap." *Social Science Quarterly*. Vol. 74, No. 4 (December 1993):850–66.

HESS, STEPHEN. "Reporters Who Cover Congress." *Society*. Vol. 28, No. 2 (January–February 1991):60–65.

HEWLETT, BARRY S. "Husband-Wife Reciprocity and the Father-Infant Relationship Among Aka Pygmies." In Barry S. Hewlett, ed., *Father-Child Relations: Cultural and Bio-Social Contexts*. New York: Aldine, 1992:153–76.

HEWLETT, SYLVIA ANN. "The Feminization of the Work Force." *New Perspectives Quarterly*. Vol. 7, No. 1 (Winter 1990):13–15.

—— . *A Lesser Life: The Myth of Women's Liberation in America*. New York: William Morrow, 1986.

HILLER, HARRY. *Canadian Society: A Macro Analysis*. 3d ed. Scarborough, Ont.: Prentice Hall Canada, 1996.

HINCH, RONALD. "Inconsistencies and contradictions in Canada's sexual assault law." *Canadian Public Policy*. Vol. XIV, No. 3 (1988): 282–294.

HIROSHI, MANNARI. *The Japanese Business Leaders*. Tokyo: University of Tokyo Press, 1974.

HIRSCHI, TRAVIS. *Causes of Delinquency*. Berkeley: University of California Press, 1969.

—— , and Michael Gottfredson. "Age and the Explanation of Crime." *American Journal of Sociology*. Vol. 89, No. 3 (November 1983):552–84.

HIV/AIDS Surveillance. Vol. 40, Nos. 51 & 52 (January 3, 1992). Atlanta: The Centers.

HOCHSCHILD, ARLIE, with ANNE MACHUNG. *The Second Shift: Working Parents and the Revolution at Home*. New York: Viking Books, 1989.

HODGE, ROBERT W., DONALD J. TREIMAN, and PETER H. ROSSI. "A Comparative Study of Occupational Prestige." In Reinhard Bendix and Seymour Martin Lipset, eds., *Class, Status, and Power: Social Stratification in Comparative Perspective*. 2d ed. New York: Free Press, 1966:309–21.

HOERR, JOHN. "The Payoff From Teamwork." *Business Week*. No. 3114 (July 10, 1989):56–62.

HOGAN, DENNIS P., and EVELYN M. KITAGAWA. "The Impact of Social Status and Neighborhood on the Fertility of Black Adolescents." *American Journal of Sociology*. Vol. 90, No. 4 (January 1985):825–55.

HOGGARTH, RICHARD. "The Abuses of Literacy." *Society*. Vol. 55, No. 3 (March–April 1995):55–62.

HOLLANDER, PAUL. "We are All (Sniffle, Sniffle) Victims Now." *Wall Street Journal* (January 18, 1995):A14.

HOLM, JEAN. *The Study of Religions*. New York: Seabury Press, 1977.

HOLMES, HELEN and DAVID TARAS. *Selling Ourselves: Media, Power and Policy in Canada*. Toronto: Harcourt Brace Jovanovich, 1992.

HOLMES, MALCOLM D., HARMON M. HOSCH, HOWARD C. DAUDISTEL, DOLORES PEREZ, and JOSEPH B. GRAVES. "Judges, Ethnicity and Minority Sentencing: Evidence Among Hispanics." *Social Science Quarterly*. Vol. 74, No. 3 (September 1993):496–506.

HOLMES, STEVEN A. "Income Disparity Between Poorest and Richest Rises." *New York Times* (June 20, 1996):A1, A18.

——. "For Hispanic Poor, No Silver Lining." *New York Times* (October 13, 1996): section 4, p. 5.

HOLMSTROM, DAVID. "Abuse of Elderly, Even by Adult Children, Gets More Attention and Official Concern." *Christian Science Monitor* (July 28, 1994):1.

HONEYWELL, ROY J. *The Educational Work of Thomas Jefferson*. Cambridge, Mass.: Harvard University Press, 1931.

HOROWITZ, IRVING LOUIS. *The Decomposition of Sociology*. New York: Oxford University Press, 1993.

HOSTETLER, JOHN A. *Amish Society*. 3d ed. Baltimore: Johns Hopkins University Press, 1980.

HOUT, MICHAEL, and ANDREW M. GREELEY. "The Center Doesn't Hold: Church Attendance in the United States, 1940–1984." *American Sociological Review*. Vol. 52, No. 3 (June 1987):325–45.

HOUT, MIKE, CLEM BROOKS, and JEFF MANZA. "The Persistence of Classes in Post-Industrial Societies." *International Sociology*. Vol. 8, No. 3 (September 1993):259–77.

HOWE, NEIL, and WILLIAM STRAUSS. "America's 13th Generation." *New York Times* (April 16, 1991).

HOWLETT, DEBBIE. "Cruzan's Struggle Left Imprint: 10,000 Others in Similar State." *USA Today* (December 27, 1990):3A.

HOYT, HOMER. *The Structure and Growth of Residential Neighborhoods in American Cities*. Washington, D.C.: Federal Housing Administration, 1939.

HSU, FRANCIS L. K. *The Challenge of the American Dream: The Chinese in the United States*. Belmont, Calif.: Wadsworth, 1971.

HUBER, JOAN, and GLENNA SPITZE. "Considering Divorce: An Expansion of Becker's Theory of Marital Instability." *American Journal of Sociology*. Vol. 86, No. 1 (July 1980):75–89.

HUCHINGSON, JAMES E. "Science and Religion." *The Herald* (Dade County, Florida). December 25, 1994:1M, 6M.

HUET-COX, ROCIO. "Medical Education: New Wine in Old Wine Skins." In Victor W. Sidel and Ruth Sidel, eds., *Reforming Medicine: Lessons of the Last Quarter Century*. New York: Pantheon Books, 1984:129–49.

HUFFMAN, MATT L., STEVEN C. VELASCO, and WILLIAM T. BIELBY. "Where Sex Composition Matters Most: Comparing the Effects of Job Versus Occupational Sex Composition of Earnings." *Sociological Focus*. Vol. 29, No. 3 (August 1996):189–207.

HULL, JON D. "A Boy and His Gun." *Time* (August 2, 1993):29–35.

HULS, GLENNA. Personal communication, 1987.

HUMPHREY, CRAIG R., and FREDERICK R. BUTTEL. *Environment, Energy, and Society*. Belmont, Calif.: Wadsworth, 1982.

HUMPHREY, DEREK. *Final Exit: The Practicalities of Self-Deliverance and Assisted Suicide for the Dying*. Eugene, Ore.: The Hemlock Society, 1991.

HUMPHRIES, HARRY LEROY. *The Structure and Politics of Intermediary Class Positions: An Empirical Examination of Recent Theories of Class*. Unpublished Ph.D. dissertation. Eugene: University of Oregon, 1984.

HUNNICUT, BENJAMIN K. "Are We All Working Too Hard? No Time for God or Family." *Wall Street Journal* (January 4, 1990).

HUNT, MORTON. *Sexual Behavior in the 1970s*. Chicago: Playboy Press, 1974.

HUNTER, FLOYD. *Community Power Structure*. Garden City, N.Y.: Doubleday, 1963; orig. 1953.

HUNTER, JAMES DAVISON. *American Evangelicalism: Conservative Religion and the Quandary of Modernity*. New Brunswick, N.J.: Rutgers University Press, 1983.

———. "Conservative Protestantism." In Philip E. Hammond, ed., *The Sacred in a Secular Age*. Berkeley: University of California Press, 1985:50–66.

———. *Evangelicalism: The Coming Generation*. Chicago: University of Chicago Press, 1987.

———. *Culture Wars: The Struggle to Define America*. New York: Basic Books, 1991.

HURLEY, ANDREW. *Environmental Inequalities: Class, Race, and Industrial Pollution in Gary, Indiana, 1945–1980*. Chapel Hill: University of North Carolina Press, 1995.

HURN, CHRISTOPHER. *The Limits and Possibilities of Schooling*. Needham Heights, Mass.: Allyn & Bacon, 1978.

HURST, L. "Tuberculosis Makes a Quiet Return." *The Toronto Star* (November 8, 1992): A1, A10.

HURTIG, MEL. *A New and Better Canada: Principles and Polices of a New Canadian Political Party*. Toronto: Stoddart, 1992.

———. *The Betrayal of Canada*. Toronto: Stoddart Publishing, 1991.

HUTCHINGSON, JAMES E. "Science and Religion." *The Herald* (Dade County, Florida) (December 25, 1994):1M, 6M.

HWANG, SEAN-SHONG, STEVEN H. MURDOCK, BANOO PARPIA, and RITA R. HAMM. "The Effects of Race and Socioeconomic Status on Residential Segregation in Texas, 1970–1980." *Social Forces*. Vol. 63, No. 3 (March 1985):732–47.

HYMAN, HERBERT H., and CHARLES R. WRIGHT. "Trends in Voluntary Association Memberships of American Adults: Replication Based on Secondary Analysis of National Sample Survey." *American Sociological Review*. Vol. 36, No. 2 (April 1971):191–206.

HYMOWITZ, CAROL. "World's Poorest Women Advance by Entrepreneurship." *Wall Street Journal* (September 9, 1995):B1.

IANNACCONE, LAURENCE R. "Why Strict Churches Are Strong." *American Journal of Sociology*. Vol. 99, No. 5 (March 1994):1180–1211.

IBM. "Focus on e-business." *The Globe and Mail* (January 28, 1998):Section C.

IBRAHIM, YOUSSEF. "Finland suddenly takes over as world's most wired country." *The Globe and Mail* (February 1, 1997):A16.

IDE, THOMAS R., and ARTHUR J. CORDELL. "Automating Work." *Society*. Vol. 31, No. 6 (September–October 1994):65–71.

ILLICH, IVAN. *Medical Nemesis: The Expropriation of Health*. New York: Pantheon Books, 1976.

"Implications for Research and Service." *Family Relations*. Vol. 32 (July 1983):395–402.

INGLE, LORNE, ED. *Meech Lake Reconsidered*. Hull, Que.: Voyageur Publishing, 1989.

INTER-PARLIAMENTARY UNION. *Men and Women in Politics: Democracy in the Making*. Geneva: 1997.

IRWIN, JOHN. *Prison in Turmoil*. Boston: Little, Brown, 1980.

ISAJIW, WSEVELOD W. "Definitions of Ethnicity." In Rita M. Bienvenue and Jay E. Goldstein. *Ethnicity and Ethnic Relations in Canada*. 2d ed. Toronto: Butterworths, 1985: 5–18.

ISAY, RICHARD A. *Being Homosexual: Gay Men and Their Development*. New York: Farrar, Straus, & Giroux, 1989.

JACOB, JOHN E. "An Overview of Black America in 1985." In James D. Williams, ed., *The State of Black America 1986*. New York: National Urban League, 1986:i–xi.

JACOBS, DAVID. "Inequality and Police Strength." *American Sociological Review*. Vol. 44, No. 6 (December 1979):913–25.

JACOBS, DAVID, and RONALD E. HELMS. "Toward a Political Model of Incarceration: A Time-Series Examination of Multiple Explanations for Prison Admission Rates." *American Journal of Sociology*. Vol. 102, No. 2 (September 1996):323–57.

JACOBS, DAVID. "Walpole Island: Sustainable Development." Pp. 179–85 in Diane Engelstad and John Bird (eds.), *Nation to Nation: Aboriginal Sovereignty and the Future of Canada*. Concord, Ontario: House of Anansi Press, 1992.

JACOBS, JAMES B. "Should Hate Be a Crime?" *The Public Interest*. No. 113 (Fall 1993):3–14.

JACOBS, JANE. *The Death and Life of Great American Cities*. New York: Random House, 1961.

———. *The Economy of Cities*. New York: Vintage Books, 1970.

———. *Cities and the Wealth of Nations*. Toronto: Random House, 1985.

JACOBSON, JODI L. "Closing the Gender Gap in Development." In Lester R. Brown et al., eds., *State of the World 1993: A Worldwatch Institute Report on Progress Toward a Sustainable Society*. New York: Norton, 1993:61–79.

JACOBY, RUSSELL, and NAOMI GLAUBERMAN, EDS. *The Bell Curve Debate*. New York: Random House, 1995.

JACQUET, CONSTANT H., and ALICE M. JONES. *Yearbook of American and Canadian Churches 1991*. Nashville, Tenn.: Abingdon Press, 1991.

JAENEN, CORNELIUS. "Mutilated Multiculturalism." In J. Donald Wilson, ed., *Canadian Education in the 1980s*. Calgary: Detselig Enterprises, 1981.

JAGAROWSKY, PAUL A., and MARY JO BANE. *Neighborhood Poverty: Basic Questions*. Discussion paper series H-90-3. John F. Kennedy School of Government. Cambridge, Mass.: Harvard University Press, 1990.

JAGGER, ALISON. "Political Philosophies of Women's Liberation." In Laurel Richardson and Verta Taylor, eds., *Feminist Frontiers: Rethinking Sex, Gender, and Society*. Reading, Mass.: Addison-Wesley, 1983.

JAMES, DAVID R. "City Limits on Racial Equality: The Effects of City-Suburb Boundaries on Public-School Desegregation, 1968–1976." *American Sociological Review*. Vol. 54, No. 6 (December 1989):963–84.

JANIS, IRVING. *Victims of Groupthink*. Boston: Houghton Mifflin, 1972.

———. *Crucial Decisions: Leadership in Policymaking and Crisis Management*. New York: Free Press, 1989.

JANUS, CHRISTOPHER G. "Slavery Abolished? Only Officially." *Christian Science Monitor* (May 17, 1996):18.

JARRETT, ROBIN L. "Living Poor: Family Life Among Single Parent, African-American Women." *Social Problems*. Vol. 41, No. 1 (February 1994):30–49.

JEFFERSON, THOMAS. Letter to James Madison, October 28, 1785. In Julian P. Boyd, ed., *The Papers of Thomas Jefferson*. Princeton, N.J.: Princeton University Press, 1953:681–83; orig. 1785.

JENCKS, CHRISTOPHER. "Genes and Crime." *The New York Review* (February 12, 1987):33–41.

JENCKS, CHRISTOPHER, ET AL. *Inequality: A Reassessment of the Effect of Family and Schooling in America*. New York: Basic Books, 1972.

JENKINS, BRIAN M. "Terrorism Remains a Threat." Syndicated column, *The Columbus Dispatch* (January 14, 1990):D1.

———. "Statements About Terrorism." In *International Terrorism, The Annals of the American Academy of Political and Social Science*. Vol. 463 (September). Beverly Hills, Calif.: Sage Publications, 1982:11–23.

JENKINS, HOLMAN, JR. "The 'Poverty' Lobby's Inflated Numbers." *Wall Street Journal* (December 14, 1992):A10.

JENKINS, J. CRAIG, and CHARLES PERROW. "Insurgency of the Powerless: Farm Worker Movements (1946–1972)." *American Sociological Review*. Vol. 42, No. 2 (April 1977):249–68.

JENKINS, J. CRAIG, and MICHAEL WALLACE. "The Generalized Action Potential of Protest Movements: The New Class, Social Trends, and Political Exclusion Explanations." *Sociological Forum*. Vol. 11, No. 2 (June 1996):183–207.

JENSEN, LIEF, DAVID J. EGGEBEEN, and DANIEL T. LICHTER. "Child Policy and the Ameliorative Effects of Public Assistance." *Social Science Quarterly*. Vol. 74, No. 3 (September 1993):542–59.

JOHNSON, BRIAN D. "Amazing Gross." *Maclean's* (October 13, 1997):57.

JOHNSON, CATHRYN. "Gender, Legitimate Authority, and Leader-Subordinate Conversations." *American Sociological Review*. Vol. 59, No. 1 (February 1994):122–35.

JOHNSON, DIRK. "Census Finds Many Claiming New Identity: Indian." *New York Times* (March 5, 1991):A1, A16.

JOHNSON, F. HENRY. *A Brief History of Canadian Education*. Toronto: McGraw-Hill, 1968.

JOHNSON, NORRIS R. "Panic at 'The Who Concert Stampede': An Empirical Assessment." *Social Problems*. Vol. 34, No. 4 (October 1987):362–73.

JOHNSON, PAUL. "The Seven Deadly Sins of Terrorism." In Benjamin Netanyahu, ed., *International Terrorism*. New Brunswick, N.J.: Transaction Books, 1981:12–22.

JOHNSTON, DAVID CAY. "Voting, America's Not Keen On. Coffee Is Another Matter." *New York Times* (November 10, 1996): section 4, p. 2.

JOHNSTON, R. J. "Residential Area Characteristics." In D. T. Herbert and R. J. Johnston, eds., *Social Areas in Cities. Vol. 1: Spatial Processes and Form*. New York: Wiley, 1976:193–235.

JOHNSTONE, RONALD L. *Religion in Society: A Sociology of Religion*. 2d ed. Englewood Cliffs, N.J.: Prentice Hall, 1983.

JOINT ECONOMIC COMMITTEE. *The Concentration of Wealth in the United States: Trends in the Distribution of Wealth Among American Families*. Washington, D.C.: United States Congress, 1986.

JOSEPHY, ALVIN M., JR. *Now That the Buffalo's Gone: A Study of Today's American Indians*. New York: Alfred A. Knopf, 1982.

JOURNAL OF THE AMERICAN MEDICAL ASSOCIATION. Data cited in Pollack, Andrew, "Overseas, Smoking Is One of Life's Small Pleasures." *New York Times* (August 17, 1996).

KADUSHIN, CHARLES. "Friendship Among the French Financial Elite." *American Sociological Review*. Vol. 60, No. 2 (April 1995):202–21.

KAELBLE, HARTMUT. *Social Mobility in the 19th and 20th Centuries: Europe and America in Comparative Perspective*. New York: St. Martin's Press, 1986.

KAIN, EDWARD L. "A Note on the Integration of AIDS Into the Sociology of Human Sexuality." *Teaching Sociology*. Vol. 15, No. 4 (July 1987):320–23.

———. *The Myth of Family Decline: Understanding Families in a World of Rapid Social Change*. Lexington, Mass.: Lexington Books, 1990.

KAIN, EDWARD L., and SHANNON HART. "AIDS and the Family: A Content Analysis of Media Coverage." Presented to National Council on Family Relations, Atlanta, 1987.

KALISH, CAROL B. "International Crime Rates." *Bureau of Justice Statistics Special Report*, May. Washington, D.C.: U. S. Government Printing Office, 1988.

KALISH, RICHARD A. "The New Ageism and the Failure Models: A Polemic." *The Gerontologist*. Vol. 19, No. 4 (August 1979):398–402.

———. *Late Adulthood: Perspectives on Human Development*. 2d ed. Monterey, Calif.: Brooks/Cole, 1982.

KALISH, SUSAN. "Interracial Births Increase as U.S. Ponders Racial Definitions." *Population Today*. Vol. 23, No. 4 (April 1995):1–2.

KALLEBERG, ARNE L., and MARK E. VAN BUREN. "Is Better Better? Explaining the Relationship Between Organization Size and Job Rewards." *American Sociological Review*. Vol. 61, No. 1 (February 1996):47–66.

KAMINER, WENDY. "Volunteers: Who Knows What's in It for Them." *Ms.* (December 1984):93–94, 96, 126–28.

———. "Demasculinizing the Army." *New York Times Review of Books* (June 15, 1997):7.

KANAMINE, LINDA. "School Operation Fails For-Profit Test." *USA Today* (November 24, 1995):6A.

KANTER, ROSABETH MOSS. *Men and Women of the Corporation*. New York: Basic Books, 1977.

———. *The Change Masters: Innovation and Entrepreneurship in the American Corporation*. New York: Simon & Schuster, 1983.

———. *When Giants Learn to Dance: Mastering the Challenges of Strategy, Management, and Careers in the 1990s*. New York: Simon & Schuster, 1989.

KANTER, ROSABETH MOSS, and BARRY A. STEIN. "The Gender Pioneers: Women in an Industrial Sales Force." In R. M. Kanter and B. A. Stein, eds., *Life in Organizations*. New York: Basic Books, 1979:134–60.

———. *A Tale of "O": On Being Different in an Organization*. New York: Harper & Row, 1980.

KANTROWITZ, BARBARA. "Mothers on Their Own." *Newsweek* (December 23, 1985):66–67.

KAPFERER, JEAN-NOEL. "How Rumors Are Born." *Society*. Vol. 29, No. 5 (July–August 1992):53–60.

KAPLAN, ELAINE BELL. "Black Teenage Mothers and Their Mothers: The Impact of Adolescent Childbearing on Daughters' Relations With Mothers." *Social Problems*. Vol. 43, No. 4 (November 1996):427–43.

KAPLAN, ERIC B., ET AL. "The Usefulness of Preoperative Laboratory Screening." *Journal of the American Medical Association*. Vol. 253, No. 24 (June 28, 1985):3576–81.

KAPTCHUK, TED. "The Holistic Logic of Chinese Medicine." In Shepard Bliss et al., eds., *The New Holistic Health Handbook*. Lexington, Mass.: The Steven Greene Press/Penguin Books, 1985:41.

KARATNYCKY, ADRIAN. "Democracies on the Rise, Democracies at Risk." *Freedom Review*. Vol. 26, No. 1 (January–February 1995):5–10.

KARP, DAVID A., and WILLIAM C. YOELS. "The College Classroom: Some Observations on the Meaning of Student Participation." *Sociology and Social Research*. Vol. 60, No. 4 (July 1976):421–39.

KASARDA, JOHN D. "Entry-Level Jobs, Mobility and Urban Minority Employment." *Urban Affairs Quarterly*. Vol. 19, No. 1 (September 1983):21–40.

KATES, ROBERT W. "Ending Hunger: Current Status and Future Prospects." *Consequences*. Vol. 2, No. 2 (1996):3–11.

KATZ, JAMES E. "The Social Side of Information Networking." *Society*. Vol. 34, No. 3 (March/April 1997):9–12.

KATZ, MICHAEL B. *In the Shadow of the Poorhouse*. New York: Basic Books, 1986.

KAUFMAN, MARC. "Becoming 'Old Old'." *Philadelphia Inquirer* (October 28, 1990):1–A, 10–A.

KAUFMAN, ROBERT L., and SEYMOUR SPILERMAN. "The Age Structures of Occupations and Jobs." *American Journal of Sociology*. Vol. 87, No. 4 (January 1982):827–51.

KAUFMAN, WALTER. *Religions in Four Dimensions: Existential, Aesthetic, Historical and Comparative*. New York: Reader's Digest Press, 1976.

KEITH, JULIE AND LAURA LAUDREY. "Well-being of Older Canadians." In Craig McKie and Keith Thompson, eds. *Canadian Social Trends*. Toronto: Thompson Educational Publishing, 1994.

KEITH, PAT M., and ROBERT B. SCHAFER. "They Hate to Cook: Patterns of Distress in an Ordinary Role." *Sociological Focus*. Vol. 27, No. 4 (October 1994):289–301.

KELLER, HELEN. *The Story of My Life*. New York: Doubleday, Page, 1903.

KELLER, SUZANNE. *The Urban Neighborhood*. New York: Random House, 1968.

KELLERT, STEPHEN R., and F. HERBERT BORMANN. "Closing the Circle: Weaving Strands Among Ecology, Economics, and Ethics." In F. Herbert Bormann and Stephen R. Kellert, eds., *Ecology, Economics, and Ethics: The Broken Circle*. New Haven, Conn.: Yale University Press, 1991:205–10.

KELLEY, JONATHAN, and M. D. R. EVANS. "Class and Class Conflict in Six Western Nations." *American Sociological Review*. Vol. 60, No. 2 (April 1995):157–78.

KEMP, ALICE ABEL, and SHELLEY COVERMAN. "Marginal Jobs or Marginal Workers: Identifying Sex Differences in Low-Skill Occupations." *Sociological Focus*. Vol. 22, No. 1 (February 1989):19–37.

KENNICKELL, ARTHUR, and JANICE SHACK-MARQUEZ. "Changes in Family Finances From 1983 to 1989: Evidence From the Survey of Consumer Finances." *Federal Reserve Bulletin* (January 1992):1–18.

KENYON, KATHLEEN. *Digging Up Jericho*. London: Ernest Benn, 1957.

KERCKHOFF, ALAN C., RICHARD T. CAMPBELL, and IDEE WINFIELD-LAIRD. "Social Mobility in Great Britain and the United States." *American Journal of Sociology*. Vol. 91, No. 2 (September 1985):281–308.

KIDD, QUENTIN, and AIE-RIE LEE. "Postmaterialist Values and the Environment: A Critique and Reappraisal." *Social Science Quarterly*. Vol. 78, No. 1 (March 1997):1–15.

KIDRON, MICHAEL, and RONALD SEGAL. *The New State of the World Atlas*. New York: Simon & Schuster, 1991.

KILBOURNE, BROCK K. "The Conway and Siegelman Claims Against Religious Cults: An Assessment of Their Data." *Journal for the Scientific Study of Religion*. Vol. 22, No. 4 (December 1983):380–85.

KILGORE, SALLY B. "The Organizational Context of Tracking in Schools." *American Sociological Review*. Vol. 56, No. 2 (April 1991):189–203.

KILLIAN, LEWIS M. "Organization, Rationality and Spontaneity in the Civil Rights Movement." *American Sociological Review*. Vol. 49, No. 6 (December 1984):770–83.

KING, KATHLEEN PIKER, and DENNIS E. CLAYSON. "The Differential Perceptions of Male and Female Deviants." *Sociological Focus*. Vol. 21, No. 2 (April 1988):153–64.

KING, MARTIN LUTHER, JR. "The Montgomery Bus Boycott." In Walt Anderson, ed., *The Age of Protest*. Pacific Palisades, Calif.: Goodyear, 1969:81–91.

KINKEAD, GWEN. *Chinatown: A Portrait of a Closed Society*. New York: HarperCollins, 1992.

KINSEY, ALFRED, ET AL. *Sexual Behavior in the Human Male*. Philadelphia: Saunders, 1948.

———. *Sexual Behavior in the Human Female*. Philadelphia: Saunders, 1953.

KIPP, RITA SMITH. "Have Women Always Been Unequal?" In Beth Reed, ed., *Towards a Feminist Transformation of the Academy: Proceedings of the Fifth Annual Women's Studies Conference*. Ann Arbor, Mich.: Great Lakes Colleges Association, 1980:12–18.

KIRK, MARSHALL, and PETER MADSEN. *After the Ball: How America Will Conquer its Fear and Hatred of Gays in the '90s*. New York: Doubleday, 1989.

KISER, EDGAR, and JOACHIM SCHNEIDER. "Bureaucracy and Efficiency: An Analysis of Taxation in Early Modern Prussia." *American Sociological Review*. Vol. 59, No. 2 (April 1994):187–204.

KISHOR, SUNITA. "'May God Give Sons to All': Gender and Child Mortality in India." *American Sociological Review*. Vol. 58, No. 2 (April 1993):247–65.

KITANO, HARRY H. L. "Japanese." In *Harvard Encyclopedia of American Ethnic Groups*. Cambridge, Mass.: Harvard University Press, 1980:561–71.

KITSON, GAY C., and HELEN J. RASCHKE. "Divorce Research: What We Know, What We Need to Know." *Journal of Divorce*. Vol. 4, No. 3 (Spring 1981):1–37.

KITTRIE, NICHOLAS N. *The Right To Be Different: Deviance and Enforced Therapy.* Baltimore: Johns Hopkins University Press, 1971.

KLUCKHOHN, CLYDE. "As An Anthropologist Views It." In Albert Deuth, ed., *Sex Habits of American Men.* New York: Prentice Hall, 1948.

KMITCH, JANET, PEDRO LABOY, and SARAH VAN DAMME. "International Comparisons of Manufacturing Compensation." *Monthly Labor Review.* Vol. 118, No. 10 (October 1995):3–9.

KNOWLES, VALERIE. *Strangers at Our Gates: Canadian Immigration and Immigration Policy, 1540–1990.* Toronto: Dundurn, 1992.

KOCH, HOWARD. *The Panic Broadcast: Portrait of an Event.* Boston: Little, Brown, 1970.

KOELLN, KENNETH, ROSE M. RUBIN, and MARION SMITH PICARD. "Vulnerable Elderly Households: Expenditures on Necessities by Older Americans." *Social Science Quarterly.* Vol. 76, No. 3 (September 1995):619–33.

KOHLBERG, LAWRENCE. *The Psychology of Moral Development: The Nature and Validity of Moral Stages.* New York: Harper & Row, 1981.

KOHLBERG, LAWRENCE, and CAROL GILLIGAN. "The Adolescent as Philosopher: The Discovery of Self in a Postconventional World." *Daedalus.* Vol. 100 (Fall 1971):1051–86.

KOHN, MELVIN L. *Class and Conformity: A Study in Values.* 2d ed. Homewood, Ill.: Dorsey Press, 1977.

KOHN, MELVIN L., and CARMI SCHOOLER. "Job Conditions and Personality: A Longitudinal Assessment of Their Reciprocal Effects." *American Journal of Sociology.* Vol. 87, No. 6 (May 1982):1257–83.

KOLATA, GINA. "When Grandmother Is the Mother, Until Birth." *New York Times* (August 5, 1991):1, 11.

KOMAROVSKY, MIRRA. *Blue Collar Marriage.* New York: Vintage Books, 1967.

———. "Cultural Contradictions and Sex Roles: The Masculine Case." *American Journal of Sociology.* Vol. 78, No. 4 (January 1973):873–84.

———. *Dilemmas of Masculinity: A Study of College Youth.* New York: Norton, 1976.

KORNHAUSER, WILLIAM. *The Politics of Mass Society.* New York: Free Press, 1959.

KOSTERS, MARVIN. "Looking for Jobs in All the Wrong Places." *The Public Interest.* Vol. 125 (Fall 1996):125–31.

KOWALEWSKI, DAVID, and KAREN L. PORTER. "Ecoprotest: Alienation, Deprivation, or Resources." *Social Sciences Quarterly.* Vol. 73, No. 3 (September 1992):523–34.

KOZOL, JONATHAN. *Prisoners of Silence: Breaking the Bonds of Adult Illiteracy in the United States.* New York: Continuum, 1980.

———. "A Nation's Wealth." *Publisher's Weekly* (May 24, 1985a):28–30.

———. *Illiterate America.* Garden City, N.Y.: Doubleday, 1985b.

———. *Rachel and Her Children: Homeless Families in America.* New York: Crown Publishers, 1988.

———. *Savage Inequalities: Children in America's Schools.* New York: Harper Perennial, 1992.

KRAFFT, SUSAN. "¿Quién es Numero Uno?" *American Demographics.* Vol. 15, No. 7 (July 1993):16–17.

KRAMARAE, CHERIS. *Women and Men Speaking.* Rowley, Mass.: Newbury House, 1981.

KRANTZ, MICHAEL. "Say It With a :-)." *Time.* Vol. 149, No. 15:29.

KRASKA, PETER B., and VICTOR E. KAPPELER. "Militarizing American Police: The Rise and Normalization of Paramilitary Units." *Social Problems.* Vol. 44, No. 1 (February 1997):1–18.

KRAYBILL, DONALD B. *The Riddle of Amish Culture.* Baltimore: Johns Hopkins University Press, 1989.

———. "The Amish Encounter With Modernity." In Donald B. Kraybill and Marc A. Olshan, eds., *The Amish Struggle With Modernity.* Hanover, N.H.: University Press of New England, 1994:21–33.

KRAYBILL, DONALD B., and MARC A. OLSHAN, EDS. *The Amish Struggle With Modernity.* Hanover, N.H.: University Press of New England, 1994.

KRIESI, HANSPETER. "New Social Movements and the New Class in the Netherlands." *American Journal of Sociology.* Vol. 94, No. 5 (March 1989):1078–116.

KRISBERG, BARRY, AND IRA SCHWARTZ. "Rethinking Juvenile Justice." *Crime and Delinquency.* Vol. 29, No. 3 (July 1983):333–64.

KRISTOF, NICHOLAS D. "Baby May Make Three, But in Japan, That's Not Enough." *New York Times* (October 6, 1996):A3.

KRISTOL, IRVING. "Life Without Father." *Wall Street Journal* (November 3, 1994):A18.

———. "Age Before Politics." *Wall Street Journal* (April 25, 1996):A20.

KÜBLER-ROSS, ELISABETH. *On Death and Dying.* New York: Macmillan, 1969.

KUHN, THOMAS. *The Structure of Scientific Revolutions.* 2d ed. Chicago: University of Chicago Press, 1970.

KUZNETS, SIMON. "Economic Growth and Income Inequality." *The American Economic Review.* Vol. XLV, No. 1 (March 1955):1–28.

———. *Modern Economic Growth: Rate, Structure, and Spread.* New Haven, Conn.: Yale University Press, 1966.

Labour Force Activity: The Nation. Ottawa: Statistics Canada, 1993.

Labour Force Annual Averages. Catalogue No. 71-529. Ottawa: Statistics Canada, 1981–88.

LABOVITZ, PRICISSA. "Immigration—Just the Facts." *New York Times* (March 25, 1996).

LACAYO, RICHARD. "Blood in the Stands." *Time.* Vol. 125, No. 23 (June 10, 1985):38–39, 41.

LADD, JOHN. "The Definition of Death and the Right to Die." In John Ladd, ed., *Ethical Issues Relating to Life and Death.* New York: Oxford University Press, 1979:118–45.

LADNER, JOYCE A. "Teenage Pregnancy: The Implications for Black Americans." In James D. Williams, ed., *The State of Black America 1986.* New York: National Urban League, 1986:65–84.

LAI, H. M. "Chinese." In *Harvard Encyclopedia of American Ethnic Groups.* Cambridge, Mass.: Harvard University Press, 1980:217–33.

LAMAR, JACOB V., JR. "Redefining the American Dilemma." *Time.* Vol. 126, No. 19 (November 11, 1985):33, 36.

LAMBERG-KARLOVSKY, C. C., and MARTHA LAMBERG-KARLOVSKY. "An Early City in Iran." In *Cities: Their Origin, Growth, and Human Impact.* San Francisco: Freeman, 1973:28–37.

LANDERS, ANN. Syndicated column: *Dallas Morning News* (July 8, 1984):4F.

LANDERS, RENE M. "Gender, Race, and the State Courts." *Radcliffe Quarterly.* Vol. 76, No. 4 (December 1990):6–9.

LANE, DAVID. "Social Stratification and Class." In Erik P. Hoffman and Robbin F. Laird, eds., *The Soviet Polity in the Modern Era.* New York: Aldine, 1984:563–605.

LANG, KURT, and GLADYS ENGEL LANG. *Collective Dynamics.* New York: Thomas Y. Crowell, 1961.

LAPPÉ, FRANCES MOORE, and JOSEPH COLLINS. *World Hunger: Twelve Myths.* New York: Grove Press/Food First Books, 1986.

LAPPÉ, FRANCES MOORE, JOSEPH COLLINS, and DAVID KINLEY. *Aid as Obstacle: Twenty Questions about Our Foreign Policy and the Hungry.* San Francisco: Institute for Food and Development Policy, 1981.

LAPRAIRIE, CAROL P. "Community Types, Crime and Police Services on Canadian Indian Reserves." *Journal of Research in Crime and Delinquency.* Vol. 25, No. 4 (1988): 375–91.

LARMER, BROOK. "Dead End Kids." *Newsweek* (May 25, 1992):38–40.

LASLETT, PETER. *The World We Have Lost: England Before the Industrial Age.* 3d ed. New York: Charles Scribner's Sons, 1984.

LATOUCHE, DANIEL. "Québec." In *The Canadian Encyclopedia.* 2d ed. Vol. 3. Edmonton: Hurtig Publishers, 1988:1793–1802.

LAUMANN, EDWARD O., JOHN H. GAGNON, ROBERT T. MICHAEL, and STUART MICHAELS. *The Social Organization of Sexuality: Sexual Practices in the United States.* Chicago: University of Chicago Press, 1994.

LAURENCE, MARGARET. *The Stone Angel.* Toronto: McClelland & Stewart, 1964.

LAW, BARBARA, ED. *Corpus Almanac and Canadian Sourcebook.* Don Mills: Southam Information and Technology Group, 1992.

LAXER, GORDON. *Open for Business: The Roots of Foreign Ownership in Canada.* Toronto: Oxford University Press, 1989.

LEACOCK, ELEANOR. "Women's Status in Egalitarian Societies: Implications for Social Evolution." *Current Anthropology.* Vol. 19, No. 2 (June 1978):247–75.

LEACOCK, STEPHEN. "My Financial Career." In Stephen Leacock, *The Best of Leacock.* Toronto: McClelland & Stewart, 1965.

LEAVITT, JUDITH WALZER. "Women and Health in America: An Overview." In Judith Walzer Leavitt, ed., *Women and Health in America.* Madison: University of Wisconsin Press, 1984:3–7.

LE BON, GUSTAVE. *The Crowd: A Study of the Popular Mind.* New York: Viking Press, 1960; orig. 1895.

LEE, BARRETT A., R. S. OROPESA, BARBARA J. METCH, and AVERY M. GUEST. "Testing the Decline of Community Thesis: Neighborhood Organization in Seattle, 1929 and 1979." *American Journal of Sociology.* Vol. 89, No. 5 (March 1984):1161–88.

LEE, SHARON M. "Poverty and the U.S. Asian Population." *Social Science Quarterly.* Vol. 75, No. 3 (September 1994):541–59.

LEERHSEN, CHARLES. "Unite and Conquer." *Newsweek* (February 5, 1990):50–55.

LEFEBVRE, HENRI. *The Production of Space.* Oxford: Blackwell, 1991.

LELAND, JOHN. "Bisexuality." *Newsweek* (July 17, 1995):44–49.

LEMERT, EDWIN M. *Social Pathology.* New York: McGraw-Hill, 1951.

———. *Human Deviance, Social Problems, and Social Control.* 2d ed. Englewood Cliffs, N.J.: Prentice Hall, 1972.

LENGERMANN, PATRICIA MADOO, and RUTH A. WALLACE. *Gender in America: Social Control and Social Change.* Englewood Cliffs, N.J.: Prentice Hall, 1985.

LENNON, MARY CLARE, and SARAH ROSENFELD. "Relative Fairness and the Doctrine of Housework: The Importance of Options." *American Journal of Sociology.* Vol. 100, No. 2 (September 1994):506–31.

LENSKI, GERHARD. *Power and Privilege: A Theory of Social Stratification.* New York: McGraw-Hill, 1966.

———. "Techniques of Child Discipline and Abuse by Parents." *Canadian Review of Sociology and Anthropology.* Vol. 27, No. 2 (1990):157-185.

LENSKI, GERHARD, PATRICK NOLAN, and JEAN LENSKI. *Human Societies: An Introduction to Macrosociology.* 7th ed. New York: McGraw-Hill, 1995.

LEONARD, EILEEN B. *Women, Crime, and Society: A Critique of Theoretical Criminology.* New York: Longman, 1982.

LERNER, DANIEL. *The Passing of Traditional Society: Modernizing the Middle East.* New York: Free Press, 1958.

LESLIE, GERALD R., and SHEILA K. KORMAN. *The Family in Social Context*. 7th ed. New York: Oxford University Press, 1989.

LESTER, DAVID. *The Death Penalty: Issues and Answers*. Springfield, Ill.: Charles C. Thomas, 1987.

LEVER, JANET. "Sex Differences in the Complexity of Children's Play and Games." *American Sociological Review*. Vol. 43, No. 4 (August 1978):471–83.

LEVIN, B. "Tuition Fees and University Accessibility." *Canadian Public Policy*. Vol. 16, No. 1 (March 1993).

LEVINE, DONALD N. *Georg Simmel: On Individuality and Social Forms*. Chicago: University of Chicago Press, 1971; orig. 1904:294–323.

LEVINE, MICHAEL. "Reducing Hostility Can Prevent Heart Disease." *Mount Vernon News* (August 7, 1990):4A.

LEVINE, MICHAEL P. *Student Eating Disorders: Anorexia Nervosa and Bulimia*. Washington, D.C.: National Educational Association, 1987.

LEVINE, ROBERT V. "Is Love a Luxury?" *American Demographics*. Vol. 15, No. 2 (February 1993):27–28.

LEVINSON, DANIEL J., with CHARLOTTE N. DARROW, EDWARD B. KLEIN, MARIA H. LEVINSON, and BRAXTON MCKEE. *The Seasons of a Man's Life*. New York: Alfred A. Knopf, 1978.

LEVITAN, SARA, and ISAAC SHAPIRO. *Working but Poor: America's Contradiction*. Baltimore: Johns Hopkins University Press, 1987.

LEVY, FRANK. *Dollars and Dreams: The Changing American Income Distribution*. New York: Russell Sage Foundation, 1987.

LEWIS, FLORA. "The Roots of Revolution." *New York Times Magazine* (November 11, 1984):70–71, 74, 77–78, 82, 84, 86.

LEWIS, OSCAR. *The Children of Sanchez*. New York: Random House, 1961.

LEWIS, PEIRCE, CASEY MCCRACKEN, and ROGER HUNT. "Politics: Who Cares?" *American Demographics*. Vol. 16, No. 10 (October 1994):20–26.

LEWTHWAITE, GILBERT A., and GREGORY KANE. "Bought and Freed." *Sun* (Baltimore: June 18, 1996):A1, A8.

LI, JIANG HONG, and ROGER A. WOJTKIEWICZ. "A New Look at the Effects of Family Structure on Status Attainment." *Social Science Quarterly*. Vol. 73, No. 3 (September 1992):581–95.

LI, PETER S. *Ethnic Inequality in a Class Society*. Toronto: Wall and Thompson, 1988.

LIAZOS, ALEXANDER. "The Poverty of the Sociology of Deviance: Nuts, Sluts and Preverts." *Social Problems*. Vol. 20, No. 1 (Summer 1972):103–20.

LICHTER, DANIEL R. "Race, Employment Hardship, and Inequality in the American Nonmetropolitan South." *American Sociological Review*. Vol. 54, No. 3 (June 1989):436–46.

LICHTER, S. ROBERT, STANLEY ROTHMAN, and LINDA R. ROTHMAN. *The Media Elite: America's New Powerbrokers*. Bethesda, Md.: Adler & Adler, 1986.

LICHTER, S. ROBERT, STANLEY ROTHMAN, and LINDA S. LICHTER. *The Media Elite: America's New Powerbrokers*. New York: Hastings House, 1990.

LIEBOW, ELLIOT. *Tally's Corner*. Boston: Little, Brown, 1967.

LIN, GE, and PETER ROGERSON. Research reported in Diane Crispell, "Sons and Daughters Who Keep in Touch." *American Demographics*. Vol. 16, No. 8 (August 1994):15–16.

LIN, NAN, and WEN XIE. "Occupational Prestige in Urban China." *American Journal of Sociology*. Vol. 93, No. 4 (January 1988):793–832.

LINDEN, EUGENE. "Can Animals Think?" *Time*. Vol. 141, No. 12 (March 22, 1993):54–61.

———. "More Power to Women, Fewer Mouths to Feed." *Time*. Vol. 144, No. 13 (September 26, 1994):64–65.

LINDSTROM, BONNIE. "Chicago's Post-Industrial Suburbs." *Sociological Focus*. Vol. 28, No. 4 (October 1995):399–412.

LING, PYAU. "Causes of Chinese Emigration." In Amy Tachiki et al., eds., *Roots: An Asian American Reader*. Los Angeles: UCLA Asian American Studies Center, 1971:134–38.

LINK, BRUCE G., BRUCE P. DOHRENWEND, and ANDREW E. SKODOL. "Socio-Economic Status and Schizophrenia: Noisome Occupational Characteristics As a Risk Factor." *American Sociological Review*. Vol. 51, No. 2 (April 1986):242–58.

LINN, MICHAEL. Noted in *Cornell Alumni News*. Vol. 99, No. 2 (September 1996):25.

LINTON, RALPH. "One Hundred Percent American." *The American Mercury*. Vol. 40, No. 160 (April 1937):427–29.

———. *The Study of Man*. New York: D. Appleton-Century, 1937.

LIPOVENKO, DOROTHY. 1996. "Golden handshakes launch new careers." *The Globe and Mail*. Monday Jan. 29:1, 6.

LIPSET, SEYMOUR MARTIN. *Political Man: The Social Bases of Politics*. Garden City, N.Y.: Anchor/Doubleday, 1963.

———. *Canada and the United States*. Charles F. Donan and John H. Sigler, eds., Englewood Cliffs, N.J.: Prentice Hall, 1985.

———. *Continental Divide: The Values and Institutions of the United States and Canada*. New York: Routledge, 1991.

LIPSET, SEYMOUR MARTIN, and REINHARD BENDIX. *Social Mobility in Industrial Society*. Berkeley: University of California Press, 1967.

LISKA, ALLEN E. *Perspectives on Deviance*. 3d ed. Englewood Cliffs, N.J.: Prentice Hall, 1991.

LISKA, ALLEN E., and MARK TAUSIG. "Theoretical Interpretations of Social Class and Racial Differentials in Legal Decision Making for Juveniles." *Sociological Quarterly*. Vol. 20, No. 2 (Spring 1979):197–207.

LISKA, ALLEN E., and BARBARA D. WARNER. "Functions of Crime: A Paradoxical Process." *American Journal of Sociology*. Vol. 96, No. 6 (May 1991):1441–63.

LITTMAN, DAVID L. "2001: A Farm Odyssey." *Wall Street Journal* (September 14, 1992):A10.

LIVINGSTONE, D.W. AND MEG LUXTON. "Gender Consciousness at Work: Modification of the Male Breadwinner Norm Among Steelworkers and Their Spouses." Pp. 172–200 in E.D. Nelson and B.W. Robinson (eds.), *Gender in the 1990s: Images, Realities, and Issues*. Scarborough, Ontario: Nelson Canada, 1995.

LO, CLARENCE Y. H. "Countermovements and Conservative Movements in the Contemporary U.S." *Annual Review of Sociology*. Vol. 8. Palo Alto, Calif.: Annual Reviews, 1982:107–34.

LOFLAND, LYN. *A World of Strangers*. New York: Basic Books, 1973.

LOGAN, JOHN R., and MARK SCHNEIDER. "Racial Segregation and Racial Change in American Suburbs, 1970–1980." *American Journal of Sociology*. Vol. 89, No. 4 (January 1984):874–88.

LOHR, STEVE. "British Health Service Faces a Crisis in Funds and Delays." *New York Times* (August 7, 1988):1, 12.

———. "Leashes Get Shorter for Executives." *New York Times* (July 18, 1997):D1, D6.

LONGINO, JR., CHARLES F. "Myths of An Aging America." *American Demographics*. Vol. 16, No. 8 (August 1994):36–42.

LORD, WALTER. *A Night to Remember*. Rev. ed. New York: Holt, Rinehart & Winston, 1976.

LORENZ, FREDERICK O., and BRENT T. BRUTON. "Experiments in Surveys: Linking Mass Class Questionnaires to Introductory Research Methods." *Teaching Sociology*. Vol. 24, No. 3 (July 1996):264–71.

LORENZ, KONRAD. *On Aggression*. New York: Harcourt, Brace & World, 1966.

LOY, PAMELA HEWITT, and LEA P. STEWART. "The Extent and Effects of Sexual Harassment of Working Women." *Sociological Focus*. Vol. 17, No. 1 (January 1984):31–43.

LUBENOW, GERALD C. "A Troubling Family Affair." *Newsweek* (May 14, 1984):34.

LUND, DALE A. "Conclusions about Bereavement in Later Life and Implications for Interventions and Future Research." In Dale A. Lund, ed., *Older Bereaved Spouses: Research With Practical Applications*. London: Taylor-Francis-Hemisphere, 1989:217–31.

LUND, DALE A., MICHAEL S. CASERTA, and MARGARET F. DIMOND. "Gender Differences Through Two Years of Bereavement Among the Elderly." *The Gerontologist*. Vol. 26, No. 3 (1986):314–20.

LUPRI, EUGENE. "Male Violence in the Home." In Craig McKie and K. Thompson, eds., Social Trends in Canada. Toronto: Thompson Educational Publishers, 1988:170–172.

LUTZ, CATHERINE A. *Unnatural Emotions: Everyday Sentiments on a Micronesia Atoll and Their Challenge to Western Theory*. Chicago: University of Chicago Press, 1988.

LUTZ, CATHERINE A., and GEOFFREY M. WHITE. "The Anthropology of Emotions." In Bernard J. Siegel, Alan R. Beals, and Stephen A. Tyler, eds., *Annual Review of Anthropology*. Palo Alto, Calif.: Annual Reviews, Vol. 15 (1986):405–36.

LUTZ, WILLIAM. Presented in "The Two Sides of Warspeak." *Time* (February 25, 1991):13.

LUXTON, MEG. *More Than a Labour of Love*. Toronto: Women's Press, 1980.

LYALL, SARAH AND ROBIN POGREBIN. "Desperately Seeking Diana." *The Globe and Mail* (September 11, 1997).

LYNCH, BARBARA DEUTSCH. "The Garden and the Sea: U.S. Latino Environment; Discourses and Mainstream Environmentalism." *Social Problems*. Vol. 40, No. 1 (February 1993):108–24.

LYNCH, GERALD. "Stephen Leacock." In *The Canadian Encyclopedia*. 2d ed. Vol. 2. Edmonton: Hurtig Publishers, 1988: 1192.

LYND, ROBERT S. *Knowledge For What? The Place of Social Science in American Culture*. Princeton, N.J.: Princeton University Press, 1967.

LYND, ROBERT S., and HELEN MERRELL LYND. *Middletown in Transition*. New York: Harcourt, Brace & World, 1937.

LYNOTT, PATRICIA PASSUTH, and BARBARA J. LOGUE. "The 'Hurried Child': The Myth of Lost Childhood on Contemporary American Society." *Sociological Forum*. Vol. 8, No. 3 (September 1993):471–91.

MA, LI-CHEN. Personal communication, 1987.

MABRY, MARCUS. "New Hope for Old Unions?" *Newsweek* (February 24, 1992):39.

MCADAM, DOUG. *Political Process and the Development of Black Insurgency, 1930–1970*. Chicago: University of Chicago Press, 1982.

———. "Tactical Innovation and the Pace of Insurgency." *American Sociological Review*. Vol. 48, No. 6 (December 1983):735–54.

———. *Freedom Summer*. New York: Oxford University Press, 1988.

———. "The Biographical Consequences of Activism." *American Sociological Review*. Vol. 54, No. 5 (October 1989):744–60.

———. "Gender as a Mediator of the Activist Experience: The Case of Freedom Summer." *American Journal of Sociology*. Vol. 97, No. 5 (March 1992):1211–40.

MCADAM, DOUG, JOHN D. MCCARTHY, and MAYER N. ZALD. "Social Movements." In Neil J. Smelser, ed., *Handbook of Sociology*. Newbury Park, Calif.: Sage, 1988:695–737.

McALL, CHRISTOPHER. *Class, Ethnicity and Social Inequality*. Montreal and Kingston: McGill-Queen's University Press, 1990.

McBROOM, WILLIAM H., and FRED W. REED. "Recent Trends in Conservatism: Evidence of Non-Unitary Patterns." *Sociological Focus*. Vol. 23, No. 4 (October 1990):355–65.

McCARTHY, JOHN D., and MAYER N. ZALD. "Resource Mobilization and Social Movements: A Partial Theory." *American Journal of Sociology*. Vol. 82, No. 6 (May 1977):1212–41.

MACCOBY, ELEANOR EMMONS, and CAROL NAGY JACKLIN. *The Psychology of Sex Differences*. Palo Alto, Calif.: Stanford University Press, 1974.

McCOLM, R. BRUCE, JAMES FINN, DOUGLAS W. PAYNE, JOSEPH E. RYAN, LEONARD R. SUSSMAN, and GEORGE ZARYCKY. *Freedom in the World: Political Rights & Civil Liberties, 1990–1991*. New York: Freedom House, 1991.

McCONNELL, SCOTT. "New Liberal Fear: Hyperdemocracy." *The New York Post* (January 18, 1995):19.

McDANIEL, SUSAN. "Emotional Support and Family Contacts of Older Canadians." In *Canadian Social Trends*, vol. 2, ed. Craig McKie and Keith Thompson, 129-32. Toronto: Thompson Educational Publishing, 1994.

MACDONALD, J. FRED. *Blacks and White TV: African Americans in Television Since 1948*. Chicago: Nelson-Hall, 1992.

McDONALD, LYNN. *The Women Founders of the Social Sciences*. Ottawa: Carleton University Press, 1994.

McDOUGALL, DEBORAH. "Gay politicians rise above stigma." *The Toronto Star* (August 2, 1997):L3.

MACE, DAVID, and VERA MACE. *Marriage East and West*. Garden City, N.Y.: Doubleday (Dolphin), 1960.

McGUIRE, MEREDITH B. *Religion: The Social Context*. 2d ed. Belmont, Calif.: Wadsworth, 1987.

McHENRY, SUSAN. "Rosabeth Moss Kanter." In *Ms*. Vol. 13 (January 1985):62–63, 107–8.

McILROY, ANNE. 1996. "Tough Reproductive Rules Proposed: Legislation Introduced in Commons Would Prohibit Selection of Baby's Sex, Sale of Eggs or Sperm." *The Globe and Mail* (June 15, 1996):A1, A4.

MACIONIS, JOHN J. "Intimacy: Structure and Process in Interpersonal Relationships." *Alternative Lifestyles*. Vol. 1, No. 1 (February 1978):113–30.

———. "The Search for Community in Modern Society: An Interpretation." *Qualitative Sociology*. Vol. 1, No. 2 (September 1978):130–43.

———. "A Sociological Analysis of Humor." Presentation to the Texas Junior College Teachers Association, Houston, 1987.

———. "Making Society (and, Increasingly, the World) Visible." In Earl Babbie, ed., *The Spirit of Sociology*. Belmont, Calif.: Wadsworth, 1993:221–24.

MACIONIS, JOHN J., and VINCENT R. PARRILLO. *Cities and Urban Life*. Upper Saddle River, N.J.: Prentice Hall, 1998.

MACKAY, DONALD G. "Prescriptive Grammar and the Pronoun Problem." In Barrie Thorne, Cheris Kramarae, and Nancy Henley, eds., *Language, Gender and Society*. Rowley, Mass.: Newbury House, 1983:38–53.

McKIE, CRAIG AND KEITH THOMPSON, EDS. *Canadian Social Trends*. Toronto: Thompson Educational Publishing, 1990.

———. *Canadian Social Trends: A Canadian Studies Reader*, vol. 2. Toronto: Thompson Educational Publishing, 1994.

MACKIE, MARLENE. "Ethnic Stereotypes and Prejudice: Alberta Indians, Hutterites and Ukrainians." *Canadian Ethnic Studies*. Vol. X (1974): 118–129.

———. *Exploring Gender Relations: A Canadian Perspective*. Toronto: Butterworths, 1983.

MACKINNON, CATHARINE A. *Feminism Unmodified: Discourses on Life and Law*. Cambridge, Mass.: Harvard University Press, 1987.

MACKLIN, ELEANOR D. "Nonmarital Heterosexual Cohabitation: An Overview." In Eleanor D. Macklin and Roger H. Rubin, eds., *Contemporary Families and Alternative Lifestyles: Handbook on Research and Theory*. Beverly Hills, Calif.: Sage, 1983:49–74.

McKUSICK, LEON, ET AL. "Reported Changes in the Sexual Behavior of Men at Risk for AIDS, San Francisco, 1982–84—The AIDS Behavioral Research Project." *Public Health Reports*. Vol. 100, No. 6 (November–December 1985):622–29.

McLANAHAN, SARA. "Family Structure and the Reproduction of Poverty." *American Journal of Sociology*. Vol. 90, No. 4 (January 1985):873–901.

McLEAN, STUART. *Welcome Home: Travels in Smalltown Canada*. Toronto: Viking, 1992.

McLEOD, JANE D., and MICHAEL J. SHANAHAN. "Poverty, Parenting, and Children's Mental Health." *American Sociological Review*. Vol. 58, No. 3 (June 1993):351–66.

McLEOD, JAY. *Ain't No Makin' It: Aspirations and Attainment in a Low-Income Neighborhood*. Boulder, Colo.: Westview Press, 1995.

McLUHAN, MARSHALL. *The Gutenberg Galaxy*. New York: New American Library, 1969.

McNEIL, DONALD G., JR. "Should Women Be Sent Into Combat?" *New York Times* (July 21, 1991):E3.

McNULTY, PAUL J. "Who's in Jail and Why They Belong There." *Wall Street Journal* (November 9, 1994):A23.

McPHAIL, CLARK. *The Myth of the Maddening Crowd*. New York: Aldine, 1991.

McPHAIL, CLARK, and RONALD T. WOHLSTEIN. "Individual and Collective Behaviors Within Gatherings, Demonstrations, and Riots." *Annual Review of Sociology*. Vol. 9. Palo Alto, Calif.: Annual Reviews, 1983:579–600.

McPHERSON, BARRY D. *Aging as a Social Process: An Introduction to Individual and Population Aging*. 2d ed. Toronto: Butterworths, 1990.

McRAE, SUSAN. *Cross-Class Families: A Study of Wives' Occupational Superiority*. New York: Oxford University Press, 1986.

McROBERTS, HUGH A., and KEVIN SELBEE. "Trends in Occupational Mobility in Canada and the United States: A Comparison." *American Sociological Review*. Vol. 46, No. 4 (August 1981):406–21.

MADDOX, SETMA. "Organizational Culture and Leadership Style: Factors Affecting Self-Managed Work Team Performance." Paper presented at the annual meeting of the Southwest Social Science Association, Dallas, February, 1995.

MADSEN, AXEL. *Private Power: Multinational Corporations for the Survival of Our Planet*. New York: William Morrow, 1980.

MAJKA, LINDA C. "Sexual Harassment in the Church." *Society*. Vol. 28. No. 4 (May-June 1991):14–21.

MALEY, DIANNE. "Canada's Top Women CEOs." *Maclean's* (October 20, 1997):52.

MALTHUS, THOMAS ROBERT. *First Essay on Population 1798*. London: Macmillan, 1926; orig. 1798.

MARCHAK, PATRICIA. *Ideological Perspectives on Canadian Society*. Toronto: McGraw Hill, 1975.

———. "The Rise and Fall of the Peripheral State: The Case of British Columbia." In Robert J. Brym, ed., *Regionalism in Canada*. Toronto: Irwin, 1986:123–160.

MARCUSE, HERBERT. *One-Dimensional Man*. Boston: Beacon Press, 1964.

MARE, ROBERT D. "Change and Stability in Educational Stratification." *American Sociological Review*. Vol. 46, No. 1 (February 1981):72–87.

———. "Five Decades of Educational Assortative Mating." *American Sociological Review*. Vol. 56, No. 1 (February 1991):15–32.

MARGOLICK, DAVID. "Rape in Marriage Is No Longer Within the Law." *New York Times* (December 13, 1984):6E.

MARÍN, GERARDO, and BARBARA VANOSS MARÍN. *Research With Hispanic Populations*. Newbury Park, Calif.: Sage, 1991.

MARKOFF, JOHN. "Remember Big Brother? Now He's a Company Man." *New York Times* (March 31, 1991):7.

MARKSON, ELIZABETH W. "Moral Dilemmas." *Society*. Vol. 29, No. 5 (July-August 1992):4–6.

MARLIOS, PETER. "Interlocking Directorates and the Control of Corporations: The Theory of Bank Control." *Social Science Quarterly*. Vol. 56, No. 3 (December 1975):425–39.

MARQUAND, ROBERT. "Worship Shift: Americans Seek Feeling of 'Awe'." *Christian Science Monitor* (May 28, 1997):1, 8.

MARQUAND, ROBERT, and DANIEL B. WOOD. "Rise in Cults as Millennium Approaches." *Christian Science Monitor* (March 28, 1997):1, 18.

MARRIOTT, MICHAEL. "Fathers Find that Child Support Means Owing More than Money." *New York Times* (July 20, 1992):A1, A13.

MARSDEN, LORNA R. AND EDWARD B. HARVEY. *Fragile Federation: Social Change in Canada*. Toronto: McGraw-Hill Ryerson, 1979.

MARSDEN, PETER. "Core Discussion Networks of Americans." *American Sociological Review*. Vol. 52, No. 1 (February 1987):122–31.

MARSHALL, SUSAN E. "Ladies Against Women: Mobilization Dilemmas of Antifeminist Movements." *Social Problems*. Vol. 32, No. 4 (April 1985):348–62.

MARTIN, DOUGLAS. "The Medicine Woman of the Mohegans." *New York Times* (June 4, 1997):B1, B7.

MARTIN, JOHN M., and ANNE T. ROMANO. *Multinational Crime: Terrorism, Espionage, Drug and Arms Trafficking*. Newbury Park, Calif.: Sage, 1992.

MARTIN, RICHARD C. *Islam: A Cultural Perspective*. Englewood Cliffs, N.J.: Prentice Hall, 1982.

MARTIN, WILLIAM. "The Birth of a Media Myth." *The Atlantic*. Vol. 247, No. 6 (June 1981):7, 10, 11, 16.

MARTINEAU, HARRIET. *How to Observe Morals and Manners*. London: Knight, 1838.

MARTINEZ, VALERIE J., R. KENNETH GODWIN, FRANK R. KEMERER, and LAURA PERNA. "The Consequences of School Choice: Who Leaves and Who Stays in the Inner City." *Social Science Quarterly*. Vol. 76, No. 1 (September 1995):485–501.

MARULLO, SAM. "The Functions and Dysfunctions of Preparations for Fighting Nuclear War." *Sociological Focus*. Vol. 20, No. 2 (April 1987):135–53.

MARX, GARY T., and JAMES L. WOOD. "Strands of Theory and Research in Collective Behavior." In Alex Inkeles et al., eds., *Annual Review of Sociology*. Vol. 1. Palo Alto, Calif.: Annual Reviews, 1975:363–428.

MARX, KARL. Excerpt from "A Contribution to the Critique of Political Economy." In Karl Marx and Friedrich Engels, *Marx and Engels: Basic Writings on Politics and Philosophy*. Lewis S. Feurer, ed. Garden City, N.Y.: Anchor Books, 1959:42–46.

———. *Karl Marx: Early Writings*. T. B. Bottomore, ed. New York: McGraw-Hill, 1964a.

———. *Karl Marx: Selected Writings in Sociology and Social Philosophy*. T. B. Bottomore, trans. New York: McGraw-Hill, 1964.

———. *Capital*. Friedrich Engels, ed. New York: International Publishers, 1967; orig. 1867.

———. "Theses on Feuer." In Robert C. Tucker, ed., *The Marx-Engels Reader*. New York: Norton, 1972:107–9; orig. 1845.

MARX, KARL, and FRIEDRICH ENGELS. "Manifesto of the Communist Party." In Robert C. Tucker, ed., *The Marx-Engels Reader*. New York: Norton, 1972:331–62; orig. 1848.

———. *The Marx-Engels Reader*. Robert C. Tucker, ed. New York: Norton, 1977.

MARX, LEO. "The Environment and the 'Two Cultures' Divide." In James Rodger Fleming and Henry A. Gemery, eds., *Science, Technology, and the Environment: Multidisciplinary Perspectives*. Akron, Ohio: University of Akron Press, 1994:3–21.

MASSEY, DOUGLAS S. Review of *The Bell Curve: Intelligence and Class Structure in American Life* by Richard J. Herrnstein and Charles Murray. *American Journal of Sociology*. Vol. 101, No. 3 (November 1995):747–53.

MASSEY, DOUGLAS S., and NANCY A. DENTON. "Hypersegregation in U.S. Metropolitan Areas: Black and Hispanic Segregation Along Five Dimensions." *Demography*. Vol. 26, No. 3 (August 1989):373–91.

MASTERS, WILLIAM H., VIRGINIA E. JOHNSON, and ROBERT C. KOLODNY. *Human Sexuality*. 3d ed. Glenview, Ill.: Scott, Foresman/Little, Brown, 1988.

MATAS, ROBERT. "B.C. gay parents gain equality." *The Globe and Mail* (February 5, 1998):A1.

MATTHEWS, RALPH. *"There's No Better Place Than Here": Social Change in Three Newfoundland Communities*. Toronto: Peter Martin Associates, 1976.

———. *The Creation of Regional Dependency*. Toronto: University of Toronto Press, 1983.

MATTHIESSEN, PETER. *In the Spirit of Crazy Horse*. New York: Viking Press, 1983.

———. *Indian Country*. New York: Viking Press, 1984.

MAUER, MARC. *Americans Behind Bars: The International Use of Incarceration, 1992–1993*. Washington, D.C.: The Sentencing Project, 1994.

MAURO, TONY. "Cruzan's Struggle Left Imprint: Private Case Triggered Public Debate." *USA Today* (December 27, 1990):3A.

MAURO, TONY. "Ruling Likely Will Add Fuel to Already Divisive Debate." *USA Today* (January 7, 1997):1A, 2A.

MAUSS, ARMAND L. *Social Problems of Social Movements*. Philadelphia: Lippincott, 1975.

MAXWELL, MARY PERCIVAL, AND JAMES D. MAXWELL. "Three Decades of Private School Females' Ambitions: Implications for Canadian Elites." *Canadian Review of Sociology and Anthropology*. Vol. 31, No. 2 (1994):139-68.

MAY, ELAINE TYLER. "Women in the Wild Blue Yonder." *New York Times* (August 7, 1991):21.

MAYO, KATHERINE. *Mother India*. New York: Harcourt, Brace, 1927.

MEAD, GEORGE HERBERT. *Mind, Self, and Society*. Charles W. Morris, ed. Chicago: University of Chicago Press, 1962; orig. 1934.

MEAD, MARGARET. *Coming of Age in Samoa*. New York: Dell, 1961; orig. 1928.

———. *Sex and Temperament in Three Primitive Societies*. New York: William Morrow, 1963; orig. 1935.

MEADOWS, DONELLA H., DENNIS L. MEADOWS, JORGAN RANDERS, and WILLIAM W. BEHRENS, III. *The Limits to Growth: A Report on the Club of Rome's Project on the Predicament of Mankind*. New York: Universe, 1972.

MEISEL, J. *Working Papers on Canadian Politics*. Montreal: McGill-Queen's University Press, 1975.

MELTZER, BERNARD N. "Mead's Social Psychology." In Jerome G. Manis and Bernard N. Meltzer, eds., *Symbolic Interaction: A Reader in Social Psychology*. 3d ed. Needham Heights, Mass.: Allyn & Bacon, 1978.

MELUCCI, ALBERTO. "The New Social Movements: A Theoretical Approach." *Social Science Information*. Vol. 19, No. 2 (May 1980):199–226.

———. *Nomads of the Present: Social Movements and Individual Needs in Contemporary Society*. Philadelphia: Temple University Press, 1989.

MERGENBAGEN, PAULA. "Rethinking Retirement." *American Demographics*. Vol. 16, No. 6 (June 1994):28–34.

———. "Sun City Gets Boomerized." *American Demographics*. Vol. 18, No. 8 (August 1996):16–20.

MERRIT, SUSAN E. *Her Story: Women from Canada's Past*. St. Catharines, Ontario: Vanwell Publishing, 1993.

MERTON, ROBERT K. "Social Structure and Anomie." *American Sociological Review*. Vol. 3, No. 6 (October 1938):672–82.

———. *Social Theory and Social Structure*. New York: Free Press, 1968.

———. "Discrimination and the American Creed." In *Sociological Ambivalence and Other Essays*. New York: Free Press, 1976:189–216.

MEYER, DAVIS S. and NANCY WHITTIER. "Social Movement Spillover." *Social Problems*. Vol. 41, No. 2 (May 1994):277–98.

MEYER, DAVID S., and SUZANNE STAGGENBORG. "Movements, Countermovements, and the Structure of Political Opportunity." *American Journal of Sociology*. Vol. 101, No. 6 (May 1996):1628–60.

MEYROWITZ, JOSHUA, and JOHN MAGUIRE. "Media, Place, and Multiculturalism." *Society*. Vol. 30, No. 5 (July-August 1993):41–48.

MICHELS, ROBERT. *Political Parties*. Glencoe, Ill.: Free Press, 1949; orig. 1911.

MICHELSON, WILLIAM. "Urbanization and Urbanism." In James Curtis and Lorne Tepperman, eds., *Understanding Canadian Society*. Toronto: McGraw-Hill Ryerson, 1988: 73–104.

MILBRATH, LESTER W. *Envisioning A Sustainable Society: Learning Our Way Out*. Albany: State University of New York Press, 1989.

MILGRAM, STANLEY. "Behavioral Study of Obedience." *Journal of Abnormal and Social Psychology*. Vol. 67, No. 4 (1963):371–78.

———. "Group Pressure and Action Against a Person." *Journal of Abnormal and Social Psychology*. Vol. 69, No. 2 (August 1964):137–43.

———. "Some Conditions of Obedience and Disobedience to Authority." *Human Relations*. Vol. 18 (February 1965):57–76.

MILIBAND, RALPH. *The State in Capitalist Society*. London: Weidenfeld and Nicolson, 1969.

MILLER, ARTHUR G. *The Obedience Experiments: A Case of Controversy in Social Science*. New York: Praeger, 1986.

MILLER, BERNA. "The Quest for Lifelong Learning." *American Demographics*. Vol. 19, No. 3 (March 1997):20, 22.

———. "Population Update for April." *American Demographics*. Vol. 19, No. 4 (April 1997):18.

MILLER, DAVID L. *Introduction to Collective Behavior*. Belmont, Calif.: Wadsworth, 1985.

MILLER, FREDERICK D. "The End of SDS and the Emergence of Weatherman: Demise Through Success." In Jo Freeman, ed., *Social Movements of the Sixties and Seventies*. New York: Longman, 1983:279–97.

MILLER, G. TYLER, JR. *Living in the Environment: An Introduction to Environmental Science*. Belmont, Calif.: Wadsworth, 1992.

MILLER, MARK. "Under Cover, In the Closet." *Newsweek* (January 14, 1991):25.

MILLER, MICHAEL. "Lawmakers Begin to Heed Calls to Protect Privacy." *Wall Street Journal* (April 11, 1991):A16.

MILLER, WALTER B. "Lower Class Culture as a Generating Milieu of Gang Delinquency." In Marvin E. Wolfgang, Leonard Savitz, and Norman Johnston, eds., *The Sociology of Crime and Delinquency*. 2d ed. New York: Wiley, 1970:351–63; orig. 1958.

MILLET, KATE. *Sexual Politics*. Garden City, N.Y.: Doubleday, 1970.

MILLMAN, JOEL, NINA MUNK, MICHAEL SCHUMAN, and NEIL WEINBERG. "The World's Wealthiest People." *Forbes*. Vol. 152, No. 1 (July 5, 1993):66–69.

MILLS, C. WRIGHT. *White Collar: The American Middle Classes*. New York: Oxford University Press, 1951.

———. *The Power Elite*. New York: Oxford University Press, 1956.

———. *The Sociological Imagination*. New York: Oxford University Press, 1959.

MINK, BARBARA. "How Modernization Affects Women." *Cornell Alumni News*. Vol. III, No. 3 (April 1989):10–11.

MINTZ, BETH, and MICHAEL SCHWARTZ. "Interlocking Directorates and Interest Group Formation." *American Sociological Review*. Vol. 46, No. 6 (December 1981):851–69.

MIROWSKY, JOHN. "The Psycho-Economics of Feeling Underpaid: Distributive Justice and the Earnings of Husbands and Wives." *American Journal of Sociology*. Vol. 92, No. 6 (May 1987):1404–34.

MIROWSKY, JOHN, and CATHERINE ROSS. "Working Wives and Mental Health." Presentation to the American Association for the Advancement of Science, New York, 1984.

———. *The Social Causes of Psychological Distress*. Hawthorne, N.Y.: Aldine, 1989.

MITCHELL, ALANNA. "Greying of Canada oversold notion." *The Globe and Mail* (July 30, 1997):A4.

———. "More children running away younger, Statscan says." *The Globe and Mail* (February 13, 1998):A3.

Mittelstaedt, Martin. "Change unavoidable for Ontario Hydro." *The Globe and Mail* (August 18, 1997):A1.

MOGELONSKY, MARCIA. "Reconfiguring the American Dream (House)." *American Demographics*. Vol. 19, No. 1 (January 1997):31–35.

MOLM, LINDA D. "Risk and Power Use: Constraints on the Use of Coercion in Exchange." *American Sociological Review*. Vol. 62, No. 1 (February 1997):113–33.

MOLOTCH, HARVEY. "The City as a Growth Machine." *American Journal of Sociology*. Vol. 82, No. 2 (September 1976):309–33.

MONEY, JOHN, and ANKE A. EHRHARDT. *Man and Woman, Boy and Girl*. New York: New American Library, 1972.

MONK-TURNER, ELIZABETH. "The Occupational Achievement of Community and Four-Year College Graduates." *American Sociological Review*. Vol. 55, No. 5 (October 1990):719–25.

MONSEBRAATEN, LAURIE. "Stuggling On in Wake of Cuts." *Toronto Star* (May 5, 1996): F6.

MONTAGU, ASHLEY. *The Nature of Human Aggression*. New York: Oxford University Press, 1976.

MONTGOMERY, LUCY MAUD. *Anne of Green Gables*. Toronto: Seal Books, 1976; orig. 1908.

MONTIGNY, GILLES. "Reading Skills." Pp. 111–19 in *Canadian Social Trends: A Canadian Studies Reader*, vol. 2, ed. Craig McKie and Keith Thompson. Toronto: Thompson Educatinal Publishing, 1994.

MONTREAL GAZETTE. "Tobacco Production Edges Up." January 25, 1992:PE1.

MOODY, JOHN. "Safe? You Bet Your Life." *Time*. Vol. 126, No. 24 (July 24, 1995):35.

MOORE, GWEN. "The Structure of a National Elite Network." *American Sociological Review*. Vol. 44, No. 5 (October 1979):673–92.

———. "Structural Determinants of Men's and Women's Personal Networks." *American Sociological Review*. Vol. 55, No. 5 (October 1991):726–35.

———. "Gender and Informal Networks in State Government." *Social Science Quarterly*. Vol. 73, No. 1 (March 1992):46–61.

MOORE, JOAN, and HARRY PACHON. *Hispanics in the United States*. Englewood Cliffs, N.J.: Prentice Hall, 1985.

MOORE, MIKE. "14 Minutes to Nuclear Midnight." *Chronicle of Higher Education.* Vol. XLII, No. 30 (April 5, 1996):A52.

MOORE, WILBERT E. "Modernization as Rationalization: Processes and Restraints." In Manning Nash, ed., *Essays on Economic Development and Cultural Change in Honor of Bert F. Hoselitz.* Chicago: University of Chicago Press, 1977:29–42.

———. *World Modernization: The Limits of Convergence.* New York: Elsevier, 1979.

MORAN, JOHN S., S. O. ARAL, W. C. JENKINS, T. A. PETERMAN, and E. R. ALEXANDER. "The Impact of Sexually Transmitted Diseases on Minority Populations." *Public Health Reports.* Vol. 104, No. 6 (November-December 1989):560–65.

MORRIS, ALDON. "Black Southern Sit-in Movement: An Analysis of Internal Organization." *American Sociological Review.* Vol. 46, No. 6 (December 1981):744–67.

MORRISON, DENTON E. "Some Notes Toward Theory on Relative Deprivation, Social Movements, and Social Change." In Louis E. Genevie, ed., *Collective Behavior and Social Movements.* Itasca, Ill.: Peacock, 1978:202–9.

MORROW, LANCE. "The Temping of America." *Time.* Vol. 131, No. 14 (March 29, 1993):40–41.

MORTON, JACKSON. "Census on the Internet." *American Demographics.* Vol. 17, No. 3 (March 1995):52–53.

MOSKOS, CHARLES C. "Female GIs in the Field." *Society.* Vol. 22, No. 6 (September-October 1985):28–33.

MOSLEY, W. HENRY, and PETER COWLEY. "The Challenge of World Health." *Population Bulletin.* Vol. 46, No. 4 (December 1991). Washington, D.C.: Population Reference Bureau.

MOTTAZ, CLIFFORD J. "Some Determinants of Work Alienation." *The Sociological Quarterly.* Vol. 22, No. 4 (Autumn 1981):515–29.

MOYNIHAN, DANIEL PATRICK. *The Negro Family: The Case for National Action.* Washington, D.C.: U.S. Department of Labor, 1965.

———. "Toward a New Intolerance." *The Public Interest.* No. 112 (Summer 1993):119–22.

MUELLER, DANIEL P., and PHILIP W. COOPER. "Children of Single Parent Families: How Do They Fare as Young Adults?" Presentation to the American Sociological Association, San Antonio, Texas, 1984.

MUFSON, STEVEN. "China's Growing Inequality." *Washington Post* (January 1, 1997):A1, A26–A27.

MULLER, EDWARD N. *Aggressive Political Participation.* Princeton, N.J.: Princeton University Press, 1979.

MUMFORD, LEWIS. *The City in History: Its Origins, Its Transformations, and Its Prospects.* New York: Harcourt, Brace & World, 1961.

MURDOCK, GEORGE PETER. "Comparative Data on the Division of Labor by Sex." *Social Forces.* Vol. 15, No. 4 (May 1937):551–53.

———. "The Common Denominator of Cultures." In Ralph Linton, ed., *The Science of Man in World Crisis.* New York: Columbia University Press, 1945:123–42.

———. *Social Structure.* New York: Free Press, 1965; orig. 1949.

MURRAY, CHARLES. *Losing Ground: American Social Policy 1950–1980.* New York: Basic Books, 1984.

———. "Keeping Priorities Straight on Welfare Reform." *Society.* Vol. 33, No. 5 (July/August 1996):10–12.

MURRAY, MEGAN BALDRIDGE. "Innovation Without Geniuses." In *Yale Alumni Magazine and Journal.* Vol. XLVII, No. 6 (April 1984):40–43.

MURRAY, PAULI. *Proud Shoes: The History of an American Family.* New York: Harper & Row, 1978.

MYERS, NORMAN. "Humanity's Growth." In Sir Edmund Hillary, ed., *Ecology 2000: The Changing Face of the Earth.* New York: Beaufort Books, 1984a:16–35.

———. "The Mega-Extinction of Animals and Plants." In Sir Edmund Hillary, ed., *Ecology 2000: The Changing Face of the Earth.* New York: Beaufort Books, 1984b:82–107.

———. "Disappearing Cultures." In Sir Edmund Hillary, ed., *Ecology 2000: The Changing Face of the Earth.* New York: Beaufort Books, 1984c:162–69.

———. "Biological Diversity and Global Security." In F. Herbert Bormann and Stephen R. Kellert, eds., *Ecology, Economics, and Ethics: The Broken Circle.* New Haven, Conn.: Yale University Press, 1991:11–25.

MYERS, SHEILA, and HAROLD G. GRASMICK. "The Social Rights and Responsibilities of Pregnant Women: An Application of Parsons' Sick Role Model." Paper presented to Southwestern Sociological Association, Little Rock, Arkansas, March 1989.

NADER, RALPH, NADIA MILLERON AND DUFF CONACHER. *Canada Firsts.* Toronto: McClelland & Stewart, 1992.

NAGEL, JOANE. "Constructing Ethnicity: Creating and Recreating Ethnic Identity and Culture." *Social Problems.* Vol. 41, No. 1 (February 1994):152–76.

———. *American Indian Ethnic Renewal: Red Power and the Resurgence of Identity and Culture.* New York: Oxford University Press, 1996.

NAJAFIZADEH, MEHRANGIZ, and LEWIS A. MENNERICK. "Sociology of Education or Sociology of Ethnocentrism: The Portrayal of Education in Introductory Sociology Textbooks." *Teaching Sociology.* Vol. 20, No. 3 (July 1992):215–21.

NASH, J. MADELEINE. "To Know Your Own Fate." *Time.* Vol. 145, No. 14 (April 3, 1995):62.

NATIONAL CENTER FOR EDUCATION STATISTICS. *Digest of Education Statistics: 1991.* Washington, D.C.: U.S. Government Printing Office, 1992.

———. *Digest of Education Statistics: 1994.* Washington, D.C.: U.S. Government Printing Office, 1995.

NATIONAL CENTER FOR HEALTH STATISTICS. *Monthly Vital Statistics Report.* Vol. 44, No. 4 (April 1995). Washington, D.C.: U.S. Government Printing Office.

NATIONAL COMMISSION ON EXCELLENCE IN EDUCATION. *A Nation at Risk.* Washington, D.C.: U.S. Government Printing Office, 1983.

NATIONAL COUNCIL OF WELFARE. *Women and Poverty Revisited.* Ottawa: Supply and Services, 1990.

NAVARRO, VICENTE. "The Industrialization of Fetishism or the Fetishism of Industrialization: A Critique of Ivan Illich." In Vicente Navarro, ed., *Health and Medical Care in the U.S.: A Critical Analysis.* Farmingdale, N.Y.: Baywood Publishing Co., 1977:38–58.

NAWAZ, MOHAMED. *Potsmoking and Illegal Conduct: Understanding the Social World of University Students.* Canada: Diliton Publications, 1978.

NEIDERT, LISA J., and REYNOLDS FARLEY. "Assimilation in the United States: An Analysis of Ethnic and Generation Differences in Status and Achievement." *American Sociological Review.* Vol. 50, No. 6 (December 1985):840–50.

NEILL, SHIRLEY. "Unionization in Canada." In Craig McKie and Keith Thompson, eds., *Canadian Social Trends.* Toronto: Thompson Educational Publishing, 1990.

NELAN, BRUCE W. "Crimes Without Punishment." *Time.* Vol. 141, No. 2 (January 11, 1993):21.

NELSON, JOEL I. "Work and Benefits: The Multiple Problems of Service Sector Employment." *Social Problems.* Vol. 42, No. 2 (May 1994):240–55.

NEMETH, MARY. "God is Alive." *Maclean's* (April 12, 1993).

NETT, EMILY M. *Canadian Families: Past and Present.* 2d ed. Toronto: Butterworths, 1993.

NEUGARTEN, BERNICE L. "Grow Old with Me. The Best Is Yet to Be." *Psychology Today.* Vol. 5 (December 1971):45–48, 79, 81.

———. "Personality and the Aging Process." *The Gerontologist.* Vol. 12, No. 1 (Spring 1972):9–15.

———. "Personality and Aging." In James E. Birren and K. Warner Schaie, eds., *Handbook of the Psychology of Aging.* New York: Van Nostrand Reinhold, 1977:626–49.

NEUHOUSER, KEVIN. "The Radicalization of the Brazilian Catholic Church in Comparative Perspective." *American Sociological Review.* Vol. 54, No. 2 (April 1989):233–44.

NEVITTE, NEIL. *The Decline of Deference.* Peterborough, Ontario: Broadview Press, 1996.

NEW HAVEN JOURNAL-COURIER. "English Social Structure Changing." November 27, 1986.

NEWMAN, JAMES L., and GORDON E. MATZKE. *Population: Patterns, Dynamics, and Prospects.* Englewood Cliffs, N.J.: Prentice Hall, 1984.

NEWMAN, KATHERINE S. *Declining Fortunes: The Withering of the American Dream.* New York: Basic Books, 1993.

NEWMAN, PETER C. *The Canadian Revolution: From Deference to Defiance.* Toronto: Penguin Books, 1996.

NEWMAN, WILLIAM M. *American Pluralism: A Study of Minority Groups and Social Theory.* New York: Harper & Row, 1973.

NIELSEN, FRANCOIS, and ARTHUR S. ALDERSON. "The Kuznets Curve: The Great U-Turn: Income Inequality in U.S. Counties, 1970 to 1990." *American Sociological Review.* Vol. 62, No. 1 (February 1997):12–33.

NIELSEN, JOYCE MCCARL, ED. *Feminist Research Methods: Exemplary Readings in the Social Sciences.* Boulder, Colo.: Westview Press, 1990.

NIN.DA.WAAB.JIG, WALPOLE ISLAND HERITAGE CENTRE. "Walpole Island in 2005: A View from the Future." Pp. 186–96 in Diane Engelstad and John Bird (eds.), *Nation to Nation: Aboriginal Sovereignty and the Future of Canada.* Concord, Ontario: House of Anansi Press, 1992.

1991 Green Book. U.S. House of Representatives. Washington, D.C.: U.S. Government Printing Office, 1991.

NISBET, ROBERT A. *The Sociological Tradition.* New York: Basic Books, 1966.

———. *The Quest for Community.* New York: Oxford University Press, 1969.

———. "Sociology as an Art Form." In *Tradition and Revolt: Historical and Sociological Essays.* New York: Vintage Books, 1970.

NOCH, D. A. "Religion." In K. Ishwaran, ed., *Sociology: An Introduction.* Don Mills, Ont.: Addison-Wesley, 1986.

NOLAN, JAMES L., JR., ed. *The American Culture Wars: Current Contests and Future Prospects.* Charlottesville, Va.: University Press of Virginia, 1996.

NORBECK, EDWARD. "Class Structure." In *Kodansha Encyclopedia of Japan.* Tokyo: Kodansha, 1983:322–25.

NORC. *General Social Surveys, 1972–1991: Cumulative Codebook.* Chicago: National Opinion Research Center, 1991.

———. *General Social Surveys, 1972–1992: Cumulative Codebook.* Chicago: National Opinion Research Center, 1992.

———. *General Social Surveys, 1972–1994: Cumulative Codebook.* University of Chicago: National Opinion Research Center, 1994.

———. *General Social Surveys, 1972–1996: Cumulative Codebook.* Chicago: National Opinion Research Center, 1996.

———. *GSS News* (August 1997):3.

NORDHEIMER, JON. "Downsized, But Not Out: A Mill Town's Tale." *New York Times* (March 9, 1997): section 3, pp. 1, 12, 13.

NORTON, PHILLIP Jackrabbit Johannsen: The pioneer of Skiing in Canada." *Canadian Geographic* (April/May 1997):18–23.

NUNN, CLYDE Z., HARRY J. CROCKETT, JR., and J. ALLEN WILLIAMS, JR. *Tolerance for Nonconformity*. San Francisco: Jossey-Bass, 1978.

OAKES, JEANNIE. "Classroom Social Relationships: Exploring the Bowles and Gintis Hypothesis." *Sociology of Education*. Vol. 55, No. 4 (October 1982):197–212.

———. *Keeping Track: How High Schools Structure Inequality*. New Haven, Conn.: Yale University Press, 1985.

OBERSCHALL, ANTHONY. *Social Conflict and Social Movements*. Englewood Cliffs, N.J.: Prentice Hall, 1973.

O'BRIEN, DAVID J., EDWARD W. HASSINGER, and LARRY DERSHEM. "Size of Place, Residential Stability, and Personal Social Networks." *Sociological Focus*. Vol. 29, No. 1 (February 1996):61–72.

O'BRIEN, MARY. *The Politics of Reproduction*. Boston: Routledge and Kegan Paul, 1981.

O'CONNOR, RORY J. "Internet Declared Protected Speech." *Post-Star* (Glens Fall, N.Y.: June 27, 1997):A1–A2.

O'DEA, THOMAS F., and JANET O'DEA AVIAD. *The Sociology of Religion*. 2d ed. Englewood Cliffs, N.J.: Prentice Hall, 1983.

ODERKIRK, JILLIAN. "Education Achievement: An International Comparison." *Canadian Social Trends* (Autumn 1993): 8-12.

OFFIR, CAROLE WADE. *Human Sexuality*. New York: Harcourt Brace Jovanovich, 1982.

OGBURN, WILLIAM F. *On Culture and Social Change*. Chicago: University of Chicago Press, 1964.

O'HARE, WILLIAM P. "In the Black." *American Demographics*. Vol. 11, No. 11 (November 1989):25–29.

———. "The Rise of Hispanic Affluence." *American Demographics*. Vol. 12, No. 8 (August 1990):40–43.

O'HARE, WILLIAM P., WILLIAM H. FREY, and DAN FOST. "Asians in the Suburbs." *American Demographics*. Vol. 16, No. 9 (May 1994):32–38.

OLSEN, GREGG M. "Re-Modeling Sweden: The Rise and Demise of the Compromise in a Global Economy." *Social Problems*. Vol. 43, No. 1 (February 1996):1–20.

OLSEN, LAWRENCE. *Costs of Children*. Toronto: D.C. Heath and Company, 1983.

OLSEN, MARVIN E., DORA G. LODWICK, and RILEY E. DUNLAP. *Viewing the World Ecologically*. Boulder, Colo.: Westview Press, 1992.

OLZAK, SUSAN. "Labor Unrest, Immigration, and Ethnic Conflict in Urban America, 1880–1914." *American Journal of Sociology*. Vol. 94, No. 6 (May 1989):1303–33.

OLZAK, SUSAN, and ELIZABETH WEST. "Ethnic Conflict and the Rise and Fall of Ethnic Newspapers." *American Sociological Review*. Vol. 56, No. 4 (August 1991):458–74.

ORBACH, S. *Fat Is a Feminist Issue*. New York: Berkeley Books, 1979.

———. *Hunger Strike: The Anorectic's Struggle as a Metaphor for our Age*. New York: Norton, 1986.

O'REILLY, JANE. "Wife Beating: The Silent Crime." *Time*. Vol. 122, No. 10 (September 5, 1983):23–24, 26.

ORLANSKY, MICHAEL D., and WILLIAM L. HEWARD. *Voices: Interviews With Handicapped People*. Columbus, Ohio: Merrill, 1981:85, 92, 133–34, 172.

ORNSTEIN, MICHAEL. "Aspects of the Political and Personal Sociology of AIDS: Knowledge, Policy Attitudes and Risk." *Canadian Review of Sociology and Anthropology*. Vol. 29, No. 3 (1992):243–65.

ORSHANSKY, MOLLIE. "How Poverty Is Measured." *Monthly Labor Review*. Vol. 92, No. 2 (February 1969):37–41.

ORWIN, CLIFFORD. "All Quiet on the Western Front?" *The Public Interest*. Vol. 123 (Spring 1996): 3–9.

OSGOOD, D. WAYNE, JANET K. WILSON, PATRICK M. O'MALLEY, JERALD G. BACHMAN, and LLOYD D. JOHNSTON. "Routine Activities and Individual Deviant Behavior." *American Sociological Review*. Vol. 61, No. 4 (August 1996):635–55.

OSSENBERG, RICHARD J. "Social Class and Bar Behavior during an Urban Festival." In James E. Curtis and William G. Scott, eds. *Social Stratification: Canada*. 2d ed. Scarborough, Ont.: Prentice Hall, 1979.

OSTLING, RICHARD N. "Jerry Falwell's Crusade." *Time*. Vol. 126, No. 9 (September 2, 1985):48–52, 55, 57.

———. "Technology and the Womb." *Time*. Vol. 129, No. 12 (March 23, 1987):58–59.

OSTRANDER, SUSAN A. "Upper Class Women: The Feminine Side of Privilege." *Qualitative Sociology*. Vol. 3, No. 1 (Spring 1980):23–44.

———. *Women of the Upper Class*. Philadelphia: Temple University Press, 1984.

OUCHI, WILLIAM. *Theory Z: How American Business Can Meet the Japanese Challenge*. Reading, Mass.: Addison-Wesley, 1981.

OWEN, DAVID. *None of the Above: Behind the Myth of Scholastic Aptitude*. Boston: Houghton Mifflin, 1985.

PAKULSKI, JAN. "Mass Social Movements and Social Class." *International Sociology*. Vol. 8, No. 2 (June 1993):131–58.

PALMORE, ERDMAN. "Predictors of Successful Aging." *The Gerontologist*. Vol. 19, No. 5 (October 1979a):427–31.

———. "Advantages of Aging." *The Gerontologist*. Vol. 19, No. 2 (April 1979b):220–23.

———. "What Can the USA Learn from Japan About Aging?" In Steven H. Zarit, ed., *Readings in Aging and Death: Contemporary Perspectives*. New York: Harper & Row, 1982:166–69.

PAMPEL, FRED C., KENNETH C. LAND, and MARCUS FELSON. "A Social Indicator Model of Changes in the Occupational Structure of the United States: 1947–1974." *American Sociological Review*. Vol. 42, No. 6 (December 1977):951–64.

PARCEL, TOBY L., CHARLES W. MUELLER, and STEVEN CUVELIER. "Comparable Worth and Occupational Labor Market: Explanations of Occupational Earnings Differentials." Paper presented to the American Sociological Association, New York, 1986.

PARENTI, MICHAEL. *Inventing Reality: The Politics of the Mass Media*. New York: St. Martin's Press, 1986.

PARK, ROBERT E. *Race and Culture*. Glencoe, Ill.: Free Press, 1950.

———. "The City: Suggestions for the Investigation of Human Behavior in the Human Environment." In Robert E. Park and Ernest W. Burgess, *The City*. Chicago: University of Chicago Press, 1967; orig. 1925:1–46.

PARKINSON, C. NORTHCOTE. *Parkinson's Law and Other Studies in Administration*. New York: Ballantine Books, 1957.

PARRILLO, VINCENT N. "Diversity in America: A Sociohistorical Analysis." *Sociological Forum*. Vol. 9, No. 4 (December 1994):42–45.

PARROTT, JULIE. "The Effects of Culture on Eating Disorders." Paper presented to Southwestern Social Science Association, Dallas, Texas, March 1987.

PARSONS, TALCOTT. "Age and Sex in the Social Structure of the United States." *American Sociological Review*. Vol. 7, No. 4 (August 1942):604–16.

———. *Essays in Sociological Theory*. New York: Free Press, 1954.

———. *The Social System*. New York: Free Press, 1964; orig. 1951.

———. *Societies: Evolutionary and Comparative Perspectives*. Englewood Cliffs, N.J.: Prentice Hall, 1966.

PARSONS, TALCOTT, and ROBERT F. BALES, EDS. *Family, Socialization and Interaction Process*. New York: Free Press, 1955.

PAUL, ELLEN FRANKEL. "Bared Buttocks and Federal Cases." *Society*. Vol. 28, No. 4 (May-June, 1991):4–7.

PEAR, ROBERT. "Women Reduce Lag in Earnings, But Disparities With Men Remain." *New York Times* (September 4, 1987):1, 7.

PEAR, ROBERT, with ERIK ECKHOLM. "When Healers Are Entrepreneurs: A Debate Over Costs and Ethics." *New York Times* (June 2, 1991):1, 17.

PEARSON, DAVID E. "Post-Mass Culture." *Society*. Vol. 30, No. 5 (July-August 1993):17–22.

———. "Community and Sociology." *Society*. Vol. 32, No. 5 (July-August 1995):44–50.

PENNINGS, JOHANNES M. "Organizational Birth Frequencies: An Empirical Investigation." *Administrative Science Quarterly*. Vol. 27, No. 1 (March 1982):120–44.

PEREZ, LISANDRO. "Cubans." In *Harvard Encyclopedia of American Ethnic Groups*. Cambridge, Mass.: Harvard University Press, 1980:256–60.

PERROLLE, JUDITH A. "Comments from the Special Issue Editor: The Emerging Dialogue on Environmental Justice." *Social Problems*. Vol. 40, No. 1 (February 1993):1–4.

PERSELL, CAROLINE HODGES. *Education and Inequality: A Theoretical and Empirical Synthesis*. New York: Free Press, 1977.

———. "The Interdependence of Social Justice and Civil Society." *Sociological Forum*. Vol. 12, No. 2 (June 1997):149–72.

PESSEN, EDWARD. *Riches, Class, and Power: America Before the Civil War*. New Brunswick, N.J.: Transaction Books, 1990.

PETER, LAURENCE J., and RAYMOND HULL. *The Peter Principle: Why Things Always Go Wrong*. New York: William Morrow, 1969.

Peters Atlas of the World. New York: Harper & Row, 1990.

PETERS, THOMAS J., and ROBERT H. WATERMAN, JR. *In Search of Excellence: Lessons From America's Best-Run Companies*. New York: Warner Books, 1982.

PETERSILIA, JOAN. "Probation in the United States: Practices and Challenges." *National Institute of Justice Journal*. No. 233 (September 1997):4.

PETERSON, RICHARD R. "A Re-Evaluation of the Economic Consequences of Divorce." *American Sociological Review*. Vol. 61, No. 3 (June 1996):528–36.

PETERSON, SCOTT. "Women Live on Own Terms Behind the Veil." *Christian Science Monitor* (July 31, 1996):1, 10.

PEVERE, GEOFF AND GREIG DYMOND. *Mondo Canuck: A Canadian Pop Culture Odyssey*. Scarborough, Ontario: Prentice Hall Canada, 1996.

PHELAN, JO, BRUCE G. LINK, ANN STUEVE, and ROBERT E. MOORE. "Education, Social Liberalism, and Economic Conservatism: Attitudes Toward Homeless People." *American Sociological Review*. Vol. 60, No. 1 (February 1995):126–40.

PHILIPSON, ILENE J., and KAREN V. HANSEN. "Women, Class, and the Feminist Imagination." In Karen V. Hansen and Ilene J. Philipson, eds., *Women, Class, and the Feminist Imagination: A Socialist-Feminist Reader*. Philadelphia: Temple University Press, 1992:3–40.

PHILLIPS, KEVIN. *Arrogant Capital: Washington, Wall Street, and the Frustration of American Politics*. Boston: Little, Brown and Company, 1994.

PHILLIPSON, CHRIS. *Capitalism and the Construction of Old Age*. London: Macmillan, 1982.

PHILP, MARGARET. "Unpaid work worth at least $234 billion." *The Globe and Mail* (December 21, 1995):A8.

PHYSICIANS' TASK FORCE ON HUNGER IN AMERICA. "Hunger Reaches Blue-Collar America." Report issued 1987.

PICHARDO, NELSON A. "The Power Elite and Elite-Driven Countermovements: The Associated Farmers of California During the 1930s." *Sociological Forum.* Vol. 10, No. 1 (March 1995):21–49.

PILLEMER, KARL. "Maltreatment of the Elderly at Home and in Institutions: Extent, Risk Factors, and Policy Recommendations." In U.S. Congress. House, Select Committee on Aging and Senate, Special Committee on Aging. *Legislative Agenda for an Aging Society: 1988 and Beyond.* Washington, D.C.: U.S. Government Printing Office, 1988.

PINES, MAYA. "The Civilization of Genie." *Psychology Today.* Vol. 15 (September 1981):28–34.

PIRANDELLO, LUIGI. "The Pleasure of Honesty." In *To Clothe the Naked and Two Other Plays.* New York: Dutton, 1962:143–98.

PITNEY, JOHN J., JR. "What Scholars Don't Know About Term Limits." *The Chronicle of Higher Education.* Vol. XLI, No. 33 (April 28, 1995):A76.

PITT, MALCOLM. *Introducing Hinduism.* New York: Friendship Press, 1955.

PIVEN, FRANCES FOX, and RICHARD A. CLOWARD. *Poor People's Movements: Why They Succeed, How They Fail.* New York: Pantheon Books, 1977.

———. *Why Americans Don't Vote.* New York: Pantheon Books, 1988.

PLATIEL, RUDY. "Natives have legal right to self-rule, inquiry finds." *The Globe and Mail* (August 19, 1993): A4.

PLOMIN, ROBERT, and TERRYL T. FOCH. "A Twin Study of Objectively Assessed Personality in Childhood." *Journal of Personality and Social Psychology.* Vol. 39, No. 4 (October 1980):680–88.

POHL, RUDIGER. "The Transition From Communism to Capitalism in East Germany." *Society.* Vol. 33, No. 4 (June 1996):62–65.

POLENBERG, RICHARD. *One Nation Divisible: Class, Race, and Ethnicity in the United States Since 1938.* New York: Pelican Books, 1980.

POLLACK, ANDREW. "Occult in the Japanese Office." *The Globe and Mail* (December 16, 1995):D8.

———. "Happy in the East (^-^) or Smiling :-) in the West." *New York Times* (August 12, 1996).

———. "Overseas, Smoking Is One of Life's Small Pleasures." *New York Times* (August 17, 1997):E5.

POLLACK, PHILIP H., III, and M. ELLIOT VITTAS. "Who Bears the Burdens of Environmental Pollution: Race, Ethnicity, and Environmental Equity in Florida." *Social Science Quarterly.* Vol. 76, No. 2 (June 1995):294–310.

POLLARD, KELVIN. "Play Ball! Demographics and Major League Baseball." *Population Today.* Vol. 24, No. 4 (April 1996):3.

———. "Speaking Graphically: Per Capita Fresh Water Availability . . ." *Population Today.* Vol. 24, No. 12 (December 1996):6.

POLSBY, NELSON W. "Three Problems in the Analysis of Community Power." *American Sociological Review.* Vol. 24, No. 6 (December 1959):796–803.

POMER, MARSHALL I. "Labor Market Structure, Intragenerational Mobility, and Discrimination: Black Male Advancement Out of Low-Paying Occupations, 1962–1973." *American Sociological Review.* Vol. 51, No. 5 (October 1986):650–59.

POMFRET, RICHARD. *The Economic Development of Canada.* Toronto: Methuen, 1981.

POOLEY, ERIC. "Death or Life?" *Time.* Vol. 149, No. 24 (June 16, 1997):30–36.

POPENOE, DAVID. *Disturbing the Nest: Family Change and Decline in Modern Societies.* New York: Aldine, 1988.

———. "Family Decline in the Swedish Welfare State." *The Public Interest.* No. 102 (Winter 1991):65–77.

———. "The Controversial Truth: Two-Parent Families Are Better." *New York Times* (December 26, 1992):21.

———. "American Family Decline, 1960–1990: A Review and Appraisal." *Journal of Marriage and the Family.* Vol. 55, No. 3 (August 1993):527–55.

———. "Parental Androgyny." *Society.* Vol. 30, No. 6 (September-October 1993):5–11.

———. "Scandinavian Welfare." *Society.* Vol. 31, No. 6 (September-October 1994):78–81.

———. Review of John Snarey's *How Fathers Care for the Next Generation: A Four Decade Study,* in *Contemporary Sociology.* Vol. 23, No. 5 (September 1994):698–700.

———. "Past and Future Population Doubling Times, Selected Countries." *Population Today.* Vol. 23, No. 2 (February 1995):6.

POPKIN, SUSAN J. "Welfare: Views From the Bottom." *Social Problems.* Vol. 17, No. 1 (February 1990):64–79.

POPULATION REFERENCE BUREAU. *1995 World Population Data Sheet.* Washington, D.C.: Population Reference Bureau, Inc., 1995.

———. "Past and Future Population Doubling Times, Selected Countries." *Population Today.* Vol. 23, No. 2 (February 1995):6.

———. "Kids Count." Washington, D.C.: 1997.

POPULATION TODAY. "Majority of Children in Poverty Live with Parents Who Work." Vol. 23, No. 4 (April 1995):6.

PORTER, JOHN. *The Vertical Mosaic: An Analysis of Social Class and Power in Canada.* Toronto: University of Toronto Press, 1965.

———, Marion Porter, and Bernard R. Blishen. *Stations and Callings.* Toronto: Methuen, 1982.

PORTES, ALEJANDRO. "The Rise of Ethnicity: Determinants of Ethnic Perceptions Among Cuban Exiles in Miami." *American Sociological Review.* Vol. 49, No. 3 (June 1984):383–97.

PORTES, ALEJANDRO, and LEIF JENSEN. "The Enclave and the Entrants: Patterns of Ethnic Enterprise in Miami Before and After Mariel." *American Sociological Review.* Vol. 54, No. 6 (December 1989):929–49.

A Portrait of Seniors in Canada. Catalogue No. 89–59. Ottawa: Statistics Canada, 1990.

POSTEL, SANDRA. "Facing Water Scarcity." In Lester R. Brown et al., eds., *State of the World 1993: A Worldwatch Institute Report on Progress Toward a Sustainable Society.* New York: Norton, 1993:22–41.

Poverty Profile: Update for 1991. Ottawa: National Council on Welfare, 1993.

POWELL, CHRIS, and GEORGE E. C. PATON, EDS. *Humour in Society: Resistance and Control.* New York: St. Martin's Press, 1988.

Power of Attorney Kit. Toronto: Ministry of the Attorney General (Ontario), 1995.

PRESSER, HARRIET B. "The Housework Gender Gap." *Population Today.* Vol. 21, No. 7/8 (July-August 1993):5.

PRESSLEY, SUE ANNE, and NANCY ANDREWS. "For Gay Couples, the Nursery Becomes the New Frontier." *Washington Post* (December 20, 1992):A1, A22–23.

PRIMEGGIA, SALVATORE, and JOSEPH A. VARACALLI. "Southern Italian Comedy: Old to New World." In Joseph V. Scelsa, Salvatore J. LaGumina, and Lydio Tomasi, eds., *Italian Americans in Transition.* New York: The American Italian Historical Association, 1990:241–52.

PRINDLE, DAVID F. *Risky Business: The Political Economy of Hollywood.* Boulder, Colo.: Westview Press, 1993.

———. "Take Three on Hollywood Liberalism." *Social Science Quarterly.* Vol. 75, No. 2 (June 1994):458–59.

PRINDLE, DAVID F., and JAMES W. ENDERSBY. "Hollywood Liberalism." *Social Science Quarterly.* Vol. 74, No. 1 (March 1993):136–49.

PUTERBAUGH, GEOFF, ED. *Twins and Homosexuality: A Casebook.* New York: Garland, 1990.

PUTKA, GARY. "SAT To Become A Better Gauge." *Wall Street Journal* (November 1, 1990):B1.

PUTKA, GARY, and STEVE STECKLOW. "Do For-Profit Schools Work? These Seem to for One Entrepreneur." *Wall Street Journal* (June 8, 1994):A1, A4.

QUEENAN, JOE. "The Many Paths to Riches." *Forbes.* Vol. 144, No. 9 (October 23, 1989):149.

QUICK, REBECCA. "Wanna Earn as Much as the Boss? Stop Surfing the Net, Get to Work." *Wall Street Journal* (April 11, 1997):B1.

QUINNEY, RICHARD. *Class, State and Crime: On the Theory and Practice of Criminal Justice.* New York: David McKay, 1977.

RABKIN, JEREMY. "The Supreme Court in the Culture Wars." *The Public Interest.* Vol. 125 (Fall 1996):3–26.

RADEMACHER, ERIC W. "The Effect of Question Wording on College Students." *The Pittsburgh Undergraduate Review.* Vol. 8, No. 1 (Spring 1992):45–81.

RADEMAEKERS, WILLIAM, and RHEA SCHOENTHAL. "Iceman." *Time.* Vol. 140, No. 17 (October 26, 1992):62–66.

RAJHATHY, JUDITH, AND DAVID ROULARD. "Victory for Health Freedom." *Health Naturally* (June/July 1994).

RALEY, R. KELLY. "A Shortage of Marriageable Men? A Note on the Role of Cohabitation in Black-White Differences in Marriage Rates." *American Journal of Sociology.* Vol. 61, No. 6 (December 1996):973–83.

RAMCHARAN, SUBHAS. *Racism: Nonwhites in Canada.* Toronto: Butterworths, 1982.

RAMO, JOSHUA COOPER. "Finding God on the Web." *Time* (December 16, 1996):60–67.

RANDALL, VICKI. *Women and Politics.* London: Macmillan, 1982.

RAPHAEL, RAY. *The Men From the Boys: Rites of Passage in Male America.* Lincoln and London: University of Nebraska Press, 1988.

RATAN, SUNEEL. "A New Divide Between Haves and Have-Nots?" *Time.* Special Issue. Vol. 145, No. 12 (Spring 1995):25–26.

RAVITCH, DIANE, and JOSEPH VITERITTI. "A New Vision for City Schools." *The Public Interest.* Vol. 122 (Winter 1996):3–16.

RAY, PAUL H. "The Emerging Culture." *American Demographics.* Vol 19, No. 2 (February 1997):29–34, 56.

RECKLESS, WALTER C., and SIMON DINITZ. "Pioneering With Self-Concept as a Vulnerability Factor in Delinquency." *Journal of Criminal Law, Criminology, and Police Science.* Vol. 58, No. 4 (December 1967):515–23.

REICH, ROBERT B. "As the World Turns." *The New Republic* (May 1, 1989):23, 26–28.

———. *The Work of Nations: Preparing Ourselves for 21st-Century Capitalism.* New York: Alfred A. Knopf, 1991.

Reid, C. "Sick to Death: The Health of Aboriginal People in Australia and Canada." in *Raval Minorities, Medicine and Health,* ed. B. Singh Bolaria and Rosemary Bolaria. Halifax: Fernwood Publishing, 1994:297–312.

REID, SUE TITUS. *Crime and Criminology.* 6th ed. Fort Worth, Tex.: Holt, Rinehart & Winston, 1991.

REIMAN, JEFFREY H. *The Rich Get Richer and the Poor Get Prison: Ideology, Class, and Criminal Justice.* 3d ed. New York: John Wiley & Sons, 1990.

REINHARZ, SHULAMIT. *Feminist Methods in Social Research.* New York: Oxford University Press, 1992.

REITZ, JEFFREY G. *The Survival of Ethnic Groups.* Toronto: McGraw-Hill Ryerson, 1980.

REITZ, JEFFREY G. AND RAYMOND BRETON. *The Illusion of Difference: Realities of Ethnicity in Canada and the United States.* Toronto: C.D. Howe Institute, 1994.

REMIS, ROBERT S. "The Epidemiology of HIV and AIDS in Canada: Current Perspectives and Future Needs." *Canadian Journal of Public Health.* Vol. 84, No. 1 (January/February 1993): 534, 536.

REMOFF, HEATHER TREXLER. *Sexual Choice: A Woman's Decision.* New York: Dutton/Lewis, 1984.

Report on the Demographic Situation in Canada. Ottawa: Statistics Canada, 1992.

RICE, TOM W., and MEREDITH L. PEPPER. "Region, Migration, and Attitudes in the United States." *Social Science Quarterly.* Vol. 78, No. 1 (March 1997):83–95.

RICHARDSON, JAMES T. "Definitions of Cult: From Sociological-Technical to Popular Negative." Paper presented to the American Psychological Association, Boston, August 1990.

RIDGEWAY, CECILIA L. *The Dynamics of Small Groups.* New York: St. Martin's Press, 1983.

———, and David Diekema. "Dominance and Collective Hierarchy Formation in Male and Female Task Groups." *American Sociological Review.* Vol. 54, No. 1 (February 1989):79–93.

RIEFF, PHILIP. "Introduction." In Charles Horton Cooley, *Social Organization.* New York: Schocken Books, 1962.

RIESMAN, DAVID. *The Lonely Crowd: A Study of the Changing American Character.* New Haven, Conn.: Yale University Press, 1970; orig. 1950.

RILEY, MATILDA WHITE, ANNE FONER, and JOAN WARING. "Sociology of Age." In Neil J. Smelser, ed., *Handbook of Sociology.* Newbury Park, Calif.: Sage, 1988:243–90.

RILEY, NANCY E. "Gender, Power, and Population Change." *Population Bulletin.* Vol. 52, No. 1 (May 1997).

RITZER, GEORGE. *Man and His Work: Conflict and Change.* New York: Appleton-Century-Crofts, 1972.

———. *Sociological Theory.* New York: Alfred A. Knopf, 1983:63–66.

———. *The McDonaldization of Society: An Investigation Into the Changing Character of Contemporary Social Life.* Thousand Oaks, Calif.: Pine Forge Press, 1993.

RITZER, GEORGE, and DAVID WALCZAK. *Working: Conflict and Change.* 4th ed. Englewood Cliffs, N.J.: Prentice Hall, 1990.

RIVERA-BATIZ, FRANCISCO L., and CARLOS SANTIAGO, cited in Sam Roberts, "Puerto Ricans on Mainland Making Gains, Study Finds." *New York Times* (October 19, 1994):A20.

ROBERGE, ROGER, JEAN MARIE BERTHELOT AND MICHAEL WOLFSAN. "Health and Socio-Economic Inequalities." *Canadian Social Trends* (Summer 1995):15-19. Statistics Canada, Catalogue No. 11-008E.

ROBERTS, J. DEOTIS. *Roots of a Black Future: Family and Church.* Philadelphia: Westminster Press, 1980.

ROBERTS, J. TIMMONS. "Psychosocial Effects of Workplace Hazardous Exposures: Theoretical Synthesis and Preliminary Findings." *Social Problems.* Vol. 40, No. 1 (February 1993):74–89.

ROBERTS, STEVEN V. "Open Arms for Online Democracy." *U.S. News and World Report.* Vol. 118, No. 2 (January 16, 1995):10.

ROBINSON, ALLAN. "Inco sends in the robo-miners." *The Globe and Mail* (January 3, 1998):B1.

ROBINSON, DAWN. "Toward a Synthesis of Sociological and Psychological Theories of Eating Disorders." Paper presented to Southwestern Social Science Association, Dallas, Texas, March 1987.

ROBINSON, JOYCE, and GLENNA SPITZE. "Whistle While You Work? The Effect of Household Task Performance on Women's and Men's Well-Being." *Social Science Quarterly.* Vol. 73, No. 4 (December 1992):844–61.

ROBINSON, VERA M. "Humor and Health." In Paul E. McGhee and Jeffrey H. Goldstein, eds., *Handbook of Humor Research, Vol. II, Applied Studies.* New York: Springer-Verlag, 1983:109–28.

ROCKETT, IAN R. H. "Population and Health: An Introduction to Epidemiology." *Population Bulletin.* Vol. 49, No. 3 (November 1994). Washington, D.C.: Population Reference Bureau.

RODGERS, JOAN R. "An Empirical Study of Intergenerational Transmission of Poverty in the United States." *Social Science Quarterly.* Vol. 76, No. 1 (March 1995):178–94.

ROESCH, ROBERTA. "Violent Families." *Parents.* Vol. 59, No. 9 (September 1984):74–76, 150–52.

ROETHLISBERGER, F. J., and WILLIAM J. DICKSON. *Management and the Worker.* Cambridge, Mass.: Harvard University Press, 1939.

ROGERS, ALISON. "The World's 101 Richest People." *Fortune.* Vol. 127, No. 13 (June 28, 1993):36–66.

ROHLEN, THOMAS P. *Japan's High Schools.* Berkeley: University of California Press, 1983.

ROKOVE, MILTON L. *Don't Make No Waves, Don't Back No Losers.* Bloomington: Indiana University Press, 1975.

ROMAN, MEL, and WILLIAM HADDAD. *The Disposable Parent: The Case for Joint Custody.* New York: Holt, Rinehart & Winston, 1978.

RÓNA-TAS, ÁKOS. "The First Shall Be Last? Entrepreneurship and Communist Cadres in the Transition From Socialism." *American Journal of Sociology.* Vol. 100, No. 1 (July 1994):40–69.

ROOF, WADE CLARK. "Socioeconomic Differentials Among White Socioreligious Groups in the United States." *Social Forces.* Vol. 58, No. 1 (September 1979):280–89.

———. "Unresolved Issues in the Study of Religion and the National Elite: Response to Greeley." *Social Forces.* Vol. 59, No. 3 (March 1981):831–36.

ROOF, WADE CLARK, and WILLIAM MCKINNEY. *American Mainline Religion: Its Changing Shape and Future.* New Brunswick, N.J.: Rutgers University Press, 1987.

ROOS, PATRICIA. "Marriage and Women's Occupational Attainment in Cross-Cultural Perspective." *American Sociological Review.* Vol. 48, No. 6 (December 1983):852–64.

ROPER CENTER FOR PUBLIC OPINION RESEARCH. *Grading the Schools.* [Online] Available http://www.pdkintl.org/kappan/kpoll97d.htm, 1998.

RORTY, RICHARD. "The Unpatriotic Academy." *New York Times* (February 13, 1994):15.

ROSE, JERRY D. *Outbreaks.* New York: Free Press, 1982.

ROSEN, ELLEN ISRAEL. *Bitter Choices: Blue-Collar Women In and Out of Work.* Chicago: University of Chicago Press, 1987.

ROSENBAUM, DAVID E. "Americans Want a Right to Die. Or So They Think." *New York Times* (June 8, 1997):E3.

ROSENBAUM, RON. "A Tangled Web for the Supreme Court." *The New York Times Magazine* (March 12, 1989):60.

ROSENFELD, RACHEL A., and ARNE L. KALLEBERG. "A Cross-National Comparison of the Gender Gap in Income." *American Journal of Sociology.* Vol. 96, No. 1 (July 1990):69–106.

ROSENTHAL, ELIZABETH. "Canada's National Health Plan Gives Care to All, With Limits." *New York Times* (April 30, 1991):A1, A16.

ROSENTHAL, JACK. "The Rapid Growth of Suburban Employment." In Lois H. Masotti and Jeffrey K. Hadden, eds., *Suburbia in Transition.* New York: New York Times Books, 1974:95–100.

ROSKIN, MICHAEL G. *Countries and Concepts: An Introduction to Comparative Politics.* Englewood Cliffs, N.J.: Prentice Hall, 1982.

ROSNOW, RALPH L., and GARY ALAN FINE. *Rumor and Gossip: The Social Psychology of Hearsay.* New York: Elsevier, 1976.

ROSS, CATHERINE E., JOHN MIROWSKY, and JOAN HUBER. "Dividing Work, Sharing Work, and In-Between: Marriage Patterns and Depression." *American Sociological Review.* Vol. 48, No. 6 (December 1983):809–23.

ROSS, DAVID P., E. RICHARD SHILLINGTON, AND CLARENCE LOCHHEAD. *The Canadian Fact of Poverty.* Ottawa: Canadian Council on Social Development, 1994.

ROSS, JOHN. "To Die in the Street: Mexico City's Homeless Population Boom as Economic Crisis Shakes Social Protections." *SSSP Newsletter.* Vol. 27, No. 2 (Summer 1996):14–15.

ROSSI, ALICE S. "Gender and Parenthood." In Alice S. Rossi, ed., *Gender and the Life Course.* New York: Aldine, 1985:161–91.

ROSSI, PETER H. Review of Christopher Jencks, *The Homeless* (Cambridge, Mass.: Harvard University Press). *Society.* Vol. 32, No. 4 (May-June 1995):80–81.

ROSTOW, WALT W. *The Stages of Economic Growth: A Non-Communist Manifesto.* Cambridge: Cambridge University Press, 1960.

———. *The World Economy: History and Prospect.* Austin: University of Texas Press, 1978.

ROSZAK, THEODORE. *The Cult of Information: The Folklore of Computers and the True Art of Thinking.* New York: Pantheon Books, 1986.

ROTHMAN, STANLEY, STEPHEN POWERS, and DAVID ROTHMAN. "Feminism in Films." *Society.* Vol. 30, No. 3 (March-April 1993):66–72.

ROUDI, NAZY. "The Demography of Islam." *Population Today.* Vol. 16, No. 3 (March 1988):6–9.

ROWE, DAVID C. "Biometrical Genetic Models of Self-Reported Delinquent Behavior: A Twin Study." *Behavior Genetics.* Vol. 13, No. 5 (1983):473–89.

ROWE, DAVID C., and D. WAYNE OSGOOD. "Heredity and Sociological Theories of Delinquency: A Reconsideration." *American Sociological Review.* Vol. 49, No. 4 (August 1984):526–40.

ROYAL COMMISSION ON THE STATUS OF WOMEN IN CANADA. *Report of the Royal Commission on the Status of Women in Canada.* Ottawa: Information Canada, 1970.

RUBENSTEIN, ELI A. "The Not So Golden Years." *Newsweek* (October 7, 1991):13.

RUBIN, BETH A. "Class Struggle American Style: Unions, Strikes and Wages." *American Sociological Review.* Vol. 51, No. 5 (October 1986):618–31.

RUBIN, KEN. "Privacy." In *The Canadian Encyclopedia.* 2d ed. Vol. 3. Edmonton: Hurtig Publishers, 1988: 1761.

RUBIN, LILLIAN BRESLOW. *Worlds of Pain: Life in the Working-Class Family.* New York: Basic Books, 1976.

RUDÉ, GEORGE. *The Crowd in History: A Study of Popular Disturbances in France and England, 1730–1848.* New York: Wiley, 1964.

RUGGLES, STEVEN. "The Origins of African-American Family Structure." *American Sociological Review.* Vol. 59, No. 1 (February 1994):136–51.

RULE, JAMES, and PETER BRANTLEY. "Computerized Surveillance in the Workplace: Forms and Delusions." *Sociological Forum.* Vol. 7, No. 3 (September 1992):405–23.

RUSSELL, CHERYL. "The Master Trend." *American Demographics.* Vol. 15, No. 10 (October 1993):28–37.

———. "Overworked? Overwhelmed?" *American Demographics.* Vol. 17, No. 3 (March 1995):8.

———. "Are We In the Dumps?" *American Demographics.* Vol. 17, No. 1 (January 1995):6.

———. "True Crime." *American Demographics*. Vol. 17, No. 8 (August 1995):22–31.

RUSSELL, DIANA E. H. *Rape in Marriage*. New York: Macmillan, 1982.

RYAN, WILLIAM. *Blaming the Victim*. Rev. ed. New York: Vintage Books, 1976.

RYMER, RUSS. *Genie*. New York: HarperPerennial, 1994.

RYTINA, JOAN HUBER, WILLIAM H. FORM, and JOHN PEASE. "Income and Stratification Ideology: Beliefs About the American Opportunity Structure." *American Journal of Sociology*. Vol. 75, No. 4 (January 1970):703–16.

SABATO, LARRY J. *PAC Power: Inside the World of Political Action Committees*. New York: Norton, 1984.

SAGAN, CARL. *The Dragons of Eden*. New York: Ballantine, 1977.

SALE, KIRKPATRICK. *The Conquest of Paradise: Christopher Columbus and the Columbian Legacy*. New York: Alfred A. Knopf, 1990.

SALHOLZ, ELOISE. "The Future of Gay America." *Newsweek* (March 12, 1990):20–25.

SALTMAN, JULIET. "Maintaining Racially Diverse Neighborhoods." *Urban Affairs Quarterly*. Vol. 26, No. 3 (March 1991):416–41.

SAMPSON, ANTHONY. *The Changing Anatomy of Britain*. New York: Random House, 1982.

SAMPSON, ROBERT J. "Urban Black Violence: The Effects of Male Joblessness and Family Disruption." *American Journal of Sociology*. Vol. 93, No. 2 (September 1987):348–82.

SAMPSON, ROBERT J., and JOHN H. LAUB. "Crime and Deviance Over the Life Course: The Salience of Adult Social Bonds." *American Sociological Review*. Vol. 55, No. 5 (October 1990):609–27.

SÀNDOR, GABRIELLE. "The Other Americans." *American Demographics*. Vol. 16, No. 6 (June 1994):36–41.

SANTOLI, AL. "Fighting Child Prostitution." *Freedom Review*. Vol. 25, No. 5 (September-October 1994):5–8.

SAPIR, EDWARD. "The Status of Linguistics as a Science." *Language*. Vol. 5 (1929):207–14.

———. *Selected Writings of Edward Sapir in Language, Culture, and Personality*. David G. Mandelbaum, ed. Berkeley: University of California Press, 1949.

SAUVÉ, ROGER. *Borderlines: What Canadians and Americans Should—But Don't—Know About Each Other*. Whitby, Ont.: McGraw-Hill Ryerson, 1994.

SAX, LINDA J., ALEXANDER W. ASTIN, WILLIAM S. KORN, and KATHRYN M. MAHONEY. *The American Freshman: National Norms for Fall 1996*. Los Angeles: UCLA Higher Education Research Institute, 1996.

SCAFF, LAWRENCE A. "Max Weber and Robert Michels." *American Journal of Sociology*. Vol. 86, No. 6 (May 1981):1269–86.

SCANLON, JAMES P. "The Curious Case of Affirmative Action for Women." *Society*. Vol. 29, No. 2 (January-February 1992):36–42.

SCHAIE, I. WARNER. "Intelligence and Problem Solving." In James E. Birren and R. Bruce Sloane, eds., *Handbook of Mental Health and Aging*. Englewood Cliffs, N.J.: Prentice Hall, 1980:262–84.

SCHEFF, THOMAS J. *Being Mentally Ill: A Sociological Theory*. 2d ed. New York: Aldine, 1984.

SCHELLENBERG, JAMES A. *Masters of Social Psychology*. New York: Oxford University Press, 1978:38–62.

SCHELLENBERG, KATHRYN. "Policing the Police: Technological Surveillance and the Predilection for Leniency." *Criminal Justice and Behavior* (forthcoming).

———. "Taking It or Leaving It: Instability and Turnover in a High-Tech Firm." *Work and Occupations*. Vol. 23, No. 2 (1996): 190-213.

SCHELLENBERG, KATHRYN AND GEORGE A. MILLER. "Turbulence and Bureaucracy." *Journal of Applied Behavioral Science*. Vol. 43, No. 2 (1998): 202–21.

SCHERER, RON. "Worldwide Trend: Tobacco Use Grows." *Christian Science Monitor* (July 17, 1996):4, 8.

SCHILLER, BRADLEY. "Who Are the Working Poor?" *The Public Interest*. Vol. 155 (Spring 1994):61–71.

SCHLESINGER, ARTHUR. "The City in American Civilization." In A. B. Callow, Jr., ed., *American Urban History*. New York: Oxford University Press, 1969:25–41.

SCHLESINGER, ARTHUR, JR. "The Cult of Ethnicity: Good and Bad." *Time*. Vol. 137, No. 27 (July 8, 1991):21.

SCHMIDT, ROGER. *Exploring Religion*. Belmont, Calif.: Wadsworth, 1980.

SCHOOLER, CARMI, JOANNE MILLER, KAREN A. MILLER, and CAROL N. RICHTAND. "Work for the Household: Its Nature and Consequences for Husbands and Wives." *American Journal of Sociology*. Vol. 90, No. 1 (July 1984):97–124.

SCHUMANN, HANS WOLFGANG. *Buddhism: An Outline of Its Teachings and Schools*. Wheaton, Ill.: The Theosophical Publishing House/Quest Books, 1974.

SCHUTT, RUSSELL K. "Objectivity Versus Outrage." *Society*. Vol. 26, No. 4 (May-June 1989):14–16.

SCHWARTZ, BARRY. "Memory As a Cultural System: Abraham Lincoln in World War II." *American Sociological Review*. Vol. 61, No. 5 (October 1996):908–27.

SCHWARTZ, FELICE N. "Management, Women, and the New Facts of Life." *Harvard Business Review*. Vol. 89, No. 1 (January-February 1989):65–76.

SCHWARTZ, JOE. "Rising Status." *American Demographics*. Vol. 11, No. 1 (January 1989):10.

SCOTT, JOHN, AND CATHERINE GRIFF. *Directors of Industry: The British Corporate Network, 1904–1976*. New York: Blackwell, 1985.

SCHWARTZ, JOHN E., and THOMAS J. VOLGY. *The Forgotten Americans: Thirty Million Working Poor in the Land of Opportunity*. New York: Norton, 1992.

SCHWARTZ, MARTIN D. "Gender and Injury in Spousal Assault." *Sociological Focus*. Vol. 20, No. 1 (January 1987):61–75.

SCHWARTZ-NOBEL, LORETTA. *Starving in the Shadow of Plenty*. New York: McGraw-Hill, 1981.

SCOMMEGNA, PAOLA. "Teens' Risk of AIDS, Unintended Pregnancies Examined." *Population Today*. Vol. 24, No. 8 (August 1996):1–2.

SCOTT, D.B. "Lean Machine." *Report on Business Magazine* (November 1992): 90-99.

SCOTT, JOHN, and CATHERINE GRIFF. *Directors of Industry: The British Corporate Network, 1904–1976*. New York: Blackwell, 1985.

SCOTT, W. RICHARD. *Organizations: Rational, Natural, and Open Systems*. Englewood Cliffs, NJ: Prentice Hall, 1981.

SEARS, DAVID O., and JOHN B. McCONAHAY. *The Politics of Violence: The New Urban Blacks and the Watts Riot*. Boston: Houghton Mifflin, 1973.

SEBASTIAN, TIM. "Massacred: 1,000; Tried, 0." *World Press Review* (June 1996):6–10.

SECRETARY OF STATE CANADA. *Profile of Higher Education in Canada* (S2-196/1991). Ottawa: Ministry of Supply and Services, 1992.

SEELEY, JOHN R. ET AL. *Crestwood Heights: A Study of the Culture of Suburban Life*. New York: Wiley, 1963.

SEGAL, MADY WECHSLER, and AMANDA FAITH HANSEN. "Value Rationales in Policy Debates on Women in the Military: A Content Analysis of Congressional Testimony, 1941–1985." *Social Science Quarterly*. Vol. 73, No. 2 (June 1992):296–309.

SEKULIC, DUSKO, GARTH MASSEY, and RANDY HODSON. "Who Were the Yugoslavs? Failed Sources of Common Identity in the Former Yugoslavia." *American Sociological Review*. Vol. 59, No. 1 (February 1994):83–97.

SELIMUDDIN, ABU K. "The Selling of America." *USA Today*. Vol. 117, No. 2525 (March 1989):12–14.

SELLIN, THORSTEN. *The Penalty of Death*. Beverly Hills, Calif.: Sage, 1980.

SELTZER, ROBERT M. *Jewish People, Jewish Thought: The Jewish Experience in History*. New York: Macmillan, 1980.

SEN, K. M. *Hinduism*. Baltimore: Penguin Books, 1961.

SENNETT, RICHARD, and JONATHAN COBB. *The Hidden Injuries of Class*. New York: Vintage Books, 1973.

SERRILL, MICHAEL S. "A Nation Blessed, A Nation Stressed." *Time* (November 20, 1995): 20-41.

SHAPIRO, JOSEPH P. "Welfare: The Myth of Reform." *U.S. News and World Report*. Vol. 188, No. 2 (January 16, 1995):30–40.

SHAPIRO, JOSEPH P., and JOANNIE M. SCHROF. "Honor Thy Children." *U.S. News and World Report*. Vol. 118, No. 8 (February 27, 1995):39–49.

SHAPIRO, MARTIN. *Getting Doctored: Critical Reflections on Becoming a Physician*. Toronto: Between the Lines, 1978.

SHAPIRO, NINA. "Botswana Test Case." *Chicago Tribune* (September 15, 1991):1.

SHARPE, ANITA. "The Rich Aren't So Different After All." *Wall Street Journal* (November 12, 1996):B1, B10.

SHAWCROSS, WILLIAM. *Sideshow: Kissinger, Nixon and the Destruction of Cambodia*. New York: Pocket Books, 1979.

SHEEHAN, TOM. "Senior Esteem as a Factor in Socioeconomic Complexity." *The Gerontologist*. Vol. 16, No. 5 (October 1976):433–40.

SHEEHY, GAIL. *Passages: Predictable Crises of Adult Life*. New York: Dutton, 1976.

SHELDON, WILLIAM H., EMIL M. HARTL, and EUGENE McDERMOTT. *Varieties of Delinquent Youth*. New York: Harper, 1949.

SHELEY, JAMES F., JOSHUA ZHANG, CHARLES J. BRODY, and JAMES D. WRIGHT. "Gang Organization, Gang Criminal Activity, and Individual Gang Members' Criminal Behavior." *Social Science Quarterly*. Vol. 76, No. 1 (March 1995):53–68.

SHENON, PHILIP. "A Pacific Island Nation Is Stripped of Everything." *New York Times* (December 10, 1995):3.

SHERMAN, LAWRENCE W., and DOUGLAS A. SMITH. "Crime, Punishment, and Stake in Conformity: Legal and Informal Control of Domestic Violence." *American Sociological Review*. Vol. 57, No. 5 (October 1992):680–90.

SHERRID, PAMELA. "Hot Times in the City of London." *U.S. News & World Report* (October 27, 1986):45–46.

SHEVKY, ESHREF, and WENDELL BELL. *Social Area Analysis*. Stanford, Calif.: Stanford University Press, 1955.

SHIBUTANI, TAMOTSU. *Improvised News: A Sociological Study of Rumor*. Indianapolis, Ind.: Bobbs-Merrill, 1966.

SHIELDS, JOHN, AND STEPHEN McBRIDE. "Dismantling a Nation: The Canadian Political Economy and Continental Free Trade." In *Power and Resistance: Critical Thinking About Canadian Social Issues*, ed. Les Samuelson, 227-60. Halifax, N.S.: Fernwood Publishing, 1994.

SHIPLER, DAVID K. *Russia: Broken Idols, Solemn Dreams*. New York: Penguin Books, 1984.

SHIPLEY, JOSEPH T. *Dictionary of Word Origins*. Totowa, N.J.: Roman & Allanheld, 1985.

SHIVELY, JOELLEN. "Cowboys and Indians: Perceptions of Western Films Among American Indians and Anglos." *American Sociological Review*. Vol. 57, No. 6 (December 1992):725–34.

SHKILNYK, ANASTASIA M. *A Poison Stronger than Love: The Destruction of an Ojibwa Community*. New Haven: Yale University Press, 1985.

SHUPE, ANSON, WILLIAM A. STACEY, and LONNIE R. HAZLEWOOD. *Violent Men, Violent Couples: The Dynamics of Domestic Violence*. Lexington, Mass.: Lexington Books, 1987.

SHUTE, JEREMY J. AND DAVID B. KNIGHT. "Obtaining an Understanding of Environmental Knowledge: Wendaban Stewardship Authority." *The Canadian Geographer*. Vol. 39, No. 2 (1995):101–11.

SIDEL, RUTH, and VICTOR W. SIDEL. *A Healthy State: An International Perspective on the Crisis in United States Medical Care*. Rev. ed. New York: Pantheon Books, 1982a.

———. *The Health Care of China*. Boston: Beacon Press, 1982b.

SILLS, DAVID L. "The Succession of Goals." In Amitai Etzioni, ed., *A Sociological Reader on Complex Organizations*. 2d ed. New York: Holt, Rinehart & Winston, 1969:175–87.

SILVERBERG, ROBERT. "The Greenhouse Effect: Apocalypse Now or Chicken Little?" *Omni* (July 1991):50–54.

SILVERSTEIN, MICHAEL. In Jon Snodgrass, ed., *A Book of Readings for Men Against Sexism*. Albion, Calif.: Times Change Press, 1977:178–79.

SIMMEL, GEORG. *The Sociology of Georg Simmel*. Kurt Wolff, ed. New York: Free Press, 1950:118–69.

———. "The Metropolis and Mental Life." In Kurt Wolff, ed., *The Sociology of Georg Simmel*. New York: Free Press, 1964:409–24; orig. 1905.

———. "Fashion." In Donald N. Levine, ed., *Georg Simmel: On Individuality and Social Forms*. Chicago: University of Chicago Press, 1971; orig. 1904.

SIMON, CARL P., and ANN D. WITTE. *Beating the System: The Underground Economy*. Boston: Auburn House, 1982.

SIMON, RITA J. AND N. SHARMA. "Women and Crime: Does the American Experience Generalize?" In F. Adler and R.J. Simon, eds., *Criminology of Deviant Women*. Boston: Houghton Mifflin, 1979.

SIMONS, CAROL. "Japan's Kyoiku Mamas." In John J. Macionis and Nijole V. Benokraitis, eds., *Seeing Ourselves: Classic, Contemporary, and Cross-Cultural Readings in Sociology*. Englewood Cliffs, N.J.: Prentice Hall, 1989:281–86.

SIMONS, MARLISE. "The Price of Modernization: The Case of Brazil's Kaiapo Indians." In John J. Macionis and Nijole V. Benokraitis, eds., *Seeing Ourselves: Classic, Contemporary, and Cross-Cultural Readings in Sociology*. 4th ed. Upper Saddle River, N.J.: Prentice Hall, 1998:494–500.

SIMPSON, GEORGE EATON, and J. MILTON YINGER. *Racial and Cultural Minorities: An Analysis of Prejudice and Discrimination*. 4th ed. New York: Harper & Row, 1972.

SIMPSON, JANICE C. "Buying Black." *Time*. Vol. 140, No. 9 (August 31, 1992):52–53.

SINGER, JEROME L., and DOROTHY G. SINGER. "Psychologists Look at Television: Cognitive, Developmental, Personality, and Social Policy Implications." *American Psychologist*. Vol. 38, No. 7 (July 1983):826–34.

SINGER, JOYCE. "Without paparazzi, Canadian stars don't shine as bright." *The Globe and Mail* (September 12, 1997):C4.

SIVARD, RUTH LEGER. *World Military and Social Expenditures, 1987–88*. 12th ed. Washington, D.C.: World Priorities, 1988.

SIZER, THEODORE R. *Horace's Compromise: The Dilemma of the American High School*. Boston: Houghton Mifflin, 1984.

SKELTON, CHAD. "Decide military's role, Ottawa told." *The Globe and Mail* (August 12, 1997): A4.

SKINNER, DAVID. "Computers: Good for Education?" *The Public Interest*. No. 128 (Summer 1997):98–109.

SKOCPOL, THEDA. *States and Social Revolutions: A Comparative Analysis of France, Russia, and China*. Cambridge: Cambridge University Press, 1979.

SKOLNICK, ARLENE. *The Psychology of Human Development*. New York: Harcourt Brace Jovanovich, 1986.

SLATER, PHILIP E. "Contrasting Correlates of Group Size." *Sociometry*. Vol. 21, No. 2 (June 1958):129–39.

———. *The Pursuit of Loneliness*. Boston: Beacon Press, 1976.

SMALL BUSINESS ADMINISTRATION. News release on census data for women-owned businesses. January 1996.

SMART, NINIAN. *The Religious Experience of Mankind*. New York: Charles Scribner's Sons, 1969.

SMELSER, NEIL J. *Theory of Collective Behavior*. New York: Free Press, 1962.

SMILGAS, MARTHA. "The Big Chill: Fear of AIDS." *Time*. Vol. 129, No. 7 (February 16, 1987):50–53.

SMITH, ADAM. *An Inquiry Into the Nature and Causes of the Wealth of Nations*. New York: The Modern Library, 1937; orig. 1776.

SMITH, DAN. *The Seventh Fire: The Struggle for Aboriginal Self-Government*. Toronto: Key Porter, 1993.

SMITH, DOROTHY E. "Women, the Family and Corporate Capitalism." In M. Stephenson, ed., *Women in Canada*, Don Mills, Ont.: General Publishing, 1977: 32–48.

———. "Women's Inequality and the Family." Department of Sociology, Ontario Institute for Studies in Education, Mimeograph, 1979.

———. "Women, Class and the Family." In R. Miliband and J. Saville, eds. *The Socialist Register*. London: Merlin Press, 1983.

———. *The Everyday World as Problematic: A Feminist Sociology*. Toronto: University of Toronto Press, 1987.

———, AND SARA J. DAVID, EDS. *Women Look at Psychiatry*. Vancouver, B.C.: Press Gang Publishers, 1975.

SMITH, DOUGLAS A. "Police Response to Interpersonal Violence: Defining the Parameters of Legal Control." *Social Forces*. Vol. 65, No. 3 (March 1987):767–82.

SMITH, DOUGLAS A., and PATRICK R. GARTIN. "Specifying Specific Deterrence: The Influence of Arrest on Future Criminal Activity." *American Sociological Review*. Vol. 54, No. 1 (February 1989):94–105.

SMITH, DOUGLAS A., and CHRISTY A. VISHER. "Street-Level Justice: Situational Determinants of Police Arrest Decisions." *Social Problems*. Vol. 29, No. 2 (December 1981):167–77.

SMITH, GWEN. "The Home Team." *Maclean's* (April 17, 1997a):68.

———. "She Shoots: She Scores!" *Elm Street* (November/December 1997b):32.

SMITH, MICHAEL. "Earth Too Small for Comfort." *Calgary Herald* (February 10, 1996): A8.

SMITH, ROBERT B. "Health Care Reform Now." *Society*. Vol. 30, No. 3 (March–April 1993):56–65.

SMITH, ROBERT ELLIS. *Privacy: How to Protect What's Left of It*. Garden City, N.Y.: Anchor/Doubleday, 1979.

SMITH, TOM W. Research results reported in "Anti-Semitism Decreases But Persists." *Society*. Vol. 33, No. 3 (March/April 1996):2.

SMITH-LOVIN, LYNN, and CHARLES BRODY. "Interruptions in Group Discussions: The Effects of Gender and Group Composition." *American Journal of Sociology*. Vol. 54, No. 3 (June 1989):424–35.

SMOLAN, RICK, and JENNIFER ERWITT. *24 Hours in Cyberspace*. New York: Que* Macmillan Publishing, 1996.

SMOLOWE, JILL. "A Heavenly Host in Georgia." *Time*. Vol. 141, No. 3 (January 18, 1993):55.

———. "When Violence Hits Home." *Time*. Vol. 144, No. 1 (July 4, 1994):18–25.

SNELL, MARILYN BERLIN. "The Purge of Nurture." *New Perspectives Quarterly*. Vol. 7, No. 1 (Winter 1990):1–2.

SNIDERMAN, PAUL M., DAVID A. NORTHRUP, JOSEPH F. FLETCHER, PETER H. RUSSELL AND PHILIP E. TETLOCK. "Psychological and Cultural Foundations of Prejudice: The Case of Anti-Semitism in Quebec." *Canadian Review of Sociology and Anthropology*. Vol. 30, No. 2 (May 1993): 242–270.

SNOW, DAVID A., E. BURKE ROCHFORD, JR., STEVEN K. WORDEN, and ROBERT D. BENFORD. "Frame Alignment Processes, Micromobilization, and Movement Participation." *American Sociological Review*. Vol. 51, No. 4 (August 1986):464–81.

SNOW, DAVID A., LOUIS A. ZURCHER, JR., and SHELDON EKLAND-OLSON. "Social Networks and Social Movements: A Macrostructural Approach to Differential Recruitment." *American Sociological Review*. Vol. 45, No. 5 (October 1980):787–801.

SNOWMAN, DANIEL. *Britain and America: An Interpretation of Their Culture 1945–1975*. New York: Harper Torchbooks, 1977.

SOUTH, SCOTT J., and STEVEN F. MESSNER. "Structural Determinants of Intergroup Association: Interracial Marriage and Crime." *American Journal of Sociology*. Vol. 91, No. 6 (May 1986):1409–30.

SOWELL, THOMAS. *Ethnic America*. New York: Basic Books, 1981.

———. *Race and Culture*. New York: Basic Books, 1994.

———. "Ethnicity and IQ." In Steven Fraser, ed., *The Bell Curve Wars: Race, Intelligence and the Future of America*. New York: Basic Books, 1995:70–79.

———. *Migrations and Cultures: A World View*. New York: Basic Books, 1996.

SOYINKA, WOLE. "Africa's Culture Producers." *Society*. Vol. 28, No. 2 (January–February 1991):32–40.

SPATES, JAMES L. "Sociological Overview." In Alan Milberg, ed., *Street Games*. New York: McGraw-Hill, 1976a:286–90.

———. "Counterculture and Dominant Culture Values: A Cross-National Analysis of the Underground Press and Dominant Culture Magazines." *American Sociological Review*. Vol. 41, No. 5 (October 1976b):868–83.

———. "The Sociology of Values." In Ralph Turner, ed., *Annual Review of Sociology*. Vol. 9. Palo Alto, Calif.: Annual Reviews, 1983:27–49.

SPATES, JAMES L., and JOHN J. MACIONIS. *The Sociology of Cities*. 2d ed. Belmont, Calif.: Wadsworth, 1987.

SPATES, JAMES L., and H. WESLEY PERKINS. "American and English Student Values." *Comparative Social Research*. Vol. 5. Greenwich, Conn.: JAI Press, 1982:245–68.

SPECTOR, LEONARD S. "Nuclear Proliferation Today." In William M. Evan and Stephen Hilgartner, eds., *The Arms Race and Nuclear War*. Englewood Cliffs, N.J.: Prentice Hall, 1988:25–29.

SPECTER, MICHAEL. "Plunging Life Expectancy Puzzles Russia." *New York Times* (August 2, 1995):A1, A2.

———. "Moscow on the Make." *New York Times Magazine* (June 1, 1997):48–55, 72, 75, 80, 84.

———. "Deep in the Russian Soul, a Lethal Darkness." *New York Times* (June 8, 1997): section 4, pp. 1, 5.

SPEER, JAMES A. "The New Christian Right and Its Parent Company: A Study in Political Contrasts." In David G. Bromley and Anson Shupe, eds., *New Christian Politics*. Macon, Ga.: Mercer University Press, 1984:19–40.

SPEER, TIBBETT L. "Are College Costs Cutting Enrollment?" *American Demographics*. Vol. 16, No. 11 (November 1994):9–10.

———. "Digging Into the Underground Economy." *American Demographics*. Vol. 17, No. 2 (February 1995):15–16.

———. "A Nation of Students." *American Demographics*. Vol. 48, No. 8 (August 1996):32–39.

———. "Taxing Times." *American Demographics*. Vol. 49, No. 4 (April 1997):41–44.

SPENCER, MARTIN E. "Multiculturalism, 'Political Correctness,' and the Politics of Identity." *Sociological Forum*. Vol. 9, No. 4 (December 1994):547–67.

SPENCER, META. *Foundations of Modern Sociology*. Canadian 2d ed. Toronto: Prentice Hall, 1981.

SPENDER, DALE. *Man Made Language*. London: Routledge & Kegan Paul, 1980.

SPITZER, STEVEN. "Toward a Marxian Theory of Deviance." In Delos H. Kelly, ed., *Criminal Behavior: Readings in Criminology*. New York: St. Martin's Press, 1980:175–91.

STACEY, JUDITH. *Patriarchy and Socialist Revolution in China*. Berkeley: University of California Press, 1983.

———. *Brave New Families: Stories of Domestic Upheaval in Late Twentieth-Century America*. New York: Basic Books, 1990.

———. "Good Riddance to 'The Family': A Response to David Popenoe." *Journal of Marriage and the Family*. Vol. 55, No. 3 (August 1993):545–47.

STACK, CAROL B. *All Our Kin: Strategies for Survival in a Black Community*. New York: Harper & Row, 1975.

STAHURA, JOHN M. "Suburban Development, Black Suburbanization and the Black Civil Rights Movement Since World War II." *American Sociological Review*. Vol. 51, No. 1 (February 1986):131–44.

STANLEY, LIZ, ED. *Feminist Praxis: Research, Theory, and Epistemology in Feminist Sociology*. London: Routledge & Kegan Paul, 1990.

STANLEY, LIZ, and SUE WISE. *Breaking Out: Feminist Consciousness and Feminist Research*. London: Routledge & Kegan Paul, 1983.

STAPLES, ROBERT, and ALFREDO MIRANDE. "Racial and Cultural Variations Among American Families: A Decennial Review of the Literature on Minority Families." *Journal of Marriage and the Family*. Vol. 42, No. 4 (August 1980):157–72.

STARK, EVAN, AND ANN FLITCRAFT. "Domestic Violence and Female Suicide Attempts." Presentation to American Public Health Association, New York, 1979.

STARK, RODNEY. *Sociology*. Belmont, Calif.: Wadsworth, 1985.

STARK, RODNEY, and WILLIAM SIMS BAINBRIDGE. "Of Churches, Sects, and Cults: Preliminary Concepts for a Theory of Religious Movements." *Journal for the Scientific Study of Religion*. Vol. 18, No. 2 (June 1979):117–31.

———. "Secularization and Cult Formation in the Jazz Age." *Journal for the Scientific Study of Religion*. Vol. 20, No. 4 (December 1981):360–73.

STARK, RODNEY, and CHARLES Y. GLOCK. *American Piety: The Nature of Religious Commitment*. Berkeley: University of California Press, 1968.

STARR, PAUL. *The Social Transformation of American Medicine*. New York: Basic Books, 1982.

STATISTICS CANADA. *1881, 1921 and 1961 Censuses of Canada and Projections*. Catalogue No. 91-520. Ottawa: Statistics Canada, 1989a.

———. *Profile of Ethnic Groups—Dimensions*. Ottawa: Statistics Canada, 1989b.

———. *Lone-Parent Families in Canada*. Catalogue No. 89-522E. Ottawa: Statistics Canada, 1992.

———. *Juristat Service Bulletin*. Catalogue No. 85-002. Ottawa: Statistics Canada, 1994.

———. "Social Indicators." *Canadian Social Trends* (Spring 1996).

Statistics of Income Bulletin. Vol. 11, No. 3 (Winter 1991–92).

STAVRIANOS, L. S. *A Global History: The Human Heritage*. 3d ed. Englewood Cliffs, N.J.: Prentice Hall, 1983.

STEARNS, LINDA BREWSTER, and KENNETH D. ALLAN. "Economic Behavior in Institutional Environments: The Corporate Merger Wave of the 1980s." *American Sociological Review*. Vol. 61, No. 4 (August, 1996):699–718.

STEELE, SCOTT. "Women at work: Room to improve." *Macleans* (August 21, 1995):28-29.

STEELE, SHELBY. *The Content of Our Character: A New Vision of Race in America*. New York: St. Martin's Press, 1990.

STEIN, MAURICE R. *The Eclipse of Community: An Interpretation of American Studies*. Princeton, N.J.: Princeton University Press, 1972.

STEINBERG, LAURENCE. "Failure Outside the Classroom." *Wall Street Journal* (July 11, 1996):A14.

STEPHENS, JOHN D. *The Transition From Capitalism to Socialism*. Urbana: University of Illinois Press, 1986.

STERNLIEB, GEORGE, and JAMES W. HUGHES. "The Uncertain Future of the Central City." *Urban Affairs Quarterly*. Vol. 18, No. 4 (June 1983):455–72.

STEVENS, GILLIAN, and GRAY SWICEGOOD. "The Linguistic Context of Ethnic Endogamy." *American Sociological Review*. Vol. 52, No. 1 (February 1987):73–82.

STEVENS, ROSEMARY. *American Medicine and the Public Interest*. New Haven, Conn.: Yale University Press, 1971.

STIEHM, JUDITH HICKS. *Arms and the Enlisted Woman*. Philadelphia: Temple University Press, 1989.

STIER, HAYA. "Continuity and Change in Women's Occupations Following First Childbirth." *Social Science Quarterly*. Vol. 77, No. 1 (March 1996):60–75.

STODDARD, SANDOL. *The Hospice Movement: A Better Way to Care for the Dying*. Briarcliff Manor, N.Y.: Stein and Day, 1978.

STONE, LAWRENCE. *The Family, Sex and Marriage in England 1500–1800*. New York: Harper & Row, 1977.

STONE, ROBYN. *The Feminization of Poverty and Older Women*. Washington, D.C.: U. S. Department of Health and Human Services, 1986.

STONE, ROBYN, GAIL LEE CAFFERATA, and JUDITH SANGL. *Caregivers of the Frail Elderly: A National Profile*. Washington, D.C.: U.S. Department of Health and Human Services, 1987.

STOUFFER, SAMUEL A., ET AL. *The American Soldier: Adjustment During Army Life*. Princeton, N.J.: Princeton University Press, 1949.

STOUT, CAM. "Common-law: A Growing Alternative." In *Canadian Social Trends* (Summer 1994):9.

STRAUS, MURRAY A., and RICHARD J. GELLES. "Societal Change and Change in Family Violence From 1975 to 1985 as Revealed by Two National Surveys." *Journal of Marriage and the Family*. Vol. 48, No. 4 (August 1986):465–79.

STREIB, GORDON F. "Are the Aged a Minority Group?" In Bernice L. Neugarten, ed., *Middle Age and Aging: A Reader in Social Psychology*. Chicago: University of Chicago Press, 1968:35–46.

STRIEGEL-MOORE, RUTH, LISA R. SILBERSTEIN, and JUDITH RODIN. "Toward an Understanding of Risk Factors for Bulimia." *American Psychologist*. Vol. 41, No. 3 (March 1986):246–63.

Student CHIP Social Survey Software. Data sets by Bruner & Macionis. Hanover, N.H.: Zeta Data. © 1992 by James A. Davis.

SUDNOW, DAVID N. *Passing On: The Social Organization of Dying*. Englewood Cliffs, N.J.: Prentice Hall, 1967.

SUMNER, WILLIAM GRAHAM. *Folkways*. New York: Dover, 1959; orig. 1906.

SUNG, BETTY LEE. *Mountains of Gold: The Story of the Chinese in America*. New York: Macmillan, 1967.

SURTEES, LAWRENCE. "Northern Telecom: The morning after." *The Globe and Mail* (July 5, 1993): B1, 4.

SUTHERLAND, EDWIN H. "White Collar Criminality." *American Sociological Review*. Vol. 5, No. 1 (February 1940):1–12.

SUTHERLAND, EDWIN H., and DONALD R. CRESSEY. *Criminology*. 10th ed. Philadelphia: J.B. Lippincott, 1978.

SWARTZ, STEVE. "Why Michael Milken Stands to Qualify for Guinness Book." *Wall Street Journal*. Vol. LXX, No. 117 (March 31, 1989):1, 4.

SYZMANSKI, ALBERT. *Class Structure: A Critical Perspective*. New York: Praeger, 1983.

SZASZ, THOMAS S. *The Manufacturer of Madness: A Comparative Study of the Inquisition and the Mental Health Movement*. New York: Dell, 1961.

———. *The Myth of Mental Illness: Foundations of a Theory of Personal Conduct*. New York: Harper & Row, 1970; orig. 1961.

———. "Mental Illness Is Still a Myth." *Society*. Vol. 31, No. 4 (May-June 1994):34–39.

———. "Idleness and Lawlessness in the Therapeutic State." *Society*. Vol. 32, No. 4 (May/June 1995):30–35.

TAEUBER, KARL, and ALMA TAEUBER. *Negroes in Cities*. Chicago: Aldine, 1965.

TAJFEL, HENRI. "Social Psychology of Intergroup Relations." *Annual Review of Psychology*. Palo Alto, Calif.: Annual Reviews, 1982:1–39.

"Taking the Pulse—From Gallup Canada." *Toronto Star* (September 7, 1992):A11.

TANNEN, DEBORAH. *You Just Don't Understand Me: Women and Men in Conversation*. New York: Wm. Morrow, 1990.

———. *Talking from 9 to 5: How Women's and Men's Conversational Styles Affect Who Gets Heard, Who Gets Credit, and What Gets Done at Work*. New York: Wm. Morrow, 1994.

TANNENBAUM, FRANK. *Slave and Citizen: The Negro in the Americas*. New York: Vintage Books, 1946.

TANNER, MICHAEL, and STEPHEN MOORE. "Why Welfare Pays." *Wall Street Journal* (September 28, 1995):A20.

TARAS, DAVID, BEVERLY RASPORICH, AND ELI MANDEL. *A Passion for Identity: An introduction to Canadian Studies*. Scarborough, Ontario: Nelson, 1993.

TARROW, SIDNEY. *Social Movements, Collective Action and Politics*. New York: Cambridge University Press, 1994.

TAVRIS, CAROL, and SUSAN SADD. *The Redbook Report on Female Sexuality*. New York: Delacorte Press, 1977.

TAX FOUNDATION. [Online] Available http://www.taxfoundation.org/prtaxfree.html, 1997.

TAYLOR, JOHN. "Don't Blame Me: The New Culture of Victimization." *New York Magazine* (June 3, 1991):26–34.

TEPPERMAN, LORNE. "A Simulation of Social Mobility in Industrial Societies." *Canadian Review of Sociology and Anthropology*. Vol. 13 (1976): 26–42.

TERKEL, STUDS. *Working*. New York: Pantheon Books, 1974:1–2, 57–59, 65, 66, 69, 221–22. Copyright © 1974 by Pantheon Books, a division of Random House, Inc.

TERRY, DON. "In Crackdown on Bias, A New Tool." *New York Times* (June 12, 1993):8.

THEEN, ROLF H. W. "Party and Bureaucracy." In Erik P. Hoffmann and Robbin F. Laird, eds., *The Soviet Polity in the Modern Era*. New York: Aldine, 1984:131–65.

THEILMANN, JOHN, and ALLEN WILHITE. "Congressional Turnover: Negating the Incumbent Advantage." *Social Science Quarterly*. Vol. 76, No. 3 (September 1995):594–606.

THERNSTROM, STEPHAN. "The Minority Majority Will Never Come." *Wall Street Journal* (July 26, 1990):A16.

THOITS, PEGGY A. "Self-labeling Processes in Mental Illness: The Role of Emotional Deviance." *American Journal of Sociology*. Vol. 91, No. 2 (September 1985):221–49.

THOMAS, EDWARD J. *The Life of Buddha as Legend and History*. London: Routledge & Kegan Paul, 1975.

THOMAS, PAULETTE. "Success at a Huge Personal Cost." *Wall Street Journal* (July 26, 1995):B1, B6.

THOMAS, PIRI. *Down These Mean Streets*. New York: Signet, 1967.

THOMAS, W. I. "The Relation of Research to the Social Process." In Morris Janowitz, ed., *W. I. Thomas on Social Organization and Social Personality*. Chicago: University of Chicago Press, 1966:289–305; orig. 1931.

———, AND F. ZNANIECKI. *The Polish Peasant in Europe and America*. New York: Octagon Books, 1971; orig 1919.

THOMMA, STEVEN. "Christian Coalition Demands Action From GOP." *Philadelphia Inquirer* (September 14, 1997):A2.

THOMPSON, LARRY. "The Breast Cancer Gene: A Woman's Dilemma." *Time*. Vol. 143, No. 3 (January 17, 1994):52.

———. "Fertility With Less Fuss." *Time*. Vol. 144, No. 20 (November 14, 1994):79.

THOMPSON, MARK. "Offensive Maneuvers." *Time*. Vol. 149, No. 18 (May 5, 1997):40–42.

THORNBERRY, TERRANCE, and MARGARET FARNSWORTH. "Social Correlates of Criminal Involvement: Further Evidence on the Relationship Between Social Status and Criminal Behavior." *American Sociological Review*. Vol 47, No. 4 (August 1982):505–18.

THORNE, BARRIE, CHERIS KRAMARAE, and NANCY HENLEY, EDS. *Language, Gender and Society*. Rowley, Mass.: Newbury House, 1983.

THORNTON, ARLAND. "Changing Attitudes Toward Separation and Divorce: Causes and Consequences." *American Journal of Sociology*. Vol. 90, No. 4 (January 1985):856–72.

THUROW, LESTER C. "A Surge in Inequality." *Scientific American*. Vol. 256, No. 5 (May 1987):30–37.

TIGER, LIONEL, and JOSEPH SHEPHER. *Women in the Kibbutz*. New York: Harcourt Brace Jovanovich, 1975.

TILLY, CHARLES. *From Mobilization to Revolution*. Reading, Mass.: Addison-Wesley, 1978.

———. "Does Modernization Breed Revolution?" In Jack A. Goldstone, ed., *Revolutions: Theoretical, Comparative, and Historical Studies*. New York: Harcourt Brace Jovanovich, 1986:47–57.

TINDALE, JOSEPH A. N.A.C.A. "Older Workers in an Aging Workforce." Ottawa: Statistics Canada, 1991.

TITTLE, CHARLES R., and WAYNE J. VILLEMEZ. "Social Class and Criminality." *Social Forces*. Vol. 56, No. 22 (December 1977):474–502.

TITTLE, CHARLES R., WAYNE J. VILLEMEZ, and DOUGLAS A. SMITH. "The Myth of Social Class and Criminality: An Empirical Assessment of the Empirical Evidence." *American Sociological Review*. Vol. 43, No. 5 (October 1978):643–56.

TOBIN, GARY. "Suburbanization and the Development of Motor Transportation: Transportation Technology and the Suburbanization Process." In Barry Schwartz, ed., *The Changing Face of the Suburbs*. Chicago: University of Chicago Press, 1976.

TOCH, THOMAS. "The Exodus." *U.S. News & World Report*. Vol. 111, No. 24 (December 9, 1991):68–77.

TOCQUEVILLE, ALEXIS DE. *The Old Regime and the French Revolution*. Stuart Gilbert, trans. Garden City, N.Y.: Anchor/Doubleday Books, 1955; orig. 1856.

TOENNIES, FERDINAND. *Community and Society (Gemeinschaft und Gesellschaft)*. New York: Harper & Row, 1963; orig. 1887.

TOFANI, LORETTA. "AIDS Ravages a Continent, and Sweeps a Family." *Philadelphia Inquirer* (March 24, 1991):1, 15–A.

TOFFLER, ALVIN, and HEIDI TOFFLER. *War and Anti-war: Survival at the Dawn of the 21st Century*. Boston: Little, Brown, 1993.

TOLSON, JAY. "The Trouble With Elites." *The Wilson Quarterly*. Vol. XIX, No. 1 (Winter 1995):6–8.

TOMLINSON, BRIAN. "Development in the 1990s: Critical Reflections on Canada's Economic Relations with the Third World." In Jamie Swift and Brian Tomlinson, eds., *Conflicts of Interest: Canada and the Third World*. Toronto: Between the Lines, 1991.

TOOMEY, BEVERLY, RICHARD FIRST, and JOHN RIFE. Research described in "Number of Rural Homeless Greater Than Expected." *Ohio State Quest* (Autumn 1990):2.

TOWNSEND, BICKLEY. "Room at the Top for Women." *American Demographics*. Vol. 18, No. 7 (July 1996):28–37.

TREAS, JUDITH. "Socialist Organization and Economic Development in China: Latent Consequences for the Aged." *The Gerontologist*. Vol. 19, No. 1 (February 1979):34–43.

———. "Older Americans in the 1990s and Beyond." *Population Bulletin*. Vol. 50, No. 2 (May 1995). Washington, D.C.: Population Reference Bureau.

TREIMAN, DONALD J. "Industrialization and Social Stratification." In Edward O. Laumann, ed., *Social Stratification: Research and Theory for the 1970s*. Indianapolis, Ind.: Bobbs-Merrill, 1970.

TRENT, KATHERINE. "Family Context and Adolescents' Expectations About Marriage, Fertility, and Nonmarital Childbearing." *Social Science Quarterly*. Vol. 75, No 2 (June 1994):319–39.

TROELTSCH, ERNST. *The Social Teaching of the Christian Churches*. New York: Macmillan, 1931.

TROIDEN, RICHARD R. *Gay and Lesbian Identity: A Sociological Analysis*. Dix Hills, N.Y.: General Hall, 1988.

TUCKER, M. BELINDA, and CLAUDIA MITCHELL-KERNAN, eds. *The Decline of Marriage Among African Americans*. New York: Russell Sage Foundation, 1995.

TUMIN, MELVIN M. "Some Principles of Stratification: A Critical Analysis." *American Sociological Review*. Vol. 18, No. 4 (August 1953):387–94.

———. *Social Stratification: The Forms and Functions of Inequality*. 2d ed. Englewood Cliffs, N.J.: Prentice Hall, 1985.

TURNER, RALPH H., and LEWIS M. KILLIAN. *Collective Behavior*. 2d ed. Englewood Cliffs, N.J.: Prentice Hall, 1972; 3d ed., 1987; 4th ed., 1993.

TYGIEL, JULES. *Baseball's Great Experiment: Jackie Robinson and His Legacy*. New York: Oxford University Press, 1983.

TYLER, S. LYMAN. *A History of Indian Policy*. Washington, D.C.: United States Department of the Interior, Bureau of Indian Affairs, 1973.

TYREE, ANDREA, MOSHE SEMYONOV, and ROBERT W. HODGE. "Gaps and Glissandos: Inequality, Economic Development, and Social Mobility in 24 Countries." *American Sociological Review*. Vol. 44, No. 3 (June 1979):410–24.

UCHITELLE, LOUIS. "But Just Who is That Fairy Godmother?" *New York Times* (September 29, 1991): Section 4, p. 1.

UJIMOTO, K. VICTOR. "Postwar Japanese Immigrants in British Columbia: Japanese Culture and Job Transferability." In Jean Leonard Elliott, ed., *Two Nations, Many Cultures: Ethnic Groups in Canada*. Scarborough, Ont.: Prentice Hall, 1979.

UNITED NATIONS DEVELOPMENT PROGRAMME. *Human Development Report 1990*. New York: Oxford University Press, 1990.

———. *Human Development Report 1991*. New York:Oxford University Press, 1991.

———. *Human Development Report 1993*. New York:Oxford University Press, 1993.

———. *Human Development Report 1994*. New York: Oxford University Press, 1994.

———. *Human Development Report 1995*. New York: Oxford University Press, 1995.

———. *Human Development Report 1996*. New York: Oxford University Press, 1996.

———. *Human Development Report 1997*. New York: Oxford University Press, 1997.

UNIVERSITY OF AKRON RESEARCH CENTER. *National Survey of Religion and Politics 1992*. Akron, Ohio: University of Akron Research Center, 1993.

UNLAND, KAREN. "Photo collection part of Quebec's gay history." *The Globe and Mail* (August 19, 1997):A2.

UNNEVER, JAMES D., CHARLES E. FRAZIER, and JOHN C. HENRETTA. "Race Differences in Criminal Sentencing." *The Sociological Quarterly*. Vol. 21, No. 2 (Spring 1980):197–205.

UNRUH, JOHN D., JR. *The Plains Across*. Urbana: University of Illinois Press, 1979.

U.S. BUREAU OF THE CENSUS. *Statistical Abstract of the United States 1970*. 90th ed. Washington, D.C.: U.S. Government Printing Office, 1970.

———. Press release on homeless count (CB91–117). Washington, D.C.: U.S. Government Printing Office, 1991.

———. *Fertility of American Women: June 1990*. Current Population Reports, Series P-20, No. 454. Washington, D.C.: U. S. Government Printing Office, 1991.

———. *Statistical Abstract of the United States: 1992*. 112th ed. Washington, D.C.: U.S. Government Printing Office, 1992.

———. *Money Income of Households, Families, and Persons in the United States: 1992*. Current Population Reports, Series P-60, No. 184. Washington, D.C.: U.S. Government Printing Office, 1993.

———. *Poverty in the United States: 1992*. Current Population Reports, Series P-60, No. 185. Washington, D.C.: U.S. Government Printing Office, 1993.

———. *Statistical Abstract of the United States: 1993*. 113th ed. Washington, D.C.: U.S. Government Printing Office, 1993.

———. *Educational Attainment in the United States: March 1993 and 1992*. Current Population Reports, Series P-20, No. 476. Washington, D.C.: U.S. Government Printing Office, 1994.

———. *School Enrollment—Social and Economic Characteristics of Students: October 1993*. Current Population Reports, Series P-20, No. 479. Washington, D.C.: U.S. Government Printing Office, 1994.

———. *Statistical Abstract of the United States: 1994*. 114th ed. Washington, D.C.: U.S. Government Printing Office, 1994.

———. *Asset Ownership of Households: 1993*. Current Population Reports, Series P-70, No. 47. Washington, D.C.: U.S. Government Printing Office, 1995.

———. *Current Population Reports*. Series P-60, No. 188. Washington, D.C.: U.S. Government Printing Office, 1995.

———. *Household and Family Characteristics: March 1994*. Current Population Reports, Series P-20, No. 483, Washington, D.C.: U.S. Government Printing Office, 1995.

———. *Income, Poverty, and Valuation of Noncash Benefits: 1993*. Current Population Reports, Series P-60, No. 188. Washington, D.C.: U.S. Government Printing Office, 1995.

———. *Statistical Abstract of the United States: 1995*. 115th ed. Washington, D.C.: U.S. Government Printing Office, 1995.

———. *Marital Status and Living Arrangements: March 1995*. PPL-52. Washington, D.C.: U.S. Government Printing Office, 1996.

———. *Money Income in the United States 1995*. Current Population Reports, P60–193. Washington, D.C.: U.S. Government Printing Office, 1996.

———. *Population Projections of the United States by Age, Sex, Race, and Hispanic Origin: 1995 to 2050*. P25–1130. Washington, D.C.: U.S. Government Printing Office, 1996.

———. Prepublication data on income and wealth provided by the Census Bureau, 1996.

———. Press release on women-owned businesses, 1996.

———. Response to telephone query, 1996.

———. *Women-Owned Businesses*. Washington, D.C.: U.S. Government Printing Office, 1996.

———. *World Population Profile 1996*. WP/96. Washington, D.C.: U.S. Government Printing Office, 1996.

———. Data on educational achievement. [Online] Available http://www.census.gov/population/socdemo/education/educ96cps.dat, 1997.

———. Data on mixed marriages. [Online] Available http://www.census.gov/population/socdemo/ms-la/95his04.tx, 1997.

———. *Educational Attainment in the United States: March 1996 (Update)*. Current Population Reports, P20–493. Washington, D.C.: U.S. Government Printing Office, 1997.

———. *Health Insurance Coverage: 1996*. Current Population Reports, P60–199. Washington, D.C.: U.S. Government Printing Office, 1997.

———. *Household and Family Characteristics: March 1996*. PPL-66. Washington, D.C.: U.S. Government Printing Office, 1997.

———. *Money Income in the United States 1996 (With Separate Data on Valuation of Noncash Benefits)*. Current Population Reports, P60–197. Washington, D.C.: U.S. Government Printing Office, 1997.

———. *Poverty in the United States: 1996*. Current Population Reports, P60–198. Washington, D.C.: U.S. Government Printing Office, 1997.

———. *School Enrollment—Social and Economic Characteristics of Students: October 1995 (Update)*. PPL-55: The Bureau, 1997.

———. *Statistical Abstract of the United States 1997*. Washington, D.C.: U.S. Government Printing Office, 1997.

———. *Table F-1: Income Limits for Each Fifth and Top 5 Percent of Families (All Races): 1947 to 1996*. [Online] Available http://www.census.gov/hhes/income/histinc/f01.htm, December 31, 1997.

———. *Table F-3: Mean Income Received by Each Fifth and Top 5 Percent of Families (All Races): 1966 to 1996*. [Online] Available http://www.census.gov/hhes/income/histinc/f03.htm, December 31, 1997.

———. *Table F-5: Race and Hispanic Origin of Householder—Families by Median and Mean Income: 1947 to 1996*. [Online] Available http://www.census.gov/hhes/income/histinc/f05.htm, December 31, 1997.

———. "Who's Minding Our Preschoolers?" *Fall 1994 (Update)*. P70–62. Washington, D.C.: U.S. Government Printing Office, 1997.

———. *Estimated Median Age at First Marriage, by Sex: 1890 to the Present*. [Online] Available http://www.census.gov/population/socdemo/ms-la/95his06.txt, January 2, 1998.

———. *International Database*. [Online] Available http://www.census.gov/cgi-bin/ipc/idbsum, January 8, 1998.

———. *Historical Income Tables—Persons. Table P-9: Age—All Persons 15 Years Old and Over by Median and Mean Income and Sex: 1974 to 1996*. [Online] Available http://www.census.gov/hhes/income/histinc/p09.htm, January 18, 1998.

———. *Resident Population of the United States: Estimates by Sex, Race, and Hispanic Origin, With Median Age*. [Online] Available http://www.census.gov/population/estimates/nation/intfile3–1.tx, January 19, 1998.

———. *Historical Income Tables—Families. Table F-2B: Share of Aggregate Income Received by Each Fifth and Top 5 Percent of Black Families: 1966 to 1996*. [Online] Available http://www.census.gov/hhes/income/histinc/f02b.htm, February 8, 1998.

U.S. BUREAU OF ECONOMIC ANALYSIS. *Foreign Direct Investment in the United States: Selected Items, by Country of Foreign Parent and by Industry of Affiliate, 1994–96*. [Online] Available http://www.bea.doc.gov/bea/di/fdius-d.htm#fdius-1, January 19, 1998.

U.S. BUREAU OF JUSTICE STATISTICS. *Sourcebook of Criminal Justice Statistics 1990*. Timothy J. Flanagan and Kathleen Maguire, eds. Washington, D.C.: U.S. Government Printing Office, 1991.

———. *Compendium of Federal Justice Statistics, 1989*. Washington D.C.: U.S. Government Printing Office, 1992.

———. *Violence Against Women*. Washington, D.C.: U.S. Government Printing Office, 1994.

———. *National Crime Victimization Survey, 1992–1993*. Washington, D.C.: U.S. Government Printing Office, 1995.

———. *Criminal Victimization 1994*. Washington, D.C.: U.S. Government Printing Office, 1996.

———. *Correctional Populations in the United States 1995*. Washington, D.C.: The Bureau, 1997.

———. *Criminal Victimization 1996*. Washington, D.C.: The Bureau, 1997.

———. *Sourcebook of Criminal Justice Statistics 1996*. Washington, D.C.: The Bureau, 1997.

U.S. BUREAU OF LABOR STATISTICS. *Employment and Earnings*. Vol. 41, No. 1 (January). Washington, D.C.: U.S. Government Printing Office, 1994.

———. *Employment and Earnings*. Vol. 42, No. 1 (January). Washington, D.C.: U.S. Government Printing Office, 1995.

———. Unpublished data on U.S. labor force, 1995.

———. *Employment and Earnings*. Vol. 43, No. 1 (January 1996).

———. Response to telephone query, 1996.

U.S. CENTERS FOR DISEASE CONTROL AND PREVENTION. Response to telephone query, 1994.

———. *HIV/AIDS Surveillance Report*. Vol. 7, No. 1. Rockville, Md.: CDC National AIDS Clearinghouse, 1995.

———. *HIV/AIDS Surveillance Report*. Vol. 9, No. 1 (Midyear ed., 1997): 8.

———. *Morbidity and Mortality Weekly Report*. Vol. 46, No. 51 (December 26, 1997).

U.S. DEPARTMENT OF AGRICULTURE. Agricultural Research Service. *Family Economics Research Group. Expenditures on a Child by Families, 1992*. Hyattsville, Md.: The Group, 1993.

U.S. DEPARTMENT OF JUSTICE. Press release, June 22, 1994.

U.S. DEPARTMENT OF LABOR. Bureau of Labor Statistics. "Portability of Pension Benefits Among Jobs." Washington, D.C.: U.S. Government Printing Office, 1994.

———. Bureau of Labor Statistics. *Employment and Earnings*. Vol. 44, No. 1 (January). Washington, D.C.: U.S. Government Printing Office, 1997.

———. Bureau of Labor Statistics. "Looking for a Job While Employed." Summary 97–14. Washington, D.C.: U.S. Government Printing Office, 1997.

———. Bureau of Labor Statistics. *Employment and Earnings*. Vol. 45, No. 1 (January). Washington, D.C.: U.S. Government Printing Office, 1998.

USEEM, BERT. "Disorganization and the New Mexico Prison Riot of 1980." *American Sociological Review*. Vol. 50, No. 5 (October 1985):677–88.

USEEM, MICHAEL. "The Social Organization of the Corporate Business Elite and Participation of Corporate Directors in the Governance of American Institutions." *American Sociological Review*. Vol. 44, No. 4 (August 1979): 553–72.

———. "Corporations and the Corporate Elite." In Alex Inkeles et al., eds., *Annual Review of Sociology*. Vol. 6. Palo Alto, Cal.: Annual Reviews, 1980:41–77.

USEEM, MICHAEL, and JEROME KARABEL. "Pathways to Corporate Management." *American Sociological Review*. Vol. 51, No. 2 (April 1986):184–200.

U.S. EQUAL EMPLOYMENT OPPORTUNITY COMMISSION. *Job Patterns for Minorities and Women in Private Industry 1994*. Washington, D.C.: The Commission, 1995.

———. Response to personal query, 1996.

———. *Job Patterns for Minorities and Women in Private Industry, 1996*. Washington, D.C.: The Commission, 1997.

U.S. FEDERAL BUREAU OF INVESTIGATION. *Crime in the United States 1993*. Washington, D.C.: U.S. Government Printing Office, 1994.

———. *Crime in the United States 1994*. Washington, D.C.: U.S. Government Printing Office, 1995.

———. *Uniform Crime Reports for the United States 1995*. Washington, D.C.: U.S. Government Printing Office, 1996.

———. *Uniform Crime Reports for the United States 1996*. Washington, D.C.: U.S. Government Printing Office, 1997.

U.S. FEDERAL ELECTION COMMISSION. *1994 Congressional Funding Sets New Record*. Washington, D.C.: The Commission, 1995.

———. "Congressional Fundraising and Spending Up Again in 1996." Washington, D.C.: The Commission, 1997.

———. "FEC Releases Semiannual Federal PAC Count." [Online] Available http://www.fec.gov/press/count98.htm, February 7, 1998.

U.S. HOUSE OF REPRESENTATIVES. "Street Children: A Global Disgrace." Hearing on November 7, 1991. Washington, D.C.: U.S. Government Printing Office, 1992.

U.S. IMMIGRATION AND NATURALIZATION SERVICE. *Statistical Yearbook*. Washington, D.C.: U.S. Government Printing Office, 1995.

———. *Table 3: Immigrants Admitted by Region and Selected Country of Birth, Fiscal Years 1984–94*. Fax received from INS January 1996.

———. *Immigrants Admitted by Region and Selected Country of Birth*. [Online] Available http://www.ins.doj.gov/stats/annual/fy94/744.htm, December 5, 1997.

———. *Table 5: Immigrants Admitted by Region and Selected Country of Birth, Fiscal Years 1994–96*. [Online] Available http://www.ins.doj.gov/stats/annual/fy96/1005.htm, December 5, 1997.

U.S. INTERNAL REVENUE SERVICE. *Statistics of Income Bulletin* (Spring 1993).

U.S. NATIONAL CENTER FOR EDUCATION STATISTICS. *Digest of Education Statistics 1996*. Washington, D.C.: The Center, 1996.

———. *Digest of Education Statistics 1997*. Washington, D.C.: U.S. Government Printing Office, 1997.

U.S. National Center for Health Statistics. *Vital Statistics of the United States, 1988, Vol. 1, Natality.* Washington, D.C.: U.S. Government Printing Office, 1990.

———. *Current Estimates From the National Health Interview Survey United States, 1993. Vital and Health Statistics.* Series 10, No. 190. Hyattsville, Md.: The Center, 1994.

———. "Annual Summary of Births, Marriages, Divorces, and Deaths: United States, 1994." *Monthly Vital Statistics Report.* Vol. 43, No. 13 (October 23, 1995). Hyattsville, Md.: The Center, 1995.

———. *Current Estimates From the National Health Interview Survey 1994.* Hyattsville, Md.: The Center, 1995.

———. *Advance Report of Final Mortality Statistics, 1993.* Hyattsville, Md.: The Center, 1996.

———. *Advance Report of Final Mortality Statistics, 1994.* Hyattsville, Md.: The Center, 1996.

———. *Monthly Vital Statistics Report.* Vol. 45, No. 11 (June 10, 1997).

———. *Monthly Vital Statistics Report.* Vol. 45, No. 12 (July 17, 1997):1.

———. "Births and Deaths: United States, 1996." *Monthly Vital Statistics Report.* Vol. 46, No. 1, Suppl. 2 (September 11, 1997).

U.S. State Department. *1996 Patterns of Global Terrorism Report.* [Online] Available http://www.state.gov/www/global/terrorism/1996report/1996index.htm, February 7, 1998.

Vallas, Stephen P., and John P. Beck. "The Transformation of Work Revisited: The Limits of Flexibility in American Manufacturing." *Social Problems.* Vol. 43, No. 3 (August 1996):339–61.

Vallee, F.G. "Porter, John Arthur." In *The Canadian Encyclopedia* (1988): 1726.

Valocchi, Steve. "The Emergence of the Integrationist Ideology in the Civil Rights Movement." *Social Problems.* Vol. 43, No. 1 (February 1996):116–30.

Valpy, Michael. "When Jamaican Children Come to Canada." *Globe and Mail* (March 5, 1996):A17.

Van Biema, David. "Parents Who Kill." *Time.* Vol. 144, No. 20 (November 14, 1994):50–51.

———. "Sparse At Seder?" *Time.* Vol. 149, No. 17 (April 28, 1997):67.

———. "Buddhism in America." *Time.* Vol. 150, No. 15 (October 13, 1997):71–81.

van den Haag, Ernest, and John P. Conrad. *The Death Penalty: A Debate.* New York: Plenum Press, 1983.

Van Loon, Richard J. and Michael S. Whittington. *The Canadian Political System: Environment, Structure and Process.* 3d ed. Toronto: McGraw-Hill Ryerson, 1981.

Vardy, Jill. "Job hopes take sharp nosedive." *The Financial Post* (August 7, 1993):1.

Vaughan, Mary Kay. "Multinational Corporations: The World as a Company Town." In Ahamed Idris-Soven et al., eds., *The World as a Company Town: Multinational Corporations and Social Change.* The Hague: Mouton Publishers, 1978:15–35.

Vayda, Eugene, and Raisa B. Deber. "The Canadian Health Care System: An Overview." *Social Science and Medicine.* Vol. 18, No. 3 (1984):191–97.

Veblen, Thorstein. *The Theory of the Leisure Class.* New York: The New American Library, 1953; orig. 1899.

Veum, Jonathan R. "Accounting for Income Mobility Changes in the United States." *Social Science Quarterly.* Vol. 73, No. 4 (December 1992):773–85.

Viguerie, Richard A. *The New Right: We're Ready to Lead.* Falls Church, Va.: The Viguerie Company, 1981.

Vincent, Isabel. "Parents Depend on Kids." *The Globe and Mail* (January 25, 1996):A1, A8.

Vines, Gail. "Whose Baby Is It Anyway?" *New Scientist.* No. 1515 (July 3, 1986):26–27.

Vinovskis, Maris A. "Have Social Historians Lost the Civil War? Some Preliminary Demographic Speculations." *Journal of American History.* Vol. 76, No. 1 (June 1989):34–58.

Vogel, Ezra F. *The Four Little Dragons: The Spread of Industrialization in East Asia.* Cambridge, Mass.: Harvard University Press, 1991.

Vogel, Lise. *Marxism and the Oppression of Women: Toward a Unitary Theory.* New Brunswick, N.J.: Rutgers University Press, 1983.

Vold, George B., and Thomas J. Bernard. *Theoretical Criminology.* 3d ed. New York: Oxford University Press, 1986.

von Hirsh, Andrew. *Past or Future Crimes: Deservedness and Dangerousness in the Sentencing of Criminals.* New Brunswick, N.J.: Rutgers University Press, 1986.

Vonnegut, Kurt, Jr. "Harrison Bergeron." In *Welcome to the Monkey House.* New York: Delacorte Press/Seymour Lawrence, 1968:7–13; orig. 1961.

Waite, Linda J., Gus W. Haggstrom, and David I. Kanouse. "The Consequences of Parenthood for the Marital Stability of Young Adults." *American Sociological Review.* Vol. 50, No. 6 (December 1985):850–57.

Waite, P.B. "Confederation." In *The Canadian Encyclopedia.* 2d ed. Edmonton: Hurtig Publishers, 1988: 488–9.

Walder, Andrew G. "Career Mobility and the Communist Political Order." *American Sociological Review.* Vol. 60, No. 3 (June 1995):309–28.

Waldfogel, Jane. "The Effect of Children on Women's Wages." *American Sociological Review.* Vol. 62, No. 2 (April 1997):209–17.

Waldie, Paul. "Report deepens Bre-X fiasco." *The Globe and Mail* (February 19, 1998).

Waldman, Steven. "Deadbeat Dads." *Newsweek* (May 4, 1992):46–52.

Walker, James W. St. G. *A History of Blacks in Canada.* Ottawa: Ministry of Supply and Services Canada, 1980.

Walker, Karen. "'Always There For Me': Friendship Patterns and Expectations Among Middle- and Working-Class Men and Women." *Sociological Forum.* Vol. 10, No. 2 (June 1995):273–96.

Wall, Thomas F. *Medical Ethics: Basic Moral Issues.* Washington, D.C.: University Press of America, 1980.

Wallace, Bruce. "Not an easy ride: Reform's Deborah Grey overcomes adversity." *Maclean's* (October 13, 1997):16.

Wallace, Ruth A., and Alison Wolf. *Contemporary Sociological Theory: Continuing the Classic Tradition.* 4th ed. Englewood Cliffs, N.J.: Prentice Hall, 1995.

Waller, Douglas. "Onward Cyber Soldiers." *Time.* Vol. 146, No. 8 (August 21, 1995):38–44.

Wallerstein, Immanuel. *The Modern World-System: Capitalist Agriculture and the Origins of the European World-Economy in the Sixteenth Century.* New York: Academic Press, 1974.

———. *The Capitalist World-Economy.* New York: Cambridge University Press, 1979.

———. "Crises: The World Economy, the Movements, and the Ideologies." In Albert Bergesen, ed., *Crises in the World-System.* Beverly Hills, Calif.: Sage, 1983:21–36.

———. *The Politics of the World Economy: The States, the Movements, and the Civilizations.* Cambridge: Cambridge University Press, 1984.

Wallerstein, Judith S., and Sandra Blakeslee. *Second Chances: Men, Women, and Children a Decade After Divorce.* New York: Ticknor & Fields, 1989.

Wallis, Claudia. "Children Having Children." *Time.* Vol. 126, No. 23 (December 9, 1985):78–82, 84, 87, 89–90.

———. "Hold the Eggs and Butter." *Time.* Vol. 123, No. 13 (March 26, 1984):56–63.

Wallis, David. "After Cyberoverkill Comes Cyberburnout." *New York Times* (August 4, 1996):43, 46.

Walters, Laurel Shaper. "World Educators Compare Notes." *The Christian Science Monitor: Global Report* (September 7, 1994):8.

Walton, John, and Charles Ragin. "Global and National Sources of Political Protest: Third World Responses to the Debt Crisis." *American Sociological Review.* Vol. 55, No. 6 (December 1990):876–90.

Warner, R. Stephen. "Work in Progress Toward a New Paradigm for the Sociological Study of Religion in the United States." *American Journal of Sociology.* Vol. 98, No. 5 (March 1993):1044–93.

Warner, Sam Bass, Jr. *Streetcar Suburbs.* Cambridge, Mass.: Harvard University and MIT Presses, 1962.

Warner, W. Lloyd, and J. O. Low. *The Social System of the Modern Factory.* Yankee City Series, Vol. 4. New Haven, Conn.: Yale University Press, 1947.

Warner, W. Lloyd, and Paul S. Lunt. *The Social Life of a Modern Community.* New Haven, Conn.: Yale University Press, 1941.

Waskul, Dennis. "Selfhood in the Age of Computer Mediated Symbolic Interaction." Paper presented to the annual meeting of the Southwest Social Science Association, New Orleans, La., March, 1997.

Waters, Melissa S., Will Carrington Heath, and John Keith Watson. "A Positive Model of the Determination of Religious Affiliation." *Social Science Quarterly.* Vol. 76, No. 1 (March 1995):105–23.

Watson, John B. *Behaviorism.* Rev. ed. New York: Norton, 1930.

Watson, William. "Economy." In *The Canadian Encyclopedia.* 2nd ed. Edmonton: Hurtig Publishers, 1988: 652–56.

Waxman, Chaim I. *The Stigma of Poverty: A Critique of Poverty Theories and Policies.* 2d ed. New York: Pergamon Press, 1983.

Wattenberg, Ben J. "The Population Explosion Is Over." *New York Times Magazine* (November 23, 1997):60–63.

We Need to Know About AIDS. Ottawa: Minister of National Health and Welfare, 1994.

Weber, Adna Ferrin. *The Growth of Cities.* New York: Columbia University Press, 1963; orig. 1899.

Weber, Max. *The Protestant Ethic and the Spirit of Capitalism.* New York: Charles Scribner's Sons, 1958; orig. 1904–5.

———. "Science as a Vocation." In H. H. Gerth and C. Wright Mills, *From Max Weber: Essays in Sociology.* New York: Oxford University Press, 1958:129–56; orig. 1918.

———. *Economy and Society.* G. Roth and C. Wittich, eds. Berkeley: University of California Press, 1978.

Webster, Pamela S., Terri Orbuch, and James S. House. "Effects of Childhood Family Background on Adult Marital Quality and Perceived Stability." *American Journal of Sociology.* Vol. 101, No. 2 (September 1995):404–32.

Wechsler, D. 1972. *The Measurement and Appraisal of Adult Intelligence.* 5th ed. Baltimore, Md.: Williams and Wilkins.

Weeks, John R. "The Demography of Islamic Nations." *Population Bulletin.* Vol. 43, No. 4 (December 1988). Washington, D.C.: Population Reference Bureau.

Weicher, John C. "Getting Richer (At Different Rates)." *Wall Street Journal* (June 14, 1995):A18.

WEIDENBAUM, MURRAY. "The Evolving Corporate Board." *Society*. Vol. 32, No. 3 (March/April 1995):9–20.

WEINBERG, GEORGE. *Society and the Healthy Homosexual*. Garden City, N.Y.: Anchor Books, 1973.

WEINER, TIM. "Head of C.I.A. Plans Center to Protect U.S. Cyberspace." *New York Times* (June 26, 1996):B7.

WEINRICH, JAMES D. *Sexual Landscapes: Why We Are What We Are, Why We Love Whom We Love*. New York: Charles Scribner's Sons, 1987.

WEISBURD, DAVID, STANTON WHEELER, ELIN WARING, and NANCY BODE. *Crimes of the Middle Class: White Collar Defenders in the Courts*. New Haven, Conn.: Yale University Press, 1991.

WEISNER, THOMAS S., and BERNICE T. EIDUSON. "The Children of the '60s as Parents." *Psychology Today* (January 1986):60–66.

WEITZMAN, LENORE J. *The Divorce Revolution: The Unexpected Social and Economic Consequences for Women and Children in America*. New York: Free Press, 1985.

———. "The Economic Consequences of Divorce Are Still Unequal: Comment on Peterson." *American Sociological Review*. Vol. 61, No. 3 (June 1996):537–38.

WEITZMAN, LENORE J., DEBORAH EIFLER, ELIZABETH HODAKA, and CATHERINE ROSS. "Sex-Role Socialization in Picture Books for Preschool Children." *American Journal of Sociology*. Vol. 77, No. 6 (May 1972):1125–50.

WELLER, JACK M., and E. L. QUARANTELLI. "Neglected Characteristics of Collective Behavior." *American Journal of Sociology*. Vol. 79, No. 3 (November 1973):665–85.

WELLFORD, CHARLES. "Labeling Theory and Criminology: An Assessment." In Delos H. Kelly, ed., *Criminal Behavior: Readings in Criminology*. New York: St. Martin's Press, 1980:234–47.

WELLMAN, BARRY. "The Community Question: Intimate Networks of East Yorkers." *American Journal of Sociology*. Vol. 84, No. 5 (March 1979):1201–31.

WELLS, JENNIFER. "Jobs." *Maclean's* (March 11, 1996):12-16.

WENKE, ROBERT J. *Patterns of Prehistory*. New York: Oxford University Press, 1980.

WERMAN, JILL. "Who Makes What?" *Working Woman* (January 1989):72–76, 80.

WERTHEIMER, BARBARA MAYER. "The Factory Bell." In Linda K. Kerber and Jane De Hart Mathews, eds., *Women's America: Refocusing the Past*. New York: Oxford University Press, 1982:130–40.

WESOLOWSKI, WLODZIMIERZ. "Transition From Authoritarianism to Democracy." *Social Research*. Vol. 57, No. 2 (Summer 1990):435–61.

WESTERN, BRUCE. "Postwar Unionization in Eighteen Advanced Capitalist Countries." *American Sociological Review*. Vol. 58, No. 2 (April 1993):266–82.

———. "A Comparative Study of Working-Class Disorganization: Union Decline in Eighteen Advanced Capitalist Countries." *American Sociological Review*. Vol. 60, No. 2 (April 1995):179–201.

WESTERN, MARK, and ERIK OLIN WRIGHT. "The Permeability of Class Boundaries to Intergenerational Mobility Among Men in the United States, Canada, Norway and Sweden." *American Sociological Review*. Vol. 59, No. 4 (August 1994):606–29.

WESTHUES, ANNE, AND JOYCE S. COHEN. "International Adoption in Canada: Predictions of Well-Being." In *Child Welfare in Canada: Research and Policy Implications*, ed. Joe Hudson and Burt Galaway. Toronto: Thompson Educational Publishing, 1994.

WHALEN, JACK, and RICHARD FLACKS. *Beyond the Barricades: The Sixties Generation Grows Up*. Philadelphia: Temple University Press, 1989.

WHEELIS, ALLEN. *The Quest for Identity*. New York: Norton, 1958.

WHITAKER, MARK. "Ten Ways to Fight Terrorism." *Newsweek* (July 1, 1985):26–29.

WHITE, JACK E. "I'm Just Who I Am." *Time*. Vol. 149, No. 18 (May 5, 1997):32–36.

WHITE, RALPH, and RONALD LIPPITT. "Leader Behavior and Member Reaction in Three 'Social Climates.'" In Dorwin Cartwright and Alvin Zander, eds., *Group Dynamics*. Evanston, Ill.: Row, Peterson, 1953:586–611.

WHITE, WALTER. *Rope and Faggot*. New York: Arno Press and New York Times, 1969; orig. 1929.

WHITMAN, DAVID. "Shattering Myths About the Homeless." *U.S. News & World Report* (March 20, 1989):26, 28.

WHITNELL, TIM. "MD wants tabloids banned." *The Burlington Post* (September 7, 1997):1.

WHORF, BENJAMIN LEE. "The Relation of Habitual Thought and Behavior to Language." In *Language, Thought, and Reality*. Cambridge, Mass.: The Technology Press of MIT/New York: Wiley, 1956:134–59; orig. 1941.

WHYTE, DONALD R. AND FRANK G. VALLEE. "Sociology." In *The Canadian Encyclopedia*. 2d ed. Edmonton: Hurtig Publishers, 1988: 2035–36.

WHYTE, WILLIAM FOOTE. *Street Corner Society*. 3d ed. Chicago: University of Chicago Press, 1981; orig. 1943.

WHYTE, WILLIAM H., JR. *The Organization Man*. Garden City, N.Y.: Anchor Books, 1957.

WIARDA, HOWARD J. "Ethnocentrism and Third World Development." *Society*. Vol. 24, No. 6 (September-October 1987):55–64.

WIATROWSKI, MICHAEL A., DAVID B. GRISWOLD, and MARY K. ROBERTS. "Social Control Theory and Delinquency." *American Sociological Review*. Vol. 46, No. 5 (October 1981):525–41.

WICKENS, BARBARA. "Bailey's Challengers." *Maclean's* (August 25, 1997): 52.

WIDDIS-BARR, CATHY. "The Importance and Potential of Leaders' Debates." In Frederick J. Fletcher, ed., Media and Voters in Canadian Election Campaigns, vol. 18 of the Research Papers of the Royal Commission on Electoral Reform and Party Finance. Ottawa and Toronto: RCERPF/Dundurn, 1991.

WIDOM, CATHY SPATZ. "Childhood Sexual Abuse and Its Criminal Consequences." *Society*. Vol. 33, No. 4 (May/June 1996):47–53.

WILCOX, CLYDE. "Race, Gender, and Support for Women in the Military." *Social Science Quarterly*. Vol. 73, No. 2 (June 1992):310–23.

WILES, P. J. D. *Economic Institutions Compared*. New York: Halsted Press, 1977.

WILKINS, R. AND O.B. ADAMS. *Healthfulness of Life: A Unified View of Mortality, Institutionalization, and Non-institutionalized Disability in Canada*. Montreal: The Institute for Research on Public Policy, 1983: 126.

WILLIAMS, RHYS H., and N. J. DEMERATH, III. "Religion and Political Process in an American City." *American Sociological Review*. Vol. 56, No. 4 (August 1991):417–31.

WILLIAMS, ROBIN M., JR. *American Society: A Sociological Interpretation*. 3d ed. New York: Alfred A. Knopf, 1970.

WILLIAMS, T. *The Impact of Television: A Natural Experiment in Three Communities*. New York: Academic Press, 1986.

WILLIAMSON, JEFFREY G., and PETER H. LINDERT. *American Inequality: A Macroeconomic History*. New York: Academic Press, 1980.

WILSON, BRYAN. *Religion in Sociological Perspective*. New York: Oxford University Press, 1982.

WILSON, EDWARD O. *Sociobiology: The New Synthesis*. Cambridge, Mass.: Belknap Press of the Harvard University Press, 1975.

———. *On Human Nature*. New York: Bantam Books, 1978.

———. "Biodiversity, Prosperity, and Value." In F. Herbert Bormann and Stephen R. Kellert, eds., *Ecology, Economics, and Ethics: The Broken Circle*. New Haven, Conn.: Yale University Press, 1991:3–10.

WILSON, JAMES Q. *Bureaucracy: What Government Agencies Do and Why They Do It*. New York: Basic Books, 1991.

———. "Crime, Race, and Values." *Society*. Vol. 30, No. 1 (November-December 1992):90–93.

WILSON, JAMES Q., and RICHARD J. HERRNSTEIN. *Crime and Human Nature*. New York: Simon and Schuster, 1985.

WILSON, LOGAN. *American Academics Then and Now*. New York: Oxford University Press, 1979.

WILSON, THOMAS C. "Urbanism and Tolerance: A Test of Some Hypotheses Drawn From Wirth and Stouffer." *American Sociological Review*. Vol. 50, No. 1 (February 1985):117–23.

———. "Urbanism, Migration, and Tolerance: A Reassessment." *American Sociological Review*. Vol. 56, No. 1 (February 1991):117–23.

———. "Urbanism and Unconventionality: The Case of Sexual Behavior." *Social Science Quarterly*. Vol. 76, No. 2 (June 1995):346–63.

WILSON, WILLIAM JULIUS. *The Declining Significance of Race*. Chicago: University of Chicago Press, 1978.

———. "The Black Underclass." *The Wilson Quarterly*. Vol. 8 (Spring 1984):88–99.

———. "Studying Inner-City Social Dislocations: The Challenge of Public Agenda Research." *American Sociological Review*. Vol. 56, No. 1 (February 1991):1–14.

———. *When Work Disappears: The World of the New Urban Poor*. New York: Alfred A. Knopf, 1996.

———. "Work." *New York Times Magazine* (August 18, 1996):26–31, 40, 48, 52, 54.

WINKLER, KAREN J. "Scholar Whose Ideas of Female Psychology Stir Debate Modifies Theories, Extends Studies to Young Girls." *Chronicle of Higher Education*. Vol. XXXVI, No. 36 (May 23, 1990):A6–A8.

WINKS, ROBIN W. "Slavery." In *The Canadian Encyclopedia*. 2d ed. Edmonton Hurtig Publishers, 1988: 2010–11.

WINN, MARIE. *Children Without Childhood*. New York: Pantheon Books, 1983.

WINNICK, LOUIS. "America's 'Model Minority'." *Commentary*. Vol. 90, No. 2 (August 1990):22–29.

WINSOR, HUGH. "Why Quebec welcomed the troops." *The Globe and Mail* (January 16, 1998):A4.

WIRTH, LOUIS. "Urbanism As a Way of Life." *American Journal of Sociology*. Vol. 44, No. 1 (July 1938):1–24.

WITKIN-LANOIL, GEORGIA. *The Female Stress Syndrome: How to Recognize and Live With It*. New York: Newmarket Press, 1984.

WOLF, DIANE L., ed. *Feminist Dilemma of Fieldwork*. Boulder, Colo.: Westview Press, 1996.

WOLF, NAOMI. *The Beauty Myth: How Images of Beauty Are Used Against Women*. New York: William Morrow, 1990.

WOLFE, DAVID B. "Targeting the Mature Mind." *American Demographics*. Vol. 16, No. 3 (March 1994):32–36.

WOLFE, TOM. *Radical Chic*. New York: Bantam, 1970.

WOLFGANG, MARVIN E., ROBERT M. FIGLIO, and THORSTEN SELLIN. *Delinquency in a Birth Cohort*. Chicago: University of Chicago Press, 1972.

WOLFGANG, MARVIN E., TERRENCE P. THORNBERRY, and ROBERT M. FIGLIO. *From Boy to Man, From Delinquency to Crime*. Chicago: University of Chicago Press, 1987.

WOLFINGER, RAYMOND E., and STEVEN J. ROSENSTONE. *Who Votes?* New Haven, Conn.: Yale University Press, 1980.

WOLFINGER, RAYMOND E., MARTIN SHAPIRO, and FRED J. GREENSTEIN. *Dynamics of American Politics.* 2d ed. Englewood Cliffs, N.J.: Prentice Hall, 1980.

WOLKOMIR, MICHELLE, MICHAEL FUTREAL, ERIC WOODRUM, and THOMAS HOBAN. "Substantive Religious Belief and Environmentalism." *Social Science Quarterly.* Vol. 78, No. 1 (March 1997):96–108.

Women in Canada: A Statistical Report. 2d ed. Ottawa: Statistics Canada, 1990.

Women in Canada: A Statistical Report. 3d ed. Catalogue No. 89-503E. Ottawa: Statistics Canada, 1995.

Women in the Labour Force. Ottawa: Statistics Canada, 1990–91.

WONG, BUCK. "Need for Awareness: An Essay on Chinatown, San Francisco." In Amy Tachiki et al., eds., *Roots: An Asian American Reader.* Los Angeles: UCLA Asian American Studies Center, 1971:265–73.

WOOD, DANIELL. "Death Wish: Would You Choose an Assisted Suicide." *Chatelaine* (July 25–29, 1993):94.

WOODWARD, C. VANN. *The Strange Career of Jim Crow.* 3d rev. ed. New York: Oxford University Press, 1974.

WOODWARD, KENNETH L. "Feminism and the Churches." *Newsweek.* Vol. 13, No. 7 (February 13, 1989):58–61.

———. "Talking to God." *Newsweek.* Vol. 119, No. 1 (January 6, 1992):38–44.

———. "The Elite, and How to Avoid It." *Newsweek* (July 20, 1992):55.

WOOLEY, ORLAND W., SUSAN C. WOOLEY, and SUE R. DYRENFORTH. "Obesity and Women—II: A Neglected Feminist Topic." *Women's Studies International Quarterly.* Vol. 2 (1979):81–92.

The World Almanac and Book of Facts 1998. Mahwah, N.J.: World Almanac Books, 1998.

THE WORLD BANK. *World Development Report 1991: The Challenge of Development.* New York: Oxford University Press, 1991.

———. *World Development Report 1993.* New York: Oxford University Press, 1993.

———. *World Development Report 1995: Workers in an Integrating World.* New York: Oxford University Press, 1995.

———. *World Development Report 1997: The State in a Changing World.* New York: Oxford University Press, 1997.

WORLD HEALTH ORGANIZATION. *Constitution of the World Health Organization.* New York: World Health Organization Interim Commission, 1946.

———. Data cited in Pollack, Andrew, "Overseas, Smoking Is One of Life's Small Pleasures," *New York Times* (August 12, 1996).

World Values Survey, 1990–1993. Ann Arbor, Mich.: Inter-university Consortium for Political and Social Research, 1994.

WORSLEY, PETER. "Models of the World System." In Mike Featherstone, ed., *Global Culture: Nationalism, Globalization, and Modernity.* Newbury Park, Calif.: Sage, 1990:83–95.

WOTHERSPOON, TERRY. "Transforming Canada's Education System: The Impact on Educational Inequalities, Opportunities and Benefits." In B. Singh Bolaria, ed., *Social Issues and Contradictions in Canadian Society.* Toronto: Harcourt Brace Jovanovich, 1991: 448–463.

———, AND VIC SATZEWICH. *First Nations: Race, Class, and Gender Relations.* Scarborough, Ont.: Nelson, 1993.

WREN, CHRISTOPHER S. "In Soweto-by-the-Sea, Misery Lives On as Apartheid Fades." *New York Times* (June 9, 1991):1, 7.

WRIGHT, ERIK OLIN. *Classes.* London: Verso, 1985.

WRIGHT, ERIK OLIN, ANDREW LEVINE, and ELLIOTT SOBER. *Reconstructing Marxism: Essays on Explanation and the Theory of History.* London: Verso, 1992.

WRIGHT, ERIK OLIN, and BILL MARTIN. "The Transformation of the American Class Structure, 1960–1980." *American Journal of Sociology.* Vol. 93, No. 1 (July 1987):1–29.

WRIGHT, ERIC R. "Personal Networks and Anomie: Exploring the Sources and Significance of Gender Composition." *Sociological Focus.* Vol. 28, No. 3 (August 1995):261–82.

WRIGHT, JAMES D. "Address Unknown: Homelessness in Contemporary America." *Society.* Vol. 26, No. 6 (September-October 1989):45–53.

———. "Ten Essential Observations On Guns in America." *Society.* Vol. 32, No. 3 (March-April 1995):63–68.

WRIGHT, QUINCY. "Causes of War in the Atomic Age." In William M. Evan and Stephen Hilgartner, eds., *The Arms Race and Nuclear War.* Englewood Cliffs, N.J.: Prentice Hall, 1987:7–10.

WRIGHT, RICHARD A. *In Defense of Prisons.* Westport, Conn.: Greenwood Press, 1994.

WRIGHT, ROBERT. "The Man Who Invented the Web." *Time,* Canadian Edition (May 19, 1997): 44.

WRIGHT, STUART A. "Social Movement Decline and Transformation: Cults in the 1980s." Paper presented to the Southwestern Social Science Association, Dallas, Texas, March 1987.

WRIGHT, STUART A., and WILLIAM V. D'ANTONIO. "The Substructure of Religion: A Further Study." *Journal for the Scientific Study of Religion.* Vol. 19, No. 3 (September 1980):292–98.

WU, LAWRENCE L. "Effects of Family Instability, Income, and Income Instability on the Risk of a Premarital Birth." *American Sociological Review.* Vol. 61, No. 3 (June 1996):386–406.

WUDUNN, SHERYL. "Toddlers on the Fast Track to Kingergarten." *The Globe and Mail* (January 24, 1996): A1, A10.

WYNTER, LEON E. "Business and Race." *Wall Street Journal* (May 10, 1995):B1.

YANDLE, TRACY, and DUDLEY BURTON. "Reexamining Environmental Justice: A Statistical Analysis of Historical Hazardous Waste Landfill Sitting in Metropolitan Texas." *Social Science Quarterly.* Vol. 77, No. 3 (September 1996):477–92.

YANKELOVICH, DANIEL. "How Changes in the Economy Are Reshaping American Values." In Henry J. Aaron, Thomas E. Mann, and Timothy Taylor, eds., *Values and Public Policy.* Washington, D.C.: The Brookings Institution, 1994:20.

YATES, RONALD E. "Growing Old in Japan; They Ask Gods for a Way Out." *Philadelphia Inquirer* (August 14, 1986):3A.

YEATTS, DALE E. "Self-Managed Work Teams: Innovation in Progress." *Business and Economic Quarterly* (Fall-Winter 1991):2–6.

———. "Creating the High Performance Self-Managed Work Team: A Review of Theoretical Perspectives." Paper presented at the annual meeting of the Social Science Association, Dallas, February 1995.

YODER, JAN D., and ROBERT C. NICHOLS. "A Life Perspective: Comparison of Married and Divorced Persons." *Journal of Marriage and the Family.* Vol. 42, No. 2 (May 1980):413–19.

YOELS, WILLIAM C., and JEFFREY MICHAEL CLAIR. "Laughter in the Clinic: Humor in Social Organization." *Symbolic Interaction.* Vol. 18, No. 1 (1995):39–58.

YORK, GEOFFREY. "UN body chastises Canada on poverty." *The Globe and Mail* (June 25, 1993): A1–2.

YOUNG, MICHAEL. "Meritocracy Revisited." *Society.* Vol. 31, No. 6 (September-October 1994):85–89.

ZACHARY, G. PASCAL. "Not So Fast: Neo-Luddites Say an Unexamined Cyberlife is a Dangerous One." *Wall Street Journal* (June 16, 1997):R18.

ZALMAN, MARVIN, and STEVEN STACK. "The Relationship Between Euthanasia and Suicide in the Netherlands: A Time Series Analysis, 1950–1990." *Social Science Quarterly.* Vol. 77, No. 3 (September 1996):576–93.

ZANGWILL, ISRAEL. *The Melting Pot.* Macmillan, 1921; orig. 1909.

ZASLAVSKY, VICTOR. *The Neo-Stalinist State: Class, Ethnicity, and Consensus in Soviet Society.* Armonk, N.Y.: M. E. Sharpe, 1982.

ZEITLIN, IRVING M. *The Social Condition of Humanity.* New York: Oxford University Press, 1981.

ZHOU, MIN, and JOHN R. LOGAN. "Returns of Human Capital in Ethnic Enclaves: New York City's Chinatown." *American Sociological Review.* Vol. 54, No. 5 (October 1989):809–20.

ZIMBARDO, PHILIP G. "Pathology of Imprisonment." *Society.* Vol. 9 (April 1972):4–8.

ZIPP, JOHN F. "Perceived Representativeness and Voting: An Assessment of the Impact of 'Choices' vs. 'Echoes.'" *The American Political Science Review.* Vol. 79, No. 1 (March 1985):50–61.

ZIPP, JOHN F., and JOEL SMITH. "A Structural Analysis of Class Voting." *Social Forces.* Vol. 60, No. 3 (March 1982):738–59.

ZUBOFF, SHOSHANA. "New Worlds of Computer-Mediated Work." *Harvard Business Review.* Vol. 60, No. 5 (September-October 1982):142–52.

ZURCHER, LOUIS A., and DAVID A. SNOW. "Collective Behavior and Social Movements." In Morris Rosenberg and Ralph Turner, eds., *Social Psychology: Sociological Perspectives.* New York: Basic Books, 1981:447–82.

PHOTO CREDITS

Frontispiece: Mark Peters

CHAPTER 1: Albina Kosiec Felski, *The Circus*, 1971, oil on canvas, 48 × 48 in. (121.9 × 121.9 cm), National Museum of American Art, Smithsonian Institution, Washington, DC/Art Resource, NY, *2*; Robert Burke/Gamma-Liaison, Inc., *3*; Paul W. Liebhardt, *4, 5*; Luc Delahaye/Magnum Photos, Inc., *7*; Corbis-Bettmann, *13*; Archive Photos, *15 (left)*; Simon Bening, *April: Farmyard with woman milking cow*, from *Da Costa Book of Hours*, Bruges, c.1515, © The Piermont Morgan Library, NY, M.399,F.5V/Art Resource, NY, *15 (right)*; National Archives of Canada PA 19694, *17 (left)*; Carleton University, *17 (centre)*; Canadian Press/CP, *17 (right)*; Amy Jones, *St. Regis Indian Reservation*, 1937, photo courtesy Janet Marqusee Fine Arts Ltd., *18*; © Paul Marcus 1995, oil on panel, *Dinner Is Served*, *19*; Louis Schanker (1903–1981), *Three Men on a Bench*, © Christie's Images, *20*; Toronto Sun/Stan Behal, *23*.

CHAPTER 2: Alex Colville, *To Prince Edward Island*, 1965, acrylic emulsion on masonite, 61.9 × 92.5 cm, National Gallery of Canada, Ottawa, © NGC/MBAC, *26*; Paul Chiasson/Canapress, *27*; Paul Gauguin (French, 1848–1903), *Where Do We Come From? What Are We? Where Are We Going?*, 1897, oil on canvas, 139.1 × 374.6 cm. (54 3/4 × 147 1/2 in.) Tompkins collections, courtesy of Museum of Fine Arts, Boston, *29*; John Eastcott/Yva Momatiuk/The Image Works, *30*; Canapress/Pierre Obendrauf, *32*; Steve McCurry/Magnum Photos, Inc., *34 (left)*; Argas/Gamma-Liaison, Inc., *34 (right)*; Mark Richards/PhotoEdit, *38 (left)*; no credit, *38 (right)*; Fred Cattroll, *39*; Canadian Press CP, *41*; Bill Keay/Vancouver Sun, *42*; Carol Beckwith & Angela Fisher/Robert Estall Photo Agency, *44 (left)*; AP/Wide World Photos, *44 (right)*.

CHAPTER 3: Larsen & Larsen Studio, Inc., *58*; Sylvain Grandadam/Photo Researchers Inc., *59*; Tomas Friedmann/Photo Researchers, Inc., *60*; Paul W. Liebhardt, *61 (top, left; center, left; bottom, middle)*; Carlos Humberto/TDC/Contact/The Stock Market, *61 (top, middle)*; Mireille Vautier/Woodfin Camp & Associates, *61 (top, right)*; David Austen/Stock Boston, *61 (center, middle)*; J. Du Boisberran/The Image Bank, *61 (center, right)*; Jack Fields/Photo Researchers, Inc., *61 (bottom, right)*; Alighierio e Boetti, *Mappa (Map)*, 1971–89, embroidery on canvas, 118 × 236 3/4 in. Collection Caterina Boetti, Rome, photo credit Cathy Carver/Dia Center for the Arts, *63*; *Mrs. Van Gogh Makes the Bed*, from *Great Housewives of Art* by Sally Swain, © 1988 by Sally Swain, used by permission of Viking Penguin, a division of Penguin Putnam Inc., *66*; Reprinted by permission of Margaret Courtney-Clarke, © 1990, *68*; Toronto Sun/Norm Betts, *71*; Canapress/E.J. Flynn, *73*; J.P Laffont/Sygma, *76*; Jeff Greenberg/Picture Cube Inc., *78 (left)*; Alex Webb/Magnum Photo Inc., *78 (centre)*; Pedrick/The Image Works, *78 (right)*; Sabina Dowell, *79 (left)*; CLEO Photo/Jeroboam, Inc., *79 (centre)*; David Young-Wolff/PhotoEdit, *79 (right)*; Paul W. Liebhardt, *80*; Andre Gallant/The Image Bank, *82 (top, left)*; Pete Turner/The Image Bank, *82 (top, middle)*; Brun/Photo Researchers, Inc., *82 (top, right)*; George Holton/Photo Researchers, Inc., *82 (bottom, left)*; Elliot Erwitt/Magnum Photos, Inc., *82 (bottom, middle)*; Bruno Hadjih/Gamma-Liaison, Inc., *82 (bottom, right)*; The Burlington Post/Peter McCusker, *83*.

CHAPTER 4: Walter Greaves (1846–1930) *Hammersmith Bridge on Boat Race Day* 1862, Tate Gallery, London, Great Britain/Art Resource, NY, *86*; © 1996, *The Washington Post*, photo by Carol Guzy, reprinted with permission, *87*; Patrick Bordes/Photo Researchers, Inc., *88*; Victor Englebert/Photo Researchers, Inc., *89*; Robert Frerck/Woodfin Camp & Associates, *90*; Rosenfeld Images Ltd./Science Photo Library/Photo Researchers, Inc., *93 (left)*; Cameramann/The Image Works, *93 (right)*; Culver Pictures, Inc., *96*; Norbert Goeneutte *The Paupers' Meal on a Winter Day in Paris*, Waterhouse and Dodd, London, Fine Art Photographic Library, London/Art Resource, NY, *98*; Charles Steiner/The Image Works, *99*; The Granger Collection, *102*; George Tooker, *Landscape with Figures* 1963, egg tempera on gesso panel, 26 × 30 inches, *103*; Elliot Landy/Magnum Photos, Inc., *104 (left)*; Robert Sorbo/AP/Wide World Photos, *104 (right)*; Paul W. Liebhardt, *105*.

CHAPTER 5: Hale Woodruff, *Girls Skipping*, 1949, oil on canvas, 24 × 32 inches, courtesy of Michael Rosenfeld Gallery, New York, *110*; Blair Seitz/Photo Researchers, Inc., *111*; Ted Horowitz/The Stock Market, *113 (left)*; Henley & Savage/The Stock Market, *113 (middle)*; Tom Pollack/Monkmeyer Press, *113 (right)*; William Kurelek, *Prairie Childhood*, by permission of the Estate of William Kurelek, courtesy of the Isaacs Gallery of Toronto, *114*;

UPI/Corbis-Bettmann, *115*; Elizabeth Crews/Elizabeth Crews Photography, *117*; Keith Carter, *118*; Rimma Gerlovina and Valeriy Gerlovin, *Manyness* 1990, © the artists, Pomona, NY, *119*; Dick Hemingway, *122*; Bernstein/Spooner/Gamma-Liaison, Inc., *127*; Patrick Zachmann/Magnum Photos, *130*; Danny Lyon/Magnum Photos, Inc., *131*; The Toronto Star/P. Edwards, *133*.

CHAPTER 6: Paul Cadmus (b. 1904) *Man With False Noses: An Allegory on Promiscuity*, 1955, pen, ink, and egg tempera on paper, 19 1/4 × 12 inches, courtesy DC Moore Gallery, NYC, © Christie's images, *136*; John Macionis, *137*; Prentice Hall Archives, *138*; Canapress/Frank Gunn, *139*; Dimaggio/Kalish/The Stock Market, *142*; Wesley Bocxe/Photo Researchers, Inc., *143*; Comstock, *145*; David Cooper/Gamma-Liaison, Inc., *147 (top, left)*; Alan Weiner/Gamma-Liaison, Inc., *147 (top, middle)*; Lynn McLaren/Picture Cube, Inc., *147 (top, right)*; Guido Rossi/The Image Bank, *147 (bottom, left)*; Richard Pan, *147 (bottom, middle)*; Costa Manos/Magnum Photos, Inc., *147 (bottom, right)*; Duke University/Hartman Center with permission of Pepsi-Cola Company, *149*; Paul W. Liebhardt, *150*; Courtesy of Salter Street Films Ltd., *154*.

CHAPTER 7: Ed McGowin, *Society Telephone Society*, 1989, oil on canvas with carved and painted wood frame, 54 in. × 54 in. © Ed McGowin 1997, *160*; Bob Carroll, *161*; Canapress/Clement Allard, *162*; Frank Siteman/Picture Cube Inc., *163*; Carol Beckwith & Angela Fisher/Robert Estall Photo Agency, *166*; Paul W. Liebhardt, *169*; Ann States/SABA Press Photos Inc., *170*; Elderfield-Liaison/PonoPresse, *172*; Biblioteque Nationale de France, Paris. From *The Horizon History of China* by the editors of Horizon Magazine, The Horizon Publishing Co., Inc., 551 5th Ave., NY 10017, © 1969, *174*; Paul W. Liebhardt, *176*; George Tooker *Government Bureau* 1956, egg tempera on gesso panel, 19 5/8 × 29 5/8 in., The Metropolitan Museum of Art, George A. Hearn Fund, 1956 (56.78), photograph © 1984 The Metropolitan Museum of Art, *177*; Gabe Palmer/The Stock Market, *180*; Bartholomew/Gamma-Liaison, Inc., *181*.

CHAPTER 8: Image by Fiona Smyth, *188*; Benito/Sygma, *189*; SIPA Press, *190*; Cliff Owen/UPI/Corbis-Bettmann, *192*; The Granger Collection, *193*; Canapress/Kevin Frayer, *196*; Canapress/Paul Chiasson, *197*; Danny Hellman, *200*; Mark Peterson/SABA Press Photos, Inc., *202*; Toronto Sun/Warren Toda, *206*; Benetton, *207*.

CYBER.SCOPE PART II: T. Crosby/Gamma-Liaison, Inc., *216*; Peter Steiner © 1993 from the New Yorker Collection, All Rights Reserved, *217*.

CHAPTER 9: Antonio Ruiz, *Verano* 1937, oil on wood 29 × 35 cm, collection of Acervo Patrimonial, SHCP, Mexico, *218*; Painting by Ken Marshall © 1992 from *Titanic: An Illustrated History*, a Hyperion/Madison Press Book, *219*; Sebastiao Salgado/Magnum Photo, Inc., *220*; Antonio Berni (1905–1981) *Los Emigrantes*, © Christie's Images, *221*; Haviv/SABA Press Photos, Inc., *222*; Fujifotos/The Image Bank, *225*; Robert Wallis/SABA Press Photos, Inc., *226*; Limbourg Brothers, *August* from *Tres Riches Heures du duc de Berry*, Musee Conde, Chantilly, France, Giraudon/Art Resource, NY, *228*; Agence France Press/Corbis-Bettmann, *230*; The Granger Collection, *232*; Egyptian Museum, Cairo, Hirmer Fotoarchive, *236*.

CHAPTER 10: William Gropper, *Sweat Shop*, oil on canvas, 18 × 30 in. (45.7 × 76.2 cm), © Christie's Images, *242*; Bob Carroll, *243*; Grapes/Michaud/Photo Researchers, Inc., *249 (left)*; Burt Glinn/Magnum Photos, Inc., *249 (right)*; First Light/P. Barton, *250*; Greg Locke, *252*; Prentice Hall Archives, *255*; Tony Stone Images/Bruce Ayres, *256*; Mary Kate Denny/PhotoEdit, *258*; Diego Rivera *Our Bread* (El pan nuestro), 1928, mural 2.04 × 1.58 m, Court of Fiestas, Level 3, South Wall, Secretaria de Educación Publica, Mexico City, Mexico, Schalkwijk/Art Resource, NY, © Estate of Diego Rivera/Licensed by VAGA, NY, *260*; Mary Ellen Mark Library, *261*.

CHAPTER 11: Diego Rivera *Formation of Revolutionary Leadership* (*Los Explotatores*), 1926–27, mural, 3.43 × 5.55 m, Chapel, Universidad Autonoma Chapingo, Chapingo, Mexico, Schalkwijk/Art Resource, NY, © Estate of Diego Rivera/Licensed by VAGA, NY, *266*; Photo by Gregory Kane, *Baltimore Sun*, *267*; Canapress, Tom Hanson, *269 (left)*; Bartholomew/Gamma-Liaison, Inc., *269 (right)*; Martin Benjamin/The Image Works, *271 (top, left)*; Peter Turnley/Black Star, *271 (top, right)*; Pablo Bartholomew/Gamma-Liaison, Inc., *271 (bottom)*; David Stewart-Smith/SABA Press Photos, Inc., *272*; Viviane Moos/SABA Press Photos, Inc., *276*; Charlesworth/SABA Photos, Inc., *277*; Peter Turnley/Black Star, *279*; Sean Sprague/Impact Visuals Photo & Graphics, Inc., *281*; Jane Ash Poitras, *Living in the Storm Too Long*, courtesy of Jane

Ash Poitras, photo by Janet Anderson, Thunder Bay Art Gallery, *283*; Ben Simmons/Stock Market, *286*.

CHAPTER 12: © Wendy Seller, 1994, *Magritte & Me*, o/c 34"H × 30"W, photo courtesy of Pepper Gallery, Boston, *292*; Catherine Leroy/SIPA Press, *293*; Richard J. Haier, Ph.D., *294*; Canapress/Kelowna Daily Courier/Gary Moore, *295*; Aspect Picture Library/The Stock Market, *298*; Explorer/Y. Layma/Photo Researchers, Inc., *299*; Joseph B. Brignolo/The Image Bank, *300*; Jacques M. Chenet/Gamma-Liaison, Inc., *303*; Ed Malitsky/Picture Cube, Inc., *304*; Phil Snell/Maclean's, *309*; Canapress/Fred Chartrand, *313*; Natsuko Utsumi/Gamma-Liaison, *314*; Liza McCoy, photographer, *316*; Jay Silverman/The Image Bank, *317*.

CHAPTER 13: Harry Roseland, *Beach Scene, Coney Island* 1891, © Christie's Images, *322*; Corbis-Bettmann, *323*; Joel Gordon/Joel Gordon Photography, *325 (top, left)*; Leong Ka Tai/Material World, *325 (top, middle)*; Robert Caputo/Stock Boston, *325 (top, right)*; Paul W. Liebhardt, *325 (bottom, left, and middle)*; Lisi Dennis/The Image Bank, *325 (bottom, right)*; Raveendran/Agence France-Presse, *327*; Peter Caton/Gerald Campbell Studios, *329*; Archive Photos, *333 (left)*; Sygma, *333 (right)*; Culver Pictures Inc., *334*; Canapress/Ryan Remiorz, *340*.

CHAPTER 14: *Gifts* © Deidre Scherer, 1966, from the collection of St. Mary's Foundation, Rochester, NY, *348*; Rob Crandall/Rob Crandall Photographer, *349*; Michael Drummond, Photographer, *354*; Elliot Erwitt/Magnum Photo, Inc., *355 (left)*; Bruno Barbey/Magnum Photos, Inc., *355 (right)*; Eve Arnold/Magnum Photos, Inc., *357*; The Whitehorse Star/Cathie Archbould, *361*; Alese and Mort Pechter/The Stock Market, *362*; Ira Wyman/Sygma, *364*; Reuters/Dutch TV/Archive Photos, *365*.

CYBER.SCOPE PART III: John Agee © 1995 from The New Yorker Collection, All Rights Reserved, *370*; Beth Kreiser/AP/World Wide Photos, *371 (top)*; Matthew McVay/Stock Boston, *371 (bottom)*.

CHAPTER 15: The Grand Design/SuperStock, Inc., *372*; Marko Shark, *373*; American Textile History Museum, Lowell, MA, *375*; Bob Schatz/Gamma-Liaison, Inc., *376*; Bellavia/REA/SABA Press Photos, Inc., *379 (left)*; John Bryson/Sygma, *379 (right)*; Patrick Ward/Stock Boston, *381*; Christopher Morris, *384*; Jose Clemente Orozco, *The Unemployed*, © Christie's Images, © Estate of Jose Clemente Orozco/Licensed by VAGA, NY, *386*; Dick Hemingway, *393*; Z. Bzdak/The Image Works, *395*.

CHAPTER 16: Christiane Pflug, *With the Black Flag*, 1971 oil on canvas, 137.2 × 142.2 cm. Art Gallery of Ontario, Toronto, gift of Dr. Michael Pflug, Toronto, 1975, donated by the Ontario Heritage Foundation, 1988 © Dr. Michael Pflug, *400*; Canapress/Jeff McIntosh, *401*; Philip Evergood, *American Tragedy* 1936, oil on canvas, 29 1/2 × 39 1/2 in. Terry Dintenfass Gallery, NY, *402*; David Ball/Picture Cube, Inc., *407*; Government of Canada, *408*; Fred Cattroll, *410*; Susan Wallace-Cox, *412*; Elections Canada, *416*; National Archives of Canada, *417*; Barry Iverson/Woodfin Camp & Associates, *422*; Baldeu/Sygma, *424*; Joe McNally, Life Magazine © Time Inc., *425*; Commission for Environmental Cooperation, *426*.

CHAPTER 17: Frida Kahlo, *My Grandparents, My Parents, and I (Family Tree)*, 1936, oil and tempera on metal panel 12 1/8 × 13 5/8 in. (30.7 × 35.5 cm), The Museum of Modern Art, NY, *430*; Toronto Sun/Craig Robertson, *431*; G. Stephen/Toronto Star, *432*; Marc Chagall *Scene Paysanne*, © 1999 Artists Rights Society (ARS), New York/ADAGP, Paris, *436*; Raghu Rai/Magnum Photos, *438*; Christian Pierre, B. 1962, *I Do*, American Private Collection, SuperStock, Inc., *439*; William Kurelek, *Manitoba Party*, National Gallery of Canada, Ottawa, by permission of the estate of William Kurelek, c/o The Isaacs Gallery of Toronto, *443*; D. Young-Wolfe/PhotoEdit, *444*; Edward Hopper (1882–1967) *Room in New York*, 1932, oil on canvas, 29 × 36 in. Sheldon Memorial Art Gallery, University of Nebraska-Lincoln, F.M. Hall Collection, 1932.H-1666, *447*; Stern (Ullah)/Black Star, *452*.

CHAPTER 18: © 1994 Dinh Le, *Interconfined*, C-print and Linen Tape, 55 × 39 in., *456*; Mark Peterson/SABA Press Photos, Inc., *457*; SuperStock, *458*; T. Matsumoto/Sygma, *459*; Mathieu Polak/Sygma, *460*; Gilles Peress/Magnum Photos Inc., *463*; William Kurelek, *Lord That I Might See*, by permission of the estate of William Kurelek, c/o The Isaacs of Toronto, *465*; Hans Hoefer/Woodfin Camp & Associates, *467*; Bradshaw/SABA Press Photos, Inc., *469*; Hans Kemp/Sygma, *470*; Nick Kelsh/Kelsh Wilson Design Inc., *477*.

CHAPTER 19: Romare Bearden, *The Piano Lesson*, 1983, collage and watercolor, 29 × 22 in. © Romare Bearden Foundation/Licensed by VAGA, NY, *480*; Richard Kalvar/Magnum Photos, Inc., *481*; Alan Oddie/PhotoEdit, *484*; Paul Liebhardt, *486*; Tony Stone Images/Arthur Tilley, *488 (left)*; Dick Hemingway, *488 (right)*; Bob Daemmrich/The Image Works, *495*; Jay Dickman, *500*.

CHAPTER 20: The Granger Collection, *504*; Susan Rosenberg/Photo Researchers, Inc., *505*; The Granger Collection, *506*; Mark Peters/Arthur Berry, *507*; Steve Lehman/SABA Press Photos, Inc., *508*; Tony Freeman/PhotoEdit, *510*; John Coletti/Picture Cube, Inc., *513*; Canapress/Andrew Vaughan, *515*; A.F. Seligmann, *Allgemeines Krankenhaus* (General Hospital) 19th cent. painting, canvas, *Professor Theodor Billroth Lectures at the General Hospital, Vienna, 1880*, Erich Lessing/Art Resource, NY, *517*; Peter Menzel/Peter Menzel Photography, *518*; ABC Television/Globe Photos, *522 (left)*; Lauren Greenfield/Sygma, *522 (right)*; Steve Murez/Black Star, *524*.

CYBER.SCOPE PART IV: Dirck Halstead/Gamma-Liaison, Inc., *528*; © Tara Sosrowardoyo/Indo-pix, *529*.

CHAPTER 21: Georgia Mills Jessup (b. 1926), *Rainy Night Downtown*, 1967, oil on canvas, 44 × 48 in. (111.8 × 121.9 cm). The National Museum of Women in the Arts, Gift of Savanna M. Clark, *530*; Charles Gupton/Stock Boston, *531*; Peter Menzel/Material World, *539 (top)*; David Reed/Material World, *539 (bottom)*; Najlah Feany/SABA Press Photos, Inc., *540*; Cotton Coulson/Woodfin Camp & Associates, *542*; First Light/Craig Hammell, *546*; Peter Breughel the Elder (c. 1525/30–1569), *Peasant Dance*, c. 1565, Kunsthistorisches Museum, Vienna/Superstock, *549 (left)*; Fernand Leger, *The City*, 1919, oil on canvas, 90 3/4 × 117 1/4, Philadelphia Museum of Art, A.E. Gallatin Collection, © 1999 Artists Rights Society (ARS), New York/ADAGP, Paris, *549 (right)*; Jonathan Nourok/PhotoEdit, *551*.

CHAPTER 22: © Anatoly Shdanow/UNEP/The Image Works, *558*; Canapress/S. Komulainen, *559*; Archive Photos, *561*; Canapress/J. Boissinot, *562*; Sabina Dowell, *564*; Canapress/Jacques Boissinot, *565*; Tom Kelly/FPG International, *567 (top, left)*; Inge Morath/Magnum Photos, Inc., *567 (top, middle)*; Owen Franken/Stock Boston, *567 (top, right)*; Willie L. Hill, Jr./Stock Boston, *567 (bottom, left)*; Michael Grecco/ Stock Boston, *567 (bottom, middle)*; J.L. Atlan/Sygma, *571*; SABA Press Photos, Inc./Michael Shumann, *572*; Reuters/Peter Jones, *576*.

CHAPTER 23: *Sociotecture*, 1991, Joan Truckenbrod, courtesy of The Williams Gallery, Princeton, NJ, © Joan Truckenbrod 1997, *580*; Mauri Rautkari/World Wide Fund for Nature, *581*; Mark Peters, *582*; Paul Gauguin, *The Day of the God (Mahana no Atua)*, 1894, oil on canvas (68.3 × 91.5 cm.), Helen Birch Bartlett Memorial Collection, 1926, photograph © 1994, The Art Institute of Chicago, All Rights Reserved, *585*; George Tooker, *The Subway*, 1950, egg tempera on composition board, 18 1/8 × 36 1/8 in., Whitney Museum of American Art, NY, purchased with funds from the Juliana Force Purchase Award, 50.23, *587*; Simon & Schuster/PH College, *588*; Edvard Munch *Workers on Their Way Home* 1913–1915, canvas, Expressionism Painting 20th Cent., Munch Musset, Oslo, Norway, Erich Lessing/Art Resource, N.Y., *590*; Edvard Munch, *The Scream*, Oslo, National Gallery, Scala/Art Resource, NY, *592 (left)*; © Paul Marcus, *Musical Chairs*, oil painting on wood, 48 in. × 72 in., *592 (right)*.

CYBER.SCOPE PART V: Peter Charlesworth/SABA Press Photos, Inc., *603*.

NAME INDEX

641

642 Name Index

SUBJECT INDEX

Authoritarian personality theory, 329
Authoritarianism, 406, 407, 422
Authority, 402
　charismatic, 403
　patterns of, 435
　and power, 401–403
　rational-legal, 402–403
　traditional, 402
Automatic teller machines, 182
Automation, 182, 376
Automobiles, 92, 546
Autonomy, 6
Average
　life spans, 130, 296, 350–352, 354, 441
　middle class, 252

B
Baby boom, 350, 536
Baby bust, 350, 536
Bangladesh, 281
Bank of Montreal, 391, 394
Bankruptcy, 385
Banks, 391
Barbie, 71
Barney, 71
Barter system, 90–91
Basic Concepts in Social Stratification, 240
The Batek, 88
Batman, 71
Bay of Pigs, 166
Beatrice Foods, 392–393, 394
Beauty myth, 304
Behaviourism, 112
Belgians, 59
Beliefs, 66–68
Bell Canada, 393
Bell Canada Enterprises, 391
The Bell Curve: Intelligence and Class Structure in American Life, 240–241
Bereavement, 366
Bernardo-Homolka murder case, 206
Bible, 457
Bible Gateway, 479
Big bang theory, 476
Bilateral descent, 435
Bilingualism, 73, 332, 340
Biological context, 190–191
Biology, 112–113, 115
Birth
　control, 276–277, 440, 539–540
　crude birth rate, 532
　into poverty, 247
　privilege of, 247
　rights conferred by, 243
Bisexuality, 295, 296
Black Loyalists, 334
Black peoples, 6
　and crime, 206
　educational attainment levels, 248, 337–338
　equity in remuneration, 338
　history of in Canada, 334
　imprisonment of, 209
　labour force participation, 248, 337–338
　managerial occupations, 177
　in sports, 23
　on television, 126
Black Pioneeers, 334
Blasé urbanite, 549
Blishen scale, 246
Bloc Québecois, 166, 342, 413, 414

Blue-collar occupations. *See* Workers
Bodhi, 469
Body language, 147–148
Bogadus scale, 330
Bonding, 115
Book of Ecclesiastes, 363
Books, 123
Boom, Bust and Echo, 353, 497
Boot camp, 132
Botswana, 299, 300
Bourgeoisie, 97, 232, 542
Brahmin, 221
Brainstorming, 166
Braniff Airlines, 76
Brazil, 208
Bre-X Minerals, 199
British North America Act, 340
British peoples
　educational attainment levels, 248
　labour force participation, 8
　managerial occupations, 177
　see also United Kingdom
Brown case, 333
Buddha, 469
Buddhism, 469
Bulimia, 513
Burakumin, 225
Bureau of the Census, 47
Bureaucracy
　alienation, 175
　characteristics, 173–174
　defined, 173
　inefficiency, 175–176
　informal side of, 174–175
　origins of, 173
　problems of, 175–177
　and rationality, 103
Bureaucratic
　bloat, 177
　inertia, 176
　ritualism, 175–176, 176
The Bushmen, 88
Buxton, 333, 335

C
Cadet Uniform Services, 183
Calculability, 182
Calgary declaration, 411
Calgary Stampede, 254, 265
Calvinism, 101–102, 108, 462
Cambodia, 59, 334
Canada
　aging in, 350
　average family income, 244–245
　billionaire families in, 592
　Black citizens of, 334
　composition by ethnic origin, 335–336
　counterrevolution, 408
　economic polarization, 236–237
　ethnicity in, 335–338
　euthanasia in, 365
　foreign ownership in, 391–392
　and free trade, 255–256, 409
　gender differences in, 229
　happiness in, 144, 576
　health in, 508–516
　House of Commons. *See* House of Commons
　humour and common identity, 156
　immigration to, 342–344
　and information technology, 598–599

　as land of opportunity, 255
　and low-income countries, 286
　medicine in, 520–521
　occupational categories, 246
　Parliament, 409
　political parties in, 410–412
　politics in, 408–418
　poverty in, 256–263
　race in, 335–338
　religion in, 470–473
　schooling in, 484–486
　Senate, 409
　social classes in, 249–253
　unemployment rates, 386–387
　White Canada immigration policy, 343
Canada Pension Plan, 360
Canada-The Aging Population, 369
Canadian Advisory Council on the Status of Women, 310
The Canadian Airborne Regiment: A Socio-Cultural Inquiry, 4
Canadian Alliance in Solidarity with Native Peoples. *See* CASNP
Canadian Association of Broadcasters, 125
Canadian Association on Gerontology, 369
Canadian Association of Retired Persons, 369
Canadian Association of University Teachers, 418
Canadian Broadcasting Corporation, 380
Canadian Child Care Federation, 455
Canadian Constitutional Documents: A Legal History, 25
Canadian Council of Christians and Jews, 346
Canadian Council on Social Development, 25, 265
Canadian Department of Heritage, 347
Canadian Education Association, 503
Canadian Hemophilia Society, 515
Canadian Home Builders' Association, 388
Canadian International Development Agency, 286
Canadian Journal of Educational Administration and Policy, 503
Canadian Labour Congress, 399
Canadian Lesbian and Gay Archives, 321
Canadian Medical Association, 517
Canadian Pacific Railway, 330, 544
Canadian Patent Office, 75
Canadian Political Science Association, 16
Canadian Radio-television and Telecommunications Commission, 125
Canadian Red Cross, 515
Canadian Revolution: From Deference to Defiance, 598
Canadian revolution, 402
Canadian Tire, 182
Canadian War Amputations, 176
Canadians, 59
　background, 336
　below poverty line, 30
　CEOs, 231

　class structure, 249–256
　genetically mixed, 324
　in labour force, 382
　vs. Americans, 67
　wealthy families, 393
Cancer, 140, 350, 508, 513
Capitalism, 37, 80, 95–96, 101, 228, 379–380
　advantages of, 381–382
　and alienation, 98
　backbone of, 200
　class, 233
　and class conflict, 97–98
　consumer sovereignty, 379
　and democracy, 404–406
　and deviance, 199
　elite, 232
　free competition, 379
　industrial, 97, 99, 103, 228–229, 315
　male domination and, 315
　market forces, 396
　and modernity, 588–589
　and naked self–interest, 591
　personal profit, 379
　political–economy of, 420
　private ownership of property, 379
　and protestantism, 101–102, 462
　and the rational bureaucracy, 103
　and rationality, 101
　and science, 591
　state, 381
　thriving, 233
　welfare, 380–381
　world, 285
Capitalist, 95
　revolution, 588
　world economy, 283–284
Care and responsibility perspective, 118
CASNP, 347, 572
Caste system, 221–222, 224–225
Category, 162
Caucasian, 324
Cause and effect, 31, 33
CAVEAT, 208, 213
Census Metropolitan Area, 545
Central Intelligence Agency, 425
Centre for the Study of Sport in Society, 23
Centre for World Indigenous Studies, 601
CERN/ANU Demography and Population Studies, 557
Chambri, 298
Change. *See* Social change
Charisma
　religious, 463
　routinization of, 403
Charismatic authority, 403
Charlottetown Accord, 166, 340, 341–342, 411, 417, 420, 598
Charter of Rights and Freedoms, 341, 346, 359, 409, 594
Charter of Rights Study Survey, 43, 187
Chi, 59
Chicago School, 549–550, 551
Child
　abuse, 360, 442, 449, 461
　custody, 318, 431, 447–448
　discipline, 442
　labour, 75–77, 125, 126, 375
　rearing, 440–441
Child & Family Canada, 455
Child-care subsidies, 260

Childhood, 125–127
Children
    and cyberculture, 216–217
    educational attainment, 255
    games, 68, 120, 302
    health, 506–507, 509
    humour, 154–155
    hurried child syndrome, 127
    language, 120
    missing, 449
    partisan preferences of, 415
    play, 120
    and politics, 416
    and poverty, 257, 275–276
    race, 324
    schooling, 122–123
    self-concept, 122
    and slavery, 267–268, 277, 278
    social development of, 122
    and social isolation, 114–115
    street, 276
    symbols, 120
    weddings, 438
    as women's responsibility, 309
    of working-class families, 253
China, 63, 76, 302, 380, 406, 470
    cost of medicine, 518
    and democracy, 404
    homogeneous cultural system,
        66
    immigration from, 343
    patriarchy, 316
Chinese, 59
    labourers, 330
    language, 64
Chinese Immigration Act, 343
Christianity, 90, 339, 464–465
    cult beginnings, 403, 464
    and patriarchy, 460
Chromosomes, 294
Chronic fatigue syndrome, 140
Chrysler, 392
Church of England, 460, 461
Chyrsler, 393
CI. *See* Continuous Improvement
Cigarette smoking, 512–513
Cities
    concentric zones, 550
    decentralization, 546
    evolution of, 541–543
    first, 541
    growth of, 14, 541–548
    industrial European, 542–543
    inner, 333
    megalopolis, 547
    metropolis. *See* Metropolis
    multicentred model, 550
    new shape of, 602
    North American, 543–546
    physical design of, 550
    pre-industrial European, 542
    preconditions of, 541
    social area analysis, 550
    suburbs, 546–548
    urban expansion, 544
    wedge-shaped sectors, 550
City-states, 403
Civil
    liberties, 422
    religion, 474
    rights, 28, 199
Civil rights movement, 572
Civilization, 62
Class, 219
    accessories of, 122
    average-middle, 252
    and Calgary Stampede, 254
    capitalism, 233
    and computers, 250

conflict, 97–98, 232
consciousness, 97
and family, 343, 441–442
and gender, 315–316
and health, 510–511
hidden injury of, 262
humanitarian, 343
independent, 343
lower, 252–253
lower-upper, 250–251
middle, 224, 251–252, 254
position, 234
and poverty, 261263
social, 71, 206, 226, 232,
    249–253, 472–473, 489
system, 222–223, 224–225,
    225, 228
upper, 249–250
upper-middle, 251–252
upper-upper, 250
working, 224, 252
Clerical work, 305–306, 308
Clitoridectomy, 293
Co-operative Commonwealth
    Federation, 411
Co-optation, 575
Code of ethics, 385
Cognitive
    ability, 241
    development, 116–117
    elite, 240–241
    performance, 241
Cohabitation, 450
Cohort, 131
Cold War, 425
    politics of, 268
Collective
    conscience, 105
    memory, 71
Collective behaviour, 560
    contagion theory, 563
    convergence theory, 563
    emergent–norm theory, 563
    study of, 560–563
Collectivism, 396
Collectivity, 560
Colombia, 208–209
Colonialism, 278, 283, 327,
    543–544
Combat culture. *See* Warrior
    culture
Comedians, 157
Commerce, 10
Commission on Systemic Racism
    in the Ontario Criminal
    Justice System, 207, 209, 215
Common sense, 29–30
Commonwealth of Independent
    States, 382
Communications, 419
    bureaucracies, 175
    nonverbal, 145–146
Communism, 96, 227
The Communist Manifesto, 240–241
Community colleges, 6
Community of communities, 345
Compaq, 370
Comparable worth, 308
Compartmentalization of lives, 141
Computer
    in affluence homes, 251–252
    age, 54
    chat, 217
    literacy, 251
    ownership, 370
    and social class, 250–251
    and work, 388–389
Concept, 31
Confederation, 408

Conflict
    analysis, 19
    class. *See* Class
    resolution of underlying, 426
    role, 141
    and social change, 583
    subcultures, 194
    theory, 330
Conformity, 193
    among high-ranking political
        leaders, 166
    electric shock experiment,
        165–166
    group, 164–166
    line measurement
        experiment, 165
    social control, 198
Confucianism, 470
Conglomerates, 392–393
Congo, 406
Conservative party. *See*
    Progressive Conservative
    party
The Constitution, 15, 330, 410
Constraints, 11, 84
    women's social experiences,
        143
Construction trades, 306
Consumption, 280–281
Contagion theory, 563
Containment theory, 191
Continuous Improvement (CI),
    183
Control, 32
    social, 69, 190, 489
    theory, 197–198, 211, 214
    through automation, 182
*Controlling Interest: Who Owns
    Canada*, 392
Convergence theory, 563
Coors, 76
Cops, 30
Cornerville, 45–47
Corporate linkages, 392–393
Corporations, 200, 389–394
    competitiveness of, 393–394
    economic concentration, 391
    elite, 392
    foreign ownership, 391–392
    and global economy, 394
    interlocking directorates, 393
    multinational. *See*
        Multinational corporations
    single family ownership of,
        233, 390
    stockholders, 390
Correlation, 32
    spurious, 32
    unmasking, 32
Cost of living, 367
Council of Ministers of
    Education, 503
Counterculture, 74–75
Counterrevolution, 408
Country Style Donuts, 182
Courts, 210–211
Courtship, 438–439
Cowboy convention, 254
Credentialism, 493–494
Crees, 411
Crime, 104, 201–209, 211
    against women, 208
    components of, 201–204
    defined, 189
    drugs. *See* Drug trafficking
    global perspective, 207–209
    homicide rates, 204, 207
    property, 202
    rape. *See* Rape

rates, 107
street, 200
types of, 202–203
victimless, 203
violent, 202, 203, 209
white-collar, 199–201, 207
Criminal
    age, 204
    ethnicity, 206–207
    gender, 204–206
    intent, 201
    justice system, 12, 190,
        209–214, 318
    profile, 204–207
    race, 206–207
    social class, 206
    statistics, 203–204
Criminal Code, 201
Crowd, 162, 561
    behaviour, 563
Crusades, 459
Cuba, 380, 404
Culinar, 183
Cult, 464
Cultural
    change, 75
    conflict, 72
    differences, 59, 77
    diversity, 70–77, 112
    goals, 193
    identities, 323
    innovation, 486–487
    integration, 75
    lag, 75, 93, 582, 603
    materialism, 80–81
    mosaic, 332
    norms. *See* Norms
    notion of male superiority,
        296–297
    patterns, 278, 328
    relativity, 75–77, 144
    symbols, 71
    theory, 329–330
    transmission, 64
    universals, 79
    values. *See* Values
Cultural Relativism, 85
Culture, 62
    aging, 352, 354–355
    components of, 62–70
    as constraint, 84
    corporate, 183
    counterculture, 74–75
    defined, 60
    as freedom, 84
    and gender, 299
    global, 77
    high, 71–72, 91
    and human intelligence,
        60–62
    ideal, 69
    and information technology,
        70
    language, 63–66
    material, 60, 69–70
    multiculturalism. *See*
        Multiculturalism
    nonmaterial, 60
    popular, 71–72
    and poverty, 279–280
    real, 69
    shared, 107
    shock, 60, 62–63
    and social change, 583
    subculture. *See* Subcultures
    symbols, 62–63
    theoretical analysis of, 78–84
    virtual, 71
Customs officers, 93

Cyber-church, 478
Cyber-school, 497
Cyber.scope, information
    revolution, 54–57
Cyberspace. *See* Internet
The Cyberzine for the Open Minded,
    478

D

Dances with Wolves, 126
Dangerous knowledge, 210
Dartmouth College, 603
Darwinism. *See* Social, Darwinism
Date rape, 202–203
David Suzuki Foundation, 427
Davis-Moore thesis, 229–232,
    233, 237
Dawn, 333, 335
Dead Sociologists Society, 109
Death, 130, 363–366
    crude death rate, 533
    ethical issues, 364–366, 516
    euthanasia. *See* Euthanasia
    historical patterns of,
        363–364
    modern separation of life and,
        364
    rates, 553
    right to die, 349, 364–366,
        516
    of spouse, 130
    see also Mortality
Death penalty, 212, 214
    public executions, 213
Debt
    bondage, 278
    foreign, 284
Deception, 147–148
Declaration of Independence,
    594–595
The Decline of Deference, 598
Deductive logical thought, 50
Degradation ceremony, 196
Dehumanization, 175
Deindustrialization, 256
Dell, 370
Demeanour, 148
Dementia, 353
Democracy, 404–406
    communicative, 419
    parliamentary, 419
Demographic transition theory,
    537–538
Demography, 531–536
Denmark, 450
Dentists, 306
Department of Finance, 389
Department of Indian Affairs and
    Northern Development, 327,
    334, 339, 411
Department of Multiculturalism
    and Citizenship, 332
Dependency theory, 282–286,
    394
    high–income countries,
        284–285
Deprivation
    relative, 569
    theory, 569–570
Descent, 435
The Descent of Man, 135
Deterrence, 212, 214, 425
Development
    cognitive, 116–117
    concrete operational stage,
        116–117
    conventional moral, 117
    Erikson's eight stages, 121
    formal operational stage, 117

human, 112–113
moral, 117–118
personality, 115, 116
postconventional moral, 117
preconventional moral, 117
preoperational stage, 116
of proletariat, 97
of the self, 119–120
sensorimotor stage, 116
social, 115, 122
Deviance
    and capitalism, 199
    defined, 189
    elite, 200
    and gender, 201
    medicalization of, 196–197
    and power, 198–199
    primary, 195–196
    secondary, 195–196
    and social diversity, 201
    social foundations of, 191
Deviant career, 196
Dharma, 469
Differential association theory,
    197, 198
Diffusion, 75
Diplomacy, 426
Disarmament, 426
Discipline
    moral, 104
    personal, 102
Discovery, 75
Discrimination, 330, 331, 444,
    568–569
Diseases of affluence, 508
Disengagement, 362
"Dismal parson", 537
Dispersed collectivities, 560,
    564–568
Distinct society, 341, 346–347
Distinctive identity, 326
Diverse world, 12
Diversity
    cultural, 70–77, 112
    human, 12
    racial, 324
    social, 122, 168–169, 201,
        331, 585
    world, 12
Division of labour, 105, 587
Divorce, 445–448
    among disadvantaged couples,
        253
    downward social mobility,
        255
    during middle adulthood, 129
    as process, 447–448
    rates, 107, 431–432
Divorce Act, 445
Divorce Online, 455
Djibouti, 299
DNA, 525
Dogs, 62–63
Domestication, of plants and
    animals, 90
Double standards, 36, 81–82, 178,
    308–309, 318
Dow Corning, 524
Downsizing, 386
Dramaturgical analysis, 144–150,
    217
Drug trafficking, 208–209
The Durkheim Pages, 109
Durkheim's dilemma, 106
Dyad, 168
Dying. *See* Death
Dysfunctions
    social, 18–19
    of sport, 22

E
E-business, 389
E-mail, 172, 175
    authors', 172
    screens, 175
East Indian people, 209
Eastern Airlines, 76
Eastern Europe, 227, 234
Eating disorders, 505, 513–514
Ecclesia, 463, 470
Economic
    conditions, and women, 37
    equality, 381
    inequality, 234
    production, 80
    productivity, 381
    regional disparities, 390
    trends, 180
Economic Council of Canada,
    485
Economic systems, 379–382
    capitalism. *See* Capitalism
    socialism. *See* Socialism
Economics, and politics, 409–410
Economy, 374
    global, 377–379, 394
    government control of, 380
    and Industrial Revolution,
        374–375
    laissez-faire, 379
    narrow, export-oriented, 284
    periphery of world, 283
    political, 404
    post-industrial, 376, 382–389
    primary sector, 376
    secondary sector, 377
    sectors of, 376–377
    semiperiphery of world, 284
    symbolic, 528
    tertiary sector, 377
    underground, 388
    urban political, 551–553
Education, 122–123, 481
    academic standards, 498
    access to higher, 491–493
    attainment of, 107
    classical, 485
    conflict analysis of, 19
    degrees in, 309
    dysfunctionality of, 19
    and economic development,
        481–482
    formal, 487
    gap, 488
    and gender, 122–123, 247,
        303
    global survey, 481–486
    heritage-centred curriculum,
        74
    higher, 5, 6
    multicultural, 74, 489
    occupational mobility, 255
    and political correctness, 501
    and politics, 416
    post–secondary, 485
    and poverty, 257
    private schools, 19
    progressive, 485
    streaming. *See* Streaming
    and work, 498–500
    see also Schooling
Efficiency, 103, 182
Egalitarian approaches, 36
Egalitarianism, 396
Ego, 115
Egypt, 76, 293
The elderly, 356
    abuse of, 360
    costs of living, 367

death of spouse, 358–359, 441
health care system, 351–352
health problems, 353
in the media, 361
as minority, 361
negative myths, 358
older, 353
younger, 353
Elders, 130, 356
Election, 401
    campaign budgets, 416
    of women, 418
Electronic church, 475–477
Electronic communication, 92
Electronic Frontier Canada, 187
Electronic Journal of Sociology, 53
Elizabeth Fry Society, 417
Embarrassment, 150
Emergent–norm theory, 563
Emotions, 146
"The Emperor's New Clothes",
    150
Empirical evidence, 29
Employment, full, 386
Empty nest, 441
Endogamy, 433
Engineers, 245, 309, 485
English language, 64
    gender-bias in, 152
Environment
    natural, 584
    and organizations, 180–181
Environmental
    factors, 240
    issues, 94, 426, 554–555
Equality, 230
    of outcome, 396
    sexual, 300
Erikson's eight stages of
    development, 121
Eros, 115
Eruocentrism, 73
"Essays on the Art of Thinking",
    37
Estate system, 224, 225
The Ethics of Genetic Control, 453
Ethiopia, 273, 406, 507
Ethnic villages, 331
Ethnicity, 6
    in Canada, 335–338
    and crime, 206–207
    and family, 442–444
    and poverty, 257–258
    religion, 473
    social significance of,
        324–325
    social standing, 248, 337–338
    struggle for cultural
        identities, 323
    see also Race
Ethnocentrism, 75–77
Ethnomethodology, 21, 142–143
Europe, 73
European Cup Finals, 561
Euthanasia, 349, 364, 365, 516
Evangelism, 477
Executives, 306, 309
Exogamy, 433–434
Experts, 29
Eye contact, 146, 148

F
Facial expressions, 148
Factories, 374, 375
Fads, 566–568
Fair-weather liberal, 330
Faith, 458
Faith and Justice Network, 479
Faith and the Media, 479

False consciousness, 96
Family, 121–122, 432–435
   as agent of socialization, 415
   alternative forms of, 449–451
   blended, 448
   differentiation of leadership, 164
   educational attainment, 255
   and ethnicity, 442–444
   extended, 433
   family-based loyalties, 184
   female heads and poverty, 258
   gay and lesbian, 295, 450–451
   and gender, 302, 444–445
   gender-based income disparity, 309
   global perspective, 433
   hereditary ruling, 402
   homelessness, 261
   immigration class, 343
   and Information Revolution, 529
   liberal feminists, 317
   life, 144
   lone-parent, 258, 449–450
   and master status, 139
   Native Canadian, 442–443
   nuclear, 433
   of procreation, 432
   and race, 442–444
   and social class, 253, 441–442
   social-exchange analysis, 437
   stages of life, 437–441
   symbolic-interaction analysis, 437
   traditional significance of, 92
   unit, 432
   violence, 448–449
   violence programs, 332
   as violent organization, 312
   working-class parents, 253
Family Compact, 543
Family Violence Awareness Page, 455
Farmers, 90
Fashions, 566–568
Faultlines, 598
Fecundity, 532
Feminism, 20–21, 316–319
   jokes about, 156
   liberal, 317
   and the media, 124
   opposition to, 318–319
   radical, 317–318
   socialist, 317
   variations within, 317–319
Feminist
   Canadian, 574
   Christians, 461
   research, 36–38
Feminist Majority Foundation, 321
Fertility, 531–533, 540
Feudalism, 96–97, 225, 228
Fieldwork. *See* Participant observation
Final Exit, 349, 364
The Financial Post 500, 181
The Financial Post, 249, 265
Fine arts, 303, 309–310
Finland, 299, 310
First Nations peoples, 62, 327, 338–340
   Christianity imposed on, 339
   families, 442–443
   health, 511
   lands of, 543
   modernity, 594
   public policy, 12

   right to self-government, 340, 410–411
   schooling, 492
   see also Aboriginal peoples
"First World" nations, 268
Flag, 458, 574
Flirting, 142
FLQ. *See* Front de Libération du Québec
Folkways, 69
Food banks, 256
For Seven Generations: An Information Legacy of the Royal Commission on Aboriginal Peoples, 39
Ford Motor Company, 223, 393
Foreign debt, 284
Forestry industry, 390
Formal organizations, 170–184
   coercive organizations, 172–173
   global perspective, 184–186
   in Japan, 182–184
   normative organizations, 170–171
   size, 174
   types of, 170–173
   utilitarian, 170
   see also Bureaucracy; Organizations
Former Soviet Union, 226, 285, 334, 380, 406, 518–519
Fourth World Documentation Project, 601
Fractured society, 73
France, 79
Francophones, 255
Free Trade Agreement, 255, 391
Freedom, 84, 144
   and democracy, 404–406
   personal, 381–382
   political, 382
Freedom House, 406
"Freedom Summer", 573–574
French peoples, 59
   educational attainment levels, 248
   labour force participation, 248
   managerial occupations, 177
French Revolution, 15, 421, 569
FreudNet, 135
Friendship, 163
From Whence These Rumblings, 579
Front de libération du Québec, 75, 199, 341, 422, 575
Function, 104
Functional illiteracy, 253, 498, 499
Functional interdependence, 105
Fundamentalism, 474–475
Fundamentalists, 285
Funeral rites, 79

G
Gangs, 207
Gathering societies, 88–89, 235, 355
Gay Games, 296
Gay rights, 124, 295, 431, 432–433, 448, 568, 584
Gemeinschaft, 548–549, 586, 587, 590, 593
Gender, 296–299
   blindness, 36
   in Canada, 229
   and class, 315–316
   and complementarity, 314–315

   criminal, 204–206
   and culture, 299
   and demeanour, 148
   and deviance, 201
   double standards. *See* Double standards
   and economic conditions, 37
   and education, 303, 309–310
   eye contact, 148
   and the family, 302
   and family, 164, 444–445
   gallantry, 219
   global perspective, 297–302
   and health, 509–510
   human nature, 30
   identity, 297, 316
   and income, 307–309
   income differences, 246
   inequality and poverty, 277, 278
   Information Revolution, 370–371
   inherent inequality, 296
   interference, 36
   in Japanese society, 226
   Joan/John case, 297
   and language, 151–152
   male dominance, 301
   and mass media, 303–304
   men and directions, 137
   moral reasoning theory, 118, 119, 302
   notion of male superiority, 296–297
   notions of motherhood and fatherhood, 75
   and occupations, 305–307
   in organizations, 177–179
   overgeneralizations, 36
   and peer group, 302
   and personal performances, 148–149
   and personal space, 148
   and politics, 310–311
   and poverty, 258
   reassignment experiment, 297
   and research, 35–36
   research on, 298–299
   reversal hypothesis, 298
   roles, 47, 302, 316
   and schools, 122–123
   sexual desire, 81
   smiling, 148–150
   and social movements, 573–574
   social standing, 247–248, 253
   socialization, 302–304
   stereotypes, 47
   stratification, 304–314, 316
   and suicide, 6, 7
   and the system, 11
   touching, 149
   and wealth, 307–309
   see also Women
Gender-Free Pronoun FAQ, 159
General Council of Medical Education and Registration in Upper Canada, 517
General Electric, 183, 392
General intelligence, 240
General Motors, 76, 223, 391, 392, 393
General Social Survey, 204, 211, 254–255, 370, 586
Generalized other, 120
Generation gap, 123
Genetics, 81
   and intelligence, 240
   mapping, 525

   research, 190
Genital herpes, 514
Genocide, 334–335
George Weston, 391
George's Page, 135
Gerontocracy, 355
Gerontology, 353
Gesco Industries, Inc., 245
Gesellschaft, 548–549, 586, 587, 592
Gestures, 78, 146
Gimme Shelter: A Resource on Literacy and Homelessness Work, 265
Glass ceiling, 309
Global
   communications, 77
   crime, 207–209
   culture, 77
   economy, 77, 255–256, 377–379
   emotions, 146
   inequality, 268–271, 394
   migration, 77
   perspective, 7–11
   political system, 406–407
   poverty, 10, 271–279
   power relationships, 278
   village, 16, 94
   wealth, 10
Global Environmental Change: Understanding the Human Dimensions, 291
Global perspective
   education, 481–486
   family, 433
   gender, 297–302
   groups, 184–186
   modernity, 595
   organizations, 184–186
   politics, 403–408
   population, 538
   stratification, 235–237
   technology, 235–237
Global Television, 125
Global THINK, 497
Global Window: A Guide to Business Success - Japan, 187
The Globe and Mail, 154
Globe and Mail's Report on Business Magazine, 498
God, 29
   belief in, 471–472
   as Creator, 90
God's will, 13, 14, 96
Goffman on the Internet, 159
Golden handshake, 359
Golden Horseshoe, 547–548
Gonorrhea, 514
Goods, 374
Goods and Services Tax, 388
Goodyear, 392
Gossip, 564–565
Government, 401
Government planning, 396
Graduate Record Examination, 240
Grand Council of the Crees, 411
Graphs, 51
Great Britain. *See* United Kingdom
Great Depression, 11, 343
Great Pyramids of Egypt, 91, 173
Great Wall of China, 91, 173
Green party, 413
Green Revolution, 284, 289
Greenpeace, 408
Grit, 411
Gross domestic product, 273, 381

ABOUT THE AUTHORS

John J. Macionis

J. Macionis (pronounced ma-SHOW-nis) grew up in Philadelphia, Pennsylvania. He received his bachelor's degree from Cornell University and his doctorate in sociology from the University of Pennsylvania. His publications are wide-ranging, focusing on community life in the United States, interpersonal intimacy in families, effective teaching, humour, and the importance of global education. He and Nijole V. Benokraitis have edited the fourth edition of *Seeing Ourselves: Classic, Contemporary, and Cross-Cultural Readings in Sociology*. John also has written a brief version of this book, *Society: The Basics*. In addition, he is co-author of a new urban studies text, *Cities and Urban Life*.

John Macionis is professor of sociology at Kenyon College. During his twenty-year career at Kenyon, he has served as chair of the Anthropology-Sociology Department, director of the college's multidisciplinary program in humane studies, and presided over the college's faculty. He has also been active in academic programs in other countries, having travelled to some fifty nations. In the fall of 1994, he directed the global education course for the University of Pittsburgh's Semester at Sea program, teaching 400 students on a floating campus that visited twelve countries as it circled the globe.

At Kenyon, Macionis offers a wide range of upper-level courses, but his favorite course is Introduction to Sociology, which he schedules every semester. The Macionis family—John, Amy, and children McLean and Whitney—live on a farm in rural Ohio.

LINDA M. GERBER

Linda M. Gerber has spent most of her life in or near Toronto. Her first degree was in nursing, then she turned her attention to graduate studies in sociology. While still a graduate student, she became involved as a consultant in highway planning doing socio-economic impact assessment. After completing her master's and doctoral degrees at the University of Toronto, she spent three years as a research associate at Harvard's Center for Population Studies before joining the faculty in the Department of Sociology and Anthropology at the University of Guelph.

Professor Gerber's research has focused upon Canada's Native peoples, Canadian politics and ethnicity, but she has a broader interest in Canadian society (its demographic processes, its identity, and its fragility). Her publications are in the areas of Native studies, voting behaviour, gerontology, ethnic relations and Quebec separatism. While she has taught a wide range of undergraduate and graduate courses over the years, she continues to teach one introductory sociology course each year.